U.S. Department
of Transportation

Federal Aviation Administration

AC 43.13-1B
Change 1

Acceptable Methods, Techniques, and Practices—Aircraft Inspection and Repair

September 8, 1998
Change 1 incorporated September 27, 2001

(Note: Advisory Circular 43.13-2A for Aircraft Alterations begins immediately following the end pages of AC 43.13-1B)

DEPARTMENT OF TRANSPORTATION
FEDERAL AVIATION ADMINISTRATION
Flight Standard Service

U.S. Department of Transportation

Federal Aviation Administration

Advisory Circular

TITLE 14 OF THE CODE OF FEDERAL REGULATIONS (14 CFR) GUIDANCE MATERIAL

Subject: ACCEPTABLE METHODS, TECHNIQUES, AND PRACTICES—AIRCRAFT INSPECTION AND REPAIR

Date: 9/8/98
Initiated by: AFS-640

AC No: 43.13-1B
Change: 1

1. **PURPOSE.** This advisory circular (AC) contains methods, techniques, and practices acceptable to the Administrator for the inspection and repair of nonpressurized areas of civil aircraft, only when there are no manufacturer repair or maintenance instructions. This data generally pertains to minor repairs. The repairs identified in this AC may only be used as a basis for FAA approval for major repairs. The repair data may also be used as approved data, and the AC chapter, page, and paragraph listed in block 8 of FAA form 337 when:

   a. the user has determined that it is appropriate to the product being repaired;

   b. it is directly applicable to the repair being made; and

   c. it is not contrary to manufacturer's data.

2. **CANCELLATION.** The AC 43.13-1A dated 1988 is canceled.

3. **REFERENCE:** Title 14 of the Code of Federal Regulations part 43, section 43.13(a) states that each person performing maintenance, alteration, or preventive maintenance on an aircraft, engine, propeller, or appliance shall use the methods, techniques, and practices prescribed in the current manufacturer's maintenance manual or Instructions for Continued Airworthiness prepared by its manufacturer, or other methods, techniques, or practices acceptable to the Administrator, except as noted in section 43.16. FAA inspectors are prepared to answer questions that may arise in this regard. Persons engaged in the inspection and repair of civil aircraft should be familiar with 14 CFR part 43, Maintenance, Preventive Maintenance, Rebuilding, and Alteration, and part 65, Subparts A, D, and E of Certification: Airmen Other Than Flight Crewmembers, and the applicable airworthiness requirements under which the aircraft was type certificated.

4. **ACKNOWLEDGMENTS.** The FAA would like to thank the following persons and organization for their assistance in producing AC 43.13-1B: Richard Finch, Richard Fischer, Michael Grimes, Ray Stits, William A. Watkins, and the SAE, Aerospace Electronics and Electrical Systems Division. Acknowledgment is also extended to all in the aviation community who commented on the document.

5. **COMMENTS INVITED.** Comments regarding this AC should be directed to DOT/FAA; ATTN: Airworthiness Programs Branch, AFS-610; PO Box 25082; Oklahoma City, OK 73125

Acting Deputy Director, Flight Standards Service

CONTENTS

Paragraph Page

CHAPTER 1. WOOD STRUCTURE

SECTION 1. MATERIALS AND PRACTICES

SECTION 2. HEALTH AND SAFETY

SECTION 3. INSPECTION

SECTION 4. REPAIRS

CONTENTS (CONTINUED)

SECTION 5. FINISHING WOOD STRUCTURES

CHAPTER 2. FABRIC COVERING

SECTION 1. PRACTICES AND PRECAUTIONS

CONTENTS (CONTINUED)

SECTION 2. APPLICATION OF DOPE

SECTION 3. INSPECTION AND TESTING

SECTION 4. REPAIRS TO FABRIC COVERING

CONTENTS (CONTINUED)

Paragraph Page

CHAPTER 3. FIBERGLASS AND PLASTICS

SECTION 1. REPAIR OF LIGHT LOAD LAMINATE STRUCTURES

SECTION 2. METALLIC SANDWICH SECONDARY STRUCTURE REPAIRS

SECTION 3. TRANSPARENT PLASTICS

CONTENTS (CONTINUED)

Paragraph Page

SECTION 4. WINDSHIELDS, ENCLOSURES, AND WINDOWS

CHAPTER 4. METAL STRUCTURE, WELDING, AND BRAZING

SECTION 1. IDENTIFICATION OF METALS

SECTION 2. TESTING OF METALS

CONTENTS (CONTINUED)

Paragraph Page

SECTION 3. PRECAUTIONARY MEASURES

SECTION 4. METAL REPAIR PROCEDURES

CONTENTS (CONTINUED)

CONTENTS (CONTINUED)

Paragraph Page

CONTENTS (CONTINUED)

Paragraph Page

SECTION 6. WELDING AND BRAZING SAFETY

CHAPTER 5. NONDESTRUCTIVE INSPECTION (NDI)

SECTION 1. GENERAL

SECTION 2. VISUAL INSPECTION

CONTENTS (CONTINUED)

Paragraph Page

CONTENTS (CONTINUED)

CONTENTS (CONTINUED)

Paragraph Page

SECTION 8. TAP TESTING

SECTION 9. ACOUSTIC-EMISSION

SECTION 10. THERMOGRAPHY

SECTION 11. HOLOGRAPHY

SECTION 12. SHEAROGRAPHY

CHAPTER 6. CORROSION, INSPECTION & PROTECTION

SECTION 1. GENERAL

SECTION 2. TYPES OF CORROSION

CONTENTS (CONTINUED)

SECTION 3. CORROSION PROTECTION MEASURES FOR BASIC MATERIALS

SECTION 4. CORROSION PREVENTIVE MAINTENANCE

SECTION 5. VISUAL CORROSION INSPECTION GUIDE FOR AIRCRAFT

CONTENTS (CONTINUED)

Paragraph Page

CONTENTS (CONTINUED)

Paragraph Page

SECTION 10. FERROUS METALS

SECTION 11. OTHER METALS AND ALLOYS

SECTION 12. PLATED PARTS

SECTION 13. CORROSION PROOFING OF LAND PLANES CONVERTED TO SEA PLANES

SECTION 14. HANDLING AND CARE OF AIRCRAFT RECOVERED FROM WATER IMMERSION

CHAPTER 7. AIRCRAFT HARDWARE, CONTROL CABLES, AND TURNBUCKLES

SECTION 1. RIVETS

SECTION 2. SCREWS

CONTENTS (CONTINUED)

CONTENTS (CONTINUED)

Paragraph Page

SECTION 5. WASHERS

SECTION 6. PINS

SECTION 7. SAFETYING

SECTION 8. INSPECTION AND REPAIR OF CONTROL CABLES AND TURNBUCKLES

CONTENTS (CONTINUED)

SECTION 9. TURNBUCKLES

SECTION 10. SAFETY METHODS FOR TURNBUCKLES

CONTENTS (CONTINUED)

Paragraph Page

SECTION 11. HARDWARE IDENTIFICATION TABLES

CHAPTER 8. ENGINES, FUEL, EXHAUST, AND PROPELLERS

SECTION 1. ENGINES

CONTENTS (CONTINUED)

CONTENTS (CONTINUED)

CONTENTS (CONTINUED)

Paragraph Page

CHAPTER 9. AIRCRAFT SYSTEMS AND COMPONENTS

SECTION 1. INSPECTION AND MAINTENANCE OF LANDING GEAR

SECTION 2. HYDRAULIC SYSTEMS

CONTENTS (CONTINUED)

Paragraph Page

CONTENTS (CONTINUED)

Paragraph Page

SECTION 2. WEIGHING PROCEDURES

CHAPTER 11. AIRCRAFT ELECTRICAL SYSTEMS

SECTION 1. INSPECTION AND CARE OF ELECTRICAL SYSTEMS

CONTENTS (CONTINUED)

Paragraph Page

SECTION 2. STORAGE BATTERIES

SECTION 3. INSPECTION OF EQUIPMENT INSTALLATION

SECTION 4. INSPECTION OF CIRCUIT-PROTECTION DEVICES

SECTION 5. ELECTRICAL WIRE RATING

CONTENTS (CONTINUED)

SECTION 6. AIRCRAFT ELECTRICAL WIRE SELECTION

SECTION 7. TABLE OF ACCEPTABLE WIRES

SECTION 8. WIRING INSTALLATION INSPECTION REQUIREMENTS

CONTENTS (CONTINUED)

Paragraph Page

SECTION 9. ENVIRONMENTAL PROTECTION AND INSPECTION

SECTION 10. SERVICE LOOP HARNESSES (PLASTIC TIE STRIPS)

SECTION 11. CLAMPING

SECTION 12. WIRE INSULATION AND LACING STRING TIE

CONTENTS (CONTINUED)

CONTENTS (CONTINUED)

Paragraph Page

SECTION 13. SPLICING

SECTION 14. TERMINAL REPAIRS

SECTION 15. GROUNDING AND BONDING

SECTION 16. WIRE MARKING

CONTENTS (CONTINUED)

SECTION 17. CONNECTORS

CONTENTS (CONTINUED)

Paragraph Page

SECTION 18. CONDUITS

SECTION 19. PROTECTION OF UNUSED CONNECTORS

SECTION 20. ELECTRICAL AND ELECTRONIC SYMBOLS

CHAPTER 12. AIRCRAFT AVIONICS SYSTEMS

SECTION 1. AVIONICS EQUIPMENT MAINTENANCE

SECTION 2. GROUND OPERATIONAL CHECKS FOR AVIONICS EQUIPMENT (ELECTRICAL)

CONTENTS (CONTINUED)

CONTENTS (CONTINUED)

Paragraph Page

SECTION 5. AVIONICS TEST EQUIPMENT

CHAPTER 13. HUMAN FACTORS

CHAPTER 1. WOOD STRUCTURE

SECTION 1. MATERIALS AND PRACTICES

1-1. GENERAL. Wood aircraft construction dates back to the early days of certificated aircraft. Today only a limited number of wood aircraft structures are produced. However, many of the older airframes remain in service. With proper care, airframes from the 1930's through the 1950's have held up remarkably well considering the state of technology and long term experience available at that time. It is the responsibility of the mechanic to carefully inspect such structures for deterioration and continuing airworthiness.

1-2. WOODS.

a. Quality of Wood. All wood and plywood used in the repair of aircraft structures should be of aircraft quality (reference Army Navy Commerce Department Bulletin ANC-19, Wood Aircraft Inspection and Fabrication). Table 1-1 lists some permissible variations in characteristics and properties of aircraft wood. However, selection and approval of woodstock for aircraft structural use are specialized skills and should be done by personnel who are thoroughly familiar with inspection criteria and methods.

b. Substitution of Original Wood. The wood species used to repair a part should be the same as that of the original whenever possible; however, some permissible substitutes are given in table 1-1. Obtain approval from the airframe manufacturer or the Federal Aviation Administration (FAA) for the replacement of modified woods or other non-wood products with a substitute material.

c. Effects of Shrinkage. When the moisture content of a wooden part is lowered, the part shrinks. Since the shrinkage is not equal in all directions, the mechanic should consider the effect that the repair may have on the completed structure. The shrinkage is greatest in a tangential direction (across the fibers and parallel to the growth rings), somewhat less in a radial direction (across the fibers and perpendicular to the growth rings), and is negligible in a longitudinal direction (parallel to the fibers). Figure 1-1 illustrates the different grain directions and the effects of shrinkage on the shape of a part. These dimensional changes can have several detrimental effects upon a wood structure, such as loosening of

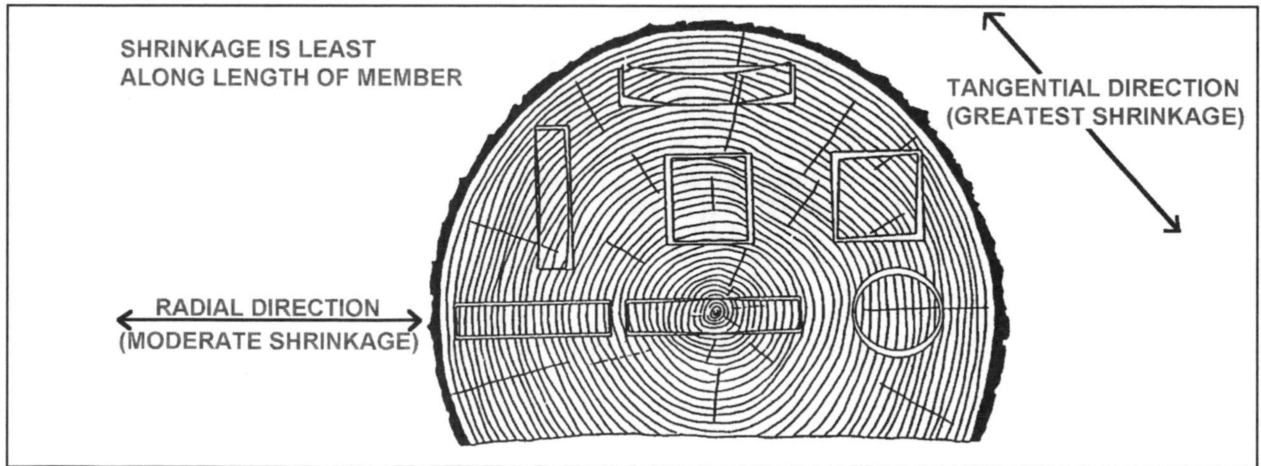

FIGURE 1-1. Relative shrinkage of wood members due to drying.

TABLE 1-1. Selection and Properties of Aircraft Wood. (See notes following table.)

Species of Wood	Strength properties as compared to spruce	Maximum permissible grain deviation (slope of grain)	Remarks
1.	2.	3.	4.
Spruce(Picea) Sitka (P. Sitchensis) Red (P. Rubra) White (P. Glauca).	100%	1:15	Excellent for all uses. Considered as standard for this table.
Douglas Fir (Pseudotsuga Taxifolia).	Exceeds spruce.	1:15	May be used as substitute for spruce in same sizes or in slightly reduced sizes providing reductions are substantiated. Difficult to work with handtools. Some tendency to split and splinter during fabrication and considerable more care in manufacture is necessary. Large solid pieces should be avoided due to inspection difficulties. Gluing satisfactory.
Noble Fir (Abies Nobiles).	Slightly exceeds spruce except 8% deficient in shear.	1:15	Satisfactory characteristics with respect to workability, warping, and splitting. May be used as direct substitute for spruce in same sizes providing shear does not become critical. Hardness somewhat less than spruce. Gluing satisfactory.
Western Hemlock (Tsuga Heterpphylla).	Slightly exceeds spruce.	1:15	Less uniform in texture than spruce. May be used as direct substitute for spruce. Upland growth superior to lowland growth. Gluing satisfactory.
Pine, Northern White (Pinus Strobus).	Properties between 85 % and 96 % those of spruce.	1:15	Excellent working qualities and uniform in properties, but somewhat low in hardness and shock-resisting capacity. Cannot be used as substitute for spruce without increase in sizes to compensate for lesser strength. Gluing satisfactory.
White Cedar, Port Orford (Charaecyparis Lawsoniana).	Exceeds spruce.	1:15	May be used as substitute for spruce in same sizes or in slightly reduced sizes providing reductions are substantiated. Easy to work with handtools. Gluing difficult, but satisfactory joints can be obtained if suitable precautions are taken.
Poplar, Yellow (Liriodendrow Tulipifera).	Slightly less than spruce except in compression (crushing) and shear.	1:15	Excellent working qualities. Should not be used as a direct substitute for spruce without carefully accounting for slightly reduced strength properties. Somewhat low in shock-resisting capacity. Gluing satisfactory.

Notes for Table 1-1

1. Defects Permitted.

a. Cross grain. Spiral grain, diagonal grain, or a combination of the two is acceptable providing the grain does not diverge from the longitudinal axis of the material more than specified in column 3. A check of all four faces of the board is necessary to determine the amount of divergence. The direction of free-flowing ink will frequently assist in determining grain direction.

b. Wavy, curly, and interlocked grain. Acceptable, if local irregularities do not exceed limitations specified for spiral and diagonal grain.

c. Hard knots. Sound, hard knots up to 3/8 inch in maximum diameter are acceptable providing: (1) they are not projecting portions of I-beams, along the edges of rectangular or beveled unrouted beams, or along the edges of flanges of box beams (except in lowly stressed portions); (2) they do not cause grain divergence **at the edges of** the board or in the flanges of a beam more than specified in column 3; and (3) they are in the center third of the beam and are not closer than 20 inches to another knot or other defect (pertains to 3/8 inch knots—smaller knots may be proportionately closer). Knots greater than 1/4 inch must be used with caution.

d. Pin knot clusters. Small clusters are acceptable providing they produce only a small effect on grain direction.

e. Pitch pockets. Acceptable in center portion of a beam providing they are at least 14 inches apart when they lie in the same growth ring and do not exceed 1-1/2 inches length by 1/8 inch width by 1/8 inch depth, and providing they are not along the projecting portions of I-beams, along the edges of rectangular or beveled unrouted beams, or along the edges of the flanges of box beams.

f. Mineral streaks. Acceptable, providing careful inspection fails to reveal any decay.

TABLE 1-1. Selection and Properties of Aircraft Wood. (See notes following table.) (continued)

2. Defects Not Permitted.

a. Cross grain. Not acceptable, unless within limitations noted in 1a.

b. Wavy, curly, and interlocked grain. Not acceptable, unless within limitations noted in 1b.

c. Hard knots. Not acceptable, unless within limitations noted in 1c.

d. Pin knot clusters. Not acceptable, if they produce large effect on grain direction.

e. Spike knots. These are knots running completely through the depth of a beam perpendicular to the annual rings and appear most frequently in quarter-sawed lumber. Reject wood containing this defect.

f. Pitch pockets. Not acceptable, unless within limitations noted in 1e.

g. Mineral streaks. Not acceptable, if accompanied by decay (see 1f).

h. Checks, shakes, and splits. Checks are longitudinal cracks extending, in general, across the annual rings. Shakes are longitudinal cracks usually between two annual rings. Splits are longitudinal cracks induced by artificially induced stress. Reject wood containing these defects.

i. Compression wood. This defect is very detrimental to strength and is difficult to recognize readily. It is characterized by high specific gravity, has the appearance of an excessive growth of summer wood, and in most species shows little contrast in color between spring wood and summer wood. In doubtful cases reject the material, or subject samples to toughness machine test to establish the quality of the wood. Reject all material containing compression wood.

j. Compression failures. This defect is caused from the wood being overstressed in compression due to natural forces during the growth of the tree, felling trees on rough or irregular ground, or rough handling of logs or lumber. Compression failures are characterized by a buckling of the fibers that appear as streaks on the surface of the piece substantially at right angles to the grain, and vary from pronounced failures to very fine hairlines that require close inspection to detect. Reject wood containing obvious failures. In doubtful cases reject the wood, or make a further inspection in the form of microscopic examination or toughness test, the latter means being the more reliable.

k. Decay. Examine all stains and discoloration carefully to determine whether or not they are harmless, or in a stage of preliminary or advanced decay. All pieces must be free from rot, dote, red heart, purple heart, and all other forms of decay.

fittings and wire bracing and checking or splitting of wood members. A few suggestions for minimizing these shrinkage effects are:

(1) Use bushings that are slightly short so that when the wood member shrinks the bushings do not protrude and the fittings may be tightened firmly against the member.

(2) Gradually drop off plywood faceplates by feathering as shown in figure 1-2.

(3) Thoroughly seal all wood surfaces, particularly end grain and bolt holes, with varnish, epoxy, or other acceptable sealer to slow or prevent moisture changes in the member. (See Section 5. Finishing Wood Structures.)

1-3. MODIFIED WOOD PRODUCTS. The most common forms of modified woods found in aircraft construction are plywood. Although not a wood product, Phenolic parts are sometimes incorporated into structures. These products are used whenever the manufacturer requires specialized strength or durability characteristics.

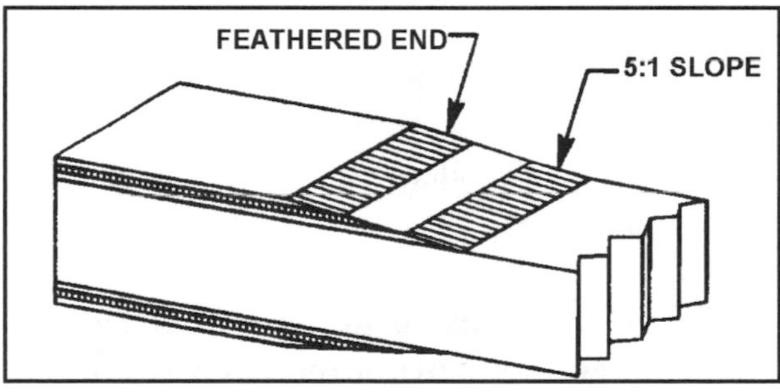

FIGURE 1-2. Tapering of faceplate.

1-4. ADHESIVES. Because of the critical role played by adhesives in aircraft structure, the mechanic must employ only those types of adhesives that meet all of the performance requirements necessary for use in certificated civil aircraft. Use each product strictly in accordance with the aircraft and adhesive manufacturer's instructions.

a. Adhesives acceptable to the FAA can be identified in the following ways:

(1) Refer to the aircraft maintenance or repair manual for specific instructions on acceptable adhesive selection for use on that type aircraft.

(2) Adhesives meeting the requirements of a Military Specification (Mil Spec), Aerospace Material Specification (AMS), or Technical Standard Order (TSO) for wooden aircraft structures are satisfactory providing they are found to be compatible with existing structural materials in the aircraft and the fabrication methods to be used in the repair.

b. Common types of adhesives that are or have been used in aircraft structure fall into two general groups: casein and synthetic-resins. Adhesive technology continues to evolve, and new types (meeting the requirements of paragraph 1-4a) may become available in the future.

(1) Casein adhesive performance is generally considered inferior to other products available today, modern adhesives should be considered first.

CAUTION: Casein adhesive deteriorates over the years after exposure to moisture in the air and temperature variations. Some modern adhesives are incompatible with casein adhesive. If a joint that has previously been bonded with casein is to be rebonded with another type adhesive, all traces of the casein must be scraped off before the new adhesive is applied. If any casein adhesive is left, residual alkalinity may cause the new adhesive to fail to cure properly.

(2) Synthetic-resin adhesives comprise a broad family which includes plastic resin glue, resorcinol, hot-pressed Phenol, and epoxy.

(3) Plastic resin glue (urea-formaldehyde resin glue) has been used in wood aircraft for many years. Caution should be used due to possible rapid deterioration (more rapidly than wood) of plastic resin glue in hot, moist environments and under cyclic swell-shrink stress. For these reasons, urea-formaldehyde should be considered obsolete for all repairs. Any proposed use of this type adhesive should be discussed with the appropriate FAA office prior to using on certificated aircraft.

(4) Federal Specification MMM-A-181D and Military Specification MIL-A-22397 both describe a required series of tests that verify the chemical and mechanical properties of resorcinol. Resorcinol is the only known adhesive recommended and approved for use in wooden aircraft structure and fully meets necessary strength and durability requirements. Resorcinol adhesive (resorcinol-formaldehyde resin) is a two-part synthetic resin adhesive consisting of resin and a hardener. The appropriate amount of hardener (per manufacturer's instruction) is added to the resin, and it is stirred until it is uniformly mixed; the adhesive is now ready for immediate use. Quality of fit and proper clamping pressure are both critical to the achievement of full joint strength. The adhesive bond lines must be very thin and uniform in order to achieve full joint strength.

CAUTION: Read and observe material safety data. Be sure to follow the manufacturer's instructions regarding mixing, open assembly and close assembly times, and usable temperature ranges.

(5) Phenol-formaldehyde adhesive is commonly used in the manufacturing of aircraft grade plywood. This product is cured at elevated temperature and pressure; therefore, it is not practical for use in structural repair.

(6) Epoxy adhesives are a two-part synthetic resin product, and are acceptable providing they meet the requirements of paragraph 1-4a. Many new epoxy resin systems appear to have excellent working properties. They have been found to be much less critical of joint quality and clamping pressure. They penetrate well into wood and plywood. However, joint durability in the presence of elevated temperature or moisture is inadequate in many epoxies. The epoxy adhesives generally consist of a resin and a hardener that are mixed together in the proportions specified by the manufacturer. Depending on the type of epoxy, pot life may vary from a few minutes to an hour. Cure times vary between products.

CAUTION: Some epoxies may have unacceptable thermal or other hidden characteristics not obvious in a shop test. It is essential that only those products meeting the requirements of paragraph 1-4a be used in aircraft repair. Do not vary the resin-to-hardener ratio in an attempt to alter the cure time. Strength, thermal, and chemical resistance will be adversely affected. Read and observe material safety data. Be sure to follow the adhesive manufacturer's instructions regarding mixing, open and closed curing time, and usable temperature ranges.

1-5. BONDING PRECAUTIONS. Satisfactory bond joints in aircraft will develop the full strength of wood under all conditions of stress. To produce this result, the bonding operation must be carefully controlled to obtain a continuous thin and uniform film of solid adhesive in the joint with adequate adhesion and penetration to both surfaces of the wood. Some of the more important conditions involve:

a. Properly prepared wood surfaces.

b. Adhesive of good quality, properly prepared, and properly selected for the task at hand.

c. Good bonding technique, consistent with the adhesive manufacturer's instructions for the specific application.

1-6. PREPARATION OF WOOD SURFACES FOR BONDING. It is recommended that no more time than necessary be permitted to elapse between final surfacing and bonding. Keep prepared surfaces covered with a clean plastic sheet or other material to maintain cleanliness prior to the bonding operation. The mating surfaces should be machined smooth and true with planers, joiners, or special miter saws. Planer marks, chipped or loosened grain, and other surface irregularities are not permitted. Sandpaper must never be used to smooth softwood surfaces that are to be bonded. Sawn surfaces must approach well-planed surfaces in uniformity, smoothness, and freedom from crushed fibers. It is advisable to clean both joint surfaces with a vacuum cleaner just prior to adhesive application. Wood surfaces ready for bonding must be free from oil, wax, varnish, shellac, lacquer, enamel, dope, sealers, paint, dust, dirt, adhesive, crayon marks, and other extraneous materials.

a. Roughening smooth, well-planed surfaces of normal wood before bonding is not recommended. Such treatment of well-planed wood surfaces may result in local irregularities and objectionable rounding of edges. When surfaces cannot be freshly machined before bonding, such as plywood or inaccessible members, very slight sanding of the surface with a fine grit such as 220, greatly improves penetration by the adhesive of aged or polished surfaces. Sanding should never be continued to the extent that it alters the flatness of the surface. Very light sanding may also improve the wetting of the adhesive to very hard or resinous materials.

b. Wetting tests are useful as a means of detecting the presence of wax, old adhesive, and finish. A drop of water placed on a surface that is difficult to wet and thus difficult to bond will not spread or wet the wood rapidly (in seconds or minutes). The surface may be difficult to wet due to the presence of wax, exposure of the surface to heat and pressure as in the manufacture of hot press bonded plywood, the presence of synthetic resins or wood extractives, or simply chemical or physical changes in the wood surface with time. Good wettability is only an indication that a surface can be bonded satisfactorily. After performing wetting tests, allow adequate time for wood to dry before bonding. Preliminary bonding tests and tests for bond strength are the only positive means of actually determining the bonding characteristics of the adhesive and material combinations. (See paragraph 1-29h.)

1-7. APPLYING THE ADHESIVE. To make a satisfactory bonded joint, spread the adhesive in a thin, even layer on both surfaces to be joined. It is recommended that a clean brush be used and care taken to see that all surfaces are covered. Spreading of adhesive on only one of the two surfaces is not recommended. Be sure to read and follow the adhesive manufacturer's application instructions.

1-8. ASSEMBLY TIME IN BONDING. Resorcinol, epoxy, and other adhesives cure as a result of a chemical reaction. Time is an important consideration in the bonding process. Specific time constraints are as follows:

a. Pot life is the usable life of the adhesive from the time that it is mixed until it must be spread onto the wood surface. Once pot life has expired, the remaining adhesive must be discarded. Do not add thinning agents to the adhesive to extend the life of the batch.

b. Open assembly time is the period from the moment the adhesive is spread until the parts are clamped together. Where surfaces are coated and exposed freely to the air, some adhesives experience a much more rapid change in consistency than when the parts are laid together as soon as the spreading has been completed.

c. Closed assembly time is the period from the moment that the structure parts are placed together until clamping pressure is applied. The consistency of the adhesive does not change as rapidly when the parts are laid together.

d. Pressing (or clamping) time is the period during which the parts are pressed tightly together and the adhesive cures. The pressing time must be sufficient to ensure that joint strength is adequate before handling or machining the bonded structure.

NOTE: Follow the adhesive manufacturer's instructions for all time limits in the bonding process. If the recommended open or closed assembly periods are exceeded, the bond process should not be continued. Discard the parts if feasible. If the parts cannot be discarded, remove the partially cured adhesive and clean the bond line per adhesive manufacturer's instructions before application of new adhesive.

1-9. BONDING TEMPERATURE. Temperature of the bond line affects the cure rate of the adhesive. Some adhesive types, such as resorcinol, require a minimum temperature which must be maintained throughout the curing process. Each type of adhesive requires a specific temperature during the cure cycle, and the manufacturer's recommendations should be followed.

1-10. CLAMPING PRESSURE.

a. Use the recommended pressure to squeeze adhesive out into a thin, continuous film between the wood layers. This forces air from the joint and brings the wood surfaces into intimate contact. Pressure should be applied to the joint before the adhesive becomes too thick to flow and is accomplished by means of clamps, presses, or other mechanical devices.

b. Nonuniform clamping pressure commonly results in weak and strong areas in the same joint. The amount of pressure required to produce strong joints in aircraft assembly operations varies with the type of adhesive used and the type of wood to be bonded. Typical pressures when using resorcinol may vary from 125 to 150 pounds per square inch for softwoods and 150 to 200 pounds per square inch for hardwoods. Insufficient pressure or poorly machined wood surfaces usually result in thick bond lines, which indicate a weak joint, and should be carefully guarded against. Some epoxy adhesives require much less clamping pressure to produce acceptable joint strength. Be sure to read and follow the manufacturer's instructions in all cases.

1-11. METHOD OF APPLYING PRESSURE. The methods of applying pressure to joints in aircraft bonding operations range from the use of brads, nails, small screws, and clamps; to the use of hydraulic and electrical power presses. The selection of appropriate clamping means is important to achieving sound bond joints.

a. Hand nailing is used rather extensively in the bonding of ribs and in the application of plywood skins to the wing, control surfaces, and fuselage frames. Small brass screws may also be used advantageously when the particular parts to be bonded are relatively small and do not allow application of pressure by means of clamps. Both nails and screws produce adverse after effects. There is considerable risk of splitting small parts when installing nails or screws. Metal fasteners also provide vulnerable points for moisture to enter during service.

b. On small joints using thin plywood for gussets or where plywood is used as an outer skin, the pressure is usually applied by nailing or stapling. Thin plywood nailing strips are often used to spread the nailing pressure over a larger area and to facilitate removal of the nails after the adhesive has cured.

c. The size of the nails must vary with the size of the members. If multiple rows of nails are required, the nails should be 1 inch apart in rows spaced 1/2 inch apart. The nails in adjacent rows should be staggered. In no case should the nails in adjacent rows be more than 3/4 inch from the nearest nail. The length of the nails should be such that they penetrate the wood below the joint at least 3/8 inch. In the case of small members, the end of the nail should not protrude through the member below the joint. Hit the nails with several light strokes, just seating the head into the surface of the gusset. Be careful not to crush the wood with a heavy hammer blow.

d. In some cases the nails are removed after adhesive cure, while in others the nails are left in place. The nails are employed for clamping pressure during adhesive cure and must not be expected to hold members together in service. In deciding whether to re move nails after assembly, the mechanic should examine adjacent structure to see whether nails remain from original manufacture.

e. On larger members (spar repairs for example), apply pressure by means of screw clamps, such as a cabinet-maker's bar or "C-clamps." Strips or blocks should be used to distribute clamping pressure and protect members from local crushing due to the limited pressure area of the clamps, especially when one member is thin (such as plywood). The strip or block should be at least twice as thick as the thinner member being bonded.

f. Immediately after clamping or nailing a member, the mechanic must examine the entire joint to assure uniform part contact and adhesive squeeze-out. Wipe away excess adhesive.

1-12.—1-17. [RESERVED.]

SECTION 2. HEALTH AND SAFETY

1-18. GENERAL. The possibility of an injury is an important consideration when working with wooden aircraft structures. The tools and machines used to shape wooden members can be very dangerous. In addition, there are potential health hazards in working with adhesives and finishes. The mechanic should follow manufacturer's instructions wherever applicable to prevent injury. Federal law mandates that individual chemical manufacturers are to provide Material Safety Data Sheets (MSDS) with health hazard data to all consumers. First aid information and handling precautions must also be identified. Most of the products used in wooden aircraft construction are flammable. Some, such as dope and paint, may be highly flammable.

1-19. SANDING IN AREAS OF EXISTING BOND JOINTS AND FINISHES. Some adhesives used in wooden aircraft construction contain biocides. A commonsense precaution when machining or sanding existing structure is to wear a respirator to avoid inhaling dust products. To lower potential fire hazards avoid using electric sanders around dope, paints, and adhesives.

1-20. HANDLING OF ADHESIVES AND FINISHES. Most adhesives and finish products present at least some toxic potential to users. Injury may occur from skin or eye contact, inhalation, or accidental ingestion. Users should be aware of the manufacturer's instructions and MSDS.

a. Appropriate skin, eye, ear, and respiratory protection should be worn whenever indicated.

b. Shop cleanliness is essential for health and fire safety.

c. Shop personnel should maintain awareness of others in the work area to assure that bystanders are not injured.

d. Proper shop ventilation is essential to disperse fumes emitted from adhesives such as resorcinol and epoxy.

1-21.—1-26. [RESERVED.]

SECTION 3. INSPECTION

1-27. GENERAL. Inspection of wooden structure includes some methods, equipment, and awareness of failure modes which are unique to wooden aircraft.

1-28. TYPES OF DETERIORATION AND DAMAGE.

a. Wood Decay. Wood is an organic product which is subject to attack by fungi. Fungi are plants that grow on and in wood. The moisture content of the wood nominally will have to be 20 percent or greater to sustain fungus growth. The result of this growth is called decay. Decayed wood exhibits softness, swelling if still wet, excessive shrinkage when dry, cracking, and discoloration. Repair or replace wood if any amount or form of decay is found.

b. Splitting. Splits or cracks in wooden members occur along grain lines. When the moisture content of wood is lowered, its dimensions decrease. The dimensional change is greatest in a tangential direction (across the fibers and parallel to the growth rings), somewhat less in a radial direction (across the fibers and perpendicular to the growth rings), and is negligible in a longitudinal direction (parallel to the fibers). These dimensional changes can have detrimental effects upon a wood structure, particularly when two parts are bonded together with grains in different directions. This effect can often be seen where a plywood doubler is bonded to a spruce member. As the spruce member dries, it attempts to shrink, but is restrained by the plywood, which shrinks less. The resulting stress in the spruce member exceeds its cross-grain strength, and a split occurs.

c. Bond Failure. Bond joint failure is generally due to improper fabrication technique or prolonged exposure to moisture in service. Although none of the older adhesives have been specifically found to fail by simple aging, the mechanic is advised to inspect all accessible joints carefully.

d. Finish Failure. The finish coat on wood structure (usually varnish) is the last line of defense to prevent water entry into wood and the resulting decay. Finish failure can be the result of prolonged water exposure, wood splitting, ultraviolet light exposure, or surface abrasion.

e. Damage. Stress, impact, or mechanical damage to a wood structure is caused by excessive aerodynamic loads or impact loads occurring while the aircraft is on the ground. Overtightening of fittings can also cause crushing of the underlying wood member and possible bending of the metal fitting.

1-29. INSPECTION METHODS. Whenever possible, the aircraft should be kept in a dry, well-ventilated hangar, with all inspection covers, access panels, etc., removed for as long as possible before final inspection. The aircraft should be given a preliminary inspection when first removing the inspection covers and access panels and inspected with a moisture meter at this time. If the moisture content is high, the aircraft should be thoroughly dried. If the aircraft is dry, this will facilitate later inspection, especially when determining the condition of bonded joints.

a. Likely locations for wood structure deterioration should be given special attention. Most damage is caused by external influence such as moisture, temperature extremes, or sunlight. Care should be taken to note all possible entry points for moisture, (i.e., cracks or breaks in the finish, fastener holes, inspection/access openings, control system openings, drain holes, and the interfaces of metal fittings and the wood structure). The mechanic should also look for evidence of swelling or warpage of the aircraft's wood structure, which would indicate underlying damage or decay. Particular attention should be paid to the wood structure immediately beneath the upper surfaces, especially under areas that are finished in dark colors, for signs of deteriorating adhesives. Cracks in wood spars are often hidden under metal fittings or metal rib flanges and leading edge skins. Any time a reinforcement plate exists that is not feathered out on its ends, a stress riser exists at the ends of the plate. A failure of the primary structure can be expected to occur at this point.

b. Tapping the wood structure with a light plastic hammer or screwdriver handle should produce a sharp solid report. If the suspect area sounds hollow and soft, further inspection is warranted by the following methods.

c. Probe the area in question, if accessible, with a sharp metal tool. The wood structure should be solid and firm. If the suspect area feels soft and mushy the mechanic should assume that the area is rotted. Disassembly of the structure is warranted at this point.

d. Prying the area of a bond joint will reveal any mechanical separation of the joint. If the mechanic detects any relative movement between two adjacent wood members, a failure of the bond is evident. Any loose fittings should arouse the mechanic's suspicion, and the fittings should be removed to check for elongated bolt holes. Disassembly is warranted for further inspection.

e. Odor is an important indicator of possible deterioration. During the initial inspection, as the access panels are being removed from the structure, the mechanic should be aware of any areas that smell musty or moldy. These odors are indicative of the presence of moisture and associated fungal growth and decay.

f. Visual inspection requires looking at the wood structure both externally and internally for visual signs of decay or physical damage. Any accumulations of dirt, bird nests, or rodent nests are likely places to hold moisture and promote decay.

(1) The mechanic should remove any such accumulations that are found and inspect the area for signs of decay. Decay will appear as a dark discoloration or gray stains running along the grain and often a swelling of the wood member if still wet. Fittings will be imbedded in the wood instead of flush.

(2) Highly suspected structurally damaged areas are shown in figure 1-3. A list of most likely areas to incur structural damage include the following:

(a) Check front and rear spars for compression cracks adjacent to the plywood reinforcing plates, where the lift struts attach, and at the rib attach points on either side of the strut attach points. Triple-check these areas and the spar to fuselage attach points for cracks if the wingtip has contacted the ground, a hangar wall, etc.

(b) Check all metal fittings which attach to wooden structure for looseness, corrosion, cracks, or warps. Areas of particular interest are strut attach fittings, spar butt fittings, aileron and flap hinges, jury strut fittings, compression struts, pulley brackets, and any landing gear fittings.

(c) Check front and rear spars for longitudinal cracks at the ends of the plywood reinforcement plates where the lift struts attach. Triple-check this area if the wing has encountered any kind of ground strike.

(d) Check ribs on either side of strut attach points for missing or loose rib-to-spar attach nails.

(e) Check ribs on either side of strut attach points for cracks where the cap strips pass over and under the spars.

(f) Check for cracked leading edge skin and/or failed nose ribs in the area directly in front of the jury strut.

(g) Check the brackets which attach the struts to the spars for cracks.

(h) Check the aileron, flap hinge, and hinge brackets for cracks and loose or missing rivets.

(i) Check all exposed end grain wood, particularly the spar butts, for cracking or checking. Checking, or splitting, of wood spar butts is common on aircraft based in arid areas.

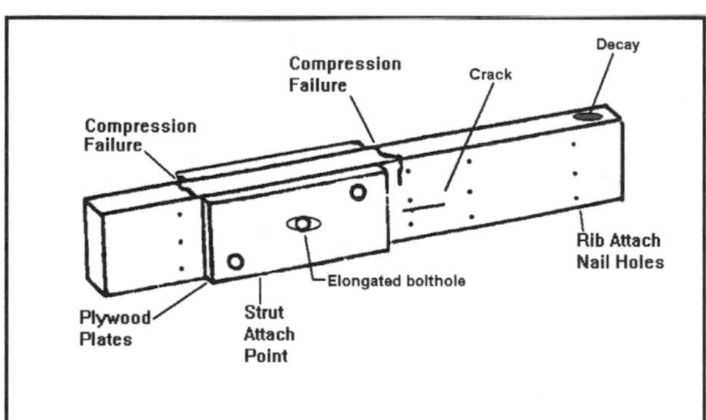

FIGURE 1-3. Likely areas to incur structural damage.

(j) Also check for any cracks that indicate a bond line failure or structural failure of the wood member. Any evidence of movement of fittings, bushings, or fasteners should be cause for concern, and further inspection is warranted. Splits in fabric covering the plywood, especially on upper surfaces exposed to ultraviolet light and water, dictate that the mechanic remove the fabric around the split so the underlying plywood may be inspected for physical damage or decay. When removing metal fasteners from wood, check for evidence of corrosion. Any corrosion present indicates the presence of moisture and the strong probability of decay in the adjoining wood structure.

(k) Any wooden member that has been overstressed is subject to compression failure (e.g., ground loop). Compression cracking and failure of the wood spars in certain aircraft are a continuing problem. Compression failures are defined as failure of wood fibers on a plane perpendicular to the wood fiber's longitudinal axis. If undetected, compression failures may result in structural failure of the wing during flight. Compression cracks have been found emanating from the upper surfaces of the wing spars and progressing downward.

(l) The usual locations for cracks have been the front spar at both ends of the reinforcement plate for the lift strut and the front spar rib attach points, both inboard and outboard of the spar reinforcement plate; and the rear spar lift strut and rib attach points. An inspection of both the front and rear spars for compression cracks is recommended.

(m) The two areas where it is possible to identify a compression crack are on the face and top surface of the spar. Using a borescope through existing inspection holes is one method of inspection. An alternate method is to cut inspection holes in the skin. If inspection holes are cut, they should be made on the aft side of the front spar and the forward side of the rear spar. This will allow the fabric to be peeled away from the spar. Longitudinal cracks may also be detected during this inspection. Loose or missing rib nails may indicate further damage and should be thoroughly investigated. The mechanic may shine a light, at a low angle and parallel with the grain, in the area of the member subjected to the compression load. An area of grain waviness would indicate a potential compression failure. In all cases the manufacturer's inspection data should be followed.

g. Moisture Meters are effective tools for detection of excessive moisture content in wood members. An instrument such as this allows the mechanic to insert a probe into the wood member and read its moisture content directly off the meter. A correction chart usually accompanies the instrument to correct for temperature and species of wood. Any reading over 20 percent indicates the probability of fungus growth in the member. Moisture content of the wood should be 8-16 percent, preferably in the 10-12 percent range (this range is during inspection). Where plywood skin covers the spar and the spar would be inaccessible without removing the skin, the moisture meter probe can be inserted through the plywood skin and into the spar to check the moisture content of the spar. The small holes made by the probe are easily sealed.

h. Destructive testing of sample bonded joints whenever a new bond joint is made, a sample joint should be made with the adhesive from the same batch used on the repair and scraps of wood left over from the repair. After curing, the sample joint should be destructively tested to ensure proper bonding of the two wood pieces. Any failure in the bond line indicates a cohesive failure of the adhesive. Any failure along the bond line indicates an adhesive failure, which is indicative of poor bonding. The ideal situation is when wood fibers are observed on both sides of the fracture surface. This indicates a failure in the wood, and indicates the bond joint is actually stronger than the wood.

1-30.—1-35. [RESERVED.]

SECTION 4. REPAIRS

1-36. GENERAL. The basic standard for any aircraft repair is that the repaired structure must be as strong as the original structure and be equivalent to the original in rigidity and aerodynamic shape. Repairs should be made in accordance with manufacturer specifications whenever such data is available.

1-37. REPLACEMENT OF DRAIN HOLES AND SKIN STIFFENERS. Whenever repairs are made that require replacing a portion that includes drain holes, skin stiffeners, or any other items, the repaired portion must be provided with similar drain holes, skin stiffeners, or items of the same dimensions in the same location. Additional drain holes may be required if reinforcement under a skin repair interferes with waterflow to existing drain holes. Make any additional drain holes the same diameter as originals, usually 1/4 inch.

1-38. CONTROL SURFACE FLUTTER PRECAUTIONS. When repairing or refinishing control surfaces, especially on high-performance airplanes, care must be exercised that the repairs do not involve the addition of weight aft of the hinge line. Such a procedure may adversely affect the balance of the surface to a degree that could induce flutter. As a general rule, it will be necessary to repair control surfaces in such a manner that the structure is identical to the original, and that the stiffness, weight distribution, and mass balance are not affected in any way. Consult the aircraft maintenance manual or seek manufacturer's direction for specific requirements on checking control surface balance after repair and refinishing of any control surface.

1-39. SCARF JOINTS. The scarf joint is the most satisfactory method of making an end joint between two solid wood members. Cut both parts accurately. The strength of the joints depends upon good joint design and a thin, uniform bond line. Make the scarf cut in the general direction of the grain slope as shown in figure 1-4.

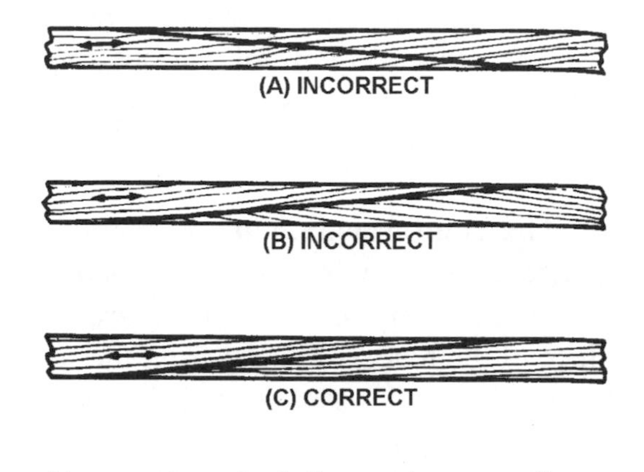

No grain deviation steeper than 1 in 15 should be present in an outer eighth of the depth of the spar. In adjacent eighths, deviations involving steeper slopes, such as a wave in a few growth layers, are unlikely to be harmful. Local grain slope deviations in excess of those specified may be permitted in spar flanges only in the inner one-fourth of the flange depth.

FIGURE 1-4. Consideration of grain direction when making scarf joints.

1-40. SPLICING OF SPARS. Unless otherwise specified by the manufacturer, a spar may be spliced at any point except under the wing attachment fittings, landing gear fittings, engine mount fittings, or lift and interplane strut fittings. These fittings may not overlap any part of the splice. A spar splice repair should not be made adjacent to a previous splice or adjacent to a reinforcing plate. Spacing between two splices or between a splice and a reinforcing plate should be no less than three times the length of the longer splice.

Splicing under minor fittings such as drag wire, antidrag wire, or compression strut fittings is acceptable under the following conditions:

a. The reinforcement plates of the splice should not interfere with the proper attachment or alignment of the fittings. Do not alter the locations of pulley support brackets, bellcrank support brackets, or control surface support brackets. Plates are to be tapered off, as depicted in figure 1-2.

b. The reinforcement plate may overlap drag wire, antidrag wire, or compression strut fittings, if the reinforcement plates are on the rear face of the rear spar or the front face of the front spar. In such cases, it will be necessary to install slightly longer bolts. The front face reinforcement plate should not overlap drag strut fittings, except when it does not require sufficient shortening of compression struts or changes in drag-truss geometry, to prevent adjustment for proper rigging. Even though take up is sufficient, it may be necessary to change the angles on the fittings. (Acceptable methods for splicing the various types of spars are shown in figure 1-4 through figure 1-9.) Reinforcement plates must be used as indicated on all scarf repairs to spars and the slopes of scarves shown are minimum slopes.

1-41. SPAR REPLACEMENT. Replacement of spars is a major repair. Spars may be replaced by new parts made by the manufacturer or the holder of a Parts Manufacturer Approval (PMA) for that part. Owner-produced spars may be installed providing they are made from a manufacturer-approved drawing. Also, a spar may be made by reference to an existing spar providing sufficient evidence is presented to verify that the existing spar is an original part, and that all materials and dimensions can be determined. The dimensions and type of wood used are critical to the structural strength of the aircraft. Care should be taken that any replacement spars accurately match the manufacturer's original design.

1-42. SPLICING OF BOX SPAR WEBS. Always splice and reinforce plywood webs with the same type of plywood as found on the original part. Do not use solid wood to replace plywood webs. Plywood is stronger in shear than solid wood of the same thickness due to the grain direction of the individual plies. The face-grain of plywood replacement webs and reinforcement plates must be in the same direction as the original member to ensure that the new web will have the required strength. (The method of splicing plywood webs is shown in figure 1-9.)

1-43. REPLACING SOLID-TYPE SPARS WITH LAMINATED-TYPE SPARS. Solid spars may be replaced with laminated spars or vice versa, provided the material is of the same high quality. External reinforcements (plywood or solid) must always be replaced as on the original member.

1-44. SPAR LONGITUDINAL CRACKS AND LOCAL DAMAGE. Cracked spars (except box spars) may be repaired by bonding plates of spruce or plywood of sufficient thickness to develop the longitudinal shear on both sides of the spar. Extend the plates well beyond the termination of the cracks, as shown in figure 1-10. A method of repairing small local damage to either the top or bottom side of a spar is also shown in figure 1-10.

a. Longitudinal Cracking of Wood Wing Spars of Aircraft Operating in Arid Regions. Aircraft having wood spars and operating in arid regions may develop longitudinal spar cracks in the vicinity of the plywood reinforcement plates. These cracks result from the tendency of the spar to shrink when drying takes place. Plywood resists this tendency to

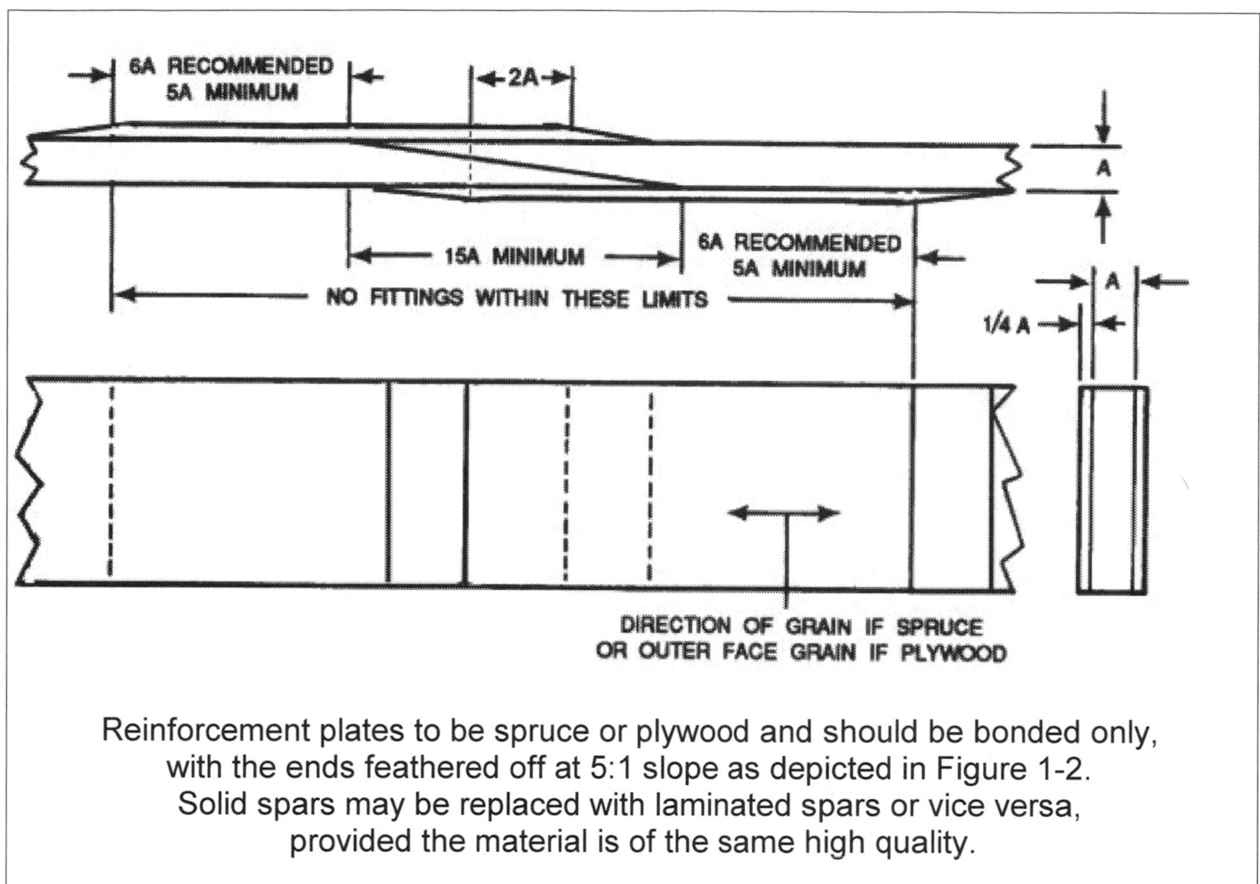
6A RECOMMENDED
5A MINIMUM
2A
A
15A MINIMUM
6A RECOMMENDED
5A MINIMUM
NO FITTINGS WITHIN THESE LIMITS
A
1/4 A
DIRECTION OF GRAIN IF SPRUCE
OR OUTER FACE GRAIN IF PLYWOOD
Reinforcement plates to be spruce or plywood and should be bonded only, with the ends feathered off at 5:1 slope as depicted in Figure 1-2. Solid spars may be replaced with laminated spars or vice versa, provided the material is of the same high quality.

FIGURE 1-5. Method of splicing solid or laminated rectangular spars.

shrink and causes the basic spar stock to split (see paragraph 1-2c). Cracks start under the plywood plates, usually (but not necessarily) at a bolt hole or cutout, and usually spread in each direction until they extend a short distance beyond the ends of the plates where the resistance to spar shrinkage disappears. Cracks have also been found in the butt end of spars. Other factors, which have been found conducive to the formation of cracks are poor protective finishes, large cutouts, and metal fittings that utilize two lines of large diameter bolts.

b. Repairing Cracks Versus Installing a New Spar. The presence of cracks does not necessarily mean that the spar must be discarded. If the crack is not too long or too close to either edge and can be reinforced properly, it will probably be more economical and satisfactory to perform repair rather than install a new spar or section. However, a generally acceptable procedure suitable for all airplane models is not available. Because of the possibility of strength deficiencies contact the manufacturer. In absence of the manufacturer, the FAA should be contacted for approval before making repairs not in accordance with the manufacturer-approved instructions or the recommendations of this advisory circular. Longitudinal cracking or the recurrence of cracking can be minimized by ensuring that the moisture content of the solid wood portion is within the proper range before bonding. In arid desert areas, during bonding the moisture content should be in the range of 6-8 percent before bonding, but in other areas 10-12 percent is satisfactory. If solid or plywood repair stock is procured from another climatic region, it should be allowed to season,

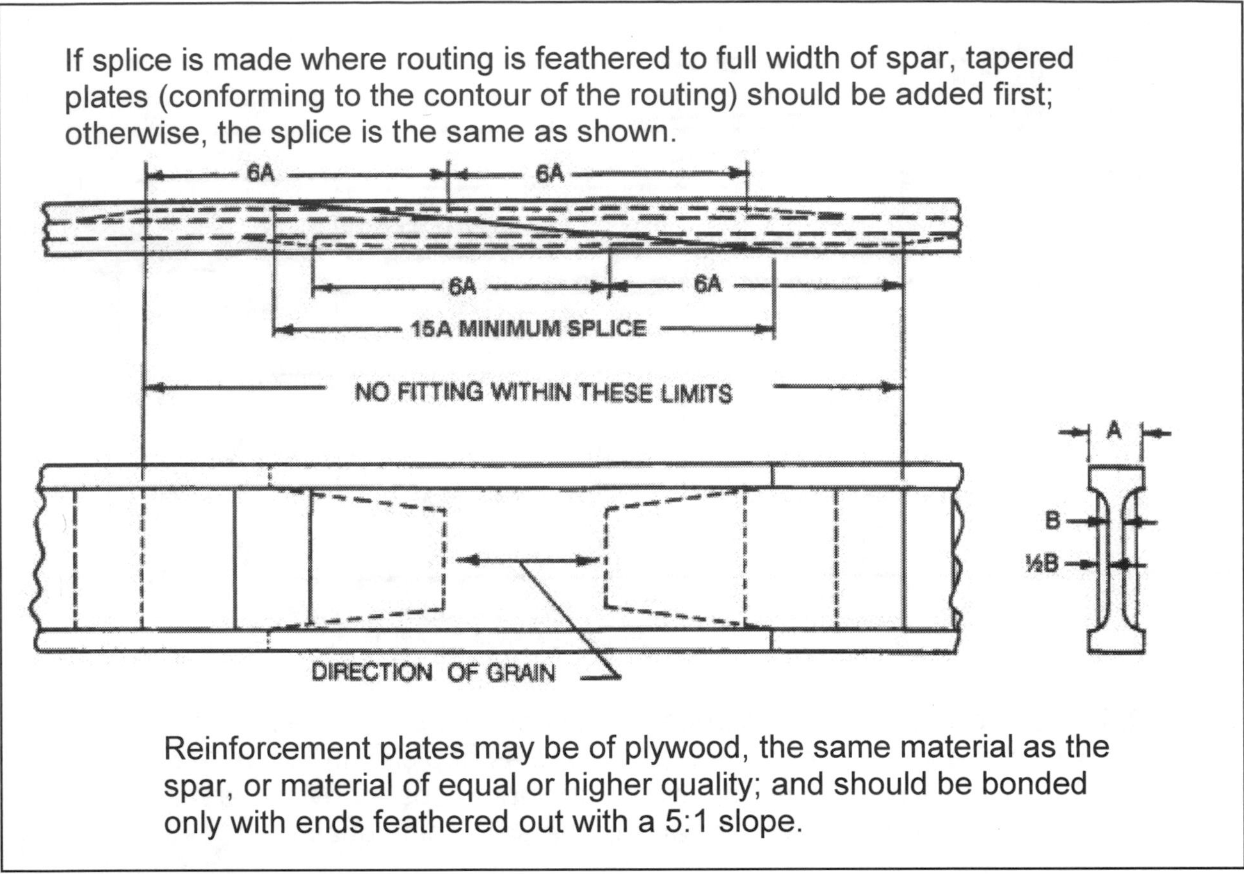
If splice is made where routing is feathered to full width of spar, tapered plates (conforming to the contour of the routing) should be added first; otherwise, the splice is the same as shown.
6A
6A
6A
6A
15A MINIMUM SPLICE
NO FITTING WITHIN THESE LIMITS
A
B
½B
DIRECTION OF GRAIN
Reinforcement plates may be of plywood, the same material as the spar, or material of equal or higher quality; and should be bonded only with ends feathered out with a 5:1 slope.

FIGURE 1-6. Method of splicing solid "I" spars.

in the same storage area as the part to be repaired, for no less than 2 weeks.

c. Preventing Cracks. An important step in the prevention of longitudinal cracking, particularly in spar butts, is to ensure that the wood is thoroughly sealed with a penetrating and highly moisture-resistant finish. Application of a thin, slow-curing epoxy adhesive or sealer can be very effective in slowing or preventing moisture changes in spar butts.

1-45. ELONGATED HOLES IN SPARS. In cases of elongated bolt holes in a spar, or cracks in the vicinity of bolt holes, splice in a new section of spar, or replace the spar entirely. If hole elongation or cracking is minimal and the bolt holes are for noncritical fittings, repair (rather than replacement) may be feasible. Obtain approval for any such repair from the manufacturer or a representative of the FAA. In many cases, it has been found advantageous to laminate the new section of the spar, particularly if the spar butts are being replaced.

1-46. RIB REPAIRS. Ribs may be replaced by new parts made by the manufacturer or the holder of a PMA for that part. Owner-produced ribs may be installed providing they are made from a manufacturer-approved drawing or by reference to an existing original rib. A rib may be made by reference to an existing rib providing sufficient evidence is presented to verify that the existing rib is an original part and that all materials and dimensions can be determined. The contour of the rib is important to the safe flying qualities of the aircraft, and care should be taken that any replacement ribs accurately match the manufacturer's original design.

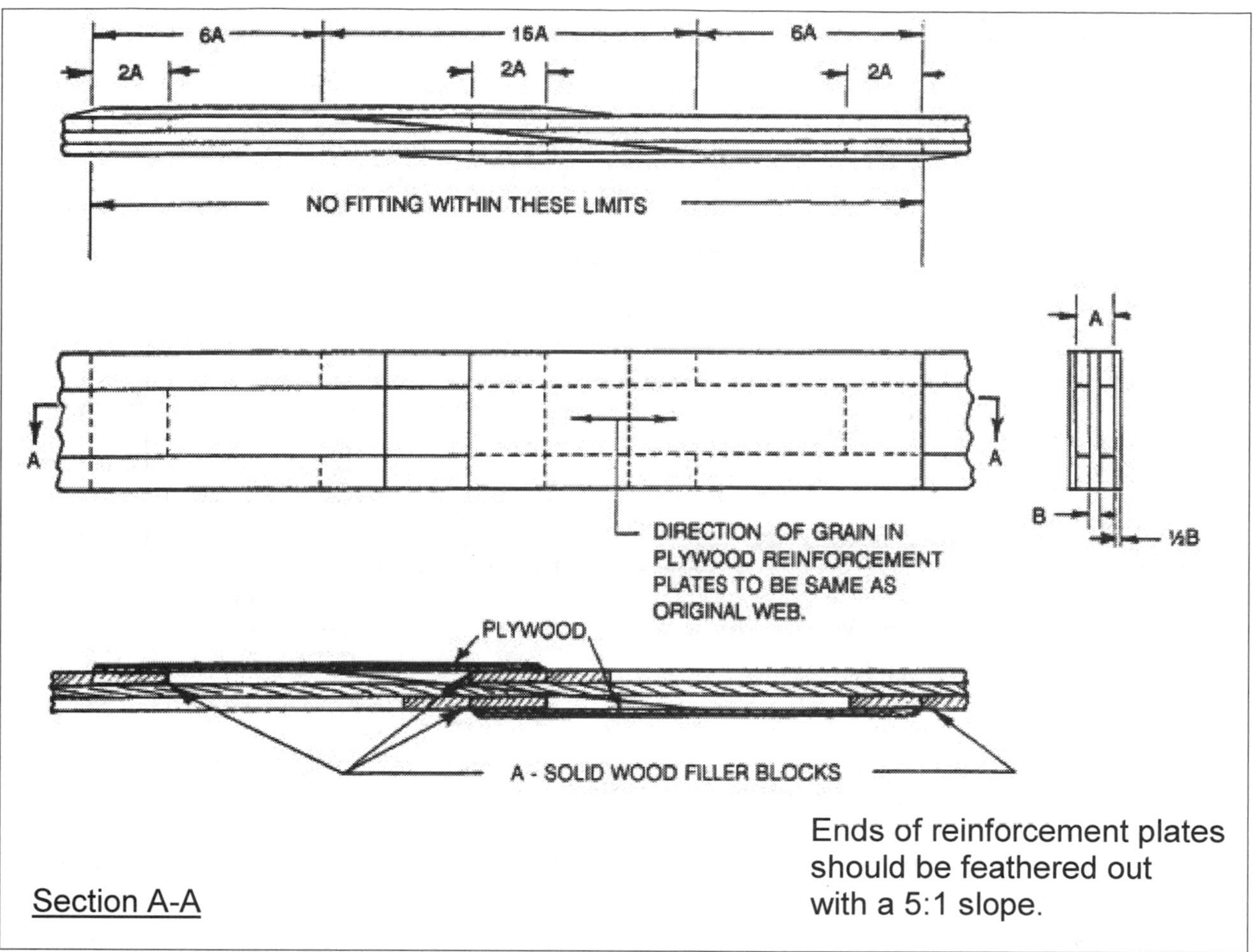

FIGURE 1-7. Repairs to built-up "I" spar.

a. Rib Repair Methods. Acceptable methods of repairing damaged ribs are shown in figure 1-11. Wood ribs should not be nailed to wood spars by driving nails through the rib cap strips, as this weakens the rib materially. The attachment should be by means of adhesive with cement coated, barbed, or spiraled nails driven through the vertical rib members on each face of the spar.

b. Compression Rib Repair. Acceptable methods of repairing damaged compression ribs are shown in figure 1-12.

(1) Figure 1-12(A) illustrates the repair of a compression rib of the "I" section type; i.e., wide, shallow cap strips, and a center plywood web with a rectangular compression member on each side of the web. The rib is assumed to be cracked through the cap strips, web member, and compression member in the illustration. Cut the compression member as shown in figure 1-12(D). Cut and replace the aft portion of the cap strips, and reinforce as shown in figure 1-11. The plywood side plates are bonded on, as indicated in figure 1-12(A). These plates are added to reinforce the damaged web.

(2) Figure 1-12(B) illustrates a compression rib of the type that is basically a standard rib with rectangular compression members added to one side and plywood web to the other side. The method used in this repair is essentially the same as in figure 1-12(A) except that the plywood reinforcement plate,

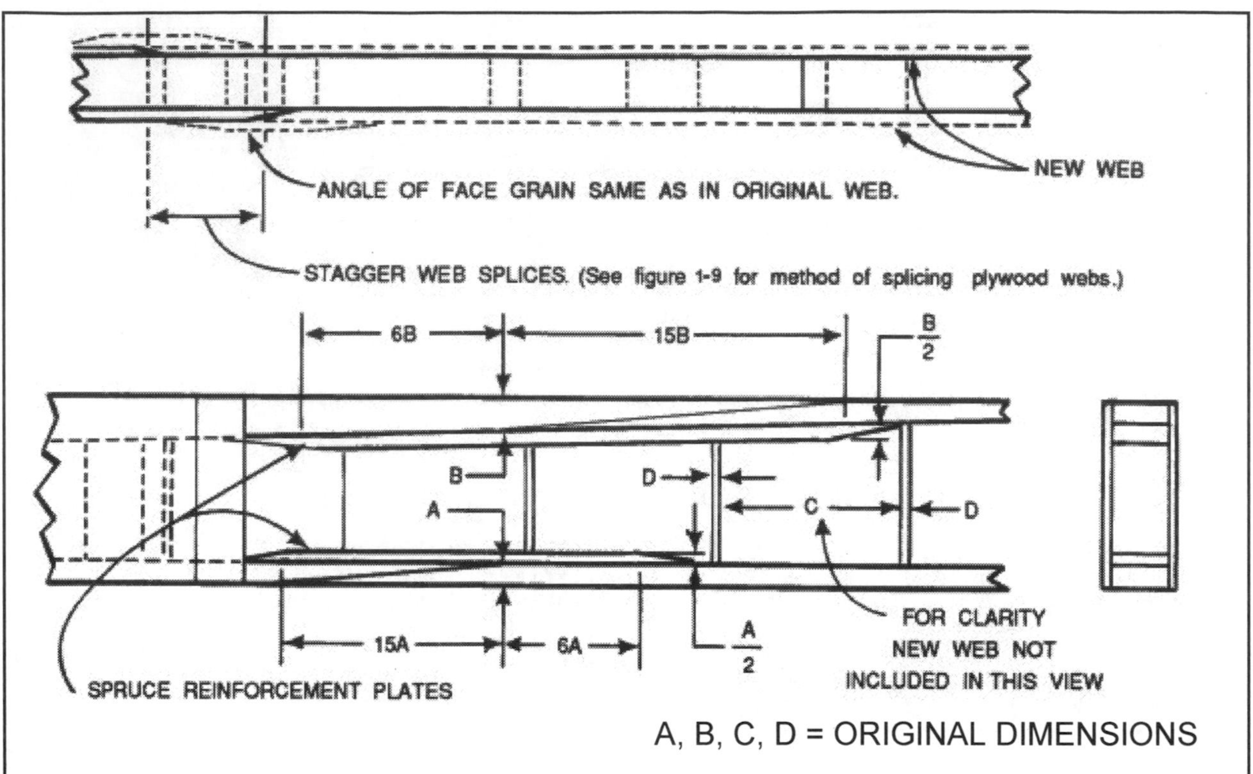

FIGURE 1-8. Method of splicing box spar flanges (plate method).

shown in section B-B, is continued the full distance between spars.

(3) Figure 1-12(C) illustrates a compression rib of the "I" type with a rectangular vertical member on each side of the web. The method of repair is essentially the same as in figure 1-12(A) except the plywood reinforcement plates on each side, shown as striped blocks in section C-C, are continued the full distance between spars.

1-47. PLYWOOD SKIN REPAIR. Make extensive repairs to damaged stressed skin plywood structures in accordance with specific recommendations from the aircraft manufacturer. It is recommended that repairs be made by replacing the entire panel, from one structural member to the next, if damage is very extensive. When damaged plywood skin is repaired, carefully inspect the adjacent internal structure for possible hidden damage. Repair any defective frame members prior to making skin repairs.

1-48. DETERMINATION OF SINGLE OR DOUBLE CURVATURE. Much of the outside surface of plywood aircraft is curved. On such areas, plywood used for repairs to the skin must be similarly curved. Curved skins are either of single curvature or of double (compound) curvature. A simple test to determine which type of curvature exists may be made by laying a sheet of heavy paper on the surface in question. If the sheet can be made to conform to the surface without wrinkling, the surface is either flat or single curvature. If the sheet cannot be made to conform to the surface without wrinkling, the surface is of double curvature.

1-49. REPAIRS TO SINGLE CURVATURE PLYWOOD SKIN. Repairs to single curvature plywood skin may usually be formed from flat plywood, either by bending it dry or after soaking it in hot water. The degree of curvature to which a piece of plywood can be bent will depend upon the direction of the grain and the thickness. Table 1-2 is a guide

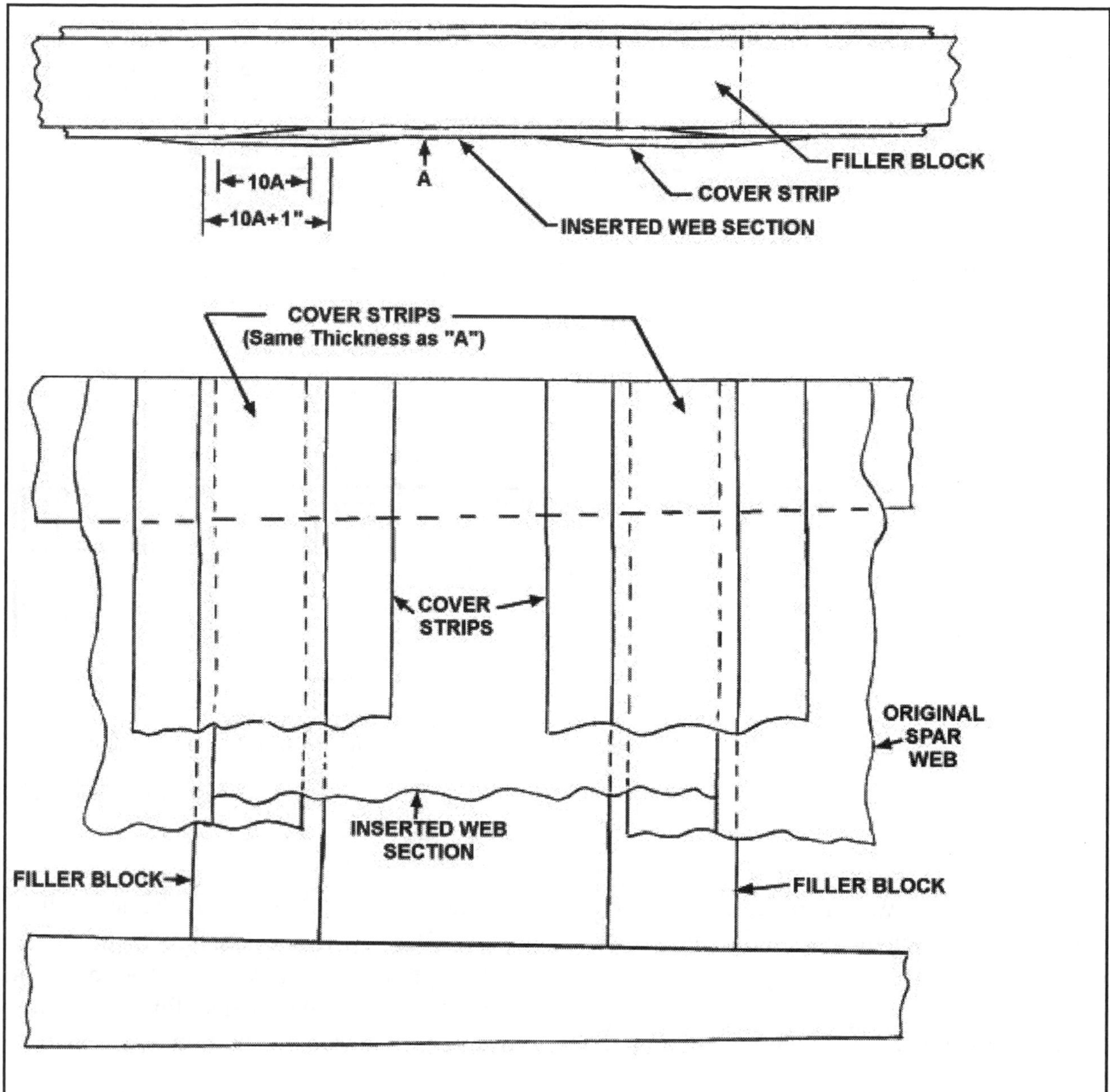

1. AFTER INSERTED WEB HAS BEEN BONDED IN PLACE, BOND COVER STRIPS OVER ENTIRE LENGTH OF WEB SPLICE JOINTS.
2. SECTIONAL SHAPE OF FILLER BLOCKS MUST CONFORM EXACTLY TO TAPER OF SPAR. THEY MUST NOT BE TOO TIGHTLY FITTED, FOR WEDGING ACTION WILL LOOSEN EXISTING BONDS OF WEBS TO FLANGES. IF TOO LOOSELY FITTED, CRUSHING OF WEB WILL OCCUR WHEN CLAMPING.
3. DIRECTION OF FACE GRAIN OF INSERTED WEB SECTION AND COVER STRIPS TO BE SAME AS ORIGINAL WEB.

FIGURE 1-9. Method of splicing box spar webs.

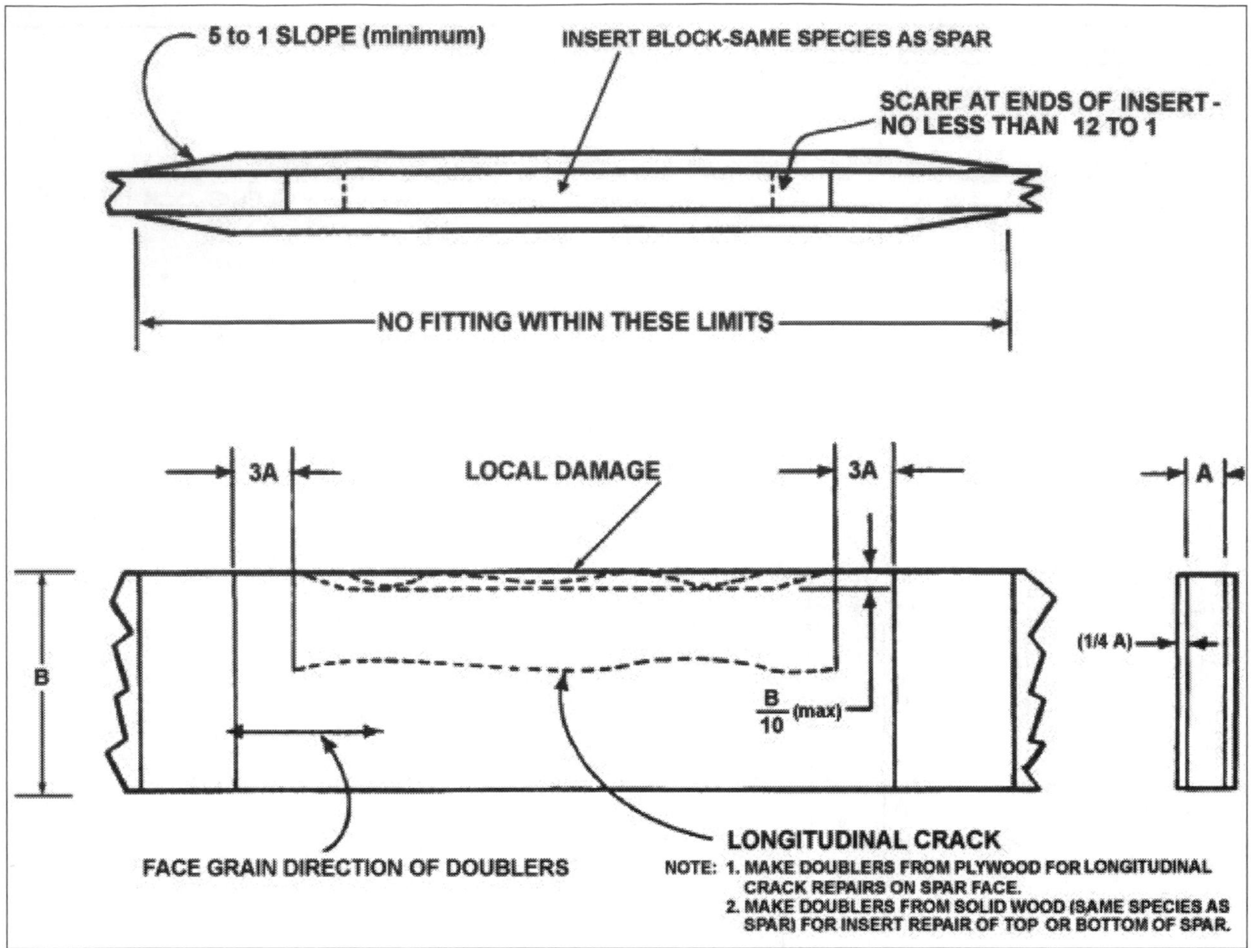

FIGURE 1-10. Method of reinforcing a longitudinal crack and/or local damage in a solid spar.

for determining which process of bending should be used for the curvature being considered.

a. Plywood, after softening, may be bent on a cold ventilated form, or it may be bent over the leading edge near the area being patched if space permits. In either method the repair part should be allowed to dry completely on the form. When bending plywood over a leading edge, drying may be hastened by laying a piece of coarse burlap over the leading edge before using it as a bending form. To speed drying, a fan may be used to circulate air around the repair part.

b. In bending pieces of small radii or to speed up the bending of a large number of parts of the same curvature, it may be necessary to use a heated bending form. The surface temperature of this form may be as high as 149 °C (300 °F), if necessary, without danger of damage to the plywood. The plywood should be left on the heated form only long enough to dry to room conditions.

1-50. REPAIRS TO DOUBLE CURVATURE PLYWOOD SKIN. The molded plywood necessary for a repair to a damaged plywood skin of double curvature cannot be made from flat plywood unless the area to be repaired is very small or is of exceedingly slight double curvature; therefore, molded plywood of the proper curvature must be on hand before the repair can be made. If molded plywood of the proper curvature is available, the repair may be made using the same procedure as on single curvature skins.

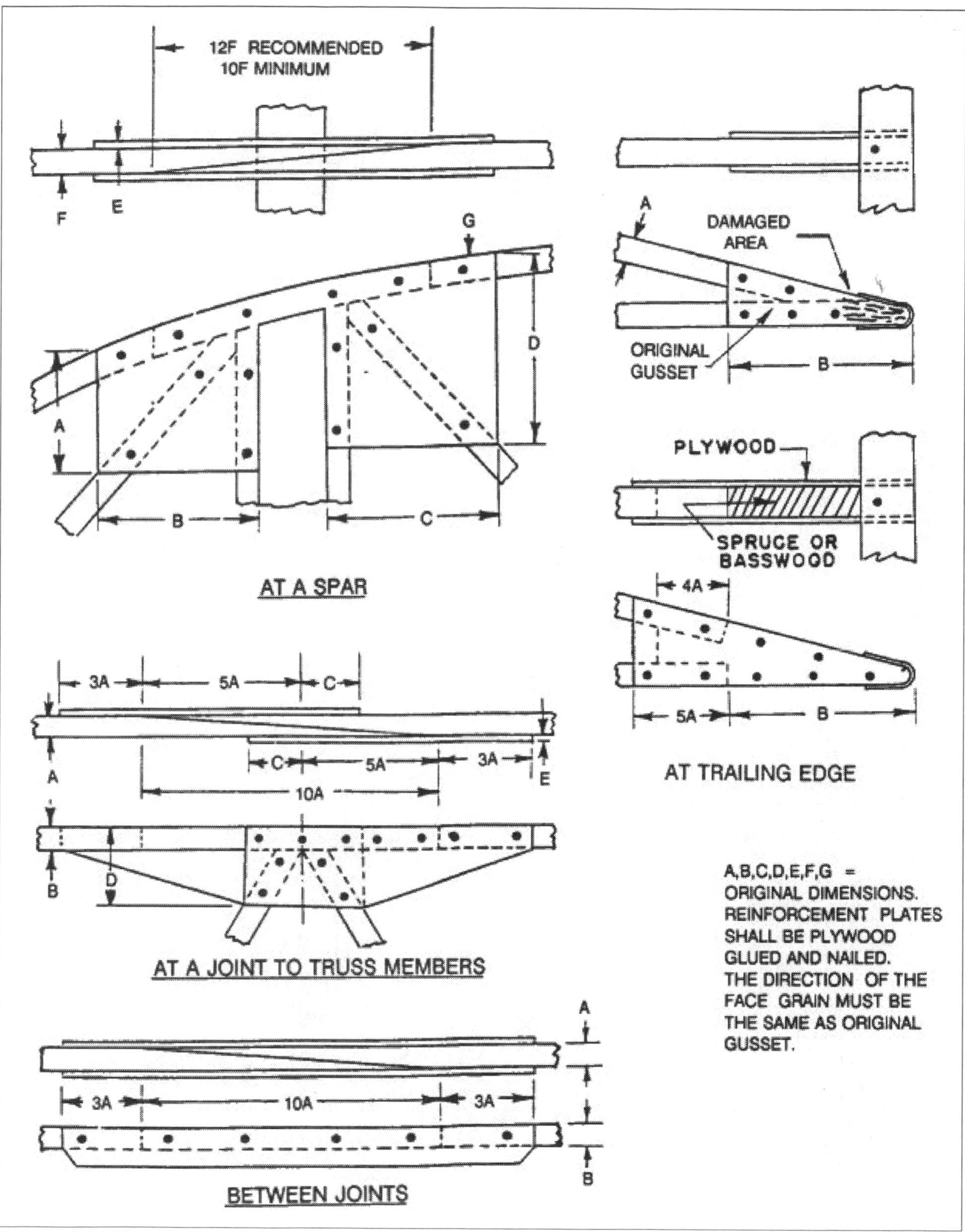

FIGURE 1-11. Repair of wood ribs.

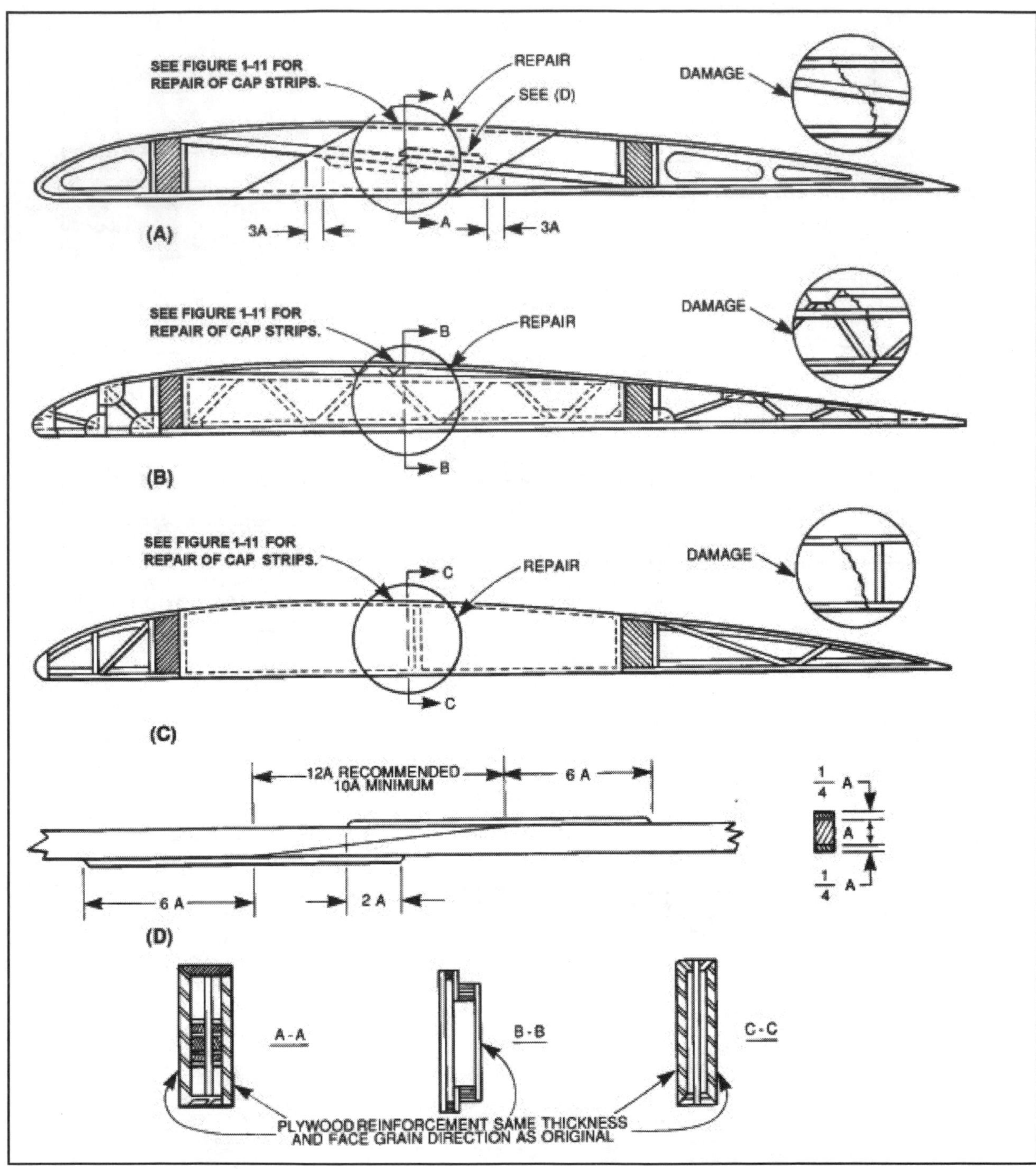

FIGURE 1-12. Typical wing compression rib repairs.

TABLE 1-2. Minimum recommended bend radii for aircraft plywood.

PLYWOOD CHARACTERISTICS		10 PERCENT MOISTURE CONTENT, BENT ON COLD MANDRELS		THOROUGHLY SOAKED IN HOT WATER AND BENT ON COLD MANDRELS	
		AT 90▪ TO FACE GRAIN	AT 0▪ OR 45▪ TO FACE GRAIN	AT 90▪ TO FACE GRAIN	AT 0▪0R 45° TO FACE GRAIN
THICKNESS (INCHES)	NUMBER OF PLIES	MINIMUM BEND RADIUS (INCHES)			
.035	3	2.0	1.1	0.5	0.1
.070	3	5.2	3.2	1.5	0.4
.100	3	8.6	5.2	2.6	0.8
.125	3	12	7.1	3.8	1.2
.155	3	16	10	5.3	1.8
.185	3	20	13	7.1	2.6
.160	5	17	11	6	2
.190	5	21	14	7	3
.225	5	27	17	10	4
.250	5	31	20	12	5
.315	5	43	28	16	7
.375	5	54	36	21	10

1-51. TYPES OF PATCHES. There are four types of patches: splayed patch, surface (or overlay) patch, scarf patch, and plug patch. They are all acceptable for repairing plywood skins.

a. Splayed Patch. Small holes with their largest dimensions not over 15 times the skin thickness, in skins not more than 1/10 inch in thickness, may be repaired by using a circular splayed patch as illustrated in figure 1-13. The term "splayed" is used to denote that the edges of the patch are tapered, but the slope is steeper than is allowed in scarfing operations.

(1) Lay out the patch according to figure 1-13. Tack a small piece of plywood over the hole for a center point and draw two circles with a divider, the inner circle to be the size of the hole and the outer circle marking the limits of the taper. The difference between the radii is 5T (5 times the thickness of the skin). If one leg of the dividers has been sharpened to a chisel edge, the dividers may be used to cut the inner circle.

(2) Taper the hole evenly to the outer mark with a chisel, knife, or rasp.

(3) Prepare a circular tapered patch to fit the prepared hole, and bond the patch into place with face-grain direction matching that of the original surface.

(4) Use waxed paper or plastic wrap, (cut larger than the size of the patch) between the patch and the plywood pressure plate. This prevents excess adhesive from bonding the pressure plate to the skin. Center the pressure plate carefully over the patch.

(5) As there is no reinforcement behind this patch, care must be used so that pressure is not great enough to crack the skin. On horizontal surfaces, weights or sandbags will be sufficient. On patches too far from any edge for the use of standard hand clamps, jaws of greater length may be improvised. Table 1-2, columns (1) and (3), may also be used for determining the maximum thickness of single laminations for curved members.

(6) Fill, sand, and refinish the patch.

b. Surface Patch. Plywood skins that are damaged between or along framing members may be repaired by surface or overlay patches as shown in figure 1-14. Surface patches located entirely aft of the 10 percent chord line, or which wrap around the leading edge and terminate aft of the 10 percent chord line, are permissible. Surface patches may have as much as a 50 inch perimeter and may cover as much as 1 frame (or rib) space. Trim the damaged skin to a rectangular or triangular shape and round the corners. The radius of rounded corners must be at least 5 times the skin thickness. Bevel the forward edges of patches located entirely aft of the 10 percent chord line to 4 times the skin thickness. The face-grain direction must be the same as the original skin. Cover completed surface patches with fabric to match surrounding area. The fabric must overlap the original fabric at least 2 inches.

c. Scarf Patch. A properly prepared and inserted scarf patch is the best repair for damaged plywood skins and is preferred for most skin repairs. Figure 1-15 shows the details and dimensions to be used when installing typical scarf skin patches, when the back of the skin is accessible. Follow figure 1-16 when the back of the skin is not accessible. The scarf slope of 1 in 12, shown in both figures, is the steepest slope permitted for all kinds of plywood. If the radius of curvature of the skin at all points on the trimmed opening is greater than 100 times the skin thickness, a scarf patch may be installed.

(1) Scarf cuts in plywood may be made by hand plane, spoke shave, scraper, or accurate sandpaper block. Rasped surfaces, except at the corners of scarf patches and sawn surfaces, are not recommended as they are likely to be rough or inaccurate.

(2) Nail strip or small screw clamping is often the only method available for bonding scarf joints in plywood skin repairs. It is essential that all scarf joints in plywood be backed with plywood or solid wood to provide adequate nail holding capacity. The face-grain direction of the plywood patch must be the same as that of the original skin.

(3) If the back of a damaged plywood skin is accessible (such as a fuselage skin), it should be repaired with a scarf patch, following the details shown in figure 1-15. Whenever possible, the edges of the patch should be supported as shown in section C-C of figure 1-15. When the damage follows or extends to a framing member, the scarf may be supported as shown in section B-B of figure 1-15. Damages that do not exceed 25 times the skin thickness in diameter after being trimmed to a circular shape and are not less than 15 times the skin thickness to a framing member, may be repaired as shown in figure 1-15, section D-D.

(a) The backing block is carefully shaped from solid wood and fitted to the inside surface of the skin, and is temporarily held in place with nails.

(b) Use waxed paper or plastic wrap to prevent bonding of the backing block to the skin.

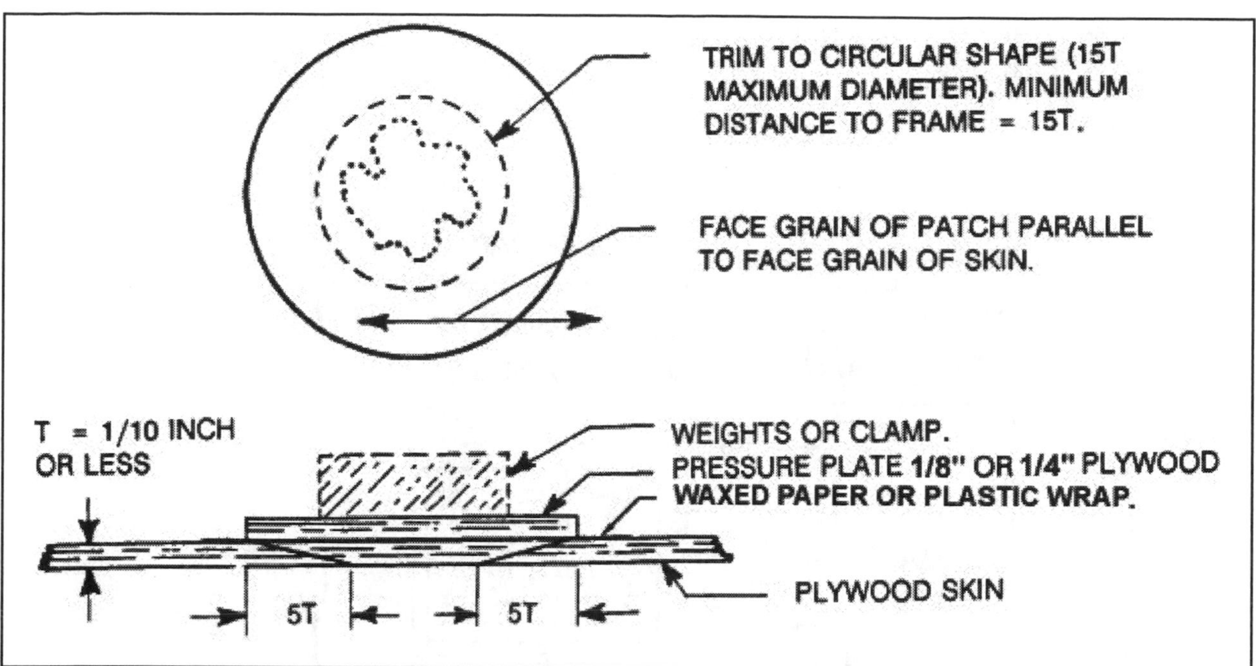

FIGURE 1-13. Splayed patch.

(c) A hole, the exact size of the inside circle of the scarf patch, is made in the block, and is centered over the trimmed area of damage.

(d) The block is removed, after the adhesive on the patch has set, leaving a flush surface to the repaired skin.

(4) Steps in making a scarf patch when the back of the skin is not accessible are as follows:

(a) After removing damaged sections, install backing strips, as shown in figure 1-16, along all edges that are not fully backed by a rib or a spar. To prevent warping of the skin, backing strips should be made of a soft-textured plywood, such as yellow poplar or spruce rather than solid wood. All junctions between backing strips and ribs or spars should have the end of the backing strip supported by a saddle gusset of plywood.

(b) If needed, nail and bond the new gusset plate to rib. It may be necessary to remove and replace the old gusset plate with a new saddle gusset, or it may be necessary to nail a saddle gusset over the original gusset.

(c) Attach nailing strips to hold backing strips in place while the adhesive sets. Use a bucking bar, where necessary, to provide support for nailing. After the backing strips are fully bonded, install the patch.

d. Plug Patch. Either oval or round plug patches may be used on plywood skins provided the damage can be covered by the patches whose dimensions are given in figure 1-17 and figure 1-18. The plug patch is strictly a skin repair, and should be used only for damage that does not involve the supporting structure under the skin. The face-grain direction of the finished patch must match the surrounding skin.

(1) Steps in making an oval plug patch are as follows:

(a) Explore the area about the hole to be sure it lies at least the width of the oval

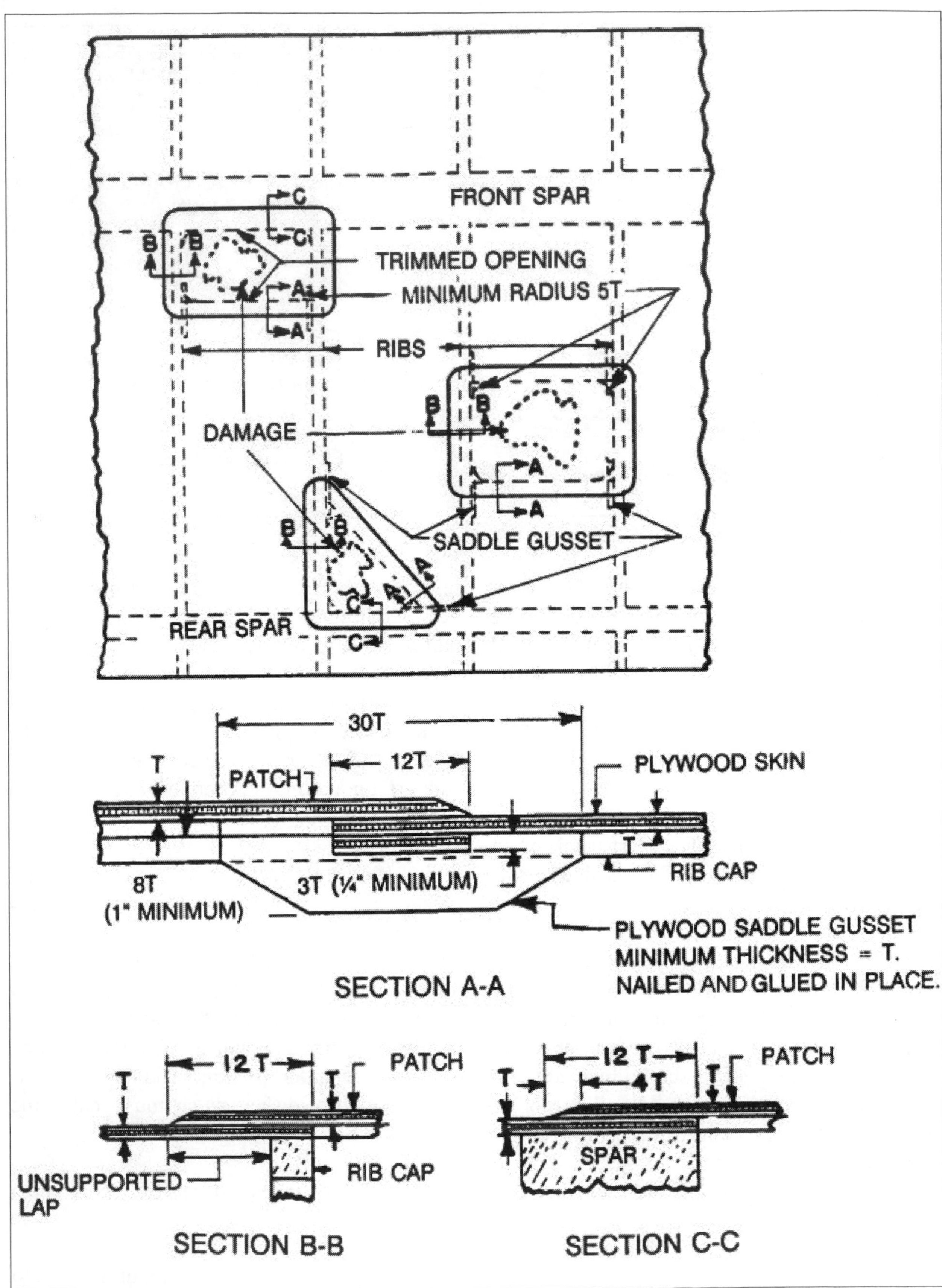

FIGURE 1-14. Surface patches.

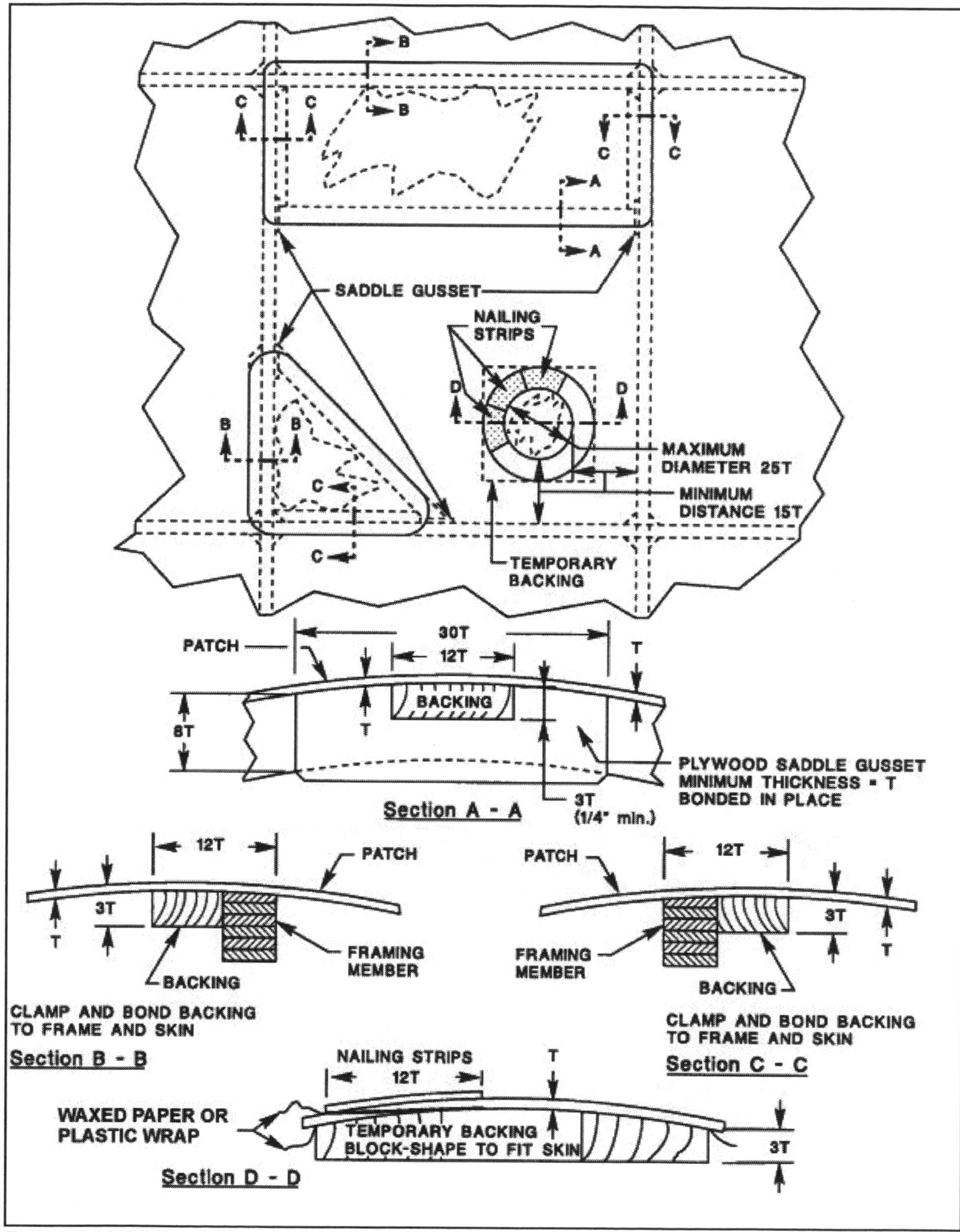

FIGURE 1-15. Scarf patches (back of skin accessible).

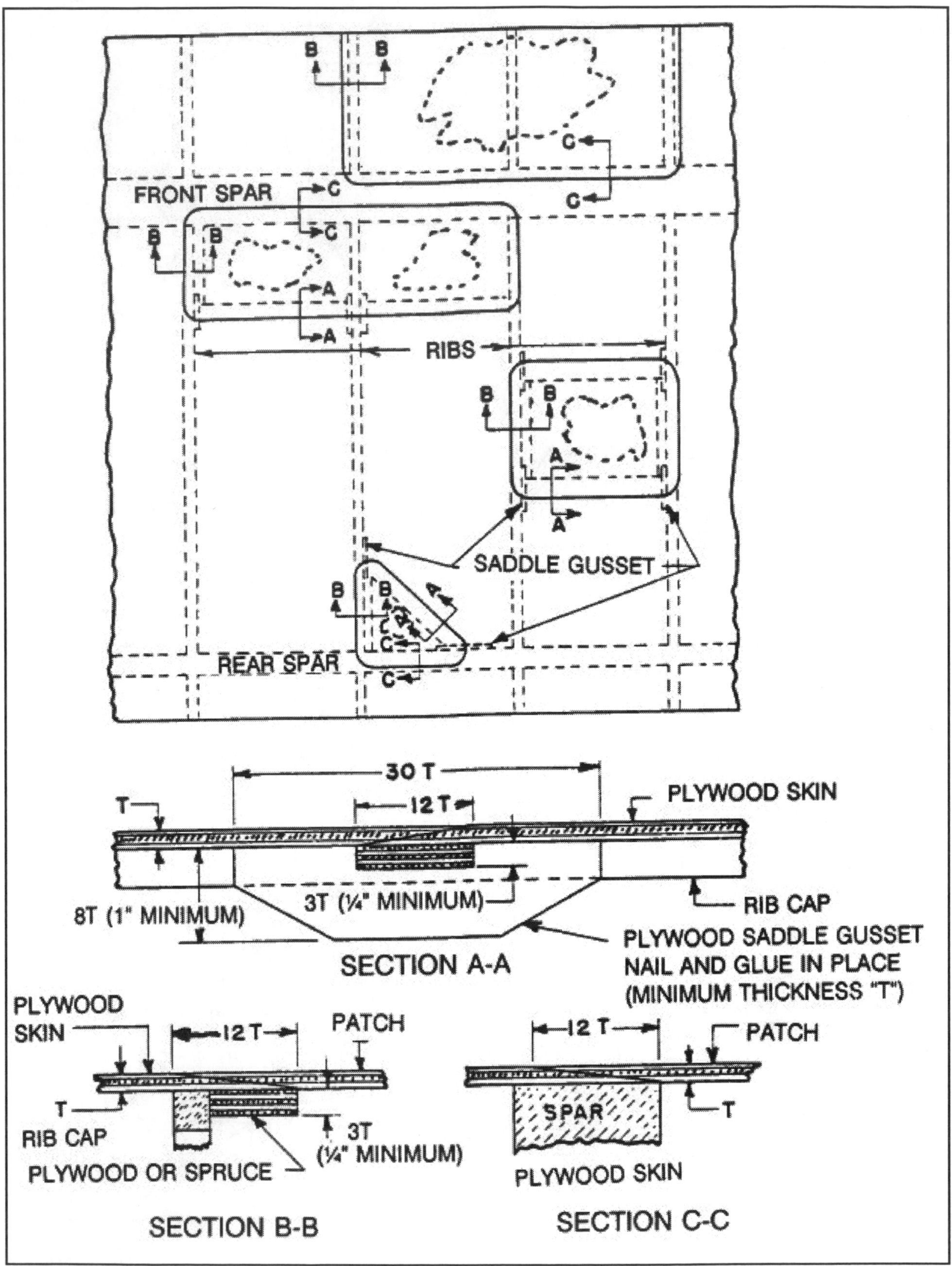

FIGURE 1-16. Scarf patches (back of skin not accessible).

doubler from a rib or a spar. Refer to figure 1-17 for repair details.

(b) Prepare a patch and a doubler of the same species plywood as the surrounding skin using the dimensions shown in figure 1-17.

(c) Lay the oval plug patch over the damage and trace the patch onto the skin. Saw to the line, and trim the hole edges with a knife and sandpaper.

(d) Mark the exact size of the patch on one surface of the oval doubler and apply adhesive to the area outside the line. Insert doubler through the hole and bring it, adhesive side up, to the underside of the skin with the pencil outline of the patch matching the edges of the hole. If the curvature of the surface to be repaired is greater than a rise of 1/8 inch in 6 inches, the doubler should be preformed by hot water or steam bending to the approximate curvature. As an alternative to preforming of the 1/4 inch stock, the doubler may be laminated from two thicknesses of 1/8 inch ply.

(e) Apply nailing strips outlining the hole to apply bonding pressure between doubler and skin. Use a bucking bar to provide support for nailing. When two rows of nails are used, stagger nail spacing. Allow adhesive to cure.

(f) Apply adhesive to remaining surface of the doubler and to the mating surface on the patch. Lay the patch in position over the doubler, and screw the pressure plate to the patch assembly using a small nail to line up the holes that have been previously made with patch and plate matching. No. 4 round head screws are used. Lead holes in the plywood doubler are not necessary. Waxed paper or plastic wrap between the plate and patch prevents adhesive from bonding the plate to the patch. No clamps or further pressure need be applied, as the nailing strips and screws exert ample pressure.

(2) Round plug patches may be made by following the steps in figure 1-18. The steps are identical to those for making the oval patch except for the insertion of the doubler. In using the round patch, where access is from only one side, the round doubler cannot be inserted unless it has been split.

1-52. FABRIC PATCH. Small holes not exceeding 1 inch in diameter, after being trimmed to a smooth outline, may be repaired by doping a fabric patch on the outside of the plywood skin. The edges of the trimmed hole should first be sealed, and the fabric patch should overlap the plywood skin by at least 1 inch. Holes nearer than 1 inch to any frame member, or in the leading edge or frontal area of the fuselage, should not be repaired with fabric patches.

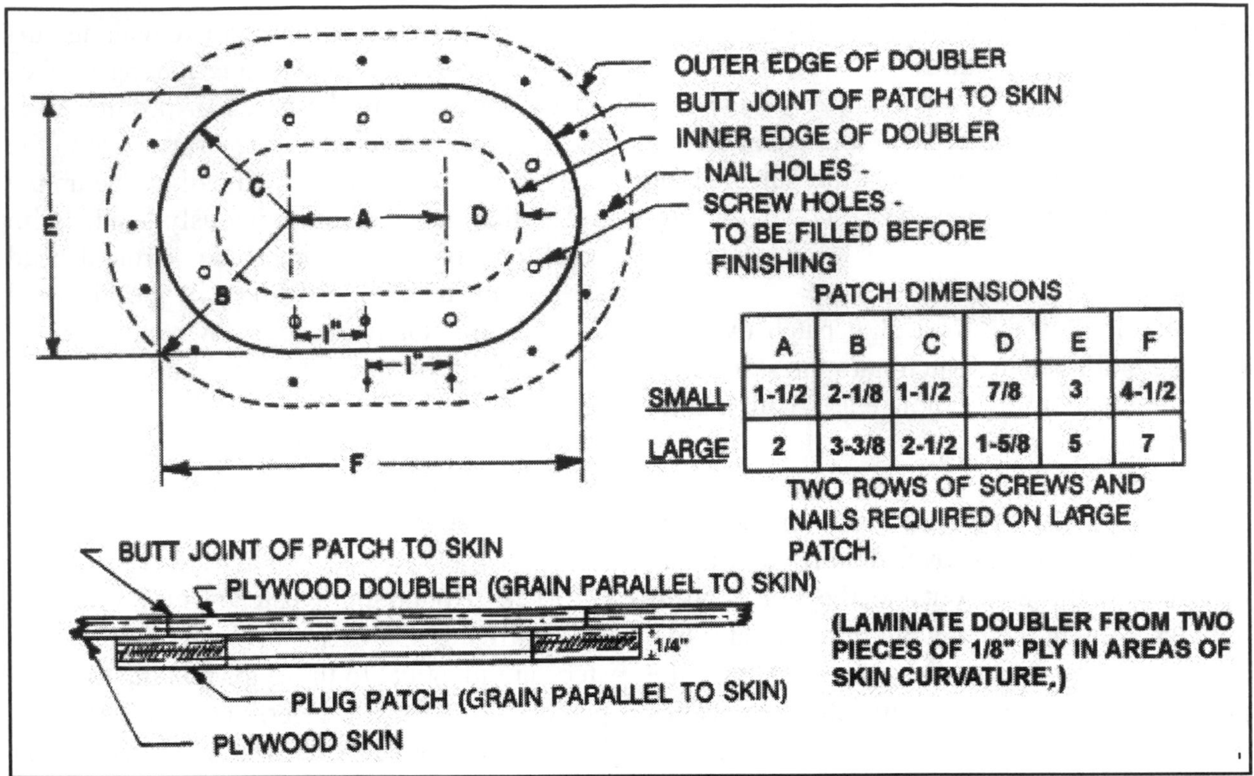

	A	B	C	D	E	F
SMALL	1-1/2	2-1/8	1-1/2	7/8	3	4-1/2
LARGE	2	3-3/8	2-1/2	1-5/8	5	7

FIGURE 1-17. Oval plug patch assembly.

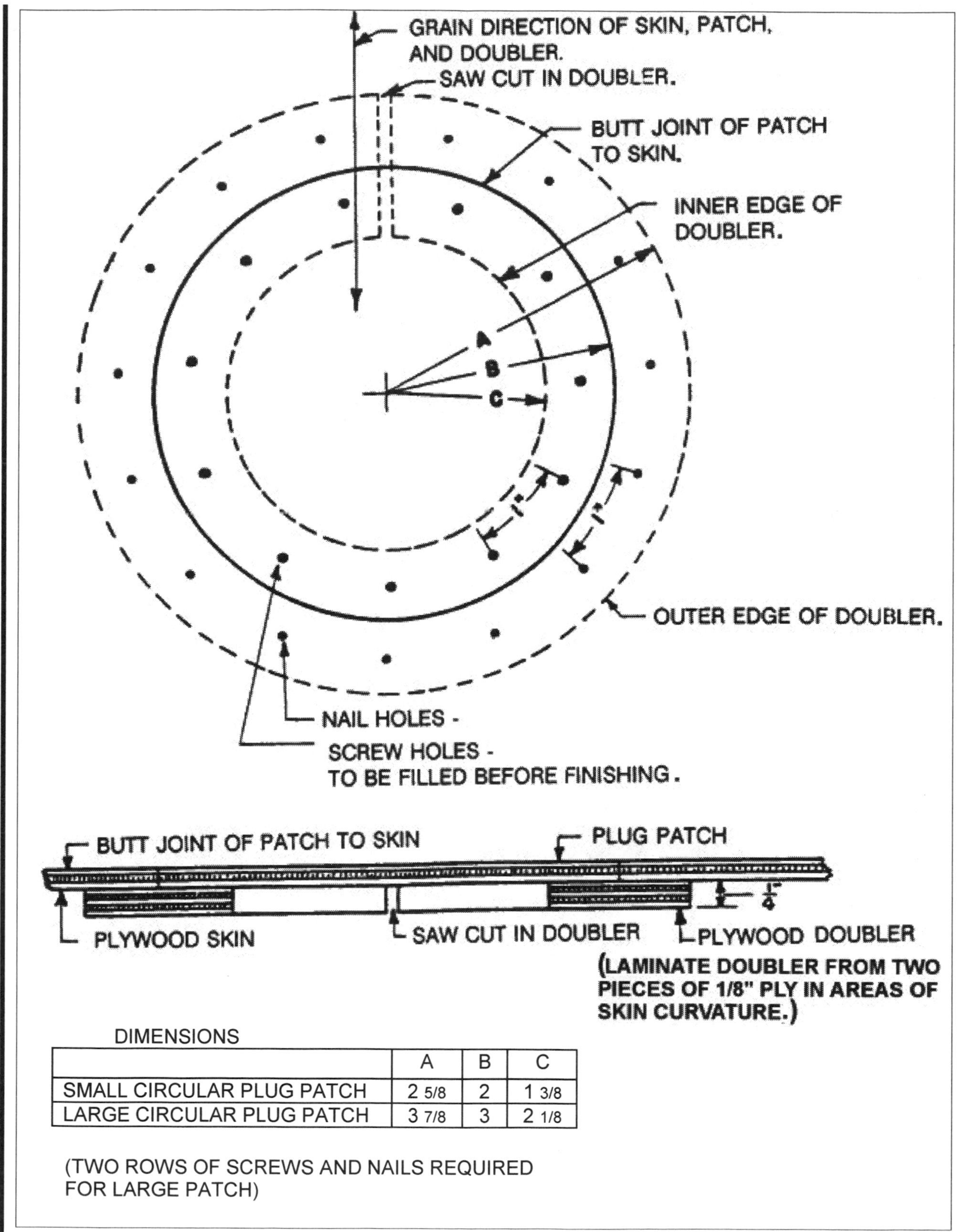

DIMENSIONS

	A	B	C
SMALL CIRCULAR PLUG PATCH	2 5/8	2	1 3/8
LARGE CIRCULAR PLUG PATCH	3 7/8	3	2 1/8

(TWO ROWS OF SCREWS AND NAILS REQUIRED FOR LARGE PATCH)

FIGURE 1-18. Round plug patch assembly.

1-53.—1-63. [RESERVED.]

SECTION 5. FINISHING WOOD STRUCTURES

1-64. GENERAL. Any repair to spars, ribs, skin surfaces, or other structural parts of the airframe involves finishing as the final step of the job. The surface finish is the final line of defense to prevent the destructive effects of moisture entry into the structure. The time and effort spent during the preparatory phase of the refinishing process will be reflected in the appearance and longevity of the finished surface. Adherence to the instructions issued by the finish manufacturer is necessary to obtain the appearance desired and protective characteristics for the product used. The primary objective of interior finishes is to afford protection of the wood against serious change in moisture content when exposed to damp air or to water that gains entrance to closed spaces by condensation or by penetration of rain, mist, or fog. Coatings, on contact areas between wood and metal protect the metal against corrosion from moisture in the wood. The primary objectives of the exterior finish are to protect the wood against weathering, provide a suitable appearance, and present a smooth surface in flight.

1-65. ACCEPTABLE FINISHES. Any varnish conforming to Federal Specification TT-V-109, as amended, or other coating approved by the airframe manufacturer or the FAA is acceptable. Exterior surfaces must be further protected from the effects of abrasion, weather, and sunlight. A number of systems for exterior finishing have STC approval and are manufactured under a PMA. (See Chapter 2, Fabric Covering.) Low viscosity epoxy adhesive (meeting the requirements of paragraph 1-4 for that purpose) may be used as an internal surface finish when subsequent bonding is necessary.

1-66. PRECAUTIONS.

a. When making repairs, avoid excessive contamination of surfaces with adhesive squeeze-out at joints and on all surfaces. Excess adhesive should always be removed before applying finish. Because many paints and adhesives are incompatible, even a slight amount of adhesive underneath the finish may cause premature deterioration of the finish.

b. Soiling substances, such as oil and grease, should be removed as completely as possible. Naphtha may be used to remove surface deposits of oil and grease; however, thinned residue may penetrate into any unprotected wood. In areas where minor amounts of oil or grease have penetrated the wood surface, removal may be accomplished by use of an absorbent type of cleaner such as gunsmith's whiting or a clothing spot lifter such as K2r™. Marks that are made by grease pencils or lumber crayons containing wax are harmful and should be removed, but marks made by ordinary soft graphite pencils and nonoily stamp pad inks may be safely finished over. All dust, dirt, and other solid particles should be removed.

c. Sawdust, shavings, and chips must be removed from enclosed spaces before they are sealed off by replacement of skin. A vacuum cleaner is useful for such cleaning.

d. Since most adhesives will not bond satisfactorily to sealers, it is necessary to avoid applying sealer over the areas where adhesive will be applied. Mark off areas to receive adhesive, and allow an additional 1/4 inch on each side of the adhesive area to provide for misalignment when mating the parts. It is preferable to leave some unsealed areas rather than risk weakening the joint by accidental overlap of the sealer into the bonded areas. Wherever possible, apply sealer to the margins after the adhesive has cured. As an example, the lower skin of a wing bay would be installed first, leaving access from above to apply sealer. All low spots (where moisture would collect) are well sealed. The top skin would be installed last, so that the only unsealed margins would be on upper surfaces where moisture is least likely to collect.

e. An alternative to the previous paragraph is to use an approved epoxy coating and compatible epoxy adhesive. Apply the coating, allowing 1/4 inch margins as in the previous paragraph. After the coating has cured, apply epoxy adhesive to joint surfaces, and overlap the adhesive onto the sealer. Close joint and clamp. The epoxy adhesive will bond satisfactorily to the coating and ensure a complete coverage of the wood surfaces. Use only approved and compatible adhesives and coatings for this method.

1-67. FINISHING OF INTERIOR SURFACES. Finish repaired ribs, spars, interior of plywood skin, and other internal members, including areas of contact between metal and wood, by applying one thinned coat (for penetration into wood grain) of varnish or other acceptable finish, followed by two full coats. Protect built-up box spars and similar closed structures on the interior in the same way. Where better protection is required, as on the surfaces of wheel wells and the bottoms of hulls below the floor boards, an additional coat of aluminized sealer consisting of 12 to 16 ounces of aluminum paste per gallon of sealer, may be applied.

1-68. FINISHING OF EXTERIOR SURFACES. Exterior surfaces require more protection than interior areas due to the effects of abrasion, weather, and sunlight. (See chapter 2.) Tests have shown that the interior temperature of wooden aircraft structures can reach 185 °F when the aircraft is finished in a dark color and parked outdoors on a hot, still day. Exposure to prolonged high temperature is detrimental to wood, adhesives, and finishes. Wood loses approximately 25 percent of its strength at 125 °F. For this reason, the mechanic should consider temperature effects when selecting finish colors or looking for areas of likely deterioration. The lowest temperatures are found when the aircraft is finished in white or very light colors, while darker colors produce higher temperatures. A general trend toward higher temperatures may be seen when exterior colors are yellow, pink, light blue, aluminum, purple, blue, light green, orange, tan, red, green, brown, and black. A lighter shade of a particular color helps to reduce temperatures.

1-69. FINISHING OF END GRAIN SURFACES. End grain portions of wooden members are much more absorbent than side grain. Because of this extreme vulnerability to moisture entry, it is necessary to take extra precautions to seal end grain.

a. Apply at least one thinned coat of acceptable sealer to ensure maximum penetration, and then follow with as many full strength coats as necessary to achieve a smooth, glossy coating. Depending on the type wood to be finished, two to four full coats will be required. A final coat of aluminized varnish may be applied to end grain surfaces. If the surfaces are to be finished with dope or lacquer, a dope-proof sealer, similar to Federal Specification TT-V-109, or epoxy sealer should be used.

b. Exposed end grain includes such surfaces as spar butts, skin edges, areas around vent holes, inspection holes, fittings, and exposed scarfed or tapered surfaces.

1-70. FINISHING WITH FABRIC OR TAPE. A number of systems for exterior finishing have STC approval and are manufactured under a PMA. Follow the product manufacturer's instructions for the system used.

a. If the finish surrounding the repair is a traditional dope system, seal the wood grain with a suitable solvent resistant one-part varnish, commonly described as "dope proof," or a two-part epoxy varnish. Follow with two coats of clear dope, and allow sufficient drying time between coats.

b. Apply a third coat of clear dope and lay a piece of pinked-edge airplane cloth into the wet film. All air bubbles should be worked out by brushing to ensure maximum adhesion. When dry, apply one brush coat, to ensure proper penetration, and at least one spray coat of clear dope. The dried spray coat may be sanded with fine sandpaper to obtain a smoother finish. Complete the refinishing of the surface by application of a topcoat as required to match the adjacent area.

1-71. SEALING OF BOLT HOLES. Bolt holes in wooden structure provide a vulnerable entry point for moisture. Variations in moisture content around bolt holes can lead to decay or splitting. In addition, excessive moisture at bolt holes promotes corrosion of the bolts. Sealing of the wood surfaces in bolt holes can be accomplished by application of varnish or other acceptable sealer into the open hole. The sealer must be allowed to dry or cure thoroughly prior to bolt installation.

1-72.—1-79. [RESERVED.]

CHAPTER 2. FABRIC COVERING

SECTION 1. PRACTICES AND PRECAUTIONS

2-1. GENERAL. Cotton and Irish linen fabrics were the airframe coverings of choice from WWI through the 1950's. However, increases in cost and the short lifespan of natural fabrics became the driving factors which resulted in almost 100 percent replacement of original airframe fabrics by man-made, STC-approved, polyester, and glass filament fabric.

2-2. PROBLEM AREAS.

a. Deterioration. Polyester fabric deteriorates only by exposure to ultraviolet radiation as used in an aircraft covering environment. When coatings completely protect the fabric its service life is infinite. Therefore, it is very important to thoroughly protect the structure from deterioration before covering and provide adequate inspection access to all areas of fabric-covered components to allow inspection for corrosion, wood rot, and mice infestation. Multiple drain holes in the lower ends of all fabric-covered sections also provide needed ventilation to remove condensation.

b. Tension. Polyester fabric obtains maximum tension on an airframe at 350 °F, and will not be excessive on aircraft originally covered with natural fabric and 12 coats of Nitrate or Butyrate Dope. However, dope applied over full heat-tauted fabric can develop excess tension after aging and damage light aircraft structures. Coatings other than dope will not increase fabric tension after aging. The heat-tauting instructions given in the manual of each STC-approved covering process should be followed.

2-3. AIRCRAFT FABRIC-SYNTHETIC.

a. STC-Approved Covering Materials. There is a wide selection of STC-approved covering materials available which utilize synthetic fabric falling within the generic class "Polyester" and may vary in characteristics. Difference in the fabric may be denier, tenacity, thread count, weight, shrink, tension, and weave style.

b. Polyester Filaments. Polyester Filaments are manufactured by polymerization of various select acids and alcohols, then extruding the resulting molten polymers through spinnerets to form filaments. The filaments are heat stretched to reduce to the desired denier or size. It is the heat stretching that imparts a memory in the filaments causing them to try and return to their original shorter length when reheated at a controlled temperature. Overheating will cancel the memory and melt the filaments.

c. Covering Procedures. Coating types, covering accessories, and covering procedures also may vary; therefore, the covering procedures given in the pertinent manuals must be followed to comply with the STC. The FAA STC-approved installation takes precedence over instructions in this advisory circular.

d. Installation. Initial installation of polyester fabric is similar to natural fabric. The fabric is installed with as little slack as possible, considering fittings and other protrusions. It may be sewn into an envelope, installed as a blanket, or installed by cementing to the airframe with a fabric cement. Each STC may differ in the cement seam overlap, type of sewn seam, heat shrinking procedures, and temperature.

2-4. AIRCRAFT FABRIC-NATURAL. Physical specifications and minimum strength requirements for natural fiber fabric, cotton and linen, used to recover or repair components of an aircraft, are listed in table 2-1. Tear resistance is an important factor when considering aircraft fabric. A test method such as ASTM D 1424 is recommended. Technical Standard Order TSO-C15d, entitled Aircraft Fabric, Grade A (AMS 3806D); and TSO-C14b, Aircraft Fabric, Intermediate Grade (AMS 3804C) current edition, respectively, describe the minimum standards that all fabric must meet to qualify as aircraft covering material.

2-5. RECOVERING AIRCRAFT. Recover or repair aircraft with a fabric of equal quality and strength to that used by the original aircraft manufacturer. It is recommended that fabric conforming to TSO-C15d or TSO-C14b be used to recover aircraft originally covered with lower strength fabric conforming to AMS 3802, current edition.

NOTE: Recovering or repairing aircraft with any type fabric and/or coating other than the type used by the original aircraft manufacturer is considered a major alteration. Obtain approval from the FAA on fabric and installation data. Cotton and linen rib lacing cord, machine and hand-sewing thread, and finishing tapes should not be used with polyester and glass fabric covering.

a. Reinforcing tape minimum tensile strength is listed in table 2-2. Reinforcing tape meeting specification MIL-T-5661, Type I, current edition, is acceptable. Reinforcing tape should have a minimum 40 lb. resistance without failure when static tested in shear against a single rib lace, or a pull-through resistance when tested against a single-wire clip, rivet, screw, or any other type of fabric-to-rib attachment. Reinforcing tape is used over the rib cab on top of the fabric and for inter-rib bracing.

b. Finishing Tape, sometimes referred to as surface tape, should have the same properties as the fabric used to cover the aircraft.

c. Lacing Cord shall have a minimum breaking strength of 40 lb. Lacing cord meeting the specifications listed in table 2-2 is acceptable. Rib lace cord should have a microcrystalline fungicidal wax, paraffin-free wax, or beeswax coating, or other approved treatment to prevent wearing and fraying when pulling through the structure.

d. Machine Thread shall have a minimum breaking strength of 5 lb. Thread meeting the specifications listed in table 2-2 is acceptable.

e. Hand-Sewing Thread shall have a minimum breaking strength of 14 lb. Thread meeting the specifications listed in table 2-2, is acceptable. When covering with STC-approved fabric covering material, use the type of sewing thread approved by the STC and manufactured under the specific PMA.

f. Flutter Precautions. When re-covering or repairing control surfaces, especially on high performance airplanes, make sure that dynamic and static balances are not adversely affected. Weight distribution and mass balance must be considered to preclude to possibility of induced flutter.

2-6. PREPARATION OF THE STRUCTURE FOR COVERING. One of the most important items when covering aircraft is the proper preparation of the structure. Before covering, the airframe must be inspected and approved by a FAA-certified mechanic or repair station.

TABLE 2-1. Cotton and linen fabrics.

Materials	Specification	Minimum Tensile Strength New (undoped)	Minimum Tearing Strength New (undoped) (ASTM D 1424)	Minimum Tensile Strength Deteriorated (undoped)	Thread Count Per Inch	Use and Remarks
Airplane cloth mercerized cotton (Grade "A").	TSO-C15d, as amended, references Society Automotive Engineers AMS 3806d, as amended or MIL-C-5646	80 pounds per inch warp and fill.	5 pounds warp and fill.	56 pounds per inch.	80 min., 84 max. warp and fill.	For use on all aircraft. Required on aircraft with wing loading of 9 p.s.f. or greater or placard never exceed speed of 160 m.p.h. or greater.
Airplane cloth mercerized cotton.	TSO-C14b, as amended, references Society Automotive Engineers AMS-3804c, as amended.	65 pounds per inch warp and fill.	4 pounds warp and fill.	46 pounds per inch.	80 min., 94 max. warp and fill.	For use on aircraft with wing loading less than 9 p.s.f. and never exceed speed of less than 160 m.p.h.
Airplane cloth mercerized cotton.	Society Automotive Engineers AMS 3802, as amended.	50 pounds per inch warp and fill.	3 pounds warp and fill.	35 pounds per inch.	110 max. warp and fill.	For use on gliders with wing loading of 8 p.s.f. or less, provided the placarded never-exceed speed is 135 m.p.h. or less.
Aircraft linen.	British 7F1.					This material meets the minimum strength Requirements of TSO-C15.

a. Battery Box Treatment. An asphaltic, rubber-based acid-proof coating should be applied to the structure in the area of a battery box, by brush, for additional protection from battery acid. Control cables routed in the area of the battery box should be coated with paralketone.

b. Worn Holes. Oversized screw holes or worn size 4 self-tapping screw holes through ribs and other structures used to attach fabric may be redrilled a minimum 1-1/2 hole diameter distance from the original hole location with a # 44 (0.086) drill bit. Size 6 screws, drill bit size # 36 (0.1065), may be installed in stripped or worn holes drilled for size 4 screws, usually without redrilling. Worn holes for wire clips and wire barbs should be redrilled a minimum 1-1/2 hole distance from the original locations using a drill jig to ensure correct spacing, with the appropriate size drill bit. Drill bit size # 30 (0.128) may be used to redrill oversize holes for 1/8-inch diameter blind rivets a minimum 1-1/2 hole diameter distance from the original location.

TABLE 2-2. Cotton and Linen, Tapes and Threads.

Materials	Specification	Yarn Size	Minimum Tensile Strength	Yards Per Pound	Use and Remarks
Reinforcing tape, cotton.	MIL-T-566 1 E, Type 1 MIL-Y-1140H		150 pounds per 1/2 inch width.		Used as reinforcing tape on fabric and under rib lacing cord. Strength of other widths approx. in proportion.
Lacing cord, prewaxed braided cotton.	Federal T-C-57 1F		40 pounds.	310 minimum.	Lacing fabric to structures. Unless already waxed, must be lightly waxed before using.
Lacing cord, braided cotton.	MIL-C-5648A		80 pounds.	170 minimum.	Lacing fabric to structures. Unless already waxed, must be lightly waxed before using.
Lacing cord thread, high tenacity cotton.	MIL-T-5660B	Ticket No. 10.	62 pounds.	480 minimum.	Lacing fabric to structures. Unless already waxed, must be lightly waxed before using.
Machine thread cotton	Federal V-T-276H	20/4 ply	5 pounds.	5,000 nominal.	Use for all machine sewing.
Hand-Sewing thread cotton.	Federal V-T-276H Type III B	8/4 ply	14 pounds.	1,650 nominal.	Use for all hand-sewing. Use fully waxed thread.
Finishing (Surface) tape cotton.	Same as fabric used.		Same as fabric used.		Use over seams, leading edges, trailing edges, outer edges and ribs, pinked, raveled or straight edges.

c. Fairing Precautions. Aluminum leading edge replacement fairings installed in short sections may telescope during normal spar bending loads or from thermal expansion and contraction. This action may cause a wrinkle to form in the fabric, at the edge of the lap joint. Leading edge fairing sections may be fastened together with rivets or screws to prevent telescoping after installation. Trailing edges should be adequately secured to prevent movement and wrinkles.

d. Dope Protection. Solvents found in nitrate and butyrate dope will penetrate, wrinkle, lift, or dissolve most one-part wood varnishes and one-part metal primers. All wood surfaces that come in contact with doped fabric should be treated with a protective coating such as aluminum foil, cellulose tape, or dope-proof paint to protect them against the action of the solvents in the dope. This can also be accomplished by recoating with a suitable, solvent resistant two-part epoxy varnish, which will be impervious to solvent penetration and damage after curing. Clad aluminum and stainless steel parts need not be dope-proofed.

(1) A solvent-sensitive primer on ferrous metal and aluminum alloy components which will be in contact with fabric may be protected from solvent damage by overcoating with a two-part epoxy primer. Epoxy primer meeting MIL-P-53022B is acceptable.

(2) Small metal or wood surfaces, such as rib caps, to which fabric will not be dope bonded as a part of the particular fabric attachment procedure may be protected from dope damage by cellophane tape or aluminum foil.

e. Chafe Protection. Fabric and finishing tape is often cut through with sandpaper over sharp edges during the coating and finishing procedure and later polishing. All sharp metal edges or protruding screws, nails, rivets, and bolt heads should be covered with an anti-chafe tape to prevent cutting and wearing through the fabric after installation. Use appropriate non-bleeding cotton adhesive coated tape, finishing tape, or strips of fabric, cut from the fabric being used to cover the aircraft, doped in place.

(1) Small holes cut through the fabric to accommodate flying wires, control cables, and fittings, must be reinforced with finishing tape or fabric patches cut from the same fabric used for the covering.

(2) Areas needing additional chafe protection such as control cables routed firm against the fabric surface should be protected with patches cut from cotton duck, leather, or plastic. These patches may be sewn, doped, or cemented in place, as appropriate.

(3) Any drag and anti-drag wires in the wings should be protected from chafing at cross points.

f. Inter-Rib Bracing. Use a woven fabric tape of the same quality and width as that used for the rib lace reinforcing, where so incorporated in the wing design by the original aircraft manufacturer. When the original routing for the inter rib bracing is not known, the tape will be routed diagonally, alternating between the top and bottom of each rib cap on each successive rib, if a single pair, half way between the front and rear spars. The number of tape pairs will duplicate the original aircraft manufacturer's installation. Tapes will be routed continuously from the wing butt to the wingtip bow, with one turn of tape around each intermediate rib cap strip. Care should be given to position the tape so as not to interfere with control cables, bellcranks or push-pull rods.

g. Preparation of Plywood Surfaces for Covering. Prior to covering plywood surfaces, prepare the surface by sanding, cleaning, and applying sealer and dope. When plywood surfaces are to be covered with light weight glass fiber deck cloth instead of fabric, no sealer or dope should be applied to the plywood as it would inhibit penetration of epoxy resin.

(1) Sand plywood surfaces as needed to remove old loose dope or varnish residue to provide a clean bonding surface. Remove any oil, grease, or other contamination with a suitable solvent such as naphtha. Small, rough areas and irregularities in the plywood surface and around any plywood repairs may be filled and smoothed with an appropriate commercial grade wood filler. Filling large warp depressions on plywood surfaces with a wood filler for cosmetic purposes is not acceptable.

(2) After cleaning and sanding all plywood surfaces, seal the wood grain with a suitable solvent resistant two-part epoxy varnish. After the varnish has thoroughly dried, apply two brush or spray coats of clear dope, allowing sufficient drying time between coats.

2-7. FABRIC SEAMS. Seams parallel to the line of flight are preferable; however, spanwise seams are acceptable.

a. Sewn Seams.

(1) Machine-sewn seams should be double stitched using any of the styles illustrated in figure 2-1 A, B, C, or D. A machine-sewn seam used to close an envelope at a wingtip, wing trailing edge, empennage and control surface trailing edge, and a fuselage longeron may be made with a single stitch when the seam will be positioned over a structure. (See figure 2-1 E.) The envelope size should accommodate fittings or other small protrusions with minimum excess for installation. Thick or protruding leading edge sewn seams should be avoided on thin airfoils with a sharp leading edge radius because they may act as a stall strip.

(2) Hand sew, with plain overthrow or baseball stitches at a minimum of four stitches per inch, or permanent tacking, to the point where uncut fabric or a machine-sewn seam is reached. Lock hand sewing at a maximum of 10 stitch intervals with a double half hitch, and tie off the end stitch with a double half hitch. At the point where the hand-sewing or permanent tacking is necessary, cut the fabric so that it can be doubled under a minimum of 3/8 inch before sewing or permanent tacking is performed. (See figure 2-2.)

(3) After hand sewing is complete, any temporary tacks used to secure the fabric over wood structures may be removed.

(4) Cover a sewn spanwise seam on a wing's leading edge with a minimum 4-inch wide pinked-edged surface tape with the tape centered on the seam.

(5) Cover a spanwise-sewn seam at the wing trailing edge with pinked-edge surface tape that is at least 3 inches wide. For aircraft with never-exceed speeds in excess of 200 mph, cut V notches at least 1 inch in depth and 1/4 inch in width in both edges of the surface tape when used to cover spanwise seams on trailing edges of control surfaces. Space notches at intervals not exceeding 6 inches. On tape less than 3 inches wide, the notches should be 1/3 the tape width. In the event the surface tape begins to separate because of poor adhesion or other causes, the tape will tear at a notched section, thus preventing progressive loosening of the entire length of the tape which could seriously affect the controllability of the aircraft. A loose tape acts as a trim tab only on a movable surface. It becomes a spoiler on a fixed surface and has no effect at the trailing edge other than drag.

(6) Make spanwise-sewn seams on the wing's upper or lower surfaces in a manner that will minimize any protrusions. Cover the seams with finishing tape at least 3 inches wide, centering the tape on the seam.

(7) Sewn seams parallel to the line of flight (chordwise) may be located over ribs. However, careful attention must be given to avoid damage to the seam threads by rib lace needles, screws, rivets, or wire clips that are used to attach the fabric to the rib. Cover chordwise seams with a finishing tape at least 3 inches wide with the tape centered on the seam.

b. Doped Seams.

(1) For an overlapped and doped spanwise seam on a wing's leading edge, overlap the fabric at least 4 inches and cover with finishing tape at least 4 inches wide, with the tape centered at the outside edge of the overlap seam.

(2) For an overlapped and doped spanwise seam at the trailing edge, lap the fabric at least 3 inches and cover with pinked-edge surface tape at least 4 inches wide, with the tape centered on the outside edge of the overlap seam.

(3) For an overlapped and doped seam on wingtips, wing butts, perimeters of wing control surfaces, perimeters of empennage surfaces, and all fuselage areas, overlap the fabric 2 inches and cover with a finishing tape that is at least 3 inches wide, centered on the outside edge of the overlap seam.

(4) For an overlapped and doped seam on a wing's leading edge, on aircraft with a velocity never exceed (Vne) speed up to and including 150 mph, overlap the fabric 2 inches and cover with a finishing tape that is at least 3 inches wide, with the tape centered on the outside edge of the overlap seam.

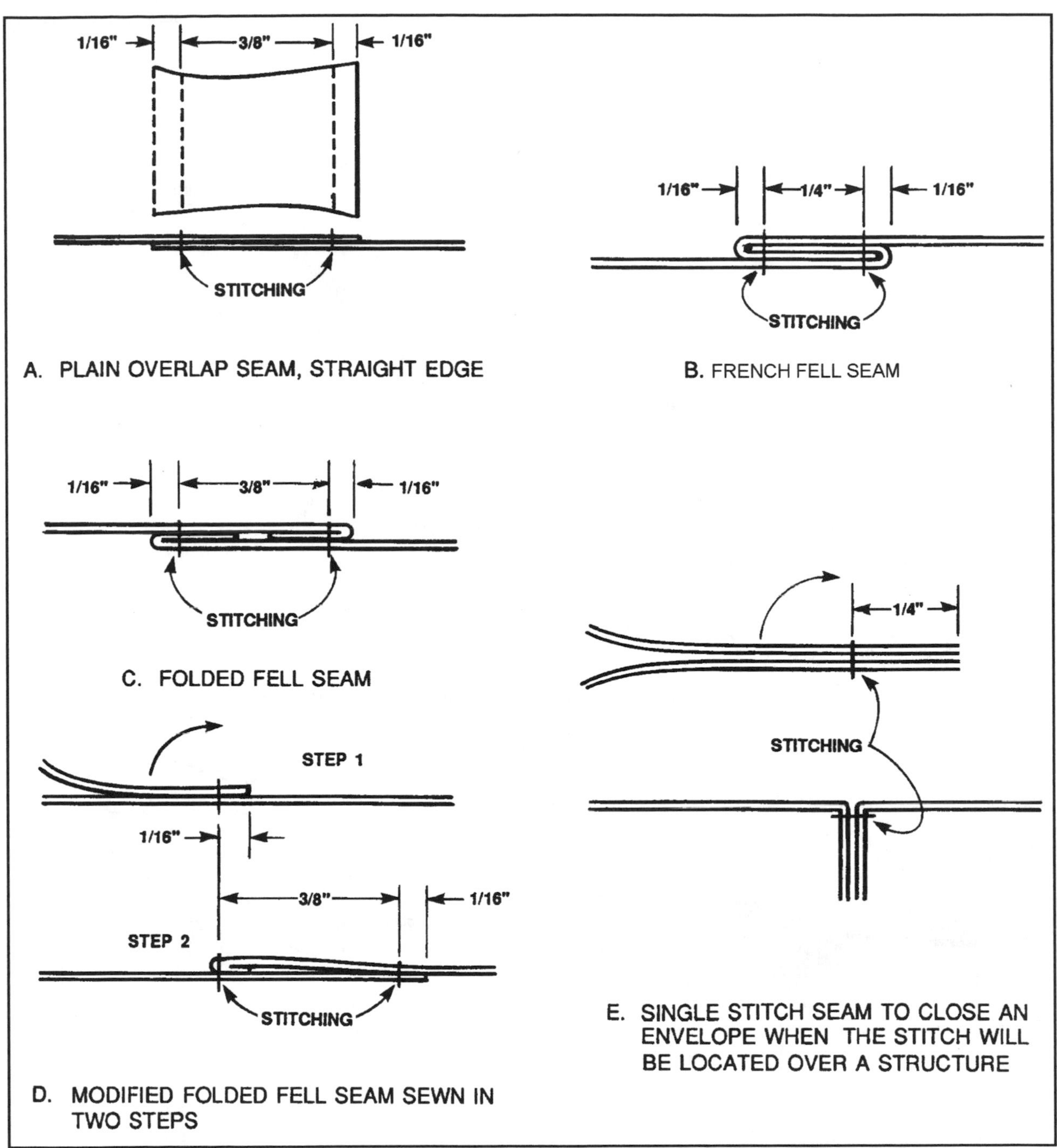

FIGURE 2-1. Fabric seams.

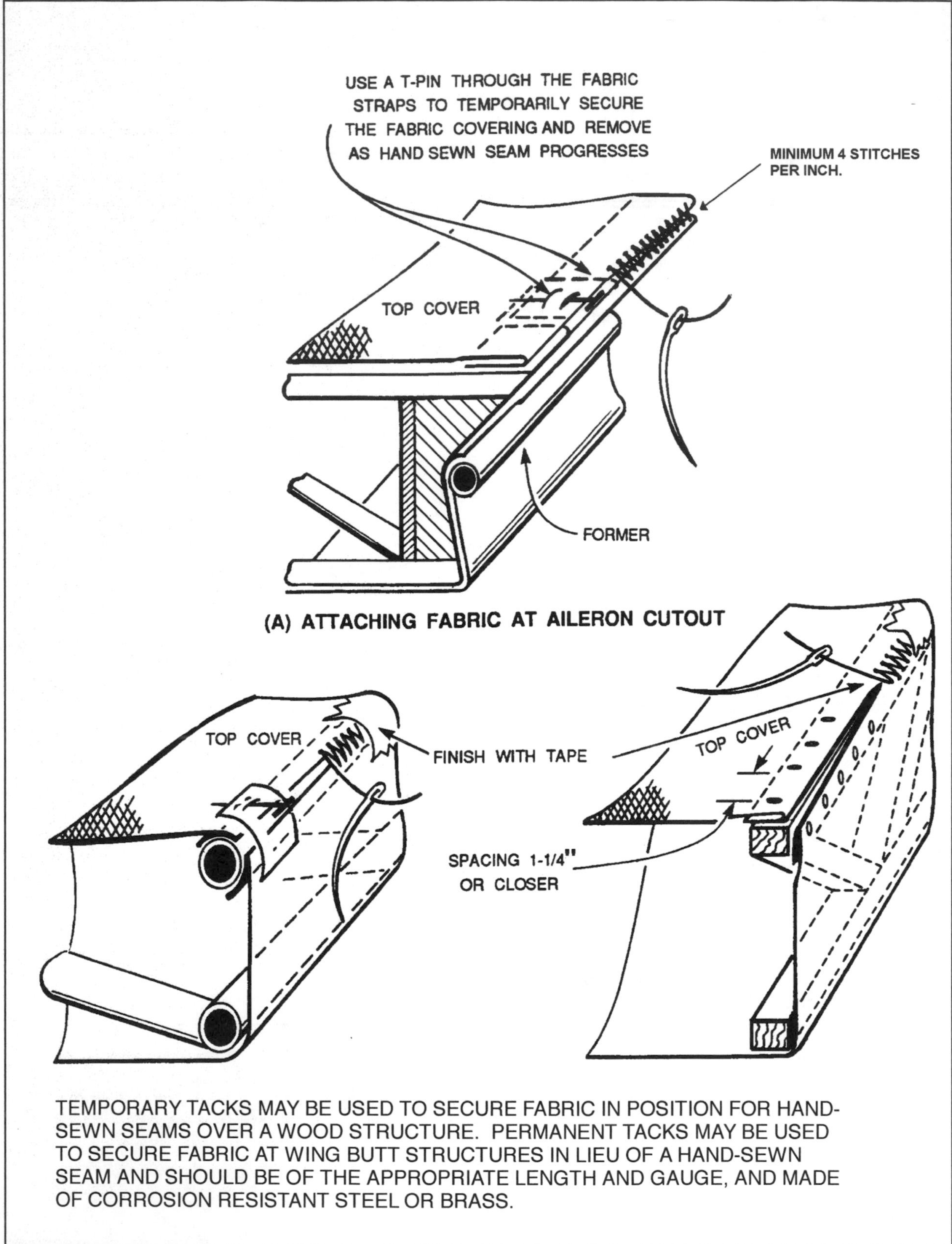
USE A T-PIN THROUGH THE FABRIC STRAPS TO TEMPORARILY SECURE THE FABRIC COVERING AND REMOVE AS HAND SEWN SEAM PROGRESSES
MINIMUM 4 STITCHES PER INCH.
TOP COVER
FORMER
(A) ATTACHING FABRIC AT AILERON CUTOUT
TOP COVER
FINISH WITH TAPE
TOP COVER
SPACING 1-1/4" OR CLOSER
TEMPORARY TACKS MAY BE USED TO SECURE FABRIC IN POSITION FOR HAND-SEWN SEAMS OVER A WOOD STRUCTURE. PERMANENT TACKS MAY BE USED TO SECURE FABRIC AT WING BUTT STRUCTURES IN LIEU OF A HAND-SEWN SEAM AND SHOULD BE OF THE APPROPRIATE LENGTH AND GAUGE, AND MADE OF CORROSION RESISTANT STEEL OR BRASS.

FIGURE 2-2. Typical methods of attaching fabric.

(5) For an overlapped and doped seam on the perimeter of a wing (except a leading edge), perimeters of wing control surfaces, perimeters of empennage surfaces, and all areas of a fuselage, on aircraft with a Vne speed up to and including 150 mph, overlap the fabric 1 inch and cover with a finishing tape that is at least 3 inches wide, centered on the outside edge of the overlap seam.

2-8. COVERING METHODS. The method of fabric attachment should be identical, as far as strength and reliability are concerned, to the method used by the manufacturer of the airplane being recovered or repaired. Carefully remove the old fabric from the airframe, noting the location of inspection covers, drain grommets, and method of attachment. Cotton or linen fabric may be applied so that either the warp or fill-threads are parallel to the line of flight. Either the envelope method or blanket method of covering is acceptable.

a. The Envelope Method. A wing envelope may be developed by two methods. Machine sew together, side by side multiple fabric sections, cut to reach chordwise around the wing, starting and ending at the trailing edge with a minimum of 1 inch excess length. The sewn envelope is then positioned around the wing and secured with closely spaced T-Head pins at the wingtip and trailing edge. Excess material may then be trimmed. Carefully remove the envelope and complete by machine sewing at the wingtip and along the trailing edge, except where the geometry of the wing (aileron and flap cut out) would prevent the sewn envelope from being reinstalled. After reinstalling the envelope, the un-sewn sections and butt end are then closed by hand-sewn or overlapped and doped seams in accordance with the aircraft Vne speed. (Refer to paragraph 2-7 b.)

(1) An alternative method, when fabric of sufficient width is available, is to sew together, side-by-side, two sections of fabric, placing the seams spanwise on the leading edge, then fit and sew the wingtip and trailing edge in the same manner as the multiple piece chordwise envelope.

(2) An envelope may be developed for the fuselage in the same manner, with a final closing along a longeron by hand-sewn or overlapped and doped seams in accordance with the aircraft Vne speed.

b. The Blanket Method. A blanket is developed by sewing together, side-by-side, multiple sections of fabric with the seams chordwise or two wide sections of fabric, side-by-side, placing the seam spanwise on the leading edge, the same as an envelope. Close the three remaining sides with a hand-sewn seam or overlapped and doped seams in accordance with the aircraft Vne speed. Small components may be covered by wrapping one piece of fabric over a straight leading or trailing edge, then closing three sides with hand-stitched or overlapped and doped seams in accordance with the aircraft Vne speed.

NOTE: All overlapped and doped seams will be made only over underlying supporting structures extending the full width of the seam.

c. Machine-sewn alternate. An alternate to machine-sewn seams on a wing envelope or blanket is to use two sections of wide fabric spanwise. Attach the fabric with overlapped and doped seams at the leading and trailing edge, wingtip and wing butt, in accordance with the aircraft Vne speeds. (Reference paragraph 2-7 b.) Smaller components may be covered in the same manner. The fuselage may be covered with multiple fabric sections with overlapped and doped seams on the longerons or other wide fabric-forming structures in accordance with the aircraft Vne speed. (Reference paragraph 2-7 b.)

d. Holes in Fabric. Never cut any holes in the fabric for inspection panels, spar fittings, or drain grommets; or attach the fabric to the airframe with rib lacing screws, rivets, clips, or rib stitch cord until the fabric has been semi-tauted and stabilized with several coats of dope.

2-9. REINFORCING TAPE.

a. Reinforcing tape should be securely bonded to the fabric surface with dope before cord lacing or installation of hardware. Where multiple attachments are in close proximity, such as on a wing rib, continuous reinforcing tape should be installed, extending at least 1 inch past the last attachment at each end. Random or wide spacing, such as on fuselage stringers or empennage surfaces, may be reinforced with 2-inch lengths of reinforcing tape centered on the attachment location.

b. Reinforcing tapes should be of the appropriate width for hardware attachment such as screws, rivets, wire clips, etc., which pierce the center of the tape. Reinforcing tape under cord lacing should be the same width as the rib to which the fabric is laced and may be comprised of multiple widths positioned side-by-side to achieve the required width.

c. When the aircraft Vne speed is over 250 mph, anti-tear strips, cut from the same quality fabric used to cover the aircraft, are recommended for use under reinforcing tape on the entire top surface of the wing and on the portion of the wing's bottom surface in the propeller slipstream. The propeller slipstream is considered to be the propeller diameter plus one outboard rib. The anti-tear strip should be installed completely around the wing, beginning and ending at the trailing edge in the propeller slipstream, and installed from the trailing edge over the leading edge and back under to the front spar on the balance of the ribs. Anti-tear strips should extend 1/2 inch past the wing rib cap edges and be thoroughly bonded to the fabric with dope before the reinforcing tape is installed. (See figure 2-3.)

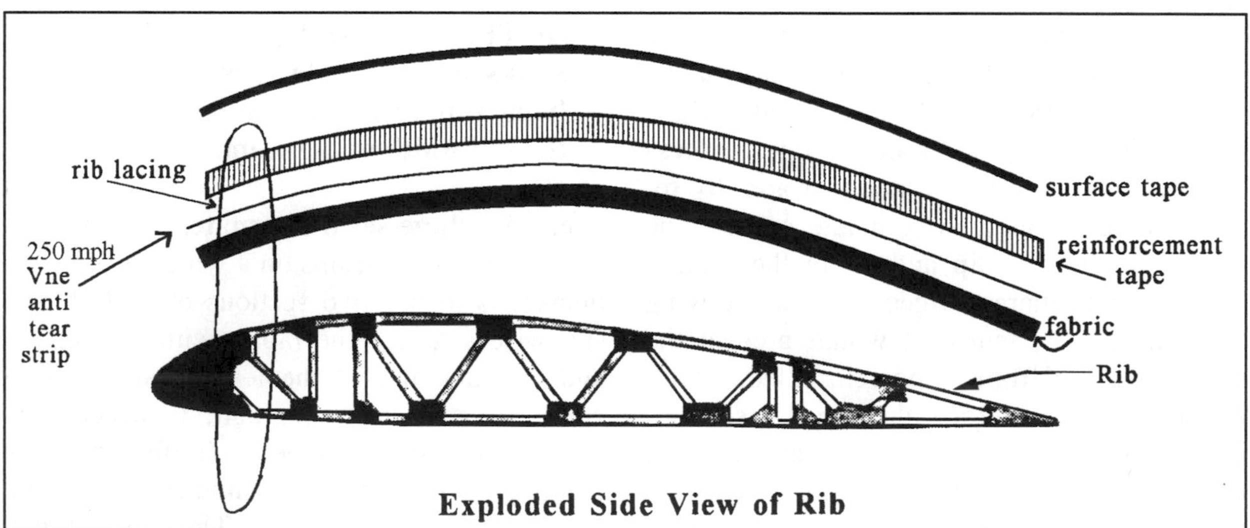

FIGURE 2-3. Exploded side view of rib.

2-10. LACING.

a. Fabric should be attached to aircraft components to prevent ballooning due to aerodynamic forces, in the identical manner and locations as used by the original aircraft manufacturer. Any deviation from the original method(s) of attachment, such as screws, rivets, wire clips, lacing cord, etc., are considered a major alteration and in conflict with the aircraft type design data. Obtain FAA approval on any deviation.

NOTE: When the type of rib lace knot used by the original aircraft manufacturer is not known, the modified seine knot shown in figure 2-4 through figure 2-9c will be used.

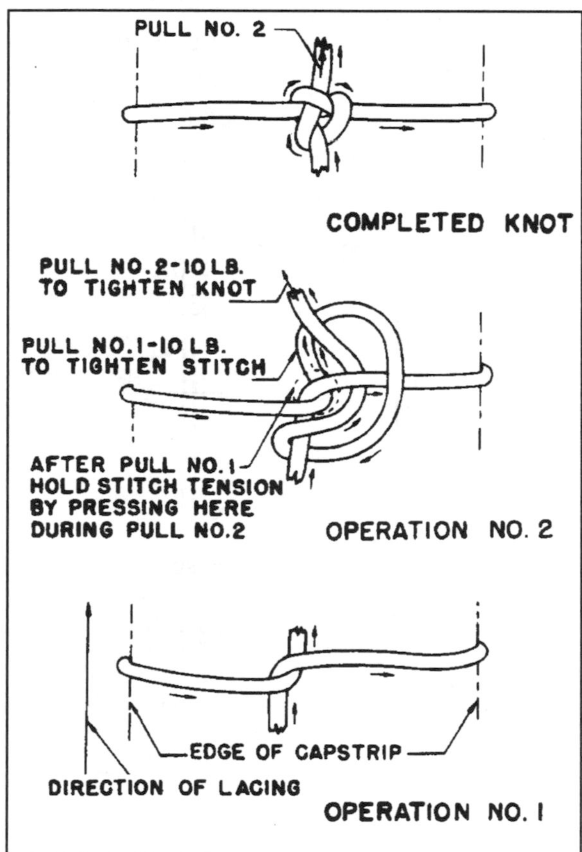

FIGURE 2-4. Standard external modified seine knot used for single and double rib lacing.

b. During the installation of lacing cord through a wing or any other component, special attention should be given to avoid interference with the routing of any control cable, bellcrank, or any other movable item. To prevent chafing and cutting of the lacing cord, control cables or any other movable items should be tensioned or positioned to their normal alignment before rib lacing and checked afterwards to ensure adequate clearance. When a lace cord will be chafed by a moving component, a blindstitch may be made around the top and bottom rib caps as illustrated in figure 2-11.

c. Stationary structures interfering with needle routing may be circumvented by aligning the needle forward or aft adjacent to the rib cap. Pull the needle through the wing and then return through the same hole and exit at the desired adjacent location.

NOTE: The first lace on a wing rib should be spaced from the leading edge fairing no more than 1/2 the required lace spacing for the balance of the rib.

d. Both surfaces of fabric covering on wings and control surfaces must be securely fastened to the ribs by lacing cord or any other method originally approved for the aircraft. Care must be taken to insure that all sharp edges against which the lacing cord may bear are protected by tape in order to prevent abrasion of the cord. Separate lengths of lacing cord may be joined by the splice knot shown in figure 2-10 or tied off. The first loop is tied with a square knot as illustrated in figure 2-5 and figure 2-9a, and the knot secured with a half hitch on each side after the lacing is pulled tight around the rib. The needle is then routed through the wing and around the rib cap at the

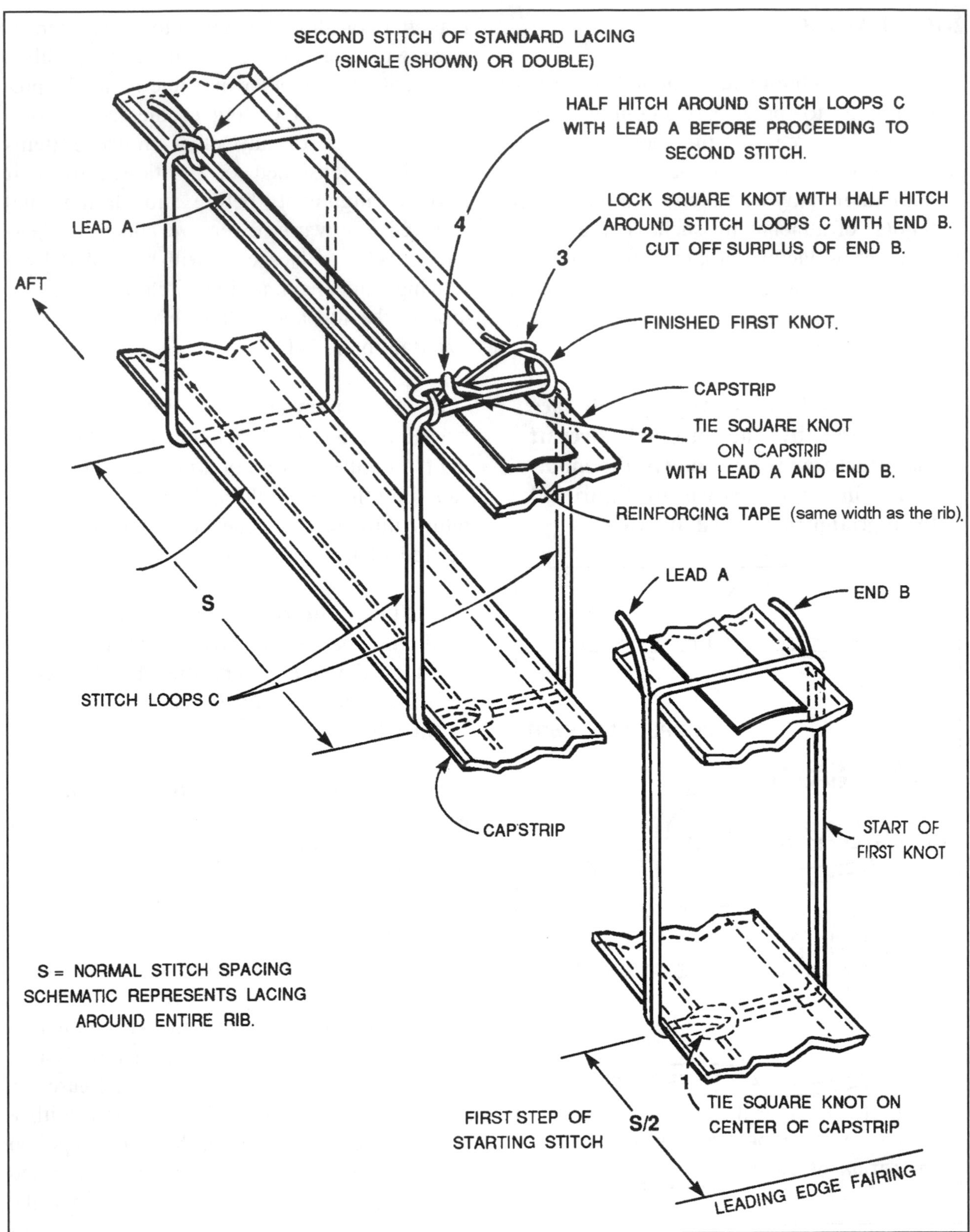

FIGURE 2-5. Starting stitch for rib lacing.

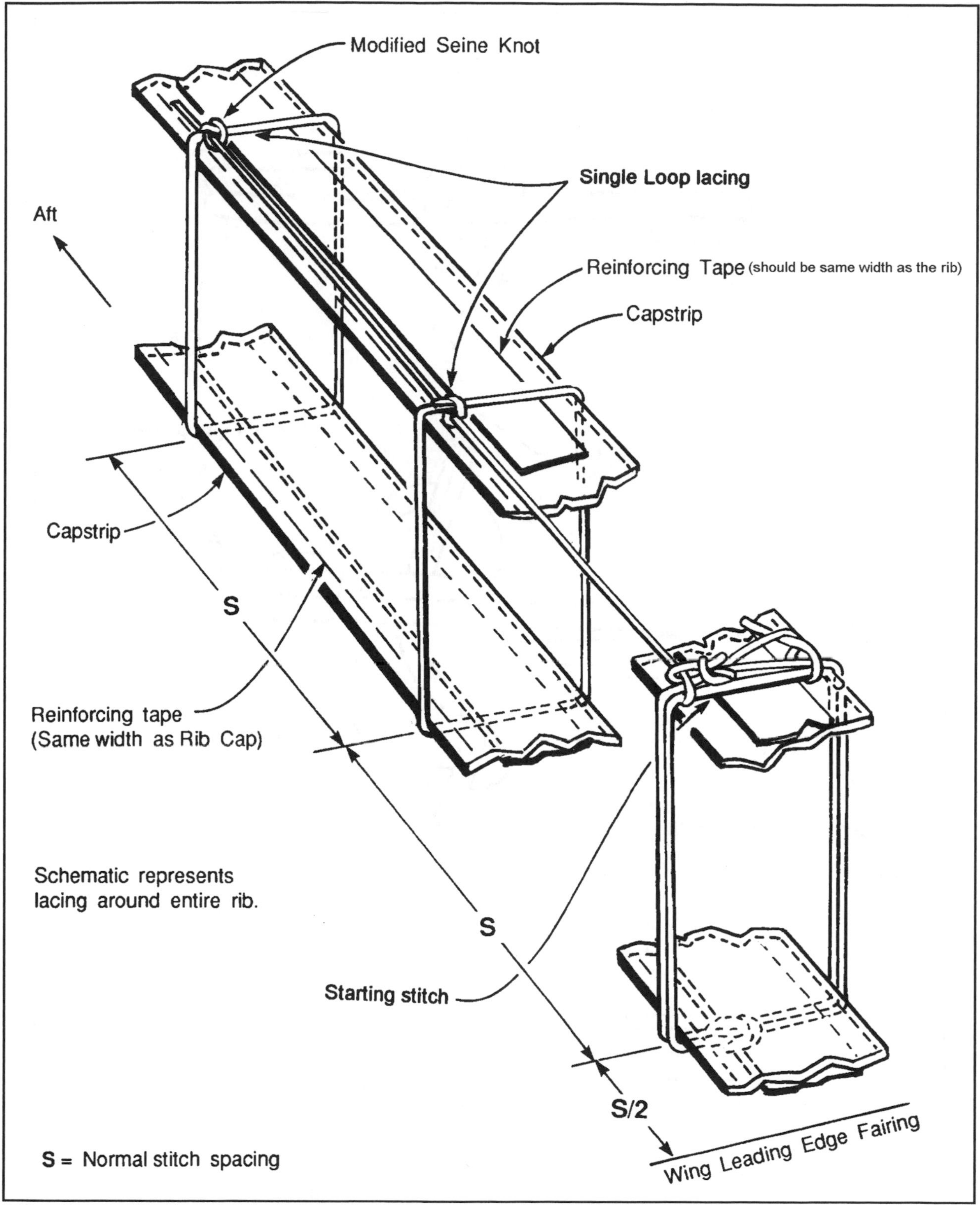

FIGURE 2-6. Standard single-loop lacing.

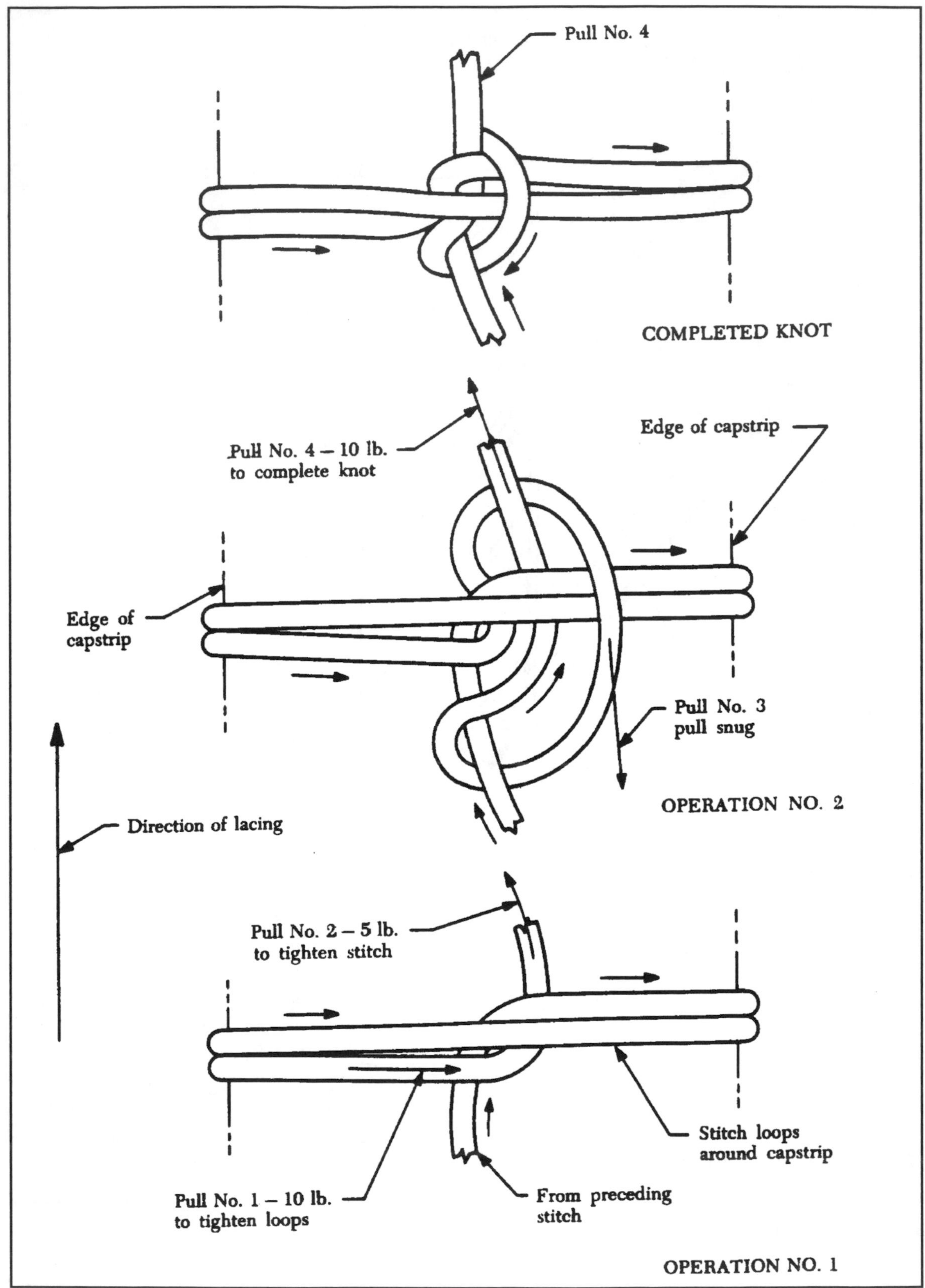

FIGURE 2-7. Standard knot for double-loop lacing.

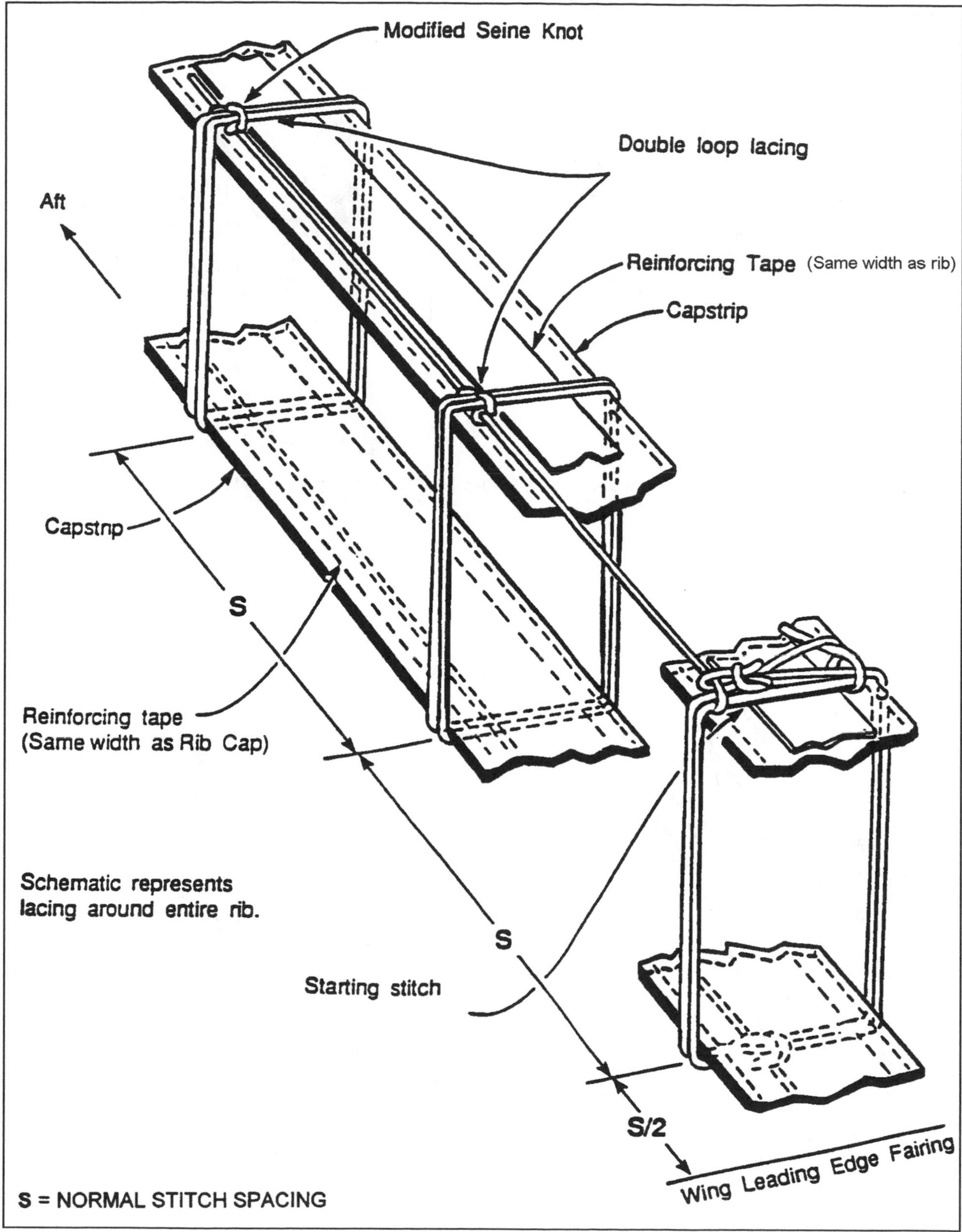

FIGURE 2-8. Standard double-loop lacing (optional).

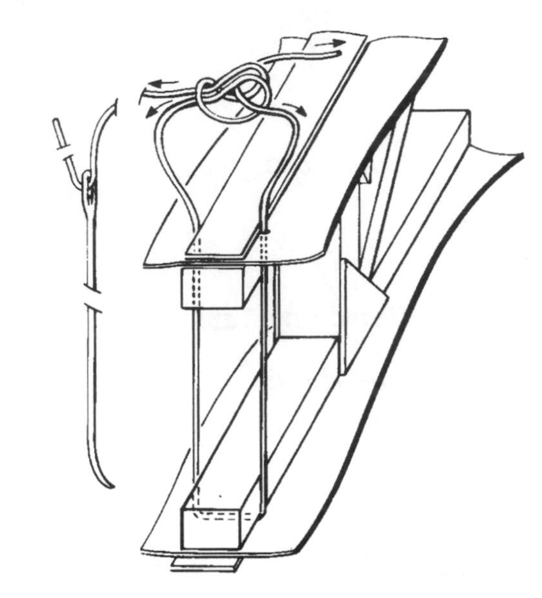

Step 1. Tie a square knot by passing the short end of the cord thru the fold-back loop, as illustrated.

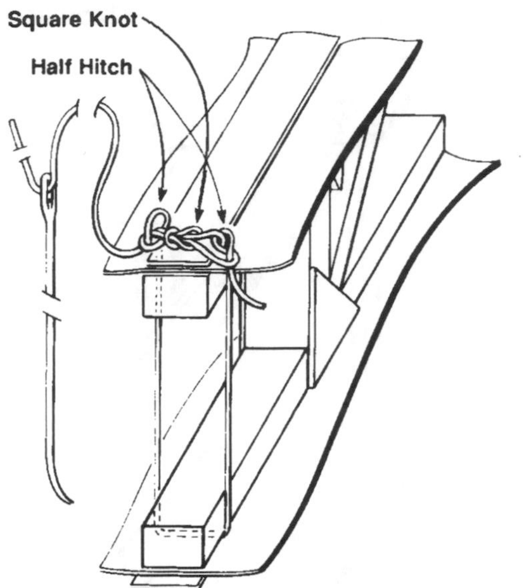

Step 2. Secure the tight square knot with a half hitch at each side.

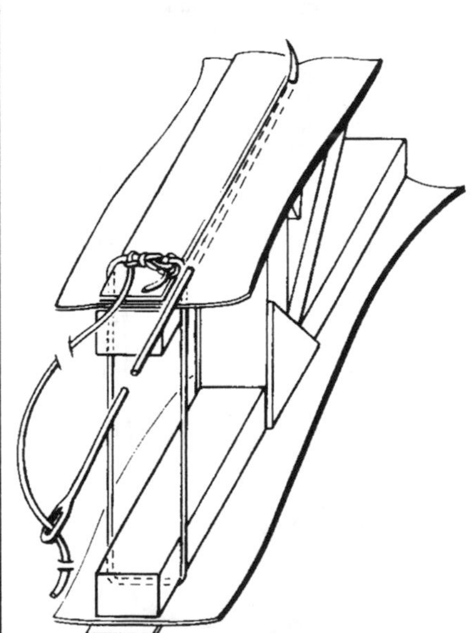

Step 3. Route the needle back thru the right hand hole and exit at the next pre-punched lacing location.

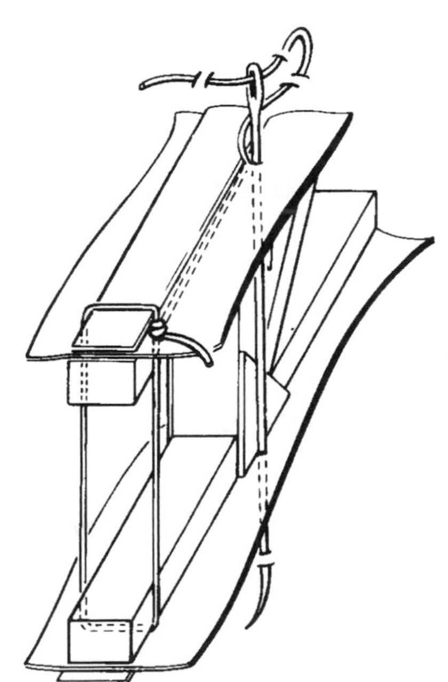

Step 4. Route the needle back thru the exit hole and thru the opposite fabric surface leaving approximately a 3" loop around a finger on the top surface.

FIGURE 2-9a. Alternate sequence to tie a modified seine knot for rib lacing.

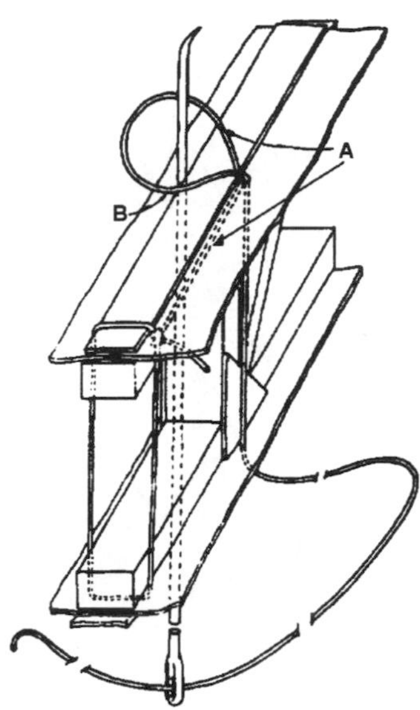

Step 5. As the needle is returned thru the top surface on the opposite side of the rib cap the loop is rotated to position cord section "A" to the forward side of the needle, then the needle is pulled thru.

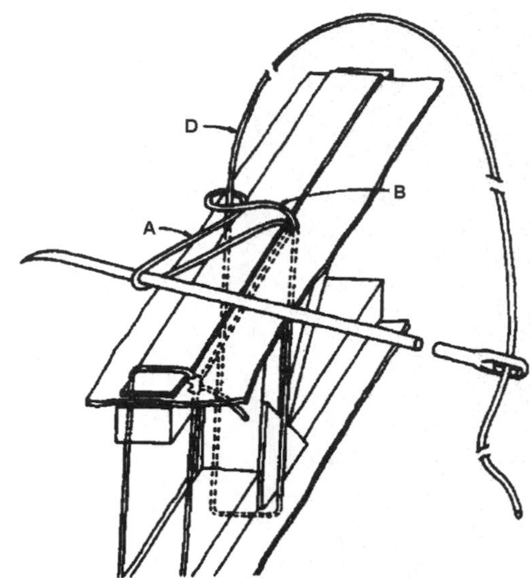

Step 6. The needle tip is routed under cord section "B" to hook and pull cord section "A" aft.

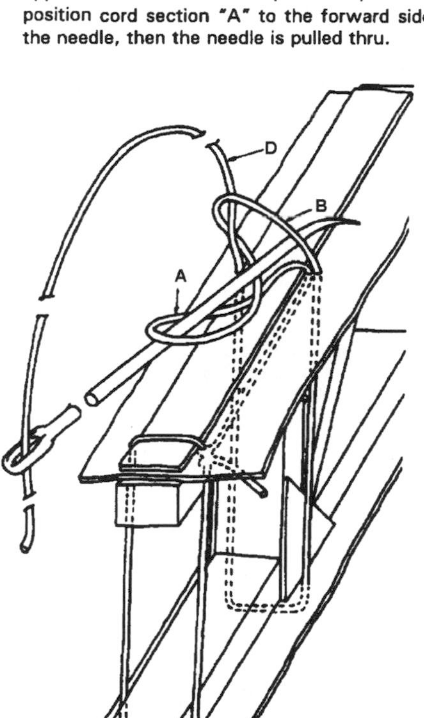

Step 7. The needle tip is then routed over the top of cord section "A" and under cord section "B."

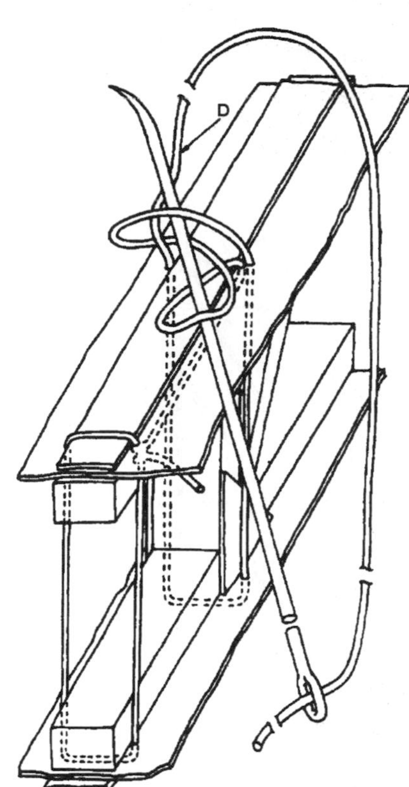

Step 8. The needle tip is then routed over cord section "D" and passed thru the lacing while holding cord section "D" perpendicular to the surface to avoid cord entanglement.

FIGURE 2-9b. Alternate sequence to tie a modified seine knot for rib lacing.

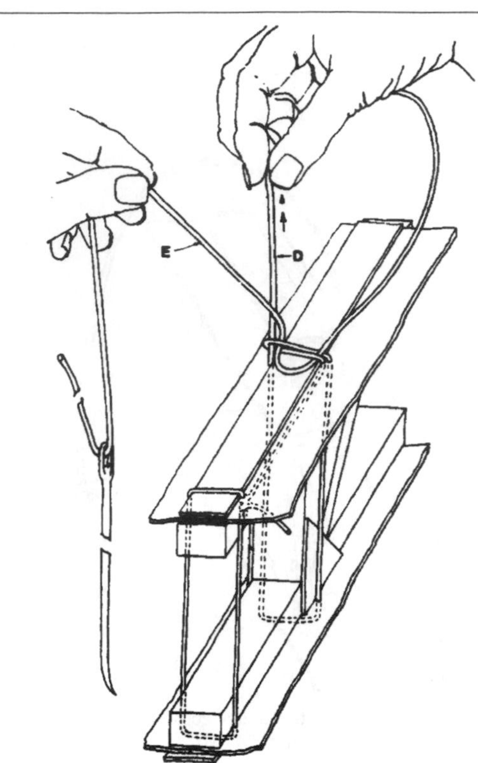

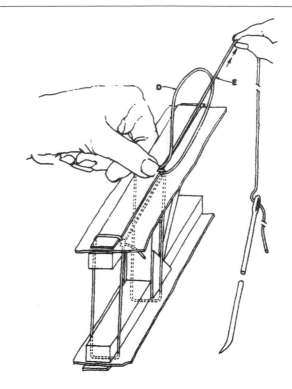

Step 9. Pull cord section "D" perpendicular to the fabric surface to remove all slack in the cord back to the last rib lacing knot while working the loose knot to the right side. Do not pull cord section "E."

Step 10. After all slack is removed by pulling cord section "D," switch hands and place a thumbnail on the loose knot formed on the right-hand side, then secure the knot by pulling firmly perpendicular to the fabric surface on cord section "E."

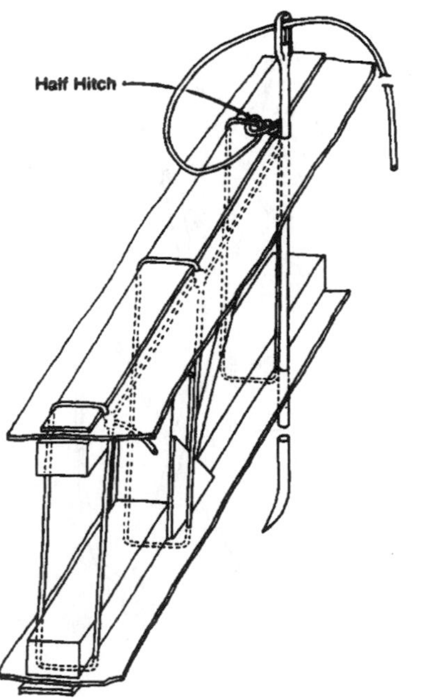

Step 11. After completing all lacing in the same sequence, the end is secured with a half hitch after the modified seine knot. The knot is pulled to the inside by routing the needle thru the wing before cutting the cord to leave the end inside.

FIGURE 2-9c. Alternate sequence to tie a modified seine knot for rib lacing.

next rib lace location with the cord and knot remaining on top of the fabric surface as illustrated in figure 2-5, figure 2-6, and figure 2-8. An alternate method is to route the needle under the fabric and out through the next lace location, then back down through the wing as illustrated in figure 2-9a through figure 2-9c. A modified seine knot is then tied as illustrated in figure 2-4 through figure 2-9c.

(1) Rotate each lace loop to place the knot at the side of the rib cap to reduce the protrusion and aerodynamic interference before moving to the next lace location, or the cord routed under the fabric to the next lace location as illustrated in figure 2-9a through figure 2-9c. The end cord is then cut off leaving a minimum of 1/4 inch stub. Lacing tension should be uniform.

(2) Repeated pulling of long lengths of lacing cord may remove wax coating from the cord and cause fraying. Convenient lengths of rib lacing cord may be used to lace long or thick ribs. The end of each length is tied off with a half hitch as illustrated in figure 2-9c, or if needed, separate lengths of lacing cord may be joined by using the splice knot illustrated in figure 2-10.

(3) Lacing is installed through other components, where applicable, in the same manner as a wing. Single, wide space lace attachments, usually used on empennage surfaces, are tied with a square knot and half hitch on each side, the same as a starting wing rib lace illustrated in figure 2-9a, steps 1 and 2. The lace may be rotated to place the knot under the fabric before cutting the cord.

e. Blind lacing on a fuselage, wing rib caps above and below a fuel tank, and any other component, when used by the original aircraft manufacturer, should be reinstalled in the same location and spacing as installed by the original aircraft manufacturer. The lace cord is routed around the stringer, rib cap, or other structure using an appropriate length, single or double pointed, curved needle as illustrated in figure 2-11. Blind laces are tied with a square knot, then pulled tight and secured with a half hitch at each side. The lace may be rotated to place the knot under the fabric surface before cutting the cord.

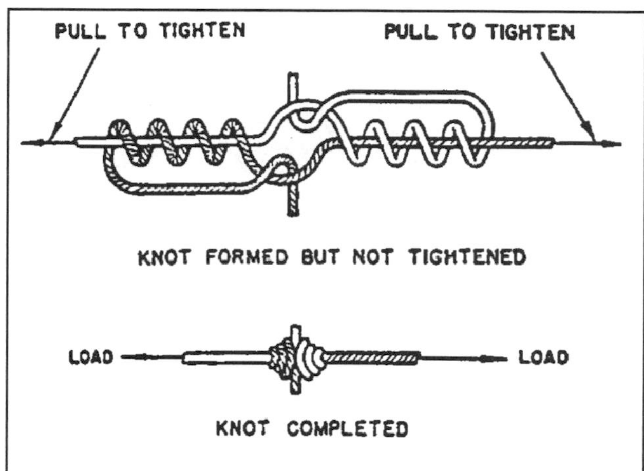

The splice knot is made by crossing the ends of the cord, and making four complete wraps with the small end of the free piece around the end of the standing piece. The end is then doubled back through the formed loop. The other free end is wrapped and doubled back. The long ends of the cords are then pulled until the knot is tight. The short ends are cut close to the knot. This finishes the splice knot.

FIGURE 2-10. Splice knot.

2-11. STITCH SPACING.

a. Rib lace spacing on wings, formerly referred to as stitch spacing, should be no greater than the spacing used by the original aircraft manufacturer. When the original spacing cannot be determined the maximum spacing illustrated in figure 2-12 should be used on the wings and wing control surfaces.

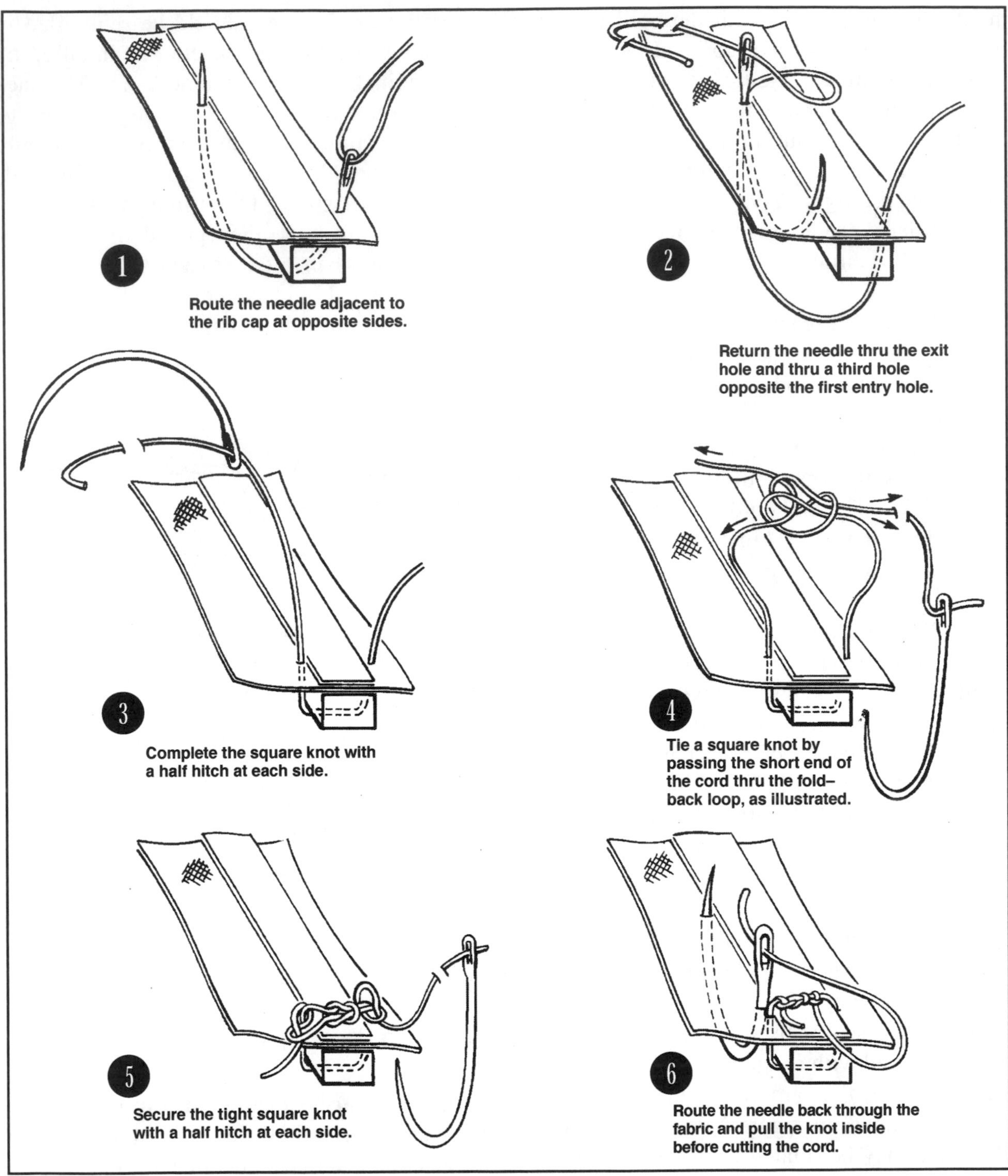

1
Route the needle adjacent to the rib cap at opposite sides.
2
Return the needle thru the exit hole and thru a third hole opposite the first entry hole.
3
Complete the square knot with a half hitch at each side.
4
Tie a square knot by passing the short end of the cord thru the fold–back loop, as illustrated.
5
Secure the tight square knot with a half hitch at each side.
6
Route the needle back through the fabric and pull the knot inside before cutting the cord.

FIGURE 2-11. Blindstitch lacing - square knot secured with half hitches.

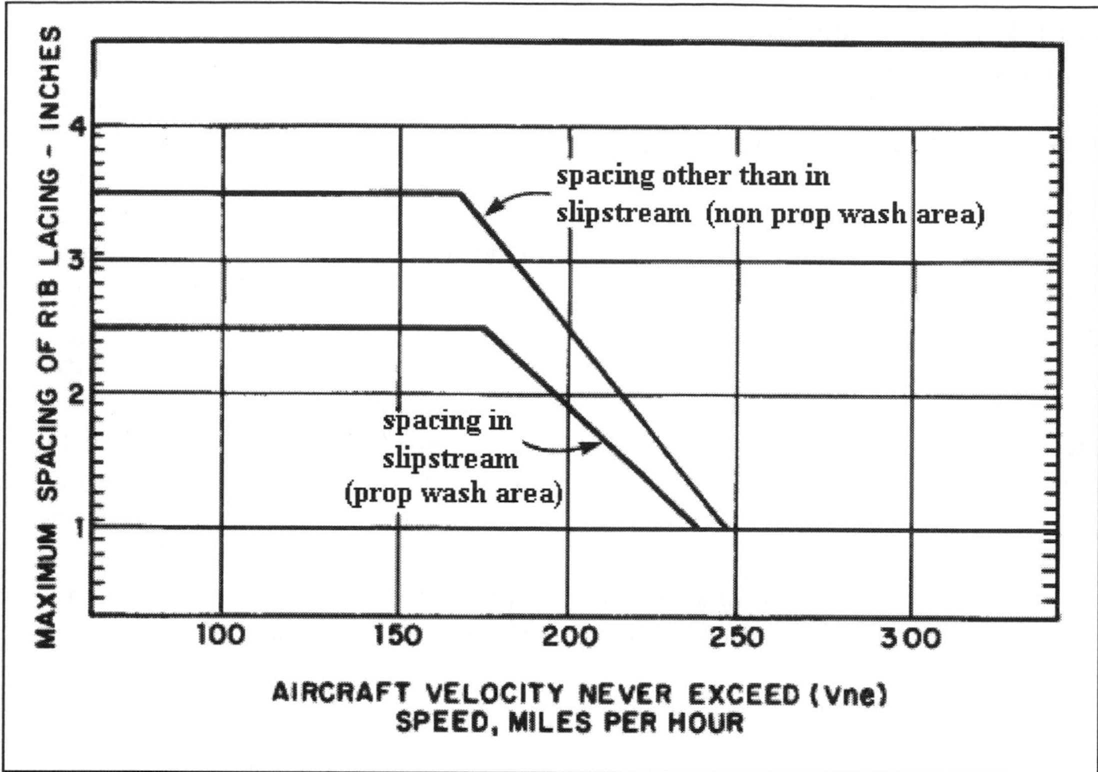

FIGURE 2-12. Fabric attachment spacing

b. When the original lace spacing on the empennage surfaces and fuselage, is not known, a maximum spacing of two times the spacing shown in figure 2-12 for the slipstream area (prop wash) on the wings may be used.

c. The installations of fabric attachments such as screws, rivets, wire clips, and rib lacing should be delayed until the fabric is stabilized and pulled taut with dope. This action is delayed to avoid pulling wing ribs and other structures out of alignment or tearing the fabric at attachment points as the fabric becomes taut. All lacing should be installed adjacent to the structure to which the fabric is being laced, to avoid tearing the fabric and/or creating slack in the cord loop when a load is applied. Where plastic washers were used by the aircraft manufacturer to provide increased pull-through resistance, under the heads of rivets or screws, the same diameter aluminum washer may be used as replacement. Aluminum washers are used because they are not affected by solvents found in adhesives or dopes, nor do they become brittle because of age or cold weather.

2-12. FASTENERS. Several light aircraft designs employ screws, rivets, or single-wire metal clips to secure the fabric to the wing.

a. Screws holding the old fabric can be removed after spinning a small sharpened tube around each screw or using a razor blade to cut and peel away the finishing tape. Care must be taken not to mark or scribe the underlying metal or wood structure. Blind rivets through ribs can be removed by drilling in the center to undercut the head.

b. Single-wire clips may be removed without damage to the rib by inserting a wide, thin screwdriver blade under the clip and carefully twisting. Apply a lifting force at the clip end to pull it up through the hole.

NOTE: It is important that any damage found to ribs, such as oversize rivet or screw holes, and cracks or breaks in the rib cap, should be tagged immediately for easy location and repair later.

c. When repairs are made to fabric surfaces attached by special mechanical methods, duplicate the original type of fastener. When self-tapping screws are used for the attachment of fabric to the rib structure, observe the following procedure:

(1) Redrill the holes where necessary due to wear, distortion, etc., and in such cases, use a screw one size larger as a replacement.

(2) Extend the length of the screw beyond the rib capstrip at least two threads.

(3) Install a thin washer, preferably aluminum, under the heads of screws and dope pinked-edge tape over each screw head.

2-13. FINISHING TAPE.

a. Finishing tape (surface tape) is installed after the fabric has been pulled taut with the initial dope application. This procedure is performed to prevent ripples from forming in fabric panels adjacent to newly applied tapes. Ripple formation is caused by the inability of the combined tape and fabric to tighten uniformly with adjacent fabric when additional dope is applied.

b. In addition to the tape widths required to be installed over fabric seams specified in paragraph 2-7, finishing tape should be installed as weather protection over all rib lacing, screws, rivets, wire clips, or other devices used to secure fabric. This includes wings, control surface ribs, empennage surface ribs, and fuselage stringers, where so installed by the original aircraft manufacturer. Tape width should be sufficient to bond the fabric a minimum of 3/8 inch on each side of all fabric attachments. Two inch width tape is normally used. Tapes over wing rib lacing should extend a minimum of 1/2 inch past each end of any reinforcing tapes. Random or widely-spaced attachments may be covered by individual sections of fabric or finishing tape.

c. Installation of finishing tapes for additional wear resistance is recommended over the edges of all fabric-forming structures. This includes fuselage stringers, longerons, leading and trailing edges, false or nose ribs, control surfaces, and empennage ribs not already covered and protected by a finishing tape that is required to be on a fabric seam or fabric attached to the structure. Compound surfaces, such as wingtip bow and empennage surfaces, are more conveniently taped using bias cut finishing tape, which easily conforms to the compound contour, rather than notching linear cut tape to fit the surface. Bias cut tape will be reduced to approximately two thirds the original cut width when pulled tight around a wingtip bow and should be considered when selecting the width of tape for the various locations.

d. Finishing tapes are applied by coating the fabric surface over which the tape will be applied with dope, applying the tape over the wet dope film, then brushing the tape firmly onto the fabric surface. This action will assure a good bond by thoroughly saturating and wetting the finishing tape.

2-14. INSPECTION RINGS AND DRAIN GROMMETS.

a. Inspection Rings. Inspection access is provided adjacent to or over every control bellcrank, drag-wire junction, cable guide, pulley, wing fitting, or any other component throughout the aircraft which will be inspected or serviced annually. They are installed only on the bottom side of the wings except where installed on the top surface by the original manufacturer.

(1) Cutting the holes may be delayed until needed; however, all covers should be finished in matching colors with any trim lines and stored until needed. Spraying matching colors a year later is expensive and time consuming.

(2) The 3-9/16 inch inside diameter cellulose acetate butyrate (CAB) plastic inspection access rings have become popular and bond satisfactorily with Nitrate Dope or Fabric Cement. Any metal inspection hole reinforcements of a particular shape or special design or size, installed by the original manufacturer, should be reinstalled after cleaning.

(3) Tapes or patches over aluminum reinforcements are optional, but recommended in the prop-wash areas on the wings and forward fuselage bottom.

(4) Fabric patches over plastic rings are strongly recommended because plastic is not a stable material, becomes brittle at low temperatures, and fatigues and cracks from prop blast vibration. Plastic rings are often cracked during removal and installation of spring, clip-held covers. Patches with a minimum 1-inch overlap, should be installed with dope.

b. Drain Grommets. Atmospheric temperature changes cause the humidity in the air to condense on the inside of aircraft surfaces and pool in all low areas. Rainwater enters through openings in the sides and top, and when flying, everywhere throughout the structure. Taxiing on wet runways also splashes water up through any bottom holes. Therefore, provisions must be made to drain water from the lowest point in each fabric panel or plywood component throughout the airframe while in a stored attitude. Drain holes also provide needed ventilation.

(1) Install drain grommets on the under side of all components, at the lowest point in each fabric panel, when the aircraft is in stored attitude. Seaplane grommets, which feature a protruding lip to prevent water splashes through the drain hole, are recommended over drain holes subject to water splashing on land planes as well as seaplanes. The appropriate-size holes must be cut through the fabric before installing seaplane grommets. Plastic drain grommets may be doped directly to the fabric surface or mounted on fabric patches then doped to the covering. Installing a small fabric patch over flat grommets to ensure security is optional. Alternate brass grommets are mounted on fabric patches, then doped to the fabric.

(2) After all coating applications and sanding are completed, open all holes through flat drain grommets by cutting through the fabric with a small-blade knife. Do not attempt to open drain holes by punching with a sharp object because the drain hole will not remain open.

2-15.—2-19. [RESERVED.]

SECTION 2. APPLICATION OF DOPE

2-20. GENERAL. Nitrate dope and butyrate dope are manufactured by treating cellulose, derived from wood pulp or cotton linter with select acids, then dissolving in a blend of solvents and adding plasticizers for flexibility. After a brush or spray application on fabric, the film develops tension and strength as the solvents evaporate. The tension and strength will increase in proportion to the total film thickness. The fabric functions as a film former and carries no load until a crack develops in the dope film. An excessively-thick dope film will develop too much tension and may warp or damage a light airframe.

a. Viscosity adjustments for brush or spray applications may also vary between brands. When the viscosity adjustment ratio is not provided or is unclear, the product manufacturer should be contacted for detailed instructions. If instructions cannot be obtained or the source of the dope is unknown, the dope should be considered suspect and its use is not advised.

b. Dope, which has been stored for an extended period of time or under adverse conditions, should be suspected of becoming acidic and should be tested before being used on cotton or linen fabric. In some cases, fresh production dope has also been found to have a high acid content and will begin to deteriorate cotton or linen in a period of a few months. The acid content of nitrate or butyrate dope should not exceed 0.06 percent, calculated as acidic acid. An acidity test can be performed by most testing laboratories if high acid content is suspected.

c. Butyrate dope is superior to nitrate dope in weather exposure tests. However, nitrate dope provides better adhesion to natural fiber than butyrate dope. The adhesion of butyrate dope to natural fibers is adequate; it is not necessary to use nitrate dope for the first application and butyrate dope for all other applications. The presence of naphtha in nitrate dope, manufactured in accordance with canceled Mil Specs formulas, causes nitrate dope to be incompatible with butyrate dope; therefore, nitrate dope should not be applied over butyrate dope for repairs or refinishing; however, butyrate dope may be applied over nitrate dope.

NOTE: Nitrate or butyrate dope thinners and retarders should not be substituted for each other, nor should automotive coating-type thinners be used.

d. Clear dope produces the most tension and strength. Aluminum-pigmented dope will weigh slightly more than clear dope and develop less tension and strength for the same film thickness. Pigmented color finishes will produce the least tension and strength due to the higher ratio of plasticizers.

e. During the coating-buildup procedure, solvents released from each succeeding coat will penetrate and be absorbed into the previous dope film, temporarily releasing the tension and increasing the drying time between coats as the dope film becomes thicker. If elapsed time between coats exceeds several weeks at temperatures above 70 F, it is recommended that several spray coats of an appropriate dope thinner or dope with retarder and/or rejuvenator added be applied to the lightly-sanded, dried dope film to open the surface and provide cohesion for the next coat. This will reduce the possibility of surface cracks caused by dissimilar tension between the old and new dope film.

f. All dope coats through the final finish may be applied with a brush; however, brush marks will be noticeable in the finish. With increasing environmental concerns, high pressure airless and high-volume low-pressure (HVLP) paint spray equipment is recommended over conventional siphon and pressure pot spraying equipment. High pressure airless and HVLP paint spraying equipment will greatly reduce paint over-spray and fogging. A spray gun, single coat is applied by overlapping each consecutive pass 50 percent of the fan width. A double coat is applied by repeating the coating application in the same direction, or at a 90° angle to the first coat (cross coat) before the first coat has flashed off or dried dust free. For safety and helpful tips for doping, see tables 2-3 and 2-4.

TABLE 2-3. Safety tips for dope/paint.

SAFETY TIPS.
Always ground the aircraft structure while sanding and painting.
Do not use an electric drill as a dope/paint mixer.
Wear leather-soled shoes in the dope/painting area.
Have an adequate, approved ventilation system.
Wear cotton clothes when doping or painting.
Wear an approved face mask or respirator when spraying.
Follow all the manufacturer's instructions.

TABLE 2-4. Tips for doping.

HELPFUL TIPS FOR DOPING.
Limits for optimum application of dope: relative humidity 20 to 60%; temperature range 65° to 75 °F.
Drying time will vary with temperature, humidity, amount of thinner used, and whether or not retarder was added to the mixture.
Do not recoat until the surface is completely dry and all active solvents have left the dope film.
Spray all coats except the first three or four clear coats, to avoid brush marks.
Over thinning is preferred to under thinning.
Addition of retarder will produce a smoother coat, but drying time between coats will be extended.
To get a clean line for the trim colors, apply a light coat of clear dope directly on the masking tape prior to painting. This will help eliminate the trim color from running under the masking tape.
Remember to always bring the dope to room temperature before using.
Rubbing compound and wax polish may be applied after all solvents have escaped (usually 2 weeks, depending upon the weather).

2-21. DOPE APPLICATION PROCEDURE (Natural Fabrics).

a. Step 1. After the cotton or linen fabric is installed in accordance with the procedures specified in paragraphs 2-7 and 2-8, the fabric is wetted with distilled water to remove wrinkles and fold creases, which will show in a gloss finish. Water may be applied by rubbing with a clean sponge or rag, or by using a paint spray gun. Do not use tap water. It may contain minerals which will contaminate the fabric.

(1) As water is absorbed by the fibers, the threads swell, resulting in temporary tauting of the fabric panel. The fabric should be allowed to dry before dope application, otherwise the water in the fibers will interfere with the dope penetration and adhesion.

(2) After the fabric has dried, the first coat of dope is applied, brushing in one direction to set the nap with a clean, non-shedding, 2-to 6-inch wide, semi-soft, long bristle paint brush.

(3) To offset the deteriorating effect of mildew or other fungus on natural fibers, especially in damp climates, it is recommended that a fungicide be added to the first coat of dope. The preferred fungicide is zinc dimethyldithiocarbamate powder, which should be prepared per the manufacturer's instructions. If no manufacturer's instructions are available the zinc powder may be stirred in at a ratio of 4 ounces, to one gallon of un-thinned nitrate or butyrate dope, after the powder is wetted to a paste with a 50/50 ratio of dope and thinner.

(4) Pre-mixed fungicidal dope, manufactured in accordance with the formula specified in MIL-D-7850, will have a transparent purple tint to indicate the fungicide additive. Dope manufactured with other colors to identify the manufacturers' products sold under proprietary trade names may or may not have a fungicidal additive.

(5) The viscosity of the dope should be adjusted to uniformly wet the fabric, indicated by the fabric becoming translucent so that it penetrates through the fabric but does not drip or run down the opposite side. Any dope-runs or pooling on the opposite side will shrink and distort the fabric, and may be visible on the finished surface.

(6) The ideal temperature for application of dope or other coatings is 65 to 75 F and the humidity should be less than 65 percent. As a general rule, each 10 F increase or decrease in ambient temperature will increase or decrease drying time by 100 percent. Dope should be allowed to warm to room temperature prior to attempting to adjust the viscosity.

b. Step 2. Depending upon the quality of the dope and the ratio of thinning, the fabric should start to become taut after the first brushed coat of dope has dried approximately 1 hour at 70 °F. A second, heavier coat is applied by cross brushing at 90°F to the first coat. Viscosity should be adjusted only as necessary to brush out a heavy uniform coat. If the fabric is not taut, with all sag removed, after the second coat has dried approximately 2 hours, a third coat may be applied.

c. Step 3. After the fabric has become semi-taut and stabilized with the initial dope application, and the rib lacing and other fabric attachments are completed as detailed in paragraphs 2-9 through 2-12, it is ready for "dressing out" as described in paragraphs 2-13 and 2-14.

d. NOTE: "Dressing out" means applying all the finishing tapes, reinforcing patches, inspection access ports, and drain grommets, etc.

e. Step 4. After the covering is a dressed out, one or more coats of clear dope are brushed over all finishing tapes and fabric reinforcing patches. This will balance the thickness of the dope film with the previously coated areas of the fabric. It is very important that the porosity of the fabric be filled while brushing to avoid pinholes showing in the finish.

f. Step 5. After drying at least 2 hours at 70 °F, a third heavy coat of clear dope is applied over the entire surface, preferably with a paint spray gun if brush marks are to be avoided. After the third coat of dope has dried at least 2 hours at 70 °F, the fabric should be taut and the dope film should show a gloss, depending upon the dope quality and the ratio of thinner added. If not, a fourth coat of clear dope may be applied, in the same manner as the third coat.

NOTE: Three to four clear coats of dope film showing a uniform gloss combined with the aluminum-pigmented coats and finish coats is considered satisfactory for light aircraft up to 9 lb. per square foot wing loading. Five to eight clear coats, depending upon the quality of the dope and resulting film thickness, are recommended for higher wing loading aircraft to assure the covering does not stretch and lose tension.

g. Step 6. After the clear coats are found to be satisfactory, two heavy cross-coats of aluminum-pigmented dope are applied with a spray gun to provide protection from ultraviolet (UV) rays. Tests have shown that UV radiation will deteriorate cotton, linen, and polyester fabric; however, polyester fabric deteriorates at a rate half that of cotton or linen under identical exposure conditions. UV radiation does not deteriorate glass fabric. Aluminum-pigmented dope blocks UV radiation and provides a sanding base. A gauge of ultraviolet protection in the field is to block all visible light from penetrating through the fabric. Drying time between the two coats should be at least 1 hour at 70 °F.

(1) An option to premixed aluminum dope is to use aluminum-pigment paste. Aluminum paste should be prepared per the manufacturer's instructions. If no manufacturer's instructions are available, mix 3 ounces (by weight), of 325-mesh aluminum-pigment paste, to 1 gallon of unthinned, clear dope. The aluminum paste should first be mixed to a cream consistency with a 50/50 ratio of dope and thinner before mixing into the unthinned clear dope. A higher ratio of aluminum-pigment added to the dope may cause a loss of primer-coat and finish-coat adhesion, and peeling may occur especially when high tack tape is used to mask for the trim colors and registration numbers.

(2) The viscosity of the mixed aluminum-pigmented dope should be adjusted for satisfactory spray gun application.

h. Step 7. After two coats of aluminum-pigmented dope have dried at least 4 hours at 70 °F, the surface may be wet sanded with # 280 grit (or finer) waterproof sandpaper. The aluminum-pigmented dope should be sanded only to develop a smooth surface, not sanded completely off to the clear dope undercoats. Do not sand over screwheads, rib lacing, or any structural sharp edges that will quickly cut through fabric and require patching. Additional coats of aluminum-pigmented dope may be applied and sanded, depending on the final finish desired. The last coat should not be sanded to assure ultraviolet protection along the edges of the finishing tapes and reinforcing patches is maintained.

i. Step 8. Three coats of pigmented color finish are applied with a paint spray gun, allowing adequate drying time between coats. The color finish may be wet sanded between coats, if desired, with a fine grit waterproof sandpaper. Adding blush retarder to the final dope finish will improve the gloss. After drying several weeks, a rubbing compound may be used to buff the finish and increase the gloss. A periodic application of a wax polish will help protect the finish from the weather and environmental pollution.

NOTE: Drain holes should be opened soon after all finishing is complete to insure drainage and to aid ventilation of the structure.

(1) When exposed to the sun, dark colors absorb more sun energy and convert that energy to heat more easily than light colors. High temperatures dry out wood structures and deteriorate organic materials in an aircraft structure. Preferably the lighter color shades are applied first and then overcoated with darker trim and registration number colors.

(2) Only high-quality, solvent-resistant crepe paper or polypropylene masking tape should be used to avoid finish bleed under the tape edge. Newspaper printing ink may transfer to a fresh finish and should not be used for masking paper. Plastic sheeting should not be used as a dust cover on a fresh finish due to possible bonding and damage.

2-22. COVERING OVER PLYWOOD. Exposed, stressed plywood surfaces, such as wings, must be protected from weather deterioration with fabric at least equal to that used by the original manufacturer. If the quality is not known, intermediate-grade fabric, meeting TSO-C14b specification, is acceptable. Fabric may be installed in sections with a 1/2 inch edge overlap without covering the overlap with finishing tape. Fabric may also be installed with the edges butted together, and the seam covered with a minimum 1-inch wide finishing tape. The seams may be oriented in any direction, in reference to the line of flight. However, overlapped seams, not covered with a finishing tape, should be oriented rearward. Fabric should be wrapped completely around a wing's leading and trailing edges and other components, where possible, to provide fabric-to-fabric continuity around all edges to avoid a poorly-bonded fabric edge from peeling from the plywood surface causing serious aerodynamic consequences.

a. After the plywood surface is prepared, and the two pre-coats of clear dope have dried as recommended in paragraph 2-6 g, the fabric is pulled snug and bonded with clear dope around the perimeter of the fabric section. The fabric is then wetted with distilled water to remove fold creases, in the same manner described for fabric panel areas. After the water has evaporated, a heavy coat of low-viscosity clear dope is brushed firmly through the fabric to soften the underlying dope pre-coat, insuring a good bond. Brushing techniques should be accomplished by moving the brush from one side across to the opposite side to remove all air bubbles and thoroughly saturate the fabric. This is indicated by the plywood grain being easily visible through the translucent fabric. Except for very small imperfections or small dents in the plywood surface, voids are not permissible between the fabric and plywood surfaces. Voids may allow the fabric to balloon from the plywood surface, creating adverse handling characteristics.

b. After the first dope coat has dried at least 1 hour at 70 °F, a second heavy coat of clear dope is applied by brush to fill the fabric weave and prevent pinholes. The installation of finish tape around the perimeter of the plywood surfaces, leading edges, and other wear points, is optional but recommended for wear and chafe protection. The application of aluminum-pigmented dope coating, sanding, and finish coats will be the same as that specified for fabric panel areas. Reinforcement grommets are not required on drain holes through plywood surfaces.

2-23. COATING APPLICATION DEFECTS.

a. Blushing. The appearance of light shaded dull areas on the surface as dope dries is the result of moisture in the atmosphere condensing on a surface due to the cooling effect of the fast-evaporating components of dope thinner escaping from the coating. Blushing can occur at any temperature when the humidity is above 65 percent. There are several ways to remedy this problem. The drying time may be slowed by adding up to 1 quart of blush retarder to 1 gallon of dope or by increasing the temperature of the dope room and eliminating any cooling draft from blowing across the surface. Blushed surfaces may be reworked by spraying several, closely-timed coats of a 50/50 blend of blush retarder and dope thinner to soften and return the dope surface to the original liquid state. Blush retarder, mixed with dope, may delay the full drying time by several days, but will eventually escape from the dope film if the room temperature is maintained an average of 70 °F.

b. Pinholes. Voids between the fabric threads that are not filled with the first coats of dope are called pinholes. They may be caused by fabric contamination, such as oil or finger prints, but are usually the result of improper dope application. Pinholes are usually found in a second layer of fabric such as finishing tapes and reinforcing patches or over underlying, non-porous structures; such as leading edges, turtle decks, and plywood surfaces. Any non-porous structure under fabric will act as a backstop and will resist complete dope penetration into the fabric. Microscopic cavities between the backstop and fabric collect escaping solvent vapors during the drying process and balloon up through the surface leaving pinholes, or become pinholes when the top of the balloon is sanded. Moisture, in the fabric or on the backstop surface, also interferes with complete dope penetration, resulting in pinholes. The remedy for pinholes, at any stage before the final finish coat, is to add blush retarder to low viscosity dope and carefully brush over the affected surfaces to penetrate into and fill the pinholes. Discontinue brushing after five or six strokes to avoid leaving brush marks.

c. Orange Peel. A rough spray gun-applied finish, similar to the texture of an orange peel, may be caused by one or more of the following conditions:

(1) Viscosity of material being sprayed is too high.

(2) Air temperature is too high.

(3) Spraying in direct sunlight, onto a hot surface or in a drafty/windy condition, which causes a fast solvent evaporation.

(4) Spray gun, tip, cap, and/or needle are not properly matched for the type material being sprayed.

(5) Volume of air available from the compressor not sufficient for spray gun.

(6) Wrong thinner used and drying too fast.

(7) Spray gun not properly adjusted. The spray gun should be adjusted to a uniform spray pattern with the material atomized to deposit fine, wet particles that merge and form a smooth film.

d. Blisters. One or more of the following conditions my cause blisters:

(1) Freshly coated surface placed in hot sunlight or high temperature area to accelerate drying time, causing the vapor from rapidly evaporating solvents to be trapped.

(2) Excessive high air pressure used to spray heavy coats which "blasts" air bubbles into the coating.

(3) Water or oil in air supply.

e. Runs, Sags, and Curtains. These defects may be caused by one or more of the following conditions:

(1) Viscosity of material being sprayed is too low.

(2) Coats applied too heavily.

(3) Insufficient drying time between coats.

(4) Spray gun held too close to work surface.

(5) Improperly adjusted spray gun.

f. Spray Gun Laps and Streaks. These defects may be caused by one or more of the following conditions:

(1) Spray gun not properly adjusted to spray a wet, smooth surface.

(2) Overspray on a partially-dried surface.

(3) Spray pattern not sufficiently overlapped on each pass.

(4) Viscosity of material being sprayed is too high.

(5) Metallic finishes sprayed too heavily allowing metallic pigments to move or flow after deposit, causing a marbled appearance.

2-24.—2-29. [RESERVED.]

SECTION 3. INSPECTION AND TESTING

2-30. GENERAL. All components of the covering should be inspected for general condition. Loose finishing tape and reinforcing patches; chafing under fairings; brittle, cracking, peeling, or deteriorated coatings; fabric tears and rock damage; broken or missing rib lacing; and rodent nests are unacceptable. The entire fabric covering should be uniformly taut with no loose or wrinkled areas, or excess tension which can warp and damage the airframe.

a. Excess Tension. There are no methods or specifications for measuring acceptable fabric tension other than observation. Excess tension may warp critical components, such as longerons, wing rib, and trailing edges out of position, weakening the airframe structure.

(1) Excess tension with cotton, linen, and glass fiber fabric covering is usually caused by excessive dope film on a new covering, or continuous shrinking of an originally satisfactory dope film as the plasticizers migrate from the dope with age. Heat from sun exposure accelerates plasticizer migration.

(2) Excess tension with polyester fabric, coated with dope, is usually caused by the combined tension of the heat tautened polyester fabric and continuous shrinking of the dope film as the plasticizers migrate from the dope with age.

b. Loose Fabric. Fabric that flutters or ripples in the propeller slipstream, balloons, or is depressed excessively in flight from the static position, is unacceptable.

(1) Loose or wrinkled cotton, linen, and glass fabric covering may be caused by inadequate dope film; poor quality dope; fabric installed with excess slack; or by a bent, broken, or warped structure.

(2) Loose or wrinkled polyester fabric covering, finished with coatings other than dope, may be caused by inadequate or excessive heat application; excess slack when the fabric was installed; or bent or warped structure. Polyester fabric which does not meet aircraft quality specifications will very likely become loose after a short period of time.

(3) Glass fabric covering should be tested with a large suction cup for rib lacing cord failure and reinforcing tape failure caused by chafing on all wing ribs and other structural attachments throughout the airframe. Particular attention should be given to the area within the propeller slipstream. If failure is indicated by the covering lifting from the static position, the rib lacing cord and reinforcing tape must be reinstalled with double the number of original laces.

NOTE: Temporary wrinkles will develop in any fabric coated and finished with dope, when moisture from rain, heavy fog, or dew is absorbed into a poor-quality dope film, causing the film to expand. Temporary wrinkles may also develop with any type of thick coatings, on any type of fabric, when an aircraft is moved from a cold storage area to a warm hangar or parked in the warming sunshine, causing rapid thermal expansion of the coating.

c. Coating Cracks. Fabric exposed through cracks in the coating may be initially tested for deterioration by pressing firmly with a thumb to check the fabric's strength. Natural fibers deteriorate by exposure to ultraviolet radiation, mildew, fungus from moisture, high acid-content rain, dew, fog, pollution, and age. Polyester filaments will deteriorate by exposure to UV radiation.

(1) Glass fabric will not deteriorate from UV exposure, but will be deteriorated by acid rain, dew fallout, and chaffing if loose in the prop blast area.

(2) Cotton, linen, and glass fabric coverings are dependent solely on the strength and tautening characteristics of the dope film to carry the airloads. Dope coatings on heat-tautened polyester fabric will also absorb all the airloads because the elongation of polyester filaments are considerably higher than the dope film. Polyester fabric that is coated with materials other than dope, is dependent solely on the heat tautening and low-elongation characteristics of the polyester filaments to develop tension and transmit the airloads to the airframe without excess distortion from a static position.

(3) Cracks in coatings will allow any type of exposed fabric to deteriorate. Cracks should be closed by sealing or removing the coatings in the immediate area and replace with new coatings, or recover the component.

2-31. FABRIC IDENTIFICATION. Cotton Fabric meeting TSO-C15 or TSO-C14 can be identified by an off-white color and thread count of 80 to 94 for TSO-C14b and 80 to 84 for TSO-C15d in both directions.

a. Aircraft linen conforming to British specification 7F1 may be identified by a slightly darker shade than cotton fabric and irregular thread spacing. The average thread count will be about the same as Grade A fabric (TSO-C15d). The non-uniformity of the linen thread size is also noticeable, with one thread half the size of the adjacent thread. When viewed under a magnifying glass, the ends of the cotton and linen fiber nap may be seen on the backside. The nap is also seen when the coating is removed from the front or outside surface. A light-purple color showing on the back side of cotton or linen fabric indicates a fungicide was present in the dope to resist deterioration by fungus and mildew.

b. Polyester fabric conforming to TSO-C14b or TSO-C15d is whiter in color than cotton or linen. The fabric styles adapted for use as aircraft covering have a variety of thread counts, up to ninety-four (94), depending on the manufacturing source, weight, and breaking strength. Polyester is a monofilament and will not have any nap or filament ends showing.

c. Glass fabric is manufactured white in color, and one source is precoated with a blue-tinted dope as a primer and to reduce weave distortion during handling. Thread count will be approximately 36 threads per inch. Glass fabrics are monofilament and will not have any nap or filament ends showing unless they are inadvertently broken.

d. When a small fabric sample can be removed from the aircraft and all the coatings removed, a burn test will readily distinguish between natural fabric, polyester, and glass fabric. Cotton and linen will burn to a dry ash, polyester filaments will melt to a liquid and continue burning to a charred ash, and glass filaments, which do not support combustion, will become incandescent over a flame.

2-32. COATING IDENTIFICATION. Nitrate or butyrate dope must be used to develop tension on cotton, linen, and glass fabrics. When a small sample can be removed, burn tests will distinguish nitrate dope-coated fabric from butyrate dope-coated fabric by its immediate ignition and accelerated combustion. Butyrate dope will burn at less than one-half the rate of nitrate dope. Coating types other than nitrate or butyrate dope may have been used as a finish over dope on cotton, linen, and glass fiber fabric coverings.

a. If the fabric type is determined to be polyester, coating identification should start by reviewing the aircraft records and inspecting the inside of the wings and the fuselage for the required fabric source identification stamps for covering materials authorized under the STC. The manual, furnished by the holder of the STC-approved fabric, should be reviewed to determine whether the coatings are those specified by the STC.

b. Coating types, other than those authorized by the original STC, may have been used with prior FAA approval, and this would be noted in the aircraft records. The presence of dope on polyester can be detected by a sample burn test.

2-33. STRENGTH CRITERIA FOR AIRCRAFT FABRIC. Minimum performance standards for new intermediate-grade fabric are specified in TSO-C14b, which references AMS 3804C. Minimum performance standards for new Grade A fabric are specified in TSO-C15d, which references AMS 3806D.

a. The condition of the fabric covering must be determined on every 100-hour and annual inspection, because the strength of the fabric is a definite factor in the airworthiness of an airplane. Fabric is considered to be airworthy until it deteriorates to a breaking strength less than 70 percent of the strength of new fabric required for the aircraft. For example, if grade-A cotton is used on an airplane that requires only intermediate fabric, it can deteriorate to 46 pounds per inch width (70 percent of the strength of intermediate fabric) before it must be replaced.

b. Fabric installed on aircraft with a wing loading less than 9 lb. per square foot (psf), and a Vne less than 160 mph, will be considered unairworthy when the breaking strength has deteriorated below 46 lb. per inch width, regardless of the fabric grade. Fabric installed on aircraft with a wing loading of 9 lb. per square foot and over, or a Vne of 160 mph and over, will be considered unairworthy when the breaking strength has deteriorated below 56 lb. per inch width.

c. Fabric installed on a glider or sailplane with a wing loading of 8 lb. per square foot and less, and a Vne of 135 mph or less, will be considered unairworthy when the fabric breaking strength has deteriorated below 35 lb. per inch width, regardless of the fabric grade.

2-34. FABRIC TESTING. Mechanical devices used to test fabric by pressing against or piercing the finished fabric are not FAA approved and are used at the discretion of the mechanic to base an opinion on the general fabric condition. Punch test accuracy will depend on the individual device calibration, total coating thickness, brittleness, and types of coatings and fabric. Mechanical devices are not applicable to glass fiber fabric that will easily shear and indicate a very low reading regardless of the true breaking strength. If the fabric tests in the lower breaking strength range with the mechanical punch tester or if the overall fabric cover conditions are poor, then more accurate field tests may be made. Cut a 1-1/4-inch wide by 4-inch long sample from a top exposed surface, remove all coatings and ravel the edges to a 1-inch width. Clamp each end between suitable clamps with one clamp anchored to a support structure while a load is applied (see table 2-1) by adding sand in a suitable container suspended a few inches above the floor. If the breaking strength is still in question, a sample should be sent to a qualified testing laboratory and breaking strength tests made in accordance with American Society of Testing Materials (ASTM) publication D5035.

NOTE: ASTM publication D1682 has been discontinued but is still referred to in some Aerospace Material Specification (AMS). The grab test method previously listed in ASTM D1682, sections 1 through 16, has been superseded by ASTM publication D5034. The strip testing method (most commonly used in aircraft) previously listed in ASTM D1682, sections 17 through 21, has been superseded by ASTM publication D5035.

2-35. REJUVENATION OF THE DOPE FILM. If fabric loses its strength, there is nothing to do but remove it and recover the aircraft. But if the fabric is good and the dope is cracked, it may be treated with rejuvenator, a mixture of very potent solvents and plasticizers, to restore its resilience. The surface of the fabric is cleaned and the rejuvenator sprayed on in a wet coat, and the solvents soften the old finish so the plasticizers can become part of the film. When the rejuvenator dries, the surface should be sprayed with two coats of aluminum-pigmented dope, then sanded and a third coat of aluminum-pigmented dope applied, followed with the colored-dope finish. When repairing, rejuvenating, and refinishing covering materials approved under an STC, instructions in the manual furnished by the material supplier should be followed.

2-36.—2-41. [RESERVED.]

SECTION 4. REPAIRS TO FABRIC COVERING

2-42. GENERAL. All materials used to make repairs to fabric covering must be of a quality at least equal to the original materials. Workmanship and repair methods must be made in a manner that will return the fabric covering to its original airworthy condition.

a. **Any combination** of seams hand-sewn and overlapped and doped may be used to make repairs and install new fabric sections. (See paragraph 2-7.)

b. **All pigmented dope coats,** including aluminum-pigmented coats, should be removed to the clear dope preliminary coats before installing a new fabric section or finishing tape on the old fabric. The appropriate dope thinner (see paragraph 2-20) may be applied with a brush to soften the old dope. The softened coats can then be removed down to the clear dope coats by scraping with a dull-bladed knife while supporting the fabric from the back side. Removing the old dope by sanding is optional.

c. **Avoid allowing dope to run down** the back side of the fabric or drip through the wing onto the back side of the opposite surface, which will cause cosmetic damage and will show in a high gloss finish.

d. **Repairing a new fabric section** over two adjacent wing ribs is considered a major repair. A log book entry and an FAA Form 337 must be processed accordingly.

e. **All fabric patch edges** not covered with a finishing tape should have a pinked edge or a 1/4-inch raveled edge.

f. **Where the edge of a new fabric section will be located** within 1 inch of a structural member to which the fabric is attached by rib lacing or other methods, the new fabric section should be extended 3 inches past the structural member.

NOTE: Before installing new finishing tape, duplicate the original rib lacing or other attachments without removing the original rib lacing or attachment. Removing the original finishing tape is optional.

g. **When installing large sections of fabric** on a wing or other components, all machine-sewn and/or overlapped and doped seams should be made in accordance with the guidelines specified in paragraphs 2-7 and 2-8.

h. **When repairing a covering material other than cotton or linen,** which was approved with the manufacturer's type certificate (TC), or approved under the authority of an STC, follow the repair instructions furnished by the aircraft manufacturer or supplier of the STC-approved covering materials.

2-43. REPAIR OF TEARS AND ACCESS OPENINGS. When all the original fabric is intact, an opening may be repaired by sewing the two sides together with a curved needle as illustrated in figures 2-13 and 2-14. The fabric edges should be pulled together uniformly with no wrinkles. Before sewing, remove the old dope coats down to the clear dope coats a distance of 2 inches on each side of the opening. The hand-sewn thread quality should be at least equal to that specified in table 2-2 and treated with wax (paraffin-free or beeswax) to prevent fraying, or use the proper thread on the STC application. After sewing, apply a coat of clear dope over the cleaned area and install a 3-inch wide finishing tape, centered over the stitches.

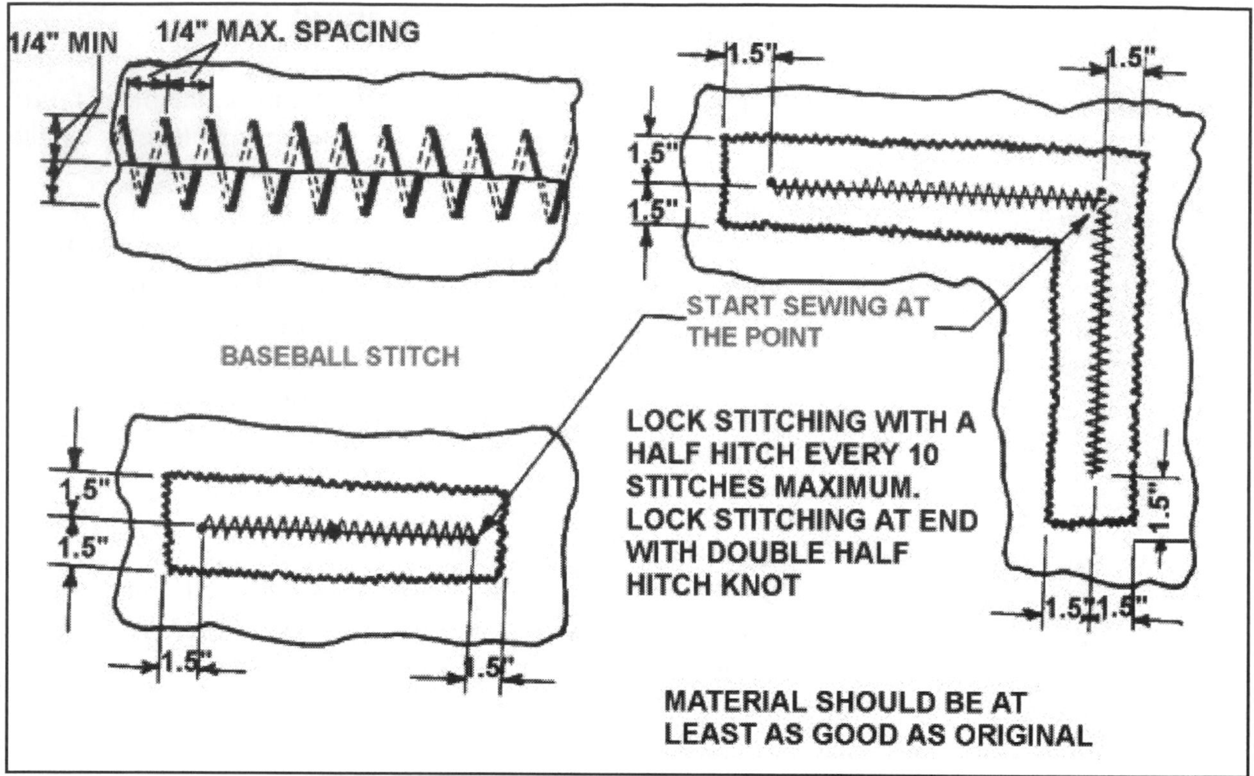

FIGURE 2-13. Repair of tears in fabric.

a. Finishing tapes should be well saturated with dope and smoothed out with no voids or wrinkles during installation. After drying for 1 hour at 70 °F, additional coats of clear dope followed with pigmented dope are applied as detailed in paragraph 2-21.

b. If the opening is more than 8 inches long but less than 16 inches long in any direction, the finishing tape width should be increased to 4 inches.

c. The finishing tape width should be increased to 6 inches if the opening is more than 16 inches long in any direction, is located on a wing top surface, or the aircraft Vne speed is greater than 150 mph.

2-44. SEWN-PATCH REPAIR. Openings that cannot be repaired by closing with stitches may be repaired by sewing in a new fabric section. The edges of the fabric around the opening should be trimmed straight on four sides to facilitate the installation of straight sections of finishing tape over the stitches.

a. After cutting out the damaged section and removing the coatings as detailed in paragraph 2-42, the new fabric section should be sized to allow folding both edges of the fabric back 1/2-inch to increase the stitch tear resistance. Temporarily attach the four corners in position with thread. Start with a double thread with a square knot at the end (see figure 2-14) and continue stitching in the manner described in figures 2-13 and 2-14. When the stitching is complete, wet the new fabric section as described in paragraph 2-21 to remove any creases. After drying, apply one coat of clear dope on the new fabric, as described in paragraph 2-21. When the first coat of dope has dried 1 hour at 70 °F, apply a 3-inch wide finishing tape, centered over the stitches. The finishing tape should be well saturated with

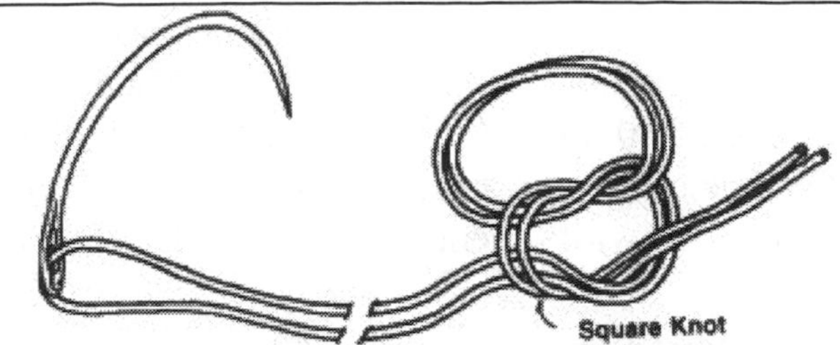

Step 1. Tie the thread ends together with a square knot.

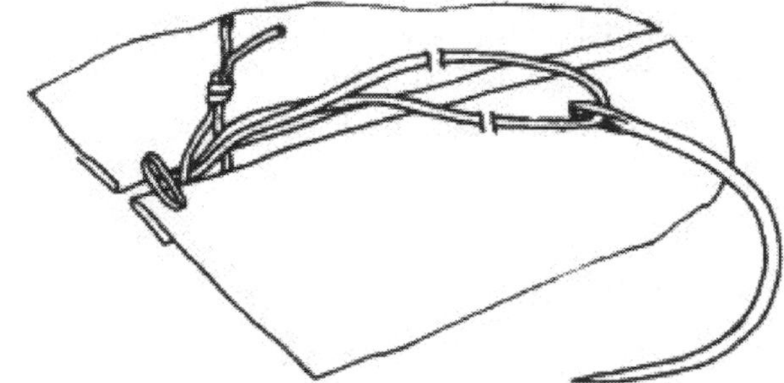

Step 2. Start the stitch by routing through the loop, positioning the square knot on the inside.

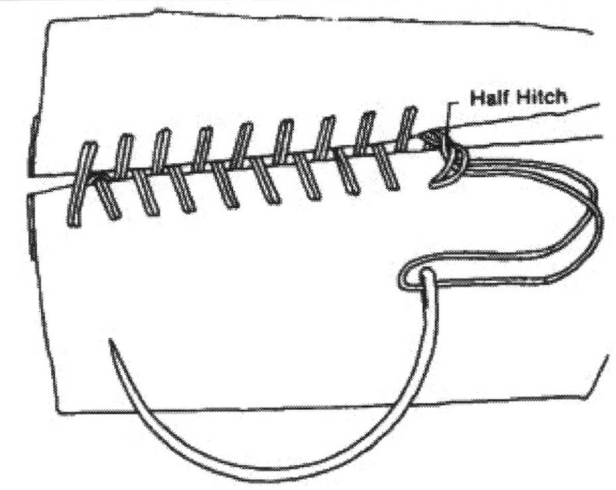

Step 3. Complete the hand-stitch and secure the stitching with a half hitch at a maximum each 10 stitches.

FIGURE **2-14.** Hand-stitch detail.

dope and smoothed out with no voids or wrinkles. Additional coats of clear dope and pigmented dope are then applied to obtain the desired tautness and finish, as described in paragraph 2-21.

b. If the opening is more than 8 inches but less than 16 inches long in any direction, the finishing tape should be 4 inches wide.

c. The finishing tape width should be 6 inches wide if the opening is over 16 inches long in any direction, is located on a wing top surface, or the aircraft Vne speed is greater than 150 mph.

2-45. DOPED-ON PATCH REPAIR. An opening not over 8 inches in length in any direction, on an aircraft with a Vne speed less than 150 mph, may be repaired with a 2-inch overlapped and doped patch. The opening should be trimmed to eliminate any irregular edges and old pigmented dope coats removed as described in paragraph 2-42.

a. When installing a fabric patch over a small opening, the loose edge of the fabric around the opening may be secured by extending a series of small threads, from the edge across the opening, to the opposite side. After the patch is completed, the threads may be clipped and removed through an access port or left in place.

b. The fabric patch is installed by applying a coat of clear dope around the opening, then positioning the patch over the opening. Brush out any void or wrinkles while saturating only the fabric overlap area. After the first coat of clear dope around the edge has dried 1 hour at 70 °F, wet the fabric patch to remove any creases as described in paragraph 2-21. After drying, apply additional coats of clear dope and pigmented dope over the entire patch as described in paragraph 2-21.

c. If the opening is less than 8 inches in length in any direction and the aircraft Vne speed is greater than 150 mph, a 2-inch wide finishing tape should be installed on all sides, centered on the edge of the 2-inch overlap patch.

d. If the opening is more than 8 inches but less than 16 inches in length, in any direction on an aircraft with a Vne speed less than

150 mph, it may be repaired with a doped patch, which is overlapped 1/4 of the opening maximum dimension. The maximum overlap should not exceed 4 inches.

e. If the opening is more than 8 inches but less than 16 inches in length in any direction, the repair is located on a wing top surface, and the aircraft Vne speed is greater than 150 mph, the patch overlap should be 4 inches and a 2-inch wide finishing tape installed on all sides, centered on the edge of the patch.

f. If the opening is more than 16 inches in length in any direction and the Vne speed is less than 150 mph, the patch overlap should be 4 inches and the finishing tape should be 4 inches in width, centered on the edge of the patch.

g. If the opening is more than 16 inches in length in any direction and the Vne speed is greater than 150 mph, the patch overlap should be 4 inches and the finishing tape should be 6 inches in width, centered on the edge of the patch.

2-46.—2-51. [RESERVED.]

CHAPTER 3. FIBERGLASS AND PLASTICS

SECTION 1. REPAIR OF LIGHT LOAD LAMINATE STRUCTURES

3-1. GENERAL. There is a wide variation in the composition and structural application of laminates, and it is essential that these factors be given major consideration when any restoration activities are undertaken. To a similar extent, there also exist many types of laminate structure repairs that may or may not be suitable for a given condition. For this reason, it is important that the aircraft or component manufacturer's repair data be reviewed when determining what specific type of repair is permissible and appropriate for the damage at hand.

NOTE: Review Material Safety Data Sheets for material to be used. When handling materials, prepreg fabrics, or parts with prepared surfaces, observe shelf life. Latex gloves and approved masks must be worn.

a. The materials used in the repair of laminate structures must preserve the strength, weight, aerodynamic characteristics, or electrical properties of the original part or assembly. Preservation is best accomplished by replacing damaged material with material of identical chemical composition or a substitute approved by the manufacturer.

b. To eliminate dangerous stress concentrations, avoid abrupt changes in cross-sectional areas. When possible, for scarf joints and facings, make small patches round or oval-shaped, and round the corners of large repairs. Smooth and properly contour aerodynamic surfaces.

c. Test specimens should be prepared during the actual repair. These can then be subjected to a destructive test to establish the quality of the adhesive bond in the repaired part. To make this determination valid, the specimens must be assembled with the same adhesive batch mixture and subjected to curing pressure, temperature, and time identical to those in the actual repair.

3-2. FIBERGLASS LAMINATE REPAIRS. The following repairs are applicable to fiberglass laminate used for non-structural fairing, covers, cowlings, honeycomb panel facings, etc. Prior to undertaking the repair, remove any paint by using normal dry sanding methods. Bead blasting may be used but caution must be exercised not to abrade the surfaces excessively.

NOTE: Chemical paint strippers must not be used.

NOTE: These repairs are not to be used on radomes or advanced composite components, such as graphite (carbon fiber) or Kevlar.

CAUTION: Sanding fiberglass laminates gives off a fine dust that may cause skin and/or respiratory irritation unless suitable skin and respiration protection is used. Sanding also creates static charges that attract dirt or other contaminants.

a. Check for voids and delamination by tap testing. (See chapter 5.) When the surface of a fiberglass laminated structure is scratched, pitted, or eroded; first wash with detergent and water to remove all of the dirt, wax, or oxide film. Then scrub the surface with an acceptable cleaner. After the surface is thoroughly cleaned, sand it with 280-grit sandpaper, and again use an acceptable cleanser to remove any sanding residue and moisture. This is essential, as any moisture remaining on the surface will inhibit the cure of the resin. Dry the fiberglass laminate thoroughly prior to bonding repair. Mix enough resin, using the manufacturer's instructions, to completely cover the damaged area, and apply one or two coats. Cover the resin with a peel ply to exclude all air from the resin while it is curing. After the resin has cured, remove the film and file or sand the surface to conform to the original shape of the part. Ensure that all edges of the laminate part are sealed to prevent water absorption. Then refinish it to match the rest of the structure.

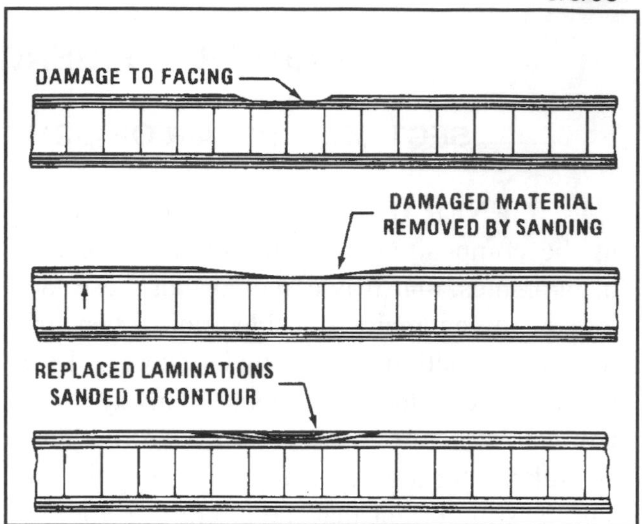

FIGURE 3-1. Typical laminate (facing) repair.

b. Superficial scars, scratches, surface abrasion, or rain erosion can generally be repaired by applying one or more coats of a suitable low temperature resin, catalyzed to cure at room temperature, to the abraded surface. The number of coats required will depend upon the type of resin and the severity of the damage.

(1) Damage not exceeding the first layer or ply of fiberglass laminate can be repaired by filling with a putty consisting of a compatible room-temperature-setting resin and clean short glass fibers. Before the resin sets, apply a sheet of peel ply over the repair area and work out any bubbles and excess resin. After the resin has cured, sand off any excess and prepare the area for refinishing.

(2) Damage deep enough to seriously affect the strength of the laminate (usually more than the first ply or layer of fabric) may be repaired as illustrated in figure 3-1. Coat the sanded area with room-temperature-setting resin and apply contoured pieces of glass fabric soaked in resin. Apply a peel ply sheet over the repair and work out any bubbles and excess resin. After the resin has cured, scrape off the excess resin and sand the surface of the repair to the original contour.

(3) Damage that extends completely through one facing and into the core requires the replacement of the damaged core and facing. A method for accomplishing this type of repair is shown in figure 3-2. An alternate method for repairing the facing is shown in figure 3-3. The damaged portion is carefully trimmed out to a circular or oval shape and the core material is removed completely to the opposite facing. Exercise caution so as not to damage the opposite facing or to start delamination between the facings and the core around the damage.

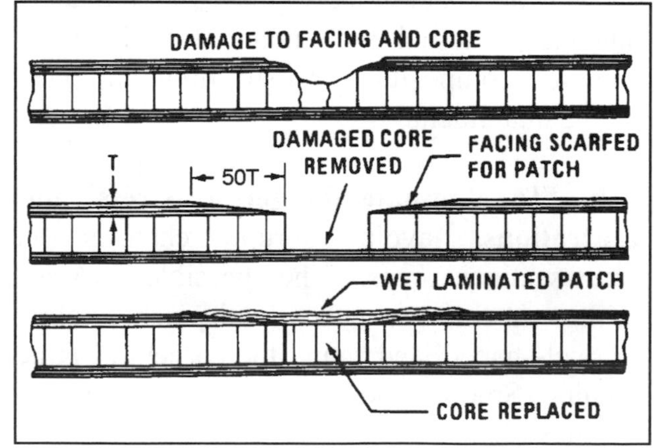

FIGURE 3-2. Typical core and facing repair.

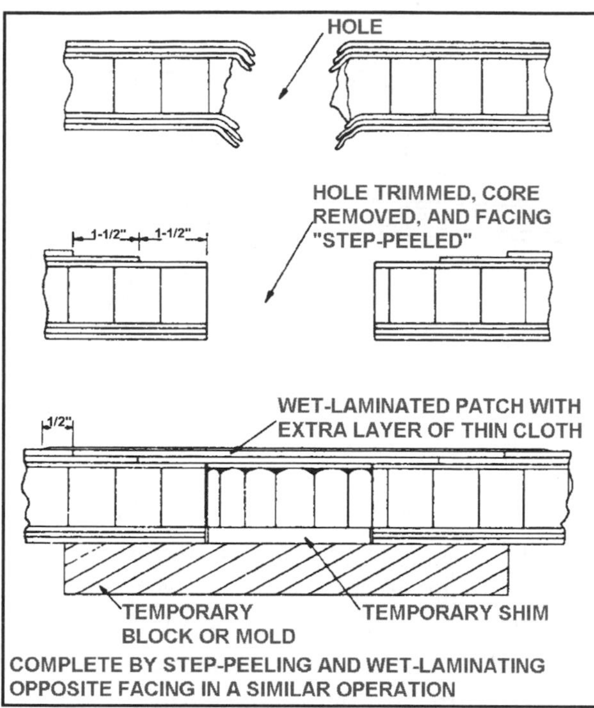

FIGURE 3-3. Typical stepped joint repair.

c. Use replacement core stock of the same material and density as the original (or an acceptable substitute) and cut it to fit snugly in the trimmed hole. Observe the direction of the original core. When all of the pieces of replacement facing laminations are cut and soaked in resin, coat all surfaces of the hole and the scarfed area with resin. Then coat all surfaces of the core replacement with resin and insert it into the hole. After all of the pieces of resin-impregnated glass-fabric facing are in place and lined up with the original fiber-orientation, cover the entire area with a piece of peel ply and carefully work down the layers of fabric to remove any air bubbles and excess resin. Apply light pressure by means of sand bags or a vacuum bag. When the resin has cured, sand the repair to match the original contour and refinish the surface.

3-3. REPAIRING HOLES.

a. Scarf Method. If the damaged area is less than 3 inches in diameter, the damage may be removed by either sanding with a power sander or hand sanding with 180-grit sandpaper.

(1) Scarf back the edges of the hole about 50 times the thickness of the face ply. Thoroughly clean out all of the sanding residue with a cloth wet with an acceptable cleanser.

(2) Prepare the patches by (see figure 3-4) laying the proper weight fiberglass cloth impregnated with resin on a piece of peel ply. A weight of resin equal to the weight of the patch provides a 50-percent ratio.

A. FILL THE GLASS CLOTH WITH RESIN.
B. COVER THE GLASS CLOTH WITH PEEL PLY AND TRIM IT TO THE PROPER SIZE WITH SCISSORS.

FIGURE 3-4. Preparing the fiberglass sandwich.

(3) Make a sandwich by laying a second layer of peel ply over the patch before cutting it to the required size and shape. Sandwiching will prevent the patch from raveling when cut. Brush a good coat of resin over the scarfed area. Remove one piece of peel ply from the first patch and lay the patch in place. Work all of the air out of the resin and remove the top peel ply. Cut the next larger patch so it will overlap the first patch by at least one-half inch. Remove one piece of peel ply from this patch and center the patch over the first one. Work all of the air out of the resin. Continue laying in patches, each overlapping the one below it by at least one-half inch, until you have the required number of layers (see figures 3-5 and 3-6) plus an extra ply to restore original strength to the repaired area.

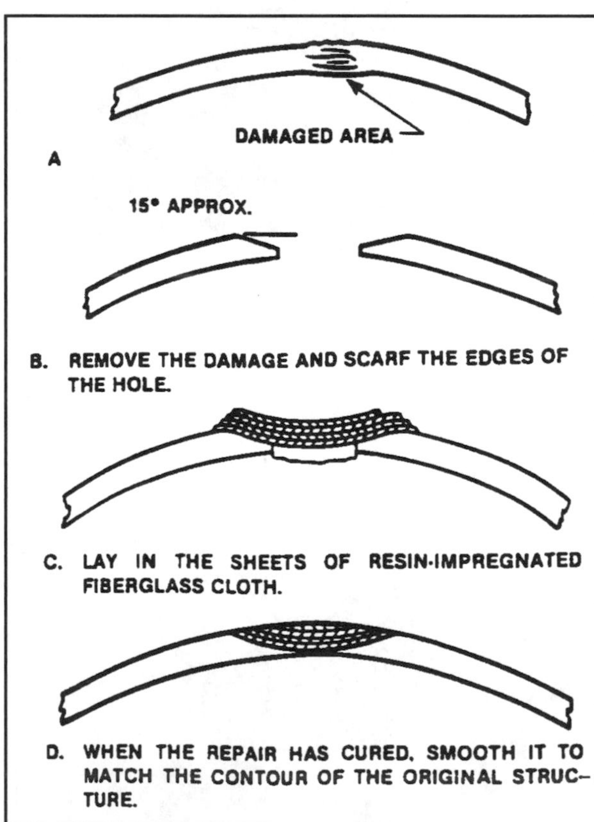

FIGURE 3-5. Scarfed repair to a nonstructural laminated fiberglass component.

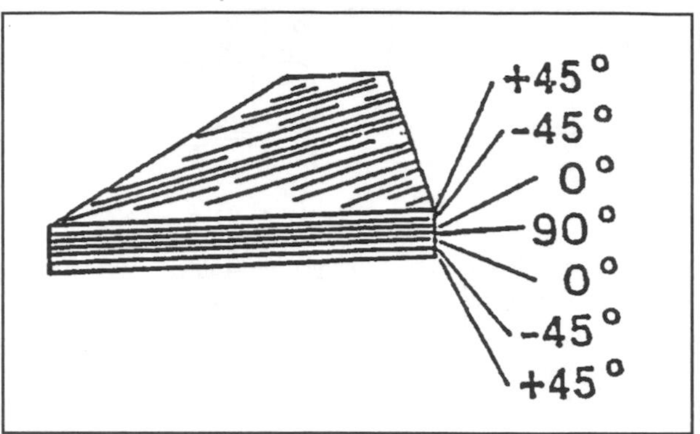

FIGURE 3-6. Symmetrical layup same as original number of plies, plus one extra ply.

(4) Cover the entire repair with peel ply and carefully work out all of the air bubbles from the resin. Apply pressure over the repair with tape or sandbags and allow it to cure. After the repair has cured, remove the excess resin by filing or sanding the surface to the contour of the original part. Smooth the surface with fine sandpaper and refinish it to match the original part.

(5) An alternate layup method that works equally well is to place the larger patch over the scarfed area first, and then each subsequent smaller patch over this. Both types of repair are finished in exactly the same way.

(6) The scarfed joint method (see figure 3-7) is normally used on small punctures up to 3 or 4 inches in maximum dimension and in facings that are made of thin fabric that is difficult to peel.

b. Step-Joint Method. The scarf method of repairing a laminated fiberglass face sheet of a honeycomb structure is the easiest method to use. In this type of repair, the damage is outlined with a compass. If a square or rectangular repair is more appropriate then the damage is outlined using a straight-edge and a compass to round out the corners.

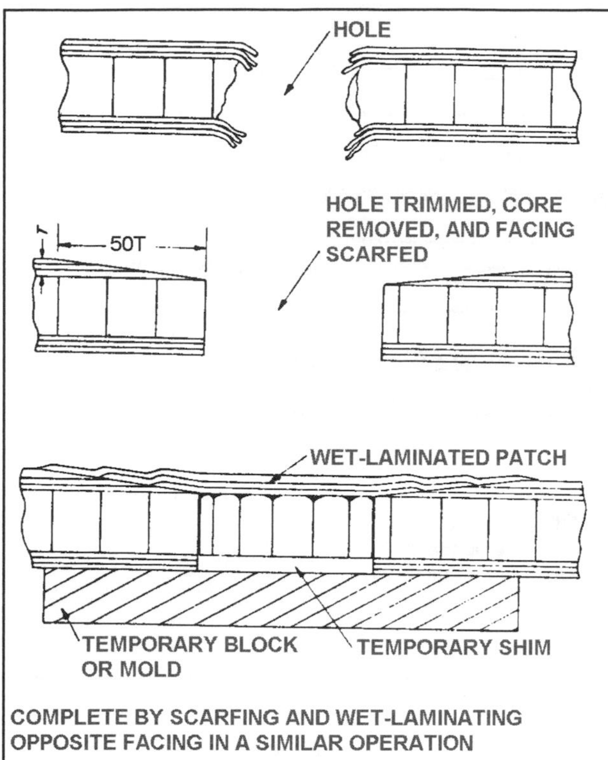

FIGURE 3-7. Typical scarf joint repair.

(1) The configuration of the repair should be that which will remove the least amount of sound material. Extend the cleaned-out area for a distance equal to the number of plies to be removed, less 1 inch. For example, if you must remove three plies, extend the repair for 2 inches beyond the cleaned-out area. Each layer should be 1 inch beyond the layer below. Use a sharp knife or other type of cutter to cut through the top layer, being careful not to damage the underneath layer. Use several passes with the knife rather than one deep cut. (See figure 3-8.)

(2) Begin with one corner of the patch and carefully pry it loose and peel it up until all of the layer is removed. Next, mark the exposed layer 1/2 inch inside the opening and carefully cut and remove it. Continue until you have removed all of the damaged or delaminated layers.

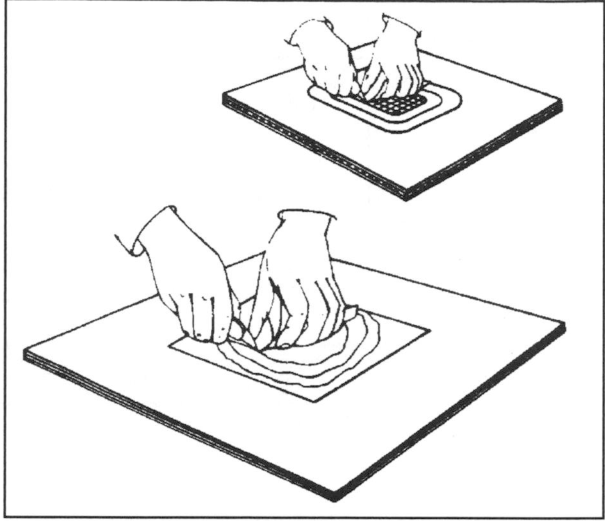

FIGURE 3-8. Carefully cut through each layer of fiberglass cloth and remove it from the damaged area.

(3) Lightly sand, then scrub the entire area with an acceptable cleanser. Prepare the patches exactly as you did for the scarf method, cutting each layer to exactly the size of the material removed. Brush in a coat of resin, lay in the patch of the smallest size, and carefully work out all of the air bubbles from the resin. Now, lay in the next larger size patch to lock the first layer of fiberglass cloth into place. Repeat the process until the damage area is filled.

(4) Butt the top layer of cloth to the opening in the face ply and cover the entire repair with peel ply. Carefully work all of the air bubbles out of the resin and put pressure on the repair with either sandbags, or another appropriate method, such as vacuum bagging. (See figure 3-9.) After the top repair has hardened, repeat the process on the bottom.

3-4. SAMPLE BAGGING AND CURING PROCESS. Figure 3-9 shows a typical bagging arrangement for a localized repair in which patch plies of prepreg are cured with a layer of adhesive, and a heating blanket is used to supply heat.

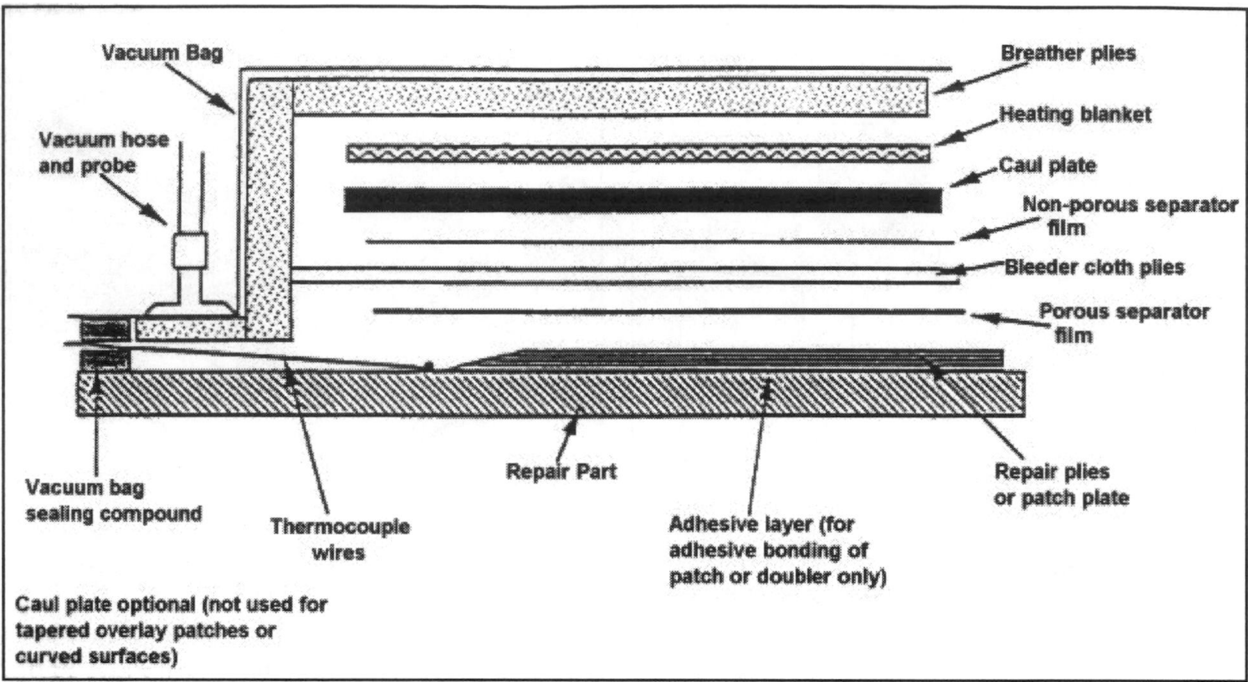

FIGURE 3-9. Sample bagging layup cross section.

a. The materials used for most bonded repairs require elevated temperatures and pressure, during their cure, to develop full strength. The following paragraphs describe the operations required to enclose the repair in a vacuum bag. When the part to be cured can be placed in an autoclave, additional pressure and heat can be applied. For cured-in-place parts, vacuum pressure and portable heat blankets usually suffice.

(1) When selecting materials, especially the parting agent film, the temperature at which the repair is to be cured must be known. Polyvinyl alcohol (PVA) film is ideal when the bonding temperature does not exceed 250 °F. PVA film has very high tear resistance and may be heat-sealed effectively. When the bond temperature is not above 180 °F, polyvinyl chloride film can be used. For temperatures up to 450 °F, a polyvinyl fluoride film is used. These three types of films are available in a variety of weights and widths. Most nylon bagging films are used for temperatures up to 400 °F.

(2) When all repair details are in place and ready to be cured, they are enclosed in a bag of plastic film or thin rubber. Air is removed from the bag by a vacuum source so that atmospheric pressure exerts a pressure on the repair as it is cured.

(3) To provide a path to draw off the air initially inside the bag, layers of fiberglass cloth or similar noncontaminating materials, known as breather plies, are placed inside the bag. When prepreg is being cured as part of the repair, it is sometimes necessary to bleed off excess resin. To do this, layers of fiberglass cloth or similar materials known as bleeder plies are placed over the prepreg. Some repairs have been made with a net resin prepreg that does not require bleeding, and therefore does not require bleeder plies. Porous separator plies or film are used between the prepreg and the bleeder and nonporous separator plies or film are used between the bleeder and breather plies to control the flow of resin.

(4) Small parts may be envelope bagged (i.e., enclosing the entire part in the bag). Larger parts with localized repairs can be bagged by sealing the surface completely around the repair areas with sealing tape and applying the bagging material to the sealing tape.

CAUTION: The whole panel must be vacuum bagged to prevent delamination in sandwich skins when using an oven or autoclave. Contoured parts must be restrained with tooling to prevent warpage.

b. When the heat for curing the repair is provided by a heat blanket, the blanket can be either inside or outside the vacuum bag. However, the blanket should be covered to minimize heat loss, and the blanket should be separated from direct contact with most bagging materials by layers of fiberglass cloth.

(1) This will prevent localized overheating that could damage the bag. It is sometimes helpful to place a thin aluminum sheet under the heating blanket to minimize localized heating. A thin rubber blanket can help smooth the surface of the material being cured. A pressure plate should be used when two or more heat blankets are applied to the same repair.

NOTE: Understanding that various resins behave differently during cure, the choice of bagging arrangements will often vary with the material being cured.

(2) The procedure for the bagging arrangement is as follows:

(a) Place a peel ply over the patch material to provide a surface finish for subsequent bonding or painting if not previously accomplished. Place a layer of porous separator cloth over the patch, extending beyond the prepreg and the adhesive. Smooth to avoid wrinkles.

(b) With the patch material in place, place the end of the thermocouple wire next to the edge of the prepreg. Tape the wire to the structure inside the bag with heat-resistant tape. The tape should not be in contact with the prepreg or the adhesive.

(c) Place bleeder plies as shown, extending 2 to 3 inches beyond the patch. The number of bleeder plies needed will vary with the type of resin and the resin content required.

(d) Place a layer of nonporous parting film over the bleeder plies, cut 1 inch smaller than the bleeder plies. This layer is intended to stop resin flow from bleeder plies into breather plies while still providing an airflow path when vacuum is applied.

(e) If a pressure plate is used, place it over the previous separator ply. The plate is frequently perforated with small holes to permit airflow to the breather plies. Bleeder plies may be necessary when using a pressure plate.

NOTE: Pressure on the repair will be reduced if the pressure plate does not conform to the repair.

(f) Place the heat blanket over the assembly, making sure it extends 3 to 4 inches beyond the material to be cured.

(g) One or more thermocouples should be in contact with the heat blanket to monitor its temperature. Additional thermocouples should be placed near the curing repair to monitor the temperature of the curing resin.

(h) When using a heat blanket as the heat source, four to six layers of fiberglass surface breather or the equivalent should be used over the heat blanket. This will insulate and prevent damage to the nylon bagging film. Ensure that the breather plies are in contact with the bleeder plies so that an air passage exists.

(i) Place a bead of sealing tape against the parent material around the edge of the breather plies. Seal the thermocouple wires to prevent vacuum leakage.

NOTE: Two layers of sealing tape may be required in order to provide a good seal.

(j) Cover with a suitable vacuum bag, smoothed to minimize wrinkles. Press the bag firmly onto the sealing tape to obtain an air-tight seal. Place pleats in vacuum bag to allow the bag material to stretch.

(k) Install two vacuum probes or sniffers through openings cut in the bag. One will be used for the vacuum gauge and the other will be connected to the vacuum source. The vacuum probe must sit on the breather plies, but must not touch the patch or adhesive.

NOTE: Place the vacuum gauge on the opposite side of the vacuum port, where applicable. Do not place vacuum probes near repair area.

(l) Connect the vacuum source and smooth the bag by hand pressure as the air is removed. Check for leaks and reseal as necessary. A minimum vacuum of 22 inches of mercury is required.

(m) Place insulating material over the vacuum bag to prevent heat loss.

(n) Apply power to the heat blanket and control its temperature as specified for the material being cured.

(o) Observe cure time requirements established by the product manufacturer.

3-5.—3-9. [RESERVED.]

SECTION 2. METALLIC SANDWICH SECONDARY STRUCTURE REPAIRS

3-10. REPAIRS TO METALLIC SANDWICH SECONDARY STRUCTURE. Magnesium, titanium, or stainless steel facings require special procedures that are not included in the following methods of repair. Aluminum alloys such as 7075-T6, 2024-T3, and 2014-T6 are commonly used for the repair of facings for sandwich structural parts having aluminum facings. For maximum corrosion resistance, use only clad aluminum for repairs to clad aluminum alloy facings.

a. Dents, scratches, or fractures, not exceeding 1/4 inch in largest dimension in aluminum facings, may be repaired with a suitable filler such as viscous epoxy resin. Dents that are delaminated shall not be filled but repaired. Thoroughly clean the repair area with fine sandpaper and acetone before applying the filler. After the resin has partially cured, remove any excess resin with a sharp plastic scraper. When the resin has completely cured, sand to the original contour. If the damage included a fracture, reclean the area around the filled hole and apply a surface patch.

b. Fractures or punctures in one facing and partial damage to the core of an aluminum-faced laminate may be repaired by several different methods. The technique used will depend upon the size of the damage, the strength required, and the aerodynamic loads of the area involved. If the repair requires aerodynamic smoothness, the facing surrounding the repair core cavity may have to be step cut to one-half its thickness. This can be done by using a router with an end mill bit and a template.

c. Damage that extends completely through the core and both facings may be repaired using the same general techniques as those used for repairing fiberglass laminates when both facings are accessible.

d. After locating the extent of the total damaged area by tapping or other nondestructive test methods, remove the damaged facing and that portion of the core material that is also affected. The depth to which the core must be removed will depend upon the type of core material and the method of repair. The replacement core material must be the same material and core cell size as the original. Fabricate core material to shape, keeping the same core ribbon or grain direction. When a substitution is permissible, wood or glass-fabric honey-comb cores are sometimes used in the repair of aluminum honeycomb cores, as they are generally easier to shape. Typical types of core replacements are shown in figure 3-10. Resin fills can be used to replace the core and facing where smaller core damage exists. Phenolic microballoons, low-density insulating materials, and/or other ingredients are added to lower the density and give greater flexibility.

e. For the repair of larger holes in which it is inconvenient to use a face patch because of aerodynamic smoothness requirements in that area, both the core and facing are sometimes replaced with glass-fiber fabric discs and resin. Undercut the core, as shown in figure 3-11, in order to obtain a better bonding of the fill with the facing. Fill the core cavity with accurately shaped resin-saturated glass cloth discs, and press each ply down to remove any air bubbles. Special care should be taken that the final plies fit well against the underside of the top facing. When the core cavity is filled, close the cutout in the facing with resin-impregnated glass fiber fabric discs that have been precut to size.

f. Overlap repairs, typically called scab patches, have a long history of use in repairing aircraft structures. These repairs simply cover the damaged area with patch material. Overlap repairs can be bonded and/or mechanically

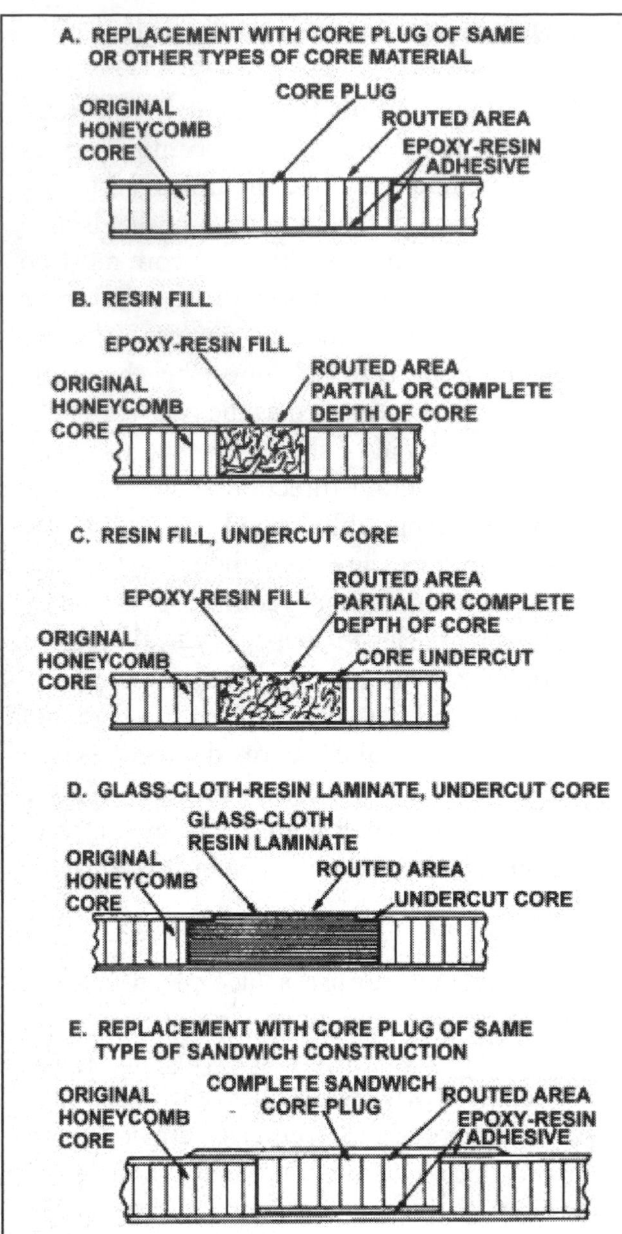

FIGURE 3-10. Typical types of core replacement.

fastened. Figure 3-12 shows a cross-section of a typical bonded and mechanically fastened repair. The damaged area may or may not need to be filled.

(1) Bonded overlap repairs work well on most structures. The overlap repair consists of a solid patch material such as metal, precured laminates, prepreg or wet layup material co-cured in place.

(2) Bolt or blind rivet. Mechanically fastened, bolted, or blind rivet repairs are primarily used for thick structures. Primary concerns include bolt/rivet spacing, fastener diameter, number of fasteners, and sealant type.

g. Core potting is the process of filling the core cutout with a curable paste filler material. If the damage is sustained in an area with an already-potted core, the replacement core should also be potted. In other cases, if the honeycomb or foam core is damaged, it may be potted rather than plugged if the damaged area is small (1 inch or less). Remove the face sheet with a power router, using a router template to prevent injury to undamaged face skin. The router may be adjusted to remove one of the face skins only, a face skin and part of the core, a face skin and all of the core, or both the face skins and the core. (See figure 3-13.)

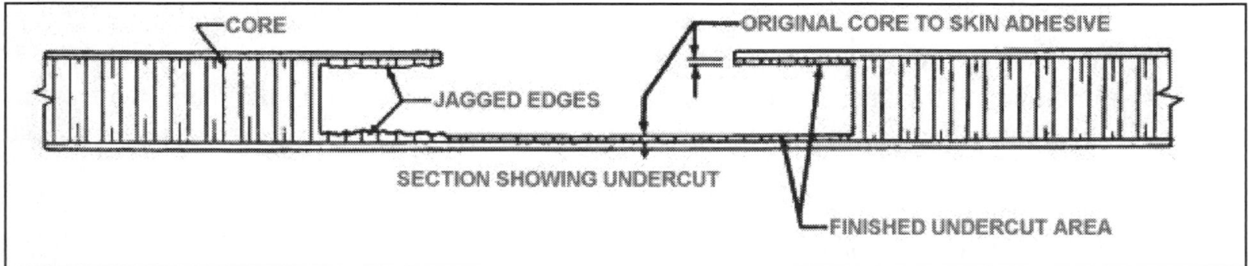

FIGURE 3-11. Typical undercut core material cavity.

(1) It may be necessary when routing a tapered section such as an aileron to use a wedge-shaped block between the routing template and the upper surface. This will allow the router to cut the core material parallel with the lower surface. (See figure 3-14.)

(2) Select the appropriate potting adhesive as recommended by the manufacturer. Mix a sufficient quantity of filler to fill the hole and add microballoons if they are needed to serve as a filler. When the resin and filler are thoroughly mixed according to the manufacturer's recommendations, pour the mixture into the hole filling all of the cells, then work out all of the bubbles with a toothpick. If performing an overlay repair fill the core cavity to slightly above the part's surface. If performing a flush repair, fill the core cavity to slightly above the original core.

(3) Cure the compound according to the manufacturer's dircctions. Trim the top of the cured potting compound flush with the surface, for the type of repair you are performing.

h. A core plug repair replaces damaged core material with a shaped piece of similar core material.

(1) Complete removal of core material to the opposite face generally requires some hand-cutting with a core knife. Figure 3-15 shows core material being removed with a core knife. The core can be peeled away from the skin bond using duckbill pliers. Sanding is then required to remove irregular accumulations of adhesive from the undamaged inner face. Remove only enough adhesive to produce a smooth finish.

CAUTION: Care should be used when peeling core material from thin-skin sandwich face sheets, because the skin can be damaged by pulling on the core.

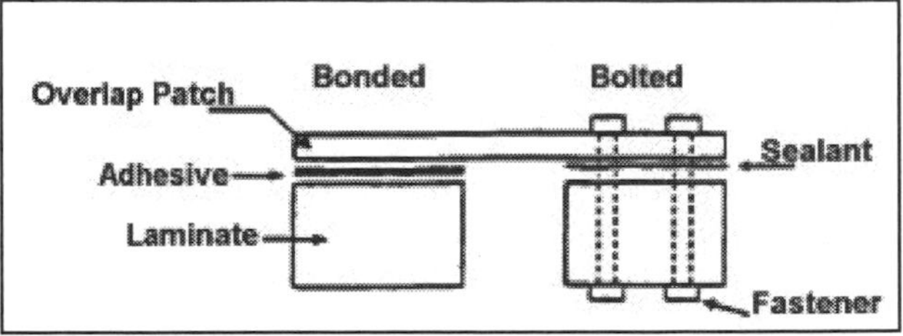

FIGURE 3-12. Cross section of bonded and bolted overlap repairs.

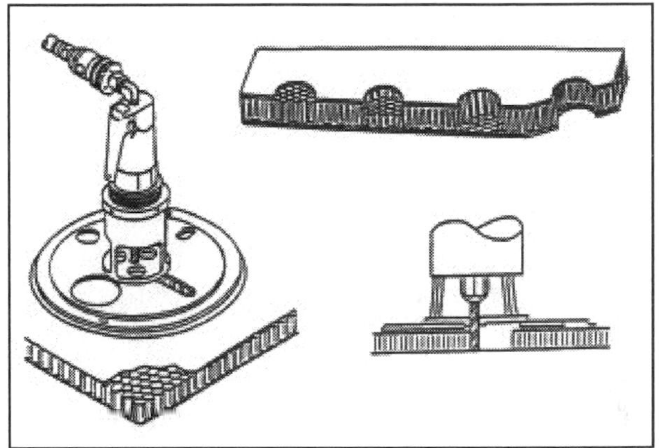

FIGURE 3-13. Honeycomb core removal.

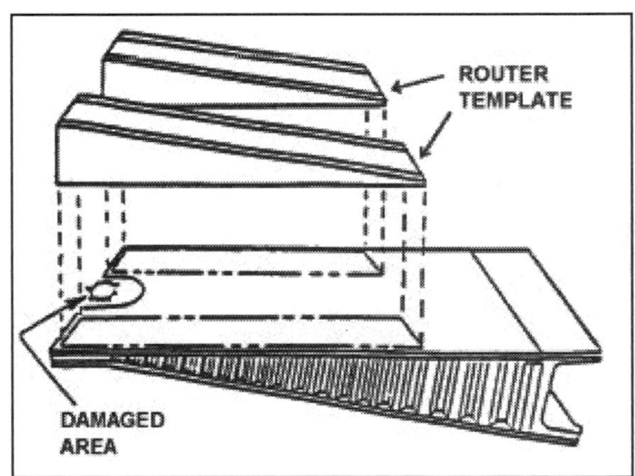

FIGURE 3.14 — Removing honeycomb core from a tapered control surface.

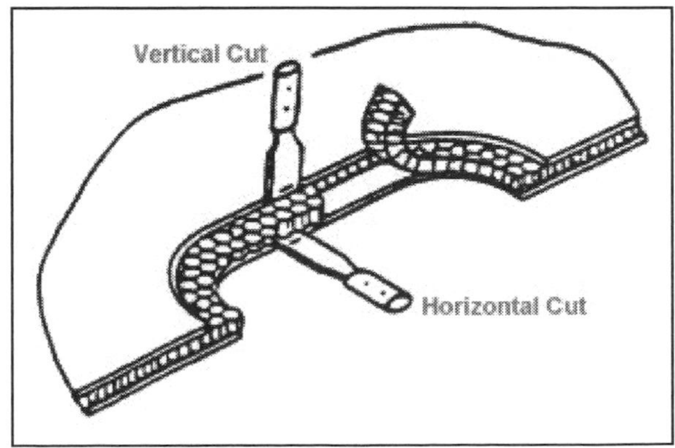

FIGURE 3-15. Removal of core with core knife.

(2) A core plug should be fabricated as follows. Select the core density. Cell size and ribbon direction and thickness should be at least the same as that used in the original construction. Trim the sides of the plug to a loose fit in the routed cavity. Trim the plug height so the top of the plug sits .001 inch higher than the level of the original surface. The core will compress and set during cure thereby requiring the extra height. Carefully remove the trimmed core plug from the machined cavity. Use a vacuum cleaning device to remove any dust or particles remaining on the core plug or in the repair area. Clean the core plug by rinsing with an approved solvent and wrap the plug in a clean polyethylene bag until needed for assembly.

CAUTION: When handling film adhesives, prepreg fabrics, or parts with prepared surfaces, latex gloves must be worn.

(3) Using a film adhesive, the core plug should be installed as follows. Select the appropriate adhesive film. Cut one disk of adhesive to the same shape and size as the perimeter of the repair cutout if the repair extends through the entire core thickness. Cut two disks if a partial depth core repair is being made. Cut one strip of core splice adhesive to wrap around the core perimeter to its full depth. For a partial depth core repair, also cut out a fiberglass or aluminum disk, again matching the size and the shape of the repair cutout. Figure 3-16 shows the details of a partial depth core repair. Preassemble the pieces.

(4) Wipe the bottom and sides of the cutout area with solvent. Allow the area to dry. Insert the core plug assembly with splice adhesive applied to the perimeter into the core cutout. Ensure the core plug ribbon direction matches that of the parent core. In the case of a partial depth core repair, the plug and disk

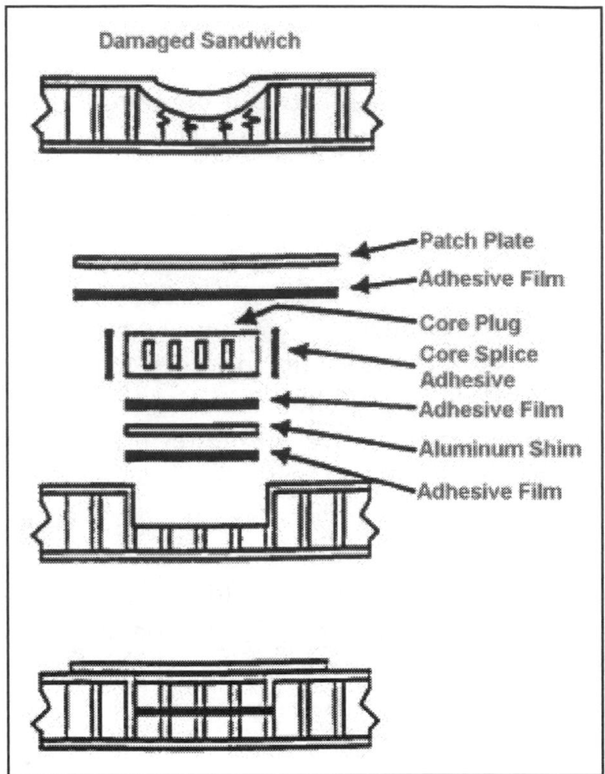

FIGURE 3-16. Details of core repair.

may be cured to save time. Some restraining method, such as vacuum bagging, may be desirable over the core splice adhesive as this material usually foams up and out during cure. Cure the adhesive according to the manufacturer's directions and allow the area to cool.

(5) Trim the top of the cured core plug flush with either the original core or the mold line, depending on the type of laminate repair to be performed. Proceed with laminate repair.

3-11. FINISHING. The type of finish coating applied to a metallic sandwich repair will normally be determined by the exposed material and the application of the part or assembly. Rain erosion of plastic parts, the need for electrical or dielectric properties, and/or the necessity for anti-corrosion coatings must be considered when the choice of finish is made. Plastic-faced parts such as radomes are finished primarily for rain erosion while aluminum- or other metal-faced laminates are finished for corrosion protection. For coatings to perform their function properly, it is essential that they be applied to surfaces that are clean, free of voids, and smooth. The edges of all parts not protected by a bonding of aluminum or glass-fabric laminate must be sealed to reduce the rate of moisture absorption.

3-12.—3-17. [RESERVED.]

SECTION 3. TRANSPARENT PLASTICS

3-18. GENERAL. Plastics cover a broad field of organic synthetic resin and may be divided into two main classifications – thermoplastics and thermosetting plastics.

a. Thermoplastics. Thermoplastics may be softened by heat and can be dissolved in various organic solvents. Two kinds of transparent thermoplastic materials are commonly employed in windows, canopies, etc. These materials are known as acrylic plastics and cellulose acetate plastics.

(1) Cellulose acetate was used in the past but since it is dimensionally unstable and turns yellow after it has been installed for a time, it has just about passed from the scene and is not considered an acceptable substitute for acrylic.

(2) Acrylic plastics are known by the trade names of Lucite or Plexiglas and by the British as Perspex and meet the military specifications of MIL-P-5425 for regular acrylic, MIL-P-8184 for craze-resistant acrylic.

b. Thermosetting Plastics. These plastics do not soften appreciably under heat but may char and blister at temperatures of 240 to 260 °C (400 to 500 °F). Most of the molded products of synthetic resin composition, such as phenolic, urea-formaldehyde, and melamine formaldehyde resins, belong to the thermosetting group. Once the plastic becomes hard, additional heat will not change it back into a liquid as it would with a thermoplastic.

3-19. STORAGE AND HANDLING. Because transparent thermoplastic sheets soften and deform when they are heated, they must be stored where the temperature will never become excessive. Store them in a cool, dry location away from heating coils, radiators, or steam pipes, and away from such fumes as are found in paint spray booths or paint storage areas.

a. Paper-masked transparent sheets must be kept out of the direct rays of the sun, because sunlight will accelerate deterioration of the adhesive, causing it to bond to the plastic and making it difficult to remove.

b. Plastic sheets should be stored with the masking paper in place, in bins that are tilted at a ten-degree angle from the vertical. This will prevent their buckling. If the sheets are stored horizontally, take care to avoid getting dirt and chips between them. Stacks of sheets must never be over 18 inches high, with the smallest sheets stacked on top of the larger ones so there will be no unsupported overhang. Leave the masking paper on the sheets as long as possible, and take care not to scratch or gouge the sheets by sliding them against each other or across rough or dirty tables.

c. Formed sections should be stored with ample support so they will not lose their shape. Vertical nesting should be avoided. Protect formed parts from temperatures higher than 120 °F (49 °C), and leave their protective coating in place until they are installed on the aircraft.

3-20. FORMING PROCEDURES AND TECHNIQUES. Transparent acrylic plastics get soft and pliable when they are heated to their forming temperatures and can be formed to almost any shape. When they cool, they retain the shape to which they were formed. Acrylic plastic may be cold-bent into a single curvature if the material is thin and the bending radius is at least 180 times the thickness of the sheet. Cold bending beyond these limits will impose so much stress on the surface of the plastic that tiny fissures or cracks, called crazing, will form.

3-21. HEATING. Before heating any transparent plastic material, remove all of the masking paper and adhesive from the sheet. If the sheet is dusty or dirty, wash it with clean water and rinse it well. Dry the sheet thoroughly by blotting it with soft absorbent paper towels.

NOTE: Wear cotton gloves when handling the plastic to eliminate finger marks on the soft surface.

a. For the best results when hot-forming acrylics, use the temperatures recommended by the manufacturer. A forced-air oven should be used–one that is capable of operating over a temperature range of 120 to 374 °F (49 to 190 °C). If the part gets too hot during the forming process, bubbles may form on the surface and impair the optical qualities of the sheet.

b. For uniform heating, it is best to hang the sheets vertically by grasping them by their edges with spring clips and suspending the clips in a rack. (See figure 3-17.) If the piece is too small to hold with clips, or if there is not enough trim area, lay the sheets on shelves or racks covered with soft felt or flannel. Be sure there is enough open space to allow the air to circulate around the sheet and heat it evenly.

c. Small forming jobs, such as landing light covers, may be heated in a kitchen baking oven. Infrared heat lamps may be used if they are arranged on 7-or 8-inch centers and enough of them are used in a bank to heat the sheet evenly. Place the lamps about 18 inches from the material.

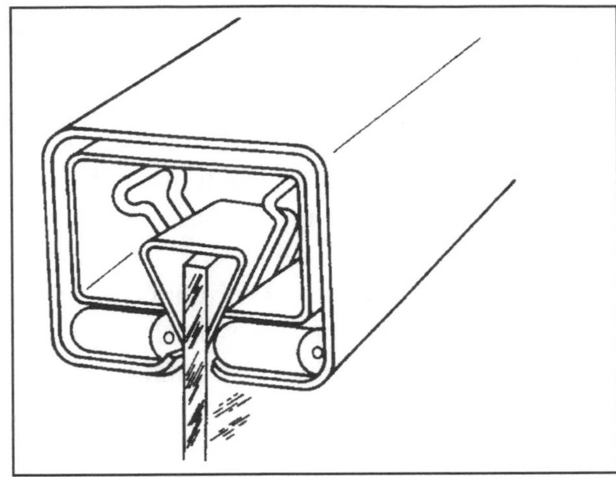

FIGURE 3-17. Hanging of acrylic sheets.

d. Never use hot water or steam directly on the plastic to heat it, because this will likely cause the acrylic to become milky or cloudy.

3-22. FORMS. Heated acrylic plastic will mold with almost no pressure, so the forms used can be of very simple construction. Forms made of pressed wood, plywood, or plaster are adequate to form simple curves, but reinforced plastic or plaster may be needed to shape complex or compound curves.

a. Since hot plastic conforms to any waviness or unevenness, the form used must be completely smooth. To ensure this, sand the form and cover it with soft cloth such as outing flannel or billiard felt.

b. The mold should be large enough to extend beyond the trim line of the part, and provisions should be made for holding the hot plastic snug against the mold as it cools.

c. A mold can be made for a complex part by using the damaged part itself. If the part is broken, tape the pieces together, wax or grease the inside so the plaster will not stick to it, and support the entire part in sand. Fill the part with plaster and allow it to harden, and then remove it from the mold. Smooth out any roughness and cover it with soft cloth. It is now ready to use to form the new part.

3-23. FORMING METHODS. (See table 3-1.)

a. Simple Curve Forming. Heat the plastic material to the recommended temperature, remove it from the heat source, and carefully drape it over the prepared form. Carefully press the hot plastic to the form and either hold or clamp the sheet in place until it cools. This process may take from ten minutes to one-half hour. Do not force-cool it.

b. Compound-Curve Forming. This type of forming is normally used for such parts as canopies or complex wingtip light covers, and it requires a great deal of specialized equipment. There are four commonly used methods, each having its advantages and disadvantages.

c. Stretch Forming. Preheated acrylic sheets are stretched mechanically over the form in much the same way as is done with the simple curved piece. Special care must be taken to preserve uniform thickness of the material, since some parts will have to stretch more than others.

d. Male And Female Die Forming. This requires expensive matching male and female dies. The heated plastic sheet is placed between the dies which are then mated. When the plastic cools, the dies are opened.

e. Vacuum-Forming Without Forms. Many aircraft canopies are formed by this method. In this process a clamp with an opening of the desired shape is placed over a vacuum box and the heated sheet of plastic is clamped in place. When the air in the box is evacuated, the outside air pressure will force the hot plastic through the opening and form the concave canopy. It is the surface tension of the plastic that shapes the canopy.

f. Vacuum-Forming With A Female Form. If the shape needed is other than that which would be formed by surface tension, a female mold, or form must be used. It is placed below the plastic sheet and the vacuum pump is connected. When air from the form is evacuated, the outside air pressure will force the hot plastic sheet into the mold and fill it.

g. Sawing And Drilling.

(1) Several types of saws can be used with transparent plastics, however circular saws are the best for straight cuts. The blades

TABLE 3-1. Typical temperatures for forming acrylic sheets.

Thickness of sheet (in.)	0.125		0.250		0.125		0.250	
Type of forming	Regular acrylic plastic. MIL-P-6886				Heat-resistant acrylic plastic, MIL-P-5425, and craze-resistant acrylic plastic, MIL-P-8184			
	°C	°F	°C	°F	°C	°F	°C	°F
Simple curve	113	235	110	230	135	275	135	275
Stretch forming (dry mold cover)	140	284	135	275	160	320	150	302
Male and female forming	140	284	135	275	180	356	170	338
Vacuum forming without form	140	284	135	275	150	302	145	293
Vacuum forming with female form	145	293	140	284	180	356	170	338

should be hollow-ground or have some set to prevent binding. After the teeth are set, they should be side-dressed to produce a smooth edge on the cut. Band saws are recommended for cutting flat acrylic sheets when the cuts must be curved or where the sheet is cut to a rough dimension to be trimmed later. Close control of size and shape may be obtained by band sawing a piece to within 1/16 inch of the desired size, as marked by a scribed line on the plastic, and then sanding it to the correct size with a drum or belt sander.

(2) Unlike soft metal, acrylic plastic is a very poor conductor of heat. Make provisions for removing the heat when drilling. Deep holes need cooling, and a water-soluble cutting oil is a satisfactory coolant since it has no tendency to attack the plastic.

(a) The drill used on acrylics must be carefully ground and free from nicks and burrs that would affect the surface finish. Grind the drill with a greater included angle than would be used for soft metal. The rake angle should be zero in order to scrape, not cut. (See figure 3-18.)

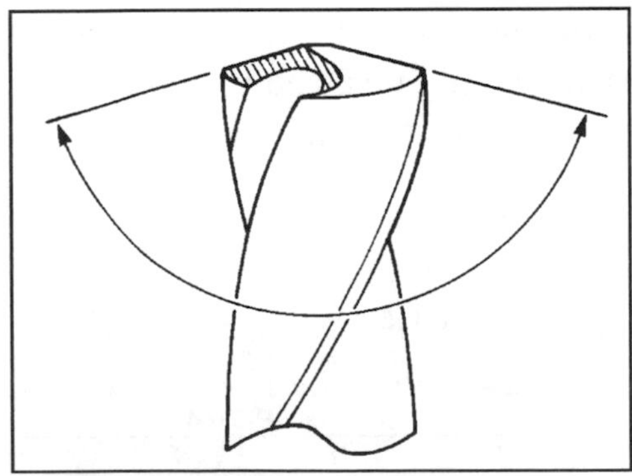

FIGURE 3-18. Drill having an included angle of approximately 150°, used to drill acrylic plastics.

(b) The patented Unibit (see figure 3-19) is good for drilling small holes in aircraft windshields and windows. It can cut holes from 1/8-to 1/2–inch in 1/32–inch increments and produces good smooth holes with no stress cracks around their edges.

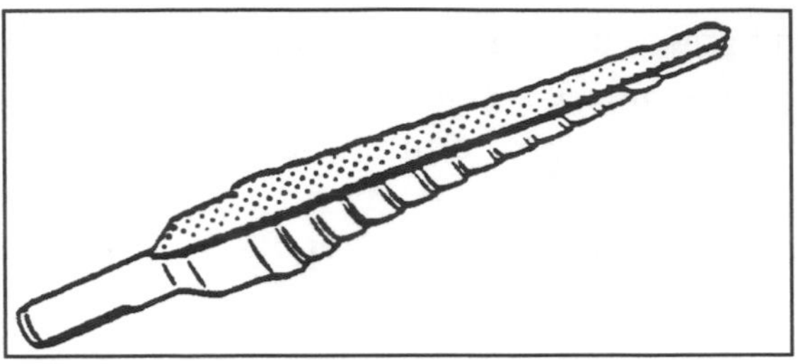

FIGURE 3-19. Unibit drill for drilling acrylic plastics.

h. Polymerizable Cements. Polymerizable cements are those in which a catalyst is added to an already thick monomerpolymer syrup to promote rapid hardening. Cement PS-30 and Weld-On 40 are polymerizable cements of this type. They are suitable for cementing all types of PLEXIGLAS acrylic cast sheet and parts molded from PLEXIGLAS molding pellets. At room temperature, the cements harden (polymerize) in the container in about 45 minutes after mixing the components. They will harden more rapidly at higher temperatures. The cement joints are usually hard enough for handling within 4 hours after assembly. The joints may be machined within 4 hours after assembly, but it is better to wait 24 hours.

(1) PS-30 and Weld-On 40 joints retain excellent appearance and color stability after outdoor exposure. These cements produce clear, transparent joints and should be used when the color and appearance of the joints are important.

(2) PS-30 and Weld-On 40 should be used at temperatures no lower than 65 °F. If cementing is done in a room cooler than 65 °F, it will require a longer time to harden and the joint strength will be reduced.

(a) The cement should be prepared with the correct proportions of components as given in the manufacturer's instructions and thoroughly mixed, making sure neither the mixing container nor mixing paddle adds color or affects the hardening of the cement.

Clean glass or polyethylene mixing containers are preferred.

(b) Because of their short pot life (approximately 45 minutes) Cement PS-30 and Weld-On 40 must be used quickly once the components are mixed. Time consumed in preparation shortens the effective working time, making it necessary to have everything ready to be cemented before the cements are mixed. For better handling pour cement within 20 minutes of mixing.

(c) For maximum joint strength, the final cement joint should be free of bubbles. It will usually be sufficient to allow the mixed cement to stand for 10 minutes before cementing to allow bubbles to rise to the surface. (See figure 3-20.)

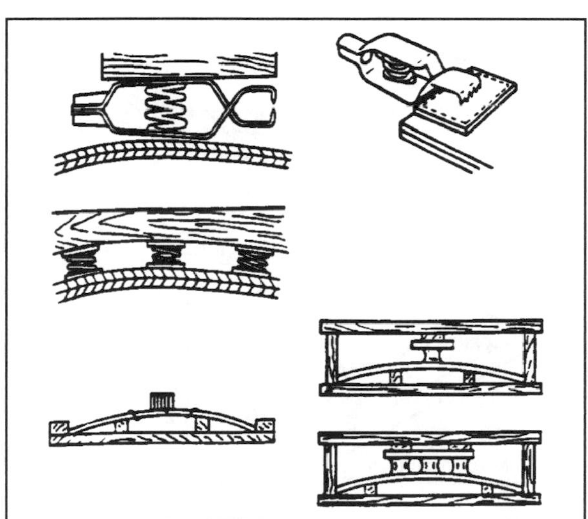

FIGURE 3-20. Applying pressure to acrylic plastics.

(d) The gap joint technique can only be used with colorless PLEXIGLAS acrylic or in cases in which joints will be hidden. If inconspicuous joints in colored PLEXIGLAS acrylic are needed, the parts must be fitted closely, using closed V groove, butt, or arc joints.

(3) Cement forms or dams may be made with masking tape as long as the adhesive surface does not contact the cement. This is easily done with a strip of cellophane tape placed over the masking tape adhesive. The tape must be chosen carefully. The adhesive on ordinary cellophane tape prevents the cure of PS-30 and Weld-On 40. Before actual fabrication of parts, sample joints should be tried to ensure that the tape system used will not harm the cement. Since it is important for all of the cement to remain in the gap, only contact pressure should be used.

(4) Bubbles will tend to float to the top of the cement bead in a gap joint after the cement is poured. These cause no problem if the bead is machined off. A small wire (not copper), or similar objects may be used to lift some bubbles out of the joint; however, the cement joint should be disturbed as little as possible.

(5) Polymerizable cements shrink as the cement hardens. Therefore, the freshly poured cement bead should be left above the surfaces being cemented to compensate for the shrinkage. If it is necessary for appearances, the bead may be machined off after the cement has set.

3-24. REPAIR OF PLASTICS. Replace, rather than repair extensively damaged transparent plastic, whenever possible, since even a carefully patched part is not the equal of a new section, either optically or structurally. At the first sign of crack development, drill a small hole with a # 30 or a 1/8-inch drill at the extreme ends of the cracks as shown in figure 3-21. This serves to localize the cracks and to prevent further splitting by distributing the strain over a large area. If the cracks are small, stopping them with drilled holes will usually suffice until replacement or more permanent repairs can be made. The following repairs are permissible; however, they are not to be located in the pilot's line of vision during landing or normal flight.

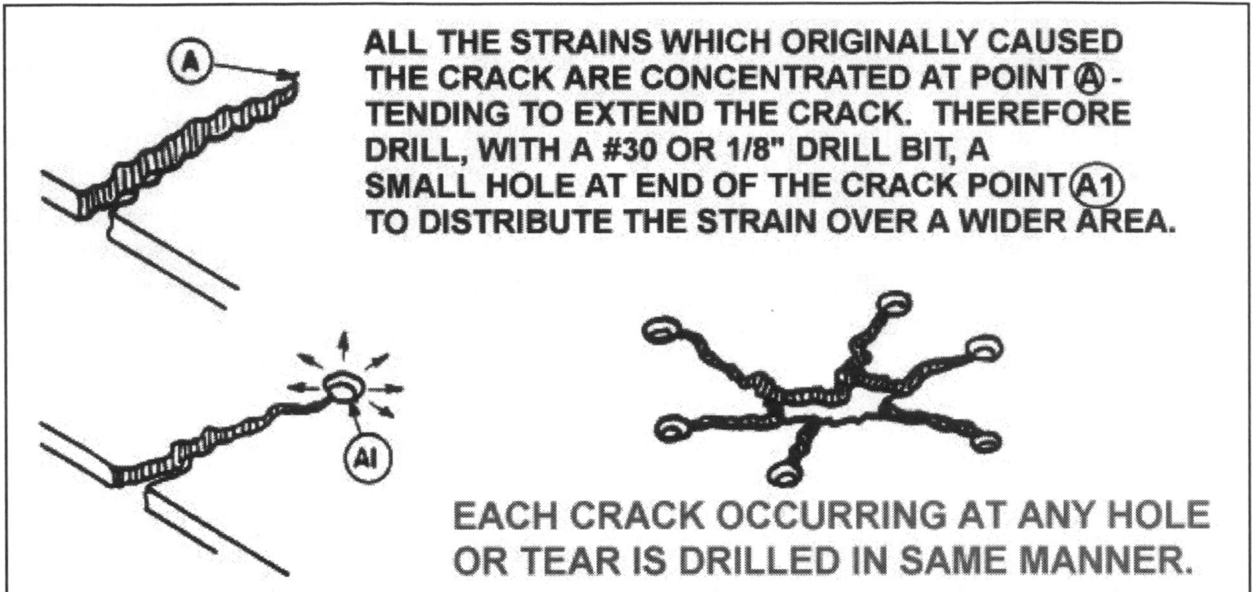

ALL THE STRAINS WHICH ORIGINALLY CAUSED THE CRACK ARE CONCENTRATED AT POINT Ⓐ - TENDING TO EXTEND THE CRACK. THEREFORE DRILL, WITH A #30 OR 1/8" DRILL BIT, A SMALL HOLE AT END OF THE CRACK POINT (A1) TO DISTRIBUTE THE STRAIN OVER A WIDER AREA.
A
AI
EACH CRACK OCCURRING AT ANY HOLE OR TEAR IS DRILLED IN SAME MANNER.

FIGURE 3-21. Stop-drilling cracks.

a. Surface Patch. If a surface patch is to be installed, trim away the damaged area and round all corners. Cut a piece of plastic of sufficient size to cover the damaged area and extend at least 3/4 inch on each side of the crack or hole. Bevel the edges as shown in figure 3-22. If the section to be repaired is curved, shape the patch to the same contour by heating it in an oil bath at a temperature of 248 to 302 °F, or it may be heated on a hot-plate until soft. Boiling water should not be used for heating. Coat the patch evenly with plastic solvent adhesive and immediately place it over the hole. Maintain a uniform pressure of 5 to 10 psi on the patch for a minimum of 3 hours. Allow the patch to dry 24 to 36 hours before sanding or polishing.

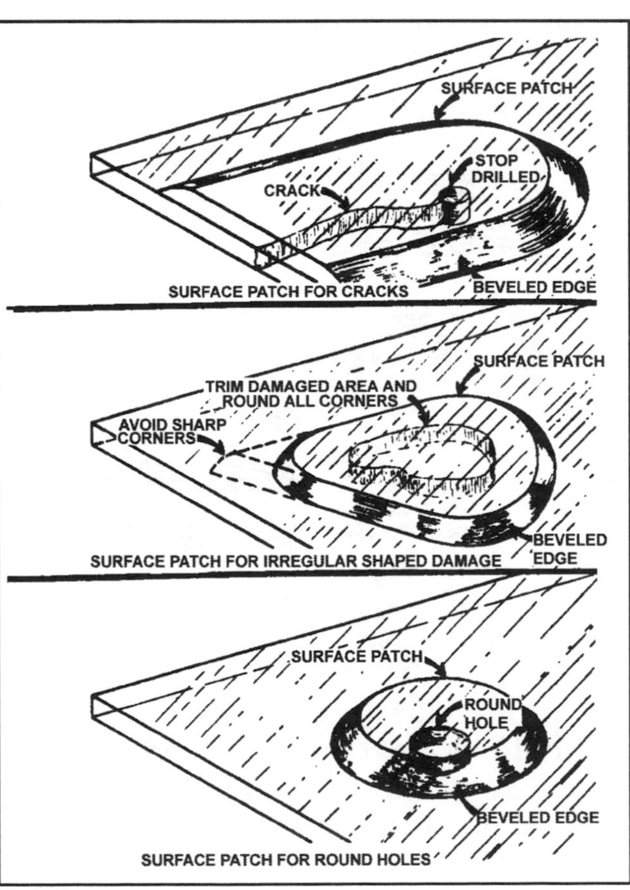

FIGURE 3-22. Surface patches.

b. Plug Patch. When using inserted patches to repair holes in plastic structures, trim the holes to a perfect circle or oval and bevel the edges slightly. Make the patch slightly thicker than the material being repaired and similarly bevel its edges. Install patches in accordance with figure 3-23. Heat the plug until soft and press it into the hole without cement and allow to cool to make a perfect fit. Remove the plug, coat the edges with adhesive, and then reinsert in the hole. Maintain a firm light pressure until the cement has set. Sand or file the edges level with the surface, then buff and polish.

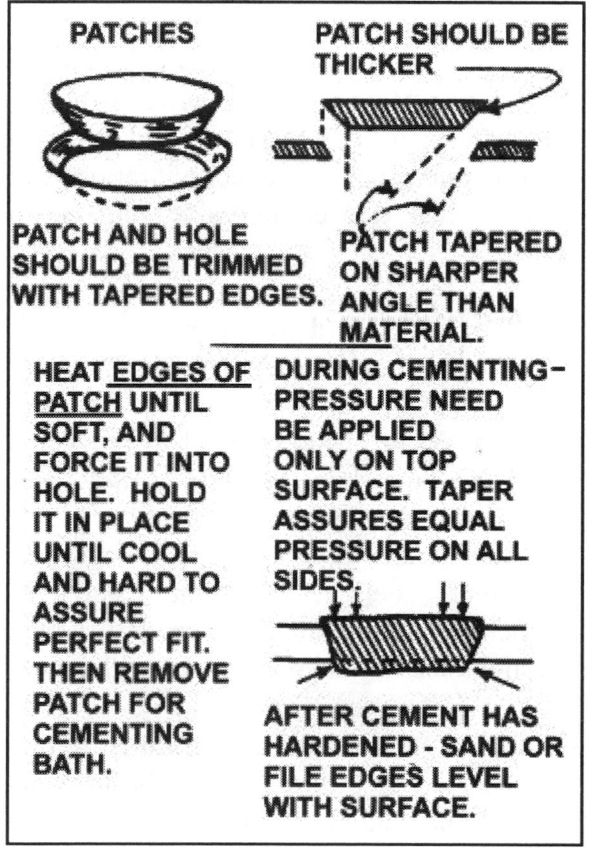

FIGURE 3-23. Plug patch repair.

3-25. CLEANING AND POLISHING TRANSPARENT PLASTIC. Plastics have many advantages over glass for aircraft use, but they lack the surface hardness of glass and care must be exercised while servicing the aircraft to avoid scratching or otherwise damaging the surface.

a. Clean the plastic by washing it with plenty of water and mild soap, using a clean, soft, grit-free cloth, sponge, or bare hands. Do not use gasoline, alcohol, benzene, acetone, carbon tetrachloride, fire extinguisher or deicing fluids, lacquer thinners, or window cleaning sprays. These will soften the plastic and cause crazing.

b. Plastics should not be rubbed with a dry cloth since this is likely to cause scratches, and also to build up an electrostatic charge that attracts dust particles to the surface. If after removing dirt and grease, no great amount of scratching is visible, finish the plastic with a good grade of commercial wax. Apply the wax in a thin even coat and bring to a high polish by rubbing lightly with a soft cloth.

c. Do not attempt hand polishing or buffing until the surface is clean. A soft, open-type cotton or flannel buffing wheel is suggested. Minor scratches may be removed by vigorously rubbing the affected area by hand, using a soft clean cloth dampened with a mixture of turpentine and chalk, or by applying automobile cleanser with a damp cloth. Remove the cleaner and polish with a soft, dry cloth. Acrylic and cellulose acetate plastics are thermoplastic. Friction created by buffing or polishing too long in one spot can generate sufficient heat to soften the surface. This condition will produce visual distortion and should be avoided.

3-26. REPLACEMENT PANELS. Use material equivalent to that originally used by the manufacturer of the aircraft for replacement panels. There are many types of transparent plastics on the market. Their properties vary greatly, particularly in regard to expansion characteristics, brittleness under low temperatures, resistance to discoloration when exposed to sunlight, surface checking, etc. Information on these properties is in MIL-HDBK-17A, Plastics for Flight Vehicles, Part II—Transparent Glazing Materials, available from the Government Printing Office (GPO). These properties are considered by aircraft manufacturers in selecting materials to be used in their designs and the use of substitutes having different characteristics may result in subsequent difficulties.

3-27. INSTALLATION PROCEDURES. When installing a replacement panel, use the same mounting method employed by the manufacturer of the aircraft. While the actual installation will vary from one type of aircraft to another, consider the following major principles when installing any replacement panel.

a. Never force a plastic panel out of shape to make it fit a frame. If a replacement panel does not fit easily into the mounting, obtain a new replacement or heat the whole panel and reform. When possible, cut and fit a new panel at ordinary room temperature.

b. In clamping or bolting plastic panels into their mountings, do not place the plastic under excessive compressive stress. It is easy to develop more than 1,000 psi on the plastic by over-torquing a nut and bolt. Tighten each nut to a firm fit, then back the nut off one full turn (until they are snug and can still be rotated with the fingers).

c. In bolted installations, use spacers, collars, shoulders, or stop-nuts to prevent tightening the bolt excessively. Whenever such devices are used by the aircraft manufacturer, retain them in the replacement installation. It is important that the original number of bolts, complete with washers, spacers, etc., be used. When rivets are used, provide adequate spacers or other satisfactory means to prevent excessive tightening of the frame to the plastic.

d. Mount plastic panels between rubber, cork, or other gasket material to make the installation waterproof, to reduce vibration, and to help to distribute compressive stresses on the plastic.

e. Plastics expand and contract considerably more than the metal channels in which they are mounted. Mount windshield panels to a sufficient depth in the channel to prevent it from falling out when the panel contracts at low temperatures or deforms under load. When the manufacturer's original design permits, mount panels to a minimum depth of 1-1/8 inch, and with a clearance of 1/8 inch between the plastic and bottom of the channel.

f. In installations involving bolts or rivets, make the holes through the plastic oversize by 1/8-inch diameter and center so that the plastic will not bind or crack at the edge of the holes. The use of slotted holes is also recommended.

3-28.—3-39. [RESERVED.]

SECTION 4. WINDSHIELDS, ENCLOSURES, AND WINDOWS

3-40. GENERAL. These repairs are applicable to plastic windshields, enclosures, and windows in *nonpressurized airplanes*. For pressurized airplanes, replace or repair plastic elements in accordance with the manufacturer's recommendation. When windshields and side windows made of acrylic plastics are damaged, they are usually replaced unless the damage is minor and a repair would not be in the line of vision. Repairs usually require a great deal of labor. Replacement parts are readily available, so replacement is normally more economical than repair.

a. Minor Repairs. There are times, however, when a windshield may be cracked and safety is not impaired. In that case, repairs can be made by stop-drilling the ends of the crack with a # 30 drill (1/8 inch) to prevent the concentration of stresses causing the crack to continue. Drill a series of number 40 holes a half-inch from the edge of the crack about a half-inch apart, and lace through these holes with brass safety wire (see figure 3-24) and seal with clear silicone to waterproof.

b. Temporary Repairs. One way to make a temporary repair is to stop-drill the ends of the crack, and then drill number 27 holes every inch or so in the crack. Use AN515-6 screws and AN365-632 nuts with AN960-6 washers on both sides of the plastic. This will hold the crack together and prevent further breakage until the windshield can be properly repaired or replaced. (See figure 3-24.)

c. Permanent Repairs. Windshields or side windows with small cracks that affect only the appearance rather than the airworthiness of a sheet, may be repaired by first stop-drilling the ends of the crack with a # 30 or a 1/8-inch drill. Then use a hypodermic syringe and needle to fill the crack with polymerizable cement such as PS-30 or Weld-On 40, and allow capillary action to fill the crack completely. Soak the end of a 1/8-inch acrylic rod in cement to form a cushion and insert it in the stop-drilled hole. Allow the repair to dry for about 30 minutes, and then trim the rod off flush with the sheet.

d. Polishing and Finishing. Scratches and repair marks, within certain limitations, can be removed from acrylic plastic. No sanding that could adversely affect the plastic's optical properties and distort the pilot's vision should be done on any portion of a windshield.

(1) If there are scratches or repair marks in an area that can be sanded, they may be removed by first sanding the area. Use 320- or 400-grit abrasive paper that is wrapped around a felt or rubber pad.

(2) Use circular rubbing motions, light pressure, and a mild liquid soap solution as a lubricant. After the sanding is complete, rinse the surface thoroughly with running water. Then, using a 500-grit paper, continue to sand lightly. Keep moving to higher grit paper and sand and rinse until all of the sanding or repair marks have been removed.

(3) After using the finest abrasive paper, use rubbing compound and buff in a circular motion to remove all traces of the sanding.

e. Cleaning. Acrylic windshields and windows may be cleaned by washing them with mild soap and running water. Rub the surface with your bare hands in a stream of water. Follow with the same procedure but with soap and water. After the soap and dirt have been flushed away, dry the surface with a soft, clean cloth or tissue and polish it with a

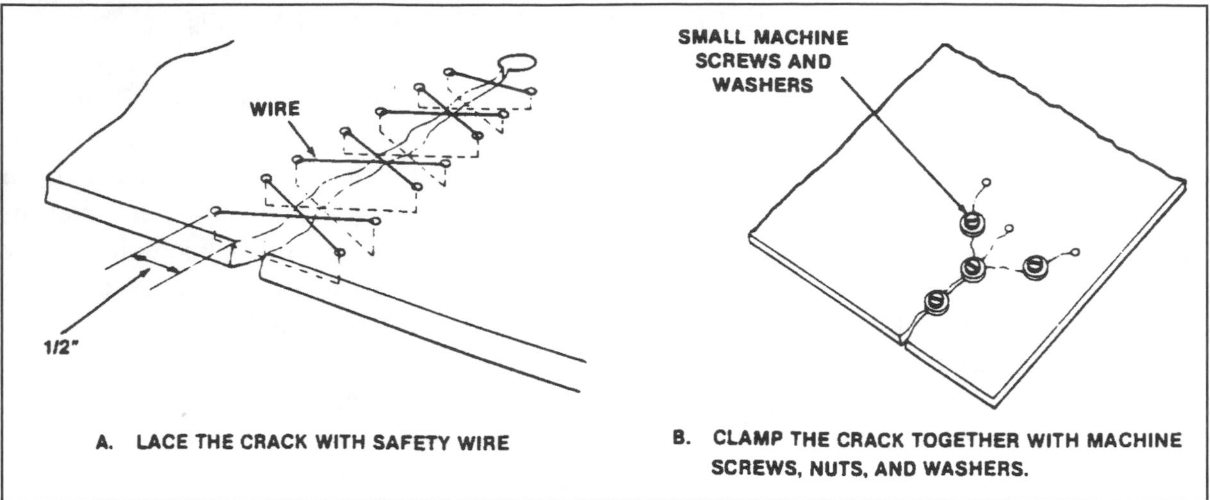

FIGURE 3-24. Temporary repairs to cracked windshields or windows.

windshield cleaner especially approved for use on aircraft transparent plastics. These cleaners may be purchased through aircraft supply houses.

f. Waxing. A thin coating of wax will fill any minute scratches that may be present and will cause rain to form droplets that are easily blown away by the wind.

3-41. PROTECTION. Acrylic windshields are often called "lifetime" windshields, to distinguish them from those made of the much shorter-lived acetate material. However, even acrylic must be protected from the ravages of the elements.

a. When an aircraft is parked in direct sunlight, the windshield will absorb heat and will actually become hotter than either the inside of the aircraft or the outside air. The sun will cause the inside of a closed aircraft to become extremely hot, and this heat is also absorbed by the plastic windshield.

b. To protect against this damage, it is wise to keep the aircraft in a hangar. If this is not possible, some type of shade should be provided to keep the sun from coming in direct contact with the windshield. Some aircraft owners use a close-fitting, opaque, reflective cover over the windshield. In many cases, this has done more harm than good. This cover may absorb moisture from the air and give off harmful vapors, and if it touches the surface of the plastic it can cause crazing or minute cracks to form in the windshield. Another hazard in using such a cover is that sand can blow up under the cover and scratch the plastic.

3-42. WINDSHIELD INSTALLATION. Aircraft windshields may be purchased either from the original aircraft manufacturer or from any of several FAA-PMA sources. These windshields are formed to the exact shape required, but are slightly larger than necessary so they may be trimmed to the exact size.

a. After removing the damaged windshield, clean all of the sealer from the grooves and cut the new windshield to fit. New windshields are covered with either protective paper or film to prevent damage during handling or installation. Carefully peel back just enough of this covering to make the installation. The windshield must fit in its channels with about 1/8- to 1/4-inch clearance to allow for expansion and contraction. If any holes are drilled in the plastic for screws, they should be about 1/8 inch oversize.

b. Place the sealing tape around the edges of the windshield and install the windshield in its frame. Screws that go through the windshield should be tightened down snug and then backed out a full turn, so the plastic can shift as it expands and contracts.

c. Do not remove the protective paper or film until the windshield is installed and all of the securing screws are in place.

3-43.—3-47. [RESERVED.]

CHAPTER 4. METAL STRUCTURE, WELDING, AND BRAZING

SECTION 1. IDENTIFICATION OF METALS

4-1. GENERAL. Proper identification of the aircraft structural material is the first step in ensuring that the continuing airworthiness of the aircraft will not be degraded by making an improper repair using the wrong materials.

a. Ferrous (iron) alloy materials are generally classified according to carbon content. (See table 4-1.)

TABLE 4-1. Ferrous (iron) alloy materials.

MATERIALS	CARBON CONTENT
Wrought iron	Trace to 0.08%
Low carbon steel	0.08% to 0.30%
Medium carbon steel	0.30% to 0.60%
High carbon steel	0.60% to 2.2%
Cast iron	2.3% to 4.5%

b. The strength and ductility, or toughness of steel, is controlled by the kind and quantity of alloys used and also by cold-working or heat-treating processes used in manufacturing. In general, any process that increases the strength of a material will also decrease its ductility.

c. Normalizing is heating steel to approximately 150 °F to 225 °F above the steel's critical temperature range, followed by cooling to below that range in still air at ordinary temperature. Normalizing may be classified as a form of annealing. This process also removes stresses due to machining, forging, bending, and welding. After the metal has been held at this temperature for a sufficient time to be heated uniformly throughout, remove the metal from the furnace and cool in still air. Avoid prolonging the soaking of the metal at high temperatures, as this practice will cause the grain structure to enlarge. The length of time required for the soaking temperature depends on the mass of the metal being treated. The soaking time is roughly ¼ hour per inch of the diameter of thickness (Ref: Military Tech Order (T.O.) 1-1A-9).

4-2. IDENTIFICATION OF STEEL STOCK. The Society of Automotive Engineers (SAE) and the American Iron and Steel Institute (AISI) use a numerical index system to identify the composition of various steels. The numbers assigned in the combined listing of standard steels issued by these groups represent the type of steel and make it possible to readily identify the principal elements in the material.

a. The basic numbers for the four digit series of the carbon and alloy steel may be found in table 4-2. The first digit of the four number designation indicates the type to which the steel belongs. Thus, "1" indicates a carbon steel, "2" a nickel steel, "3" a nickel chromium steel, etc. In the case of simple alloy steels, the second digit indicates the approximate percentage of the predominant alloying element. The last two digits usually indicate the mean of the range of carbon content. Thus, the designation "1020" indicates a plain carbon steel lacking a principal alloying element and containing an average of 0.20 percent (0.18 to 0.23) carbon. The designation "2330" indicates a nickel steel of approximately 3 percent (3.25 to 3.75) nickel and an average of 0.30 percent, (0.28 to 0.33) carbon content. The designation "4130" indicates a chromium-molybdenum steel of approximately 1 percent (0.80 to 1.10) chromium, 0.20 percent (0.15 to 0.25) molybdenum, and 0.30 percent (0.28 to 0.33) carbon.

b. There are numerous steels with higher percentages of alloying elements that do not fit into this numbering system. These include a large group of stainless and heat resisting alloys in which chromium is an essential alloying element. Some of these alloys are identified by three digit AISI numbers and many others by designations assigned by the steel company that produces them. The few examples in table 4-3 will serve to illustrate the kinds of designations used and the general alloy content of these steels.

c. "1025" welded tubing as per Specification MIL-T-5066 and "1025" seamless tubing conforming to Specification MIL-T-5066A are interchangeable.

4-3. INTERCHANGEABILITY OF STEEL TUBING.

a. "4130" welded tubing conforming to Specification MIL-T-6731, and "4130" seam-less tubing conforming to Specification MIL-T-6736 are interchangeable.

b. NE-8630 welded tubing conforming to Specification MIL-T-6734, and NE-8630 seamless tubing conforming to Specification MIL-T-6732 are interchangeable.

4-4. IDENTIFICATION OF ALUMINUM. To provide a visual means for identifying the various grades of aluminum and aluminum alloys, such metals are usually marked with symbols such as a Government Specification Number, the temper or condition furnished, or the commercial code marking. Plate and sheet are usually marked with specification numbers or code markings in rows approximately 5 inches apart. Tubes, bars, rods, and extruded shapes are marked with specification numbers or code markings at intervals of 3 to 5 feet along the length of each piece.

The commercial code marking consists of a number which identifies the particular composition of the alloy. In addition, letter suffixes (see table 4-4) designate the basic temper designations and subdivisions of aluminum alloys.

TABLE 4-2. Numerical system for steel identification.

TYPES OF STEELS	NUMERALS AND DIGITS
Plain carbon steel	10XX
Carbon steel with additional sulfur for easy machining.	11XX
Carbon steel with about 1.75% manganese	13XX
.25% molybdenum.	40XX
1% chromium, .25% molybdenum	41XX
2% nickel, 1% chromium, .25% molybdenum	43XX
1.7% nickel, .2% molybdenum	46XX
3.5% nickel, .25% molybdenum	48XX
1% chromium steels	51XX
1% chromium, 1.00% carbon	51XXX
1.5% chromium steels	52XX
1.5% chromium, 1.00% carbon	52XXX
1% chromium steel with .15% vanadium	61XX
.5% chromium, .5% nickel, .20% molybdenum	86XX
.5% chromium, .5% nickel, .25% molybdenum	87XX
2% silicon steels, .85% manganese	92XX
3.25% nickel, 1.20% chromium, .12% molybdenum	93XX

TABLE 4-3. Examples of stainless and heat-resistant steels nominal composition (percent)

ALLOY DESIGNATION	CARBON	CHROMIUM	NICKEL	OTHER	GENERAL CLASS OF STEEL
302	0.15	18	9		Austenitic
310	0.25	25	20		Austenitic
321	0.08	18	11	Titanium	Austenitic
347	0.08	18	11	Columbium or Tantalum	Austenitic
410	0.15	12.5			Martensitic, Magnetic
430	0.12	17			Ferritic, Magnetic
446	0.20	25		Nitrogen	Ferritic, Magnetic
PH15-7 Mo	0.09	15	7	Molybdenum, Aluminum	Precipitation Hardening
17-4 PH	0.07	16.5	4	Copper, Columbium or Tantalum	Precipitation Hardening

TABLE 4-4. Basic temper designations and subdivisions from aluminum alloys.

NON HEAT-TREATABLE ALLOYS		HEAT-TREATABLE ALLOYS	
Temper Designation	**Definition**	**Temper Designation**	**Definition**
-0	Annealed recrystallized (wrought products only) applies to softest temper of wrought products.	-0	Annealed recrystallized (wrought products only) applies to softest temper of wrought products.
-H1	Strain-hardened only. Applies to products which are strain-hardened to obtain the desired strength without supplementary thermal treatment.	-T1	Cooled from an elevated temperature shaping process (such as extrusion or casting) and naturally aged to a substantially stable condition.
-H12	Strain-hardened one-quarter-hard temper.	-T2	Annealed (castings only).
-H14	Strain-hardened half-hard temper.	-T3	Solution heat-treated and cold-worked by the flattening or straightening operation.
-H16	Strain-hardened three-quarters-hard temper.	-T36	Solution heat-treated and cold-worked by reduction of 6 percent
-H18	Strain-hardened full-hard temper.	-T4	Solution heat-treated.
-H2	Strain-hardened and then partially annealed. Applies to products which are strain-hardened more than the desired final amount and then reduced in strength to the desired level by partial annealing.	-T42	Solution heat-treated by the user regardless of prior temper (applicable only to 2014 and 2024 alloys).
-H22	Strain-hardened and partially annealed to one-quarter-hard temper.	-T5	Artificially aged only (castings only).
-H24	Strain-hardened and partially annealed to half-hard temper.	-T6	Solution heat-treated and artificially aged.
-H26	Strain-hardened and partially annealed to three-quarters-hard temper.	-T62	Solution heat-treated and aged by user regardless of prior temper (applicable only to 2014 and 2024 alloys).
-H28	Strain-hardened and partially annealed to full-hard temper.	-T351, -T451, -T3510, -T3511, -T4510, -T4511.	Solution heat-treated and stress relieved by stretching to produce a permanent set of 1 to 3 percent, depending on the product.
-H3	Strain-hardened and then stabilized. Applies to products which are strain-hardened and then stabilized by a low temperature heating to slightly lower their strength and increase ductility.	-T651, -T851, -T6510, -T8510, -T6511, -T8511.	Solution heat-treated, stress relieved by stretching to produce a permanent set of 1 to 3 percent, and artificially aged.
-H32	Strain-hardened and then stabilized. Final temper is one-quarter hard.	-T652	Solution heat-treated, compressed to produce a permanent set and then artificially aged.
-H34	Strain-hardened and then stabilized. Final temper is one-half hard.	-T8	Solution heat-treated, cold-worked and then artificially aged.
-H36	Strain-hardened and then stabilized. Final temper is three-quarters hard.	-T/4	Solution heat-treated, cold-worked by the flattening or straightening operation, and then artificially aged.
-H38	Strain-hardened and then stabilized. Final temper is full-hard.	-T86	Solution heat-treated, cold-worked by reduction of 6 percent, and then artificially aged.
-H112	As fabricated; with specified mechanical property limits.	-T9	Solution heat-treated, artificially aged and then cold-worked.
-F	For wrought alloys; as fabricated. No mechanical properties limits. For cast alloys; as cast.	-T10	Cooled from an elevated temperature shaping process artificially aged and then cold-worked.
		-F	For wrought alloys; as fabricated. No mechanical properties limits. For cast alloys; as cast.

4-5. - 4-15. [RESERVED.]

SECTION 2. TESTING OF METALS

4-16. HARDNESS TESTING. If the material type is known, a hardness test is a simple way to verify that the part has been properly heat-treated. Hardness testers such as Rockwell, Brinell, and Vickers can be useful to check metals for loss of strength due to exposure to fire or abusive heating. Also, understrength bolts can be found and removed from the replacement part inventory by checking the hardness of the bolt across the hex flats. Although hardness tests are generally considered nondestructive, hardness testing does leave a small pit in the surface; therefore, hardness tests should not be used on sealing surfaces, fatigue critical parts, load bearing areas, etc., that will be returned to service. These hardness tests provide a convenient means for determining, within reasonable limits, the tensile strength of steel. It has several limitations in that it is not suitable for very soft or very hard steels. Hardness testing of aluminum alloys should be limited to distinguishing between annealed and heat-treated material of the same aluminum alloy. In hardness testing, the thickness and the edge distance of the specimen being tested are two factors that must be considered to avoid distortion of the metal. Several readings should be taken and the results averaged. In general, the higher the tensile strength, the greater its hardness. Common methods of hardness testing are outlined in the following paragraphs. These tests are suitable for determining the tensile properties resulting from the heat treatment of steel. Care should be taken to have case-hardened, corroded, pitted, decarburized, or otherwise nonuniform surfaces removed to a sufficient depth. Exercise caution not to cold-work, and consequently harden, the steel during removal of the surface.

4-17. ROCKWELL HARDNESS TEST. The Rockwell hardness test is the most common method for determining hardness of ferrous and many nonferrous metals. (See table 4-5.) It differs from Brinell hardness testing in that the hardness is determined by the depth of indentation made by a constant load impressing on an indenter. In this test, a standard minor load is applied to set a hardened steel ball or a diamond cone in the surface of the metal, followed by the application of a standard major load. The hardness is measured by depth of penetration. Rockwell superficial hardness tests are made using light minor and major loads and a more sensitive system for measuring depth of indentation. It is useful for thin sections, very small parts, etc. Calibration of Rockwell hardness testers is done in accordance with American Society of Testing Materials (ASTM E-18) specifications.

4-18. BRINELL HARDNESS TEST. In this test a standard constant load, usually 500 to 3,000 kg, is applied to a smooth flat metal surface by a hardened steel-ball type indenter, 10 mm in diameter. The 500-kg load is usually used for testing nonferrous metals such as copper and aluminum alloys, whereas the 3,000-kg load is most often used for testing harder metals such as steels and cast irons. The numerical value of Brinell Hardness (HB), is equal to the load, divided by the surface area of the resulting spherical impression.

$$HB = \frac{P}{(\pi \frac{D}{2}[D - \sqrt{(D^2 - d^2)}])}$$

Where *P* is the load, in kg; *D* is the diameter of the ball, in mm; and *d* is the diameter of the indentation, in mm.

a. General Precautions. To avoid misapplication of Brinell hardness testing, the fundamentals and limitations of the test procedure must be clearly understood. To avoid inaccuracies, the following rules should be followed.

(1) Do not make indentations on a curved surface having a radius of less than 1 inch.

(2) Do make the indentations with the correct spacing. Indentations should not be made too close to the edge of the work piece being tested.

(3) Apply the load steadily to avoid overloading caused by inertia of the weights.

(4) Apply the load so the direction of loading and the test surface are perpendicular to each other within 2 degrees.

(5) The thickness of the work piece being tested should be such that no bulge or mark showing the effect of the load appears on the side of the work piece opposite the indentation.

(6) The indentation diameter should be clearly outlined.

b. Limitations. The Brinell hardness test has three principal limitations.

(1) The work piece must be capable of accommodating the relatively large indentations.

(2) Due to the relatively large indentations, the work piece should not be used after testing.

(3) The limit of hardness, 15 HB with the 500-kg load to 627 HB with the 3,000-kg load, is generally considered the practical range.

c. Calibration. A Brinell Hardness Tester should be calibrated to meet ASTM standard E10 specifications.

4-19. VICKERS HARDNESS TEST. In this test, a small pyramidal diamond is pressed into the metal being tested. The Vickers Hardness number (HV) is the ratio of the load applied to the surface area of the indention. This is done with the following formula.

$$HV = P / 0.5393d^2$$

a. The indenter is made of diamond, and is in the form of a square-based pyramid having an angle of 136 degrees between faces. The facets are highly-polished, free from surface imperfections, and the point is sharp. The loads applied vary from 1 to 120 kg; the standard loads are 5, 10, 20, 30, 50, 100, and 120 kg. For most hardness testing, 50 kg is maximum.

b. A Vickers hardness tester should be calibrated to meet ASTM standard E10 specifications, acceptable for use over a loading range.

4-20. MICROHARDNESS TESTING. This is an indentation hardness test made with loads not exceeding 1 kg (1,000 g). Such hardness tests have been made with a load as light as 1 g, although the majority of microhardness tests are made with loads of 100 to 500 g. In general, the term is related to the size of the indentation rather than to the load applied.

a. Fields of Application. Microhardness testing is capable of providing information regarding the hardness characteristics of materials which cannot be obtained by hardness tests such as the Brinell or Rockwell, and are as follows.

(1) Measuring the hardness of precision work pieces that are too small to be measured by the more common hardness-testing methods.

(2) Measuring the hardness of product forms such as foil or wire that are too thin or too small in diameter to be measured by the more conventional methods.

(3) Monitoring of carburizing or nitriding operations, which is sometimes accomplished by hardness surveys taken on cross sections of test pieces that accompanied the work pieces through production operations.

(4) Measuring the hardness of individual microconstituents.

(5) Measuring the hardness close to edges, thus detecting undesirable surface conditions such as grinding burn and decarburization.

(6) Measuring the hardness of surface layers such as plating or bonded layers.

b. Indenters. Microhardness testing can be performed with either the Knoop or the Vickers indenter. The Knoop indenter is used mostly in the United States; the Vickers indenter is the more widely used in Europe.

(1) Knoop indentation testing is performed with a diamond, ground to pyramidal form, that produces a diamond-shaped indentation with an approximate ratio between long and short diagonals of 7 to 1. The indentation depth is about one-thirtieth of its length. Due to the shape of the indenter, indentations of accurately measurable length are obtained with light loads.

(2) The Knoop hardness number (HK) is the ratio of the load applied to the indenter to the unrecovered projected area of indentation. The formula for this follows.

$$HK = P / A = P / Cl^2$$

Where P is the applied load, in kg; A is the unrecovered projected area of indentation, in square mm; l is the measured length of the long diagonal, in mm; and C is 0.07028, a constant of the indenter relating projected area of the indentation to the square of the length of the long diagonal.

4-21. INDENTATIONS. The Vickers indenter penetrates about twice as far into the work piece as does the Knoop indenter. The diagonal of the Vickers indentation is about one-third of the total length of the Knoop indentation. The Vickers indenter is less sensitive to minute differences in surface conditions than is the Knoop indenter. However, the Vickers indentation, because of the shorter diagonal, is more sensitive to errors in measuring than is the Knoop indentation. (See figure 4-1.)

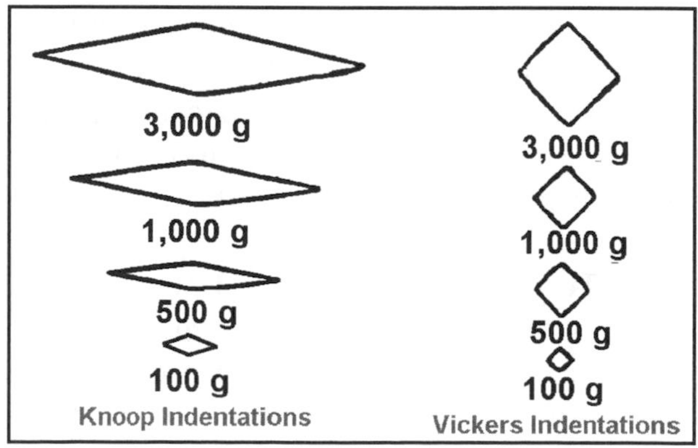

FIGURE 4-1. Comparison of indentation made by Knoop and Vickers indenters in the same work metal and at the same loads.

4-22. MAGNETIC TESTING. Magnetic testing consists of determining whether the specimen is attracted by a magnet. Usually, a metal attracted by a magnet is iron, steel, or an iron-base alloy containing nickel, cobalt, or chromium. However, there are exceptions to this rule since some nickel and cobalt alloys may be either magnetic or nonmagnetic. Never use this test as a final basis for identification. The strongly attracted metals could be pure iron, pure nickel, cobalt, or iron-nickel-cobalt alloys. The lightly attracted metals could be cold-worked stainless steel, or monel. The nonmagnetic metals could be aluminum, magnesium, silver, or copper-base alloy, or an annealed 300-type stainless steel.

4-23. ALUMINUM TESTING. Hardness tests are useful for testing aluminum alloy chiefly as a means of distinguishing between annealed, cold-worked, heat-treated, and heat-treated and aged material. It is of little value in indicating the strength or quality of heat treatment. Typical hardness values for aluminum alloys are shown in table 4-5.

a. Clad aluminum alloys have surface layers of pure aluminum or corrosion-resistant aluminum alloy bonded to the core material to inhibit corrosion. Presence of such a coating may be determined under a magnifying glass by examination of the edge surface which will show three distinct layers. In aluminum alloys, the properties of any specific alloy can be altered by work hardening (often called strain-hardening), heat treatment, or by a combination of these processes.

b. Test for distinguishing heat-treatable and nonheat-treatable aluminum alloys. If for any reason the identification mark of the alloy is not on the material, it is possible to distinguish between some heat-treatable alloys and some nonheat-treatable alloys by immersing a sample of the material in a 10 percent solution of caustic soda (sodium hydroxide). Those heat-treated alloys containing several percent of copper (2014, 2017, and 2024) will turn black due to the copper content. High-copper alloys when clad will not turn black on the surface, but the edges will turn black at the center of the sheet where the core is exposed. If the alloy does not turn black in the caustic soda solution it is not evidence that the alloy is nonheat-treatable, as various high-strength heat-treatable alloys are not based primarily on the use of copper as an alloying agent. These include among others 6053, 6061, and 7075 alloys. The composition and heat-treating ability of alloys which do not turn black in a caustic soda solution can be established only by chemical or spectro-analysis.

TABLE 4-5. Hardness values for aluminum alloys. (Reference MIL-H-6088G.)

Material Commercial Designation	Hardness Temper	Brinell number 500 kg. load 10 mm. ball
1100	0	23
	H18	44
3003	0	28
	H16	47
2014	0	45
	T6	135
2017	0	45
	T6	105
2024	0	47
	T4	120
2025	T6	110
6151	T6	100
5052	0	47
	H36	73
6061	0	30
	T4	65
	T6	95
7075	T6	135
7079	T6	135
195	T6	75
220	T4	75
C355	T6	80
A356	T6	70

4-24.—4-35. [RESERVED.]

SECTION 3. PRECAUTIONARY MEASURES

4-36. FLUTTER AND VIBRATION PRECAUTIONS. To prevent the occurrence of severe vibration or flutter of flight control surfaces during flight, precautions must be taken to stay within the design balance limitations when performing maintenance or repair.

a. Balance Changes. The importance of retaining the proper balance and rigidity of aircraft control surfaces cannot be overemphasized. The effect of repair or weight change on the balance and center of gravity is proportionately greater on lighter surfaces than on the older heavier designs. As a general rule, repair the control surface in such a manner that the weight distribution is not affected in any way, in order to preclude the occurrence of flutter of the control surface in flight. Under certain conditions, counter-balance weight is added forward of the hinge line to maintain balance. Add or remove balance weights only when necessary in accordance with the manufacturer's instructions. Flight testing must be accomplished to ensure flutter is not a problem. Failure to check and retain control surface balance within the original or maximum allowable value could result in a serious flight hazard.

b. Painting and Refinishing. Special emphasis is directed to the effect of too many extra coats of paint on balanced control surfaces. Mechanics must avoid adding additional coats of paint in excess of what the manufacturer originally applied. If available consult the aircraft manufacturer's instructions relative to finishing and balance of control surfaces.

c. Trapped Water or Ice. Instances of flutter have occurred from unbalanced conditions caused by the collection of water or ice within the surface. Therefore, ventilation and drainage provisions must be checked and retained when maintenance is being done.

d. Trim Tab Maintenance. Loose or vibrating trim tabs will increase wear of actuating mechanisms and hinge points which may develop into serious flutter conditions. When this happens, primary control surfaces are highly susceptible to wear, deformation, and fatigue failures because of the buffeting nature of the airflow over the tab mechanism. Trailing-edge play of the tab may increase, creating an unsafe flutter condition. Careful inspection of the tab and its mechanism should be conducted during overhaul and annual inspection periods. Compared to other flight control systems on the aircraft, only a minor amount of tab-mechanism wear can be tolerated.

(1) Free play and stiffness may best be measured by a simple static test where "upward" and "downward" (or "leftward" and "rightward") point forces are applied near the trailing edge of the tab at the span-wise attachment of the actuator (so as not to twist the tab). The control surface to which the trim tab is attached should be locked in place. Rotational deflection readings are then taken near the tab trailing edge using an appropriate measuring device, such as a dial gauge. Several deflection readings should be taken using loads first applied in one direction, then in the opposite. If the tab span does not exceed 35 percent of the span of the supporting control surface, the total free play at the tab trailing edge should not exceed 2 percent of the tab chord. If the tab span equals or exceeds 35 percent of the span of the supporting control surface, the total free play at the tab trailing edge should not exceed 1 percent of the distance from the tab hinge line to the trailing edge of the tab perpendicular to the tab hinge line. For example, a tab that has a chord of

4 inches and less than or equal to 35 percent of the control surface span would have a maximum permissible free play of 4 inches x 0.020 or 0.080 inches (total motion up and down) measured at the trailing edge. Correct any free play in excess of this amount.

(2) Care must also be exercised during repair or rework to prevent stress concentration points or areas that could increase the fatigue susceptibility of the trim tab system. Advisory Circular (AC) 23.629-1A, Means of Compliance with Section 23.629, "Flutter," contains additional information on this subject.

NOTE: If the pilot has experienced flutter, or thinks he/she has, then a complete inspection of the aircraft flight control system and all related components including rod ends, bearings, hinges, and bellcranks must be accomplished. Suspected parts should be replaced.

4-37. LOAD FACTORS FOR REPAIRS. In order to design an effective repair to a sheet metal aircraft, the stresses that act on the structure must be understood.

a. Six types of major stresses are known and should be considered when making repairs. These are tension, compression, bending, torsion, shear, and bearing

b. The design of an aircraft repair is complicated by the requirement that it be as light as possible. If weight were not critical, repairs could be made with a large margin of safety. But in actual practice, repairs must be strong enough to carry all of the loads with the required factor of safety, but they must not have too much extra strength. A joint that is too weak cannot be tolerated, but neither can one that is too strong because it can create stress risers that may cause cracks in other locations.

4-38. TRANSFER OF STRESSES WITHIN A STRUCTURE. An aircraft structure must be designed in such a way that it will accept all of the stresses imposed upon it by the flight and ground loads without any permanent deformation. Any repair made must accept the stresses, carry them across the repair, and then transfer them back into the original structure. These stresses are considered as flowing through the structure, so there must be a continuous path for them, with no abrupt changes in cross-sectional areas along the way. Abrupt changes in cross-sectional areas of aircraft structure that are subject to cycle loading/stresses will result in stress concentration that may induce fatigue cracking and eventual failure. A scratch or gouge in the surface of a highly-stressed piece of metal will cause a stress concentration at the point of damage.

a. Multirow Fastener Load Transfer. When multiple rows of rivets are used to secure a lap joint, the transfer of stresses is not equal in each row. The transfer of stress at each row of rivets may be thought of as transferring the maximum amount capable of being transferred without experiencing rivet shear failure.

b. Use Of Stacked Doublers. A stacked doubler is composed of two or more sheets of material that are used in lieu of a single, thicker sheet of material. Because the stress transferred at each row of rivets is dependent upon the maximum stress that can be transferred by the rivets in that row, the thickness of the sheet material at that row need only be thick enough to transfer the stress applied. Employing this principle can reduce the weight of a repair joint.

4-39.—4-49. [RESERVED.]

SECTION 4. METAL REPAIR PROCEDURES

4-50. GENERAL. The airframe of a fixed-wing aircraft is generally considered to consist of five principal units; the fuselage, wings, stabilizers, flight control surfaces, and landing gear.

a. Aircraft principal structural elements (PSE) and joints are designed to carry loads by distributing them as stresses. The elements and joints as originally fabricated are strong enough to resist these stresses, and must remain so after any repairs. Long, thin elements are called members. Some examples of members are the metal tubes that form engine mount and fuselage trusses and frames, beams used as wing spars, and longerons and stringers of metal-skinned fuselages and wings. Longerons and stringers are designed to carry principally axial loads, but are sometimes required to carry side loads and bending moments, as when they frame cutouts in metal-skinned structures. Truss members are designed to carry axial (tension and compression) loads applied to their ends only. Frame members are designed to carry side loads and bending moments in addition to axial loads. Beam members are designed to carry side loads and bending moments that are usually large compared to their axial loads. Beams that must resist large axial loads, particularly compression loads, in combination with side loads and bending moments are called beam-columns. Other structural elements such as metal skins, plates, shells, wing ribs, bulkheads, ring frames, intercostal members, gussets, and other reinforcements, and fittings are designed to resist complex stresses, sometimes in three dimensions.

b. Any repair made on an aircraft structure must allow all of the stresses to enter, sustain these stresses, and then allow them to return into the structure. The repair must be equal to the original structure, but not stronger or stiffer, which will cause stress concentrations or alter the resonant frequency of the structure.

c. All-metal aircraft are made of very thin sheet metal, and it is possible to restore the strength of the skin without restoring its rigidity. All repairs should be made using the same type and thickness of material that was used in the original structure. If the original skin had corrugations or flanges for rigidity, these must be preserved and strengthened. If a flange or corrugation is dented or cracked, the material loses much of its rigidity; and it must be repaired in such a way that will restore its rigidity, stiffness, and strength.

4-51. RIVETED (OR BOLTED) STEEL TRUSS-TYPE STRUCTURES. Repairs to riveted structures may be made employing the general principles outlined in the following paragraphs on aluminum alloy structures. Repair methods may also be found in text books on metal structures. Methods for repair of the major structural members must be specifically approved by the Federal Aviation Administration (FAA).

4-52. ALUMINUM ALLOY STRUCTURES. Extensive repairs to damaged stressed skin on monocoque-types of aluminum alloy structures must be made in accordance with FAA-approved manufacturer's instructions or other FAA-approved source.

a. Rivet Holes. Rivet holes are slightly larger than the diameter of the rivet. When driven, solid rivets expand to fill the hole. The strength of a riveted joint is based upon the expanded diameter of the rivet. Therefore, it is important that the proper drill size be used for each rivet diameter.

(1) The acceptable drill size for rivets may be found in Metallic Materials and Elements for Flight Vehicle Structure (MIL-HDBK-5).

(2) Avoid drilling oversized holes or otherwise decreasing the effective tensile areas of wing-spar capstrips, wing, fuselage, fin-longitudinal stringers, or highly-stressed tensile members. Make all repairs, or reinforcements, to such members in accordance with factory recommendations or with the specific approval of an FAA representative.

b. Disassembly Prior to Repairing. If the parts to be removed are essential to the rigidity of the complete structure, support the structure prior to disassembly in such a manner as to prevent distortion and permanent damage to the remainder of the structure. When rivets are removed, undercut rivet heads by drilling. Use a drill of the same size as the diameter of the rivet. Drilling must be exactly centered and to the base of the head only. After drilling, break off the head with a pin punch and carefully drive out the shank. On thin or unsupported metal skin, support the sheet metal on the inside with a bucking bar. Removal of rivet heads with a cold chisel and hammer is not recommended because skin damage and distorted rivet holes will probably result. Inspect rivet joints adjacent to damaged structure for partial failure by removing one or more rivets to see if holes are elongated or the rivets have started to shear.

c. Effective Tools. Care must also be taken whenever screws must be removed to avoid damage to adjoining structure. When properly used, impact wrenches can be effective tools for removal of screws; however, damage to adjoining structure may result from excessive vertical loads applied through the screw axis. Excessive loads are usually related to improperly adjusted impact tools or attempting to remove screws that have seized from corrosion. Remove seized screws by drilling and use of a screw extractor. Once the screw has been removed, check for structural cracks that may appear in the adjoining skin doubler, or in the nut or anchor plate.

4-53. SELECTION OF ALUMINUM FOR REPLACEMENT PARTS. All aluminum replacement sheet metal must be identical to the original or properly altered skin. If another alloy is being considered, refer to the information on the comparative strength properties of aluminum alloys contained in MIL-HDBK-5.

a. Temper. The choice of temper depends upon the severity of the subsequent forming operations. Parts having single curvature and straight bend lines with a large bend radius may be advantageously formed from heat-treated material; while a part, such as a fuselage frame, would have to be formed from a soft, annealed sheet, and heat-treated after forming. Make sure sheet metal parts which are to be left unpainted are made of clad (aluminum coated) material. Make sure all sheet material and finished parts are free from cracks, scratches, kinks, tool marks, corrosion pits, and other defects which may be factors in subsequent failure.

b. Use of Annealed Alloys for Structural Parts. The use of annealed aluminum alloys for structural repair of an aircraft is not recommended. An equivalent strength repair using annealed aluminum will weigh more than a repair using heat-treated aluminum alloy.

4-54. HEAT TREATMENT OF ALUMINUM ALLOY PARTS. All structural aluminum alloy parts are to be heat-treated in accordance with the heat-treatment instruction issued by the manufacturers of the part. In the case of a specified temper, the sequence of heat-treating operations set forth in

MIL-HDBK-5 and corresponding specifications. If the heat-treatment produces warping, straighten the parts immediately after quenching. Heat-treat riveted parts before riveting, to preclude warping and corrosion.

a. Quenching. Quench material from the solution heat-treating temperature as rapidly as possible after removal from the furnace. Quenching in cold water is preferred, although less drastic chilling (hot or boiling water, or airblast) is sometimes employed for bulk sections, such as forgings, to minimize quenching stresses.

b. Reheating at Temperatures Above Boiling Water. Reheating of 2017 and 2024 alloys above 212 °F tend to impair the original heat treatment. Therefore, reheating above 212 °F, including the baking of primers, is not acceptable without subsequent complete and correct heat treatment.

4-55. BENDING METAL. When describing a bend in aviation, the term "bend radii" is used to refer to the inside radius. Requirements for bending the metal to various shapes are frequently encountered. When a metal is bent, it is subjected to changes in its grain structure, causing an increase in its hardness.

a. The minimum radius is determined by the composition of the metal, its temper, and thickness. Table 4-6 shows the recommended radius for different types of aluminum. Note that the smaller the thickness of the material, the smaller the recommended minimum bend radius, and that as the material increases in hardness, the recommended bend radii increases.

b. When using layout techniques, the mechanic must be able to calculate exactly how much material will be required for the bend. It is easier to lay out the part on a flat sheet before the bending or shaping is performed. Before bending, smooth all rough edges, remove burrs, and drill relief holes at the ends of bend lines and at corners; to prevent cracks from starting. Bend lines should preferably be made to lie at an angle to the grain of the metal (preferably 90 degrees).

c. Bend radii (BR) in inches for a specific metal composition (alloy) and temper is determined from table 4-6. For example, the minimum bend radii for 0.016 thick 2024-T6 (alloy and temper) is found is found to be 2 to 4 times the material thickness or 0.032 to 0.064.

4-56. SETBACK.

a. Setback is a measurement used in sheet metal layout. It is the distance the jaws of a brake must be setback from the mold line to form a bend. For a 90 degree bend, the point is back from the mold line to a distance equal to the bend radius plus the metal thickness. The mold line is an extension of the flat side of a part beyond the radius. The mold line dimension of a part, is the dimension made to the intersection of mold lines, and is the dimension the part would have if its corners had no radius. (See figure 4-2.)

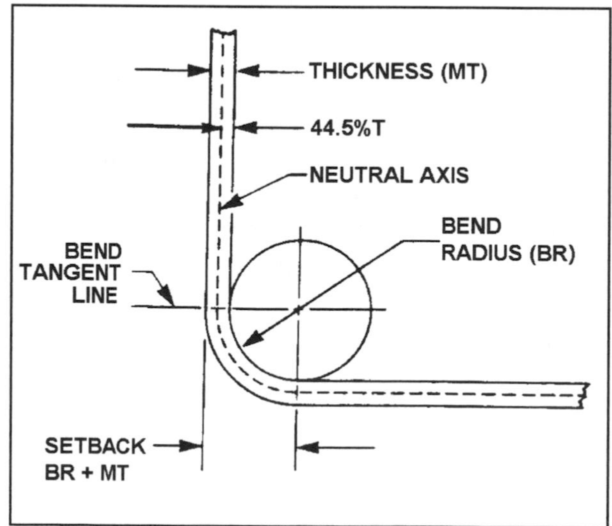

FIGURE 4-2. Setback for a 90-degree bend.

TABLE 4-6. Recommended radii for 90-degree bends in aluminum alloys.

Alloy and temper	Approximate sheet thickness (t) (inch)					
	0.016	**0.032**	**0.064**	**0.128**	**0.182**	**0.258**
2024-0[1]	0	0-1t	0-1t	0-1t	0-1t0-1t	0-1t
2024-T3[1,2]	1½t-3t	2t-4t	3t-5t	4t-6t	4t-6t	5t-7t
2024-T6[1]	2t-4t	3t-5t	3t-5t	4t-6t	5t-7t	6t-10t
5052-0	0	0	0-1t	0-1t	0-1t	0-1t
5052-H32	0	0	½t-1t	½t-1½t	½t-1½t	½t-1½t
5052-H34	0	0	½t-1½t	1½t-2½t	1½t-2½t	2t-3t
5052-H36	0-1t	½t-1½t	1t-2t	1½t-3t	2t-4t	2t-4t
5052-H38	½t-1½t	1t-2t	1½t-3t	2t-4t	3t-5t	4t-6t
6061-0	0	0-1t	0-1t	0-1t	0-1t	0-1t
6061-T4	0-1t	0-1t	½t-1½t	1t-2t	1½t-3t	2½t-4t
6061-T6	0-1t	½t-1½t	1t-2t	1½t-3t	2t-4t	3t-4t
7075-0	0	0-1t	0-1t	½t-1½t	1t-2t	1½t-3t
7075-T6[1]	2t-4t	3t-5t	4t-6t	5t-7t	5t-7t	6t-10t

[1] **Alclad sheet may be bent over slightly smaller radii than the corresponding tempers of uncoated alloy.**
[2] **Immediately after quenching, this alloy may be formed over appreciably smaller radii.**

b. To determine setback for a bend of more or less than 90 degrees, a correction known as a K-factor must be applied to find the setback.

(1) Table 4-7 shows a chart of K-factors. To find the setback for any degree of bend, multiply the sum of the bend radius and metal thickness by the K-value for the angle through which the metal is bent.

(2) Figure 4-3 shows an example of a piece of 0.064 inch sheet metal bent through 45 degrees to form an open angle of 135 degrees. For 45 degrees, the K-factor is 0.41421. The setback, or the distance from the mold point to the bend tangent line, is:

$$\begin{aligned} \text{Setback} &= K(BR + MT) \\ &= 0.41421\ (0.25 + 0.064) \\ &= 0.130 \text{ inches} \end{aligned}$$

(3) If a closed angle of 45 degrees is formed, the metal must be bent through 135 degrees. The K-factor for 135 degrees is 2.4142, so the setback, or distance from the mold point to the bend tangent line, is 0.758 inch.

4-57. RIVETING.

a. The two major types of rivets used in aircraft are the common solid shank rivet, which must be driven using an air-driven rivet gun and bucking bar; and special (blind) rivets, which are installed with special installation tools. Design allowables for riveted assemblies are specified in MIL-HDBK-5.

(1) Solid shank rivets are used widely during assembly and repair work. They are identified by the material of which they are made, the head type, size of shank, and temper condition.

TABLE 4-7. K-chart for determining setback for bends other than 90 degrees.

Deg.	K	Deg.	K	Deg.	K	Deg.	K	Deg:	K
1	0.0087	37	0.3346	73	0.7399	109	1.401	145	3.171
2	0.0174	38	0.3443	74	0.7535	110	1,428	146	3.270
3	0.0261	39	0.3541	75	0.7673	111	1.455	147	3.375
4	0.0349	40	0.3639	76	0.7812	112	1.482	148	3.487
5	0.0436	41	0.3738	77	0.7954	113	1.510	149	3.605
6	0.0524	42	0.3838	78	0.8097	114	1.539	150	3.732
7	0.0611	43	0.3939	79	0.8243	115	1.569	151	3.866
8	0.0699	44	0.4040	80	0.8391	116	1.600	152	4.010
9	0.0787	45	0.4142	81	0.8540	117	1.631	153	4.165
10	0.0874	46	0.4244	82	0.8692	118	1.664	154	4.331
11	0.0963	47	0.4348	83	0.8847	119	1.697	155	4.510
12	0.1051	48	0.4452	84	0.9004	120	1.732	156	4.704
13	0.1139	49	0.4557	85	0.9163	121	1.767	157	4.915
14	0.1228	50	0.4663	86	0.9324	122	1.804	158	5.144
15	0.1316	51	0.4769	87	0.9489	123	1.841	159	5.399
16	0.1405	52	0.4877	88	0.9656	124	1.880	160	5.671
17	0.1494	53	0.4985	89	0.9827	125	1.921	161	5.975
18	0.1583	54	0.5095	90	1.000	126	1.962	162	6.313
19	0.1673	55	0.5205	91	1.017	127	2.005	163	6.691
20	0.1763	56	0.5317	92	1.035	128	2.050	164	7.115
21	0.1853	57	0.5429	93	1.053	129	2.096	165	7.595
22	0.1943	58	0.5543	94	1.072	130	2.144	166	8.144
23	0.2034	59	0.5657	95	1.091	131	2.194	167	8.776
24	0.2125	60	0.5773	96	1.110	132	2.246	168	9.514
25	0.2216	61	0.5890	97	1-130	133	2.299	169	10.38
26	0.2308	62	0.6008	98	1.150	134	2.355	170	11.43
27	0.2400	63	0.6128	99	1.170	135	2.414	171	12.70
28	0.2493	64	0.6248	100	1.191	136	2.475	172	14.30
29	0.2586	65	0.6370	101	1.213	137	2.538	173	16.35
30	0.2679	66	0.6494	102	1.234	138	2.605	174	19.08
31	0.2773	67	0.6618	103	1.257	139	2.674	175	22.90
32	0.2867	68	0.6745	104	1.279	140	2.747	176	26.63
33	0.2962	69	0.6872	105	1.303	141	2.823	177	38.18
34	0.3057	70	0.7002	106	1.327	142	2.904	178	57.29
35	0.3153	71	0.7132	107	1.351	143	2.988	179	114.59
36	0.3249	72	0.7265	108	1.376	144	3.077	180	Inf.

(2) The material used for the majority of solid shank rivets is aluminum alloy. The strength and temper conditions of aluminum alloy rivets are identified by digits and letters similar to those used to identify sheet stock. The 1100, 2017-T, 2024-T, 2117-T, and 5056 rivets are the six grades usually available. AN-type aircraft solid rivets can be identified by code markings on the rivet heads. A rivet made of 1100 material is designated as an "A" rivet, and has no head marking. The 2017-T alloy rivet is designated as a "D" rivet and has a raised teat on the head. Two dashes on a rivet head indicate a 2024-T alloy designated as a "DD" rivet. The 2117-T rivet is designated as an "AD" rivet, and has a dimple on the head. A "B" designation is given to a rivet of 5056 material and is marked with a raised cross on the rivet head. Each type of rivet is identified by a part number to allow the user to select the correct rivet. The numbers are in series and each series represents a particular type of head. (See figure 4-4 and table 4-8.)

(3) An example of identification marking of rivet follows.

MS 20470AD3-5	Complete part number
MS	Military standard number
20470	Universal head rivet
AD	2117-T aluminum alloy
3	3/32nds in diameter
5	5/16ths in length

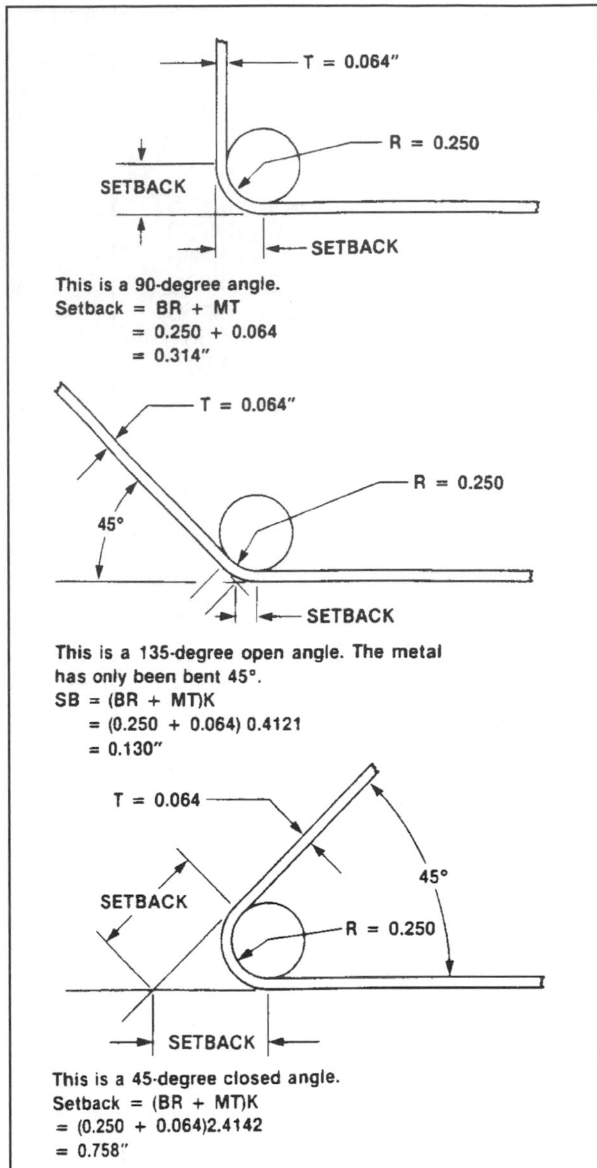

FIGURE 4-3. Methods of determining setback for bends other than 90 degree.

(4) Countersunk head rivets (MS20426 supersedes AN426 100-degree) are used where a smooth finish is desired. The 100-degree countersunk head has been adopted as the standard in the United States. The universal head rivet (AN470 superseded by MS20470) has been adopted as the standard for protruding-head rivets, and may be used as a replacement for the roundhead, flathead, and brazier head rivet. These rivets can also be purchased in half sizes by designating a "0.5" after the main length (i.e., MS20470 AD4-3.5).

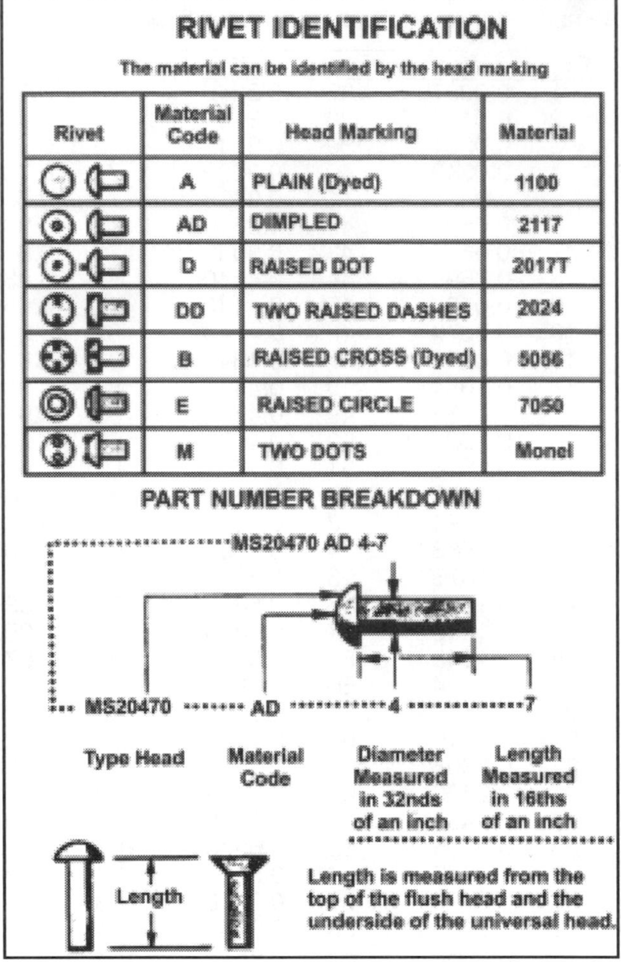

RIVET IDENTIFICATION

The material can be identified by the head marking

Rivet	Material Code	Head Marking	Material
	A	PLAIN (Dyed)	1100
	AD	DIMPLED	2117
	D	RAISED DOT	2017T
	DD	TWO RAISED DASHES	2024
	B	RAISED CROSS (Dyed)	5056
	E	RAISED CIRCLE	7050
	M	TWO DOTS	Monel

FIGURE 4-4. Rivet identification and part number breakdown.

b. Replace rivets with those of the same size and strength whenever possible. If the rivet hole becomes enlarged, deformed, or otherwise damaged; drill or ream the hole for the next larger size rivet. However, make sure that the edge distance and spacing is not less than minimums listed in the next paragraph. Rivets may not be replaced by a type having lower strength properties, unless the lower strength is adequately compensated by an increase in size or a greater number of rivets. It is acceptable to replace 2017 rivets of 3/16 inch diameter or less, and 2024 rivets of 5/32 inch diameter or less with 2117 rivets for general repairs, provided the replacement rivets are 1/32 inch greater in diameter than the rivets they replace.

TABLE 4-8. Aircraft rivet identification.

Material	1100	2117T	2017T	2017T-HD	2024T	5056T	7075-T73
Head Marking	Plain	Dimpled	Raised Dot	Raised Dot	Raised Double Dash	Raised Cross	Three Raised Dashes
AN Material Code	A	AD	D	D	DD	B	
AN425 78▪ Counter-Sunk Head	X	X	X	X	X		X
AN426 100▪ Counter-Sunk Head MS20426	X	X	X	X	X	X	X
AN427 100▪ Counter-Sunk Head MS20427							
AN430 Round Head MS20470	X	X	X	X	X	X	X
AN435 Round Head MS20613 MS20615							
AN 441 Flat Head							
AN 442 Flat Head MS20470	X	X	X	X	X	X	X
AN 455 Brazier Head MS20470	X	X	X	X	X	X	X
AN 456 Brazier Head MS20470	X	X	X	X	X	X	X
AN 470 Universal Head MS20470	X	X	X	X	X	X	X
Heat Treat Before Using	No	No	Yes	No	Yes	No	No
Shear Strength psi	10000	30000	34000	38000	41000	27000	
Bearing Strength psi	25000	100000	113000	126000	136000	90000	

TABLE 4-8. Aircraft rivet identification. (continued)

Material	Carbon Steel	Corrosion-Resistant Steel	Copper	Monel	Monel Nickel-Copper Alloy	Brass	Titanium
Head Marking	Recessed Triangle	Recessed Dash	Plain	Plain	Recessed Double Dots	Plain	Recessed Large and Small Dot
AN Material Code		F	C	M	C		
AN425 78° Counter-Sunk Head							
AN426 100° Counter-Sunk Head MS20426							MS 20426
AN427 100° Counter-Sunk Head MS20427	X	X	X	X			
AN430 Round Head MS20470							
AN435 Round Head MS20613 MS20615	X MS20613	X MS20613	X		X MS20615	X MS20615	
AN 441 Flat Head	X		X	X			X
AN 442 Flat Head MS20470							
AN 455 Brazier Head MS20470							
AN 456 Brazier Head MS20470							
AN 470 Universal Head MS20470							
Heat Treat Before Using	No	No	No	No	No	No	No
Shear Strength psi	35000	65000	23000	49000	49000		95000
Bearing Strength psi	90000	90000					

c. Rivet edge distance is defined as the distance from the center of the rivet hole to the nearest edge of the sheet. Rivet spacing is the distance from the center of the rivet hole to the center of the adjacent rivet hole. Unless structural deficiencies are suspected, the rivet spacing and edge distance should duplicate those of the original aircraft structure. If structural deficiencies are suspected, the following may be used in determining minimum edge distance and rivet spacing.

(1) For single row rivets, the edge distance should not be less than 2 times the diameter of the rivet and spacing should not be less than 3 times the diameter of the rivet.

(2) For double row rivets, the edge distance and spacing should not be less than the minimums shown in figure 4-5.

(3) For triple or multiple row rivets, the edge distance and spacing should not be less than the minimums shown in figure 4-5.

d. The 2117 rivets may be driven in the condition received, but 2017 rivets above 3/16 inch in diameter and all 2024 rivets are to be kept packed in dry ice or refrigerated in the "quenched" condition until driven, or be reheat treated just prior to driving, as they would otherwise be too hard for satisfactory riveting. Dimensions for formed rivet heads are shown in figure 4-6(a), together with commonly found rivet imperfections.

e. When solid shank rivets are impractical to use, then special fasteners are used. Special fastening systems used for aircraft construction and repair are divided into two types, special and blind fasteners. Special fasteners are sometimes designed for a specific purpose in an aircraft structure. The name "special fasteners" refers to its job requirement and the tooling needed for installation. Use of special fasteners may require an FAA field approval.

f. Blind rivets are used under certain conditions when there is access to only one side of the structure. Typically, the locking characteristics of a blind rivet are not as good as a driven rivet. Therefore, blind rivets are usually not used when driven rivets can be installed.

Blind rivets shall not be used:

(1) in fluid-tight areas;

(2) on aircraft in air intake areas where rivet parts may be ingested by the engine, on aircraft control surfaces, hinges, hinge brackets, flight control actuating systems, wing attachment fittings, landing gear fittings, on floats or amphibian hulls below the water level, or other heavily-stressed locations on the aircraft;

CAUTION: For metal repairs to the airframe, the use of blind rivets must be specifically authorized by the airframe manufacturer or approved by a representative of the FAA.

(3) Self plugging friction-lock cherry rivets. This patented rivet may be installed when there is access to only one side of the structure. The blind head is formed by pulling the tapered stem into the hollow shank. This swells the shank and clamps the skins tightly together. When the shank is fully upset, the stem pulls in two. The stem does not fracture flush with the rivet head and must be trimmed and filed flush for the installation to be complete. Because of the friction-locking stem, these rivets are very sensitive to vibrations. Inspection is visual, with a loose rivet standing out in the standard "smoking rivet" pattern. Removal consists of punching out the friction-

locked stem and then treating it like any other rivet. (See figure 4-7.)

(4) Mechanical-lock rivets have a device on the puller or rivet head which locks the center stem into place when installed. Many friction-lock rivet center stems fall out due to vibrations; this in turn, greatly reduces its shear strength. The mechanical-lock rivet was developed to prevent that problem. Various manufacturers make mechanical-lock fasteners such as: Bulbed Cherrylock, CherryMax, Olympic-Loks, and Huck-Loks.

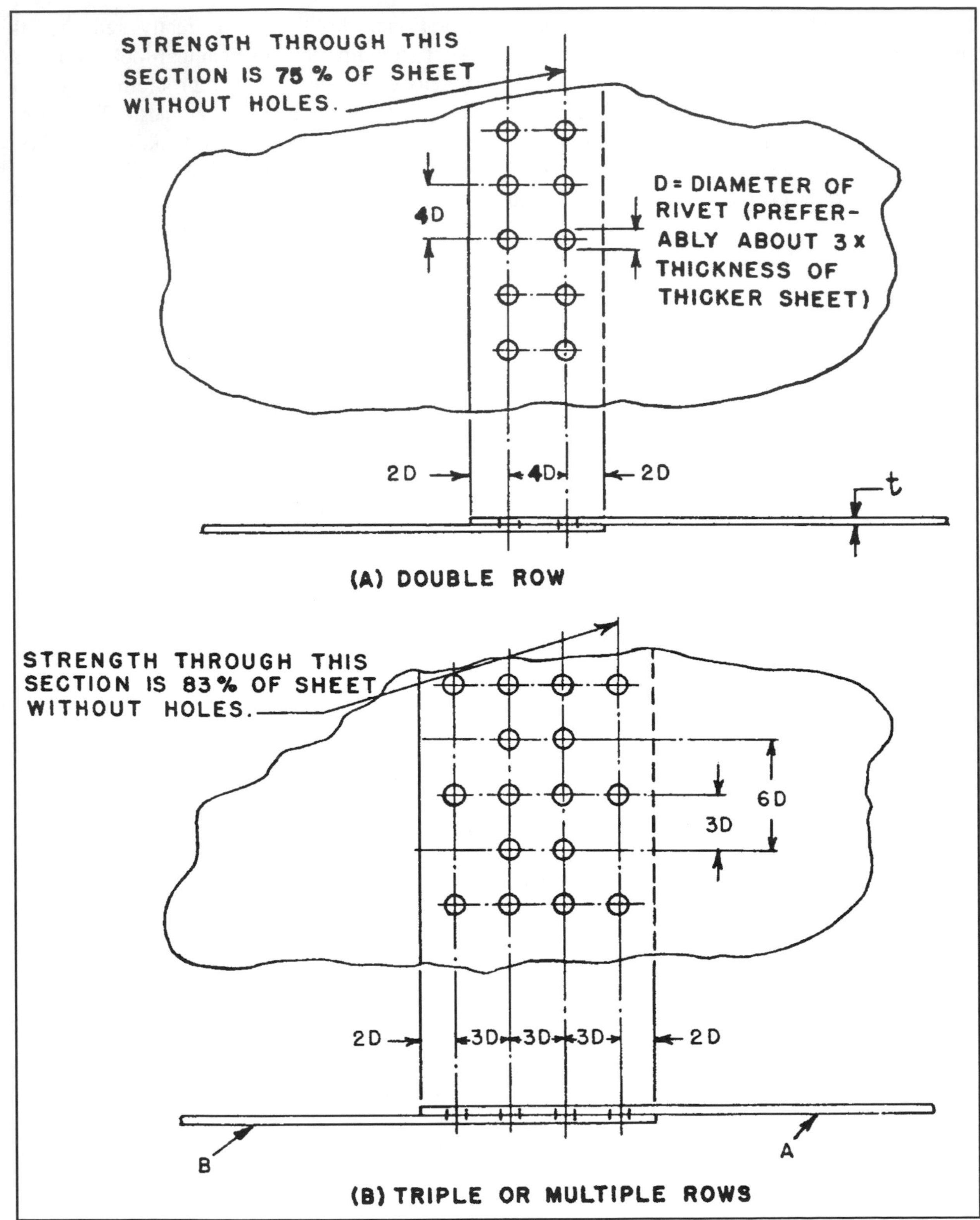

FIGURE 4-5. Rivet hole spacing and edge distance for single-lap sheet splices.

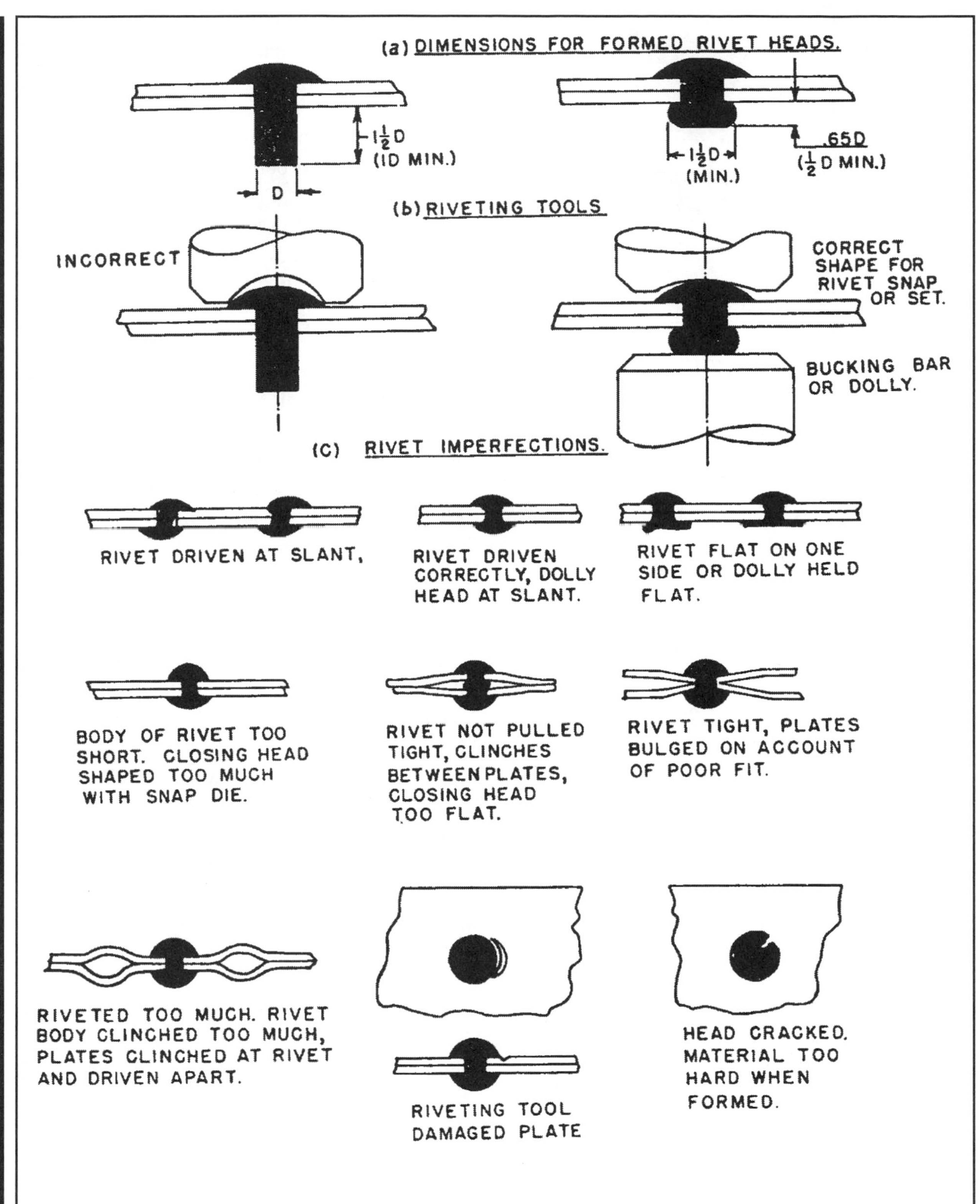

FIGURE 4-6. Riveting practice and rivet imperfections.

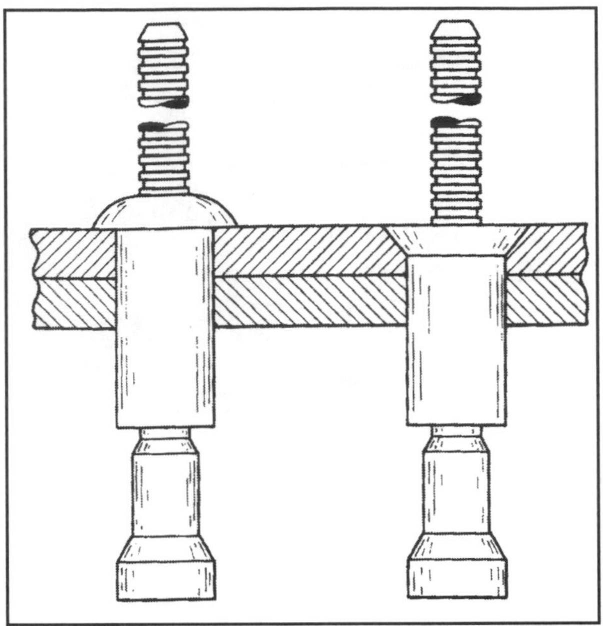

FIGURE 4-7. Self plugging friction-lock Cherry rivets.

(5) Bulbed Cherrylock Rivets. One of the earlier types of mechanical-lock rivets developed were Bulbed Cherrylock blind rivets. These blind rivets have as their main advantage the ability to replace a solid shank rivet size for size. (See figure 4-8.)

(a) A Bulbed Cherrylock consists of three parts; a rivet shell, a puller, and a lockring. The puller or stem has five features which are activated during installation; a header, shank expanding section, lockring indent, weak or stem fracture point, and a serrated pulling stem. Carried on the pulling stem, near the manufactured head, is the stem lockring. When the rivet is pulled the action of the moving stem clamps together the sheets of metal and swells the shank to fill the drilled hole. When the stem reaches its preset limit of travel, the upper stem breaks away (just above the lockring) as the lockring snaps into the recess on the locking stem. The rough end of the retained stem in the center on the manufactured head must never be filed smooth, because it will weaken the strength of the lockring and the center stem could fall out. (See figure 4-8.)

(b) The Bulbed Cherrylock rivets are available in two head styles: universal and 100° countersunk. Their lengths are measured in increments of 1/16 inch. It is important to select a rivet with a length related to the grip length of the metal being joined.

(c) The Bulbed Cherrylock rivet can be installed using a G35 cherry rivet hand puller or a pneumatic Bulbed Cherrylock pulling tool.

(6) The CherryMax (see figure 4-9) rivet uses one tool to install three standard rivet diameters and their oversize counterparts. This makes the use of CherryMax rivets very popular with many small general aviation repair shops. CherryMax rivets are available in four nominal diameters 1/8, 5/32, 3/16, and 1/4 inch and three oversized diameters. CherryMax rivets are manufactured with two head styles, universal and countersunk. The CherryMax rivets consists of five parts; bulbed blind header, hollow rivet shell, locking (foil) collar, driving anvil, and pulling stem. The blind bulbed header takes up the extended shank and forms the bucktail on a CherryMax rivet stem. Rivet sleeves are made from 5056 aluminum, monel, and INCO 600. The stems are made from alloy steel, CRES, and INCO X-750 stem. CherryMax rivets have an ultimate shear strength ranging from 50 KSI to 75 KSI.

(7) An Olympic-Lok (see figure 4-10) rivet is a light three-piece mechanically locked, spindle-type blind rivet. It carries its stem lock integral to the manufactured head. While installing, the lockring is pressed into a groove on the pulling stem just as the rivet completes drawing the metal together. After installation is completed, never file the stem of an Olympic-Lok rivet, because it will weaken the lockring attachment. The Olympic-Lok fastener is available in three head styles:

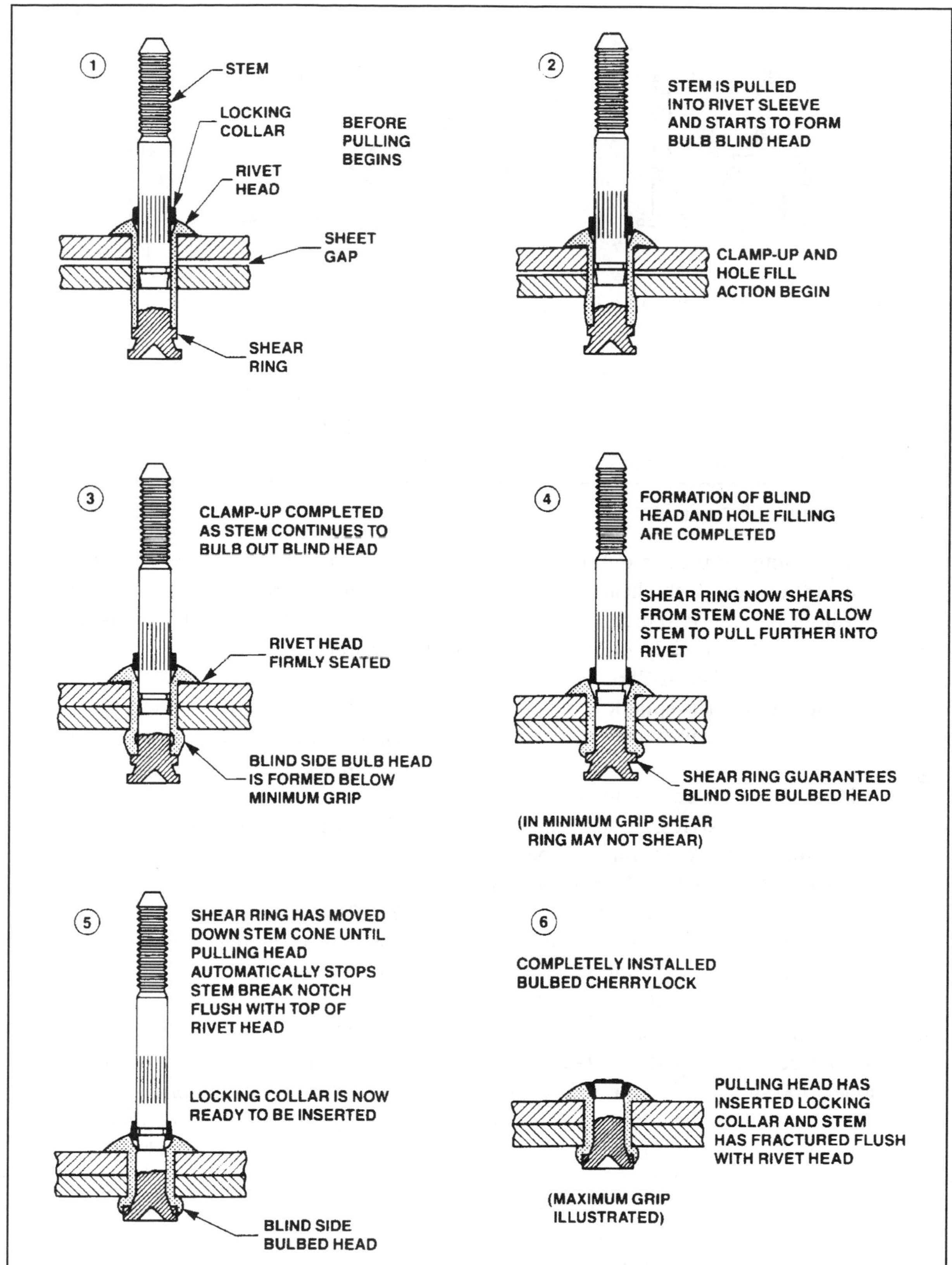

FIGURE 4-8. Mechanical-lock (Bulbed Cherrylock) Cherry rivet.

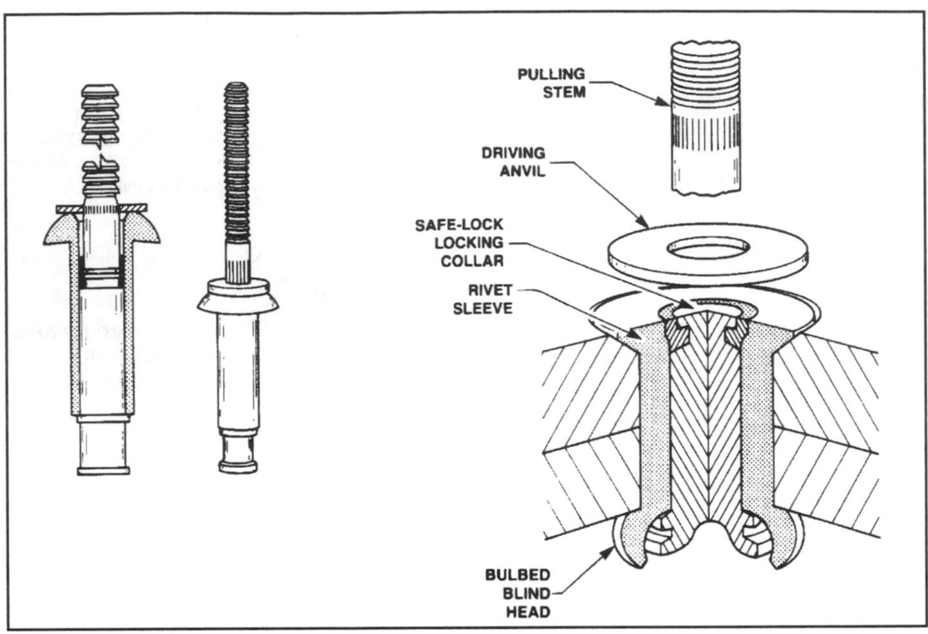

FIGURE 4-9. CherryMax rivet.

universal protruding, 100-degree flush countersink, and 100-degree flush shear; and three diameters 1/8, 5/32, and 3/16 inch. The three diameters are available in eight different alloy combinations of 2017-T4, A-286, 5056, and monel. Olympic-Lok lock spindles are made from the same material as the sleeves.

(8) Huck rivets (see figure 4-11) are available in two head styles, protruding and flush. They are available in four diameters 1/8, 5/32, 3/16, and 1/4 inch. Their diameters are measured in increments of 1/32 inch and lengths are measured in 1/16 inch increments. They are manufactured in three different combinations of alloys: 5056 aluminum sleeve with 2024 aluminum alloy pin, A-286 corrosion-resistant steel sleeve with an A-286 pin, and a monel 400 sleeve with an A-286 pin. The Huck fastener has the ability to tightly draw-up two or more sheets of metal together while being installed. After the take-up of the Huck fastener is completed, the lockring is squeezed into a groove on the pulling stem. The anvil or footer (of the installation tool) packs the ring into the groove of the pulling stem by bearing against the lockring.

(9) Common pull-type Pop rivets, produced for nonaircraft related applications, are not approved for use on certificated aircraft structures or components.

g. Design a new or revised rivet pattern for strength required in accordance with one of the following:

(1) The aircraft manufacturer's maintenance manuals.

(2) The techniques found in structural text books and using the mechanical properties found in MIL-HDBK-5.

(3) The specific instructions in paragraphs 4-58g through 4-58n. When following the instruction in paragraphs 4-58g through 4-58n, the general rule for the diameter of the rivets used to join aluminum sheets is to use a diameter approximately three times the thickness of the thicker sheet. Do not use rivets where they would be placed in tension, tending to pull the heads off; and backup a lap joint of thin sheets with a stiffener section.

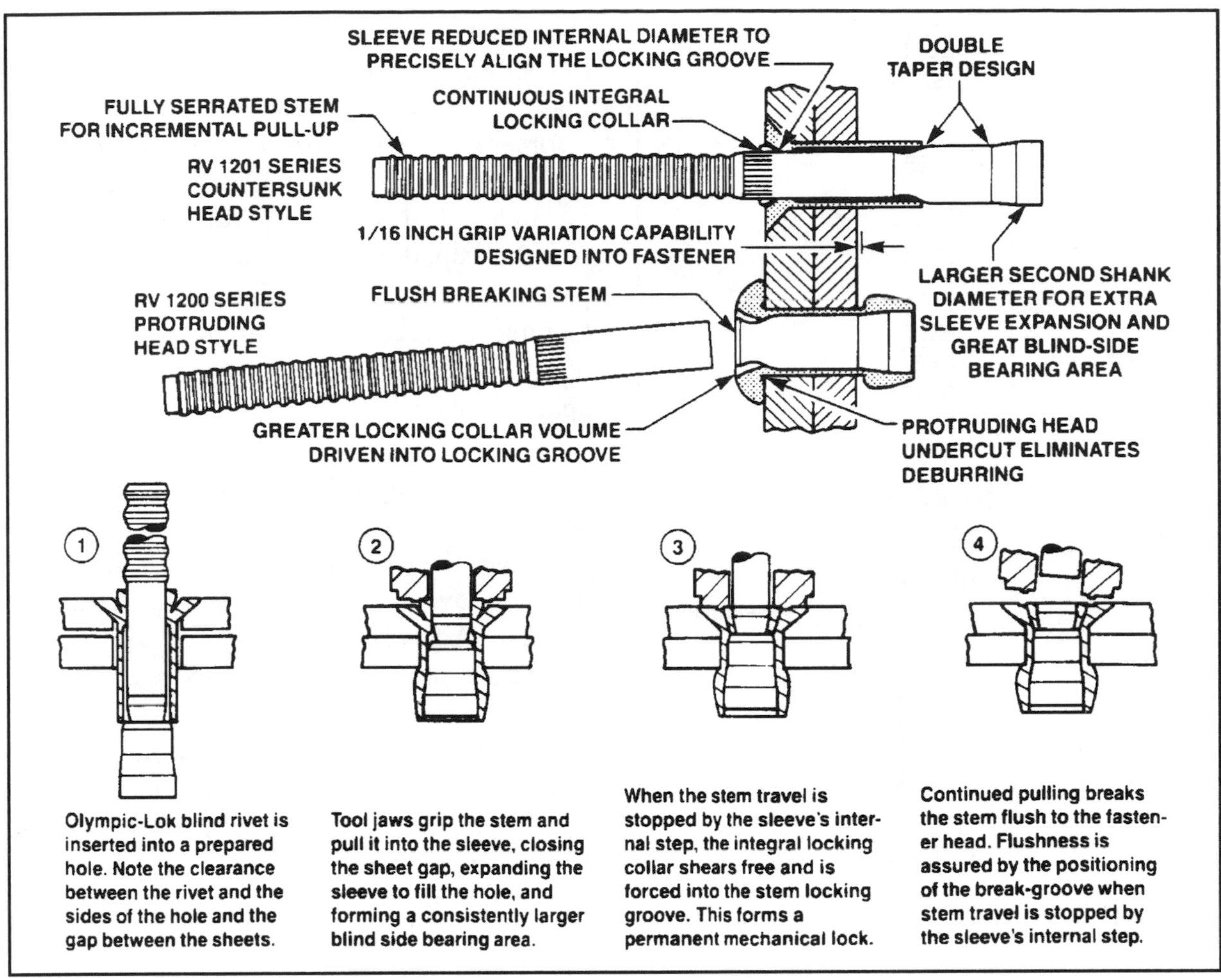

FIGURE 4-10. Olympic-Lok rivet.

4-58. REPAIR METHODS AND PRECAUTIONS FOR ALUMINUM STRUCTURE. Carefully examine all adjacent rivets outside of the repair area to ascertain that they have not been harmed by operations in adjacent areas. Drill rivet holes round, straight, and free from cracks. Deburr the hole with an oversize drill or deburring tool. The rivet-set used in driving the rivets must be cupped slightly flatter than the rivet head. (See figure 4-6.) Rivets are to be driven straight and tight, but not overdriven or driven while too hard, since the finished rivet must be free from cracks. Information on special methods of riveting, such as flush riveting, usually may be obtained from manufacturer's service manuals.

a. Splicing of Tubes. Round or streamline aluminum alloy tubular members may be repaired by splicing. (See figure 4-12.) Splices in struts that overlap fittings are not acceptable. When solid rivets go completely through hollow tubes, their diameter must be at least one-eighth of the outside diameter of the outer tube. Rivets which are loaded in shear should be hammered only enough to form a small head and no attempt made to form the standard roundhead. The amount of hammering required to form the standard roundhead often causes the rivet to buckle inside the tube. (Correct and incorrect examples of this type of rivet application are incorporated in figure 4-12.)

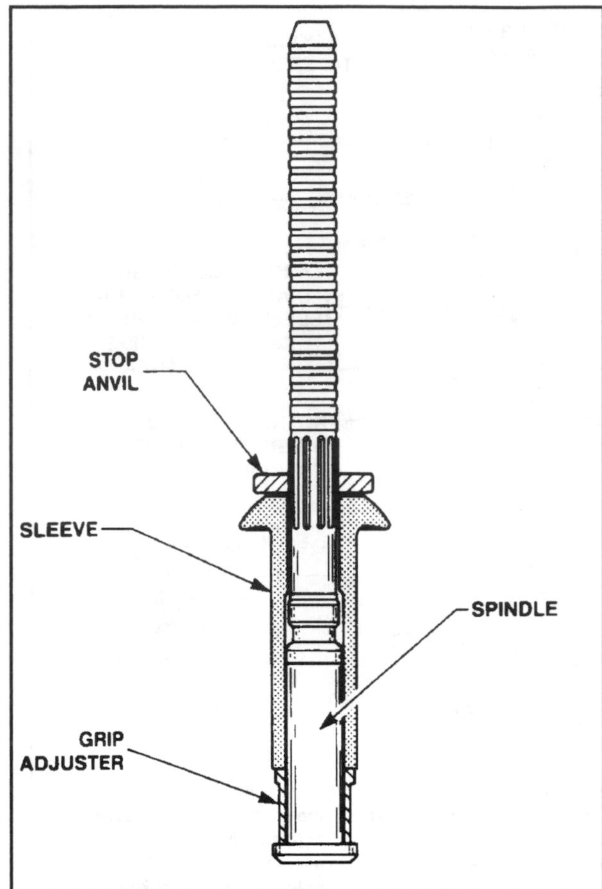

FIGURE 4-11. Huck rivet.

b. Repairs to Aluminum Alloy Members. Make repairs to aluminum alloy members with the same material or with suitable material of higher strength. The 7075 alloy has greater tensile strength than other commonly used aluminum alloys such as 2014 and 2024, but is subject to somewhat greater notch sensitivity. In order to take advantage of its strength characteristics, pay particular attention to design of parts to avoid notches, small radii, and large or rapid changes in cross-sectional areas. In fabrication, exercise caution to avoid processing and handling defects, such as machine marks, nicks, dents, burrs, scratches, and forming cracks. Cold straightening or forming of 7075-T6 can cause cracking; therefore, it may be advisable to limit this processing to minor cold straightening.

c. Wing and Tail Surface Ribs. Damaged aluminum alloy ribs either of the stamped sheet-metal type or the built-up type employing special sections, square or round tubing, may be repaired by the addition of suitable reinforcement. (Acceptable methods of repair are shown in figures 4-13 and 4-14.) These examples deal with types of ribs commonly found in small and medium size aircraft. Repair schemes developed by the aircraft manufacturer are acceptable, but any other methods of reinforcement are major repairs and require approved data.

d. Trailing and Leading Edges and Tip Strips. Repairs to wing, control surface trailing edges, leading edges, and tip strips should be made by properly executed and reinforced splices. Acceptable methods of trailing edge repairs are shown in figure 4-15.

e. Repair of Damaged Skin. In cases where metal skin is damaged extensively, repair by replacing an entire sheet panel from one structural member to the next. The repair seams are to lie along stiffening members, bulkheads, etc.; and each seam must be made exactly the same in regard to rivet size, splicing, and rivet pattern as the manufactured seams at the edges of the original sheet. If the two manufactured seams are different, the stronger one will be copied. (See figure 4-16 for typical acceptable methods of repairs.)

f. Patching of Small Holes. Small holes in skin panels which do not involve damage to the stiffening members may be patched by covering the hole with a patch plate in the manner shown in figure 4-16. Flush patches also may be installed in stressed-skin type construction. An acceptable and easy flush patch may be made by trimming out the damaged area and then installing a conventional patch on the underneath side or back of the sheet being repaired. A plug patch plate of the same size and skin thickness as the opening may then be inserted and riveted to the patch plate. Other types of flush patches similar to those used for patching plywood may be used. The rivet pattern used, however, must follow standard practice to maintain satisfactory strength in the sheet.

g. Splicing of Sheets. The method of copying the seams at the edges of a sheet may not always be satisfactory. For example, when the sheet has cutouts, or doubler plates at an edge seam, or when other members transmit loads into the sheet, the splice must be designed as illustrated in the following examples.

(1) Material: Clad 2024 sheet, 0.032 inch thickness. Width of sheet (i.e., length at splice) = "W" = 10 inches.

(2) Determine rivet size and pattern for a single lap joint similar to figure 4-5.

(a) Use rivet diameter of approximately three times the sheet thickness, 3 x 0.032 = 0.096-inch. Use 1/8-inch 2117-T4 (AD) rivets (5/32-inch 2117-T4 (AD) would be satisfactory).

(b) Use the number of rivets required per inch of width "W" from table 4-10. (Number per inch 4.9 x .75 = 3.7 or the total number of rivets required = 10 x 3.7 or 37 rivets.) See notes in table.

(c) Lay out rivet pattern with spacing not less than shown in figure 4-5. Referring to figure 4-5(A), it seems that a double row pattern with the minimum spacing will give a total of 40 rivets. However, as only 37 rivets are required, two rows of 19 rivets each equally spaced over the10 inches will result in a satisfactory splice.

h. Straightening of Stringers or Intermediate Frames. Members which are slightly bent may be straightened cold and examined with a magnifying glass for cracks or tears to the material. Reinforce the straightened part to its original shape, depending upon the condition of the material and the magnitude of any remaining kinks or buckles. If any strain cracks are apparent, make complete reinforcement in sound metal beyond the damaged portion.

i. Local Heating. Do not apply local heating to facilitate bending, swaging, flattening, or expanding operations of heat-treated aluminum alloy members, as it is difficult to control the temperatures closely enough to prevent possible damage to the metal, and it may impair its corrosion resistance.

j. Splicing of Stringers and Flanges. It is recommended that all splices be made in accordance with the manufacturer's recommendations. If the manufacturer's recommendations are not available, the typical splices for various shapes of sections are shown in figures 4-17 through 4-19. Design splices to carry both tension and compression, and use the splice shown in figure 4-18 as an example illustrating the following principles.

(1) To avoid eccentric loading and consequent buckling in compression, place splicing or reinforcing parts as symmetrically as possible about the centerline of the member, and attach to as many elements as necessary to prevent bending in any direction.

(2) To avoid reducing the strength in tension of the original bulb angle, the rivet holes at the ends of the splice are made small (no larger than the original skin attaching rivets), and the second row of holes (those through the bulbed leg) are staggered back from the ends. In general, arrange the rivets in the splice so that the design tensile load for the member and splice plate can be carried into the splice without failing the member at the outermost rivet holes.

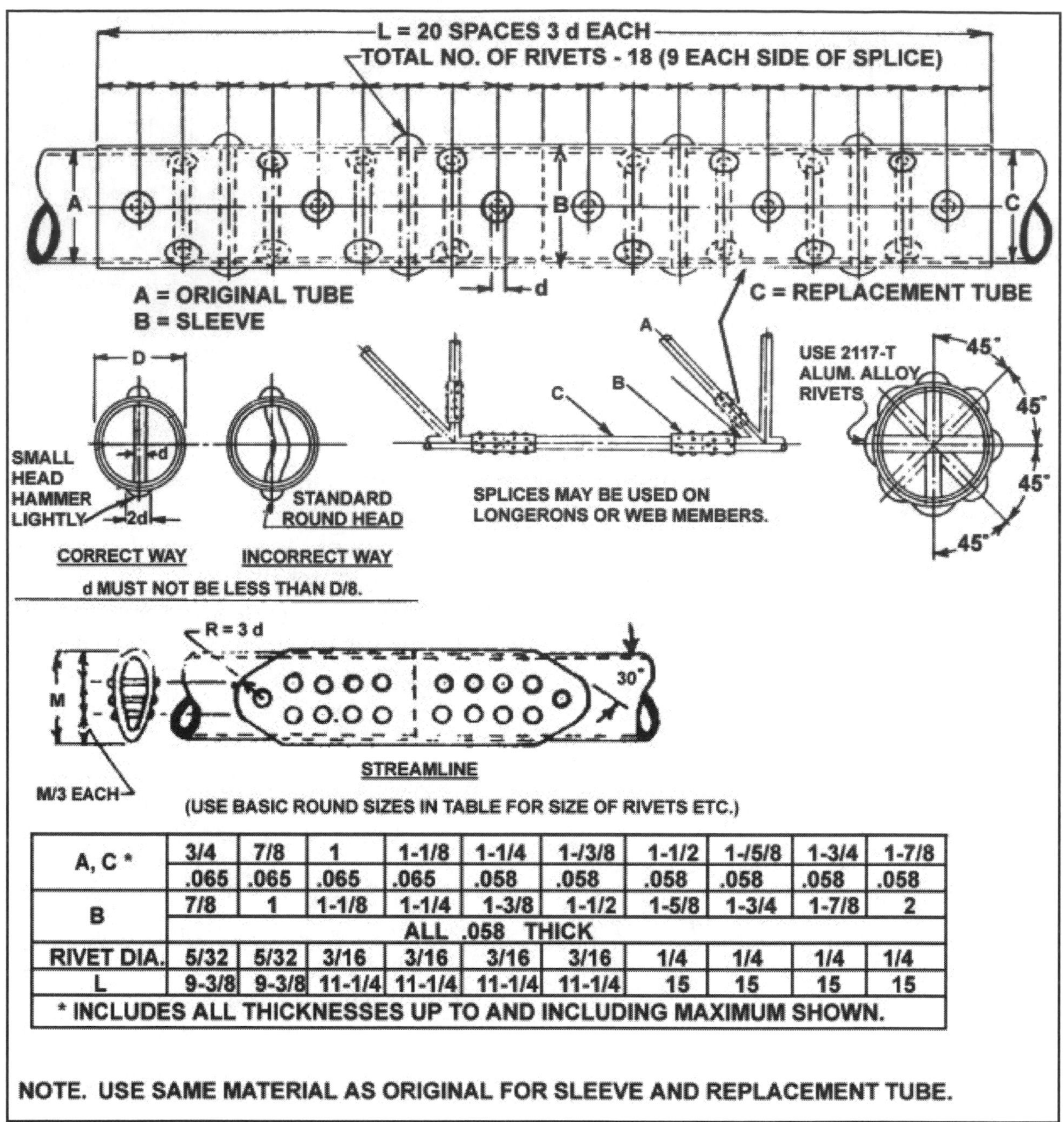

A, C *	3/4	7/8	1	1-1/8	1-1/4	1-/3/8	1-1/2	1-/5/8	1-3/4	1-7/8
	.065	.065	.065	.065	.058	.058	.058	.058	.058	.058
B	7/8	1	1-1/8	1-1/4	1-3/8	1-1/2	1-5/8	1-3/4	1-7/8	2
	ALL .058 THICK									
RIVET DIA.	5/32	5/32	3/16	3/16	3/16	3/16	1/4	1/4	1/4	1/4
L	9-3/8	9-3/8	11-1/4	11-1/4	11-1/4	11-1/4	15	15	15	15
* INCLUDES ALL THICKNESSES UP TO AND INCLUDING MAXIMUM SHOWN.										

NOTE. USE SAME MATERIAL AS ORIGINAL FOR SLEEVE AND REPLACEMENT TUBE.

FIGURE 4-12. Typical repair method for tubular members of aluminum alloy.

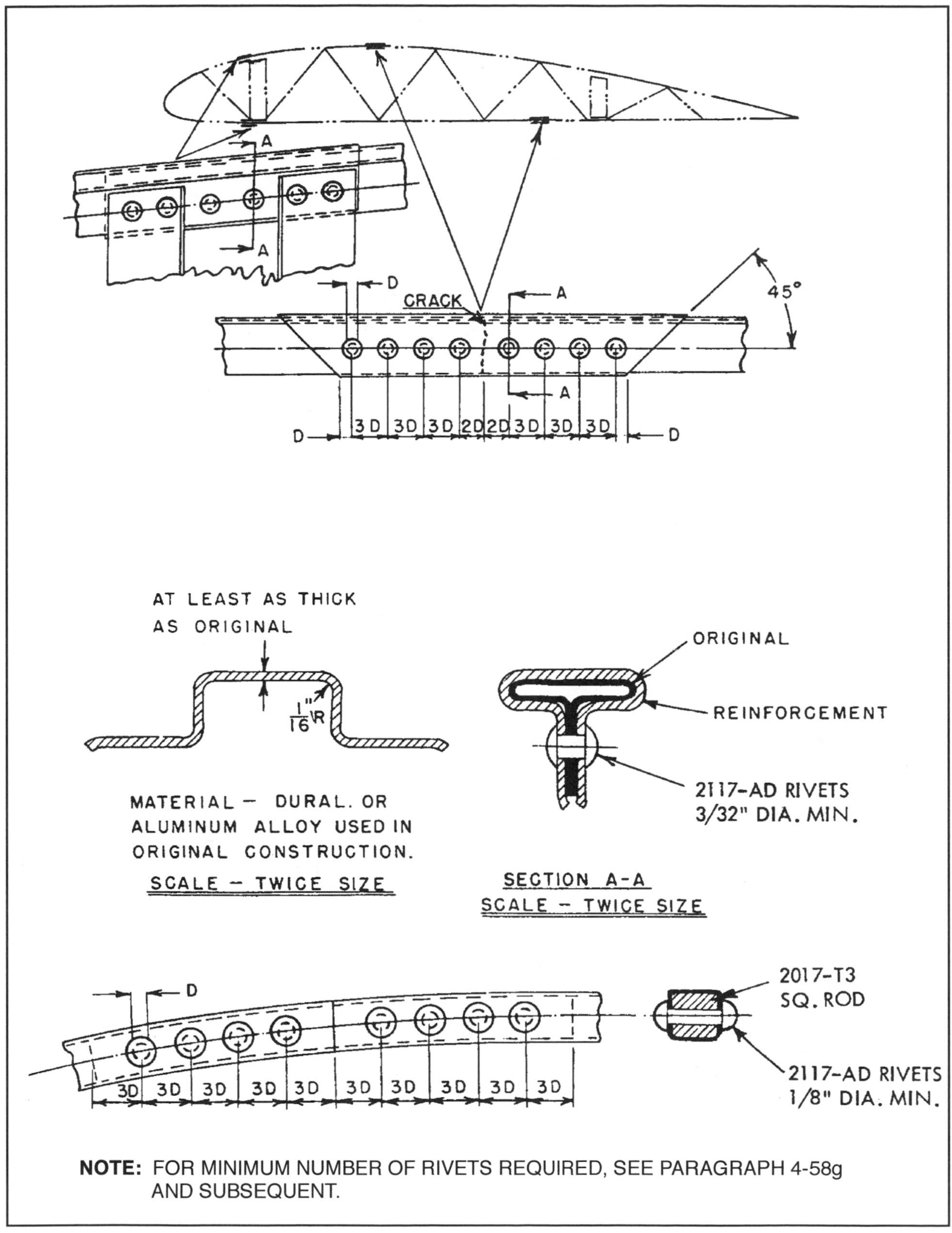

NOTE: FOR MINIMUM NUMBER OF RIVETS REQUIRED, SEE PARAGRAPH 4-58g AND SUBSEQUENT.

FIGURE 4-13. Typical repair for buckled or cracked metal wing rib capstrips.

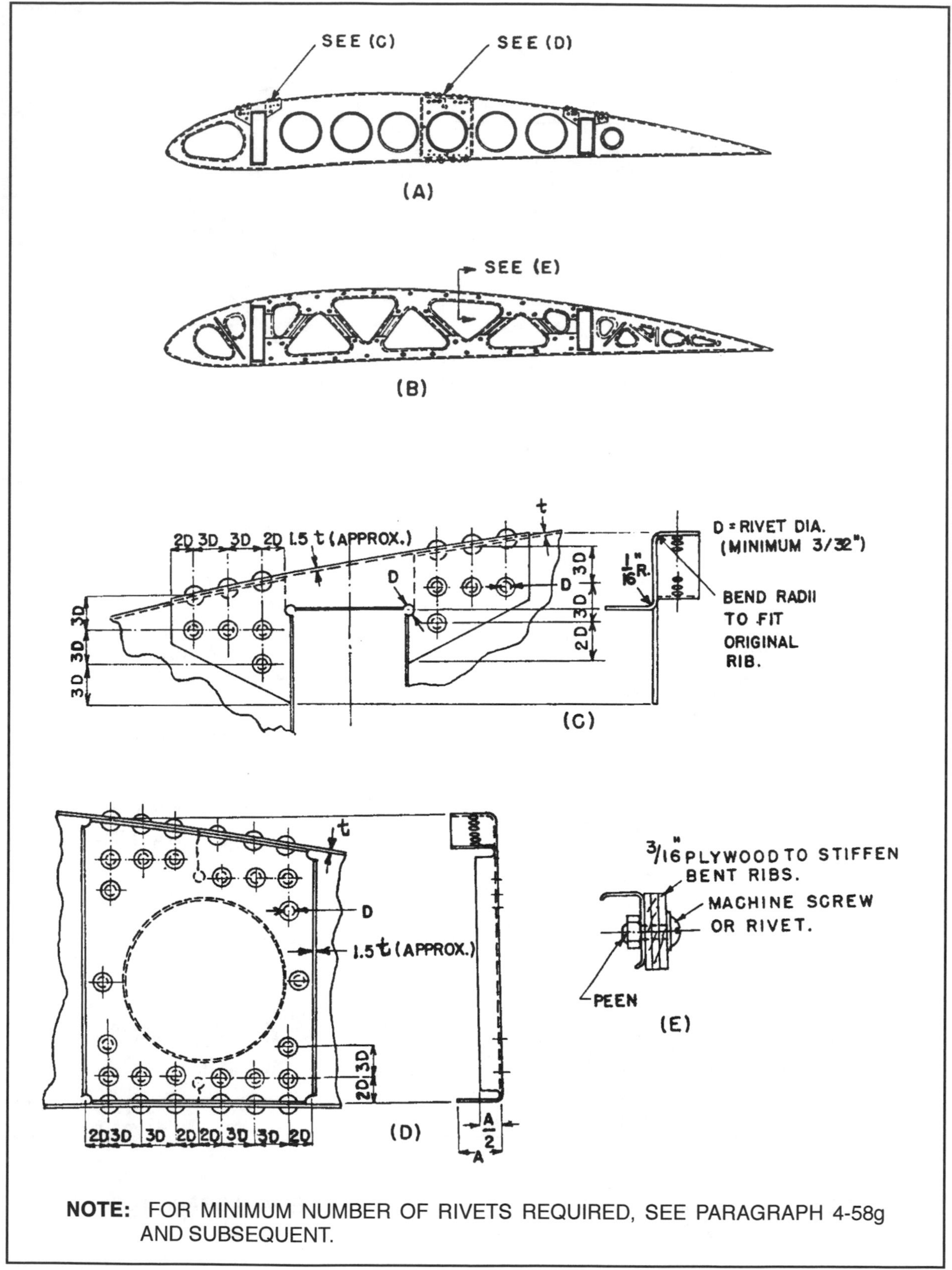

NOTE: FOR MINIMUM NUMBER OF RIVETS REQUIRED, SEE PARAGRAPH 4-58g AND SUBSEQUENT.

FIGURE 4-14. Typical metal rib repairs (usually found on small and medium-size aircraft).

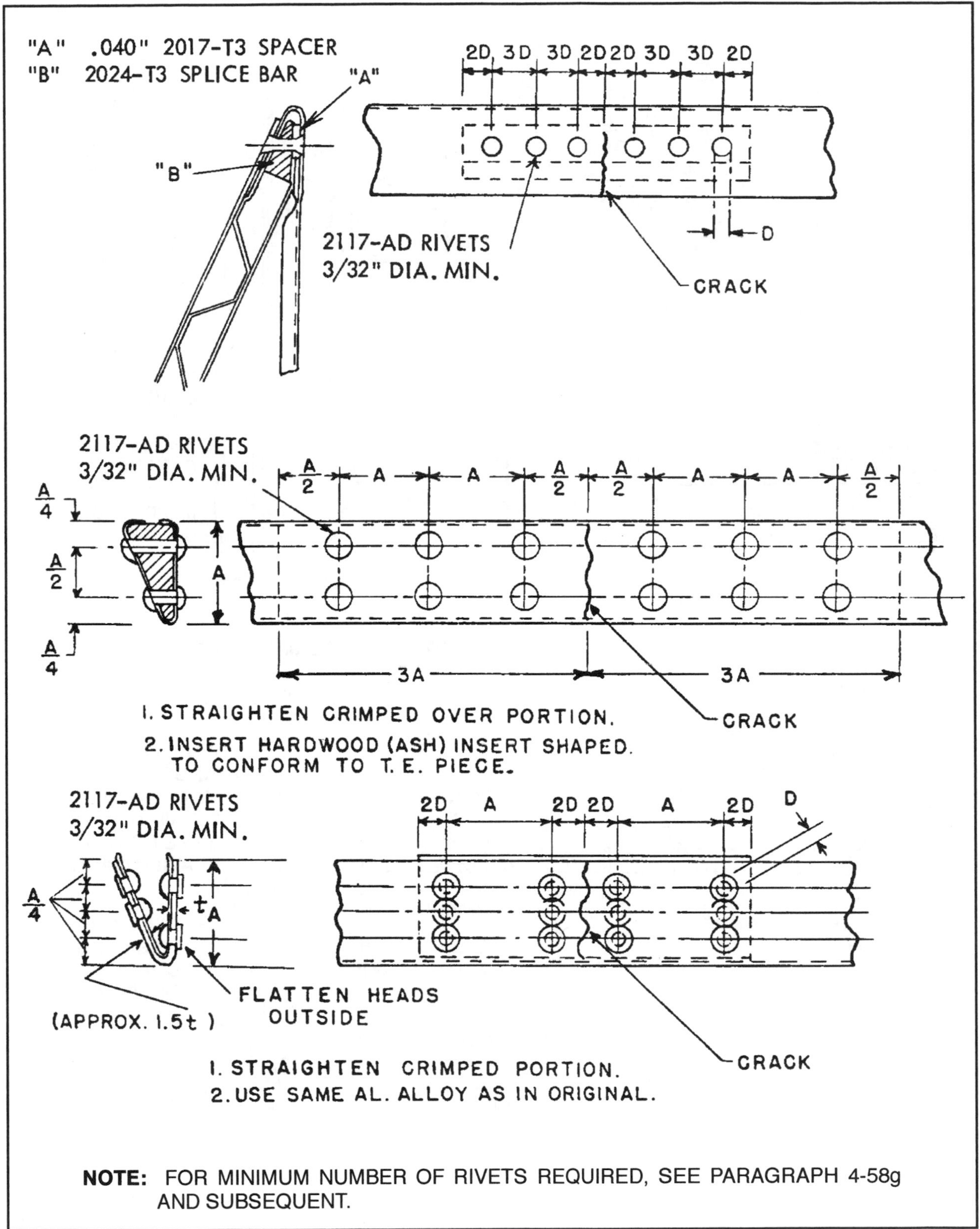

FIGURE 4-15. Typical repairs of trailing edges.

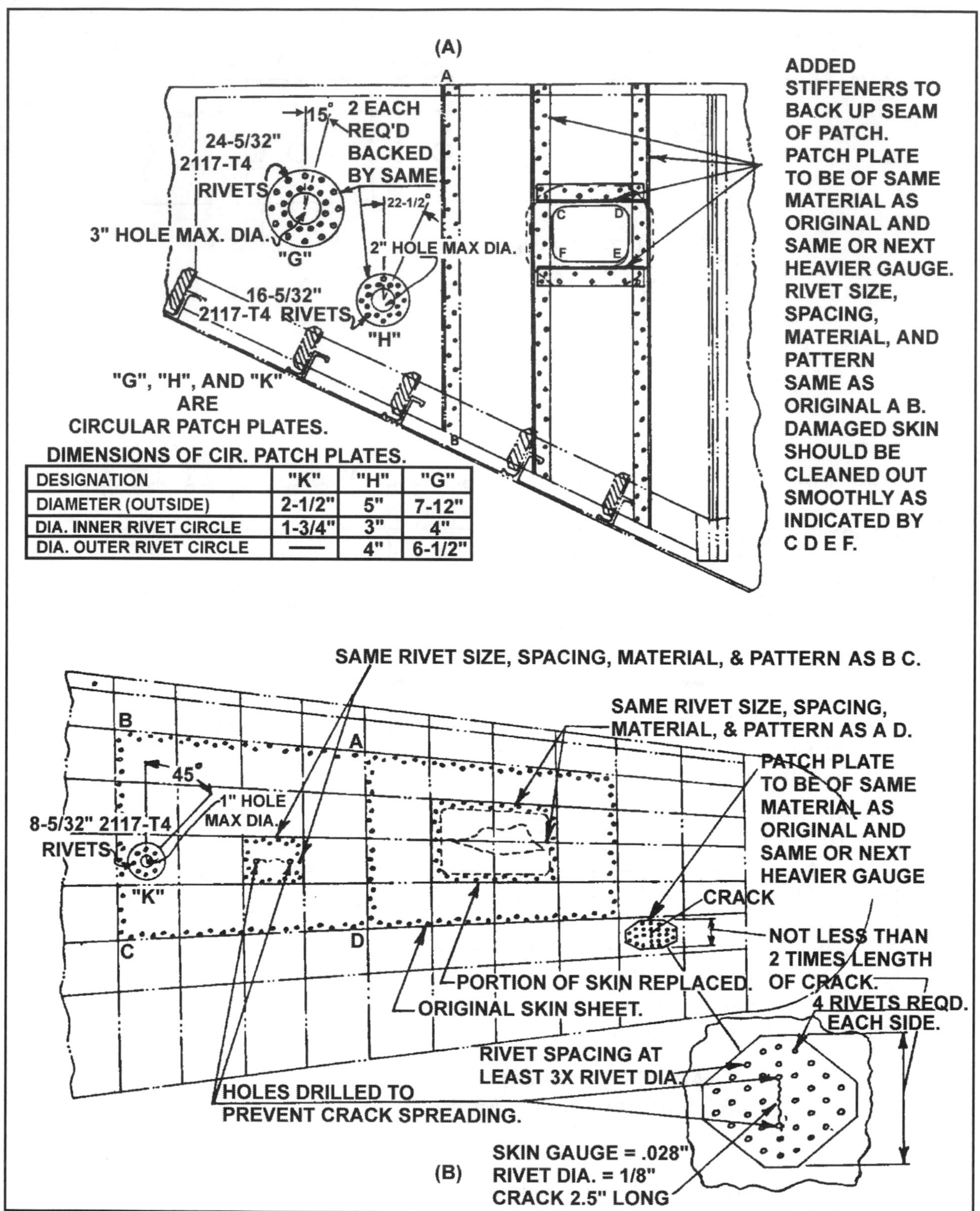

DESIGNATION	"K"	"H"	"G"
DIAMETER (OUTSIDE)	2-1/2"	5"	7-12"
DIA. INNER RIVET CIRCLE	1-3/4"	3"	4"
DIA. OUTER RIVET CIRCLE	—	4"	6-1/2"

FIGURE 4-16. Typical repairs of stressed sheet metal coverings. (Refer to tables 4-9, 4-10, and 4-11 to calculate number of rivets to be used.)

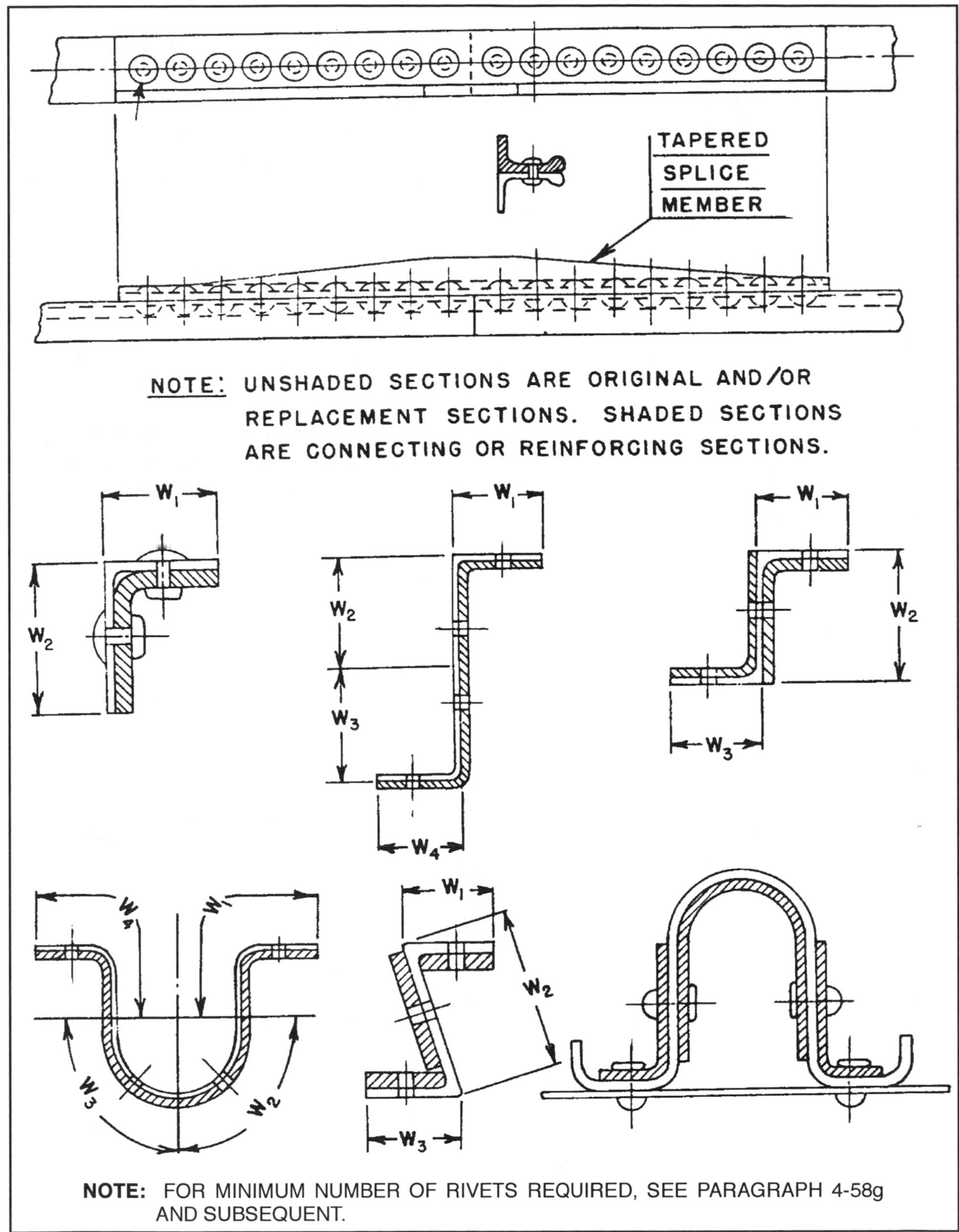
TAPERED
SPLICE
MEMBER
NOTE: UNSHADED SECTIONS ARE ORIGINAL AND/OR REPLACEMENT SECTIONS. SHADED SECTIONS ARE CONNECTING OR REINFORCING SECTIONS.
W1
W2
W3
W4
NOTE: FOR MINIMUM NUMBER OF RIVETS REQUIRED, SEE PARAGRAPH 4-58g AND SUBSEQUENT.

FIGURE 4-17. Typical stringer and flange splices.

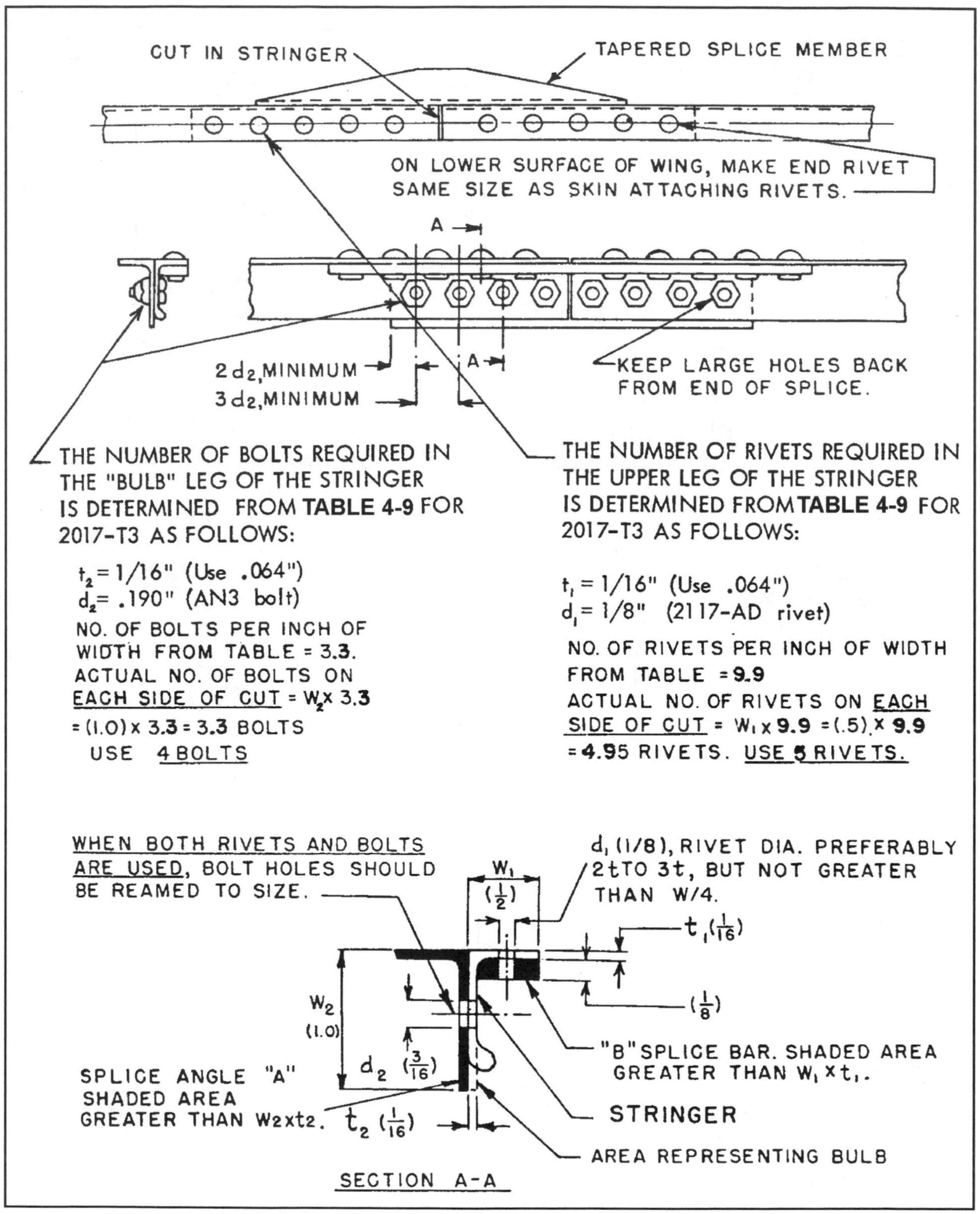

FIGURE 4-18. Example of stringer splice (material-2017 alloy).

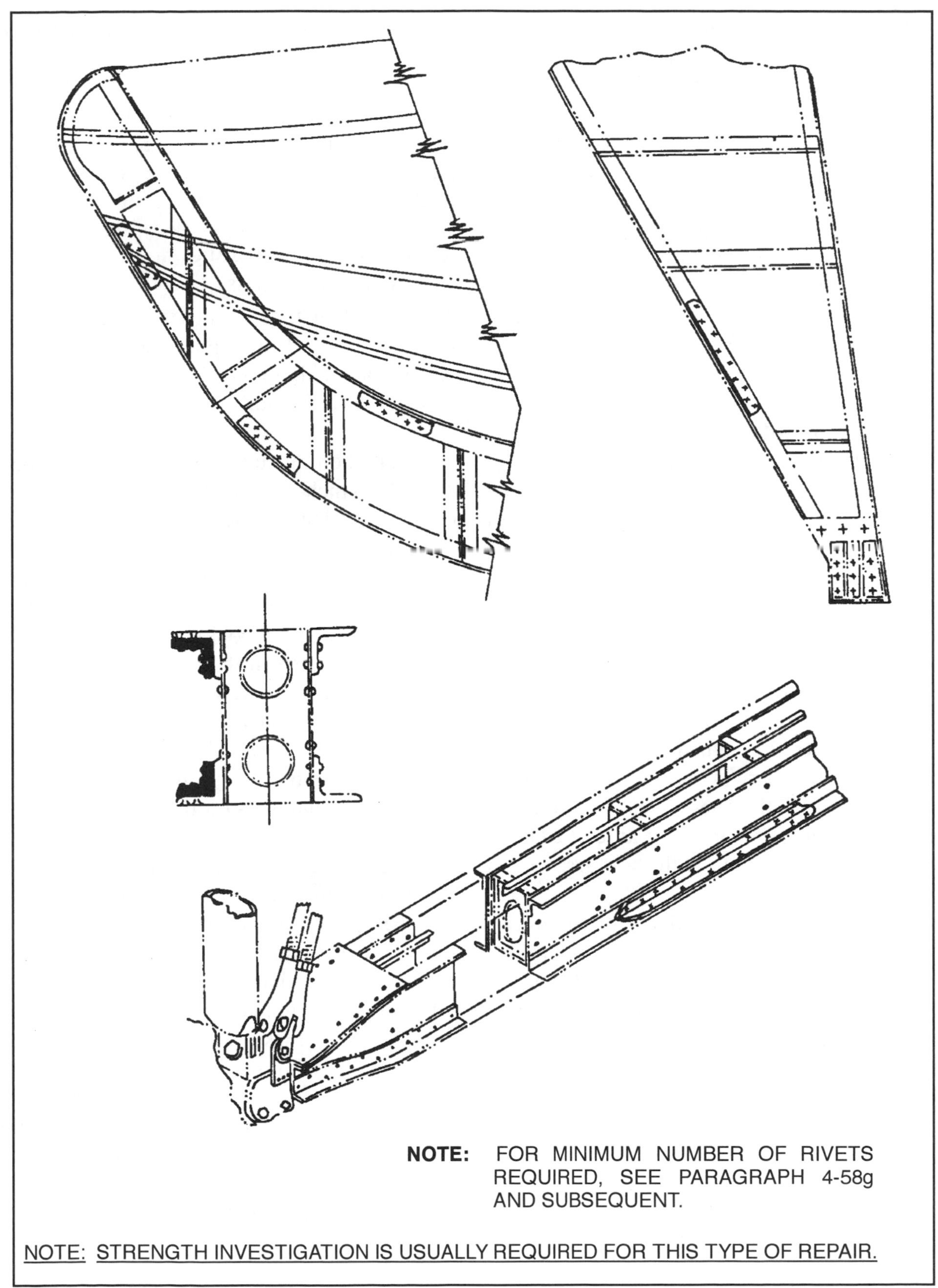

NOTE: FOR MINIMUM NUMBER OF RIVETS REQUIRED, SEE PARAGRAPH 4-58g AND SUBSEQUENT.
NOTE: STRENGTH INVESTIGATION IS USUALLY REQUIRED FOR THIS TYPE OF REPAIR.

FIGURE 4-19. Application of typical flange splices and reinforcement.

(3) To avoid concentration of load on the end rivet and consequent tendency toward progressive rivet failure, the splice is tapered at the ends by tapering the backing angle and by making it shorter than the splice bar. (See figure 4-18.)

(4) The preceding principles are especially important in splicing stringers on the lower surface of stressed skin wings, where high-tension stresses may exist. When several adjacent stringers are spliced, stagger the splices if possible.

k. Size of Splicing Members. When the same material is used for the splicing members as for the original member, the cross-section area (i.e., the shaded areas in figure 4-17), of the splice material will be greater than the area of the section element which it splices. The area of a section element (e.g., each leg of an angle or channel) is equal to the width multiplied by the thickness. For example, the bar "B" in figure 4-18 is assumed to splice the upper leg of the stringer, and the angle "A" is assumed to splice the bulbed leg of the stringer. Since the splice bar "B" is not as wide as the adjacent leg, its thickness must be increased such that the area of bar "B" is at least equal to the area of the upper leg of the stringer.

l. The Diameter of Rivets in Stringers. The diameter of rivets in stringers might preferably be between two and three times the thickness "t" of the leg, but must not be more than 1/4th the width "W" of the leg. Thus, 1/8-inch rivets are chosen in the example, figure 4-18. If the splices were in the lower surface of a wing, the end rivets would be made the same size as the skin-attaching rivets, or 3/32 inch.

m. The Number of Rivets. The number of rivets required on each side of the cut in a stringer or flange may be determined from standard text books on aircraft structures, or may be found in tables 4-9 through 4-11.

(1) In determining the number of rivets required in the example, figure 4-18, for attaching the splice bar "B" to the upper leg, the thickness "t" of the element of area being spliced is 1/16 inch (use 0.064), the rivet size is 1/8 inch, and table 4-9 shows that 9.9 rivets are required per inch of width. Since the width "W" is 1/2 inch, the actual number of rivets required to attach the splice bar to the upper leg on each side of the cut is 9.9 (rivets per inch) x 0.5 (inch width) = 4.95 (use 5 rivets).

(2) For the bulbed leg of the stringer "t" = 1/16 inch (use 0.064); AN-3 bolts are chosen, and the number of bolts required per inch of width = 3.3. The width "W" for this leg, however, is 1 inch; and the actual number of bolts required on each side of the cut is 1 x 3.3 = 3.3 (use 4 bolts). When both rivets and bolts are used in the same splice, the bolt holes must be accurately reamed to size. It is preferable to use only one type of attachment, but in the above example, the dimensions of the legs of the bulb angle indicated rivets for the upper leg and bolts for the bulb leg.

n. Splicing of Intermediate Frames. The same principles used for stringer splicing may be applied to intermediate frames when the following point is considered. Conventional frames of channel or Z sections are relatively deep and thin compared to stringers, and usually fail by twisting or by buckling of the free flange. Reinforce the splice joint against this type of failure by using a splice plate heavier than the frame and by splicing the free flange of the frame with a flange of the splice plate. (See figure 4-20.) Since a frame is likely to be subjected to bending loads, make the length of splice plate "L" more than twice the width "W_2," and the rivets spread out to cover the plate.

TABLE 4-9. Number of rivets required for splices (single-lap joint) in bare 2014-T6, 2024-T3, 2024-T36, and 7075-T6 sheet, clad 2014-T6, 2024-T3, 2024-T36, and 7075-T6 sheet, 2024-T4, and 7075-T6 plate, bar, rod, tube, and extrusions, 2014-T6 extrusions.

Thickness "t" in inches	No. of 2117-T4 (AD) protruding head rivets required per inch of width "W"					No. of Bolts
	Rivet size					
	3/32	1/8	5/32	3/16	1/4	AN-3
.016	6.5	4.9	- -	- -	- -	- -
.020	6.9	4.9	3.9	- -	- -	- -
.025	8.6	4.9	3.9	- -	- -	- -
.032	11.1	6.2	3.9	3.3	- -	- -
.036	12.5	7.0	4.5	3.3	2.4	- -
.040	13.8	7.7	5.0	3.5	2.4	3.3
.051	- -	9.8	6.4	4.5	2.5	3.3
.064	- -	12.3	8.1	5.6	3.1	3.3
.081	- -	- -	10.2	7.1	3.9	3.3
.091	- -	- -	11.4	7.9	4.4	3.3
.102	- -	- -	12.8	8.9	4.9	3.4
.128	- -	- -	- -	11.2	6.2	3.2

NOTES:

a. For stringers in the upper surface of a wing, or in a fuselage, 80 percent of the number of rivets shown in the table may be used.

b. For intermediate frames, 60 percent of the number shown may be used.

c. For single lap sheet joints, 75 percent of the number shown may be used.

ENGINEERING NOTES:

a. The load per inch of width of material was calculated by assuming a strip 1 inch wide in tension.

b. Number of rivets required was calculated for 2117-T4 (AD) rivets, based on a rivet allowable shear stress equal to 40 percent of the sheet allowable tensile stress, and a sheet allowable bearing stress equal to 160 percent of the sheet allowable tensile stress, using nominal bolt diameters for rivets.

c. Combinations of sheet thickness and rivet size above the underlined numbers are critical in (i.e., will fail by) bearing on the sheet; those below are critical in shearing of the rivets.

d. The number of AN-3 bolts required below the underlined number was calculated based on a sheet allowable tensile stress of 70,000 psi and a bolt allowable single shear load of 2,126 pounds.

TABLE 4-10. Number of rivets required for splices (single-lap joint) in 2017, 1017 ALCLAD, 2024-T3 ALCLAD sheet, plate, bar, rod, tube, and extrusions.

Thickness "t" in inches	No. of 2117-T4 (AD) protruding head rivets required per inch of width "W"					No. of Bolts
	Rivet size					
	3/32	1/8	5/32	3/16	1/4	AN-3
.016	6.5	4.9	- -	- -	- -	- -
.020	6.5	4.9	3.9	- -	- -	- -
.025	6.9	4.9	3.9	- -	- -	- -
.032	8.9	4.9	3.9	3.3	- -	- -
.036	10.0	5.6	3.9	3.3	2.4	- -
.040	11.1	6.2	4.0	3.3	2.4	- -
.051	- -	7.9	5.1	3.6	2.4	3.3
.064	- -	9.9	6.5	4.5	2.5	3.3
.081	- -	12.5	8.1	5.7	3.1	3.3
.091	- -	- -	9.1	6.3	3.5	3.3
.102	- -	- -	10.3	7.1	3.9	3.3
.128	- -	- -	12.9	8.9	4.9	3.3

NOTES:

a. For stringers in the upper surface of a wing, or in a fuselage, 80 percent of the number of rivets shown in the table may be used.

b. For intermediate frames, 60 percent of the number shown may be used.

c. For single lap sheet joints, 75 percent of the number shown may be used.

ENGINEERING NOTES:

a. The load per inch of width of material was calculated by assuming a strip 1 inch wide in tension.

b. Number of rivets required was calculated for 2117-T4 (AD) rivets, based on a rivet allowable shear stress equal to percent of the sheet allowable tensile stress, and a sheet allowable bearing stress equal to 160 percent of the sheet allowable tensile stress, using nominal hole diameters for rivets.

c. Combinations of sheet thickness and rivet size above the underlined numbers are critical in (i.e., will fail by) bearing on the sheet; those below are critical in shearing of the rivets.

d. The number of AN-3 bolts required below the underlined number was calculated based on a sheet allowable tensile stress of 55,000 psi and a bolt allowable single shear load of 2,126 pounds.

TABLE 4-11. Number of rivets required for splices (single-lap joint) in 5052 (all hardnesses) sheet.

Thickness "t" in inches	No. of 2117-T4 (AD) protruding head rivets required per inch of width "W" — Rivet size					No. of Bolts
	3/32	1/8	5/32	3/16	1/4	AN-3
.016	6.3	4.7		- -	- -	- -
.020	6.3	4.7	3.8	- -	- -	- -
.025	6.3	4.7	3.8	- -	- -	- -
.032	6.3	4.7	3.8	3.2	- -	- -
.036	7.1	4.7	3.8	3.2	2.4	- -
.040	7.9	4.7	3.8	3.2	2.4	- -
.051	10.1	5.6	3.8	3.2	2.4	- -
.064	12.7	7.0	4.6	3.2	2.4	- -
.081	- -	8.9	5.8	4.0	2.4	3.2
.091	- -	10.0	6.5	4.5	2.5	3.2
.102	- -	11.2	7.3	5.1	2.8	3.2
.128	- -	- -	9.2	6.4	3.5	3.2

NOTES:

a. For stringers in the upper surface of a wing, or in a fuselage, 80 percent of the number of rivets shown in the table may be used.

b. For intermediate frames, 60 percent of the number shown may be used.

c. For single lap sheet joints, 75 percent of the number shown may be used.

ENGINEERING NOTES:

a. The load per inch of width of material was calculated by assuming a strip 1 inch wide in tension.

b. Number of rivets required was calculated for 2117-T4 (AD) rivets, based on a rivet allowable shear stress equal to 70 percent of the sheet allowable tensile stress, and a sheet allowable bearing stress equal to 160 percent of the sheet allowable tensile stress, using nominal hole diameters for rivets.

c. Combinations of sheet thickness and rivet size above the underlined numbers are critical in (i.e., will fail by) bearing on the sheet, those below are critical in shearing of the rivets.

4-59. REPAIRING CRACKED MEMBERS. Acceptable methods of repairing various types of cracks in structural elements are shown in figures 4-21 through 4-24. The following general procedures apply in repairing such defects.

a. Drill small holes 3/32 inch (or 1/8 inch) at the extreme ends of the cracks to minimize the possibility of their spreading further.

b. Add reinforcement to carry the stresses across the damaged portion and to stiffen the joints. (See figures 4-14 through 4-17.) The condition causing cracks to develop at a particular point is stress concentration at that point in conjunction with repetition of stress, such as produced by vibration of the structure. The stress concentration may be due to the design or to defects such as nicks, scratches, tool marks, and initial stresses or cracks from forming or heat-treating operations. It should be noted, that an increase in sheet thickness alone is usually beneficial but does not necessarily remedy the conditions leading to cracking.

4-60. STEEL AND ALUMINUM FITTINGS.

a. Steel Fittings. Inspect for the following defects.

(1) Fittings are to be free from scratches, vise and nibbler marks, and sharp bends or edges. A careful examination of the fitting with a medium power (at least 10 power) magnifying glass is acceptable as an inspection.

(2) When repairing aircraft after an accident or in the course of a major overhaul, inspect all highly-stressed main fittings, as set forth in the manufacturer's instruction manual.

(3) Replace torn, kinked, or cracked fittings.

(4) Elongated or worn bolt holes in fittings, which were designed without bushings, are not to be reamed oversize. Replace such fittings, unless the method of repair is approved by the FAA. Do not fill holes with welding rod. Acceptable methods of repairing elongated or worn bolt holes in landing gear, stabilizer, interplane, or cabane-strut ends are shown in figure 4-25.

b. Aluminum and Aluminum Alloy Fittings.

(1) Replace damaged fittings with new parts that have the same material specifications.

(2) Repairs may be made in accordance with data furnished by the aircraft manufacturer, or data substantiating the method of repair may be submitted to the FAA for approval.

4-61. CASTINGS. Damaged castings are to be replaced and not repaired unless the method of repair is specifically approved by the aircraft manufacturer or substantiating data for the repair has been reviewed by the FAA for approval.

4-62. SELECTIVE PLATING IN AIRCRAFT MAINTENANCE. Selective plating is a method of depositing metal from an electrolyte to the selected area. The electrolyte is held in an absorbent material attached to an inert anode. Plating contact is made by brushing or swabbing the part (cathode) with the electrolyte-bearing anode.

a. Selective Plating Uses. This process can be utilized for any of the following reasons.

THE NUMBER OF RIVETS REQUIRED IN EACH LEG ON EACH SIDE OF THE CUT IS DETERMINED BY THE WIDTH "W," THE THICKNESS OF THE FRAME "t," AND THE RIVET DIAMETER "d" USING TABLE 4-10 IN A MANNER SIMILAR TO THAT FOR STRINGERS IN FIGURE 4-20.

NOTE b. IN TABLE 4-10 INDICATES THAT ONLY 60 PERCENT OF THE NUMBER OF RIVETS SO CALCULATED NEED BE USED IN SPLICES IN INTERMEDIATE.

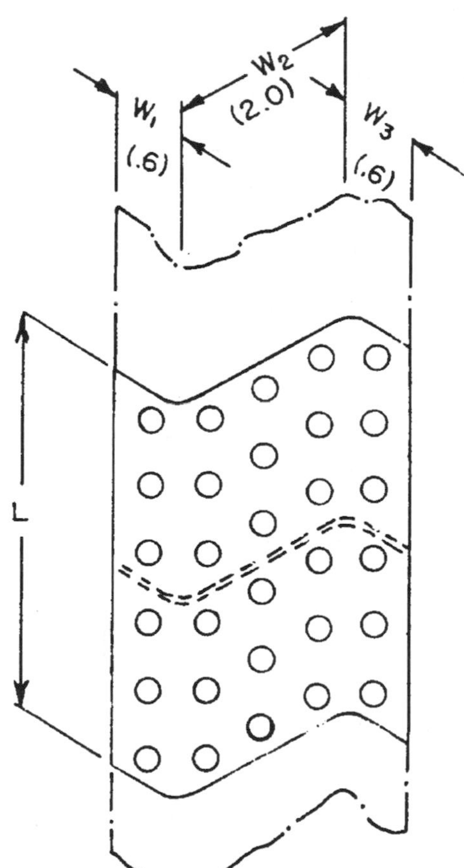

EXAMPLE: (FOR 2017-T3 aluminum alloy frame)

FLANGE LEG

t = .040"
d = 1/8" 2117-T4 (AD)
W_1 & W_3 = .6 inch

NO. OF RIVETS PER INCH OF WIDTH FROM TABLE 4-10 = 6.2

No. of rivets required = W x 6.2 =
.6 x 6.2 = 3.72 or 4 rivets.
60 percent of 4 rivets = 2.4 rivets.
USE 3 RIVETS ON EACH SIDE OF THE CUT IN EACH FLANGE LEG.

WEB OF ZEE (OR CHANNEL)

t = .040"
d = 1/8" 2117-T4 (AD) rivet
W = 2.0 inches

NO. OF RIVETS PER INCH OF WIDTH FROM TABLE 4-10 = 6.2

No. of rivets required = W x 6.2 =
2.0 x 6.2 = 12.4 or 13 rivets.
60 percent of 13 rivets = 7.8 rivets.
USE 8 RIVETS ON EACH SIDE OF CUT IN THE WEB OF ZEE (OR CHANNEL).

"L" SHOULD BE MORE THAN TWICE W_2

Thickness of splice plate to be greater than that of the frame to be spliced.

FIGURE 4-20. Example of intermediate frame stringer splice (material 2017-T3 AL alloy).

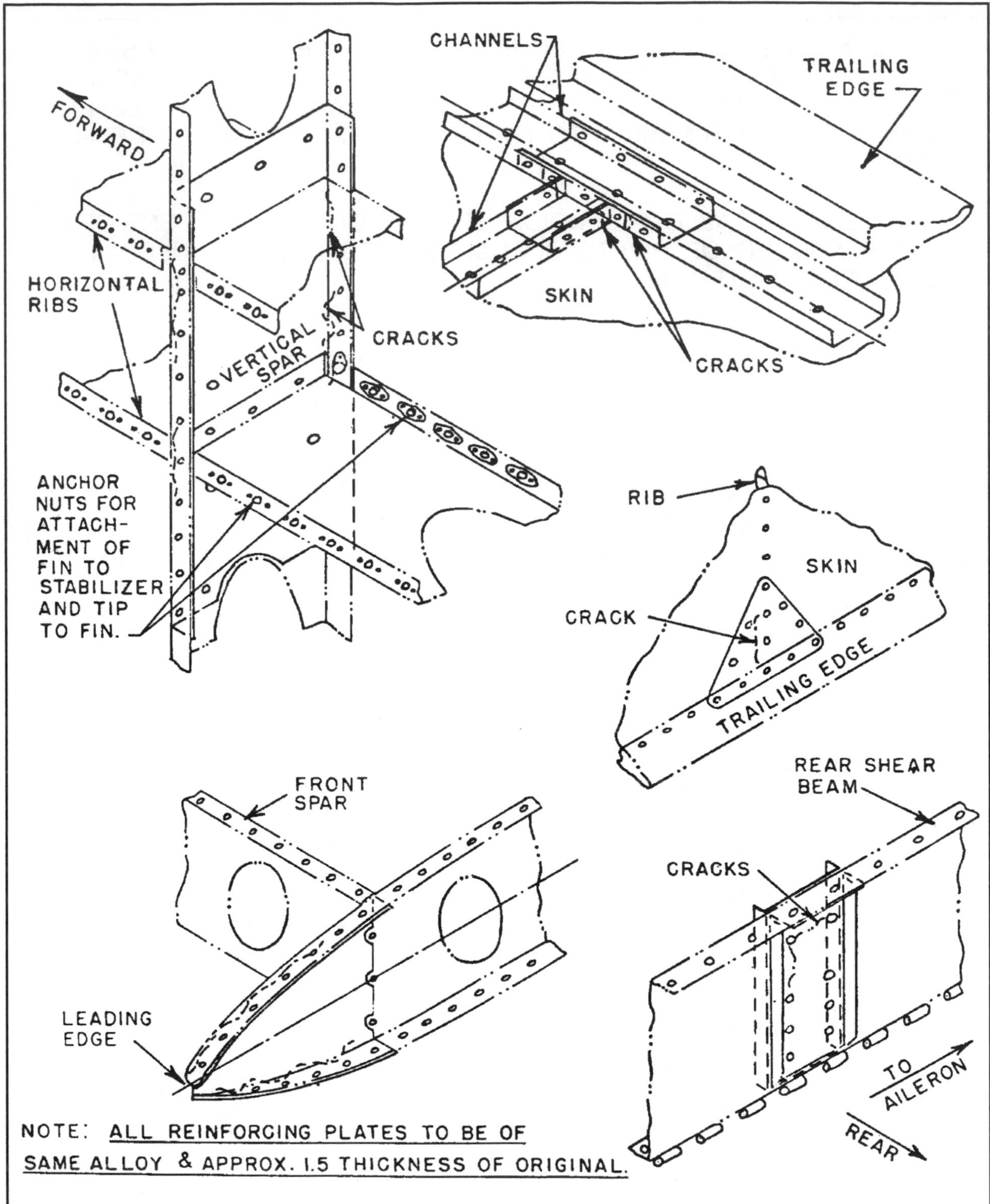

FIGURE 4-21. Typical methods of repairing cracked leading and trailing edges and rib intersections.

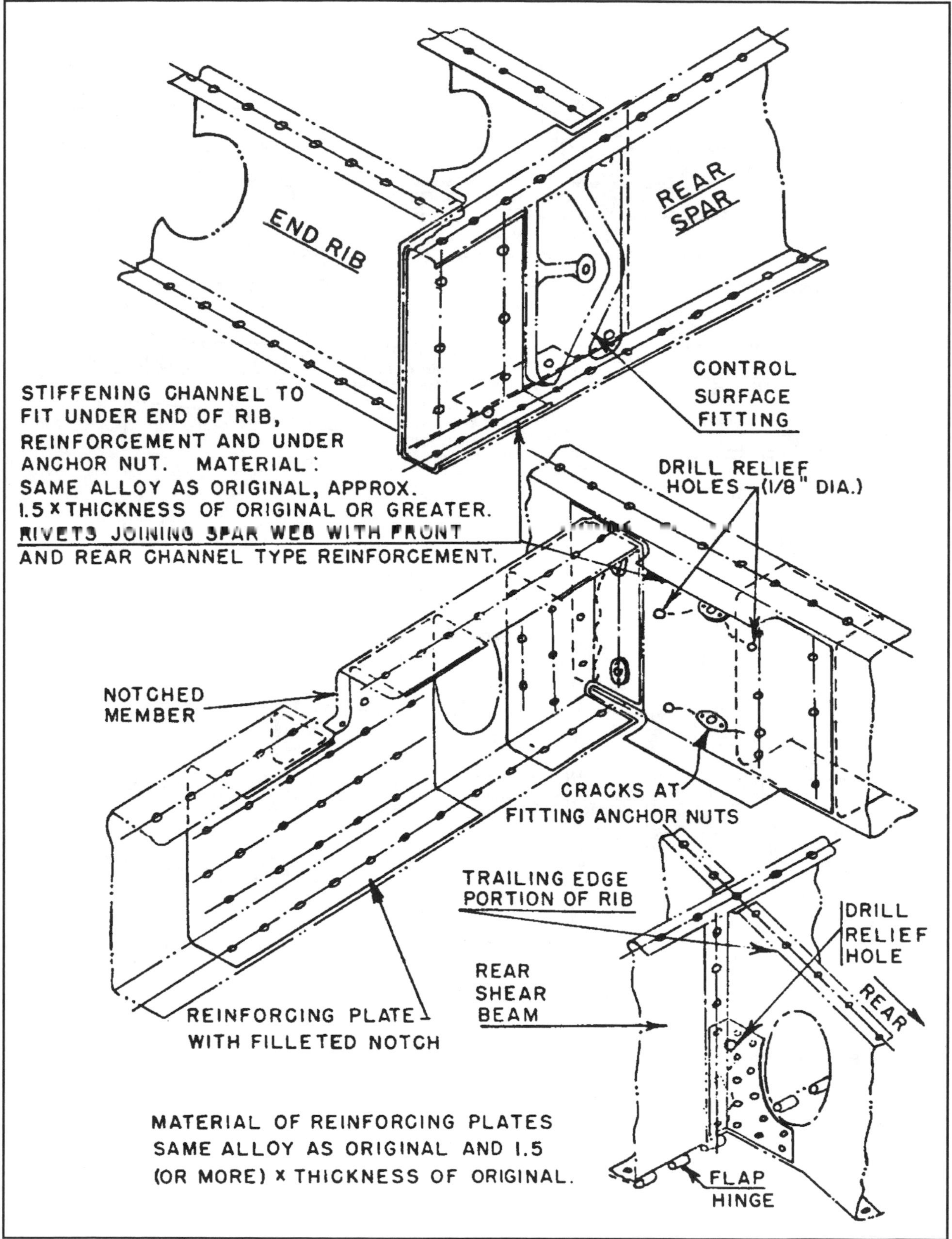

FIGURE 4-22. Typical methods of replacing cracked members at fittings.

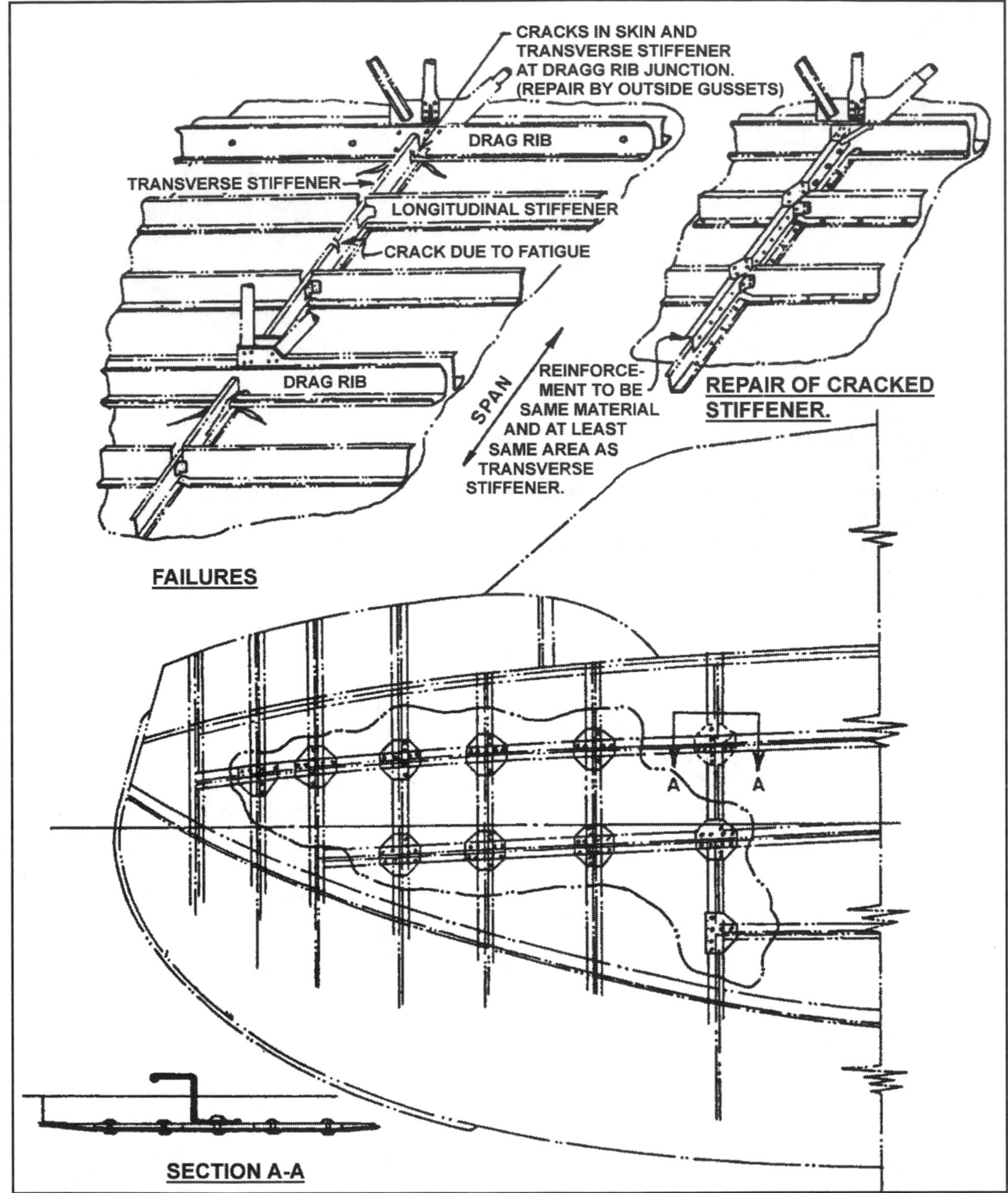

FIGURE 4-23. Typical methods of repairing cracked frame and stiffener combination.

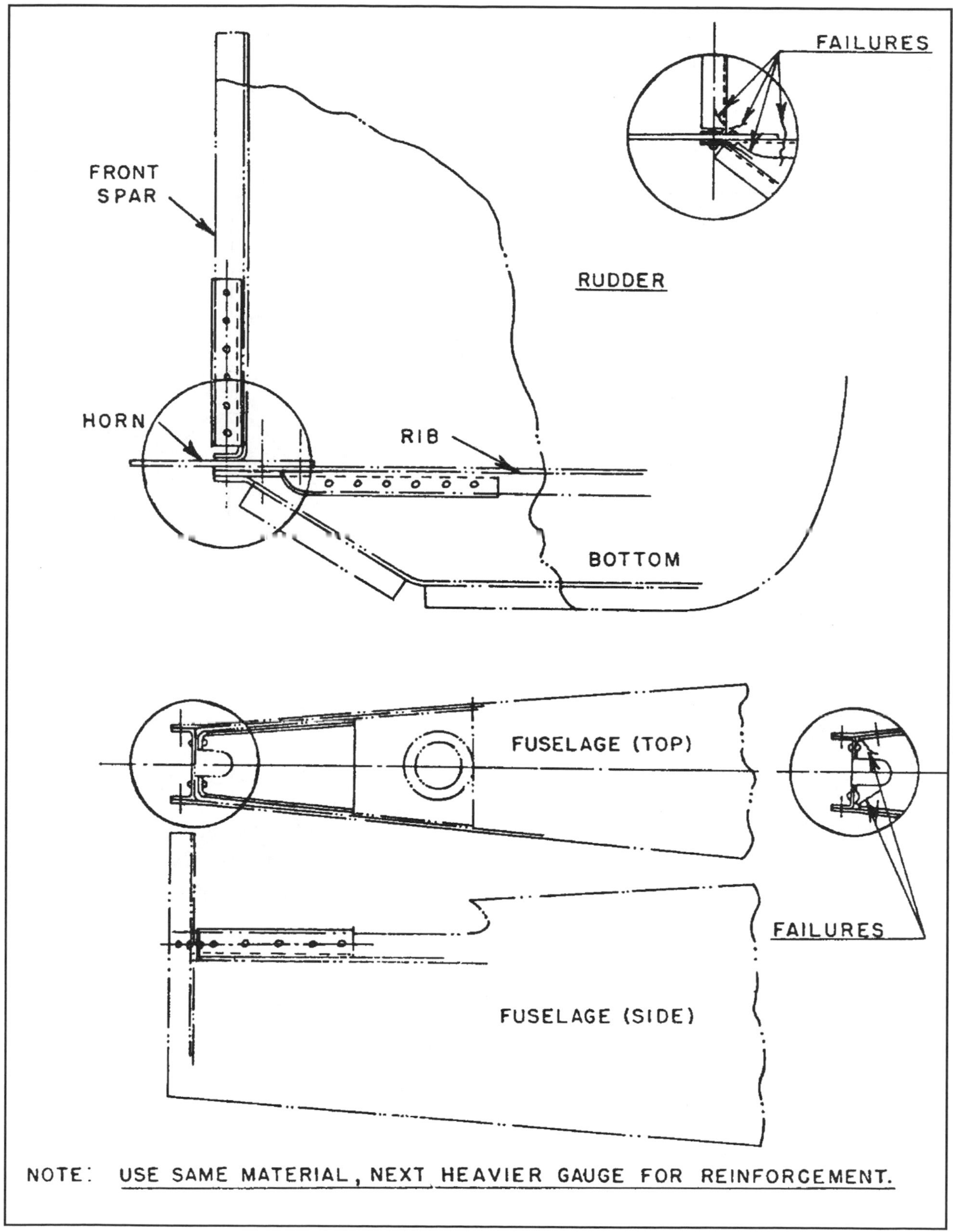

FIGURE 4-24. Typical repairs to rudder and to fuselage at tail post.

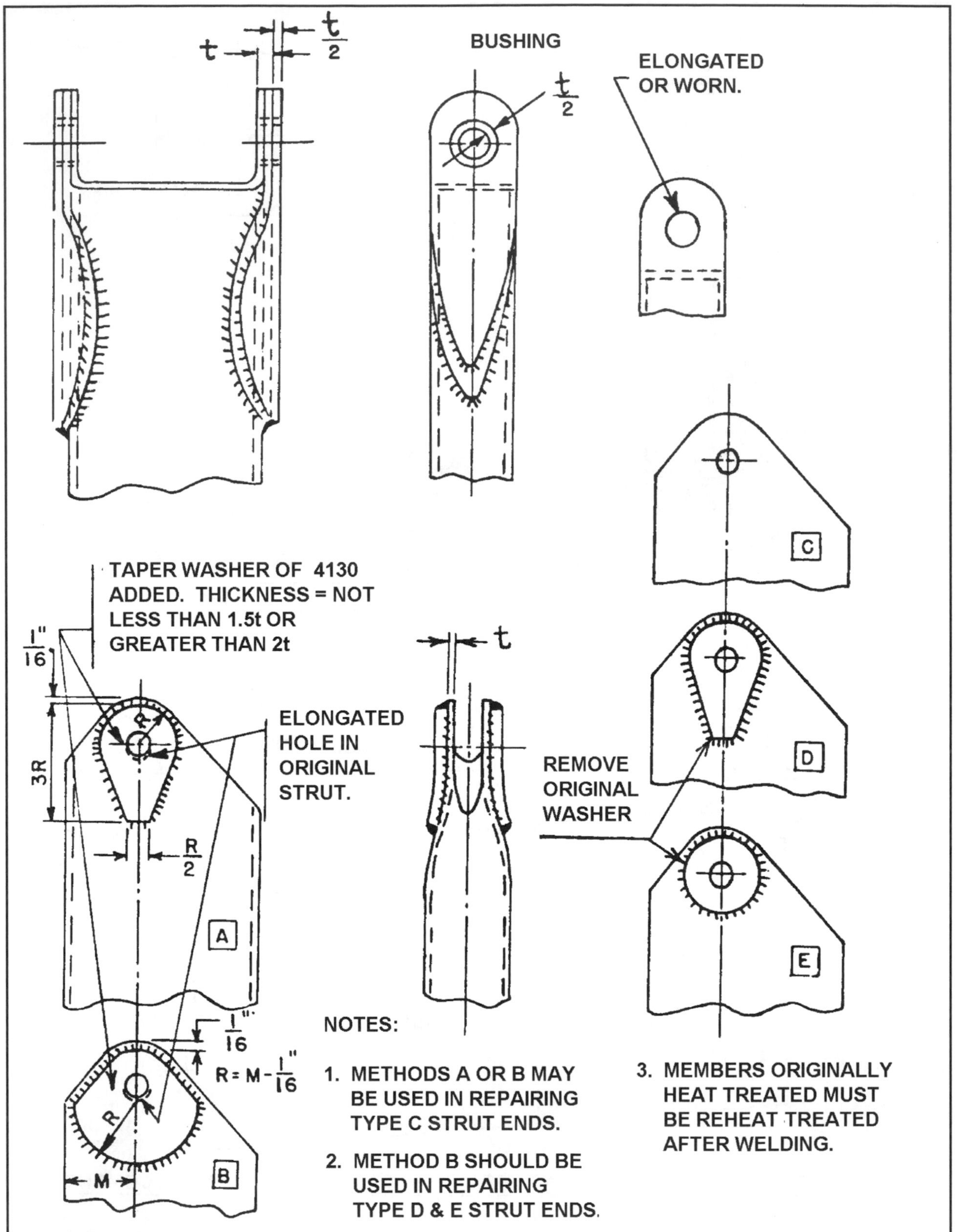

FIGURE 4-25. Typical methods of repairing elongated or worn bolt holes.

(1) To prevent or minimize disassembly, or reassembly.

(2) Resizing worn components (plate to size).

(3) Filling in damaged or corroded areas.

(4) To plate small areas of extremely large parts.

(5) To plate electrical contacts.

(6) To plate parts too large for existing baths.

(7) To supplement conventional plating.

(8) To plate components which become contaminated if immersed in a plating bath.

(9) To cadmium-plate ultrahigh strength steels without hydrogen embrittlement.

(10) On-site plating.

(11) Reverse current applications (e.g., stain removal, deburring, etching, and dynamic balancing).

b. Specifications. Selective plating (electrodepositions), when properly applied, will meet the following specifications and standards.

(1) QQ-C-320, Chromium Plating.

(2) QQ-N-290, Nickel Plating.

(3) QQ-P-416, Cadmium Plating.

(4) QQ-S-365, Silver Plating.

(5) QQ-Z-325, Zinc Plating.

(6) MIL-T-10727, Tin Plating.

(7) MIL-C-14550, Copper Plating.

(8) MIL-G-45204, Gold Plating.

c. General Requirements.

(1) Areas to be repaired by this process should be limited to small areas of large parts, particularly electrical or electronic parts.

(2) All solutions should be kept clean and free from contamination. Care should be taken to insure that the solutions are not contaminated by used anodes or other plating solutions. Brush-plating solutions are not designed to remove large amounts of scale, oil, or grease. Mechanical or chemical methods should be used to remove large amounts of scale or oxide. Use solvents to remove grease or oil.

(3) Brush-plating solutions are five to fifty times as concentrated as tank solutions. The current densities used range from 500 to 4,000 amps/feet^2. The voltages listed on the solution bottles have been precalculated to give proper current densities. Too high a current density burns the plating, while too low a current density produces stressed deposits and low efficiencies. Agitation is provided by anode/cathode motion. Too fast a motion results in low efficiencies and stressed deposits, and too slow a motion causes burning. A dry tool results in burnt plate, coarse grain structure, and unsound deposits. The tool cannot be too wet. Solution temperatures of 110 °F to 120 °F are reached during operation.

(4) Materials such as stainless steel, aluminum, chromium, and nickel (which have a passive surface) will require an activating operation to remove the passive surface. During the activating process, do not use solutions that have been previously used with reverse current (because of solution contamination).

d. Equipment. The power source should operate on either 110 or 220-volt alternating current (AC), 60 Hertz, single-phase input. It should have a capability to produce direct current (DC) having smooth characteristics with controlled ripple and be able to output a current of at least 25 amperes at 0 to 25 volts. Minimum instrumentation of the power source should include a voltmeter, ammeter, and ampere-hour meter.

(1) The ammeter should provide a full-scale reading equal to the maximum capacity of the power source, and with an accuracy of ±5 percent of the current being measured.

(2) The voltmeter should have sufficient capacity to provide a full-scale reading equal to the maximum capacity of the power source and an accuracy of ±1.0 volt.

(3) An ampere-hour meter should be readable to 0.001 ampere-hour and have an accuracy of ±0.01 ampere-hour.

(4) The stylus should be designed for rapid cooling and to hold anodes of various sizes and configurations. For safety, the anode holder should be insulated.

(5) The containers for holding and catching runoff solutions should be designed to the proper configuration and be inert to the specific solution.

(6) The mechanical cleaning equipment and materials should be designed and selected to prevent contamination of the parts to be cleaned.

e. Materials. The anodes should be of high-purity dense graphite or platinum-iridium alloys. Do not mix solutions from different suppliers. This could result in contamination.

f. Detail Requirements. On large parts, no area greater than approximately 10 percent of the total area of the part should be plated by this selective plating process. Small parts may be partially or completely plated. Special cases exceeding these limitations should be coordinated with the manufacturer of the plating equipment being used and their recommendations should be followed.

g. Anode Selection. As a general guide, the contact area of the anode should be approximately one-third the size of the area to be plated. When selecting the anode, the configuration of the part will dictate the shape of the anode.

h. Required Ampere-Hour Calculation. The selected plating solution has a factor which is equal to the ampere-hours required to deposit 0.0001 inch on 1 square inch of surface. Determine the thickness of plating desired on a certain area, and multiply the solution factor times the plating thickness times the area in square inches to determine the ampere-hours required. This factor may vary because of temperature, current density, etc.

i. Cleaning. Remove corrosion, scale, oxide, and unacceptable plating prior to processing. Use a suitable solvent or cleaner to remove grease or oil.

j. Plating on Aluminum and Aluminum Base Alloys.

(1) Electroclean the area using direct current until water does not break on the surface. This electroclean process should be accomplished at 10 to 15 volts, using the appropriate electroclean solution.

(2) Rinse the area in cold, clean tap water.

(3) Activate the area with reverse current, 7 to 10 volts, in conjunction with the proper activating solution until a uniform, gray-to-black surface is obtained.

(4) Rinse thoroughly in cold, clean tap water.

(5) Immediately electroplate to color while the area is still wet, using the appropriate nickel solution.

(6) Rinse thoroughly.

(7) Immediately continue plating with any other solution to desired thickness.

(8) Rinse and dry.

k. Plating on Copper and Copper Base Alloys.

(1) Electroclean the area using direct current until water does not break on the surface. The electroclean process should be accomplished at 8 to 12 volts using the appropriate electroclean solution.

(2) Rinse the area in cold, clean tap water.

(3) Immediately electroplate the area with any of the plating solutions, except silver. Silver requires an undercoat.

(4) Rinse and dry.

l. Plating on 300 and 400 Series Stainless Steels, Nickel Base Alloys, Chrome Base Alloys, High Nickel Ferrous Alloys, Cobalt Base Alloys, Nickel Plate, and Chrome Plate.

(1) Electroclean the area using direct current until water does not break on the surface. This electroclean process should be accomplished at 12 to 20 volts using the appropriate electrocleaning solution.

(2) Rinse the area in cold, clean tap water.

(3) Activate the surface using direct current for 1 to 2 minutes, using the activating solution, and accomplish at 6 to 20 volts.

(4) Do not rinse.

(5) Immediately nickel-flash the surface to a thickness of 0.00005 to 0.0001 inch, using the appropriate nickel solution.

(6) Rinse thoroughly.

(7) Immediately continue plating with any other solution to desired thickness.

(8) Rinse and dry.

m. Plating on Low-Carbon Steels (Heat Treated to 180,000 psi).

(1) Electroclean the area using direct current until water does not break on the surface. This electroclean process should be accomplished at 12 to 20 volts, using the appropriate electrocleaning solution.

(2) Rinse the area in cold, clean tap water.

(3) Reverse-current etch at 8 to 10 volts, using the appropriate activating solution, until a uniform gray surface is obtained.

(4) Rinse thoroughly.

(5) Immediately electroplate the part using any solutions, except copper or silver. Both of these require undercoats.

(6) Rinse and dry.

n. Plating on Cast Iron and High-Carbon Steels (Steels Heat Treated to 180,000 psi).

(1) Electroclean the area using direct current until water does not break on the surface. This electroclean process should be accomplished at 12 to 20 volts, using the appropriate electrocleaning solution.

(2) Rinse the area thoroughly in cold, clean tap water.

(3) Reverse-current etch at 8 to 10 volts, using the appropriate etching solution, until a uniform gray is obtained.

(4) Rinse thoroughly.

(5) Remove surface smut with 15 to 25 volts using the appropriate activating solution.

(6) Rinse thoroughly.

(7) Electroplate immediately, using any of the solutions, except copper or silver (both of these require undercoats).

(8) Rinse and dry.

o. Plating on Ultrahigh Strength Steels (Heat Treated Above 180,000 psi).

(1) Electroclean the area using reverse current until water does not break on the surface. This electroclean process should be accomplished at 8 to 12 volts using the appropriate electroclean solution.

(2) Rinse the area thoroughly in cold, clean tap water.

(3) Immediately electroplate the part, using either nickel, chromium, gold, or cadmium. Other metals require an undercoat of one of the above. Plate initially at the highest voltage recommended for the solution so as to develop an initial barrier layer. Then reduce to standard voltage.

(4) Rinse and dry.

(5) Bake the part for 4 hours at 375 °F ± 25 °F.

NOTE: Where the solution vendor provides substantiating data that hydrogen embrittlement will not result from plating with a particular solution, then a postbake is not required. This substantiating data can be in the form of aircraft industry manufacturer's process specifications, military specifications, or other suitable data.

NOTE: Acid etching should be avoided, if possible. Where etching is absolutely necessary, it should always be done with reverse current. Use alkaline solutions for initial deposits.

p. Dissimilar Metals and Changing Base. As a general rule, when plating two dissimilar metals, follow the plating procedure for the one with the most steps or activation. If activating steps have to be mixed, use reverse-current activation steps prior to direct-current activation steps.

q. Plating Solution Selection.

(1) Alkaline and neutral solutions are to be used on porous base metals, white metals, high-strength steel, and for improved coating ability. Acid solutions are to be used for rapid buildup and as a laminating structure material in conjunction with alkaline-type solutions.

(2) Chrome brush-plating solutions do not yield as hard a deposit as bath-plating solutions. The hardness is about 600 Brinell as compared to 1,000 Brinell for hard chrome deposited from a tank.

(3) Silver-immersion deposits will form with no current flowing on most base metals from the silver brush-plating solutions. Such deposits have poor adhesion to the base metal. Consequently, a flash of a more noble metal should be deposited prior to silver plating to develop a good bond.

(4) In general, brush plating gives less hydrogen embrittlement and a lower fatigue strength loss than does equivalent tank deposits. However, all brush-plated, ultrahigh strength steel parts (heat treated above 180,000 psi) should be baked, as mentioned, unless it is specifically known that embrittlement is not a factor.

r. Qualification Tests. All brush-plated surfaces should be tested for adhesion of the electrodeposit. Apply a 1-inch wide strip of Minnesota Mining and Manufacturing tape code 250, or an approved equal, with the adhesive side to the freshly plated surface. Apply the tape with heavy hand pressure and remove it with one quick motion perpendicular to the plated surface. Any plating adhering to the tape should be cause for rejection.

s. Personnel Training for Quality Control. Manufacturers of selective-plating equipment provide training in application techniques at their facilities. Personnel performing selective plating must have adequate knowledge of the methods, techniques, and practices involved. These personnel should be certified as qualified operators by the manufacturers of the products used.

4-63.—4-73. [RESERVED.]

SECTION 5. WELDING AND BRAZING

4-74. GENERAL. This section covers weld repairs to aircraft and component parts only. Observe the following procedures when using such equipment as gas tungsten arc welding (GTAW), gas metal arc welding (GMAW), plasma arc welding, and oxyacetylene gas welding. When repairs of any of these flight-critical parts are required, it is extremely important to make the weld repairs equal to the original weld. Identifying the kind of metal to be welded, identifying the kind of welding process used in building the part originally, and determining the best way to make welded repairs are of utmost importance.

a. Welding is one of the three commonly used methods of joining metals without the use of fasteners. Welding is done by melting the edges of two pieces of metal to be joined and allowing the molten material to flow together so the two pieces will become one.

b. Brazing is similar to welding in that heat is used to join the material; but rather than melting, the metal is heated only enough to melt a brazing rod having a much lower melting point. When this brazing rod melts, it wets the surfaces to be joined, and when it cools and solidifies, it bonds the pieces together.

c. Soldering is similar to brazing except that brazing materials normally melt at temperatures above 425 °C (800 °F), while solders melt at temperatures considerably lower.

d. The next step in making airworthy weld repairs is to decide the best process to use, considering the available state-of-the-art welding equipment, and then deciding the correct weld-filler material to use. Before any weld repairs can be made, the metal parts to be welded must be cleaned properly, fitted and jigged properly, and all defective welds must be removed to prepare for an aircraft quality weld repair.

e. Finally, after the weld is completed, the weld must be inspected for defects. All these things are necessary in order to make an airworthy weld repair.

f. Aircraft welding Qualifications. Four groups of metals a person can be certified and qualified to use are:

(1) Group 1, 4130 Steel.
(2) Group 2, Stainless Steel.
(3) Group 3, Aluminum
(4) Group 4, Titanium.

g. For other group listing of metal the welder may qualify, refer to Mil-Std-1595A.

h. Most large business or agencies conduct their own certification tests, or they have an outside testing lab validate the certification tests.

4-75. EQUIPMENT SELECTION. Use the welding equipment manufacturer's information to determine if the equipment will satisfy the requirements for the type of welding operation being undertaken. Disregarding such detailed operating instructions may cause substandard welds. For example, when using GTAW equipment, a weld can be contaminated with tungsten if the proper size electrode is not used when welding with direct current reverse polarity. Another example, the depletion of the inert gas supply below the critical level causes a reduction in the gas flow and will increase the danger of atmospheric contamination.

(a) Electric welding equipment versatility requires careful selection of the type current and polarity to b used. Since the composition and thickness of metals are deciding factors, the selection may vary with each specific application. Metals having refractory surface oxide films (i.e., magnesium alloys and aluminum and its alloys), are generally welded with alternating current (AC), while direct current (DC) is used for carbon, low alloy, noncorrodible, and heat-resisting steels. General recommendations covering current and polarity are shown in table 4-12.

(b) Oxyacetylene gas equipment is suitable for welding most metals. It is not, however, the best method to use on such materials as stainless steel, magnesium, and aluminum alloys; because of base metal oxidization, distortion, and loss of ductility.

> **NOTE: If oxyacetylene is used for welding stainless steel or aluminum, all flux must be removed, as it may cause corrosion.**

4-76. ACCURATELY IDENTIFY THE TYPE OF MATERIAL TO BE REPAIRED. If positive identification of the material is not possible, contact the aircraft manufacturer or subject the item to a metallurgical laboratory analysis. Before any welding is attempted, carefully consider the weldability of the alloy, since all alloys are not readily weldable. The following steels are readily weldable; plain carbon (of the 1000 series), nickel steel (of the Society of Automotive Engineers (SAE) 2300 series), chrome-nickel alloys (of the SAE 3100 series), chrome-molybdenum steels (of the SAE 4100 series), and low nickel-chrome-molybdenum steel (of the SAE 8600 series).

4-77. PREPARATION FOR WELDING.

a. Hold elements to be welded in a welding jig or fixture which is sufficiently rigid to prevent misalignment due to expansion and contraction of the heated material and which positively and accurately positions the pieces to be welded.

b. Clean parts to be welded with a wire brush or other suitable method prior to welding. Do not use a brush of dissimilar metal, such as brass or bronze on steel. The small deposit left by a brass or bronze brush will materially weaken the weld, and may cause cracking or subsequent failure of the weld. If the members are metallized, the surface metal may be removed by careful sandblasting followed by a light buffing with emery cloth.

4-78. INSPECTION OF A COMPLETED WELD. Visually inspect the completed weld for the following:

(a) The weld has a smooth seam and uniform thickness. Visual inspection shall be made of the completed weld to check for undercut and/or smooth blending of the weld contour into the base metal.

(b) The weld is tapered smoothly into the base metal.

(c) No oxide has formed on the base metal more than 1/2 inch from the weld.

(d) There are no signs of blowholes, porosity, or projecting globules. Many military specifications, as well as American Society of Testing Materials (ASTM) codes, specify acceptable limits of porosity and other types of defects that are acceptable.

(e) The base metal shows no signs of pitting, burning, cracking, or distortion.

(f) The depth of penetration insures fusion of base metal and filler rod.

(g) The welding scale is removed. The welding scale can be removed using a wire brush or by sandblasting. Remove any roll over, cold lab, or unfued weld metal. Check underside of welded joint for defects.

TABLE 4-12. Current and polarity selection for inert gas welding.

MATERIAL	ALTERNATING CURRENT With High-Frequency Stabilization	DIRECT CURRENT STRAIGHT Polarity
Magnesium up to 1/8 in. thick	1	N.R.
Magnesium above 3/16 in. thick	1	N.R.
Magnesium Castings	1	N.R.
Aluminum up to 3/32 in. thick	1	N.R.
Aluminum over 3/32 in. thick	1	N.R.
Aluminum Castings	1	N.R.
Stainless Steel		1
Low Carbon Steel, 0.015 to 0.030 in.		1
Low Carbon Steel, 0.030 to 0.125 in.	N.R.	1
1 Recommended N.R. Not Recommended		

4-79. MICROFISSURES Cracks in parts and materials can vary from tiny microfissures, that are visible only with magnification, to those easily identified by unaided eyes. Microfissures are the worst type of defect for two reasons; they are often hard to detect, and they produce the worst form of notch effect/stress concentration. Once they form, they propagate with repeated applications of stress and lead to early failures. Every possible means should be used to detect the presence of cracks, and ensure their complete removal before welding operations proceed. (See figure 4-26.)

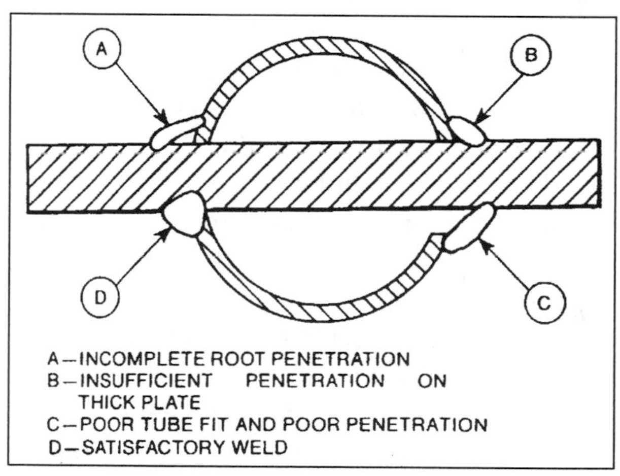

FIGURE 4-26. Common defects to avoid when fitting and welding aircraft certification cluster.

4-80. NONDESTRUCTIVE TESTING or evaluation is advisable in critical applications. Nondestructive testing methods such as; magnetic particle, liquid penetrant, radiography, ultrasonic, eddy current, and acoustic emission can be used; however, they require trained and qualified people to apply them.

4-81. PRACTICES TO GUARD AGAINST Do not file or grind welds in an effort to create a smooth appearance, as such treatment causes a loss of strength. Do not fill welds with solder, brazing metal, or any other filler. When it is necessary to weld a joint which was previously welded, remove all of the old weld material before rewelding. Avoid welding over a weld, because reheating may cause the material to lose its strength and become brittle. Never weld a joint which has been previously brazed.

4-82. TORCH SIZE (Oxyacetylene welding). When using oxyacetylene welding, the torch tip size depends upon the thickness of the material to be welded. Commonly used sizes, proven satisfactory by experience, are shown in table 4-13.

TABLE 4-13. Torch tip sizes.

Thickness of steel (in inches)	Diameter of hole in tip	Drill size
0.015 to 0.031	0.026	71
0.031 to 0.065	.031	68
0.065 to 0.125	.037	63
0.125 to 0.188	.042	58
0.188 to 0.250	.055	54
0.250 to 0.375	.067	51

4-83. WELDING RODS AND ELECTRODES Use welding rods and electrodes that are compatible with the materials to be welded. Welding rods and electrodes for various applications have special properties suitable for the application intended.

Lap welds are used in shear applications. The weld throat of the fillet weld is considered the plane 45 degrees to the surface plane of the sheet being welded and is equal to 0.707 times the thickness of the sheet stock. (See figure 4-27.)

$$P_{WS} = 0.707 \times t \times l \times F_{wsu}$$

where: P_{WS} = *the allowable tensile strength of the joint.*

t = *the thickness of the sheet stock (the throat of the weld joint.*

l = *the length of the weld joint.*

F_{wsu} = *the shear strength of the filled rod material.*

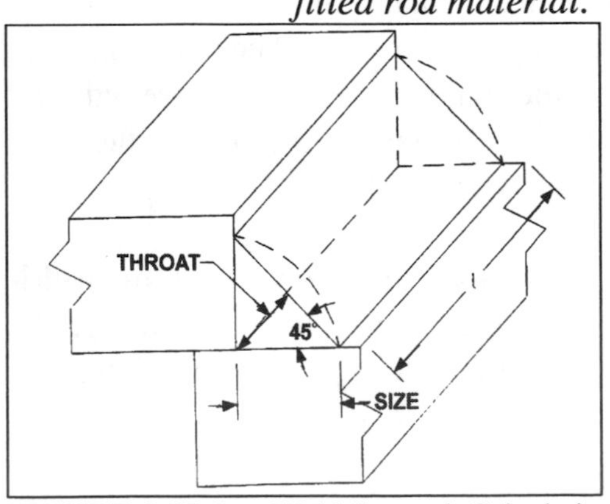

FIGURE 4-27. Lap Weld Strength Calculation

4-84. ROSETTE WELDS are generally employed to fuse an inner reinforcing tube (liner) with the outer member. Where a rosette weld is used, drill a hole, (in the outside tube only) of sufficient size to insure fusion of the inner tube. A hole diameter of approximately one-fourth the tube diameter of the outer tube serves adequately for this purpose. In cases of tight-fitting sleeves or inner liners, the rosettes may be omitted. Rosette weld edge distance is 1/2 the diameter of the tube, as measured from the edge of the rosette hole to the end of the inside and outside tube. Rosettes shall not be considered when determining the strength of a welded form. Drill an 1/8-inch hole in the lower tube in the center of the intended rosette weld so the heat does not burn away the outer tube. This small hole tends to bleed off the heat from the torch and keeps the size of the rosette small.

4-85. HEAT-TREATED MEMBERS Certain structural parts may be heat treated and, therefore, could require special handling. In general, the more responsive an alloy steel is to heat treatment, the less suitable it is for welding because of its tendency to become brittle and lose its ductility in the welded area. Weld the members which depend on heat treatment for their original physical properties by using a welding rod suitable for producing heat-treated values comparable to those of the original members. (See paragraph 4-74.) After welding, heat treat the affected members to the manufacturer's specifications.

4-86. TYPES OF WELDING.

a. Gas Welding. A fuel gas such as acetylene or hydrogen is mixed inside a welding torch with oxygen to produce a flame with a temperature of around 6,300 °F (3,482 °C).

This flame is used to melt the materials to be welded. A filler rod is melted into the puddle of molten metal to reinforce the weld. When highly-reactive metals such as aluminum are gas welded, they must be covered with flux to exclude oxygen from the molten metal and keep oxides from forming which would decrease the strength of the weld. (An illustration of a carburizing flame, a neutral flame, and an oxidizing flame is shown in figure 4-28.)

b. Shielded Metal Arc Welding (SMAW). This method is the most familiar and common type and is known in the trade as stick welding. A metal wire rod coated with a welding flux is clamped in an electrode holder connected to the power supply with a heavy electrical cable. The metal to be welded is also attached to the power supply. The electrical power is supplied to the work at a low voltage

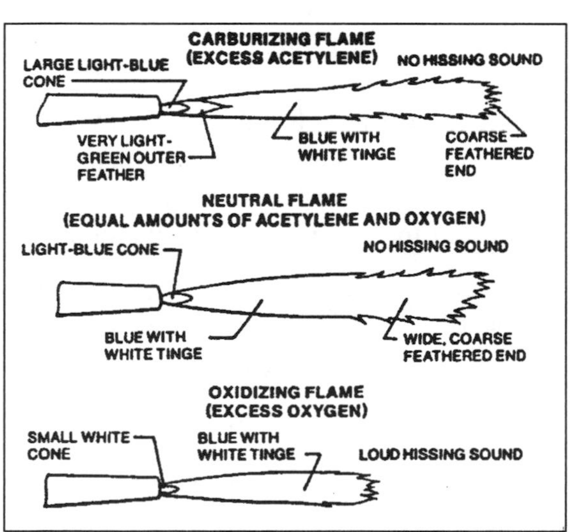

FIGURE 4-28. Basic gas-welding flames: Each has distinctive shape, color and sound. Neutral flame is the most used.

and high current and may be either AC or DC, depending upon the type of welding being done. An arc is struck between the rod and the work and produces heat in excess of 10,000 °F, which melts both the material and the rod. As the flux melts, it releases an inert gas which shields the molten puddle from oxygen in the air and prevents oxidation. The molten flux covers the weld and hardens to an airtight slag cover that protects the weld bead as it cools. This slag must be chipped off to examine the weld.

c. Gas Metal Arc Welding (GMAW). This method of welding was formerly called Metal Inert Gas (MIG) welding and is an improvement over stick welding because an uncoated wire electrode is fed into the torch and an inert gas such as argon, helium, or carbon dioxide flows out around the wire to protect the puddle from oxygen. The power supply connects between the torch and the work, and the arc produces the intense heat needed to melt the work and the electrode. Low-voltage high-current DC is used almost exclusively with GMAW welding. GMAW is used more for large-volume production work than for aircraft repair.

d. Gas Tungsten Arc Welding (GTAW). This is the form of electric arc welding that fills most of the needs in aircraft maintenance. It is more commonly known as Tungsten Inert Gas (TIG) welding and by the trade names of Heliarc or Heliweld. These trade names were derived from the fact that the inert gas originally used was helium.

(1) Rather than using a consumable electrode such as is used in both of the other two methods we have discussed, the electrode in TIG welding is a tungsten rod. (In earlier procedures using this form of welding, a carbon electrode was used, but it has been replaced almost exclusively with tungsten.)

(2) The 250+ amp arc between the electrode and the work melts the metal at 5,432 °F, and a filler rod is manually fed into the molten puddle. A stream of inert gas such as argon or helium flows out of the torch and envelopes the arc, thereby preventing the formation of oxides in the puddle.

(3) The versatility of TIG welding is increased by the power supply that is used. Direct current of either polarity or alternating current may be used. (See figures 4-29 and 4-30.)

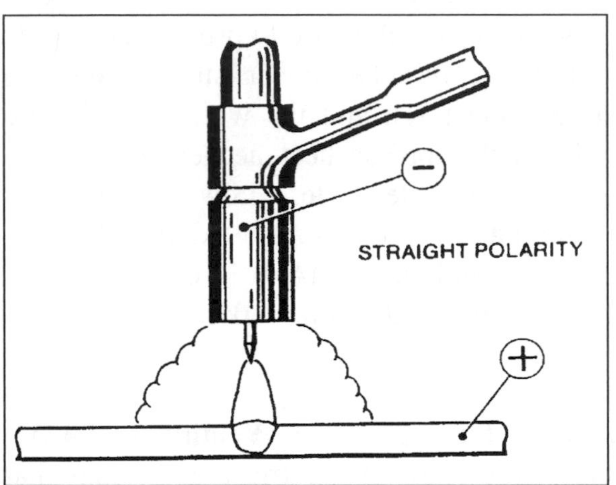

FIGURE 4-29. Set TIG welder to DC current, straight polarity for welding mild steel, stainless steel and titanium

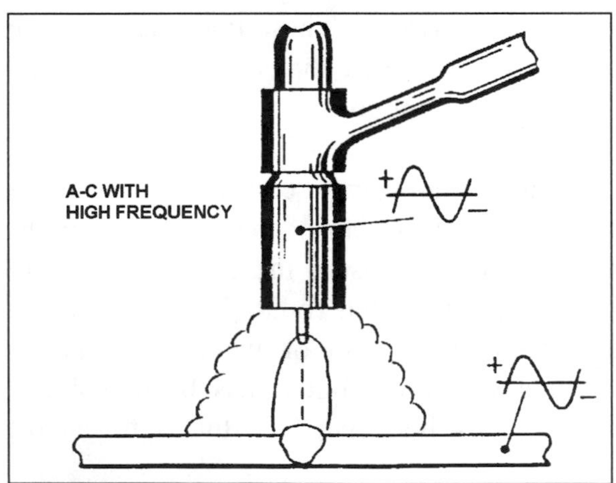

FIGURE 4-30. Set TIG to AC current for welding aluminum and magnesium.

4-87. ELECTRIC-RESISTANCE WELDING. Many thin sheet metal parts for aircraft, especially stainless steel parts, are joined by one of the forms of electric resistance welding, either spot welding or seam welding.

a. Spot Welding. Two copper electrodes are held in the jaws of the spot welding machine, and the material to be welded is clamped between them. Pressure is applied to hold the electrodes tightly together, and electrical current flows through the electrodes and the material. The resistance of the material being welded is so much higher than that of the copper electrodes that enough heat is generated to melt the metal. The pressure on the electrodes forces the molten spots in the two pieces of metal to unite, and this pressure is held after the current stops flowing long enough for the metal to solidify. Refer to MIL HDBK-5 for joint construction and strength data. The amount of current, pressure, and dwell time are all carefully controlled and matched to the type of material and the thickness to produce the correct spot welds. (See figure 4-31.)

b. Seam Welding. Rather than having to release the electrodes and move the material to form a series of overlapping spot welds, a seam-welding machine is used to manufacture fuel tanks and other components where a continuous weld is needed. Two copper wheels

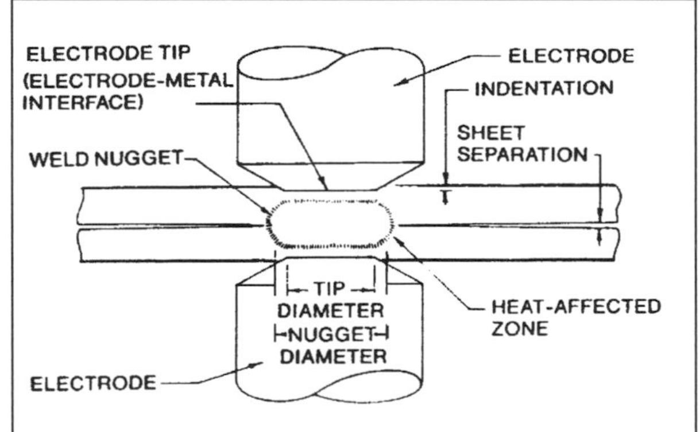

FIGURE 4-31. In spot welding, heat is produced by electrical resistance between copper electrodes. Pressure is simultaneously applied to electrode tips to force metal together to complete fusing process. Spot-weld-nugget size is directly related to tip size.

replace the bar-shaped electrodes. The metal to be welded is moved between them, and electric pulses create spots of molten metal that overlap to form the continuous seam.

4-88. BRAZING. Brazing refers to a group of metal-joining processes in which the bonding material is a nonferrous metal or alloy with a melting point higher than 425 C (800 F), but lower than that of the metals being joined. Brazing includes silver brazing (erroneously called silver soldering or hard soldering), copper brazing, and aluminum brazing.

NOTE: Never weld over a previously brazed joint.

a. Brazing requires less heat than welding and can be used to join metals that are damaged by high heat. However, because the strength of brazed joints is not as great as welded joints, brazing is not used for structural repairs on aircraft. In deciding whether brazing of a joint is justified, it should be remembered that a metal, which will be subjected to a sustained high temperature in use, should not be brazed.

b. A brazing flux is necessary to obtain a good union between the clean base metal and the filler metal. There are a number of readily available manufactured fluxes conforming to AWS and AMT specifications.

c. The base metal should be preheated slowly with a mild flame. When it reaches a dull-red heat (in the case of steel), the rod should be heated to a dark (or purple) color and dipped into the flux. Since enough flux adheres to the rod, it is not necessary to spread it over the surface of the metal.

d. A neutral flame is used in most brazing applications. However, a slightly oxidizing flame should be used when copper-zinc, copper-zinc-silicon, or copper-zinc-nickel-silicon filler alloys are used. When brazing aluminum and its alloys, a neutral flame is preferred, but if difficulties are encountered, a slightly reduced flame is preferred to an oxidizing flame.

e. The filler rod can now be brought near the tip of the torch, causing the molten bronze to flow over a small area of the seam. The base metal must be at the flowing temperature of the filler metal before it will flow into the joint. The brazing metal melts when applied to the steel and runs into the joint by capillary attraction. In braze welding, the rod should continue to be added, as the brazing progresses, with a rhythmic dipping action; so that the bead will be built to a uniform width and height. The job should be completed rapidly and with as few passes of the rod and torch as possible.

f. When the job is finished, the metal should be allowed to cool slowly. After cooling, remove the flux from the parts by immersing them for 30 minutes in a lye solution.

(1) Copper brazing of steel is normally done in a special furnace having a controlled atmosphere, and at a temperature so high that field repairs are seldom feasible. If copper brazing is attempted without a controlled atmosphere, the copper will probably not completely wet and fill the joint. Therefore, copper brazing in any conditions other than appropriately controlled conditions is not recommended.

(a) The allowable shear strength for copper brazing of steel alloys should be 15 thousand pounds per square inch (kpsi), for all conditions of heat treatment.

(b) The effect of the brazing process on the strength of the parent or base metal of steel alloys should be considered in the structural design. Where copper furnace brazing is employed, the calculated allowable strength of the base metal, which is subjected to the temperatures of the brazing process, should be in accordance with table 4-14.

TABLE 4-14. Calculated allowable strength of base metal.

Material	Allowable Strength
Heat-treated material (including normalized) used in "as-brazed" condition	Mechanical properties of normalized material
Heat-treated material (including normalized) reheat-treated during or after brazing	Mechanical properties corresponding to heat treatment performed

(2) Alloys commonly referred to as silver solders melt above 425 °C (800 °F), and when using them the process should be called silver brazing.

(a) The principal use of silver brazing in aircraft work is in the fabrication of high-pressure oxygen lines and other parts which must withstand vibration and high temperatures. Silver brazing is used extensively to join copper (and its alloys), nickel, silver, various combinations of these metals, and thin steel parts. Silver brazing produces joints of higher strength than those produced by other brazing processes.

(b) It is necessary to use flux in all silver-brazing operations, because of the necessity for having the base metal chemically clean, (without the slightest film of oxide to prevent the silver-brazing alloy from coming into intimate contact with the base metal).

(c) The joint must be physically and chemically clean, which means it must be free of all dirt, grease, oil, and paint. After removing the dirt, grease, and paint, any oxide should be removed by grinding or filing the piece until bright metal can be seen. During the soldering operation, the flux continues the process of keeping oxide away from the metal and aids the flow of solder.

(d) In figure 4-32, three types of joints for silver brazing are shown; flanged butt, lap, and edge joints. If a lap joint is used, the amount of lap should be determined according to the strength needed in the joint. For strength equal to that of the base metal in the heated zone, the amount of lap should be four to six times the metal thickness.

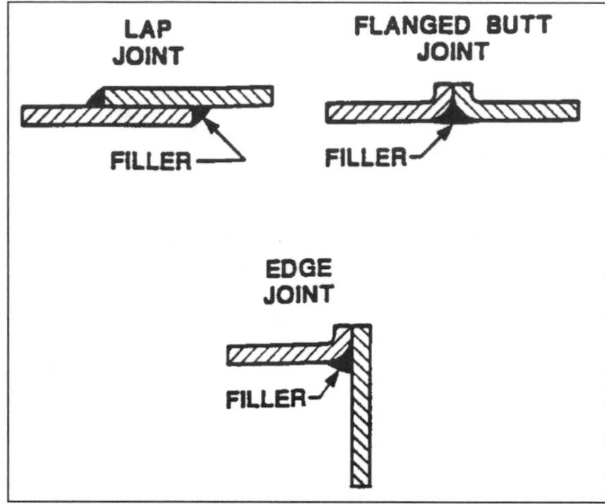

FIGURE 4-32. Silver brazing joints.

(e) The oxyacetylene flame for silver brazing should be neutral, but may have a slight excess of acetylene. It must be soft, not harsh. During both preheating and application of the solder, the tip of the inner cone of the flame should be held about 1/2 inch from the work. The flame should be kept moving so that the metal will not become overheated.

(f) When both parts of the base metal are at the right temperature (indicated by the flow of flux), brazing alloy can be applied to the surface of the under or inner part at the edge of the seam. It is necessary to simultaneously direct the flame over the seam, and keep moving it so that the base metal remains at an even temperature.

(3) The torch can be shut off simply by closing the acetylene off first and allowing the gas remaining in the torch tip to burn out. Then turn off the oxygen valve. If the torch is not to be used again for a long period, the pressure should be turned off at the cylinder. The hose lines should then be relieved of pressure by opening the torch needle valves and the working pressure regulator, one at a time, allowing the gas to escape. Again, it is a good practice to relieve the oxygen pressure and then the acetylene pressure. The hose should then be coiled or hung carefully to prevent damage or kinking.

(4) Soft soldering is used chiefly for copper, brass, and coated iron in combination with mechanical seams; that is, seams that are riveted, bolted, or folded. It is also used where a leak-proof joint is desired, and sometimes for fitting joints to promote rigidity and prevent corrosion. Soft soldering is generally performed only in very minor repair jobs. This process is used to join electrical connections because it forms a strong union with low electrical resistance.

(a) Soft solder gradually yields under a steadily applied load and should not be used unless the transmitted loads are very low. It should never be used as a means of joining structural members.

(b) A soldering iron is the tool used in soldering. Its purpose is to act as a source of heat for the soldering operation. The bit, or working face, is made from copper since this metal will readily absorb heat and transmit it to the work. Figure 4-33 shows a wedge-shaped bit.

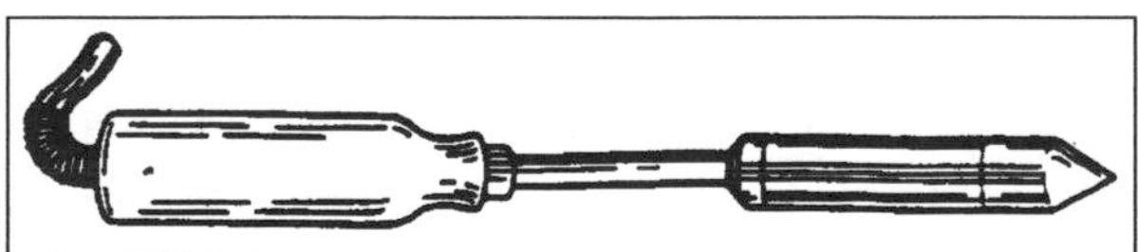

FIGURE 4-33. Electric soldering iron.

(c) To tin the soldering iron, it is first heated to a bright red, and then the point is cleaned (by filing) until it is smooth and bright. No dirt or pits should remain on its surface. After the soldering iron has been mechanically cleaned, it should be reheated sufficiently to melt solder and chemically cleaned by rubbing it firmly on a block of sal ammoniac (ammonium chloride). Rosin flux paste may also be used. Solder is then applied to the point and wiped with a clean cloth.

(d) A properly tinned copper iron has a thin unbroken film of solder over the entire surface of its point.

(e) Soft solders are chiefly alloys of tin and lead. The percentages of tin and lead vary considerably in various solder, with a corresponding change in their melting points, ranging from 145-311 °C (293-592 °F). Half-and-half (50/50) solder is a general purpose solder and is most frequently used. It contains equal proportions of tin and lead, and it melts at approximately 182 °C (360 °F).

(f) The application of the melted solder requires somewhat more care than is apparent. The parts to be soldered should be locked together or held mechanically or manually while tacking. To tack the seam, the hot copper iron is touched to a bar of solder, then the drops of solder adhering to the copper iron are used to tack the seam at a number of points. The film of solder between the surfaces of a joint must be kept thin to make the strongest joint.

(g) A hot, well-tinned soldering copper iron should be held so that its point lies flat on the metal (at the seam), while the back of the copper iron extends over the seam proper at a 45-degree angle, and a bar of solder is touched to the point. As the solder melts, the copper iron is drawn slowly along the seam. As much solder as necessary is added without raising the soldering copper iron from the job. The melted solder should run between the surfaces of the two sheets and cover the full width of the seam. Work should progress along the seam only as fast as the solder will flow into the joint.

4-89. AIRCRAFT PARTS NOT TO BE WELDED.

a. Brace Wires and Cables. Do not weld aircraft parts whose proper function depends upon strength properties developed by cold-working. Among parts in this classification are streamlined wire and cables.

b. Brazed and Soldered Parts. Do not weld brazed or soldered parts as the brazing mixture or solder will penetrate and weaken the hot steel.

c. Alloy Steel Parts. Do not weld alloy steel parts such as aircraft bolts, turnbuckle ends, etc., which have been heat treated to improve their mechanical properties.

d. Nos. 2024 and 7075 Aluminum. Do not weld these two aluminum alloys (that are often used in aircraft construction) because the heat from the welding process will cause severe cracking. The 2024 aluminum is most often used in wing skins, fuselage skins, and in most structured airframe parts. The 7075 aluminum is most often used in machined fittings such as wing-spar attachments, landing-gear attachments, and other structural parts.

4-90. WELDING ROD SELECTION. Most aircraft repair shops that are prepared to make weld repairs should have the basic selection of welding rods available. The best rods to stock, the metals they weld, and the AWS specification number are shown in table 4-15.

4-91. REPAIR OF TUBULAR MEMBERS.

a. Inspection. Prior to repairing tubular members, carefully examine the structure surrounding any visible damage to insure that no secondary damage remains undetected. Secondary damage may be produced in some structure, remote from the location of the primary damage, by the transmission of the damaging load along the tube. Damage of this nature usually occurs where the most abrupt change in direction of load travel is experienced. If this damage remains undetected, subsequent normal loads may cause failure of the part.

b. Location and Alignment of Welds. Unless otherwise noted, welded steel tubing may be spliced or repaired at any location along the length of the tube. To avoid distortion, pay particular attention to the proper fit and alignment.

c. Members Dented at a Cluster. Repair dents at a steel-tube cluster joint by welding a specially formed steel patch plate over the dented area and surrounding tubes. (See figure 4-34.) To prepare the patch plate, cut a section of steel sheet of the same material and thickness as the heaviest tube damaged. Trim the reinforcement plate so that the fingers extend over the tubes a minimum of 1.5 times the respective tube diameter. (See figure 4-34.) Remove all the existing finish on the damaged cluster-joint area to be covered by the reinforcement plate. The reinforcement plate may be formed before any welding is attempted, or it may be cut and tack-welded to one or more of the tubes in the cluster joint, then heated and formed around the joint to produce a smooth contour. Apply sufficient heat to the plate while forming so that there is generally a gap of no more than 1/16 inch from the contour of the joint to the plate. In this operation avoid unnecessary heating, and exercise care to prevent damage at the point of the angle formed by any two adjacent fingers of the plate. After the plate is formed and tack welded to the cluster joint, weld all the plate edges to the cluster joint.

TABLE 4-15. Chart showing Welding Filler Rod selection.

Welding Rod #	AMS Spec.	AWS Spec.	Welds these Metals
4130	AMS 6457	AWS A5.18	Mild Steel, 4130 steel
4140	AMS 6452	AWS A5.28	4140 Steel
4043	AMS 4190	AWS A5.10	Most weldable Aluminum
308L	AMS 5692	AWS A5.9	304 Stainless steel
316L	AMS 5692	AWS A5.9	316 Stainless steel
AZ61A	AMS 4350	AWS A5.19	AZ61A Magnesium
ERTi-5	AMS 4954	AWS A5-16	Titanium

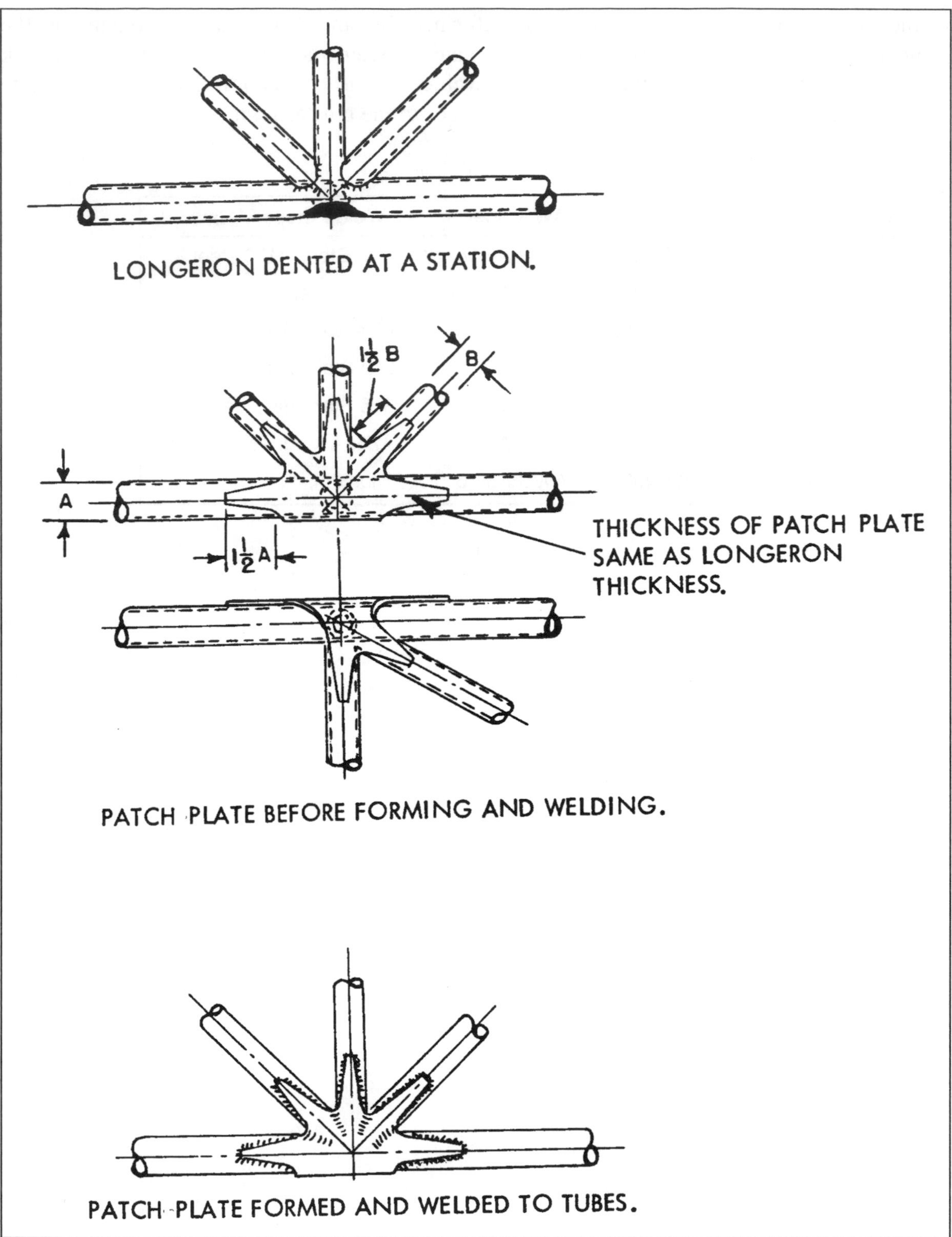

FIGURE 4-34. Finger patch repairs for members dented at a cluster.

d. Members Dented in a Bay. Repair dented, bent, cracked, or otherwise damaged tubular members by using a split-sleeve reinforcement. Carefully straighten the damaged member, and in the case of cracks, drill No. 40 (0.098) inch stop holes at the ends of the crack.

4-92. REPAIR BY WELDED SLEEVE. This repair is outlined in figure 4-35. Select a length of steel tube sleeve having an inside diameter approximately equal to the outside diameter of the damaged tube and of the same material, and at least the same wall thickness. Diagonally cut the sleeve reinforcement at a 30-degree angle on both ends so that the minimum distance of the sleeve from the edge of the crack or dent is not less than 1-1/2 times the diameter of the damaged tube. Cut through the entire length of the reinforcement sleeve, and separate the half-sections of the sleeve. Clamp the two sleeve sections to the proper positions on the affected areas of the original tube. Weld the reinforcement sleeve along the length of the two sides, and weld both ends of the sleeve to the damaged tube. (See figure 4-35.) The filling of dents or cracks with welding rod in lieu of reinforcing the member is not acceptable.

4-93. REPAIR BY BOLTED SLEEVE. Do not use bolted-sleeve repairs on welded steel-tube structure unless specifically authorized by the manufacturer or the FAA. The tube area removed by the bolt holes, in this type of repair, may prove critical.

4-94. WELDED-PATCH REPAIR. Dents or holes in tubing may be repaired by using a patch of the same material, one gauge thicker. (See figure 4-36.)

a. Dented Tubing.

(1) Dents are not deeper than 1/10 of tube diameter, do not involve more than 1/4 of the tube circumference, and are not longer than tube diameter.

(2) Dents are free from cracks, abrasions, and sharp corners.

(3) The dented tubing can be substantially reformed, without cracking, before application of the patch.

b. Punctured Tubing. Holes are not longer than tube diameter and involve not more than 1/4 of tube circumference.

4-95. SPLICING TUBING BY INNER-SLEEVE METHOD. If the damage to a structural tube is such that a partial replacement of the tube is necessary, the inner-sleeve splice is recommended; especially where a smooth tube surface is desired. (See figure 4-37.)

a. Make a diagonal cut when removing the damaged portion of the tube, and remove the burr from the edges of the cut by filing or similar means. Diagonally cut a replacement steel tube of the same material and diameter, and at least the same wall thickness, to match the length of the removed portion of the damaged tube. At each end of the replacement tube allow a 1/8-inch gap from the diagonal cuts to the stubs of the original tube. Select a length of steel tubing of the same material, and at least the same wall thickness, and of an outside diameter equal to the inside diameter of the damaged tube. Fit this inner-sleeve tube material snugly within the original tube, with a maximum diameter difference of 1/16 inch. From this inner-sleeve tube material cut two sections of tubing, each of such a length that the ends of the inner sleeve will be a minimum distance of 1-1/2-tube diameters from the nearest end of the diagonal cut.

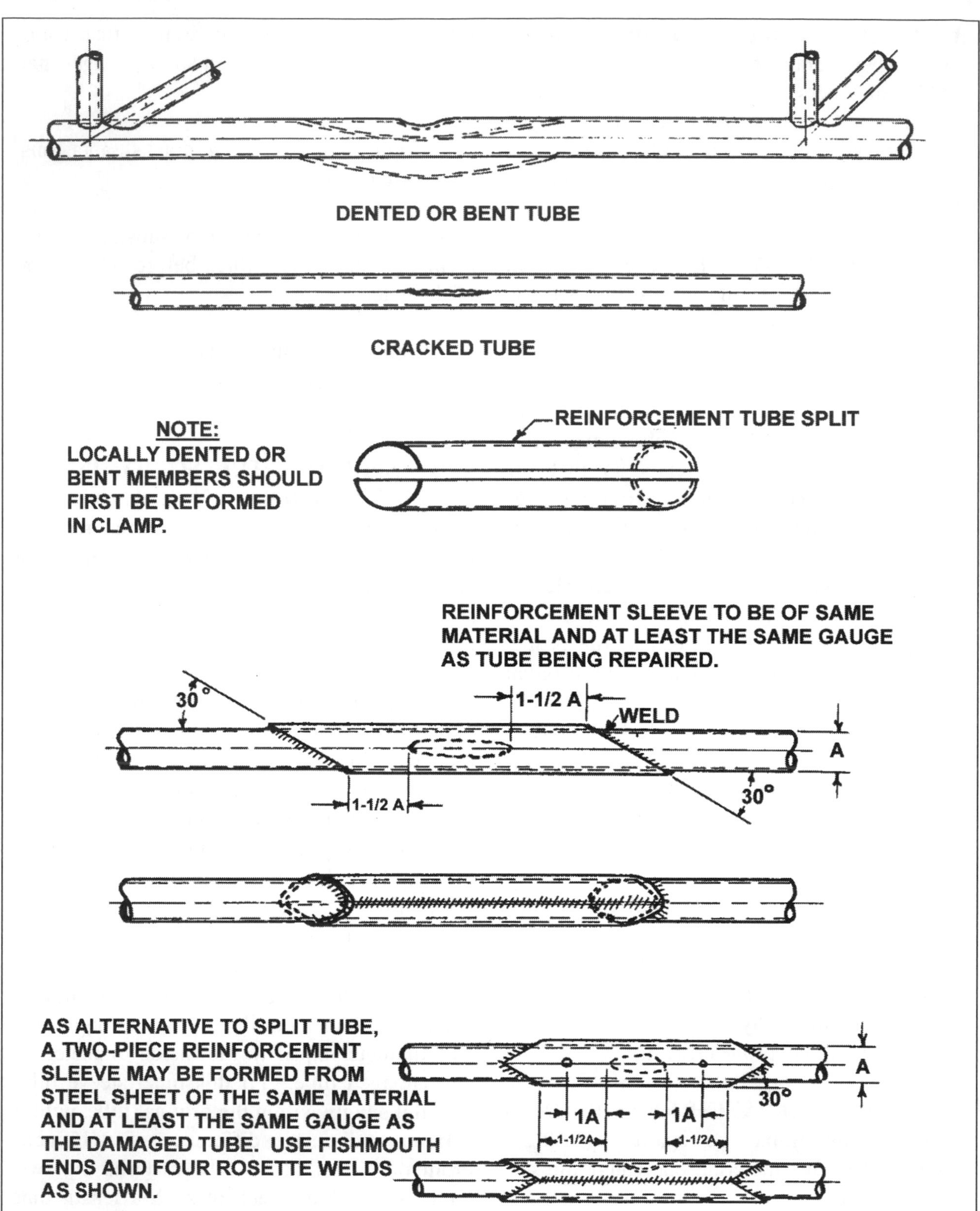
DENTED OR BENT TUBE
CRACKED TUBE
NOTE:
LOCALLY DENTED OR BENT MEMBERS SHOULD FIRST BE REFORMED IN CLAMP.
REINFORCEMENT TUBE SPLIT
REINFORCEMENT SLEEVE TO BE OF SAME MATERIAL AND AT LEAST THE SAME GAUGE AS TUBE BEING REPAIRED.
30°
1-1/2 A
WELD
A
30°
1-1/2 A
AS ALTERNATIVE TO SPLIT TUBE, A TWO-PIECE REINFORCEMENT SLEEVE MAY BE FORMED FROM STEEL SHEET OF THE SAME MATERIAL AND AT LEAST THE SAME GAUGE AS THE DAMAGED TUBE. USE FISHMOUTH ENDS AND FOUR ROSETTE WELDS AS SHOWN.
A
30°
1A
1A
1-1/2A
1-1/2A

FIGURE 4-35. Members dented in a bay (repairs by welded sleeve).

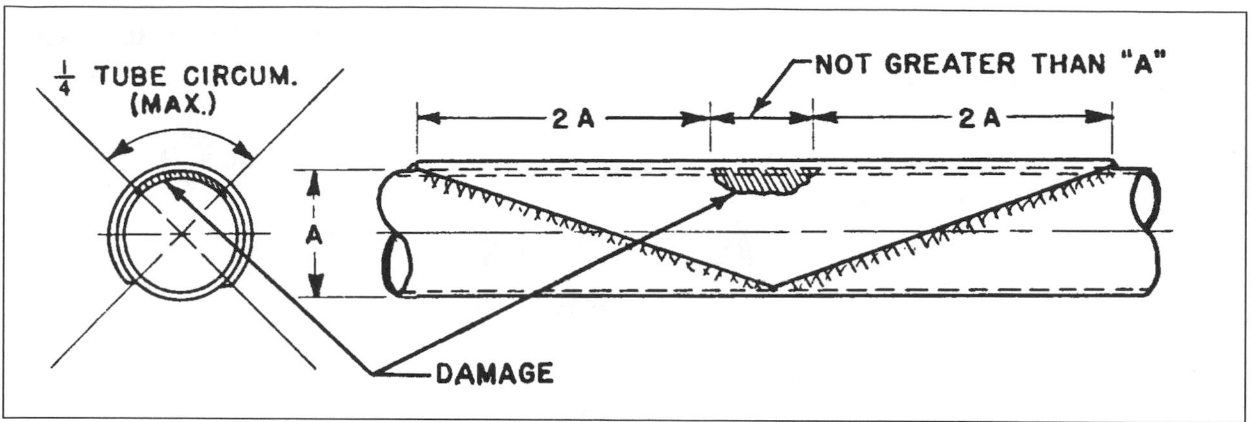

FIGURE 4-36. Welded patch repair.

b. If the inner sleeve fits very tightly in the replacement tube, chill the sleeve with dry ice or cold water. If this is insufficient, polish down the diameter of the sleeve with emery cloth. Tack the outer and inner replacement tubes using rosette welds. Weld the inner sleeve to the tube stubs through the 1/8-inch gap, forming a weld bead over the gap.

4-96. SPLICING TUBING BY OUTER-SLEEVE METHOD. If partial replacement of a tube is necessary, make the outer-sleeve splice using a replacement tube of the same diameter. Since the outer-sleeve splice requires the greatest amount of welding, it should be used only when the other splicing methods are not suitable. Information on the replacement by use of the outer-sleeve method is given in figure 4-38 and figure 4-39.

a. Remove the damaged section of a tube utilizing a 90-degree cut. Cut a replacement steel tube of the same material, diameter, and at least the same wall thickness to match the length of the removed portion of the damaged tube. This replacement tube must bear against the stubs of the original tube with a total tolerance not to exceed 1/32 inch. The outer-sleeve tube material selected must be of the same material and at least the same wall thickness as the original tube. The clearance between inside diameter of the sleeve and the outside diameter of the original tube may not exceed 1/16 inch.

b. From this outer-sleeve tube material, cut diagonally (or fishmouth) two sections of tubing, each of such length that the nearest end of the outer sleeve is a minimum distance of 1-1/2-tube diameters from the end of the cut on the original tube. Use a fishmouth sleeve wherever possible. Deburr the edges of the sleeves, replacement tube, and the original tube stubs.

c. Slip the two sleeves over the replacement tube, align the replacement tube with the original tube stubs, and slip the sleeves over the center of each joint. Adjust the sleeves to suit the area and provide maximum reinforcement.

d. Tack weld the two sleeves to the replacement tube in two places before welding. Apply a uniform weld around both ends of one of the reinforcement sleeves and allow the weld to cool; then, weld around both ends of the remaining reinforcement tube. Allow one sleeve weld to cool before welding the remaining tube to prevent undue warping.

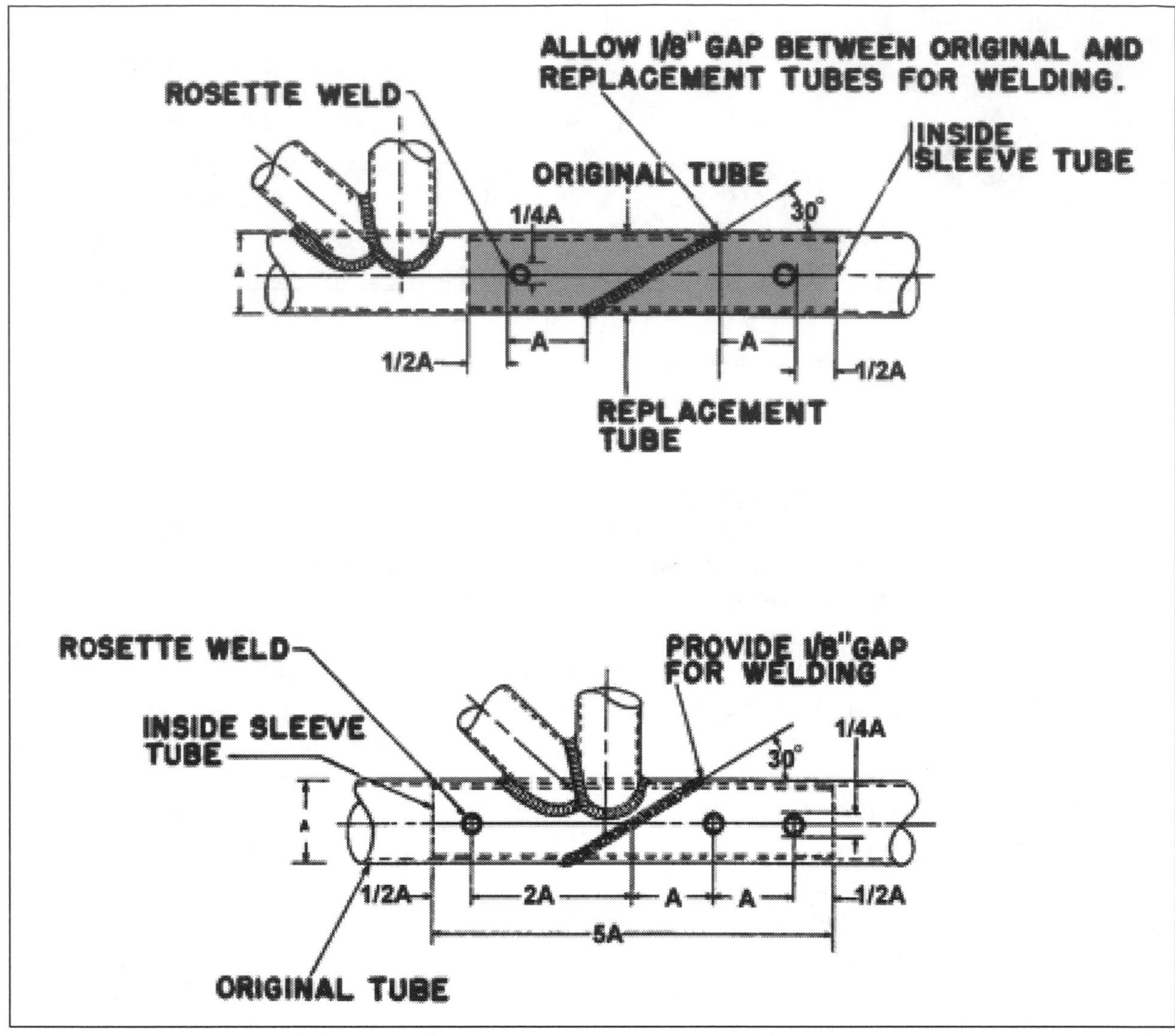

FIGURE 4-37. Splicing by inner-sleeve method.

4-97. SPLICING USING LARGER DIAMETER REPLACEMENT TUBES. The method of splicing structural tubes, as shown in figure 4-40, requires the least amount of cutting and welding. However, this splicing method cannot be used where the damaged tube is cut too near the adjacent cluster joints, or where bracket-mounting provisions make it necessary to maintain the same replacement tube diameter as the original. As an aid to installing the replacement tube, squarely cut the original damaged tube leaving a minimum short stub equal to 2-1/2-tube diameters on one end and a minimum long stub equal to 4-1/2-tube diameters on the other end. Select a length of steel tube of the same material and at least the same wall thickness, having an inside diameter approximately equal to the outside diameter of the damaged tube. Fit this replacement tube material snugly around the original tube with a maximum diameter difference of 1/16 inch. From this replacement tube material, cut a section of tubing diagonally (or fishmouth) of such a length that each end of the tube is a minimum distance of 1-1/2-tube diameters from the end of the cut on the original tube. Use a fishmouth cut replacement tube wherever possible. Deburr the edges of the replacement tube and original tube stubs. If a fishmouth cut is used, file out the sharp radius of the cut with a small round file.

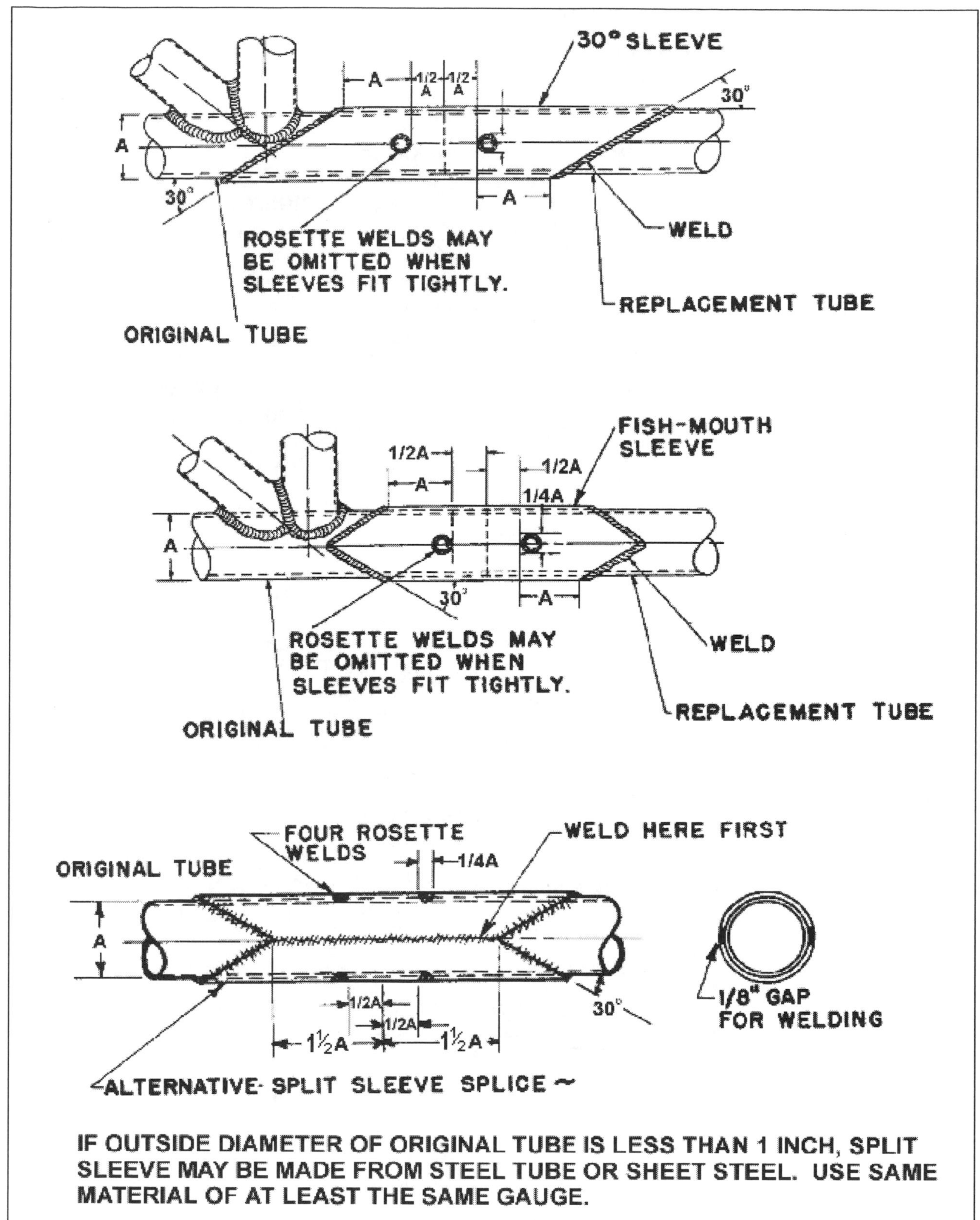

FIGURE 4-38. Splicing by outer-sleeve method (replacement by welded outside sleeve).

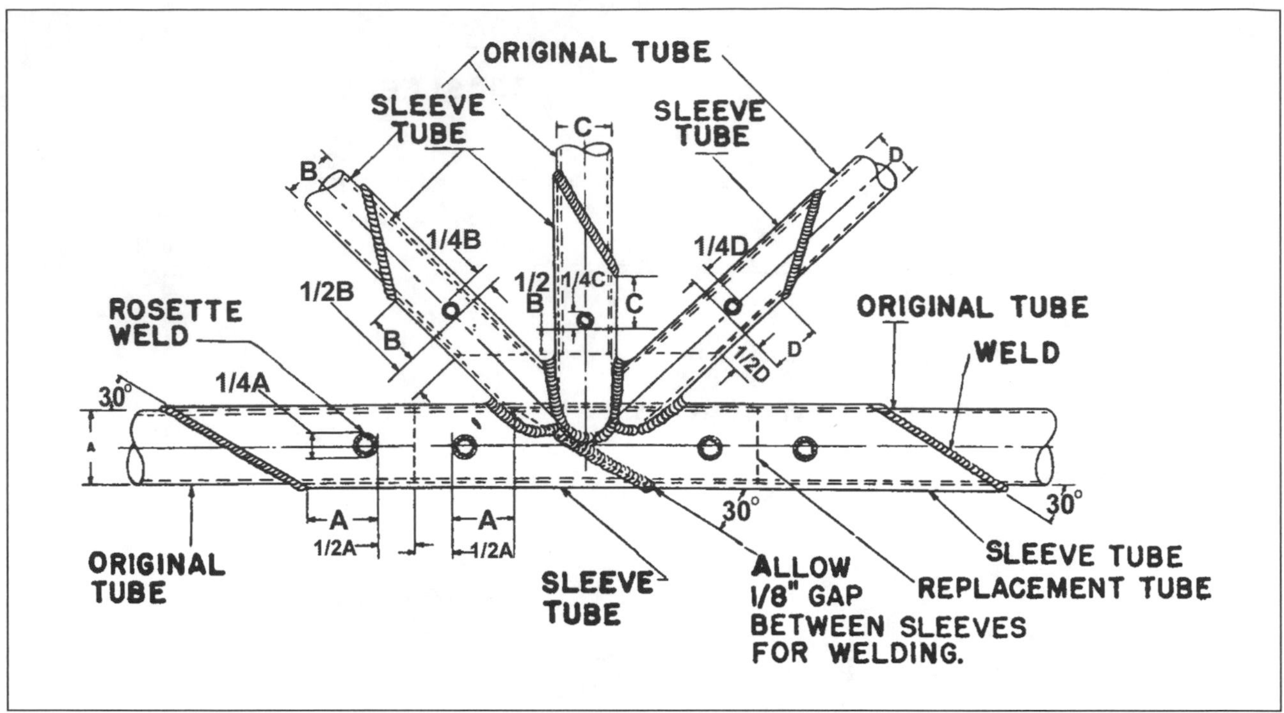

FIGURE 4-39. Tube replacement at a station by welded outer sleeves.

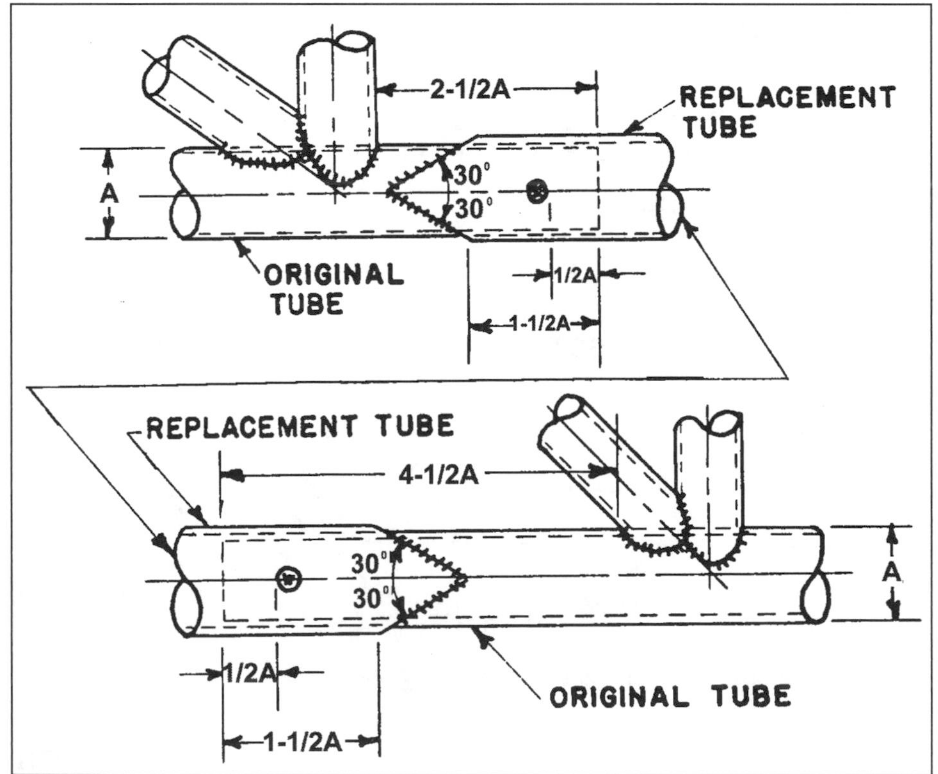

FIGURE 4-40. Splicing using larger diameter replacement tube.

Spring the long stub of the original tube from the normal position, slip the replacement tube over the long stub, and then back over the short stub. Center the replacement tube between the stubs of the original tube. Tack weld one end of the replacement tube in several places, then weld completely around the end. In order to prevent distortion, allow the weld to cool completely, then weld the remaining end of the replacement tube to the original tube.

4-98. REPAIRS AT BUILT-IN FUSELAGE FITTINGS. Make splices in accordance with the methods described in paragraphs 4-86 through 4-92. Repair built-in fuselage fittings in the manner shown in figure 4-41. The following paragraphs outline the different methods as shown in figure 4-41.

a. Tube of Larger Diameter Than Original. A tube (sleeve) of larger diameter than the original is used in the method shown in figure 4-41 (A). The forward splice is a 30-degree scarf splice. Cut the rear longeron (right) approximately 4 inches from the centerline of the joint and fit a 1 inch long spacer over the longeron, and edge weld this spacer and longeron. Make a tapered "V" cut approximately 2 inches long in the aft end of the outer sleeve, and swage the end of the outer sleeve to fit the longeron and weld.

b. Tube of Same Diameter as Original. In the method shown in figure 4-41 (B) the new section is the same size as the longeron forward (left) of the fitting. The rear end (right) of the tube is cut at 30 degrees and forms the outside sleeve of the scarf splice. A sleeve is centered over the forward joint as indicated.

c. Simple Sleeve. In figure 4-41 (C), it is assumed the longeron is the same size on each side of the fitting. It is repaired by a sleeve of larger diameter than the longeron.

d. Large Difference in Longeron Diameter Each Side of Fitting. Figure 4-41 (D) assumes that there is 1/4-inch difference in the diameter of the longeron on the two sides of the fitting. The section of longeron forward (left) of the fitting is cut at 30 degrees, and a section of tubing of the same size as the tube and of such length as to extend well to the rear (right) of the fitting is slipped through it. One end is cut at 30 degrees to fit the 30-degree scarf at left, and the other end fishmouthed. This makes it possible to insert a tube of proper diameter to form an inside sleeve for the tube on the left of the fitting and an outside sleeve for the tube on the right of the fitting.

4-99. ENGINE-MOUNT REPAIRS. All welding on an engine mount must be of the highest quality, since vibration tends to accentuate any minor defect. Engine-mount members should preferably be repaired by using a larger diameter replacement tube, telescoped over the stub of the original member, and using fishmouth and rosette welds. However, 30-degree scarf welds in place of the fishmouth welds will be considered acceptable for engine-mount repair work.

a. Repaired engine mounts must be checked for accurate alignment. When tubes are used to replace bent or damaged ones, the original alignment of the structure must be maintained. When drawings are not available, this can be done by measuring the distance between points of corresponding members that have not been distorted.

b. Grind out all cracked welds.

c. Use only high-grade metallurgically controlled (mc) welding rods for engine-mount repairs.

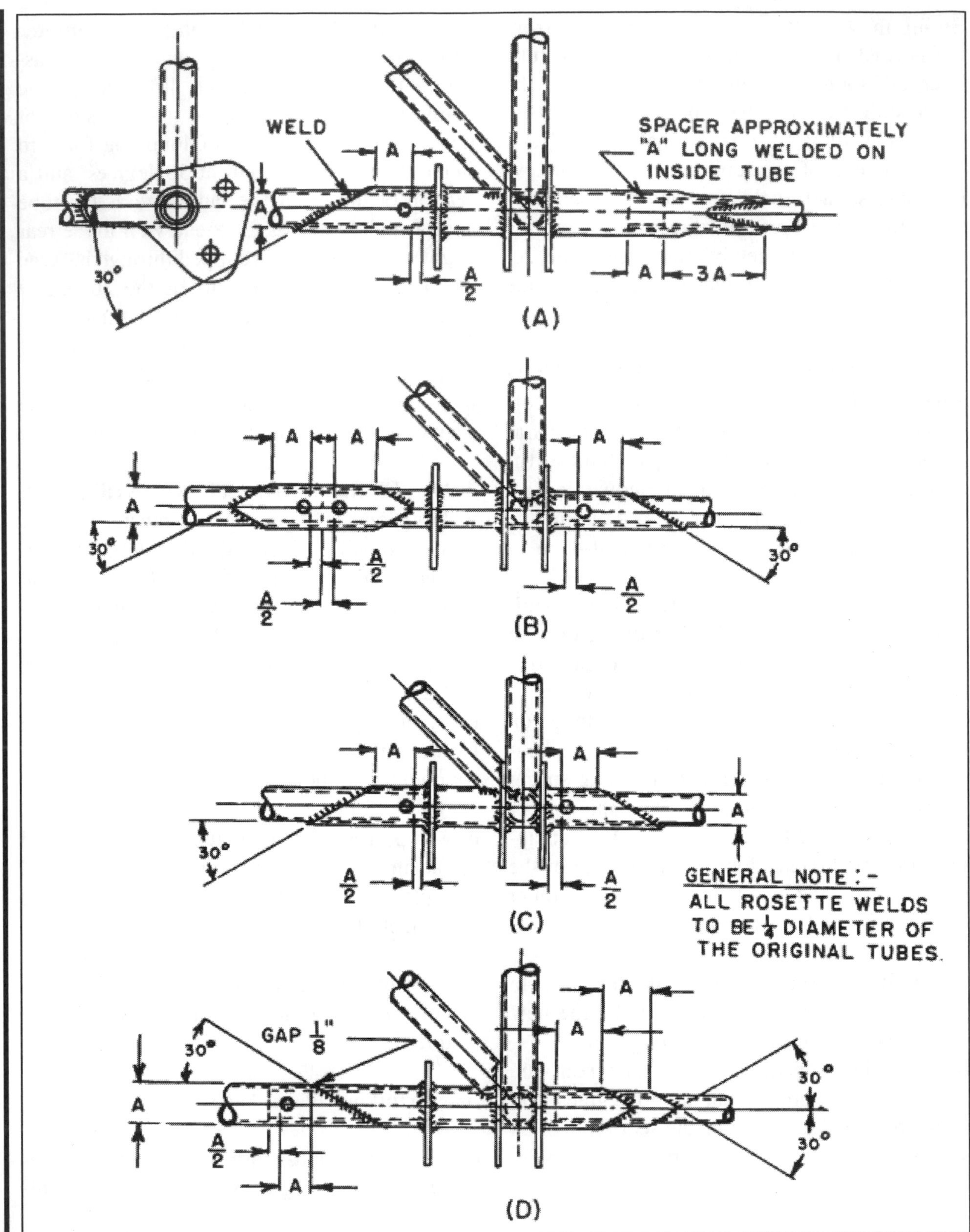

FIGURE 4-41. Repairs at built-in fuselage fittings.

d. If all members are out of alignment, reject the engine mount and replace with one supplied by the manufacturer or one which was built to conform to the manufacturer's drawings. The method of checking the alignment of the fuselage or nacelle points should be requested from the manufacturer.

e. Repair minor damage, such as a crack adjacent to an engine-attachment lug, by rewelding the ring and extending a gusset or a mounting lug past the damaged area. Engine-mount rings which are extensively damaged must not be repaired, unless the method of repair is specifically approved by the FAA, or the repair is accomplished in accordance with FAA-approved instructions.

f. If the manufacturer stress relieved the engine mount after welding it, the engine mount should be re-stress relieved after the weld repairs are made.

4-100. BUILT-UP TUBULAR WING OR TAIL-SPARS. Repair built-up tubular wing or tail-spars by using any of the applicable splices and methods of repair shown in figure 4-35 through figure 4-45, provided the spars are not heat treated. In the case of heat-treated spars, the entire spar assembly would have to be reheat treated to the manufacturer's specifications after completion of the repair. In general, this will be found less practicable than replacing the spar with one furnished by the manufacturer or holder of the PMA for the part.

4-101. WING-BRACE STRUTS AND TAIL-BRACE STRUTS. In general, it will be found advantageous to replace damaged wing-brace struts made either from rounded or streamlined tubing with new members purchased from the original manufacturer. However, there is no objection, from an airworthiness point of view, to repairing such members in a proper manner. An acceptable method of repair, if streamlined tubing is used, will be found in figure 4-43. Repair similar members made of round tubes using a standard splice, as shown in figure 4-35, figure 4-37, or figure 4-38.

a. Location of Splices. Steel-brace struts may be spliced at any point along the length of the strut provided the splice does not overlap part of an end fitting. The jury-strut attachment is not considered an end fitting; therefore, a splice may be made at this point. The repair procedure and workmanship minimize distortion due to welding and the necessity for subsequent straightening operations. Observe every repaired strut carefully during initial flights to ascertain that the vibration characteristics of the strut and attaching components are not adversely affected by the repair. A wide range of speed and engine-power combination must be covered during this check.

b. Fit and Alignment. When making repairs to wing and tail surface brace members, ensure to proper fit and alignment to avoid distortion.

4-102. LANDING GEAR REPAIR.

a. Round Tube Construction. Repair landing gears made of round tubing using standard repairs and splices as shown in figure 4-35 and figure 4-41.

b. Streamline Tube Construction. Repair landing gears made of streamlined tubing by either one of the methods shown in figure 4-42, figure 4-44, or figure 4-45.

c. Axle Assemblies. Representative types of repairable and nonrepairable landing gear axle assemblies are shown in figures 4-46 and 4-47. The types as shown in A, B, and C of this figure are formed from steel tubing and may be repaired by the applicable method

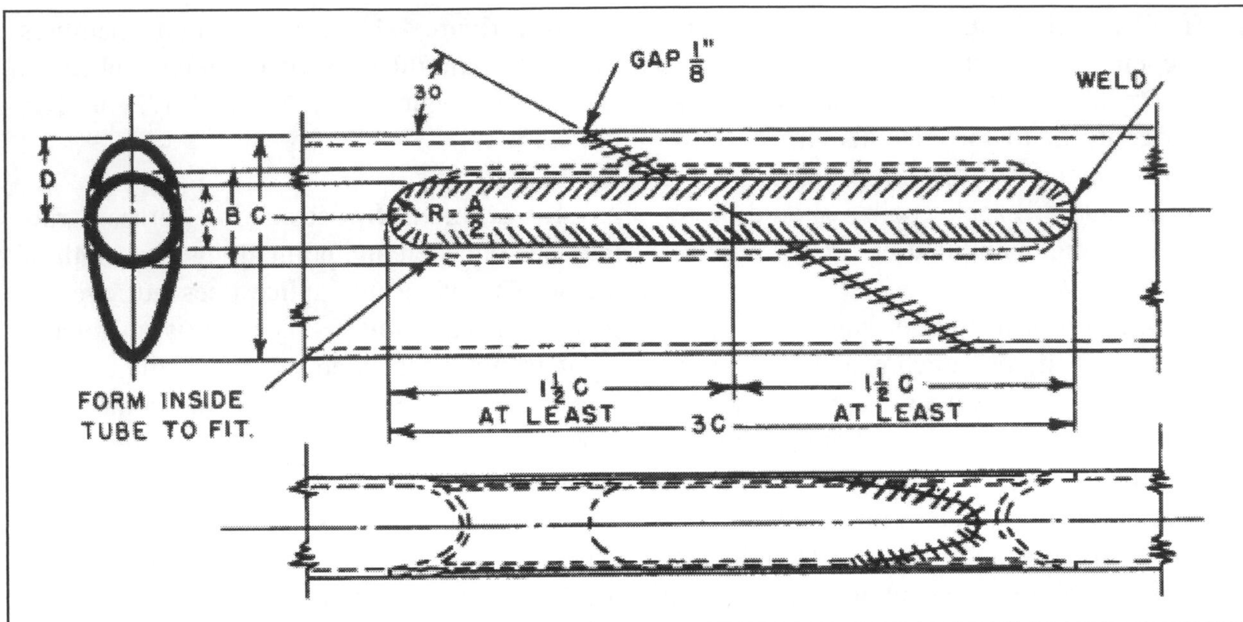

A- Slot Width (Original Tube).
B- Outside Diameter (Insert Tube).
C- Streamline Tube Length of Major Axis.

S.L. Size	A	B	C	D
1"	.375	.563	1.340	.496
1-¼	.375	.688	1.670	.619
1-½	.500	.875	2.005	.743
1-¾	.500	1.000`	2.339	.867
2	.500	1.125	2.670	.991
2-¼	.500	1.250	3.008	1.115
2-½	.500	1.375	3.342	1.239

ROUND INSERT TUBE (B) SHOULD BE AT LEAST OF SAME MATERIAL AND ONE GAUGE THICKER THAN ORIGINAL STREAMLINE TUBE (C).

FIGURE 4-42. Streamline tube splice using round tube (applicable to landing gear).

d. shown in figure 4-35 through figure 4-45. However, it will always be necessary to ascertain whether or not the members are heat treated. The axle assembly as shown in figure 4-47 is, in general, of a nonrepairable type for the following reasons.

(1) The axle stub is usually made from a highly heat-treated nickel alloy steel and carefully machined to close tolerances. These stubs are usually replaceable and must be replaced if damaged.

(2) The oleo portion of the structure is generally heat treated after welding, and is perfectly machined to ensure proper functioning of the shock absorber. These parts would be distorted by welding after machining.

4-103. REPAIRS TO WELDED ASSEMBLIES. These repairs may be made by the following methods.

a. A welded joint may be repaired by cutting out the welded joint and replacing it with one properly gusseted. Standard splicing procedures should be followed.

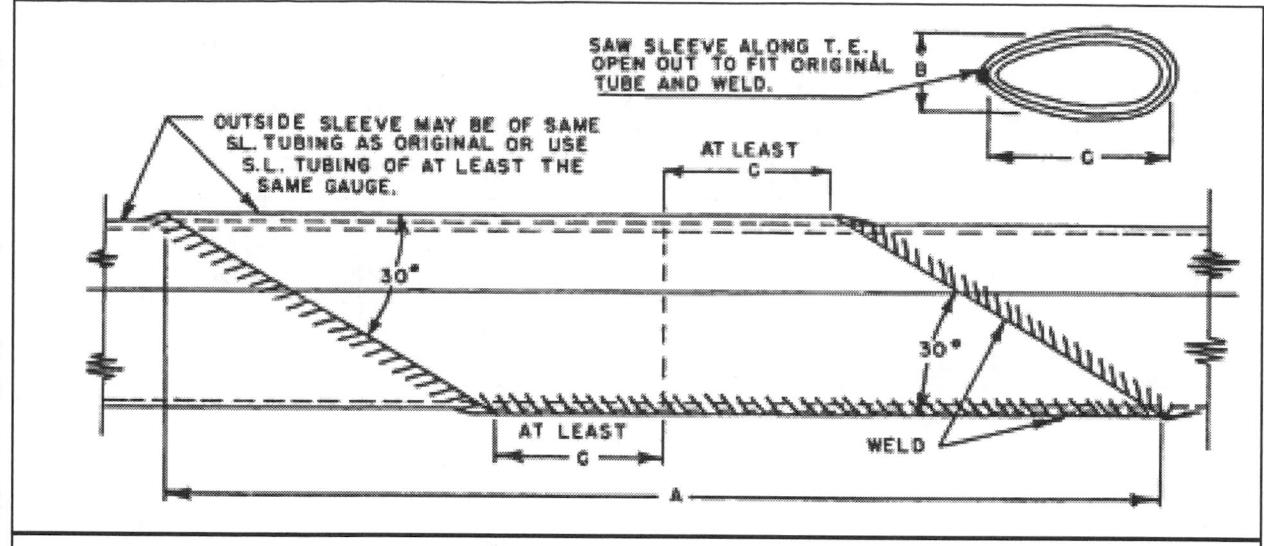

A- Minimum Length of Sleeve.
B- Streamline Tube Length of Minor Axis.
C- Streamline Tube Length of Major Axis.

S.L. Size	A	B	C
1"	7.324	.572	1.340
1-¼	9.128	.714	1.670
1-½	10.960	.858	2.005
1-¾	12.784	1.000	2.339
2	14.594	1.144	2.670
2-¼	16.442	1.286	3.008
2-½	18.268	1.430	3.342

FIGURE 4-43. Streamline tube splice using split sleeve (applicable to wing and tail surface brace struts and other members).

b. Replacing weld deposit by chipping out the metal deposited by the welding process and rewelding after properly reinforcing the joint by means of inserts or external gussets.

4-104. STAINLESS STEEL STRUCTURE. Repair structural components made from stainless steel, particularly the "18-8" variety (18 percent chromium, 8 percent nickel), joined by spot welding, in accordance with the instructions furnished by the manufacturer, DER, or FAA. Substitution of bolted or riveted connections for spot-welded joints are to be specifically approved by a DER or the FAA. Repair secondary structural and nonstructural elements such as tip bows or leading and trailing edge tip strips of wing and control surfaces by soldering with a 50-50 lead-tin solder or a 60-40 lead-tin solder. For best results, use a flux of phosphoric acid (syrup). Since the purpose of flux is to attack the metal so that the soldering will be effective, remove excess flux by washing the joint. Due to the high-heat conductivity of the stainless steel, use a soldering iron large enough to do the work properly.

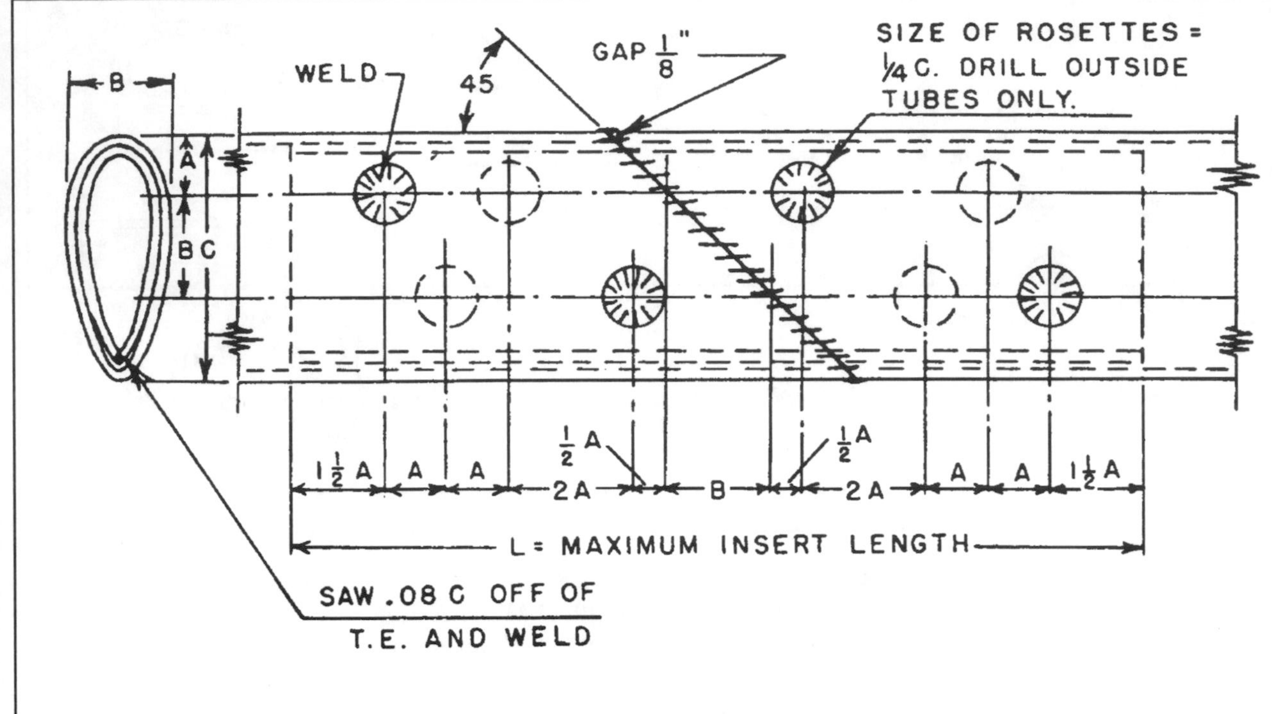

INSERT TUBE IS OF SAME STREAMLINE TUBING AS ORIGINAL.

A- Is 2/3 B.

B- Is Minor Axis Length of Original Streamline Tube.
C- Is Major Axis Length of Original Streamline Tube.

S.L. Size	A	B	C	L
1"	.382	.572	1.340	5.160
1-¼	.476	.714	1.670	6.430
1-½	.572	.858	2.005	7.720
1-¾	.667	1.000	2.339	9.000
2	.763	1.144	2.670	10.300
2-¼	.858	1.286	3.008	11.580
2-½	.954	1.430	3.342	12.880

FIGURE 4-44. Streamline tube splice using split insert (applicable to landing gear).

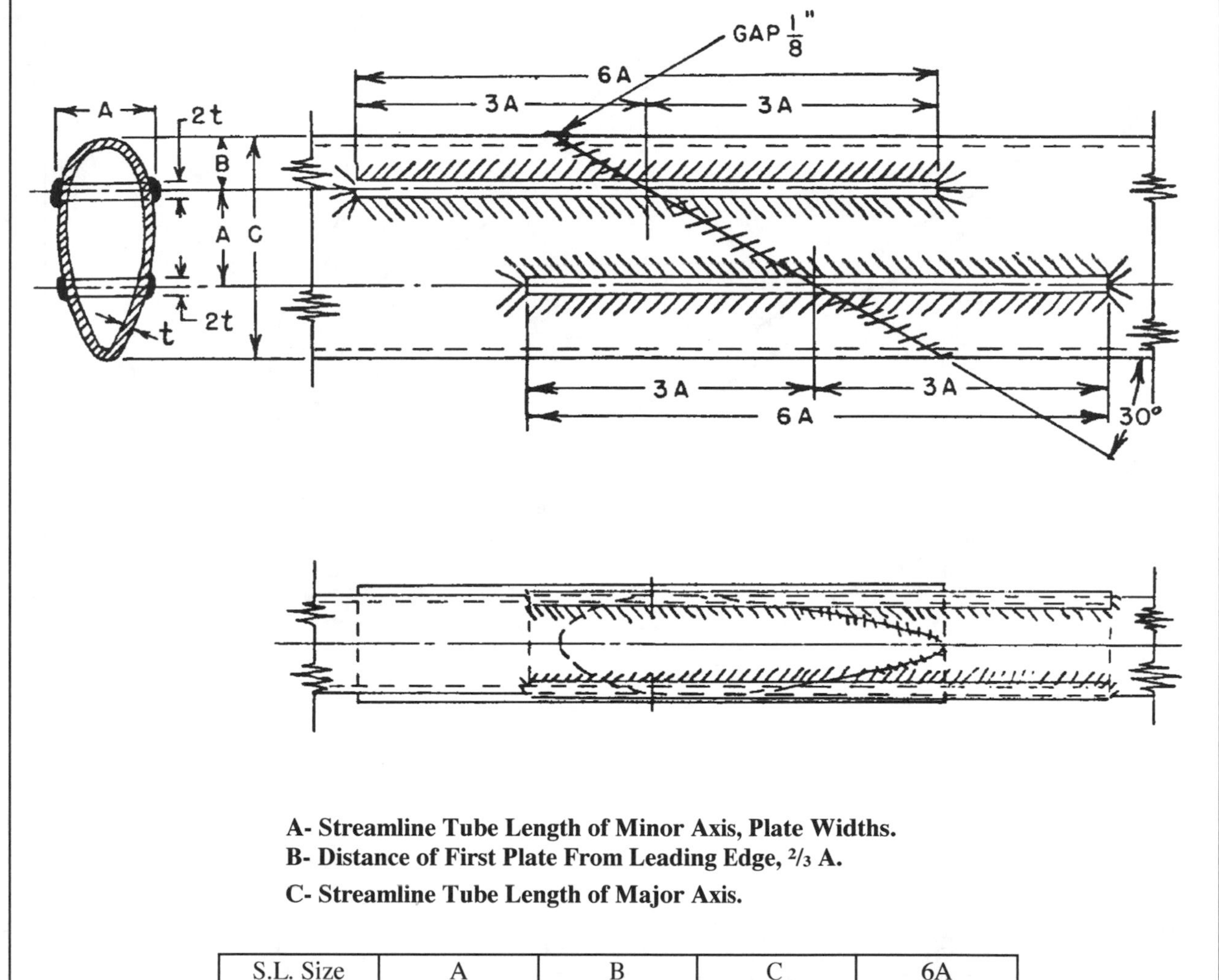

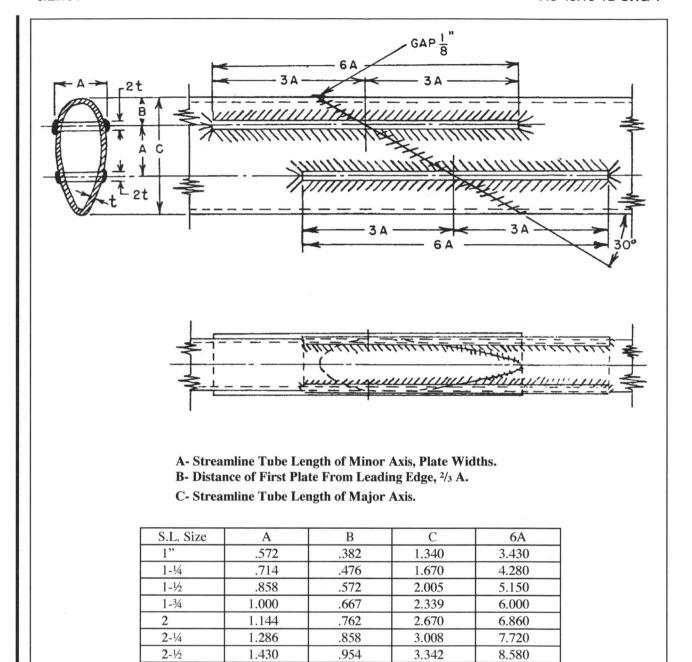

A- Streamline Tube Length of Minor Axis, Plate Widths.
B- Distance of First Plate From Leading Edge, ²/₃ A.
C- Streamline Tube Length of Major Axis.

S.L. Size	A	B	C	6A
1"	.572	.382	1.340	3.430
1-¼	.714	.476	1.670	4.280
1-½	.858	.572	2.005	5.150
1-¾	1.000	.667	2.339	6.000
2	1.144	.762	2.670	6.860
2-¼	1.286	.858	3.008	7.720
2-½	1.430	.954	3.342	8.580

FIGURE 4-45. Streamline tube splice using plates (applicable to landing gear).

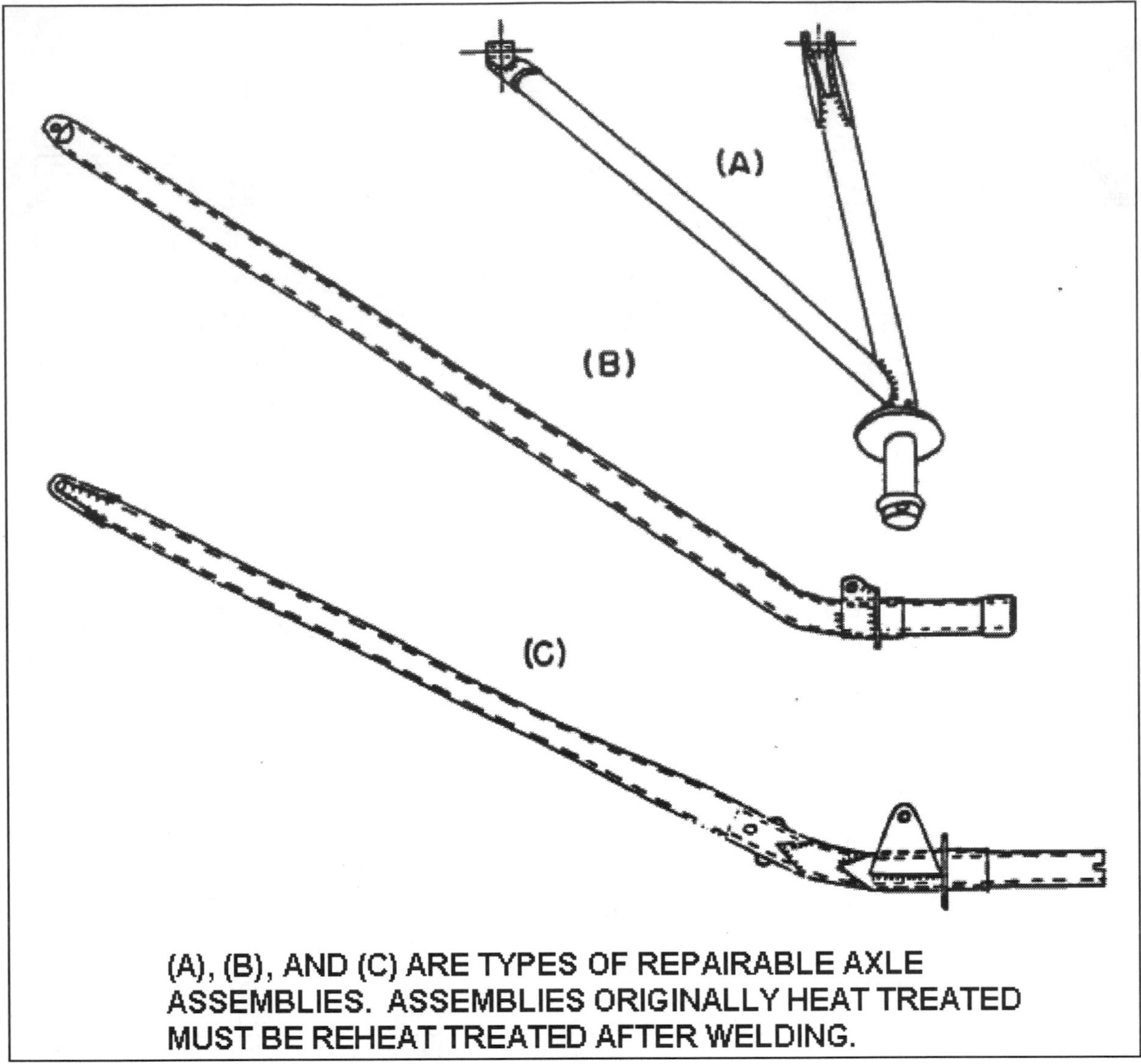

(A)
(B)
(C)
(A), (B), AND (C) ARE TYPES OF REPAIRABLE AXLE ASSEMBLIES. ASSEMBLIES ORIGINALLY HEAT TREATED MUST BE REHEAT TREATED AFTER WELDING.

FIGURE 4-46. Representative types of repairable axle assemblies.

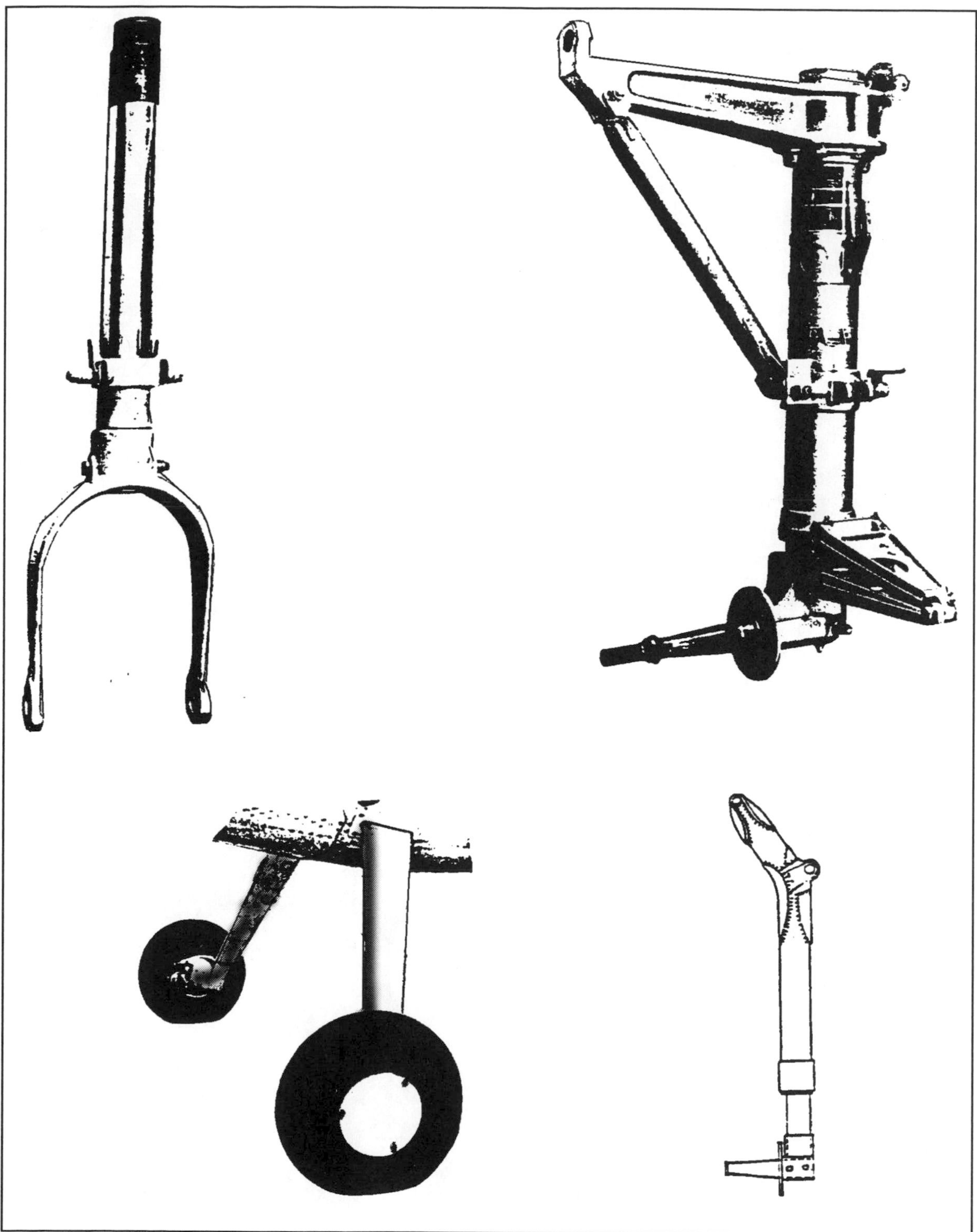

FIGURE 4-47. Landing gear assemblies that CANNOT be repaired by welding.

4-105.—4-110. [RESERVED.]

SECTION 6. WELDING AND BRAZING SAFETY

4-111. GENERAL. A number of inherent hazards exist in the use of oxy-fuel welding and cutting apparatus. It is necessary that proper safety and operating procedures are understood. A thorough understanding of the proper safety and operating procedures minimizes the hazards involved and adds to the pleasure and efficiency of your work.

4-112. FIRE AND EXPLOSION SAFETY. Fires occur in welding areas because flammables are left where they can be ignited by welding sparks or gas welding flames. Before welding, clear the welding area of all flammables such as rags, paper, wood, paint cans, solvent, and trash containers. Do not weld in areas where flammables are present.

a. Unless absolutely necessary, never weld any tank or radiator that has had a flammable in it, including gasoline, av-gas, motor oil, hydraulic fluid, or any other liquid that could ignite if the vapor and temperature reach a flashpoint. Explosions often occur when empty tanks are being welded or cut open with a torch.

b. If welding such tanks or radiator coolers is absolutely necessary, the tank must first be washed with a caustic-based, water-soluble liquid, rinsed with plenty of clear water, and then dried. Before welding, the tank or container should be thoroughly purged with argon, or other inert gas, while the welding is in process.

4-113. WELDING WORK AREA.

a. The work area must have a fireproof floor, concrete floors are recommend.

b. Use heat-resistant shields to protect nearby walls or unprotected flooring from sparks and hot metal.

c. Maintain an adequate suction ventilation system to prevent the concentration of oxygen/fuel gas, flammable gases, and/or toxic fumes. It is important to remember that oxygen will not burn. The presence of oxygen, however, serves to accelerate combustion, and causes materials to burn with great intensity.

CAUTION: Oil and grease in the presence of oxygen can ignite and burn violently.

d. A completely clean welding shop area with white walls, ceiling, and floor; and with plenty of light, is better for welding. The better the lighting conditions, the easier it is to see the weld puddle and make excellent aircraft-quality welds.

e. During oxy-fuel processes use work benches or tables with fireproof tops. Fire bricks commonly top these surfaces and support the work.

f. Chain or otherwise secure oxygen and fuel gas cylinders to a wall, bench, post, cylinder cart, etc. This will protect them from falling and hold them upright.

4-114. FIRE PROTECTION. Practice fire prevention techniques whenever oxy-fuel operations are in progress. Simple precautions prevent most fires, and minimize damage in the event a fire does occur. Always practice the following rules and safety procedures.

a. Inspect oxy-fuel apparatus for oil, grease, or damaged parts. DO NOT use the oxy-fuel apparatus if oil or grease is present or if damage is evident. Have the oxy-fuel apparatus cleaned and/or repaired by a qualified repair technician before it is used.

b. Never use oil or grease on or around any oxy-fuel apparatus. Even a trace of oil or grease can ignite and burn violently in the presence of oxygen.

c. Keep flames, heat, and sparks away from cylinders and boxes.

d. Flying sparks can travel as much as 35 feet. Move combustibles a safe distance away from areas where oxy-fuel operations are performed.

e. Use approved heat-resistant shields to protect nearby walls, floor, and ceiling.

f. Have a fire extinguisher of the proper class (ABC) and size in the work area. Inspect it regularly to ensure that it is in proper working order. Know how it is used.

g. Use oxy-fuel equipment only with the gases for which it is intended.

h. DO NOT open an acetylene cylinder valve more than approximately 1-1/2 turns and preferably no more than 3/4 of a turn. Keep the cylinder wrench, if one is required, on the cylinder valve so, if necessary, the cylinder may be turned off quickly.

i. On all gases except acetylene, open the cylinder valve completely to seal the cylinder back-seal packing.

j. Never test for gas leaks with a flame. Use an approved leak-detector solution.

k. When work is complete, inspect the area for possible fires or smoldering materials.

l. Special care should be taken when welding structural tubing that has been coated on the inside with linseed oil. Smoke and fire may be generated by the heat of the torch. Ensure that an observer with a fire extinguisher is close.

4-115. PROTECTIVE APPAREL.

a. Protect yourself from sparks, flying slag, and flame brilliance at all times.

(1) For gas welding and brazing, use number 3 or 4 green-shaded tempered lenses.

(2) When gas welding aluminum, use cobalt-blue tint lenses.

(3) When arc welding, including TIG, MIG, and plasma cutting; use number 9 to 12 green lenses and a full face-and-neck covering helmet.

(4) Electronically darkening lenses provide number 3 to 12 automatic darkening as soon as the arc is ignited.

b. Wear protective gloves, sleeves, aprons, and lace-up shoes to protect skin and clothing from sparks and slag.

CAUTION: Keep all clothing and protective apparel absolutely free of oil or grease.

4-116. FIRST-AID KITS. Always keep a special welder's first-aid kit where it is easily accessible. Burns are the most common welding accidents.

4-117.—4-128. [RESERVED.]

CHAPTER 5. NONDESTRUCTIVE INSPECTION (NDI)

SECTION 1. GENERAL

5-1. GENERAL. The field of NDI is too varied to be covered in detail in this Advisory Circular (AC). This chapter provides a brief description of the various Nondestructive Testing (NDT) used for inspection of aircraft, powerplant, and components in aircraft inspection. The effectiveness of any particular method of NDI depends upon the skill, experience, and training of the person(s) performing the inspection process. Each process is limited in its usefulness by its adaptability to the particular component to be inspected. Consult the aircraft or product manufacturer's manuals for specific instructions regarding NDI of their products. (Reference AC 43-3, Nondestructive Testing in Aircraft, for additional information on NDI.

The product manufacturer or the Federal Aviation Administration (FAA) generally specifies the particular NDI method and procedure to be used in inspection. These NDI requirements will be specified in the manufacturer's inspection, maintenance, or overhaul manual; FAA Airworthiness Directives (AD); Supplemental Structural Inspection Documents (SSID); or manufacturer's service bulletins (SB). However, in some conditions an alternate NDI method and procedure can be used. This includes procedures and data developed by FAA certificated repair stations under Title 14 of the Code of Federal Regulations, (14 CFR), part 145.

5-2. APPROVED PROCEDURES. Title 14 CFR, part 43 requires that all maintenance be performed using methods, techniques, and practices prescribed in the current manufacturer's maintenance manual or instructions for continued airworthiness prepared by its manufacturer, or other methods, techniques, and practices acceptable to the administrator. If the maintenance instructions include materials, parts, tools, equipment, or test apparatus necessary to comply with industry practices then those items are required to be available and used as per part 43.

5-3. NDT LEVELS. Reference Air Transport Association (ATA) Specification 105-Guidelines For Training and Qualifying Personnel In Nondestructive Testing Methods.

a. Level I Special.

Initial classroom hours and on-the-job training shall be sufficient to qualify an individual for certification for a specific task. The individual must be able to pass a vision and color perception examination, a general exam dealing with standards and NDT procedures, and a practical exam conducted by a qualified Level II or Level III certificated person.

b. Level I/Level II.

The individual shall have an FAA Airframe and Powerplant Mechanic Certificate, complete the required number of formal classroom hours, and complete an examination.

c. Level III.

(1) The individual must have graduated from a 4 year college or university with a degree in engineering or science, plus 1 year of minimum experience in NDT in an assignment comparable to that of a Level II in the applicable NDT methods: or

(2) The individual must have 2 years of engineering or science study at a university, college, or technical school, plus 2 years of experience as a Level II in the applicable NDT methods: or

(3) The individual must have 4 years of experience working as a Level II in the applicable NDT methods and complete an examination.

5-4. TRAINING, QUALIFICATION, AND CERTIFICATION. The success of any NDI method and procedure depends upon the knowledge, skill, and experience of the NDI personnel involved. The person(s) responsible for detecting and interpreting indications, such as eddy current, X-ray, or ultrasonic NDI, must be qualified and certified to specific FAA, or other acceptable government or industry standards, such as MIL-STD-410, Nondestructive Testing Personnel Qualification and Certification, or Air Transport Association (ATA) Specification 105-Guidelines for Training and Qualifying Personnel in Nondestructive Testing Methods. The person should be familiar with the test method, know the potential types of discontinuities peculiar to the material, and be familiar with their effect on the structural integrity of the part.

5-5. FLAWS. Although a specific discussion of flaws and processes will not be given in this AC, the importance of this area should not be minimized. Inspection personnel should know where flaws occur or can be expected to exist and what effect they can have in each of the NDI test methods. Misinterpretation and/or improper evaluation of flaws or improper performance of NDI can result in serviceable parts being rejected and defective parts being accepted.

All NDI personnel should be familiar with the detection of flaws such as: corrosion, inherent flaws, primary processing flaws, secondary processing or finishing flaws, and in-service flaws. The following paragraphs classify and discuss the types of flaws or anomalies that may be detected by NDI.

a. Corrosion. This is the electrochemical deterioration of a metal resulting from chemical reaction with the surrounding environment. Corrosion is very common and can be an extremely critical defect. Therefore, NDI personnel may devote a significant amount of their inspection time to corrosion detection.

b. Inherent Flaws. This group of flaws is present in metal as the result of its initial solidification from the molten state, before any of the operations to forge or roll it into useful sizes and shapes have begun. The following are brief descriptions of some inherent flaws.

(1) Primary pipe is a shrinkage cavity that forms at the top of an ingot during metal solidification, which can extend deep into the ingot. Failure to cut away all of the ingot shrinkage cavity can result in unsound metal, called pipe, that shows up as irregular voids in finished products.

(2) Blowholes are secondary pipe holes in metal that can occur when gas bubbles are trapped as the molten metal in an ingot mold solidifies. Many of these blowholes are clean on the interior and are welded shut into sound metal during the first rolling or forging of the ingot. However, some do not weld and can appear as seams or laminations in finished products.

(3) Segregation is a nonuniform distribution of various chemical constituents that can occur in a metal when an ingot or casting solidifies. Segregation can occur anywhere in the metal and is normally irregular in shape. However, there is a tendency for some constituents in the metal to concentrate in the liquid that solidifies last.

(4) Porosity is holes in a material's surface or scattered throughout the material, caused by gases being liberated and trapped as the material solidifies.

(5) Inclusions are impurities, such as slag, oxides, sulfides, etc., that occur in ingots and castings. Inclusions are commonly caused by incomplete refining of the metal ore or the incomplete mixing of deoxidizing materials added to the molten metal in the furnace.

(6) Shrinkage cracks can occur in castings due to stresses caused by the metal contracting as it cools and solidifies.

c. Primary Processing Flaws. Flaws which occur while working the metal down by hot or cold deformation into useful shapes such as bars, rods, wires, and forged shapes are primary processing flaws. Casting and welding are also considered primary processes although they involve molten metal, since they result in a semi-finished product. The following are brief descriptions of some primary processing flaws:

(1) Seams are surface flaws, generally long, straight, and parallel to the longitudinal axis of the material, which can originate from ingot blowholes and cracks, or be introduced by drawing or rolling processes.

(2) Laminations are formed in rolled plate, sheet, or strip when blowholes or internal fissures are not welded tight during the rolling process and are enlarged and flattened into areas of horizontal discontinuities.

(3) Cupping is a series of internal metal ruptures created when the interior metal does not flow as rapidly as the surface metal during drawing or extruding processes. Segregation in the center of a bar usually contributes to the occurrence.

(4) Cooling cracks can occur in casting due to stresses resulting from cooling, and are often associated with changes in cross sections of the part. Cooling cracks can also occur when alloy and tool steel bars are rolled and subsequently cooled. Also, stresses can occur from uneven cooling which can be severe enough to crack the bars. Such cracks are generally longitudinal, but not necessarily straight. They can be quite long, and usually vary in depth along their length.

(5) Flakes are internal ruptures that can occur in metal as a result of cooling too rapidly. Flaking generally occurs deep in a heavy section of metal. Certain alloys are more susceptible to flaking than others.

(6) Forging laps are the result of metal being folded over and forced into the surface, but not welded to form a single piece. They can be caused by faulty dies, oversized dies, oversized blanks, or improper handling of the metal in the die. They can occur on any area of the forging.

(7) Forging bursts are internal or external ruptures that occur when forging operations are started before the material to be forged reaches the proper temperature throughout. Hotter sections of the forging blank tend to flow around the colder sections causing internal bursts or cracks on the surface. Too rapid or too severe a reduction in a section can also cause forging bursts or cracks.

(8) A hot tear is a pulling apart of the metal that can occur in castings when the metal contracts as it solidifies.

(9) A cold shut is a failure of metal to fuse. It can occur in castings when part of the metal being poured into the mold cools and does not fuse with the rest of the metal into a solid piece.

(10) Incomplete weld penetration is a failure of the weld metal to penetrate completely through a joint before solidifying.

(11) Incomplete weld fusion occurs in welds where the temperature has not been high enough to melt the parent metal adjacent to the weld.

(12) Weld undercutting is a decrease in the thickness of the parent material at the toe of the weld caused by welding at too high a temperature.

(13) Cracks in the weld metal can be caused by the contraction of a thin section of the metal cooling faster than a heavier section or by incorrect heat or type of filler rod. They are one of the more common types of flaws found in welds.

(14) Weld crater cracks are star shaped cracks that can occur at the end of a weld run.

(15) Cracks in the weld heat-affected zone can occur because of stress induced in the material adjacent to the weld by its expansion and contraction from thermal changes.

(16) A slag inclusion is a nonmetallic solid material that becomes trapped in the weld metal or between the weld metal and the base metal.

(17) Scale is an oxide formed on metal by the chemical action of the surface metal with oxygen from the air.

d. Secondary Processing or Finishing Flaws. This category includes those flaws associated with the various finishing operations, after the part has been rough-formed by rolling, forging, casting or welding. Flaws may be introduced by heat treating, grinding, and similar processes. The following are brief descriptions of some secondary processing or finishing flaws.

(1) Machining tears can occur when working a part with a dull cutting tool or by cutting to a depth that is too great for the material being worked. The metal does not break away clean, and the tool leaves a rough, torn surface which contains numerous short discontinuities that can be classified as cracks.

(2) Heat treating cracks are caused by stresses setup by unequal heating or cooling of portions of a part during heat treating operations. Generally, they occur where a part has a sudden change of section that could cause an uneven cooling rate, or at fillets and notches that act as stress concentration points.

(3) Grinding cracks are thermal type cracks similar to heat treating cracks and can occur when hardened surfaces are ground. The overheating created by the grinding can be caused by the wheel becoming glazed so that it rubs instead of cutting the surface; by using too little coolant; by making too heavy a cut; or by feeding the material too rapidly. Generally, the cracks are at right angles to the direction of grinding and in severe cases a complete network of cracks can appear. Grinding cracks are usually shallow and very sharp at their roots, which makes them potential sources of fatigue failure.

(4) Etching cracks can occur when hardened surfaces containing internal residual stresses are etched in acid.

(5) Plating cracks can occur when hardened surfaces are electroplated. Generally, they are found in areas where high residual stresses remain from some previous operation involving the part.

e. In-Service Flaws. These flaws are formed after all fabrication has been completed and the aircraft, engine, or related component has gone into service. These flaws are attributable to aging effects caused by either time, flight cycles, service operating conditions, or combinations of these effects. The following are brief descriptions of some in-service flaws.

(1) Stress corrosion cracks can develop on the surface of parts that are under tension stress in service and are also exposed to a corrosive environment, such as the inside of wing skins, sump areas, and areas between two metal parts of faying surfaces.

(2) Overstress cracks can occur when a part is stressed beyond the level for which it was designed. Such overstressing can occur as the result of a hard landing, turbulence, accident, or related damage due to some unusual or emergency condition not anticipated by the designer, or because of the failure of some related structural member.

(3) Fatigue cracks can occur in parts that have been subjected to repeated or changing loads while in service, such as riveted lap joints in aircraft fuselages. The crack usually starts at a highly-stressed area and propagates through the section until failure occurs. A fatigue crack will start more readily where the design or surface condition provides a point of stress concentration. Common stress concentration points are: fillets; sharp radii; or poor surface finish, seams, or grinding cracks.

(4) Unbonds, or disbonds, are flaws where adhesive attaches to only one surface in an adhesive-bonded assembly. They can be the result of crushed, broken, or corroded cores in adhesive-bonded structures. Areas of unbonds have no strength and place additional stress on the surrounding areas making failure more likely.

(5) Delamination is the term used to define the separation of composite material layers within a monolithic structure. Ultrasonic is the primary method used for the detection of delamination in composite structures.

5-6. SELECTING THE NDI METHOD. The NDI method and procedure to be used for any specific part or component will generally be specified in the aircraft or component manufacturer's maintenance or overhaul manuals, SSID's, SB's, or in AD's.

NOTE: Some AD's refer to SB's which may, in turn, refer to manufacturer's overhaul or maintenance manuals.

a. Appropriate Method. The appropriate NDI method may consist of several separate inspections. An initial inspection may indicate the presence of a possible flaw, but other inspections may be required to confirm the original indication. Making the correct NDI method selection requires an understanding of the basic principles, limitations, and advantages and disadvantages of the available NDI methods and an understanding of their comparative effectiveness and cost.

b. Other Factors. Other factors affecting the inspection are:

(1) The critical nature of the component;

(2) The material, size, shape, and weight of the part;

(3) The type of defect sought;

(4) Maximum acceptable defect limits in size and distribution;

(5) Possible locations and orientations of defects;

(6) Part accessibility or portability; and

(7) The number of parts to be inspected.

c. Degree of Inspection. The degree of inspection sensitivity required is an important factor in selecting the NDI method. Critical parts that *cannot* withstand small defects and could cause *catastrophic failure* require the use of the more sensitive NDI methods. Less critical parts and general hardware generally require less-sensitive NDI methods.

d. Material Safety Data Sheets (MSDS). The various materials used in NDI may contain chemicals, that if improperly used, can be hazardous to the health and safety of operators and the safety of the environment, aircraft, and engines. Information on safe handling of materials is provided in MSDS. MSDS, conforming to Title 29 of the Code of Federal Regulations (29 CFR), part 1910, section 1200, or its equivalent, must be provided by the material supplier to any user and must be prepared according to FED-STD-313.

e. Advantages and Disadvantages. Table 5-1 provides a list of the advantages and disadvantages of common NDI methods. Table 5-1, in conjunction with other information in the AC, may be used as a guide for evaluating the most appropriate NDI method when the manufacturer or the FAA has not specified a particular NDI method to be used.

5-7. TYPES OF INSPECTIONS. Nondestructive testing methods are techniques used both in the production and in-service environments without damage or destruction of the item under investigation. Examples of NDI methods are as follows:

a. Visual inspection

b. Magnetic particle

c. Penetrants

d. Eddy current

e. Radiography

f. Ultrasonic

g. Acoustic emission

h. Thermography

i. Holography

j. Shearography

k. Tap testing

TABLE 5-1. Advantages and disadvantages of NDI methods.

METHOD	ADVANTAGES	DISADVANTAGES
VISUAL	Inexpensive Highly portable Immediate results Minimum training Minimum part preparation	Surface discontinuities only Generally only large discontinuities Misinterpretation of scratches
DYE PENETRANT	Portable Inexpensive Sensitive to very small discontinuities 30 min. or less to accomplish Minimum skill required	Locate surface defects only Rough or porous surfaces interfere with test Part preparation required (removal of finishes and sealant, etc.) High degree of cleanliness required Direct visual detection of results required
MAGNETIC PARTICLE	Can be portable Inexpensive Sensitive to small discontinuities Immediate results Moderate skill required Detects surface and subsurface discontinuities Relatively fast	Surface must be accessible Rough surfaces interfere with test Part preparation required (removal of finishes and sealant, etc.) Semi-directional requiring general orientation of field to discontinuity Ferro-magnetic materials only Part must be demagnetized after test.
EDDY CURRENT	Portable Detects surface and subsurface discontinuities Moderate speed Immediate results Sensitive to small discontinuities Thickness sensitive Can detect many variables	Surface must be accessible to probe Rough surfaces interfere with test Electrically conductive materials Skill and training required Time consuming for large areas
ULTRASONIC	Portable Inexpensive Sensitive to very small discontinuities Immediate results Little part preparation Wide range of materials and thickness can be inspected	Surface must be accessible to probe Rough surfaces interfere with test Highly sensitive to sound beam - discontinuity orientation High degree of skill required to set up and interpret Couplant usually required
X-RAY RADIOGRAPHY	Detects surface and internal flaws Can inspect hidden areas Permanent test record obtained Minimum part preparation	Safety hazard Very expensive (slow process) Highly directional, sensitive to flaw orientation High degree of skill and experience required for exposure and interpretation Depth of discontinuity not indicated
ISOTOPE RADIOGRAPHY	Portable Less expensive than X-ray Detects surface and internal flaws Can inspect hidden areas Permanent test record obtained Minimum part preparation	Safety hazard Must conform to Federal and State regulations for handling and use Highly directional, sensitive to flaw orientation High degree of skill and experience required for exposure and interpretation Depth of discontinuity not indicated

5-8.—5-14. [RESERVED.]

SECTION 2. VISUAL INSPECTION

5-15. GENERAL. Visual inspection is the oldest and most common form of NDI for aircraft. Approximately 80 percent of all NDI procedures are accomplished by the direct visual methods. This inspection procedure may be greatly enhanced by the use of appropriate combinations of magnifying instruments, borescopes, light sources, video scanners, and other devices discussed in this AC. Visual inspection provides a means of detecting and examining a wide variety of component and material surface discontinuities, such as cracks, corrosion, contamination, surface finish, weld joints, solder connections, and adhesive disbonds. Visual inspection is widely used for detecting and examining aircraft surface cracks, which are particularly important because of their relationship to structural failures. Visual inspection is frequently used to provide verification when defects are found initially using other NDI techniques. The use of optical aids for visual inspection is beneficial and recommended. Optical aids magnify defects that cannot be seen by the unaided eye and also permit visual inspection in inaccessible areas.

5-16. SIMPLE VISUAL INSPECTION AIDS. It should be emphasized that the eye-mirror-flashlight is a critical visual inspection process. Aircraft structure and components that must be routinely inspected are frequently located beneath skin, cables, tubing, control rods, pumps, actuators, etc. Visual inspection aids such as a powerful flashlight, a mirror with a ball joint, and a 2 to 10 power magnifying glass are essential in the inspection process.

a. Flashlights. Flashlights used for aircraft inspection should be suitable for industrial use and, where applicable, safety approved by the Underwriters Laboratory or equivalent agency as suitable for use in hazardous atmospheres such as aircraft fuel tanks. Military Specification MIL-F-3747E, flashlights: plastic case, tubular (regular, explosion-proof, explosion-proof heat resistant, traffic directing, and inspection-light), provides requirements for flashlights suitable for use in aircraft inspection. However, at the present time, the flashlights covered by this specification use standard incandescent lamps and there are no standardized performance tests for flashlights with the brighter bulbs: Krypton, Halogen, and Xenon. Each flashlight manufacturer currently develops its tests and provides information on its products in its advertising literature. Therefore, when selecting a flashlight for use in visual inspection, it is sometimes difficult to directly compare products. The following characteristics should be considered when selecting a flashlight: foot-candle rating; explosive atmosphere rating; beam spread (adjustable, spot, or flood); efficiency (battery usage rate); brightness after extended use; and rechargeable or standard batteries. (If rechargeable, how many hours of continuous use and how long is required for recharging?) If possible, it would be best to take it apart and inspect for quality of construction and to actually use the flashlight like it would be used in the field. Inspection flashlights are available in several different bulb brightness levels:

(1) Standard incandescent (for long-battery life).

(2) Krypton (for 70 percent more light than standard bulbs).

(3) Halogen (for up to 100 percent more light than standard bulbs).

(4) Xenon (for over 100 percent more light than standard bulbs).

b. Inspection Mirrors. An inspection mirror is used to view an area that is not in the normal line of sight. The mirror should be of the appropriate size to easily view the component, with the reflecting surface free of dirt, cracks, worn coating, etc., and a swivel joint tight enough to maintain its setting.

c. Simple Magnifiers. A single converging lens, the simplest form of a microscope, is often referred to as a simple magnifier. Magnification of a single lens is determined by the equation M = 10/f. In this equation, "M" is the magnification, "f" is the focal length of the lens in inches, and "10" is a constant that represents the average minimum distance at which objects can be distinctly seen by the unaided eye. Using the equation, a lens with a focal length of 5 inches has a magnification of 2, or is said to be a two-power lens.

5-17. BORESCOPES. These instruments are long, tubular, precision optical instruments with built-in illumination, designed to allow remote visual inspection of internal surfaces or otherwise inaccessible areas. The tube, which can be rigid or flexible with a wide variety of lengths and diameters, provides the necessary optical connection between the viewing end and an objective lens at the distant, or distal tip of the borescope. Rigid and flexible borescopes are available in different designs for a variety of standard applications and manufacturers also provide custom designs for specialized applications. Figure 5-1 shows three typical designs of borescopes.

a. Borescopes Uses. Borescopes are used in aircraft and engine maintenance programs to reduce or eliminate the need for costly teardowns. Aircraft turbine engines have access ports that are specifically designed for borescopes. Borescopes are also used extensively in a variety of aviation maintenance programs to determine the airworthiness of difficult-to-reach components. Borescopes typically are used to inspect interiors of hydraulic cylinders and valves for pitting, scoring, porosity, and tool marks; inspect for cracked cylinders in aircraft reciprocating engines; inspect turbojet engine turbine blades and combustion cans; verify the proper placement and fit of seals, bonds, gaskets, and subassemblies in difficult to reach areas; and assess Foreign Object Damage (FOD) in aircraft, airframe, and powerplants. Borescopes may also be used to locate and retrieve foreign objects in engines and airframes.

b. Optical Designs. Typical designs for the optical connection between the borescope viewing end and the distal tip are:

(1) A rigid tube with a series of relay lenses;

(2) A flexible or rigid tube with a bundle of optical fibers; and

(3) A flexible or rigid tube with wiring that carries the image signal from a Charge Couple Device (CCD) imaging sensor at the distal tip.

These designs can have either fixed or adjustable focusing of the objective lens at the distal tip. The distal tip may also have prisms and mirrors that define the direction and field of view. A fiber optic light guide with white light is generally used in the illumination system, but ultraviolet light can also be used to inspect surfaces treated with liquid fluorescent penetrant or to inspect for contaminants that fluoresce. Some borescopes with long working lengths use light-emitting diodes at the distal tip for illumination.

5-18. VISUAL INSPECTION PROCEDURES. Corrosion can be an extremely critical defect. Therefore, NDI personnel should be familiar with the appearance of common types of corrosion and have training and

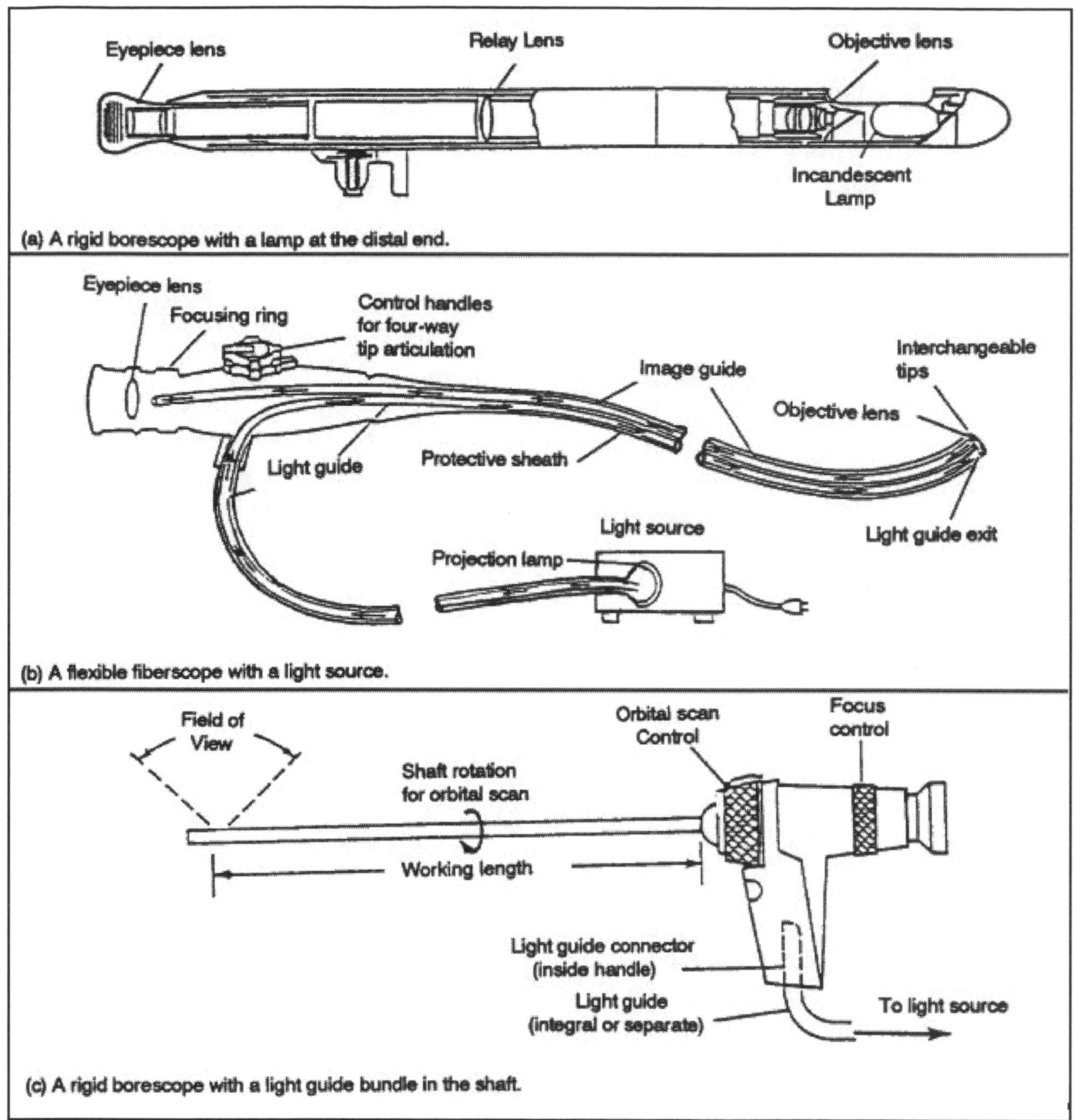

FIGURE 5-1. Typical borescope designs.

experience on corrosion detection on aircraft structure and engine materials. (Reference: AC 43-4A, Corrosion Control for Aircraft, for additional information on corrosion.

a. Preliminary Inspection. Perform a preliminary inspection of the overall general area for cleanliness, presence of foreign objects, deformed or missing fasteners, security of parts, corrosion, and damage. If the configuration or location of the part conceals the area to be inspected, use visual aids such as a mirror or borescope.

b. Corrosion Treatment. Treat any corrosion found during preliminary inspection after completing a visual inspection of any selected part or area.

NOTE: Eddy current, radiography, or ultrasonic inspection can determine the loss of metal to corrosion.

c. Lighting. Provide adequate lighting to illuminate the selected part or area.

d. Personal Comfort. Personal comfort (temperature, wind, rain, etc.) of the inspector can be a factor in visual inspection reliability.

e. Noise. Noise levels while conducting a visual inspection are important. Excessive noise reduces concentration, creates tension, and prevents effective communication. All these factors will increase the likelihood of errors.

f. Inspection Area Access. Ease of access to the inspection area has been found to be of major importance in obtaining reliable visual inspection results. Access consists of the act of getting into an inspection position (primary access) and doing the visual inspection (secondary access). Poor access can affect the inspector's interpretation of discontinuities, decision making, motivation, and attitude.

g. Precleaning. Clean the areas or surface of the parts to be inspected. Remove any contaminates that might hinder the discovery of existing surface indications. Do not remove the protective finish from the part or area prior to inspection. Removal of the finish may be required at a later time if other NDI techniques are required to verify any visual indications of flaws that are found.

h. Inspection. Carefully inspect the area for discontinuities, using optical aids as required. An inspector normally should have available suitable measuring devices, a flashlight, and a mirror.

(1) Surface cracks. When searching for surface cracks with a flashlight, direct the light beam at a 5 to 45 degree angle to the inspection surface, towards the face. (See figure 5-2.) Do not direct the light beam at such an angle that the reflected light beam shines directly into the eyes. Keep the eyes above the reflected light beam during the inspection. Determine the extent of any cracks found by directing the light beam at right angles to the crack and tracing its length. Use a 10-power magnifying glass to confirm the existence of a suspected crack. If this is not adequate, use other NDI techniques, such as penetrant, magnetic particle, or eddy current to verify cracks.

(2) Other surface discontinuities. Inspect for other surface discontinuities, such as: discoloration from overheating; buckled, bulging, or dented skin; cracked, chafed, split, or dented tubing; chafed electrical wiring; delaminations of composites; and damaged protective finishes.

i. Recordkeeping. Document all discrepancies by written report, photograph, and/or video recording for appropriate evaluation. The full value of visual inspection can be realized only if records are kept of the discrepancies found on parts inspected. The size and shape of the discontinuity and its location on the part should be recorded along with other pertinent information, such as rework performed or disposition. The inclusion on a report of some visible record of the discontinuity makes the report more complete.

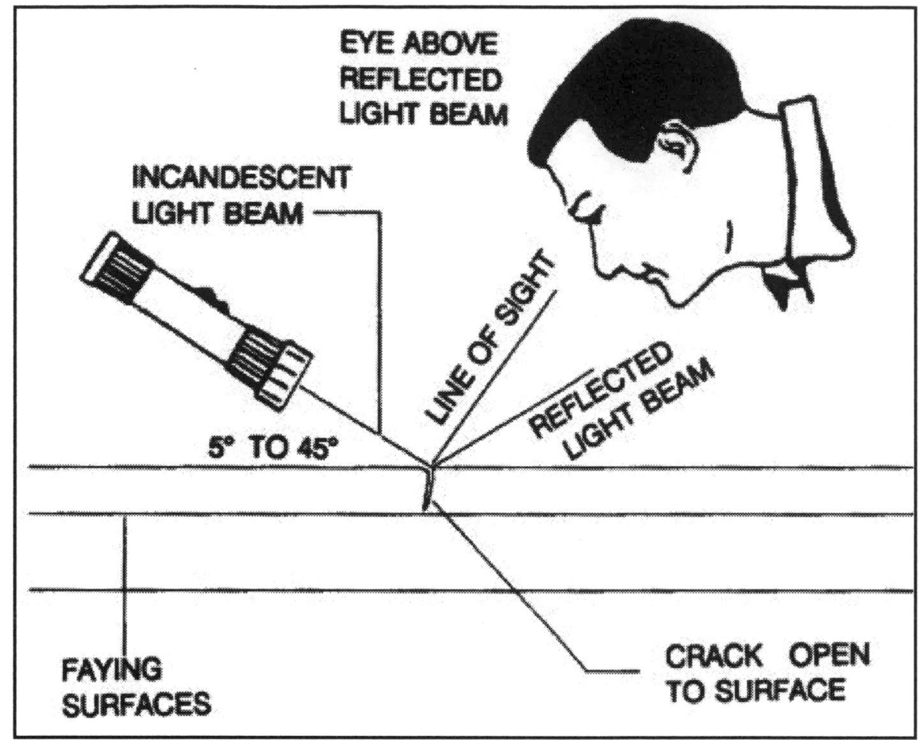

FIGURE 5-2. Using a flashlight to inspect for cracks.

5-19.—5-24. [RESERVED.]

SECTION 3. EDDY CURRENT INSPECTION

5-25. EDDY CURRENT INSPECTION. Eddy current is used to detect surface cracks, pits, subsurface cracks, corrosion on inner surfaces, and to determine alloy and heat-treat condition.

a. Eddy Current Instruments. A wide variety of eddy current test instruments are available. The eddy current test instrument performs three basic functions: generating, receiving, and displaying. The generating portion of the unit provides an alternating current to the test coil. The receiving section processes the signal from the test coil to the required form and amplitude for display. Instrument outputs or displays consist of a variety of visual, audible, storage, or transfer techniques utilizing meters, video displays, chart recorders, alarms, magnetic tape, computers, and electrical or electronic relays.

b. Principles of Operations. Eddy currents are induced in a test article when an alternating current is applied to a test coil (probe). The alternating current in the coil induces an alternating magnetic field in the article which causes eddy currents to flow in the article. (See figure 5-3.)

(1) Flaws in or thickness changes of the test-piece influence the flow of eddy currents and change the impedance of the coil accordingly. (See figure 5-4.) Instruments display the impedance changes either by impedance plane plots or by needle deflection.

(2) Figure 5-5 shows typical impedance plane display and meter display instrument responses for aluminum surface cracks, subsurface cracks, and thickness.

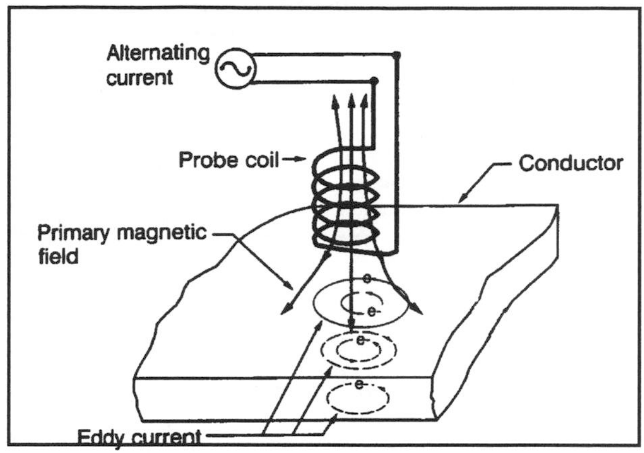

FIGURE 5-3. Generating an eddy current.

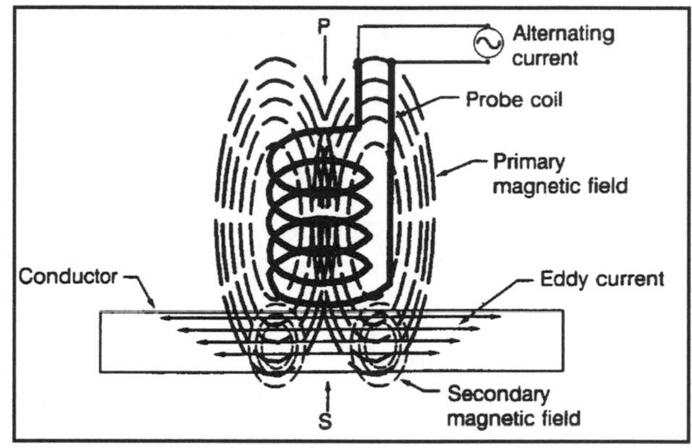

FIGURE 5-4. Detecting an eddy current.

5-26. EDDY CURRENT COILS AND PROBES. A wide variety of eddy current coils and probes is available. Coils and probes are not always interchangeable between various types of instruments and, for best results, should be matched to a specific instrument and frequency range. Special probe holders can be fabricated to facilitate eddy current inspection of contoured or shaped parts including part edges.

5-27. FIELD APPLICATION OF EDDY CURRENT INSPECTION. Eddy current techniques are particularly well-suited for detection of service-induced cracks in the field.

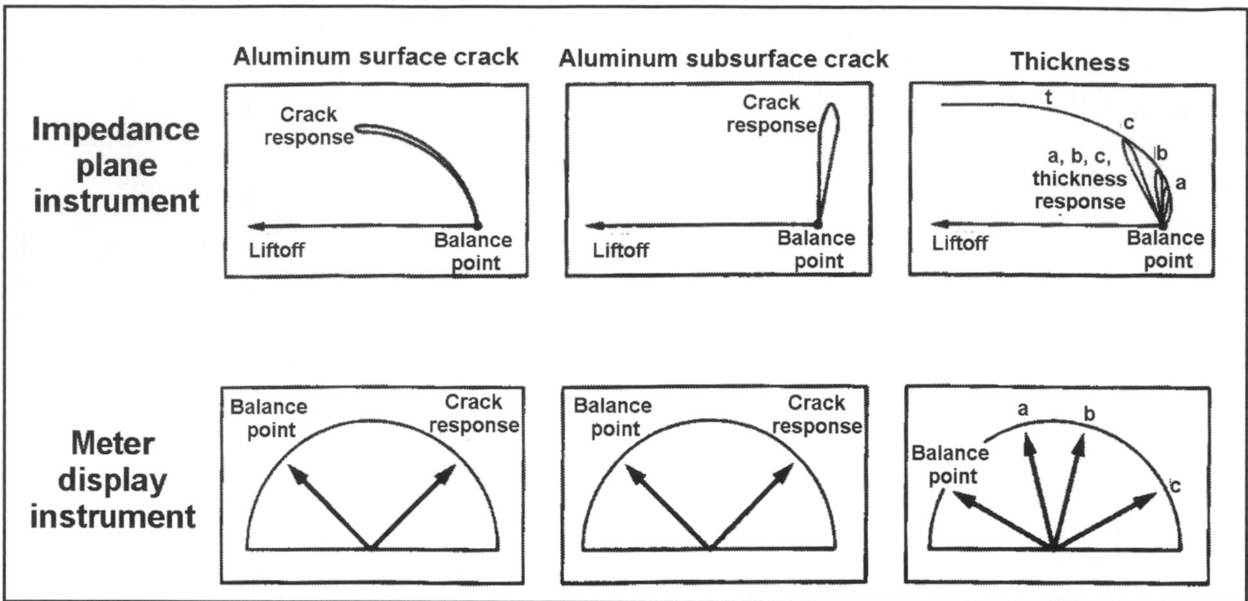

FIGURE 5-5. Typical instrument displays.

Service-induced cracks in aircraft structures are generally caused by fatigue or stress corrosion. Both types of cracks initiate at the surface of a part. If this surface is accessible, a high-frequency eddy current inspection can be performed with a minimum of part preparation and a high degree of sensitivity. If the surface is less accessible, such as in a subsurface layer of structure, low-frequency eddy current inspection can usually be performed. Eddy current inspection can usually be performed without removing surface coatings such as primer, paint, and anodic films. Eddy current inspection has the greatest application for inspecting small localized areas where possible crack initiation is suspected rather than for scanning broad areas for randomly-oriented cracks. However, in some instances it is more economical to scan relatively large areas with eddy current rather than strip surface coatings, inspect by other methods, and then refinish.

5-28. SURFACE INSPECTION. Eddy current inspection techniques are used to inspect for surface cracks such as those shown in figure 5-6.

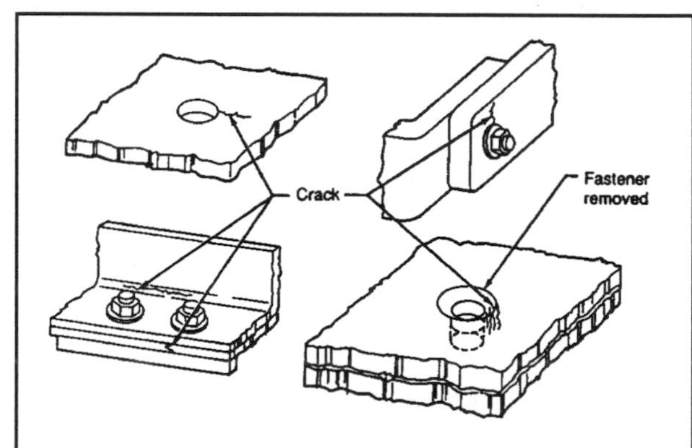

FIGURE 5-6. Typical surface cracks.

a. Equipment Requirements. The following are typical eddy current equipment requirements for surface crack inspections.

(1) Instruments must meet the liftoff and sensitivity requirements of the applicable NDI procedures. The frequency requirement is generally 100 Hz to 200 kHz.

(2) Many types of probes are available such as: flat-surface; spring-loaded; pencil; shielded pencil; right-angle pencil; or fastener hole probes.

(3) A reference standard is required for the calibration of Eddy Current test equipment. A reference standard is made from the same material as that which is to be tested. A reference standard contains known flaws or cracks and could include items such as: a flat surface notch, a fastener head, a fastener hole, or a countersink hole.

5-29. SUBSURFACE INSPECTION. Eddy current inspection techniques are used to inspect for subsurface cracks such as those shown in figure 5-7. The following are typical eddy current equipment requirements for subsurface crack inspections.

a. Use a variable frequency instrument with frequency capability from 100 Hz to 500 MHz.

b. The probe used would be a low-frequency; spot, ring, or sliding probe.

c. Use a reference standard appropriate for the inspection being performed.

5-30. CORROSION INSPECTION. Eddy current inspection is used to detect the loss of metal as a result of corrosion. An estimation of material loss due to corrosion can be made by comparison with thickness standards. Figure 5-8 shows typical structural corrosion that may be detected by the use of eddy current inspection. Remove all surface corrosion before performing the eddy current corrosion inspection. The following are typical eddy current equipment requirements for corrosion inspection.

a. Use a variable frequency instrument with frequency capability from 100 Hz to 40 kHz.

b. Use a shielded probe with coil diameter between 0.15 and 0.5 inch and designed to operate at the lower frequencies.

c. A reference standard made from the same alloy, heat treatment, and thickness as the test structure will be required.

5-31. ESTABLISHING EDDY CURRENT INSPECTION PROCEDURES. When establishing eddy current inspection procedures, where no written procedures are available, the following factors must be considered: type of material to be inspected; accessibility of the inspection area; material or part geometry, the signal-to-noise ratio, test system; lift-off effects, location and size of flaws to be detected; scanning pattern; scanning speed; and reference standards. All of these factors are interrelated. Therefore, a change in one of the factors may require changes in other factors to maintain the same level of sensitivity and reliability of the eddy current inspection procedure. Written procedures should elaborate on these factors and place them in their proper order.

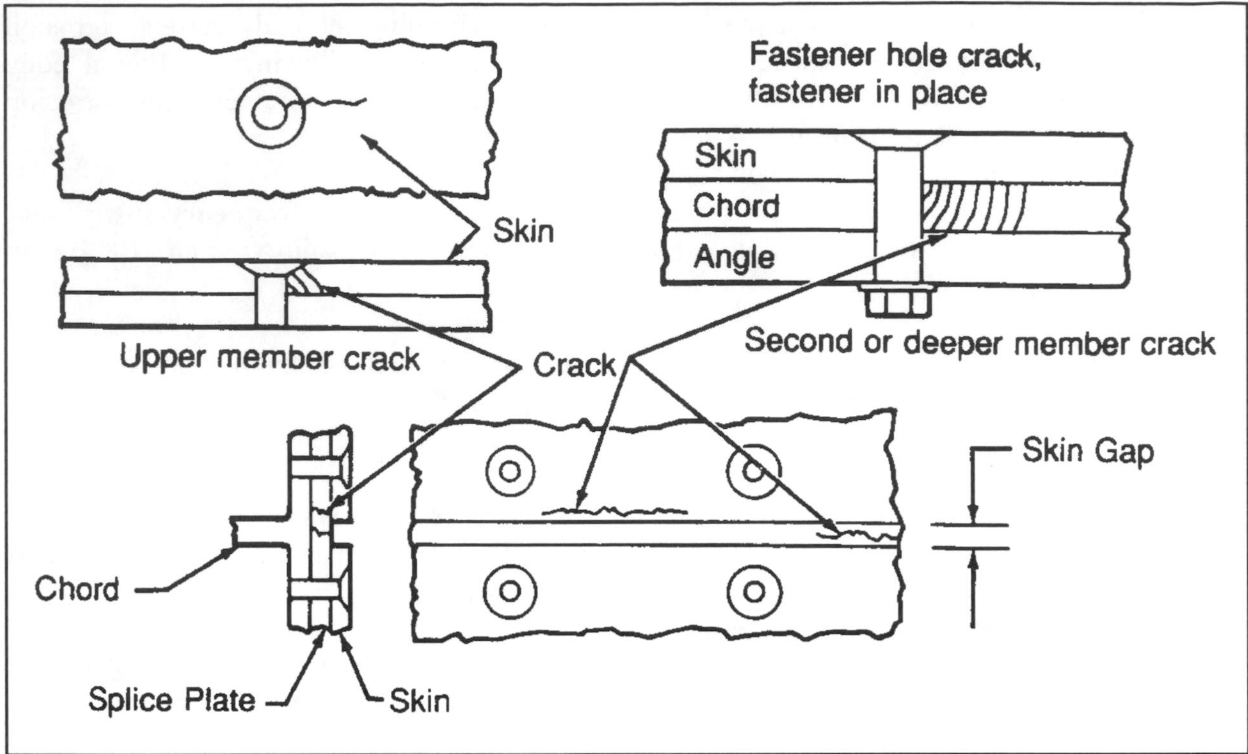

FIGURE 5-7. Typical subsurface cracks.

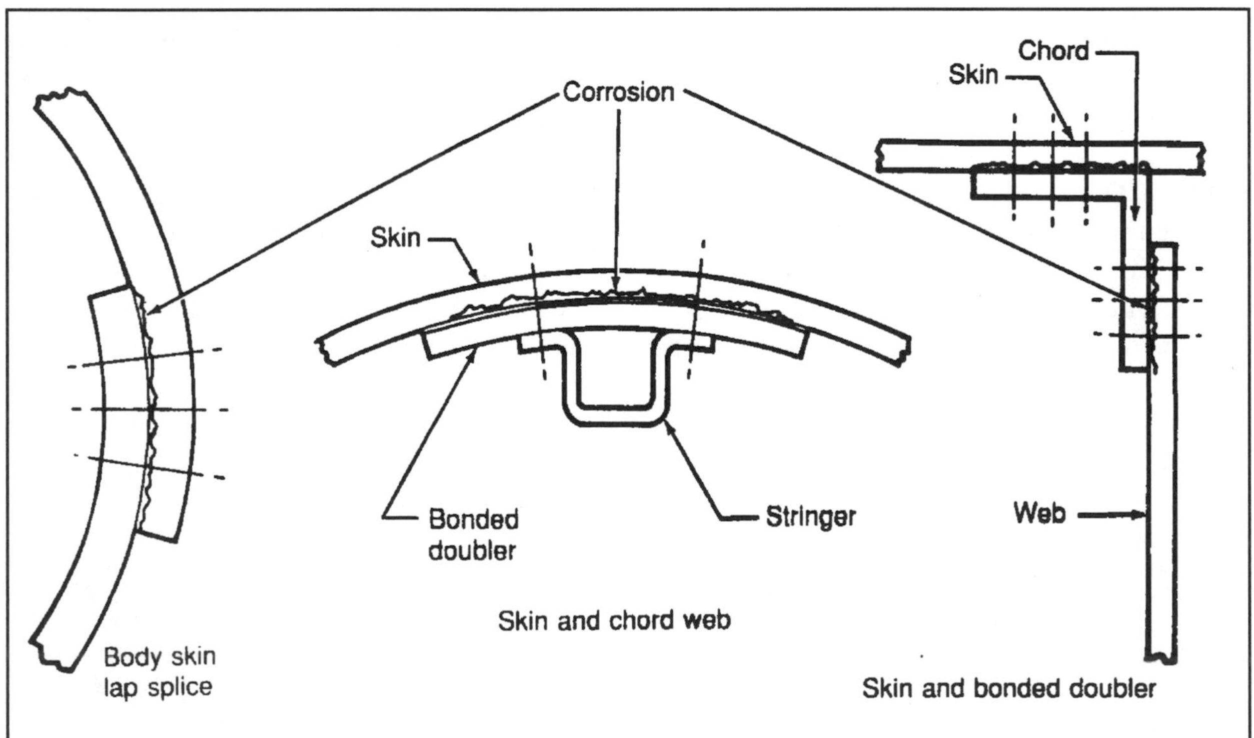

FIGURE 5-8. Typical structural corrosion.

5-32.—5-39. [RESERVED.]

SECTION 4. MAGNETIC PARTICLE INSPECTION

5-40. GENERAL. Magnetic particle inspection is a method for detecting cracks, laps, seams, voids, pits, subsurface holes, and other surface, or slightly subsurface, discontinuities in ferro-magnetic materials. Magnetic particle inspection can be used only on ferro-magnetic materials (iron and steel). It can be performed on raw material, billets, finished and semi-finished materials, welds, and in-service assembled or disassembled parts. Magnetic particles are applied over a surface either dry, as a powder, or wet, as particles in a liquid carrier such as oil or water.

Common uses for magnetic particle inspection are; final inspection, receiving inspection, in-process inspection; and quality control, maintenance, and overhaul.

5-41. PRINCIPLES OF OPERATION. Magnetic particle inspection uses the tendency of magnetic lines of force, or flux, of an applied field to pass through the metal rather than through the air. A defect at or near the metal's surface distorts the distribution of the magnetic flux and some of the flux is forced to pass out through the surface. (See figure 5-9.) The field strength is increased in the area of the defect and opposite magnetic poles form on either side of the defect. Fine magnetic particles applied to the part are attracted to these regions and form a pattern around the defect. The pattern of particles provides a visual indication of a defect. (See figure 5-10.)

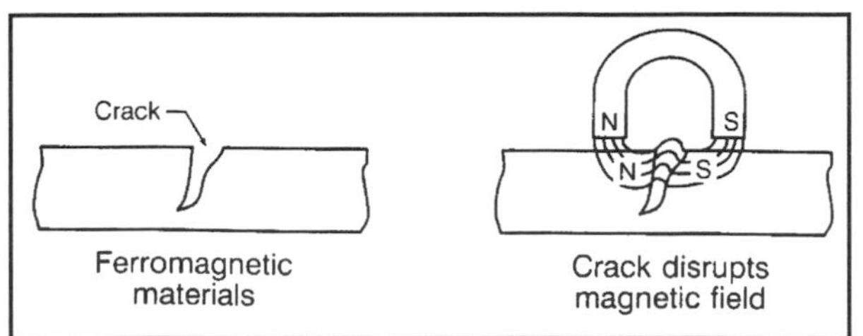

FIGURE 5-9. Magnetic field disrupted.

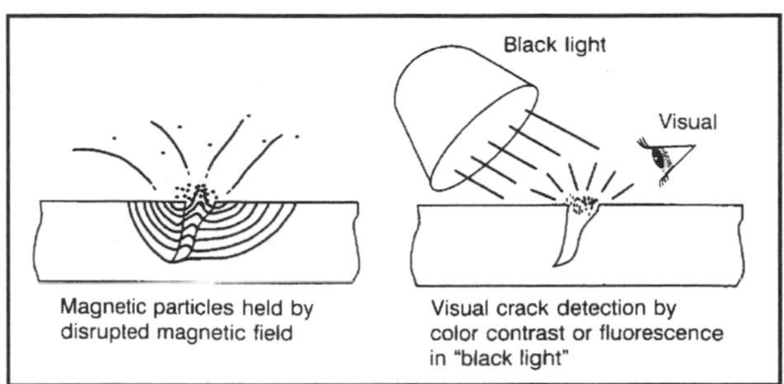

FIGURE 5-10. Crack detection by magnetic particle inspection.

a. To locate a defect, it is necessary to control the direction of magnetization, and flux lines must be perpendicular to the longitudinal axes of expected defects. Examination of critical areas for defects may require complete disassembly. Two methods of magnetization, circular and longitudinal, are used to magnetize the part and induce perpendicular flux paths. Parts of complex configuration may require local magnetization to ensure proper magnetic field direction and adequate removal of surface coatings, sealants, and other similar compounds. Possible adverse influence of the applied or residual magnetic fields on delicate parts such as instruments, bearings, and mechanisms may require removal of these parts before performing the inspection.

b. Certain characteristics inherent in the magnetic particle method may introduce errors in examination results. Nonrelevant errors are caused by magnetic field distortions due to intentional design features, such as:

(1) Sharp radii, less than 0.10 inch radius, in fillets;

(2) Thread roots, keyways, and drilled holes; and

(3) Abrupt changes in geometry or in magnetic properties within the part.

c. Operators must understand nonrelevant error indications and recognize them during examination. Proper analysis of indications in these regions will require considerable skill and experience, and supplemental methods may be required before a final evaluation can be made. Special techniques for examination of these areas are given in subsequent paragraphs.

5-42. APPLICATIONS. Use magnetic particle inspection on any well-cleaned surface that is accessible for close visual examination. Typical parts deserving magnetic particle examination are: steel fasteners and pins; critical structural elements; linkages; landing gear components; splice and attach fittings; and actuating mechanisms.

a. During field repair operations, disassembly is often not necessary, except when the parts have critical areas or delicate installed components. However, for overhaul operations, a more thorough and critical examination may be obtained with stationary equipment in a shop environment with completely disassembled, and thoroughly cleaned and stripped parts.

b. Magnetic rubber examination material is useful for in-field service examinations of fastener holes in areas where the accessibility is limited or restricted, where particle suspensions may cause unwanted contamination, when a permanent record is desired, and when the examination area cannot be observed visually.

5-43. ELECTRICAL MAGNETIZING EQUIPMENT. Stationary equipment in the range of 100 to 6000 amperes is normal for use within the aerospace industry for overhaul operations. Mobile equipment with similar amperage outputs is available for field examination of heavy structures, such as landing gear cylinders and axles. Small parts and local areas of large components can be adequately checked with the use of small, inexpensive permanent magnets or electromagnetic yokes. In procuring magnetizing equipment, the maximum rated output should be greater than the required examination amperage. Actual current flow through a complex part may be reduced as much as 20 percent by the resistance load of the rated output.

5-44. MATERIALS USED IN MAGNETIC PARTICLE INSPECTION. The particles used in magnetic particle inspection are finely divided ferro-magnetic materials that have been treated with color or fluorescent dyes to improve visibility against the various surface backgrounds of the parts under inspection. Magnetic particles, particle-suspension vehicles, and cleaners are required for conducting magnetic particle inspection. Requirements for magnetic particle inspection materials, other than cleaners, are contained in the aerospace industry standard, ASTM-E1444, Inspection, Magnetic Particle (as revised). A certification statement which will certify that the material meets applicable specification requirements will generally be received when a magnetic particle inspection material is purchased. Magnetic particle inspection materials for use on a specific part or component will generally be specified by the aircraft or component manufacturer or the FAA in documents such as; maintenance or overhaul manuals, AD's, SSID's, or manufacturer's SB's. However, if the magnetic particle inspection materials are not specified for the specific part or component to be inspected, it is recommended that personnel use materials meeting the aircraft or component manufacturers' specifications or materials meeting the requirements of ASTM-E1444. Other FAA engineering-approved materials may also be used. Table 5-2 provides a partial listing of commonly accepted standards and specifications for magnetic particle inspection.

TABLE 5-2. Listing of commonly accepted standards and specifications for magnetic particle inspection.

NUMBER	TITLE
ASTM STANDARDS	
ASTM A275/A275 M-96	Standard Test Method for Magnetic Particle Examination of Steel Forgings. 1995
ASTM A456/A456 M Rev. A.	Standard Specification for Magnetic Particle Examination of Large Crankshaft Forgings. 1995
ASTM D96	Standard Test Methods for Water and Sediment in Crude Oils by Centrifuge Method (Field Procedure). 1988
ASTM E125-63 (1993)	Standard Reference Photographs for Magnetic Particle Indications on Ferrous Castings. (Revised 1993) 1963
ASTM E1316-95C	Standard Terminology for Nondestructive Examination. 1995 (Replaces ASTM E269).
SAE-AMS SPECIFICATIONS	
AMS 2300G	Premium Aircraft-Quality Steel Cleanliness Magnetic Particle Inspection Procedure. 1991 (Revised 1995)
MAM 2300A	Premium Aircraft Quality Steel Cleanliness Magnetic Particle Inspection Procedure Metric (SI) Measurement. 1992
AMS 2303C	Aircraft Quality Steel Cleanliness Martensitic Corrosion Resistant Steels Magnetic Particle Inspection Procedure. 1993
MAM 2303A	Aircraft Quality Steel Cleanliness Martensitic Corrosion Resistant Steels Magnetic Particle Inspection Procedure Metric (SI) Measurement. 1993
AMS 2641	Vehicle, Magnetic Particle Inspection Petroleum Base. 1988
AMS 3040B	Magnetic Particles, Nonfluorescent, Dry Method. 1995
AMS 3041B	Magnetic Particles, Nonfluorescent, Wet Method, Oil Vehicle, Ready-To-Use. 1988
AMS 3042B	Magnetic Particles, Nonfluorescent, Wet Method, Dry Powder. 1988
AMS 3043A	Magnetic Particles, Nonfluorescent, Wet Method, Oil Vehicle, Aerosol Packaged. 1988
AMS 3044C	Magnetic Particles, Fluorescent, Wet Method, Dry Powder. 1989
AMS 3045B	Magnetic Particles, Fluorescent, Wet Method, Oil Vehicle Ready-to-Use. 1989
AMS 3046B	Magnetic Particles, Fluorescent, Wet Method, Oil Vehicle, Aerosol Packaged. 1989
U.S. GOVERNMENT SPECIFICATIONS	
DOD-F-87935	Fluid, Magnetic Particle Inspection, Suspension. 1993
Mil-Std-271F	Requirements for Nondestructive Testing Methods. 1993
Mil-Std-410E	Nondestructive Testing Personnel Qualifications and Certifications. 1991
MIL-HDBK-728/1	Nondestructive Testing. 1985
MIL-HDBK-728/4A	Magnetic Particle Testing. 1993
OTHER PUBLICATIONS	
SNT-TC-1A	American Society for Nondestructive Testing. Recommended Practice . 1992 (Personnel Qualification and Certification in Nondestructive Testing and Recommended Training Courses) Note: Updated every 4 years - 1996 edition due in early 1997.
ATA No. 105	Air Transport Association of America. Guidelines for Training and Qualifying Personnel in Nondestructive Testing Methods, (Revision 4 1993)
ASM Handbook, Volume 17	Nondestructive Evaluation and Quality Control. 1989

5-45. PREPARATION OF SURFACE.

a. Remove protective coatings according to the manufacturer's instructions if necessary. Unless otherwise specified, magnetic particle examination should not be performed with coatings in place that could prevent the detection of surface defects in the ferro-magnetic substrate. Such coatings include paint or chromeplate thicker than 0.003 inch, or ferromagnetic coatings such as electroplated nickel thicker than 0.001 inch.

b. Parts should be free of grease, oil, rust, scale, or other substances which will interfere with the examination process. If required, clean by vapor degrease, solvent, or abrasive means per the manufacturer's instructions. Use abrasive cleaning only as necessary to completely remove scale or rust. Excessive blasting of parts can affect examination results.

c. Exercise extreme care to prevent any cleaning material or magnetic particles from becoming entrapped where they cannot be removed. This may require extracting components such as bushings, bearings, or inserts from assemblies before cleaning and magnetic particle examination.

d. A water-break-free surface is required for parts to be examined by water suspension methods. If the suspension completely wets the surface, this requirement is met.

e. Magnetic particle examination of assembled bearings is not recommended because the bearings are difficult to demagnetize. If a bearing cannot be removed, it should be protected from the magnetic particle examination materials and locally magnetized with a magnetic yoke to limit the magnetic field across the bearing.

5-46. METHODS OF EXAMINATION. Magnetic particle examination generally consists of: the application of magnetic particles; magnetization; determination of field strength; special examination techniques; and demagnetization and post-examination cleaning. Each of these steps will be described in the following paragraphs.

5-47. APPLICATION OF MAGNETIC PARTICLES. The magnetic particles used can be nonfluorescent or fluorescent (dependent on the examination required) and are applied suspended in a suitable substance. Fluorescent particles are preferred due to their higher sensitivity.

a. Wet Continuous Method. Unless otherwise specified, use only the wet continuous method. In the wet continuous method, the particle suspension is liberally applied to wet all surfaces of the part. The magnetizing current is applied at the instant the suspension is diverted from the part. Apply two shots of magnetizing current, each at least 1/2 second long.

(1) Wet suspensions of fluorescent particles, either in water or oil, should be used for most overhaul and in-service examinations except where the material, size, or shape of the part prohibits its use.

(2) Water, with a suitable rust inhibitor and wetting agent, may be used as a liquid vehicle, provided that magnetic examination equipment is designed for use or is satisfactorily converted for use with water.

b. Dry Continuous Method. This method is not recommended for use on aerospace components because of its lower sensitivity level.

c. Residual Magnetization Method. In this method, the part is magnetized and the magnetizing current is then cut off. If the amperage has been correctly calculated and quality indicator has verified the technique, then one shot will correctly magnetize the part. The magnetic particles are applied to the part after the magnetization. This method is dependent upon the retentiveness of the part, the strength of the applied field, the direction of magnetization, and the shape of the part.

5-48. MAGNETIZATION.

a. Circular. Circular magnetization is induced in the part by the central-conductor method or the direct-contact method. (See figure 5-11.)

(1) Indirect Induction (central-conductor method). Pass the current through a central conductor that passes through the part. When several small parts are examined at one time, provide sufficient space between each piece to permit satisfactory coverage (with particles), magnetization, and examination.

(2) Direct Induction (contact method). Pass current through the part mounted horizontally between contact plates. As an example, circular magnetization of a round steel bar would be produced by placing the ends of the steel bar between the heads of the magnetic inspection machine and passing a current through the bars. Magnetic particles applied either during or after passage of the current, or after passage of the current in magnetically-retentive steels, would disclose discontinuities parallel to the axis of the bar.

NOTE: Exercise extreme caution to prevent burning of the part at the electrode contact areas. Some causes of overheating and arcing are: insufficient contact area, insufficient contact pressure, dirty or coated contact areas, electrode removal during current flow, and too high an amperage setting.

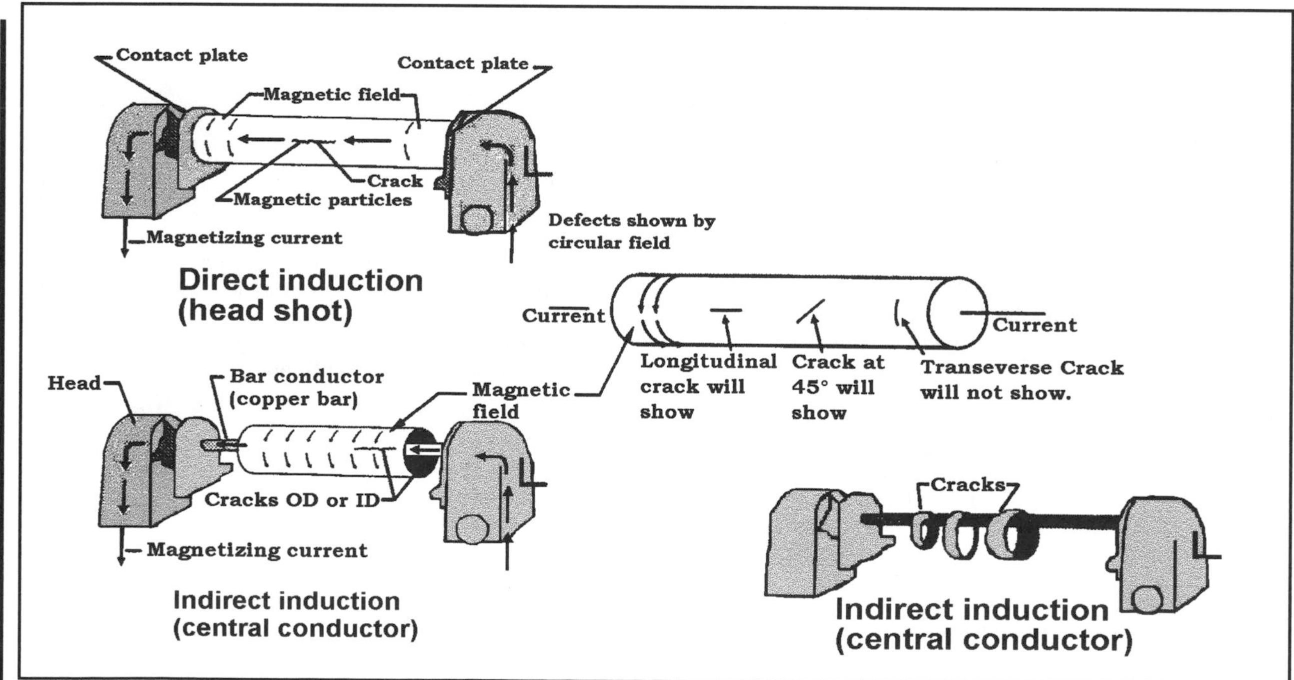

FIGURE 5-11. Circular magnetization.

b. Longitudinal. Longitudinal magnetization is induced in a part by placing the part in a strong magnetic field, such as the center of a coil or between the poles of an electromagnetic yoke. (See figure 5-12.) When using a coil, optimum results are obtained when the following conditions are met.

(1) The part to be examined is at least twice as long as it is wide.

(2) The long axis of the part is parallel to the axis of the coil opening.

(3) The area of the coil opening is at least 10 times the cross-sectional areas of the part.

(4) The part is positioned against the inner wall of the coil.

(5) Three to five turns are employed for hand-held coils formed with cables.

(6) For the 10-to-1 fill factor, the effective region of inspection is 1 coil radius on either side of the coil with 10 percent overlap. (Refer to ASTME-1444.)

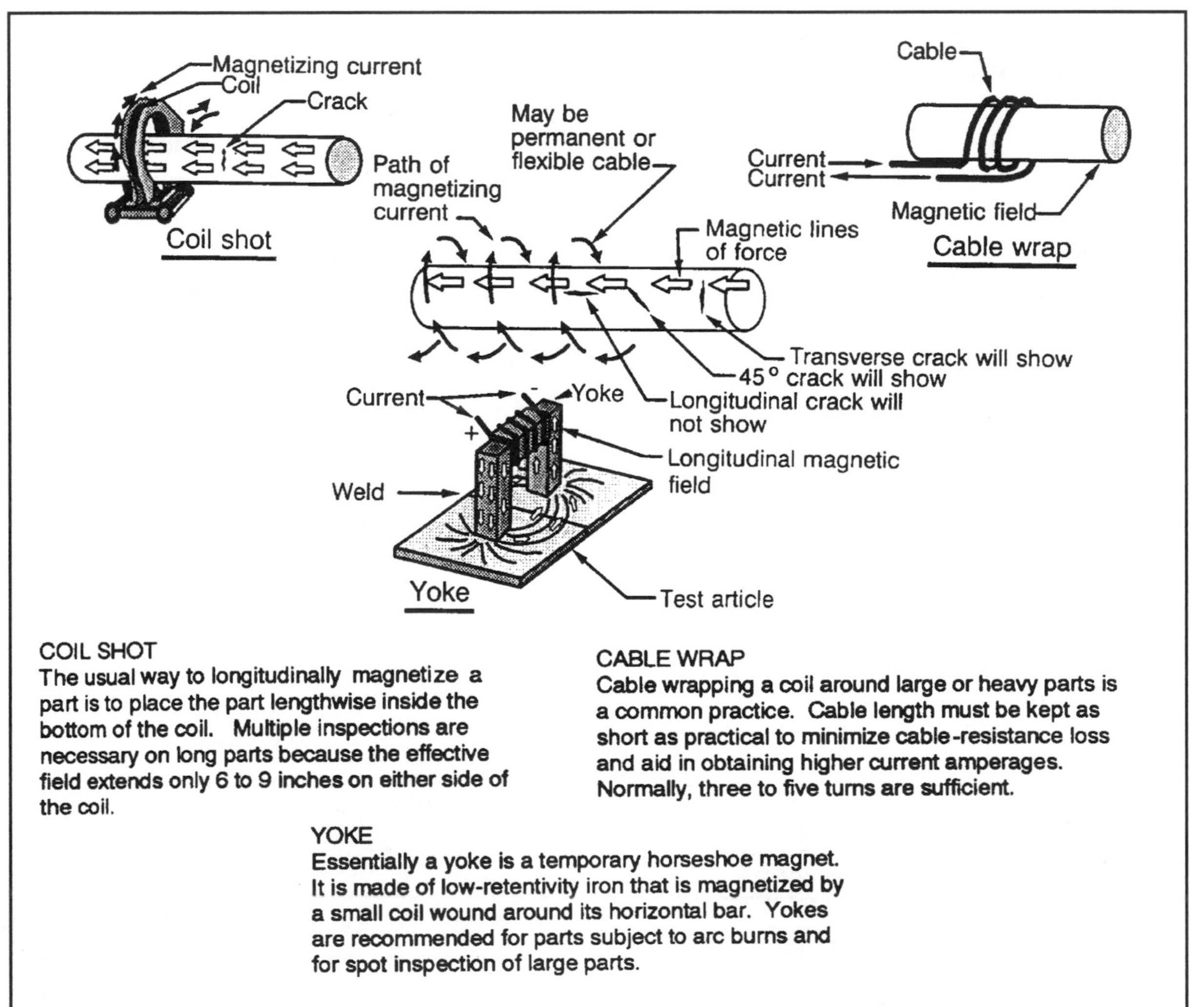
Magnetizing current
Coil
Crack
Coil shot
Path of magnetizing current
May be permanent or flexible cable
Magnetic lines of force
Cable
Current
Current
Magnetic field
Cable wrap
Transverse crack will show
45° crack will show
Longitudinal crack will not show
Longitudinal magnetic field
Current
Yoke
Weld
Yoke
Test article
COIL SHOT
The usual way to longitudinally magnetize a part is to place the part lengthwise inside the bottom of the coil. Multiple inspections are necessary on long parts because the effective field extends only 6 to 9 inches on either side of the coil.
CABLE WRAP
Cable wrapping a coil around large or heavy parts is a common practice. Cable length must be kept as short as practical to minimize cable-resistance loss and aid in obtaining higher current amperages. Normally, three to five turns are sufficient.
YOKE
Essentially a yoke is a temporary horseshoe magnet. It is made of low-retentivity iron that is magnetized by a small coil wound around its horizontal bar. Yokes are recommended for parts subject to arc burns and for spot inspection of large parts.

FIGURE 5-12. Longitudinal magnetization.

(7) The intensity of the longitudinal shots is kept just below the level at which leakage fields develop across sharp changes of section, such as radii under bolt heads, threads, and other sharp angles in parts. This does not apply when checking chrome-plated parts for grinding cracks.

(a) For example, longitudinal magnetization of a round steel bar would be produced by placing the DC coil around the bar. After application of the magnetic particles, either during or subsequent to magnetization, discontinuities perpendicular to the longitudinal axis of the bar would be disclosed.

(b) When a yoke is used, the portion of the part between the ends of the yoke completes the path of the magnetic lines of force. This results in a magnetic field between the points of contact.

c. Permanent Magnets and Electromagnetic Yoke. The stability of the magnetic field generated by permanent magnets requires some agitation of the oxide particles within the field. The wet method is considered most satisfactory. Use a well-agitated plastic squirt bottle for the most effective application of the magnetic particle suspension. When the direction of possible cracks in a suspect area is not known, or would not necessarily be normal to the lines of force between the poles of the magnet, reposition the magnet to the best advantage and recheck. Usually, two shots, 90 degrees apart are required. The part must be demagnetized between each magnetization when the field direction is changed unless the next shot is at least 10 percent stronger than the previous shot, if this is the case demagnetization is not necessary.

5-49. DETERMINATION OF FIELD STRENGTH. Factors such as part size, shape, magnetic properties of the material, and the method of magnetization will affect the field strength induced within a part by a given applied magnetizing force. The factors vary considerably, making it difficult to establish rules for magnetizing during examination. Technique requirements are best determined on actual parts having known defects.

a. A magnetization indicator, such as a Quantitative Quality Indicator (QQI), should be used to verify that adequate magnetic flux strength is being used. It effectively indicates the internally-induced field, the field direction, and the quality of particle suspension during magnetization.

b. The level of magnetization required for detection of service-related defects in most cases can be lower than that required for material and manufacturing control. Contact the manufacturer for correct specifications.

NOTE: If the examination must be performed with less current than is desired because of part size or equipment limitations, the lower field strength can be partially accommodated by reducing the area of examination for each magnetization, or the examination can be supplemented by using electromagnetic yokes. Examine only 4 inches on either side of a coil instead of 6, or apply additional magnetization around the periphery of a hollow cylinder when using an internal conductor.

5-50. SPECIAL EXAMINATION TECHNIQUES.

a. Magnetic Rubber. Magnetic rubber formulations using finely divided magnetic particles in a silicone rubber base are used for the inspection of screw, bolt, or other bore holes, which are not easily accessible. The liquid silicone rubber mixture is poured into holes in magnetic parts to be inspected.

Curing time for silicone rubbers varies from about 30 minutes and up depending upon the particular silicone rubber, the catalyst, and the amount of catalyst used to produce the curing reaction.

b. Curing. While curing is taking place, the insides of the hole must be maintained in the required magnetized state. This can be accomplished using a permanent magnet, a DC yoke, an electromagnet, or some other suitable means. Whatever method of magnetization is used, the leakage fields at any discontinuities inside the holes must be maintained long enough to attract and hold in position the magnetic particles until a partial cure takes place. A two-step magnetizing procedure has been developed.

(1) The first magnetization is accomplished for a short time in one direction followed by a second at 90 degrees to the first for the same length of time. This procedure must be repeated for whatever period of time is needed until the cure prevents particle mobility. Magnetization in two directions 90 degrees apart ensures formation of indications at discontinuities in all directions inside the holes.

(2) After curing, the rubber plugs, which are exact replicas of the holes, are removed and visibly examined for indications which will appear as colored lines against the lighter colored background of the silicone rubber. Location of any discontinuities or other surface imperfections in the holes can be determined from the location of the indications on the plugs. The magnetic rubber inspection method is covered in detail in Air Force Technical Order 33B-1-1, section XI.

c. Critical Examination for Sharp Radii Parts. A critical examination is required for cracks in sharp radii; such as threaded parts, splines, gear teeth roots, and abrupt changes in sections, that cause obscuring and nonrelevant indications during normal examination practices. The procedure provided herein is the most sensitive method for detecting the early beginnings of in-service fatigue cracks in the sharp, internal radii of ferro-magnetic parts. Magnetic particle examination equipment may be used; however, alternating fields are not reliable to provide the necessary high level of residual magnetism. Optical aids are necessary to realize the maximum sensitivity provided by this magnetic particle procedure. Low-power (10x-30x) binocular microscopes are recommended. As a minimum, pocket magnifiers of 7 to 10 power may be used with the following procedure.

(1) Thoroughly clean the part at the sharp radii and fillets where soils, greases, and other contaminants tend to accumulate and at other places where they might be overlooked during a casual or hasty examination.

(2) The residual method should be used as an aid in particular problem areas, even though it is not considered the best practice in most of the instances. The conventional wet continuous methods should be used initially for overall examination and the residual technique should be applied only for supplemental, local examination of the sharp radii. It should not be applied except in those cases where nonrelevant indications have proven to be a problem in the initial examination.

(3) Methods of magnetization should be done according to standard procedures; however, alternating fields should not be used, and the level of magnetizing force imposed should usually be increased above the normal levels to ensure a higher residual field within the part.

(4) Following magnetization, apply particles in liquid suspension. The application should be liberal and in a manner to cause maximum particle buildup. Immersion of small parts such as rod end fittings in a container of suspension, which has just been stirred for about 30 seconds, is an excellent method.

(5) Check for the presence of particle accumulation in the sharp radii. It is necessary that the level of magnetization and the particle application result in the formation of nonrelevant indications. Lack of indications will require remagnetization to a higher level, more care in applying the particles, or both.

(6) Wash the parts in a clean suspension vehicle only enough to remove the weakly-held particle accumulations causing the nonrelevant indications. Particles at true cracks will be more strongly held and will persist if the washing is gently done. This can be accomplished by flowing or directing a stream of liquid vehicle over the part, or for a small component, by gently stirring in a container of the vehicle. Closely observe the removal of the nonrelevant particle accumulations in the region to be examined to avoid excessive washing. If washing is prolonged beyond the minimum needed to remove the nonrelevant indications, the small defect indications may also be washed away. A few trials will help to develop the best method and time required for washing.

(7) Check for crack indications with optical magnification and ample lighting. The smaller indications that are attainable by this procedure cannot be reliably seen or evaluated with the unaided eye.

5-51. DEMAGNETIZATION AND POST-EXAMINATION CLEANING. Parts should be magnetized longitudinally last before demagnetizing.

NOTE: Circular magnetism cannot be read with a field meter since it is an internal magnetic field. However, if the last shot, was a coil shot the meter can read it if a magnetic field is present.

a. Demagnetization. Demagnetize between successive magnetization of the same part, to allow finding defects in all directions, and whenever the residual magnetism interferes with the interpretation of the indications. Also, demagnetize all parts and materials after completion of magnetic particle examination. Test all parts at several locations and parts for residual magnetism of complex configuration at all significant changes in geometry. Repeat demagnetization if there is any appreciable deflection of the field indicator needle.

(1) AC method. Hold the part in the AC demagnetizing coils and then move the part slowly and steadily through the coils and approximately 3 to 4 feet past the coils. Repeat this process until the part loses its residual magnetism. Rotate and tumble parts of complex configuration as they are passed through the coils.

(2) DC method. Place the part in the same relative position as when magnetized and apply reversing DC current. Gradually reduce the current to zero and repeat the process until the residual magnetic field is depleted.

b. Post-Examination Cleaning.

(1) When oil suspensions are used, solvent clean or remove the part until all magnetic particles and traces of oil are removed.

(2) When parts or materials have been examined using water suspension methods, completely remove the water by any suitable means, such as an air blast, to ensure that the parts are dried immediately after cleaning. Thoroughly rinse the part with a detergent-base cleaner until all magnetic particles are removed. Then rinse in a solution of water and rust inhibitor.

(3) For cadmium-plated parts an air-water vapor blast may be used to remove any remaining magnetic particle residue.

(4) After final cleaning and drying, use temporary protective coatings, when necessary, to prevent corrosion.

(5) After magnetic particle examination has been completed, restore any removed finishes according to the manufacturer's repair manual.

NOTE: Visible penetrant is often used interchangeably by NDI personnel with fluorescent penetrant. However, the chemical within most common red dye penetrants will neutralize the fluorescence of the chemicals used in that method. Therefore, a thorough cleaning of all magnetic particles is mandatory.

5-52.—5-59. [RESERVED.]

SECTION 5. PENETRANT INSPECTION

5-60. GENERAL. Penetrant inspection is used on nonporous metal and nonmetal components to find material discontinuities that are open to the surface and may not be evident to normal visual inspection. The part must be clean before performing a penetrant inspection. The basic purpose of penetrant inspection is to increase the visible contrast between a discontinuity and its background. This is accomplished by applying a liquid of high penetrating power that enters the surface opening of a discontinuity. Excess penetrant is removed and a developer material is then applied that draws the liquid from the suspected defect to reveal the discontinuity. The visual evidence of the suspected defect can then be seen either by a color contrast in normal visible white light or by fluorescence under black ultraviolet light. (See figure 5-13.)

a. The penetrant method does not depend upon ferro-magnetism like magnetic particle inspection, and the arrangement of the discontinuities is not a factor. The penetrant method is effective for detecting surface defects in nonmagnetic metals and in a variety of nonmetallic materials. Penetrant inspection is also used to inspect items made from ferromagnetic steels and its sensitivity is generally greater than that of magnetic particle inspection. Penetrant inspection is superior to visual inspection but not as sensitive as other advanced forms of tests for detection of in-service surface cracks.

b. The major limitations of the penetrant inspection is that it can detect only those discontinuities that are open to the surface; some other method must be used for detecting subsurface defects. Surface roughness or porosity can limit the use of liquid penetrants. Such surfaces can produce excessive background indications and interfere with the inspection. Penetrant inspection can be used on most airframe parts and assemblies accessible to its application. The basic steps to perform penetrant inspections are briefly described in the following paragraphs.

5-61. EQUIPMENT USED IN THE PENETRANT INSPECTION PROCESS. Equipment varies from simple aerosol cans used in portable systems to fully automated computer-controlled systems. Whether fluorescent or visible penetrants are used, different penetrant bases are available but may require different cleaning methods. Water-washable penetrants can often be removed by a simple water washing process, whereas oil-base penetrants may require special solvents for removal. Some oil-base penetrants have emulsifiers, either added to the penetrant before it is applied or added afterwards, that allow water washing to be used. Developers used, can be applied either by a wet or dry bath. Therefore, each penetrant inspection process may require different cleaning facilities and procedures. (See table 5-3.)

5-62. BASIC STEPS TO PERFORM PENETRATION INSPECTION. Table 5-4 shows a general process, in the procedures flow sheet, for commonly used penetrant inspection processes. It is important to ensure that parts are thoroughly cleaned and dried before doing penetrant inspection. All surfaces to be inspected should be free of contaminants, paint, and other coatings that could prevent penetrant from entering discontinuities. Table 5-5 shows applications of various methods of precleaning for penetrant inspection.

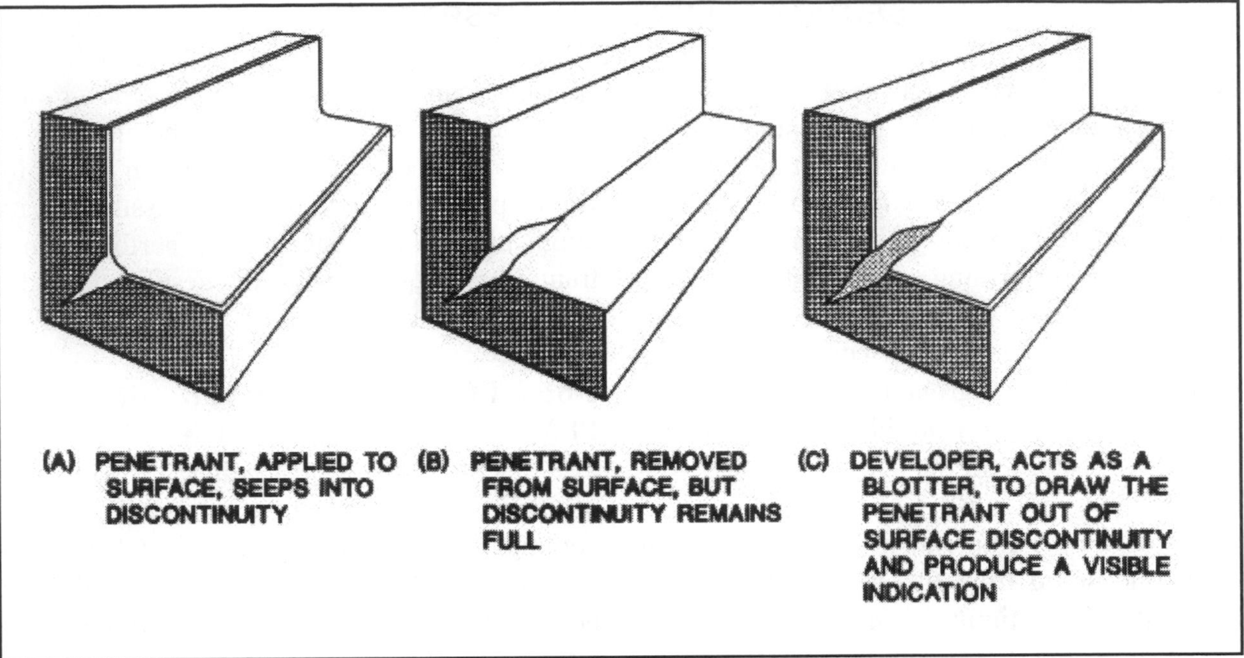

FIGURE 5-13. Penetrant and developer action.

TABLE 5-3. Classification of penetrant inspection materials covered by MIL-I-25135E.

PENETRANT SYSTEMS	DEVELOPERS	SOLVENT REMOVERS
Type I Fluorescent Dye Type II Visible Dye Type III Visible and Fluorescent Dye (dual mode)	Form a Dry Powder Form b Water Soluble Form c Water Suspendible Form d Nonaqueous Form e Specific Application	Class (1) Halogenated (chlorinated) Class (2) Nonhalogenated (nonchlorinated) Class (3) Specific Application
Method A Water Washable Method B Post emulsifiable, Lipophilic Method C Solvent Removable Method D Post Emulsifiable, Hydrophilic		
Sensitivity Level 1/2 Ultralow Sensitivity Level 1 Low Sensitivity Level 2 Medium Sensitivity Level 3 High Sensitivity Level 4 Ultrahigh		

TABLE 5-4. Fluorescent and visible penetrant inspection general processing procedures flowsheet.

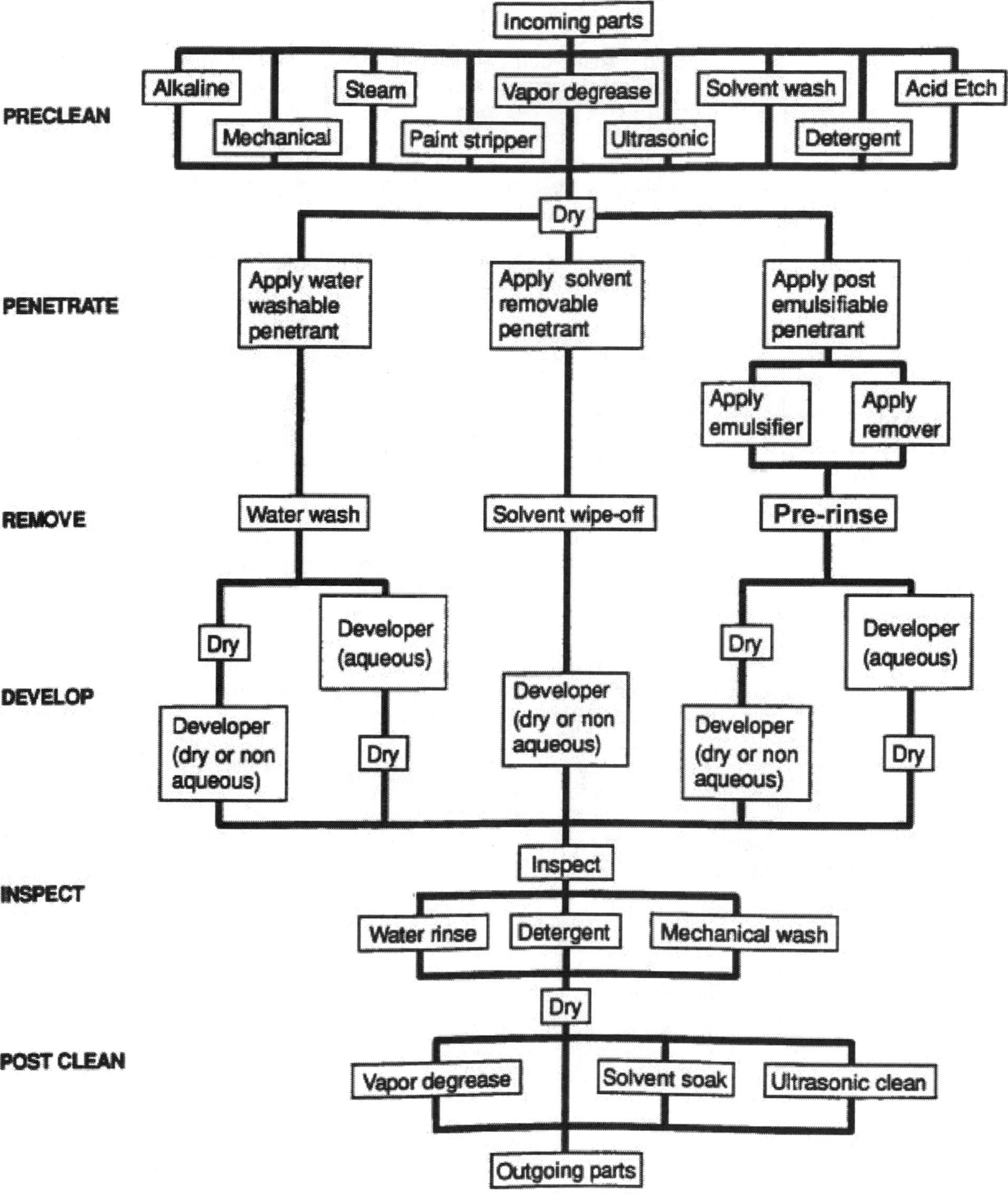

TABLE 5-5. Pre-cleaning methods for penetrant inspection.

METHOD	USE
Mechanical Methods	
Abrasive tumbling	Removing light scale, burrs, welding flux, braze stopoff, rust, casting mold, and core material; should not be used on soft metals such as aluminum, magnesium, or titanium.
Dry abrasive grit blasting	Removing light or heavy scale, flux, stopoff, rust, casting mold and core material, sprayed coatings, carbon deposits: In general, any brittle deposit. Can be fixed or portable (may peen metal over defect).
Wet abrasive grit blast	Same as dry except, where deposits are light, better surface and better control of dimensions are required.
Wire brushing	Removing light deposits of scale, flux, and stopoff (may mask defect by displacing metal).
High pressure water and steam	Ordinarily used with an alkaline cleaner or detergent; removing typical machine shop contamination, such as cutting oils, polishing compounds, grease, chips, and deposits from electrical discharge machining; used when surface finish must be maintained.
Ultrasonic cleaning	Ordinarily used with detergent and water or with a solvent; removing adhering shop contamination from large quantities of small parts.
Chemical Methods	
Alkaline cleaning	Removing braze stopoff, rust, scale, oils, greases, polishing material, and carbon deposits; ordinarily used on large articles where hand methods are too laborious; also used on aluminum for gross metal removal.
Acid cleaning	Strong solutions for removing heavy scale; mild solutions for light scale; weak (etching) solutions for removing lightly smeared metal.
Molten salt bath cleaning	Conditioning and removing heavy scale; not suitable for aluminum, magnesium, or titanium.
Solvent Methods	
Solvent wiping	Same as for vapor degreasing except a hand operation; may employ nonhalogenated (nonchlorinated) solvents; used for localized low-volume cleaning.

CAUTION: Improper cleaning methods can cause severe damage or degradation of the item being cleaned. Personnel must select and apply cleaning processes in accordance with aircraft, engine, propeller, or appliance manufacturer's recommendations.

5-63. CLEANERS AND APPLICATIONS. Use a cleaner to remove contaminants from parts prior to the application of penetrant inspection materials. After the inspection is completed, penetrant inspection material residues are removed. The following cleaners are commonly used during the penetrant inspection process.

a. Detergents. Detergent cleaners are water-based chemicals called surfactants, which surround and attach themselves to particles of contaminants allowing them to be washed away.

b. Solvents. Solvents dissolve contaminants such as oils, greases, waxes, sealants, paints, and general organic matter so they can easily be wiped away or absorbed on a cloth. They are also used to remove Method C penetrant material prior to developer application.

c. Alkalies. Alkaline cleaners are water solutions of chemicals that remove contaminants by chemical action or displacement rather than dissolving the contaminant.

d. Paint Removers. The general types of removers used for conventional paint coatings are solvent, bond release, and disintegrating.

e. Salt Baths. Molten salt baths are used in removing heavy, tightly-held scale and oxide from low alloy steels, nickel, and cobalt-base alloys, and some types of stainless steel. They cannot be used on aluminum, magnesium, or titanium alloys.

f. Acids. Solutions of acids or their salts are used to remove rust, scale, corrosion products, and dry shop contamination. The type of acid used and its concentration depends on the part material and contaminants to be removed.

g. Etching Chemicals. Etching chemicals contain a mixture of acids or alkalies plus inhibitors. They are used to remove a thin layer of surface material, usually caused by a mechanical process, that may seal or reduce the opening of any discontinuities. The type of etching solution used depends on the part material and condition.

h. Penetrant Application. Apply the penetrant by spraying, brushing, or by completely submerging the part in a container of penetrant. Wait the recommended amount of time after the penetrant has been applied to allow it to enter any discontinuities

(1) Removal of Excess Penetrant. Excess penetrant must be removed from the part's surface to prevent a loss of contrast between indications of discontinuities and the background during the inspection. Removal may require actually washing or spraying the part with a cleansing liquid, or may simply require wiping the part clean with a solvent-moistened cloth. The removal method is determined by the type of penetrant used.

(2) Drying. If removal of the excess penetrant involves water or other cleaning liquids, drying of the part may be required prior to developer application. When drying is required, the time can be decreased by using ovens or ventilation systems.

i. Developer Application. Apply developer after excess penetrant is removed and, where required, the surface is dried. Apply the developer in a thin uniform layer over the surface to be inspected. Developer acts like a blotter to assist the natural capillary action bleed-out of the penetrant from discontinuities and to spread the penetrant at discontinuity surface edges to enhance bleed-out indications. After the developer is applied, allow sufficient time for the penetrant to be drawn out of any discontinuities. Follow the manufacturer's recommendations.

j. Inspection for Discontinuities. After the penetrant has sufficiently developed, visually inspect the surface for indications from discontinuities. Evaluate each indication observed to determine if it is within acceptable limits. Visible penetrant inspection is performed in normal visible white light, whereas fluorescent penetrant inspection is performed in black (ultraviolet) light.

k. Post-Cleaning. Remove inspection material residues from parts after completion of penetrant inspection. This residue could interfere with subsequent part processing, or if left on some alloys, it could increase their susceptibility to hydrogen embrittlement, intergranular corrosion, and stress corrosion during service.

5-64. TECHNICAL STANDARDS. Two of the more generally accepted aerospace industry standards are the MIL-I-25135E, Inspection Materials, Penetrants (see table 5-6) and ASTM-E-1417. The penetrant materials specification (MIL-I-25135E) is used to procure penetrant materials and the process control specification (MIL-STD-6866) is used to establish minimum requirements for conducting a penetrant inspection. Table 5-6 provides a partial listing of commonly-accepted standards and specifications for penetrant inspection.

TABLE 5-6. Listing of commonly accepted standards and specifications for penetrant inspection.

NUMBER	TITLE
ASTM STANDARDS	
ASTM-E-165	Standard Practice for Liquid Penetrant Inspection Method
ASTM -E-270	Standard Definitions of Terms Relating to Liquid Penetrant Inspection
ASTM -E-1135	Standard Method for Comparing the Brightness of Fluorescent Penetrants
ASTM -E-1208	Standard Method for Fluorescent Liquid Penetrant Examination Using the Lipophilic Post-Emulsification Process
ASTM -E-1209	Standard Method for Fluorescent Penetrant Examination Using the Water Washable Process
ASTM -E-1210	Standard Method for Fluorescent Penetrant Examination Using the Hydrophilic Post-Emulsification Process
ASTM -E-1219	Standard Method for Fluorescent Penetrant Examination Using the Solvent Removable Process
ASTM -E-1220	Standard Method for Visible Penetrant Examination Using the Solvent Removable Method
ASTM -E-2512	Compatibility of Materials with Liquid Oxygen (Impact-Sensitivity Threshold Technique)
SAE-AMS SPECIFICATIONS	
AMS-2647	Fluorescent Penetrant Inspection - Aircraft and Engine Component Maintenance
US GOVERNMENT SPECIFICATIONS	
MIL-STD-271	Requirements for Nondestructive Testing
MIL-STD-410	Nondestructive Testing Personnel Qualifications and Certifications
MIL-STD-1907	Inspection, Liquid Penetrant and Magnetic Particle, Soundness Requirements for Materials, Parts and Welds
MIL-STD-6866	Inspection, Liquid Penetrant
MIL-STD-728/1	Nondestructive Testing
MIL-STD-728/3	Liquid Penetrant Testing
MIL-STD-25135E	Inspection Materials, Penetrants
QPL-25135	Qualified Products List of Materials Qualified Under MIL-I-25135
T.O. 33B-1-1	U.S. Air Force/Navy Technical Manual, Nondestructive Testing Methods
OTHER PUBLICATIONS	
SNT-TC-1A	Personnel Qualification and Certification in Nondestructive Testing and Recommended Training Courses
ATA No. 105	Guidelines for Training and Qualifying Personnel in Nondestructive Methods,
Metals Handbook, Ninth Edition, Volume 17	Nondestructive Evaluation, and Quality Control

5-65.—5-72. [RESERVED.]

SECTION 6. RADIOGRAPHY (X-RAY) INSPECTION

5-73. GENERAL. Radiography (x-ray) is an NDI method used to inspect material and components, using the concept of differential adsorption of penetrating radiation. Each specimen under evaluation will have differences in density, thickness, shapes, sizes, or absorption characteristics, thus absorbing different amounts of radiation. The unabsorbed radiation that passes through the part is recorded on film, fluorescent screens, or other radiation monitors. Indications of internal and external conditions will appear as variants of black/white/gray contrasts on exposed film, or variants of color on fluorescent screens. (See figure 5-14.)

5-74. LIMITATIONS. Compared to other nondestructive methods of inspection, radiography is expensive. Relatively large costs and space allocations are required for a radiographic laboratory. Costs can be reduced considerably when portable x-ray or gamma-ray sources are used in film radiography and space is required only for film processing and interpretation. Operating costs can be high because sometimes as much as 60 percent of the total inspection time is spent in setting up for radiography. With real-time radiography, operating costs are usually much lower, because setup times are shorter and there are no extra costs for processing or interpretation of film.

5-75. FILM OR PAPER RADIOGRAPHY. In film or paper radiography, a two-dimensional latent image from the projected radiation is produced on a sheet of film or paper that has been exposed to the unabsorbed radiation passing through the test piece. This technique requires subsequent development of the exposed film or paper so that the latent image becomes visible for viewing.

5-76. REAL-TIME RADIOGRAPHY. A two-dimensional image that can be immediately displayed on a viewing screen or television monitor. This technique converts unabsorbed radiation into an optical or electronic signal which can be viewed immediately or can be processed with electronic or video equipment.

5-77. ADVANTAGE OF REAL-TIME RADIOGRAPHY OVER FILM RADIOGRAPHY. The principal advantage of real-time radiography over film radiography is the opportunity to manipulate the test piece during radiographic inspection. This capability allows the inspection of internal mechanisms and enhances the detection of cracks and planar defects by allowing manipulation of the part to achieve the best orientation for flaw detection. Part manipulation during inspection also simplifies three-dimensional dynamic imaging for the determination of flaw location and size. In film radiography, depth parallel to the radiation beam is not recorded. Consequently, the position of a flaw within the volume of a test piece cannot be determined exactly with a single radiograph. To determine flaw location and size more exactly with film radiography, other film techniques; such as stereo-radiography, triangulation, or simply making two or more film exposures with the radiation beam being directed at the test piece from a different angle for each exposure, must be used.

5-78. COMPUTED TOMOGRAPHY (CT). CT is another important radiological technique with enhanced flaw detection and location capabilities. Unlike film and real-time radiography, CT involves the generation of cross-sectional views instead of a planar

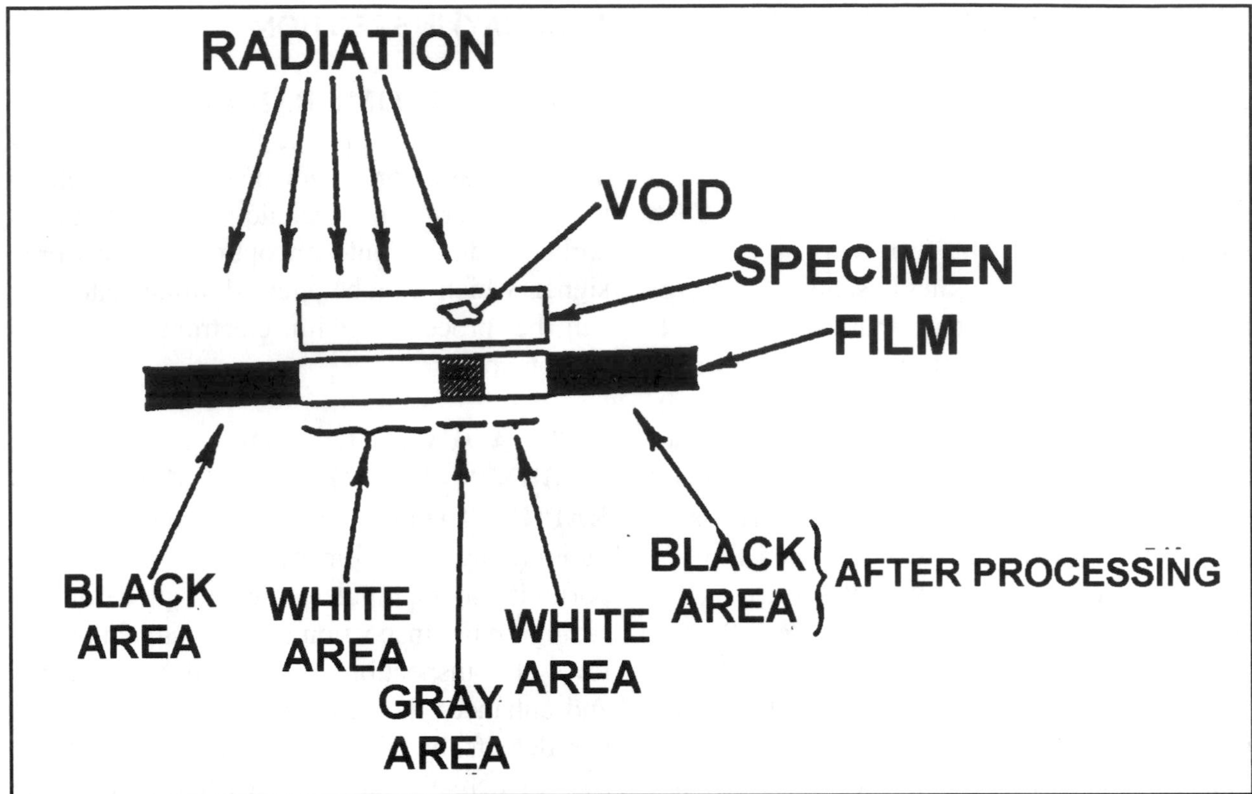

FIGURE 5-14. Radiography.

projection. The CT image is comparable to that obtained by making a radiograph of a physically sectioned thin planar slab from an object. This cross-sectional image is not obscured by overlying and underlying structures and is highly sensitive to small differences in relative density. Computed tomography images are also easier to interpret than radiographs.

5-79. USES OF RADIOGRAPHY. Radiography is used to detect the features of a component or assembly that exhibit a difference in thickness or density as compared to surrounding material. Large differences are more easily detected than small ones. In general, radiography can detect only those features that have an appreciable thickness in a direction along the axis of the radiation beam. Therefore, the ability of radiography to detect planar discontinuities, such as cracks, depends on proper orientation of the test piece during inspection. Discontinuities which have measurable thickness in all directions, such as voids and inclusions, can be detected as long as they are not too small in relation to section thickness. In general, features that exhibit a 2 percent or more difference in radiation adsorption compared to the surrounding material can be detected.

5-80. COMPARISON WITH OTHER NDI METHODS. Radiography and ultrasonic are the two generally-used, nondestructive inspection methods that can satisfactorily detect flaws that are completely internal and located well below the surface of the test part. Neither method is limited to the detection of specific types of internal flaws. However, radiography is more effective when the flaws are not planar, while ultrasonic is more effective when flaws are planar. In comparison to other generally-used NDI methods (e.g., magnetic particle, liquid penetrant, and eddy current inspection), radiography has the following advantages.

a. The ability to inspect for both internal and external flaws.

b. The ability to inspect covered or hidden parts or structures.

c. The ability to detect significant variations in composition.

d. Provides a permanent recording of raw inspection data.

5-81. FLAWS. Certain types of flaws are difficult to detect by radiography. Cracks cannot be detected unless they are essentially along the axis of the radiation beam. Tight cracks in thick sections may not be detected at all, even when properly oriented. Minute discontinuities such as: inclusions in wrought material, flakes, microporosity, and microfissures may not be detected unless they are sufficiently segregated to yield a detectable gross effect. Delaminations are nearly impossible to detect with radiography. Because of their unfavorable orientation, delaminations do not yield differences in adsorption that enable laminated areas to be distinguished from delaminated areas.

5-82. FIELD INSPECTION. The field inspection of thick sections can be a time-consuming process, because the effective radiation output of portable sources may require long exposure times of the radiographic film. This limits field usage to sources of lower activity that can be transported. The output of portable x-ray sources may also limit field inspection of thick sections, particularly if a portable x-ray tube is used. Portable x-ray tubes emit relatively low-energy (300 kev) radiation and are limited in the radiation output. Both of these characteristics of portable x-ray tubes combine to limit their application to the inspection of sections having the adsorption equivalent of 75 mm (3 inches) of steel maximum. Portable linear accelerators and betatrons that provide high-energy (> 1 MeV) x-rays can be used for the radiographic field inspection of thicker sections.

5-83. SAFETY. Radiographic safety requirements can be obtained from; the OEM's manual, FAA requirements, cognizant FAA ACO engineers, and radiation safety organizations such as the Nuclear Regulatory Commission (NRC). Information in radiation safety publications can be used as a guide to ensure that radiation exposure of personnel involved in radiographic operations is limited to safe levels, and to afford protection for the general public.

5-84.—5-88. [RESERVED.]

SECTION 7. ULTRASONIC INSPECTION

5-89. GENERAL. Ultrasonic inspection is an NDI technique that uses sound energy moving through the test specimen to detect flaws. The sound energy passing through the specimen will be displayed on a Cathode Ray Tube (CRT), a Liquid Crystal Display (LCD) computer data program, or video/camera medium. Indications of the front and back surface and internal/external conditions will appear as vertical signals on the CRT screen or nodes of data in the computer test program. There are three types of display patterns; "A" scan, "B" scan, and "C" scan. Each scan provides a different picture or view of the specimen being tested. (See figure 5-15.)

5-90. SOUND REFLECTION. The amount of reflection that occurs when a sound wave strikes an interface depends largely on the physical state of the materials forming the interface and to a lesser extent on the specific physical properties of the material. For example: sound waves are almost completely reflected at metal/gas interfaces; and partial reflection occurs at metal/liquid or metal/solid interfaces.

5-91. ULTRASONIC INSPECTION TECHNIQUES. Two basic ultrasonic inspection techniques are employed: pulse-echo and through-transmission. (See figure 5-16.)

a. Pulse-Echo Inspection. This process uses a transducer to both transmit and receive the ultrasonic pulse. The received ultrasonic pulses are separated by the time it takes the sound to reach the different surfaces from which it is reflected. The size (amplitude) of a reflection is related to the size of the reflecting surface. The pulse-echo ultrasonic response pattern is analyzed on the basis of signal amplitude and separation.

b. Through-Transmission Inspection. This inspection employs two transducers, one to generate and a second to receive the ultrasound. A defect in the sound path between the two transducers will interrupt the sound transmission. The magnitude (the change in the sound pulse amplitude) of the interruption is used to evaluate test results. Through-transmission inspection is less sensitive to small defects than is pulse-echo inspection.

5-92. FLAW DETECTION. Ultrasonic inspection can easily detect flaws that produce reflective interfaces. Ultrasonic inspection is used to detect surface and subsurface discontinuities, such as: cracks, shrinkage cavities, bursts, flakes, pores, delaminations, and porosity. It is also used to measure material thickness and to inspect bonded structure for bonding voids. Ultrasonic inspection can be performed on raw material, billets, finished, and semi-finished materials, welds, and in-service assembled or disassembled parts. Inclusions and other nonhomogeneous areas can also be detected if they cause partial reflection or scattering of the ultrasonic sound waves or produce some other detectable effect on the ultrasonic sound waves. Ultrasonic inspection is one of the more widely-used methods of NDI.

5-93. BASIC EQUIPMENT. Most ultrasonic inspection systems include the following basic equipment; portable instruments (frequency range 0.5 to 15 MHz), transducers (longitudinal and shear wave), positioners, reference standards, and couplant.

a. Ultrasonic Instruments. A portable, battery-powered ultrasonic instrument is used for field inspection of airplane structure. (See figure 5-17.) The instrument generates an

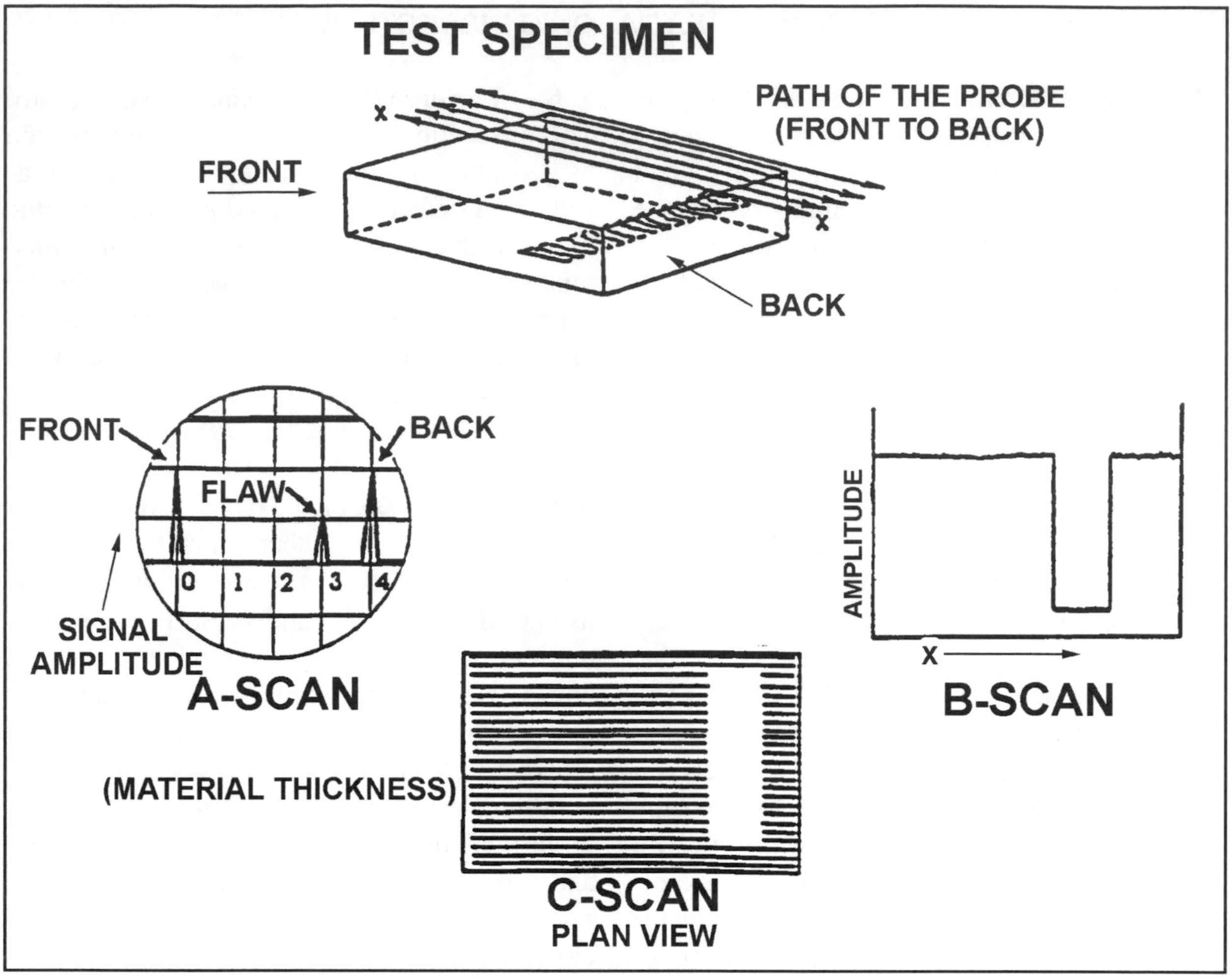

TEST SPECIMEN
PATH OF THE PROBE (FRONT TO BACK)
X
FRONT
X
BACK
FRONT
BACK
FLAW
0 1 2 3 4
SIGNAL AMPLITUDE
A-SCAN
(MATERIAL THICKNESS)
C-SCAN
PLAN VIEW
AMPLITUDE
X
B-SCAN

FIGURE 5-15. Ultrasound.

Receive
Generate
Generate and receive
Pulse-echo
Sound path
Receive
Generate
Generate
Receive
Through-transmission

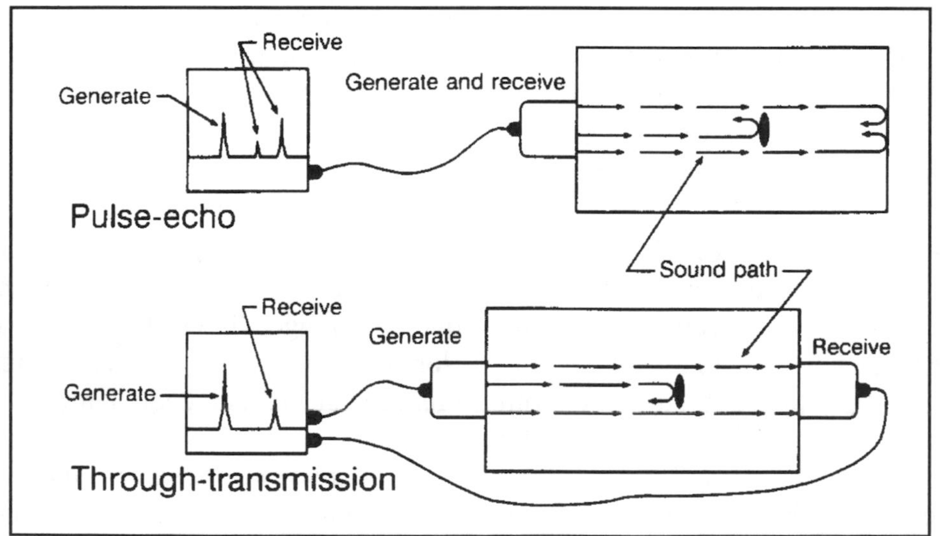

FIGURE 5-16. Pulse-echo and through-transmission ultrasonic inspection techniques.

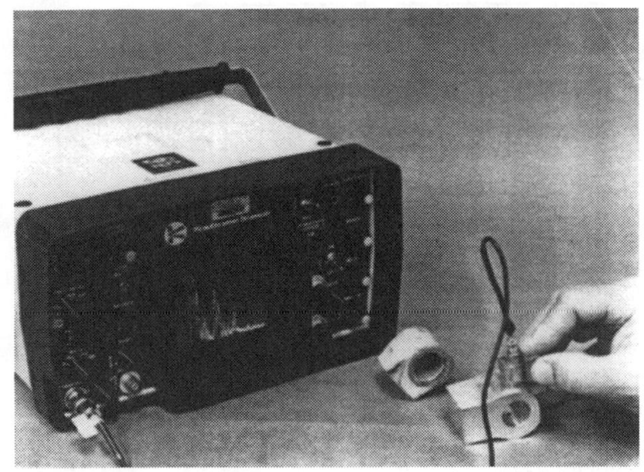

FIGURE 5-17. Typical portable ultrasonic inspection instrument.

ultrasonic pulse, detects and amplifies the returning echo, and displays the detected signal on a cathode ray tube or similar display. Piezoelectric transducers produce longitudinal or shear waves, which are the most commonly used wave forms for aircraft structural inspection.

b. Positioning Fixtures. To direct ultrasound at a particular angle, or to couple it into an irregular surface, transducer positioning fixtures and sound-coupling shoes are employed. (See figure 5-18.) Shoes are made of a plastic material that has the necessary sound-transmitting characteristics. Positioning fixtures are used to locate the transducer at a prescribed point and can increase the sensitivity of the inspection. (See figure 5-19.) If a transducer shoe or positioning fixture is required, the inspection procedure will give a detailed description of the shoe or fixture.

c. Reference Standards. Reference standards are used to calibrate the ultrasonic instrument (see figure 5-20), reference standards serve two purposes to provide an ultrasonic response pattern that is related to the part being inspected, and to establish the required inspection sensitivity. To obtain a representative response pattern, the reference standard configuration is the same as that of the test structure, or is a configuration that provides an ultrasonic response pattern representative of the test structure. The reference standard contains a simulated defect (notch) that is positioned to provide a calibration signal representative of the expected defect. The notch size is chosen to establish inspection sensitivity (response to the expected defect size). The inspection procedure gives a detailed description of the required reference standard.

d. Couplants. Inspection with ultrasonics is limited to the part in contact with the transducer. A layer of couplant is required to couple the transducer to the test piece because ultrasonic energy will not travel through air. Some typical couplants used are: water, glycerin, motor oils, and grease.

5-94. INSPECTION OF BONDED STRUCTURES. Ultrasonic inspection is finding increasing application in aircraft bonded construction and repair. Detailed techniques for specific bonded structures should be obtained from the OEM's manuals, or FAA requirements. In addition, further information on the operation of specific instruments should be obtained from the applicable equipment manufacturer manuals.

a. Types of Bonded Structures. Many configurations and types of bonded structures are in use in aircraft. All of these variations complicate the application of ultrasonic inspections. An inspection method that works well on one part or one area of the part may not be applicable for different parts or areas of the same part. Some of the variables in the types of bonded structures are as follows.

(1) Top skin material is made from different materials and thickness.

(2) Different types and thickness of adhesives are used in bonded structures.

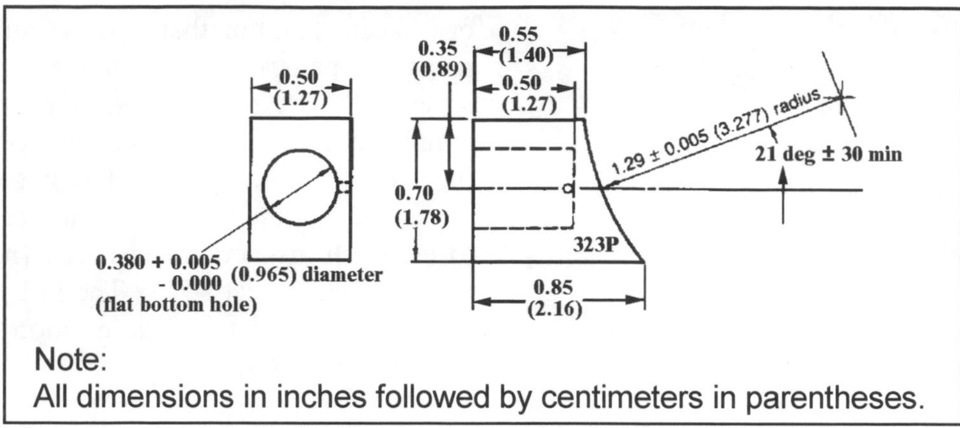

FIGURE 5-18. Example of position fixture and shoe.

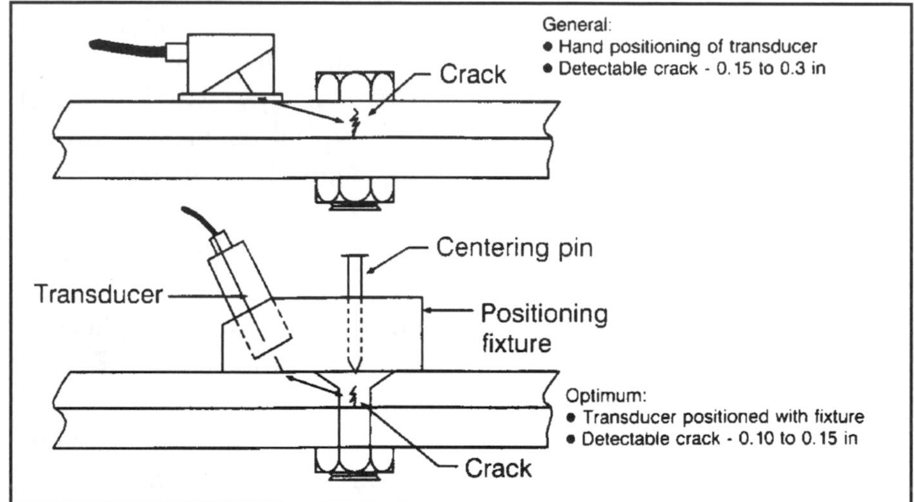

FIGURE 5-19. Example of the use if a transducer positioning fixture.

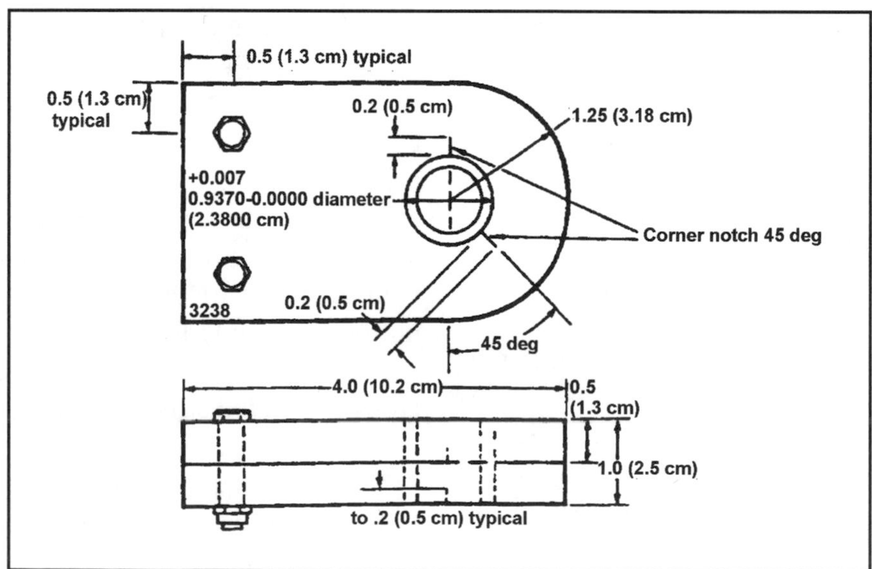

FIGURE 5-20. Example of a typical reference standard.

(3) Underlying structures contain differences in; core material, cell size, thickness, and height, back skin material and thickness, doublers (material and thickness), closure member attachments, foam adhesive, steps in skins, internal ribs, and laminates (number of layers, layer thickness, and layer material).

(4) The top only or top and bottom skin of a bonded structure may be accessible.

b. Application of Ultrasonic Inspection. Application to bonded structures must be examined in detail because of the many inspection methods and structural configurations. The advantages and limitations of each inspection method should be considered, and reference standards (representative of the structure to be inspected) should be ultrasonically inspected to verify proposed techniques.

c. Internal Configuration. Complete information on the internal configuration of the bonded test part must be obtained by the inspector. Drawings should be reviewed, and when necessary, radiographs of the test part should be taken. Knowledge of details such as the location and boundaries of doublers, ribs, etc., is required for valid interpretation of ultrasonic inspection results. The boundaries of internal details should be marked on the test part using a grease pen or other easily removable marking.

d. Reference Standards. Standards can be a duplicate of the test part except for the controlled areas of unbond. As an option, simple test specimens, which represent the varied areas of the test part and contain controlled areas of unbond, can be used. Reference standards must meet the following requirements.

(1) The reference standard must be similar to the test part regarding material, geometry, and thickness. This includes containing: closure members, core splices, stepped skins, and internal ribs similar to the test part if bonded areas over or surrounding these details are to be inspected.

(2) The reference standard must contain bonds of good quality except for controlled areas of unbond fabricated as explained below.

(3) The reference standard must be bonded using the adhesive and cure cycle prescribed for the test part.

e. Types of Defects. Defects can be separated into five general types to represent the various areas of bonded sandwich and laminate structures as follows:

(1) Typc I. Unbonds or voids in an outer skin-to-adhesive interface.

(2) Type II. Unbonds or voids at the adhesive-to-core interface.

(3) Type III. Voids between layers of a laminate.

(4) Type IV. Voids in foam adhesive or unbonds between the adhesive and a closure member at core-to-closure member joints.

(5) Type V. Water in the core.

f. Fabrication of NDI Reference Standards. Every ultrasonic test unit should have sample materials that contain unbonds equal to the sizes of the minimum rejectable unbonds for the test parts. Information on minimum rejectable unbond sizes for test parts should be obtained from the OEM's manuals, FAA requirements, or the cognizant FAA Aircraft Certification Office (ACO) engineer. One or more of the following techniques can be used in fabricating reference defects; however, since bonding materials vary, some of the methods may not work with certain materials.

(1) Standards for Types I, II, III, and IV unbonds can be prepared by placing discs of 0.006 inch thick (maximum) Teflon sheets over the adhesive in the areas selected for unbonds. For Type II unbonds, the Teflon is placed between the core and adhesive. The components of the standard are assembled and the assembly is then cured.

(2) Types I, II, and III standards can also be produced by cutting flat-bottomed holes of a diameter equal to the diameter of the unbonds to be produced. The holes are cut from the back sides of bonded specimens, and the depths are controlled to produce air gaps at the applicable interfaces. When using this method, patch plates can be bonded to the rear of the reference standard to cover and seal each hole.

(3) Type II standards can be produced by locally undercutting (before assembly) the surface of the core to the desired size unbond. The depth of the undercut should be sufficient to prevent adhesive flow causing bonds between the undercut core and the skin.

(4) Type IV standards can be produced by removing the adhesive in selected areas prior to assembly.

(5) Type V standards can be produced by drilling small holes in the back of the standard and injecting varying amounts of water into the cells with a hypodermic needle. The small holes can then be sealed with a small amount of water-resistant adhesive.

g. Inspection Coverage. Examples of several different configurations of bonded structure along with suggested inspection coverages with standard ultrasonic test instruments are shown in figure 5-21. In many cases, access limitations will not permit application of the suggested inspections in all of the areas shown. The inspection coverages and suggested methods contained in figure 5-21 and table 5-7 are for reference only. Details of the inspection coverage and inspections for a particular assembly should be obtained from the OEM's manuals, or other FAA-approved requirements.

h. Inspection Methods. Table 5-8 lists the various inspection methods for bonded structures along with advantages and disadvantages of each inspection method.

5-95. BOND TESTING INSTRUMENTS. Standard ultrasonic inspection instruments can be used for bond testing as previously noted; however, a wide variety of bond testing instruments are available for adaptation to specific bonded structure inspection problems.

a. General Principle. Two basic operating principles are used by a variety of bond testers for single-sided bond inspection.

(1) Ultrasonic resonance. Sound waves from a resonant transducer are transmitted into and received from a structure. A disbond in the structure will alter the sound wave characteristics, which in turn affect the transducer impedance.

(2) Mechanical impedance. Low-frequency, pulsed ultrasonic energy is generated into a structure. Through ultrasonic mechanical vibration of the structure, the impedance or stiffness of the structure is measured, analyzed, and displayed by the instrumentation.

b. Operation. In general, operation of the adhesive bond test instruments noted is similar. The test probe is moved over the surface in smooth overlapping strokes. The direction of the stroke with regard to the surface is generally immaterial; however, when using the Sondicator models, the direction of the stroke becomes critical when the test probe is

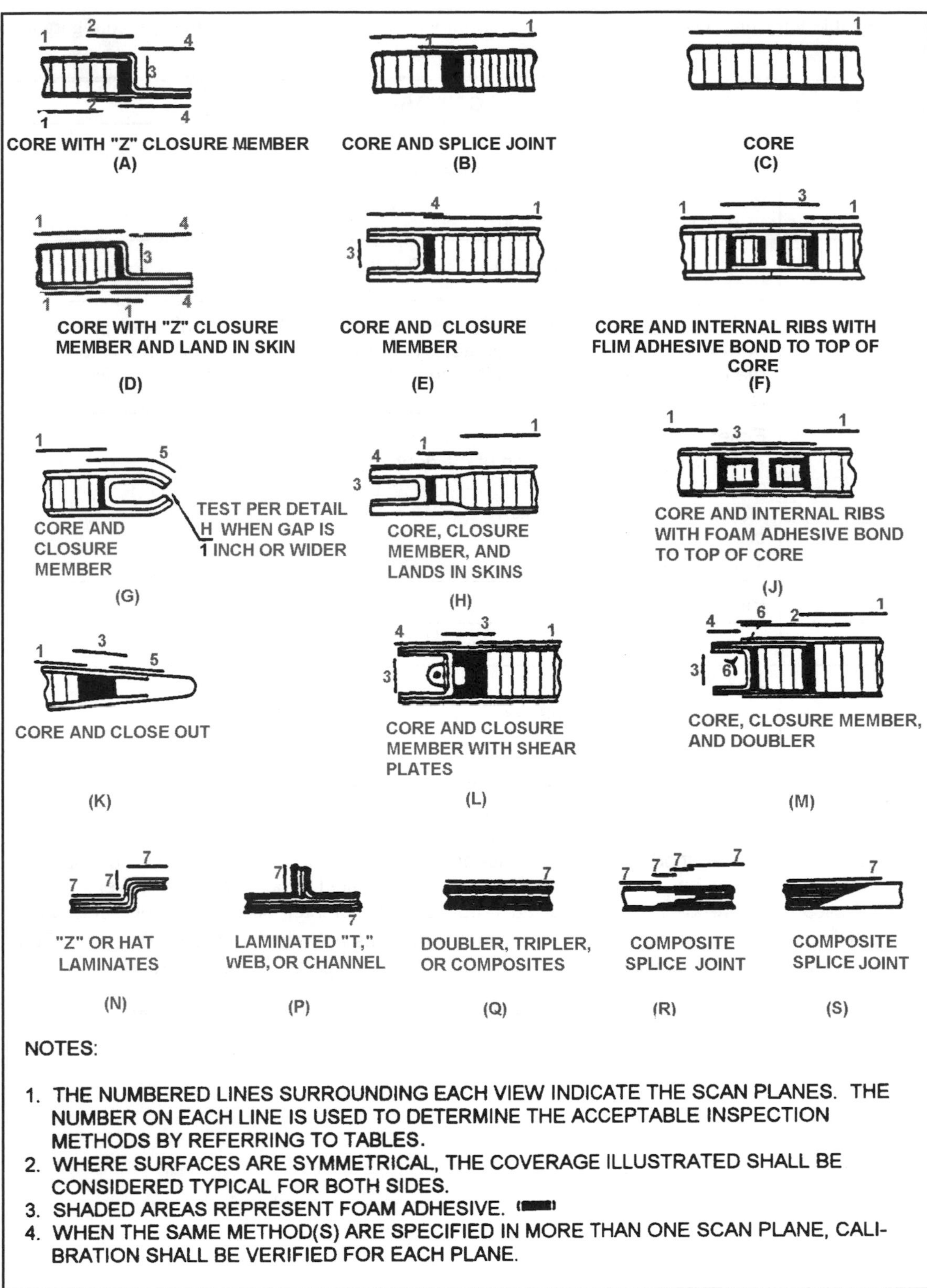

NOTES:

1. THE NUMBERED LINES SURROUNDING EACH VIEW INDICATE THE SCAN PLANES. THE NUMBER ON EACH LINE IS USED TO DETERMINE THE ACCEPTABLE INSPECTION METHODS BY REFERRING TO TABLES.
2. WHERE SURFACES ARE SYMMETRICAL, THE COVERAGE ILLUSTRATED SHALL BE CONSIDERED TYPICAL FOR BOTH SIDES.
3. SHADED AREAS REPRESENT FOAM ADHESIVE.
4. WHEN THE SAME METHOD(S) ARE SPECIFIED IN MORE THAN ONE SCAN PLANE, CALIBRATION SHALL BE VERIFIED FOR EACH PLANE.

FIGURE 5-21. Examples of bonded structure configurations and suggested inspection coverage.

TABLE 5-7. Acceptable ultrasonic inspection methods associated with the example bonded structure configurations shown in figure 5-21.

NUMBER	ACCEPTABLE METHODS
1	Either (a) Pulse-echo straight or angle beam, on each side or (b) Through-transmission.
2	Pulse-echo, straight beam, on each skin.
3	Refer to 1 for methods. If all these methods fail to have sufficient penetration power to detect reference defects in the reference standard, then the ringing method, applied from both sides, should be used. Otherwise, the ringing method is unacceptable.
4	Either (a) Ringing, on each skin of the doubler. or (b) Through-transmission or (c) Damping.
5	Ringing.
6	Through-transmission. Dotted Line represents beam direction.
7	Either (a) Through-transmission or (b) Damping.

NOTE

A variety of ultrasonic testing methods and instruments are available for adaptation to specific inspection problems. Other bond inspection instruments can be used if detailed procedures are developed and proven on the applicable reference standards for each configuration of interest. Some representative instruments, which can be used for the inspection of bonded structures are; the Sondicator, Harmonic Bond Tester, Acoustic Flaw Detector, Audible Bond Tester, Fokker Bond Tester, 210 Bond Tester, and Bondascope 2100.

TABLE 5-8. Ultrasonic inspection methods for bonded structures.

	INSPECTION METHOD			
	THROUGH-TRANSMISSION	PULSE-ECHO	RINGING	DAMPING
Advantages	Applicable to structures with either thick or thin facing sheets. Applicable to structures with multiple layers bonded over honeycomb core. Detects unbonds on either side Detects broken, crushed, and corroded core. In some cases water in core can be detected.	Applicable to structures with either thick or thin facing sheets. Determines which side is unbonded. Detects small unbonds. Detects broken, crushed, and corroded core. In some cases water in core can be detected.	Applicable to complex shapes. Detects small near surface unbonds (larger than diameter of search unit).	Applicable to structures with either thick or thin facing sheets. Applicable to multiple-layered (more than two layers) structures. Detects unbonds on either side. Detects small unbonds (larger than diameter of receiving search unit).
Disadvantages	Access to both sides of part is required. Does not determine layer position of unbonds. Alignment of search units is critical. Couplant is required. Inspection rate is slow.	Inspection from both sides required, does not detect far side unbonds. Applicable only to skin-to-honeycomb core structures. Reduced effectiveness on structures with multiple skins over honeycomb core. Couplant required.	Applicable only to near surface unbonds, works best on unbonds between top sheet and adhesive, may miss other unbonds. Reduced effectiveness on thick skins. Couplant required.	Applicable only to doublers and laminate-type structures. Access to both sides required. Does not determine layer positions of unbonds. Couplant required.

operated near a surface edge. Edge effects on vibration paths give a test reading that may be misinterpreted. To avoid edge effects, the test probe should be moved so that the inspection path follows the surface edge, giving a constant edge for the test probe to inspect. Edge effects are more pronounced in thicker material. To interpret meter readings correctly, the operator should determine whether there are variations in the thickness of the material.

c. Probe Sending Signal. With the exception of the Sondicator models, the test probes of the testers emit a sending signal that radiates in a full circle. The sending signal of the Sondicator probe travels from one transducer tip to the other. For this reason, the test probe should be held so that the transducer tips are at right angles to the inspection path. When inspecting honeycomb panels with a Sondicator model, the transducer tips should be moved consistently in the direction of the ribbon of the honeycomb or at right angles to the ribbon so that a constant subsurface is presented.

5-96. THICKNESS MEASUREMENTS. Ultrasonic inspection methods can be used for measurement of material thickness in aircraft parts and structures.

a. Applications. Ultrasonic thickness measurements are used for many applications, such as: checking part thickness when access to the back side is not available; checking large panels in interior areas where a conventional micrometer cannot reach; and in maintenance inspections for checking thickness loss due to wear and/or corrosion.

b. Pulse-Echo Method. The most commonly used ultrasonic thickness measurement method. The ultrasonic instrument measures time between the initial front and back surface signals or subsequent multiple back reflection signals. Since the velocity for a given material is a constant, the time between these signals is directly proportional to the thickness. Calibration procedures are used to obtain direct readout of test part thickness.

c. Thickness Measurement Instrument Types. Pulse-echo instruments designed exclusively for thickness measurements are generally used in lieu of conventional pulse-echo instruments; however, some conventional pulse-echo instruments also have direct thickness measurement capabilities. Conventional pulse-echo instruments without direct thickness measuring capabilities can also be used for measuring thickness by using special procedures.

d. Thickness Measurement Ranges. Dependent upon the instrument used and the material under test, material thickness from 0.005 inches to 20 inches (or more) can be measured with pulse-echo instruments designed specifically for thickness measuring.

5-97. LEAK TESTING. The flow of a pressurized gas through a leak produces sound of both sonic and ultrasonic frequencies. If the gas leak is large, the sonic frequency sound it produces can probably be detected with the ear or with such instruments as stethoscopes or microphones; however, the ear and these instruments have limited ability to detect and locate small leaks. Ultrasonic leak detectors are frequently used to detect leaks that cannot be detected by the above methods, because they are very sensitive to ultrasonic energy and, under most conditions, background noise at other frequencies does not affect them.

a. Standard Method. A standard method of testing for leaks using ultrasonics is provided in ASTM E 1002. The method covers procedures for calibration, location, and estimated measurements of leakage by the ultrasonic technique (sometimes called ultrasonic translation).

b. Detection Distance. Ultrasonic energy in the relatively low-frequency range of 30-50 KHz travels easily through air; therefore, an ultrasonic leak detector can detect leakage with the probe located away from the leak. The maximum detection distance depends on the leakage rate.

c. Typical Applications. Some typical applications for the ultrasonic leak detector on aircraft are: fuel system pressurization tests, air ducts and air conditioning systems, emergency evacuation slides, tire pressure retention, electrical discharge, oxygen lines and valves, internal leaks in hydraulic valves and actuators, fuel cell testing, identifying cavitation in hydraulic pumps, arcing in wave guides, cabin and cockpit window and door seals, and cabin pressurization testing.

5-98.—5-104. [RESERVED.]

SECTION 8. TAP TESTING

5-105. GENERAL. Tap testing is widely used for a quick evaluation of any accessible aircraft surface to detect the presence of delamination or debonding.

a. The tap testing procedure consists of lightly tapping the surface of the part with a coin, light special hammer with a maximum of 2 ounces (see figure 5-22), or any other suitable object. The acoustic response is compared with that of a known good area.

b. A "flat" or "dead" response is considered unacceptable. The acoustic response of a good part can vary dramatically with changes in geometry, in which case a standard of some sort is required. The entire area of interest must be tapped. The surface should be dry and free of oil, grease, and dirt. Tap testing is limited to finding relatively shallow defects in skins with a thickness less than .080 inch. In a honeycomb structure, for example, the far side bondline cannot be evaluated, requiring two-side access for a complete inspection. This method is portable, but no records are produced. The accuracy of this test depends on the inspector's subjective interpretation of the test response; therefore, only qualified personnel should perform this test.

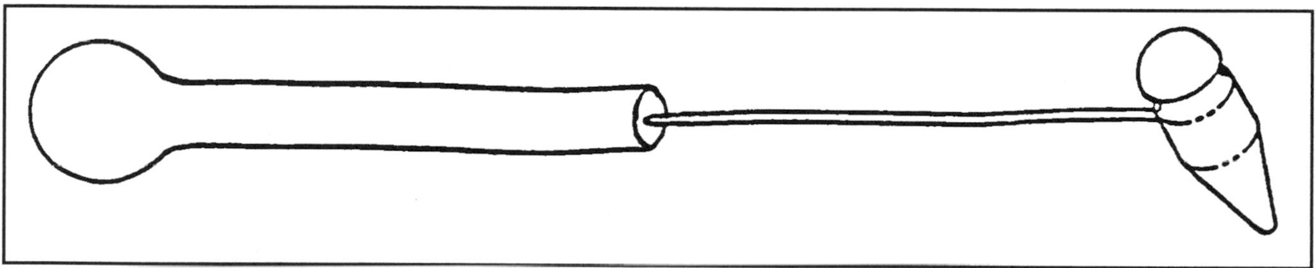

FIGURE 5-22. Sample of special tap hammer.

5-106.—5-111. [RESERVED.]

SECTION 9. ACOUSTIC-EMISSION

5-112. GENERAL. Acoustic-Emission is an NDI technique that involves the placing of acoustical-emission sensors at various locations on the aircraft structure and then applying a load or stress. The level of stress applied need not reach general yielding, nor does the stress generally need to be of a specific type. Bending stress can be applied to beamed structures, torsional stress can be applied to rotary shafts, thermal stresses can be applied with heat lamps or blankets, and pressure-induced stress can be applied to pressure-containment systems such as the aircraft fuselage. The materials emit sound and stress waves that take the form of ultrasonic pulses that can be picked up by sensors. Cracks and areas of corrosion in the stressed airframe structure emit sound waves (different frequencies for different size defects) which are registered by the sensors. These acoustic-emission bursts can be used both to locate flaws and to evaluate their rate of growth as a function of applied stress. Acoustic-emission testing has an advantage over other NDI methods in that it can detect and locate all of the activated flaws in a structure in one test. Acoustic-emission testing does not now provide the capability to size flaws, but it can greatly reduce the area required to be scanned by other NDI methods.

5-113. APPLICATIONS. A wide variety of structures and materials, such as: wood, plastic, fiberglass, and metals can be inspected by the acoustic-emission technique by applying stress on the test material. The emission-producing mechanism in each type of material may differ, but characteristic acoustic-emissions are produced and can be correlated to the integrity of the material. Acoustic-emission technology has been applied quite successfully in monitoring proof tests of pressure vessels and tests of fiber-reinforced plastic structures of all kinds. There are now ASTM standards and ASME codes applying to its use in testing gas cylinders and both metal and fiber-reinforced plastic vessels, tanks, and piping.

For a welded structure such as a pressure vessel, acoustic-emission testing works well with relatively simple instrumentation. However, slight movement of bolted or riveted joints can also generate acoustic signals. Thus a complex structure may have many acoustic sources besides flaws in its components. These unwanted emission sources greatly complicate acoustic-emission tests of complex structures. The difficulties are not prohibitive, but they put a premium on the intelligent use of signal processing and interpretation. Therefore, because of the complexity of aircraft structures, application of acoustic-emission testing to aircraft has required a new level of sophistication, both in testing techniques and data interpretation. Research and testing programs are currently in progress to determine the feasibility of acoustic-emission testing on several different types of aircraft.

5-114.—5-119. [RESERVED.]

SECTION 10. THERMOGRAPHY

5-120. GENERAL. Thermography is an NDI technique that uses radiant electromagnetic thermal energy to detect flaws. The presence of a flaw is indicated by an abnormal temperature variant when the item is subjected to normal heating and cooling conditions inherent to the in-service life, and/or when artificially heated or cooled. The greater the material's resistance to heat flow, the more readily the flow can be identified due to temperature differences caused by the flaw.

5-121.—5-126. [RESERVED.]

SECTION 11. HOLOGRAPHY

5-127. GENERAL. Holography is an NDI technique that uses visible light waves coupled with photographic equipment to create a three-dimensional image. The process uses two laser beams, one called a reference beam and the other called an object beam. The two laser beams are directed to an object, between beam applications the component is stressed. The beams are then compared and recorded on film, or other electronic recording medium, creating a double image. Indications of applied stresses or defects are shown as virtual images with a system of fringe lines overlaying the part. Holography is most commonly used for rapid assessment of surface flaws in composite structures.

5-128.—5-133. [RESERVED.]

SECTION 12. SHEAROGRAPHY

5-134. GENERAL. Shearography was developed for strain measurements. The process now provides a full-field video strain gauge, in real time, over large areas. It is an enhanced form of holography, which requires the part to be under stress. A laser is used for illumination of the part while under stress. The output takes the form of an image processed video display. This technique has been used effectively in locating defects, such as disbonds and delaminations, through multiple bondlines. It is capable of showing the size and shape of subsurface anomalies when the test part is properly stressed. Shearography has been developed into a useful tool for NDI. It can be used easily in a hangar environment, while meeting all laser safety concerns. Other applications include the testing of honeycomb structures, such as flaps and control surfaces. Shearography offers a great increase in the speed of inspection by allowing on-aircraft inspections of structures without their removal, as well as inspections of large areas in just seconds.

5-135.—5-140. [RESERVED.]

CHAPTER 6. CORROSION, INSPECTION & PROTECTION

SECTION 1. GENERAL

6-1. GENERAL. The purpose of this chapter is to provide information that will help maintenance personnel prevent, control, identify, and treat various types of corrosion. (Refer to AC 43-4A, Corrosion Control For Aircraft for a more in-depth study on the detection and treatment of corrosion.)

a. Corrosion is a natural occurrence that attacks metal by chemical or electrochemical action and converts it back to a metallic compound.

b. Four conditions must exist before electrochemical corrosion can occur. (See figure 6-1.) They are:

(1) A metal subject to corrosion (Anode);

(2) A dissimilar conductive material (Cathode), which has less tendency to corrode;

(3) Presence of a continuous, conductive liquid path (Electrolyte); and

(4) Electrical contact between the anode and the cathode (usually in the form of metal-to-metal contact such as rivets, bolts, and corrosion).

c. Elimination of any one of these conditions will stop electrochemical corrosion. (See figure 6-2.)

NOTE: Paint can mask the initial stages of corrosion. Since corrosion products occupy more volume than the original metal, painted surfaces should be inspected often for irregularities such as blisters, flakes, chips, and lumps.

6-2. FACTORS INFLUENCING CORROSION.

a. Some factors which influence metal corrosion and the rate of corrosion are:

(1) Type of metal;

(2) Heat treatment and grain direction;

(3) Presence of a dissimilar, less corrodible metal;

(4) Anodic and cathodic surface areas (in galvanic corrosion);

(5) Temperature;

(6) Presence of electrolytes (hard water, salt water, battery fluids, etc.);

(7) Availability of oxygen;

(8) Presence of biological organisms;

(9) Mechanical stress on the corroding metal; and,

(10) Time of exposure to a corrosive environment.

(11) Lead/graphite pencil marks on aircraft surface metals.

b. Most pure metals are not suitable for aircraft construction and are used only in combination with other metals to form alloys. Most alloys are made up entirely of small crystalline regions, called grains. Corrosion can occur on surfaces of those regions which are less resistant and also at boundaries between regions, resulting in the formation of pits and intergranular corrosion. Metals have a wide range of corrosion resistance. The most active metals, (those which lose electrons easily), such as magnesium and aluminum, corrode easily. The most noble metals (those which do not lose electrons easily), such as gold and silver, do not corrode easily.

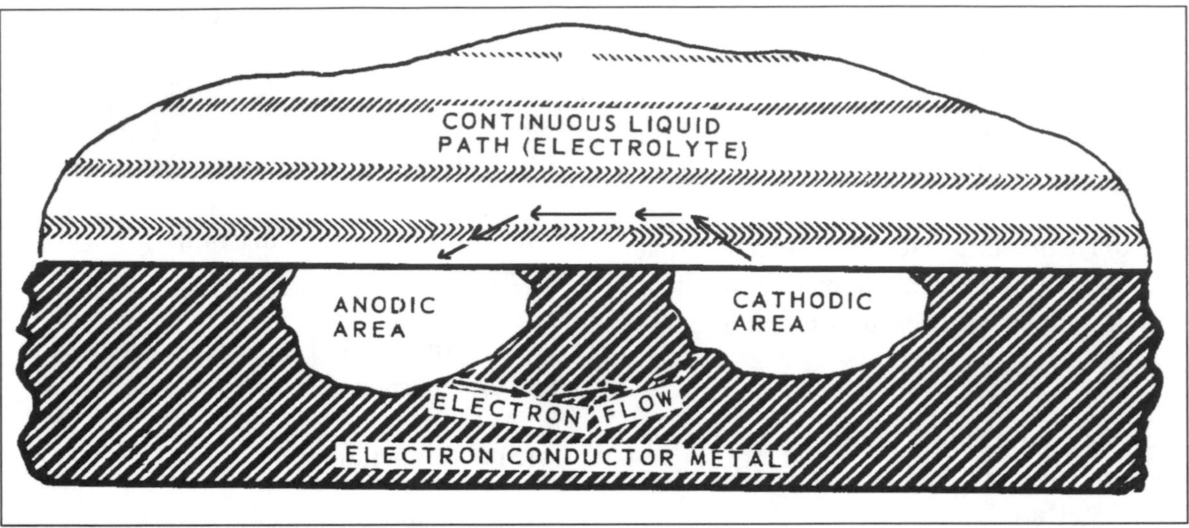

FIGURE 6-1. Simplified corrosion cell showing conditions which must exist for electrochemical corrosion.

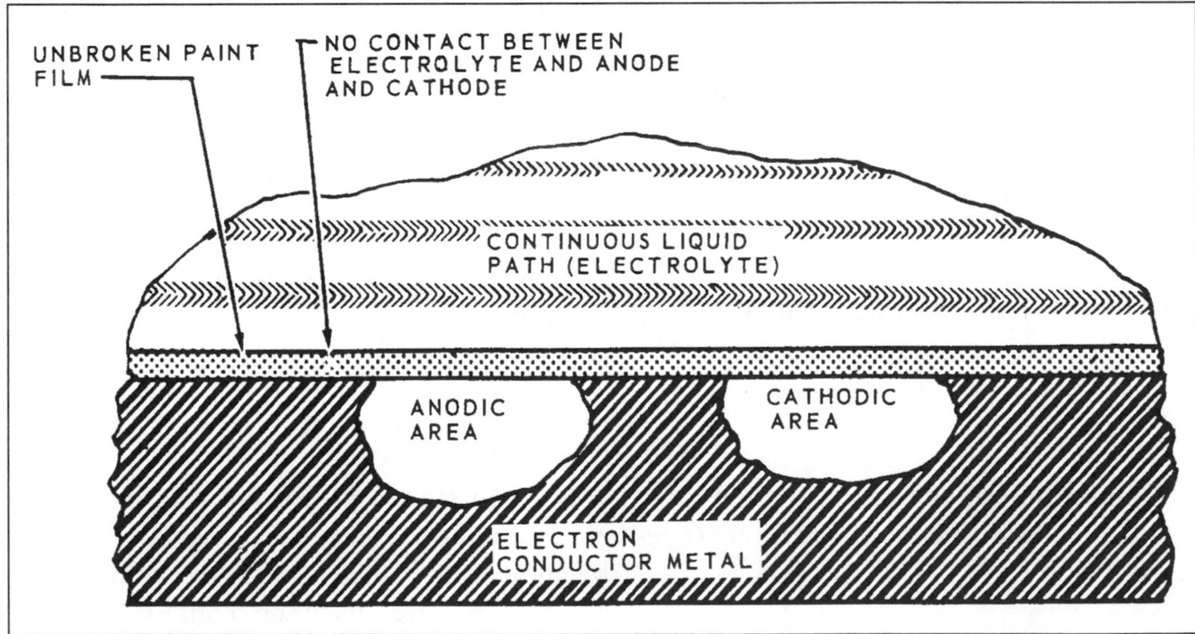

FIGURE 6-2. Elimination of corrosion by application of an organic film to metal surface.

c. Corrosion is quickened by high-temperature environments that accelerate chemical reactions and increase the concentration of water vapor in the air.

d. Electrolytes (electrically-conducting solutions) form on surfaces when condensation, salt spray, rain, or rinse water accumulate. Dirt, salt, acidic gases, and engine exhaust gases can dissolve on wet surfaces, increasing the electrical conductivity of the electrolyte, thereby increasing the rate of corrosion.

e. When some of the electrolyte on a metal surface is partially confined, (such as between faying surfaces or in a deep crevice) the metal around this area corrodes more rapidly. This type of corrosion is called an oxygen concentration cell. Corrosion occurs more rapidly because the reduced oxygen content of the confined electrolyte causes the adjacent metal to become anodic to other metal surfaces on the same part that are immersed in electrolyte or exposed to air.

f. Slime, molds, fungi, and other living organisms (some microscopic) can grow on damp surfaces. Once they are established, the area usually remains damp, increasing the possibility of corrosion.

g. Manufacturing processes such as machining, forming, welding, or heat treatment can leave residual stress in aircraft parts and can cause cracking in a corrosive environment.

6-3. COMMON CORROSIVE AGENTS.

Substances that cause corrosion are called corrosive agents. The most common corrosive agents are acids, alkalies, and salts. The atmosphere and water, the two most common media for these agents, may also act as corrosive agents.

a. Any acid will severely corrode most of the alloys used in airframes. The most destructive are sulfuric acid (battery acid), halogen acids (hydrochloric, hydrofluoric, and hydrobromic), nitrous oxide compounds, and organic acids found in the wastes of humans and animals.

b. Alkalies, as a group, are not as corrosive as acids. Aluminum and magnesium alloys are exceedingly prone to corrosive attack by many alkaline solutions unless the solutions contain a corrosion inhibitor. Substances particularly corrosive to aluminum are washing soda, potash (wood ashes), and lime (cement dust).

c. The major atmospheric corrosive agents are oxygen and airborne moisture. Corrosion often results from the direct action of atmospheric oxygen and moisture on metal nd the presence of additional moisture often accelerates corrosive attack, particularly on ferrous alloys. The atmosphere may also contain other corrosive gases and contaminants, particularly industrial and marine salt spray.

d. The corrosiveness of water depends on the type and quantity of dissolved mineral and organic impurities and dissolved gasses (particularly oxygen) in the water. One characteristic of water that makes it corrosive is its conductivity. Physical factors, such as water temperature and velocity also have a direct bearing on its corrosiveness.

6-4. MICRO-ORGANISMS.

a. Bacteria may be either aerobic or anaerobic. Aerobic bacteria require oxygen to live. They accelerate corrosion by oxidizing sulfur to produce sulfuric acid. Bacteria living adjacent to metals may promote corrosion by depleting the oxygen supply or by releasing metabolic products. Anaerobic bacteria, on the other hand, can survive only when free oxygen is not present. The metabolism of these bacteria requires them to obtain part of their sustenance by oxidizing inorganic compounds, such as iron, sulfur, hydrogen, and carbon monoxide. The resultant chemical reactions cause corrosion.

b. Fungi are the growths of micro-organisms that feed on organic materials. While low humidity does not kill microbes, it slows their growth and may prevent corrosion damage. Ideal growth conditions for most micro-organisms are temperatures between 68 and 104 °F (20 and 40 °C) and relative humidity between 85 and 100 percent.

c. Damage resulting from microbial growth can occur when any of three basic mechanisms, or a combination of these, is brought into play. First, fungi have a tendency to hold moisture, which contributes to other forms of corrosion. Second, because fungi are living organisms, they need food to survive. This food is obtained from the material on which the fungi are growing. Third, these micro-organisms secrete corrosive fluids that attack many materials, including some that are not fungi nutrient.

d. Microbial growth must be removed completely to avoid corrosion. Microbial growth should be removed by hand with a firm non-metallic bristle brush and water. Removal of microbial growth is easier if the growth is kept wet with water. Microbial growth may also be removed with steam at 100 psi. Protective clothing must be used when using steam for removing microbial growth.

6-5.—6-10. [RESERVED.]

SECTION 2. TYPES OF CORROSION

6-11. GENERAL. All corrosive attacks begin on the surface of the metal making the classification of corrosion by physical appearance a convenient means of identification. (See figure 6-3.)

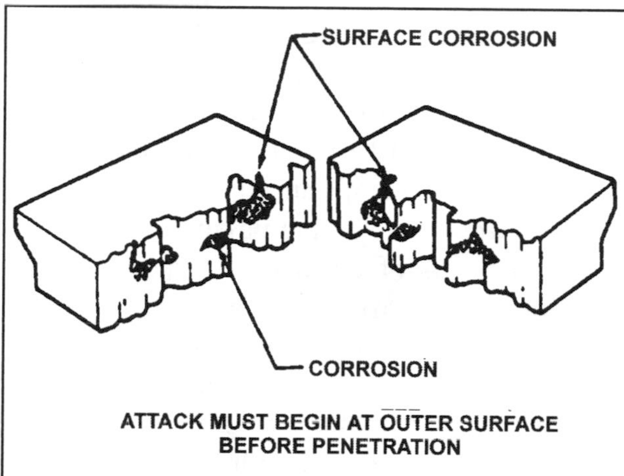

FIGURE 6-3. Corrosion attack.

6-12. GENERAL SURFACE CORROSION. General surface corrosion (also referred to as Uniform Etch or Uniform Attack Corrosion) is the most common form of corrosion and results from a direct chemical attack on a metal surface and involves only the metal surface. (See figure 6-4.) General surface corrosion usually occurs over a wide area and is more or less equal in dispersion. On a polished surface, this type of corrosion is first seen as a general dulling of the surface, and if allowed to continue, the surface becomes rough and possibly frosted in appearance. The discoloration or general dulling of metal created by exposure to elevated temperatures is not to be considered general surface corrosion.

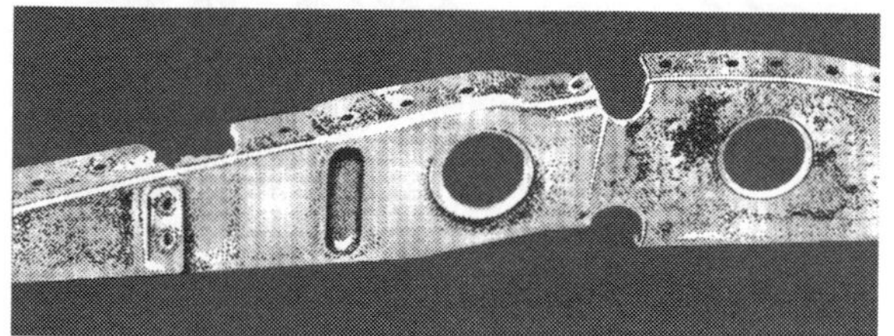

FIGURE 6-4. General surface corrosion.

6-13. PITTING CORROSION. Pitting corrosion is one of the most destructive and intense forms of corrosion. It can occur in any metal but is most common on metals that form protective oxide films, such as aluminum and magnesium alloys. It is first noticeable as a white or gray powdery deposit, similar to dust, which blotches the surface. When the deposit is cleaned away, tiny holes or pits can be seen in the surface. (See figures 6-5(a) and 6-5(b).) These small surface openings may penetrate deeply into structural members and cause damage completely out of proportion to its surface appearance.

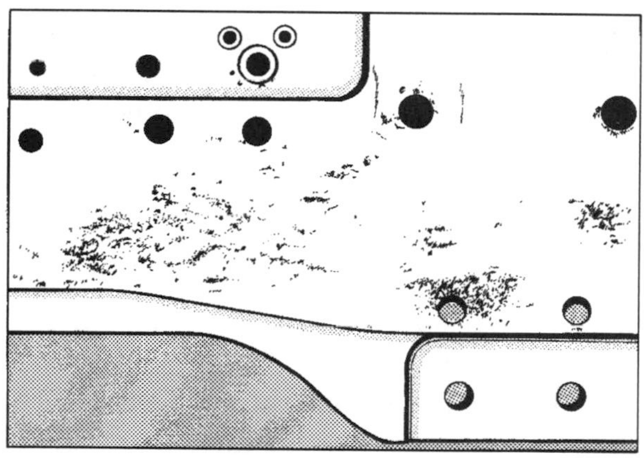

FIGURE 6-5(a). Pitting corrosion (external view).

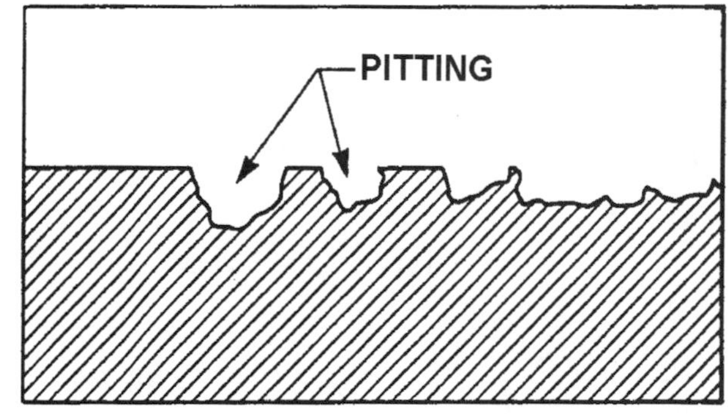

FIGURE 6-5(b). Pitting corrosion (magnified cross section).

6-14. CONCENTRATION CELL CORROSION. Concentration cell corrosion, (also known as Crevice Corrosion) is corrosion of metals in a metal-to-metal joint, corrosion at the edge of a joint even though the joined metals are identical, or corrosion of a spot on the metal surface covered by a foreign material. Metal ion concentration cells and oxygen concentration cells are the two general types of concentration cell corrosion. (See figure 6-6.)

a. Metal Ion Concentration Cells. The solution may consist of water and ions of the metal which is in contact with water. A high concentration of the metal ions will normally exist under faying surfaces where the solution is stagnant, and a low concentration of metal ions will exist adjacent to the crevice which is created by the faying surface. An electrical potential will exist between the two points; the area of the metal in contact with the low concentration of metal ions will be anodic and corrode, and the area in contact with the high metal ion concentration will be cathodic and not show signs of corrosion.

b. Oxygen Concentration Cells. The solution in contact with the metal surface will normally contain dissolved oxygen. An oxygen cell can develop at any point where the oxygen in the air is not allowed to diffuse into the solution, thereby creating a difference in oxygen concentration between two points. Typical locations of oxygen concentration cells are under gaskets, wood, rubber, and other materials in contact with the metal surface. Corrosion will occur at the area of low oxygen concentration (anode). Alloys such as stainless steel are particularly susceptible to this type of crevice corrosion.

6-15. ACTIVE-PASSIVE CELLS. Metals which depend on a tightly adhering passive film, usually an oxide, for corrosion protection are prone to rapid corrosive attack by active-passive cells. Active-passive cells are often referred to as a type of concentration cell corrosion. However, the active-passive cell is actually two forms of corrosion working in conjunction. The corrosive action usually starts as an oxygen concentration cell. As an example, salt deposits on the metal surface in the presence of water containing oxygen can create the oxygen cell. The passive film will be broken beneath the salt crystals. Once the passive film is broken, the active metal beneath the film will be exposed to corrosive attack. (See figure 6-7.) Rapid pitting of the active metal will result. This reaction can become locally intense due to several factors. First the reaction is augmented by the affected area, since the proportion of the exposed base metal is small compared to the surrounding non-reactive metal. This effectively concentrates the focal point of the reaction, often resulting in deep pits in a short time and a greater rate of corrosion.

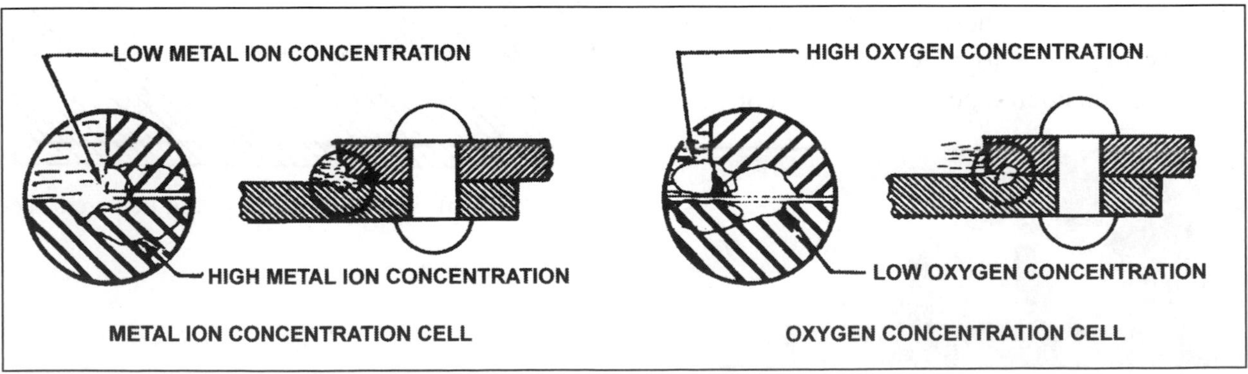

FIGURE 6-6. Concentration cell corrosion.

6-16. FILIFORM CORROSION. Filiform corrosion is a special form of oxygen concentration cell which occurs on metal surfaces having an organic coating system. It is recognized by its characteristic worm-like trace of corrosion products beneath the paint film. (See figure 6-8.) Polyurethane finishes are especially susceptible to filiform corrosion. Filiform occurs when the relative humidity of the air is between 78 and 90 percent and the surface is slightly acidic. This corrosion usually attacks steel and aluminum surfaces. The traces never cross on steel, but they will cross under one another on aluminum which makes the damage deeper and more severe for aluminum. If the corrosion is not removed, the area treated, and a protective finish applied, the corrosion can lead to inter-granular corrosion, especially around fasteners and at seams. Filiform corrosion can be removed using glass bead blasting material with portable abrasive blasting equipment or sanding. Filiform corrosion can be prevented by storing aircraft in an environment with a relative humidity below 70 percent, using coating systems having a low rate of diffusion for oxygen and water vapors, and by washing the aircraft to remove acidic contaminants from the surface.

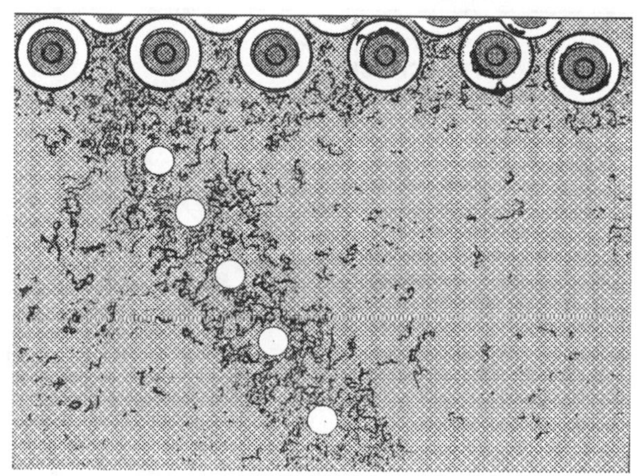

FIGURE 6-8. Filiform corrosion.

6-17. INTERGRANULAR CORROSION. Inter-granular corrosion is an attack on the grain boundaries of a metal. A highly magnified cross section of any commercial alloy shows the granular structure of the metal. It consists of quantities of individual grains, and each of these tiny grains has a clearly defined boundary which chemically differs from the metal within the grain. The grain boundary and the grain center can react with each other as anode and cathode when in contact with an electrolyte. (See figure 6-9.) Rapid selective corrosion of the grain boundaries can occur. High-strength aluminum alloys such as 2014 and 7075 are more susceptible to inter-granular corrosion if they have been improperly heat-treated and then exposed to a corrosive environment.

6-18. EXFOLIATION CORROSION. Exfoliation corrosion is an advanced form of inter-granular corrosion and shows itself by lifting up the surface grains of a metal by the force of expanding corrosion products occurring at the grain boundaries just below the surface. (See figure 6-10.) It is visible evidence of inter-granular corrosion and is most often seen on extruded sections where grain thickness are usually less than in rolled forms.

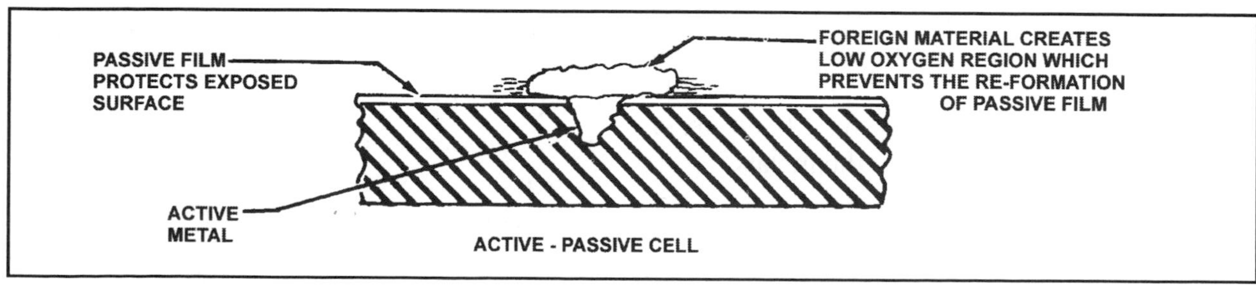

FIGURE 6-7. Active-passive cell.

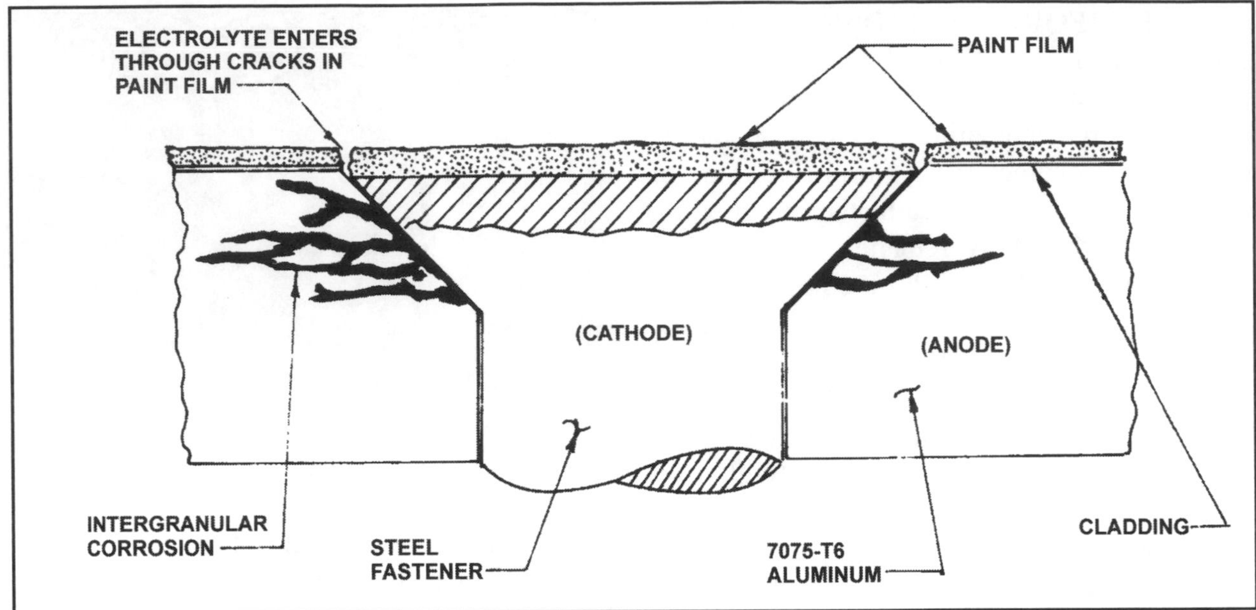

FIGURE 6-9. Inter-granular Corrosion of 7075-T6 aluminum adjacent to steel fastener.

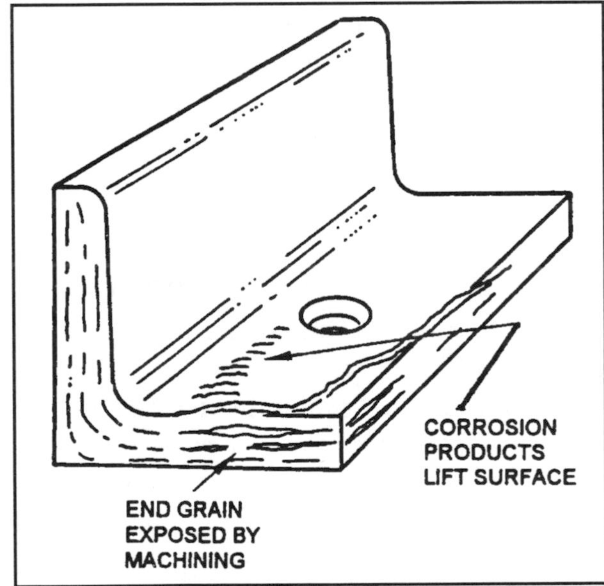

FIGURE 6-10. Exfoliation corrosion.

6-19. GALVANIC CORROSION. Galvanic corrosion occurs when two dissimilar metals make contact in the presence of an electrolyte. (See figure 6-11.) It is usually recognizable by the presence of a build-up of corrosion at the joint between the metals.

6-20. STRESS CORROSION CRACKING. This form of corrosion involves a constant or cyclic stress, acting in conjunction with a damaging chemical environment. The stress may be caused by internal or external loading.

a. Internal stress may be trapped in a part of structure during manufacturing processes such as cold working or by unequal cooling from high temperatures. Most manufacturers follow up these processes with a stress relief operation. Even so, sometimes stress remains trapped. The stress may be externally introduced in part structure by riveting, welding, bolting, clamping, press fit, etc. If a slight mismatch occurs, or a fastener is over-torque, internal stress will be present.

b. Internal stress is more important than design stress, because stress corrosion is difficult to recognize before it has overcome the design safety factor. The level of stress varies from point to point within the metal. Stresses near the yield strength are generally necessary to promote stress corrosion cracking. (See figure 6-12.) However, failures may occur at lower stresses. Specific environments have been identified which cause stress corrosion cracking of certain alloys.

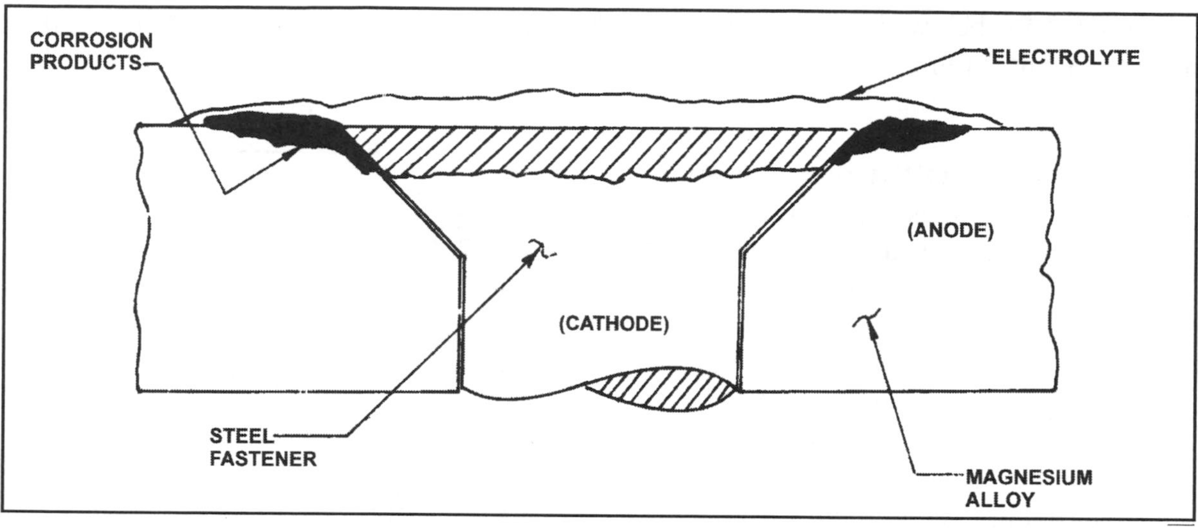

FIGURE 6-11. Galvanic corrosion of magnesium adjacent to steel fastener.

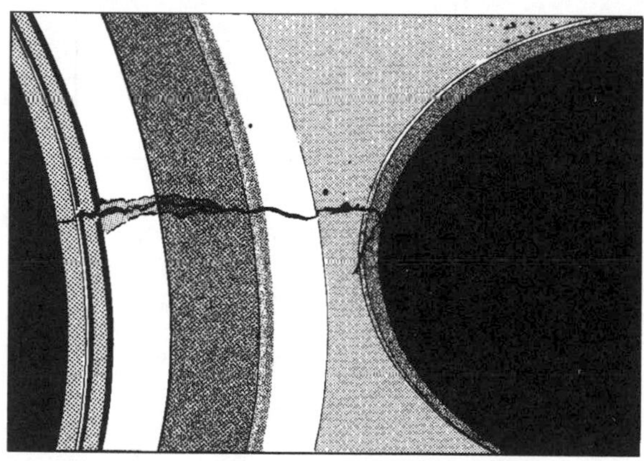

FIGURE 6-12. Stress corrosion cracking.

(1) Salt solutions and sea water cause stress corrosion cracking of high-strength, heat-treated steel and aluminum alloys.

(2) Methyl alcohol-hydrochloric acid solutions will cause stress corrosion cracking of some titanium alloys.

(3) Magnesium alloys may stress-corrode in moist air.

(4) Stress Corrosion may be reduced by

- applying protective coatings,
- stress relief heat treatments,
- using corrosion inhibitors, or
- controlling the environment.

6-21. FATIGUE CORROSION. Fatigue corrosion involves cyclic stress and a corrosive environment. Metals may withstand cyclic stress for an infinite number of cycles so long as the stress is below the endurance limit of the metal. Once the limit has been exceeded, the metal will eventually crack and fail from metal fatigue. However, when the part or structure undergoing cyclic stress is also exposed to a corrosive environment, the stress level for failure may be reduced many times. Thus, failure occurs at stress levels that can be dangerously low depending on the number of cycles assigned to the life-limited part.

a. Fatigue corrosion failure occurs in two stages. During the first stage the combined action of corrosion and cyclic stress damages the metal by pitting and crack formations to such a degree that fracture by cyclic stress will occur, even if the corrosive environment is completely removed.

b. The second stage is essentially a fatigue stage in which failure proceeds by propagation of the crack (often from a corrosion pit or pits). It is controlled primarily by stress concentration effects and the physical properties of the metal. Fracture of a metal part due to fatigue corrosion, generally occurs at a stress level far below the fatigue limit of an uncorroded part, even though the amount of corrosion is relatively small.

6-22. FRETTING CORROSION. Fretting corrosion,(also known as wear corrosion or friction oxidation) can occur at the interface of two highly-loaded surfaces which are not supposed to move against each other. However, vibration may cause the surfaces to rub together resulting in an abrasive wear known as fretting. (See figure 6-13.) The protective film on the metallic surfaces is removed by this rubbing action. With continued rubbing, metal particles sheared from the surface of the metal combine with oxygen to form metal oxide. As these oxides accumulate, they cause damage by abrasive action and increased local stress. The most common example of fretting corrosion is the *smoking rivet* found on engine cowling and wing skins. This is one corrosion reaction that is not driven by an electrolyte, and in fact, moisture may inhibit the reaction. Application of a lubricant or installation of a fretting-resistant material between the two surfaces can reduce fretting corrosion.

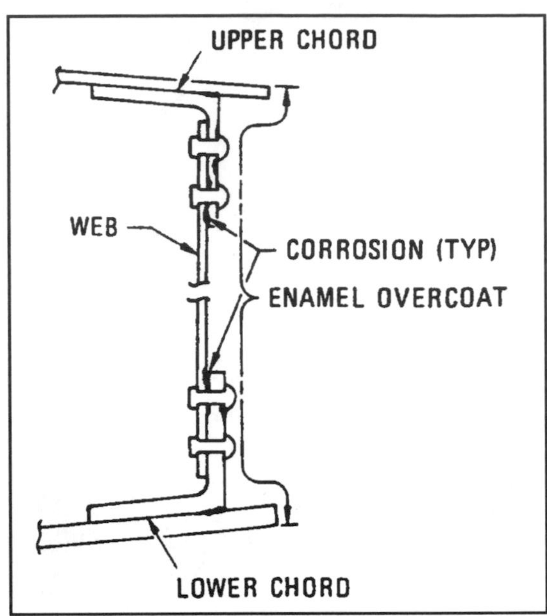

FIGURE 6-13. Fretting corrosion.

6-23.—6-28. [RESERVED.]

SECTION 3. CORROSION PROTECTION MEASURES FOR BASIC MATERIALS

6-29. GENERAL. In the repair of aircraft, apply corrosion proofing of the same type or equivalent to that originally applied unless the repair would result in increased susceptibility to corrosion, in which case use additional corrosion protection measures. The following is a list of the most commonly-used corrosion-proofing techniques.

6-30. ANODIZING AND RELATED PROCESSES. In anodizing, aluminum alloys are placed in an electrolytic bath causing a thin film of aluminum oxide to form on the surface of the aluminum. This is resistant to corrosion and affords a good paint base. However, other processes, which do not provide as good a corrosive protection as anodizing, are good paint bases. The processes are:

a. Alkaline cleaning followed by chromic acid dip;

b. Alcoholic phosphoric acid cleaner; and

c. Alkaline dichromate treatment.

6-31. PLATING. Steels are commonly plated with other metals to prevent corrosion. Plating is accomplished by placing the article in an electrolytic bath. Metals used in plating vary in the corrosion protection they afford steel. For instance, in platings that corrode before steel, such as zinc or cadmium, slight breaks or cracks throughout the plating will not result in rusting of the exposed steel. With the surface metal corroded, the steel is protected. However, when the steel corrodes faster than the plate metal, such as chromium, the amount of protection depends on the tightness of the plating. Post-plate bake treatment to relieve hydrogen embrittlement is a necessary part of replating procedures for high-strength steel parts. High-strength nuts and bolts are susceptible to failure from hydrogen embrittlement. Because of the potential failures of embrittled parts, careful control over the heat treatment, grinding, preplate cleaning, plating, and post-plate baking of high-strength parts is necessary.

6-32. PHOSPHATE RUST-PROOFING. This process is commercially known as Parkerizing, Bonderizing, Granodizing, etc. The coating placed on the part is used to protect steel parts after machining and before painting.

6-33. CHROME-PICKLE TREATMENT. Magnesium parts which have been immersed or brushed with a solution of nitric acid and sodium dichromate will be protected for temporary storage. The coating will also serve as a bond for subsequent organic finishes. Sealed chrome-pickle treatment is used on magnesium parts for long term protection. Diluted chromic acid is a touch-up treatment. It is less critical to apply and can be applied over previously-applied thin chromate films.

6-34. DICHROMATE TREATMENT. This treatment consists of boiling magnesium parts in a solution of sodium dichromate. It provides good paint base and protective qualities on all standard wrought magnesium alloys except the magnesium-thorium alloys. Acid pickling of the magnesium surface prior to application of the dichromate treatment is required if maximum corrosion resistance of the finish is expected.

6-35. STANNATE IMMERSION TREATMENT. Stannate immersion treatment deposits a layer of tin. It is a protective paint base for magnesium alloy parts which contain inserts and fasteners of a dissimilar metal such as brass, copper, or steel. This treatment cannot be used with parts containing aluminum inserts or fasteners because the high alkalinity of the bath attacks the aluminum.

6-36. GALVANIC ANODIZING TREATMENT. An electrolytic process that provides a paint base and corrosion-preventive film on magnesium alloys containing manganese.

6-37. CLADDING. Aluminum alloys which are susceptible to corrosion are frequently clad with pure aluminum. Slight pits, scratches, or other defects through the cladding material must be avoided, since the aluminum alloy core will corrode rapidly.

6-38. METAL SPRAYING. Metal is melted and sprayed on the surface to be protected. The surface must be properly prepared and thoroughly cleaned to prevent peeling of the sprayed coat.

6-39. SHOT-PEENING. Shot-peening and other treatments, by which the surface can be placed in compression, are effective in preventing stress corrosion.

6-40. ORGANIC COATINGS. Zinc chromate primer, enamels, chlorinated rubber compounds, etc., are organic coatings commonly used to protect metals.

6-41. DOPE PROOFING. When doped fabrics are applied over an organic finished metal structure, the dope will have a tendency to loosen the finish on the metal. For this reason, organic coatings on the metal are usually covered with a dope-proof paint, with metal foil, or with cellulose tape to prevent the dope from soaking through.

6-42. TUBE INTERIORS. Protect the interiors of structural steel and aluminum tubing against corrosion. A small amount of water entrapped in a tube can corrode entirely through the tube thickness in a short period. Coat the tube interior by flushing with hot linseed oil, paralketone, or other approved corrosion inhibitor. The flushing liquid is usually introduced through small holes drilled in the tubing. Allow the flushing liquid to drain and plug the holes with a screw or by other means to prevent entry of moisture. Air and watertight sealing of the tubing will also give adequate protection against corrosion if the tubing is internally dry before being sealed.

6-43.—6-49. [RESERVED.]

SECTION 4. CORROSION PREVENTIVE MAINTENANCE

6-50. GUIDELINES: ALL AIRCRAFT. Corrosion prevention depends on a comprehensive prevention and control plan, implemented from the start of operation of an aircraft, which includes:

a. Adequately-trained personnel in

(1) recognition of corrosion-inducing conditions;

(2) corrosion identification techniques;

(3) corrosion detection, cleaning, and treating; and

(4) lubrication and preservation of aircraft structure and components.

b. Inspection for corrosion on a scheduled basis.

c. Thorough cleaning, inspection, lubrication, and preservation at prescribed intervals.

d. Prompt corrosion treatment after detection.

e. Accurate record-keeping and reporting of material or design deficiencies to the manufacturer and the Federal Aviation Administration (FAA).

f. Use of appropriate materials, equipment, and technical publications.

g. Maintenance of the basic finish systems.

h. Keeping drain holes and passages open and functional. Sealants, leveling compounds, miscellaneous debris, or corrosion inhibitors should not block drain paths.

i. Replacing deteriorated or damaged gaskets and sealants (using non-corrosive type sealants) to avoid water intrusion and entrapment that leads to corrosion.

j. Minimizing the exposure of aircraft to adverse environments by keeping the aircraft in a hangar.

k. Periodic and frequent inspection of areas where there are foamed plastics or other absorbent material.

l. Daily draining of fuel cavities to remove accumulated water and other foreign matter.

m. Daily wipe-down of exposed critical surfaces of hydraulic cylinders.

6-51. GUIDELINES: AIRCRAFT OPERATING OVER SALT WATER. In addition to the inspection and treatment prescribed above, the following treatment shall be applied:

a. Remove all traces of salt water and salt water residue by thoroughly washing the aircraft with fresh water.

(1) After drying, coat the propeller, hubs, blades and other unpainted or unprotected parts of the engine and its installation parts by spraying or rubbing lightly with corrosion preventive compound, Specification MIL-C-16173, Grade 4.

(2) Apply this mixture on parts that move or require some lubrication and on all fittings subject to corrosion such as landing gear retracting plungers, control surface hinges, control cables, exposed rivets and bolts, and other similar parts not protected by paint. Apply with a cloth or a soft brush soaked in the mixture.

(3) Wipe off excess mixture. When applying the mixture take care that as little as possible is deposited on exhaust pipes or collector rings to avoid a fire hazard when the engine is started. Keep the ignition wires, propeller anti-icer feed hose, tires, and other rubber parts free of the mixture.

b. Where maximum corrosion protection is desired on stationary parts, use exterior surface corrosion preventive compound, Specification MIL-C-16173, grade I.

c. Wipe the exposed portion of the landing gear shock strut piston with a cloth soaked in the applicable hydraulic fluid.

d. Most parts of landing gear wheels are made from magnesium or aluminum alloys which corrode rapidly unless carefully protected. When the aircraft operates near salt water and off coral beaches, the corrosion can be very rapid. Inspect wheels to determine the paint condition.

e. Refinish portions of a wheel where paint has deteriorated, peeled, or chipped.

f. Except for friction and bearing surfaces, apply a protective coating to all parts of wheels and brake assemblies.

6-52.—6-62. [RESERVED.]

SECTION 5. VISUAL CORROSION INSPECTION GUIDE FOR AIRCRAFT

6-63. GENERAL. This guide provides a general inspection checklist for those parts or surfaces that can be visually inspected without disassembly of the aircraft. It is intended for use in establishing corrosion inspection areas for which the manufacturer has not provided a recommended corrosion inspection program. The manufacturer's recommended corrosion inspection program will take precedence over this guideline. These inspections should be accomplished in conjunction with other preventive maintenance.

6-64. EXHAUST TRAIL AREAS.

a. Visually inspect paint in areas of the exhaust trails for damage.

b. Visually inspect under fairings, around rivet heads, and in skin crevices, for corrosion in areas of engine exhaust trail.

6-65. BATTERY COMPARTMENTS AND BATTERY VENT OPENINGS.

a. Inspect battery compartment for electrolyte spillage, corrosion, and condition of protective paint.

b. Inspect area around battery vent for corrosion.

6-66. LAVATORIES AND GALLEYS. Inspection areas around lavatories, sinks, and ranges for spillage and corrosion. Pay particular attention to floor area and the area behind and under lavatories, sinks, and ranges.

6-67. BILGE AREAS.

a. Inspect bilge areas for waste hydraulic fluids, water, dirt, loose fasteners, drill chips, and other debris.

b. Remove any foreign material from bilge and inspect for corrosion.

6-68. WHEEL WELLS AND LANDING GEAR. Inspect wheel well area and landing gear components for damage to exterior finish coating and corrosion. Particular attention should be given to exposed surfaces of struts, oleos, arms, links, and attaching hardware; axle interiors, exposed position indicator switches and other electrical equipment; crevices between stiffeners, ribs, and lower skin surfaces; magnesium wheels, particularly around bolt heads, lugs, and wheel web areas; and exposed rigid tubing at "B" nuts and ferrules under clamps, and tubing identification tapes.

6-69. EXTERNAL SKIN AREAS.

a. Inspect external skin surfaces for damage to protective finishes and corrosion.

b. Inspect around fasteners for damage to protective finishes and corrosion.

c. Inspect lap joints for bulging of skin surface, which may indicate the presence of corrosion between the faying surfaces. Skin cracks and/or dished or missing fastener heads may also indicate severe corrosion in bonded joints.

d. Inspect area around spot welds for bulges, cracks, or corrosion.

e. Inspect piano type hinges for corrosion. When piano hinges are inspected they should be lubricated and actuated through several cycles to ensure complete penetration of the lubricant.

f. Inspect thick alloy skin surfaces for pitting, intergranular corrosion, and exfoliation of the metal. Look for white or gray deposits around countersunk fastener heads and raised areas or bumps under the paint film.

g. Inspect composite skins for corrosion of attachment fasteners.

6-70. WATER ENTRAPMENT AREAS. Inspect area around edge of drain holes for corrosion and ensure that drain holes are not blocked by debris.

6-71. ENGINE FRONTAL AREAS.

a. Inspect reciprocating engine cylinder fins, engine cases, and cooling air ducts for damage to exterior finish and corrosion.

b. Inspect radiator cooler cores for corrosion.

6-72. ELECTRONIC PACKAGE COMPARTMENTS.

a. Inspect circuit-breakers, contact points, and switches for evidence of moisture and corrosive attack.

b. Treatment of corrosion in electrical and electronic components should be done by or supervised by qualified personnel familiar with the function of the unit involved.

6-73. FLEXIBLE HOSE ASSEMBLIES.

a. Inspect hose assemblies for chafing, weather-checking, hardening, discoloration, evidence of fungus, torn weather protective coatings or sleeves, and corrosion of fittings.

b. Replace any defective, damaged, twisted, or bulging hoses.

6-74. SANDWICH PANELS. Inspect edges of sandwich panels for damage to the corrosion protection finish or sealant and for corrosion.

6-75. CONTROL CABLES.

a. Inspect control cables for bare spots in the preservative coating and corrosion.

b. If external corrosion is found, relieve tension on the cable and check internal strands for corrosion. Cables with corrosion on internal strands should be replaced. External corrosion should be removed by a clean, dry, coarse rag or fiber brush. A preservative should be applied after removal of external corrosion.

6-76. INTEGRAL FUEL CELLS.

a. Inspect top coat finish for breaks, peeling, lifting of surface, or other damage.

b. Inspect aircraft structure for top coat finish damage from pitting or intergranular corrosion.

6-77. ELECTRICAL CONNECTORS.

a. Inspect electrical connectors for breaks in potting compound and corrosion of pins and wires.

b. If the electrical connector is suspected of having moisture intrusion, disassemble the connector, clean the connector, and inspect it for corrosion.

6-78.—6-88. [RESERVED.]

SECTION 6. CORROSION REMOVAL PROCEDURES

6-89. GENERAL. General safety precautions for handling materials with hazardous physical properties are outlined in the following paragraphs. They also address emergency procedures for immediate treatment of personnel who have inadvertently come into contact with harmful materials. All personnel responsible for using or handling hazardous materials should be thoroughly familiar with the information in the following paragraphs.

6-90. SAFETY PRECAUTIONS.

a. Chemical. When required to use or handle solvents, special cleaners, paint strippers (strong alkalies and acids), etchants (corrosion removers containing acids), or surface activation material (Alodine 1200), observe the following safety precautions:

(1) Avoid prolonged breathing of solvent or acid vapors.

(2) Never add water to acid. Always add acid to water.

(3) Mix all chemicals per the manufacturer's instructions.

(4) Clean water for emergency use should be available in the immediate work area before starting work.

(5) Avoid prolonged or repeated contact with the skin of solvents, cleaners, etchants (acid), or conversion coating material (Alodine solution). Rubber or plastic gloves should be worn. Goggles or plastic face shields and suitable protective clothing should be worn when cleaning, stripping, etching, or conversion coating overhead surfaces.

(6) When mixing alkalies with water or other substance, use containers that are made to withstand heat generated by this process.

(7) Wash any paint stripper, etchant, or conversion coating material immediately from body, skin, or clothing.

(8) Materials splashed into the eyes should be promptly flushed out with water, and medical aid obtained immediately.

(9) Do not eat or keep food in areas where poisons may be absorbed. Always wash hands before eating or smoking.

(10) Verify that the area within 50 feet of any cleaning or treating operations where low flash point (140 °F or below) materials are being used, is clear and remains clear of all potential ignition sources.

(11) Suitable fire-extinguishing equipment should be available to the cleaning/treating area.

(12) Equipment should be effectively grounded where any flammable materials are being used.

(13) If materials (acid, alkali, paint remover, or conversion coatings) are spilled on equipment and/or tools, treat immediately by rinsing with clean water, if possible, and /or neutralizing acids with baking soda and alkalies with a weak (5 percent) solution of acetic acid in water.

(14) In confined location, do not use solvents with a low flash point, (below 100 °F) such as Methyl Ethyl Ketone (MEK) and acetone.

(15) All equipment should be cleaned after work has been completed.

(16) Check and follow all applicable restrictions and requirements on the use of solvents, primers, and top coats.

(17) Check and follow all applicable restrictions and requirements for use and disposal of waste material.

b. Blasting. The following precautions should be taken when using any type of blasting equipment:

(1) Operators should be adequately protected with complete face and head covering equipment, and provided with pure breathing air.

(2) Static-ground the dry abrasive blaster and the material to be blasted.

(3) Magnesium cuttings and small shavings can ignite easily and are an extreme hazard. Fires of this metal must be extinguished with absolutely dry talc, calcium carbonate, sand, or graphite by applying the powder to a depth of 1/2 inch over the metal.

(4) Titanium alloys and high-tensile-strength steel create sparks during dry abrasive blasting. Care should be taken to ensure that hazardous concentrations of flammable vapors do not exist.

6-91. CORROSION CONTROL WORK PROCEDURES. The effectiveness of corrosion control depends on how well basic work procedures are followed. The following common work practices are recommended:

a. If rework procedures or materials are unknown, contact the aircraft manufacturer or FAA authorized Designated Engineering Representative (DER) before proceeding.

b. The work areas, equipment, and components should be clean and free of chips, grit, dirt, and foreign materials.

c. Do not mark on any metal surface with a graphite pencil or any type of sharp, pointed instrument. Temporary markings (defined as markings soluble in water or methyl chloroform) should be used for metal layout work or marking on the aircraft to indicate corroded areas.

d. Graphite should not be used as a lubricant for any component. Graphite is cathodic to all structural metals and will generate galvanic corrosion in the presence of moisture, especially if the graphite is applied in dry form.

e. Footwear and clothing should be inspected for metal chips, slivers, rivet cuttings, dirt, sand, etc., and all such material removed before walking or working on metal surfaces such as wings, stabilizers, fuel tanks, etc.

f. Do not abrade or scratch any surface unless it is an authorized procedure. If surfaces are accidentally scratched, the damage should be assessed and action taken to remove the scratch and treat the area.

g. Coated metal surfaces should not be polished for aesthetic purposes. Buffing would remove the protective coating and a brightly polished surface is normally not as corrosion resistant as a non-polished surface unless it is protected by wax or paint.

h. Protect surrounding areas when welding, grinding, or drilling, to prevent contamination with residue from these operations. In those areas where protective covering cannot be used, remove the residue by cleaning.

i. Severely corroded screws, bolts, and washers should be replaced. When a protective coating, such as a cadmium plating on bolts, or screws, is damaged, immediately apply an appropriate protective finish to prevent additional corrosion damage.

6-92.—6-112. [RESERVED.]

SECTION 7. BASIC CORROSION REMOVAL TECHNIQUES

6-113. GENERAL. When active corrosion is found, a positive inspection and rework program is necessary to prevent any further deterioration. The following methods of assessing corrosion damage and procedures for rework of corroded areas could be used during cleanup programs. In general, any rework would involve the cleaning and stripping of all finish from the corroded area, removal of corrosion products, and restoration of surface protective film.

a. Repair of corrosion damage includes removal of all corrosion and corrosion products. When the corrosion damage is severe and exceeds the damage limits set by the aircraft or parts manufacturer, the part must be replaced.

b. If manufacturer information and limits are not available, then a DER must be consulted before the aircraft or part is returned to service.

6-114. PREPARATIONS FOR REWORK. All corrosion products should be removed completely when corroded structures are reworked. Before starting rework of corroded areas, carry out the following:

a. Document corrosion damage.

b. Position the aircraft in a wash rack or provide washing apparatus for rapid rinsing of all surfaces.

c. Connect a static ground line from the aircraft to a grounding point.

d. Prepare the aircraft for safe ground maintenance.

(1) Remove battery(s), liquid oxygen generator container (if installed), and external hydraulic and electric power.

(2) Install all applicable safety pins, flags, and jury struts.

e. Protect the pitot-static ports, louvers, airscoops, engine opening, wheels, tires, magnesium skin panels, and airplane interior from moisture and chemical brightening agents.

f. Protect the surfaces adjacent to rework areas from chemical paint strippers, corrosion removal agents, and surface treatment materials.

6-115. FAIRING OR BLENDING REWORKED AREAS. All depressions resulting from corrosion rework should be faired or blended with the surrounding surface. Fairing can be accomplished as follows:

a. Remove rough edges and all corrosion from the damaged area. All dish-outs should be elliptically shaped with the major axis running spanwise on wings and horizontal stabilizers, longitudinally on fuselages, and vertically on vertical stabilizers. (Select the proper abrasive for fairing operations from table 6-1.)

b. In critical and highly stressed areas, all pits remaining after the removal of corrosion products should be blended out to prevent stress risers that may cause stress corrosion cracking. (See figure 6-14.) On a non-critical structure, it is not necessary to blend out pits remaining after removal of corrosion products by abrasive blasting, since this results in unnecessary metal removal.

TABLE 6-1. Abrasives for corrosion removal.

METALS OR MATERIALS TO BE PROCESSED	RESTRICTIONS	OPERATION	ABRASIVE PAPER OR CLOTH			ABRASIVE FABRIC OR PAD	ALUMINUM	STAINLESS STEEL	PUMICE 350 MESH OR FINER	ABRASIVE WHEEL
			ALUMINUM OXIDE	SILICON CARBIDE	GARNET					
FERROUS ALLOYS		CORROSION REMOVAL OR FAIRING	150 GRIT OR FINER	180 GRIT OR FINER		FINE TO ULTRA FINE	X	X	X	X
		FINISHING	400				X	X	X	
ALUMINUM ALLOYS EXCEPT CLAD ALUMINUM	DO NOT USE SILICON CARBIDE ABRASIVE	CORROSION REMOVAL OR FAIRING	150 GRIT OR FINER		7/0 GRIT OR FINER	VERY FINE AND ULTRA FINE	X		X	X
		FINISHING	400				X		X	
CLAD ALUMINUM	SANDING LIMITED TO THE REMOVAL OF MINOR SCRATCHES	CORROSION REMOVAL OR FAIRING	240 GRIT OR FINER		7/0 GRIT OR FINER	VERY FINE AND ULTRA FINE			X	X
		FINISHING	400						X	
MAGNESIUM ALLOYS		CORROSION REMOVAL OR FAIRING	240 GRIT OR FINER			VERY FINE AND ULTRA FINE	X		X	X
		FINISHING	400				X		X	
TITANIUM		CLEANING AND FINISHING	150 GRIT OR FINER	180 GRIT OR FINER				X	X	X

c. Rework depressions by forming smoothly blended dish-outs, using a ratio of 20:1, length to depth. (See figure 6-15.) In areas having closely spaced multiple pits, intervening material should be removed to minimize surface irregularity or waviness. (See figure 6-16.) Steel nut-plates and steel fasteners should be removed before blending corrosion out of aluminum structure. Steel or copper particles embedded in aluminum can become a point of future corrosion. All corrosion products must be removed during blending to prevent reoccurrence of corrosion.

6-116. CORROSION REMOVAL BY BLASTING. Abrasive blasting is a process for cleaning or finishing ferrous metals by directing a stream of abrasive particles against the surface of the parts. Abrasive blasting is used for the removal of rust and corrosion and for cleaning prior to painting or plating. The following standard blast-cleaning practices should be adopted.

a. The part to be blast-cleaned should be removed from the aircraft, if possible. Otherwise, areas adjacent to the part should be masked or protected from abrasive impingement and system (hydraulic, oil, fuel, etc.) contamination.

b. Parts should be dry and clean of oil, grease, or dirt, prior to blast cleaning.

c. Close-tolerance surfaces, such as bushings and bearing shafts, should be masked.

d. Blast-clean only enough to remove corrosion coating. Proceed immediately with surface treatments as required.

6-117. CLEANERS, POLISHES, AND BRIGHTENERS. It is important that aircraft be kept thoroughly clean of contaminating deposits such as oil, grease, dirt, and other foreign materials.

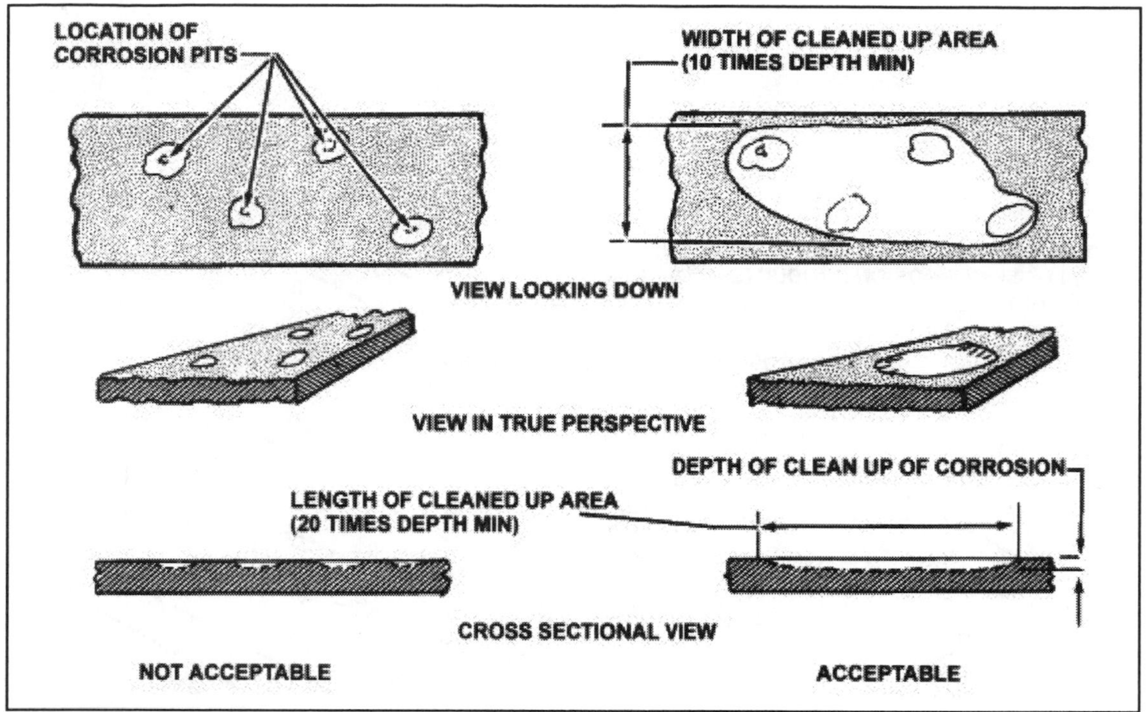

FIGURE 6-14. Typical example of acceptable cleanup of corrosion pits.

a. Materials. Do not use harmful cleaning, polishing, brightening, or paint-removing materials. Use only those compounds that conform to existing government or established industry specifications or that have been specifically recommended by the aircraft manufacturer. Observe the product manufacturer's recommendations concerning use.

b. Chemical Cleaners. Chemicals must be used with great care in cleaning assembled aircraft. The danger of entrapping corrosive materials in faying surfaces and crevices counteracts any advantages in their speed and effectiveness. Use materials that are relatively neutral and easy to remove.

c. Removal of spilled battery acid. The battery, battery cover, battery box and adjacent areas will be corroded if battery acid spills onto them. To clean spilled battery acid, brush off any salt residue and sponge the area with fresh water. For lead-acid batteries, sponge the area with a solution of 6 ounces of sodium bicarbonate (baking soda) per gallon of fresh water. Apply generously until bubbling stops and let solution stay on the area for 5 to 6 minutes, but do not allow it to dry. For nickel-cadmium batteries, sponge the area with a solution of 6 ounces of monobasic sodium phosphate per gallon of fresh water. Sponge area again with clean fresh water and dry surface with compressed air or clean wiping cloths.

6-118. STANDARD METHODS. Several standard mechanical and chemical methods are available for corrosion removal. Mechanical methods include hand sanding using abrasive mat, abrasive paper, or metal wool; and powered mechanical sanding, grinding, and buffing, using abrasive mat, grinding wheels, sanding discs, and abrasive rubber mats. The method used depends upon the metal and degree of corrosion. The removal method to use on each metal for each particular degree of corrosion is outlined in the following section.

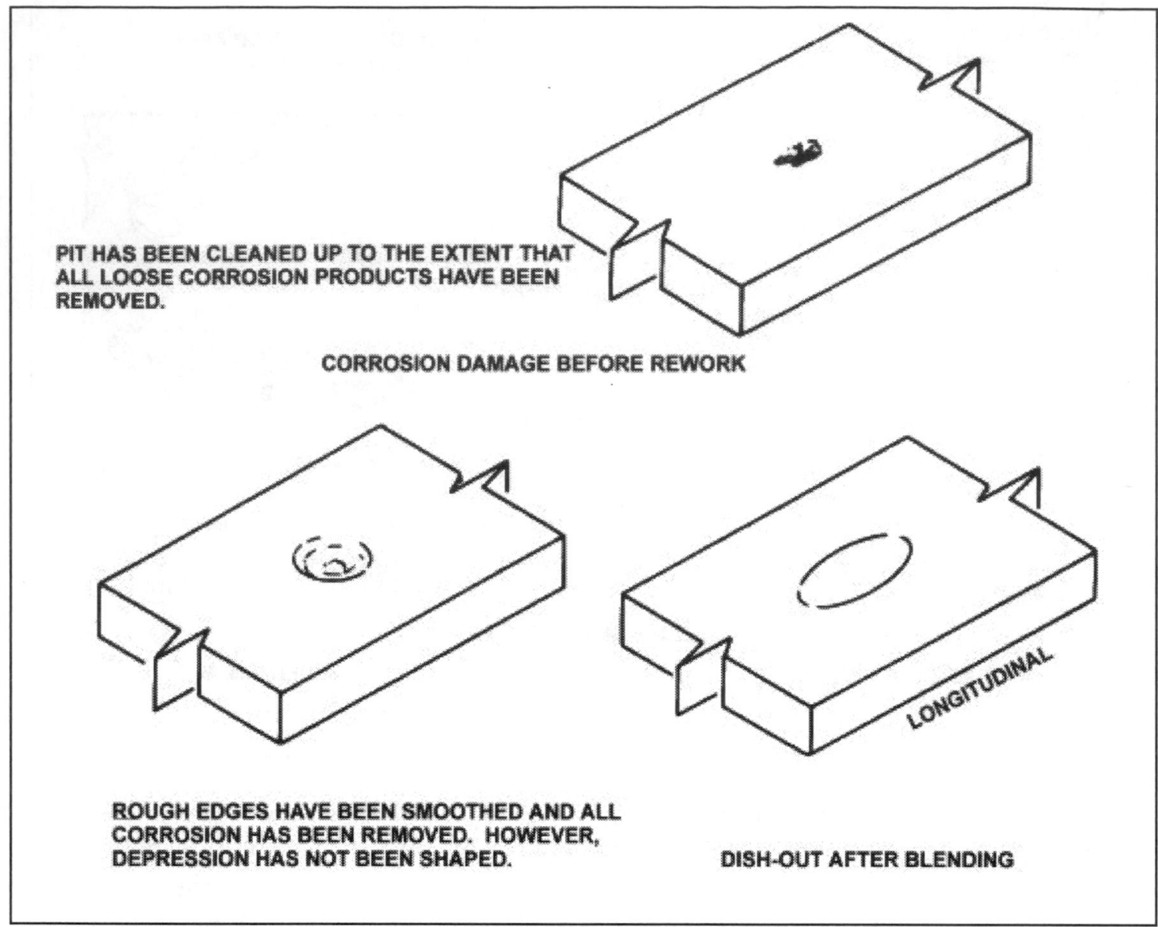
PIT HAS BEEN CLEANED UP TO THE EXTENT THAT ALL LOOSE CORROSION PRODUCTS HAVE BEEN REMOVED.
CORROSION DAMAGE BEFORE REWORK
LONGITUDINAL
ROUGH EDGES HAVE BEEN SMOOTHED AND ALL CORROSION HAS BEEN REMOVED. HOWEVER, DEPRESSION HAS NOT BEEN SHAPED.
DISH-OUT AFTER BLENDING

FIGURE 6-15. Blendout of corrosion as a single depression.

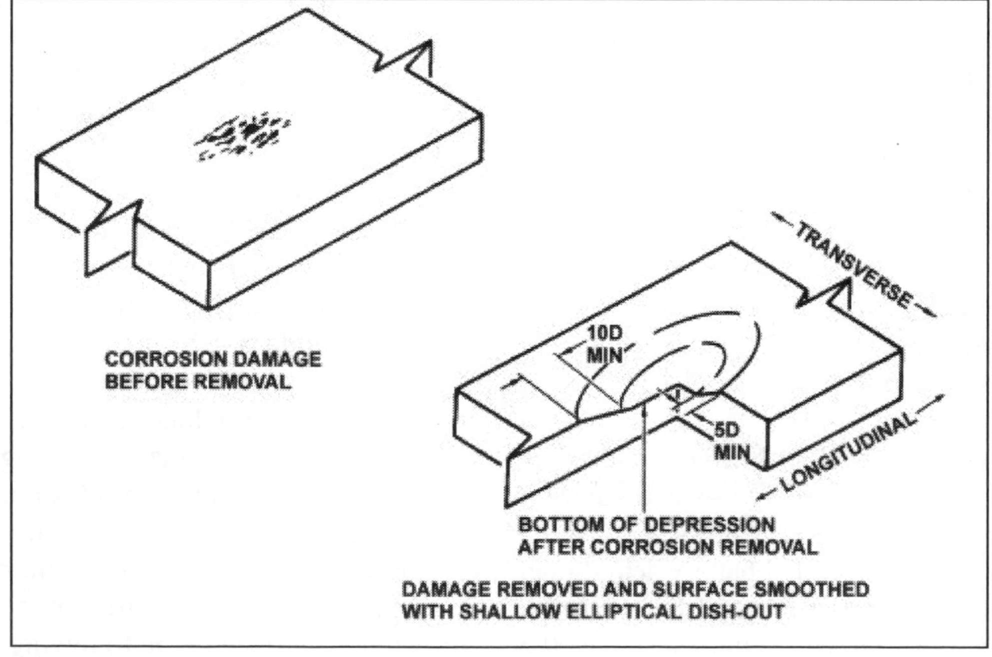
TRANSVERSE
10D MIN
CORROSION DAMAGE BEFORE REMOVAL
5D MIN
LONGITUDINAL
BOTTOM OF DEPRESSION AFTER CORROSION REMOVAL
DAMAGE REMOVED AND SURFACE SMOOTHED WITH SHALLOW ELLIPTICAL DISH-OUT

FIGURE 6-16. Blendout of multiple pits in a corroded area.

6-119.—6-131. [RESERVED.]

SECTION 8. ALUMINUM AND ALUMINUM ALLOYS

6-132. GENERAL. Aluminum and aluminum alloys are the most widely used material for aircraft construction. Aluminum appears high in the electro-chemical series of elements and corrodes very easily. However, the formation of a tightly-adhering oxide film offers increased resistance under most corrosive conditions. Most metals in contact with aluminum form couples that undergo galvanic corrosion attack. The alloys of aluminum are subject to pitting, intergranular corrosion and intergranular stress corrosion cracking. In some cases the corrosion products of metal in contact with aluminum are corrosive to aluminum. Therefore, aluminum and its alloys must be cleaned and protected.

6-133. SPECIAL TREATMENT OF ANODIZED SURFACES. Anodizing is the most common surface treatment of aluminum alloy surfaces. The aluminum sheet or casting is made the positive pole in an electrolyte bath in which chromic acid or other oxidizing agents produce a supplemental protective oxide film on the aluminum surface. The anodized surface coating offers the alloy a great deal of protection as long as it is not damaged. Once the film is damaged, it can only be partially restored by chemical surface treatment. Therefore exercise care to avoid breaking of the protective film, particularly at the edges of the sheet.

6-134. REPAIR OF ALUMINUM ALLOY SHEET METAL. After extensive corrosion removal the following procedures should be followed:

a. If water can be trapped in blended areas, chemical conversion coat in accordance with MIL-C-81706 and fill the blended area with structural adhesive or sealant to the same level and contour as the original skin. When areas are small enough that structural strength has not been significantly decreased, no other work is required prior to applying the protective finish.

b. When corrosion removal exceeds the limits of the structural repair manual, contact a DER or the aircraft manufacturer for repair instructions.

c. Where exterior doublers are installed, it is necessary to seal and insulate them adequately to prevent further corrosion.

d. Doublers should be made from alclad, when available, and the sheet should be anodized (preferred) or a chemical conversion coat applied after all cutting, drilling, and countersinking has been accomplished.

e. All rivet holes should be drilled, countersunk, surface treated, and primed prior to installation of the doubler.

f. Apply a suitable sealing compound in the area to be covered by the doubler. Apply sufficient thickness of sealing compound to fill all voids in the area being repaired.

g. Install rivets wet with sealant. Sufficient sealant should be squeezed out into holes so that all fasteners, as well as all edges of the repair plate, will be sealed against moisture.

h. Remove all excess sealant after fasteners are installed. Apply a fillet sealant bead around the edge of the repair. After the sealant has cured apply the protective paint finish to the reworked area.

6-135. CORROSION REMOVAL AROUND COUNTERSUNK FASTENERS IN ALUMINUM ALLOY. Intergranular corrosion in aluminum alloys often originates at countersunk areas where steel fasteners are used.

a. When corrosion is found around a fixed fastener head, the fastener must be removed to ensure corrosion removal. All corrosion must be removed to prevent further corrosion and loss of structural strength. To reduce the recurrence of corrosion, the panel should receive a chemical conversion coating, be primed, and have the fasteners installed wet with sealant.

b. Each time removable steel fasteners are removed from access panels, they should be inspected for condition of the plating. If mechanical or plating damage is evident, replace the fastener. One of the following fastener installation methods should be used:

(1) Brush a corrosion-preventive compound on the substructure around and in the fastener hole, start the fastener, apply a bead of sealant to the fastener countersink, set and torque the fastener within the working time of the sealant (this is the preferred method).

(2) Apply the corrosion preventive compound to the substructure and fastener, set and torque the fastener.

(3) Apply a coating of primer to the fastener, and while wet with primer, set and torque the fastener.

6-136. EXAMPLES OF REMOVING CORROSION FROM ALUMINUM AND ALUMINUM ALLOYS.

a. Positively identify the metal as aluminum.

b. Clean the area to be reworked. Strip paint if required.

c. Determine extent of corrosion damage.

d. Remove light to moderate corrosion with one of the following.

(1) Non-Powered Corrosion Removal.

(a) The removal of corrosion products by hand can be accomplished by use of aluminum grit and silicon carbide abrasive, such as non-woven, non-metallic, abrasive mat (Spec. MIL-A-9962), abrasive cloth, and paper. Aluminum wool, fiber bristle brushes, and pumice powder are also acceptable methods.

(b) Stainless steel brush (Spec. H-B-178, type III, class 2) may be used as long as the bristles do not exceed 0.010 inch in diameter. After use of this brush the surface should be polished with 60 grit aluminum oxide abrasive paper, then with 400 grit aluminum oxide paper. Care should be exercised in any cleaning process to avoid breaking the protective film.

(c) Steel wool, emery cloth, steel wire brushes (except stainless steel brush) copper alloy brushes, rotary wire brushes, or severe abrasive materials should not be used on any aluminum surface.

(2) Chemical Corrosion Removal.

(a) The corrosion removal compound aluminum pretreatment MIL-C-38334, an acid material, may be used to remove corrosion products from aluminum alloy materials or items (e.g., skins, stringer, ribs in wings, tubing, or ducts). MIL-C-38334 is available in two types:

1 Type I Liquid concentrate materials should be diluted in accordance with the manufacture's instructions before use. Type I has a 1 year shelf life; therefore it shall not be used after 1 year from the date of manufacture.

2 Type II Powdered concentrate materials should be dissolved in the volume of water specified on the kit. These materials have an indefinite shelf life in the dry state. Once mixed, they should be used within 90 days.

(b) Mix MIL-C-38334 in wood, plastic, or plastic-lined containers only. Wear acid-resistant gloves, protective mask and protective clothing when working with this acid compound. If acid contacts the skin or eyes, flush immediately with water.

(c) Apply MIL-C-38334 solution by flowing, mopping, sponging, brushing, or wiping. When applying the solution to large areas, begin the application at the lowest area and work upward, applying the solution with a circular motion to disturb the surface film and ensure proper coverage. If pumping is required, pumps, valves, and fittings should be manufactured from 18-8 stainless steel or plastic.

CAUTION: When working with MIL-C-38334, keep the solution away from magnesium surfaces. The solution must be confined to the area being treated. All parts and assemblies including cadmium-plated items and hinges susceptible to damage from acid should be masked and/or protected. Also mask all openings leading to the primary structure that could trap the solution and doors or other openings that would allow the solution (uncontrolled) to get into the aircraft or equipment interior. It is a good practice to keep a wet rag on hand at all times, for removal of spills or splashes.

(d) Allow the solution to remain on the surface for approximately 12 minutes and then rinse away with clean tap water. For pitted or heavily-corroded areas the compound will be more effective if applied warm (140 °F) followed by vigorous agitation with a non-metallic acid-resisting brush or aluminum oxide abrasive nylon mat. Allow sufficient dwell time, 12 to 15 minutes, before rinsing. After each application examine the pits and/or corroded area to determine if another application is required with a 4 to 10 power magnifying glass. (Select the power depending on the distance available to make the inspection.) Corrosion still on the area will appear as a powdery crust slightly different in color than the uncorroded base metal. Darkening of area due to shadows and reaction from the acid remover should not be considered.

(e) Once the corrosion has been removed and the area well-rinsed with clean water, a chromate conversion coating such as MIL-C-81706 or MIL-C-5541 alodine 1200, must be applied immediately thereafter.

e. Remove moderate to heavy corrosion with one of the following.

(1) Powered Corrosion Removal.

(a) Where the problem is severe enough to warrant the use of power tools, a pneumatic drill motor driving either an aluminum-oxide-impregnated nylon abrasive wheel, flap brush or rubber grinding wheel may be used with an abrasive value to approximately 120 grit, as needed. Corrosion-removal accessories, such as flap brushes or rotary files, should be used on one type of metal only. For example, a flap brush used to remove aluminum should not be used to remove magnesium, steel, etc. Pneumatic sanders may be used with disk and paper acceptable for use on aluminum.

(b) When mechanically removing corrosion from aluminum, especially aircraft skin thinner than 0.0625 inch, extreme care must be used. Vigorous, heavy, continuous abrasive grinding can generate enough heat to cause metallurgical change. If heat damage is suspected, hardness tests or conductivity tests must be accomplished to verify condition of the metal. The use of powered rotary files should be limited to heavy corrosion and should not be used on skin thinner than 0.0625 inch.

(2) Blasting.

(a) Abrasive blasting may be used on aluminum alloys using glass beads (Spec. MIL-G-9954) sizes 10 to 13, or grain abrasive (Spec. MIL-G-5634) types I and III may be used as an alternate method of removing corrosion from clad and non-clad aluminum alloys. Abrasive blasting should not be used to remove heavy corrosion products. Direct pressure machines should have the nozzle pressure set at 30 to 40 psi for clad aluminum alloys and 40 to 45 psi for non-clad aluminum alloys. Engineering approval should be obtained prior to abrasive blasting metal thinner than 0.0625 inch.

(b) When using abrasive blasting on aluminum alloys, do not allow the blast stream to dwell on the same spot longer than 15 seconds. Longer dwell times will cause excessive metal removal. Intergranular exfoliation corrosion is not to be removed by abrasive blasting; however, blasting may be used with powered corrosion removal to determine whether all exfoliation corrosion has been removed.

f. Inspect the area for remaining corrosion. Repeat procedure if any corrosion remains.

NOTE: If corrosion remains after the second attempt, use a stronger method, e.g., chemical to mechanical.

g. Using a blend ratio of 20:1 (length to depth) blend and finish the corrosion rework area with progressively finer abrasive paper until 400-grit paper is used.

h. Clean reworked area using dry cleaning solvent. Do not use kerosene or any other petroleum base fuel as a cleaning solvent.

i. Determine depth of faired depressions to ensure that rework limits have not been exceeded.

j. Apply chemical conversion coating, MIL-C-81706, immediately after reworking. If 48 hours or more have elapsed since the conversion coating was first applied and the primer or final paint system has not yet been applied, then reapply the conversion coating before continuing.

NOTE: These solutions should not be allowed to come in contact with magnesium or high-strength steels (180,000 psi). Do not permit solutions or materials to contact paint thinner, acetone or other combustible material: FIRE MAY RESULT.

k. Apply paint finish to area.

6-137.—6-147. [RESERVED.]

SECTION 9. MAGNESIUM AND MAGNESIUM ALLOYS

6-148. GENERAL. Magnesium and magnesium alloys are the most chemically active of the metals used in aircraft construction and are the most difficult to protect. However, corrosion on magnesium surfaces is probably the easiest to detect in its early stages. Since magnesium corrosion products occupy several times the volume of the original magnesium metal destroyed, initial signs show a lifting of the paint films and white spots on the magnesium surface. These rapidly develop into snow-like mounds or even white whiskers. The prompt and complete correction of the coating failure is imperative if serious structural damage is to be avoided.

6-149. TREATMENT OF WROUGHT MAGNESIUM SHEETS AND FORGINGS. Corrosive attack on magnesium skins will usually occur around the edges of skin panels, underneath hold-down washers, or in areas physically damaged by shearing, drilling, abrasion, or impact. Entrapment of moisture under and behind skin crevices is frequently a contributing factor. If the skin section can be easily removed, this should be accomplished to ensure complete inhibition and treatment.

a. Complete mechanical removal of corrosion products should be practiced when practical. Mechanical cleaning should normally be limited to the use of stiff bristle brushes and similar nonmetallic cleaning tools.

b. Any entrapment of steel particles from steel wire brushes, steel tools, or contamination of treated surfaces, or dirty abrasives, can cause more trouble than the initial corrosive attack. The following procedural summary is recommended for treatment of corroded magnesium areas when accomplished under most field conditions.

c. When aluminum insulating washers are used and they no longer fasten tightly to magnesium panels, corrosion is likely to occur under the washers if corrective measures are not taken.

(1) When machine screw fasteners are used, aluminum insulating washers must be removed from all locations to surface treat the magnesium panel.

(2) Where permanent fasteners other than machine screws are used, the insulating washer and fastener must be removed.

(3) When located so water can be trapped in the counter-bored area where the washer was located, use sealants to fill the counterbore. If necessary, fill several areas adjacent to each other. It may be advantageous to cover the entire row of fasteners with a strip of sealant.

6-150. REPAIR OF MAGNESIUM SHEET METAL AFTER EXTENSIVE CORROSION REMOVAL. The same general instructions apply when making repairs in magnesium as in aluminum alloy skin, except that two coats of epoxy primer may be required on both the doubler and skin being patched instead of one. Where it is difficult to form magnesium alloys in the contour, aluminum alloy may be utilized. When this is done, it is necessary to ensure effective dissimilar metal insulation. Vinyl tape will ensure positive separation of dissimilar metals, but edges will still have to be sealed to prevent entrance of moisture between mating surfaces at all points where repairs are made. It is recommended that only non-corrosive type sealant be used, since it serves a dual purpose of material separation and sealing.

6-151. IN-PLACE TREATMENT OF MAGNESIUM CASTINGS. Magnesium castings, in general, are more porous and more prone to penetrating attack than wrought magnesium skin. However, treatment in the field is, for all practical purposes, the same for all magnesium. Bellcranks, fittings, and numerous covers, plates, and handles may also be magnesium castings. When attack occurs on a casting, the earliest practical treatment is required to prevent dangerous corrosive penetration. Engine cases in salt water can develop moth holes and complete penetration overnight.

a. If at all practical, faying surfaces involved shall be separated to treat the existing attack effectively and prevent its further progress. The same general treatment sequence as detailed for magnesium skin should be followed. Where engine cases are concerned, baked enamel overcoats are usually involved rather than other top coat finishes. A good air drying enamel can be used to restore protection.

b. If extensive removal of corrosion products from a structural casting is involved, a decision from the aircraft manufacturer or a DER may be necessary to evaluate the adequacy of structural strength remaining. Refer to the aircraft manufacturer if any questions of safety are involved.

6-152. EXAMPLE OF REMOVING CORROSION FROM MAGNESIUM. If possible, corroded magnesium parts shall be removed from aircraft. When impossible to remove the part, the following procedure will be used.

a. Positively identify metal as magnesium.

b. Clean area to be reworked.

c. Strip paint if required.

d. Determine the extent of corrosion damage.

e. Remove light to moderate corrosion by one of the following means.

(1) Non-Powered Corrosion Removal.

(a) Non-powered removal can be accomplished using abrasive mats, cloth, and paper with aluminum oxide grit (do not use silicon carbide abrasive). Metallic wools and hand brushes compatible with magnesium such as stainless steel and aluminum, may be used.

(b) When a brush is used the bristles should not exceed 0.010 inch in diameter. After using a brush, the surface should be polished with 400 grit aluminum oxide abrasive paper, then with 600 grit aluminum oxide abrasive paper.

(c) Pumice powder may be used to remove stains or to remove corrosion on thin metal surfaces where minimum metal removal is allowed.

(2) Chemical Corrosion Removal.

(a) Chemical corrosion removal on magnesium alloys is usually done with a chromic acid pickle solution. Chemical corrosion removal methods are not considered adequate for areas that have:

1 Deep pitting,

2 Heavy corrosion and corrosion by products,

3 Previously had corrosion removed by mechanical means, or

4 Previously been sand blasted.

(b) Do not use this method for parts containing copper and steel-based inserts (unless the inserts are masked off) and where it might come into contact with adhesive bonded skins or parts.

(3) The following solution may be used to remove surface oxidation and light corrosion products from magnesium surfaces.

(a) Solution Composition and Operation:

1 Chromium Trioxide. 24 oz.

2 (O-C-303, Type II). Water to Make 1 gal. Reaction Time 1 to 15 min.

3 Operation Temperature. (Solution can be operated at room temperature for a longer reaction time if desired.) 190 to 202 °F.

4 Container Construction. Lead-lined steel, stainless steel, or 1100 aluminum.

(b) Mask off nearby operating mechanisms, cracks and plated steel to keep the solution from attacking them.

(c) Apply chromic acid solution carefully to the corroded area with an acid-resistant brush.

(d) Allow the solution to remain on the surface for approximately 15 minutes. Agitation may be required.

(e) Thoroughly rinse the solution from the surface with plenty of clean water.

(f) Repeat the preceding sequence as necessary until all corrosion products have been removed and the metal is a bright metallic color.

f. Remove moderate to heavy corrosion by one of the following means.

(1) Powered Corrosion Removal.

(a) Powered corrosion removal can be accomplished using pneumatic drill motor with either an aluminum-oxide-impregnated abrasive wheel, flap brush, or rubber grinding wheel with an abrasive value to approximately 120 grain size.

(b) Also a rotary file with fine flutes can be used for severe or heavy corrosion product buildup on metals thicker than 0.0625 inch. If a flap brush or rotary file is used, it should only be used on one type of metal. Do not use either a hand or rotary carbon steel brush on magnesium.

(c) Pneumatic sanders are acceptable if used with disk or paper of aluminum oxide. When using sanders, use extra care to avoid over heating aircraft skins thinner than 0.0625 inch.

(d) Do not use rotary wire brushes on magnesium.

WARNING: Cuttings and small shavings from magnesium can ignite easily and are an extreme fire hazard. Fires of this metal must be extinguished with absolutely dry talc, calcium carbonate, sand, or graphite by applying the powder to a depth of 1/2 inch over the metal.

(2) Blasting. Abrasive blasting is an approved method of corrosion removal on magnesium alloys of a thickness greater than 0.0625 inch. Remove heavy corrosion products by hand brushing with a stainless steel or fiber brush followed by vacuum abrasive blasting with glass beads, (Spec. MIL-G-9954) sizes 10-13; or grain abrasive (Spec. MIL-G-5634), types I or III at an air pressure of 10 to 35 psi (if suction equipment is used, use a 50 percent higher pressure). Upon completion of blasting, inspect for the presence of corrosion in the blast area. Give particular attention to areas where pitting has progressed into intergranular attack. This is necessary because abrasive blasting has a tendency to close up streaks of intergranular corrosion rather than remove them if the operator uses an improper impingement angle. If the corrosion has not been removed in a total blasting time of 60 seconds on any one specific area, other mechanical methods of removal should be utilized.

CAUTION: When blasting magnesium alloys, do not allow the blast stream to dwell on the same spot longer than 15 seconds. Longer dwell times will cause excessive metal removal.

g. Inspect the reworked area to ensure that no corrosion products remain. If corrosion products are found, repeat method used and re-inspect.

h. Fair depressions resulting from rework using a blend ratio of 20:1. Clean rework area using 240 grit abrasive paper. Smooth with 300 grit and finally polish with 400 grit abrasive paper.

i. Determine depth of faired depressions to ensure that rework limits have not been exceeded. Refer to the manufacture's specifications.

j. Clean reworked area using a solvent to provide a water-break-free surface. Do not use kerosene or another petroleum base fuel as a cleaning solvent.

k. Apply Chromic Acid Brush-on Pretreatment.

(1) Chemical pretreatment such as the following chromic acid solution (Conversion coat conforming to Spec. MIL-M-3171, type VI) provides a passive surface layer with an inhibitive characteristic that resists corrosive attack and also provides a bond for subsequent coatings. Properly-applied magnesium pretreatment tend to neutralize corrosion media in contact with the surface.

(2) The chromic acid brush-on pretreatment may be applied to all magnesium parts that require touch-up. This treatment is generally used in refinishing procedures or when parts and assemblies are too large to be immersed. This treatment is less critical to apply than the other brush-on treatments. It is relatively inexpensive and not as harmful when trapped in faying surfaces.

(a) Solution Composition and Operation:

1 Distilled Water 1 gal.

2 Chromic Acid (CrO_3) 1.3 oz.

3 (99.5 pure), Calcium Sulfate 1 oz. ($CaSo_4.2H_2O$)

4 Operating Temp. 70-90 °F.

5 Container: Stainless Steel, Aluminum, Vinyl, Polyethylene, or Rubber.

NOTE: Good application requires proper preparation of the chromic acid coating solution and cleaning of the surface where the solution will be applied. A water-break test is recommended if the cleanliness of the surface is in doubt.

(b) Add chemicals to water in the order shown.

(c) Stir vigorously for at least 15 minutes, either mechanically or by air agitation, to ensure that the solution is saturated with calcium sulfate. (Let solution stand for 15 minutes before decanting.)

(d) Prior to use, decant solution (avoid transfer of undissolved calcium sulfate) into suitable containers (polyethylene or glass).

(e) Apply solution by brush, swab, or flow on using low-pressure spray (non-atomizing) until the metal surface becomes a dull color (the color can vary from green-brown, brassy, yellow-brown to dark-brown). For good paint adhesion, a dark-brown color free of powder is considered best. The color may vary in using different vendors' materials.

NOTE: Too long an exposure to the brush-on solution produces coatings that will powder and impair adhesion of applied paint finish/films.

(f) Observe the coating closely during the treatment for color changes, rinsed with cold running watcr when the desired condition/color is reached and air dried. Preparation and use of test panels made of the same material and under the same conditions, before starting the actual treating operation may be used as to determine the application time required to produce the required coating. A good coating is uniform in color/density, adheres well and is free of loose powder.

l. Apply primer and top coat finish

m. Remove masking and protective coverings.

6-153.—6-163. [RESERVED.]

SECTION 10. FERROUS METALS

6-164. GENERAL. One of the most familiar kinds of corrosion is red iron rust. Red iron rust results from atmospheric oxidation of steel surfaces. Some metal oxides protect the underlying base metal, but red rust is not a protective coating. Its presence actually promotes additional attack by attracting moisture from the air and acts as a catalyst to promote additional corrosion.

a. Red rust first shows on bolt heads, hold down nuts, and other unprotected aircraft hardware. Red rust will often occur under nameplates that are secured to steel parts. Its presence in these areas is generally not dangerous. It has no immediate effect on the structural strength of any major components. However, it shows a general lack of maintenance and may indicate attack in more critical areas.

b. When paint failures occur or mechanical damage exposes highly-stressed steel surfaces to the atmosphere, even the smallest amount of rusting is potentially dangerous and should be removed immediately.

6-165. SPECIAL TREATMENT OF HIGH-STRENGTH STEEL. (High-strength steels heat treated above Rockwell C40, 180,000 psi tensile strength). Any corrosion on the surface of a highly-stressed steel part is potentially dangerous, and the careful removal of corrosion products is mandatory. Surface scratches or change in surface structure from overheating can cause sudden failure of these parts. The removal of corrosion products is required and will be performed carefully and completely.

a. Acceptable methods include careful use of mild abrasive mats, cloths, and papers, such as fine grit aluminum oxide, metallic wool, or fine buffing compounds.

b. Undesirable methods include the use of any power tool because the danger of local overheating and the formation of notches that could lead to failure. The use of chemical corrosion removers is prohibited, without engineering authorization, because high-strength steel parts are subject to hydrogen embrittlement.

6-166. SPECIAL TREATMENT OF STAINLESS STEEL. Stainless steels are of two general types: magnetic and nonmagnetic.

a. Magnetic steels are of the ferritic or martensitic types and are identified by numbers in the 400-series. Corrosion often occurs on 400-series stainless steels and treatment is the same as specified in high-strength steels. (See paragraph 6-165.)

b. Non-magnetic stainless steels are of the austenitic type and are identified by numbers in the 300-series. They are much more corrosion resistant than the 400-series steels, particularly in a marine environment.

(1) Austenitic steels develop corrosion resistance by an oxide film, which should not be removed even though the surface is discolored. The original oxide film is normally formed at time of fabrication by passivation. If this film is broken accidentally or by abrasion, it may not restore itself without repassivation.

(2) If any deterioration or corrosion does occur on austenitic steels, and the structural integrity or serviceability of the part is affected, it will be necessary to remove the part.

6-167. EXAMPLE OF REMOVING CORROSION FROM FERROUS METALS. If possible, corroded steel parts should be removed from the aircraft. When impractical to remove the part, follow the procedure below.

a. Prepare the area for rework.

b. Positively identify the metal as steel and establish its heat-treated value.

c. Clean the area and strip paint if required.

NOTE: Use of acid-based strippers, chemical removers, or chemical conversion coatings are not permitted on steel parts without engineering authorization.

d. Determine extent of corrosion damage.

e. Remove residual corrosion by hand sanding with mild abrasive mats, cloths, and papers, such as fine aluminum oxide grit.

f. Remove heavy deposits of corrosion products by approved mechanical methods for that particular form of steel and/or stainless steel.

g. Inspect the area for remaining corrosion. Repeat procedure if any corrosion remains and the structural integrity of the part is not in danger, and the part meets the rework limits established by the manufacturer or FAA authorized DER.

h. Fair depressions using a blend ratio of 20:1. Clean area using 240-grit paper. Smooth area with 300-grit paper and give final polish with 400-grit paper.

i. Determine depth of faired depression to ensure that rework limits have not been exceeded.

j. Clean reworked area with dry cleaning solvent. Do not use kerosene.

k. Apply protective finish or specific organic finish as required.

NOTE: Steel surfaces are highly-reactive immediately following corrosion removal; consequently, primer coats should be applied within 1 hour after sanding.

l. Remove masking and protective coverings.

6-168.—6-178. [RESERVED.]

SECTION 11. OTHER METALS AND ALLOYS

6-179. NOBLE METAL COATINGS - CLEANUP AND RESTORATION. Silver, platinum, and gold finishes are used in aircraft assemblies because of their resistance to ordinary surface attack and their improved electrical or heat conductivity. Silver-plated electrodes can be cleaned of brown or black sulfide tarnish, by placing them in contact with a piece of magnesium sheet stock while immersed in a warm water solution of common table salt mixed with baking soda or by using a fine grade abrasive mat or pencil eraser followed by solvent cleaning. If assemblies are involved, careful drying and complete displacement of water is necessary. In general, cleaning of gold or platinum coatings is not recommended in the field.

6-180. COPPER AND COPPER ALLOYS are relatively corrosion resistant, and attack on such components will usually be limited to staining and tarnish. Such change in surface condition is not dangerous and should ordinarily have no effect on the function of the part. However, if it is necessary to remove such staining, a chromic acid solution of 8 to 24 ounces per gallon of water containing a small amount of battery electrolyte (not to exceed 50 drops per gallon) is an effective brightening bath. Staining may also be removed using a fine grade abrasive mat or pencil eraser followed by solvent cleaning.

a. Immerse the stained part in the cold solution. Surfaces can also be treated in place by applying the solution to the stained surface with a small brush.

b. Avoid any entrapment of the solution after treatment. Clean the part thoroughly following treatment with all residual solution removed.

c. Serious copper corrosion is evident by the accumulation of green-to-blue copper salts on the corroded part. Remove these products mechanically using a stiff bristle brush, brass wire brush, 400-grit abrasive paper or bead blast with glass beads, (specification MIL-G-9954, size 13). Air pressure when blasting should be 20 to 30 psi for direct pressure machines. Do not bead blast braided copper flexible lines. Reapply a surface coating over the reworked area. Chromic acid treatment will tend to remove the residual corrosion products.

WARNING: Brushing, sanding, and abrasive blasting of copper and copper alloys can be dangerous due to the creation of toxic airborne particles. Take necessary precautions to ensure safety.

6-181. TITANIUM AND TITANIUM ALLOYS are highly corrosion resistant because an oxide film forms on their surfaces upon contact with air.

a. When titanium is heated, different oxides having different colors form on the surface. A blue oxide coating will form at 700 to 800 °F; a purple oxide at 800 to 950 °F; and a gray or black oxide at 1000 °F or higher. These coatings are protective discolorations and should not be removed.

b. Corrosive attack on titanium surfaces is difficult to detect. It may show deterioration from the presence of salt deposits and metal impurities at elevated temperatures so periodic removal of surface deposits is required. However, if corrosion develops on titanium, it usually occurs as pitting. Acceptable methods for corrosion removal are:

(1) Stainless steel wool or hand brush.

(2) Abrasive mats, cloths, and papers with either aluminum oxide or silicon carbide grit.

(3) Dry abrasive blasting using glass beads (spec. MIL-G-9954) sizes 10-13 or Aluminum oxide (spec. MIL-G-21380, type I, grades A or B) at a blast pressure of 40 to 50 psi (if using suction equipment use 50 percent higher pressure).

WARNING: Dry abrasive blasting of titanium alloys creates sparking. Ensure that hazardous concentrations of flammable vapors are not present.

(4) Hand polish with aluminum polish and soft cloth.

c. Titanium surfaces are susceptible to hydrogen embrittlement that can induce stress corrosion and associated pitting. Therefore, chemicals such as fire-resistant hydraulic fluids must be controlled. Chlorinated hydrocarbon solvents and chemical corrosion removers are prohibited from use on titanium and titanium alloys.

6-182.—6-192. [RESERVED.]

SECTION 12. PLATED PARTS

6-193. CHROMIUM AND NICKEL-PLATED PARTS. Nickel and chromium platings are used extensively as protective and wear-resistant coatings over high-strength steel parts (landing gear journals, shock strut pistons, etc.). Chromium and nickel plate provide protection by forming a somewhat impervious physical coat over the underlying base metal. When breaks occur in the surface, the protection is destroyed.

a. The amount of reworking that can be performed on chromium and nickel-plated components is limited.

b. The rework should consist of light buffing to remove corrosion products and produce the required smoothness. The buffing should not take the plating below the minimum allowable thickness.

c. Whenever a chromium or nickel-plated component requires buffing, coat the area with a corrosion-preventive compound, if possible.

d. When buffing exceeds the minimum thickness of the plating, or the base metal has sustained corrosive attack, the component should be removed and replaced.

e. The removed component can be restored to serviceable condition by having the old plating completely stripped and replated in accordance with acceptable methods and specifications.

6-194. CADMIUM AND ZINC-PLATED PARTS. Cadmium plating is used extensively in aircraft construction as a protective finish over both steel and copper alloys. Protection is provided by a sacrificial process in which the cadmium is attacked rather than the underlying base material. Properly functioning cadmium surface coatings may show mottling, ranging from white to brown to black spots on their surfaces. These show the sacrificial protection being offered by the cadmium coat, and under no condition should such spotting be removed merely for appearance sake. In fact, cadmium will continue to protect even when actual breaks in the coating develop and bare steel or exposed copper surfaces appear.

a. When the breakdown of the cadmium plating occurs and the initial appearance of corrosion products on the base metal develops, some mechanical cleaning of the area may be necessary but shall be limited to removal of the corrosion products from the underlying base material.

b. Under no condition should such a coating be cleaned with a wire brush. If protection is needed, a touch-up with primer or a temporary preservative coating should be applied. Restoration of the plate coating cannot be done in the field.

c. Zinc coatings offer protection in an identical manner to cadmium, and the corrective treatment for failure is generally the same as for cadmium-plated parts. However, the amount of zinc on aircraft structures is very limited and usually does not present a maintenance problem.

6-195.—6-205. [RESERVED.]

SECTION 13. CORROSION PROOFING OF LAND PLANES CONVERTED TO SEA PLANES

6-206. GENERAL. A special problem is encountered in the conversion of land planes to seaplanes. In general, land planes do not receive corrosion proofing to the same extent as do seaplanes. Corrosion-proofing standards for land planes converted to seaplanes are divided into two classes, necessary minimum precautions and recommended precautions. Regardless of such precautions, it is imperative that the exterior surfaces of seaplanes be washed with clear fresh water immediately following extended water operation, or at least once a day when operated in salty or brackish water. Wash interior surfaces of seaplanes exposed to spray, taking care to prevent damage to electrical circuits or other items subject to injury.

6-207. NECESSARY MINIMUM PRECAUTIONS. The following procedures are considered the minimum to safeguard the airworthiness of converted aircraft and are not in themselves intended to maintain airworthiness for an indefinite period.

a. Unless already protected, treat exposed fittings or fittings that can be reached through inspection openings with two coats of zinc chromate primer, paralketone, nonwater-soluble heavy grease, or comparable materials. This applies to items such as wing-root fittings, wing-strut fittings, control-surface hinges, horns, mating edges of fittings, and attached bolts.

b. Coat non-stainless control cables with grease or paralketone or other comparable protective coating, if not replaced with corrosion-resistant cables.

c. Inspect all accessible sections of aircraft structure. Clean structural parts showing corrosion and refinish if corrosion attack is superficial. If a part is severely corroded, replace with an adequately corrosion-proofed part.

6-208. RECOMMENDED PRECAUTIONS. Recommended precautions are those which are suggested as a means of maintaining such aircraft in condition for safe operation over extended periods.

a. Provide additional inspection openings to assist in detecting corrosion. Experience has shown openings to allow inspection of the lower and rearward portion of the fuselage to be particularly desirable.

b. Incorporate additional provisions for free drainage and ventilation of all interiors to prevent collection of moisture (scoop-type marine drain grommets).

c. Protect the interior of structural steel tubing. This may be done by air and watertight sealing or by flushing with hot linseed oil and plugging the openings. Inspect tubing for missing sealing screws, presence of entrapped water, local corrosion around sealing screws, welded clusters, and bolted fittings, which may be indicative of entrapped moisture.

d. Slit the fabric of fabric-covered aircraft longitudinally on the bottom of the fuselage and tail structure for access to these sections. Coat the lower structural members with zinc chromate primer (two coats); follow by a coat of dope-proof paint or wrap with cellophane tape and rejoin the fabric. This precaution is advisable within a few months after start of operation as a seaplane.

e. Spray the interior of metal-covered wings and fuselages with an adherent corrosion inhibitor.

f. Place bags of potassium or sodium dichromate in the bottom of floats and boat hulls to inhibit corrosion.

g. Prevent the entry of water by sealing, as completely as possible, all openings in wings, fuselage, control-surface members, openings for control cables, tail-wheel wells, etc.

6-209.—6-219. [RESERVED.]

SECTION 14. HANDLING AND CARE OF AIRCRAFT RECOVERED FROM WATER IMMERSION.

6-220. GENERAL. Aircraft recovered from partial or total immersion in standing water or flash floods require an in-depth inspection and cleaning of both the exterior and interior areas. Water-immersion increases the probability of corrosive attack, it removes lubricants, deteriorates aircraft materials, and destroys electrical and avionics components.

a. Sea water, because of salt content, is more corrosive than fresh water. However, fresh water may also contain varying amounts of salt and, as drying occurs, the salt concentration is increased and corrosive attack accelerated.

b. Prompt action is the most important factor following recovery of an aircraft from water-immersion. Components of the aircraft which have been immersed, such as the powerplant, accessories, airframe sections, actuating mechanisms, screws, bearings, working surfaces, fuel and oil systems, wiring, radios, and radar should be disassembled, as necessary, and the contaminants completely removed.

6-221. INITIAL FRESH WATER OR DETERGENT WASH. As soon as possible after the aircraft is recovered from water-immersion, thoroughly wash all internal and external areas of the aircraft using a water/detergent solution as follows:

a. Mix liquid detergent (MIL-D-16791, type I) and isopropyl alcohol (TT-I-735) in ratio of eight parts detergent, to 20 parts of alcohol. Add the detergent/alcohol mixture to 72 parts of tap water and mix thoroughly. For use, add one part of the preceding concentrate to nine parts of tap water (warm water if available) and mix thoroughly.

b. If the above specified detergent/alcohol materials are not available, use water-emulsion cleaning compound (MIL-C-43616). Add one part compound to nine parts water. If the MIL cleaning compound is not available, use any available mild household detergent solution with fresh tap water.

6-222. RECIPROCATING ENGINES AND PROPELLERS. Remove the propeller from the engine and the engine from the aircraft. The exterior of the engine and propeller should be washed with steam, or fresh water, preferably hot.

a. Major accessories, engine parts, etc., should be removed and all surfaces flushed with fresh water, preferably hot. If facilities are available, immerse the removed parts, time permitting, in hot water or hot oil, 180 °F, for a short time. Soft water is preferred. Change the water frequently. All parts must be completely dried by air blast or other means. If no heat-drying facility is available, wipe the cleaned parts with suitable drying cloths.

b. The constant-speed propeller mechanism should be disassembled, as required, to permit complete decontamination. Clean parts with steam or fresh water, preferably hot. Dry the cleaned parts in an oven, but if a heat-drying facility is not available, wipe the cleaned parts with suitable drying cloths.

6-223. AIRFRAME. The salvable components of the fuselage, wings, empennage, seaplane and amphibian hulls and floats, and movable surfaces should be processed as follows:

a. The fabric from fabric-covered surfaces should be removed and replaced.

b. Clean the aircraft interior and exterior using steam under pressure with steam cleaning compound. Direct the steam into all seams and crevices where corrosive water may have penetrated. Avoid steam cleaning electrical equipment, such as terminal boards and relays.

c. Areas that have been steam cleaned should be rinsed immediately with either hot or cold fresh water.

d. Touch up all scratches and scars on painted surfaces using zinc chromate primer or preservative.

e. Undrained hollow spaces or fluid entrapment areas should be provided temporary draining facilities by drilling out rivets at the lowest point. Install new rivets after drainage.

f. Remove and replace all leather, fabric upholstery, and insulation. Plastic or rubber foam that cannot be cleaned of all corrosive water must be replaced.

g. All drain plugs or drive screws in tubular structures should be removed and the structure blown out with compressed air. If water has reached the tubular interiors, carefully flush with hot fresh water and blow out water with compressed air. Roll the structure as necessary to remove water from pockets. Fill the tubes with hot linseed oil, approximately 180 °F, drain oil and replace drain plugs or drive screws.

h. Clean sealed wood, metallic, and other non-metallic areas, excluding acrylic plastics, with warm water. Replace wood, metalite, and other porous materials exposed to water-immersion unless surfaces are adequately sealed to prevent penetration by water. Virtually all solvents and phenolic type cleaning agents are detrimental to acrylics and will either soften the plastic or cause crazing.

i. Remove instruments and radios and applicable cables and plumbing, and repair and inspect as necessary.

6-224.—6-234. [RESERVED.]

CHAPTER 7. AIRCRAFT HARDWARE, CONTROL CABLES, AND TURNBUCKLES

SECTION 1. RIVETS

7-1. GENERAL.

a. Standard solid-shank rivets and the universal head rivets (AN470) are used in aircraft construction in both interior and exterior locations. All protruding head rivets may be replaced by MS20470 (supersedes AN470) rivets. This has been adopted as the standard for protruding head rivets in the United States.

b. Roundhead rivets (AN430) are used in the interior of aircraft except where clearance is required for adjacent members.

c. Flathead rivets (AN442) are used in the interior of the aircraft where interference of adjacent members does not permit the use of roundhead rivets.

d. Brazierhead rivets (AN455 and AN456) are used on the exterior surfaces of aircraft where flush riveting is not essential.

e. Countersunk head rivets MS20426 (supersedes AN426 100-degree) are used on the exterior surfaces of aircraft to provide a smooth aerodynamic surface, and in other applications where a smooth finish is desired. The 100-degree countersunk head has been adopted as the standard in the United States. Refer to MIL-HD BK5 Metallic Materials and Elements for Fight Vehicle Structures, and U.S.A.F./Navy T./O. 1-1A-8, Structural Hardware."

f. Typical rivet types are shown in table 7-10.

7-2. MATERIAL APPLICATIONS.

a. Rivets made with 2117-T4 are the most commonly used rivets in aluminum alloy structures. The main advantage of 2117-T4 is that it may be used in the condition received without further treatment.

b. The 2017-T3, 2017-T31, and 2024-T4 rivets are used in aluminum alloy structures where strength higher than that of the 2117-T4 rivet is needed. See Metallic Materials and Elements for Flight Vehicle Structures (MIL-HDBK-5) for differences between the types of rivets specified here.

c. The 1100 rivets of pure aluminum are used for riveting nonstructural parts fabricated from the softer aluminum alloys, such as 1100, 3003, and 5052.

d. When riveting magnesium alloy structures, 5056 rivets are used exclusively due to their corrosion-resistant qualities in combination with the magnesium alloys.

e. Mild steel rivets are used primarily in riveting steel parts. **Do not** use galvanized rivets on steel parts subjected to high heat.

f. Corrosion-resistant steel rivets are used primarily in riveting corrosion-resistant steel parts such as firewalls, exhaust stack bracket attachments, and similar structures.

g. Monel rivets are used in special cases for riveting high-nickel steel alloys and nickel alloys. They may be used interchangeably with stainless steel rivets as they are more easily driven. However, it is preferable to use stainless steel rivets in stainless steel parts.

h. Copper rivets are used for riveting copper alloys, leather, and other nonmetallic materials. This rivet has only limited usage in aircraft.

i. Hi-Shear rivets are sometimes used in connections where the shearing loads are the primary design consideration. Its use is restricted to such connections. It should be noted that Hi-Shear rivets are not to be used for the installation of control surface hinges and hinge brackets. Do not paint the rivets before assembly, even where dissimilar metals are being joined. However, it is advisable to touch up each end of the driven rivet with primer to allow the later application of the general airplane finish.

j. Blind rivets in the NASM20600 through NASM20603 series rivets and the mechanically-locked stem NAS 1398, 1399, 1738, and 1739 rivets sometimes may be substituted for solid rivets. They should not be used where the looseness or failure of a few rivets will impair the airworthiness of the aircraft. Design allowable for blind rivets are specified in MIL-HDBK-5. Specific structural applications are outlined in NASM33522. Nonstructural applications for such blind rivets as NASM20604 and NASM20605 are contained in NASM33557.

CAUTION: For sheet metal repairs to airframe, the use of blind rivets must be authorized by the airframe manufacturer or approved by a representative of the FAA.

For more information on blind rivets, see page 4-19, f. of this document.

7-3.—7-13. [RESERVED.]

SECTION 2. SCREWS

7-14. GENERAL. In general, screws differ from bolts by the following characteristics.

a. Screws usually have lower material strength, a looser thread fit, head shapes formed to engage a screwdriver, and the shank may be threaded along its entire length without a clearly defined grip. Screws may be divided into three basic groups: structural screws, machine screws, and self-tapping screws. Screws are marked as required by the applicable Army Navy (AN), National Aerospace Standard (NAS), or Military Standard (MS) drawing. Normally a manufacturer places his trademark on the head of the screw. Several types of structural screws are available that differ from the standard structural bolts only in the type of head.

b. It would be impossible to cover all screws that are available to the aviation market; therefore, only the most frequently used screws will be discussed in this text. Design specifications are available in MIL-HDBK-5, or U.S.A.F./Navy T.O.1-1A-8/NAVAIR 01-1A-8, Structural Hardware.

c. Typical screw types are shown in table 7-11.

7-15. STRUCTURAL SCREWS. NAS502, NAS503, AN509, NAS220 through NAS227, and NAS583 through NAS590, may be used for structural applications, similar to structural bolts or rivets. These screws are fabricated from a material with a high-tensile strength and differ from structural bolts only in the type of head.

7-16. MACHINE SCREWS. These screws are available in four basic head styles: flathead (countersunk), roundhead, fillister, and socket head.

a. Flathead machine screws (AN505, AN510, AN507, NAS200, NAS514, NAS517, and NAS662) are used in countersunk holes where a flush surface is desired.

b. Roundhead machine screws (AN515 and AN520) are general-purpose screws for use in nonstructural applications.

c. Fillister head machine screws (AN500 through AN503, AN116901 through AN116912, AN116913 through AN116924, AN116962 through AN116990, AN117002 through AN117030, and AN117042 through AN117070) are general-purpose screws that may be used as capscrews in light mechanical applications and are usually drilled for safety wire.

d. Socket head machine screws (NAS608 and NAS609) are designed to be driven into tapped holes by means of internal wrenches. They may be used in applications requiring high strength, compactness of assembled parts, or sinking of heads below surfaces into fitted holes.

7-17. PANHEAD SCREWS (NAS600 THROUGH NAS606, NAS610 THROUGH NAS616, NAS623, AND NAS1402 THROUGH NAS1406). Flathead screws (MS35188 through MS35203), panhead machine screws (MS35024 through MS35219), and truss-head screws (AN526) are general-purpose screws used where head height is not important.

7-18. SELF-TAPPING SCREWS. The self-tapping screw taps their own mating thread when driven into untapped or punched holes slightly smaller than the diameter of the screw. Self-tapping machine screws (AN504 and AN530), may be used to attach minor nonstructural parts. Self-tapping sheet metal screws (AN504, AN530, AN531 and NAS548) may be used in blind applications for the temporary attachment of sheet metal for riveting and the permanent assembly of nonstructural assemblies. The MS21318 is a roundhead drive screw used in the attachment of nameplates or in sealing drain holes, and is not intended to be removed after installation. They are normally installed by driving the screw into a drilled hole with a hammer.

CAUTION: Self-tapping screws should never be used as a replacement for standard screws, nuts, bolts, or rivets in any aircraft structure.

7-19. WOOD SCREWS AN545 and AN550, MS35492 and MS35493 are screws used in wood structures of aircraft.

7-20.—7-33. [RESERVED.]

SECTION 3. BOLTS

7-34. GENERAL. "Hardware" is the term used to describe the various types of fasteners and small items used to assemble and repair aircraft structures and components. Only hardware with traceability to an approved manufacturing process or source should be used. This traceability will ensure that the hardware is at least equal to the original or properly-altered condition. Hardware that is not traceable or is improperly altered, may be substandard or counterfeit, since their physical properties cannot be substantiated. Selection and use of fasteners are as varied as the types of aircraft; therefore, care should be taken to ensure fasteners are approved by the Federal Aviation Administration (FAA) for the intended installation, repair, or replacement. Threaded fasteners (bolts/screws) and rivets are the most commonly used fasteners because they are designed to carry shear and/or tensile loads.

7-35. BOLTS. Most bolts used in aircraft structures are either general-purpose, internal-wrenching, or close-tolerance AN, NAS, or MS bolts. In certain cases, fastener manufacturers produce bolts of different dimensions or greater strength than the standard types. *Such bolts are made for a particular application, and it is of extreme importance to use like bolts in replacement.* Design specifications are available in MIL-HDBK-5 or USAF/Navy T.O. 1-1A-8/NAVAIR 01-1A-8. References should be made to military specifications and industry design standards such as NAS, the Society of Automotive Engineers (SAE), and Aerospace Material Standards (AMS). Typical bolt types are shown in table 7-12.

7-36. IDENTIFICATION. Aircraft bolts may be identified by code markings on the bolt heads. These markings generally denote the material of which the bolt is made, whether the bolt is a standard AN-type or a special-purpose bolt, and sometimes include the manufacturer.

a. AN standard steel bolts are marked with either a raised dash or asterisk, corrosion-resistant steel is marked by a single dash, and AN aluminum-alloy bolts are marked with two raised dashes.

b. Special-purpose bolts include high-strength, low-strength, and close-tolerance types. These bolts are normally inspected by magnetic particle inspection methods. Typical markings include "SPEC" (usually heat-treated for strength and durability), and an aircraft manufacturer's part number stamped on the head. Bolts with no markings are low strength. Close-tolerance NAS bolts are marked with either a raised or recessed triangle. The material markings for NAS bolts are the same as for AN bolts, except they may be either raised or recessed. Bolts requiring non-destructive inspection (NDI) by magnetic particle inspection are identified by means of colored lacquer, or head markings of a distinctive type. (See figure 7-1.)

7-37. GRIP LENGTH. In general, bolt grip lengths of a fastener is the thickness of the material the fastener is designed to hold when two or more parts are being assembled. Bolts of slightly greater grip length may be used, provided washers are placed under the nut or bolthead. The maximum combined height of washers that should be used is 1/8 inch. This limits the use of washers necessary to compensate for grip, up to the next standard grip size. Over the years, some fasteners specifications have been changed. For this reason, it is recommended when making repairs to an aircraft, whose original hardware is being replaced, that you must first measure the bolt before ordering, rather than relying on the parts manual for

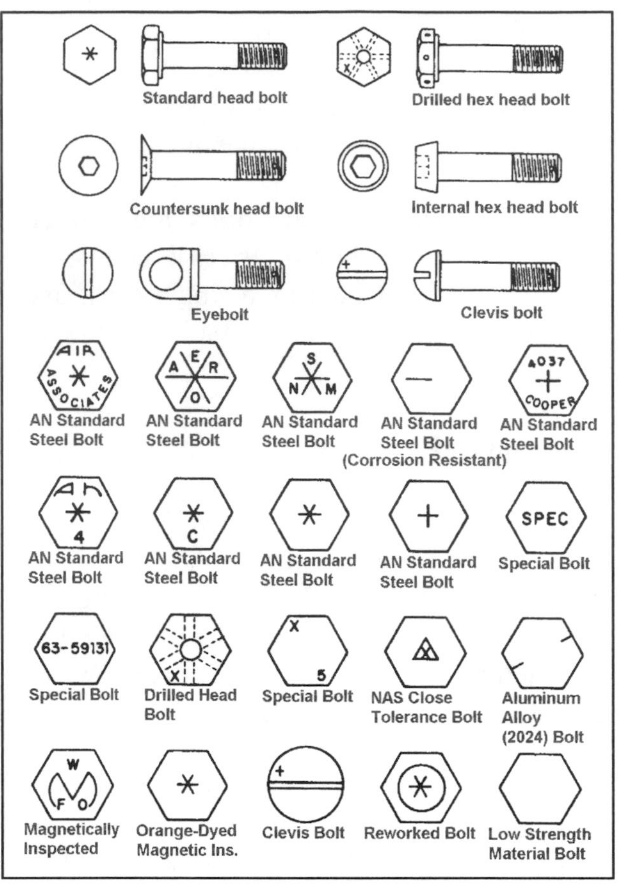

FIGURE 7-1. Typical aircraft bolt markings.

identification. In the case of plate nuts, if proper bolt grip length is not available, add shims under the plate. All bolt installations which involve self-locking or plain nuts should have at least one thread of the bolt protruding through the nut.

7-38. LOCKING OR SAFETYING OF BOLTS. Lock or safety all bolts and/or nuts, except self-locking nuts. Do not reuse cotter pins or safety wire.

7-39. BOLT FIT. Bolt holes, particularly those of primary connecting elements, have close tolerances. Generally, it is permissible to use the first-lettered drill size larger than the nominal bolt diameter, except when the AN hexagon bolts are used in light-drive fit (reamed) applications and where NAS close-tolerance bolts or AN clevis bolts are used. A light-drive fit can be defined as an interference of 0.0006 inch for a 5/8 inch bolt. Bolt holes should be flush to the surface, and free of debris to provide full bearing surface for the bolt head and nut. In the event of over-sized or elongated holes in structural members, reaming or drilling the hole to accept the next larger bolt size may be permissible. Care should be taken to ensure items, such as edge distance, clearance, and structural integrity are maintained. Consult the manufacturer's structural repair manual, the manufacturer's engineering department, or the FAA before drilling or reaming any bolt hole in a critical structural member.

7-40. TORQUES. The importance of correct torque application cannot be overemphasized. Undertorque can result in unnecessary wear of nuts and bolts, as well as the parts they secure. Overtorque can cause failure of a bolt or nut from overstressing the threaded areas. Uneven or additional loads that are applied to the assembly may result in wear or premature failure. The following are a few simple, but important procedures, that should be followed to ensure that correct torque is applied.

NOTE: Be sure that the torque applied is for the size of the bolt shank not the wrench size.

a. Calibrate the torque wrench at least once a year, or immediately after it has been abused or dropped, to ensure continued accuracy.

b. Be sure the bolt and nut threads are clean and dry, unless otherwise specified by the manufacturer.

c. Run the nut down to near contact with the washer or bearing surface and check the friction drag torque required to turn the nut. Whenever possible, apply the torque to the nut and not the bolt. This will reduce rotation of the bolt in the hole and reduce wear.

d. Add the friction drag torque to the desired torque. This is referred to as "final torque," which should register on the indicator or setting for a snap-over type torque wrench.

e. Apply a smooth even pull when applying torque pressure. If chattering or a jerking motion occurs during final torque, back off the nut and retorque.

NOTE: Many applications of bolts in aircraft/engines require stretch checks prior to reuse. This requirement is due primarily to bolt stretching caused by overtorquing.

f. When installing a castle nut, start alignment with the cotter pin hole at the minimum recommended torque plus friction drag torque.

NOTE: Do not exceed the maximum torque plus the friction drag. If the hole and nut castellation do not align, change washer or nut and try again. Exceeding the maximum recommended torque is not recommended.

g. When torque is applied to bolt heads or capscrews, apply the recommended torque plus friction drag torque.

h. If special adapters are used which will change the effective length of the torque wrench, the final torque indication or wrench setting must be adjusted accordingly. Determine the torque wrench indication or setting with adapter installed as shown in figure 7-2.

i. Table 7-1 shows the recommended torque to be used when specific torque is not supplied by the manufacturer. The table includes standard nut and bolt combinations, currently used in aviation maintenance. For further identification of hardware, see chapter 7, section 11.

7-41. STANDARD AIRCRAFT HEX HEAD BOLTS (AN3 THROUGH AN20). These are all-purpose structural bolts used for general applications that require tension or shear loads. Steel bolts smaller than No. 10-32, and aluminum alloy bolts smaller than 1/4 inch diameter, should not be used in primary structures. Do not use aluminum bolts or nuts in applications requiring frequent removal for inspection or maintenance.

7-42. DRILLED HEAD BOLTS (AN73 THROUGH AN81). The AN drilled head bolt is similar to the standard hex bolt, but has a deeper head which is drilled to receive safety wire. The physical differences preventing direct interchangeability are the slightly greater head height, and longer thread length of the AN73 through AN81 series. The AN73 through AN81 drilled head bolts have been superseded by MS20073, for fine thread bolts and MS20074 for coarse thread bolts. AN73, AN74, MS20073, and MS20074 bolts of like thread and grip lengths are universally, functionally, and dimensionally interchangeable.

7-43. ENGINE BOLTS. These are hex head bolts (AN101001 through AN101900), drilled shank hex head bolts (AN101901 through AN102800), drilled hex head (one hole) bolts (AN102801 through AN103700), and drilled hex head (six holes) bolts (AN103701 through AN104600). They are similar to each other except for the holes in the head and shank. Hex head bolts (AN104601 through AN105500), drilled shank hex head bolts (AN105501 through AN106400), drilled hex head (one hole) bolts (AN106401 through AN107300), and drilled hex head (six holes) bolts (AN107301 through AN108200) are similar to the bolts described in paragraph 7-42, except that this series is manufactured from corrosion-resistant steel.

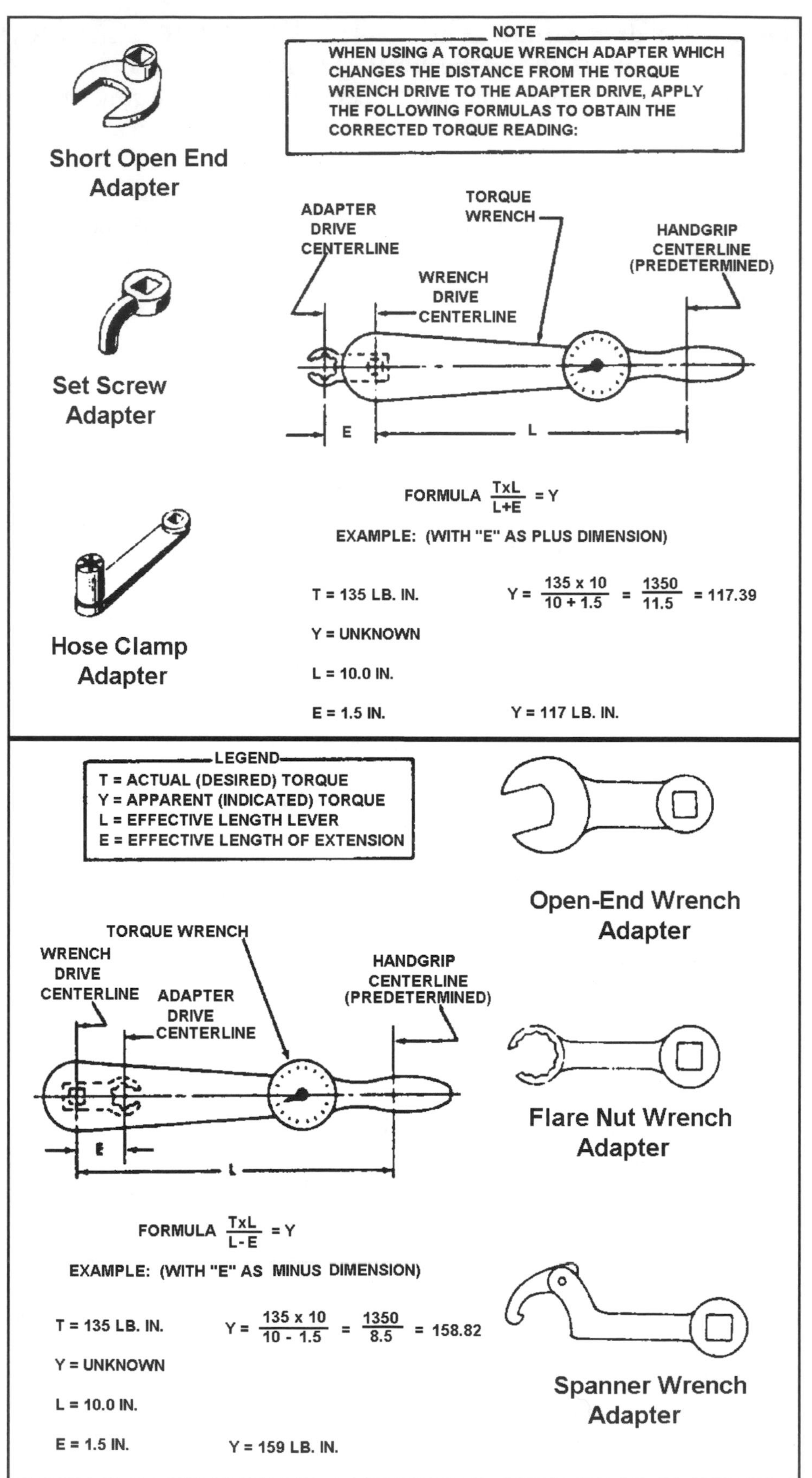

FIGURE 7-2. Torque wrench with various adapters.

TABLE 7-1. Recommended torque values (inch-pounds).

CAUTION THE FOLLOWING TORQUE VALUES ARE DERIVED FROM OIL FREE CADMIUM PLATED THREADS.				
	TORQUE LIMITS RECOMMENDED FOR INSTALLATION (BOLTS LOADED PRIMARILY IN SHEAR)		MAXIMUM ALLOWABLE TIGHTENING TORQUE LIMITS	
Thread Size	Tension type nuts MS20365 and AN310 (40,000 psi in bolts)	Shear type nuts MS20364 and AN320 (24,000 psi in bolts)	Nuts MS20365 and AN310 (90,000 psi in bolts)	Nuts MS20364 and AN320 (54,000 psi in bolts)
FINE THREAD SERIES				
8-36	12-15	7-9	20	12
10-32	20-25	12-15	40	25
1/4-28	50-70	30-40	100	60
5/16-24	100-140	60-85	225	140
3/8-24	160-190	95-110	390	240
7/16-20	450-500	270-300	840	500
1/2-20	480-690	290-410	1100	660
9/16-18	800-1000	480-600	1600	960
5/8-18	1100-1300	600-780	2400	1400
3/4-16	2300-2500	1300-1500	5000	3000
7/8-14	2500-3000	1500-1800	7000	4200
1-14	3700-5500	2200-3300*	10,000	6000
1-1/8-12	5000-7000	3000-4200*	15,000	9000
1-1/4-12	9000-11,000	5400-6600*	25,000	15,000
COARSE THREAD SERIES				
8-32	12-15	7-9	20	12
10-24	20-25	12-15	35	21
1/4-20	40-50	25-30	75	45
5/16-18	80-90	48-55	160	100
3/8-16	160-185	95-100	275	170
7/16-14	235-255	140-155	475	280
1/2-13	400-480	240-290	880	520
9/16-12	500-700	300-420	1100	650
5/8-11	700-900	420-540	1500	900
3/4-10	1150-1600	700-950	2500	1500
7/8-9	2200-3000	1300-1800	4600	2700
The above torque values may be used for all cadmium-plated steel nuts of the fine or coarse thread series which have approximately equal number of threads and equal face bearing areas. * Estimated corresponding values.				

7-44. CLOSE-TOLERANCE BOLTS.

Close-tolerance, hex head, machine bolts (AN173 through AN186), 100-degree countersunk head, close-tolerance, high-strength bolts (NAS333 through NAS340), hex head, close-tolerance, short thread, titanium alloy bolts (NAS653 through NAS658), 100-degree countersunk flathead, close-tolerance titanium alloy bolts (NAS663 through NAS668), and drilled hex head close-tolerance titanium alloy bolts (NAS673 through NAS678), are used in applications where two parts bolted together are subject to severe load reversals and vibration. Because of the interference fit, this type of bolt may require light tapping with a mallet to set the bolt shank into the bolt hole.

NOTE: Elimination of friction in interference fit applications may sometimes be attained by placing the bolt in a freezer prior to installation. When this procedure is used, the bolt should be allowed to warm up to ambient temperature before torquing.

CAUTION: Caution must be exercised in the use of close-tolerance bolts for all critical applications, such as

landing gear, control systems, and helicopter rotary controls. Do not substitute for close-tolerance fasteners without specific instructions from the aircraft manufacturer or the FAA.

7-45. INTERNAL WRENCHING BOLTS (NAS144 THROUGH NAS158 AND NAS172 THROUGH NAS176). These are high-strength bolts used primarily in tension applications. Use a special heat-treated washer (NAS143C) under the head to prevent the large radius of the shank from contacting only the sharp edge of the hole. Use a special heat-treated washer (NAS143) under the nut.

7-46. INTERNAL WRENCHING BOLTS (MS20004 THROUGH MS20024) AND SIX HOLE, DRILLED SOCKET HEAD BOLTS (AN148551 THROUGH AN149350). These are very similar to the bolts in paragraph 7-45, except these bolts are made from different alloys. The NAS144 through NAS158 and NAS172 through NAS176 are interchangeable with MS20004 through MS20024 in the same thread configuration and grip lengths. The AN148551 through AN149350 have been superseded by MS9088 through MS9094 with the exception of AN149251 through 149350, which has no superseding MS standard.

7-47. TWELVE POINT, EXTERNAL WRENCHING BOLTS, (NAS624 THROUGH NAS644). These bolts are used primarily in high-tensile, high-fatigue strength applications. The twelve point head, heat-resistant machine bolts (MS9033 through MS9039), and drilled twelve point head machine bolts (MS9088 through MS9094), are similar to the (NAS624 through NAS644); but are made from different steel alloys, and their shanks have larger tolerances.

7-48. CLOSE-TOLERANCE SHEAR BOLTS (NAS464). These bolts are designed for use where stresses normally are in shear only. These bolts have a shorter thread than bolts designed for torquing.

7-49. NAS6200 SERIES BOLTS. These are close tolerance bolts and are available in two oversized diameters to fit slightly elongated holes. These bolts can be ordered with an “X” or “Y” after the length, to designate the oversized grip portion of the bolt (i.e., NAS6204-6X for a 1/4 inch bolt with a 1/64 inch larger diameter). The elongated hole may have to be reamed to insure a good fit.

7-50. CLEVIS BOLTS (AN21 THROUGH AN36). These bolts are only used in applications subject to shear stress, and are often used as mechanical pins in control systems.

7-51. EYEBOLTS (AN42 THROUGH AN49). These bolts are used in applications where external tension loads are to be applied. The head of this bolt is specially designed for the attachment of a turnbuckle, a clevis, or a cable shackle. The threaded shank may or may not be drilled for safetying.

7-52.—7-62. [RESERVED.]

SECTION 4. NUTS

7-63. GENERAL. Aircraft nuts are available in a variety of shapes, sizes, and material strengths. The types of nuts used in aircraft structures include castle nuts, shear nuts, plain nuts, light hex nuts, checknuts, wingnuts, and sheet spring nuts. Many are available in either self-locking or nonself-locking style. Typical nut types are shown in table 7-13. Refer to the aircraft manufacturer's structural repair manual, the manufacturer's engineering department, or the FAA, before replacing any nut with any other type.

7-64. SELF-LOCKING NUTS. These nuts are acceptable for use on certificated aircraft subject to the aircraft manufacturer's recommended practice sheets or specifications. Two types of self-locking nuts are currently in use, the all-metal type, and the fiber or nylon type.

a. DO NOT use self-locking nuts on parts subject to rotation.

b. Self-locking castellated nuts with cotter pins or lockwire may be used in any system.

c. Self-locking nuts should not be used with bolts or screws on turbine engine airplanes in locations where the loose nut, bolt, washer, or screw could fall or be drawn into the engine air intake scoop.

d. Self-locking nuts should not be used with bolts, screws, or studs to attach access panels or doors, or to assemble any parts that are routinely disassembled before, or after each flight. They may be used with anti-friction bearings and control pulleys, provided the inner race of the bearing is secured to the supporting structure by the nut and bolt.

e. Metal locknuts are constructed with either the threads in the locking insert, out-of-round with the load-carrying section, or with a saw-cut insert with a pinched-in thread in the locking section. The locking action of the all-metal nut depends upon the resiliency of the metal when the locking section and load-carrying section are engaged by screw threads. Metal locknuts are primarily used in high temperature areas.

f. Fiber or nylon locknuts are constructed with an unthreaded fiber or nylon locking insert held securely in place. The fiber or nylon insert provides the locking action because it has a smaller diameter than the nut. Fiber or nylon self-locking nuts are not installed in areas where temperatures exceed 250 °F. After the nut has been tightened, make sure the bolt or stud has at least one thread showing past the nut. DO NOT reuse a fiber or nylon locknut, if the nut cannot meet the minimum prevailing torque values. (See table 7-2.)

g. Self-locking nut plates are produced in a variety of forms and materials for riveting or welding to aircraft structures or parts. Certain applications require the installation of self-locking nuts in channel arrangement permitting the attachment of many nuts in a row with only a few rivets.

7-65. NUT IDENTIFICATION FINISHES. Several types of finishes are used on self-locking nuts. The particular type of finish is dependent on the application and temperature requirement. The most commonly used finishes are described briefly as follows.

TABLE 7-2. Minimum prevailing torque values for re-used self-locking nuts.

FINE THREAD SERIES	
THREAD SIZE	MINIMUM PREVAILING TORQUE
7/16 - 20	8 inch-pounds
1/2 - 20	10 inch-pounds
9/16 - 18	13 inch-pounds
5/8 -18	18 inch-pounds
3/4 - 16	27 inch-pounds
7/8 - 14	40 inch-pounds
1 - 14	55 inch-pounds
1-1/8 - 12	73 inch-pounds
1-1/4 - 12	94 inch-pounds
COARSE THREAD SERIES	
THREAD SIZE	MINIMUM PREVAILING TORQUE
7/16 - 14	8 inch-pounds
1/2 - 13	10 inch-pounds
9/16 - 12	14 inch-pounds
5/8 - 11	20 inch-pounds
3/4 - 10	27 inch-pounds
7/8 - 9	40 inch-pounds
1 - 8	51 inch-pounds
1-1/8 - 8	68 inch-pounds
1-1/4 - 8	88 inch-pounds

a. Cadmium-Plating. This is an electrolytically deposited silver-gray plating which provides exceptionally good protection against corrosion, particularly in salty atmosphere, but is not recommended in applications where the temperature exceeds 450 °F. The following additional finishes or refinements to the basic cadmium can be applied.

(1) Chromic Clear Dip. Cadmium surfaces are passivated, and cyanide from the plating solution is neutralized. The protective film formed gives a bright, shiny appearance, and resists staining and finger marks.

(2) Olive Drab Dichromate. Cadmium-plated work is dipped in a solution of chromic acid, nitric acid, acetic acid, and a dye which produces corrosion resistance.

(3) Iridescent Dichromate. Cadmium-plated work is dipped in a solution of sodium dichromate and takes on a surface film of basic chromium chromate which resists corrosion. Finish is yellow to brown in color.

NOTE: Cadmium-plated nuts are restricted for use in temperatures not to exceed 450 °F. When used in temperatures in excess of 450 °F, the cadmium will diffuse into the base material causing it to become very brittle and subject to early failure.

b. Silver plating. Silver plating is applied to locknuts for use at higher temperatures. Important advantages are its resistance to extreme heat (1,400 °F) and its excellent lubricating characteristics. Silver resists galling and seizing of mating parts when subjected to heat or heavy pressure.

c. Anodizing for Aluminum. An inorganic oxide coating is formed on the metal by connecting the metals and anodes in a suitable electrolyte. The coating offers excellent corrosion resistance and can be dyed in a number of colors.

d. Solid Lubricant Coating. Locknuts are also furnished with molybdenum disulfide for lubrication purposes. It provides a clean, dry, permanently-bonded coating to prevent seizing and galling of threads. Molybdenum disulfide is applied to both cadmium and silver-plated parts. Other types of finishes are available, but the finishes described in this chapter are the most widely used.

7-66. CASTLE NUT (AN310). The castle nut is used with drilled shank hex head bolts, clevis bolts, drilled head bolts, or studs that are subjected to tension loads. The nut has slots or castellations cut to accommodate a cotter pin or safety wire as a means of safetying.

7-67. CASTELLATED SHEAR NUT (AN320). The castellated shear nut is designed for use with hardware subjected to shear stress only.

7-68. PLAIN NUT (AN315 AND AN335). The plain nut is capable of withstanding large tension loads; however, it requires an auxiliary locking device, such as a checknut or safety wire. Use of this type on aircraft structures is limited.

7-69. LIGHT HEX NUTS (AN340 AND AN345). These nuts are used in nonstructural applications requiring light tension. Like the AN315 and AN335, they require a locking device to secure them.

7-70. CHECKNUT (AN316). The checknut is used as a locking device for plain nuts, screws, threaded rod ends, and other devices.

7-71. WINGNUTS (AN350). The wingnut is used where the desired torque is obtained by use of the fingers or handtools. Wingnuts are normally drilled to allow safetying with safety wire.

7-72. SHEET SPRING NUTS (AN365). Sheet spring nuts are commonly called speed nuts. They are used with standard and sheet metal self-tapping screws in nonstructural applications. They are used to support line and conduit clamps, access doors, etc. Their use should be limited to applications where they were originally used in assembly of the aircraft.

7-73.—7-84. RESERVED.

SECTION 5. WASHERS

7-85. GENERAL. The type of washers used in aircraft structure are plain washers, , and special washers. Typical washer types are shown in table 7-14.

7-86. PLAIN WASHERS (AN960 AND AN970). Plain washers are widely used with hex nuts to provide a smooth bearing surface, act as a shim to obtain the proper grip length, and to position castellated nuts in relation to drilled cotter pin holes in bolts. Use plain washers under lock washers to prevent damage to bearing surfaces. Cadmium-plated steel washers are recommended for use under boltheads and nuts used on aluminum alloy or magnesium structures to prevent corrosion. The AN970 steel washer provides a larger bearing surface than the plain type, and is often used in wooden structures under boltheads and nuts to prevent local crushing of the surface.

7-87. LOCKWASHERS (AN935 AND AN936). Lock washers may be used with machine screws or bolts whenever the self-locking or castellated type nut is not applicable. Do not use lock washers where frequent removal is required, in areas subject to corrosion, or in areas exposed to airflow. Use a plain washer between the lock washer and material to prevent gouging the surface of the metal.

CAUTION: Lock washers are not to be used on primary structures, secondary structures, or accessories where failure might result in damage or danger to aircraft or personnel.

7-88. BALL SOCKET AND SEAT WASHERS (AN950 AND AN955). Ball socket and seat washers are used in special applications where the bolt is installed at an angle to the surface or when perfect alignment with the surface is required. These washers are used together as a pair.

7-89. TAPER PIN WASHERS (AN975). Taper pin washers are used with the threaded taper pin. NAS143 and MS20002 washers are used with NAS internal wrenching bolts and internal wrenching nuts. They may be plain or countersunk. The countersunk washer (designated as NAS143C and MS20002C) is used to seat the bolthead shank radius, and the plain washer is used under the nut.

7-90.—7-100. [RESERVED.]

SECTION 6. PINS

7-101. TAPER PINS. Plain (AN385) and threaded (AN386) taper pins are used in joints which carry shear loads and where the absence of play is essential. The plain taper pin is usually drilled and secured with wire. The threaded taper pin is used with a taper-pin washer (AN975) and shear nut (safetied with a cotter pin) or self-locking nut (if undrilled). Typical pin types are shown in table 7-15.

7-102. FLATHEAD PINS (AN392 THROUGH AN406). Commonly called a clevis pin, this pin is used in conjunction with tie-rod terminals and in secondary controls which are not subject to continuous operation. The pin is normally installed with the head up, or forward, to prevent loss should the cotter pin fail or work out.

7-103. COTTER PINS (AN380). Cotter pins are used for securing bolts, screws, nuts, and pins. Use AN381 or MS24665 cotter pins in locations where nonmagnetic material or resistance to corrosion is desired. Cotter pins should not be reused.

7-104. SPRING PINS. The spring pin is designed for use in double-shear applications. The pins are manufactured with the diameter greater than the holes in which they are to be used. Spring pins are stronger than mild carbon steel straight pins, taper pins, or grooved pins of the equivalent size. The spring pin is compressed as it is driven into the hole, and exerts continuous spring pressure against the sides of the hole to prevent loosening by vibration. Spring pins require no other means of securing, and can be used inside one another to increase shear strength.

a. Be careful when using these pins, since spring-pin performance depends entirely on the fit and the durability of the fit under vibration or repeated load conditions (especially in soft materials, such as aluminum alloys and magnesium). They should not be used in an aircraft component or system where the loss or failure of the pin might endanger safe flight.

b. The joints where spring pins are used for fastening shall be designed like riveted and bolted joints. Spring pins should not be mixed with other structural fasteners in the same joint. These pins, for primary structural applications, should be used only where there will be no rotation or relative movement of the joint. Spring pins may be reused if a careful inspection reveals no deformation of the pin or hole.

c. Be careful to observe that the hole has not enlarged or deformed preventing proper functioning of the spring pin. Where hole misalignment results in the pin gap closing or necessitates excess inserting force, the spring pin will not be used. The spring pin should not be used as a substitute for a cotter pin. When a spring pin is used in a clevis joint, it is recommended that the pin be held by the outer members of the unit for maximum efficiency and reduced maintenance.

7-105. QUICK-RELEASE PINS. These pins are used in some applications where rapid removal and replacement of equipment is necessary. When equipment is secured with these pins, no binding of the spindle should be present. Spindle binding could cause the locking balls to remain in the open position which could result in the pin falling out under vibration.

7-106—7-121. [RESERVED.]

SECTION 7. SAFETYING

7-122. GENERAL. The word *safetying* is a term universally used in the aircraft industry. Briefly, safetying is defined as: "Securing by various means any nut, bolt, turnbuckle etc., on the aircraft so that vibration will not cause it to loosen during operation." These practices are not a means of obtaining or maintaining torque, rather a safety device to prevent the disengagement of screws, nuts, bolts, snap rings, oil caps, drain cocks, valves, and parts. Three basic methods are used in safetying; safety-wire, cotter pins, and self-locking nuts. Retainer washers and pal nuts are also sometimes used.

a. Wire, either soft brass or steel is used on cylinder studs, control cable turnbuckles, and engine accessory attaching bolts.

b. Cotter pins are used on aircraft and engine controls, landing gear, and tailwheel assemblies, or any other point where a turning or actuating movement takes place.

c. Self-locking nuts are used in applications where they will not be removed often. Repeated removal and installation will cause the self-locking nut to lose its locking feature. They should be replaced when they are no longer capable of maintaining the minimum prevailing torque. (See table 7-2.)

d. Pal or speed nuts include designs which force the nut thread against the bolt or screw thread when tightened. These nuts should never be reused and should be replaced with new ones when removed.

7-123. SAFETY WIRE. Do not use stainless steel, monel, carbon steel, or aluminum alloy safety wire to secure emergency mechanisms such as switch handles, guards covering handles used on exits, fire extinguishers, emergency gear releases, or other emergency equipment. Some existing structural equipment or safety-of-flight emergency devices require copper or brass safety wire (.020 inch diameter only). Where successful emergency operation of this equipment is dependent on shearing or breaking of the safety wire, particular care should be used to ensure that safetying does not prevent emergency operation.

a. There are two methods of safety wiring; the double-twist method that is most commonly used, and the single-wire method used on screws, bolts, and/or nuts in a closely-spaced or closed-geometrical pattern such as a triangle, square, rectangle, or circle. The single-wire method may also be used on parts in electrical systems and in places that are difficult to reach. (See figures 7-3 and 7-3a.)

b. When using double-twist method of safety wiring, .032 inch minimum diameter wire should be used on parts that have a hole diameter larger than .045 inch. Safety wire of .020 inch diameter (double strand) may be used on parts having a nominal hole diameter between .045 and .062 inch with a spacing between parts of less than 2 inches. When using the single-wire method, the largest size wire that the hole will accommodate should be used. Copper wire (.020 inch diameter), aluminum wire (.031 inch diameter), or other similar wire called for in specific technical orders, should be used as seals on equipment such as first-aid kits, portable fire extinguishers, emergency valves, or oxygen regulators.

CAUTION: Care should be taken not to confuse steel with aluminum wire.

c. A secure seal indicates that the component has not been opened. Some emergency devices require installation of brass or soft

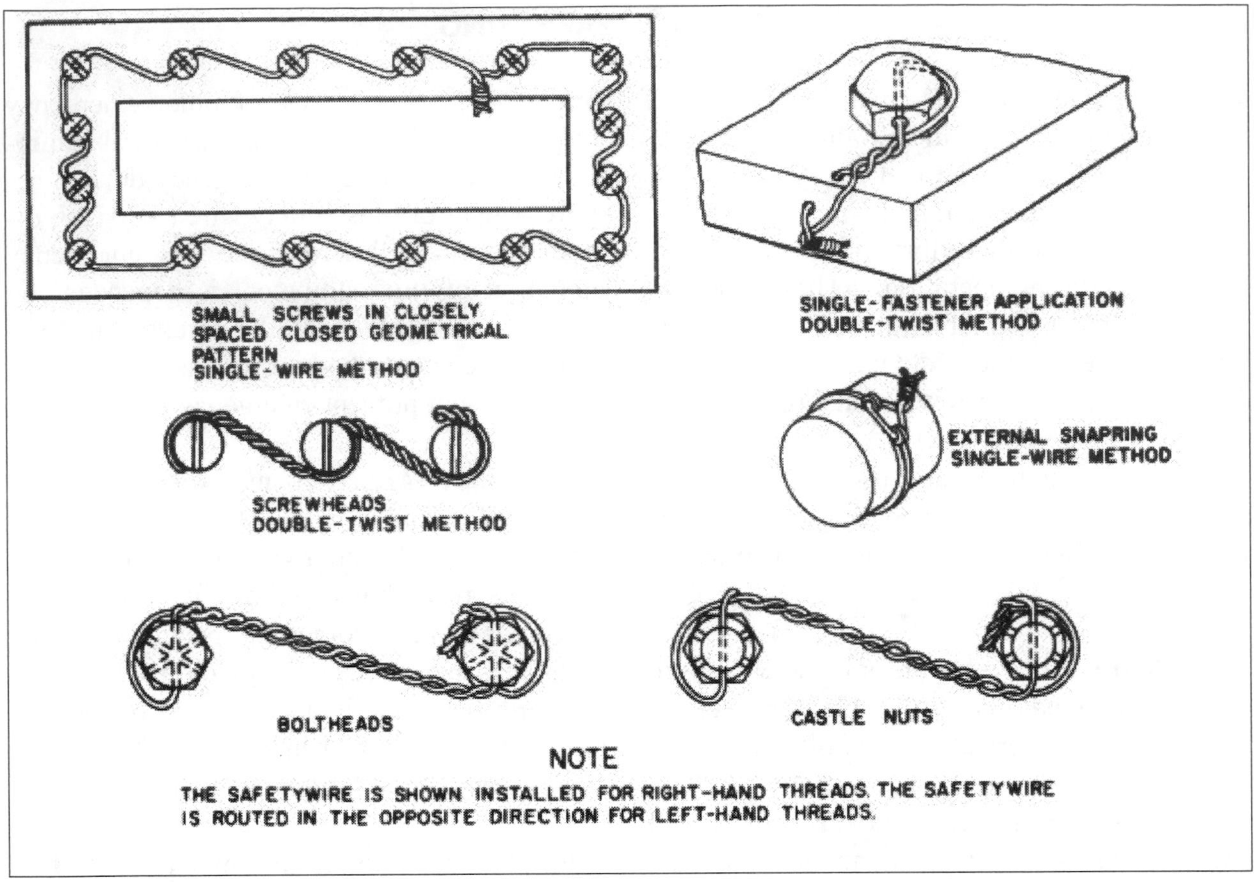

SMALL SCREWS IN CLOSELY SPACED CLOSED GEOMETRICAL PATTERN SINGLE-WIRE METHOD

SINGLE-FASTENER APPLICATION DOUBLE-TWIST METHOD

SCREWHEADS DOUBLE-TWIST METHOD

EXTERNAL SNAPRING SINGLE-WIRE METHOD

BOLTHEADS

CASTLE NUTS

NOTE

THE SAFETYWIRE IS SHOWN INSTALLED FOR RIGHT-HAND THREADS. THE SAFETYWIRE IS ROUTED IN THE OPPOSITE DIRECTION FOR LEFT-HAND THREADS.

FIGURE 7-3. Securing screws, nuts, bolts, and snaprings.

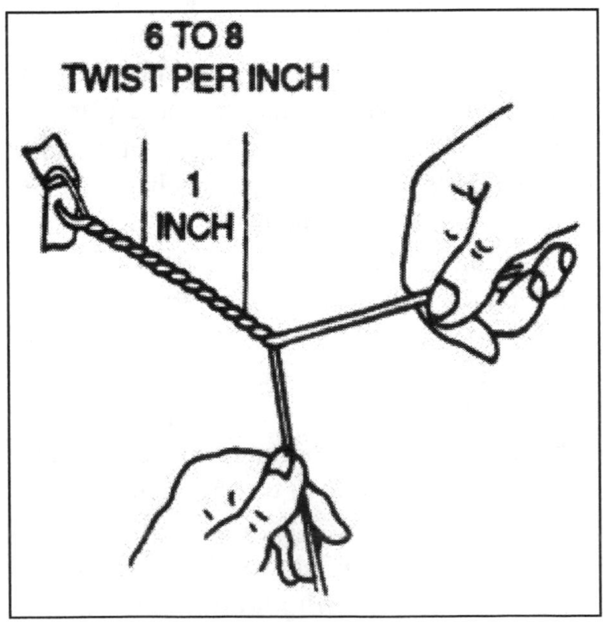

FIGURE 7-3a. Wire twisting by hand.

copper shear safety wire. Particular care should be exercised to ensure that the use of safety wire will not prevent emergency operation of the devices.

7-124. SAFETY-WIRING PROCEDURES. There are many combinations of safety wiring with certain basic rules common to all applications. These rules are as follows.

a. When bolts, screws, or other parts are closely grouped, it is more convenient to safety wire them in series. The number of bolts, nuts, screws, etc., that may be wired together depends on the application.

b. Drilled boltheads and screws need not be safety wired if installed with self-locking nuts.

c. To prevent failure due to rubbing or vibration, safety wire must be tight after installation.

d. Safety wire must be installed in a manner that will prevent the tendency of the part to loosen.

e. Safety wire must never be overstressed. Safety wire will break under vibrations if twisted too tightly. Safety wire must be pulled taut when being twisted, and maintain a light tension when secured. (See figure 7-3a.)

f. Safety-wire ends must be bent under and inward toward the part to avoid sharp or projecting ends, which might present a safety hazard.

g. Safety wire inside a duct or tube must not cross over or obstruct a flow passage when an alternate routing can be used.

(1) Check the units to be safety wired to make sure that they have been correctly torqued, and that the wiring holes are properly aligned to each other. When there are two or more units, it is desirable that the holes in the units be aligned to each other. Never overtorque or loosen to obtain proper alignment of the holes. It should be possible to align the wiring holes when the bolts are torqued within the specified limits. Washers may be used (see paragraph 7-37) to establish proper alignment. However, if it is impossible to obtain a proper alignment of the holes without undertorquing or overtorquing, try another bolt which will permit proper alignment within the specified torque limits.

(2) To prevent mutilation of the twisted section of wire, when using pliers, grasp the wires at the ends. Safety wire must not be nicked, kinked, or mutilated. Never twist the wire ends off with pliers; and, when cutting off ends, leave at least four to six complete turns (1/2 to 5/8 inch long) after the loop. When removing safety wire, never twist the wire off with pliers. Cut the safety wire close to the hole, exercising caution.

h. Install safety wire where practicable with the wire positioned around the head of the bolt, screw, or nut, and twisted in such a manner that the loop of the wire fits closely to the contour of the unit being safety wired.

7-125. TWISTING WITH SPECIAL TOOLS. Twist the wire with a wire twister as follows. (See figure 7-4.)

CAUTION: When using wire twisters, and the wire extends 3 inches beyond the jaws of the twisters, loosely wrap the wire around the pliers to prevent whipping and possible personal injury. Excessive twisting of the wire will weaken the wire.

a. Grip the wire in the jaws of the wire twister and slide the outer sleeve down with your thumb to lock the handles or lock the spring-loaded pin.

b. Pull the knob, and the spiral rod spins and twists the wire.

c. Squeeze handles together to release wire.

7-126. SECURING OIL CAPS, DRAIN COCKS, AND VALVES. (See figure 7-4a.) When securing oil caps and drain cocks, the safety wire should be anchored to an adjacent fillister-head screw. This method of safety wiring is applied to wingnuts, filler plugs, single-drilled head bolts, fillister-head screws, etc.; which are safety wired individually. When securing valve handles in the vertical position, the wire is looped around the threads of the pipe leading into one side of the valve,

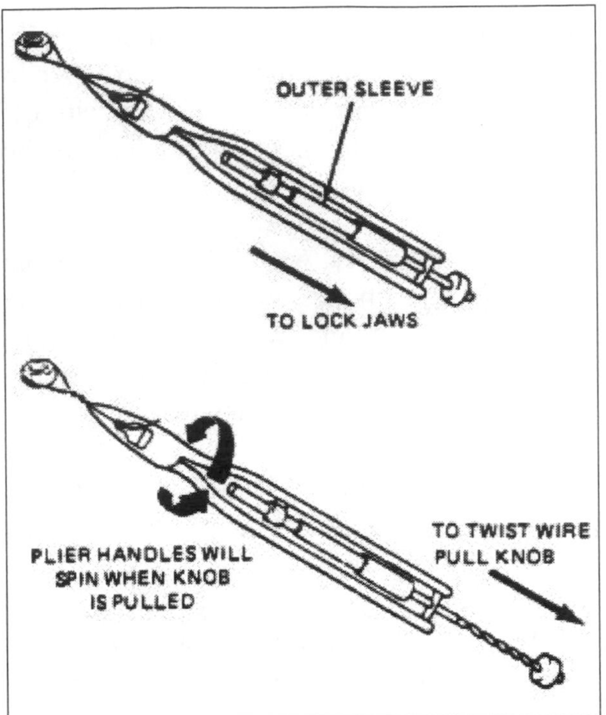

FIGURE 7-4. Use of a typical wire twister.

double-twisted around the valve handle, and anchored around the threads of the pipe leading into the opposite side of the valve. When castellated nuts are to be secured with safety wire, tighten the nut to the low side of the selected torque range, unless otherwise specified; and, if necessary, continue tightening until a slot lines with the hole. In blind tapped hole applications of bolts or castellated nuts on studs, the safety wiring should be in accordance with the general instructions of this chapter. Hollow-head bolts are safetied in the manner prescribed for regular bolts.

NOTE: Do not loosen or tighten properly tightened nuts to align safety-wire holes.

NOTE: Although there are numerous safety wiring techniques used to secure aircraft hardware, practically all are derived from the basic examples shown in figures 7-5 through 7-5b.

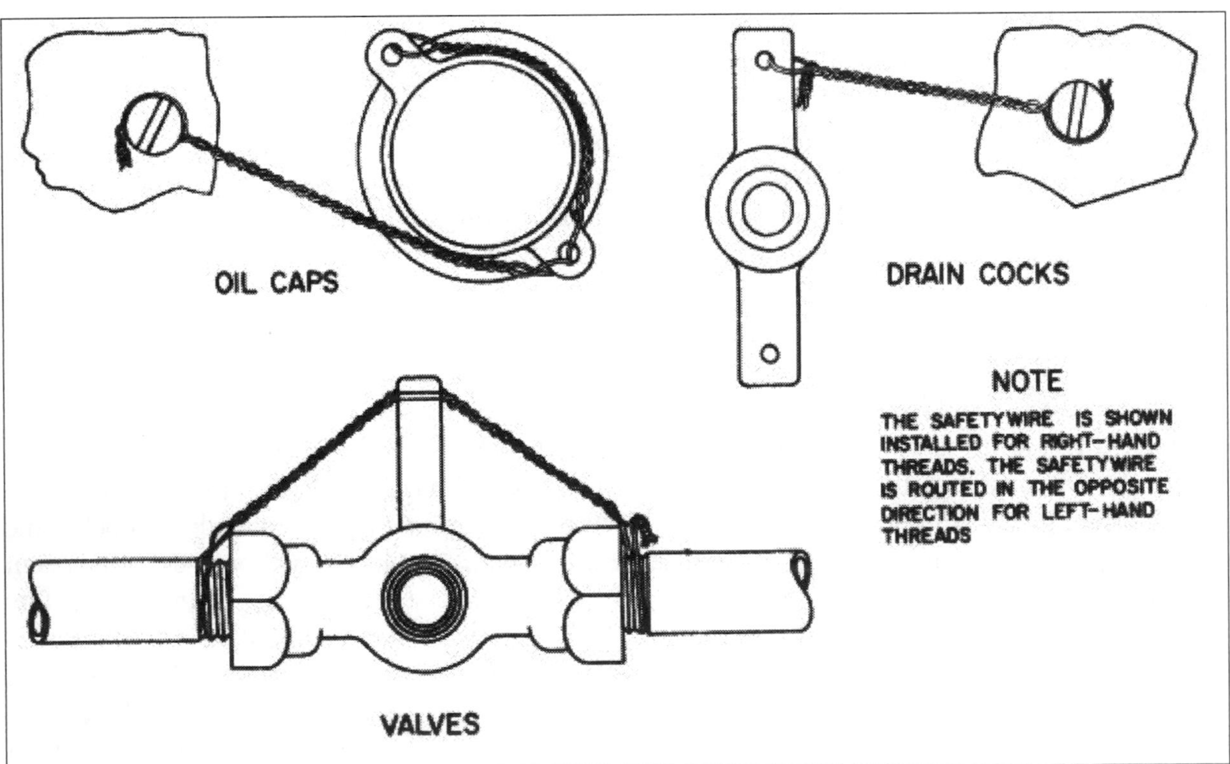

FIGURE 7-4a. Securing oil caps, drain cocks, and valves.

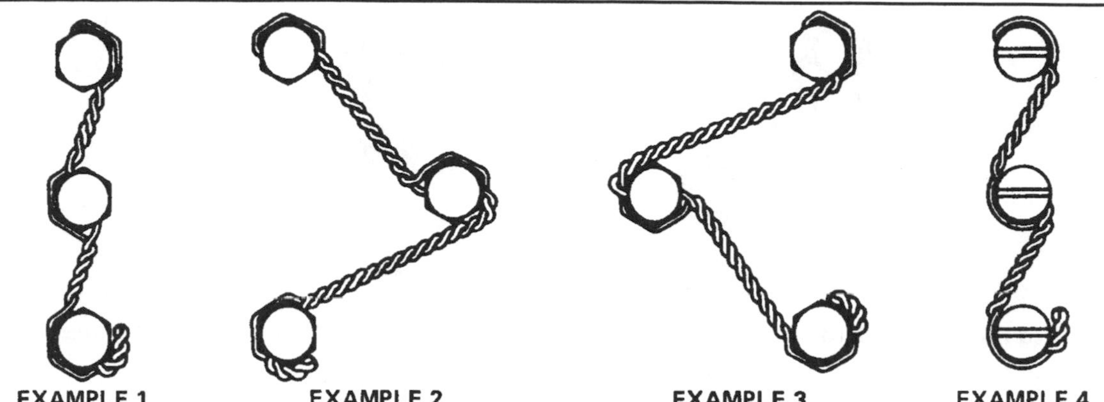

EXAMPLE 1 EXAMPLE 2 EXAMPLE 3 EXAMPLE 4

Examples 1, 2, 3, and 4 apply to all types of bolts, fillister-head screws, square-head plugs, and other similar parts which are wired so that the loosening tendency of either part is counteracted by tightening of the other part. The direction of twist from the second to the third unit is counterclockwise in examples 1, 3, and 4 to keep the loop in position against the head of the bolt. The direction of twist from the second to the third unit in example 2 is clockwise to keep the wire in position around the second unit. The wire entering the hole in the third unit will be the lower wire, except example 2, and by making a counterclockwise twist after it leaves the hole, the loop will be secured in place around the head of that bolt.

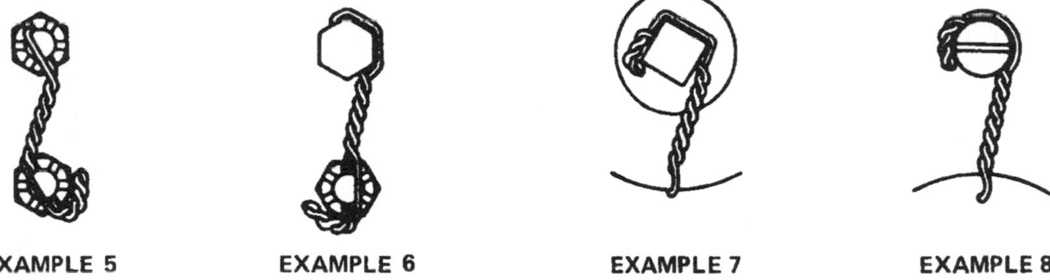

EXAMPLE 5 EXAMPLE 6 EXAMPLE 7 EXAMPLE 8

Examples 5, 6, 7, & 8 show methods for wiring various standard items, NOTE: Wire may be wrapped over the unit rather than around it when wiring castellated nuts or on other items when there is a clearance problem.

EXAMPLE 9

Example 9 shows the method for wiring bolts in different planes. Note that wire should always be applied so that tension is in the tightening direction.

EXAMPLE 10

Hollow-head plugs shall be wired as shown with the tab bent inside the hole to avoid snags and possible injury to personnel working on the engine.

EXAMPLE 11

Correct application of single wire to closely spaced multiple group.

FIGURE 7-5. Safety-wiring procedures.

EXAMPLE 12 **EXAMPLE 13**

Examples 12 and 13 show methods for attaching lead seal to protect critical adjustments.

EXAMPLE 14

Example 14 shows bolt wired to a right-angle bracket with the wire wrapped around the bracket.

EXAMPLE 15

Example 15 shows correct method for wiring adjustable connecting rod.

EXAMPLE 16

Example 16 shows correct method for wiring the coupling nut on flexible line to the straight connector brazed on rigid tube.

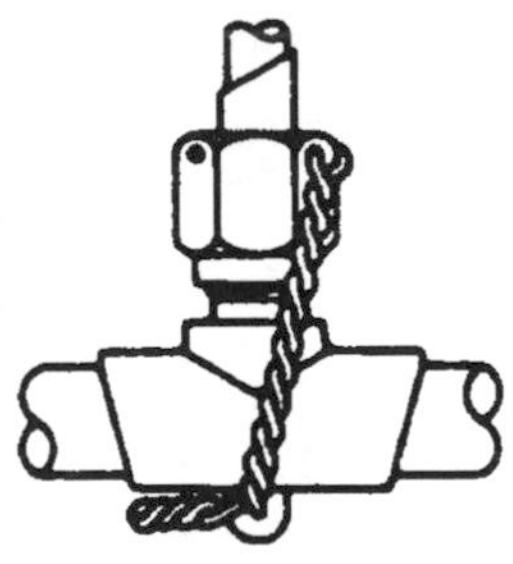

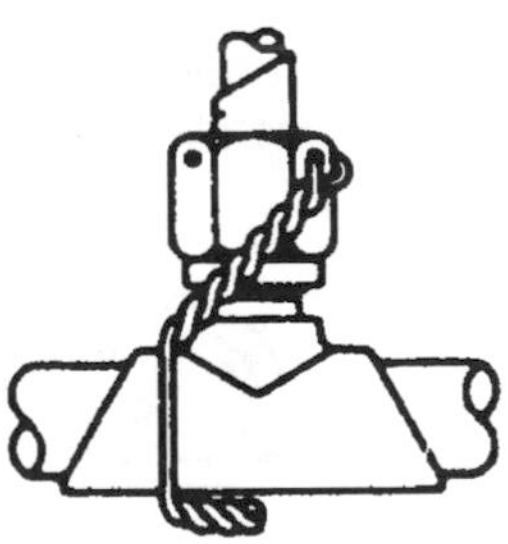

EXAMPLE 17 **EXAMPLE 18** **EXAMPLE 19** **EXAMPLE 20** **EXAMPLE 21**

Fittings incorporating wire lugs shall be wired as shown in Examples 17 and 18. Where no lock-wire lug is provided, wire should be applied as shown in examples 19 and 20 with caution being exerted to ensure that wire is wrapped tightly around the fitting.

Small size coupling nuts shall be wired by wrapping the wire around the nut and inserting it through the holes as shown.

FIGURE 7-5a. Safety-wiring procedures.

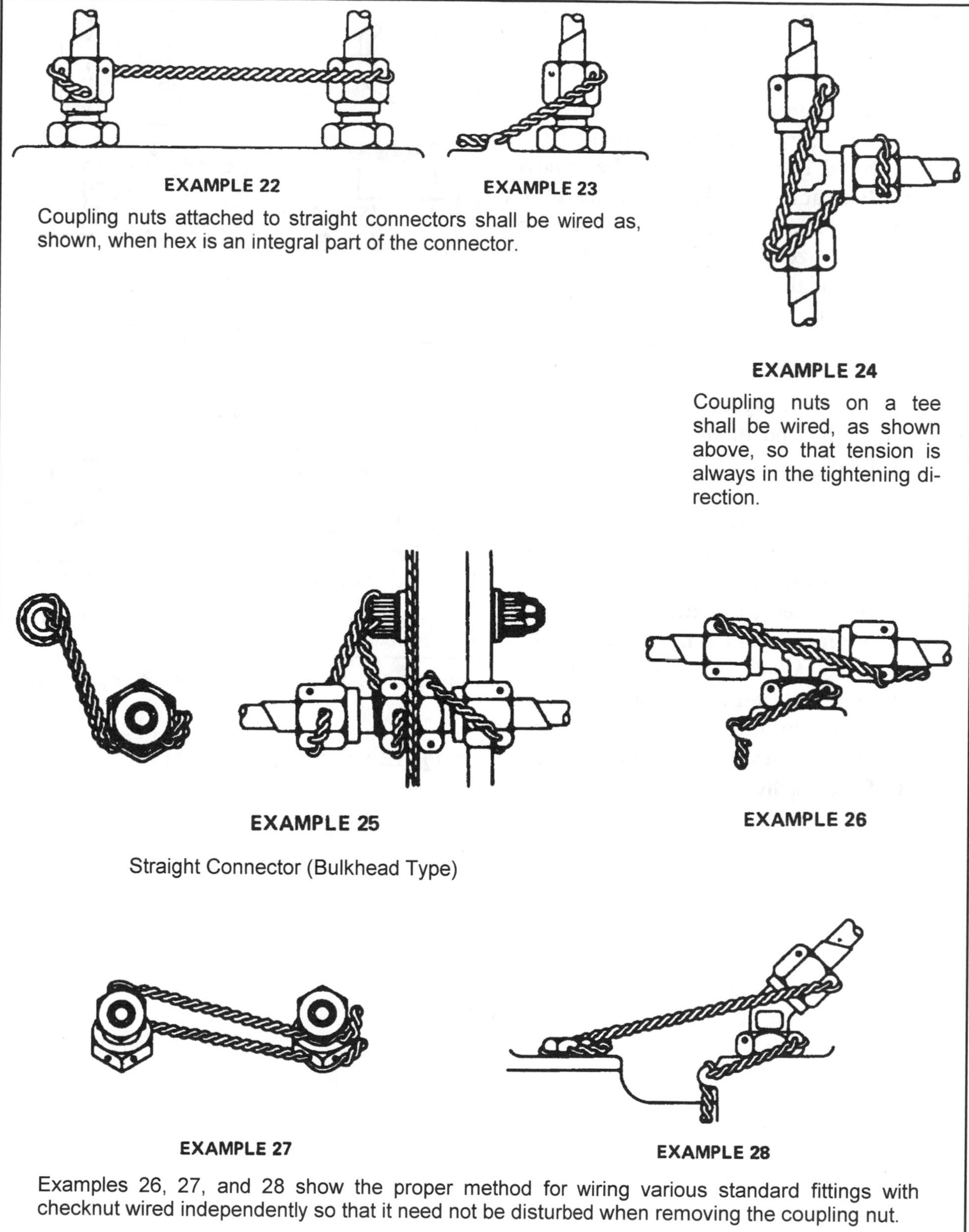

EXAMPLE 22
EXAMPLE 23
Coupling nuts attached to straight connectors shall be wired as, shown, when hex is an integral part of the connector.
EXAMPLE 24
Coupling nuts on a tee shall be wired, as shown above, so that tension is always in the tightening direction.
EXAMPLE 25
Straight Connector (Bulkhead Type)
EXAMPLE 26
EXAMPLE 27
EXAMPLE 28
Examples 26, 27, and 28 show the proper method for wiring various standard fittings with checknut wired independently so that it need not be disturbed when removing the coupling nut.

FIGURE 7-5b. Safety-wiring procedures.

7-127. SECURING WITH COTTER PINS.

a. Cotter pins are used to secure such items as bolts, screws, pins, and shafts. Their use is favored because they can be removed and installed quickly. The diameter of the cotter pins selected for any application should be the largest size that will fit consistent with the diameter of the cotter pin hole and/or the slots in the nut. Cotter pins should not be re-used on aircraft.

b. To prevent injury during and after pin installation, the end of the cotter pin can be rolled and tucked.

NOTE: In using the method of cotter pin safetying, as shown in figures 7-6 and 7-7, ensure the prong, bent over the bolt, is seated firmly against the bolt shank, and does not exceed bolt diameter. Also, when the prong is bent over the nut, ensure the bent prong is down and firmly flat against the nut and does not contact the surface of the washer.

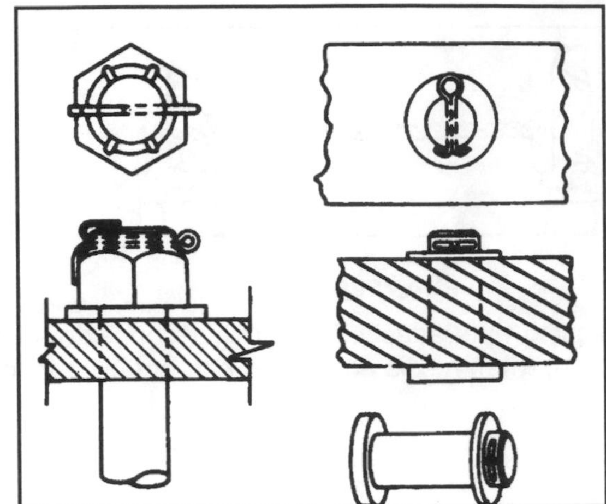

FIGURE 7-6. Securing with cotter pins.

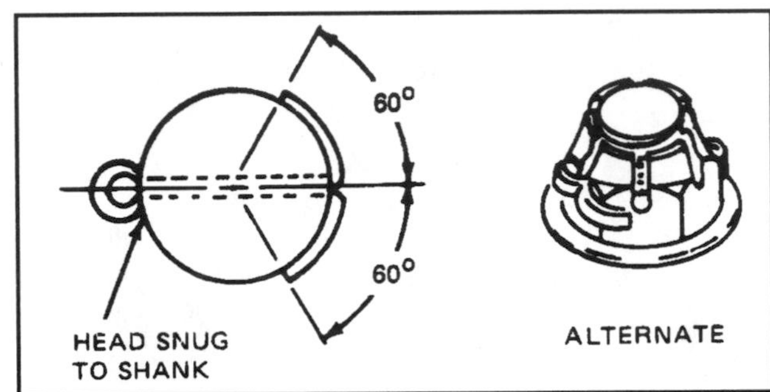

FIGURE 7-7. Alternate method for securing with cotter pins.

7-128.—7-139. [RESERVED.]

SECTION 8. INSPECTION AND REPAIR OF CONTROL CABLES AND TURNBUCKLES

7-140. GENERAL. Aircraft control cables are generally fabricated from carbon steel or corrosion-resistant steel wire of either flexible or nonflexible-type construction.

7-141. CABLE DEFINITIONS. The following cable components are defined in accordance with Military Specifications MIL-W-83420, MIL-C-18375, and MIL-W-87161.

a. Wire Center. The center of all strands shall be an individual wire and shall be designated as a wire center.

b. Strand Center or Core. A strand center is a single, straight strand made of preformed wires, similar to the other strands comprising the cable, in arrangement and number of wires.

c. Independent Wire Rope Center (IWRC) 7 by 7. A 7 by 7 independent wire rope center as specified herein shall consist of a cable or wire rope of six strands of seven wires each, twisted or laid around a strand center or core consisting of seven wires.

7-142. FLEXIBLE CABLES. Flexible, preformed, carbon steel, Type I, composition A cables, MIL-W-83420, are manufactured from steel made by the acid-open-hearth, basic-open hearth, or electric-furnace process. The wire used is coated with pure tin or zinc. Flexible, preformed, corrosion-resistant, Type I, composition B cables, MIL-W-87161, MIL-W-83420, and MIL-C-18375 are manufactured from steel made by the electric-furnace process. (See table 7-3 and figure 7-8.) These cables are of the 3 by 7, 7 by 7, 7 by 19, or 6 by 19 IWRC construction, according to the diameter as specified in table 7-3. The 3 by 7 cable consists of three strands of seven wires each. There is no core in this construction. The 3 by 7 cable has a length of lay of not more than eight times or less than five times the nominal cable diameter. The 7 by 7 cable consists of six strands, of seven wires each, laid around a center strand of seven wires. The wires are laid so as to develop a cable which has the greatest bending and wearing properties. The 7 by 7 cable has a length of lay of not more than eight times or less than six times the cable diameter. The 7 by 19 cable consists of six strands laid around a center strand in a clockwise direction. The wires composing the seven individual strands are laid around a center wire in two layers. The center core strand consists of a lay of six wires laid around the central wire in a clockwise direction and a layer of 12 wires laid around this in a clockwise direction. The six outer strands of the cable consist of a layer of six wires laid around the center wire in a counterclockwise direction and a layer of 12 wires laid around this in a counterclockwise direction. The 6 by 19 cable consists of six strands of 19 wires each, laid around a 7 by 7. MIL-C-18375 cable, although not as strong as MIL-W-83420, is equal in corrosion resistance and superior in non-magnetic and coefficient of thermal expansion properties.

7-143. NYLON-COATED CABLES.

a. Nylon-coated cable is made by extruding a flexible nylon coating over corrosion-resistant steel (CRES) cable. The bare CRES cable must conform and be qualified to MIL-W-83420. After coating, the jacketed cable must still conform to MIL-W-83420.

b. The service life of nylon-coated cable is much greater than the service life of the same cable when used bare. Most cable wear occurs at pulleys where the cable bends. Wear

TABLE 7-3. Flexible cable construction and physical properties.

				MINIMUM BREAKING STRENGTH (Pounds)		
NOMINAL DIAMETER OF WIRE ROPE CABLE	CONSTRUCTION	TOLERANCE ON DIAMETER (PLUS ONLY)	ALLOWABLE INCREASE OF DIAMETER AT CUT END	MIL-W-83420 COMP A	MIL-W-83420 COMP B (CRES)	MIL-C-18375 (CRES)
INCHES		INCHES	INCHES	LBS	LBS	LBS
1/32	3 x 7	0.006	0.006	110	110	
3/64	7 x 7	0.008	0.008	270	270	
1/16	7 x 7	0.010	0.009	480	480	360
1/16	7 x 19	0.010	0.009	480	480	
3/32	7 x 7	0.012	0.010	920	920	700
3/32	7 x 19	0.012	0.010	1,000	920	
1/8	7 x 19	0.014	0.011	2,000	1,760	1,300
5/32	7 x 19	0.016	0.017	2,800	2,400	2,000
3/16	7 x 19	0.018	0.019	4,200	3,700	2,900
7/32	7 x 19	0.018	0.020	5,600	5,000	3,800
1/4	7 x 19	0.018	0.021	7,000	6,400	4,900
9/32	7 x 19	0.020	0.023	8,000	7,800	6,100
5/16	7 x 19	0.022	0.024	9,800	9,000	7,600
11/32	7 x 19	0.024	0.025	12,500		
3/8	7 x 19	0.026	0.027	14,400	12,000	11,000
7/16	6 x 19 IWRC	0.030	0.030	17,600	16,300	14,900
1/2	6 x 19 IWRC	0.033	0.033	22,800	22,800	19,300
9/16	6 x 19 IWRC	0.036	0.036	28,500	28,500	24,300
5/8	6 x 19 IWRC	0.039	0.039	35,000	35,000	30,100
3/4	6 x 19 IWRC	0.045	0.045	49,600	49,600	42,900
7/8	6 x 19 IWRC	0.048	0.048	66,500	66,500	58,000
1	6 x 19 IWRC	0.050	0.050	85,400	85,400	75,200
1 - 1/8	6 x 19 IWRC	0.054	0.054	106,400	106,400	
1 - 1/4	6 x 19 IWRC	0.057	0.057	129,400	129,400	
1 - 3/8	6 x 19 IWRC	0.060	0.060	153,600	153,600	
1 - 1/2	6 x 19 IWRC	0.062	0.062	180,500	180,500	

is caused by friction between strands and between wires. In bare cable, this is aggravated by dirt and grit working its way into the cable; and the lubricant working its way out leaving dry, dirty wires rubbing against each other. In long, straight runs of cable, vibration work-hardens the wires causing the brittle wires to fracture with eventual failure of the cable.

c. The nylon-jacket protects the cable in a threefold manner. It keeps the lubricant from oozing out and evaporating, it keeps dirt and grit out, and it dampens the vibrations, thereby, greatly reducing their effect on the cable.

7-144. NONFLEXIBLE CABLES. (Refer to table 7-4 and figure 7-9.) Nonflexible, preformed, carbon steel cables, MIL-W-87161, composition A, are manufactured by the same processes as MIL-W-83420, composition B, flexible corrosion-resistant steel cables. The nonflexible steel cables are of the 1 by 7 (Type I) or 1 by 19 (Type II) construction according to the diameter as specified in table 7-4. The 1 by 7 cable consists of six

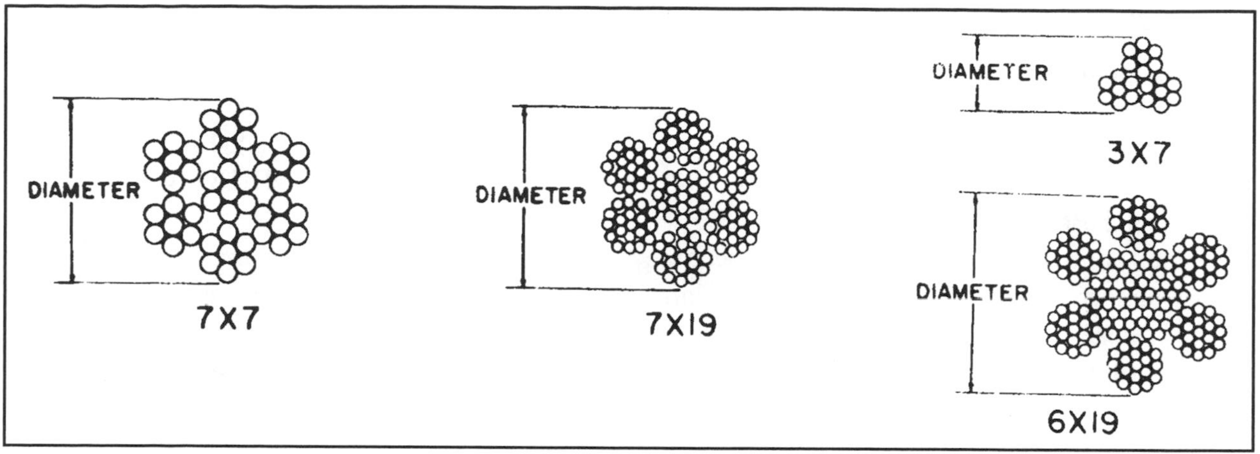

FIGURE 7-8. Flexible cable cross section.

TABLE 7-4. Nonflexible cable construction and physical properties.

STRAND TYPE	NOMINAL DIAMETER OF WIRE STRAND In.	TOLERANCE ON DIAMETER (Plus Only) In.	ALLOWABLE INCREASE IN DIAMETER AT THE END In.	CONSTRUCTION	MIL-W-87161 MINIMUM BREAK STRENGTH COMP A & B Lbs.
I	1/32	0.003	0.006	1 x 7	185
I	3/64	0.005	0.008	1 x 7	375
II	3/64	0.005	0.008	1 x 19	375
I	1/16	0.006	0.009	1 x 7	500
II	1/16	0.006	0.009	1 x 19	500
II	5/64	0.008	0.009	1 x 19	800
II	3/32	0.009	0.010	1 x 19	1,200
II	7/64	0.009	0.010	1 x 19	1,600
II	1/8	0.013	0.011	1 x 19	2,100
II	5/32	0.013	0.016	1 x 19	3,300
II	3/16	0.013	0.019	1 x 19	4,700
II	7/32	0.015	0.020	1 x 19	6,300
II	1/4	0.018	0.021	1 x 19	8,200
II	5/16	0.022	0.024	1 x 19	12,500
II	3/8	0.026	0.027	1 x 19	17,500

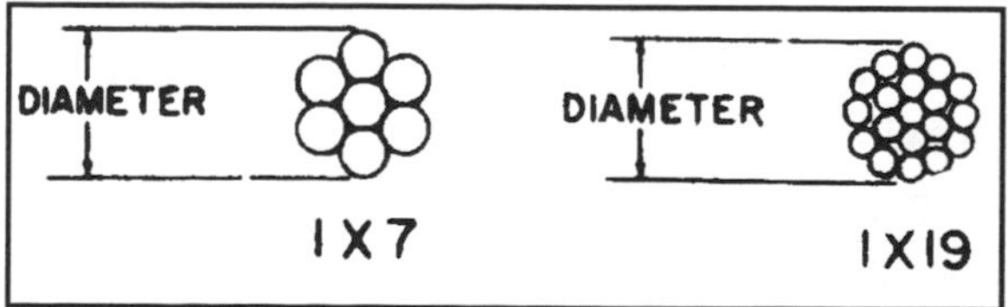

FIGURE 7-9. Nonflexible cable cross section.

wires laid around a center wire in a counterclockwise direction. The 1 by 19 cable consists of a layer of six wires laid around a center wire in a clockwise direction plus twelve wires laid around the inner strand in a counterclockwise direction.

7-145. CABLE SPECIFICATIONS. Cable diameter and strength data are given in table 7-3 and table 7-4. These values are acceptable for repair and modification of civil aircraft.

7-146. CABLE PROOF LOADS. Cable terminals and splices should be tested for proper strength before installation. Gradually apply a test load equal to 60 percent of the cable-breaking strengths given in table 7-3 and table 7-4, for a period of 3 minutes. Place a suitable guard over the cable during the test to prevent injury to personnel in the event of cable failure.

7-147. REPLACEMENT OF CABLES. Replace control cables when they become worn, distorted, corroded, or otherwise damaged. If spare cables are not available, prepare exact duplicates of the damaged cable. Use materials of the same size and quality as the original. Standard swaged cable terminals develop the full cable strength and may be substituted for the original terminals wherever practical. However, if facilities and supplies are limited and immediate corrective action is necessary, repairs may be made by using cable bushings, eye splices, and the proper combination of turnbuckles in place of the original installation. (See figure 7-12(c).)

a. Location of Splices. Locate splices so that no portion of the splice comes closer than 2 inches to any fair-lead or pulley. Locate connections at points where jamming cannot occur during any portion of the travel of either the loaded cable or the slack cable in the deflected position.

b. Cutting and Heating. Cut cables to length by mechanical means. The use of a torch, in any manner, is not permitted. Do not subject wires and cables to excessive temperature. Soldering the bonding braid to the control cable is not permitted.

c. Ball-and-Socket Type Terminals. Do not use ball-and-socket type terminals or other types for general replacement that do not positively prevent cable untwisting, except where they were utilized on the original installation by the aircraft manufacturer.

d. Substitution of Cable. Substitution of cable for hard or streamlined wires will not be acceptable unless specifically approved by a representative of the FAA.

7-148. MECHANICALLY-FABRICATED CABLE ASSEMBLIES.

a. Swage-Type Terminals. Swage-type terminals, manufactured in accordance with AN, are suitable for use in civil aircraft up to, and including, maximum cable loads. When swaging tools are used, it is important that all the manufacturers' instructions, including "go and no-go" dimensions, be followed in detail to avoid defective and inferior swaging. Observance of all instructions should result in a terminal developing the full-rated strength of the cable. Critical dimensions, both before and after swaging, are shown in table 7-5.

(1) Terminals. When swaging terminals onto cable ends, observe the following procedures.

(a) Cut the cable to the proper length allowing for growth during swaging. Apply a preservative compound to the cable ends before insertion into the terminal barrel.

NOTE: Never solder cable ends to prevent fraying, since the presence of the solder will greatly increase the tendency of the cable to pull out of the terminal.

(b) Insert the cable into the terminal approximately 1 inch, and bend toward the terminal, then push the cable end entirely into the terminal barrel. The bending action puts a kink or bend in the cable end, and provides enough friction to hold the terminal in place until the swaging operation can be performed. Bending also tends to separate the strands inside the barrel, thereby reducing the strain on them.

TABLE 7-5. Straight-shank terminal dimensions. (Cross reference AN to MS: AN-666 to MS 21259, AN-667 to MS 20667, AN-668 to MS 20668, AN-669 to MS 21260.)

		Before swaging				After swaging	
Cable size (inches)	Wire strands	Outside diameter	Bore diameter	Bore length	Swaging length	Minimum breaking strength (pounds)	Shank diameter *
1/16	7 x 7	0.160	0.078	1.042	0.969	480	0.138
3/32	7 x 7	.218	.109	1.261	1.188	920	.190
1/8	7 x 19	.250	.141	1.511	1.438	2,000	.219
5/32	7 x 19	.297	.172	1.761	1.688	2,800	.250
3/16	7 x 19	.359	.203	2.011	1.938	4,200	.313
7/32	7 x 19	.427	.234	2.261	2.188	5,600	.375
1/4	7 x 19	.494	.265	2.511	2.438	7,000	.438
9/32	7 x 19	.563	.297	2.761	2.688	8,000	.500
5/16	7 x 19	.635	.328	3.011	2.938	9,800	.563
3/8	7 x 19	.703	.390	3.510	3.438	14,400	.625

*Use gauges in kit for checking diameters.

NOTE: If the terminal is drilled completely through, push the cable into the terminal until it reaches the approximate position shown in figure 7-10. If the hole is not drilled through, insert the cable until the end rests against the bottom of the hole.

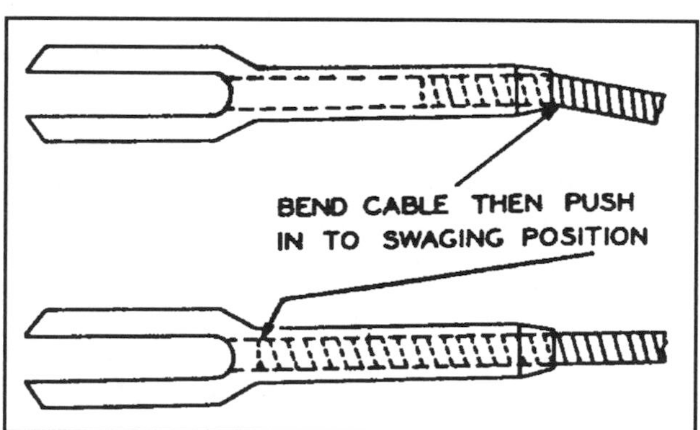

FIGURE 7-10. Insertion of cable into terminal.

(c) Accomplish the swaging operation in accordance with the instructions furnished by the manufacturer of the swaging equipment.

(d) Inspect the terminal after swaging to determine that it is free from the die marks and splits, and is not out-of-round. Check for cable slippage in the terminal and for cut or broken wire strands.

(e) Using a "go no-go" gauge or a micrometer, check the terminal shank diameter as shown in figure 7-11 and table 7-5.

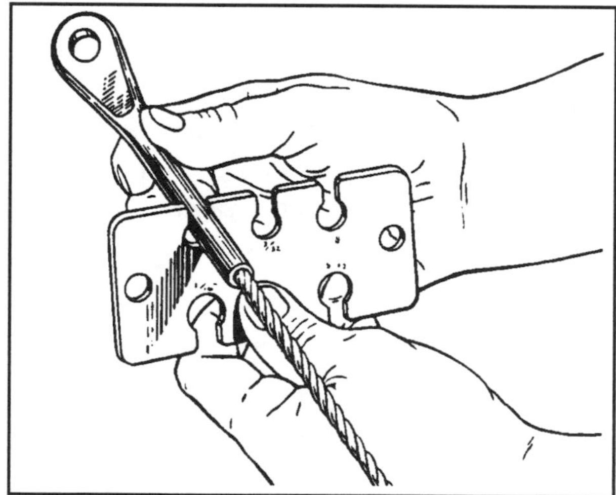

FIGURE 7-11. Gauging terminal shank after swaging.

(f) Test the cable by proof-loading it to 60 percent of its rated breaking strength.

(2) Splicing. Completely severed cables, or those badly damaged in a localized area, may be repaired by the use of an eye terminal bolted to a clevis terminal. (See figure 7-12(a).) However, this type of splice can only be used in free lengths of cable which do not pass over pulleys or through fair-leads.

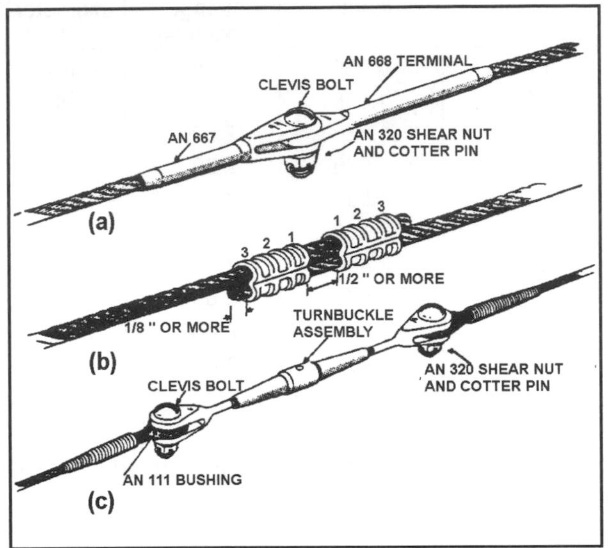

FIGURE 7-12. Typical cable splices.

(3) Swaged ball terminals. On some aircraft cables, swaged ball terminals are used for attaching cables to quadrants and special connections where space is limited. Single shank terminals are generally used at the cable ends, and double shank fittings may be used at either the end or in the center of the cable. Dies are supplied with the swaging machines for attaching these terminals to cables by the following method.

(a) The steel balls and shanks have a hole through the center, and are slipped over the cable and positioned in the desired location.

(b) Perform the swaging operation in accordance with the instructions furnished by the manufacturer of the swaging equipment.

(c) Check the swaged fitting with a "go no-go" gauge to see that the fitting is properly compressed, and inspect the physical condition of the finished terminal. (See figure 7-13.)

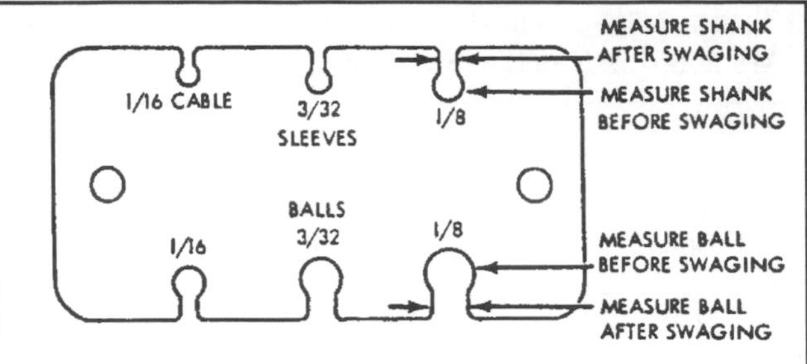

FIGURE 7-13. Typical terminal gauge.

(4) Cable slippage in terminal. Ensure that the cable is properly inserted in the terminal after the swaging operation is completed. Instances have been noted wherein only 1/4 inch of the cable was swaged in the terminal. Observance of the following precautions should minimize this possibility.

(a) Measure the length of the terminal end of the fitting to determine the proper length of cable to be inserted into the barrel of the fitting.

(b) Lay off this length at the end of the cable and mark with masking tape. Since the tape will not slip, it will provide a positive marking during the swaging process.

(c) After swaging, check the tape marker to make certain that the cable did not slip during the swaging operation.

(d) Remove the tape and paint the junction of the swaged fitting and cable with red tape.

(e) At all subsequent service inspections of the swaged fitting, check for a gap in the painted section to see if cable slippage has occurred.

b. Nicopress Process. A patented process using copper sleeves may be used up to the full rated strength of the cable when the cable is looped around a thimble. This process may also be used in place of the five-tuck splice on cables up to and including 3/8 inch diameter. The use of sleeves that are fabricated of materials other than copper will require engineering approval for the specific application by the FAA.

(1) Before undertaking a nicopress splice, determine the proper tool and sleeve for the cable to be used. Refer to table 7-6 and table 7-7 for details on sleeves, tools, and the number of presses required for the various sizes of aircraft cable. The tool must be in good working condition and properly adjusted to ensure a satisfactory splice.

(2) To compress a sleeve, have it well-centered in the tool groove with the major axis of the sleeve at right angles to the tool. If the sleeve appears to be out of line after the press is started, open the tool, re-center the sleeve, and complete the press.

c. Thimble-Eye Splice. Before undertaking a thimble-eye splice, initially position the cable so the end will extend slightly beyond the sleeve, as the sleeve will elongate somewhat when it is compressed. If the cable end is inside the sleeve, the splice may not hold the full strength of the cable. It is desirable that the oval sleeve be placed in close proximity to the thimble points, so that when compressed, the sleeve will contact the thimble as shown in figure 7-14. The sharp ends of the thimble may be cut off before being used; however, make certain the thimble is firmly secured in the cable loop after the splice has been completed. When using a sleeve requiring three compressions, make the center compression first, the compression next to the thimble second, and the one farthest from the thimble last.

d. Lap Splice. Lap or running splices may also be made with copper oval sleeves. When making such splices, it is usually necessary to use two sleeves to develop the full strength of the cable. The sleeves should be positioned as shown in figure 7-12(b), and the compressions made in the order shown. As in the case of eye splices, it is desirable to have the cable ends extend beyond the sleeves sufficiently to allow for the increased length of the compressed sleeves.

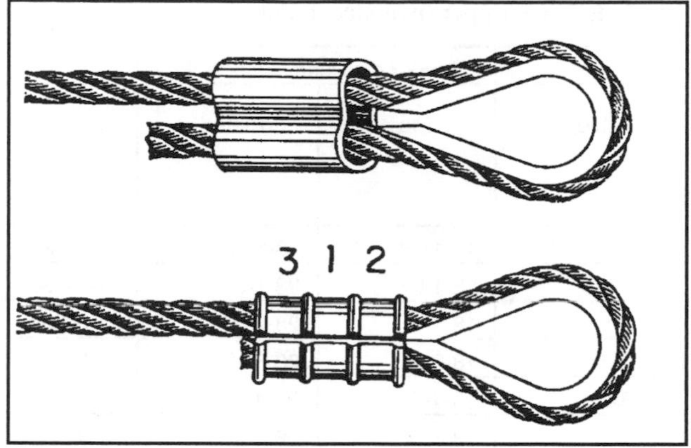

FIGURE 7-14. Typical thimble-eye splice.

e. Stop Sleeves. Stop sleeves may be used for special cable end and intermediate fittings. They are installed in the same manner as nicopress oval sleeves.

NOTE: All stop sleeves are plain copper. Certain sizes are colored for identification.

f. Terminal Gauge. To make a satisfactory copper sleeve installation, it is important that the amount of sleeve pressure be kept uniform. The completed sleeves should be checked periodically with the proper gauge. Hold the gauge so that it contacts the major axis of the sleeve. The compressed portion at the center of the sleeve should enter the gauge opening with very little clearance, as shown in figure 7-15. If it does not, the tool must be adjusted accordingly.

g. Other Applications. The preceding information regarding copper oval sleeves and stop sleeves is based on tests made with flexible aircraft cable. The sleeves may also be

TABLE 7-6. Copper oval sleeve data.

	Copper oval sleeve stock No.						
Cable size	Plain	Plated*	Manual tool No.	Sleeve length before compression (approx.) (inches)	Sleeve length after compression (approx.) (inches)	Number of presses	Tested strength (pounds)
3/64	18-11-B4	28-11-B4	51-B4-887	3/8	7/16	1	340
1/16	18-1-C	28-1-C	51-C-887	3/8	7/16	1	550
3/32	18-2-G	28-2-G	51-G-887	7/16	1/2	1	1,180
1/8	18-3-M	28-3-M	51-M-850	9/16	3/4	3	2,300
5/32	18-4-P	28-4-P	51-P-850	5/8	7/8	3	3,050
3/16	18-6-X	28-6-X	51-X-850	1	1 1/4	4	4,350
7/32	18-8-F2	28-8-F2	51-F2-850	7/8	1 1/16	4	5,790
1/4	18-10-F6	28-10-F6	3-F6-950	1 1/8	1 1/2	3	7,180
5/16	18-13-G9	28-13-G9	3-G9-950	1 1/4	1 5/8	3	11,130
			No. 635 Hydraulic tool dies				
3/8	18-23-H5	28-23-H5	Oval H5	1 1/2	1 7/8	1	16,800
7/16	18-24-J8	28-24-J8	Oval J8	1 3/4	2 1/8	2	19,700
1/2	18-25-K8	28-25-K8	Oval K8	1 7/8	2 1/2	2	25,200
9/16	18-27-M1	28-27-M1	Oval M1	2	2 5/8	3	31,025
5/8	18-28-N5	28-28-N5	Oval N5	2 3/8	3 1/8	3	39,200

*Required on stainless cables due to electrolysis caused by different types of metals.

TABLE 7-7. Copper stop sleeve data.

Cable size (inch)	Sleeve No.	Tool No.	Sleeve	Sleeve	Tested strength (pounds)
3/64	871-12-B4	51-B4-887	7/32	11/64	280
1/16	871-1-C	51-C-887	7/32	13/64	525
3/32	871-17-J (Yellow)	51-MJ	5/16	21/64	600
1/8	S71-18-J (Red)	51-MJ	5/16	21/64	800
5/32	871-19-M	51-MJ	5/16	27/64	1,200
3/16	871-20-M (Black)	51-MJ	5/16	27/64	1,600
7/32	871-22-M	51-MJ	5/8	7/16	2,300
1/4	871-23-F6	3-F6-950	11/16	21/32	3,500
5/16	871-26-F6	3-F6-950	11/16	21/32	3,800

NOTE: All stop sleeves are plain copper. Certain sizes are colored for identification.

used on wire ropes of other construction, if each specific type of cable is proof-tested initially. Because of variation in rope strengths, grades, construction, and actual diameters, the test is necessary to insure proper selection of materials, the correct pressing procedure, and an adequate margin of safety for the intended use.

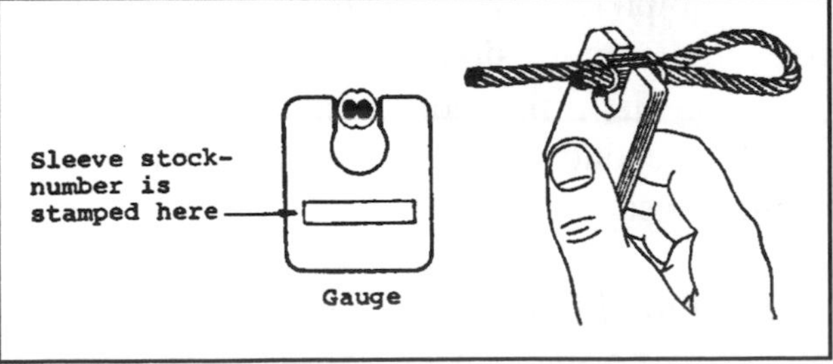

FIGURE 7-15. Typical terminal gauge.

7-149. CABLE SYSTEM INSPECTION. Aircraft cable systems are subject to a variety of environmental conditions and deterioration. Wire or strand breakage is easy to visually recognize. Other kinds of deterioration such as wear, corrosion, and/or distortion are not easily seen; therefore, control cables should be removed periodically for a more detailed inspection.

a. At each annual or 100 hour inspection, all control cables must be inspected for broken wires strands. Any cable assembly that has one broken wire strand located in a critical fatigue area must be replaced.

b. A critical fatigue area is defined as the working length of a cable where the cable runs over, under, or around a pulley, sleeve, or through a fair-lead; or any section where the cable is flexed, rubbed, or worked in any manner; or any point within 1 foot of a swaged-on fitting.

c. A swaged-on fitting can be an eye, fork, ball, ball and shank, ball and double shank, threaded stud, threaded stud and turnbuckle, compression sleeve, or any hardware used as a termination or end fitting on the cable. These fittings may be attached by various swaging methods such as rotary swaging, roll swaging, hydraulic pressing, and hand swaging tools. (See MIL-T-781.) The pressures exerted on the fittings during the swaging process sometimes pinch the small wires in the cable. This can cause premature failure of the pinched wires, resulting in broken wires.

d. Close inspection in these critical fatigue areas, must be made by passing a cloth over the area to snag on broken wires. This will clean the cable for a visual inspection, and detect broken wires if the cloth snags on the cable. Also, a very careful visual inspection must be made since a broken wire will not always protrude or stick out, but may lie in the strand and remain in the position of the helix as it was manufactured. Broken wires of this type may show up as a hairline crack in the wire. If a broken wire of this type is suspected, further inspection with a magnifying glass of 7 power or greater, is recommended. Figure 7-16 shows a cable with broken wires that was not detected by wiping, but was found during a visual inspection. The damage became readily apparent when the cable was removed and bent as shown in figure 7-16.

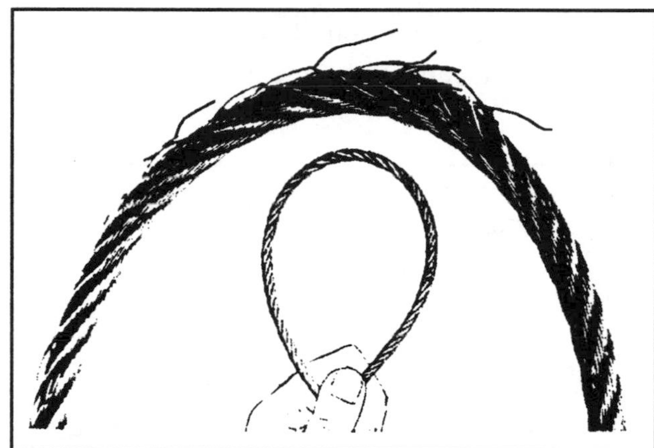

FIGURE 7-16. Cable inspection technique.

e. Kinking of wire cable can be avoided if properly handled and installed. Kinking is caused by the cable taking a spiral shape as the result of unnatural twist. One of the most common causes for this twist is improper unreeling and uncoiling. In a kinked cable, strands and wires are out of position, which creates unequal tension and brings excessive wear at this part of the cable. Even though the kink may be straightened so that the damage appears to be slight, the relative adjustment between the strands has been disturbed so that the cable cannot give maximum service and should be replaced. Inspect cables for a popped core or loose strands. Replace any cable that has a popped core or loose strands regardless of wear or broken wires.

f. Nylon-jacketed cable with any cracks or necking down in the diameter of the jacket shall be replaced. Usable cable life is over when these conditions begin to appear in the nylon jacket.

g. External wear patterns will extend along the cable equal to the distance the cable moves at that location and may occur on one side of the cable or on its entire circumference. Replace flexible and nonflexible cables when the individual wires in each strand appear to blend together (outer wires worn 40 to 50 percent) as depicted in figure 7-17. Actual instances of cable wear beyond the recommended replacement point are shown in figure 7-18.

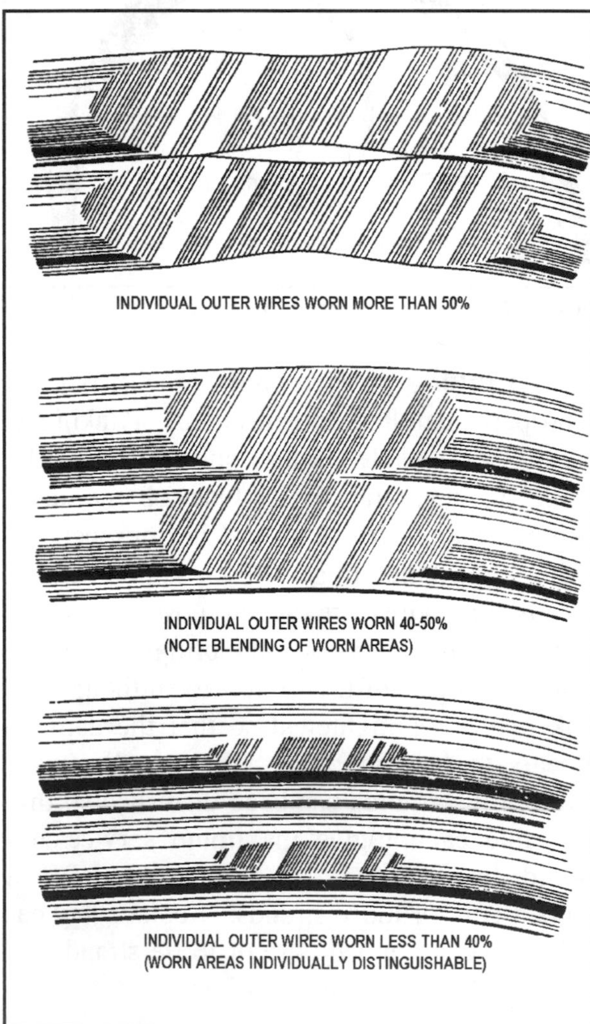

FIGURE 7-17. Cable wear patterns.

h. As wear is taking place on the exterior surface of a cable, the same condition is taking place internally, particularly in the sections of the cable which pass over pulleys and quadrants. This condition (shown in figure 7-19) is not easily detected unless the strands of the cable are separated. This type of wear is a result of the relative motion between inner wire surfaces. Under certain conditions, the rate of this type of wear can be greater than that occurring on the surface.

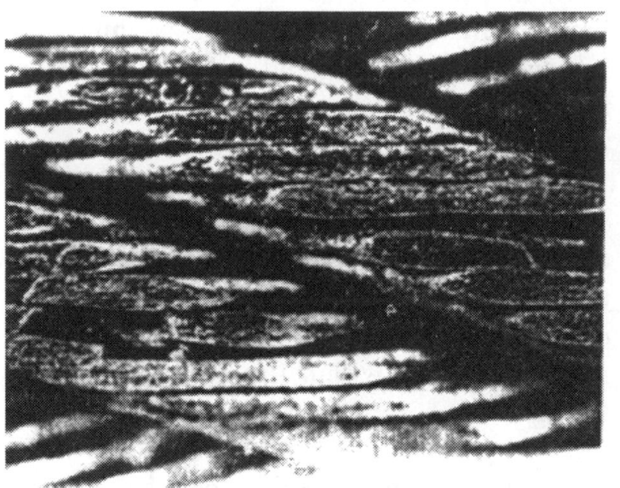

FIGURE 7-18. Worn cable (replacement necessary).

i. Areas especially conducive to cable corrosion are battery compartments, lavatories, wheel wells, etc.; where a concentration of corrosive fumes, vapors, and liquids can accumulate. Carefully examine any cable for corrosion, when it has a broken wire in a section that is not in contact with a wear-producing airframe component, such as a pulley, fair-lead, etc. If the surface of the cable is corroded, relieve cable tension and carefully force the cable open by reverse twisting and visually inspect the interior. Corrosion on the interior strands of the cable constitutes failure, and the cable must be replaced. If no internal corrosion is detected, remove loose external rust and corrosion with a clean, dry, coarse-weave rag, or fiber brush. Do not use metallic

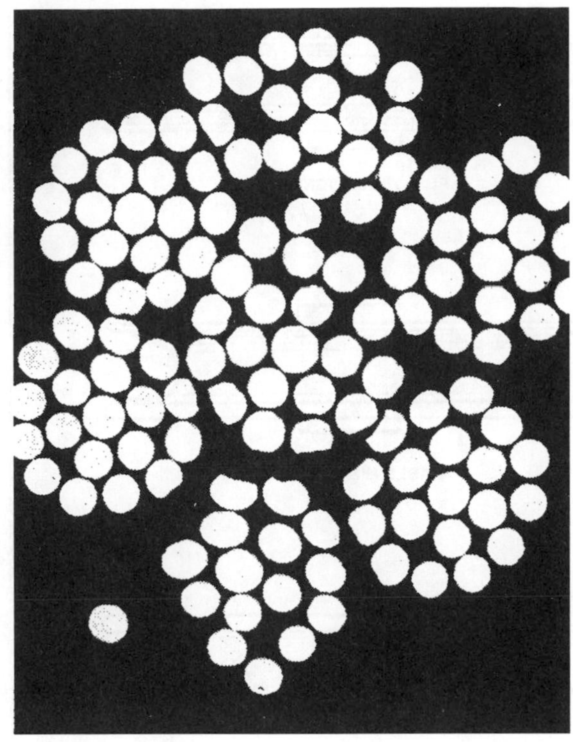

FIGURE 7-19. Internal end view of cable wear.

wool or solvents to clean installed cables. Use of metallic wool will embed dissimilar metal particles in the cables and create further corrosion problems. Solvents will remove internal cable lubricant allowing cable strands to abrade and further corrode. After thorough cleaning, sparingly apply specification MIL-C-16173, grade 4, corrosion-preventive compound to cable. Do not apply the material so thick that it will interfere with the operation of cables at fair-leads, pulleys, or grooved bellcrank areas.

j. Examine cable runs for incorrect routing, fraying, twisting, or wear at fair-leads, pulleys, antiabrasion strips, and guards. Look for interference with adjacent structure, equipment, wiring, plumbing, and other controls. Inspect cable systems for binding, full travel, and security of attaching hardware. Check for slack in the cable system by attempting to move the control column and/or pedals while the gust locks are installed on the control surfaces. With the gust locks removed, actuate the controls and check for friction or hard movement. These are indications that excessive cable tension exists.

NOTE: If the control movement is stiff after maintenance is performed on control surfaces, check for parallel cables twisted around each other, or cables connected in reverse.

k. Check swaged terminal reference marks for an indication of cable slippage within the fitting. Inspect the fitting assembly for distortion and/or broken strands at the terminal. Ensure that all bearings and swivel fittings (bolted or pinned) pivot freely to prevent binding and subsequent failure. Check turnbuckles for proper thread exposure and broken or missing safety wires/clips.

l. Inspect pulleys for roughness, sharp edges, and presence of foreign material embedded in the grooves. Examine pulley bearings to ensure proper lubrication, smooth rotation; and freedom from flat spots, dirt, and paint spray. During the inspection, rotate the pulleys, which only turn through a small arc, to provide a new bearing surface for the cable. Maintain pulley alignment to prevent the cable from riding on the flanges and chafing against guards, covers, or adjacent structure. Check all pulley brackets and guards for damage, alignment, and security.

m. Various cable system malfunctions may be detected by analyzing pulley conditions. These include such discrepancies as too much tension, misalignment, pulley bearing problems, and size mismatches between cables and pulleys. Examples of these condition are shown in figure 7-20.

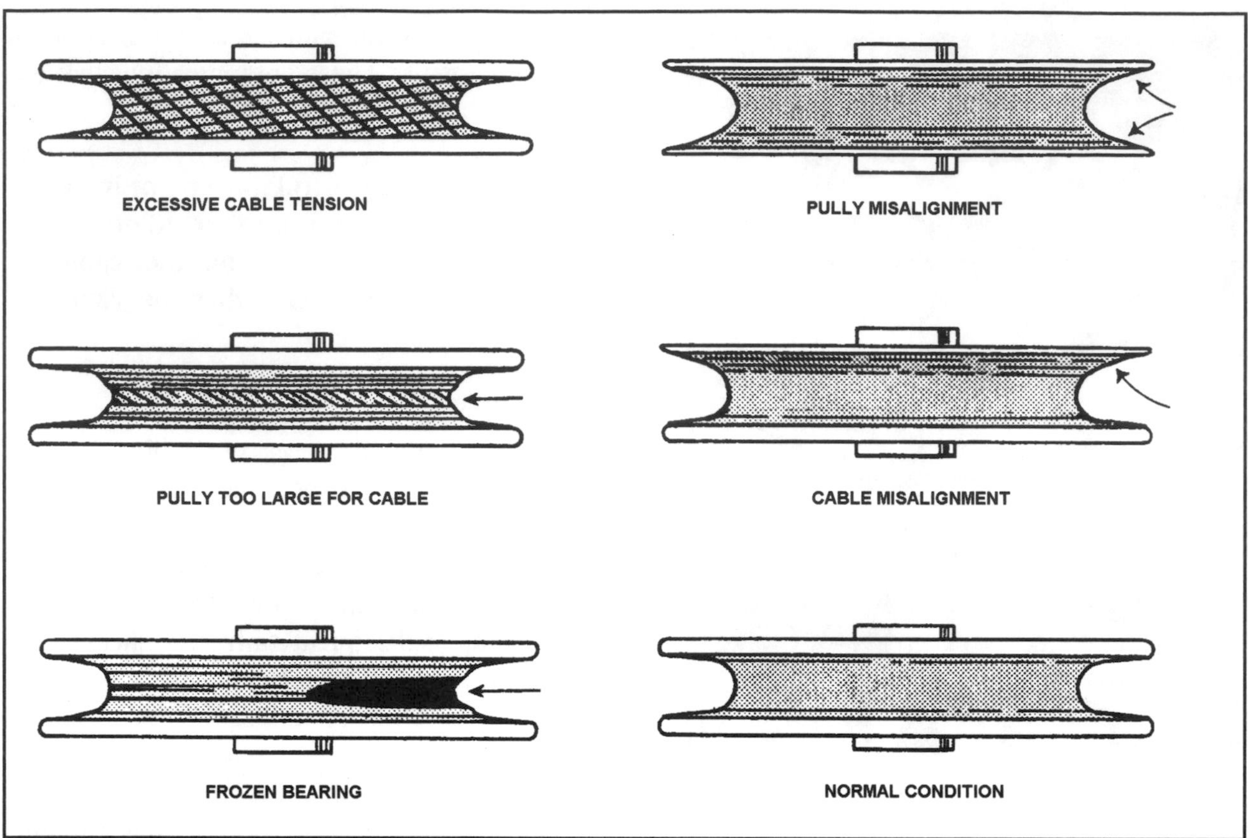

FIGURE 7-20. Pulley wear patterns.

n. Inspect fair-leads for wear, breakage, alignment, cleanliness, and security. Examine cable routing at fair-leads to ensure that defection angles are no greater than 3°€maximum. Determine that all guides and anti-abrasion strips are secure and in good condition.

o. Examine pressure seals for wear and/or material deterioration. Seal guards should be positioned to prevent jamming of a pulley in case pressure seal fails and pieces slide along the cable.

7-150. CORROSION AND RUST PREVENTION. To ensure a satisfactory service life for aircraft control cables, use a cable lubricant to reduce internal friction and prevent corrosion.

a. If the cable is made from tinned steel, coat the cable with rust-preventive oil, and wipe off any excess. It should be noted that corrosion-resistant steel cable does not require this treatment for rust prevention.

b. Lubrication and corrosion preventive treatment of carbon steel cables may be effected simultaneously by application of compound MIL-C-16173, grade 4, or MIL-C-11796, Class I. MIL-C-16173 compound should be brushed, sprayed, or wiped on the cable to the extent it penetrates into the strands and adequately covers the cable surfaces. It will dry "tack free" in 24 hours at 77 °F. MIL-C-11796 compound is applied by dipping the cable for 1/2 minute into a tank of compound heated to 77 ° ± 5 °C (170 ° ± 9 °F) for 1/2 minute then removing it and wiping off the excess oil. (An example of cable corrosion, attributable to battery acid, is shown in figure 7-21.)

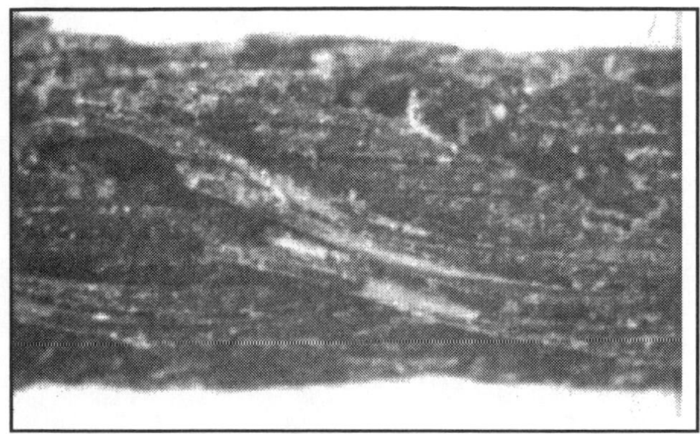

FIGURE 7-21. Corrosion.

7-151. WIRE SPLICES. Standard manufacturing splices have been mistaken for defects in the cable because individual wire end splices were visible after assembly of a finished cable length. In some instances, the process of twisting outer strands around the core strand may also slightly flatten individual outer wires, particularly in the area of a wire splice. This flattening is the result of die-sizing the cable, and does not affect the strength of the cable. These conditions (as shown in figure 7-22) are normal, and are not a cause for cable rejection.

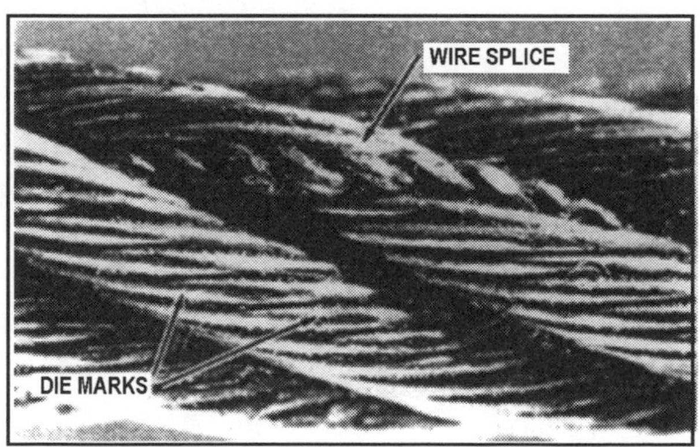

FIGURE 7-22. Manufacturer's wire splice.

7-152. CABLE MAINTENANCE. Frequent inspections and preservation measures such as rust-prevention treatments for bare carbon steel cable areas, will help to extend cable service life. Where cables pass through fair-leads, pressure seals, or over pulleys, remove accumulated heavy coatings of corrosion-prevention compound. Provide corrosion protection for these cable sections by lubricating with a light coat of grease or general-purpose, low-temperature oil.

7-153. CABLE TENSION ADJUSTMENT. Carefully adjust, control cable tension in accordance with the airframe manufacturer's recommendations. On large aircraft, take the temperature of the immediate area into consideration when using a tension meter. For long cable sections, use the average of two or three temperature readings to obtain accurate tension values. If necessary, compensate for extreme surface temperature variations that may be encountered if the aircraft is operated primarily in unusual geographic or climatic conditions such as arctic, arid, or tropic locations. Use rigging pins and gust locks, as necessary, to ensure satisfactory results. At the completion of rigging operations, check turnbuckle adjustment and safetying in accordance with section 10 of this chapter.

7-154.—7-164. [RESERVED.]

SECTION 9. TURNBUCKLES

7-165. GENERAL. A turnbuckle is a device used in cable systems to provide a means of adjusting tension. Turnbuckles have barrel-shaped sleeves with internal left- and right-hand threads at opposite ends. The cables, with terminals attached, are made to such a length that, when the turnbuckle is adjusted to give the specified cable tension, a sufficient number of threads on the terminal ends are screwed into the barrel to hold the load. The clip-locking turnbuckle and its associated parts are identical to standard AN and MS parts except for a slot grooved on the interior of the barrel and the shanks of the forks, eyes, etc. The clip-locking turnbuckle parts have the following drawing numbers: MS21251, turnbuckle body; MS21252, turnbuckle clevis end; MS21253, turnbuckle clevis end (for bearing); NAS649 and NAS651, turnbuckle clip; MS21254 and NAS648, turnbuckle eye (for pin); MS21255 and NAS647, turnbuckle eye end (for wire rope); NAS645 and NAS646, turnbuckle fork; MS21256, turnbuckle barrel locking clip; AN130-170, turnbuckle assemblies; and, MS21259 and MS21260, terminal, wire rope, stud.

NOTE: Turnbuckles showing signs of thread distortion/bending should be replaced. Turnbuckle ends are designed for providing the specified cable tension on a cable system, and a bent turnbuckle would place undesirable stress on the cable, impairing the function of the turnbuckle.

7-166. TURNBUCKLE INSTALLATION. (See figure 7-25.) When installing cable system turnbuckles, it is necessary to screw both threaded terminals into the turnbuckle barrel an equal amount. It is essential that turnbuckle terminals be screwed into the barrel so that not more than three threads on the terminal are exposed. (See figure 7-23A.) On initial installation, the turnbuckle terminals should not be screwed inside the turnbuckle barrel more than four threads. (See figure 7-23B.)

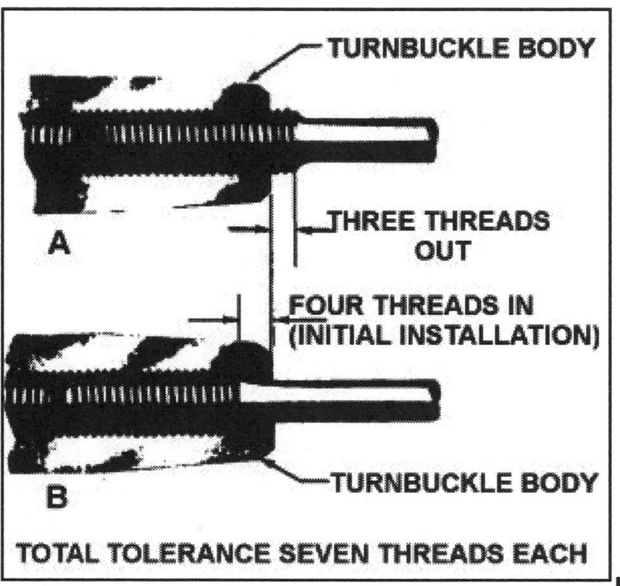

FIGURE 7-25. Turnbuckle thread tolerance.

7-167. WITNESS HOLE. Some manufacturers of turnbuckles incorporate a "witness hole," in the turnbuckle barrel to ensure that the threaded cable terminals are screwed in far enough into the barrel. The "witness hole" can be inspected visually, or by using a piece of safety wire as a probe.

7-168.—7-178. [RESERVED.]

SECTION 10. SAFETY METHODS FOR TURNBUCKLES

7-179. GENERAL. Safety all turnbuckles with safety wire using either the double or single-wrap method, or with any appropriately approved special safetying device complying with the requirements of FAA Technical Standard Order TSO-C21. The swaged and unswaged turnbuckle assemblies are covered by AN standard drawings. Do not reuse safety wire. Adjust the turnbuckle to the correct cable tension so that no more than three cable threads are exposed on either side of the turnbuckle barrel.

7-180. DOUBLE-WRAP METHOD. Of the methods using safety wire for safetying turnbuckles, the method described here is preferred, although either of the other methods described is satisfactory. The method of double-wrap safetying is shown in figure 7-26(A).

a. Use two separate lengths of wire. Run one end of the wire through the hole in the barrel of the turnbuckle and bend the ends of the wire toward opposite ends of the turnbuckle.

b. Pass the second length of the wire into the hole in the barrel and bend the ends along the barrel on the side opposite the first. Spiral the two wires in opposite directions around the barrel to cross each other twice between the center hole and the ends.

c. Then pass the wires at the end of the turnbuckle in opposite directions through the hole in the turnbuckle eyes or between the jaws of the turnbuckle fork, as applicable, laying one wire along the barrel and wrapping the other at least four times around the shank of the turnbuckle and binding the laid wires in place before cutting the wrapped wire off.

d. Wrap the remaining length of safety wire at least four turns around the shank and cut it off. Repeat the procedure at the opposite end of the turnbuckle.

e. When a swaged terminal is being safetied, pass the ends of both wires through the hole provided in the terminal for this purpose and wrap both ends around the shank as previously described. If the hole is not large enough to allow passage of both wires, pass the wire through the hole and loop it over the free end of the other wire, and then wrap both ends around the shank as previously described. Another satisfactory double-wrap method is similar to the previous method, except that the spiraling of the wires is omitted as shown in figure 7-26(B).

7-181. SINGLE-WRAP METHOD. The single-wrap methods described in the following paragraphs and as illustrated in figure 7-26(C) and (D) are acceptable, but are not the equal of the double-wrap methods.

a. Pass a single length of wire through the cable eye or fork, or through the hole in the swaged terminal at either end of the turnbuckle assembly. Spiral each of the wire ends in opposite directions around the first half of the turnbuckle barrel, so as to cross each other twice. Thread both wire ends through the hole in the middle of the barrel so that the third crossing of wire ends is in the hole, again, spiral the two wire ends in opposite directions around the remaining half of the turnbuckle, crossing them twice. Then, pass one wire end through the cable eye or fork, or through the hole in the swaged terminals, in the manner previously described. Wrap both wire ends around the shank for at least four turns each, cutting off excess wire. This method is shown in figure 7-26(C).

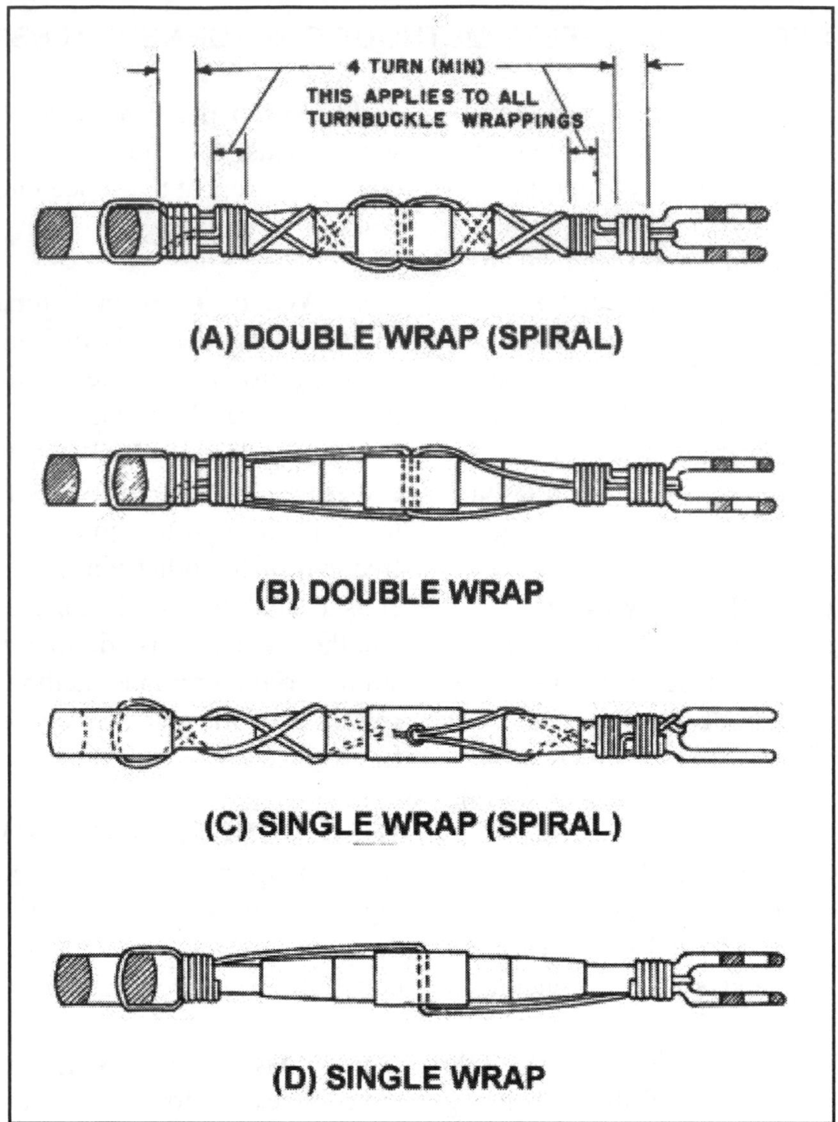

FIGURE 7-26. Safetying turnbuckles.

b. For the method shown in figure 7-26D, pass one length of wire through the center hole of the turnbuckle and bend the wire ends toward opposite ends of the turnbuckle. Then pass each wire end through the cable eye or fork, or through the hole in the swaged terminal, and wrap each wire around the shank for at least four turns, cutting off excess wire. After safetying, no more than three threads of the turnbuckle threaded terminal should be exposed.

7-182. SAFETY-WIRE SECURED TURNBUCKLES. (See figure 7-27.) Before securing turnbuckles, threaded terminals should be screwed into the turnbuckle barrel until no more than three threads of either terminal are outside the barrel. After the turnbuckle has been adjusted for proper cable tension, two pieces of safety wire are inserted, half the wire length into the hole in the center of the turnbuckle barrel. The safety-wires are bent so that each wire extends half the length of the turnbuckle on top and half on bottom. The ends of the wires are passed through the hole in the turnbuckle eyes or between the jaws of the turnbuckle fork, as applicable. The wires are then bent toward the center of the turnbuckle and each wire is wrapped around the shank four times, binding the wrapping wires in place as shown in figure 7-27.

a. When a swaged terminal is being secured, one wire is passed through the hole in the terminal and is looped over the free end of the other wire and both ends wrapped around the shank. All lock wire used in the safetying of turnbuckles should be carbon steel, corrosion-resistant steel, nickel-chromium iron alloy (inconel), nickel-copper alloy (monel) or aluminum alloy. For safety cable diameter of safety wire size and material, refer to table 7-8.

b. Care should be exercised when safety wiring, particularly where corrosion will present a problem, because smaller wire sizes tend to crack when twisted.

TABLE 7-8. Turnbuckle safetying guide.

Cable Size	Type of Wrap	Diameter of Safety Wire	Material (Annealed Condition)
1/16	Single	0.040	Copper, brass.[1]
3/32	Single	0.040	Copper, brass.[1]
1/8	Single	0.040	Stainless steel, Monel and "K" Monel.
1/8	Double	0.040	Copper, brass.[1]
1/8	Single	0.057 min.	Copper, brass.[1]
5/32 and greater.	Double	0.040	Stainless steel, Monel and "K" Monel.[1]
5/32 and greater	Single	0.057 min.	Stainless steel, Monel or "K" Monel.[1]
5/32 and greater	Double	0.0512	Copper, brass.

[1]Galvanized or tinned steel, or soft iron wires are also acceptable.

7-183. SPECIAL LOCKING DEVICES. Several turnbuckle locking devices are available for securing turnbuckle barrels such as wire-locking clips. Persons intending to use a special device must ensure the turnbuckle assembly has been designed to accommodate such devices. A typical unit is shown in figure 7-28. When special locking devices are not readily available, the use of safety wire is acceptable.

7-184. ASSEMBLING AND SECURING CLIP-LOCKING TURNBUCKLES. (See table 7-9 and figure 7-29.) Wire clip-locking turnbuckles are assembled and secured in the following ways.

a. Engage threads of turnbuckle barrel with threads of cable terminal and turn barrel until proper cable tension is reached.

b. Align slot in barrel with slot in cable terminal.

c. Hold lock clip between thumb and forefinger at loop end and insert straight end of clip into opening formed by aligned slots.

d. Bring hook end of lock clip over hole in center of turnbuckle barrel and seat hook loop into hole.

e. Apply pressure to hook shoulder to engage hook lip in turnbuckle barrel and to complete safety locking of one end of turnbuckle.

NOTE: Repeat the above steps to safety lock the opposite end of turnbuckle. Both lock clips may be inserted in the same turnbuckle barrel hole or they may be inserted in opposite holes. However, do not reverse wire locking clips

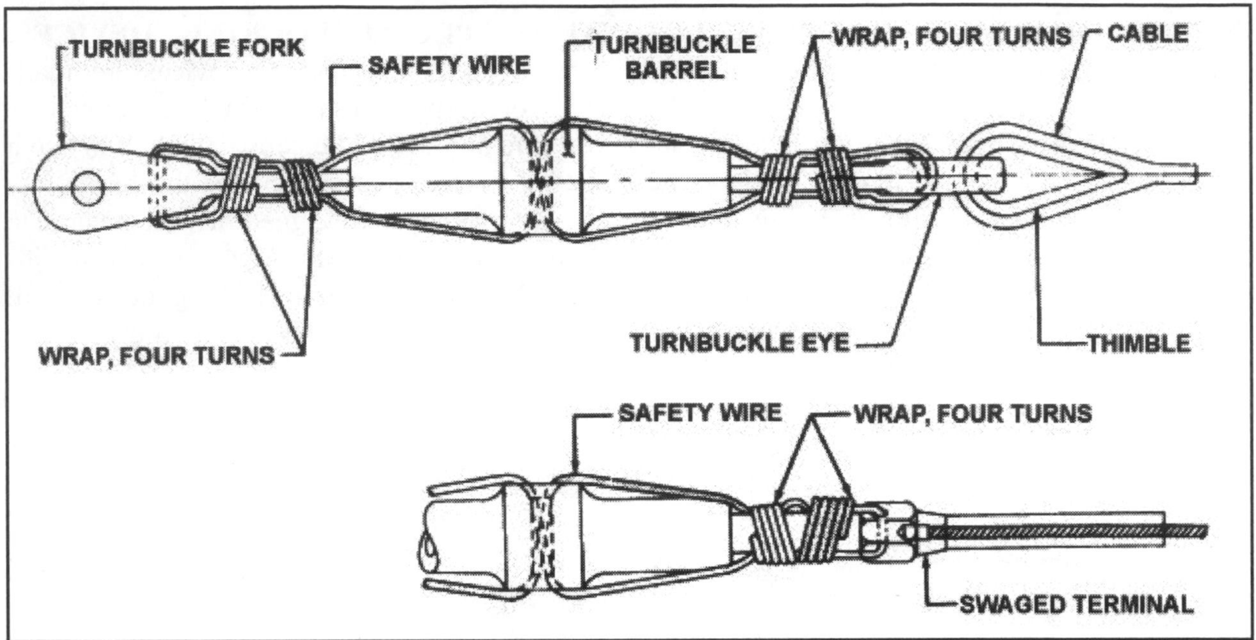

FIGURE 7-27. Securing turnbuckles.

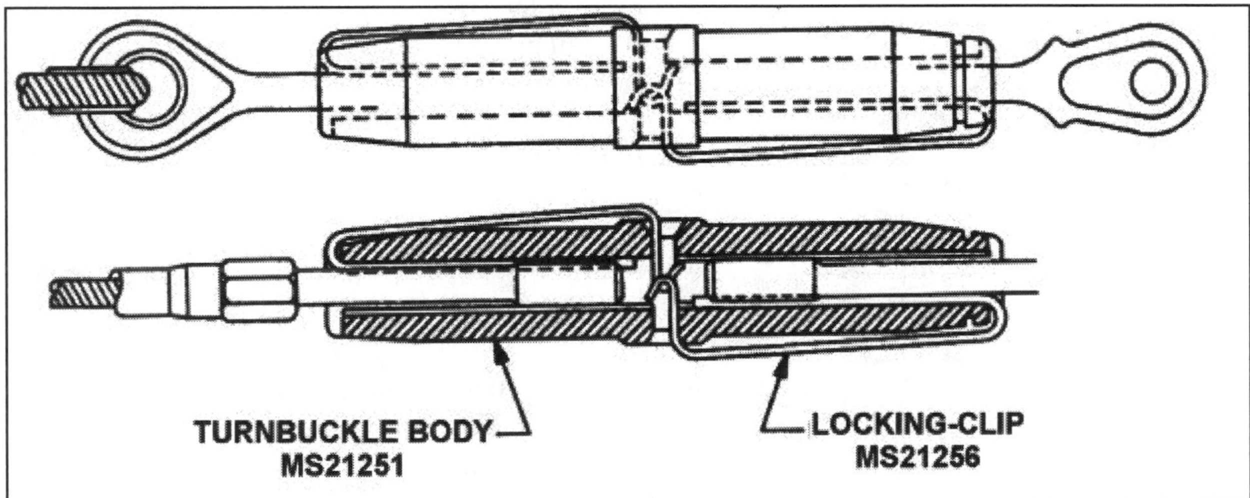

FIGURE 7-28. Clip-type locking device.

TABLE 7-9. Locking-clip application.

NOMINAL CABLE DIA.	THREAD UNF-3	LOCKING CLIP MS21256	TURNBUCKLE BODY MS21251
1/16	No. 6-40	-1	-2S
3/32	No. 10-32		-3S
		-2	-3L
1/8	1/4-28	-1	-4S
		-2	-4L
5/32		-1	-5S
		-2	-5L
3/16	5/16-24	-1	-6S
		-2	-6L
7/32	3/8-24		-7L
1/4			-8L
9/32	7/16-20	-3	-9L
5/16	1/2-20		-10L

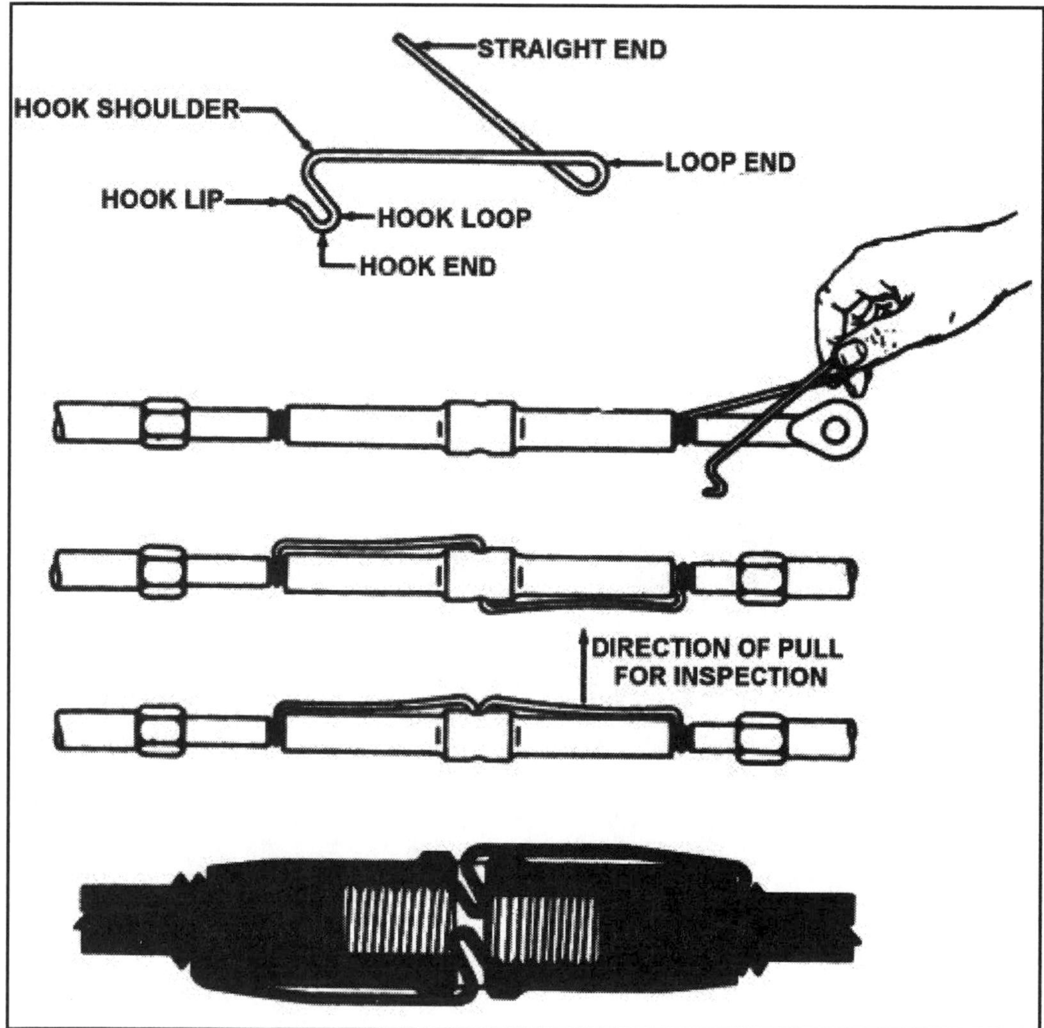

FIGURE 7-27. Assembling and securing clip-locking turnbuckles

7-185.—7-195. [RESERVED.]

SECTION 11. HARDWARE IDENTIFICATION TABLES

TABLE 7-10. TABLE OF RIVETS.

Rivet Number	Description
AN427 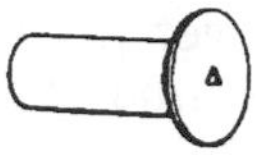	Rivet, 100▪csk. Head steel, monel, copper
AN430 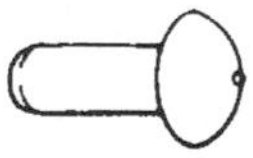	Rivet, round head al. Alloy
AN441 	Rivet, tinners Head, steel, ss, monel
AN456 	Rivet, brazier head, aluminum alloy
AN123151-123750 	Rivet, universal head & 100▪ steel, Inconel
NAS 1200 	Rivet, solid, 100▪ flush shear head
NAS 1241 	Rivet, solid, 100▪ flush head
NAS 1242 	Rivet, solid universal head
NAS 1398 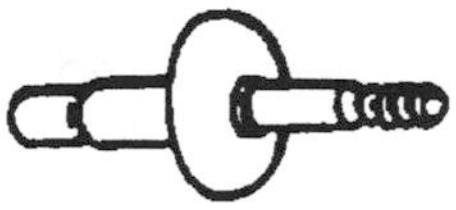	Rivet, blind, protruding head, locked spindle
NAS 1399 	Rivet, blind, 100▪ csk. Head, locked spindle

TABLE 7-10. (CONTINUED)

Rivet Number	Description
NAS 1738-1739 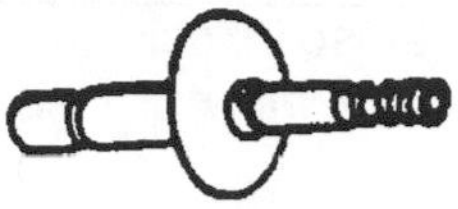	Rivet, blind, protruding & flush hd., mech. locked spindle, bulbed
NAS1806-1816 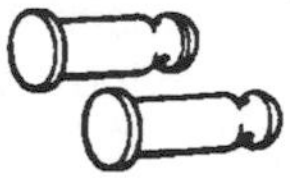	Rivet, hi-shear, flathead., ti. alloy
NAS1906-1916 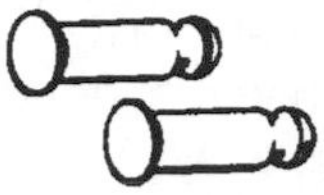	Rivet, hi-shear, 100° hd., ti. alloy
AN124951-125550 	Rivet, solid universal head & 100° csk. head, cres. steel, inconel
AN125551-1255700 	Rivet, solid universal head, steel
AN426 MS20426 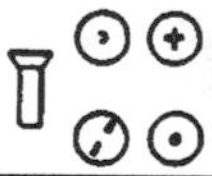	Rivet, solid, csk. 100° head al. alloy
AN470 MS20470 	Rivet, solid, universal head, al. & al. alloy
MS9319 	Rivet, solid univ. head, AMS 7233
MS9403 	Rivet, solid, universal head, AMS 5737
MS16535 	Rivet, tubular, oval head

TABLE 7-10. (CONTINUED)

Rivet Number	Description
MS16536 	Rivet, tubular, 100° flat csk. head
MS20426 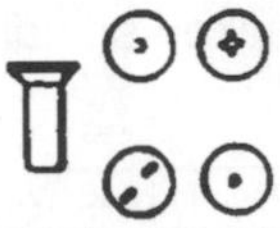	Rivet, solid, csk., 100° al. alloy
MS20427 	Rivet, solid, csk., 100° flush hd., AMS 7233
MS20470 	Rivet, solid, universal head, al. alloy
MS20600 	Rivet, blind, pull stem, protruding head
MS20601 	Rivet, blind, pull stem, 100°, flush head
MS20602-20603 	Rivet, blind, explosive
MS20604-20605 	Rivet, blind nonstructural univ. and 100° flush head
MS20613-20615 	Rivet, solid, monel, universal hd., steel, ss, brass, copper
NAS452-453 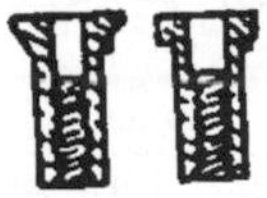	Rivnut, 100° csk. head & flathead
NAS454-455 	Rivet blind, al. alloy

TABLE 7-10. (CONTINUED)

Rivet Number	Description
NAS508 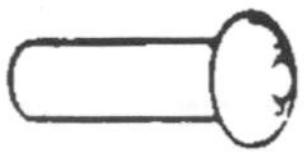	Rivet, universal head, monel
NAS1054 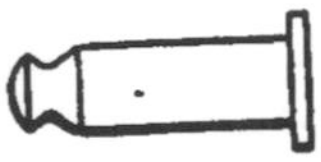	Rivet, hi-shear, protruding head
NAS1055	Rivet, hi-shear, 100° flush head
NAS1097 	Rivet, solid, 100° flush shear head, al. Alloy
NAS1198 	Rivet, solid, universal head
NAS1199 	Rivet, solid, 100° flush head

TABLE 7-11. TABLE OF SCREWS.

Screw MS, AN, or NAS Number	Description
AN255 	Screw, external relieved body
AN500 & 501 	Screw, machine fillister head
AN502 & 503 	Screw, machine, fill. Head, drilled, coarse & fine
AN504 	Screw, tapping, thread cutting rnd. Head, mach. Thread

TABLE 7-11. (CONTINUED)

Screw MS, AN, or NAS Number	Description
AN505 	Screw, machine, flathead, 82° coarse thread
AN506 	Screw, tapping, type F, coarse & fine
AN507 	Screw, machine, flathead, 100°
AN508 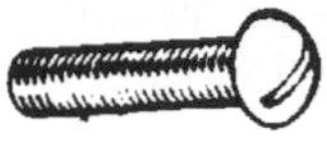	Screw, machine, round head
AN509 	Screw machine, 100° structural
AN510 	Screw, machine, flathead, 82° fine thread
AN515 & AN520 	Screw, machine, round head
AN525 	Screw, washer head
AN526 	Screw, machine buttonhead
AN530 	Screw-tapping, thread cutting, rnd. hd.
AN531 	Screw, tapping, thread forming or cutting, 82° flathead.

TABLE 7-11. (CONTINUED)

Screw MS, AN, or NAS Number	Description
AN535 	Drive screw, round head
AN545 	Screw, wood, round head
AN550 	Screw, wood, flathead, 82°
AN565 	Setscrew, hex. & fluted socket
AN115401-115600 	Screws, flat fill. head, steel, .190-.375
AN115601-115800 	Drilled shank Screw flat fill. head, steel, .190-.375
AN115801-116150 	Screw, flat fill. head, steel. .190-.375
AN116901-117080 	Screw, oval fill. head, steel
MS9016 	Bushing Screw, plain
MS9017 	Bushing Screw, slotted
MS9122-9123 	Screw, machine slotted hex. hd.

TABLE 7-11. (CONTINUED)

Screw MS, AN, or NAS Number	Description
MS9177-9178 	Screw, dbl. hex. head, cres.
MS9183-9186 	Screw, machine, steel, drilled 12 pt. hd., cad. plate
MS9187-9188 	Screw, drilled dbl. hex. head, cres.
MS9189-9192 	Screw, machine, steel, 12 pt. hd., black oxide
MS9206-9214 	Screw, dbl. hex. ext. washer head, diffused nickel cad. plate
MS9215-9223 	Screw, dbl. hex. ext. washer head, diffused nickel cad. plate, drilled
MS9281-9291 	Screw, machine, hex. hd., AMS 6322 black oxide
MS9292-9302 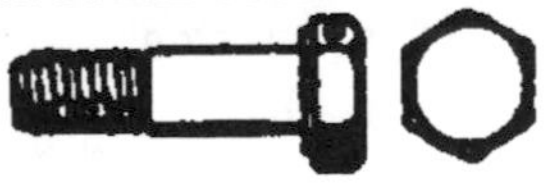	Screw, machine, hex. hd., AMS 6322 blk. oxide, drilled
MS9316-9317 	Screw, machine, steel slotted hex. head
MS9438-9439 	Screw, mach. steel AMS 6304 diffused nickel cad. hex. hd., one hole
MS9631-9639 	Screw, mach., hex. hd. one hole, full shank, titanium AMS 4967

TABLE 7-11. (CONTINUED)

Screw MS, AN, or NAS Number	Description
MS16198 	Screw, wood, slotted RH austenitic corr. res. steel
MS16199 	Screw, wood, slot flat-head, copper silicone
MS16995 	Screw, cap, socket head hex., corr. resisting steel UNC-3A
MS16996 	Screw, cap, socket head, hex., corr. resisting steel UNF-3A
MS16997 	Screw, cap, socket head, hex., alloy steed cad. UNC-3A
MS16998 	Screw, cap, socket head, hex., alloy steel, cad. UNF-3A
MS18063-18068 	Setscrew, self-locking, cup, flat, cone pts., steel & stainless
MS18211 	Screw, machine, flat-head, plastic, nylon
MS18212 	Screw, machine, pan-head, plastic, nylon
MS21090 	Screw, self-lock, pan-head, cross recessed
MS21207 	Screw, tapping, 100° clk. flathead., steel, cres. steel

TABLE 7-11. (CONTINUED)

Screw MS, AN, or NAS Number	Description
MS21262 	Screw, self-lock, int. wrenching
MS21277-21285 	Screw, machine, double hex., ext. washer head
MS21286-21294 	Screw, machine, double hex., ext. washer head
MS21295 	Screw, self-lock, int. wrenching
MS21318 	Screw, drive, round head, Type U
MS21342 	Setscrew, fluted socket, cup and flat point
MS24615-24618 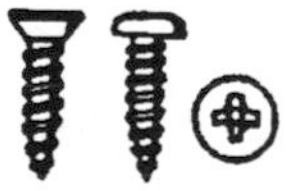	Screw, tapping, phillips recessed, pan & 82° flathead Type A
MS24619-24622 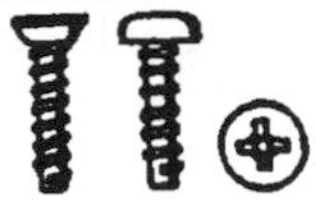	Screw, tapping, phillips recessed, pan & 82° flathead Type B
MS24623-24626 	Screw, tapping, cross recessed pan & 82° flathead, Type BF or BT
MS24627-24630 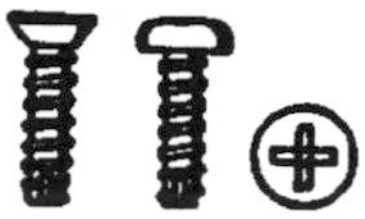	Screw, tapping, thread cutting cross recessed pan & 82° flathead, Type F
MS24667 & 24671 	Screw, cap socket hd., flat, csk.

TABLE 7-11. (CONTINUED)

Screw MS, AN, or NAS Number	Description
MS24673-24678 	Screw, cap socket hd., flat, drilled
MS24693 	Screw, machine, flat csk. head, 100° cross recess
MS24694 	Screw, machine, csk. flathead., 100° cross recess, structural
MS27039 	Screw, machine, panhead, structural, cross recessed
MS35190-35203 	Screw, machine 82° flathead., cross recessed, steel, brass, alum.
MS35206-35219 	Screw, machine, panhead, cross recessed, steel, brass, alum.
MS35223-35234 	Screw, machine, panhead, slotted, SS steel, steel
MS35239-35243 	Screw, machine, flathead., slotted, steel
MS35265-35278 	Screw, machine, drilled fillister head, slotted, SS steel, brass, alum.
MS35492-35493 	Screw, wood, flathead, cross recessed
MS35494-35495 	Screw. wood, flat & round hd., slotted

TABLE 7-11. (CONTINUED)

Screw MS, AN, or NAS Number	Description
MS35914 	Insert, screw, thread, self-tapping
MS51017-51047 	Setscrew, hex. socket SS & steel half dog, cone, flat, cup pt.
MS51861 	Screw, tapping, type AB, panhead, cross recessed
MS51862 	Screw, tapping, type AB, flathead., cross recessed
MS51957-51958 	Screw, machine, panhead, cross recessed
MS51959-51960 	Screw, machine, flathead, cross recessed
MS51963-51966 	Setscrew, hex. socket, cup & flat point
MS51973-51974 	Setscrew, hex. socket, cone point
MS51975 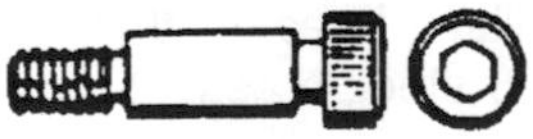	Screw, shoulder, socket head
MS51976-51977 	Setscrew, hex. socket, half dog point
MS51981-51982 	Setscrew, hex. socket, oval point

TABLE 7-11. (CONTINUED)

Screw MS, AN, or NAS Number	Description
NAS220-237 	Screw, brazier hd. phillips recessed
NAS384-385 	Screw, oval head, phillips recessed 100°, 82°, steel
NAS387-388 	Screw, machine, oval hd., 100°, 82°, steel
NAS514	Screw, machine, 100° flathead., fully threaded, al. steel
NAS517 	Screw, 100° flathead, close tol. 160,000 psi
NAS548 	Screw, 100° flathead, type B tapping
NAS560 	Screw, machine, 100° structural, hi-temp
NAS600-606 	Screw, machine, aircraft, panhead phillips recessed, full thr., steel
NAS608-609 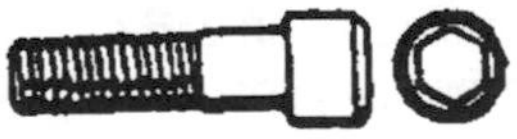	Screw, hex. socket cap, plain & self-locking, drilled head
NAS623 	Screw, panhead. thr. short, 160,000 psi
NAS720 	Screw, panhead, assembled

TABLE 7-11. (CONTINUED)

Screw MS, AN, or NAS Number	Description
NAS1081 	Setscrew, hex. socket, self-locking
NAS1096 	Screw, hex. head, recess, full thr.
NAS1100 	Screw, machine, panhead, full thread, torq.-set
NAS1101 	Screw, machine, flat fill hd. full thread
NAS1102 	Screw, machine, 100° flathead. full thr. torq.-set
NAS1121-1128 	Screw, machine, flat fill hd., short thread, torq.-set
NAS1131-1138 	Screw, machine, pan hd., short thread, torq.-set
NAS1141-1148 	Screw, machine, panhead. modified, short thread torq.-set
NAS1151-1158 	Screw, machine, 100° flathead., sort thread, torq.-set
NAS1161-1168 	Screw, machine, 100° flathead., shear, torq.-set
NAS1171-1178 	Screw, panhead., shear, self-lock., torq.-set

TABLE 7-11. (CONTINUED)

Screw MS, AN, or NAS Number	Description
NAS1181-1188 	Screw, flat fill hd., self-locking, torq.-set
NAS1189 	Screw, flat 100° hd., full thread, self-locking
NAS1190 	Screw, panhead., self-locking, full thread
NAS1191 	Screw, flat fill. hd., full thread, self-locking
NAS1216 	Screw, panhead hi-torque, full thread
NAS1217 	Screw, panhead, hi-torque, short thread
NAS1218 	Screw, panhead, hi-torque, short thread
NAS1219 	Screw, 100° csk. hd., hi-torque, full thread
NAS1220 	Screw, 100° csk. hd., hi-torque, short thread
NAS1221 	Screw, 100° clk. hd., hi-torque, long thread
NAS1298 	Screw, shoulder, brazier head

TABLE 7-11. (CONTINUED)

Screw MS, AN, or NAS Number	Description
NAS1299 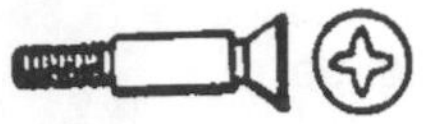	Screw, shoulder, 100° flathead
NAS1300 	Thumbscrew, drilled/undrilled
NAS1301 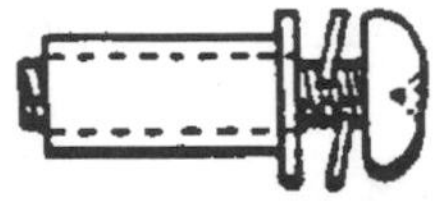	Screw, panhead, assembled washers phillips recess
NAS1351-1352 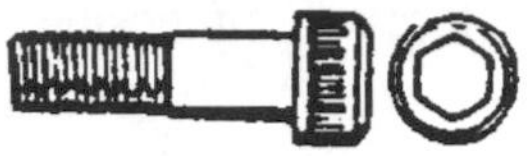	Socket Capscrew, hex. head, drilled/undrilled
NAS1393 	Screw, 82° flathead, torq-set
NAS1402-1406 	Screw, panhead, phillips recess
NAS1579 	Screw, panhead., full thread, 1200° F
NAS1603-1610 	Screw, flush head, .0312 O.S.
NAS1620-1628 	Screw, machine, 100° flat short thread, torq-set
NAS1630-1634 	Screw, machine, panhead., short thread, torq.-set
NAS1635 	Screw, panhead cross recessed, full thread

TABLE 7-11. (CONTINUED)

Screw MS, AN, or NAS Number	Description
NAS5000-5006 	Screw, panhead, tri-wing recess, short thr., alloy stl.
NAS5100-5106 	Screw, panhead, tri-wing recess, short thr., cres.
NAS5200-5206 	Screw, panhead, tri-wing recess, short thr., cres.
NAS5300-5306 	Screw, fillister head, tri-wing recess, full thr., alloy stl.
NAS5400-5406 	Screw, fillister hd., tri-wing recess, full thr., cres.
NAS5500-5506 	Screw, fillister hd., tri-wing recess, full thr., titanium
NAS5600-5606 	Screw, 100° head, tri-wing recess, full thr., alloy stl.
NAS5700-5706 	Screw, 100° head, tri-wing recess, full thr., cres.
NAS5800-5806 	Screw, 100° head, tri-wing recess, full thr., titanium
NAS5900-5903 	Screw, hex. Head, tri-wing recess, full thr., alloy stl.
NAS6000-6003 	Screw, hex. Head, tri-wing recess, full thr., cres.

TABLE 7-11. (CONTINUED)

Screw MS, AN, or NAS Number	Description
NAS6100-6103 	Screw, hex head, tri-wing recess, full thr., titanium
NAS6500-6506 	Screw, 100° oval hd., tri-wing recess, full thr., cres.
NAS6900-6904 	Screw, panhead, tri-wing recess, full thr., cres.

TABLE 7-12. TABLE OF BOLTS.

Bolt Number	Description
AN3-20 	Bolt, machine
AN21-36 	Bolt, clevis
AN42-49 	Bolt, eye
AN73-81 	Bolt, machine, drilled
AN173-186 	Bolt, aircraft Close tolerance
AN774 	Bolt, flared tube
AN775 	Bolt, universal fitting

TABLE 7-12. (CONTINUED)

Bolt Number	Description
AN148551-149350 	Bolt, socket head, 6-hole drilled, .190-.625
AN101001-101900 	Bolt, hex, steel, head
AN101901-102800 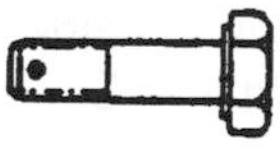	Bolt, hex., drilled shank, steel
AN102801-103700 	Bolt. Drilled hex. Head, (one hole), steel
AN103701-104600 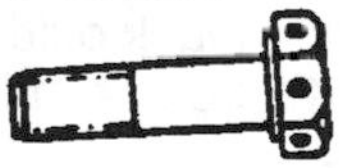	Bolt, drilled hex. Head, steel, (six holes)
AN104601-105500 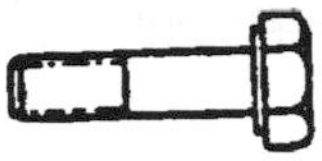	Bolt, hex. Head, corrosion-resistant steel
AN105501-106400 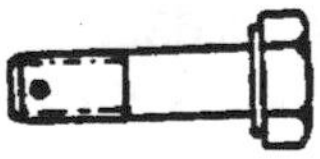	Bolt, hex. Head, drilled shank, corrosion-resistant steel
AN106401-107300 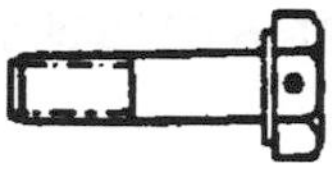	Bolt, hex., drilled head, (one holes), corrosion-resistant steel
AN107301-108200 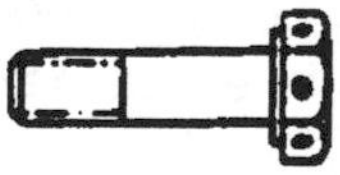	Bolt, hex., drilled head, (six holes), corrosion-resistant steel
MS9033-9039 	Bolt, machine 12pt. Head, 130,000 psi min. T.S.
MS9060-9066 	Bolt, machine 12pt. Double hex. 130,000 psi min. T.S. ext. washer head, drilled

TABLE 7-12. (CONTINUED)

Bolt Number	Description
MS9088-9094 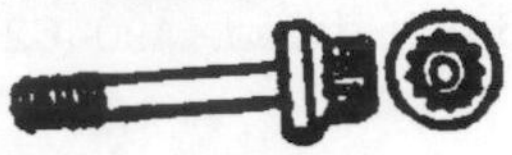	Bolt, machine, steel, drilled 12 pt. head
MS9110-9113 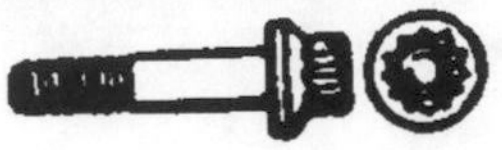	Bolt, machine, double hex., ext. washer head, close tolerance
MS9146-9152 	Bolt, steel, 12 pt. hd. black oxide 125,000 psi min. T.S.
MS9157-9163 	Bolt, steel, 12pt. hd. black oxide 125,000 psi min. T.S.
MS9169-9175 	Bolt, steel, 12 pt. drilled hd., black oxide 125,000 psi min. T.S.
MS9224 	Bolt, 12 pt. head, heat resistant
MS9397-9402 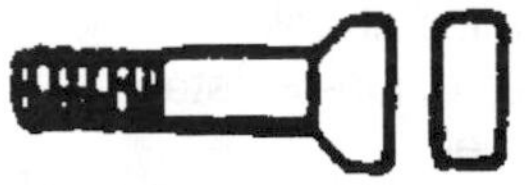	Bolt, tee head, AMS 6322, chamfered cad. pl.
MS9432-9437 	Bolt, tee head AMS 5735 chamfered
MS9440-9448 	Bolt, mach. steel. AMS 6304 diffused nickel cad. hex. hd., 3 holes
MS9449-9459 	Bolt, mach. steel, AMS 6304 diffused nickel cad., hex. head
MS9487-9497 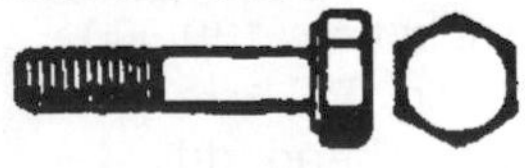	Bolt, mach. hex. hd. full shank, AMS 5731

TABLE 7-12. (CONTINUED)

Bolt Number	Description
MS9498-9508 	Bolt, mach. hex. hd., 1 hole, full shank
MS9516-9526 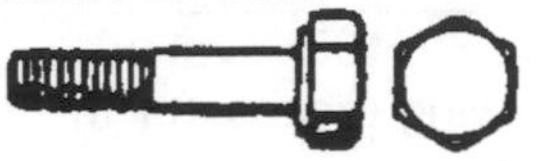	Bolt, mach., steel AMS 6322 cad. 1 hole hex. hd.
MS9527-9537 	Bolt, mach., steel AMS 6322 cad. 1 hole hex. hd.
MS9554-9562 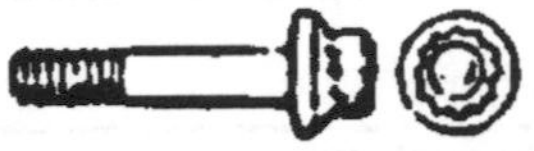	Bolt, mach., dbl. hex. ext. wash. hd., PD shank, AMS 5731
MS9563-9571 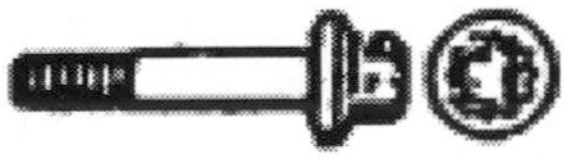	Bolt, mach., dbl. hex. ext. wash. hd. drilled, AMS 5731
MS9572-9580 	Bolt, mach., dbl. hex. ext. wash. hd., drilled, PD shank AMS 5731 silver plated
MS9583-9591 	Bolt, mach., hex. hd. 6 holes full shank, AMS 5731
MS9622-9630 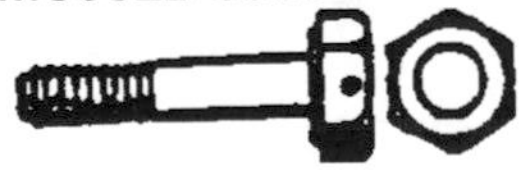	Bolt, mach., hex. hd. 1 hole, PD shank, titanium AMS 4967
MS9641-9648 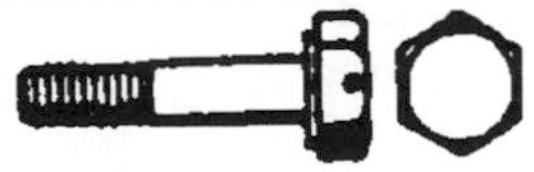	Bolt, mach., hex. hd., 1 hole, full shank titanium AMS 4967
MS9649-9652 	Bolt, mach., hex. hd. full shank, titanium AMS 4967
MS9676-9679 	Bolt, mach., dbl. hex. ext. wash. hd., cup washer locked, cres. AMS 5731

TABLE 7-12. (CONTINUED)

Bolt Number	Description
MS9680-9683 	Bolt, mach., dbl. hex. ext. wash. hd., cup washer locked, steel AMS 6322 cad.
MS9685-9693 	Bolt, mach., hex. hd. 1 hole, PD shank, steel AMS 6304 diffused nickel cad.
MS9694-9702 	Bolt mach. dbl. hex. ext. wash. hd. AMS 5708
MS9703-9711 	Bolt, mach., dbl. hex. ext. wash. hd., drilled, AMS 5708
MS9712-9720 	Bolt, mach. dbl. hex. ext. wach. hd. drilled, AMS 5708 silver plate
MS9730-9738 	Bolt, mach., dbl. hex. ext. wash. hd. PD shank, cres. AMS 5643
MS9739-9747 	Bolt, mach. dbl. hex. est. wash, hd. drilled, PD shank, cres. AMS 5643
MS9748-9756 	Bolt, mach. dbl. hex. ext. wash. hd. PD shank, titanium AMS 4967
MS9757-9765 	Bolt, mach., dbl. hex. ext. wash. hd., PD shank, drilled, titanium AMS 4967
MS9781-9791 	Bolt, hex. hd., mach. full shank, AMS 5643
MS9792-9802 	Bolt, mach., hex. hd. 1 hole, full shank, AMS 5643

TABLE 7-12. (CONTINUED)

Bolt Number	Description
MS9803-9813 	Bolt, mach., hex. Hd. 1 hole, full shank, AMS 5643
MS9814-9824 	Bolt, mach., hex. Hd. 1 hole, PD shank, AMS 5643
MS9883-9891 	Bolt, mach., dbl. Hex. Ext. wash. Hd., AMS 5616
MS9892-9900 	Bolt mach., dbl. Hex. Ext. wash. Hd., AMS 5616 drilled
MS9912-9920 	Bolt, mach., dbl. Hex. Ext. wash. Hd., PD shank, steel AMS 6322 cad.
MS9921-9929 	Bolt, mach., dbl. Hex. Ext. wash hd. PD shank, steel AMS 6322 cad. Drilled
MS9930-9938 	Bolt, mach., dbl. Hex. Ext. wash. Hd., full shank, steel AMS 6322 cad.
MS9939-9946 	Bolt, mach., dbl. Hex. Ext. wash. Hd., drilled, full shank, steel AMS 6322 cad.
MS20004-20024 	Bolt, int. wrench, 160 KSI
MS20033-20046 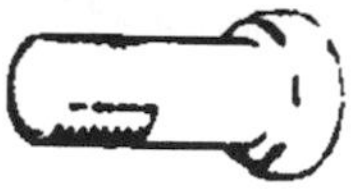	Bolt, machine, hex. Head, 1200 °F
MS20073-20074 	Bolt, machine, aircraft, drilled hd., fine & coarse thr.

TABLE 7-12. (CONTINUED)

Bolt Number	Description
MS21091-21093 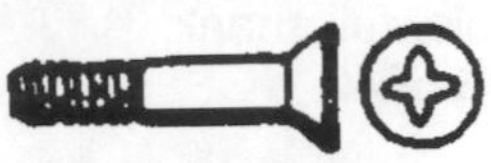	Bolt, self-lock., 100° flush head, cross recessed
MS21094-21095 	Bolt, self-lock., hex. head
MS21096-21097 	Bolt, self-lock., pan-head, crass recessed
MS21098-21099 	Bolt, self-lock., 12 pt. ext. wrenching
MS21250 	Bolt, 12 pt., ext. wrenching
NAS144-158 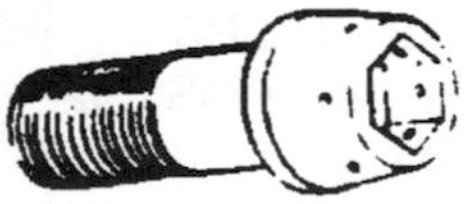	Bolt, internal wrenching, steel, 1/4-28 thru 1-1/8-12
NAS333-340 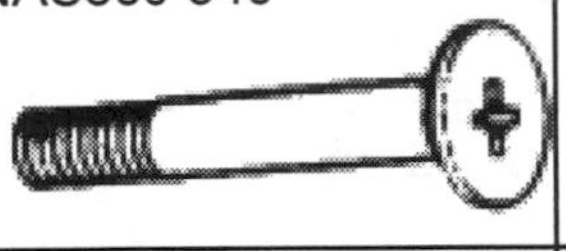	Bolt, 100°, close tolerance, hi-strength
NAS428 	Bolt, adjusting, crowned hex. hd.
NAS464 	Bolt, shear, close tolerance
NAS501 	Bolt, hex. head, drilled & undrilled
NAS551 	Bolt, universal fitting

TABLE 7-12. (CONTINUED)

Bolt Number	Description
NAS563-572 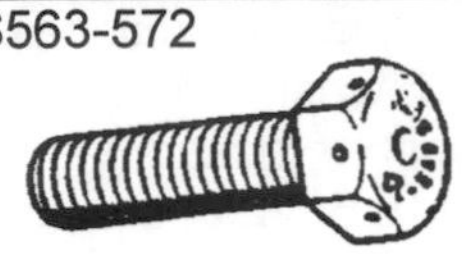	Bolt, full thread, fully identified head
NAS583-590 	Bolt, 100° head, hi-torque, close tol. 160,000 psi
NAS624-644 	Bolt, twelve point external wrench, 180000 psi
NAS653-658 	Bolt, hex. head, close tolerance, ti. alloy
NAS663-668 	Bolt, full thread, fully identified head
NAS673-678 	Bolt, hex. head, close tolerance, ti. alloy
NAS1003-1020 	Bolt, machine, hex. head
NAS1053 	Eye Bolt Assembly, Shoulder nut
NAS1083 	Bolt, 100° flathead, titanium alloy
NAS1103-1120 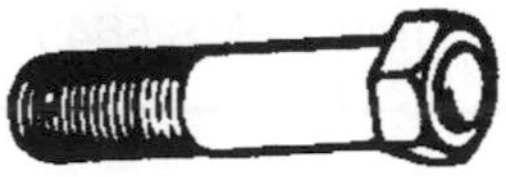	Bolt, machine, hex. head
NAS1202-1210 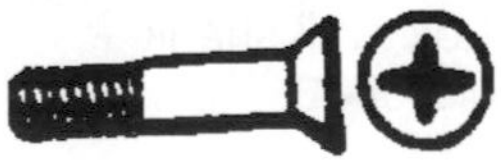	Bolt, 100° phil. recessed, close tolerance, 16,000 psi

TABLE 7-12. (CONTINUED)

Bolt Number	Description
NAS1223-1235	Bolt, self-locking, hex. head 250 °F
NAS1236	Bolt, universal, Tube-end, flareless
NAS1243-1250	Bolt, 100° head, hi-torq. 1600 psi
NAS1253-1260	Bolt, 100° head, flush hd., .0312 O.S. hi-torque
NAS1261-1270	Bolt, hex. head, short thread
NAS1271-1280	Bolt, 12 point hd., external wrenching
NAS1297	Bolt, shoulder, hex. head
NAS1303-1320	Bolt, hex. head, close tolerance, 160,000 psi
NAS1414-1422	Lock bolt, shear 100° head, all. steel
NAS1424-1432	Lock bolt, shear protruding head, steel
NAS1503-1510	Bolt, 100° flush head, hi-torq.

TABLE 7-12. (CONTINUED)

Bolt Number	Description
NAS1516-1522	Lock Bolt, 100° head, pull type, al. Alloy
NAS1578	Bolt, shear panhead, 1200 °F
NAS1580	Bolt, tension, flush hd., 1200 °F
NAS1581	Bolt, shear reduced 100 °F flush head, 1200 °F
NAS1586	Bolt-tension, 1200 °F, 12 point, external wrenching
NAS1588	Bolt, tension, flush hd., 1200 °F
NAS1703-1710	Bolt, 100° head, .0156 O.S. shank,
NAS2005-2012	Bolt lock, protruding head, ti. Alloy
NAS2105-2112	Bolt, lock, 100° head, ti. Alloy
NAS2206-2210	Bolt, lock, stump type, protruding head, ti. Alloy
NAS2306-2310	Bolt, lock, stump type, 100° head, ti. Alloy

TABLE 7-12. (CONTINUED)

Bolt Number	Description
NAS2406-2412 	Bolt, lock, shear protruding head, ti. alloy
NAS2506-2512 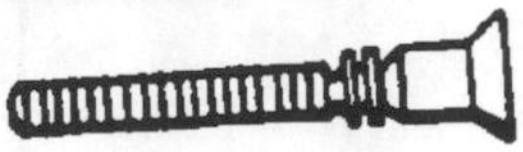	Bolt, lock, 100°head, ti. alloy
NAS2606-2612 	Bolt, lock, shear protruding head, ti. alloy
NAS2706-2712 	Bolt, lock, shear 100° head, ti. alloy
NAS2803-2810 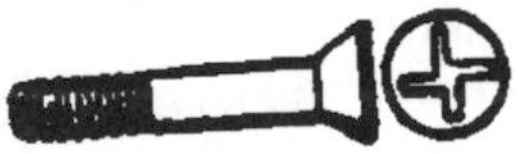	Bolt, lock, 100° hd., torq-set 180,000 psi
NAS2903-2920 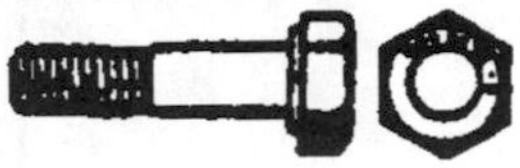	Bolt, hex. head, .0156 O.S. shank, 160,000 psi
NAS3003-3020 	Bolt, hex. head, .0312 O.S. shank, 160,000 psi
NAS3103-3110 	Bolt, U type
NAS3203-3210 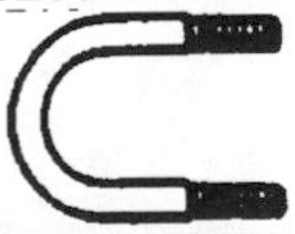	Bolt, hook
NAS3303-3305 	Bolt, U strap type
NAS4104-4116 	Bolt, 100° head, tri-wing recess, long thr., alloy stl.

TABLE 7-12. (CONTINUED)

Bolt Number	Description
NAS4204-4216 	Bolt, 100°head, tri-wing recess, long thr., cres.
NAS4304-4316 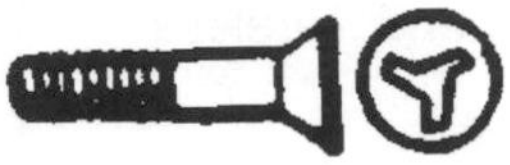	Bolt, 100° head, tri-wing recess, long thr., titanium
NAS4400-4416 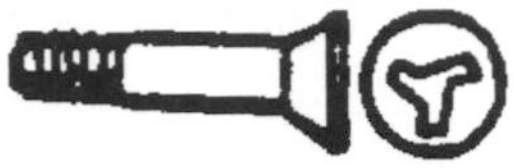	Bolt, 100° head, tri-wing recess, short thr., alloy stl.
NAS4500-4516 	Bolt, 100° head, tri-wing recess, short thr., cres.
NAS4600-4616 	Bolt, 100° head, tri-wing recess, short thr., titanium
NAS4703-4716 	Bolt, 100° reduced, tri-wing recess, short thr., alloy stl.
NAS4803-4816 	Bolt, 100° reduced, tri-wing recess, short thr., cres.
NAS4903-4916 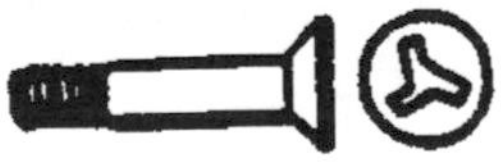	Bolt, 100° reduced, tri-wing recess, short thr., titanium
NAS6203-6220 	Bolt, hex. head, short thread, alloy steel
NAS6303-6320 	Bolt, hex. head, short thread, cres.
NAS6403-6420 	Bolt, hex. head, short thread, titanium

TABLE 7-12. (CONTINUED)

Bolt Number	Description
NAS6604-6620 	Bolt, hex head, long thread, alloy steel
NAS6704-6720 	Bolt, hex. head, long thread, cres.

TABLE 7-13. TABLE OF NUTS.

Nut Part Number	Description
AN256 	Nut, self-lock right angle plate
AN310 	Nuts, castellated
AN315 	Nut, plain
AN316 	Nut, check
AN320 	Nut, castle shear
AN335 	Nut, plain, hex, nonstructural
AN340 	Nut, plain, hex., n-s, course thread
AN341 	Nut, plain, hex.

TABLE 7-13. (CONTINUED)

Nut Part Number	Description
AN345 	Nut, plain, hex., n-s, fine thread
AN350 	Nut, plain, wing
AN355 	Nut, engine, slotted
AN356 	Nut, stamped
AN360 	Nut, plain, engine
AN361 	Self-locking nut plate, countersunk 100°, 550 °F.
AN362 	Nut, plate, self-locking, noncounters., 550°F.
AN363 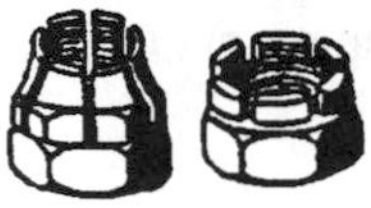	Nut, self-locking, 550 °F.
AN364 	Nut, self-locking, thin, 250 °F.
AN365 	Nut, self-locking 250°F.
AN366 	Nut, plate, noncounters., 250°F.

TABLE 7-13. (CONTINUED)

Nut Part Number	Description
AN373	Countersunk nut, plate 100°, 250°F.
AN805	Nut, union
AN817	Nut, coupling
AN818	Nut, coupling
AN924	Nut, flared tube
AN3054	Nut, coupling, elec. conduit
AN3066	Nut, plain, hex. conduit coupling
AN6289	Nut, flared tube universal fitting
AN121501-121550	Nut, plain or cres. steel
AN121551-121600	Nut, castel., hex.
MS9099-9100	Nut, hex., boss connection, aluminum & cres.

TABLE 7-13. (CONTINUED)

Nut Part Number	Description
MS9197-9199	Nut, tube coupling
MS9200-9201	Nut, plain, hex., boss connection
MS9356-9357	Nut, plain hex., A-286
MS9358-9359	Nut, castellated hex., A-286
MS9360	Nut, plain hex. Drilled, A-286
MS9361-9362	Nut, plain hex. Check, A-286
MS9363-9364	Nut, slotted hex. Shear hd., A-286
MS9553	Nut, hex. Boss connection, cres.
MS9766-9767	Nut, dbl. Hex. Cup washer locked, AMS 5737 cres. And AMS 6322 cad.
MS9881	Nut, plain, hex. AMS 6322, cad. Plate
MS9882	Nut, plain, hex., drilled, AMS 6322, cad. Plate

TABLE 7-13. (CONTINUED)

Nut Part Number	Description
MS9951 	Nut, spanner, end slots, cup washer locked, AMS 6322
MS16203 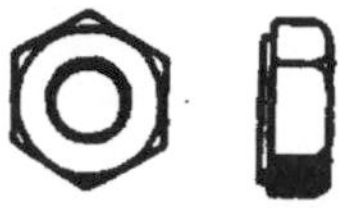	Nut, plain, hex. Nonmagnetic
MS17825-17826 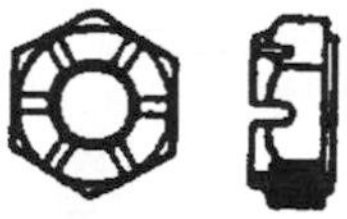	Nut, self-locking, castle, hex. Regular and thin
MS17828 	Nut, self-locking, nylon insert, 250°, regular ht., monel
MS17829-17830 	Nut, self-locking, nylon insert, 250°, regular ht., cres. Steel, steel
MS19067-19068 	Nut, plain, round, retaining
MS20341 	Nut, electrical, plain, hex.
MS20364 	Nut, self-locking, 250 °F, thin
MS20365 	Nut, self-locking, 250° F, regular
MS20501 	Nut, plate, self-locking, two lug
MS21025 	Nut, castellated bearing, retaining

TABLE 7-13. (CONTINUED)

Nut Part Number	Description
MS21047-21048 	Nut, self-locking, plate, two lug, low ht.
MS21049-21050 	Nut, self-locking, plate, two lug, 100° csk., low ht.
MS21051-21052 	Nut, self-locking, plate, one lug, low ht.
MS21053-21054 	Nut, self-locking, plate, one lug, 100° csk.
MS21055-21056 	Nut, self-locking, plate, corner, low ht.
MS21057-21058 	Nut, self-locking, plate, corner, 100° csk.
MS21059-21060 	Nut, self-locking, plate, two lug, floating, low ht.
MS21061-21062 	Nut, self-locking, plate, floating low ht., one lug
MS21069-21070 	Nut, self-locking, plate, two lug, low ht., reduced rivet spacing
MS21071-21072 	Nut, self-locking, plate, one lug, low ht., reduced rivet spacing
MS21073-21074 	Nut, self-locking, plate, corner, reduced rivet spacing

TABLE 7-13. (CONTINUED)

Nut Part Number	Description
MS21078	Nut, self-locking, plate, two lug, nylon insert
MS21080	Nut, self-locking, plate, one lug, nylon insert
MS21081	Nut, self-locking, plate, corner, nylon insert
MS21083	Nut, self-locking, hex., nylon insert
MS21340	Nut, plain, hex., electrical, thin, wire holes
MS21917	Nut, sleeve coupling, flareless
MS21921	Nut, sleeve coupling, flareless
MS24679-24680	Nut, plain cap, low & high crown
MS25082	Nut, plain, thin, hex., electrical
MS27040	Nut, plain square
MS27128	Nut, plain, welding

TABLE 7-13. (CONTINUED)

Nut Part Number	Description
MS27130-27131	Nut, blind, rivet, flathead., open and closed end
MS27151	Nut, stamped
MS27955	Nut, spanner, plain, round
MS35425-35426	Nut, wing, plain & drilled
MS35649-35650	Nut, plain hex.
MS35690-35691	Nut, plain hex.
MS35692	Nut, slotted hex.
MS51967-51972	Nut, plain, hex.
MS90415	Nut, self-locking, 12 point captive washer
MS172236-172270	Nut, spanner, bearing, retaining
MS172321-172370	Nut, spanner

TABLE 7-13. (CONTINUED)

Nut Part Number	Description
NAS395-396 	Nut, U type
NAS443 	Nut, self-locking, int. wrenching
NAS444-445 	Nut, double lug, anchor type, offset
NAS446 	Nut, flat type
NAS447-448 	Nut, plate, self-locking
NAS449 	Nut, anchor type
NAS450 	Nut, plate, self-locking
NAS463 	Shim, plain anchor nut
NAS487 	Nut, instrument mount
NAS500 	Shim, anchor nut, csk.
NAS509 	Nut, drilled

TABLE 7-13. (CONTINUED)

Nut Part Number	Description
NAS577-578 	Nut, self-locking floating barrel retainer
NAS671 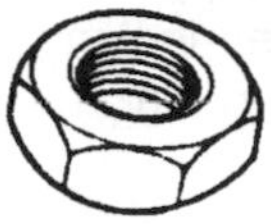	Nut, plain hex., small pattern
NAS680-681 	Nut, plate, self-locking, two lug
NAS682-683 	Nut, plate, self-locking, one lug
NAS684-685 	Nut, plate, corner, self-locking
NAS686 	Nut, plate, self-locking, two lug, floating
NAS687 	Nut, plate, self-locking, one lug
NAS688-695 	Nut Assembly, self-locking, gang channel
NAS696 	Nut, plate self-locking, one lug, miniature
NAS697 	Nut, plate, self-locking, two lug, miniature
NAS698 	Nut, plate, corner, self-locking, miniature

TABLE 7-13. (CONTINUED)

Nut Part Number	Description
NAS1021-1022	Self-locking Nut, hex., regular and low ht.
NAS1023-1024	Nut, plate, self-locking, two lug
NAS1025-1026	Nut, plate, self-locking, one lug
NAS1027-1028	Nut, plate, corner, self-locking
NAS1029-1030	Nut, plate, self-locking, one lug, two lug
NAS1031	Nut, plate, self-locking, two lug, floating
NAS1032	Nut, plate, self-locking, one lug, floating
NAS1033	Nut, plate, right angle, floating, self-locking
NAS1034-1041	Nut Assembly, self-locking, gang channel
NAS1067	Nut, plate, self-locking, one lug, miniature
NAS1068	Nut, plate, floating, self-locking, two lug, miniature

TABLE 7-13. (CONTINUED)

Nut Part Number	Description
NAS1098	Nut, tube fitting
NAS1287-1288	Nut, hexagonal, self-locking, nut and washer shear pin
NAS1291	Nut, hexagonal, self-locking, low height
NAS1329	Nut, blind rivet, flathead, internal thread
NAS1330	Nut, blind rivet, csk. Head, internal thread
NAS1408-1409	Nut, hexagonal, self-locking, regular height, coarse and fine thr.
NAS1410	Nut, tube fitting
NAS1423	Nut, plain, thin hex., drilled jamnut
NAS1473	Nut, plate, self-locking, two lug, cap floating
NAS1474	Nut, plate, self-locking, two lug, cap floating, reduced rivet spacing
NAS1512-1513	Nut, plate, self-locking gang channel

TABLE 7-13. (CONTINUED)

Nut Part Number	Description
NAS8679	Nut, self-locking, low height 550 °F, 800 °F

TABLE 7-14. TABLE OF WASHERS.

Washer Number	Description
AN935	Washer, lock, spring
AN936	Washer, tooth lock
AN950 and 955	Washer, ball socket, ball seat
AN960	Washer, flat
AN961	Washer, flat electrical (Brass, silver or tin-plated)
AN970	Washer, flat, wood
AN975	Washer, flat
AN8013	Washer, insulator
AN122576-122600	Washer, plain steel

TABLE 7-14. (CONTINUED)

Washer Number	Description
MS9081	Washer, key dbl. Bearing retaining
MS9274	Washer, key, dbl. Bearing ret. Cres.
MS9276	Washer, key, cres. AMS 5510 180° locking
MS9320-9321	Washer, flat AMS 6350 and 5510
MS9482	Washer, flat, steel AMS 6437 or AMS 6485 diffused nickel cad. Csk.
MS9549	Washer, flat, AMS 5510
MS9581	Washer, key, cres. AMS 5510 90° locking
MS9582	Washer, key, cres. AMS 5510 270° locking
MS9684	Washer, cup, lock cres. AMS 5510
MS9768	Washer, flat, cres. AMS 5525 and AMS 5737 csk.
MS9880	Washer, cup, lock cres. AMS 5510

TABLE 7-14. (CONTINUED)

Washer Number	Description
MS9952 	Washer, cup, lock, spanner nut, cres. AMS 5646
MS15795 	Washer, flat, metal
MS17811 	Washer, thrust, steel
MS19069-19070 	Washer, key, retaining
MS20002 	Washer, plain, csk., hi-strength
MS21258 	Washer, key, retaining, steel
MS25081 	Washer, key
MS27051 	Washer, slotted
MS27111 	Washer, finishing, countersunk
MS27129 	Washer, finishing, csk., 80°, 82°
MS27183 	Washer, flat, round

TABLE 7-14. (CONTINUED)

Washer Number	Description
MS28777 	Washer, hydraulic, packing backup
MS35333-35334 	Washer, lock, flat internal tooth, light and heavy
MS35335-35336 	Washer, lock, flat and csk., external tooth
MS35337-35340 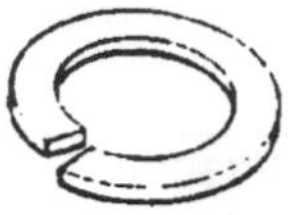	Washer, lock, med., light, heavy
MS35790 	Washer, lock, 100° csk., ext. tooth
MS122026-122075 	Washer, lock spring
MS172201-172235 	Washer, key, single bearing, retaining
MS172271-172320 	Washer, key, single
NAS70 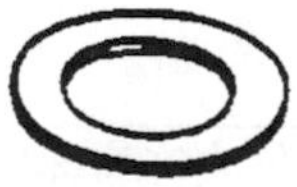	Washer, plain
NAS143 	Washer, csk. and plain
NAS390-391 	Washer, finishing

TABLE 7-14. (CONTINUED)

Washer Number	Description
NAS460 	Washer, tab type
NAS513 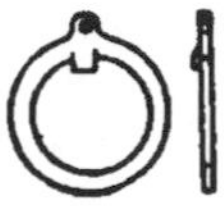	Washer, rod end locking, steel
NAS549 	Washer, flat, resin fiber
NAS620 	Washer, flat, reduced O.D.
NAS1061 	Washer, hi-temp, lock, spring
NAS1099 	Washer, bevel 9 1/2°
NAS1169 	Washer, dimpled 100°
NAS1197 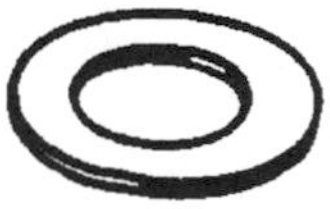	Washer, flat, 5052 aluminum
NAS1252 	Washer, flat
NAS1401 	Washer, radius, al. Alloy, steel, cres. Steel
NAS1515 	Washer, plastic and rubber

TABLE 7-14. (CONTINUED)

Washer Number	Description
NAS1587 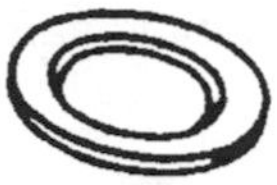	Washer, 1200 °F, plain and csk.
NAS1598 	Washer, sealing
NAS1636 	Washer, key dual tab
NAS1640 	Washer, lock, spring, nonmagnetic

TABLE 7-15. TABLE OF PINS.

Pin Number	Description
AN253 	Pin, hinge
AN380 & 381	Pin, cotter
AN385 	Pin, plain taper
AN386	Threaded taper pin
AN392-406 	Pin, flathead
AN415 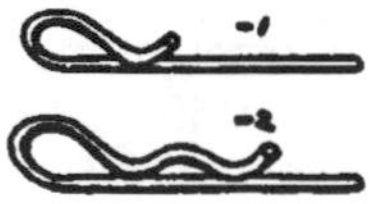 -1 -2	Pin, lock

TABLE 7-15. (CONTINUED)

Pin Number	Description
AN416 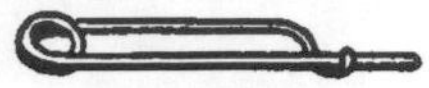	Pin, retaining safety
AN122676-122775 	Pin, dowel steel
AN121601-121925 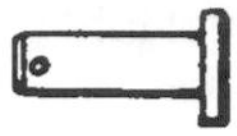	Pin, flathead clevis .125 -.500 drilled shank
AN150201-150400 	Pin, lock, steel, brass
MS9047 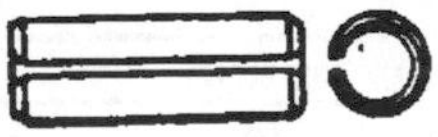	Pin, spring, steel, phoshated finish
MS9048 	Pin, spring, steel, cad-mium plate
MS9105 	Pin, lock
MS9164	Pin, straight, steel, headless, oversize
MS9245 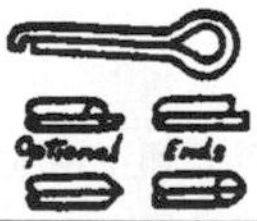	Pin, cotter, cres. AMS 7211
MS9389 	Pin, straight, headless, lock, AMS 5735
MS9390 	Pin, straight, headless, cres. AMS 5735, dowel std. & O.S.

TABLE 7-15. (CONTINUED)

Pin Number	Description
MS9462-9468	Pin, straight hd. AMS 5735
MS9486	Pin, straight, headless, lock, AMS 5132
MS9842-9848 	Pin, straight, headed, AMS 5616
MS16555 	Pin, straight, headless .0002 over nominal size
MS16556 	Pin, straight, headless .001 over nominal size
MS16562 	Pin, spring, tubular, slotted
MS17984-17990 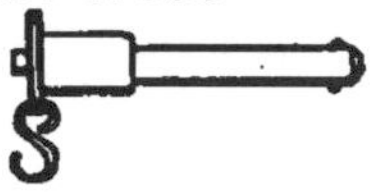	Pin, quick release, positive lock
MS20253 	Pin, hinge
MS20392 	Pin, straight, headed, drilled
MS24665	Pin, cotter
MS35671-35679	Pin, grooved, headless, tapered groove

TABLE 7-15. (CONTINUED)

Pin Number	Description
MS35810 	Pin, clevis, headed
MS39086	Pin, spring, tubular coiled
MS51923	Pin, spring, tubular coiled
MS51987 	Pin, tubular coiled
MS171401-171900 	Pin, spring, SS, steel
NAS427 	Pin, pulley guard, steel, al. Alloy
NAS561 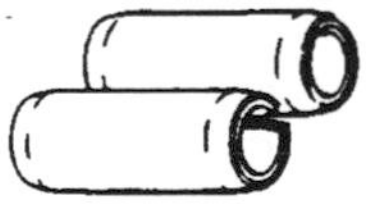	Pin, spring slotted and coiled, heavy duty
NAS574 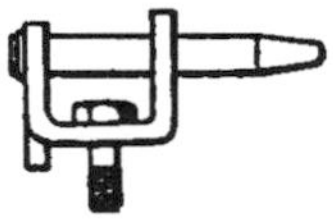	Pin, rear mounting
NAS607	Pin, headless, dowel, steel
NAS1292-1296 	Pin, shear thread 100° flush head
NAS1322 	Pin, shear thread, protruding head

TABLE 7-15. (CONTINUED)

Pin Number	Description
NAS1332-1346 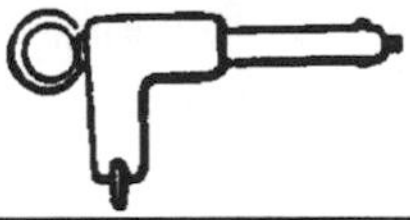	Pin, quick release
NAS1353-1366 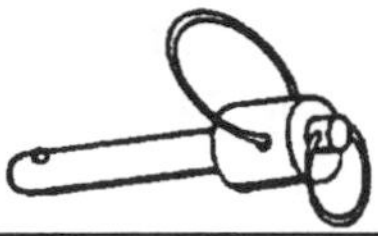	Pin, quick release, positive locking, double acting
NAS1407	Pin, spring, coiled
NAS1436-1442 	Pin, swage lock, 100° shear head, pull type, steel
NAS1446-1452 	Pin, swage lock, protruding head, pull type, steel
NAS1456-1462 	Pin, swage lock, 100° head, pull type, steel
NAS1465-1472 	Pin, swage lock, protruding head, pull type, steel
NAS1475-1482 	Pin, swage lock, 100° head, pull type, steel
NAS1486-1492 	Pin, swage lock, 100° head, stump type, steel
NAS1496-1502 	Pin, swage lock, protruding head, stump type, steel
NAS1525-1532 	Pin, swage lock, protruding head, al. alloy

TABLE 7-15. (CONTINUED)

Pin Number	Description
NAS1535-1542 	Pin, swage lock, 100° hd., tension, pull type, alum.
NAS1546-1552 	Pin, swage lock, 100° hd., tension, stump type, alum.
NAS1583 	Pin, 100° csk. hd., hi-shear rivet, 1200 °F
NAS1584	Pin, flathead, hi-shear rivet, 1200 °F

7-196.—7-206. [RESERVED.]

CHAPTER 8. ENGINES, FUEL, EXHAUST, AND PROPELLERS

SECTION 1. ENGINES

8-1. GENERAL. Consult the manufacturer's manuals, service bulletins, and instruction books regarding the repair and overhaul, inspection, installation, and maintenance of aircraft engines, for that particular make, model, and type of engine. This section lists acceptable inspection and repair procedures that may be used in the absence of an engine manufacturer's maintenance information.

8-2. SPECIAL INSPECTION. A visual inspection is needed to determine the condition of the engine and its components. An annual or 100-hour inspection should include the engine and nacelle group as follows.

a. Cold Cylinder Check. If an engine is running rough the cause may be a bad ignition lead, a spark plug not firing, a partially clogged fuel injector, or a bad magneto. The dead cylinder will be colder than the surrounding cylinders and can be quickly determined by using the recommended cold cylinder checks. This should be done using a thermocouple probe which is very sensitive to small differences in temperature, which is the case with a partially-clogged injector. For a carbureted engine, the following check may be helpful:

(1) Using experienced personnel, run the engine on the bad magneto for approximately 30 seconds at 1200 rpm. Without switching the magneto switch back to both shut off the engine. Have another mechanic use a grease pencil (non-carbon), and quickly mark each exhaust stack approximately 1 inch from the flange that holds the exhaust stack to the cylinder. Next, check the exhaust stacks and look for the exhaust stack whose grease pencil mark has not turned to a grayish-white or ash color. This is the cold cylinder.

(2) The probable cause of the cold cylinder is either a defective spark plug or ignition lead. Switch spark plugs to another cylinder and run the test again. If the problem stays with the original cylinder, the problem is either the ignition lead or the magneto.

b. Piston Engine Sudden Stoppage Inspection. Sudden stoppage is a very rapid and complete stoppage of the engine. It can be caused by engine seizure or by one or more of the propeller blades striking an object in such a way that rpm goes to zero in less than one complete revolution of the propeller. Sudden stoppage can cause internal damage to constant-speed propellers; reduction drive; gear train damage in the accessory section; crankshaft misalignment; or damage to accessories such as magnetos, generators, vacuum pumps, and tach generators.

(1) Every engine that suffers a sudden stoppage must be inspected in accordance with the manufacturer's maintenance instructions before being returned to service.

(2) If the engine manufacturer does not provide the required information, then the engine case must be opened and every major component part must be inspected using visual and/or nondestructive inspection (NDI) procedures as applicable.

(3) The sudden-stoppage inspections include: checking for cowling, spinner, and airframe cracks and hidden damage; and alignment of the engine mount to the airframe, the mounting hardware, isolation mounts, and bushings. The aircraft's firewall must also be checked for distortion, cracks, and elongated bolt holes. The damaged propeller must be sent to an FAA-certificated repair station for complete NDI and repair.

(4) Engine accessories such as: magnetos, starters, fuel pumps, turbochargers, alternators, or generators must be inspected in accordance with the manufacturer's maintenance manual on sudden stoppage or overhaul procedures to determine the product's airworthiness.

c. Reciprocating Engine (Direct Drive). Preliminary inspection before tear down.

(1) Remove the engine cowling and examine the engine for visible external damage and audible internal damage.

(2) Rotate the propeller shaft to determine any evidence of abnormal grinding or rubbing sounds.

(3) With the propeller removed, inspect the crankshaft flange or splines for signs of twisting, cracks, or other deformation. Remove the thrust-bearing nut and seal and thoroughly inspect the threaded area of the shaft for evidence of cracks.

(4) Rotate the shaft slowly in 90-degree increments while using a dial indicator or an equivalent instrument to check the concentricity of the shaft.

(5) Remove the oil sump drain plug and check for metal chips and foreign material.

(6) Remove the oil screens and inspect for metal particles and contamination.

(7) Visually inspect engine case exterior for signs of oil leaks and cracks. Give particular attention to the propeller thrust-bearing area of the nose case section.

(8) Inspect cylinders and cylinder hold-down area for cracks and oil leaks. Thoroughly investigate any indication of cracks, oil leaks, or other damage.

d. Internal Inspection Requirements.

(1) On engines equipped with crankshaft vibration dampers, remove and inspect the cylinders, and inspect the crankshaft dampers in accordance with the engine manufacturer's inspection and overhaul manual. When engine design permits, remove the damper pins, and examine the pins and damper liners for signs of nicks or brinelling.

(2) After removing the engine-driven accessories, remove the accessory drive case and examine the accessory and supercharger drive gear train, couplings, and drive case for evidence of damage.

(a) Check for cracks in the case in the area of accessory mount pads and gear shaft bosses.

(b) Check the gear train for signs of cracked, broken, or brinelled teeth.

(c) Check the accessory drive shaft couplings for twisted splines, misalignment, and run-out.

(d) Check connecting rods for cracks and straightness.

e. Reciprocating Engine (Gear-Drive). Inspect the engine, propeller, (refer to section 4 on propeller inspection), and components as described in the preceding paragraphs.

(1) Remove the propeller reduction gear housing and inspect for:

(a) Loose, sheared, or spalled cap screws or bolts.

(b) Cracks in the case.

(2) Disassemble the gear train and inspect the propeller shaft, reduction gears and accessory drive gears for nicks, cracks, or spalling.

f. Engine-Mount Inspection.

(1) Examine the engine flex mounts when applicable, for looseness of engine to mount, distortion, or signs of wear.

(2) Inspect the engine-mount structure for bent, cracked, or buckled tubes.

(3) Check the adjacent airframe structure firewall for cracks, distortion, or wrinkles.

(4) Remove engine-mount bolts and mount hold-down bolts and replace.

g. Exhaust-driven Supercharger (Turbo) Inspection. Sudden stoppage of the powerplant can cause the heat in turbine parts to heat-soak the turbine seals and bearings. This excessive heat causes carbon to develop in the seal area and varnish to form on the turbine bearings and journals.

(1) Inspect all air ducts and connections for air leaks, warpage, or cracks.

(2) Remove compressor housing and check the turbine wheel for rubbing or binding, and coke or varnish buildup.

NOTE: Turbine turbo supercharger disk seal rubbing is not unusual and may be a normal condition. Consult the engine manufacturer's inspection procedures and table of limits.

h. Accessory and Drive Inspection. Check the drive shaft of each accessory, i.e., magnetos, generators, external superchargers, and pumps for evidence of damage.

8-3. CRANKSHAFT INSPECTION AND REPAIR REQUIREMENTS. Carefully inspect for misalignment and replace if bent beyond the manufacturer's permissible service limit. Worn journals may be repaired by regrinding in accordance with manufacturers' instructions. It is recommended that grinding operations be performed by appropriately-rated repair stations or the original engine manufacturer. Common errors that occur in crankshaft grinding are the removal of nitrided journal surface, improper journal radii, unsatisfactory surfaces, and grinding tool marks on the journals. If the fillets are altered, do not reduce their radii. Polish the reworked surfaces to assure removal of all tool marks. Most opposed engines have nitrided crankshafts, and engine manufacturers specify that these crankshafts must be re-nitrided after grinding.

NOTE: Rapid deceleration or momentary slowing of a propeller may occur due to contact with tall grass, water, or snow. If this occurs, the engine and propeller should be inspected in accordance with the manufacturer's instruction or service bulletins.

8-4. REPLACEMENT PARTS IN CERTIFICATED ENGINES. Engine replacement parts must be approved under Title 14 of the Code of Federal Regulations (14 CFR), part 21. Serviceable parts obtained from the engine manufacturer, authorized service facility, and those which are approved Federal Aviation Administration (FAA)/Parts Manufacture Approval (PMA), or Technical Standard Order (TSO), and meet the requirements of part 21 are acceptable for use as replacement parts. Used engine parts can be installed if that part either conforms to new part tolerances or meets the manufacturer's service limits. Ensure that used parts are airworthy and properly identified as a PMA or TSO part.

8-5. OIL SYSTEM LINES INSPECTION. The inspection of the plumbing for an oil system is similar to the inspection of any other plumbing system. The tubing, hose, tube fittings, hose fittings, hose clamps, and all other components of the system are inspected for cracks, holes, dents, bulges, and other signs of damage that might restrict the oil flow or cause a leak. All lines are inspected to ensure that they are properly supported and are not rubbing against a structure. Fittings should be checked for signs of improper installation, over-torquing, excessive tension, or other conditions which may lead to failure.

8-6. OIL FILTER INSPECTION. The oil filter provides an excellent method for discovering internal engine damage. During the inspection of the engine oil filter, the residue on the screens, disks, or disposable filter cartridge and the residue in the filter housing are carefully examined for metal particles. A new engine or a newly-overhauled engine will often have a small amount of fine metal particles in the screen or filter, but this is not considered abnormal. After the engine has been operated for a time and the oil has been changed one or more times, there should not be an appreciable amount of metal particles in the oil screen. If an unusual residue of metal particles is found in the oil screen, the engine must be taken out of service and disassembled to determine the source of the particles. As an additional precaution, an oil analysis/trend analysis may prevent an engine failure in flight.
At oil changes, oil samples are often taken and sent to laboratories to be analyzed for wear by determining the amount of metal in the sample. Over time, a trend is developed and the engine can be removed from service before failure.

8-7. CYLINDER HOLD-DOWN NUTS AND CAP SCREWS. Great care is required in tightening cylinder hold-down nuts and cap screws. They must be tightened to recommended torque limits to prevent improper stressing and to ensure even loading on the cylinder flange. The installation of baffles, brackets, clips, and other extraneous parts under nuts and cap screws is not a good practice and is discouraged. If these baffles, brackets, etc., are not properly fabricated or made of suitable material, they may cause loosening of the nuts or cap screws even though the nuts or cap screws were properly tightened and locked at installation. Improper pre-stressing or loosening of any one of these nuts or cap screws will introduce the danger of progressive stud failure with the possible loss of the engine cylinder in flight.

8-8. REUSE OF SAFETYING DEVICES. Do not use cotter pins and safety wire a second time. Flat, steel-type wrist pin retainers and lock washers, likewise, must be replaced at overhaul unless the manufacturer's recommendations permit their reuse.

8-9. SELF-LOCKING NUTS FOR AIRCRAFT ENGINES AND ACCESSORIES. Self-locking nuts may be used on aircraft engines provided the following criteria are met:

a. When their use is specified by the engine manufacturer in the assembly drawing, parts list, and bills of material.

b. When the nuts will not fall inside the engine should they loosen and come off.

c. When there is at least one full thread protruding beyond the nut.

d. Where the temperature will not exceed the maximum limits established for the self-locking material used in the nut. On many engines the cylinder baffles, rocker box covers, drive covers and pads, and accessory and supercharger housings are fastened with fiber insert lock nuts which are limited to a maximum temperature of 250 °F. Above this temperature, the fiber insert will usually char and, consequently, lose its locking characteristic. For locations such as the exhaust pipe attachment to the cylinder, a locknut which has good locking features at elevated temperatures will give invaluable service. In a few instances, fiber insert lock nuts have been approved for use on cylinder hold-down studs. This practice is not generally recommended, since especially tight stud fits to the crankcase must be provided, and extremely good cooling must prevail so that low temperatures exist where the nut is installed.

e. Information concerning approved self-locking nuts and their use on specific engines are usually found in engine manufacturer's manuals or bulletins. If the desired information is not available, it is suggested that the engine manufacturer be contacted.

f. Refer to Chapter 7, Aircraft Hardware, Control Cables, and Turnbuckles, for additional information on self-locking nuts.

8-10. METALLIZING. Metallizing internal parts of aircraft engines is not acceptable unless it is proven to the FAA that the metallized part will not adversely affect the airworthiness of the engine. Metallizing the finned surfaces of steel cylinder barrels with aluminum is acceptable, since many engines are originally manufactured in this manner.

8-11. PLATING. Before restoring the plating on any engine part in accordance with the manufacturer's instructions, the part should be visually inspected and have an NDI performed before any cylinder reconditioning. In general, chromium plating would not be applied to highly-stressed engine parts. Certain applications of this nature have been found to be satisfactory; however, engineering evaluation of the details for the processes used should be obtained.

a. Dense chromium plating of the crankpin and main journals of some small engine crankshafts has been found satisfactory, except where the crankshaft is already marginal in strength. Plating to restore worn, low-stress engine parts, such as accessory drive shafts and splines, propeller shaft ends, and seating surfaces of roller and ball-type bearing races is acceptable but requires compliance with FAA-approved data.

b. Porous chromium-plated walls of cylinder barrels have been found to be satisfactory for practically all types of engines. Dense or smooth chromium plating, without roughened surfaces on the other hand, has not been found to be satisfactory.

(1) Cylinder barrel pre-grinding and chromium plating techniques used by the military are considered acceptable for all engines, and military-approved facilities engaged in doing this work in accordance with military specifications are eligible for approval by the FAA.

(2) Chromium-plated cylinder barrels have been required for some time to be identified in such a manner that the markings are visible with the cylinder installed. Military-processed cylinders are banded with orange enamel above the mounting flange. It has been the practice to etch on either the flange edge or on the barrel skirt the processor's initials and the cylinder oversize. Most plating facilities use the orange band as well as the permanent identification marks.

(3) A list of engine and maximum permissible cylinder barrel oversize are referenced in table 8-1.

TABLE 8-1. Current engine and maximum permissible cylinder barrel oversize.

Engine manufacturer	Engine series	Max. oversize (in.)
Air Cooled Motors (Franklin)	No oversize for sleeved cylinders.	
	Solid cylinders..........	0.017
Continental Motors	R-670, W-670, R9A....	0.010 to 0.020
		0.005
	GTSIO-520, 550........	0.015
	All others..................	
Jacobs	All............................	0.015
Kinner	All............................	0.015
Pigman, LeBlond, Rearwin, Ken Royce	All............................	0.025
Lycoming	All............................	0.010 to 0.020
Menasco	All............................	0.010
Pratt & Whitney	R-2800B, C, CA, CB..	0.025
	*R-959 and R-1830....	0.030
	All others..................	0.020
Ranger	6-410 early cyls. 6-390	0.010
	6-410 late cyls. 6-440 (L-440) series..	0.120
Warner	All............................	0.015
Wright	All............................	0.020

*(The above oversize limits correspond to the manufacturer's requirements, except for P&W R-985 and R-1830 series engines.)

NOTE: (Check for latest manufacturer specifications.)

(4) Cylinder barrels which have been plated by an agency whose process is approved by the FAA and which have not been worked beyond maximum permissible limits, will be considered acceptable for installation on certificated engines. It will be the responsibility of the owner or the repairing agency to provide this proof. In some cases, it may be necessary to remove cylinders to determine the amount of oversize since this information may be etched on the mating surface of the cylinder base flange.

8-12. CORROSION. Accomplish corrosion preventive measures for temporary and long-term storage in accordance with the instructions issued by the pertinent engine manufacturer. Avoid the use of solutions which contain strong caustic compounds and all solutions, polishes, cleaners, abrasives, etc., which might possibly promote corrosive action. (Refer to Chapter 6, Corrosion, Inspection, and Protection.)

8-13. ENGINE RUN-IN. After an aircraft engine has been overhauled, it is recommended that the pertinent aircraft engine manufacturer's run-in instructions be followed. Observe the manufacturer's recommendations concerning engine temperatures and other criteria. Repair processes employed during overhaul often necessitate amending the manufacturer's run-in procedures. Follow the approved amended run-in procedures in such instances.

NOTE: Do not run up engines on the ground for long periods of time with the cowling off. The engine will overheat because cylinder cooling has been disrupted.

8-14. COMPRESSION TESTING OF AIRCRAFT ENGINE CYLINDERS. A test to determine the internal condition of the combustion chamber cylinder assembly by ascertaining if any appreciable internal leakage is occurring is compression testing of aircraft engine cylinders. If a cylinder has less than a 60/80 reading on the differential test gauges on a hot engine, and procedures in paragraphs 8-15b(5)(i) and (j) fail to raise the compression reading, the cylinder must be removed and inspected. To determine the cylinder's problem area, have someone hold the propeller at the weak cylinder's top dead center and with compressed air still being applied, listen. If air is heard coming out of the exhaust pipe, the cylinder's exhaust-valve is not seating properly. If air is heard leaking out of the air cleaner/carburetor heat box, the intake valve is leaking. With the oil dipstick removed, and air is rushing out, the piston rings are defective. Remove and repair/overhaul the defective cylinder.

a. Differential Compression Test. The most common type of compression tester currently in use is the differential pressure-type tester. It provides a cross-reference to validate the readings obtained and tends to assure that the cylinder is defective before it is removed. Before beginning a compression test, consider the following points:

(1) When the spark plugs are removed from the engine, identify them to coincide with the cylinder and location from which they were removed. Close examination of the plugs will reveal the actual operating conditions and aid in diagnosing problems within each individual cylinder.

(2) The operating and maintenance records of the engine should be reviewed. Records of previous compression tests are of assistance in determining progressive wear conditions and help to establish the necessary maintenance corrective actions.

b. Differential Pressure Compression Test. The differential pressure tester is designed to check the compression of aircraft engines by measuring the leakage through the cylinders caused by worn or damaged components. The operation of the compression tester is based on the principle that, for any given airflow through a fixed orifice, a constant pressure drop across that orifice will result. The restrictor orifice dimensions in the differential pressure tester should be sized for the particular engine as follows:

(1) For an engine cylinder having less than a 5.00-inch bore; 0.040-inch orifice diameter; .250 inch long; and a 60-degree approach angle.

(2) For an engine cylinder with 5.00 inch bore and over: 0.060 inch orifice diameter, .250 inch long, 60 degree approach angle.

(3) A typical schematic diagram of the differential pressure tester is shown in figure 8-1.

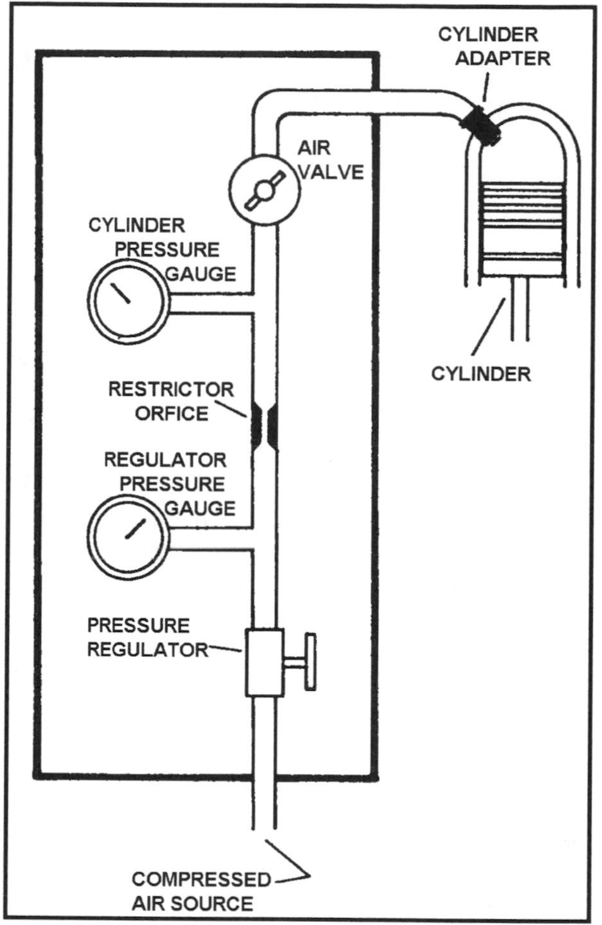

FIGURE 8-1. Schematic of differential pressure compression tester.

(4) As the regulated air pressure is applied to one side of the restrictor orifice with the air valve closed, there will be no leakage on the other side of the orifice and both pressure gauges will read the same. However, when the air valve is opened and leakage through the cylinder increases, the cylinder pressure gauge will record a proportionally lower reading.

(5) While performing the check the following procedures are listed to outline the principles involved, and are intended to supplement the manufacturer's instructions for the particular tester being used.

(a) Perform the compression test as soon as possible after the engine is shut down to ensure that the piston rings, cylinder walls, and other engine parts are well-lubricated.

(b) Remove the most accessible spark plug from each cylinder.

(c) With the air valve closed, apply an external source of clean air (approximately 100 to 120 psi) to the tester.

(d) Install an adapter in the spark plug bushing and connect the compression tester to the cylinder.

(e) Adjust the pressure regulator to obtain a reading of 20 psi on the regulator pressure gauge. At this time, the cylinder pressure gauge should also register 20 psi.

(f) Turn the crankshaft, by hand, in the direction of rotation until the piston (in the cylinder being checked) is coming up on its compression stroke. Slowly open the air valve and pressurize the cylinder to 80 psi.

CAUTION: Care must be exercised in opening the air valve since sufficient air pressure will have built up in the cylinder to cause it to rapidly rotate the propeller if the piston is not at top dead center (TDC).

(g) Continue rotating the engine against this pressure until the piston reaches TDC. Reaching TDC is indicated by a flat spot or sudden decrease in force required to turn the crankshaft. If the crankshaft is rotated too far, back up at least one-half revolution and start over again to eliminate the effect of backlash in the valve operating mechanism and to keep piston rings seated on the lower ring lands.

(h) Open the air valve completely. Check the regulated pressure and readjust, if necessary, to read 80 psi.

(i) Observe the pressure indication of the cylinder pressure gauge. The difference between this pressure and the pressure shown by the regulator pressure gauge is the amount of leakage through the cylinder. A loss in excess of 25 percent of the input air pressure is cause to suspect the cylinder of being defective; however, recheck the readings after operating the engine for at least 3 minutes to allow for sealing of the rings with oil.

(j) If leakage is still occurring after a recheck, it may be possible to correct a low reading. This is accomplished by placing a fiber drift on the rocker arm directly over the valve stem and tapping the drift several times with a hammer to dislodge any foreign material between the valve face and seat.

NOTE: When correcting a low reading in this manner, rotate the propeller so the piston will not be at TDC. This is necessary to prevent the valve from striking the top of the piston in some engines. Rotate the engine before rechecking compression to reseat the valves in the normal manner.

8-15. SPARK PLUGS. The spark plug provides the high-voltage electrical spark to ignite the fuel/air mixture in the cylinder. The types of spark plugs used in different engines will vary with regard to heat range, reach, thread size, and other characteristics required by the particular installation.

a. Heat Range. The heat range of a spark plug is the principal factor governing aircraft performance under various service conditions. The term "heat range" refers to the classification of spark plugs according to their ability to transfer heat from the firing end of the spark plug to the cylinder head.

(1) Spark plugs have been classified as "hot," "normal," and "cold." However, these terms may be misleading because the heat range varies through many degrees of temperature from extremely hot to extremely cold. Thus the words "hot," "cold," and "normal" do not necessarily tell the whole story.

(2) Since the insulator is designed to be the hottest part of the spark plug, its temperature can be related to the pre-ignition and fouling regions as shown in figure 8-2. Pre-ignition is likely to occur if surface areas in the combustion chamber exceed critical limits or if the spark plug core nose temperature exceeds 1,630 °F (888 °C). However, fouling or short-circuiting of the plug due to carbon deposits is likely to occur if the insulator tip temperature drops below approximately 800 °F (427 °C). Since spark plugs must operate between fairly well-defined temperature limits, they must be supplied in various heat ranges to meet the requirements of different engines under a variety of operating conditions.

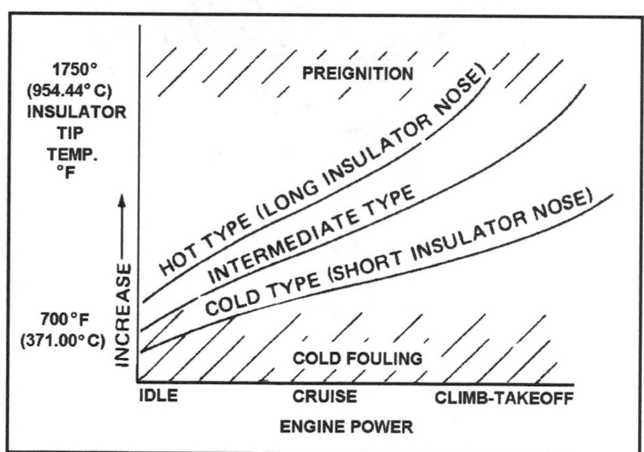

FIGURE 8-2. Chart of spark plug temperature ranges.

(3) From the engineering standpoint, each individual plug must be designed to offer the widest possible operating range. This means that a given type of spark plug should operate as hot as possible at low speeds and light loads and as cool as possible under cruising and takeoff power. Plug performance, therefore, depends on the operating temperature of the insulator nose, with the most desirable temperature range falling between 1,000 °F and 1,250 °F (538 °C and 677 °C).

(4) Fundamentally, an engine which runs hot requires a relatively cold spark plug, whereas an engine which runs cool requires a relatively hot spark plug. If a hot spark plug is installed in an engine which runs hot, the spark plug tip will be overheated and cause pre-ignition. If a cold spark plug is installed in an engine which runs cool, the tip of the spark plug will collect unburned carbon, causing fouling of the plug. The principal factors governing the heat range of aircraft spark plugs are:

(a) the distance between the copper sleeve around the insulator and the insulator tip;

(b) the thermal conductivity of the insulating material;

(c) the thermal conductivity of the electrode;

(d) the rate of heat transfer between the electrode and the insulator;

(e) the shape of the insulator tip;

(f) the distance between the insulator tip and the shell; and

(g) the type of outside gasket used.

(5) "Hot" plugs have a long insulator nose; thereby, creating a long heat transfer path, whereas "cold" plugs have a relatively short insulator to provide a rapid transfer of heat to the cylinder head. (See figure 8-3.)

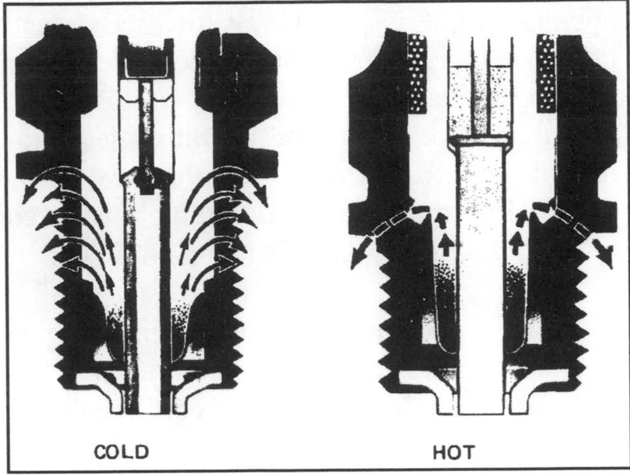

FIGURE 8-3. Hot and cold spark plugs.

b. Reach. The spark plug reach (see figure 8-4) is the threaded portion which is inserted into the spark plug bushing of the cylinder. A plug with the proper reach will ensure that the electrode end inside the cylinder is in the best position to achieve ignition. Spark plug seizure or improper combustion within the cylinder will probably occur if a plug with the wrong reach is used. Shell threads of spark plugs are classified as 14- or 18-mm spark plug diameter, long reach or short reach, thus:

Diameter	Long reach	Short reach
14 mm	1/2 in (12.7 mm)	3/8 in (9.53 mm)
18 mm	13/16 in. (20.64 mm)	1/2 in (12.7 mm)

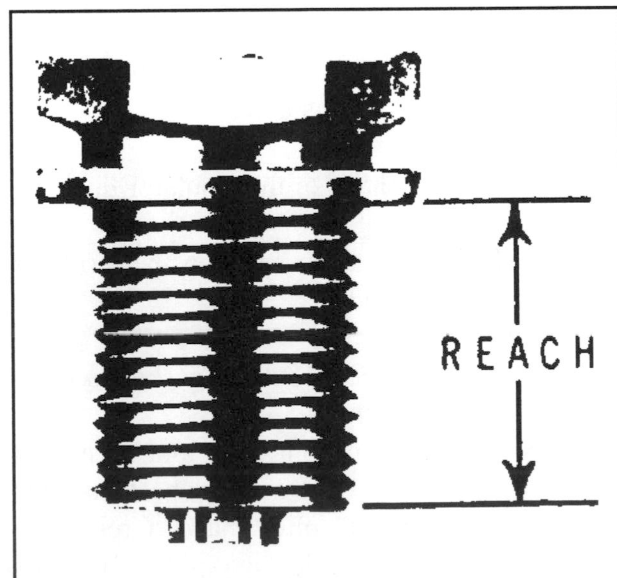

FIGURE 8-4. Spark plug reach.

c. Installation Procedures. When installing spark plugs, observe the following procedure.

(1) Visually inspect the plug for cleanliness and condition of the threads, ceramic, and electrodes.

NOTE: Never install a spark plug which has been dropped and always use new gaskets every time you install a spark plug.

(2) Check the plug for the proper gap setting, using a round wire feeler gauge as shown in figure 8-5. In the case of used plugs, procedures for cleaning and regapping are usually contained in the various manufacturers' manuals.

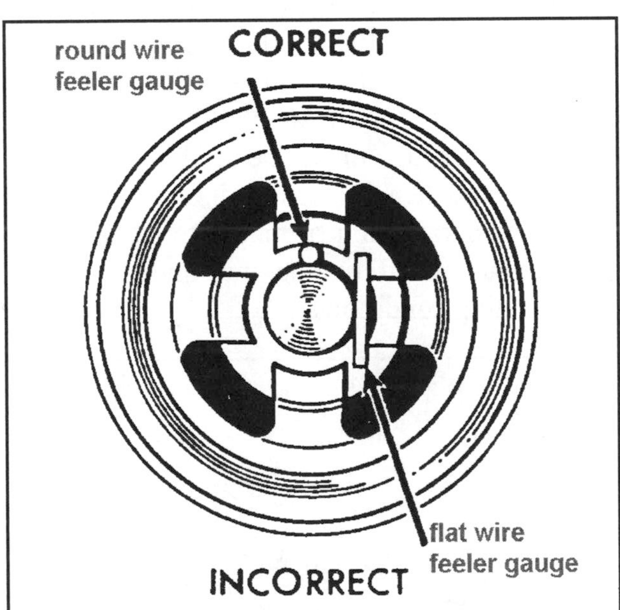

FIGURE 8-5. Method of checking spark plug gap.

(3) Check the plug and cylinder bushing to ascertain that only one gasket is used per spark plug. When a thermocouple-type gasket is used, no other gasket is required.

(4) Apply anti-seize compound sparingly to the shell threads, but do not allow the compound to contact the electrodes since the material is conductive and will short out the plug. If desired, the use of anti-seize compound may be eliminated on engines equipped with stainless steel spark plug bushings or inserts.

(5) Screw the plug into the cylinder head as far as possible by hand. If the plug will not turn easily to within two or three threads of the gasket, it may be necessary to clean the threads.

NOTE: Cleaning inserts with a tap is not recommended as permanent damage to the insert may result.

(6) Seat the proper socket securely on the spark plug and tighten to the torque limit specified by the engine manufacturer before proceeding to the next plug.

CAUTION: A loose spark plug will not transfer heat properly, and during engine operation, may overheat to the point the nose ceramic will become a "hot spot" and cause pre-ignition. However, avoid over-tightening as damage to the plug and bushing may result.

(7) Connect the ignition lead after wiping clean with a dry, lint-free cloth. Insert the terminal assembly into the spark plug in a straight line. (Care should be taken as improper techniques can damage the terminal sleeves.) Screw the connector nut into place until finger tight, then tighten an additional one quarter turn while holding the elbow in the proper position.

(8) Perform an engine run-up after installing a new set of spark plugs. When the engine has reached normal operating temperatures, check the magnetos and spark plugs in accordance with the manufacturer's instructions.

8-16. OPERATIONAL PROBLEMS.

Whenever problems develop during engine operation, which appear to be caused by the ignition system, it is recommended that the spark plugs and ignition harnesses be checked first before working on the magnetos. The following are the more common spark plug malfunctions and are relatively easy to identify.

a. Fouling.

(1) Carbon fouling (see figure 8-6) is identified by the dull black, sooty deposits on the electrode end of the plug. Although the primary causes are excessive ground idling and rich idle mixtures, a cold heat range may also be a contributing factor.

(2) Lead fouling is characterized by hard, dark, cinder-like globules which gradually fill up the electrode cavity and short out the plug. (See figure 8-6a.) The primary cause for this condition is poor fuel vaporization combined with a high tetraethyl-lead content fuel. A cold heat range may also contribute to this condition.

(3) Oil fouling is identified by a wet, black carbon deposit over the entire firing end of the plug as shown in figure 8-6b. This condition is fairly common on the lower plugs in horizontally-opposed engines, and both plugs in the lower cylinders of radial engines. Oil fouling is normally caused by oil drainage past the piston rings after shutdown. However, when both spark plugs removed from the same cylinder are badly fouled with oil and carbon, some form of engine damage should be suspected, and the cylinder more closely inspected. Mild forms of oil fouling can usually be cleared up by slowly increasing power, while running the engine until the deposits are burned off and the misfiring stops.

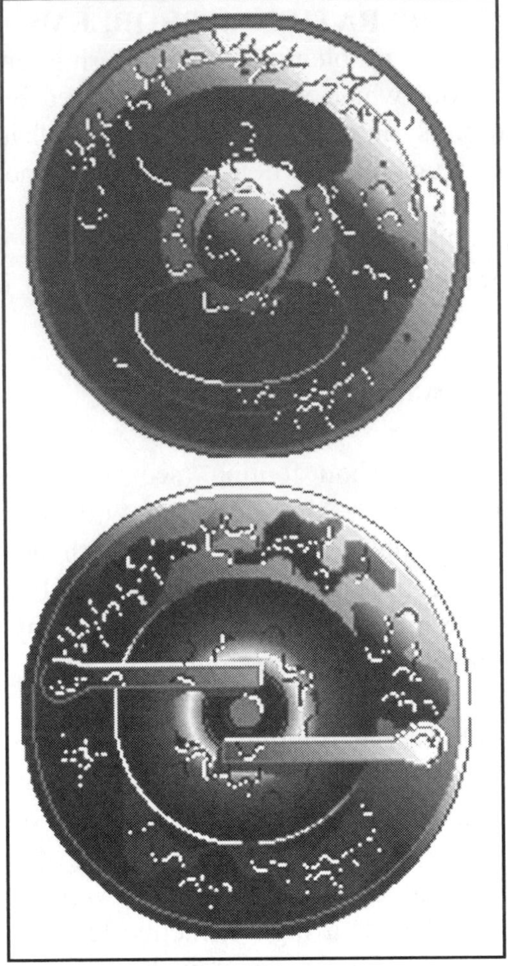

FIGURE 8-6. Typical carbon-fouled spark plug.

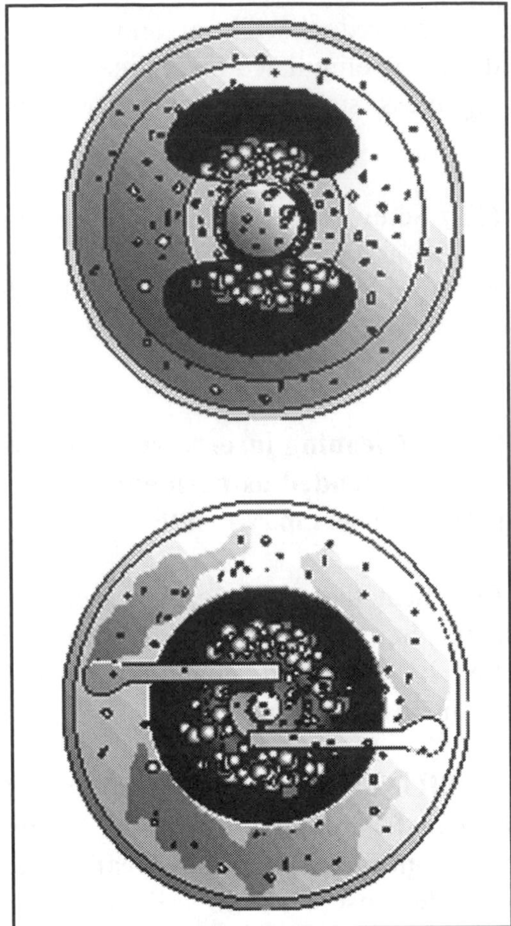

FIGURE 8-6a. Typical lead-fouled spark plug.

b. Fused Electrodes. There are many different types of malfunctions which result in fused spark plug electrodes; however, most are associated with pre-ignition either as the cause or the effect. For this reason, any time a spark plug is found with the following defects, further investigation of the cylinder and piston should be conducted.

(1) Occasionally, the ceramic nose core will crack, break away, and remain trapped behind the ground electrode. This piece of insulation material will then buildup heat to the point it will ignite the fuel/air mixture prematurely. The high temperatures and pressures encountered during this condition can cause damage to the cylinder and piston and ultimately lead to fusing and shorting out of the plug. (See figure 8-6c.)

(2) Corrosive gases formed by combustion and the high voltage spark have eroded the electrodes. Spark plugs in this condition require more voltage to fire—often more than the ignition system can produce. (See figure 8-6d.)

c. Bridged Electrodes. Occasionally, free combustion chamber particles will settle on the electrodes of a spark plug and gradually bridge the electrode gap, resulting in a shorted plug. Small particles may be dislodged by slowly cycling the engine as described for the oil-fouled condition; however, the only remedy for more advanced cases is removal and replacement of the spark plug. This condition is shown in figure 8-6e.

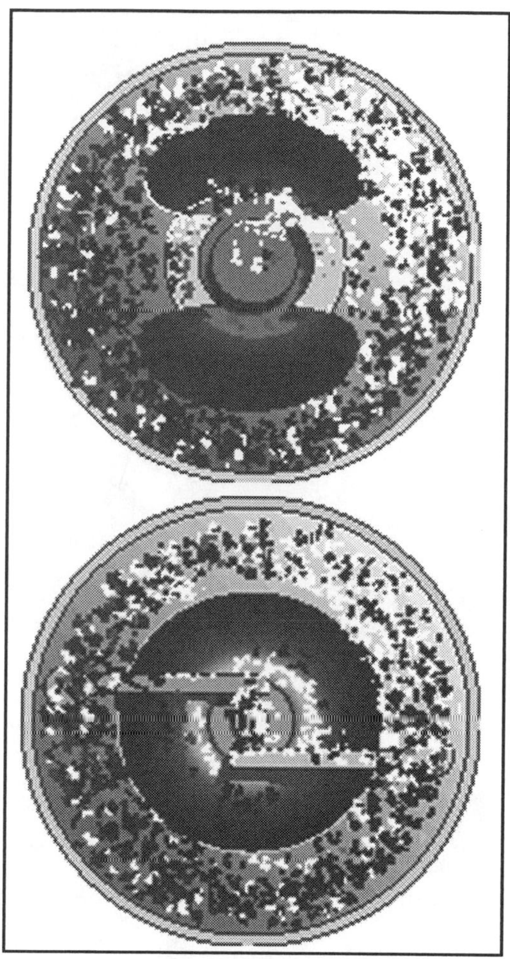

FIGURE 8-6b. Typical oil-fouled spark plug.

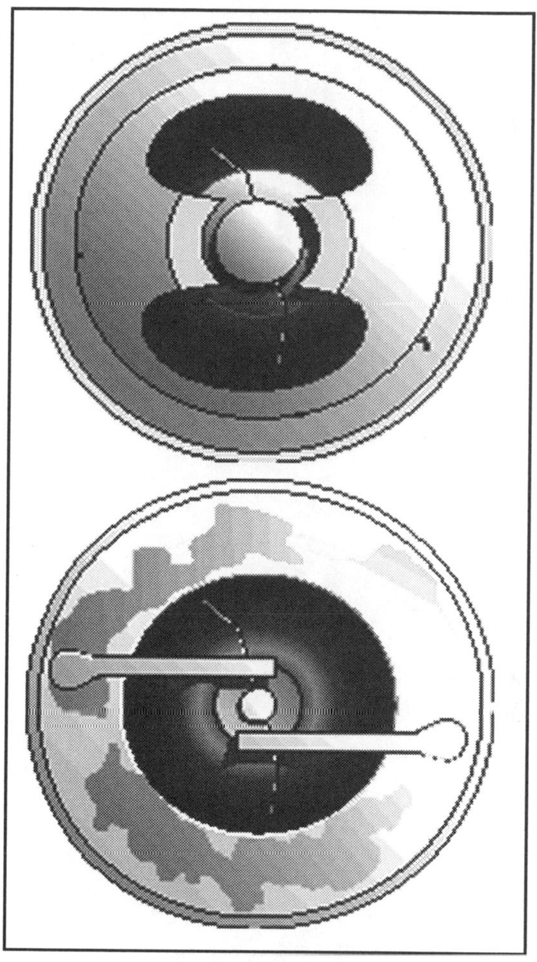

FIGURE 8-6c. Typical spark plug with cracked core nose.

d. Metal Deposits. Whenever metal spray is found on the electrodes of a spark plug, it is an indication that a failure of some part of the engine is in progress. The location of the cylinder in which the spray is found is important in diagnosing the problem, as various types of failures will cause the metal spray to appear differently. For example, if the metal spray is located evenly in every cylinder, the problem will be in the induction system, such as an impeller failure. If the metal spray is found only on the spark plugs in one cylinder, the problem is isolated to that cylinder and will generally be a piston failure.

In view of the secondary damage which occurs whenever an engine part fails, any preliminary indication such as metal spray should be thoroughly investigated to establish and correct the cause.

e. Flashover. It is important that spark plug terminal contact springs and moisture seals be checked regularly for condition and cleanliness to prevent "flashover" in the connector well. Foreign matter or moisture in the terminal connector well can reduce the insulation value of the connector to the point the ignition system voltages at higher power settings may flash over the connector well surface to ground and cause the plug to misfire. If moisture is the cause, hard starting can also result. The cutaway spark plug shown in figure 8-7 illustrates this malfunction. Any spark plug found with a dirty connector well may have this condition, and should be reconditioned before reuse.

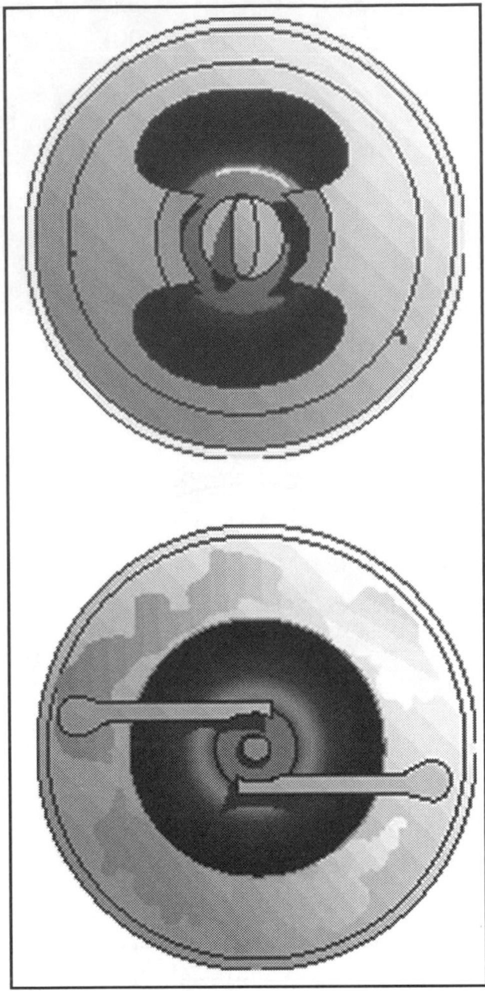

FIGURE 8-6d. Typical worn out spark plug.

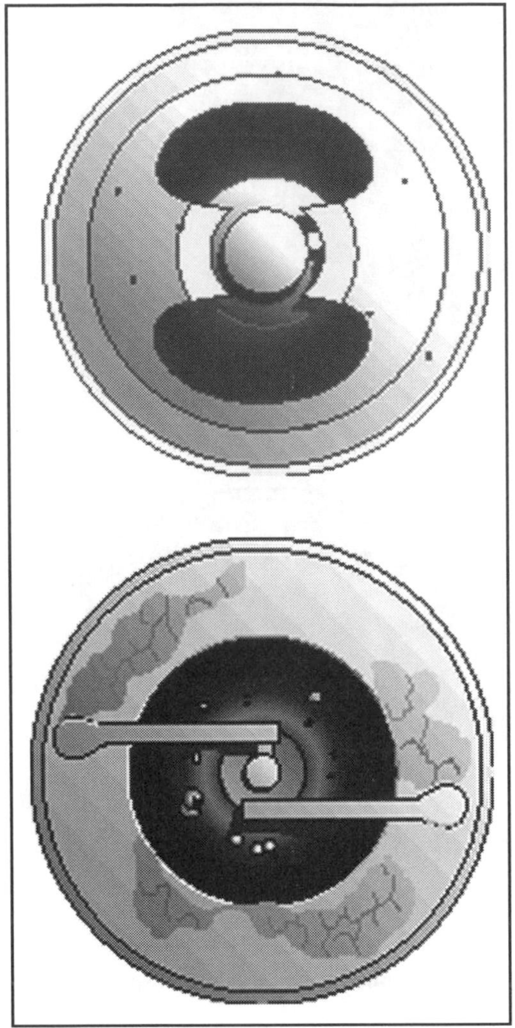

FIGURE 8-6e. Typical spark plug with bridged electrodes.

8-17. SPARK PLUG PRE-RECONDITIONING INSPECTION. All spark plugs should be inspected visually before reconditioning to eliminate any plug with obvious defects. A partial checklist of common defects includes:

a. Chipped or cracked ceramic either at the nose core or in the connector well.

b. Damaged or badly worn electrodes.

c. Badly nicked, damaged, or corroded threads on shell or shielding barrel.

d. Dented, bent, or cracked shielding barrel.

e. Connector seat at the top of the shielding barrel badly nicked or corroded.

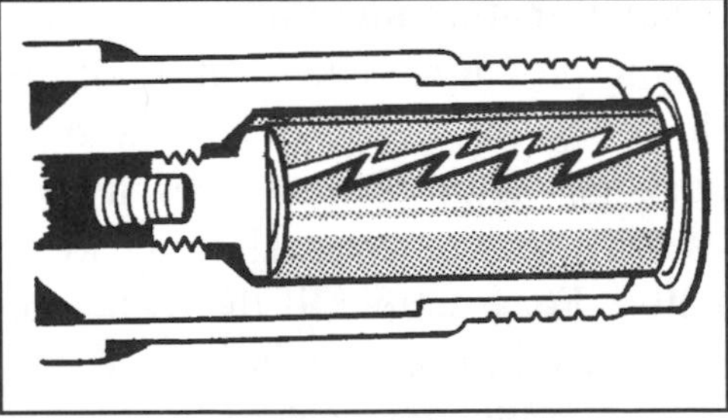

FIGURE 8-7. Spark plug well flashover.

8-18. IGNITION HARNESSES INSPECTION. Aircraft-quality ignition harness is usually made of either medium or high-temperature wire. The type used will depend upon the manufacturing specification for the particular engine. In addition to the applicable manufacturer's maintenance and repair procedures, the following is a quick-reference checklist for isolating some of the malfunctions inherent to ignition harnesses.

a. Carefully inspect the lead conduit or shielding. A few broken strands will not affect serviceability, but if the insulation in general looks worn, replace the lead.

b. When replacing a lead, if the dressing procedure is not accomplished properly, strands of shielding may be forced through the conductor insulation. If this occurs, a short will exist in the conductor; therefore, it is essential this task be performed properly.

c. The high-temperature coating used on some lightweight harnesses is provided for vibration abrasion resistance and moisture protection. Slight flaking or peeling of this coating is not serious, and a harness assembly need not be removed from service because of this condition.

d. Check the spark plug contact springs for breaks, corrosion, or deformation. If possible, check the lead continuity from the distributor block to the contact spring.

e. Check the insulators at the spark plug end of the lead for cracks, breaks, or evidence of old age. Make sure they are clean.

f. Check to see that the leads are positioned as far away from the exhaust manifold as possible and are supported to prevent any whipping action.

g. When lightweight harnesses are used and the conduit enters the spark plug at a severe angle, use clamps as shown in figure 8-8 to prevent overstressing the lead.

8-19. MAGNETO INSPECTION. Whenever ignition problems develop and it is determined that the magneto is the cause of the difficulty, the following are a few simple inspection procedures which may locate the malfunction quickly. However, conduct any internal inspection or repair of a magneto in accordance with the manufacturer's maintenance and overhaul manuals.

a. Inspect the distributor block contact springs. If broken or corroded, replace.

b. Inspect the felt oil washer, if applicable. It should be saturated with oil. If it is dry, check for a worn bushing.

c. Inspect the distributor block for cracks or a burned area. The wax coating on the block should not be removed. Do not use any solvents for cleaning.

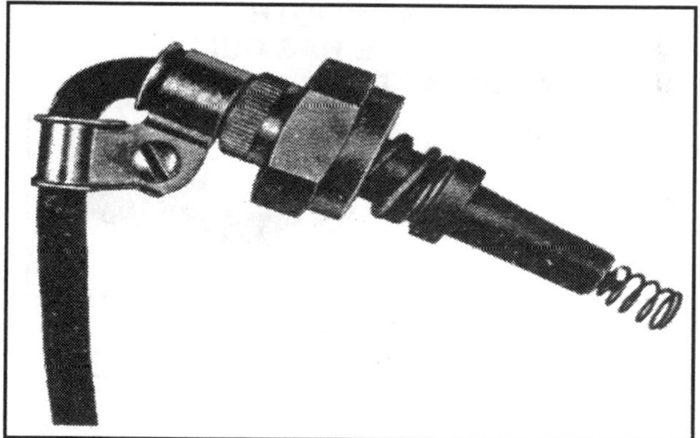

FIGURE 8-8. Typical method of clamping leads.

d. Look for excess oil in the breaker compartment. If oil is present, it may indicate a bad oil seal or bushing at the drive end. This condition could require complete overhaul, as too much oil may foul and cause excessive burning of the contact points.

e. Look for frayed insulation on the leads in the breaker compartment of the magneto. See that all terminals are secure. Be sure that wires are properly positioned.

f. Inspect the capacitor visually for general condition, and check the mounting bracket for cracks or looseness. If possible, check the capacitor for leakage, capacity, and series resistance.

g. Examine the points for excessive wear or burning. Discard points which have deep pits or excessively burned areas. Desired contact surfaces have a dull gray, sandblasted (almost rough) or frosted appearance over the area where electrical contact is made. Figure 8-9 shows how the normal contact point will look when surfaces are separated for inspection. Minor irregularities or roughness of point surfaces are not harmful (see figure 8-10), neither are small pits or mounds, if not too pronounced. If there is a possibility of the pit becoming deep enough to penetrate the pad (see figure 8-11), reject the contact assembly.

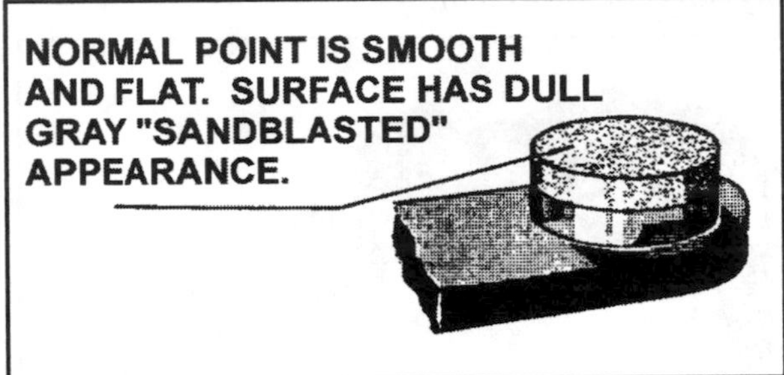

FIGURE 8-9. Normal contact point.

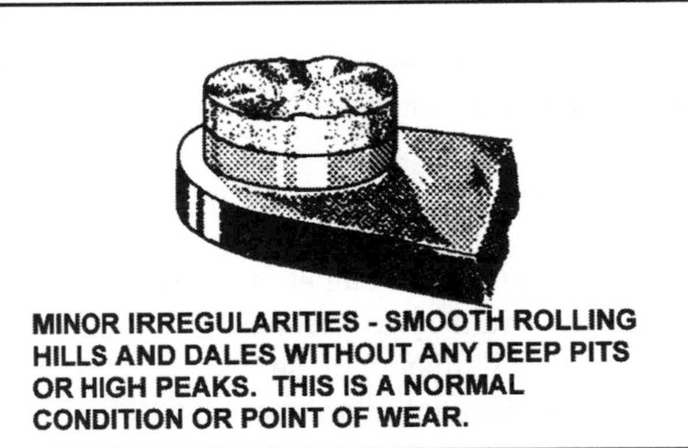

FIGURE 8-10. Point with minor irregularities.

h. Generally, no attempt should be made to dress or stone contact point assemblies; however, if provided, procedures and limits contained in the manufacturer's manuals may be followed.

FIGURE 8-11. Point with well-defined mound.

CAUTION: When inspecting the contact points for condition, do not open further than absolutely necessary. Excess tension on the spring will weaken it and adversely affect the performance of the magneto.

i. Adjustment of magneto point gaps must be correct for proper internal timing of a magneto. See applicable manufacturer's publications for internal timing procedures.

j. Check the breaker cam to assure cleanness and smoothness. Check the cam screw for tightness. If new points have been installed, blot a little oil on the cam. In addition, check contact point assembly to ascertain that the cam follower is securely fastened.

k. If the impulse coupling is accessible, inspect for excessive wear on the contact edges of the body and flyweights. In addition, check the flyweights for looseness on the axles.

l. Further examination of the impulse coupling body may disclose cracks caused by exceedingly-tight flyweight axle rivets.

m. Check the magneto ventilators for proper functioning and obstructions. If drilled plugs are used, they should be in the lowest vent hole of the magneto to serve as a drain for condensation and oil.

8-20. MAGNETO-TO-ENGINE TIMING. While the actual process of timing magnetos to an engine is covered in the engine manufacturer's technical manuals, the following general procedures may be applied.

a. Before installing a new magneto, the correct "E" gap setting specified by the magneto manufacturer should be verified.

b. When setting or checking the magneto-to-engine timing, always turn the crankshaft steadily in the normal direction of rotation to eliminate any error caused by gear backlash.

c. Recheck magneto-to-engine timing after any point-gap adjustment, or after replacement of the breaker points.

d. Never advance the magneto timing beyond the engine timing specification recommended by the engine manufacturer.

e. The possibility of a timing error exists if a timing indicator which attaches to the propeller shaft or spinner of geared engines is used. Engine timing specifications are always given in degrees of crankshaft travel and cannot be applied directly to geared propeller shafts because of the gear ratio. Therefore, the correct position of the propeller shaft, if used for timing, must be determined by multiplying the crankshaft timing angle in degrees before top center (BTC) by the propeller gear ratio.

8-21.—8-29. [RESERVED.]

SECTION 2. FUEL SYSTEMS

8-30. GENERAL. Maintain, service, and adjust aircraft fuel systems and fuel system components in accordance with the applicable manufacturer's maintenance instructions. Certain general fuel system maintenance principles are outlined in the following paragraphs..

8-31. FUEL LINES AND FITTINGS. When fuel system lines are to be replaced or repaired, consider the following fundamentals in addition to the applicable airworthiness requirements. Additional inspection and repair practices for aircraft tubing systems may be found in the Chapter 9, Aircraft Systems and Components.

a. Compatibility of Fittings. All fittings are to be compatible with their mating parts. Although various types of fittings appear to be interchangeable in many cases they have different thread pitch or minor design differences which prevent proper mating and may cause the joint to leak or fail.

b. Routing. Make sure that the line does not chafe against control cables, airframe structure, etc., or come in contact with electrical wiring or conduit. Where physical separation of the fuel lines from electrical wiring or conduit is impracticable, locate the fuel line below the wiring and clamp it securely to the airframe structure. In no case should wiring be supported by the fuel line.

c. Alignment. Locate bends accurately so that the tubing is aligned with all support clamps and end fittings and is not drawn, pulled, or otherwise forced into place by them. Never install a straight length of tubing between two rigidly-mounted fittings. Always incorporate at least one bend between such fittings to absorb strain caused by vibration and temperature changes.

d. Bonding. Bond metallic fuel lines at each point where they are clamped to the structure. Integrally bonded and cushioned line support clamps are preferred to other clamping and bonding methods.

e. Support of Line Units. To prevent possible failure, all fittings heavy enough to cause the line to sag should be supported by means other than the tubing.

f. Support clamps.

(1) Place support clamps or brackets for metallic lines as follows.

Tube O.D.	Approximate distance between supports
1/8"-3/16"--------------------------------	9"
1/4"-5/16"--------------------------------	12"
3/8"-1/2"----------------------------------	16"
5/8"-3/4"----------------------------------	22"
1"-1 1/4"----------------------------------	30"
1 1/2"-2"----------------------------------	40"

(2) Locate clamps or brackets as close to bends as possible to reduce overhang. (See figure 8-12.)

8-32. FUEL TANKS AND CELLS. Welded or riveted fuel tanks that are made of commercially pure aluminum, 3003, 5052, or similar alloys, may be repaired by welding. Tanks made from heat-treatable aluminum alloys are generally assembled by riveting. In case it is necessary to rivet a new piece in a tank, use the same material as used in the tank undergoing repair, and seal the seams with a compound that is insoluble in gasoline. Special sealing compounds are available and should be used in the repair of tanks. Inspect fuel tanks and cells for general condition, security of attachment, and evidence of leakage. Examine fuel tank or cell vent line, fuel line, and sump drain attachment fittings closely.

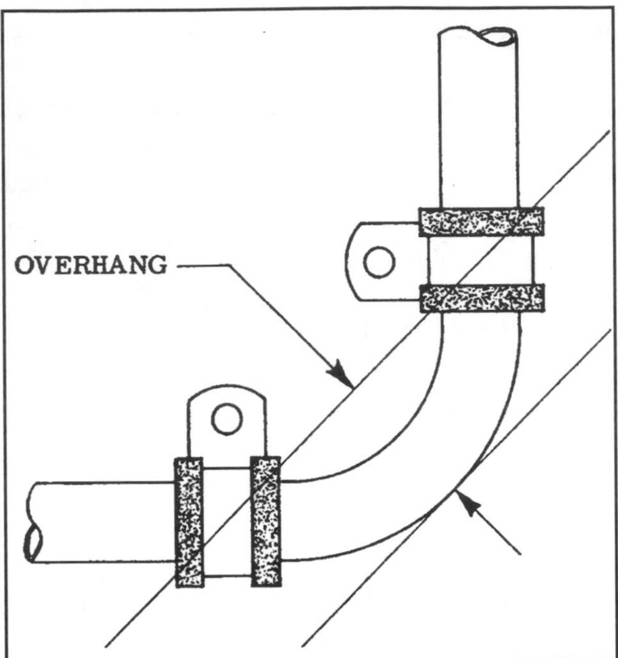

FIGURE 8-12. Location of clamps at tube bends.

CAUTION: Purge de-fueled tanks of explosive fuel/air mixtures in accordance with the manufacturer's service instructions. In the absence of such instructions, utilize an inert gas such as CO_2 as a purgative to assure the total deletion of fuel/air mixtures.

a. Integral Tanks. Examine the interior surfaces and seams for sealant deterioration and corrosion (especially in the sump area). Follow the manufacturer's instructions for repair and cleaning procedures.

b. Internal Metal Tanks. Check the exterior for corrosion and chafing. Dents or other distortion, such as a partially-collapsed tank caused by an obstructed fuel tank vent, can adversely affect fuel quantity gauge accuracy and tank capacity. Check the interior surfaces for corrosion. Pay particular attention to the sump area, especially for those of which sumps are made of cast material. Repairs to the tank may be accomplished in accordance with the practices outlined in the chapter 4, Metal Structure, Welding and Brazing of this AC.

c. Removal of Flux After Welding. It is especially important, after repair by welding, to completely remove all flux in order to avoid possible corrosion. Promptly upon completion of welding, wash the inside and outside of the tank with liberal quantities of hot water and then drain. Next, immerse the tank in either a 5 percent nitric or 5 percent sulfuric acid solution. If the tank cannot be immersed, fill the tank with either solution, and wash the outside with the same solution. Permit the acid to remain in contact with the weld about one hour and then rinse thoroughly with clean water. Test the efficiency of the cleaning operation by applying some acidified 5 percent silver nitrate solution to small quantity of the rinse water used last to wash the tank. If a heavy white precipitate is formed, the cleaning is insufficient and the washing should be repeated.

d. Flexible Fuel Cells. Inspect the interior for checking, cracking, porosity, or other signs of deterioration. Make sure the cell retaining fasteners are properly positioned. If repair or further inspection is required, follow the manufacturer's instructions for cell removal, repair, and installation. Do not allow flexible fuel cells to dry out. Preserve them in accordance with the manufacturer's instructions.

8-33. FUEL TANK CAPS, VENTS, AND OVERFLOW LINES. Inspect the fuel tank caps to determine they are the correct type and size for the installation, and that "O" rings are in good condition.

a. Unvented caps, substituted for vented caps, will cause fuel starvation and possible collapse of the fuel tank or cell. Malfunctioning of this type occurs when the pressure within the tank decreases as the fuel is withdrawn. Eventually, a point is reached where the fuel will no longer flow, and/or the outside atmospheric pressure collapses the tank. Thus, the effects will occur sooner with a full fuel tank than with one partially filled.

b. Check tank vents and overflow lines thoroughly for condition, obstructions, correct installation, and proper operation of any check valves and ice protection units. Pay particular attention to the location of the tank vents when such information is provided in the manufacturer's service instructions. Inspect for cracked or deteriorated filler opening recess drains, which may allow spilled fuel to accumulate within the wing or fuselage. One method of inspection is to plug the fuel line at the outlet and observe fuel placed in the filler opening recess. If drainage takes place, investigate condition of the line and purge any excess fuel from the wing.

c. Assure that filler opening markings are affixed to, or near, the filler opening; marked according to the applicable airworthiness requirements; and are complete and legible.

8-34. FUEL CROSS-FEED, FIREWALL SHUTOFF, AND TANK SELECTOR VALVES. Inspect these valves for leakage and proper operation as follows.

a. Internal leakage can be checked by placing the appropriate valve in the "off" position, draining the fuel strainer bowl, and observing if fuel continues to flow into it. Check all valves located downstream of boost pumps with the pump(s) operating. Do not operate the pump(s) longer than necessary.

b. External leakage from these units can result in a severe fire hazard, especially if the unit is located under the cabin floor or within a similarly-confined area. Correct the cause of any fuel stains associated with fuel leakage.

c. Selector Handles. Check the operation of each handle or control to see that it indicates the actual position of the selector valve to the placard location. Movement of the selector handle should be smooth and free of binding. Assure that stops and detents have positive action and smooth operational feel. Worn or missing detents and stops can cause unreliable positioning of the fuel selector valve.

d. Worn Linkage. Inaccurate positioning of fuel selector valves can also be caused by worn mechanical linkage between the selector handle and the valve unit. An improper fuel valve position setting can seriously reduce engine power by restricting the available fuel flow. Check universal joints, pins, gears, splines, cams, levers, etc., for wear and excessive clearance which prevent the valve from positioning accurately or from obtaining fully "off" and "on" positions.

e. Assure that required placards are complete and legible. Replace those that are missing or cannot be read easily.

8-35. FUEL PUMPS. Inspect, repair, and overhaul boost pumps, emergency pumps, auxiliary pumps, and engine-driven pumps in accordance with the appropriate manufacturer's instructions.

8-36. FUEL FILTERS, STRAINERS, AND DRAINS. Check each strainer and filter element for contamination. Determine and correct the source of any contaminants found. Replace throw-away filter elements with the recommended type. Examine fuel strainer bowls to see that they are properly installed according to the direction of the fuel flow. Check the operation of all drain devices to see that they operate properly and have positive shutoff action.

8-37. INDICATOR SYSTEMS. Inspect, service, and adjust the fuel indicator systems according to the manufacturer's instructions. Determine that the required placards and instrument markings are complete and legible.

8-38. FUEL SYSTEM PRECAUTIONS. In servicing fuel systems, remember that fuel is flammable and that the danger of fire or explosion always exists. The following precautions should be taken:

a. Aircraft being serviced or having the fuel system repaired must be properly grounded.

b. Spilled fuel must be neutralized or removed as quickly as possible.

c. Open fuel lines must be capped.

d. Fire-extinguishing equipment must always be available.

e. Metal fuel tanks must not be welded or soldered unless they have been adequately purged of fuel fumes. Keeping a tank or cell filled with carbon dioxide will prevent explosion of fuel fumes.

f. Do not use Teflon tape on any fuel lines to avoid getting the tape between the flare and fitting, which can cause fluid leaks.

8-39.—8-44. [RESERVED.]

SECTION 3. EXHAUST SYSTEMS

8-45. GENERAL. Any exhaust system failure should be regarded as a severe hazard. Depending upon the location and type of failure, it can result in carbon monoxide (CO) poisoning of crew and passengers, partial or complete engine power loss, or fire. Exhaust system failures generally reach a maximum rate of occurrence at 100 to 200 hours' operating time, and over 50 percent of the failures occur within 400 hours.

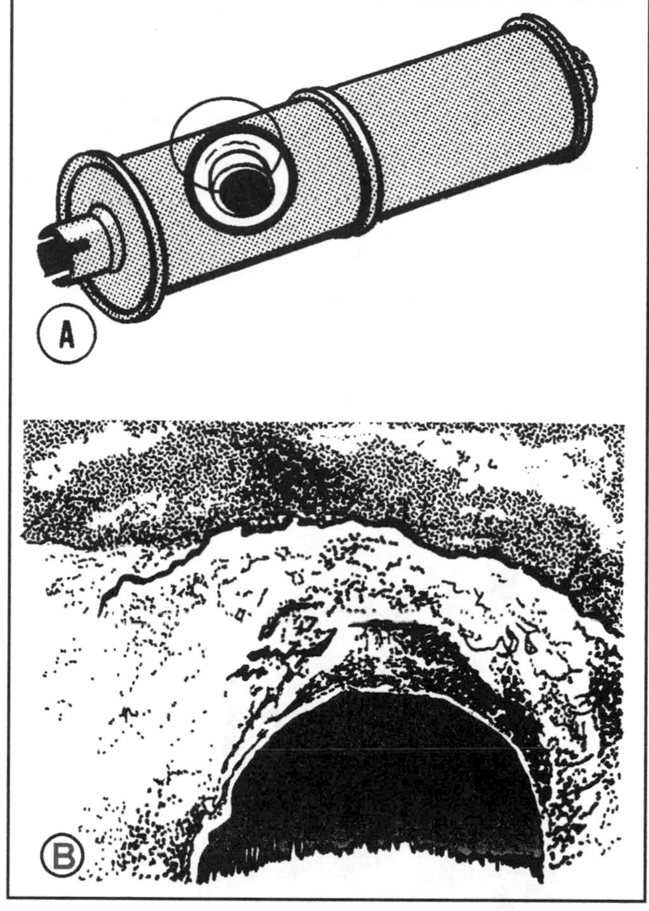

FIGURE 8-13. Typical muffler wall fatigue failure at exhaust outlet. (A. Complete muffler assembly with heat shroud removed; B. Detail view of failure.)

8-46. MUFFLER/HEAT EXCHANGER FAILURES. Approximately one-half of all exhaust system failures are traced to cracks or ruptures in the heat exchanger surfaces used for cabin and carburetor air heat sources.

a. Failures in the heat exchanger's surface (usually the muffler's outer wall) allow exhaust gases to escape directly into the cabin heat system. The failures are, for the most part, attributed to thermal and vibration fatigue cracking in the areas of stress concentration; e.g., tailpipe and stack, inlet-attachment areas. (See figures 8-13 through 8-16.)

b. Failures of the spot welds which attach heat transfer pins, as shown in figure 8-14A, can result in exhaust gas leakage. In addition to the CO hazard, failure of heat exchanger surfaces can permit exhaust gases to be drawn into the engine induction system and cause engine overheating and power loss.

8-47. MANIFOLD/STACK FAILURES. Exhaust manifold and stack failures are also usually fatigue-type failures which occur at welded or clamped joints; e.g., stack-to-flange, stack-to-manifold, muffler connections, or crossover pipe connections. Although these failures are primarily a fire hazard, they also present a CO problem. Exhaust gases can enter the cabin via defective or inadequate seals at firewall openings, wing strut fittings, doors, and wing root openings. Manifold/stack failures, which account for approximately 20 percent of all exhaust system failures, reach a maximum rate of occurrence at about 100 hours' operating time. Over 50 percent of the failures occur within 300 hours.

8-48. INTERNAL MUFFLER FAILURES. Internal failures (baffles, diffusers, etc.) can cause partial or complete engine power loss by restricting the flow of the exhaust gases. (See figures 8-17 through 8-20.)

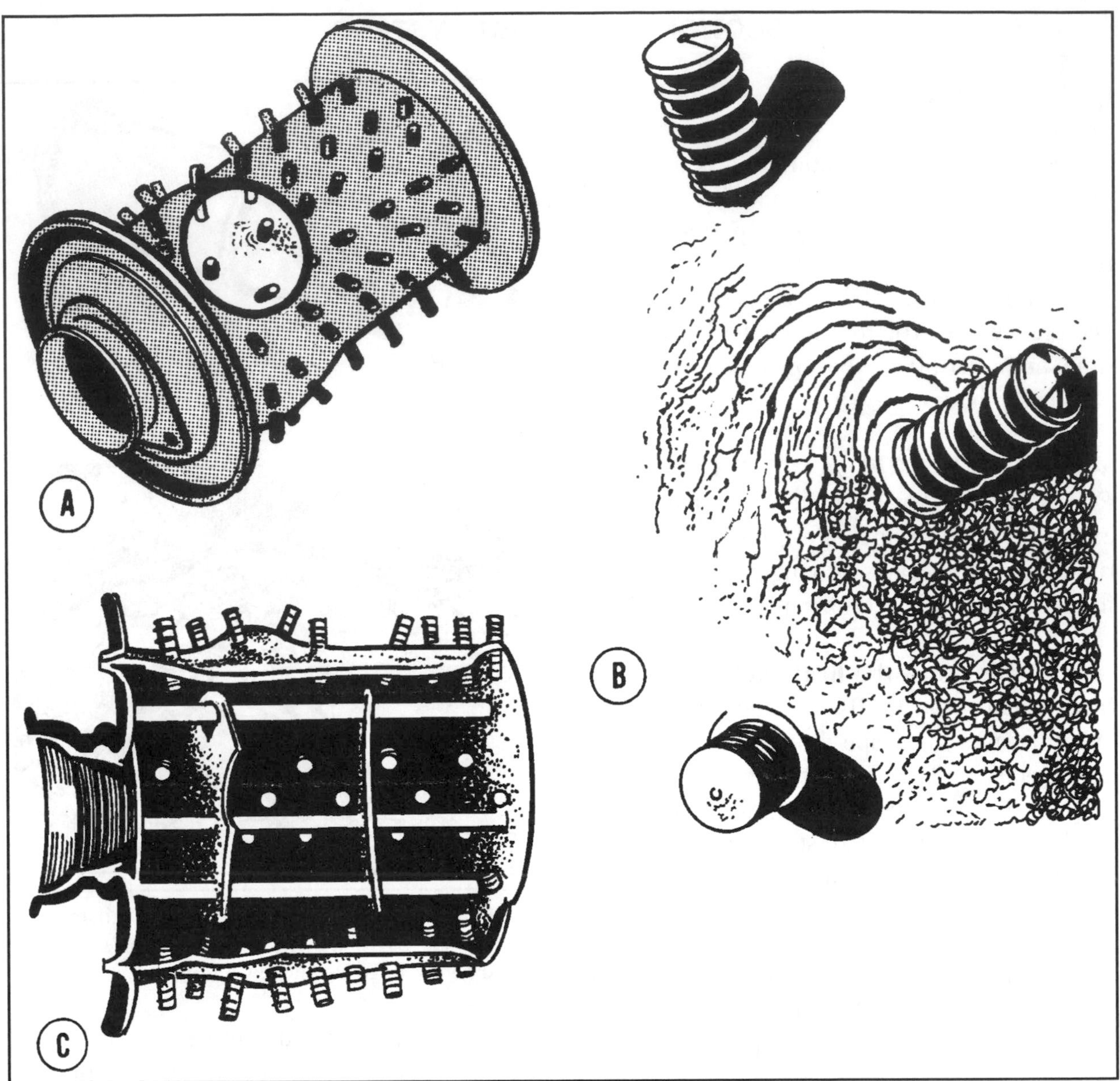

FIGURE 8-14. Typical muffler wall failure. (A. Complete muffler assembly with heat shroud removed; B. Detail view of failure; C. Cross section of failed muffler.)

As opposed to other failures, erosion and carbonizing caused by the extreme thermal conditions are the primary causes of internal failures. Engine after-firing and combustion of unburned fuel within the exhaust system are probable contributing factors.

a. In addition, local hot spot areas caused by uneven exhaust gas flow, result in burning, bulging, and rupture of the outer muffler wall. (See figure 8-14.) As might be expected, the time required for these failures to develop is longer than that for fatigue failures. Internal muffler failures account for nearly 20 percent of the total number of exhaust system failures.

b. The highest rate of internal muffler failures occurs between 500 and 750 hours of operating time. Engine power loss and excessive back-pressure caused by exhaust outlet blockage may be averted by the installation

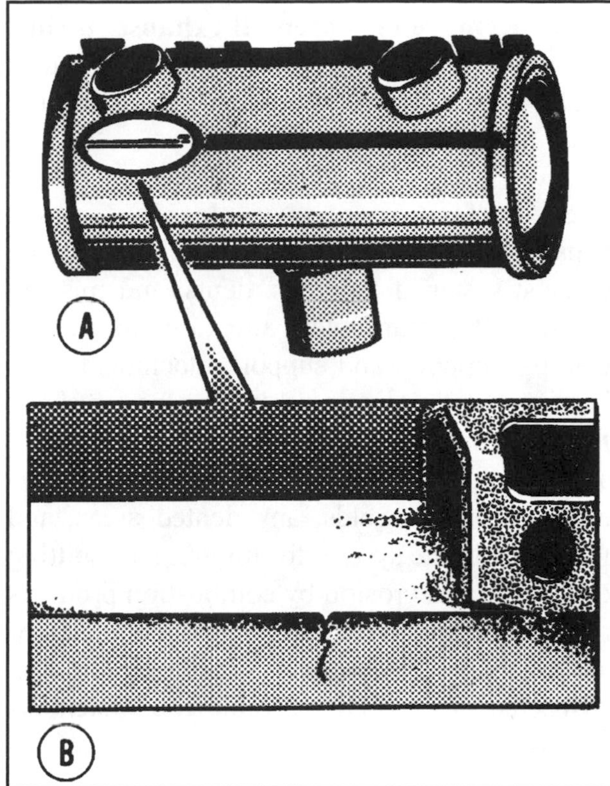

FIGURE 8-15. Typical muffler wall fatigue failure. (A. Complete muffler assembly with heat shroud partially removed; B. Detailed view of failure.)

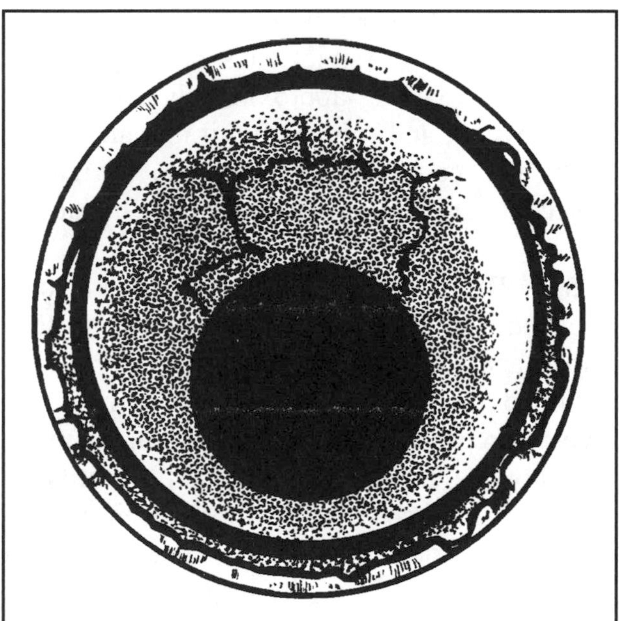

FIGURE 8-16. Typical fatigue failure of muffler end plate at stack inlet.

FIGURE 8-17. Section of a muffler showing typical internal baffle failure.

FIGURE 8-18. Loose pieces of a failed internal baffle.

of an exhaust outlet guard as shown in figures 8-21a and 8-21b. The outlet guard may be fabricated from a 3/16-inch stainless steel welding rod.

Form the rod into two "U" shaped segments, approximately 3 inches long and weld onto the exhaust tail pipe as shown in figure 8-21b so that the guard will extend 2 inches inside the exhaust muffler outlet port. Installation of an exhaust outlet guard does not negate the importance of thorough inspection of the internal parts of the muffler or the necessity of replacing defective mufflers.

8-49. INSPECTION. Inspect exhaust systems frequently to ascertain complete system integrity.

CAUTION: Marking of exhaust system parts. Never use lead pencils, carbon based pencils, etc., to mark exhaust system parts. Carbon deposited by those tools will cause cracks from heat concentration and carbonization of the metal. If exhaust system parts must be marked, use chalk, Prussian blue, India ink, or a grease pencil that is carbon-free.

a. Before any cleaning operation, remove the cowling as required to expose the complete exhaust system. Examine cowling and nacelle areas adjacent to exhaust system components for telltale signs of exhaust gas soot indicating possible leakage points. Check to make sure no portion of the exhaust system is being chafed by cowling, engine control cables, or other components. The exhaust system often operates at red-hot temperatures of 1,000 °F or more; therefore, parts such as ignition leads, hoses, fuel lines, and flexible air ducts, should be protected from radiation and convection heating by heat shields or adequate clearance.

b. Remove or loosen all exhaust shields, carburetor and cabin heater muffs, shrouds, heat blankets, etc., required to permit inspection of the complete system.

c. Perform necessary cleaning operations and inspect all external surfaces of the exhaust system for cracks, dents, and missing parts. Pay particular attention to welds, clamps, supports and support attachment lugs, bracing, slip joints, stack flanges, gaskets, flexible couplings, and etc. (See figures 8-22 and 8-23.) Examine the heel of each bend, areas adjacent to welds, any dented areas, and low spots in the system for thinning and pitting due to internal erosion by combustion products or accumulated moisture. An ice pick (or similar pointed instrument) is useful in probing suspected areas. Disassemble the system as necessary to inspect internal baffles or diffusers.

d. Should a component be inaccessible for a thorough visual inspection or hidden by non-removable parts, remove the component and check for possible leaks by plugging its openings, applying approximately 2 psi internal pressure, and submerging it in water. Any leaks will cause bubbles that can be readily detected. Dry thoroughly before reinstallation.

8-50. REPAIRS. It is generally recommended that exhaust stacks, mufflers, tailpipes, and etc., be replaced with new or reconditioned components rather than repaired. Welded repairs to exhaust systems are complicated by the difficulty of accurately identifying the base metal so that the proper repair materials can be selected. Changes in composition and grain structure of the original base metal further complicates the repair. However, when welded repairs are necessary, follow the general procedures outlined in Chapter 4; Metal Structure, Welding, and Brazing; of this AC. Retain the original contours and make sure that

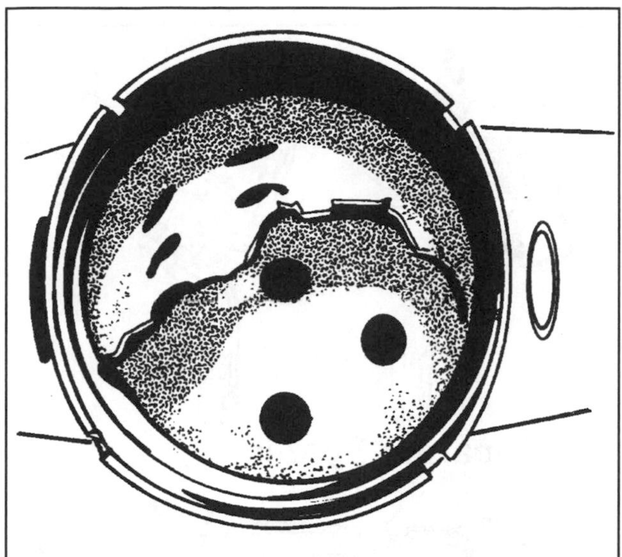

FIGURE 8-19. Failed internal baffle partially obstructing the muffler outlet.

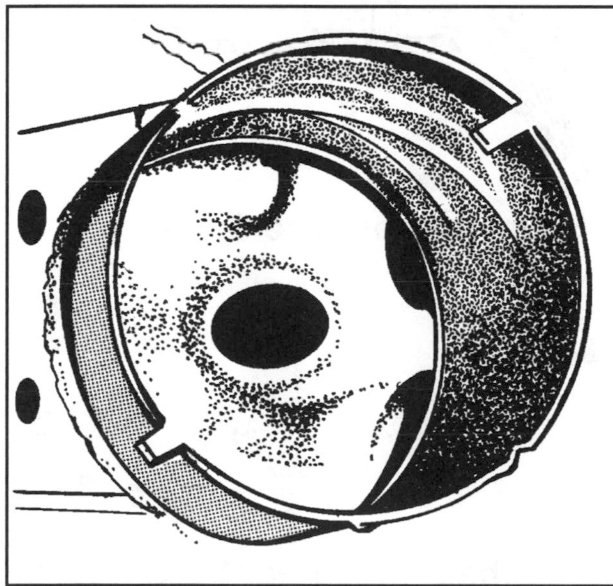

FIGURE 8-20. Failed internal baffle completely obstructing the muffler outlet.

the completed repair has not warped or otherwise affected the alignment of the exhaust system. Repairs or sloppy weld beads, which protrude internally, are not acceptable since they cause local hotspots and may restrict exhaust gas flow. All repairs must meet the manufacturer's specifications. When repairing or replacing exhaust system components, be sure that the proper hardware and clamps are used. Do not substitute steel or low-temperature self-locking nuts for brass or special high-temperature locknuts used by the manufacturer. Never reuse old gaskets or old star lock washers. When disassembly is necessary replace gaskets with new ones of the same type provided by the manufacturer.

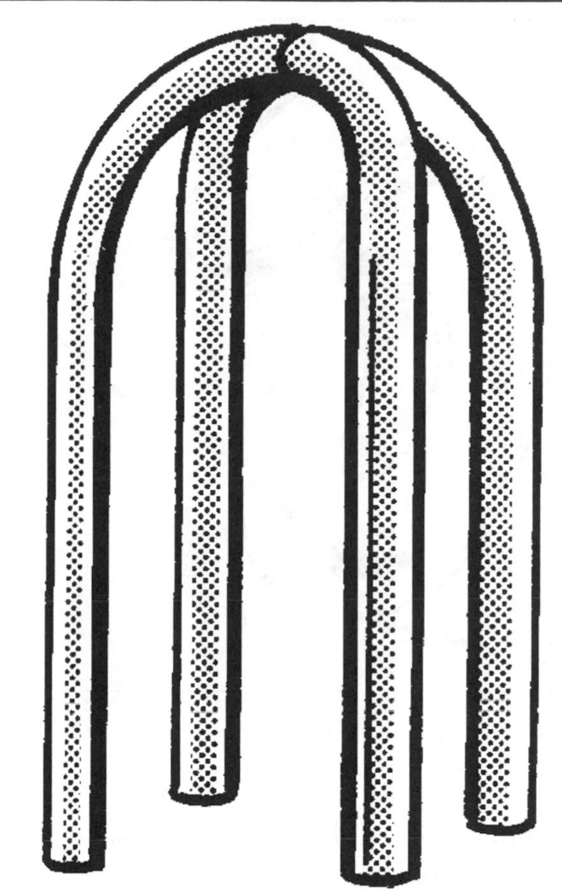

FIGURE 8-21a. Example of exhaust outlet guard.

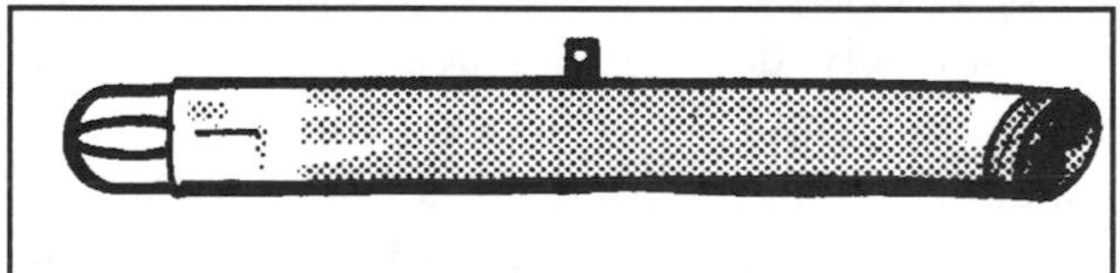

FIGURE 8-21b. Example of exhaust outlet guard installed.

8-51. TURBO-SUPERCHARGER. When a turbo-supercharger is included, the exhaust system operates under greatly-increased pressure and temperature conditions. Extra precautions should be taken in the exhaust system's care and maintenance. During

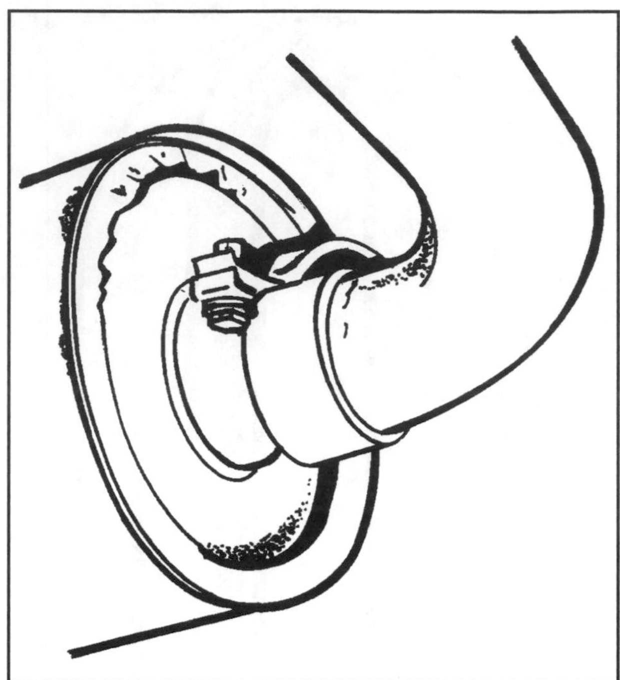

FIGURE 8-22. Effect of improperly positioned exhaust pipe/muffler clamp.

high-altitude operation, the exhaust system pressure is maintained at, or near, sea level values. Due to the pressure differential, any leaks in the system will allow the exhaust gases to escape with a torch-like intensity that can severely damage adjacent structures. A common cause of turbo-supercharger malfunction is coke deposits (carbon buildup) in the waste gate unit causing erratic system operation. Excessive deposit buildups may cause the waste gate valve to stick in the closed position, causing an overboost condition. Coke deposit buildup in the turbo-supercharger itself will cause a gradual loss of power in flight and low deck pressure reading before takeoff. Experience has shown that periodic decoking, or removal of carbon deposits, is necessary to maintain peak efficiency. Clean, repair, overhaul, and adjust turbo-supercharger system components and controls in accordance with the applicable manufacturer's instructions.

8-52. AUGMENTOR SYSTEMS. Inspect augmentor tubes periodically for proper alignment, security of attachment, and general

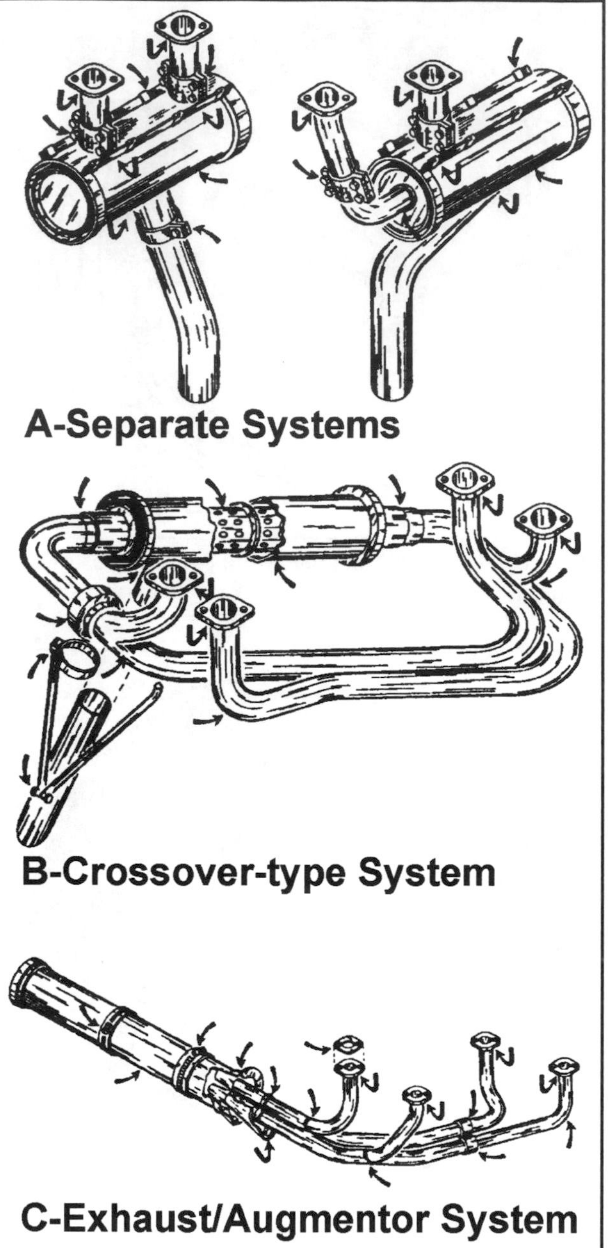

FIGURE 8-23. Primary inspection areas.

overall condition. Regardless of whether or not the augmentor tubes contain heat exchanger surfaces, they should be inspected for cracks along with the remainder of the exhaust system. Cracks can present a fire or CO hazard by allowing exhaust gases to enter nacelle, wing, or cabin areas.

8-53.—8-70. [RESERVED.]

SECTION 4. REPAIR OF METAL PROPELLERS

8-71. GENERAL. Reject damaged blades with model numbers which are on the manufacturer's list of blades that cannot be repaired. Follow the propeller manufacturer's recommendations in all cases, and make repairs in accordance with latest techniques and best industry practices.

NOTE: Title 14 of the Code of Federal Regulations, 14 CFR, part 65 does not allow an airframe and power plant mechanic to perform major repairs to propellers.

8-72. STEEL BLADES. Due to the critical effects of surface injuries and their repair on the fatigue life of steel blades, all repairs must be made in accordance with the manufacturer's instructions.

8-73. ALUMINUM PROPELLER REPAIRS. Aluminum-alloy propellers and blades with dents, cuts, scars, scratches, nicks, leading-edge pitting, etc., may be repaired, provided the removal or treatment does not materially affect the strength, weight, or performance of the blade. Remove these damages or otherwise treat as explained below, unless it is contrary to the manufacturer's instructions or recommendations. More than one injury is not sufficient cause alone for rejection of a blade. A reasonable number of repairs per blade may be made and not necessarily result in a dangerous condition, unless their location with respect to each other is such to form a continuous line of repairs that would materially weaken the blade. Suitable sandpaper or fine-cut files may be used for removing the necessary amount of metal. In each case, the area involved will be smoothly finished with #00 sandpaper or crocus cloth, and each blade from which any appreciable amount of metal has been removed will be properly balanced before it is used. Etch all repairs. To avoid removal of an excessive amount of metal, local etching should be accomplished at intervals during the process of removing suspected scratches. Upon completion of the repair, carefully inspect the entire blade by etching or anodizing. Remove all effects of the etching process with fine emery paper. Blades identified by the manufacturer as being cold-worked (shot-blasted or cold-rolled) may require peening after repair. Accomplish repair and peening operations on this type of blade in accordance with the manufacturer's instructions. However, it is not permissible in any case to peen down the edges of any injury wherein the operation will lap metal over the injury.

a. Flaws in Edges. Round out nicks, scars, cuts, etc., occurring on the leading edge of aluminum-alloy blades as shown in figure 8-24 (view B). Blades that have the leading edges pitted from normal wear in service may be reworked by removing sufficient material to eliminate the pitting. In this case, remove the metal by starting a sufficient distance from the edge, as shown in figure 8-25, and working forward over the edge in such a way that the contour will remain substantially the same, avoiding abrupt changes in contour. Trailing edges of blades may be treated in substantially the same manner. On the thrust and camber face of blades, remove the metal around any dents, cuts, scars, scratches, nicks, and pits to form shallow saucer-shaped depressions as shown in figure 8-24 (view C). Exercise care to remove the deepest point of the injury and also remove any raised metal around the edges of the injury as shown in figure 8-24 (view A). When repairing blades, figures 8-26 and 8-27 show the maximum reduction in width and thickness that is allowable below the minimum dimensions required by the blade drawing and blade manufacturing specification. Beyond the 90

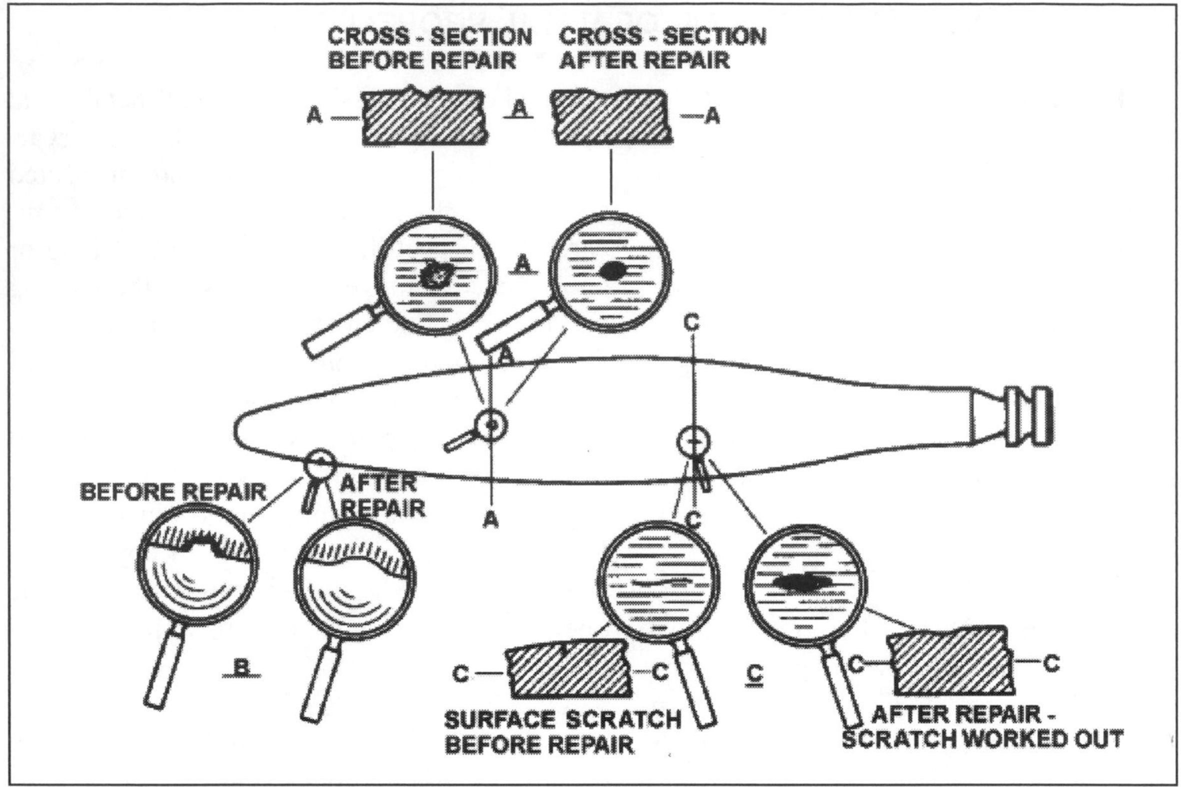

FIGURE 8-24. Method of repairing surface scratches, nicks, etc., on aluminum-alloy propellers.

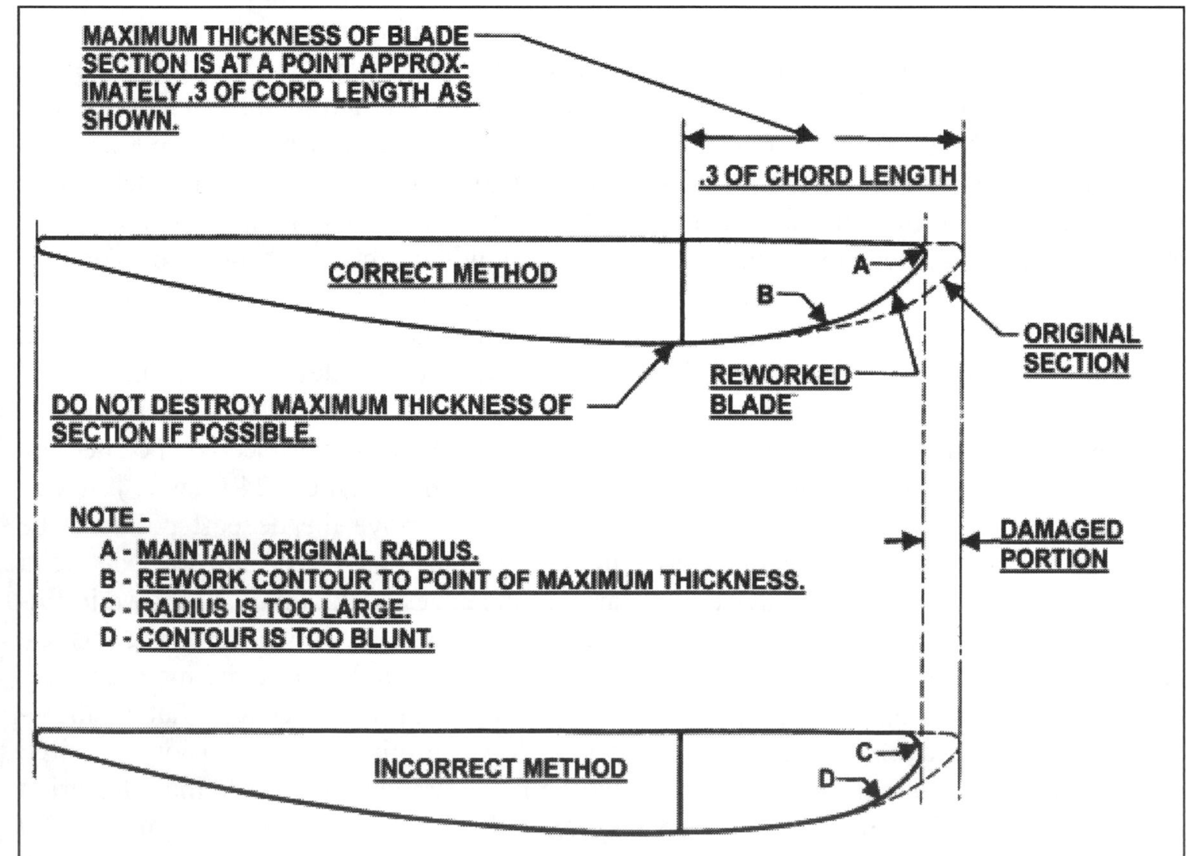

FIGURE 8-25. Correct and incorrect method of reworking leading edge of aluminum-alloy propellers.

90 percent blade radius point, the blade width and thickness may be modified as per the manufacturer's instructions.

b. Shortening Blades. Shortening propeller blades is a major repair. When the removal or treatment of defects on the tip necessitates shortening a blade, shorten each blade used with it and keep such sets of blades together. (See figure 8-26 for acceptable methods.) Mark the shortened blades to correspond with the manufacturer's system of model designation to indicate propeller diameter. In making the repair, it is not permissible to reduce the propeller diameter below the minimum diameter limit shown on the pertinent specification or type certificate data sheet.

c. Straighten Propeller Blades. Never straighten a damaged propeller. Even partial straightening of blades to permit shipment to a certificated propeller repair facility may result in hidden damage not being detected and an unairworthy propeller being returned to service.

8-74. REPAIR LIMITS. The following limits are those listed in the blade manufacturing specification for aluminum-alloy blades and govern the width and thickness of new blades. These limits are to be used with the pertinent blade drawing to determine the minimum original blade dimensions to which the reduction of figure 8-27 and figure 8-28. may be applied. When repairs reduce the width or thickness of the blade below these limits, reject the blade. The face alignment or track of the propeller should fall within the limits recommended by the manufacturer for new propellers

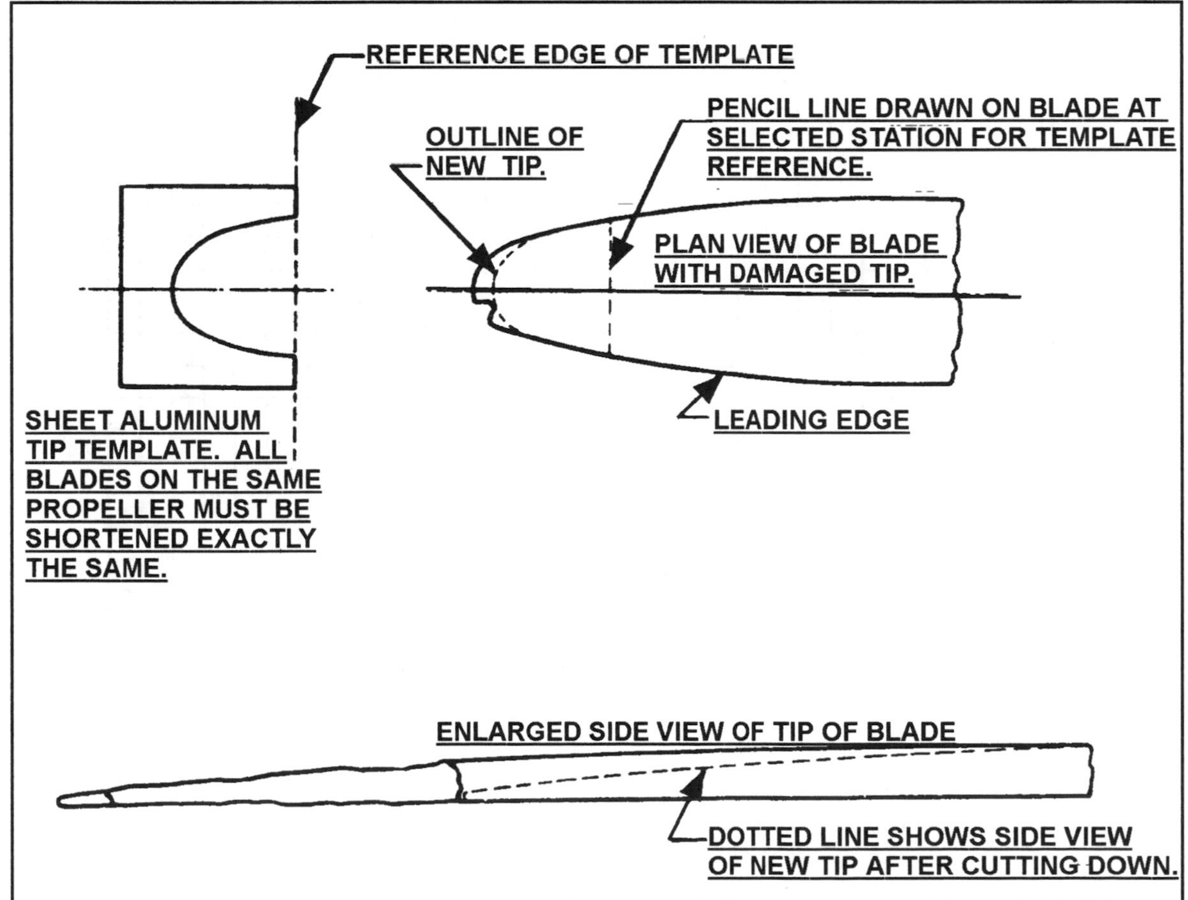

FIGURE 8-26. Method of repairing damaged tip of aluminum-alloy propellers.

a. No repairs are permitted to the shanks (roots or hub ends) of aluminum-alloy, adjustable-pitch blades. The shanks must be within manufacturer's limits.

b. The following two examples show how to determine the allowable repair limits on aluminum alloy blades.

(1) Example 1. Determine the blade width repair allowable (Δw) and minimum blade width limit, (w_1) for a blade having a diameter (d) of 10 ft. 6 in. The repair location (r_1) is 24 in. from the shank and the original, as manufactured, blade width (w) at the repair location is 1.88 in.

(a) Step 1. Calculate the blade radius (r)

$$r = d/2 = (10 \text{ ft } 6 \text{ in})/2 = 126/2 = 63 \text{ in.}$$

(b) Step 2. Calculate percent of blade radius to repair ($r\%$)

$$r\% = r_1/r \times 100 = (24/63) \times 100 = 38$$

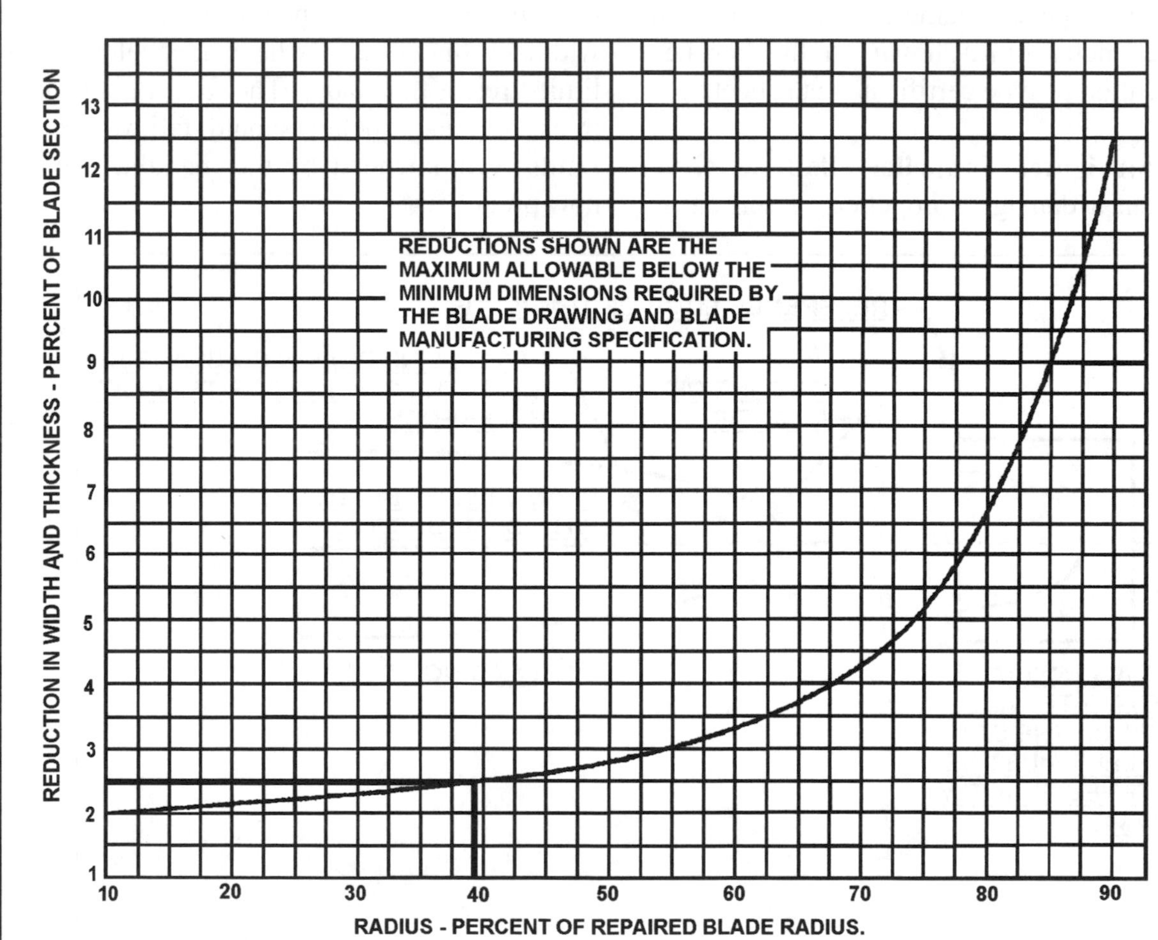

a. Draw a vertical line at the value of $r\% = 38$ on the horizontal axis.
b. Where the vertical line intersects the curve, draw a horizontal line to the right to intersect the vertical axis.
c. Read the percent reduction in width ($\Delta w\%$) on the vertical axis at this intersection.

$$\Delta w\% = 2.5$$

FIGURE 8-27. Example 1. Determine the repair width limits.

(c) Step 3. Determine percent reduction in width ($\Delta w\%$) from figure 8-27.

(d) Step 4. Calculate the blade width repair allowable (Δw)

$\Delta w = (\Delta w\%) \times (w) \times (0.01) = (2.5) \times (1.88) \times (0.01) = 0.05$ in.

(e) Step 5. Calculate the minimum blade width limit (w_1) at the repair location

$w_1 = w - \Delta w = 1.88 - 0.05 = 1.83$ in.

(2) Example 2. Determine the blade thickness repair allowable (Δt) and minimum blade thickness limit (t_1) for a blade having a diameter (d) of 10 ft. 6 in. The repair location (r_1) is 43 in. from the shank and the original, as manufactured, blade thickness (t) at the repair location is 0.07 in.

(a) Step 1. Calculate the blade radius (r)

$r = d/2 = (10 \text{ ft } 6 \text{ in})/2 = 126/2 = 63$ in.

(b) Step 2. Calculate percent of blade radius to repair (r%)

r% = r/r x 100 = (43/63) x 100 = 68

(c) Step 3. Determine percent reduction in thickness ($\Delta t\%$) from figure 8-28.

(d) Step 4. Calculate the blade thickness repair allowable (Δt)

$\Delta t = (\Delta t\%) \times (t)\,(0.01) = (4.0) \times (0.07) \times (0.01) = 0.003$ in.

(e) Step 5. Calculate the minimum blade thickness limit (t_1) at the repair location

$t_1 = t - \Delta t = 0.07 - 0.003 = 0.067$ in.

8-75. STEEL HUBS AND HUB PARTS. Repairs to steel hubs and parts must be accomplished only in accordance with the manufacturer's recommendations. Welding and remachining is permissible only when covered by manufacturer's service bulletins (SB).

8-76. PROPELLER HUB AND FLANGE REPAIR. When the fixed-pitch propeller bolt holes in a hub or crankshaft become damaged or oversized, it is permissible to make repairs by using methods (A) or (B) in figure 8-29, or by use of aircraft standard bolts 1/16-inch larger than the original bolts. Make the repairs in accordance with the recommendations of the propeller metal hub manufacturer or the engine manufacturer, as applicable. Obtain from the engine or propeller hub manufacturer suitable flange bushings with threaded or smooth bores, as illustrated in methods (A) or (B) of figure 8-29. Drill the flange and insert the bushings as recommended by the propeller to accommodate the bushings, and protect the holes with 2 coats of aluminum paint or other high moisture-resistant coating. Use bolts of the same size as those originally used. Any of the following combinations may be used: (1) drilled head bolt and castellated nut, (2) drilled head bolt and threaded bushing, or (3) undrilled bolt and self-locking nut. Where it is desirable to use oversized bolts, obtain suitable aircraft-standard bolts 1/16-inch larger than the original bolts. Enlarge the crankshaft propeller flange holes and the propeller hub holes sufficiently to accommodate the new bolts without more than 0.005-inch clearance. Such reboring will be permitted only once. Further repairs of bolt holes may be in accordance with the methods listed in (A) or (B) of figure 8-29.

NOTE: Method (A) or (B) is preferred over the oversized bolt method, because a propeller hub flange redrilled in accordance with this latter

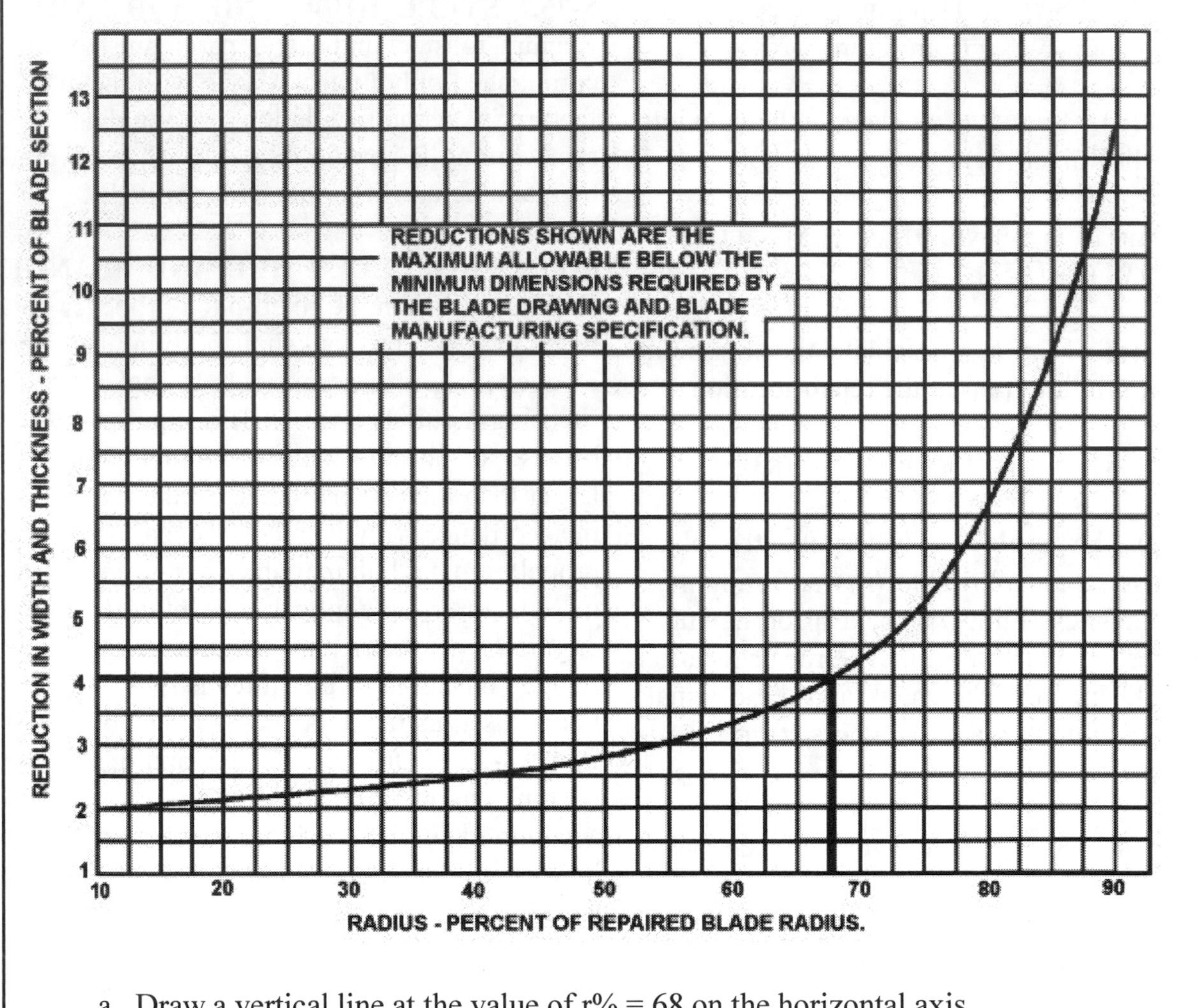

a. Draw a vertical line at the value of r% = 68 on the horizontal axis.

b. Where the vertical line intersects the curve, draw a horizontal line to the right to intersect the vertical axis.

c. Read the percent reduction in thickness ($\Delta t\%$) on the vertical axis intersection

$$\Delta t\% = 4.0$$

FIGURE 8-28. Example 2. Determine the repair thickness limits.

method will always require the re-drilling of all new propellers subsequently used with the re-drilled flange.

8-77. CONTROL SYSTEMS. Components used to control the operation of certificated propellers should be inspected, repaired, assembled, and/or tested in accordance with the manufacturer's recommendations. Only those repairs which are covered by the manufacturer's recommendations should be made, and only those replacement parts which are approved under 14 CFR, part 21 should be used.

8-78. DEICING SYSTEMS. Components used in propeller deicing systems should be inspected, repaired, assembled, and/or tested in accordance with the manufacturer's recommendations. Only those repairs which are covered by the manufacturer's recommendations should be made, and only those replacement parts which are approved under 14 CFR, part 21 should be used.

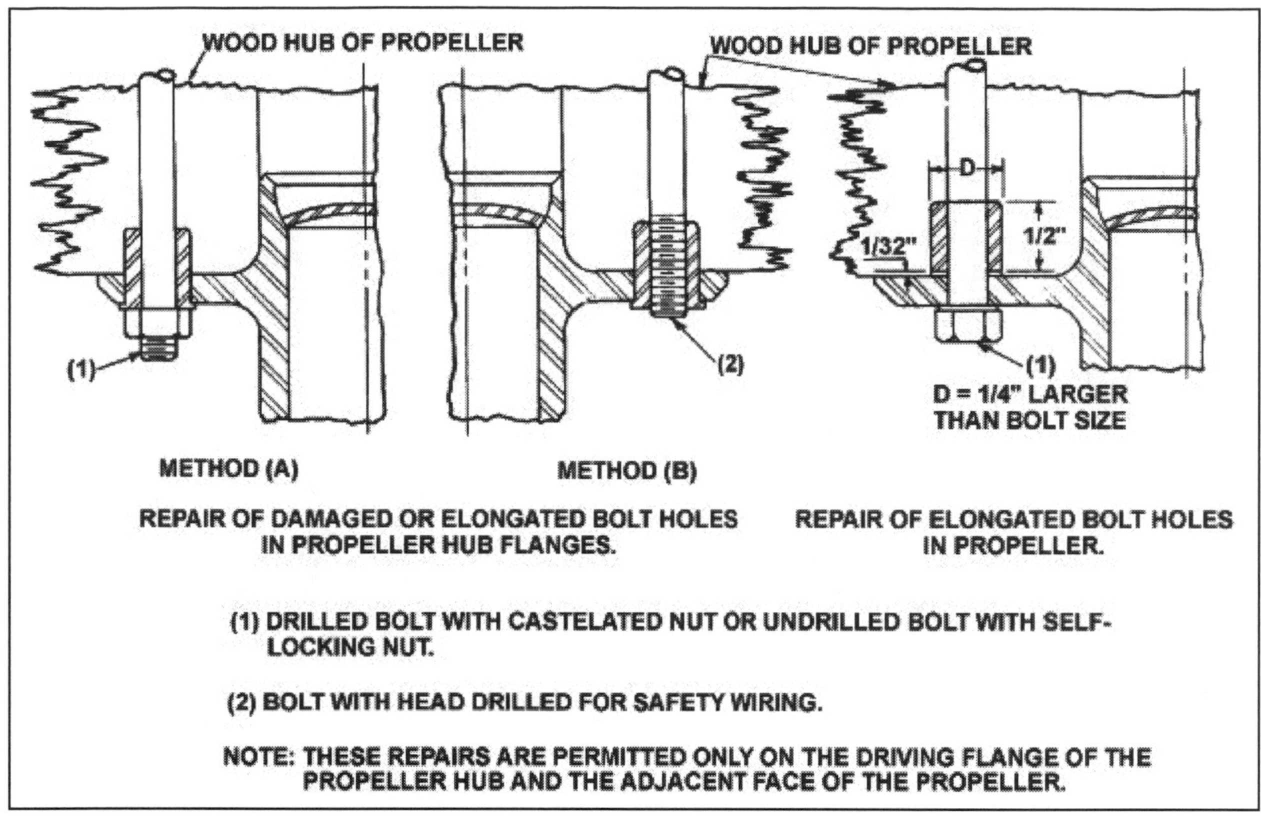
WOOD HUB OF PROPELLER
WOOD HUB OF PROPELLER
(1)
(2)
D
1/32"
1/2"
(1)
D = 1/4" LARGER THAN BOLT SIZE
METHOD (A)
METHOD (B)
REPAIR OF DAMAGED OR ELONGATED BOLT HOLES IN PROPELLER HUB FLANGES.
REPAIR OF ELONGATED BOLT HOLES IN PROPELLER.
(1) DRILLED BOLT WITH CASTELATED NUT OR UNDRILLED BOLT WITH SELF-LOCKING NUT.
(2) BOLT WITH HEAD DRILLED FOR SAFETY WIRING.
NOTE: THESE REPAIRS ARE PERMITTED ONLY ON THE DRIVING FLANGE OF THE PROPELLER HUB AND THE ADJACENT FACE OF THE PROPELLER.

FIGURE 8-29. Repair of fixed-pitch hub and propeller with elongated or damaged bolt holes.

8-79.—8-90. [RESERVED.]

SECTION 5. INSPECTION OF PROPELLERS

8-91. GENERAL. All propellers, regardless of the material from which they are made, should be regularly and carefully inspected for any possible defect. Any doubtful condition, such as looseness of parts, nicks, cracks, scratches, bruises, or loss of finish should be carefully investigated and the condition checked against repair and maintenance specifications for that particular type of propeller. Any propeller that has struck a foreign object during service should be promptly inspected for possible damage in accordance with the propeller manufacturer's prescribed procedures and, if necessary, repaired according to the manufacturer's instructions. If the propeller is damaged beyond the repair limits established by the propeller manufacturer, and a replacement is necessary, install the same make/model approved or alternate as specified in the equipment list, applicable FAA Aircraft Specification, Type Certificate Data Sheet (TCDS), or Supplemental Type Certificate (STC). A sample manufacturer's propeller inspection checklist is shown in table 8-2. It shows the items to be inspected and the inspection intervals.

8-92. WOOD OR COMPOSITION PROPELLERS AND BLADES. Wood propellers are usually found on low-power, reciprocating engines while composition (Carbon fiber, Kevlar) propellers are used on high horsepower reciprocating and turbine engines. Due to the nature of wood, these propellers should be inspected frequently to assure airworthiness. Inspect for defects such as cracks, dents, warpage, glue failure, delamination defects in the finish, and charring of the wood between the propeller and the flange due to loose propeller mounting bolts. Composition propellers should be inspected in accordance with the propeller manufacturer's instructions.

a. Fixed-pitch propellers are normally removed from the engine at engine overhaul periods. Whenever the propeller is removed, visually inspect the rear surface for any indication of cracks. When any defects are found, disassemble the metal hub from the propeller. Inspect the hub bolts for wear and cracks at the head and threads, and if cracked or worn, replace with new equivalent bolts. Inspect for elongated bolt holes, enlarged hub bore, and for cracks inside the bore or anywhere on the propeller. Repair propellers found with any of these defects. If no defects are found, the propeller may be reinstalled on the engine. Before installation, touch up with varnish all places where the finish is worn thin, scratched, or nicked. Track and balance the propeller, and coat the hub bore and bolt holes with some moisture preventive such as asphalt varnish. In case the hub flange is integral with the crankshaft of the engine, final track the propeller after it is installed on the engine. In all cases where a separate metal hub is used, make a final balance and track with the hub installed on the propeller.

b. On new, fixed-pitch propeller installations, inspect the bolts for proper torque after the first flight and after the first 25 hours of flying. Thereafter, inspect and check the bolts for proper torque at least every 50 hours. No definite time interval can be specified, since a bolt's proper torque is affected by changes in the wood caused by the moisture content of the air where the airplane is flown and stored. During wet weather, some moisture is apt to enter the propeller wood through the holes drilled in the hub. The wood then swells, and because expansion is limited by the bolts extending between the two flanges, some of the wood fibers become crushed. Later, when the propeller dries out during dry weather or due

TABLE 8-2. Sample manufacturer's propeller inspection checklist.

Nature of Inspection	Engine Operating Hours			
PROPELLER GROUP	50	100	500	1000
1. Inspect spinner and back plate for cracks	0	0	0	0
2. Inspect blades for nicks and cracks	0	0	0	0
3. Check for grease and oil leaks	0	0	0	0
4. Lubricate propeller per Lubrication Chart	0	0	0	0
5. Check spinner mounting Brackets for cracks		0	0	0
6. Check propeller mounting bolts and safety (Check torque if safety is broken)		0	0	0
7. Inspect hub parts for cracks and corrosion		0	0	0
8. Rotate blades of constant speed propeller and check for tightness in hub pilot tube		0	0	0
9. Remove constant speed propeller; remove sludge from propeller and crankshaft			0	0
10. Inspect complete propeller and spinner assembly for security, chafing, cracks, deterioration, wear and correct installation		0	0	0
11. Check propeller air pressure (at least once a month)	0	0	0	0
12. Overhaul propeller				0

to heat from the engine, a certain amount of propeller hub shrinkage takes place, and the wood no longer completely fills the space between the two hub flanges. Consequently, the hub bolts become loose.

c. In-flight tip failures may be avoided by frequent inspections of the metal cap, leading edge strip, and surrounding areas. Inspect for such defects as looseness or slipping, separation of soldered joints, loose screws, loose rivets, breaks, cracks, eroded sections, and corrosion. Inspect for separation between the metal leading edge and the cap, which would indicate the cap is moving outward in the direction of centrifugal force. This condition is often accompanied by discoloration and loose rivets. Inspect the tip for cracks by grasping it with the hand and slightly twisting about the longitudinal blade centerline and by slightly bending the tip backward and forward. If the leading edge and the cap have separated, carefully inspect for cracks at this point. Cracks usually start at the leading edge of the blade. A fine line appearing in the fabric or plastic may indicate a crack in the wood. Check the trailing edge of the propeller blades for bonding, separation, or damage.

d. Examine the wood close to the metal sleeve of wood blades for cracks extending outward on the blade. These cracks sometimes occur at the threaded ends of the lag screws and may be an indication of internal cracking of the wood. Check the tightness of the lag screws, which attach the metal sleeve to the wood blade, in accordance with the manufacturer's instructions. Inspect and protect the shank areas of composition blades next to the metal sleeve in the same manner as that used for wood blades.

8-93. METAL PROPELLERS AND BLADES. These propellers and blades are generally susceptible to fatigue failure resulting from the concentration of stresses at the bottoms of sharp nicks, cuts, and scratches. It is necessary, therefore, to frequently and carefully inspect them for such injuries. Propeller manufacturers publish SB's and instructions which prescribe the manner in which these inspections are to be accomplished. Additional information is also available in AC 20-37D, Aircraft Metal Propeller Maintenance.

a. Steel Blade Inspection. The inspection of steel blades may be accomplished by either visual, fluorescent penetrant (see chapter 5), or magnetic particle inspection. The visual inspection is easier if the steel blades are covered with engine oil or rust-preventive compound. The full length of the leading edge, especially near the tip, the full length of the trailing edge, the grooves and shoulders on the shank, and all dents and scars should be examined with a magnifying glass to decide whether defects are scratches or cracks.

b. Aluminum Propellers and Blades. Carefully inspect aluminum propellers and blades for cracks and other flaws. A transverse crack or flaw of any size is cause for rejection. Multiple deep nicks and gouges on the leading edge and face of the blade is cause for rejection. Use dye penetrant or fluorescent dye penetrant to confirm suspected cracks found in the propeller. Refer any unusual condition or appearance revealed by these inspections to the manufacturer.

c. Limitations.

(1) Corrosion may be present on propeller blades in varying amounts. Before performing any inspection process, maintenance personnel must examine the specific type and extent of the corrosion. (See chapter 6, and/or refer to AC 43-4A, Corrosion Control For Aircraft.)

(2) Corrosion, other than small areas (6 square inches or less) of light surface type corrosion, may require propeller removal and reconditioning by a qualified propeller repair facility. When intergranular corrosion is present, the repair can be properly accomplished only by an appropriately certificated propeller repair facility. Corrosion pitting under propeller blade decals should be removed as described in the propeller manufacturer's SB's and applicable airworthiness directives (AD).

(3) Unauthorized straightening of blade, following a ground strike or other damage, can create conditions that lead to immediate blade failure. These unapproved major repairs may sometimes be detected by careful inspection of the leading edges and the flat face portion of the blade. Any deviation of the flat portion, such as bows or kinks, may indicate unauthorized straightening of the blade. Sighting along the leading edge of a propeller blade for any signs of bending can provide evidence of unapproved blade straightening. Blades should be examined for any discoloration that would indicate unauthorized heating. Blades that have been heated for any repair must be rejected, since only cold straightening is authorized. All blades showing evidence of unapproved repairs should be rejected. When bent propellers are shipped to an approved repair facility for inspection and repair, the propeller should never be straightened by field service personnel to facilitate shipping, because this procedure can conceal damage. Propeller tip damage will sometimes lead maintenance personnel to consider removing damaged material from the blade tips. However, propellers are often manufactured with a particular diameter to minimize vibration. Unless the TCDS and both the engine and propeller manufacturers specifically permit shortening of the blades on a particular propeller, any shortening of the blades would probably create an unairworthy condition. When conditions warrant, inspect the blade tips for evidence of shortening and, if necessary, measure the propeller diameter to determine if it has been changed by an unauthorized repair.

8-94. PROPELLER HUB.

a. Fixed Pitch.

(1) Inspection procedures require removal of the propeller spinner for examination of the prop hub area. Cracks may be present in the hub area between or adjacent to bolt holes and along the hub pilot bore. Cracks in these areas cannot be repaired and require immediate scrapping of the propeller.

(2) Propeller attach bolts should be examined for looseness or an unsafetied or cracked condition. Cracked or broken bolts are usually the result of overtorquing. Correct torquing procedures require all bolt threads to be dry, clean, and free of any lubrication before torquing.

b. Controllable Pitch.

(1) Inspect controllable pitch propellers frequently to determine that all parts are lubricated properly. It is especially recommended that all lubrication be accomplished in accordance with the propeller manufacturer's instructions.

(2) Complete inspection/servicing requires the removal of the spinner for examination and servicing of the propeller hub and blade clamp area. All inspections and servicing of the pitch control mechanism should follow the recommendations of the propeller, engine, and airframe manufacturers. Propellers must be in compliance with applicable AD's and manufacturer's SB's.

(3) The hub, blade clamps, and pitch change mechanisms should be inspected for corrosion from all sources, including rain, snow, and bird droppings that may have entered through the spinner openings. Examine the hub area for oil and grease leaks, missing grease-fitting caps, and leaking or missing grease fittings.

(4) Propeller domes should be checked for leaks, both at the seals and on the fill valve (if so equipped). The dome valve may be leak-tested by applying soapy water over the fill valve end. Domes should be serviced only with nitrogen or dry air in accordance with the manufacturer's recommendations. When propeller domes are inspected and found filled with oil, the propeller should be removed and inspected/repaired by an appropriately-rated repair facility.

(5) It is especially recommended that all lubrication be accomplished at the periods and in the manner specified by the propeller manufacturer. On makes and models with a grease fitting on the hub, before greasing the hub remove the grease fitting opposite the one to which you are going to add grease. This will allow the excess grease and pressure to exit through the grease fitting hole rather than the hub seal.

(6) Fiber-block, pitch-change mechanisms should be inspected for deterioration, fit, and the security of the pitch-clamp forks.

(7) Certain models of full-feathering propellers use spring-loaded pins to retain the feathered blade position. Spring and pin units should be cleaned, inspected, and relubricated per the manufacturer's recommendations and applicable AD's.

(8) Pitch change counterweights on blade clamps should be inspected for security, safety, and to ensure that adequate counterweight clearance exists within the spinner.

8-95. TACHOMETER INSPECTION. Due to the exceptionally high stresses that may be generated by particular propeller/engine combinations at certain engine revolutions per minute (RPM), many propeller and aircraft manufacturers have established areas of RPM restrictions and other restrictions on maximum RPM for some models. Some RPM limits do not exceed 3 percent of the maximum RPM permitted, and a slow-running tachometer can cause an engine to run past the maximum RPM limits. Since there are no post-manufacture accuracy requirements for engine tachometers, tachometer inaccuracy could lead to propeller failure, excessive vibration, or unscheduled maintenance. If the tachometer exceeds 2 percent (plus or minus) of the tested RPM, replace it.

8-96.—8-106. [RESERVED.]

SECTION 6. PROPELLER TRACKING AND VIBRATION

8-107. GENERAL. To ensure smooth powerplant operations, first start with a properly-installed propeller. Each propeller should be checked for proper tracking (blades rotating in the same plane of rotation). Manufacturer's recommendations should in all cases be followed.

8-108. PROPELLER TRACKING CHECK. The following is a simple procedure that can be accomplished in less than 30 minutes:

a. Chock the aircraft so it cannot be moved.

b. Remove one spark plug from each cylinder. This will make the propeller easier and safer to turn.

c. Rotate one of the blades so it is pointing down.

d. Place a solid object (e.g. a heavy wooden block that is at least a couple of inches higher off the ground than the distance between the propeller tip and the ground) next to the propeller tip so that it just touches (see figure 8-30), or attach a pointer/indicator to the cowling itself.

e. Rotate the propeller slowly to see if the next blade "tracks" through the same point (touches the block/pointer). Each blade track should be within 1/16-inch (plus or minus) from the opposite blade's track.

f. If the propeller is out of track, it may be due to one or more propeller blades being bent, a bent propeller flange, or propeller mounting bolts that are either over or under-torqued. An out-of-track propeller will cause vibration and stress to the airframe and engine, and may cause premature propeller failure.

8-109. VIBRATION. Although vibration can be caused by the propeller, there are numerous other possible sources of vibration which can make troubleshooting difficult.

a. If a propeller vibrates, whether due to balance, angle, or track problems, it typically vibrates, throughout the entire RPM range, although the intensity of the vibration may vary with the RPM. If a vibration occurs only at one particular RPM or within a limited RPM range (e.g. 2200-2350 RPM), the vibration is not normally a propeller problem but a problem with a poor engine/propeller match.

b. If a propeller vibration is suspected but cannot be positively determined, if possible, the ideal troubleshooting method is to temporarily replace the propeller with one which is known to be airworthy and test fly the aircraft.

c. There are numerous allowable tolerances in blade angles, balance, track, and blade width and thickness dimensions. These tolerances have been established through many years of experience. The degree to which these factors affect vibration is sometimes disputed and can involve significant repair bills, which may or may not cure a vibration problem. Reliance upon experienced, reputable propeller repair stations is the owner's best method of dealing with these problems.

d. Blade shake is not the source of vibration problems. Once the engine is running, centrifugal force holds the blades firmly (approximately 30-40,000 lbs.) against blade bearings.

e. Cabin vibration can sometimes be improved by reindexing the propeller to the crankshaft. The propeller can be removed, rotated 180▪, and re-installed.

f. The propeller spinner can be a contributing factor to an out-of-balance condition. An indication of this would be a noticeable spinner "wobble" while the engine is running. This condition is normally caused by inadequate shimming of the spinner front support or a cracked or deformed spinner.

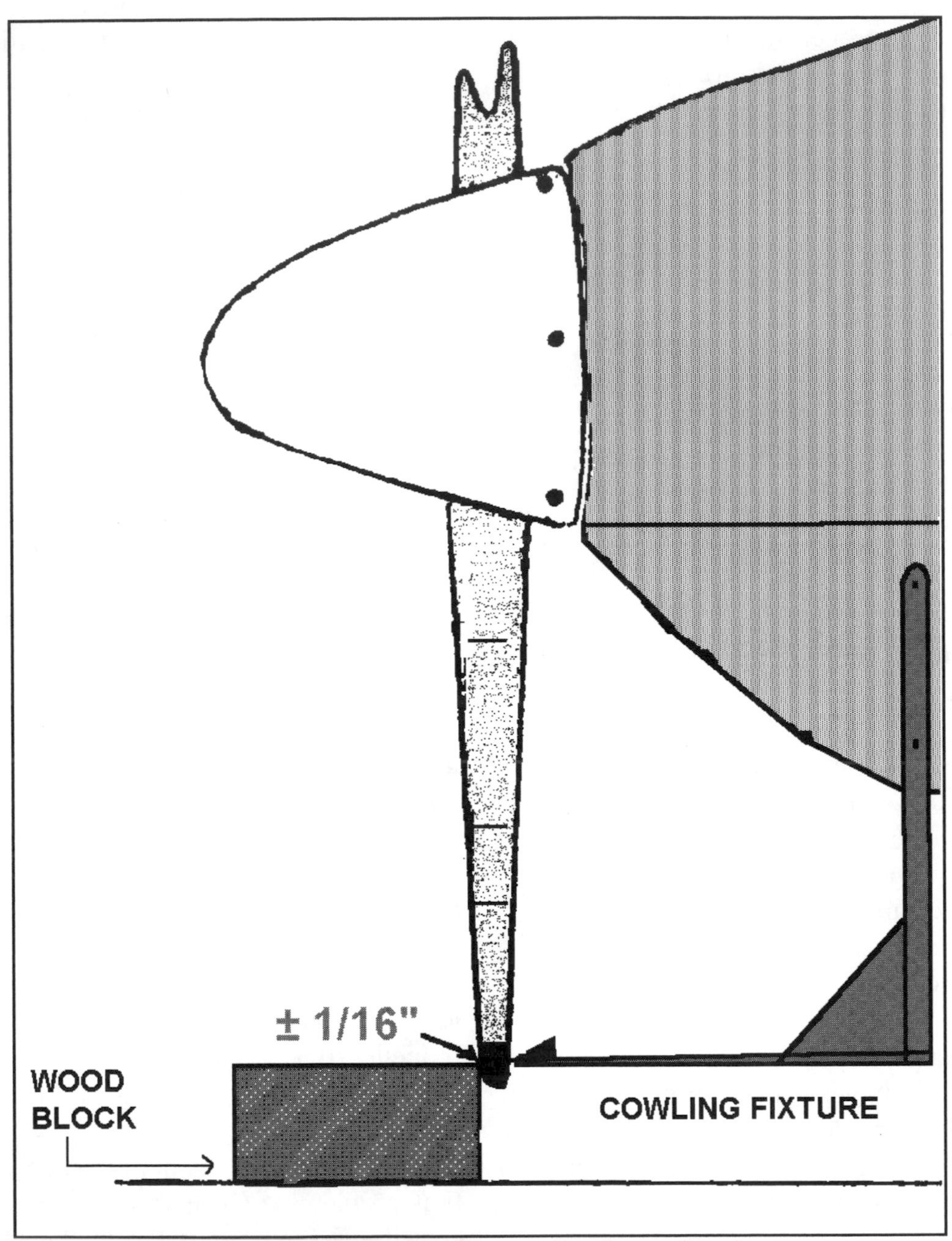

FIGURE 8-30. Propeller tracking (wood block or cowling fixture shown).

8-110.—8-129. [RESERVED.]

CHAPTER 9. AIRCRAFT SYSTEMS AND COMPONENTS

SECTION 1. INSPECTION AND MAINTENANCE OF LANDING GEAR

9-1. GENERAL.

a. The landing gear on aircraft may be fixed or retractable. A fixed gear may be wheels, floats, or skis; and for amphibians a combination of floats and wheels.

b. Retractable gear on aircraft is usually operated with hydraulic or electric power, although some models of light general aviation aircraft have manual retract systems operated by a lever in the cockpit.

(1) In addition to the normal operating system, emergency systems are usually provided to ensure that the landing gear can be lowered in case of main-system failure.

(2) Emergency systems consist of backup hydraulic systems, or stored nitrogen gas bottles that can be directed into actuating cylinders, mechanical systems that can be operated manually, or free-fall gravity systems.

9-2. GENERAL INSPECTION. A thorough inspection of the landing gear involves the entire structure of the gear, including attachments, struts, wheels, brakes, actuating mechanisms for retractable gears, gear hydraulic system and valves, gear doors, and all associated parts. The manufacturer's inspection procedures should be followed where applicable.

9-3. CLEANING AND LUBRICATING. It is recommended that only easily removable neutral solutions be used when cleaning landing gear components. Any advantage, such as speed or effectiveness, gained by using cleaners containing corrosive materials, can be quickly counteracted if these materials become trapped in close-fitting surfaces and crevices. Wear points, such as landing gear up-and-down latches, jack-screws, door hinges, pulleys, cables, bellcranks, and all pressure-type grease fittings, should be lubricated after every cleaning operation.

To prevent possible failure of a component due to incompatibility or breakdown of the grease, the following should be observed:

1. Use only greases approved for use by the product manufacturer.
2. Never mix different kinds of grease without approval from the product manufacturer.
3. Follow the manufacturer's instructions or FAA approved process for cleaning, purging, and lubricating of the component.

To obtain proper lubrication of the main support bushings, it may be necessary to jack the aircraft.

NOTE: Any time the aircraft is on jacks, check the landing gear main support bushings for wear. Consult the aircraft manufacturer's overhaul manual for specific wear tolerances.

During winter operation, excess grease may congeal and cause increased loads on the gear retraction system, electric motors, and hydraulic pumps. This condition can lead to component malfunctions; therefore, it is recommended that cleanliness be stressed during and after lubrication.

9-4. FIXED-GEAR INSPECTION. Fixed landing gear should be examined regularly for wear, deterioration, corrosion, alignment, and other factors that may cause failure or unsatisfactory operation. During a 100-hour or annual inspection of the fixed gear, the aircraft should be jacked up to relieve the aircraft weight. The gear struts and wheels should be checked for abnormal play and corrected.

a. Old aircraft landing gear that employs a rubber shock (bungee) cord for shock absorption must be inspected for age, fraying of the braided sheath, narrowing (necking) of the cord, and wear at points of contact with the structure and stretch. If the age of the shock cord is near 5 years or more, it is advisable to replace it with a new cord. A cord that shows other defects should be replaced, regardless of age.

b. The cord is color-coded to indicate when it was manufactured and to determine the life of the shock cord. According to MIL-C-5651A, the color code for the year of manufacture is repeated in cycles of 5 years. Table 9-1 shows the color of the code thread for each year and quarter year.

TABLE 9-1. Bungee cord color codes.

YEARS ENDING WITH	COLOR	QUARTER	COLOR
0 or 5	Black	1st	Red
1 or 6	Green	2nd	Blue
2 or 7	Red	3rd	Green
3 or 8	Blue	4th	Yellow
4 or 9	Yellow	1st	Red

c. The color coding is composed of threads interwoven in the cotton sheath that holds the strands of rubber cord together. Two spiral threads are used for the year coding and one thread is used for the quarter of the year sheath, e.g. yellow and blue would indicate that the cord was manufactured in 1994 during April, May, or June.

d. Shock struts of the spring-oleo type should be examined for leakage, smoothness of operation, looseness between the moving parts, and play at the attaching points. The extension of the struts should be checked to make sure that the springs are not worn or broken. The piston section of the strut should be free of nicks, cuts, and rust.

e. Air-oil struts should undergo an inspection similar to that recommended for spring-oleo struts. In addition, the extension of the strut should be checked to see that it conforms to the distance specified by the manufacturer. If an air-oil strut "bottoms"–that is, it is collapsed–the gas charge and hydraulic fluid has been lost from the air chamber. This is probably due to a loose or defective air valve or to defective O-ring seals.

CAUTION: Before an air-oil strut is removed or disassembled, the air valve should be opened to make sure that all air pressure is removed. Severe injury and/or damage can occur as the result of disassembling a strut when even a small amount of air pressure is still in the air chamber.

f. The method for checking the fluid level of an air-oil strut is given in the manufacturer's maintenance manual. An alternate means of servicing an oil strut is to jack up the aircraft, remove the strut's valve cap, release the air charge in the strut by depressing the valve core, remove the strut's valve core, attach a clean two-foot rubber or plastic hose to the threaded portion that houses the valve core, and secure with a hose clamp. Put the other end of the hose into a clean two quart container filled with the correct hydraulic fluid for the strut. Cover the container with a clean rag to prevent spillage. Now, slowly raise the gear/strut assembly either manually or with another jack under the strut. This will drive the remaining air out of the strut into the container of hydraulic fluid. Once the gear is fully retracted, slowly lower the gear. The hydraulic fluid in the can will be sucked into the strut. Repeat this procedure until you cannot hear any more air bubbles in the container when the wheel strut is fully retracted. With the strut fully retracted, remove the hose, insert the valve core, lower the gear, and service the strut with nitrogen to get the proper strut extension.

g. The entire structure of the landing gear should be closely examined for cracks, nicks, cuts, corrosion damage, or any other condition that can cause stress concentrations and eventual failure. The exposed lower end of the air-oleo piston is especially susceptible to damage and corrosion, which can lead to seal damage, because the strut is compressed and the piston moves past the strut lower seal, causing the seal to leak fluid and air. Small nicks or cuts can be filed and burnished to a smooth contour, eliminating the point of stress concentration. If a crack is found in a landing-gear member, the part must be replaced.

h. All bolts and fittings should be checked for security and condition. Bolts in the torque links and shimmy damper tend to wear and become loose due to the operational loads placed on them. The nose-wheel shimmy damper should be checked for proper operation and any evidence of leaking. All required servicing should be performed in accordance with the aircraft service manual.

9-5. INSPECTION OF RETRACTABLE LANDING GEAR. Inspection of the retractable landing gear should include all applicable items mentioned in the inspection for the fixed gear. In addition, the actuating mechanisms must be inspected for wear looseness in any joint, trunnion, or bearing; leakage of fluid from any hydraulic line or unit; and, smoothness of operation. The operational check is performed by jacking the aircraft according to the manufacturer's instructions and then operating the gear retracting and extending system.

a. During the operational test, the smoothness of operation, effectiveness of up-and-down locks, operation of the warning horn, operation of indicating systems, clearance of tires in wheel wells, and operation of landing-gear doors should be checked. Improper adjustment of sequence valves may cause doors to rub against gear structures or wheels. The manufacturer's checklist should be followed to ensure that critical items are checked. While the aircraft is still on jacks, the gear can be tested for looseness of mounting points, play in torque links, condition of the inner strut cylinder, play in wheel bearings, and play in actuating linkages. Emergency blow down gear bottles should be inspected for damage and corrosion and weighed to see if the bottle is still retaining the charge.

b. Mechanics should be aware that retread tires can be dimensionally bigger than a "new" tire. While this does not pose a problem on fixed landing gear aircraft, it may present a serious problem when installed on retractable landing gear aircraft. It is strongly recommended that if a retread tire is installed on a retractable landing gear aircraft, a retraction test be performed. With the gear in the up-and-lock position, the mechanic should determine that if the tire expands due to high ambient temperature, heat generated from taxi and take-off, repeated landings, or heavy braking, the tire will not expand to the point that it becomes wedged in the wheel well.

c. The proper operation of the anti-retraction system should be checked in accordance with the manufacturer's instructions. Where safety switches are actuated by the torque links, the actual time of switch closing or opening can be checked by removing all air from the strut and then collapsing the strut. In every case, the adjustment should be such that the gear control cannot be placed in the UP position or that the system cannot operate until the shock strut is at the full extended position.

9-6. EMERGENCY SYSTEMS. Exercise emergency landing gear systems periodically to ensure proper operation and to prevent inactivity, dirt, and corrosion from rendering the system inoperative when needed. Most emergency systems employ either mechanical, pressure-bottle, or free-fall extension capabilities. Check for the proper safeties on triggering mechanisms, and for the presence of required placards, and necessary accessories such as cranks, levers, handles, etc. Emergency blow-down bottles should be checked for corrosion damage, and then weighed to see if the bottle is still retaining the charge.

9-7. LANDING GEAR COMPONENTS. The following items are susceptible to service difficulties and should be inspected.

a. Shock Absorbers. Inspect the entire shock-strut for evidence of leaks, cracks, and possible bottoming of the piston, as this condition causes overloading of landing-gear components and contributes to fatigue cracks. Check all bolts, bolt holes, pins, and bushings for condition, lubrication, and proper torque values. Grease fitting holes (pressure-type) are especially vulnerable to cracks and cross-threading damage. Check all safety wire and other locking devices, especially at the main packing gland nuts.

(1) When assembling shock-struts, use the correct type and number of new "O"-rings, Chevron seals, and backup rings. Use only the correct filler valve core assembly, and follow the manufacturer's instructions when servicing with fluid and air. Either too much or too little air or oil will affect aircraft handling characteristics during taxi, takeoff, and landing, and can cause structural overloads.

(2) Shock cords and rubber discs deteriorate with age and exposure. When this type of shock absorber is used, inspect for general condition; i.e., cleanliness, stretching, fraying, and broken strands. These components should be kept free of petroleum products as they accelerate deterioration of the rubber.

b. Nose Gear Assembly. Inspection of the steering mechanism should include torque-links (scissors), torque-tubes, control rods and rod-end bearings, shimmy dampers, cables, and turning stops. In addition, check all nose landing gear components, including mud scrapers and slush deflectors, for damage.

(1) Towing of some aircraft with the rudder locks installed, may cause damage to the steering linkage and rudder control system. Exceeding the steering or towing stop limits should be followed by a close inspection of the entire nose steering assembly. A broken steering stop will allow turning beyond the design limit, transmitting excessive loads to structures, and to the rudder control system. It is recommended that the nose steering arc limits be painted on the steering collar or fuselage.

(2) Inspect shimmy dampers for leakage around the piston shaft and at fluid line connections, and for abnormal wear or looseness around the pivot points. Also check for proper rigging, "bottoming" of the piston in the cylinder, and the condition of the external stops on the steering collar.

c. Tail Wheels. Disassembly, cleaning, and re-rigging of tail wheels are periodically necessary. Inspect them for loose or broken bolts, broken springs, lack of lubrication, and general condition. Check steerable tail wheels for proper steering action, steering-horn wear, clearances, and for security and condition of steering springs and cables.

d. Gear Doors. Inspect gear doors frequently for cracks, deformation, proper rigging, and general condition. Gear door hinges are especially susceptible to progressive cracking, which can ultimately result in complete failure, allowing the door to move and cause possible jamming of the gear. This condition could also result in the loss of the door during flight. In addition, check for proper safetying of the hinge pins and for distorted, sheared, loose, or cracked hinge rivets. Inspect the wheel wells for improper location or routing of components and related tubing or wiring. This could interfere with the travel of the gear door actuating mechanisms.

e. Wheels. Inspect the wheels periodically for cracks, corrosion, dents, distortion, and faulty bearings in accordance with the manufacturer's service information. In split-type wheels, recondition bolt holes which have become elongated due to some play in the through-bolt, by the use of inserts or other FAA-approved means. Pay particular attention to the condition of the through-bolts and nuts. Carefully inspect the wheels used with tubeless tires for damage to the wheel flange and for proper sealing of the valve. The sealing ring used between the wheel halves should be free of damage and deformation. When bolting wheel halves together, tighten the nuts to the proper torque value. Periodically accomplish an inspection to ensure the nuts are tight and that there is no movement between the two halves of the wheel. Maintain grease retaining felts in the wheel assembly in a soft, absorbent condition. If any have become hardened, wash them with a petroleum-base cleaning agent; if this fails to soften them, they should be replaced.

(1) Corrosion of wheels. Remove all corrosion from the wheel half, and inspect it to ensure that the wheel halves are serviceable. Apply corrosion prevention treatments as applicable. Prime with a zinc chromate primer or equivalent, and apply at least two finish coats.

(2) Dented or distorted wheels. Replace wheels which wobble excessively due to deformation resulting from a severe side-load impact. In questionable cases, consult the local representative of the FAA concerning the airworthiness of the wheels. Minor dents do not affect the serviceability of a wheel.

(3) Wheel bearings. When inspecting wheel bearings for condition, replace damaged or excessively worn parts. Maintain bearings and races as matched sets. Pack bearings only with the grease type called for in the manufacturer's maintenance manual prior to their installation. Avoid pre-loading the wheel bearing when installing it on the aircraft by tightening the axle nut just enough to prevent wheel drag or side play.

f. Brakes. Disassemble and inspect the brakes periodically and examine the parts for wear, cracks, warpage, corrosion, elongated holes, etc. Discolored brake disks are an indication of overheated brakes and should be replaced. If any of these or other faults are indicated, repair, recondition, or replace the affected parts in accordance with the manufacturer's recommendations.

g. Hydraulic Brakes. For proper maintenance, periodically inspect the entire hydraulic system from the reservoir to the brakes. Maintain the fluid at the recommended level with proper brake fluid. When air is present in the brake system, bleed in accordance with the manufacturer's instructions. Replace flexible hydraulic hoses which have deteriorated due to long periods of service and replace hydraulic piston seals when there is evidence of leakage.

h. Micro-Switches. Inspect micro-switches for security of attachment, cleanliness, general condition, and proper operation. Check the associated wiring for chafing, proper routing, and to determine that protective covers are installed on wiring terminals, if required. Check the condition of the rubber dust boots which protect the micro-switch plungers from dirt and corrosion.

9-8. FLOATS AND SKIS. Aircraft operated from water may be provided with either a single float or a double float, depending upon the design and construction; however, if an aircraft is an amphibian, it has a hull for flotation and then may need only wingtip floats.

Amphibious aircraft have floats or a hull for operating on water and retractable wheels for land operation.

a. Skis are used for operating on snow and ice. The skis may be made of wood, metal, or composite materials. There are three basic styles of skis. A conventional ski, shown in figure 9-1, replaces the wheel on the axle. The shock cord is used to hold the toe of the ski up when landing. The safety cable and check cable prevent the ski from pivoting through too great an angle during flight.

b. The wheel ski is designed to mount on the aircraft along with the tire. The ski has a portion cut out that allows the tire to extend slightly below the ski, so that the aircraft can be operated from conventional runways with the wheels or from snow or ice surfaces using the ski. This arrangement has a small wheel mounted on the heel of the ski, so that it does not drag on conventional runways.

c. In retractable wheel-ski arrangements, the ski is mounted on a common axle with the wheel. In this arrangement, the ski can be extended below the level of the wheel for landing on snow or ice. The ski can be retracted above the bottom of the wheel for operations from conventional runways. A hydraulic system is commonly used for the retraction-system operation.

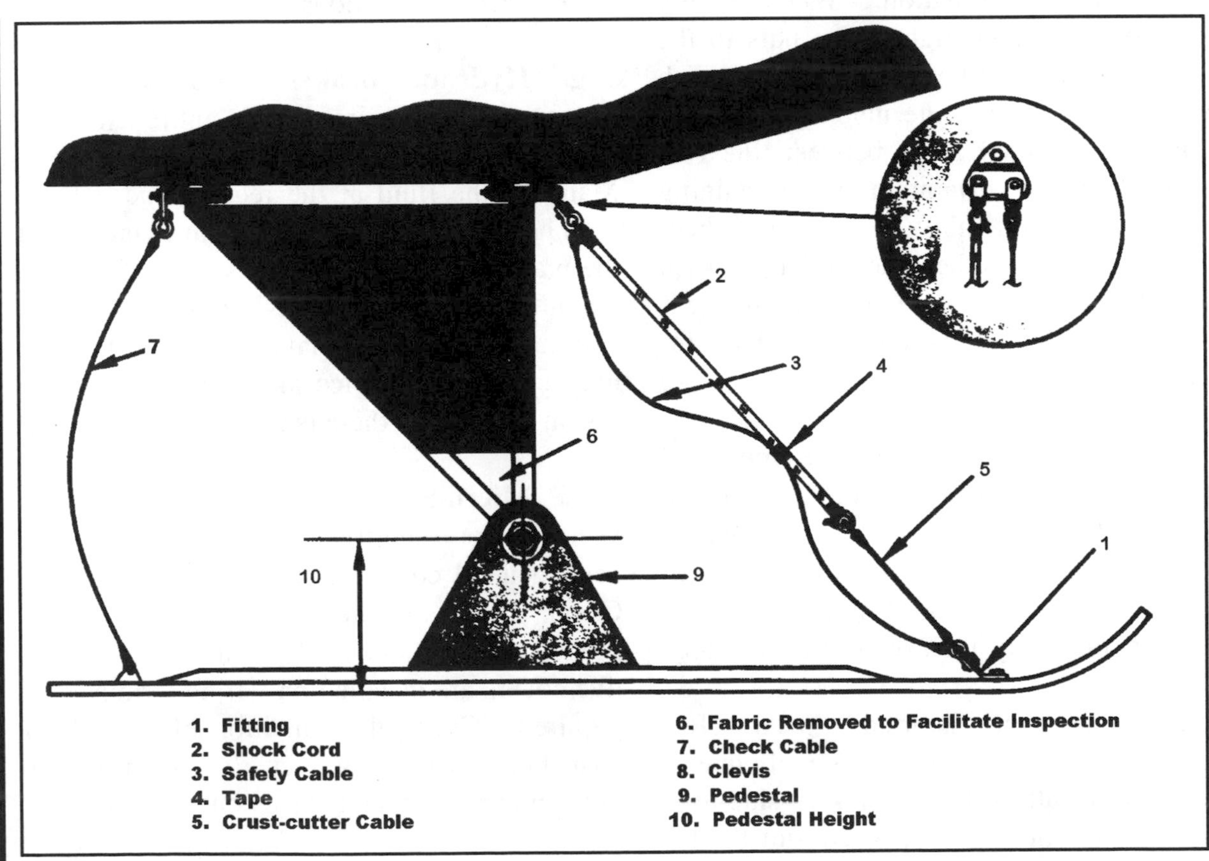

FIGURE 9-1. A typical ski installation.

9-9. INSPECTION AND REPAIR OF FLOATS AND SKIS. Inspection of floats and skis involves examination for damage due to corrosion, collision with other objects, hard landings, and other conditions that may lead to failure. Tubular structures for such gear may be repaired as described in the section covering welded repairs of tubular structures.

a. Floats. To maintain the float in an airworthy condition, periodic and frequent inspections should be made because of the rapidity of corrosion on metal parts, particularly when the aircraft is operated in salt water. Examine metal floats and all metal parts on wooden or fiberglass floats for corrosion, and take corrective action in accordance with the procedures described in Chapter 6, Corrosion, Inspection & Protection. Chapter 4, Metal Structure, Welding, and Brazing, outlines methods for repairing damage to metal floats of aluminum and aluminum alloy structures.

Note: Blind rivets should not be used on floats or amphibian hulls below the water line.

In the case of wooden floats, make repairs in accordance with general procedures outlined in Chapter 1, Wood Structure. Repair fiberglass floats in accordance with the manufacturer's instructions.

(1) If small blisters are noticed on the paint, either inside or outside the float, the paint should be removed and the area examined. If corrosion is found, the area should be cleaned thoroughly, and a coat of corrosion-inhibiting material applied. If the corrosion penetrates the metal to an appreciable depth, replace the metal. Special attention should be given to brace wire fittings and water rudder-control systems.

(2) If the hull or floats have retractable landing gear, a retraction check should be performed along with the other recommendations mentioned for retractable landing-gear systems. Sheet-metal floats should be repaired using approved practices; however, the seams between sections of sheet metal should be waterproofed with suitable fabric and sealing compound. A float that has undergone hull repairs should be tested by filling it with water and allowing it to stand for at least 24 hours to see if any leaks develop.

b. Skis and Ski Installation. Skis should be inspected for general condition of the skis, cables, bungees, and fuselage attachments. If retractable skis are used, checks in accordance with the general practices for retractable gear should be followed. Ski manufacturers usually furnish acceptable repair procedures. It is advisable to examine ski installations frequently to keep them maintained in airworthy condition. If shock cord is used to keep the ski runner in proper trim, periodically examine to ensure that the cord has enough elasticity to keep the runner in its required attitude and the cord is not becoming loose or badly frayed. Replace old or weak shock cords. When other means of restraint are provided, examine for excessive wear and binding, and replace or repair as required. Examine the points of cable attachment, both on the ski and the aircraft structure, for bent lugs due to excessive loads that have been imposed while taxiing over rugged terrain or by trying to break loose frozen skis. If skis that permit attachment to the wheels and tires are used, maintain proper tire pressure as under-inflated tires may push off the wheels if appreciable side loads are developed in landing or taxiing.

c. Repair of Ski Runners. Repair limits are found in the applicable manufacturer's manual. Fractured wooden ski runners usually require replacement. If a split at the rear end of the runner does not exceed 10 percent of the ski length, it may be repaired by attaching one or more wooden crosspieces across the top of the runner using glue and bolts. Bent or torn metal runners may be straightened if minor bending has taken place and minor tears may be repaired in accordance with procedures recommended in Chapter 4, Metal Structure, Welding, and Brazing.

d. Ski Pedestals.

(1) Tubular Pedestals. Damaged pedestals made of steel tubing may be repaired by using tube splices as shown in the chapter on welding.

(2) Cast Pedestals. Consult a Federal Aviation Administration (FAA) representative on the repair of cast pedestals.

9-10. TYPES OF LANDING GEAR PROBLEMS. During inspection and before removing any accumulated dirt, closely observe the area being inspected while the wingtips are gently rocked up and down. Excessive motion between normally close-fitting landing gear components may indicate wear, cracks, or improper adjustment. If a crack exists, it will generally be indicated by dirt or metallic particles which tend to outline the fault. Seepage of rust inhibiting oils, used to coat internal surfaces of steel tubes, also assists in the early detection of cracks. In addition, a sooty, oily residue around bolts, rivets, and pins is a good indication of looseness or wear.

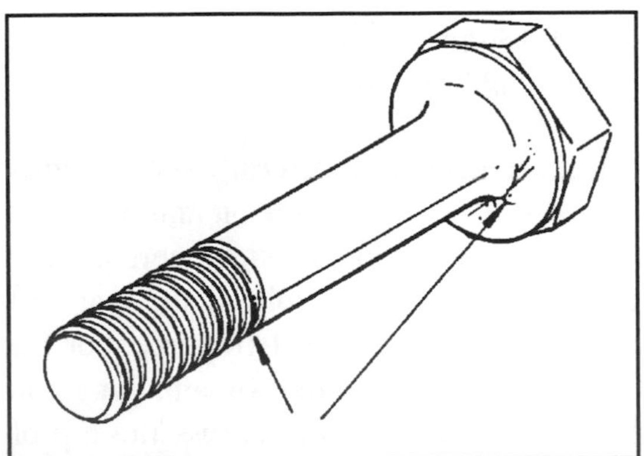

FIGURE 9-2. Typical bolt cracks.

a. Thoroughly clean and re-inspect the landing gear to determine the extent of any damage or wear. Some components may require removal and complete disassembly for detailed inspection. Others may require a specific check using an inspection process such as dye penetrant, magnetic particle, radiographic, ultrasonic, or eddy current. The frequency, degree of thoroughness, and selection of inspection methods are dependent upon the age, use, and general condition of the landing gear.

b. Inspect the aircraft or landing gear structure surrounding any visible damage to ensure that no secondary damage remains undetected. Forces can be transmitted along the affected member to remote areas where subsequent normal loads can cause failure at a later date.

c. Prime locations for cracks on any landing gear are bolts, bolt holes, pins, rivets, and welds. The following are typical locations where cracks may develop.

d. Most susceptible areas for bolts are at the radius between the head and the shank, and in the location where the threads join the shank, as shown in figure 9-2.

e. Cracks primarily occur at the edge of bolt holes on the surface and down inside the bore. (See figures 9-3 and 9-4.)

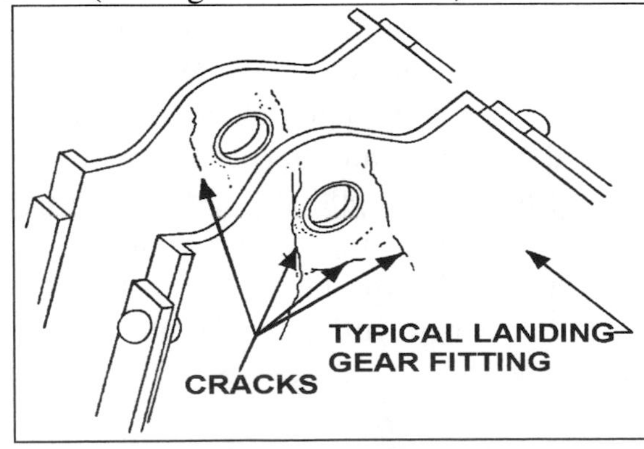

FIGURE 9-3. Typical cracks near bolt holes.

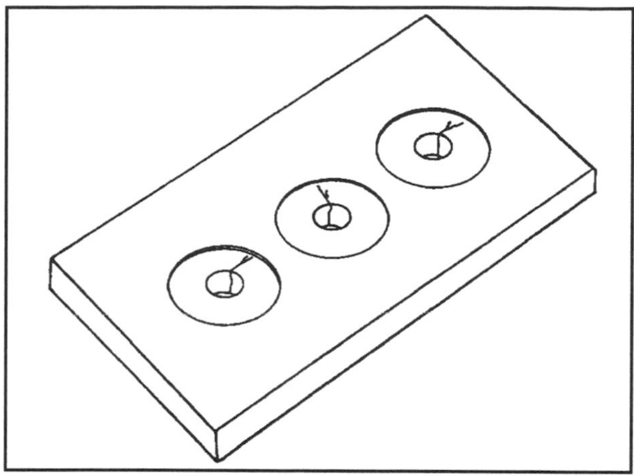

FIGURE 9-4. Typical bolt hole cracks.

f. The usual types of failure in riveted joints or seams are deformation of the rivet heads and skin cracks originating at the rivets' holes.

g. Cracks and subsequent failures of rod ends usually begin at the thread end near the bearing and adjacent to or under the jam nut. (See figure 9-5.)

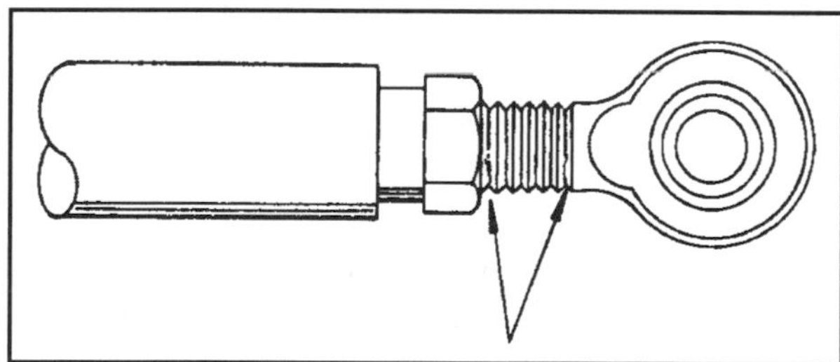

FIGURE 9-5. Typical rod-end cracks.

h. Cracks develop primarily along the edge of the weld adjacent to the base metal and along the centerline of the bead.

i. Elongated holes are especially prevalent in taper-pin holes and bolt holes or at the riveted joints of torque tubes and push-pull rods. (See figure 9-6.)

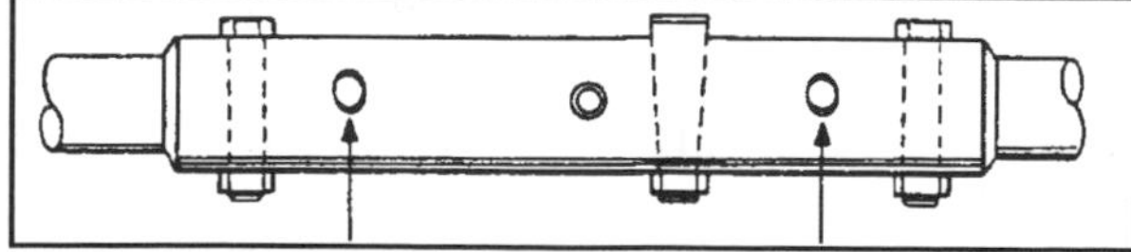

FIGURE 9-6. Typical torque tube bolt hole elongation.

j. Deformation is common in rods and tubes and usually is noticeable as stretched, bulged, or bent sections. Because deformations of this type are difficult to see, feel along the tube for evidence of this discrepancy. Deformation of sheet-metal web sections, at landing-gear component attachment points, usually can be seen when the area is highlighted with oblique lighting.

9-11. SPECIAL INSPECTIONS. When an aircraft experiences a hard or overweight landing, the mechanic should perform a special structural inspection of the aircraft, including the landing gear. Landing gear support trusses should be inspected for cracked welds, sheared bolts and rivets, and buckled structures. Wheels and tires should be inspected for cracks and cuts, and upper and lower wing surfaces should be inspected for wrinkles, deformation, and loose or sheared rivets. If any damage is found, a detailed inspection is recommended.

9-12. RETRACTION TESTS. Periodically perform a complete operational check of the landing gear retraction system. Inspect the normal extension and retraction system, the emergency extension system, and the indicating and emergency warning system. Determine that the actuating cylinders, linkage, slide tubes, sprockets, chain or drive gears, gear doors, and the up-and-down locks are in good condition and properly adjusted and lubricated, and the wheels have adequate clearance in the wheel wells. In addition, an electrical continuity check of micro-switches and associated wiring is recommended. Only qualified personnel should attempt adjustments to the gear position and warning system micro-switches. Follow the manufacturer's recommendations.

9-13. TIRE AND TUBE MAINTENANCE. A program of tire maintenance can minimize tire failures and increase tire service life.

a. Correct balance is important since a heavy spot on an aircraft tire, tube, or wheel assembly is likely to cause that heavy spot to hit the ground first when landing. This results in excessive wear at one spot and an early failure at that part of the tire. A severe case of imbalance causes excessive vibration during take-off and landing, especially at high speed.

b. A protective cover should be placed over a tire while servicing units that might drip fluid on the tire.

9-14. TIRE INSPECTION AND REPAIR. Tires should be inspected frequently for cuts, worn spots, bulges on the side walls, foreign bodies in the treads, and tread condition. Defective or worn tires may be repaired or retreaded. The term, retread, refers to several means of restoring a used tire, whether by applying a new tread alone or tread and side wall material in varying amounts. The following guidelines should be used for tire inspection:

a. Tread Wear. Inspect the tires visually for remaining tread. Tires should be removed when tread has worn to the base of any groove at any spot, or to a minimum depth as specified by the tire or aircraft manufacturer. Tires worn to fabric in the tread area should be removed regardless of the amount of tread remaining.

b. Uneven Wear. If tread wear is excessive on one side, the tire can be dismounted and turned around, providing there is no exposed fabric. Gear misalignment causing this condition should be corrected.

WARNING: Do not probe cuts or embedded foreign objects while tire is inflated.

c. Tread Cuts. Inspect tread for cuts and other foreign object damage, and mark with crayon or chalk. Remove tires that have the following:

(1) Any cuts into the carcass ply.

(2) Cuts extending more than half of the width of a rib and deeper than 50 percent of the remaining groove depth.

(3) Weather checking, cracking, cuts, and snags extending down to the carcass ply in the sidewall and bead areas.

(4) Bulges in any part of tire tread, sidewall, or bead areas that indicate a separation or damaged tire.

(5) Cracking in a groove that exposes fabric or if cracking undercuts tread ribs.

d. Flat Spots. Generally speaking, tires need not be removed because of flat spots due to skid or hydroplane burns unless fabric is exposed. If objectionable unbalance results, remove the tire from service.

e. Beads. Inspect bead areas next to wheel flanges for damage due to excessive heat, especially if brake drag or severe braking has been reported during taxi, takeoff or landing.

f. Tire Clearance. Look for marks on tires, the gear, and in the wheel wells that might indicate rubbing due to inadequate clearance.

g. Surface Condition. The surface condition of a tire can be inspected with the tire on the aircraft. The tread should be checked for abnormal wear. If the tread is worn in the center of the tire but not on the edges, this indicates that the tire is over-inflated and the operational air pressure should be reduced. On the other hand, a tire worn on the edges, but not in the center, indicates under-inflation. These indications are shown in figure 9-7.

9-15. INFLATION OF TIRES. There is serious danger involved with inflating and tire assembly. The tire should not be inflated beyond the recommended pressure (when it is not being installed in a safety cage). Over-inflation can cause damage to the aircraft, as well as personal injury. Under-inflation will cause excessive tire wear and imbalance. The airframe manufacturer's load and pressure chart should be consulted before inflating tires. Sufficiently inflate the tires to seat the tire beads; then deflate them to allow the tube to assume its position. Inflate to the recommended pressure with the tire in a horizontal position.

Tire check of storage aircraft should be done in accordance with the applicable aircraft storage manual.

9-16. PERSONAL SAFETY. When servicing aircraft tires, personnel should stand either in the front or rear of the wheel and avoid approaching from either side of the tire. See illustration below:

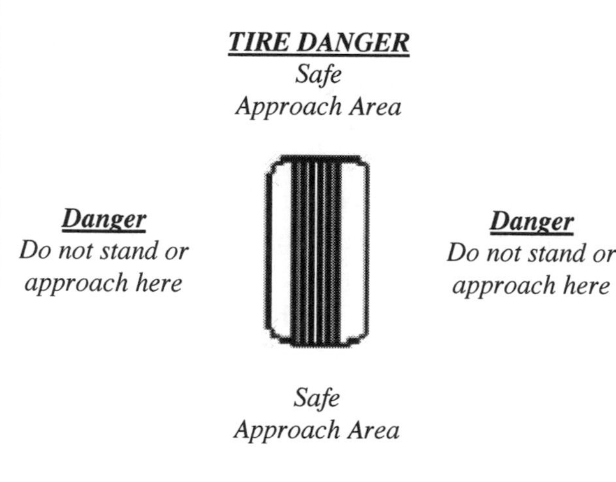

Personnel should wear protective eye gear to reduce the risk of eye injury due to inflation and deflation of tires.

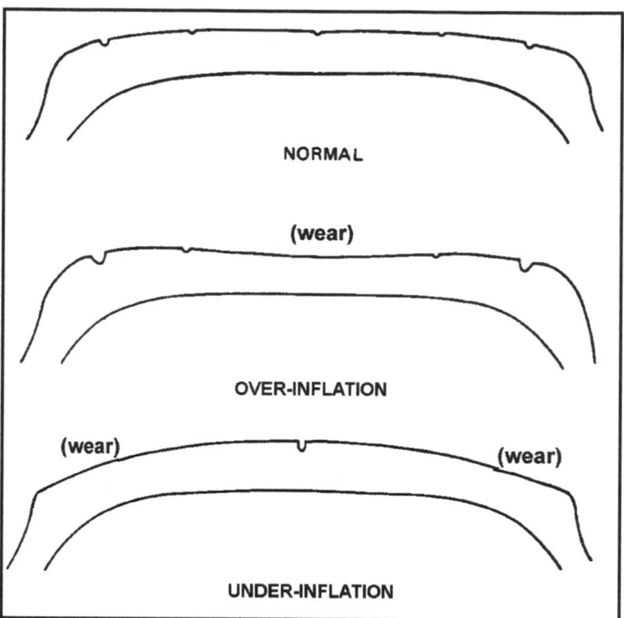

FIGURE 9-7. Examples of tread wear indicating over-inflation and under-inflation.

NOTE: The use of nitrogen to inflate tires is recommended. Do not use oxygen to inflate tires. Deflate tires prior to removing them from the aircraft or when built-up tire assemblies are being shipped.

9-17. DISASSEMBLE THE WHEEL in accordance with aircraft manufacturer's instructions.

Do not attempt to disassemble wheel until the tire has been completely deflated: otherwise serious injury or damage to equipment can result.

Do not attempt to remove valve core until tire has been completely deflated. Valve cores will eject at high velocity if unscrewed before air pressure has been released.

Never attempt to remove wheel bolts or break tire beads loose until tire has been completely deflated: otherwise, explosive separation of wheel components will result.

Do not pry between wheel flanges and tire beads as this can damage the wheel and tire.

Use caution when removing wheel bolts or nuts.

Remove tire from wheel using a wheel demounting fixture.

Valve stem, fusible plugs, wheel keys, heat shields, balance weights, and associated hardware should not be removed if demountable flange only is to be removed for tire change.

Fusible plugs and bearing cups should not be removed unless replacement is necessary, if paint is to be stripped, or if a thorough inspection of the wheel is to be made.

When removal and replacement of fusible plugs is required, remove by pressing out with a blunt instrument such as a wooden rod. Exercise caution to ensure wheel sealing surfaces are not damaged.

9-18. REASSEMBLING THE WHEEL. The correct assembly of the wheel affects the balance of the tire. After the wheel halves and bolts/nuts have been inspected and found serviceable, put a little talc on the tube and insert it in the tire. Align the heavy spot of the tube (usually marked with a yellow line) with the light spot of the tire (usually marked with a red dot). If the tube does not have a balance mark, align the valve of the tube with the balance mark on the line. Remove the valve core and inflate the tube momentarily to "seat" the tube and let the air run out. Put one wheel half in the tire and align the wheel half with the valve hole up with the valve on the tube. Insert the other wheel half in the tire and align the bolt holes. Insert the wheel bolts and torque to the manufacturer's recommended value.

NOTE: It is highly recommended that the tire be placed in a cage so that if the wheel fails, the mechanic is protected from injury.

Again inflate the tube with 5 or 10 psi and let the air out to re-seat the tube. Install the valve core, and fill the tire to the recommended pressure.

9-19. SLIPPAGE. To reduce the possibility of tire and tube failure due to slippage, and to provide a means of detecting tire slippage, tires should be marked and indexed with the wheel rim. Paint a mark one inch wide and two inches long across the tire side wall and wheel rim. Use a permanent type paint in a contrasting color, such as white, red, or orange. Pre-flight inspection must include a check of slippage marks for alignment. If the slippage marks are not in alignment, a detailed inspection must be made, the reason determined, and if necessary, the condition corrected before the next flight.

NOTE: Mechanics should be aware that retread tires can be diametrically bigger than a "new" tire. While this does not pose a problem on fixed landing gear aircraft, it may pose a problem on retractable gear aircraft. Due to a 5 to 8 percent expansion of the tire caused by the ambient temperature, if a retread tire is installed on a retractable gear aircraft, it is strongly recommended that a retraction test be performed. This is to ensure the tire will not become wedged in the wheel well during take-off and landing operation.

9-20. WHEEL INSPECTION. Check wheels for damage. Wheels that are cracked or damaged must be taken out of service for repair or replacement in accordance with the manufacturer's instruction manual.

9-21. WHEEL INSTALLATION. Various procedures are used for installing wheel assemblies on an aircraft.

a. The axle should first be cleaned and inspected for surface damage, damage to the axle threads, and the general condition and security of bolts holding the axle onto the landing-gear leg. The wheel bearings should be cleaned and packed with approved grease. The wheel bearing and tire must be inspected and assembled. Many aircraft have specific torque requirements for the wheel-retaining nuts. These torque requirements may have two values specified. The retaining nut is first tightened to the higher value to seat the bearing. It is then backed off and tightened to the lower value specified. While tightening the wheel retaining nuts, the wheel should be rotated.

b. Great care should be exercised to see that the wheel-retaining nuts are not over-tightened. In the absence of specific instructions, the wheel-retaining nut is tightened until bearing drag is felt. The nut is then backed off about one serration (castellation) or one-sixth turn before bending up the tab on the tab-lock washer or installing the cotter pin.

c. The grease cover or wheel cover, if used, is then installed. During this installation any required brake, air-pressure sensors, and speed-sensor components should be installed and connected, as appropriate, for the specific aircraft.

9-22.—9.24. [RESERVED.]

SECTION 2. HYDRAULIC SYSTEMS

9-25. GENERAL. Hydraulic systems in aircraft provide a means for the operation of aircraft components. The operation of landing gear, flaps, flight control surfaces and brakes is largely accomplished with hydraulic power systems. Hydraulic system complexity varies from small aircraft that require fluid only for manual operation of the wheel brakes to large transport aircraft where the systems are large and complex. To achieve the necessary redundancy and reliability, the system may consist of several subsystems. Each subsystem has a power generating device (pump) reservoir, accumulator, heat exchanger, filtering system, etc. System operating pressure may vary from a couple hundred psi in small aircraft and rotorcraft to several thousand psi in large transports. Generally, the larger the aircraft, the more mechanical work is required to control the aircraft's various functions. Consequently, the system operating pressure increases accordingly. Primarily, hydraulic power is generated by either engine driven or electric motor driven pumps. The majority of hydraulic pumps are pressure compensated to provide a constant output pressure at a flow-rate demanded by the system. Some constant displacement pumps with a relief valve are used on the smaller aircraft.

9-26. PURPOSES OF HYDRAULIC SYSTEMS. Hydraulic systems make possible the transmission of pressure and energy at the best weight per horsepower ratio.

9-27. TYPES OF HYDRAULIC FLUID. There are three principal categories of hydraulic fluids; mineral base fluids, polyalphaolefin base, and phosphate ester base fluids. When servicing a hydraulic system, the technician must be certain to use the correct category of replacement fluid. Hydraulic fluids are not necessarily compatible. For example, contamination of the fire-resistant fluid MIL-H-83282 with MIL-H-5606 may render the MIL-H-83282 non fire-resistant.

a. Mineral-Base Fluids. MIL-H-5606, mineral oil-based hydraulic fluid is the oldest, dating back to the 1940's. It is used in many systems, especially where the fire hazard is comparatively low. MIL-H-6083 is simply a rust-inhibited version of MIL-H-5606. They are completely interchangeable. Suppliers generally ship hydraulic components with MIL-H-6083.

b. Polyalphaolefin-Based Fluids. MIL-H-83282, is a fire-resistant hydrogenated polyalphaolefin-based fluid developed in the 1960's to overcome the flammability characteristics of MIL-H-5606. MIL-H-83282 is significantly more flame resistant than MIL-H-5606, but a disadvantage is the high viscosity at low temperature. It is generally limited to -40 ▪F. However, it can be used in the same system and with the same seals, gaskets, and hoses as MIL-H-5606. MIL-H-46170 is the rust-inhibited version of MIL-H-83282. Small aircraft predominantly use MIL-H-5606 but some have switched to MIL-H-83282, if they can accommodate the high viscosity at low temperature.

c. Phosphate Ester-Based Fluid (Skydrol/Hyjet). These fluids are used in most commercial transport category aircraft, and are extremely fire-resistant. However, they are not fireproof and under certain conditions, they will burn. The earliest generation of these fluids was developed after World War II as a result of the growing number of aircraft hydraulic brake fires which drew the collective concern of the commercial aviation industry.

(1) Progressive development of these fluids occurred as a result of performance requirements of newer aircraft designs. The airframe manufacturers dubbed these new generations of hydraulic fluid as "types" based on their performance. Today, types IV and V fluids are used. Two distinct classes of type IV fluids exist based on their density: class I fluids are low density and class II are standard density. The class I fluids provide weight savings advantages versus class II. Monsanto and Exxon are the suppliers of the type IV phosphate ester-based aviation hydraulic fluids.

(2) In addition to the type IV fluids that are currently in use, type V fluids are being developed in response to industry demands for a more thermally stable fluid at higher operating temperatures. Type V fluids will be more resistant to hydrolytic and oxidative degradation at high temperature than the type IV fluids.

d. Materials of Construction. Hydraulic systems require the use of special accessories that are compatible with the hydraulic fluid. Appropriate seals, gaskets, and hoses must be specifically designated for the type of fluid in use. Care must be taken to ensure that the components installed in the system are compatible with the fluid. When gaskets, seals, and hoses are replaced, positive identification should be made to ensure that they are made of the appropriate material.

(1) Phosphate ester-based hydraulic fluids have good solvency properties and may act as plasticizer for certain polymers. Care should be taken in handling to keep the fluid from spilling on plastic materials and paint finishes.

(2) If a small amount of the fluid is spilled during handling, it must be cleaned up immediately with a dry cloth. When larger quantities are spilled, an absorbent sweeping compound is recommended. A final cleaning with an approved solvent or detergent should remove any traces of fluid.

9-28. HANDLING HYDRAULIC FLUID. In addition to any other instructions provided in the aircraft maintenance manual or by the fluid supplier, the following general precautions must be observed in the handling of hydraulic fluids:

a. Ensure that each aircraft hydraulic system is properly identified to show the kind of fluid to be used in the system. Identification at the filler cap or valve must clearly show the type of fluid to be used or added.

b. Never allow different categories of hydraulic fluids to become mixed. Chemical reactions may occur, fire resistant fluids may lose their fire resistance, seals may be damaged, etc.

c. Never, under any circumstances, service an aircraft system with a fluid different from that shown on the instruction plate.

d. Make certain that hydraulic fluids and fluid containers are protected from contamination of any kind. Dirt particles may cause hydraulic units to become inoperative, cause seal damage, etc. If there is any question regarding the cleanliness of the fluid, do not use it. Containers for hydraulic fluid must never be left open to air longer than necessary.

e. Do not expose fluids to high temperature or open flames. Mineral-based fluids are highly flammable.

f. The hydrocarbon-based hydraulic fluids are, in general, safe to handle. To work with these fluids, reasonable handling procedures must always be followed. Take precaution to avoid fluid getting in the eyes. If fluid contacts the eye, wash immediately with water.

g. When handling Skydrol/Hyjet hydraulic fluids, gloves that are impervious to the fluid must be worn. If skin contact occurs, wash with soap and water.

h. When handling phosphate ester-based fluid use eye protection. If the eye is exposed to fluid, severe eye pain will occur.

i. When Skydrol/Hyjet mist or vapor exposure is possible, a respirator capable of removing organic vapors and mists must be worn.

j. Ingestion of any hydraulic fluid should be avoided. Although small amounts do not appear to be highly hazardous, any significant amount should be tested in accordance with manufacturer's direction, followed with hospital supervised stomach treatment.

9-29. HYDRAULIC SYSTEM MAINTENANCE PRACTICES. The maintenance of hydraulic and pneumatic systems should be performed in accordance with the aircraft manufacturer's instructions. The following is a summary of general practices followed when dealing with hydraulic and pneumatic systems.

a. Service. The servicing of hydraulic and pneumatic systems should be performed at the intervals specified by the manufacturer. Some components, such as hydraulic reservoirs, have servicing information adjacent to the component. When servicing a hydraulic reservoir, make certain to use the correct type of fluid. Hydraulic fluid type can be identified by color and smell; however, it is good practice to take fluid from the original marked container and then to check the fluid by color and smell for verification. Fluid containers should always be closed, except when fluid is being removed.

b. Contamination Control. Contamination, both particulate and chemical, is detrimental to the performance and life of components in the aircraft hydraulic system. Contamination enters the system through normal wear of components, by ingestion through external seals, during servicing, or maintenance when the system is opened to replace/repair components, etc. To control the particulate contamination in the system, filters are installed in the pressure line, in the return line, and in the pump case drain line of each system. The filter rating is given in terms of "micron," and is an indication of the particle size that will be filtered out. The replacement interval of these filters is established by the manufacturer and is included in the maintenance manual. However, in the absence of specific replacement instructions, a recommended service life of the filter elements is:

Pressure filters—3000 hrs.
Return Filters—1500 hrs.
Case drain filters—600 hrs.

(1) When replacing filter elements, be sure that there is no pressure on the filter bowl. Protective clothing and a face shield must be used to prevent fluid from contacting the eye. Replace the element with one that has the proper rating. After the filter element has been replaced, the system must be pressure tested to ensure that the sealing element in the filter assembly is intact.

(2) In the event of a major component failure, such as a pump, consideration must be given to replacing the system filter elements, as well as the failed component. System filters may also be equipped with differential pressure (ΔP) indicators. These indicators are designed to "pop-up" when the pressure drop across the element reaches a predetermined value caused by contamination held by the element. The indicators are designed to prevent false indications due to cold start, pump ripple, and shock loads. Consequently, a filter whose indicator has been activated must be replaced. In fact, some indicator designs are such that the indicator cannot be reset, unless the filter bowl is removed and the element replaced.

c. Flushing a Hydraulic System. When inspection of hydraulic filters or hydraulic fluid evaluation indicates that the fluid is contaminated, flushing the system may be necessary. This must be done according to the manufacturer's instructions; however, a typical procedure for flushing is as follows:

(1) Connect a ground hydraulic test stand to the inlet and outlet test ports of the system. Verify that the ground unit fluid is clean and contains the same fluid as the aircraft.

(2) Change the system filters.

(3) Pump clean, filtered fluid through the system, and operate all subsystems until no obvious signs of contamination are found during inspection of the filters. Dispose of contaminated fluid and filter. (Note: A visual inspection of hydraulic filters is not always effective.)

(4) Disconnect the test stand and cap the ports.

(5) Ensure that the reservoir is filled to the FULL line or proper service level.

d. Inspections. Hydraulic and pneumatic systems are inspected for leakage, worn or damaged tubing, worn or damaged hoses, wear of moving parts, security of mounting for all units, safetying, and any other condition specified by the maintenance manual. A complete inspection includes considering the age, cure date, stiffness of the hose, and an operational check of all subsystems.

(1) Leakage from any stationary connection in a system is not permitted, and if found, it should be repaired. A small amount of fluid seepage may be permitted on actuator piston rods and rotating shafts. In a hydraulic system, a thin film of fluid in these areas indicates that the seals are being properly lubricated. When a limited amount of leakage is allowed at any point, it is usually specified in the appropriate manual.

(2) Tubing should not be nicked, cut, dented, collapsed, or twisted beyond approved limits. The identification markings or lines on a flexible hose will show whether the hose has been twisted. (See figure 9.9.)

(3) All connections and fittings associated with moving units must be examined for play evidencing wear. Such units should be in an unpressurized condition when they are checked for wear.

(4) Accumulators must be checked for leakage, air or gas preload, and position. If the accumulator is equipped with a pressure gauge, the preload can be read directly.

(5) An operational check of the system can be performed using the engine-driven pump, an electrically-operated auxiliary pump (if such a pump is included in the system), or a ground test unit. The entire system and each subsystem should be checked for smooth operation, unusual noises, and speed of operation for each unit. The pressure section of the system should be checked with no subsystems to see that pressure holds for the required time without the pump supplying the system. System pressure should be observed during operation of each subsystem to ensure that the engine-driven pump maintains the required pressure.

e. Troubleshooting. Hydraulic system troubleshooting varies according to the complexity of the system and the components in the system. It is, therefore, important that the technician refer to the troubleshooting information furnished by the manufacturer.

(1) Lack of pressure in a system can be caused by a sheared pump shaft, defective relief valve, the pressure regulator, an unloading valve stuck in the "kicked-out" position, lack of fluid in the system, the check valve installed backward, or any condition that permits free flow back to the reservoir or overboard. If a system operates satisfactorily with a ground test unit but not with the system pump, the pump should be examined.

(2) If a system fails to hold pressure in the pressure section, the likely cause is the pressure regulator, an unloading valve, a leaking relief valve, or a leaking check valve.

(3) If the pump fails to keep pressure up during operation of the subsystem, the pump may be worn or one of the pressure-control units may be leaking.

(4) High pressure in a system may be caused by a defective or improperly-adjusted pressure regulator, an unloading valve, or by an obstruction in a line or control unit.

(5) Unusual noise in a hydraulic system, such as banging and chattering, may be caused by air or contamination in the system. Such noises can also be caused by a faulty pressure regulator, another pressure-control unit, or a lack of proper accumulator action.

(6) Maintenance of hydraulic system components involves a number of standard practices together with specialized procedures set forth by manufacturers such as the replacement of valves, actuators, and other units, including tubing and hoses. Care should be exercised to prevent system contamination damage to seals, packings, and other parts, and to apply proper torque in connecting fittings. When installing fittings, valves, etc. always lubricate the threads with hydraulic fluid.

(7) Overhaul of hydraulic and pneumatic units is usually accomplished in approved repair facilities; however, replacement of seals and packings may be done from time to time by technicians in the field. When a unit is disassembled, all O-ring and Chevron seals should be removed and replaced with new seals. The new seals must be of the same material as the original and must carry the correct manufacturer's part number. No seal should be installed unless it is positively identified as the correct part and the shelf life has not expired.

(8) When installing seals, care should be exercised to ensure that the seal is not scratched, cut, or otherwise damaged. When it is necessary to install a seal over sharp edges, the edges must be covered with shim stock, plastic sheet, or electrical tape.

(9) The replacement of hydraulic units and tubing usually involves the spillage of some hydraulic fluid. Care should be taken to ensure that the spillage of fluid is kept to a minimum by closing valves, if available, and by plugging lines immediately after they are disconnected. All openings in hydraulic systems should be capped or plugged to prevent contamination of the system.

(10) The importance of the proper torque applied to all nuts and fittings in a system cannot be over-emphasized. Too much torque will damage metal and seals, and too little torque will result in leaks and loose parts. The proper torque wrenches with the appropriate range should be used in assembling system units.

f. Disposal of Used Hydraulic Fluids. In the absence of organizational guidelines, the technician should be guided by local, state, and federal regulations, with regard to means of disposal of used hydraulic fluid. Presently, the most universally accepted procedure for disposal of phosphate ester-based fluid is incineration.

9-30. HYDRAULIC LINES AND FITTINGS. Carefully inspect all lines and fittings at regular intervals to ensure airworthiness. Investigate any evidence of fluid loss or leaks. Check metal lines for leaks, loose anchorage, scratches, kinks, or other damage. Inspect fittings and connections for leakage, looseness, cracks, burrs, or other damage. Replace or repair defective elements. Make sure the lines and hoses do not chafe against one another and are correctly secured and clamped.

a. Replacement of Metal Lines. When inspection shows a line to be damaged or defective, replace the entire line or, if the damaged section is localized, a repair section may be inserted. In replacing lines, always use tubing of the same size and material as the original line. Use the old tubing as a template in bending the new line, unless it is too greatly damaged, in which case a template can be made from soft iron wire. Soft aluminum tubing (1100, 3003, or 5052) under ¼-inch outside diameter may be bent by hand.. For all other tubing use an acceptable hand or power tube-bending tool. Bend tubing carefully to avoid excessive flattening, kinking, or wrinkling. Minimum bend radii values are shown in table 9-2. A small amount of flattening in bends is acceptable, but do not exceed 75 percent of the original outside diameter. Excessive flattening will cause fatigue failure of the tube. When installing the replacement tubing, line it up correctly with the mating part so that it is not forced into alignment by tightening of the coupling nuts.

b. Tube Connections. Many tube connections are made using flared tube ends with standard connection fittings: AN-818 (MS 20818) nut and AN-819 (MS 20819) sleeve. In forming flares, cut the tube ends square, file smooth, remove all burrs and sharp edges, and thoroughly clean. The tubing is then flared using the correct 37-degree aviation flare forming tool for the size of tubing and type of fitting. A double flare is used on soft aluminum tubing 3/8-inch outside diameter and under, and a single flare on all other tubing. In making the connections, use hydraulic fluid as a lubricant and then tighten. Overtightening will damage the tube or fitting, which may cause a failure. Under-tightening may cause leakage which could result in a system failure.

CAUTION: Mistaken use of 45-degree automotive flare forming tools may result in improper tubing flare shape and angle; causing misfit, stress and strain, and probable system failure.

c. Repair of Metal Tube Lines. Minor dents and scratches in tubing may be repaired. Scratches or nicks not deeper than 10 percent of the wall thickness in aluminum alloy tubing, that are not in the heel of a bend, may be repaired by burnishing with hand tools. Replace lines with severe die marks, seams, or splits in the tube. Any crack or deformity in a flare is unacceptable and cause for rejection. A dent less than 20 percent of the tube diameter is not objectionable unless it is in the heel of a bend. A severely-damaged line should be replaced; however, it may be repaired by cutting out the damaged section and inserting a tube section of the same size and material. Flare both ends of the undamaged and replacement tube sections and make the connection by using standard unions, sleeves, and tube nuts. If the damaged portion is short enough, omit the insert tube and repair by using one union and two sets of connection fittings.

TABLE 9-2. Tube data.

Dash Nos. Ref.	Tubing OD inches	Wrench torque for tightening AN-818 Nut (pound inch)						Minimum bend radii measured to tubing centerline. Dimension in inches.	
		Aluminum-alloy tubing		Steel tubing		Aluminum-alloy tubing (Flare MS33583) for use on oxygen lines only			
		Minimum	Maximum	Minimum	Maximum	Minimum	Maximum	Alum. Alloy	Steel
-2	1/8	20	30	75	85	--	--	3/8	--
-3	3/16	25	35	95	105	--	--	7/16	21/32
-4	1/4	50	65	135	150	--	--	9/16	7/8
-5	5/16	70	90	170	200	100	125	3/4	1-1/8
-6	3/8	110	130	270	300	200	250	15/16	1-5/16
-8	1/2	230	260	450	500	300	400	1-1/4	1-3/4
-10	5/8	330	360	650	700	--	--	1-1/2	2-3/16
-12	3/4	460	500	900	1000	--	--	1-3/4	2-5/8
-16	1	500	700	1200	1400	--	--	3	3-1/2
-20	1-1/4	800	900	1520	1680	--	--	3-3/4	4-3/8
-24	1-1/2	800	900	1900	2100	--	--	5	5-1/4
-28	1-3/4	--	--	--	--	--	--	--	--
-32	2	1800	2000	2660	2940	--	--	8	7

d. Replacement of Flexible Lines. When replacement of a flexible line is necessary, use the same type, size, part number, and length of hose as the line to be replaced. Check TSO requirements. If the replacement of a hose with a swaged-end type fitting is necessary, obtain a new hose assembly of the correct size and composition. Certain synthetic oils require a specially compounded synthetic rubber hose, which is compatible. Refer to the aircraft manufacturer's service information for the correct part number for the replacement hose. If the fittings on each end are of the correct type or sleeve type, a replacement may be fabricated as shown in figure 9-8. Before cutting new flexible wire braided hose to the proper size, tape the hose tightly with masking tape and cut in the center of the masking tape to prevent fraying. The use of a mandrel will prevent cutting the inside of the hose when inserting the fittings. Typical aircraft hose specifications and their uses are shown in table 9-3. Install hose assemblies without twisting. (See figure 9-9.) A hose should not be stretched tight between two fittings as this will result in overstressing and eventual failure. The length of hose should be sufficient to provide about 5 to 8 percent slack. Avoid tight bends in flex lines as they may result in failure. Never exceed the minimum bend radii as indicated in figure 9-10.

(1) Teflon hose is used in many aircraft systems because it has superior qualities for certain applications. Teflon is compounded from tetrafluoroethylene resin which is unaffected by fluids normally used in aircraft. It has an operating range of -65°F to 450 °F. For these reasons, Teflon is used in hydraulic and engine lubricating systems where temperatures and pressures preclude the use of rubber hose. Although Teflon hose has excellent performance qualities, it also has peculiar characteristics that require extra care in handling. It tends to assume a permanent set when exposed to high pressure or temperature. Do not attempt to straighten a hose that has been in service. Any excessive bending or twisting may cause kinking or weakening of the tubing wall. Replace any hose that shows signs of leakage, abrasion, or kinking. Any hose suspected of kinking may be checked with a steel ball of proper size. Table 9-4 shows hose and ball sizes. The ball will not pass through if the hose is distorted beyond limits.

(2) If the hose fittings are of the reusable type, a replacement hose may be fabricated as described in figure 9-8. Refer to figure 9-10 for minimum bend radii. When a hose assembly is removed, the ends should be tied as shown in figure 9-11, so that the preformed shape will be maintained. Refer to figure 9-12 for minimum bend radii for teflon hose.

(3) All flexible hose installations should be supported at least every 24 inches. Closer supports are preferred. They should be carefully routed and securely clamped to avoid abrasion, kinking, or excessive flexing. Excessive flexing may cause weakening of the hose or loosening at the fittings.

e. O-Ring Seals. An understanding of O-ring seal applications is necessary to determine when replacement should be made. The simplest application is where the O-ring merely serves as a gasket when it is compressed within a recessed area by applying pressure with a packing nut or screw cap. Leakage is not normally acceptable in this type of installation. In other installations, the O-ring seals depend primarily upon their resiliency to accomplish their sealing action. When moving parts are involved, minor seepage may be normal and acceptable. A moist surface found on moving parts of hydraulic units is an indication the seal is being properly lubricated. In pneumatic systems, seal lubrication is provided by the installation of a grease-impregnated felt wiper ring. When systems are static, seepage past the seals is not normally acceptable.

f. Storage of replacement seals.

(1) Store O-ring seals where temperature does not exceed 120° F.

(2) Keep seals packaged to avoid exposure to ambient air and light, particularly sunlight.

g. During inspection, consider the following to determine whether seal replacement is necessary.

(1) How much fluid is permitted to seep past the seals? In some installations minor seepage is normal. Refer to the manufacturer's maintenance information.

(2) What effect does the leak have on the operation of the system? Know the system.

(3) Does the leak of fluid create a hazard or affect surrounding installations? A check of the system fluid and a knowledge of previous fluid replenishment is helpful.

(4) Will the system function safely without depleting the reservoirs until the next inspection?

h. Do's and Don'ts that apply to O-ring seals.

(a) Correct all leaks from static seal installations.

(b) Don't retighten packing gland nuts; retightening will, in most cases, increase rather than decrease the leak.

(c) Never reuse O-ring seals because they tend to swell from exposure to fluids, and become set from being under pressure. They may have minor cuts or abrasions that are not readily discernible by visual inspection.

(d) Avoid using tools that might damage the seal or the sealing surface.

(e) Do not depend upon color-coding. Coding may vary with manufacturer

(f) Be sure that part number is correct

(g) Retain replacement seals in their package until ready for use. This provides proper identification and protects the seal from damage and contamination.

(h) Assure that the sealing surfaces are clean and free of nicks or scratches before installing seal.

(i) Protect the seal from any sharp surfaces that it may pass over during installation. Use an installation bullet or cover the sharp surfaces with tape.

(j) Lubricate the seal so it will slide into place smoothly.

(k) Be sure the seal has not twisted during installation.

i. Hydraulic System Pressure Test. When a flexible hose has been repaired or overhauled using existing hardware and new hose material, before the hose is installed on the aircraft it is recommended that the hose is tested to at least 1.5 system pressure. A new hose can be operationally checked after it is installed in the aircraft using system pressure.

j. Hydraulic Components. Hydraulic components such as pumps, actuating cylinders, selector valves, relief valves, etc., should be repaired or adjusted following the airplane and component manufacturer's instructions. Inspect hydraulic filter elements at frequent intervals and replace as necessary.

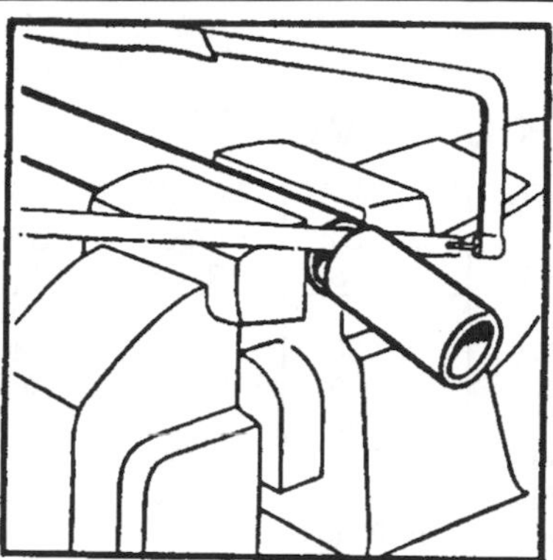

1. Place hose in vise and cut to desired length using fine tooth hacksaw or cut off wheel.

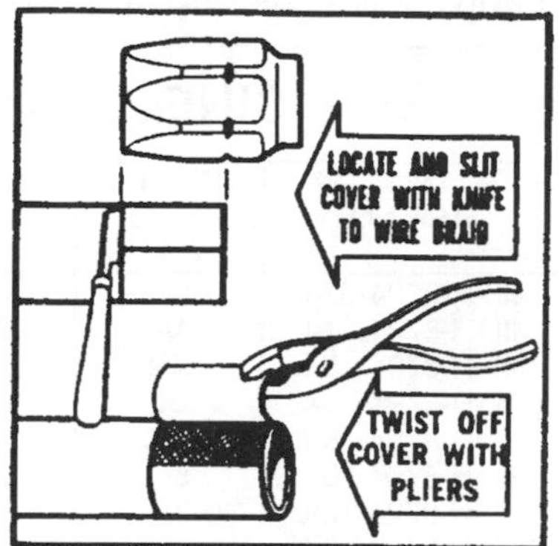

2. Locate length of hose to be cut off and slit cover with knife to wire braid. After slitting cover, twist off with pair of pliers. (see note below)

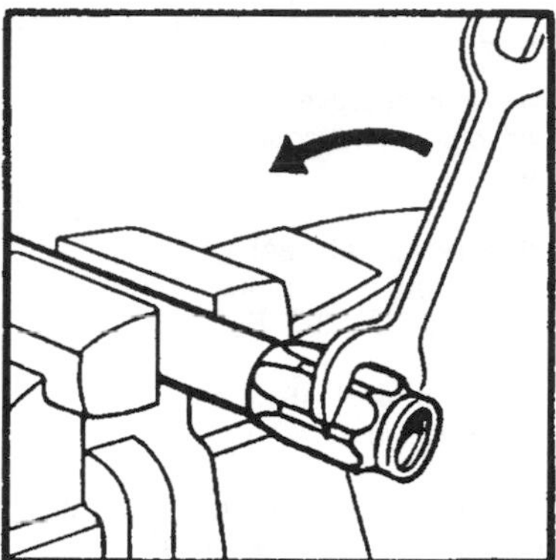

3. Place hose in vise and screw socket on hose counterclockwise.

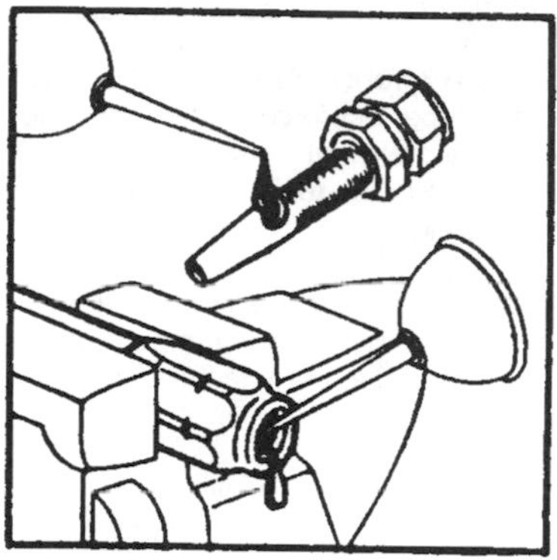

4. *Lubricate inside of hose and nipple threads liberally.

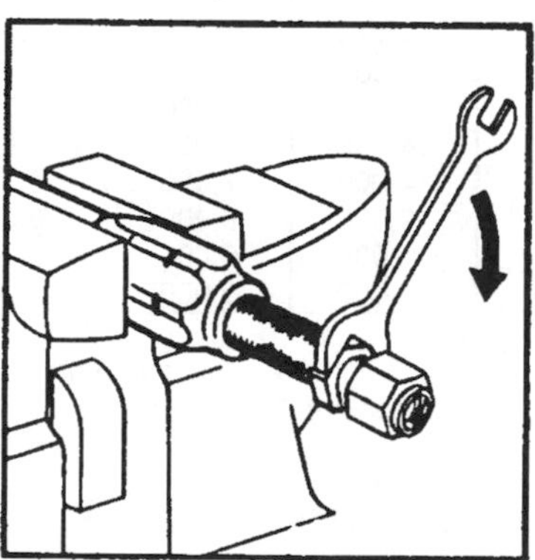

5. Screw nipple into socket using wrench on hex of nipple and leave .005 inches to .031 inches clearance between nipple hex and socket.

NOTE:
Hose assemblies fabricated per MIL-H-8790 must have the exposed wire braid coated with a special sealant.

NOTE:
Step 2 applies to high pressure hose only.

***CAUTION:**
Do not use any petroleum product with hose designed for synthetic fluids, "SKYDROL and /or HYJET product." For a lubricant during assembly use a vegetable soap liquid.

DISASSEMBLE IN REVERSE ORDER

FIGURE 9-8. Hose assembly instructions (can be used for low pressure hydraulic fluid, and oil line applications).

TABLE 9-3. Aircraft hose specifications.

SINGLE WIRE BRAID FABRIC COVERED

MIL. PART NO.	TUBE SIZE O.D.	HOSE SIZE I.D.	HOSE SIZE O.D.	RECOMM. OPER. PRESS.	MIN. BURST PRESS.	MAX. PROOF PRESS.	MIN BEND RADIUS
MIL-H-8794- 3-L	3/16	1/8	.45	3,000	12,000	6,000	3.00
MIL-H-8794- 4-L	1/4	3/16	.52	3,000	12,000	6,000	3.00
MIL-H-8794- 5-L	5/16	1/4	.58	3,000	10,000	5,000	3.38
MIL-H-8794- 6-L	38	5/16	.67	2,000	9,000	4,500	4.00
MIL-H-8794- 8-L	1/2	13/32	.77	2,000	8,000	4,000	4.63
MIL-H-8794-10-L	5/8	1/2	.92	1,750	7,000	3,500	5.50
MIL-H-8794-12-L	3/4	5/8	1.08	1,750	6,000	3,000	6.50
MIL-H-8794-16-L	1	7/8	1.23	800	3,200	1,600	7.38
MIL-H-8794-20-L	1 1/4	1 1/8	1.50	600	2,500	1,250	9.00
MIL-H-8794-24-L	1 1/2	1 3/8	1.75	500	2,000	1,000	11.00
MIL-H-8794-32-L	2	1 13/16	2.22	350	1,400	700	13.25
MIL-H-8794-40-L	2 1/2	2 3/8	2.88	200	1,000	300	24.00
MIL-H-8794-48-L	3	3	3.56	200	800	300	33.00

Construction: Seamless synthetic rubber inner tube reinforced with one fiber braid, one braid of high tensile steel wire and covered with an oil resistant rubber impregnated fiber braid.

Identification: Hose is identified by specification number, size number, quarter year and year, hose manufacturer's identification.

Uses: Hose is approved for use in aircraft hydraulic, pneumatic, coolant, fuel and oil systems.

Operating Temperatures:
Sizes-3 through 12: Minus 65 °F. to plus 250 °F.

Sizes - 16 through 48: Minus 40 °F. to plus 275 °F.

Note: Maximum temperatures and pressures should not be used simultaneously.

MULTIPLE WIRE BRAID RUBBER COVERED

MIL PAR NO.	TUBE SIZE O.D.	HOSE SIZE I.D.	HOSE SIZE O.D.	RECOMM. OPER. PRESS.	MIN. BURST PRESS.	MIN. PROOF PRESS.	MIN. BEND RADIUS
MIL-H-8788- 4-L	1/4	7/32	0.63	3,000	16,000	8,000	3.00
MIL-H-8788- 5-L	5/16	9/32	0.70	3,000	14,000	7,000	3.38
MIL-H-8788- 6-L	3/8	11/32	0.77	3,000	14,000	7,000	5.00
MIL-H-8788- 8-L	1/2	7/16	0.86	3,000	14,000	7,000	5.75
MIL-H-8788-10-L	5/8	9/16	1.03	3,000	12,000	6,000	6.50
MIL-H-8788-12-L	3/4	11/16	1.22	3,000	12,000	6,000	7.75
MIL-H-8788-16-L	1	7/8	1.50	3,000	10,000	5,000	9.63

Hose Construction: Seamless synthetic rubber inner tube reinforced with one fabric braid, two or more steel wire braids, and covered with a synthetic rubber cover (for gas applications request perforated cover).

Identification: Hose is identified by specification number, size number, quarter year and year, hose manufacturer's identification.

Uses: High pressure hydraulic, pneumatic, coolant, fuel and oil.

Operating Temperatures:
Minus 65 °F. to plus 200 °F.

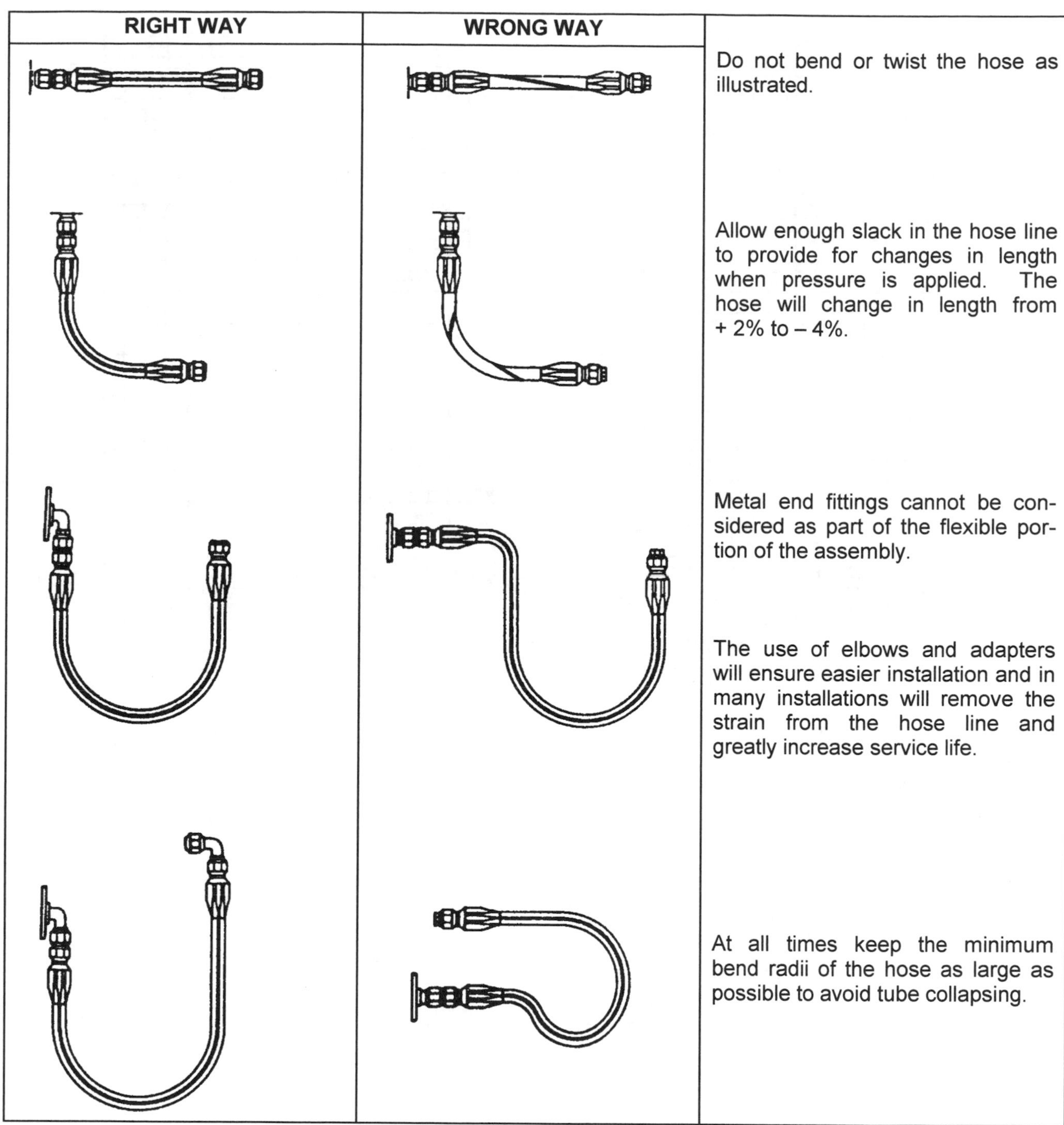

FIGURE 9-9. Proper hose installations.

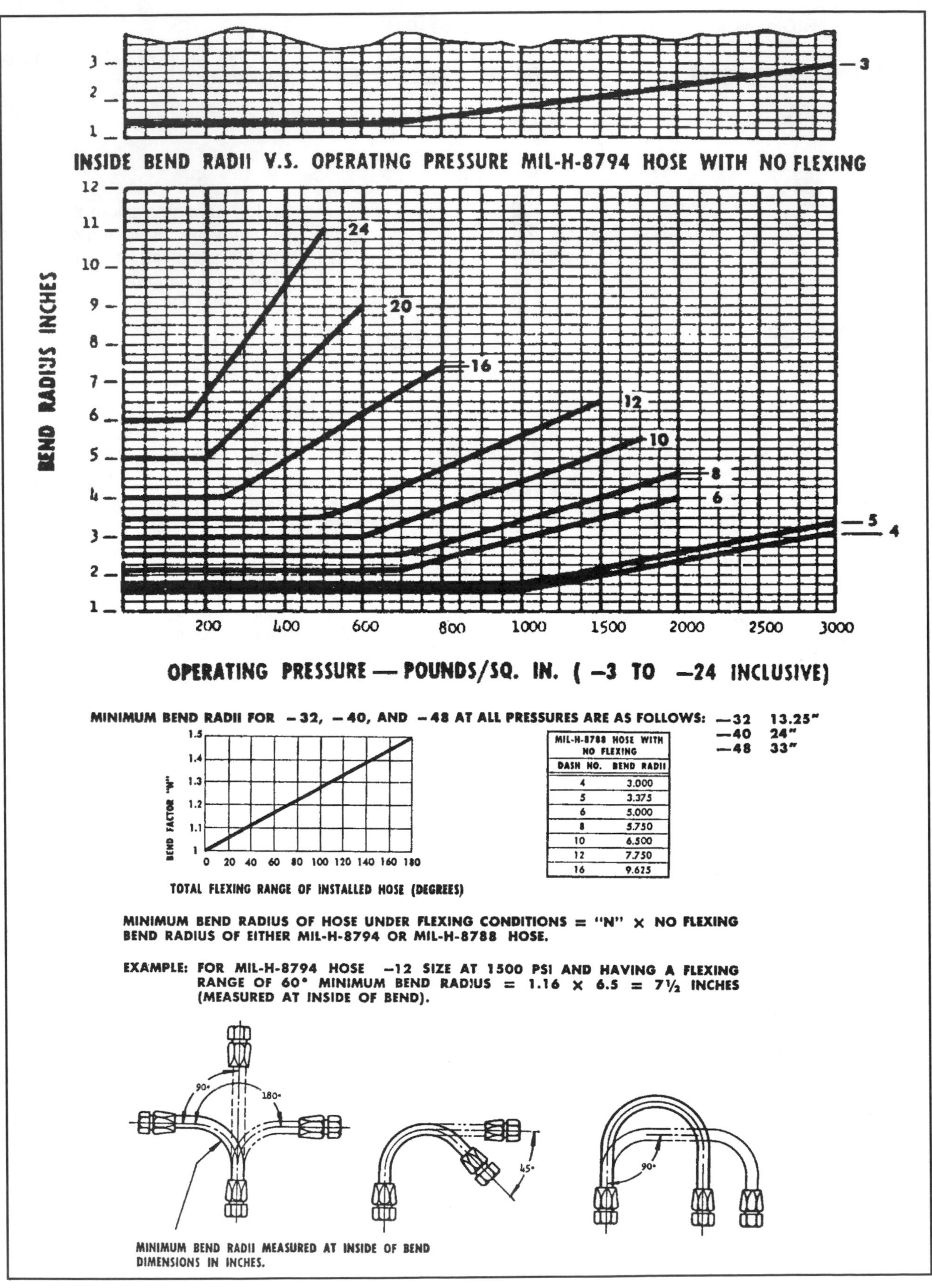

MIL-H-8788 HOSE WITH NO FLEXING	
DASH NO.	BEND RADII
4	3.000
5	3.375
6	5.000
8	5.750
10	6.500
12	7.750
16	9.625

FIGURE 9-10. Minimum bend radii.

TABLE 9-4. Ball diameters for testing hose restrictions or kinking.

HOSE SIZE	BALL SIZE
-4	5/64
-5	9/64
-6	13/64
-8	9/32
-10	3/8
-12	1/2
-16	47/64
-20	61/64

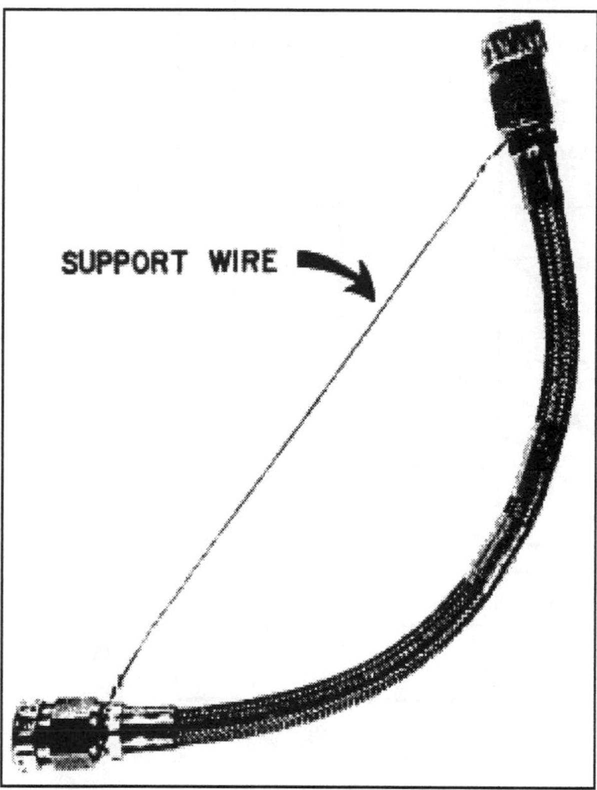

FIGURE 9-11. Suggested handling of preformed hose.

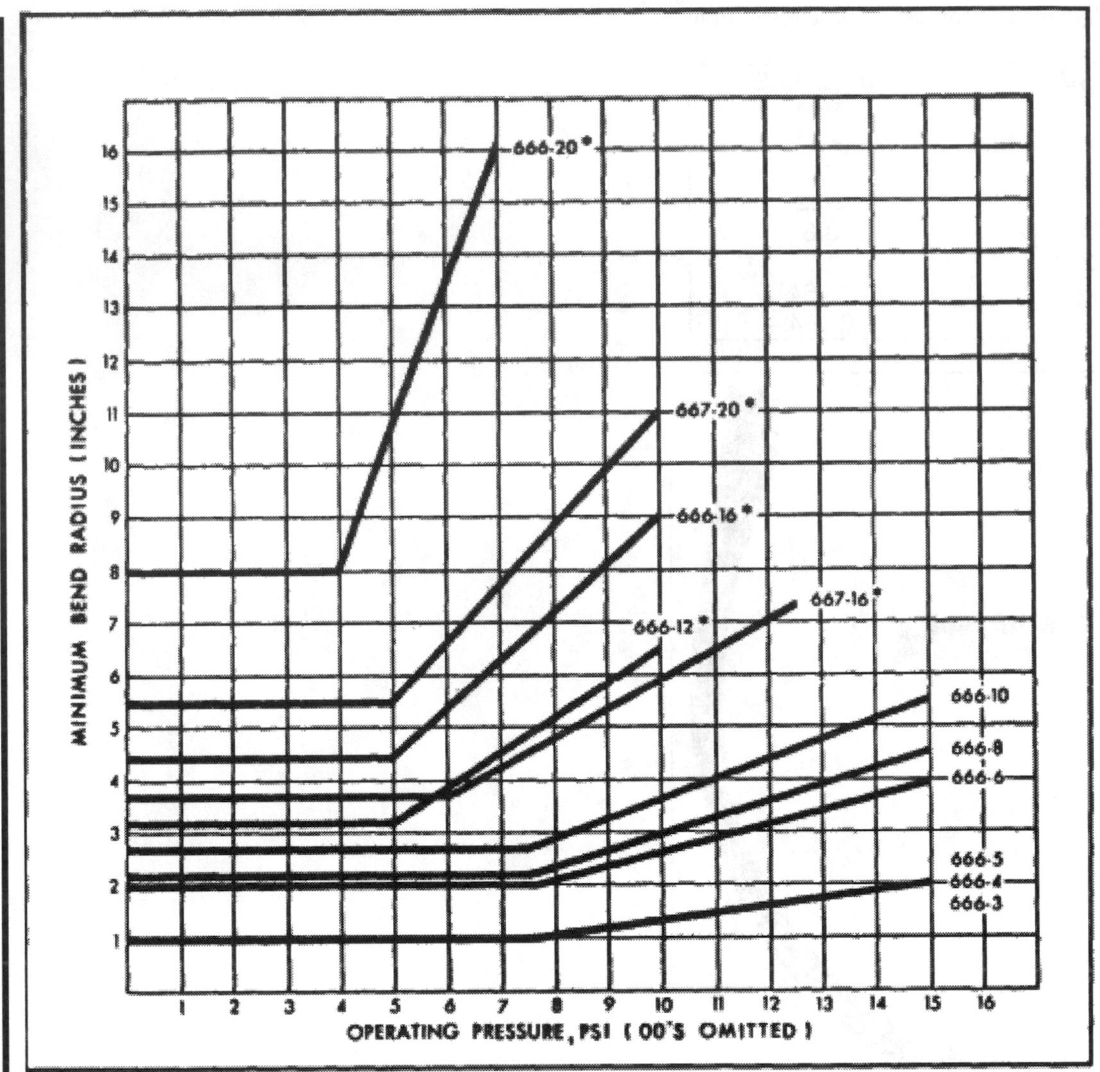

Figure 9-12. Minimum bend radii–Teflon hose.

9.31.—9.36 [RESERVED.]

SECTION 3. EMERGENCY EQUIPMENT

9-37. LIFE RAFTS. Inflatable life rafts are subject to general deterioration due to aging. Experience has indicated that such equipment may be in need of replacement at the end of 5 years due to porosity of the rubber-coated material. Wear of such equipment is accelerated when stowed on board aircraft because of vibration which causes chafing of the rubberized fabric. This ultimately results in localized leakage. Leakage is also likely to occur where the fabric is folded because sharp corners are formed. When these corners are in contact with the carrying cases or with adjacent parts of the rubberized fabric, they tend to wear through due to vibration (Ref: TSO-C70a).

a. When accomplishing maintenance, repair, and inspection of unpacked rafts, personnel should not step on any part of the raft or flotation tubes while wearing shoes. Rafts should not be thrown or dropped, since damage to the raft or accessories may result. Particular care should be exercised at all times to prevent snagging, cutting, and contact with gasoline, acids, oils, and grease. High standards of performance for proper maintenance, inspection, and repair cannot be overemphasized, since the lives of passengers could be involved.

b. Inspection and inflation tests, when applicable, will be accomplished during storage and after installation in an aircraft in accordance with the manufacturer's specifications and/or FAA-approved procedures. Accessory items will be installed during these inspections. A raft knife will be attached by a 24-inch nylon lanyard to the mooring eye located above the CO_2 cylinder case to enable rapid cutting of the mooring line.

9-38. LIFE RAFT INSPECTIONS. Inspection of life rafts should be performed in accordance with the manufacturer's specifications. General inspection procedures to be performed on most life rafts are as follows.

CAUTION: Areas where life rafts are inspected or tested must be smooth, free of splinters, sharp projections, and oil stains. Floors with abrasive characteristics, such as concrete or rough wood, will be covered with untreated tarpaulins or heavy clean paper.

a. Inspect life rafts for cuts, tears, or other damage to the rubberized material. If the raft is found to be in good condition, remove the CO_2 bottle(s) and inflate the raft with air to a pressure of 2 psi. The air should be introduced at the fitting normally connected to the CO_2 bottle(s). After at least 1 hour, to allow for the air within the raft to adjust itself to the ambient temperature, check pressure and adjust, if necessary, to 2 psi and allow the raft to stand for 24 hours. If, after 24 hours, the pressure is less than 1 psi, examine the raft for leakage by using soapy water. In order to eliminate pressure variations due to temperature differences at the time the initial and final reading are taken, test the raft in a room where the temperature is fairly constant. If the pressure drop is satisfactory, the raft should be considered as being in an airworthy condition and returned to service after being fitted with correctly charged CO_2 bottles as determined by weighing them. Rafts more than 5 years old are likely to be unairworthy due to deterioration. It is suggested that serviceable rafts be marked to indicate the date of inspection and that soapstone be used when folding them preparatory to insertion into the carrying case. Take care to see that all of the raft's required equipment is on board and properly stowed. If the raft lanyard, used to prevent the raft from floating away from the airplane, is in need of replacement, use a lanyard not less than 20 feet long and having a breaking strength of about 75 pounds.

b. It is recommended that the aforementioned procedure be repeated every 18 months using the CO_2 bottle(s) for inflation. If a single bottle is used for inflating both compartments, it should be noted whether the inflation is proceeding equally to both compartments. Occasionally, the formation of "carbon-dioxide snow" may occur in one passage of the distribution manifold and divert a larger volume of gas to one compartment, which may burst if the mattress valve is not open to relieve the pressure. If the pressure is satisfactory, return the raft to service in accordance with the procedure outlined.

c. Inspect the CO_2 cylinder for evidence of cross-threading or stripping.

d. Inspect the CO_2 bottle inflation valve cable rigging as follows.

(1) Remove the screws that attach the cover plate to the valve and remove the cover plate.

(2) Inspect the firing line cable ball swage for engagement in the correct recess for either "Upward Pull" or "Downward Pull." The cable will be wrapped around the sheave approximately 270 degrees.

(3) Reposition the cable ball swage as required. (See figure 9-12.)

(4) Replace the cover plate. The green dot on the sheave should be visible through the window in the cover plate, indicating a charged cylinder.

e. Check the CO_2 cylinder release cable and housing for condition and security.

f. Make sure the safety deflector is removed from the cylinder outlet before connecting the cylinder to the raft. (See figure 9-12.)

g. Stencil the life raft's inspection date on the raft.

9-39. SURVIVAL KIT INSPECTION.

a. Survival Kit Contents. Each raft accommodating passengers or crew members should contain, as a minimum, the following:

Hand Pump (if required)
Desalting Kit, First-Aid Kit
Mirror/Reflector
Emergency Rations
Tarpaulins
Fishing Kit
Raft Knife
Compass
Protective Ointment (Sunburn)
Oars
Emergency Water Containers
Repair Kits
Signal Flares
Carrying Case
Locator Beacon and Battery
Lines and Anchor
Police Whistle
Flashlight
Thermal Protective Aid
Light-sticks
Solar Still Kit
Survival Manual
Duct Tape
Plastic Trash Bags
Accessory Containers
 - Bailing Bucket
 - Sponge
Dye Marker

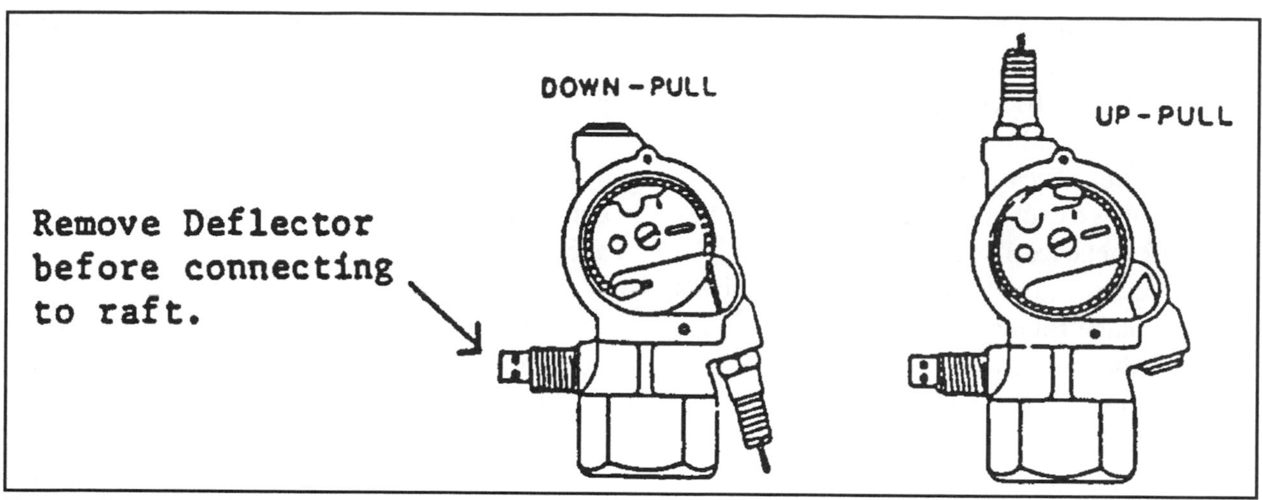

FIGURE 9-12. Inflation valve.

b. Exposure Suits. Quick-donning exposure suits should be provided in sufficient quantity to accommodate the passengers and crew on extended over-water missions whenever any of the following conditions exist.

(1) The water temperature is 59 ▪F or below, or

(2) The Outside Air Temperature (OAT) is 32 ▪F or below.

c. Physical Inspection. Make a physical inspection of the life raft's accessories and/or contents, in accordance with manufacturer's specifications, to ascertain that all items required are in a serviceable condition.

(1) Pumps and Hoses.

(a) Check the air pump for condition and security.

(b) Check the air pump hose and hose fittings for ease of attachment to the pump and mattress valves.

(c) Operate the pump to ensure that it delivers air.

(d) Close the outlet and check the seal of the piston.

(e) Blow into the outlet to determine if the pump check valve will seal.

(2) Desalting Kit.

(a) Check the desalting kit expiration date, if applicable.

(b) Replace the severely dented or punctured cans.

NOTE: Type MK-2 desalter kits have an indefinite shelf and service life and do not have to be age-controlled.

(3) First-Aid Kit. Inspect each kit prior to flight to ensure that the seal is intact; the kits have not been tampered with or opened; and check the date when the kit contents should be inspected (120-day interval), and containing the following:

1 Case First-Aid Kit, empty;
1 Bottle Benzalkonium Chloride Zinc; Tinted, 1:1000 2cc
1 Package Sodium Chloride; (Sodium Bicarbonate Mix) 4.5 gm;
1 Bandage each, Gauze, & Compress (2 inches x 6 yd);
2 Dressings, First-Aid, 4 inches x 7 inches;
1 Package Bandages; Absorbent & Adhesive, 3/4-inch x 3 inches;
3 Bottles, Snap-On Cap, Plastic Tablet and Capsule, Round, (issued empty; to be used as needed by user);
1 Tube Lipstick, Anti-Chap; and
1 bottle Water Purification Tablets, Iodine 8 mg (50).

(a) If the seal is found to be broken, or there is evidence of tampering, the kit should be opened and inspected to ensure that all components are included and undamaged. After such inspection, the kit should be resealed.

(b) To reseal the kit, use a wire and lead seal according to the manufacturer's specifications. Pass the wire through grommets or opposite flaps, bend the wire back and force each end through the middle of the lacing cord on each side of the square knot. Pass the ends of the wire through the holes in the lead seal, draw the wire taut, and compress the seal.

(4) Mirror/Reflector. Check the reflector for defective reflection surface and the reflector lanyard for defective conditions and security of attachment.

(5) Emergency Rations. Check the food ration cans for obvious damage, severe dents, and an expiration date. Replace items when severely damaged, dented, or when the date is expired. Ensure that the opening key is attached.

(6) Tarpaulins. Spread out and check for tears, mildew, corroded grommets, and general condition.

(7) Fishing Kit. Check for damaged container or for tampering. Replace if damaged or incomplete.

(8) Raft Knife. Check for corrosion and ease of opening and security of the knife lanyard to the raft.

(9) Compass. Check for proper operation and condition.

(10) Protective Ointment (Sunburn).

(a) Check the sunburn ointment containers for cracks or crushed condition.

(b) Install the ointment in a 6 inch mailing tube and tape the ends to prevent crushing. Stow it where it will be subjected to the least amount of pressure in the kit.

(11) Oars.

(a) Check for serviceability.

(b) Wrap the oars separately in craft paper and seal with tape.

(c) Stencil *inspected* in letters not less than 1/2-inch high on each package.

(12) Emergency Water Containers. Check for open seams, holes, etc. Replace defective containers.

(13) Repair Kit. Check for proper wrapping and missing items. Four plugs are wrapped in a single container. This container and the pliers are wrapped in waterproof paper and sealed with waterproof tape. The package is stenciled *repair plugs and pliers* with letters not less than 1/2-inch high.

(14) Signal Flares. Check the flares for obvious damage and suspended lot numbers. Replace if lot number is over-age or obvious damage exists.

(15) Carrying Case. Check for snags, abrasions, and defective snaps. Repair or replace as necessary.

(16) Locator Beacon and Battery.

(a) Check for corrosion and obvious damage per the manufacturer's manual.

(b) Assemble as an operating unit. Perform an operational test, prepare the beacon for water activation by pulling out the battery switch plug from the end of the transmitter section, and package as instructed on the container.

(17) Lines and Anchor. Check all lines and sea anchors for conditions and security.

(18) Police Whistle. Inspect and test.

(19) Flashlight. Test the flashlight switch for operation; remove old batteries and inspect the case for corrosion and condition; and install new batteries and test momentarily for operation.

(20) Space Blankets. Check space blankets (if required) for rips, tears, and obvious damage.

(21) Light-sticks. Inspect light-sticks for condition and check expiration date.

(22) Solar Still Kit. Check the solar still kit for condition.

(23) Survival Manual. Inspect the survival manual for condition and completeness.

(24) Duct Tape. Check the duct tape for deterioration.

(25) Plastic Trash Bags. Assure that three (each) plastic trash bags are serviceable.

(26) Accessory Containers.

(a) Check the containers for condition and security.

(b) Repack the accessories, secure, and record the inspection data on data cards. Record the Inspection date.

(27) Dye Marker. Check for dents and overall condition.

(28) Shark Chaser. Check for dents and overall condition.

d. After Inspection. Replace accessories in the container, close, and tie securely with tying tapes. Draw a 25-pound breaking strength cord tightly around the center and one approximately 5 inches from each end of the container, tie with square knots, and seal with a lead seal.

e. Folding Life Rafts. Fold the life rafts per the manufacturer's folding diagram using soapstone and secure the raft in its container. Check the container for obvious damage.

9-40. SPECIAL INSPECTIONS. Life rafts in storage or in service shall be unpacked and thoroughly inspected for mildew whenever weather or other conditions warrant. The extent of a special inspection will be determined by the inspector or maintenance chief following a review of the circumstances or conditions to which the life rafts have been subjected. The inspector or maintenance chief may direct a complete overall inspection and inflation test of the life rafts, regardless of the last date of inspection, if it is considered that another inspection is warranted.

9-41. INSPECTION RECORD. The date the inspection was completed will be stenciled on the flotation tube at the left of the cylinder. The size of lettering will not be less than 1/4-inch or greater than 1/2-inch in height. Previous inspection dates will not be removed or obliterated, but will be arranged in columnar form with the latest date at the top. After the inspection is completed, fill out the raft's inspection record in accordance with part 43 section 43.9, and attach the parts tag to the survival equipment. The date on the tag will reflect the same date as stenciled on the flotation tube and will be used to determine the next due date of inspection and test.

9-42. RAFT REPAIRS.

a. Repairs. The service life for flotation equipment will be determined by condition rather than age. Equipment passing tests and inspections may remain in service indefinitely since the inflation tests and material inspections will identify and condemn equipment having more than minor installation defects. However, the service life for life rafts operating under normal usage and environmental conditions is anticipated by the manufacturers to be 8 to 10 years, and it is appropriate to base life raft's parts replacement programs upon this estimate. It is not considered advisable or economical to perform major repairs on life rafts.

b. Life Rafts. Life rafts with any of the following conditions should be condemned rather than repaired:

(1) Life rafts over 3-1/2 years of age and requiring major repair or more than two minor repairs.

(2) A rip or tear across an air retaining seam.

(3) Rafts on which oil, grease, or any other foreign substance has caused a deterioration of the rubberized fabric.

(4) Rafts on which a heavy mildew condition has caused deterioration of the rubberized fabric.

(5) Rafts on which porous flotation tubes allow diffusion of air. A porous area is located by a soap test on the inflated raft. Higher diffusion is indicated by the excessive loss of pressure after a soap test has failed to locate a specific area of injury on the raft.

(6) Rafts requiring internal repair or opening of air retaining seams for repair.

(7) Rafts with an excessive number of injuries that would not, in the judgment of competent inspectors, justify repair.

c. Patches. Holes or abrasions which are 2 inches or less, in diameter (in air retaining chambers) will be repaired by the application of an outside patch. Holes exceeding 2 inches in length or diameter, will require an inside patch as well as an outside patch. Inside and outside patches should be round or rectangular and manufactured of fabric (specification MIL-C-6819). Cement should conform to Class 1 of specification MIL-C-5539. Patch as follows:

(1) Outside patches.

(a) With a rubber solvent thoroughly clean the area to be patched.

(b) From the material referenced, fabricate a patch as shown in figure 9-13.

(c) When two fabric surfaces are to be bonded, apply two coats of extra light cement, two coats of light cement, and three coats of heavy cement to each surface. Rubber-coated tape and seam crossover patches with protective backing do not require cement. Each coat of cement should be thoroughly dry to the touch before the next coat is applied. Start the bonding of fabric surfaces while the last coat of cement is slightly tacky. To ensure proper adhesion when bonding two cemented surfaces, the areas to be bonded should remain tacky during application. This is accomplished by brushing the cemented area with a cloth moistened with solvent.

NOTE: If difficulty in the drying of heavy cement is encountered due to atmospheric conditions, six additional coats of light cement may be substituted for the three coats of heavy cement.

(d) After applying the patch, thoroughly roll it with a hand roller, rolling from the center to the outer edge, to ensure that all air pockets are removed and a firm bond is secured.

(e) Thoroughly dust with talc. Allow to cure for 60 hours before performing leak tests and storing.

(2) Inside Patches.

(a) Cut a rectangular patch as shown in figure 9-13, allowing at least 1-1/2 inches to extend beyond the edge of the injury in all directions.

(b) Mark the center line on the side of the patch that is to be attached to the raft. Mark cross lines on each end of the patch 1-1/2 inches from the ends. When the patch is applied to the injury on the inside, the longitudinal edges of the injury will coincide with the center line, and cross lines on the ends of the patch will coincide with the ends of the injury.

(c) To ensure that the inside surface of the raft is properly powdered in the area of repair, pass a small handful of talc through the opening in the raft and place it approximately 12 inches from the injury. This should be accomplished before the inside area is cemented, exercising care to prevent distribution of the talc prior to completion of the repair.

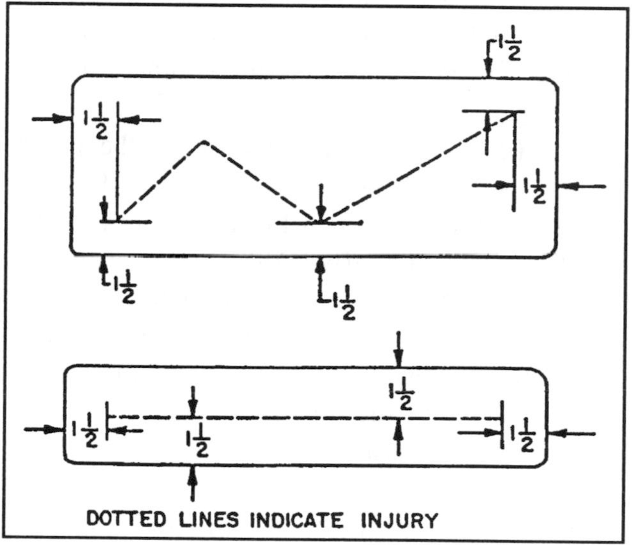

FIGURE 9-13. Repair dimensions.

(d) Using cleaning solvent, cleanse an area on the inside surface of the fabric slightly larger than the patch to be applied. Ensure that the repaired area is thoroughly dry, both inside and outside; apply two coats of extra light cement, two coats of light cement, and three coats of heavy cement (or six additional coats of light cement in lieu of the heavy cement) to the cleansed area, allowing each coat to dry thoroughly before applying successive coats.

NOTE: Since it is impossible for the repairman to visually observe the cementing that is being accomplished on the inside of the raft, exercise care to ensure that each coat of cement completely covers the area to be repaired.

(e) The inside patch should be cemented simultaneously with the application of cement to the inside of the raft. Apply the same number of coats as directed in paragraph 9 42b(2)(d) to the side of the patch that is applied to the injured fabric of the raft. Ensure that each coat is thoroughly dry before applying the next coat.

(f) To aid in adhesion, prior to applying the patch, the inside area to be repaired and cemented surface of the patch should be cleaned with a cloth moistened with rubber solvent. The cement will then become tacky.

(g) Apply the patch. Fold the patch lengthwise in the shape of the letter "U" and insert the patch between the torn edges of the injury on the life rafts. Position the patch so that the fabric at the end of the tear will coincide with a cross line and the center line on the patch follows one edge of the torn fabric. Attach one edge of the torn fabric along the center line on the patch.

(h) Inspect the repair for wrinkles. Working from the attached edge of the fabric to the edge of the patch, remove the wrinkles with a stitcher. Lay the opposite edge of the torn fabric on the patch so that it butts the edge of the torn fabric that has already been applied to the patch. Remove the wrinkles. Thoroughly roll the patch with a 2 inch rubber roller.

NOTE: The surface under the patch should be as smooth as possible so that the torn edge of the fabric may be attached to the patch instead of attempting to attach the patch to the fabric.

(i) Scatter the handful of talc that was placed inside the tube by grasping the sides of the flotation tube and pulling them apart.

(j) Prepare and attach the outside patch as outlined in "OUTSIDE PATCHES," sub-paragraphs 9-42b(1)(a)-(e).

(k) Allow to cure for at least 60 hours before performing leak tests and storing.

(3) Seams and Tapes.

(a) Remove all old or dead cement from the area that will require recementing. Dampen the repair area with a solvent-moistened cloth; then roll or rub off the old cement.

(b) Apply cement to the surface as outlined in "OUTSIDE PATCHES," sub-paragraph 9-42b(1)(a)-(e).

(c) Roll thoroughly with a roller to ensure that all air pockets are removed and a firm bond is secured.

(d) Allow to dry and apply talc over the seam as previously outlined.

(e) Allow to cure for at least 60 hours before performing leak tests and storing.

9-43. LIFE PRESERVERS. Inflatable life preservers are subject to general deterioration due to aging. Experience has indicated that such equipment may be in need of replacement at the end of 5 years due to porosity of the rubber-coated material. Wear of such equipment is accelerated when stowed on board aircraft because of vibration which causes chafing of the rubberized fabric. This ultimately results in localized leakage. Leakage is also likely to occur where the fabric is folded because sharp corners are formed. When these corners are in contact with the carrying cases, or with adjacent parts of the rubberized fabric, they tend to wear through due to vibration.

Life preservers should be inspected in accordance with the manufacturer's specification, unless climate, storage, or operational conditions indicate the need for more frequent inspections (Ref: TSO-C13).

9-44. LIFE PRESERVER INSPECTION. Life preservers should be inspected at 12-month intervals for cuts, tears, or other damage to the rubberized material. Check the mouth valves and tubing for leakage, corrosion, and deterioration. Remove the CO_2 cylinder and check the discharge mechanism by operating the lever to ascertain that the pin operates freely. Check the gaskets and valve cores of the cylinder container and the pull cord for deterioration. If no defects are found, inflate the preserver with air to a 2 psi pressure and allow to stand for 12 hours. If the preserver still has adequate rigidity at the end of that time, deflate and fit with CO_2 cylinders having weights not less than that indicated on them by the manufacturer. All cylinders made in accordance with joint Army/Navy Specification MIL-C-00601D are so stamped and have a minimum permissible weight stamped on them. The use of such CO_2 cylinders is recommended. Having fitted the preserver with an adequately-charged cylinder, mark the preserver to indicate the date of inspection and patch it to the container. It is recommended that the aforementioned procedure be repeated every 12-month period, utilizing the CO_2 cartridge for inflation. Carbon dioxide permeates the rubberized fabric at a faster rate than air and will indicate if the porosity of the material is excessive. The following checks and inspections should be completed:

a. Check for abrasions, chafing, and soiling across folded cell areas and around metal parts. Condemn the life preserver when unsuitable conditions are found.

b. Check for separation of cell fabric and loose attachments along the edges of patches and sealing tapes. Repair if practicable.

c. Check for deterioration in areas where oil and grease are noted. Condemn deteriorated cells. If deterioration is not noted, clean the areas with mild soap and water and rinse with clear water.

d. Inspect the snaps and/or buckles to ensure proper operation.

e. Inspect the instruction panel for readability.

f. Inspect all stitching for gaps, pulls, and tears.

g. Visually inspect the cell containers for snags, cuts, loose stitching, and oil and grease spots. Repair or replace as necessary.

h. Inspect the hardware for rusted or broken parts and cotter pins for damage. Ensure that pins are smooth and free of burrs.

i. Check the inflator discharge lever for proper operation. Move the inflator discharge lever slowly through a normal cycle of operation to ensure freedom of operation and to make certain that the piercing pin has sufficient movement to discharge the CO_2 cylinder. The point of the pin should move past the surface of the gasket in the inflator. In the unoperated position, the end point should be slightly below the gasket surface.

j. Check the installation of the inflator stem gaskets and check the stem caps for tightness. Ensure that the inflator is centered on the stem.

k. Check rescue light. Inspect and test.

(1) Replace the battery if it shows any signs of encrustation.

(2) Inspect for proper installation and physical condition of the lamp, wire, and battery.

(3) Check the light assembly for proper operation and water insulation and flotation.

(4) Pull the sealing plug (where applicable) from the battery. Let water flow through the open ports. Make sure the battery is activated and power is supplied to the light.

(5) Fill out the inspection record and serviceable parts tag. Attach to the vest.

l. Deflate the life preserver and repack in container and secure.

m. The accessories listed below will be required for all life preservers:

(1) One Recognition Light: Remove when returning to serviceable or reparable storage. Remove for replacement of defective light, repair, or salvage of preserver.

(2) One Recognition Light Battery: Remove when returning to serviceable or reparable storage.

n. Record the inspection data on data cards.

o. Life preserver inspected and found sea worthy. Include the inspector's signature.

p. Inspection record. Upon completion of 12-month inspection and tests, each flotation cell will be marked to indicate the date the inspection was accomplished. The inspection stencil will consist of 1/8-inch letters and numerals and will be applied to the patches on the cells (example: 4/3/97). To facilitate determination of the next 12-month inspection period, enter the date it is due in the blank beside the word *inspect* on the inspection data card provided in the inspection data pocket on the cell container. Repack, close, and seal the container.

9-45. REPAIR OF LIFE PRESERVERS. Leaks may be disclosed by immersion in soapy water. Repair leaks by the use of patches in accordance with the recommendations of the manufacturer. Clean corroded metal parts and replace missing or weakened lanyards. Life preservers which do not retain sufficient rigidity after the 12-hour period, because of general deterioration and porosity of the fabric, are beyond economical repair and should be replaced.

9-46. MISCELLANEOUS EQUIPMENT.

a. Parachutes. With reasonable care, parachutes can remain in service indefinitely. They should not be carelessly tossed about, left in aircraft to become wet, or left where someone may tamper with them. They should not be placed where they may fall on oily floors or be subject to acid fumes from adjacent battery chargers.

(1) When repacking is scheduled, to comply with the 120-day requirement in Title 14 of the Code of Federal Regulation (14 CFR) part 105 section 105.43 a careful inspection of the parachute shall be made by a qualified parachute technician (rigger). If repairs or replacements of parts are necessary to maintain the airworthiness of the parachute assembly, such work must be done by the original parachute manufacturer or by a qualified parachute rigger, certificated in accordance with 14 CFR, part 65.

(2) The lead seal should be inspected periodically to ensure the thread has not been broken. If broken, or broken and retied or

appears to have been tampered with, the parachute must be repacked by a properly certified rigger.

b. Safety Belts shall be of an approved type. All seat belts and restraint systems must conform to standards established by the FAA. These standards are contained in Technical Standard Order TSO C22 for seat belts and TSO C114 for restraint systems.

(1) Safety belts eligible for installation in aircraft must be identified by the proper TSO markings on the belt. Each safety belt must be equipped with an approved metal to metal latching device. Airworthy type-certificated safety belts currently in aircraft may be removed for cleaning and reinstalled. However, when a TSO safety belt is found unairworthy, replacement with a new TSO-approved belt or harness is required.

(2) The webbing of safety belts, even when mildew-proofed, is subject to deterioration due to constant use, cleaning, and the effects of aging. Fraying of belts is an indication of wear, and such belts are likely to be unairworthy because they can no longer hold the minimum required tensile load.

(3) Safety belts shall be repaired in accordance with specifications approved by the responsible FAA ACO.

9-47. OXYGEN SYSTEMS. The following instructions are to serve as a guide for the inspection and maintenance of aircraft oxygen systems. The information is applicable to both portable and permanently-installed equipment.

a. Aircraft Gaseous Oxygen Systems. The oxygen in gaseous systems is supplied from one or more high- or low-pressure oxygen cylinders. Since the oxygen is compressed within the cylinder, the amount of pressure indicated on the system gauge bears a direct relationship to the amount of oxygen contained in the cylinder. The pressure-indicating line connection is normally located between the cylinder and a pressure-reducing valve.

NOTE: Some of the gaseous oxygen systems do not use pressure-reducing valves. The high pressure is reduced to a useable pressure by a regulator. This regulator is located between the high- and low-pressure system.

CAUTION: Oxygen rich environments are dangerous.

b. Portable Oxygen Systems. The three basic types of portable oxygen systems are: demand, pressure demand, and continuous flow. The components of these systems are identical to those of a permanent installation with the exception that some parts are miniaturized as necessary. This is done in order that they may be contained in a case or strapped around a person's shoulder. It is for this portability reason that special attention be given to assuring that any storage or security provision for portable oxygen equipment in the aircraft is adequate, in good condition, and accessible to the user.

NOTE: Check portable equipment including its security provisions frequently, since it is more susceptible to personnel abuse than a permanently-installed system.

9-48. INSPECTION. Hands, clothing, and tools must be free of oil, grease, and dirt when working with oxygen equipment. Traces of these organic materials near compressed oxygen may result in spontaneous combustion, explosions, and/or fire.

a. Oxygen Tanks and Cylinders. Inspect the entire exterior surface of the cylinder for indication of abuse, dents, bulges, and strap chafing.

(1) Examine the neck of cylinder for cracks, distortion, or damaged threads.

(2) Check the cylinder to determine if the markings are legible.

(3) Check the date of the last hydrostatic test. If the periodic retest date is past, do not return the cylinder to service until the test has been accomplished.

(4) Inspect the cylinder mounting bracket, bracket hold-down bolts, and cylinder-holding straps for cracks, deformation, cleanliness, and security of attachment.

(5) In the immediate area where the cylinder is stored or secured, check for evidence of any types of interference, chafing, deformation, or deterioration.

b. Lines and Fittings.

(1) Inspect oxygen lines for chafing, corrosion, flat spots and irregularities, i.e., sharp bends, kinks, and inadequate security.

(2) Check fittings for corrosion around the threaded area where lines are joined. Pressurize the system and check for leaks. (See paragraph 9-49b(2)(d).)

CAUTION: In pressurizing the system, actuate the valve slowly to avoid surging which could rupture the line.

c. Regulators, Valves, and Gauges.

(1) Examine all parts for cracks, nicks, damaged threads or other apparent damage.

(2) Actuate the regulator controls and the valve to check for ease of operation.

(3) Determine if the gauge is functioning properly by observing the pressure build-up and the return to zero when the system oxygen is bled off.

d. Masks and Hoses.

(1) Check the oxygen mask for fabric cracks and rough face seals. If the mask is a full-face model, inspect the glass or plastic for cleanliness and state of repair.

(2) When appropriate, with due regard to hygienic considerations, the sealing qualities of an oxygen mask may be tested by placing a thumb over the connection at the end of the mask tube and inhaling very lightly. Remove the thumb from the disconnect after each continuous inhalation. If there is no leakage, the mask will adhere tightly to the face during inhalation, and definite resistance to inhalation will be noticeable.

(3) Flex the mask hose gently over its entirety and check for evidence of deterioration or dirt.

(4) Examine the mask and hose storage compartment for cleanliness and general condition.

(5) If the mask and hose storage compartment is provided with a cover or release mechanism, thoroughly check the operation of the mechanism.

9-49. MAINTENANCE.

a. Oxygen Tanks, Cylinders, and Hold-Down Brackets.

(1) Remove from service any cylinders that show signs of abuse, dents, bulges, cracks, distortion, damaged thread, or defects which might render them unsafe. Typical examples

of oxygen cylinder damage are shown in figure 9-14.

(2) When replacing an oxygen cylinder, be certain that the replacement cylinder is of the same size and weight as the one removed.

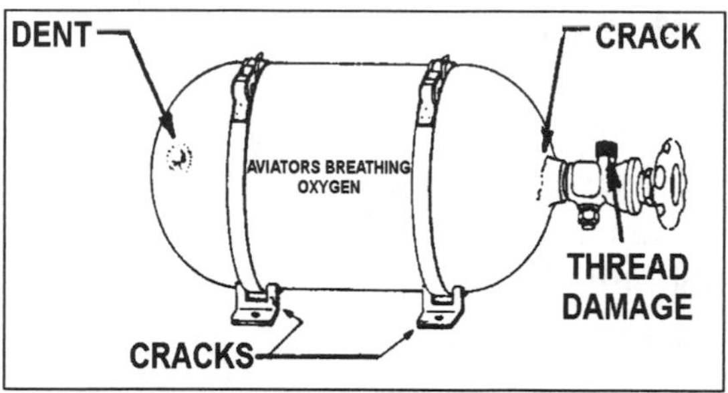

FIGURE 9-14. Oxygen cylinder damage.

NOTE: Cylinders having greater weight or size will require strengthened cylinder mounting brackets and a reevaluation to determine that the larger or heavier cylinder will not interfere with adjacent systems, components, or structural members, and that the strength of attaching structure is adequate and any additional weight will be computed into the aircraft's weight and balance report.

(3) Replace or repair any cylinder mounting brackets that show signs of wear. Visible cracks may be welded in accordance with manufacturer's standards. Replace the cylinder straps or clamps that show wear or abuse. For typical mounting bracket cracks and failure, see figure 9-15.

b. Lines and Fittings.

(1) Replace any oxygen line that is chafed, rusted, corroded, dented, cracked, or kinked.

(2) Clean oxygen system fittings showing signs of rusting or corrosion in the threaded area. To accomplish this, use a cleaner recommended by manufacturers of oxygen equipment. Replace lines and fittings that cannot be cleaned.

(a) The high-pressure lines which are located between the oxygen bottle (outside the oxygen service filler) and the regulator are normally fabricated from stainless steel or thick-wall, seamless copper alloy tubing. The fittings on high-pressure lines are normally silver brazed.

NOTE: Use silver alloys free of cadmium when silver brazing. The use of silver brazing alloys, which contain cadmium, will emit a poisonous gas when heated to a molten state. This gas is extremely hazardous to health if inhaled.

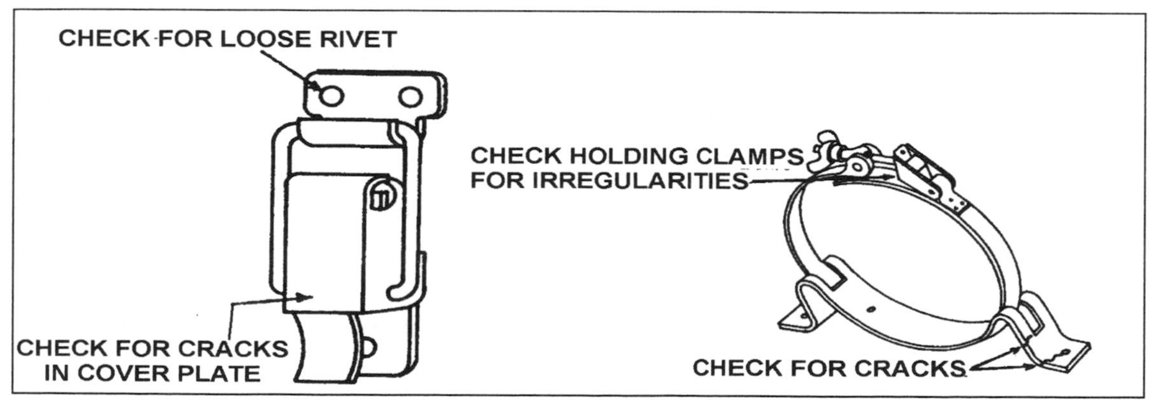

FIGURE 9-15. Cylinder brackets and clamps.

(b) The low-pressure lines extend from the pressure regulator to each passenger and crew oxygen outlet. These lines are fabricated from seamless aluminum alloy, copper, or flexible hose. Normally, flare- or flange-type connections are used.

CAUTION: Do not allow oil, grease, flammable solvent, or other combustibles such as lint or dust to come in contact with threads or any parts that will be exposed to pressurized oxygen.

(c) It is advisable to purge the oxygen system any time work has been accomplished on any of the lines and fittings. Use dry nitrogen or dry air for purging the system. All open lines should be capped immediately after purging.

(d) When oxygen is being lost from a system through leakage, a sequence of steps may be necessary to locate the opening. Leakage may often be detected by listening for the distinct hissing sound of escaping gas. If this check proves negative, it will be necessary to soap-test all lines and connections with a castile soap and water solution or specially compounded leak-test material. Make the solution thick enough to adhere to the contours of the fittings. At the completion of the leakage test, remove all traces of the soap and water.

CAUTION: Do not attempt to tighten any connections while the system is charged.

c. Regulators, Valves, and Gauges. Line maintenance of oxygen regulators, valves, and gauges does not include major repair. These components are precision made and their repair usually requires the attention of a repair station or the manufacturer. Care must be taken when reinstalling these components to ascertain if the threaded area is free of nicks, burrs, and contaminants that would prevent the connections from sealing properly.

CAUTION: Do not use petroleum lubricants on these components.

d. Masks and Hoses.

(1) Troubleshooting. If a mask assembly is defective (leaks, does not allow breathing, or contains a defective microphone), it is advisable to return the mask assembly to the manufacturer or a repair station.

(2) Maintenance Practice and Cleaning.

(a) Clean and disinfect the mask assemblies after use, as appropriate.

NOTE: Use care to avoid damaging the microphone assembly while cleaning and sterilizing.

(b) Wash the mask with a mild soap solution and rinse it with clear water.

(c) To sterilize, swab the mask thoroughly with a gauze or sponge soaked in a water merthiolate solution. This solution should contain 1/5-teaspoon of merthiolate per 1 quart of water. Wipe the mask with a clean cloth and air dry.

(d) Replace the hose if it shows evidence of deterioration.

(e) Hoses may be cleaned in the same manner as the mask.

(f) Observe that each mask breathing tube end is free of nicks, and that the tube end will slip into the cabin oxygen receptacle with ease and not leak.

9-50. FUNCTIONAL TESTING AFTER REPAIR. Following repair, and before inspection plates, cover plates, or upholstering are replaced, test the entire system.

a. **Open the cylinder valve** slowly and observe the pressure gauge on a high-pressure system. A pressure of approximately 1,800 psi (at 70 °F) should be indicated on the gauge. (Cylinder pressure will vary considerably with radical temperature changes.)

(1) Check the system by installing one of the mask hose fittings (minus the mask) in each of the cabin wall outlets to determine whether there is a flow. If a demand mask is used, check by breathing through the mask and, if appropriate, clean the mask according to paragraph 9-49d.

(2) Check the complete system for leaks in accordance with the procedure outlined in paragraph 9-49b(2)(d).

(3) If leaks are found, close the cylinder valve and open an outlet to reduce the pressure in the system to zero.

b. **The following checks** may be made for a pressure drop check of the system.

(1) Open the cylinder valve and pressurize the system. Observe the pressure gauge (a pressure of approximately 1,800 psi at 70 °F should be indicated). For the light weight ICC 3HT 1850 cylinders, pressurize the system to approximately 1,850 psi at 70 °F.

(2) Close the cylinder valve and wait approximately 5 minutes for temperatures to stabilize.

(3) Record the pressure gauge reading and temperature and after 1 hour, record the pressure gauge reading and temperature again.

(4) A maximum pressure drop of 100 psi is permissible.

NOTE: Conduct the above tests in an area where changes of temperature will be less than 10 °F. If a leak occurs during the 1-hour period, suitable corrections would be required, or reconduct the test under conditions of unvarying temperatures.

9-51. SERVICE OXYGEN CYLINDERS. REQUIREMENTS (Ref 49 CFR 173.34 e, 16). Standard-weight cylinders must be hydrostatic tested at the end of each 5-year period (10 years if it meets the requirements in 49 CFR 173.34 e, 16). This is a Department of Transportation (DOT) requirement. These-cylinders carry an ICC or DOT 3AA 1800 classification and are suitable for the use intended.

Lightweight cylinders must be hydrostatic tested every 3 years, and must be retired from service after 24 years or 4,380 pressurizations, whichever occurs first. These cylinders carry an ICC or DOT 3 HT 1850 classification and must be stamped with the approval after being inspected. (Ref. 49 CFR 173.34 e, 15).

CAUTION: Use only aviation breathing oxygen when having the oxygen bottle charged.

a. **Charging High-Pressure Oxygen Cylinders.** The following are recommended procedures for charging high-pressure oxygen cylinders from a manifold system, either permanently-installed or trailer-mounted.

CAUTION: Never attempt to charge a low-pressure cylinder directly from a high-pressure manifold system or cylinder.

(1) Inspection. Do not attempt to charge oxygen cylinders if any of the following discrepancies exist:

(a) Inspect for contaminated fittings on the manifold, cylinder, or outside filler valve. If cleaning is needed, wipe with stabilized trichlorethylene and let air dry. Do not permit the solvent to enter any internal parts.

(b) Check the hydrostatic test date of the cylinder. DOT regulations require ICC or DOT 3AA *1800* designation cylinders to be hydrostatic tested to 5/3 their working pressure, every 5 years (10 years if they meet the requirements in 49 CFR 173.34,e, 16).

Cylinders bearing designation ICC or DOT 3HT *1850* (Ref. 49 CFR 173.34,e, 15) must be hydrostatic tested to 5/3 their working pressure every 3 years, and retired from service 24 years or 4,380 filling cycles after the date of manufacture, whichever occurs first.

(c) If the cylinder is completely empty, do not charge. An empty cylinder must be removed, inspected, and cleaned before charging.

(2) Charging.

(a) Connect the cylinder valve outlet or the outside filler valve to the manifold.

(b) Slowly open the valve of the cylinder to be charged and observe the pressure on the gauge of the manifold system.

(c) Slowly open the valve of the cylinder on the manifold system having the lowest pressure and allow the pressure to equalize.

(d) Close the cylinder valve on the manifold system and slowly open the valve of the cylinder having the next highest pressure. Continue this procedure until the cylinder has been charged in accordance with table 9-5.

(e) Close all valves on the manifold system.

(f) Close the valve on the filled cylinder and remove the cylinder from the manifold.

(g) Using a leak detector, test for leakage around the cylinder valve threaded connections. (If leakage is present, discharge the oxygen and return the cylinder to the facility for repair.)

(h) Let the cylinder stabilize for a period of at least 1 hour, and then recheck the pressure.

(i) Make any necessary adjustments in the pressure.

b. Charging of Low-Pressure Oxygen Systems and Portables. For recharging a low-pressure aircraft oxygen system, or portable cylinders, it is essential that the oxygen trailer or cart have a pressure-reducing regulator. Military types E-2 or C-1 reducing regulators are satisfactory. These types of regulators reduce the large cylinder pressure from 2,000 psi to a line pressure of 450 psi. (A welding pressure-reducing regulator is not satisfactory.)

CAUTION: When refilling the low-pressure system or portable cylinders, open the oxygen filler tank valve slowly to allow the system or portable cylinders to be filled at a slow rate. After the refilling operation is completed, check for leaks with a leak detector. If a leak is detected, paragraph 9-49b(2)(d) should be referred to for corrective action.

TABLE 9-5. Table of filling pressures.

Initial Temp (° F)	Filling Pressure (psi)
0	1,650
10	1,700
20	1,725
30	1,775
40	1,825
50	1,875
60	1,925
70	1,975
80	2,000
90	2,050
100	2,100
110	2,150
120	2,200
130	2,250

Initial Temperature-Refers to the ambient temperature in the filling room.

Filling Pressure-Refers to the pressure to which aircraft cylinders should be filled. This table gives approximations only, and assumes a rise in temperature of approximately 25 °F. due to the heat of compression. This table also assumes the aircraft cylinders will be filled as quickly as possible and that they will only be cooled by ambient air, with no water bath or other means of cooling being used.

Example: If ambient temperature is 70 °F, fill aircraft cylinders to approximately 1,975 psi-as close to this pressure as the gauge may be read. Upon cooling, cylinders should have approximately 1,850 psi pressure

9-52.—9-59. [RESERVED.]

SECTION 4. CABIN INTERIOR

9-60. GENERAL. Only materials that are flash-resistant should be used in cabin interiors. The requirements related to fire protection qualities of cabin interior materials are specified in CAR 3.388, fire precautions or 14 CFR part 23, section 23.853 compartment interiors

9-61. CAR-3 AIRCRAFT INTERIOR. The requirement for an interior of a CAR-3 aircraft that is used only in 14 CFR, part 91 operations, where smoking is not permitted, is that the materials shall be flash-resistant. (Reference CAR-3.388.)

a. For compartments in CAR-3 aircraft where smoking is permitted, the wall and ceiling linings, the covering of all upholstering, floors, and furnishings shall be flame-resistant. Such compartments should be equipped with an adequate number of self-contained ash trays. All other compartments shall be placarded against smoking. (Refer to CAR-3.388.)

(1) If fabric is bought in bulk to refurbish the interior, seats, and ceiling liners for a CAR-3 aircraft used in part 91 operations, a manufacturer's statement, declaring that the material meets the American Society for Testing and Materials (ASTM) or similar national standard for either flash resistance or flame resistance, would be acceptable, but only for a CAR-3 aircraft installation. (Refer to 14 CFR part 43, section 43.13(a).) A manufacturer's statement is acceptable due to neither the Civil Aeronautics Administration (CAA) nor the Federal Aviation Administration (FAA) having published an FAA fire standard for either flash or flame resistance for interior materials for CAR-3 aircraft. Since the FAA would accept and recognize a national standard, the mechanic would reference the manufacturer's statement and the national standard that the material meets in the aircraft's maintenance records.

(2) If an annual inspection is performed on a CAR-3 aircraft with a new interior and there is no mention of a manufacturer's statement that the fabric is flash or flame resistant as applicable, the possibility exists that the fabric is an unapproved part. The mechanic should take the necessary steps to ensure that the fabric meets or exceeds the ASTM or national standards. (Refer to 14 CFR part 23, appendix F.)

(3) If an FAA-approved STC interior kit is installed in a CAR-3 aircraft, and the material and fabric in the kit are PMA or TSO approved, the mechanic should include the STC number in block 8 of FAA Form 337.

b. It is recommended that for all CAR-3 interiors to use only fabric and materials that meets the more stringent requirements of part 23, appendix F.

9-62. PART 23 AIRCRAFT INTERIOR. Materials used in part 23 aircraft interiors must meet the requirements of section 23.853, and the burn test requirements called out in part 23, appendix F.

a. If the fabric is bought in bulk to refurbish a part 23 aircraft then the fabric must meet the part 23 burn requirements. A burn test would have to be done on samples of the material and fabrics by an approved and rated FAA Repair Station. That FAA Repair Station would certify that all the material and fabrics meet part 23, appendix F requirements. The mechanic would include that repair station's statement in the aircraft's records.

b. If STC-approved interior kit with either PMA or TSO-approved materials for a part 23 aircraft is bought, the mechanic would only have to reference the STC number on FAA Form 337 and the aircraft's records. Part 23, appendix F would not be required.

c. If an annual inspection is to be performed on a part 23 aircraft in which a new interior was installed, but the aircraft's records do not reflect that a burn test was performed on the interior's materials and fabric by an FAA Approved Repair Station, or there is no mention of an STC or FAA Form 337 in the aircraft records, then a burn test that meets, part 23, appendix F must be accomplished before the aircraft is approved for return to service.

9-63. SOURCE OF INFORMATION. If information regarding the original or properly altered fire protection qualities of certain cabin interior materials is not available, requests for this information should be made to the aircraft manufacturer or the local FAA regional office, specifying the model aircraft and the aircraft manufacturer. The date the aircraft was manufactured or the serial number, and the 14 CFR part under which the aircraft is operated (i.e., CAR-3, 14 CFR part 91, or part 121, etc.).

9-64. UPHOLSTERY AND/OR BELTS. Upholstery and/or belts that have been washed may lose some or all of their fire-resistant qualities. Unless the soap is completely removed from the cloth, the strength of the material may be significantly reduced. Consult the manufacturer to determine how to maintain the fire-resistant qualities.

9-65.—9-70. [RESERVED.]

CHAPTER 10. WEIGHT AND BALANCE

SECTION 1 TERMINOLOGY

10-1. GENERAL. The removal or addition of equipment results in changes to the center of gravity (c.g.). The empty weight of the aircraft, and the permissible useful load are affected accordingly. Investigate the effects of these changes, since the aircraft flight characteristics may be adversely affected. Information on which to base the record of weight and balance changes to the aircraft may be obtained from the pertinent Aircraft Specifications, Type Certificate Data Sheet (TCDS), prescribed aircraft operating limitations, aircraft flight manual, aircraft weight and balance report, and maintenance manual. Removal of standard parts with negligible weight or addition of minor items of equipment such as nuts, bolts, rivets, washers, and similar standard parts of negligible weight on fixed-wing aircraft do not require a weight and balance check. Rotorcraft are, in general, more critical with respect to control with changes in the c.g. position. Refer to the procedures and instructions in that particular model's maintenance or flight manual.

10-2. TERMINOLOGY. The following terminology is used in the practical application of weight and balance control.

a. Maximum Weight. The maximum weight is the maximum authorized weight of the aircraft and its contents as listed in the specifications.

b. Empty Weight. The empty weight of an aircraft includes all operating equipment that has a fixed location and is actually installed in the aircraft. It includes the weight of the airframe, powerplant, required equipment, optional and special equipment, fixed ballast, full engine coolant, hydraulic fluid, residual fuel, and oil. Additional information regarding fluids that may be contained in the aircraft systems and must be included in the empty weight will be indicated in the pertinent Aircraft Specifications or TCDS.

c. Negligible Weight Change is any change of one pound or less for aircraft whose weight empty is less than 5,000 pounds; two pounds or less for aircraft whose weight empty is more than 5,000 and 50,000 pounds; and five pounds or less for aircraft whose weight empty is more than 50,000 pounds. Negligible c. g. change is any change of less than 0.05% MAC for fixed wing aircraft, 0.2 percent of the maximum allowable c. g. range for rotary wing aircraft.

d. Useful Load. The useful load is the empty weight subtracted from the maximum weight of the aircraft. This load consists of the pilot, crew (if applicable), maximum oil, fuel, passengers, and baggage unless otherwise noted.

e. Weight Check. The weight check consists of checking the sum of the weights of all items of useful load against the authorized useful load (maximum weight less empty weight) of the aircraft.

f. Datum. The datum is an imaginary vertical plane from which all horizontal measurements are taken for balance purposes with the aircraft in level flight attitude. The datum is indicated in most Aircraft Specifications or TCDS. On some of the older aircraft, when the datum is not indicated, any convenient datum may be selected. Once the datum is selected, all moment arms and the location of the permissible c.g. range must be taken with reference to it. Examples of typical locations of the datum are shown in figure 10-1.

g. Arm (or Moment Arm). The arm (or moment arm) is the horizontal distance in inches from the datum to the c.g. of an item. The algebraic sign is plus (+) if measured aft of the datum, and minus (-) if measured forward of the datum. Examples of plus and minus arms are shown in figure 10-2.

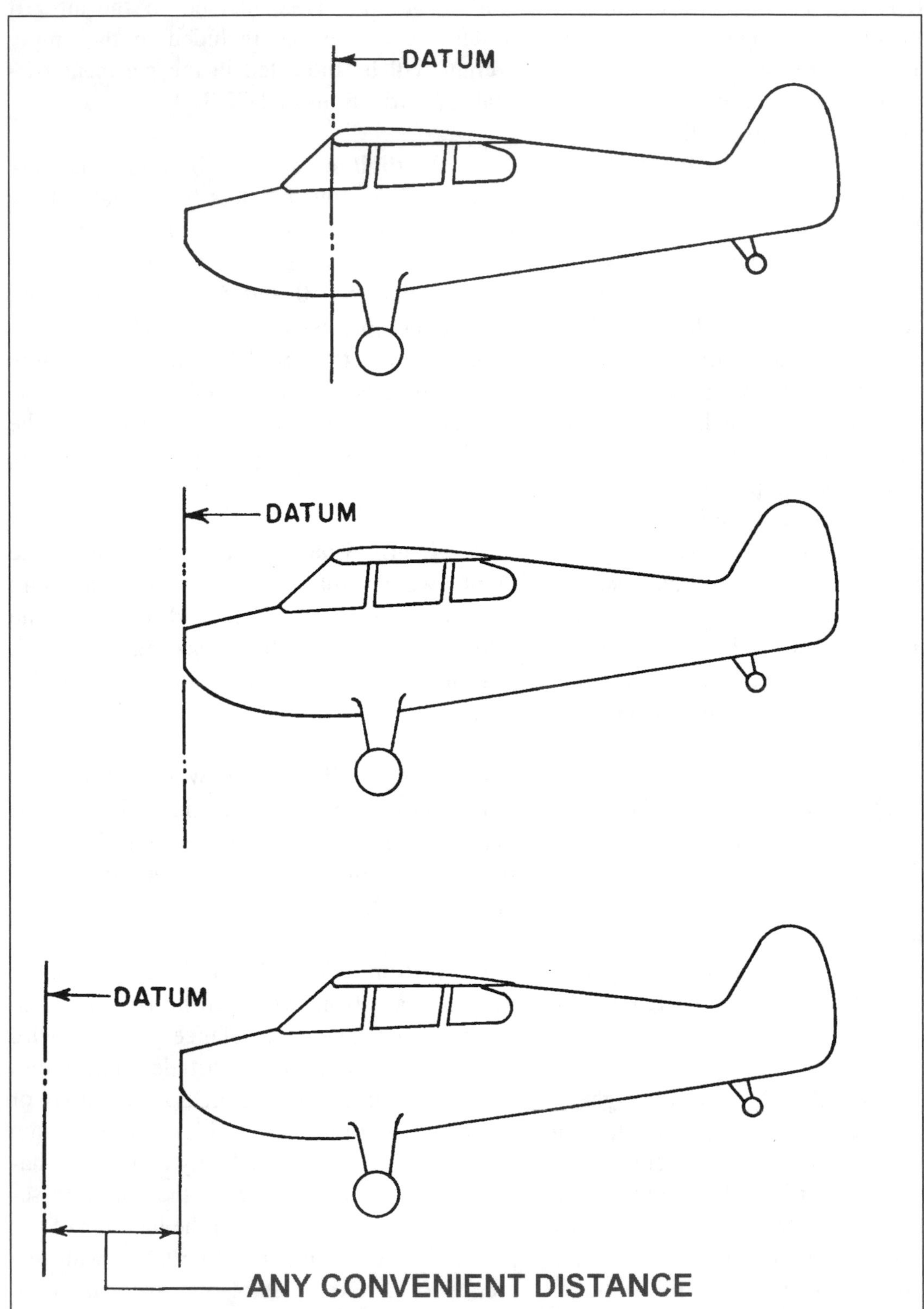

FIGURE 10-1. Typical datum locations.

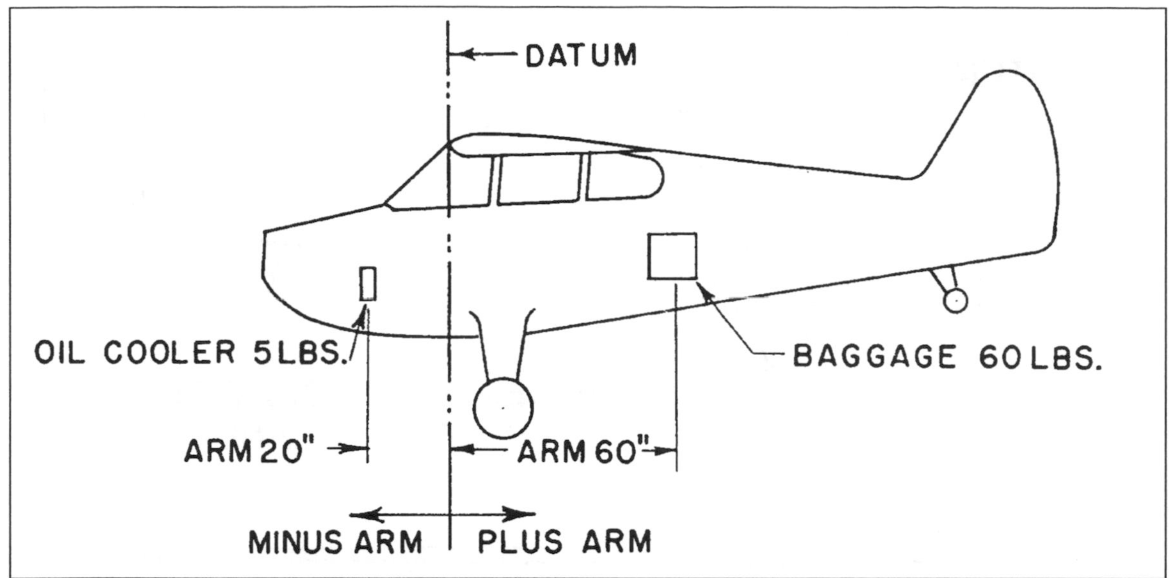

FIGURE 10-2. Illustration of arm (or moment arm).

h. Moment. The moment is the product of a weight multiplied by its arm. The moment of an item about the datum is obtained by multiplying the weight of the item by its horizontal distance from the datum. A typical moment calculation is given in figure 10-3.

i. Center of Gravity. The c.g. is a point about which the nose-heavy and tail-heavy moments are exactly equal in magnitude. If the aircraft is suspended from the c.g., it will not have a tendency to pitch in either direction (nose up or down). The weight of the aircraft (or any object) may be assumed to be concentrated at its c.g. (See figure 10-3.)

j. Empty Weight Center of Gravity. The empty weight c.g. is the c.g. of an aircraft in its empty weight condition, and is an essential part of the weight and balance record. Formulas for determining the c.g. for tail and nosewheel type aircraft are given in figure 10-4. Typical examples of computing the empty weight and empty weight c.g. for aircraft are shown in figures 10-5 and 10-6.

k. Empty Weight Center of Gravity Range. The empty weight c.g. range is determined so that the empty weight c.g. limits will not be exceeded under standard specifications loading arrangements. Calculations as outlined in paragraph 10-16 should be completed when it is possible to load an aircraft in a manner not covered in the Aircraft Specifications or TCDS (extra tanks, extra seats, etc.). The empty weight c.g. range, when applicable, is listed in the Aircraft Specifications or TCDS. Calculation of empty weight c.g. is shown in figures 10-5 and 10-6.

l. Operating Center of Gravity Range. The operating c.g. range is the distance between the forward and rearward c.g. limits indicated in the pertinent Aircraft Specifications or TCDS. These limits are determined for the most forward and most rearward loaded c.g. positions at which the aircraft meets the requirements of Title 14 of the Code of Federal Regulation (14 CFR). The limits are indicated in the specifications in either percent of mean aerodynamic chord (MAC) or inches from the

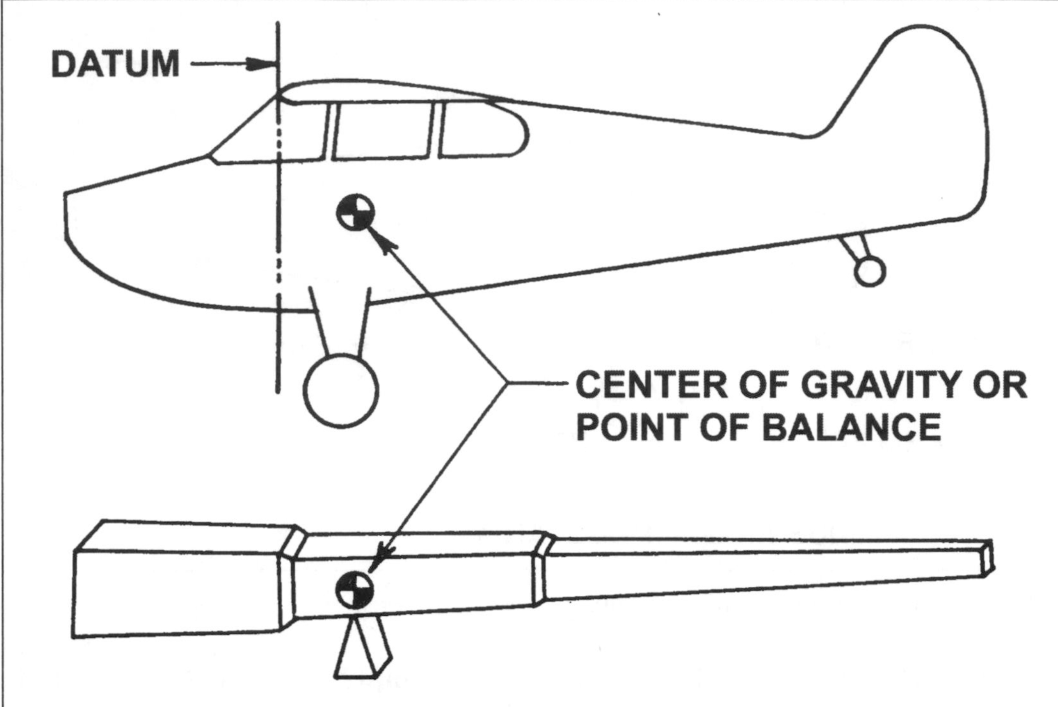

The entire aircraft weight may be considered to be concentrated at the center of gravity. Therefore, the moment of the aircraft about the datum is the weight of the aircraft times the horizontal distance between the C.G. and the datum.

Example: If the weight of this airplane is 2000 lbs. and the arm from the datum to the center of gravity is 16 inches, the moment of the aircraft about the datum is 2000 x 16 or 32,000 in. lbs.

FIGURE 10-3. Example of moment computation.

datum. The c.g. of the loaded aircraft must be within these limits at all times as illustrated in figure 10-7.

m. Mean Aerodynamic Chord (MAC). The MAC is established by the manufacturer who defines its leading edge and its trailing edge in terms of inches from the datum. The c.g. location and various limits are then expressed in percentages of the chord. The location and dimensions of the MAC can be found in the Aircraft Specifications, the TCDS, the aircraft flight manual, or the aircraft weight and balance report.

n. Weighing Point. If the c.g. location is determined by weighing, it is necessary to obtain horizontal measurements between the points on the scale at which the aircraft's weight is concentrated. If weighed using

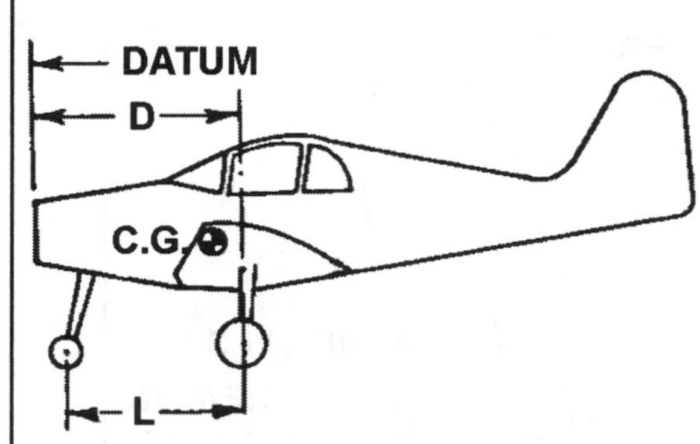

NOSE WHEEL TYPE AIRCRAFT

DATUM LOCATED FORWARD OF THE MAIN WHEELS

$$C.G. = D - \left(\frac{F \times L}{W}\right)$$

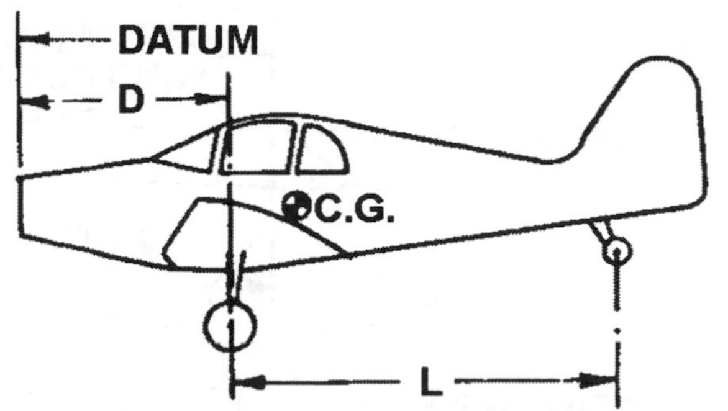

TAIL WHEEL TYPE AIRCRAFT

DATUM LOCATED FORWARD OF THE MAIN WHEELS

$$C.G. = D + \left(\frac{R \times L}{W}\right)$$

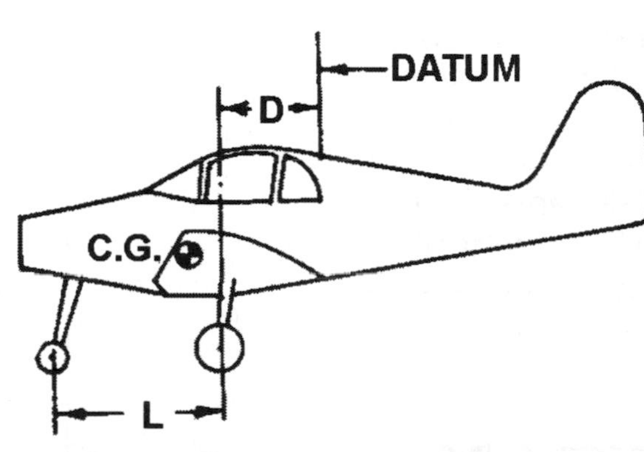

NOSE WHEEL TYPE AIRCRAFT

DATUM LOCATED AFT OF THE MAIN WHEELS

$$C.G. = -\left(D + \frac{F \times L}{W}\right)$$

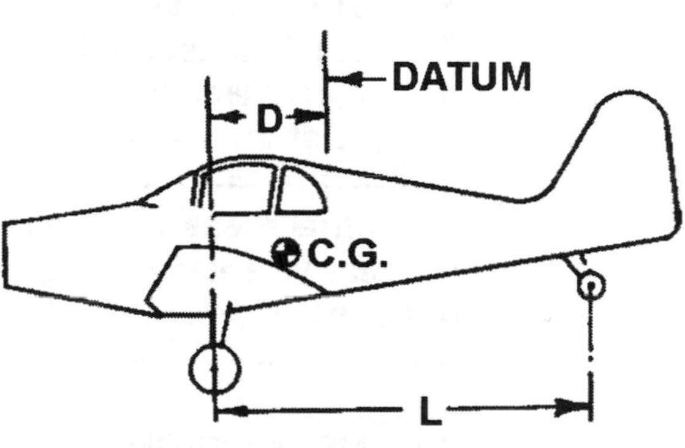

TAIL WHEEL TYPE AIRCRAFT

DATUM LOCATED AFT OF THE MAIN WHEELS

$$C.G. = -D + \left(\frac{R \times L}{W}\right)$$

C.G. = Distance from datum to center of gravity of the aircraft.
W = The weight of the aircraft at the time of weighing.
D = The horizontal distance measured from the datum to the main wheel weighing point.
L = The horizontal distance measured from the main wheel weighing point to the nose or tail weighing point.
F = The weight at the nose weighing point.
R = The weight at the tail weighing point.

FIGURE 10-4. Empty weight center of gravity formulas.

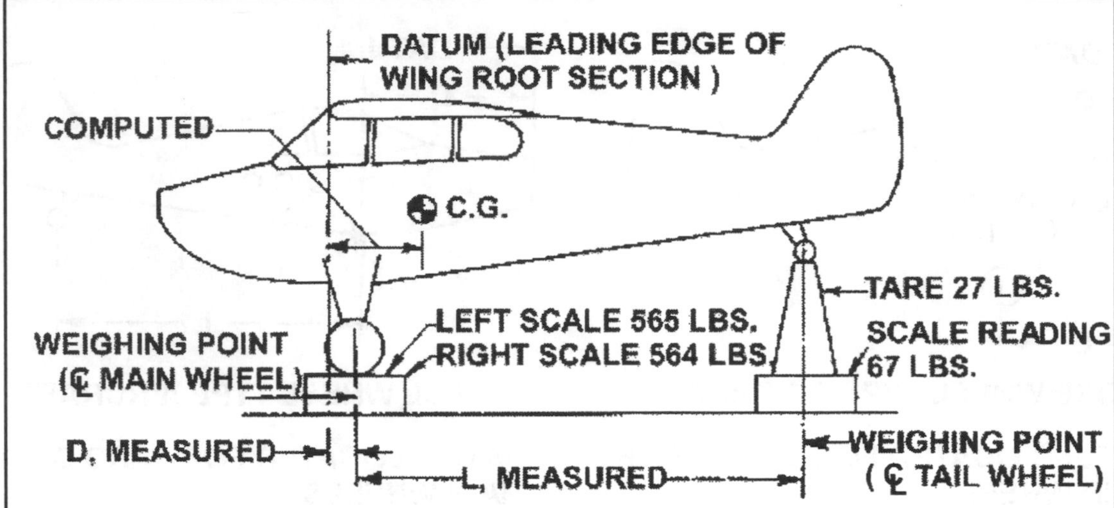

TO FIND: EMPTY WEIGHT AND EMPTY WEIGHT CENTER OF GRAVITY

Datum is the leading edge of the wing (from aircraft specification)

(D) Actual measured horizontal distance from the main wheel weighing point (℄ main wheel) to the Datum -- 3"

(L) Actual measured horizontal distance from the rear wheel weighing point (℄ rear wheel) to the main wheel weighing point -- 222"

SOLVING : EMPTY WEIGHT

Weighing Point	Scale Reading #	Tare #	Net Weight #
Right	564	0	564
Left	565	0	565
Rear	67	27	40
Empty Weight (W)			1169

SOLVING: EMPTY WEIGHT CENTER OF GRAVITY

Formula: $C.G. = D + \frac{R \times L}{W} = 3" + \frac{40 \times 222}{1169} = 3" + 7.6" = 10.6"$

Reference for formula, Figure 10-4.

This case is shown properly entered on a sample weight and balance report form, Figure 10-17

FIGURE 10-5. Empty weight and empty center of gravity - tail-wheel type aircraft.

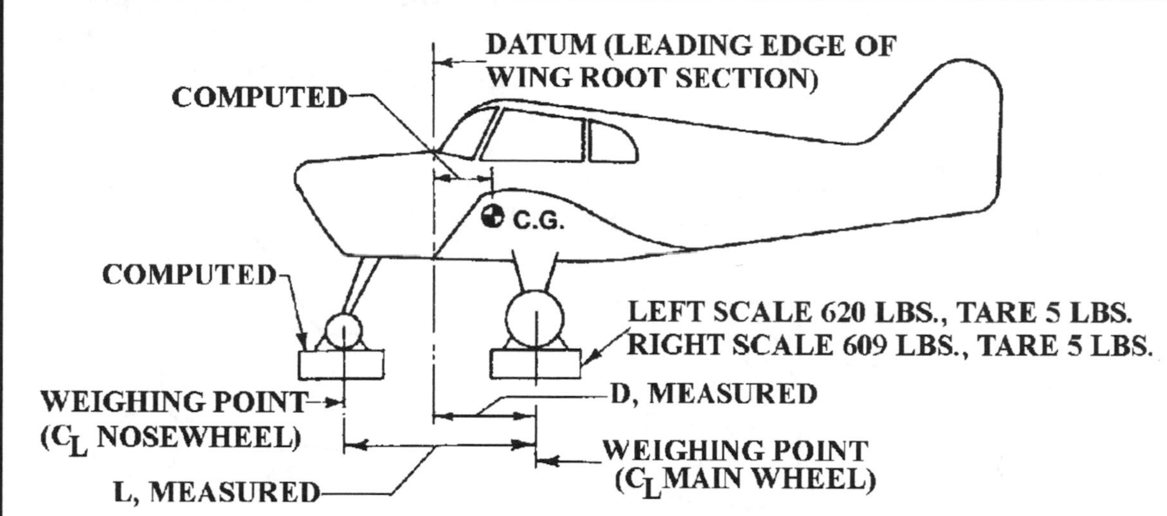

TO FIND: EMPTY WEIGHT AND EMPTY WEIGHT CENTER OF GRAVITY

Datum is the leading edge of the wing (from aircraft specification)
(D) Actual measured horizontal distance from the main wheel weighing point (C_L main wheel) to the Datum -- 34.0"
(L) Actual measured horizontal distance from the front wheel weighing point (C_L front wheel) to the main wheel weighing point -- 67.8"

SOLVING: EMPTY WEIGHT

Weighing Point	Scale Reading	Tare	Net Weight
Right	609	5	604
Left	620	5	615
Front	464	10	454
Empty Weight (W)			1673

SOLVING: EMPTY WEIGHT CENTER OF GRAVITY

Formula: $C.G. = D - \frac{F \times L}{W} = 34'' - \frac{454 \times 67.8}{1673} = 34'' - 18.4'' = 15.6''$

Reference for formula, Figure 10-4.

FIGURE 10-6. Empty weight and empty weight center of gravity - nosewheel-type aircraft.

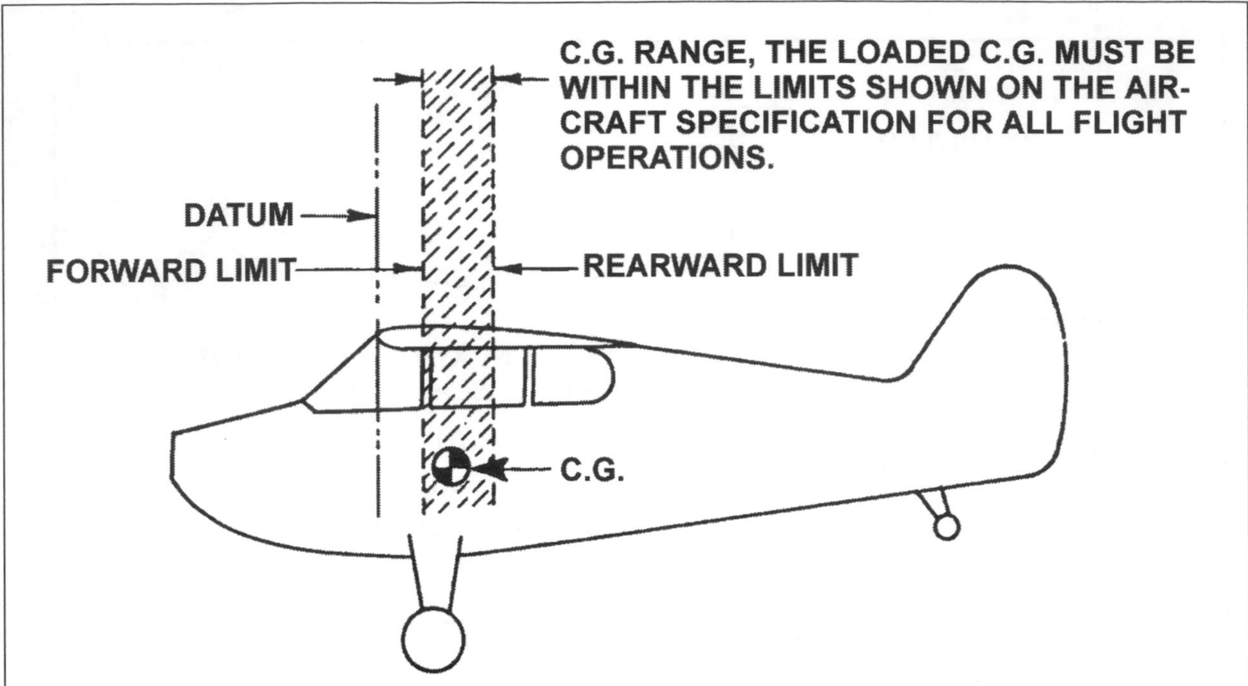

FIGURE 10-7. Operating center of gravity range.

scales under the landing gear tires, a vertical line passing through the centerline of the axle will locate the point on the scale at which the weight is concentrated. This point is called the "weighing point." Other structural locations capable of supporting the aircraft, such as jack pads on the main spar, may also be used if the aircraft weight is resting on the jack pads. Indicate these points clearly in the weight and balance report when used instead of the landing gear. Typical locations of the weighing points are shown in figure 10-8.

o. Zero Fuel Weight. The maximum permissible weight of a loaded aircraft (passengers, crew, cargo, etc.) less its fuel is zero fuel weight. All weights in excess of maximum zero fuel weight must consist of usable fuel.

p. Minimum Fuel. The minimum fuel for balance purposes is 1/12 gallon per maximum-except-take-off horsepower (METO). Minimum fuel is the maximum amount of fuel which can be used in weight and balance computations when low fuel might adversely affect the most critical balance conditions. To determine the weight of fuel in pounds divide the METO horsepower by two.

q. Full Oil. The full oil is the quantity of oil shown in the Aircraft Specifications or TCDS as oil capacity. Use full oil as the quantity of oil when making the loaded weight and balance computations.

r. Tare. The weight of chocks, blocks, stands, etc., used when weighing aircraft is called tare and is included in the scale readings. Tare is deducted from the scale reading at each respective weighing point when tare is involved, to obtain the actual aircraft weight.

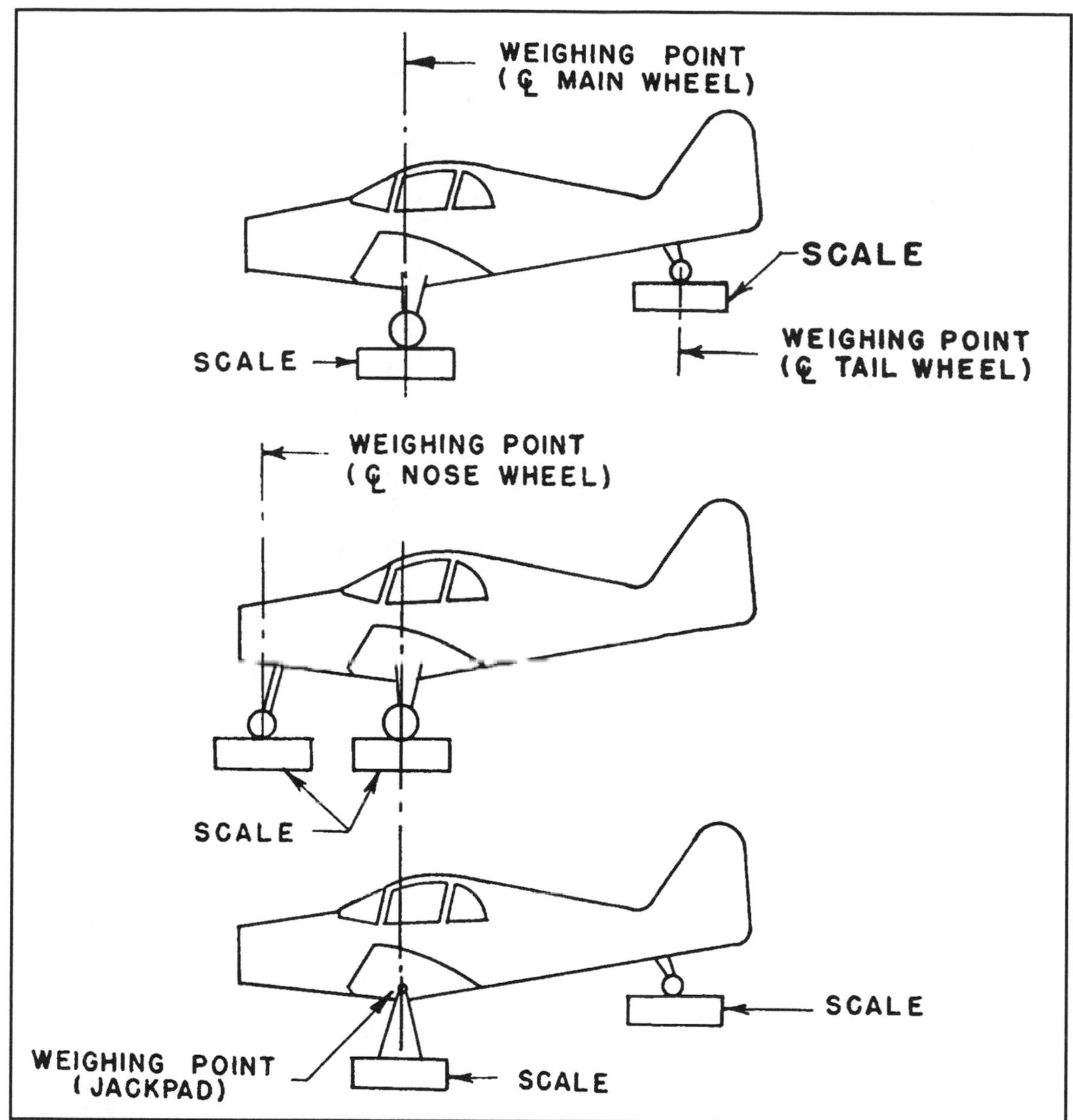

FIGURE 10-8. Weighing point centerline.

10-3.—10-13. [RESERVED.]

SECTION 2 WEIGHING PROCEDURES

10-14. GENERAL. Weighing procedures may vary with the aircraft and the type of weighing equipment employed. The weighing procedures contained in the manufacturer's maintenance manual should be followed for each particular aircraft.

10-15. PROCEDURES. Accepted procedures when weighing an aircraft are:

a. **Remove** excessive dirt, grease, moisture, etc., from the aircraft before weighing.

b. **Weigh the aircraft** inside a closed building to prevent error in scale reading due to wind.

c. **Determine the empty weight c. g.** by placing the aircraft in a level flight attitude.

d. **Have all items of equipment** that are included in the certificated empty weight report installed in the aircraft when weighing. These items of equipment are a part of the current weight and balance report.

e. **The scales** should have a current calibration before weighing begins. Zero and use the scales in accordance with the scale manufacturer's instructions. Platform scales and suitable support for the aircraft, if necessary, are usually placed under the wheels of a landplane, the keel of a seaplane float, or the skis of a skiplane. Other structural locations capable of supporting the aircraft, such as jack pads, may be used. Clearly indicate these points and the alternate equipment used in the weight and balance report.

f. **Drain the fuel system** until the quantity indicator reads *zero* or until the tanks are empty with the aircraft in level flight attitude, unless otherwise noted in the TCDS or Aircraft Specifications. The amount of fuel remaining in the tank, lines, and engine is termed residual fuel and is to be included in the empty weight. In special cases, the aircraft may be weighed with full fuel in tanks provided a definite means of determining the exact weight of the fuel is available.

g. **The oil system** should be filled to the quantity noted in the TCDS or Aircraft Specifications.

NOTE: On Civil Aeronautics Regulations (CAR-3) Certified Aircraft, the weight of the oil was subtracted mathematically to get the empty weight. In 14 CFR, part 23 aircraft, the weight of the oil is included in the empty weight.

When weighed with full oil, actual empty weight equals the actual recorded weight less the weight of the oil in the oil tank(oil weight = oil capacity in gallons x 7.5 pounds). Indicate on all weight and balance reports whether weights include full oil or oil drained. (See figure 10-9.)

h. **Do not set brakes** while taking scale reading.

i. **Note any tare reading** when the aircraft is removed from the scales.

10-15a. REPAIRS AND ALTERATIONS are the major sources of weight changes, and it is the responsibility of the aircraft mechanic making any repairs or alteration to know the weight and location of these changes, and to compute the new CG and record the new empty (EW) weight and EWCG data in the aircraft flight manual.

10-15b. ANNUAL OR 100-HOUR INSPECTION. After conducting an annual or 100-hour inspection, the aircraft mechanic must ensure the weight and balance data in the aircraft records is current and accurate.

10-16. WEIGHT AND BALANCE COMPUTATIONS. It is often necessary after completing an extensive alteration to establish by computation that the authorized weight and c.g. limits as shown in the TCDS and Aircraft Specifications are not exceeded. Paragraph b(2) explains the significance of algebraic signs used in balance computations.

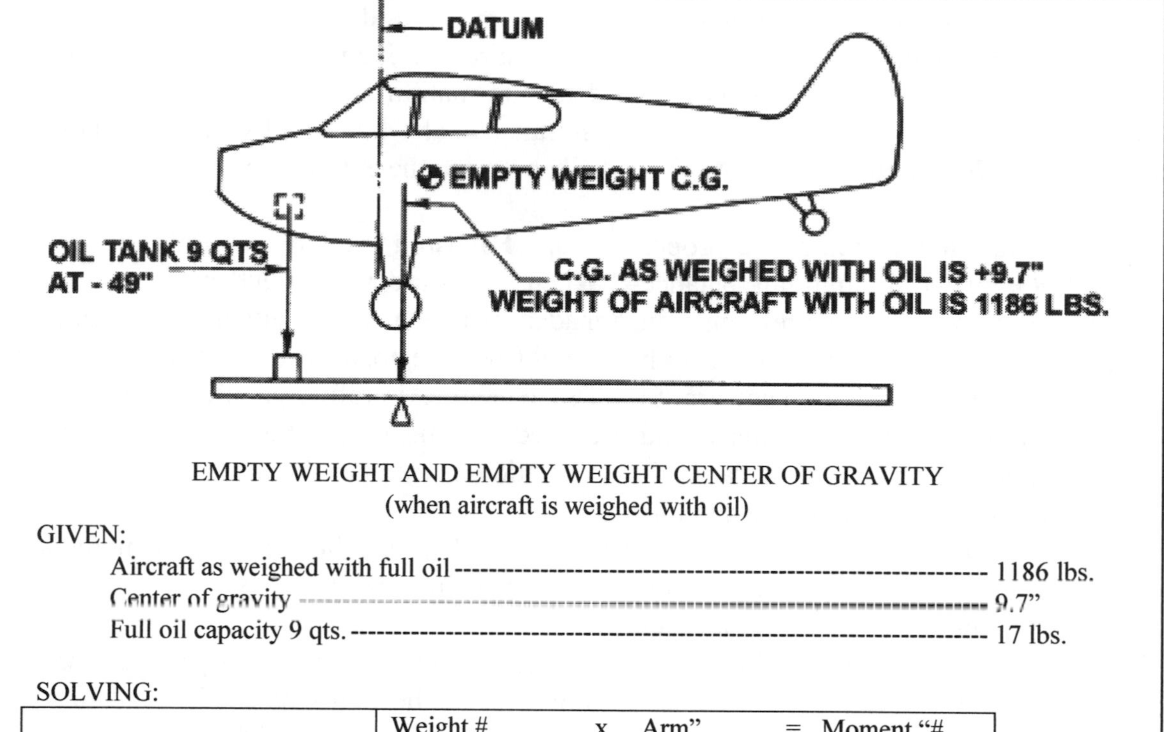

EMPTY WEIGHT AND EMPTY WEIGHT CENTER OF GRAVITY
(when aircraft is weighed with oil)

GIVEN:

Aircraft as weighed with full oil -- 1186 lbs.
Center of gravity --- 9.7"
Full oil capacity 9 qts. -- 17 lbs.

SOLVING:

	Weight #	x Arm"	= Moment "#
Aircraft as weighed	+ 1186	+ 9.7	+ 11504
Less oil	- 17	- 49.0	+ 833
Total	+ 1169(A)		+ 12337(B)

Empty Weight (A) = 1169 pounds

Empty Weight Center of Gravity $\frac{B}{A} = \frac{12337}{1169} = +10.6"$

FIGURE 10-9. Empty weight and empty weight center of gravity when aircraft is weighed with oil.

a. The TCDS or Aircraft Specifications contain the following information relating to the subject:

(1) Center of gravity range.

(2) Empty weight c.g. range when applicable.

(3) Leveling means.

(4) Datum.

(5) Maximum weights.

(6) Number of seats and arm.

(7) Maximum baggage and arm.

(8) Fuel capacity and arm.

(9) Oil capacity and arm.

(10) Equipment items and arm.

b. The TCDS do not list the basic required equipment prescribed by the applicable airworthiness regulations for certification. Refer to the manufacturer's equipment list for such information.

(1) Unit weight for weight and balance purposes.

Gasoline ----------- 6 pounds per U.S. gal.
Turbine Fuel ------ 6.7 pounds per U.S. gal.
Lubricating oil ---- 7.5 pounds per U.S. gal.
Crew and
passengers ----- 170 pounds per person.

(2) It is important to retain the proper algebraic sign (+ or -) through all balance computations. For the sake of uniformity in these computations, visualize the aircraft with the nose to the left. In this position any arm to the left (forward) of the datum is "minus" and any arm to the right (rearward) of the datum is "plus." Any item of weight added to the aircraft either side of the datum is plus weight, any weight item removed is a minus weight. When multiplying weights by arms, the answer is plus if the signs are the same, and minus if the signs are different. The following combinations are possible:

Items added forward of the datum-

(+) weight x (-) arm = (-) moment.

Items added to the rear of the datum-

(+) weight x (+) arm = (+) moment.

Items removed forward of the datum-

(-) weight x (-) arm = (+) moment.

Items removed rear of the datum-

(-) weight x (+) arm = (-) moment.

(3) The total weight of the airplane is equal to the weight of the empty aircraft plus the weight of the items added minus the weight of the items removed.

(4) The total moment of the aircraft is the algebraic sum of the empty weight moment of the aircraft and all of the individual moments of the items added and/or removed.

10-17. WEIGHT AND BALANCE EXTREME CONDITIONS. The weight and balance extreme conditions represent the maximum forward and rearward c.g. position for the aircraft. Include the weight and balance data information showing that the c.g. of the aircraft (usually in the fully loaded condition) falls between the extreme conditions.

a. Forward Weight and Balance Check. When a forward weight and balance check is made, establish that neither the maximum weight nor the forward c.g. limit listed in the TCDS and Aircraft Specifications are exceeded. To make this check, the following information is needed:

(1) The weights, arms, and moment of the empty aircraft.

(2) The maximum weights, arms, and moments of the items of useful load that are located ahead of the forward c.g. limit.

(3) The minimum weights, arms, and moments of the items of useful load that are located aft of the forward c.g. limit. A typical example of the computation necessary to make this check, using this data, is shown in figure 10-10.

b. Rearward Weight and Balance Check. When a rearward weight and balance check is made, establish that neither the maximum weight nor the rearward c.g. limit listed in the TCDS and Aircraft Specifications are exceeded. To make this check, the following information is needed:

(1) The weight, arms, and moments of the empty aircraft.

(2) The maximum weights, arms, and moments of the items of useful load that are located aft of the rearward c.g. limit.

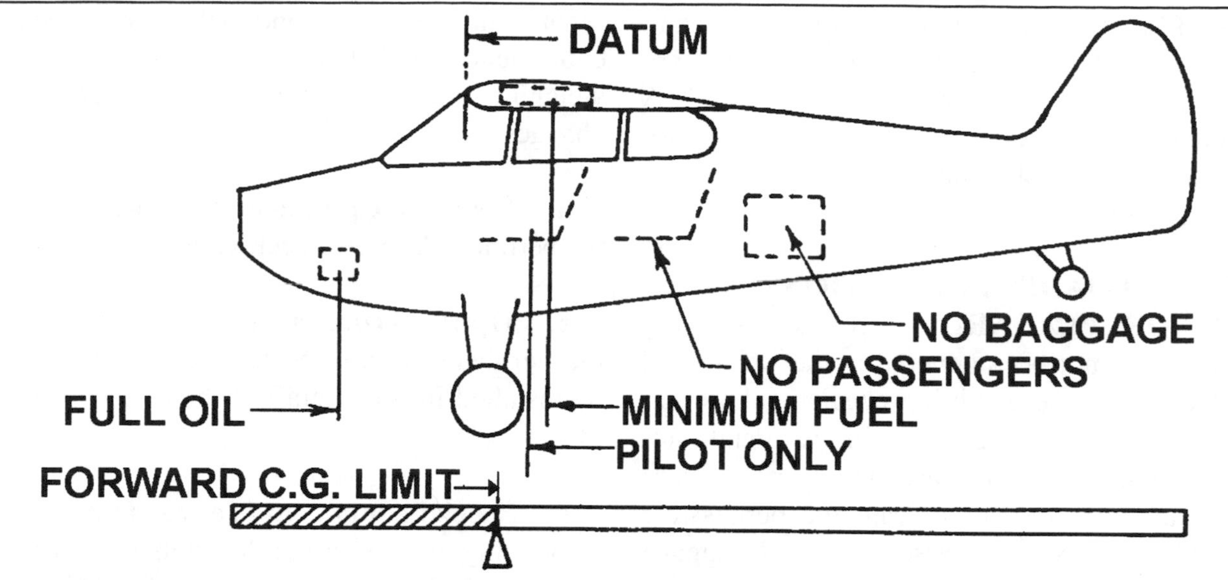

TO CHECK: MOST FORWARD WEIGHT AND BALANCE EXTREME.

GIVEN;
Actual empty weight of the aircraft---------- 1169#
Empty weight center of gravity---------- + 10.6"
*Maximum weight----------2100#
*Forward C.G.. limit ---------- + 8.5"
*Oil capacity, 9 qts. ---------- 17# at -49"
*Pilot in farthest forward seat equipped with controls (unless otherwise placarded) ---------- 170# at +16"
*Since the fuel tank is located to the rear of the forward C.G. limit, minimum fuel should be included.

$\frac{\text{METO HP}}{12} = \frac{165}{12}$ = 13.75 gal. x 6#---------- 83# at +22"

* Information should be obtained from the aircraft specification.

Note: Any items or passengers must be used if they are located ahead of the forward C.G. limit. Full fuel must be used if the tank is located ahead of the forward C.G. limit.

CHECK OF FORWARD WEIGHT AND BALANCE EXTREME

	Weight (#) x	Arm (") =	Moment ("#)
Aircraft empty	+ 1169	+ 10.6	+ 12391
Oil	+ 17	- 49	- 833
Pilot	+ 170	+ 16	+ 2720
Fuel	+ 83	+ 22	+ 1826
Total	+ 1439 (TW)		+ 16104 (TM)

Divide the TM (total moment) by the TW (total weight) to obtain the forward weight and balance extreme.

$$\frac{TM}{TW} = \frac{16104}{1439} = +11.2''$$

Since the forward C.G. limit and the maximum weight are not exceeded, the forward weight and balance extreme condition is satisfactory.

FIGURE 10-10. Example of check of most forward weight and balance extreme.

(3) The minimum weights, arms, and moments of the items of useful load that are located ahead of the rearward c.g. limit. A typical example of the computation necessary to make this check, using this data, is shown in figure 10-11.

10-18. LOADING CONDITIONS AND/OR PLACARDS. If the following items have not been covered in the weight and balance extreme condition checks and are not covered by suitable placards in the aircraft, additional computations are necessary. These computations should indicate the permissible distribution of fuel, passengers, and baggage that may be carried in the aircraft at any one time without exceeding either the maximum weight or c.g. range. The conditions to check are:

a. With full fuel, determine the number of passengers and baggage permissible.

b. With maximum passengers, determine the fuel and baggage permissible.

c. With maximum baggage, determine the fuel and the number and location of passengers.

d. Examples of the computations for the above items are given in figures 10-12, 10-13, and 10-14 respectively. The above cases are mainly applicable to the lighter type personal aircraft. In the case of the larger type transport aircraft, a variety of loading conditions is possible and it is necessary to have a loading schedule.

10-19. EQUIPMENT LIST. A list of the equipment included in the certificated empty weight may be found in either the approved aircraft flight manual or the weight and balance report. Enter into the weight and balance report all required, optional, and special equipment installed in the aircraft at time of weighing and/or subsequent equipment changes.

a. Required equipment items are listed in the pertinent Aircraft Specifications.

b. Optional equipment items are listed in the pertinent Aircraft Specifications and may be installed in the aircraft at the option of the owner.

c. Special equipment is any item not corresponding exactly to the descriptive information in the Aircraft Specifications. This includes items such as emergency locator transmitter (ELT), tail or logo lights, instruments, ashtrays, radios, navigation lights, and carpets.

d. Required and optional equipment may be shown on the equipment list with reference to the pertinent item number listed in the applicable specifications only when they are identical to that number item with reference to description, weight, and arm given in the specifications. Show all special equipment items with reference to the item by name, make, model, weight, and arm. When the arm for such an item is not available, determine by actual measurement.

10-20. EQUIPMENT CHANGE. The person making an equipment change is obligated to make an entry on the equipment list indicating items added, removed, or relocated with the date accomplished, and identify himself by name and certificate number in the aircraft records. Examples of items so affected are the installation of extra fuel tanks, seats, and baggage compartments. Figure 10-15 illustrates the effect on balance when equipment items are added within the acceptable c.g. limits and fore and aft of the established c.g. limits.

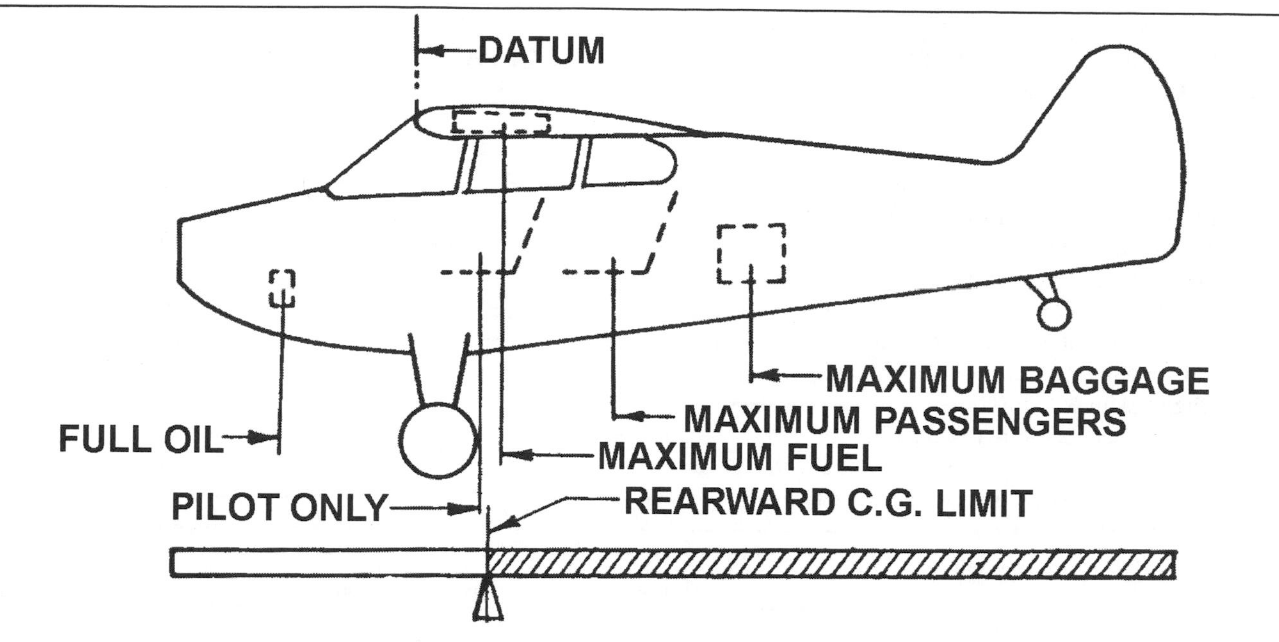

TO CHECK: MOST REARWARD WEIGHT AND BALANCE EXTREME.

GIVEN:
Actual empty weight of the aircraft---------- 1169#
Empty weight center of gravity---------- 10.6"
*Maximum weight---------- 2100#
*Rearward C.G.. limit---------- 21.9"
*Oil capacity, 9 qts. ---------- 17# at -49"
*Baggage, placarded do not exceed 100 lbs ---------- 100# at +75.5"
*Two passengers in rear seat, 170# x 2 ---------- 340# at +48"
*Pilot in most rearward seat equipped with controls (unless otherwise placarded) ---------- 170# at +16"
*Since the fuel tank is located aft of the rearward C.G. limit full fuel must be used---------- 240# at +22"

* Information should be obtained from the aircraft specification.

Note: If fuel tanks are located ahead of the rearward C.G. limit minimum fuel should be used.

CHECK OF REARWARD WEIGHT AND BALANCE EXTREME

	Weight (#) x Arm (") = Moment ("#)		
Aircraft empty	+ 1169	+ 10.6	+ 12391
Oil	+ 17	- 49	- 833
Pilot (1)	+ 170	+ 16	+ 2720
Passenger (2)	+ 340	+ 48	+ 16320
Fuel (40 gals.)	+ 240	+ 22	+ 5280
Baggage	+ 100	+ 75.5	+ 7550
Total	+ 2036 (TW)		+ 43428 (TM)

Divide the TM (total moment) by the TW (total weight) to obtain the rearward weight and balance extreme.

$$\frac{TM}{TW} = \frac{43428}{2036} = +21.3"$$

Since the rearward C.G. limit and the maximum weight are not exceeded, the rearward weight and balance extreme condition is satisfactory.

FIGURE 10-11. Example of check of most rearward weight and balance extreme.

EXAMPLE OF THE DETERMINATION OF THE NUMBER OF PASSENGERS AND BAGGAGE PERMISSIBLE WITH FULL FUEL

GIVEN:
Actual empty weight of the aircraft ---------- 1169#
Empty weight center of gravity ---------- 10.6"
Maximum weight---------- 2100#
Datum is leading edge of the wing
Forward center of gravity limit ---------- 8.5"
Rearward center of gravity limit---------- 21.9"
Oil capacity, 9 qts.; show full capacity ---------- 17# at -49"
Baggage, maximum---------- 100# at +75.5"
Two passengers in rear seat, 170# x 2 ---------- 340# at +48"
Pilot in most rearward seat equipped with
controls (unless otherwise placarded) ---------- 170# at +16"
Full fuel, 40 gals. x 6#---------- 240# at +22"

	Weight (#)	x Arm (") =	Moment ("#)
Aircraft empty	+ 1169	+ 10.6	+ 12391
Oil	+ 17	- 49	- 833
Full Fuel	+ 240	+ 22	+ 5280
Passengers 2 rear	+ 340*	+ 48	+16320
Pilot	+ 170	+ 16	+ 2720
Baggage	+ 100	+ 75.5	+ 7550
Total	+ 2036 (TW)		+ 43428 (TM)

Divide the TM (total moment) by the TW (total weight) to obtain the loaded center of gravity.

$$\frac{TM}{TW} = \frac{43428}{2036} = +21.3''$$

The above computations show that with full fuel, 100 pounds of baggage and two passengers in the rear seat may be carried in this aircraft without exceeding either the maximum weight or the approved C. G. range.

This condition may be entered in the loading schedule as follows:

GALLONS OF FUEL	NUMBER OF PASSENGERS	POUNDS OF BAGGAGE
Full	2 Rear	100

* Only two passengers are listed to prevent the maximum weight of 2100 lbs. from being exceeded.

FIGURE 10-12. Loading conditions: determination of the number of passengers and baggage permissible with full fuel.

EXAMPLE OF THE DETERMINATION OF THE POUNDS OF FUEL AND BAGGAGE PERMISSIBLE WITH MAXIMUM PASSENGERS

	Weight (#)	x Arm (") =	Moment ("#)
Aircraft empty	+ 1169	+ 10.6	+ 12391
Oil	+ 17	- 49	- 833
Pilot	+ 170	+ 16	+ 2720
Passenger (1) front	+ 170	+ 16	+ 2720
Passenger (2) rear	+ 340	+ 48	+16320
Fuel (39 gals.)	+ 234	+ 22	+ 5148
Baggage	----	----	----
Total	+ 2100		+ 38466

Divide the TM (total moment) by the TW (total weight) to obtain the loaded center of gravity.

$$\frac{TM}{TW} = \frac{38466}{2100} = +18.6''$$

The above computations show that with the maximum number of passengers, 39 gallons of fuel and zero pounds of baggage may be carried in this aircraft without exceeding either the maximum weight or the approved C. G. range.

This condition may be entered in the loading schedule as follows:

GALLONS OF FUEL	NUMBER OF PASSENGERS	POUNDS OF BAGGAGE
*Full	*2 Rear	* 100
39	1(F) 2(R)	None

* Conditions as entered from Figure 10-12
(F) Front seat
(R) Rear seat

FIGURE 10-13. Loading conditions: determination of the fuel and baggage permissible with maximum passengers.

EXAMPLE OF THE DETERMINATION OF THE FUEL AND THE NUMBER AND LOCATION OF PASSENGERS PERMISSIBLE WITH MAXIMUM BAGGAGE

	Weight (#) x	Arm (") =	Moment ("#)
Aircraft empty	+ 1169	+ 10.6	+ 12391
Oil	+ 17	- 49	- 833
Pilot	+ 170	+ 16	+ 2720
Passenger (1) rear	+ 170	+ 48	+ 8160
Passenger (1) front	+ 170	+ 16	+ 2720
Fuel (40 gals.)	+ 240	+ 22	+ 5280
Baggage	+ 100	+ 75.5	+ 7550
Total	+ 2036		+ 37988

Divide the TM (total moment) by the TW (total weight) to obtain the loaded center of gravity.

$$\frac{TM}{TW} = \frac{37988}{20366} = +18.7$$

The above computations show that with maximum baggage, full fuel and 2 passengers (1 in the front seat and 1 in the rear seat) may be carried in this aircraft without exceeding either the maximum weight or the approved C. G. range.

This condition may be entered in the loading schedule as follows:

GALLONS OF FUEL	NUMBER OF PASSENGERS	POUNDS OF BAGGAGE
*Full	*2 Rear	* 100
** 39	*1(F) 2(R)	**None
Full	1(F) 1(R)	Full

* Conditions as entered from Figure 10-12
** Conditions as entered from Figure 10-13
(F) Front seat
(R) Rear seat

FIGURE 10-14. Loading conditions: determination of the fuel and the number and location of passengers permissible with maximum baggage.

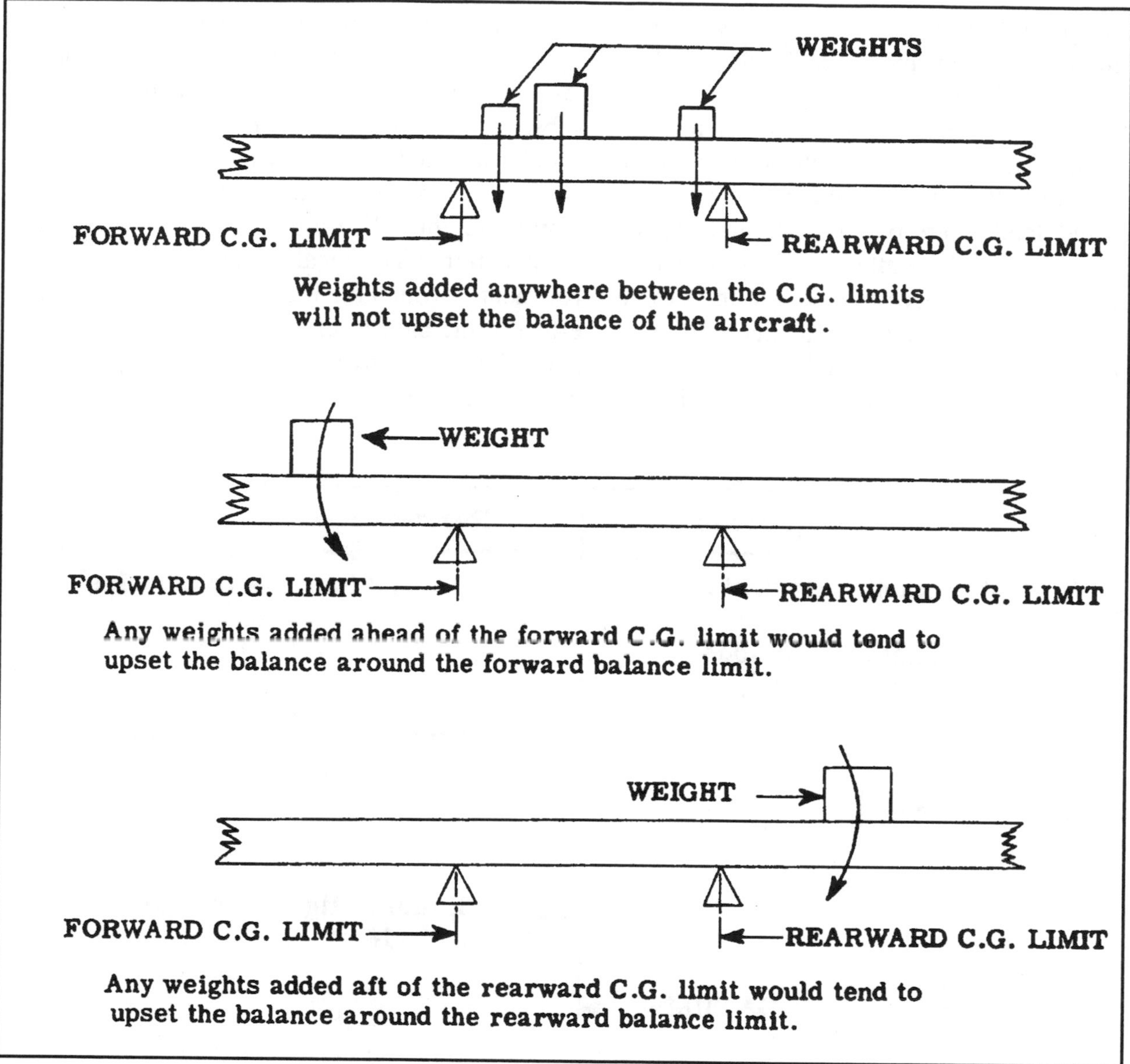

FIGURE 10-15. Effects of the addition of equipment items on balance.

Moment computations for typical equipment changes are given in figure 10-16 and are also included in the sample weight and balance sheet in figure 10-18.

10-21. SAMPLE WEIGHT AND BALANCE REPORT. Suggested methods of tabulating the various data and computations for determining the c.g., both in the empty weight condition and the fully loaded condition, are given in figures 10-17 and 10-18, respectively, and represent a suggested means of recording this information. The data presented in figure 10-17 have previously been computed in figures 10-10 and 10-11 for the extreme load conditions and figure 10-16 for equipment change, and represents suggested means of recording this information.

10-22. INSTALLATION OF BALLAST. Ballast is sometimes permanently installed for c.g. balance purposes as a result of installation or removal of equipment items and is not used to correct a nose-up or nose-down tendency of an aircraft. It is usually located as far aft or as far forward as possible in order to bring the c.g. position within acceptable limits with a minimum of weight increase. Permanent ballast is often lead plate wrapped around and bolted to the fuselage primary structure (e.i., tail-post, longerons, or bulkhead members). Permanent ballast invariably constitutes a concentrated load; therefore, the strength of the local structure and the attachment of the ballast thereto should be investigated for the design loading conditions pertinent to that particular aircraft. Placard permanent ballast with *Permanent ballast - do not remove.* It is not desirable to install permanent ballast by pouring melted lead into the tail-post or longerons due to difficulties that may be encountered in subsequent welding repair operations. It should be noted that the installation of permanent ballast results in an increase of aircraft empty weight. See figure 10-19 for ballast computation. The local strength of the compartment in which the ballast is carried and the effect of the ballast on aircraft weight and balance should be investigated when disposable ballast is carried.

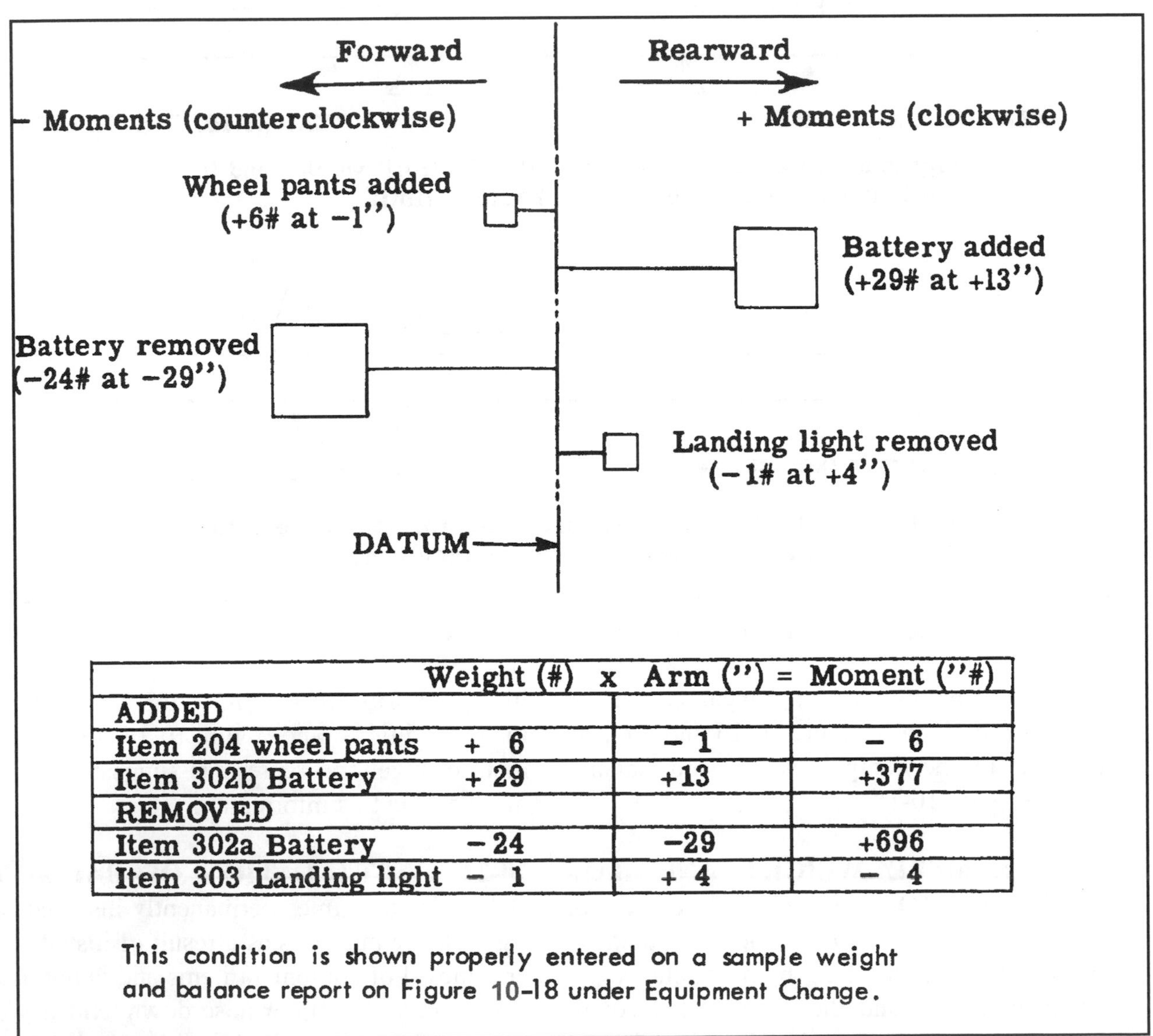

	Weight (#)	x Arm (")	= Moment ("#)
ADDED			
Item 204 wheel pants	+ 6	− 1	− 6
Item 302b Battery	+ 29	+13	+377
REMOVED			
Item 302a Battery	− 24	−29	+696
Item 303 Landing light	− 1	+ 4	− 4

This condition is shown properly entered on a sample weight and balance report on Figure 10-18 under Equipment Change.

FIGURE 10-16. Example of moment and weight changes resulting from equipment changes.

MAKE__MA-700__MODEL__A__SERIAL #__0000__REGISTRATION #__N1234__.
DATUM IS__leading edge of wing__.

COMPUTE AS FOLLOWS IF AIRCRAFT WEIGHED

1. Leveling means: level top longeron between front and rear seats.
2. Main wheel weighing point is located (_____ "FORWARD) (+__3__" AFT) of datum.
3. Actual measured distance from the main weight point centerline to the tail (or nose) point centerline __222__ ".
4. Oil over and above "ZERO" tank reading = (a. ---- Gals.) (b. ---- Lbs.) (c. ---- In.)

ACTUAL EMPTY WEIGHT

Weight Point	Scale Reading -	Tare =	Net Weight
5. Right	564	0	564
6. Left	565	0	565
7. Tail	67	27	40
8. Nose	----	----	-----
9. Total Net Weight	X	X	1169

CENTER OF GRAVITY AS WEIGHED

10. C.G. relative to main wheel weighing point:

(a) Tail wheel airc. $\frac{(\text{Item 3, 222}) \times (\text{Item 7, 40})}{(\text{Item 9, 1169})}$ = + __7.6__ = C.G.

(b) Nose wheel airc. $\frac{(\text{Item 3 ----}) \times (\text{Item 8 ----})}{(\text{Item 9 ----})}$ = _____ = C.G.

11. C.G. relative to datum:

(a) Tail wheel airc. (Item 10a, + 7.6) added to (Item 2, + 3) = __+10.6"__ = C.G.

(b) Nose wheel airc. (Item 10b,) added to (Item 2,) = _____ = C.G.

COMPUTE IF AIRCRAFT WEIGHED WITH OIL (Item 4)

	Weight x	Arm =	Moment
Aircraft Less Oil	(9) (4b)	(11) (4c)	
Empty Totals	(a)	X	(b)

12. $\frac{(b)}{(a)}$ ------------------- = (c) ------------------" = Empty weight C.G.

REPAIR AGENCY ____________ ____________ DATE ____________
Name Number

FIGURE 10-17. Sample weight and balance report to determine empty weight center of gravity.

EQUIPMENT LIST

*Required or Optional Item Numbers as Shown in Aircraft Specification						
1	2	101	102	103	104	105
106	201	202	203	301	302(a)	303
401(a)	402	----	----	----	----	----

Special Equipment				
Item	Make	Model	Weight	Arm
3 Flares 1-1/2 Min.	XYZ	03	25#	105"
Enter above those items included in the empty weight.				

WEIGHT AND BALANCE EXTREME CONDITIONS

Approved fwd limit 8.5" Approved max. weight 2100# Approved aft limit 21.9"

Item	FORWARD CHECK			REARWARD CHECK		
	Weight X	Arm =	Moment	Weight X	Arm =	Moment
Airo. Empty	+ 1169 (9 or 12a)	+ 10.6 (11 or 12c)	+ 12391	+ 1169 (9 or 12a)	+ 10.6 (11 or 12c)	+ 12391
Oil	+ 17	- 49	- 833	+ 17	- 49	- 833
Pilot	+ 170	+ 16	+ 2720	+ 170	+ 16	+ 2720
Fuel	+ 83	+ 22	+ 1826	+ 240	+ 22	+ 5280
Passenger (s)				+ 340	+ 48	+ 16320
Baggage				+ 100	+ 75.5	+ 7550
TOTAL	+ 1439 = TW	X	+ 16104 = TM	+ 2036 = TW	X	+43428=TM

TM = 16104 / TW 1439 = +11.2" = Most Forward C.G. location

TM = 43428 / TW 2036 = +21.3" = Most Rearward C.G. location

LOADING SCHEDULE

Gallons of Fuel	Number of Passengers	Pounds of Baggage
40	2(R)	100
The above includes pilot and capacity oil.		

EQUIPMENT CHANGE

Computing New C.G.			
Item, Make, and Model*	Weight X	Arm	Moment
Airc. Empty	+ 1169 (9 or 12a)	+ 10.6 (11 or 12c)	+ 12391
204 added	+ 6	- 1	- 6
302(b) added	+ 29	+ 13	+ 377
302(a) removed	- 24	+ 29	+ 696
303 removed	- 1	+ 4	- 4
NET TOTALS	- 1179 = NW	X	+ 13454 = NM

NM = 13454 / NW 1179 = +11.4" = New C.G.

*ITEM NUMBERS WHEN LISTED IN PERTINENT AIRCRAFT SPECIFICATION MAY BE USED IN LIEU OF "ITEM, MAKE, AND MODEL".

PREPARED BY________________ DATE________________

FIGURE 10-18. Sample weight and balance report including an equipment change for aircraft fully loaded.

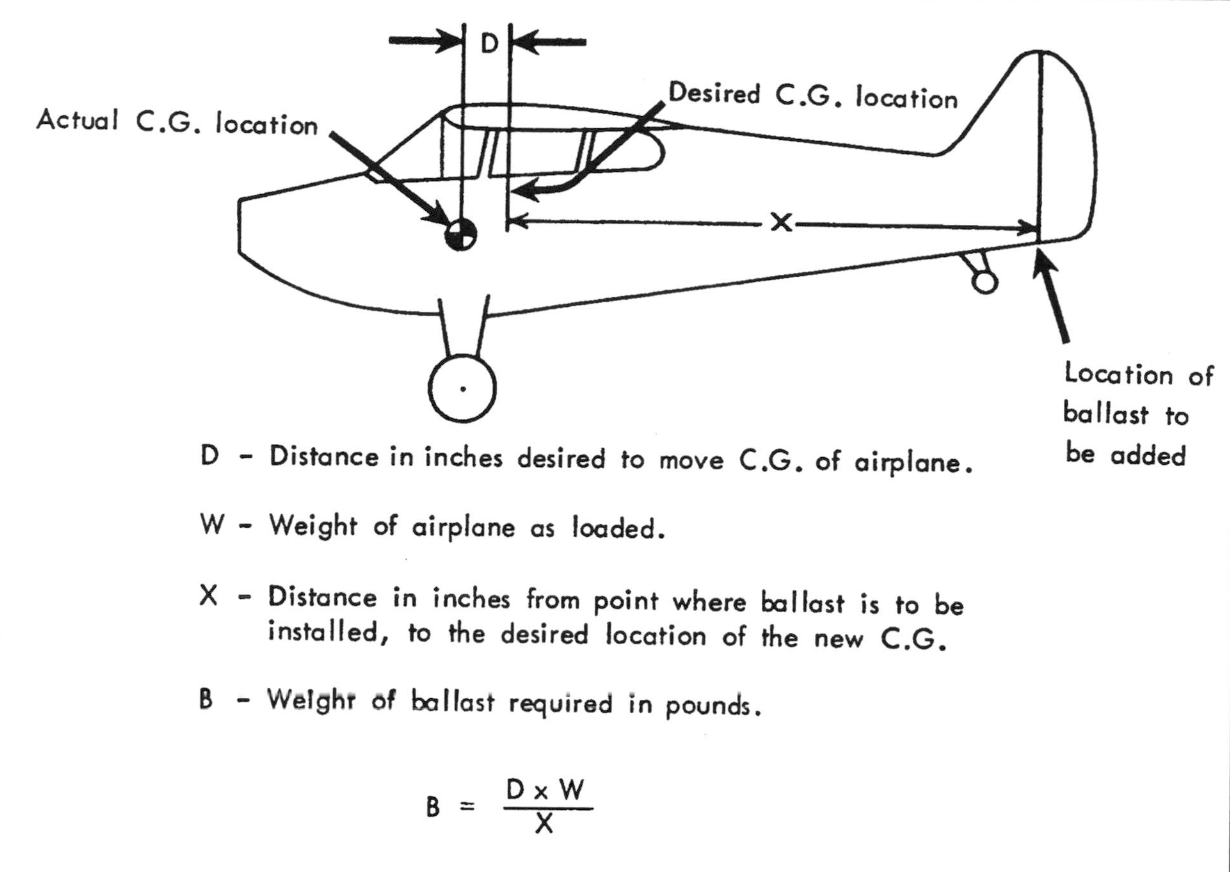

D
Desired C.G. location
Actual C.G. location
X
Location of ballast to be added
D - Distance in inches desired to move C.G. of airplane.
W - Weight of airplane as loaded.
X - Distance in inches from point where ballast is to be installed, to the desired location of the new C.G.
B - Weight of ballast required in pounds.
B = D x W / X
Compute the new C.G. of the aircraft with ballast installed.
NOTE: If greater accuracy is desired, repeat the entire formula using the NEW aircraft weight and the NEW C.G. in the second operation.

FIGURE 10-19. Permanent ballast computation formula.

10-23. LOADING SCHEDULE. The loading schedule should be kept with the aircraft and form a part of the aircraft flight manual. It includes instructions on the proper load distribution such as filling of fuel and oil tanks, passenger seating, restrictions of passenger movement, and distribution of cargo.

a. Other means of determining safe loading conditions such as the use of a graphical index and load adjuster are acceptable and may be used in lieu of the information in paragraph 10-18.

b. Compute a separate loading condition when the aircraft is to be loaded in other than the specified conditions shown in the loading schedule.

10-24.—10-34. [RESERVED.]

CHAPTER 11. AIRCRAFT ELECTRICAL SYSTEMS

SECTION 1. INSPECTION AND CARE OF ELECTRICAL SYSTEMS

11-1. GENERAL. The term "electrical system" as used in this AC means those parts of the aircraft that generate, distribute, and use electrical energy, including their support and attachments. The satisfactory performance of an aircraft is dependent upon the continued reliability of the electrical system. Damaged wiring or equipment in an aircraft, regardless of how minor it may appear to be, cannot be tolerated. Reliability of the system is proportional to the amount of maintenance received and the knowledge of those who perform such maintenance. It is, therefore, important that maintenance be accomplished using the best techniques and practices to minimize the possibility of failure. This chapter is not intended to supersede or replace any government specification or specific manufacturer's instruction regarding electrical system inspection and repair.

11-2. INSPECTION AND OPERATION CHECKS. Inspect equipment, electrical assemblies, and wiring installations for damage, general condition, and proper functioning to ensure the continued satisfactory operation of the electrical system. Adjust, repair, overhaul, and test electrical equipment and systems in accordance with the recommendations and procedures in the aircraft and/or component manufacturer's maintenance instructions. Replace components of the electrical system that are damaged or defective with identical parts, with aircraft manufacturer's approved equipment, or its equivalent to the original in operating characteristics, mechanical strength, and environmental specifications. A list of suggested problems to look for and checks (Refer to the glossary for a description of the check types) to be performed are:

a. Damaged, discolored, or overheated equipment, connections, wiring, and installations.

b. Excessive heat or discoloration at high current carrying connections.

c. Misalignment of electrically driven equipment.

d. Poor electrical bonding (broken, disconnected or corroded bonding strap) and grounding, including evidence of corrosion.

e. Dirty equipment and connections.

f. Improper, broken, inadequately supported wiring and conduit, loose connections of terminals, and loose ferrules.

g. Poor mechanical or cold solder joints.

h. Condition of circuit breaker and fuses.

i. Insufficient clearance between exposed current carrying parts and ground or poor insulation of exposed terminals.

j. Broken or missing safety wire, broken bundle lacing, cotter pins, etc.

k. Operational check of electrically operated equipment such as motors, inverters, generators, batteries, lights, protective devices, etc.

l. Ensure that ventilation and cooling air passages are clear and unobstructed.

m. Voltage check of electrical system with portable precision voltmeter.

n. Condition of electric lamps.

o. Missing safety shields on exposed high-voltage terminals (i.e., 115/200V ac).

11-3. FUNCTIONAL CHECK OF STAND-BY OR EMERGENCY EQUIPMENT. An aircraft should have functional tests performed at regular intervals as prescribed by the manufacturer. The inspections or functional check periods should be clearly stated in the aircraft maintenance manual, along with the overhaul intervals.

11-4. CLEANING AND PRESERVATION. Annual cleaning of electrical equipment to remove dust, dirt, and grime is recommended. Suitable solvents or fine abrasives that will not score the surface or remove the plating may be used to clean the terminals and mating surfaces if they are corroded or dirty. Only cleaning agents that do not leave any type of residue must be used. Components must be cleaned and preserved in accordance with the aircraft handbooks or manufacturer's instructions. Avoid using emery cloth to polish commutators or slip rings because particles may cause shorting and burning. Be sure that protective finishes are not scored or damaged when cleaning. Ensure that metal-to-metal electrically bonded surfaces are treated at the interface with a suitable anti-corrosive conductive coating, and that the joint is sealed around the edges by restoring the original primer and paint finish. Connections that must withstand a highly corrosive environment may be encapsulated with an approved sealant in order to prevent corrosion.

CAUTION: Turn power off before cleaning.

11-5. BATTERY ELECTROLYTE CORROSION. Corrosion found on or near lead-acid batteries can be removed mechanically with a stiff bristle brush and then chemically neutralized with a 10 percent sodium bicarbonate and water solution. For Nickel Cadmium (NiCad) batteries, a 3 percent solution of acetic acid can be used to neutralize the electrolyte. After neutralizing, the battery should be washed with clean water and thoroughly dried.

11-6. ADJUSTMENT AND REPAIR. Accomplish adjustments to items of equipment such as regulators, alternators, generators, contactors, control devices, inverters, and relays at a location outside the aircraft, and on a test stand or test bench where all necessary instruments and test equipment are at hand. Follow the adjustment and repair procedures outlined by the equipment or aircraft manufacturer. Replacement or repair must be accomplished as a part of routine maintenance. Adjustment of a replacement voltage regulator is likely since there will always be a difference in impedance between the manufacturer's test equipment and the aircraft's electrical system.

11-7. INSULATION OF ELECTRICAL EQUIPMENT. In some cases, electrical equipment is connected into a heavy current circuit, perhaps as a control device or relay. Such equipment is normally insulated from the mounting structure since grounding the frame of the equipment may result in a serious ground fault in the event of equipment internal failure. Stranded 18 or 20 AWG wire should be used as a grounding strap to avoid shock hazard to equipment and personnel. If the end connection is used for shock hazard, the ground wire must be large enough to carry the highest possible current (0.1 to 0.2 ohms max.).

11-8. BUS BARS. Annually check bus bars for general condition, cleanliness, and security of all attachments and terminals. Grease, corrosion, or dirt on any electrical junction may cause the connections to overheat and eventually fail. Bus bars that exhibit corrosion, even in limited amounts, should be disassembled, cleaned and brightened, and reinstalled.

11-9.—11-14. [RESERVED.]

SECTION 2. STORAGE BATTERIES

11-15. GENERAL. Aircraft batteries may be used for many functions, e.g., ground power, emergency power, improving DC bus stability, and fault-clearing. Most small private aircraft use lead-acid batteries. Most commercial and military aircraft use NiCad batteries. However, other types are becoming available such as gel cell and sealed lead-acid batteries. The battery best suited for a particular application will depend on the relative importance of several characteristics, such as weight, cost, volume, service or shelf life, discharge rate, maintenance, and charging rate. Any change of battery type may be considered a major alteration.

a. Storage batteries are usually identified by the material used for the plates. All battery types possess different characteristics and, therefore, must be maintained in accordance with the manufacturer's recommendations..

WARNING: It is extremely dangerous to store or service lead-acid and NiCad batteries in the same area. Introduction of acid electrolytes into alkaline electrolyte will destroy the NiCad and vice-versa.

11-16. BATTERY CHARGING. Operation of storage batteries beyond their ambient temperature or charging voltage limits can result in excessive cell temperatures leading to electrolyte boiling, rapid deterioration of the cells, and battery failure. The relationship between maximum charging voltage and the number of cells in the battery is also significant. This will determine (for a given ambient temperature and state of charge) the rate at which energy is absorbed as heat within the battery. For lead-acid batteries, the voltage per cell must not exceed 2.35 volts. In the case of NiCad batteries, the charging voltage limit varies with design and construction. Values of 1.4 and 1.5 volts per cell are generally used. In all cases, follow the recommendations of the battery manufacturer.

11-17. BATTERY FREEZING. Discharged lead-acid batteries exposed to cold temperatures are subject to plate damage due to freezing of the electrolyte. To prevent freezing damage, maintain each cell's specific gravity at 1.275, or for sealed lead-acid batteries check "open" circuit voltage. (See table 11-1.) NiCad battery electrolyte is not as susceptible to freezing because no appreciable chemical change takes place between the charged and discharged states. However, the electrolyte will freeze at approximately minus 75 °F.

NOTE: Only a load check will determine overall battery condition.

TABLE 11-1. Lead-acid battery electrolyte freezing points.

Specific	*Freeze point*		*State of Charge (SOC) for sealed lead-acid batteries at 70°*		
Gravity	*C.*	*F.*	SOC	12 volt	24 volt
1.300	-70	-95	100%	12.9	25.8
1.275	-62	-80	75%	12.7	25.4
1.250	-52	-62	50%	12.4	24.8
1.225	-37	-35	25%	12.0	24.0
1.200	-26	-16			
1.175	-20	-4			
1.150	-15	+5			
1.125	-10	+13			
1.100	-8	+19			

11-18. TEMPERATURE CORRECTION. U.S. manufactured lead-acid batteries are considered fully charged when the specific gravity reading is between 1.275 and 1.300. A 1/3 discharged battery reads about 1.240 and a 2/3 discharged battery will show a specific gravity reading of about 1.200, when tested by a hydrometer and the electrolyte temperature is 80 ▪F. However, to determine precise specific gravity readings, a temperature correction (see table 11-2) should be applied to the hydrometer indication. As an example, a hydrometer reading of 1.260 and the temperature of the electrolyte at 40 °F, the corrected specific gravity reading of the electrolyte is 1.244.

TABLE 11-2. Sulfuric acid temperature correction.

Electrolyte Temperature		Points to be subtracted or added to specific gravity readings
°C	°F	
60	140	+24
55	130	+20
49	120	+16
43	110	+12
38	100	+8
33	90	+4
27	80	0
23	70	-4
15	60	-8
10	50	-12
5	40	-16
-2	30	-20
-7	20	-24
-13	10	-28
-18	0	-32
-23	-10	-36
-28	-20	-40
-35	-30	-44

11-19. BATTERY MAINTENANCE.

Battery inspection and maintenance procedures vary with the type of chemical technology and the type of physical construction. Always follow the battery manufacturer's approved procedures. Battery performance at any time in a given application will depend upon the battery's age, state of health, state of charge, and mechanical integrity.

a. Age. To determine the life and age of the battery, record the install date of the battery on the battery. During normal battery maintenance, battery age must be documented either in the aircraft maintenance log or in the shop maintenance log.

b. State of Health. Lead-acid battery state of health may be determined by duration of service interval (in the case of vented batteries), by environmental factors (such as excessive heat or cold), and by observed electrolyte leakage (as evidenced by corrosion of wiring and connectors or accumulation of powdered salts). If the battery needs to be refilled often, with no evidence of external leakage, this may indicate a poor state of the battery, the battery charging system, or an over charge condition.

(1) Use a hydrometer to determine the specific gravity of the battery electrolyte, which is the weight of the electrolyte compared to the weight of pure water.

(2) Take care to ensure the electrolyte is returned to the cell from which it was extracted. When a specific gravity difference of 0.050 or more exists between cells of a battery, the battery is approaching the end of its useful life and replacement should be considered. Electrolyte level may be adjusted by the addition of distilled water.

c. State of Charge. Battery state of charge will be determined by the cumulative effect of charging and discharging the battery. In a normal electrical charging system the battery's generator or alternator restores a battery to full charge during a flight of one hour to ninety minutes.

d. Mechanical Integrity. Proper mechanical integrity involves the absence of any physical damage as well as assurance that hardware is correctly installed and the battery is properly connected. Battery and battery compartment venting system tubes, nipples and attachments, when required, provide a means of avoiding the potential buildup of explosive gases, and should be checked periodically to ensure that they are securely connected and oriented in accordance with the maintenance manual's installation procedures. Always follow procedures approved for the specific aircraft and battery system to ensure that the battery system is capable of delivering specified performance.

e. Battery and Charger Characteristics. The following information is provided to acquaint the user with characteristics of the more common aircraft battery and battery charger types. Products may vary from these descriptions due to different applications of available technology. Consult the manufacturer for specific performance data.

NOTE: Under no circumstances connect a lead-acid battery to a charger, unless properly serviced.

(1) Lead-acid vented batteries have a two volt nominal cell voltage. Batteries are constructed so that individual cells cannot be removed. Occasional addition of water is required to replace water loss due to overcharging in normal service. Batteries that become fully discharged may not accept recharge.

(2) Lead-acid sealed batteries are similar in most respects to lead-acid vented batteries, but do not require the addition of water.

(3) The lead-acid battery is economical and has extensive application, but is heavier than an equivalent performance battery of another type. The battery is capable of a high rate of discharge and low temperature performance. However, maintaining a high rate of discharge for a period of time usually warps the cell plates, shorting out the battery. Its electrolyte has a moderate specific gravity, and state of charge can be checked with a hydrometer.

(4) Do not use high amperage automotive battery chargers to charge aircraft batteries.

(5) NiCad vented batteries have a 1.2 volt nominal cell voltage. Occasional addition of distilled water is required to replace water loss due to overcharging in normal service. Cause of failure is usually shorting or weakening of a cell. After replacing the bad cell with a good cell, the battery's life can be extended for five or more years. Full discharge is not harmful to this type of battery.

(6) NiCad sealed batteries are similar in most respects to NiCad vented batteries, but do not normally require the addition of water. Fully discharging the battery (to zero volts) may cause irreversible damage to one or more cells, leading to eventual battery failure due to low capacity.

(7) The state of charge of a NiCad battery cannot be determined by measuring the specific gravity of the potassium hydroxide electrolyte. The electrolyte specific gravity does not change with the state of charge. The only accurate way to determine the state of charge of a NiCad battery is by a measured discharge with a NiCad battery charger and following the manufacturer's instructions. After the battery has been fully charged and allowed to stand for at least two hours, the fluid level may be adjusted, if necessary, using distilled or demineralized water. Because the fluid level varies with the state of charge, water should never be added while the battery is installed in the aircraft. Overfilling the battery will result in electrolyte spewage during charging. This will cause corrosive effects on the cell links, self-discharge of the battery, dilution of the electrolyte density, possible blockage of the cell vents, and eventual cell rupture.

(8) Lead-acid batteries are usually charged by regulated DC voltage sources. This allows maximum accumulation of charge in the early part of recharging.

(9) Constant-current battery chargers are usually provided for NiCad batteries because the NiCad cell voltage has a negative temperature coefficient. With a constant-voltage charging source, a NiCad battery having a shorted cell might overheat due to excessive overcharge and undergo a thermal runaway, destroying the battery and creating a possible safety hazard to the aircraft.

DEFINITION: Thermal runaway can result in a chemical fire and/or explosion of the NiCad battery under recharge by a constant-voltage source, and is due to cyclical, ever-increasing temperature and charging current. One or more shorted cells or an existing high temperature and low charge can produce the cyclical sequence of events: (1) excessive current, (2) increased temperature, (3) decreased cell(s) resistance, (4) further increased current, and (5) further increased temperature. This will not become a self-sustaining thermal-chemical action if the constant-voltage charging source is removed before the battery temperature is in excess of 160 °F.

(10) Pulsed-current battery chargers are sometimes provided for NiCad batteries.

CAUTION: It is important to use the proper charging procedures for batteries under test and maintenance. These charging regimes for reconditioning and charging cycles are defined by the aircraft manufacturer and should be closely followed.

f. Shop-Level Maintenance Procedures. Shop procedures must follow the manufacturer's recommendations. Careful examination of sealed batteries and proper reconditioning of vented batteries will ensure the longest possible service life.

g. Aircraft Battery Inspection.

(1) Inspect battery sump jar and lines for condition and security.

(2) Inspect battery terminals and quick-disconnect plugs and pins for evidence of corrosion, pitting, arcing, and burns. Clean as required.

(3) Inspect battery drain and vent lines for restriction, deterioration, and security.

(4) Routine pre-flight and post-flight inspection procedures should include observation for evidence of physical damage, loose connections, and electrolyte loss.

11-20. ELECTROLYTE SPILLAGE.

Spillage or leakage of electrolyte may result in serious corrosion of the nearby structure or control elements as both sulfuric acid and potassium hydroxide are actively corrosive. Electrolyte may be spilled during ground servicing, leaked when cell case rupture occurs, or sprayed from cell vents due to excessive charging rates. If the battery is not case enclosed, properly treat structural parts near the battery that may be affected by acid fumes. Treat all case and drain surfaces, that have been affected by electrolyte, with a solution of sodium bicarbonate (for acid electrolyte) or boric acid, vinegar, or a 3 percent solution of acetic acid (for potassium hydroxide electrolyte).

CAUTION: Serious burns will result if the electrolyte comes in contact with any part of the body. Use rubber gloves, rubber apron, and protective goggles when handling electrolyte. If sulfuric acid is splashed on the body,

neutralize with a solution of baking soda and water, and shower or flush the affected area with water. For the eyes, use an eye fountain and flush with an abundance of water. If potassium hydroxide contacts the skin, neutralize with 9 percent acetic acid, vinegar, or lemon juice and wash with water. For the eyes, wash with a weak solution of boric acid or a weak solution of vinegar and flush with water.

11-21. NOXIOUS FUMES. When charging rates are excessive, the electrolyte may boil to the extent that fumes containing droplets of the electrolyte are emitted through the cell vents. These fumes from lead-acid batteries may become noxious to the crew members and passengers; therefore, thoroughly check the venting system. NiCad batteries will emit gas near the end of the charging process and during overcharge. The battery vent system in the aircraft should have sufficient air flow to prevent this explosive mixture from accumulating. It is often advantageous to install a jar in the battery vent discharge system serviced with an agent to neutralize the corrosive effect of battery vapors.

11-22. INSTALLATION PRACTICES.

a. External Surface. Clean the external surface of the battery prior to installation in the aircraft.

b. Replacing Lead-Acid Batteries. When replacing lead-acid batteries with NiCad batteries, a battery temperature or current monitoring system must be installed. Neutralize the battery box or compartment and thoroughly flush with water and dry. A flight manual supplement must also be provided for the NiCad battery installation. Acid residue can be detrimental to the proper functioning of a NiCad battery, as alkaline will be to a lead-acid battery.

c. Battery Venting. Battery fumes and gases may cause an explosive mixture or contaminated compartments and should be dispersed by adequate ventilation. Venting systems often use ram pressure to flush fresh air through the battery case or enclosure to a safe overboard discharge point. The venting system pressure differential should always be positive, and remain between recommended minimum and maximum values. Line runs should not permit battery overflow fluids or condensation to be trapped and prevent free airflow.

d. Battery Sump Jars. A battery sump jar installation may be incorporated in the venting system to dispose of battery electrolyte overflow. The sump jar should be of adequate design and the proper neutralizing agent used. The sump jar must be located only on the discharge side of the battery venting system. (See figure 11-1.)

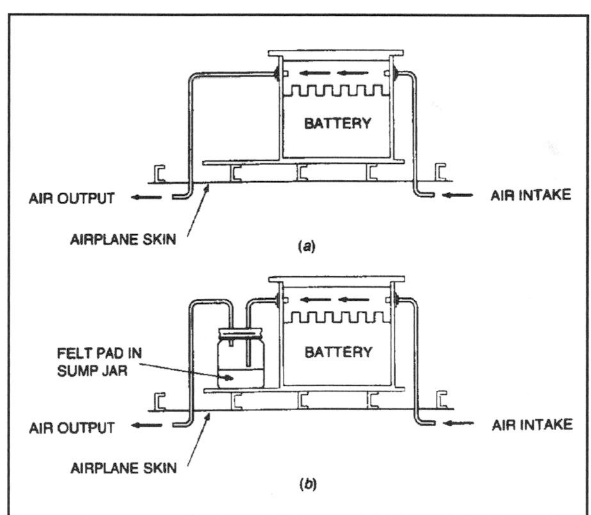

FIGURE 11-1. Battery ventilating systems.

e. Installing Batteries. When installing batteries in an aircraft, exercise care to prevent inadvertent shorting of the battery terminals. Serious damage to the aircraft structure (frame, skin and other subsystems, avionics, wire, fuel etc.) can be sustained by the resultant high discharge of electrical energy. This condition may normally be avoided by insulating the terminal posts during the installation process.

Remove the grounding lead first for battery removal, then the positive lead. Connect the grounding lead of the battery last to minimize the risk of shorting the "hot terminal" of the battery during installation.

f. Battery Hold Down Devices. Ensure that the battery hold down devices are secure, but not so tight as to exert excessive pressure that may cause the battery to buckle causing internal shorting of the battery.

g. Quick-Disconnect Type Battery. If a quick-disconnect type of battery connector, that prohibits crossing the battery lead is not employed, ensure that the aircraft wiring is connected to the proper battery terminal. Reverse polarity in an electrical system can seriously damage a battery and other electrical components. Ensure that the battery cable connections are tight to prevent arcing or a high resistance connection.

11-23.—11-29. [RESERVED.]

SECTION 3. INSPECTION OF EQUIPMENT INSTALLATION

11-30. GENERAL. When installing equipment which consumes electrical power in an aircraft, it should be determined that the total electrical load can be safely controlled or managed within the rated limits of the affected components of the aircraft's electrical power supply system. Addition of most electrical utilization equipment is a major alteration and requires appropriate FAA approval. The electrical load analysis must be prepared in general accordance with good engineering practices. Additionally, an addendum to the flight manual is generally required.

11-31. INSTALLATION CLEARANCE PROVISIONS. All electrical equipment should be installed so that inspection and maintenance may be performed and that the installation does not interfere with other systems, such as engine or flight controls.

11-32. WIRES, WIRE BUNDLES, AND CIRCUIT PROTECTIVE DEVICES. Before any aircraft electrical load is increased, the new total electrical load (previous maximum load plus added load) must be checked to determine if the design levels are being exceeded. Where necessary, wires, wire bundles, and circuit protective devices having the correct ratings should be added or replaced.

11-33. ALTERNATOR DIODES. Alternators employ diodes for the purpose of converting the alternating current to direct current. These diodes are solid-state electronic devices and are easily damaged by rough handling, abuse, over heating, or reversing the battery connections. A voltage surge in the line, if it exceeds the design value, may destroy the diode. The best protection against diode destruction by voltage surges is to make certain that the battery is never disconnected from the aircraft's electrical system when the alternator is in operation. The battery acts as a large capacitor and tends to damp out voltage surges. The battery must never be connected with reversed polarity as this may subject the diodes to a forward bias condition, allowing very high current conduction that will generally destroy them instantly.

11-34. STATIC ELECTRICAL POWER CONVERTERS. Static power converters employ solid-state devices to convert the aircraft's primary electrical source voltage to a different voltage or frequency for the operation of radio and electronic equipment. They contain no moving parts (with the exception of a cooling fan on some models) and are relatively maintenance free. Various types are available for ac to dc or dc to ac conversion.

a. Location of static converters should be carefully chosen to ensure adequate ventilation for cooling purposes. Heat-radiating fins should be kept clean of dirt and other foreign matter that may impair their cooling properties.

b. Static power converters often emit unacceptable levels of EMI that may disrupt communication equipment and navigation instruments. Properly shielded connectors, terminal blocks, and wires may be required, with all shields well grounded to the airframe.

CAUTION: Do not load converters beyond their rated capacity.

11-35. ACCEPTABLE MEANS OF CONTROLLING OR MONITORING THE ELECTRICAL LOAD.

a. Output Rating. The generator or alternator output ratings and limits prescribed by the manufacturer must be checked against the electrical loads that can be imposed on the affected generator or alternator by installed equipment. When electrical load calculations show that the total continuous electrical load can exceed 80 percent output load limits of the generator or alternator, and where special placards or monitoring devices are not installed, the electrical load must be reduced or the generating capacity of the charging system must be increased. (This is strictly a "rule of thumb" method and should not be confused with an electrical load analysis, which is a complete and accurate analysis, which is a complete and accurate of the composite aircraft power sources and all electrical loads) When a storage battery is part of the electrical power system, the battery will be continuously charged in flight.

b. The use of placards is recommended to inform the pilot and/or crew members of the combination(s) of loads that may be connected to each power source. Warning lights can be installed that will be triggered if the battery bus voltage drops below 13 volts on a 14-volt system or 26 volts on a 28-volt system.

c. For installations where the ammeter is in the battery lead, and the regulator system limits the maximum current that the generator or alternator can deliver, a voltmeter can be installed on the system bus. As long as the ammeter never reads "discharge" (except for short intermittent loads such as operating the gear and flaps) and the voltmeter remains at "system voltage," the generator or alternator will not be overloaded.

d. In installations where the ammeter is in the generator or alternator lead and the regulator system does not limit the maximum current that the generator or alternator can deliver, the ammeter can be redlined at 100 percent of the generator or alternator rating. If the ammeter reading is never allowed to exceed the red line, except for short intermittent loads, the generator or alternator will not be overloaded.

e. Where the use of placards or monitoring devices is not practical or desired, and where assurance is needed that the battery will be charged in flight, the total continuous connected electrical load should be held to approximately 80 percent of the total generator output capacity. When more than one generator is used in parallel, the total rated output is the combined output of the installed generators.

f. When two or more generators and alternators are operated in parallel and the total connected system load can exceed the rated output of a single generator, a method should be provided for quickly coping with a sudden overload that can be caused by generator or engine failure. A quick load reduction system or procedure should be identified whereby the total load can be reduced by the pilot to a quantity within the rated capacity of the remaining operable generator or generators.

11-36. ELECTRICAL LOAD DETERMINATION. The connected load of an aircraft's electrical system may be determined by any one or a combination of several acceptable methods, techniques, or practices. However, those with a need to know the status of a particular aircraft's electrical system should have accurate and up-to-date data concerning the capacity of the installed electrical power source(s) and the load(s) imposed by installed electrical power-consuming devices. Such data should provide a true picture of the status of the electrical system. New or additional electrical devices should not be installed in an aircraft, nor the capacity changed of any power source, until the status of the electrical system in the aircraft has been determined accurately and found not to adversely affect the integrity of the electrical system.

11-37. JUNCTION BOX CONSTRUCTION. Replacement junction boxes should be fabricated using the same material as the original or from a fire-resistant, nonabsorbent material, such as aluminum, or an acceptable plastic material. Where fire-proofing is necessary, a stainless steel junction box is recommended. Rigid construction will prevent "oil-canning" of the box sides that could result in internal short circuits. In all cases, drain holes should be provided in the lowest portion of the box. Cases of electrical power equipment must be insulated from metallic structure to avoid ground fault related fires. (See paragraph 11-7.)

a. Internal Arrangement. The junction box arrangement should permit easy access to any installed items of equipment, terminals, and wires. Where marginal clearances are unavoidable, an insulating material should be inserted between current carrying parts and any grounded surface. It is not good practice to mount equipment on the covers or doors of junction boxes, since inspection for internal clearance is impossible when the door or cover is in the closed position.

b. Installation. Junction boxes should be securely mounted to the aircraft structure in such a manner that the contents are readily accessible for inspection. When possible, the open side should face downward or at an angle so that loose metallic objects, such as washers or nuts, will tend to fall out of the junction box rather than wedge between terminals.

c. Wiring. Junction box layouts should take into consideration the necessity for adequate wiring space and possible future additions. Electrical wire bundles should be laced or clamped inside the box so that cables do not touch other components, prevent ready access, or obscure markings or labels. Cables at entrance openings should be protected against chafing by using grommets or other suitable means.

11-38.—11-46. [RESERVED.]

SECTION 4. INSPECTION OF CIRCUIT-PROTECTION DEVICES

11-47. GENERAL. All electrical wires must be provided with some means of circuit protection. Electrical wire should be protected with circuit breakers or fuses located as close as possible to the electrical power source bus. Normally, the manufacturer of electrical equipment will specify the fuse or breaker to be used when installing the respective equipment, or SAE publication, ARP 1199, may be referred to for recommended practices.

11-48. DETERMINATION OF CIRCUIT BREAKER RATINGS. Circuit protection devices must be sized to supply open circuit capability. A circuit breaker must be rated so that it will open before the current rating of the wire attached to it is exceeded, or before the cumulative rating of all loads connected to it are exceeded, whichever is lowest. A circuit breaker must always open before any component downstream can overheat and generate smoke or fire. Wires must be sized to carry continuous current in excess of the circuit protective device rating, including its time-current characteristics, and to avoid excessive voltage drop. Refer to section 5 for wire rating methods.

11-49. DC CIRCUIT PROTECTOR CHART. Table 11-3 may be used as a guide for the selection of circuit breaker and fuse rating to protect copper conductor wire. This chart was prepared for the conditions specified. If actual conditions deviate materially from those stated, ratings above or below the values recommended may be justified. For example, a wire run individually in the open air may possibly be protected by the circuit breaker of the next higher rating to that shown on the chart. In general, the chart is conservative for all ordinary aircraft electrical installations.

TABLE 11-3. DC wire and circuit protector chart.

Wire AN gauge copper	Circuit breaker amp.	Fuse amp.
22	5	5
20	7.5	5
18	10	10
16	15	10
14	20	15
12	30	20
10	40	30
8	50	50
6	80	70
4	100	70
2	125	100
1		150
0		150

Basis of chart:
(1) Wire bundles in 135 °F. ambient and altitudes up to 30,000 feet.
(2) Wire bundles of 15 or more wires, with wires carrying no more than 20 percent of the total current carrying capacity of the bundle as given in Specification MIL-W-5088 (ASG).
(3) Protectors in 75 to 85 °F. ambient.
(4) Copper wire Specification MIL-W-5088.
(5) Circuit breakers to Specification MIL-C-5809 or equivalent.
(6) Fuses to Specification MIL-F-15160 or equivalent.

11-50. RESETTABLE CIRCUIT PROTECTION DEVICES.

a. All resettable type circuit breakers must open the circuit irrespective of the position of the operating control when an overload or circuit fault exists. Such circuit breakers are referred to as "trip free."

b. Automatic reset circuit breakers, that automatically reset themselves periodically, are not recommended as circuit protection devices for aircraft.

11-51. CIRCUIT BREAKER USAGE. Circuit breakers are designed as circuit protection for the wire (see paragraph 11-48 and 11-49), not for protection of black boxes or components. Use of a circuit breaker as a switch is not recommended. Use of a circuit breaker as a switch will decrease the life of the circuit breaker.

11-52. CIRCUIT BREAKER MAINTENANCE. Circuit breakers should be periodically cycled with no load to enhance contact performance by cleaning contaminants from the contact surfaces.

11-53. SWITCHES. In all circuits where a switch malfunction can be hazardous, a switch specifically designed for aircraft service should be used. These switches are of rugged construction and have sufficient contact capacity to break, make, and continuously carry the connected load current. The position of the switch should be checked with an electrical meter.

a. Electrical Switch Inspection. Special attention should be given to electrical circuit switches, especially the spring-loaded type, during the course of normal airworthiness inspection. An internal failure of the spring-loaded type may allow the switch to remain closed even though the toggle or button returns to the "off" position. During inspection, attention should also be given to the possibility that improper switch substitution may have been made.

(1) With the power off suspect aircraft electrical switches should be checked in the ON position for opens (high resistance) and in The OFF position for shorts (low resistance), with an ohmmeter.

(2) Any abnormal side to side movement of the switch should be an alert to imminent failure even if the switch tested was shown to be acceptable with an ohmmeter.

b. Electromechanical Switches. Switches have electrical contacts and various types of switch actuators (i.e., toggle, plunger, push-button, knob, rocker).

(1) Contacts designed for high-level loads must not be subsequently used for low-level applications, unless testing has been performed to establish this capability.

(2) Switches are specifically selected based on the design for the aircraft service current ratings for lamp loads, inductive loads, and motor loads and must be replaced with identical make and model switches.

c. Proximity Switches. These switches are usually solid-state devices that detect the presence of a predetermined target without physical contact and are usually rated 0.5 amps or less.

d. Switch Rating. The nominal current rating of the conventional aircraft switch is usually stamped on the switch housing and represents the continuous current rating with the contacts closed. Switches should be derated from their nominal current rating for the following types of circuits:

(1) Circuits containing incandescent lamps can draw an initial current that is 15 times greater than the continuous current. Contact burning or welding may occur when the switch is closed.

(2) Inductive circuits have magnetic energy stored in solenoid or relay coils that is released when the control switch is opened and may appear as an arc.

(3) Direct-current motors will draw several times their rated current during starting, and magnetic energy stored in their armature and field coils is released when the control switch is opened.

e. Switch Selection. Switches for aircraft use should be selected with extreme caution. The contact ratings should be adequate for all load conditions and applicable voltages, at both sea level and the operational altitude. Consideration should be given to the variation in the electrical power characteristics, using MIL-STD-704 as a guide.

f. Derating Factors. Table 11-4 provides an approximate method for derating nominal ratings to obtain reasonable switch efficiency and service life under reactive load conditions.

WARNING: Do not use AC derated switches in DC circuits. AC switches will not carry the same amperage as a DC switch.

TABLE 11-4. Switch derating factors.

Nominal System Voltage	Type of Load	Derating Factor
28 VDC	Lamp	8
28 VDC	Inductive (relay-solenoid)	4
28 VDC	Resistive (Heater)	2
28 VDC	Motor	3
12 VDC	Lamp	5
12 VDC	Inductive (relay-solenoid)	2
12 VDC	Resistive (Heater)	1
12 VDC	Motor	2

NOTES:

1. To find the nominal rating of a switch required to operate a given device, multiply the continuous current rating of the device by the derating factor corresponding to the voltage and type of load.
2. To find the continuous rating that a switch of a given nominal rating will handle efficiently, divide the switch nominal rating by the derating factor corresponding to the voltage and type of load.

g. Low Energy Loads. Switches rated for use at 28 VDC or more, and at 1.0 amp or more, generally have silver contacts. In general, silver contacts should not be used to control devices which have either a voltage less than 8 volts or a continuous current less than 0.5 amps unless the switch is specifically rated for use with low-energy loads. Table 11-5 provides general guidelines for selecting contact materials for low-energy loads, but is not applicable to hermetically sealed switches.

(1) Typical logic load devices have a voltage of 0.5 volts to 28 volts and a continuous current of less than 0.5 amps. A suitable method of rating switches for use on logic load devices is specified in ANSI/EIA 5200000. (General specification for special use electromechanical switches of certified quality.)

TABLE 11-5. Selection of contact material.

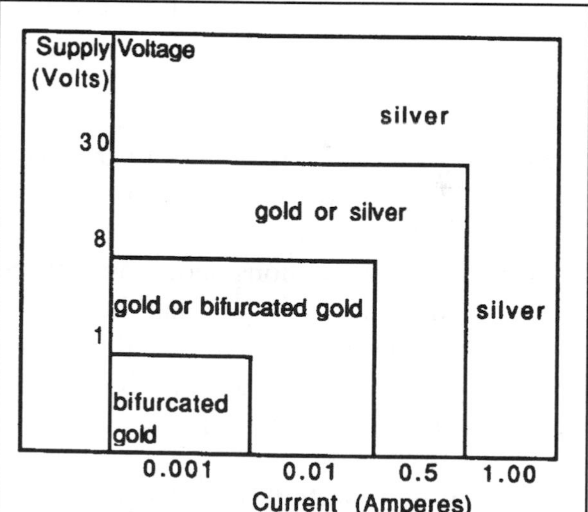

NOTES:
1. If sulfide, moisture, or any form of contamination is present, a sealed switch should be used. The degree of sealing required (environmental or hermetic) is dependent upon the environment in which the switch is intended to be operated.
2. If particle contamination in any form is likely to reach the contacts, bifurcated contacts should be used.
3. Low-voltage high-current loads are difficult to predict and may result in a combined tendency of noncontact, sticking, and material transfer.
4. High-voltage high-current applications may require the use of Silver Nickel contacts.

(2) Typical low-level load devices have a voltage of less than 0.5 volts and a continuous current of less than 0.5 amps. A suitable method of rating switches for use on logic load devices is specified in ANSI/EIA 5200000.

h. Shock and Vibration.

(1) Electromechanical switches (toggle switches) are most susceptible to shock and vibration in the plane that is parallel to contact motion. Under these conditions the switch contacts may momentarily separate. ANSI/EIA 5200000 specifies that contact separations greater than 10 microseconds and that closing of open contacts in excess of 1 microsecond are failures. Repeated contact separations during high levels of vibration or shock may cause excessive electrical degradation of the contacts. These separations can also cause false signals to be registered by electronic data processors without proper buffering.

(2) Although proximity switches do not have moving parts, the reliability of the internal electronic parts of the switch may be reduced. Reliability and mean time between-failure (MTBF) calculations should reflect the applicable environment. Note that the mounting of both the proximity sensor and its target must be rigid enough to withstand shock or vibration to avoid creating false responses.

i. Electromagnetic/Radio Frequency Interference (EMI/RFI).

(1) DC operated electromechanical switches are usually not susceptible to EMI/RFI. Proximity switches are susceptible to an EMI/RFI environment and must be evaluated in the application. Twisting lead wires, metal overbraids, lead wire routing, and the design of the proximity switch can minimize susceptibility.

(2) The arcing of electromechanical switch contacts generates short duration EMI/RFI when controlling highly inductive electrical loads. Twisting lead wires, metal overbraids, and lead wire routing can reduce or eliminate generation problems when dealing with arcing loads. Proximity sensors generally use a relatively low-energy electromagnetic field to sense the target. Adequate spacing is required to prevent interference between adjacent proximity sensors or other devices susceptible to EMI/RFI. Refer to manufacturer's instructions.

b. Temperature.

(1) Electromechanical switches can withstand wide temperature ranges and rapid gradient shifts without damage. Most aircraft switches operate between -55 °C and 85 °C with designs available from -185 °C to 260 °C or more. Higher temperatures require more exotic materials, which can increase costs and limit life. It should be noted that o-ring seals and elastomer boot seals tend to stiffen in extreme cold. This can increase operating forces and reduce release forces or stop the switch from releasing.

(2) Proximity sensors are normally designed for environments from -55 °C to 125 °C. During temperature excursions, the operating and release points may shift from 5 percent to 10 percent. Reliability of the proximity sensor will typically be highest at room temperature. The reliability and MTBF estimates should be reduced for use under high temperatures or high thermal gradients.

c. Sealing.

NOTE: The materials used for sealing (o-rings, potting materials, etc.) should be compatible with any aircraft fluids to which the switch may be exposed.

(1) Electromechanical switches range in sealing from partially sealed to hermetically sealed. Use a sealed switch when the switch will be exposed to a dirty environment during storage, assembly, or operation. Use a higher level of sealing when the switch will not have an arcing load to self-clean the contacts. Low-energy loads tend to be more susceptible to contamination.

(2) Proximity switches for aircraft applications typically have a metal face and potting material surrounding any electronics and lead wire exits. The potting material should be compatible with the fluids the switch will be exposed to in the environment. The plastic sensing face of some proximity switches may be subject to absorption of water that may cause the operating point to shift should be protected.

d. Switch Installation. Hazardous errors in switch operation may be avoided by logical and consistent installation. "On-off" two-position switches should be mounted so that the "on" position is reached by an upward or forward movement of the toggle. When the switch controls movable aircraft elements, such as landing gear or flaps, the toggle should move in the same direction as the desired motion. Inadvertent operation of switches can be prevented by mounting suitable guards over the switches.

11-48. RELAYS. A relay is an electrically controlled device that opens and closes electrical contacts to effect the operation of other devices in the same or in another electrical circuit. The relay converts electrical energy into mechanical energy through various means, and through mechanical linkages, actuates electrical conductors (contacts) that control electrical circuits. Solid-state relays may also be used in electrical switching applications.

a. Use of Relays. Most relays are used as a switching device where a weight reduction can be achieved, or to simplify electrical controls. It should be remembered that the relay is an electrically operated switch, and therefore subject to dropout under low system voltage conditions.

b. Types of Connections. Relays are manufactured with various connective means from mechanical to plug-in devices. Installation procedures vary by the type of connection and should be followed to ensure proper operation of the relay.

c. Repair. Relays are complicated electromechanical assemblies and most are not repairable.

d. Relay Selection.

(1) Contact ratings, as described on the relay case, describe the make, carry, and break capability for resistive currents only. Consult the appropriate specification to determine the derating factor to use for other types of current loads. (Ref. MIL-PRF-39016, MIL-PRF-5757, MIL-PRF-6016, MIL-PRF-835836.)

(2) Operating a relay at less than nominal coil voltage may compromise its performance and should never be done without written manufacturer approval.

e. Relay Installation and Maintenance. For installation and maintenance, care should be taken to ensure proper placement of hardware, especially at electrical connections. The use of properly calibrated torque wrenches and following the manufacturer's installation procedures is strongly recommended. This is especially important with hermetically sealed relays, since the glass-to-metal seal (used for insulation of the electrically "live" components) is especially vulnerable to catastrophic failure as a result of overtorquing.

(1) When replacing relays in alternating current (ac) applications, it is essential to maintain proper phase sequencing. For any application involving plug-in relays, proper engagement of their retaining mechanism is vital.

(2) The proximity of certain magnetically permanent, magnet assisted, coil operated relays may cause them to have an impact on each other. Any manufacturer's recommendations or precautions must be closely followed.

11-49. LOAD CONSIDERATIONS. When switches or relays are to be used in applications where current or voltage is substantially lower than rated conditions, additional intermediate testing should be performed to ensure reliable operation. Contact the manufacturer on applications different from the rated conditions.

11-50. OPERATING CONDITIONS FOR SWITCHES AND RELAYS. Switches and relays should be compared to their specification rating to ensure that all contacts are made properly under all conditions of operation, including vibration equivalent to that in the area of the aircraft in which the switch or relay is to be installed.

11-57.—11-65. [RESERVED.]

SECTION 5. ELECTRICAL WIRE RATING

11-66. GENERAL. Wires must be sized so that they: have sufficient mechanical strength to allow for service conditions; do not exceed allowable voltage drop levels; are protected by system circuit protection devices; and meet circuit current carrying requirements.

a. Mechanical Strength of Wires. If it is desirable to use wire sizes smaller than #20, particular attention should be given to the mechanical strength and installation handling of these wires, e.g., vibration, flexing, and termination. Wire containing less than 19 strands must not be used. Consideration should be given to the use of high-strength alloy conductors in small gauge wires to increase mechanical strength. As a general practice, wires smaller than size #20 should be provided with additional clamps and be grouped with at least three other wires. They should also have additional support at terminations, such as connector grommets, strain relief clamps, shrinkable sleeving, or telescoping bushings. They should not be used in applications where they will be subjected to excessive vibration, repeated bending, or frequent disconnection from screw termination.

b. Voltage Drop in Wires. The voltage drop in the main power wires from the generation source or the battery to the bus should not exceed 2 percent of the regulated voltage when the generator is carrying rated current or the battery is being discharged at the 5-minute rate. The tabulation shown in table 11-6 defines the maximum acceptable voltage drop in the load circuits between the bus and the utilization equipment ground.

TABLE 11-6. Tabulation chart (allowable voltage drop between bus and utilization equipment ground).

Nominal system voltage	Allowable voltage drop continuous operation	Intermittent operation
14	0.5	1
28	1	2
115	4	8
200	7	14

c. Resistance. The resistance of the current return path through the aircraft structure is generally considered negligible. However, this is based on the assumption that adequate bonding to the structure or a special electric current return path has been provided that is capable of carrying the required electric current with a negligible voltage drop. To determine circuit resistance check the voltage drop across the circuit. If the voltage drop does not exceed the limit established by the aircraft or product manufacturer, the resistance value for the circuit may be considered satisfactory. When checking a circuit, the input voltage should be maintained at a constant value. Tables 11-7 and 11-8 show formulas that may be used to determine electrical resistance in wires and some typical examples.

d. Resistance Calculation Methods. Figures 11-2 and 11-3 provide a convenient means of calculating maximum wire length for the given circuit current.

(1) Values in tables 11-7 and 11-8 are for tin-plated copper conductor wires. Because the resistance of tin-plated wire is slightly higher than that of nickel or silver-plated wire, maximum run lengths determined from these charts will be slightly less than the allowable limits for nickel or silver-plated copper wire and are therefore safe to use. Figures 11-2 and 11-3 can be used to derive slightly longer maximum run lengths for silver or nickel-plated wires by multiplying the maximum run length by the ratio of resistance of tin-plated wire, divided by the resistance of silver or nickel-plated wire.

TABLE 11-7. Examples of determining required tin-plated copper wire size and checking voltage drop using figure 11-2

Voltage drop	Run Lengths (Feet)	Circuit Current (Amps)	Wire Size From Chart	Check-calculated voltage drop (VD)= (Resistance/Ft) (Length) (Current)
1	107	20	No. 6	VD= (.00044 ohms/ft) (107)(20)= 0.942
0.5	90	20	No. 4	VD= (.00028 ohms/ft) (90)(20)= 0.504
4	88	20	No. 12	VD= (.00202 ohms/ft) (88)(20)= 3.60
7	100	20	No. 14	VD= (.00306 ohms/ft) (100)(20)= 6.12

TABLE 11-8. Examples of determining maximum tin-plated copper wire length and checking voltage drop using figure 11-2.

Maximum Voltage drop	Wire Size	Circuit Current (Amps)	Maximum Wire Run Length (Feet)	Check-calculated voltage drop (VD)= (Resistance/Ft) (Length) (Current)
1	No. 10	20	39	VD= (.00126 ohms/ft) (39)(20)= .98
0.5	----		19.5	VD= (.00126 ohms/ft) (19.5)(20)= .366
4	----		156	VD= (.00126 ohms/ft) (156)(20)= 3.93
7	----		273	VD= (.00126 ohms/ft) (273)(20)= 6.88

(2) As an alternative method or a means of checking results from figure 11-2, continuous flow resistance for a given wire size can be read from table 11-9 and multiplied by the wire run length and the circuit current. For intermittent flow, use figure 11-3.

(3) Voltage drop calculations for aluminum wires can be accomplished by multiplying the resistance for a given wire size, defined in table 11-10, by the wire run length and circuit current.

(4) When the estimated or measured conductor temperature (T2) exceeds 20 °C, such as in areas having elevated ambient temperatures or in fully loaded power-feed wires, the maximum allowable run length (L2), must be shortened from L1 (the 20 °C value) using the following formula for copper conductor wire:

$$L_2 = \frac{(254.5\,°C)(L_1)}{(234.5\,°C)+)(T_2)}$$

For aluminum conductor wire, the formula is:

$$L_2 = \frac{(258.1\,°C)(L_1)}{(238.1\,°C)+(T_2)}$$

These formulas use the reciprocal of each material's resistively temperature coefficient to take into account increased conductor resistance resulting from operation at elevated temperatures.

(5) To determine T2 for wires carrying a high percentage of their current carrying capability at elevated temperatures, laboratory testing using a load bank and a high-temperature chamber is recommended. Such tests should be run at anticipated worse case ambient temperature and maximum current-loading combinations.

(6) Approximate T2 can be estimated using the following formula:

$$T_2 = T_1 + (T_R - T_1)(\sqrt{I_2 / I_{\max}})$$

Where:

T_1 = Ambient Temperature
T_2 = Estimated Conductor Temperature
T_R = Conductor Temperature Rating
I_2 = Circuit Current (A=Amps)
I_{max} = Maximum Allowable Current (A=Amps) at T_R

This formula is quite conservative and will typically yield somewhat higher estimated temperatures than are likely to be encountered under actual operating conditions.

Note: Aluminum wire-From Table 11-9 and 11-10 note that the conductor resistance of aluminum wire and that of copper wire (two numbers higher) are similar. Accordingly, the electric wire current in Table 11-9 can be used when it is desired to substitute aluminum wire and the proper size can be selected by reducing the copper wire size by two numbers and referring to Table 11-10. The use of aluminum wire size smaller than No. 8 is not recommended.

TABLE 11-9. Current carrying capacity and resistance of copper wire.

Wire Size	Continuous duty current (amps)-Wires in bundles, groups, harnesses, or conduits. (See Note #1) Wire Conductor Temperature Rating			Max. resistance ohms/1000ft@20 °C tin plated conductor (See Note #2)	Nominal conductor area - circ.mils
	105 °C	150 °C	200 °C		
24	2.5	4	5	28.40	475
22	3	5	6	16.20	755
20	4	7	9	9.88	1,216
18	6	9	12	6.23	1,900
16	7	11	14	4.81	2,426
14	10	14	18	3.06	3,831
12	13	19	25	2.02	5,874
10	17	26	32	1.26	9,354
8	38	57	71	0.70	16,983
6	50	76	97	0.44	26,818
4	68	103	133	0.28	42,615
2	95	141	179	0.18	66,500
1	113	166	210	0.15	81,700
0	128	192	243	0.12	104,500
00	147	222	285	0.09	133,000
000	172	262	335	0.07	166,500
0000	204	310	395	0.06	210,900

Note #1: Rating is for 70°C ambient, 33 or more wires in the bundle for sizes 24 through 10, and 9 wires for size 8 and larger, with no more than 20 percent of harness current carrying capacity being used, at an operating altitude of 60,000 feet. For rating of wires under other conditions or configurations see paragraph 11-69.

Note #2: For resistance of silver or nickel-plated conductors see wire specifications.

TABLE 11-10. Current carrying capacity and resistance of aluminum wire.

Wire Size	Continuous duty current (amps) Wires in bundles, groups or harnesses or conduits (See table 11-9 Note #1)		Max. resistance ohms/1000ft
	Wire conductor temperature rating		@ 20 °C
	105 °C	150 °C	
8	30	45	1.093
6	40	61	0.641
4	54	82	0.427
2	76	113	0.268
1	90	133	0.214
0	102	153	0.169
00	117	178	0.133
000	138	209	0.109
0000	163	248	0.085
Note: Observe design practices described in paragraph 11-67 for aluminum conductor			

11-67. METHODS FOR DETERMINING CURRENT CARRYING CAPACITY OF WIRES. This paragraph contains methods for determining the current carrying capacity of electrical wire, both as a single wire in free air and when bundled into a harness. It presents derating factors for altitude correction and examples showing how to use the graphical and tabular data provided for this purpose. In some instances, the wire may be capable of carrying more current than is recommended for the contacts of the related connector. In this instance, it is the contact rating that dictates the maximum current to be carried by a wire. Wires of larger gauge may need to be used to fit within the crimp range of connector contacts that are adequately rated for the current being carried. Figure 11-5 gives a family of curves whereby the bundle derating factor may be obtained.

a. Effects of Heat Aging on Wire Insulation. Since electrical wire may be installed in areas where inspection is infrequent over extended periods of time, it is necessary to give special consideration to heat-aging characteristics in the selection of wire. Resistance to heat is of primary importance in the selection of wire for aircraft use, as it is the basic factor in wire rating. Where wire may be required to operate at higher temperatures due either to high ambient temperatures, high-current loading, or a combination of the two, selection should be made on the basis of satisfactory performance under the most severe operating conditions.

b. Maximum Operating Temperature. The current that causes a temperature steady state condition equal to the rated temperature of the wire should not be exceeded. Rated temperature of the wire may be based upon the ability of either the conductor or the insulation to withstand continuous operation without degradation.

c. Single Wire in Free Air. Determining a wiring system's current carrying capacity begins with determining the maximum current that a given-sized wire can carry without exceeding the allowable temperature difference (wire rating minus ambient °C). The curves are based upon a single copper wire in free air. (See figures 11-4a and 11-4b.)

d. Wires in a Harness. When wires are bundled into harnesses, the current derived for a single wire must be reduced as shown in figure 11-5. The amount of current derating is a function of the number of wires in the bundle and the percentage of the total wire bundle capacity that is being used.

e. Harness at Altitude. Since heat loss from the bundle is reduced with increased altitude, the amount of current should be derated. Figure 11-6 gives a curve whereby the altitude-derating factor may be obtained.

f. Aluminum Conductor Wire. When aluminum conductor wire is used, sizes should be selected on the basis of current ratings shown in table 11-10. The use of sizes smaller than #8 is discouraged (Ref. AS50881A). Aluminum wire should not be attached to engine mounted accessories or used in areas having corrosive fumes, severe vibration, mechanical stresses, or where there is a need for frequent disconnection. Use of aluminum wire is also discouraged for runs of less than 3 feet (AS50991A). Termination hardware should be of the type specifically designed for use with aluminum conductor wiring.

11-68. INSTRUCTIONS FOR USE OF ELECTRICAL WIRE CHART.

a. Correct Size. To select the correct size of electrical wire, two major requirements must be met:

(1) The wire size should be sufficient to prevent an excessive voltage drop while carrying the required current over the required distance. (See table 11-6, Tabulation Chart, for allowable voltage drops.)

(2) The size should be sufficient to prevent overheating of the wire carrying the required current. (See paragraph 11-69 for allowable current carrying calculation methods.)

b. Two Requirements. To meet the two requirements (see paragraph 11-66b) in selecting the correct wire size using figure 11-2 or figure 11-3, the following must be known:

(1) The wire length in feet.

(2) The number of amperes of current to be carried.

(3) The allowable voltage drop permitted.

(4) The required continuous or intermittent current.

(5) The estimated or measured conductor temperature.

(6) Is the wire to be installed in conduit and/or bundle?

(7) Is the wire to be installed as a single wire in free air?

c. Example No. 1. Find the wire size in figure 11-2 using the following known information:

(1) The wire run is 50 feet long, including the ground wire.

(2) Current load is 20 amps.

(3) The voltage source is 28 volts from bus to equipment.

(4) The circuit has continuous operation.

(5) Estimated conductor temperature is 20 °C or less.

The scale on the left of the chart represents maximum wire length in feet to prevent an excessive voltage drop for a specified voltage source system (e.g., 14V, 28V, 115V, 200V). This voltage is identified at the top of scale and the corresponding voltage drop limit for continuous operation at the bottom. The scale (slant lines) on top of the chart represents amperes. The scale at the bottom of the chart represents wire gauge.

STEP 1: From the left scale find the wire length, 50 feet under the 28V source column.

STEP 2: Follow the corresponding horizontal line to the right until it intersects the slanted line for the 20-amp load.

STEP 3: At this point, drop vertically to the bottom of the chart. The value falls between No. 8 and No. 10. Select the next larger size wire to the right, in this case No. 8. This is the smallest size wire that can be used without exceeding the voltage drop limit expressed at the bottom of the left scale. This example is plotted on the wire chart, figure 11-2. Use figure 11-2 for continuous flow and figure 11-3 for intermittent flow.

d. Procedures in Example No. 1 paragraph 11-68c, can be used to find the wire size for any continuous or intermittent operation (maximum two minutes). Voltage (e.g. 14 volts, 28 volts, 115 volts, 200 volts) as indicated on the left scale of the wire chart in figure 11-2 and 11-3.

e. Example No. 2. Using figure 11-2, find the wire size required to meet the allowable voltage drop in table 11-6 for a wire carrying current at an elevated conductor temperature using the following information:

(1) The wire run is 15.5 feet long, including the ground wire.

(2) Circuit current (I2) is 20 amps, continuous.

(3) The voltage source is 28 volts.

(4) The wire type used has a 200 °C conductor rating and it is intended to use this thermal rating to minimize the wire gauge. Assume that the method described in paragraph 11-66d(6) was used and the minimum wire size to carry the required current is #14.

(5) Ambient temperature is 50 °C under hottest operating conditions.

f. Procedures in example No. 2.

STEP 1: Assuming that the recommended load bank testing described in paragraph 11-66d(5) is unable to be conducted, then the estimated calculation methods outlined in paragraph 11-66d(6) may be used to determine the estimated maximum current (Imax). The #14 gauge wire mentioned above can carry the required current at 50 °C ambient (allowing for altitude and bundle derating).

(1) Use figure 11-4a to calculate the Imax a #14 gauge wire can carry.

Where:

T_2 = estimated conductor temperature

T_1 = 50 °C ambient temperature

T_R = 200 °C maximum conductor rated temperature

(2) Find the temperature differences (T_R-T_1) = (200 °C-50 °C) = 150 °C.

(3) Follow the 150 °C corresponding horizontal line to intersect with #14 wire size, drop vertically and read 47 Amps at bottom of chart (current amperes).

(4) Use figure 11-5, left side of chart reads 0.91 for 20,000 feet, multiple 0.91 x 47 Amps = 42.77 Amps.

(5) Use figure 11-6, find the derate factor for 8 wires in a bundle at 60 percent. First find the number of wires in the bundle (8) at bottom of graph and intersect with the 60 percent curve meet. Read derating factor, (left side of graph) which is 0.6. Multiply 0.6 x 42.77 Amps = 26 Amps.

I_{max} = 26 amps (this is the maximum current the #14 gauge wire could carry at 50°C ambient

L_1=15.5 feet maximum run length for size #14 wire carrying 20 amps from figure 11-2

STEP 2: From paragraph 11-66d (5) and (6), determine the T_2 and the resultant maximum wire length when the increased resistance of the higher temperature conductor is taken into account.

$$T_2 = T_1 + (T_R - T_1)\left(\sqrt{I_2 / I_{max}}\right)$$

$$T_2 = 50\,^{\circ}C + (200\ C - 50\ C)(\sqrt{20A/26A}$$
$$= 50\,^{\circ}\text{C} + (150\,^{\circ}\text{C})(.877)$$
$$T_2 = 182\,^{\circ}\text{C}$$

$$L_2 = \frac{(254.5\,^{\circ}\text{C})(L_1)}{(234.5\,^{\circ}\text{C}) + (T_2)} =$$

$$L_2 = \frac{(254.5\,^{\circ}\text{C})(15.5\text{Ft})}{(234.5\,^{\circ}\text{C}) + (182\,^{\circ}\text{C})}$$

$$L_2 = 9.5\text{ ft}$$

The size #14 wire selected using the methods outlined in paragraph 11-66d is too small to meet the voltage drop limits from figure 11-2 for a 15.5 feet long wire run.

STEP 3: Select the next larger wire (size #12) and repeat the calculations as follows:

L_1=24 feet maximum run length for 12 gauge wire carrying 20 amps from figure 11-2.

I_{max} = 37 amps (this is the maximum current the size #12 wire can carry at 50 °C ambient. Use calculation methods outlined in paragraph 11-69 and figure 11-4a.

$$T_2 = 50\ ^\circ\mathrm{C} + (200\ ^\circ\mathrm{C} - 50\ ^\circ\mathrm{C})(\sqrt{20A/37A} =$$

$$50\ ^\circ\mathrm{C} + (150\ ^\circ\mathrm{C})(\text{-}540) = 131\ ^\circ\mathrm{C}$$

$$L_2 = \frac{254.5\ ^\circ\mathrm{C}(L_1)}{234.5\ ^\circ\mathrm{C} + (T_2)}$$

$$L_2 = \frac{(254.5\ ^\circ\mathrm{C})(24\mathrm{ft})}{(234.5\ ^\circ\mathrm{C}) + (131\ ^\circ\mathrm{C})} = \frac{6108}{366}$$

$$L_2 = \frac{(254.5\ ^\circ\mathrm{C})(24\mathrm{ft})}{366} = 16.7\ \mathrm{ft}$$

The resultant maximum wire length, after adjusting downward for the added resistance associated with running the wire at a higher temperature, is 15.4 feet, which will meet the original 15.5 foot wire run length requirement without exceeding the voltage drop limit expressed in figure 11-2.

11-69. COMPUTING CURRENT CARRYING CAPACITY.

a. Example 1. Assume a harness (open or braided), consisting of 10 wires, size #20, 200 °C rated copper and 25 wires, size #22, 200 °C rated copper, will be installed in an area where the ambient temperature is 60 °C and the vehicle is capable of operating at a 60,000-foot altitude. Circuit analysis reveals that 7 of the 35 wires in the bundle (7/35 = 20 percent) will be carrying power currents nearly at or up to capacity.

STEP 1: Refer to the "single wire in free air" curves in figure 11-4a. Determine the change of temperature of the wire to determine free air ratings. Since the wire will be in an ambient of 60 °C and rated at 200° C, the change of to temperature is 200 °C - 60 °C = 140 °C. Follow the 140 °C temperature difference horizontally until it intersects with wire size line on figure 11-4a. The free air rating for size #20 is 21.5 amps, and the free air rating for size #22 is 16.2 amps.

STEP 2: Refer to the "bundle derating curves" in figure 11-5, the 20 percent curve is selected since circuit analysis indicate that 20 percent or less of the wire in the harness would be carrying power currents and less than 20 percent of the bundle capacity would be used. Find 35 (on the abscissa) since there are 35 wires in the bundle and determine a derating factor of 0.52 (on the ordinate) from the 20 percent curve.

STEP 3: Derate the size #22 free air rating by multiplying 16.2 by 0.52 to get 8.4 amps in-harness rating. Derate the size #20 free air-rating by multiplying 21.5 by 0.52 to get 11.2 amps in-harness rating.

STEP 4: Refer to the "altitude derating curve" of figure 11-6, look for 60,000 feet (on the abscissa) since that is the altitude at which the vehicle will be operating. Note that the wire must be derated by a factor of 0.79 (found on the ordinate). Derate the size #22 harness rating by multiplying 8.4 amps by 0.79 to get 6.6 amps. Derate the size #20 harness rating by multiplying 11.2 amps by 0.79 to get 8.8 amps.

STEP 5: To find the total harness capacity, multiply the total number of size #22 wires by the derated capacity (25 x 6.6 = 165.0 amps) and add to that the number of size #20 wires multiplied by the derated capacity (10 x 8.8 = 88 amps) and multiply the sum by the 20 percent harness capacity factor. Thus, the total harness capacity is (165.0 + 88.0) x 0.20 = 50.6 amps. It has been determined that the total harness current should not exceed 50.6 A, size #22 wire should not carry more than 6.6 amps and size #20 wire should not carry more than 8.8 amps.

STEP 6: Determine the actual circuit current for each wire in the bundle and for the whole bundle. If the values calculated in step #5 are exceeded, select the next larger size wire and repeat the calculations.

b. Example 2. Assume a harness (open or braided), consisting of 12, size #12, 200 °C rated copper wires, will be operated in an ambient of 25 °C at sea level and 60 °C at a 20,000-foot altitude. All 12 wires will be operated at or near their maximum capacity.

STEP 1: Refer to the "single wire in free air" curve in figure 11-4a, determine the temperature difference of the wire to determine free air ratings. Since the wire will be in ambient of 25 °C and 60 °C and is rated at 200 °C, the temperature differences are 200 °C-25 °C = 175 °C and 200 °C-60 °C = 140 °C respectively. Follow the 175 °C and the 140 °C temperature difference lines on figure 11-4a until each intersects wire size line, the free air ratings of size #12 are 68 amps and 61 amps, respectively.

STEP 2: Refer to the "bundling derating curves" in figure 11-5, the 100 percent curve is selected because we know all 12 wires will be carrying full load. Find 12 (on the abscissa) since there are 12 wires in the bundle and determine a derating factor of 0.43 (on the ordinate) from the 100 percent curve.

STEP 3: Derate the size #12 free air ratings by multiplying 68 amps and 61 amps by 0.43 to get 29.2 amps and 26.2 amps, respectively.

STEP 4: Refer to the "altitude derating curve" of figure 11-6, look for sea level and 20,000 feet (on the abscissa) since these are the conditions at which the load will be carried. The wire must be derated by a factor of 1.0 and 0.91, respectively.

STEP 5: Derate the size #12 in a bundle ratings by multiplying 29.2 amps at sea level and 26.6 amps at 20,000 feet by 1.0 and 0.91, respectively, to obtained 29.2 amps and 23.8 amps. The total bundle capacity at sea level and 25 °C ambient is 29.2x12=350.4 amps. At 20,000 feet and 60 °C ambient the bundle capacity is 23.8x12=285.6 amps. Each size #12 wire can carry 29.2 amps at sea level, 25 °C ambient or 23.8 amps at 20,000 feet, and 60 °C ambient.

STEP 6: Determine the actual circuit current for each wire in the bundle and for the bundle. If the values calculated in Step #5 are exceeded, select the next larger size wire and repeat the calculations.

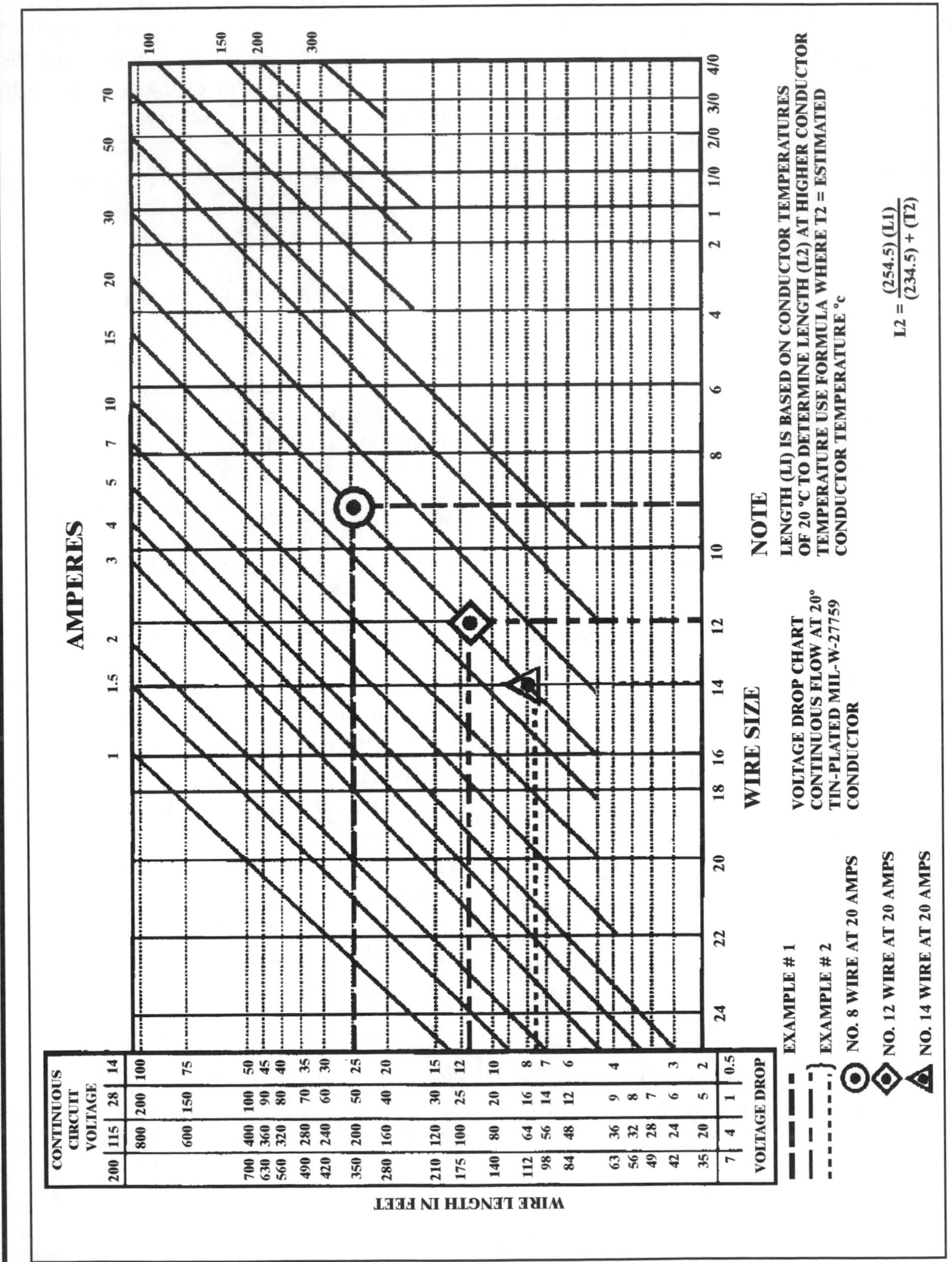

FIGURE 11-2. Conductor chart, continuous flow.

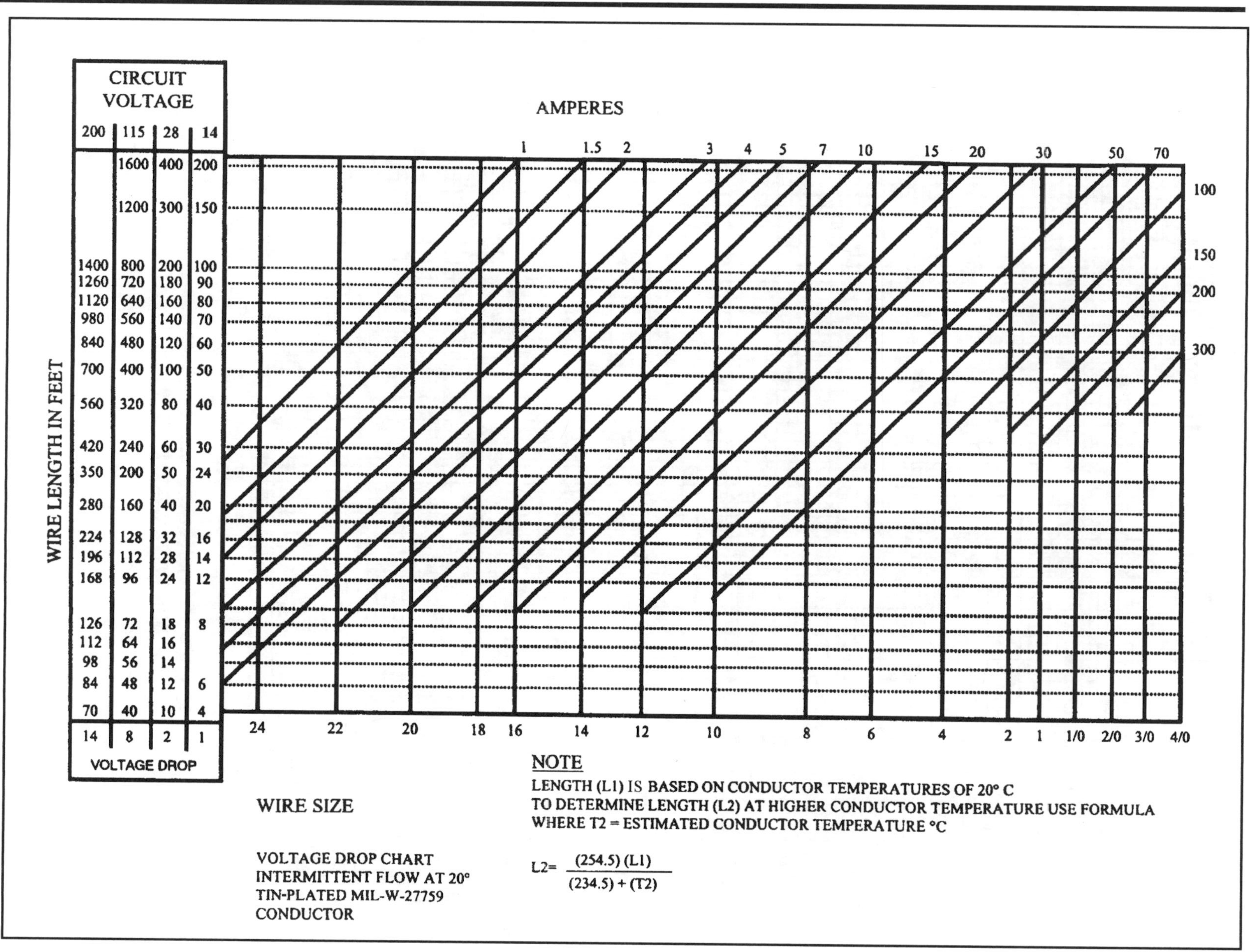

200	115	28	14
	1600	400	200
	1200	300	150
1400	800	200	100
1260	720	180	90
1120	640	160	80
980	560	140	70
840	480	120	60
700	400	100	50
560	320	80	40
420	240	60	30
350	200	50	24
280	160	40	20
224	128	32	16
196	112	28	14
168	96	24	12
126	72	18	8
112	64	16	
98	56	14	
84	48	12	6
70	40	10	4
14	8	2	1

FIGURE 11-3. Conductor chart, intermittent flow.

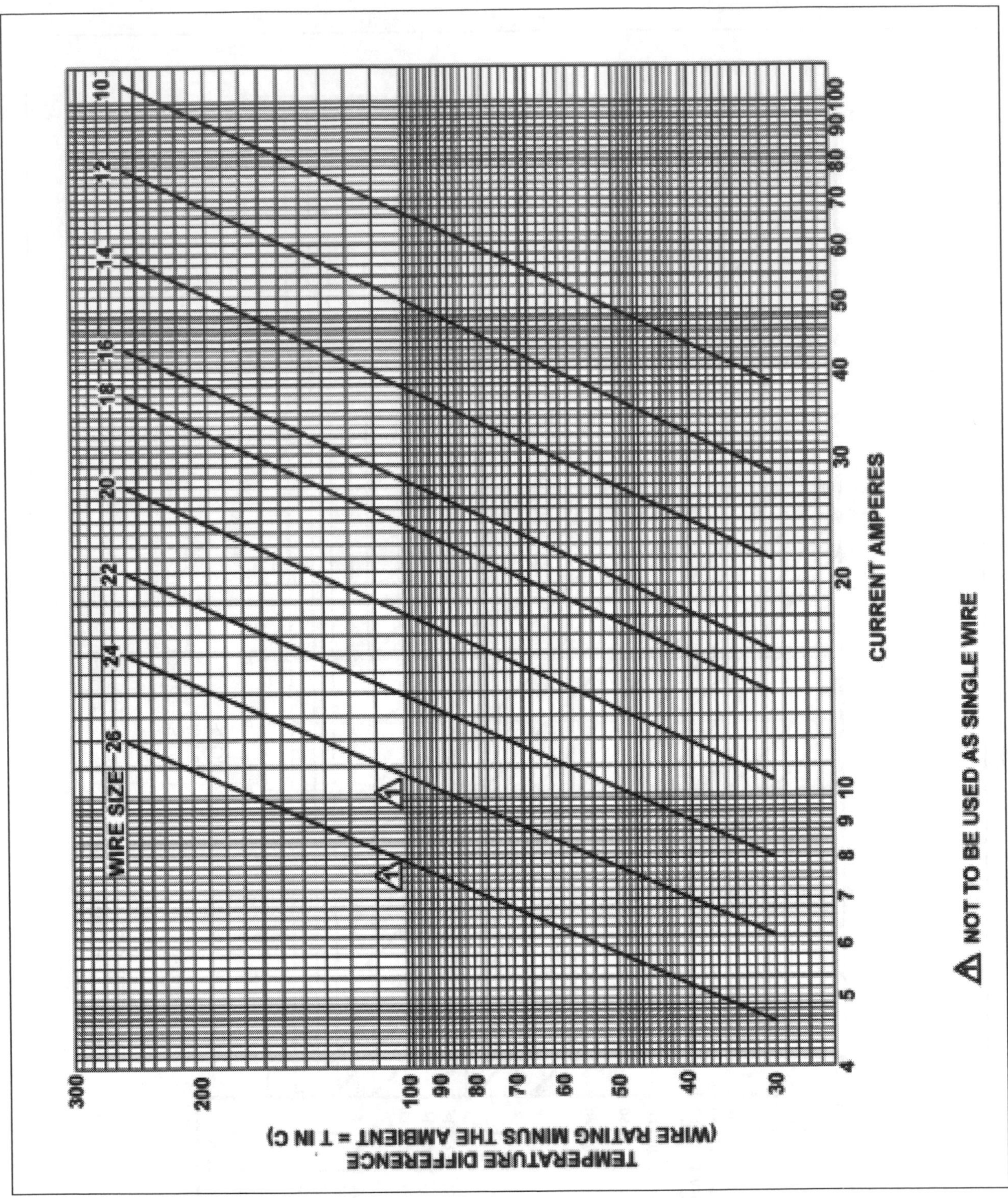

FIGURE 11-4a. Single copper wire in free air.

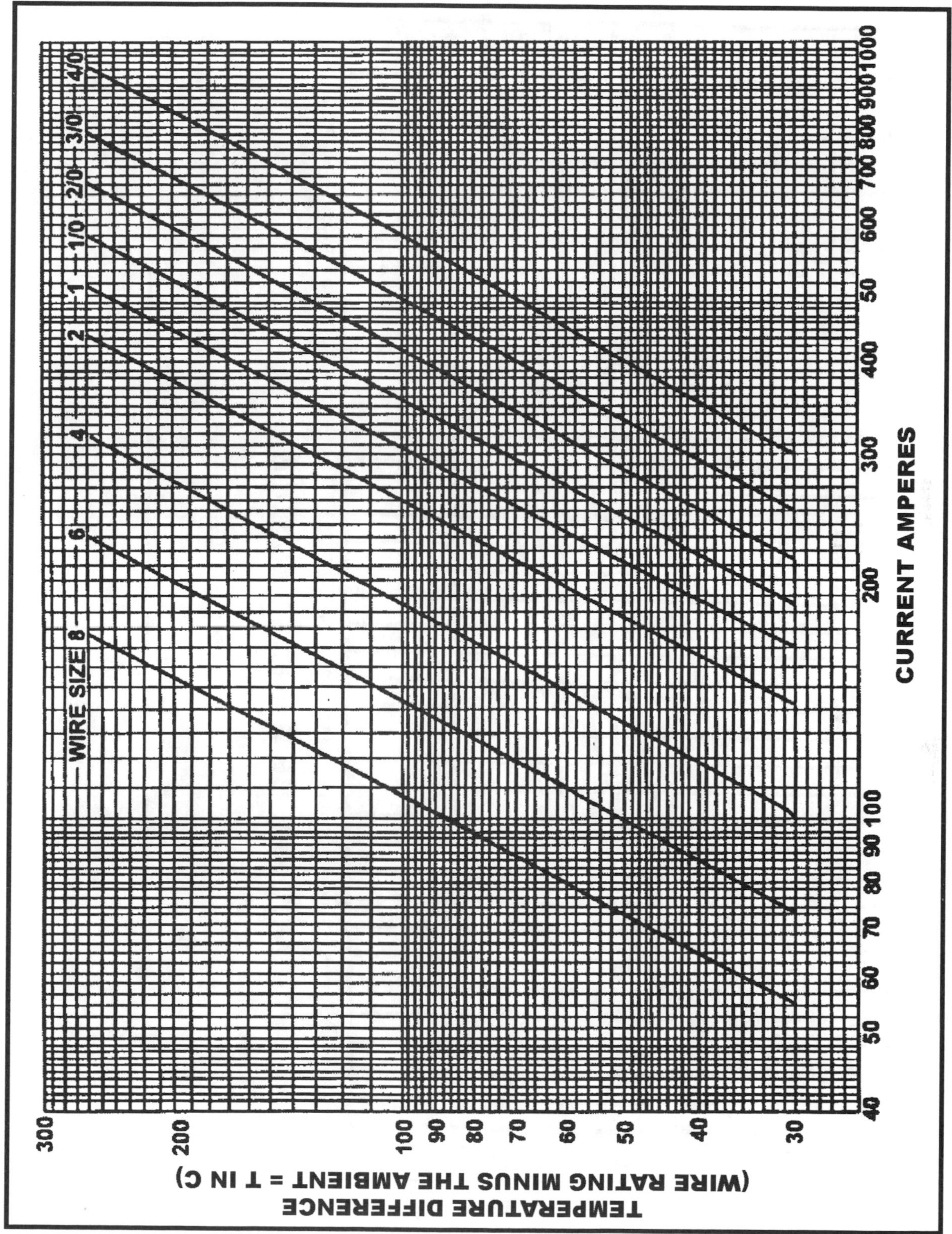

FIGURE 11-4b. Single copper wire in free air.

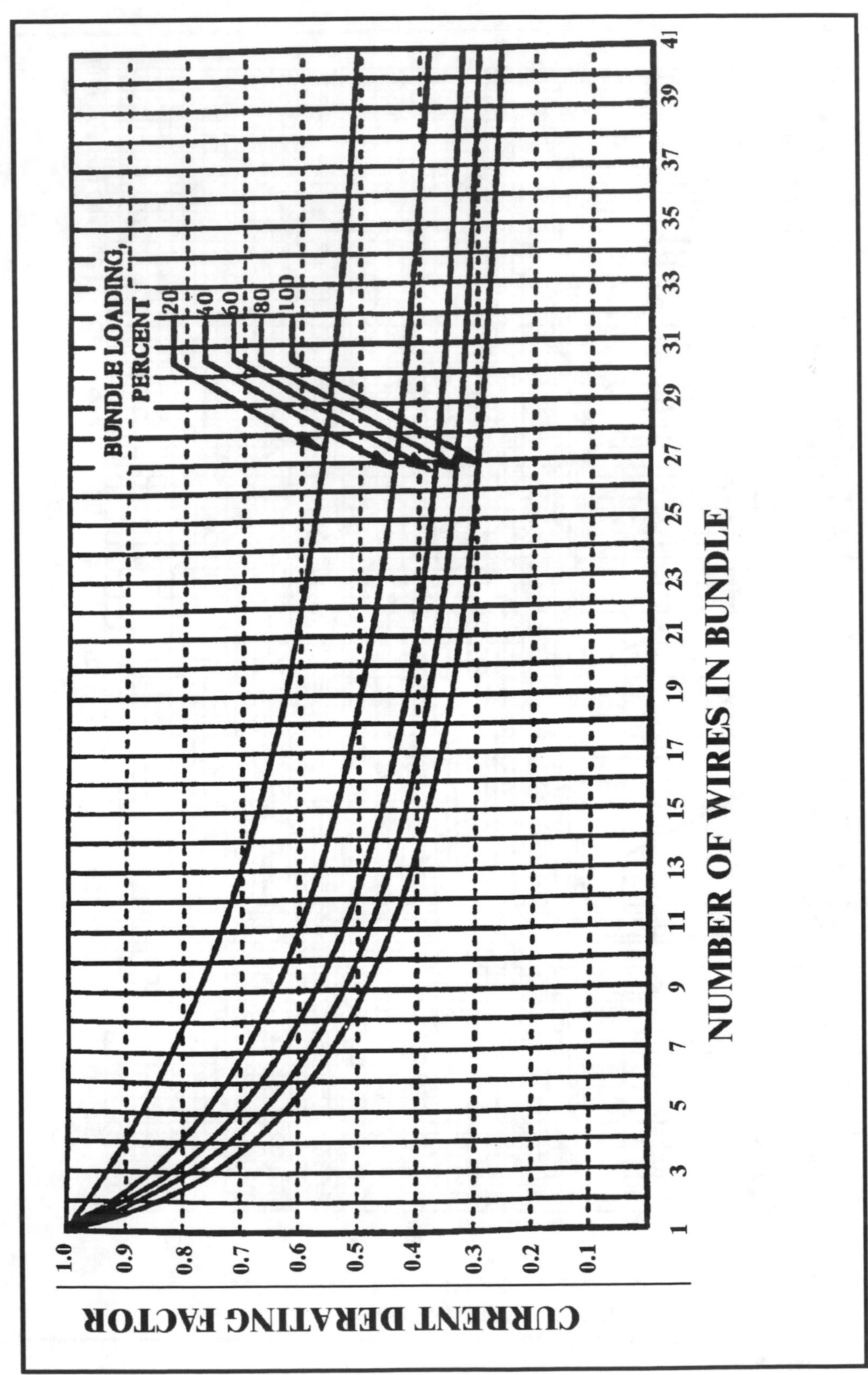

FIGURE 11-5. Bundle derating curves.

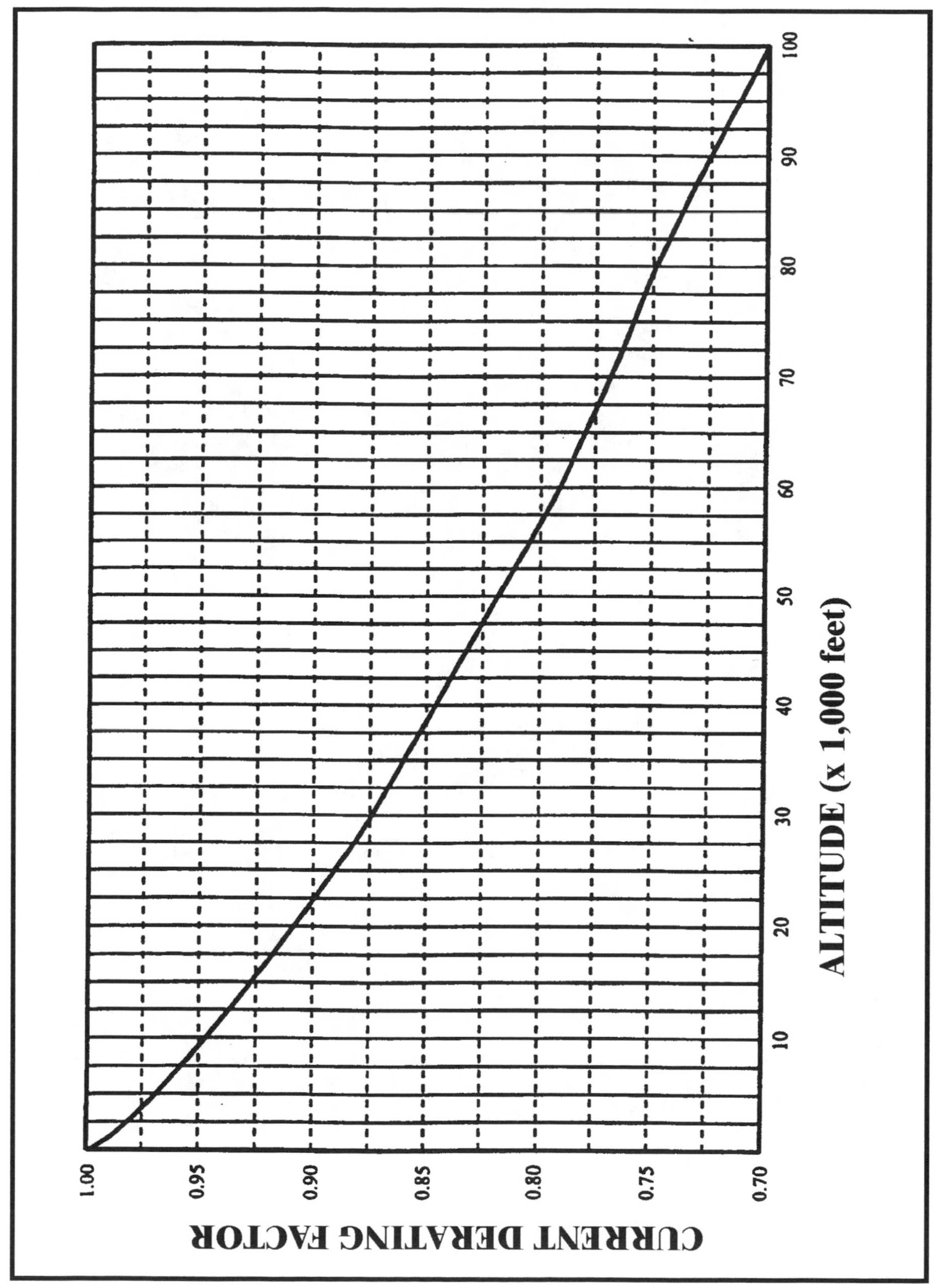

FIGURE 11-6. Altitude derating curve.

11-70. – 11-75. [RESERVED.]

SECTION 6. AIRCRAFT ELECTRICAL WIRE SELECTION

11-76. GENERAL. Aircraft service imposes severe environmental condition on electrical wire. To ensure satisfactory service, inspect wire annually for abrasions, defective insulation, condition of terminations, and potential corrosion. Grounding connections for power, distribution equipment, and electromagnetic shielding must be given particular attention to ensure that electrical bonding resistance has not been significantly increased by the loosening of connections or corrosion.

a. Wire Size. Wires must have sufficient mechanical strength to allow for service conditions. Do not exceed allowable voltage drop levels. Ensure that the wires are protected by system circuit protection devices, and that they meet circuit current carrying requirements. If it is desirable to use wire sizes smaller than #20, particular attention should be given to the mechanical strength and installation handling of these wires, e.g. vibration, flexing, and termination. When used in interconnecting airframe application, #24 gauge wire must be made of high strength alloy.

b. Installation Precautions for Small Wires. As a general practice, wires smaller than size #20 must be provided with additional clamps, grouped with at least three other wires, and have additional support at terminations, such as connector grommets, strain-relief clamps, shrinkable sleeving, or telescoping bushings. They should not be used in applications where they will be subjected to excessive vibration, repeated bending, or frequent disconnection from screw terminations.

c. Identification. All wire used on aircraft must have its type identification imprinted along its length. It is common practice to follow this part number with the five digit/letter Commercial and Government Entity (C.A.G.E). code identifying the wire manufacturer. Existing installed wire that needs replacement can thereby be identified as to its performance capabilities, and the inadvertent use of a lower performance and unsuitable replacement wire avoided.

(1) In addition to the type identification imprinted by the original wire manufacturer, aircraft wire also contains its unique circuit identification coding that is put on at the time of harness assembly. The traditional "Hot Stamp" method has not been totally satisfactory in recent years when used on modern, ultra-thin-walled installations. Fracture of the insulation wall and penetration to the conductor of these materials by the stamping dies have occurred. Later in service, when these openings have been wetted by various fluids, serious arcing and surface tracking have damaged wire bundles.

(2) Extreme care must be taken during circuit identification by a hot stamp machine on wire with a 10 mil wall or thinner. Alternative identification methods, such as "Laser Printing" and "Ink Jet," are coming into increasing use by the industry. When such modern equipment is not available, the use of stamped identification sleeving should be considered on thin-walled wire, especially when insulation wall thickness falls below 10 mils.

11-77. AIRCRAFT WIRE MATERIALS. Only wire, specifically designed for airborne use, must be installed in aircraft.

a. Authentic Aircraft Wire. Most aircraft wire designs are to specifications that require manufacturers to pass rigorous testing of wires before being added to a Qualified Products List (QPL) and being permitted to produce the wire. Aircraft manufacturers who maintain their own wire specifications invariably exercise close control on their approved sources. Such military or original equipment manufacturer (OEM) wire used on aircraft should only have originated from these defined wire mills. Aircraft wire from other unauthorized firms, and fraudulently marked with the specified identification, must be regarded as "unapproved wire," and usually will be of inferior quality with little or no process control testing. Efforts must be taken to ensure obtaining authentic, fully tested aircraft wire.

b. ***Plating.*** Bare copper develops a surface oxide coating at a rate dependent on temperature. This oxide film is a poor conductor of electricity and inhibits determination of wire. Therefore, all aircraft wiring has a coating of tin, silver, or nickel, that have far slower oxidation rates.

(1) Tin coated copper is a very common plating material. Its ability to be successfully soldered without highly active fluxes diminishes rapidly with time after manufacture. It can be used up to the limiting temperature of 150 °C.

(2) Silver-coated wire is used where temperatures do not exceed 200 °C (392 °F).

(3) Nickel coated wire retains its properties beyond 260 °C, but most aircraft wire using such coated strands have insulation systems that cannot exceed that temperature on long-term exposure. Soldered terminations of nickel-plated conductor require the use of different solder sleeves or flux than those used with tin or silver-plated conductor.

c. Conductor Stranding. Because of flight vibration and flexing, conductor round wire should be stranded to minimize fatigue breakage.

d. Wire Construction Versus Application. The most important consideration in the selection of aircraft wire is properly matching the wire's construction to the application environment. Wire construction that is suitable for the most severe environmental condition to be encountered should be selected. Wires are typically categorized as being suitable for either "open wiring" or "protected wiring" applications. MIL-W-5088L, replaced by AS50881A, wiring aerospace vehicle, Appendix A table A-I lists wires considered to have sufficient abrasion and cut-through resistance to be suitable for open-harness construction. MIL-W-5088L, replaced by *AS50881A*, wiring aerospace vehicle, Appendix A table A-II lists wires for protected applications. These wires are not recommended for aircraft interconnection wiring unless the subject harness is covered throughout its length by a protective jacket. The wire temperature rating is typically a measure of the insulation's ability to withstand the combination of ambient temperature and current related conductor temperature rise.

e. ***Insulation.*** There are many insulation materials and combinations used on aircraft electrical wire. Characteristics should be chosen based on environment; such as abrasion resistance, arc resistance, corrosion resistance, cut-through strength, dielectric strength, flame resistant, mechanical strength, smoke emission, fluid resistance, and heat distortion. An explanation of many of the abbreviations is identified in the glossary.

11-78. SUBSTITUTIONS. In the repair and modification of existing aircraft, when a replacement wire is required, the maintenance manual for that aircraft must first be reviewed to determine if the original aircraft manufacturer (OAM) has approved any substitution. If not, then the OAM must be contacted for an acceptable replacement.

a. MIL-W-5088L, replaced by *AS50881A*, wiring aerospace vehicle, Appendix A lists wire types that have been approved for military aerospace applications in open and protected wiring applications. These wires could potentially be used for substitution when approved by the OAM.

b. Areas designated as severe wind and moisture problem (SWAMP) areas differ from aircraft to aircraft but generally are considered to be areas such as wheel wells, near wing flaps, wing folds, pylons, and other exterior areas that may have a harsh environment. Wires for these applications often have design features incorporated into their construction that may make the wire unique; therefore an acceptable substitution may be difficult, if not impossible, to find. It is very important to use the wire type recommended in the aircraft manufacturer's maintenance handbook.

c. The use of current military specification, multi-conductor cables in place of OEM installed constructions may create problems such as color sequence. Some civilian aircraft are wired with the older color sequence employing "Red-Blue-Yellow" as the first three colors. Current military specification, multi-conductor cables, in accordance with MIL-C-27500, use "White-Blue-Orange" for the initial three colors. Use of an alternative color code during modification without adequate notation on wiring diagrams could severely complicate subsequent servicing of the aircraft. At the time of this writing, MIL-C-27500 is being revised to include the older color sequence and could eliminate this problem in the future.

11-79.—11-84. [RESERVED.]

Table 11-2b. Comparable properties of wire insulation systems.

	Most desirable → Least			
Relative Ranking	1	2	3	4
Weight	PI	ETFE	COMP	PTFE
Temperature	PTFE	COMP	PI	ETFE
Abrasion resistance	PI	ETFE	COMP	PTFE
Cut-through resistance	PI	COMP	ETFE	PTFE
Chemical resistance	PTFE	ETFE	COMP	PI
Flammability	PTFE	COMP	PI	ETFE
Smoke generation	PI	COMP	PTFE	ETFE
Flexibility	PTFE	ETFE	COMP	PI
Creep (at temperature)	PI	COMP	PTFE	ETFE
Arc propagation resistance	PTFE	ETFE	COMP	PI

SECTION 7. TABLE OF ACCEPTABLE WIRES

11-85. AIRCRAFT WIRE TABLE. Tables 11-11 and 11-12 list wires used for the transmission of signal and power currents in aircraft. It does not include special purpose wires such as thermocouple, engine vibration monitor wire, fiber optics, data bus, and other such wire designs. Fire resistant wire is included because it is experiencing a wider application in aircraft circuits beyond that of the fire detection systems.

a. All wires in tables 11-11 and 11-12 have been determined to meet the flammability requirements of Title 14 of the Code of Federal Regulation (14 CFR) part 25, section 25.869(a)(4) and the applicable portion of part 1 of Appendix F of part 25.

b. The absence of any wire from tables 11-11 and 11-12 are not to be construed as being unacceptable for use in aircraft. However, the listed wires have all been reviewed for such use and have been found suitable, or have a successful history of such usage.

c. Explanations of the various insulation materials mentioned in table 11-11, by abbreviations, can be found in the glossary.

11-86. OPEN AIRFRAME INTERCONNECTING WIRE. Interconnecting wire is used in point to point open harnesses, normally in the interior or pressurized fuselage, with each wire providing enough insulation to resist damage from handling and service exposure. (See table 11-11.) Electrical wiring is often installed in aircraft without special enclosing means. This practice is known as open wiring and offers the advantages of ease of maintenance and reduced weight.

11-87. PROTECTED WIRE. Airborne wire that is used within equipment boxes, or has additional protection, such as an exterior jacket, conduit, tray, or other covering is known as protected wire. (See table 11-12.)

11-88. SEVERE WIND AND MOISTURE PROBLEMS (SWAMP). Areas such as wheel wells, wing fold and pylons, flap areas, and those areas exposed to extended weather shall dictate selection and will require special consideration. Insulation or jacketing will vary according to the environment. Suitable wire types selected from MIL-W-22759 shall be used in these applications. (See table 11-11.)

Suitable wire types selected from MIL-W-22759 are preferred for areas that require repeated bending and flexing of the wire. Consideration should be made to areas that require frequent component removal or repair. (See table 11-11.)

11-89. SHIELDED WIRE. With the increase in number of highly sensitive electronic devices found on modern aircraft, it has become very important to ensure proper shielding for many electric circuits. Shielding is the process of applying a metallic covering to wiring and equipment to eliminate interference caused by stray electromagnetic energy. Shielded wire or cable is typically connected to the aircraft's ground at both ends of the wire, or at connectors in the cable. Electromagnetic Interference (EMI) is caused when electromagnetic fields (radio waves) induce high-frequency (HF) voltages in a wire or component. The induced voltage can cause system inaccuracies or even failure, therefore putting the aircraft and passengers at risk. Shielding helps to eliminate EMI by protecting the primary conductor with an outer conductor. Refer to MIL-DTL-27500, Cable, Power, Electrical and Cable Special Purpose, Electrical Shielded and Unshielded General Specifications.

TABLE 11-11. Open Wiring.

Document	Voltage rating (maximum)	Rated wire temperature (°C)	Insulation Type	Conductor type
MIL-W-22759/1	600	200	Fluoropolymer insulated TFE and TFE coated glass	Silver coated copper
MIL-W-22759/2	600	260	Fluoropolymer insulated TFE and TFE coated glass	Nickel coated copper
MIL-W-22759/3	600	260	Fluoropolymer insulated TFE -glass-TFE	Nickel coated copper
MIL-W-22759/4	600	200	Fluoropolymer insulated TFE -glass-FEP	Silver coated copper
MIL-W-22759/5	600	200	Fluoropolymer insulated extruded TFE	Silver coated copper
MIL-W-22759/6	600	260	Fluoropolymer insulated extruded TFE	Nickel coated copper
MIL-W-22759/7	600	200	Fluoropolymer insulated extruded TFE	Silver coated copper
MIL-W-22759/8	600	260	Fluoropolymer insulated extruded TFE	Nickel coated copper
MIL-W-22759/9	1000	200	Fluoropolymer insulated extruded TFE	Silver coated copper
MIL-W-22759/10	1000	260	Fluoropolymer insulated extruded TFE	Nickel coated copper
MIL-W-22759/13	600	135	Fluoropolymer insulated FEP PVF2	Tin coated copper,
MIL-W-22759/16	600	150	Fluoropolymer insulated extruded ETFE	Tin coated copper,
MIL-W-22759/17	600	150	Fluoropolymer insulated extruded ETFE	Silver coated high strength copper alloy
MIL-W-22759/20	1000	200	Fluoropolymer insulated extruded TFE	Silver coated high strength copper alloy
MIL-W-22759/21	1000	260	Fluoropolymer insulated extruded TFE	Nickel coated high strength copper alloy
MIL-W-22759/34	600	150	Fluoropolymer insulated crosslinked modified ETFE	Tin coated copper
MIL-W-22759/35	600	200	Fluoropolymer insulated crosslinked modified ETFE	Silver coated high strength copper alloy
MIL-W-22759/41	600	200	Fluoropolymer insulated crosslinked modified ETFE	Nickel coated copper
MIL-W-22759/42	600	200	Fluoropolymer insulated crosslinked modified ETFE	Nickel coated high strength copper alloy
MIL-W-22759/43	600	200	Fluoropolymer insulated crosslinked modified ETFE	Silver coated copper
MIL-W-25038/3/2/	600	260	See specification sheet *	See specification sheet
MIL-W-81044/6	600	150	Crosslinked polyalkene	Tin coated copper
MIL-W-81044/7	600	150	Crosslinked polyalkene	Silver coated high strength copper alloy
MIL-W-81044/9	600	150	Crosslinked polyalkene	Tin coated copper
MIL-W-81044/10	600	150	Crosslinked polyalkene	Silver coated high strength copper alloy

* Inorganic Fibers - Glass - TFE

TABLE 11-12. Protected wiring.

Document	Voltage rating (maximum)	Rated wire temperature (°C)	Insulation Type	Conductor type
MIL-W-22759/11	600	200	Fluoropolymer insulated extruded TFE	Silver coated copper
MIL-W-22759/12	600	260	Fluoropolymer insulated extruded TFE	Nickel coated copper
MIL-W-22759/14	600	135	Fluoropolymer insulated FEP-PVF2	Tin coated copper
MIL-W-22759/15	600	135	Fluoropolymer insulated FEP-PVF2	Silver plated high strength copper alloy
MIL-W-22759/18	600	150	Fluoropolymer insulated extruded ETFE	Tin coated copper
MIL-W-22759/19	600	150	Fluoropolymer insulated extruded ETFE	Silver coated high strength copper alloy
MIL-W-22759/22	600	200	Fluoropolymer insulated extruded TFE	Silver coated high strength copper alloy
MIL-W-22759/23	600	260	Fluoropolymer insulated extruded TFE	Nickel coated high strength copper alloy
MIL-W-22759/32	600	150	Fluoropolymer insulated crosslinked modified ETFE	Tin coated copper
MIL-W-22759/33	600	200	Fluoropolymer insulated crosslinked modified ETFE	Silver coated high strength copper alloy
MIL-W-22759/44	600	200	Fluoropolymer insulated crosslinked modified ETFE	Silver coated copper
MIL-W-22759/45	000	200	Fluoropolymer insulated crosslinked modified ETFE	Nickel coated copper
MIL-W-22759/46	600	200	Fluoropolymer insulated crosslinked modified ETFE	Nickel coated high strength copper alloy
MIL-W-81044/12	600	150	Crosslinked polyalkene - PVF2	Tin coated copper
MIL-W-81044/13	600	150	Crosslinked polyalkene - PVF2	Silver coated high strength copper alloy
MIL-W-81381/17	600	200	Fluorocarbon polyimide	Silver coated copper
MIL-W-81381/18	600	200	Fluorocarbon polyimide	Nickel coated copper
MIL-W-81381/19	600	200	Fluorocarbon polyimide	Silver coated high strength copper alloy
MIL-W-81381/20	600	200	Fluorocarbon polyimide	Nickel coated high strength copper alloy
MIL-W-81381/21	600	150	Fluorocarbon polyimide	Tin coated copper

11-90.—11-95. [RESERVED.]

SECTION 8. WIRING INSTALLATION INSPECTION REQUIREMENTS

11-96. GENERAL. Wires and cables should be inspected for adequacy of support, protection, and general condition throughout. The desirable and undesirable features in aircraft wiring installations are listed below and indicate conditions that may or may not exist. Accordingly, aircraft wiring must be visually inspected for the following requirements:

CAUTION: For personal safety, and to avoid the possibility of fire, turn off all electrical power prior to starting an inspection of the aircraft electrical system or performing maintenance.

a. Wires and cables are supported by suitable clamps, grommets, or other devices at intervals of not more than 24 inches, except when contained in troughs, ducts, or conduits. The supporting devices should be of a suitable size and type, with the wires and cables held securely in place without damage to the insulation.

b. Metal stand-offs must be used to maintain clearance between wires and structure. Employing tape or tubing is not acceptable as an alternative to stand-offs for maintaining clearance.

c. Phenolic blocks, plastic liners, or rubber grommets are installed in holes, bulkheads, floors, or structural members where it is impossible to install off-angle clamps to maintain wiring separation. In such cases, additional protection in the form of plastic or insulating tape may be used.

d. Wires and cables in junction boxes, panels, and bundles are properly supported and laced to provide proper grouping and routing.

e. Clamp retaining screws are properly secured so that the movement of wires and cables is restricted to the span between the points of support and not on soldered or mechanical connections at terminal posts or connectors.

f. Wire and cables are properly supported and bound so that there is no interference with other wires, cables, and equipment.

g. Wires and cables are adequately supported to prevent excessive movement in areas of high vibration.

h. Insulating tubing is secured by tying, tie straps or with clamps.

i. Continuous lacing (spaced 6 inches apart) is not used, except in panels and junction boxes where this practice is optional. When lacing is installed in this manner, outside junction boxes should be removed and replaced with individual loops.

j. Do not use tapes (such as friction or plastic tape) which will dry out in service, produce chemical reactions with wire or cable insulation, or absorb moisture.

k. Insulating tubing must be kept at a minimum and must be used to protect wire and cable from abrasion, chafing, exposure to fluid, and other conditions which could affect the cable insulation. However; the use of insulating tubing for support of wires and cable in lieu of stand-offs is prohibited.

l. Do not use moisture-absorbent material as “fill” for clamps or adapters.

m. Ensure that wires and cables are not tied or fastened together in conduit or insulating tubing.

n. Ensure cable supports do not restrict the wires or cables in such a manner as to interfere with operation of equipment shock mounts.

o. Do not use tape, tie straps, or cord for primary support.

p. Make sure that drain holes are present in drip loops or in the lowest portion of tubing placed over the wiring.

q. Ensure that wires and cables are routed in such a manner that chafing will not occur against the airframe or other components.

r. Ensure that wires and cables are positioned in such a manner that they are not likely to be used as handholds or as support for personal belongings and equipment.

s. Ensure that wires and cables are routed, insofar as practicable, so that they are not exposed to damage by personnel moving within the aircraft.

t. Ensure that wires and cables are located so as not to be susceptible to damage by the storage or shifting of cargo.

u. Ensure that wires and cables are routed so that there is not a possibility of damage from battery electrolytes or other corrosive fluids.

v. Ensure that wires and cables are adequately protected in wheel wells and other areas where they may be exposed to damage from impact of rocks, ice, mud, etc. (If rerouting of wires or cables is not practical, protective jacketing may be installed). This type of installation must be held to a minimum.

w. Where practical, route electrical wires and cables above fluid lines and provide a 6 inch separation from any flammable liquid, fuel, or oxygen line, fuel tank wall, or other low voltage wiring that enters a fuel tank and requires electrical isolation to prevent an ignition hazard. Where 6 inch spacing cannot practically be provided, a minimum of 2 inches must be maintained between wiring and such lines, related equipment, fuel tank walls and low voltage wiring that enters a fuel tank. Such wiring should be closely clamped and rigidly supported and tied at intervals such that contact betwe4en such lines, related equipment, fuel tank walls or other wires, would not occur, assuming a broken wire and a missing wire tie or clamp.

x. Ensure that a trap or drip loop is provided to prevent fluids or condensed moisture from running into wires and cables dressed downward to a connector, terminal block, panel, or junction box.

y. Wires and cables installed in bilges and other locations where fluids may be trapped are routed as far from the lowest point as possible or otherwise provided with a moisture-proof covering.

z. Separate wires from high-temperature equipment, such as resistors, exhaust stacks, heating ducts, etc., to prevent insulation breakdown. Insulate wires that must run through hot areas with a high-temperature insulation material such as fiberglass or PTFE. Avoid high-temperature areas when using cables having soft plastic insulation such as polyethylene, because these materials are subject to deterioration and deformation at elevated temperatures. Many coaxial cables have this type of insulation.

aa. The minimum radius of bends in wire groups or bundles must not be less than 10 times the outside diameter of the largest wire or cable, except that at the terminal strips where wires break out at terminations or reverse direction in a bundle. Where the wire is suitably supported, the radius may be 3 times the diameter of the wire or cable. Where it is not practical to install wiring or cables within the radius requirements, the bend should be enclosed in insulating tubing. The radius for thermocouple wire should be done in accordance with the manufacturer's recommendation and shall be sufficient to avoid excess losses or damage to the cable.

bb. Ensure that RF cables, e.g., coaxial and triaxial are bent at a radius of no less than 6 times the outside diameter of the cable.

cc. Ensure that wires and cables, that are attached to assemblies where relative movement occurs (such as at hinges and rotating pieces; particularly doors, control sticks, control wheels, columns, and flight control surfaces), are installed or protected in such a manner as to prevent deterioration of the wires and cables caused by the relative movement of the assembled parts.

dd. Ensure that wires and electrical cables are separated from mechanical control cables. In no instance should wire be able to come closer than 1/2 inch to such controls when light hand pressure is applied to wires or controls. In cases where clearance is less than this, adequate support must be provided to prevent chafing.

ee. Ensure that wires and cables are provided with enough slack to meet the following requirements:

(1) Permit ease of maintenance.

(2) Prevent mechanical strain on the wires, cables, junctions, and supports.

(3) Permit free movement of shock and vibration mounted equipment.

(4) Allow shifting of equipment, as necessary, to perform alignment, servicing, tuning, removal of dust covers, and changing of internal components while installed in aircraft.

ff. Ensure that unused wires are individually dead-ended, tied into a bundle, and secured to a permanent structure. Each wire should have strands cut even with the insulation and a pre-insulated closed end connector or a 1-inch piece of insulating tubing placed over the wire with its end folded back and tied.

gg. Ensure that all wires and cables are identified properly at intervals of not more than 15 inches. Coaxial cables are identified at both equipment ends.

11-97. WIRING REPLACEMENT. Wiring must be replaced with equivalent wire (see paragraph 11-78) when found to have any of the following defects:

a. Wiring that has been subjected to chafing or fraying, that has been severely damaged, or that primary insulation is suspected of being penetrated.

b. Wiring on which the outer insulation is brittle to the point that slight flexing causes it to crack.

c. Wiring having weather-cracked outer insulation.

d. Wiring that is known to have been exposed to electrolyte or on which the insulation appears to be, or is suspected of being, in an initial stage of deterioration due to the effects of electrolyte.

e. Check wiring that shows evidence of overheating (even if only to a minor degree) for the cause of the overheating.

f. Wiring on which the insulation has become saturated with engine oil, hydraulic fluid, or another lubricant.

g. Wiring that bears evidence of having been crushed or severely kinked.

h. Shielded wiring on which the metallic shield is frayed and/or corroded. Cleaning agents or preservatives should not be used to minimize the effects of corrosion or deterioration of wire shields.

i. Wiring showing evidence of breaks, cracks, dirt, or moisture in the plastic sleeves placed over wire splices or terminal lugs.

j. Sections of wire in which splices occur at less than 10-foot intervals, unless specifically authorized, due to parallel connections, locations, or inaccessibility.

k. When replacing wiring or coaxial cables, identify them properly at both equipment and power source ends.

l. Wire substitution-In the repair and modification of existing aircraft, when a replacement wire is required, the maintenance manual for that aircraft should first be reviewed to determine if the original aircraft manufacturer (OAM) has approved any substitution. If not, then the OAM should be contacted for an acceptable replacement.

m. Testing of the electrical and chemical integrity of the insulation of sample wires taken from areas of the aircraft that have experienced wiring problems in the past, can be used to supplement visual examination of the wire. The test for chemical integrity should be specific for the degradation mode of the insulation. If the samples fail either the electrical or chemical integrity tests, then the wiring in the area surrounding the sampling area is a candidate for replacement.

11-98. TERMINALS AND TERMINAL BLOCKS. Inspect to ensure that the following installation requirements are met:

a. Insulating tubing is placed over terminals (except pre-insulated types) to provide electrical protection and mechanical support and is secured to prevent slippage of the tubing from the terminal.

b. Terminal module blocks are securely mounted and provided with adequate electrical clearances or insulation strips between mounting hardware and conductive parts, except when the terminal block is used for grounding purposes.

c. Terminal connections to terminal module block studs and nuts on unused studs are tight.

d. Evidence of overheating and corrosion is not present on connections to terminal module block studs.

e. Physical damage to studs, stud threads, and terminal module blocks is not evident. Replace cracked terminal strips and those studs with stripped threads.

f. The number of terminal connections to a terminal block stud does not exceed four, unless specifically authorized.

g. Shielding should be dead-ended with suitable insulated terminals.

h. All wires, terminal blocks, and individual studs are clearly identified to correspond to aircraft wiring manuals.

i. Terminations should be made using terminals of the proper size and the appropriate terminal crimping tools.

11-99. FUSES AND FUSE HOLDERS. Inspect as follows:

a. Check security of connections to fuse holders.

b. Inspect for the presence of corrosion and evidence of overheating on fuses and fuse holders. Replace corroded fuses and clean fuse holders. If evidence of overheating is found, check for correct rating of fuse.

c. Check mounting security of fuse holder.

d. Inspect for replenishment of spare fuses used in flight. Replace with fuses of appropriate current rating only.

e. Inspect for exposed fuses susceptible to shorting. Install cover of nonconducting material if required.

11-100. CONNECTORS. Ensure reliability of connectors by verifying that the following conditions are met or that repairs are effected as required.

a. Inspect connectors for security and evidence of overheating (cause of over-heating must be corrected), and exteriors for corrosion and cracks. Also, wires leading to connectors must be inspected for deterioration due to overheating. Replace corroded connections and overheated connectors.

b. Ensure installation of cable clamp (reference MIL-C-85049) adapters on applicable MS connectors, except those that are moisture-proof.

c. See that silicone tape is wrapped around wires in MS3057 cable clamp adapters so that tightening of the cable clamp adapter cap provides sufficient grip on the wires to keep tension from being applied to the connector pins.

d. Make sure unused plugs and receptacles are covered to prevent inclusion of dust and moisture. Receptacles should have metal or composite dust caps attached by their normal mating method. Plugs may have a dust cap similar to above or have a piece of polyolefin shrink sleeving shrunk over the connector, starting from the backshell threads, with a tail sufficiently long enough to double-back over the connector and be tied with polyester lacing tape behind the coupling nut. The cable identification label should be visible behind the connector or a tag should be attached identifying the associated circuit or attaching equipment. The connector should be attached to structure by its normal mounting means or by the use of appropriate clamps.

e. Ensure that connectors are fully mated by checking position and tightness of coupling ring or its alignment with fully mated indicator line on receptacle, if applicable.

f. Ensure that the coupling nut of MS connectors is safetied, by wire or other mechanical locking means, as required by applicable aircraft instructional manuals.

g. Ensure that moisture-absorbent material is not used as "fill" for MS3057 clamps or adapters.

h. Ensure that there is no evidence of deterioration such as cracking, missing, or disintegration of the potting material.

i. Identical connectors in adjacent locations can lead to incorrect connections. When such installations are unavoidable, the attached wiring must be clearly identified and must be routed and clamped so that it cannot be mismatched.

j. Connectors in unpressurized areas should be positioned so that moisture will drain out of them when unmated. Wires exiting connectors must be routed so that moisture drains away from them.

11-101. JUNCTION BOXES, PANELS, SHIELDS, AND MICROSWITCH HOUSINGS. Examine housing assemblies to ascertain the following:

a. Verify that one or more suitable holes, about 3/8-inch diameter, but not less than 1/8-inch diameter, are provided at the lowest point of the box, except vapor-tight boxes, to allow for drainage with the aircraft on the ground or in level flight.

b. Verify that vapor tight or explosion proof boxes are externally labeled **VAPOR-TIGHT or EXPLOSION PROOF.**

c. Verify that boxes are securely mounted.

d. Verify that boxes are clean internally and free of foreign objects.

e. Verify that safety wiring is installed on all lid fasteners on J-boxes, panels, shields, or microswitch housings which are installed in areas not accessible for inspection in flight, unless the fasteners incorporate self-locking devices.

f. Verify that box wiring is properly aligned.

g. Verify that there are no unplugged, unused holes (except drainage holes) in boxes.

11-102. CONDUIT - RIGID METALLIC, FLEXIBLE METALLIC AND RIGID NONMETALLIC. Inspection of conduit assemblies should ascertain that:

a. Conduit is relieved of strain and flexing of ferrules.

b. Conduit is not collapsed or flattened from excessive bending.

c. Conduits will not trap fluids or condensed moisture. Suitable drain holes should be provided at the low points.

d. Bonding clamps do not cause damage to the conduit.

e. Weatherproof shields on flexible conduits of the nose and main landing gear and in wheel wells are not broken; that metallic braid of weatherproof conduit is not exposed; and that conduit nuts, ferrules, and conduit fittings are installed securely.

f. Ends of open conduits are flared or routed to avoid sharp edges that could chafe wires exiting from the conduit.

11-103. JUNCTIONS. Ensure that only aircraft manufacturer approved devices, such as solderless type terminals, terminal blocks, connectors, disconnect splices, permanent splices, and feed-through bushings are used for cable junctions. Inspect for the provisions outlined below:

a. Electrical junctions should be protected from short circuits resulting from movement of personnel, cargo, cases, and other loose or stored materials. Protection should be provided by covering the junction, installing them in junction boxes, or by locating them in such a manner that additional protection is not required, etc.

b. Exposed junctions and buses should be protected with insulating materials. Junctions and buses located within enclosed areas containing only electrical and electronic equipment are not considered as exposed.

c. Electrical junctions should be mechanically and electrically secure. They should not be subject to mechanical strain or used as a support for insulating materials, except for insulation on terminals.

11-104. CIRCUIT BREAKERS. Note those circuit breakers which have a tendency to open circuits frequently, require resetting more than normal, or are subject to nuisance tripping. Before considering their replacement, investigate the reason.

11-105. SYSTEM SEPARATION. Wires of redundant aircraft systems should be routed in separate bundles and through separate connectors to prevent a single fault from disabling multiple systems. Wires not protected by a circuit-protective device, such as a circuit breaker or fuse, should be routed separately from all other wiring. Power feeders from separate sources should be routed in separate bundles from each other and from other aircraft wiring, in order to prevent a single fault from disabling more than one power source. The ground wires from aircraft power sources should be attached to the airframe at separate points so that a single failure will not disable multiple sources. Wiring that is part of electro-explosive subsystems, such as cartridge-actuated fire extinguishers, rescue hoist shear, and emergency jettison devices, should be routed in shielded and jacketed twisted-pair cables, shielded without discontinuities, and kept separate from other wiring at connectors. To facilitate identification of specific separated system bundles, use of colored plastic cable ties or lacing tape is allowed. During aircraft maintenance, colored plastic cable straps or lacing tape should be replaced with the same type and color of tying materials.

11-106. ELECTROMAGNETIC INTERFERENCE (EMI). Wiring of sensitive circuits that may be affected by EMI must be routed away from other wiring interference, or provided with sufficient shielding to avoid system malfunctions under operating conditions. EMI between susceptible wiring and wiring which is a source of EMI increases in proportion to the length of parallel runs and decreases with greater separation. EMI should be limited to negligible levels in wiring related to critical systems, that is, the function of the critical system should not be affected by the EMI generated by the adjacent wire. Use of shielding with 85 percent coverage or greater is recommended. Coaxial, triaxial, twinaxial, or quadraxial cables should be used, wherever appropriate, with their shields connected to ground at a single point or multiple points, depending upon the purpose of the shielding. The airframe grounded structure may also be used as an EMI shield.

11-107. INTERFERENCE TESTS. Perform an interference test for installed equipment and electrical connections as follow:

a. The equipment must be installed in accordance with manufacturer's installation instructions. Visually inspect all the installed equipment to determine that industry standard workmanship and engineering practices were used. Verify that all mechanical and electrical connections have been properly made and that the equipment has been located and installed in accordance with the manufacturer's recommendations. The wire insulation temperature rating should also be considered.

b. Power input tests must be conducted with the equipment powered by the airplane's electrical power generating system, unless otherwise specified.

c. All associated electrically operated equipment and systems on the airplane must be on and operating before conducting interference tests, unless otherwise specified.

d. The effects on interference must be evaluated as follows:

(1) The equipment shall not be the source of harmful conducted or radiated interference or adversely affect other equipment or systems installed in the airplane.

(2) With the equipment energized on the ground, individually operate other electrically operated equipment and systems on the airplane to determine that no significant conducted or radiated interference exists. Evaluate all reasonable combinations of control settings and operating modes. Operate communication and navigation equipment on at least one low, high and mid-band frequency. Make note of systems or modes of operation that should also be evaluated during flight.

(3) For airplane equipment and systems that can be checked only in flight, determine that no operationally significant conducted or radiated interference exists. Evaluate all reasonable combinations of control settings and operating modes. Operate communications and navigation equipment on at least one low, high and mid-band frequency.

NOTE: Electromagnetic compatibility problems which develop after installation of this equipment may result from such factors as design characteristics of previously installed systems or equipment, and the physical installation itself. It is not intended that the equipment manufacturer should design for all installation environments. The installing facility will be responsible for resolving any incompatibility between this equipment and previously installed equipment in the airplane. The various factors contributing to the incompatibility should be considered.

NOTE: Ground EMI test have consistently been found adequate for follow-on approvals of like or identical equipment types, irrespective of the airplane model used for the initial approval. Radio frequency transmission devices, such as wireless telephones, must also be tested with respect to their transmission frequencies and harmonics.

11-108. IDENTIFICATION STENCILS AND PLACARDS ON ELECTRICAL EQUIPMENT. Replace worn stencils and missing placards.

11-109.—11-114. [RESERVED.]

SECTION 9. ENVIRONMENTAL PROTECTION AND INSPECTION

11-115. MAINTENANCE AND OPERATIONS. Wire bundles must be routed in accessible areas that are protected from damage from personnel, cargo, and maintenance activity. They should not be routed in areas in where they are likely to be used as handholds or as support for personal equipment or where they could become damaged during removal of aircraft equipment. Wiring must be clamped so that contact with equipment and structure is avoided. Where this cannot be accomplished, extra protection, in the form of grommets, chafe strips, etc., should be provided. Protective grommets must be used, wherever wires cannot be clamped, in a way that ensures at least a 3/8-inch clearance from structure at penetrations. Wire must not have a preload against the corners or edges of chafing strips or grommets. Wiring must be routed away from high-temperature equipment and lines to prevent deterioration of insulation. Protective flexible conduits should be made of a material and design that eliminates the potential of chafing between their internal wiring and the conduit internal walls. Wiring that must be routed across hinged panels, must be routed and clamped so that the bundle will twist, rather than bend, when the panel is moved.

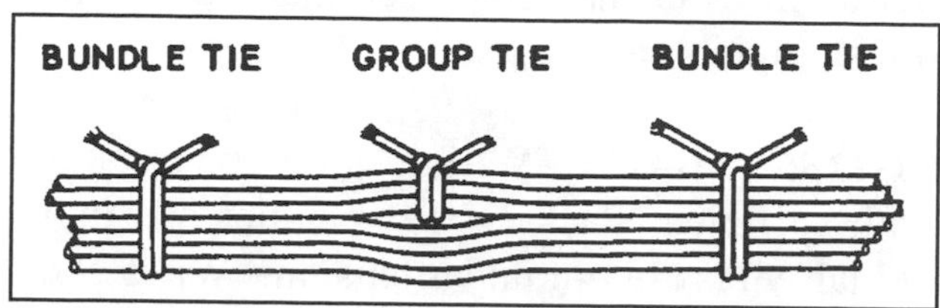

FIGURE 11-7. Group and bundle ties.

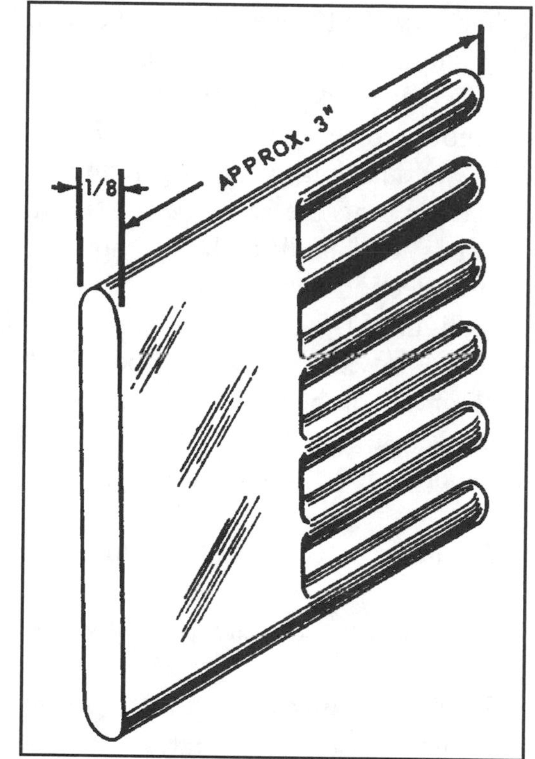

FIGURE 11-8. Comb for straightening wires in bundles.

11-116. GROUP AND BUNDLE TIES. A wire bundle consists of a quantity of wires fastened or secured together and all traveling in the same direction. Wire bundles may consist of two or more groups of wires. It is often advantageous to have a number of wire groups individually tied within the wire bundle for ease of identification at a later date. (See figure 11-7.) Comb the wire groups and bundles so that the wires will lie parallel to each other and minimize the possibility of insulation abrasion. A combing tool, similar to that shown in figure 11-8, may be made from any suitable insulating material, taking care to ensure all edges are rounded to protect the wire insulation.

11-117. MINIMUM WIRE BEND RADII. The minimum radii for bends in wire groups or bundles must not be less than 10 times the outside diameter of their largest wire. They may be bent at six times their outside diameters at breakouts or six times the diameter where they must reverse direction in a bundle, provided that they are suitably supported.

a. RF cables should not bend on a radius of less than six times the outside diameter of the cable.

b. Care should be taken to avoid sharp bends in wires that have been marked with the hot stamping process.

11-118. SLACK. Wiring should be installed with sufficient slack so that bundles and individual wires are not under tension. Wires connected to movable or shock-mounted equipment should have sufficient length to allow full travel without tension on the bundle. Wiring at terminal lugs or connectors should have sufficient slack to allow two reterminations without replacement of wires. This slack should be in addition to the drip loop and the allowance for movable equipment. Normally, wire groups or bundles should not exceed 1/2-inch deflection between support points, as shown in figure 11-9a. This measurement may be exceeded provided there is no possibility of the wire group or bundle touching a surface that may cause abrasion. Sufficient slack should be provided at each end to:

a. Permit replacement of terminals.

b. Prevent mechanical strain on wires.

c. Permit shifting of equipment for maintenance purposes.

11-118A. DRIP LOOP IN WIRE BUNDLE. A drip loop is an area where wire is dressed downward to a connector, terminal block, panel, or junction bo. In additional to the service termination and strain relief, a trap or drip loop shall be provided in the wiring to prevent fluid or condensate from running into the above devices. (see Figure 11-9b) Wires or groups of wires should enter a junction box or piece of equipment in an upward direction where practicable. Where wires must be routed downwards to a junction box or unit of electric equipment, the entry should be sealed or adequate slack should be provided to form a trap or drip loop to prevent liquid from running down the wires in the box or electric unit.

11-119. POWER FEEDERS. The power feeder wires should be routed so that they can be easily inspected or replaced. They must be given special protection to prevent potential chafing against other wiring, aircraft structure, or components.

11-120. RF CABLE. All wiring needs to be protected from damage. However, coaxial and triaxial cables are particularly vulnerable to certain types of damage. Personnel should exercise care while handling or working around coaxial. Coaxial damage can occur when clamped too tightly, or when they are bent sharply (normally at or near connectors). Damage can also be incurred during unrelated maintenance actions around the coaxial cable. Coaxial can be severely damaged on the inside without any evidence of damage on the outside. Coaxial cables with solid center conductors should not be used. Stranded center coaxial cables can be used as a direct replacement for solid center coaxial.

11-121. PRECAUTIONS.

a. Never kink coaxial cable.

b. Never drop anything on coaxial cable.

c. Never step on coaxial cable.

d. Never bend coaxial cable sharply.

e. Never loop coaxial cable tighter than the allowable bend radius.

f. Never pull on coaxial cable except in a straight line.

g. Never use coaxial cable for a handle, lean on it, or hang things on it (or any other wire).

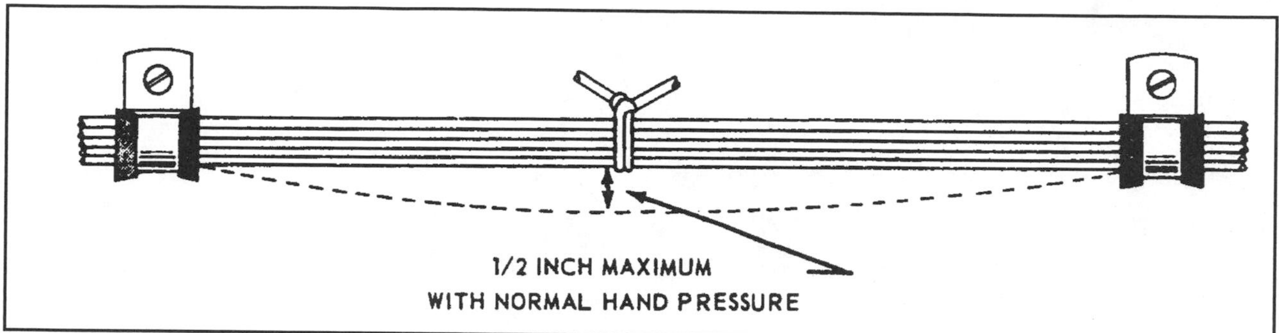

FIGURE 11-9a. Slack between supports

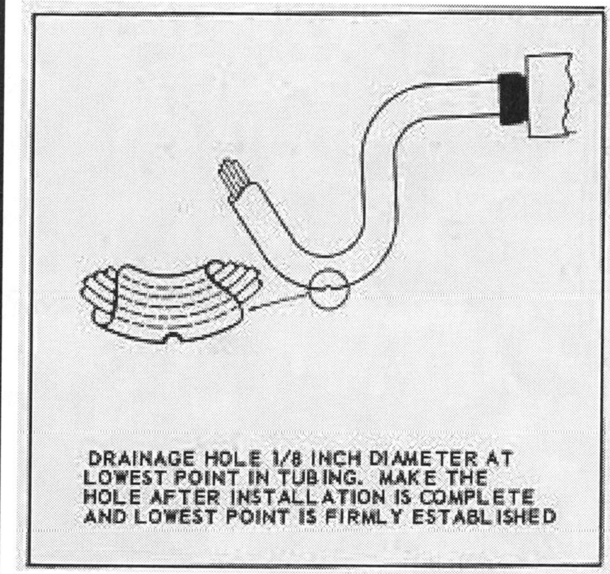

DRAINAGE HOLE 1/8 INCH DIAMETER AT
LOWEST POINT IN TUBING. MAKE THE
HOLE AFTER INSTALLATION IS COMPLETE
AND LOWEST POINT IS FIRMLY ESTABLISHED

FIGURE 11-9b. Drainage hole in low point of tubing.

11-122. MOISTURE PROTECTION, WHEEL WELLS, AND LANDING GEAR AREAS.

a. Wires located on landing gear and in the wheel well area can be exposed to many hazardous conditions if not suitably protected. Where wire bundles pass flex points, there must not be any strain on attachments or excessive slack when parts are fully extended or retracted. The wiring and protective tubing must be inspected frequently and replaced at the first sign of wear.

b. Wires should be routed so that fluids drain away from the connectors. When this is not practicable, connectors must be potted. Wiring which must be routed in wheel wells or other external areas must be given extra protection in the form of harness jacketing and connector strain relief. Conduits or flexible sleeving used to protect wiring must be equipped with drain holes to prevent entrapment of moisture.

11-123. PROTECTION AGAINST PERSONNEL AND CARGO. Wiring must be installed so the structure affords protection against its use as a handhold and damage from cargo. Where the structure does not afford adequate protection, conduit must be used, or a suitable mechanical guard must be provided.

11-124. HEAT PRECAUTIONS. Wiring must be routed away from high-temperature equipment and lines to prevent deterioration of insulation. Wires must be rated (reference paragraph 11-66 and 11-67) so that the conductor temperature remains within the wire specification maximum when the ambient temperature, and heat rise, related to current carrying capacity are taken into account. The residual heating effects caused by exposure to sunlight when aircraft are parked for extended periods should also be taken into account. Wires such as in fire detection, fire extinguishing, fuel shutoff, and fly-by-wire flight control systems that must operate during and after a fire, must be selected from types that are qualified to provide circuit integrity after exposure to fire for a specified period. Wire insulation deteriorates rapidly when subjected to high temperatures. Do not use wire with soft polyethylene insulation in areas subject to high temperatures. Use only wires or cables with heat resistance shielding or insulation.

11-125. MOVABLE CONTROLS WIRING PRECAUTIONS. Clamping of wires routed near movable flight controls must be attached with steel hardware and must be spaced so that failure of a single attachment point can not result in interference with controls. The minimum separation between wiring and movable controls must be at least 1/2 inch when the bundle is displaced by light hand pressure in the direction of the controls.

11-126. FLAMMABLE FLUIDS AND GASES. An arcing fault between an electrical wire and a metallic flammable fluid line may puncture the line and result in a fire. Every effort must be made to avoid this hazard by physical separation of the wire from lines and equipment containing oxygen, oil, fuel, hydraulic fluid, or alcohol. Wiring must be routed above these lines and equipment with a minimum separation of 6 inches or more whenever possible. When such an arrangement is not practicable, wiring must be routed so that it does not run parallel to the fluid lines. A minimum of 2 inches must be maintained between wiring and such lines and equipment, except when the wiring is positively clamped to maintain at least 1/2-inch separation, or when it must be connected directly to the fluid-carrying equipment. Install clamps as shown in figure 11-10. These clamps should not be used as a means of supporting the wire bundle. Additional clamps should be installed to support the wire bundle and the clamps fastened to the same structure used to support the fluid line(s) to prevent relative motion.

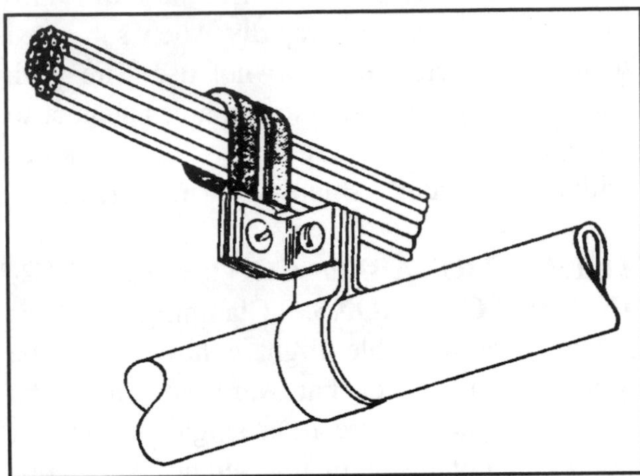

FIGURE 11-10. Separation of wires from plumbing lines.

11-127.—11-134. [RESERVED.]

SECTION 10. SERVICE LOOP HARNESSES (Plastic Tie Strips)

11-135. GENERAL. The primary function of a service loop harness is to provide ease of maintenance. The components, mounted in the instrument panel and on the lower console and other equipment that must be moved to access electrical connectors, are connected to aircraft wiring through service loops. Chafing in service loop harnesses is controlled using the following techniques.

11-136. SUPPORT. Only string ties or plastic cable straps in accordance with paragraph 11-158 should be used on service loop harnesses. A 90° or "Y" type spot tie should be installed at the harness breakout point on the harness bundle. Ties should be installed on service loop harnesses at 4 to 6-inch intervals.

11-137. ANTI-CHAFING MATERIAL. When service loops are likely to be in contact with each other, expandable sleeving or equivalent chafe protection jacket material must be installed over service loop harnesses to prevent harness-to-harness chafing. The sleeve should be held in place with string ties at 6 to 8-inch intervals. Harness identification labels should be installed, with string tie, within 3 inches of the service loop harness installation.

11-138. STRAIN RELIEF. The strain relief components may be installed to control routing where close clearance exists between termination and other components or bulkheads. Strain relief components provide support of the service loop harness at the termination point. Connector strain relief adapters, heat-shrinkable boot, or a length of heat-shrinkable tubing should be installed. The heat-shrinkable boots will provide preselected angles of wire harness termination when heat is applied. Heat-shrinkable tubing should be held at the desired angle until cool.

11-139. "SERVICE LOOP." Primary support for service loop harness(es) should be a cushion clamp and a connector at the harness termination. Service loop harnesses should be inspected for the following:

a. Adequate Length. Components should extend out from their mounting position a distance that permits rotating and unlocking (or locking) the electrical connector. Usually a distance of 3 to 6 inches, with all other components installed, should be sufficient.

b. Bundle BreakOut Point.

(1) Bundle breakout point should be adequately supported with string tie.

(2) Service loop must maintain a minimum bend radius of 3 times the harness diameter.

(3) The breakout point should be located directly behind, beside, below, or above the component so that the service loop harness does not bind other components.

(4) Plastic ties should not be used between the service loop breakout and the electrical connector when they are likely to chafe against adjacent wire.

c. Service Loop Routing. The service loop harness should be routed directly from the breakout point to the component. The harness should not contact moving mechanical components or linkage, and should not be wrapped or tangled with other service loop harnesses.

d. Service Loop Harness Termination. Strain relief should be provided at the service loop harness termination, and is normally provided by the connector manufacturer's backshell, heat-shrinkable boot, or tubing.

11-140.—11-145. [RESERVED.]

SECTION 11. CLAMPING

11-146. GENERAL. Wires and wire bundles must be supported by using clamps meeting Specification MS-21919, or plastic cable straps in accessible areas if correctly applied within the restrictions of paragraph 11-158. Clamps and other primary support devices must be constructed of materials that are compatible with their installation and environment, in terms of temperature, fluid resistance, exposure to ultraviolet (UV) light, and wire bundle mechanical loads. They should be spaced at intervals not exceeding 24 inches. Clamps on wire bundles should be selected so that they have a snug fit without pinching wires, as shown in figure 11-11 through figure 11-13.

CAUTION: The use of metal clamps on coaxial RF cables may cause problems if clamp fit is such that RF cable's original cross-section is distorted.

a. Clamps on wire bundles should not allow the bundle to move through the clamp when a slight axial pull is applied. Clamps on RF cables must fit without crushing and must be snug enough to prevent the cable from moving freely through the clamp, but may allow the cable to slide through the clamp when a light axial pull is applied. The cable or wire bundle may be wrapped with one or more turns of electrical tape when required to achieve this fit. Plastic clamps or cable ties must not be used where their failure could result in interference with movable controls, wire bundle contact with movable equipment, or chafing damage to essential or unprotected wiring. They must not be used on vertical runs where inadvertent slack migration could result in chafing or other damage. Clamps must be installed with their attachment hardware positioned above them, wherever practicable, so that they are unlikely to rotate as the result of wire bundle weight or wire bundle chafing. (See figure 11-11.).

b. Clamps lined with nonmetallic material should be used to support the wire bundle along the run. Tying may be used between clamps, but should not be considered as a substitute for adequate clamping. Adhesive tapes are subject to age deterioration and, therefore, are not acceptable as a clamping means.

c. The back of the clamp, whenever practical, should be rested against a structural member. Stand-offs should be used to maintain clearance between the wires and the structure. Clamps must be installed in such a manner that the electrical wires do not come in contact with other parts of the aircraft when subjected to vibration. Sufficient slack should be left between the last clamp and the electrical equipment to prevent strain at the terminal and to minimize adverse effects on shock-mounted equipment. Where wires or wire bundles pass through bulkheads or other structural members, a grommet or suitable clamp should be provided to prevent abrasion.

d. When wire bundle is clamped into position, if there is less than 3/8-inch clearance between the bulkhead cutout and the wire bundle, a suitable grommet should be installed as indicated in figure 11-14. The grommet may be cut at a 45 degree angle to facilitate installation, provided it is cemented in place and the slot is located at the top of the cutout.

11-147. WIRE AND CABLE CLAMPS INSPECTION. Inspect wire and cable clamps for proper tightness. Where cables pass through structure or bulkheads, inspect for proper clamping and grommets. Inspect for sufficient slack between the last clamp and the electronic equipment to prevent strain at the cable terminals and to minimize adverse effects on shock-mounted equipment.

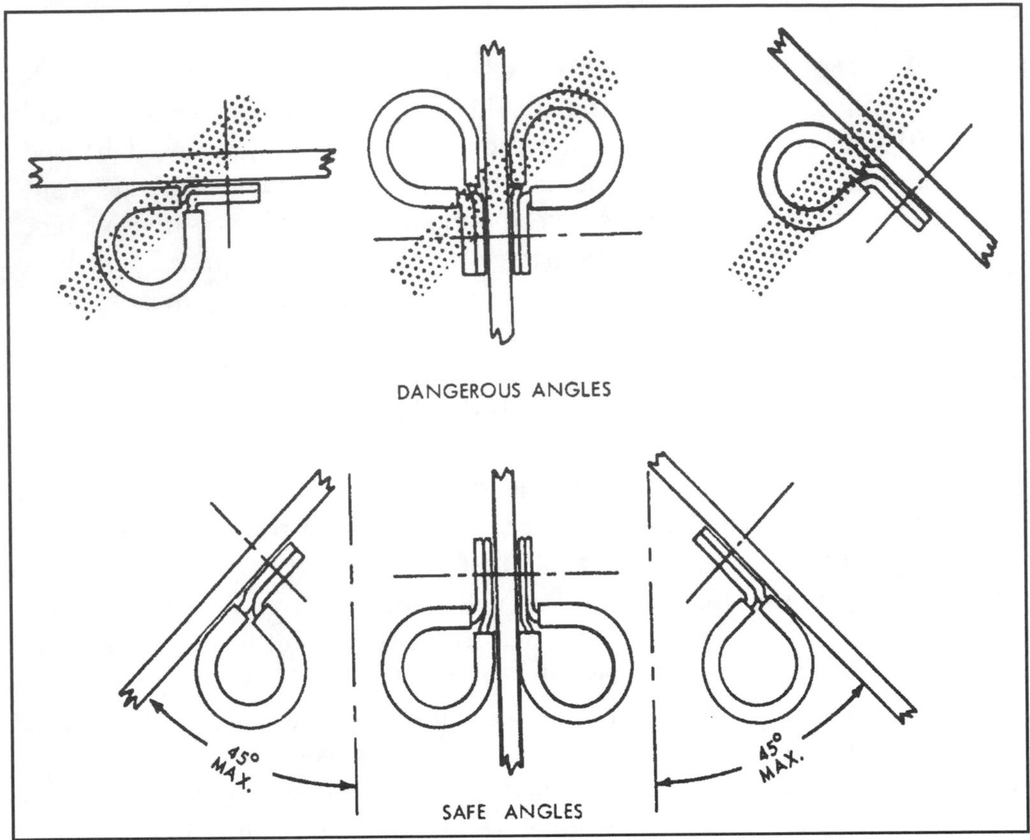

FIGURE 11-11. Safe angle for cable clamps.

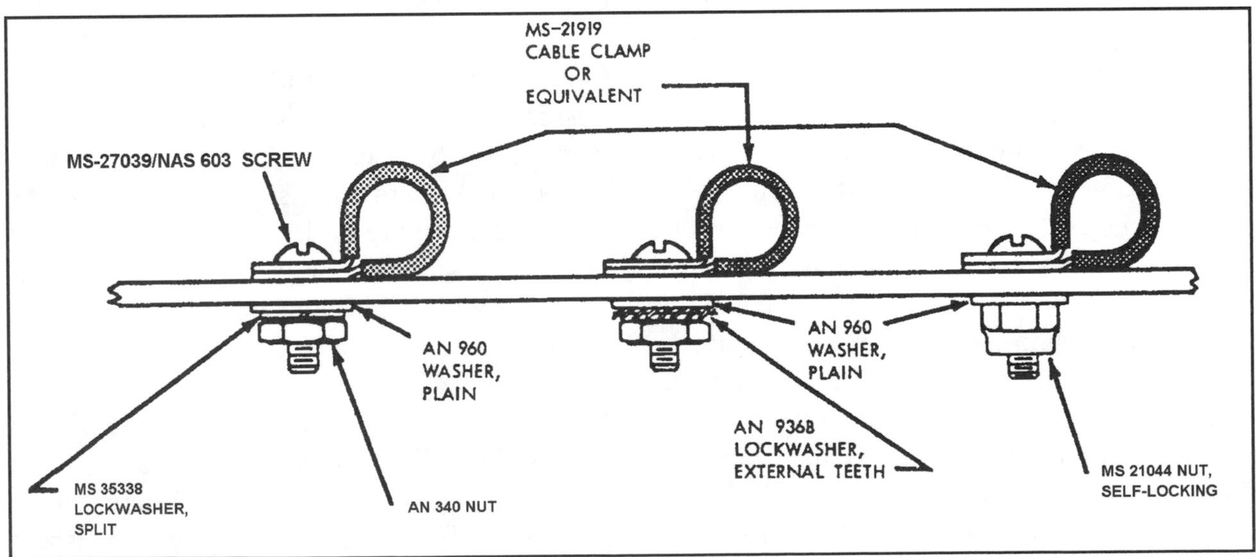

FIGURE 11-12. Typical mounting hardware for MS-21919 cable clamps.

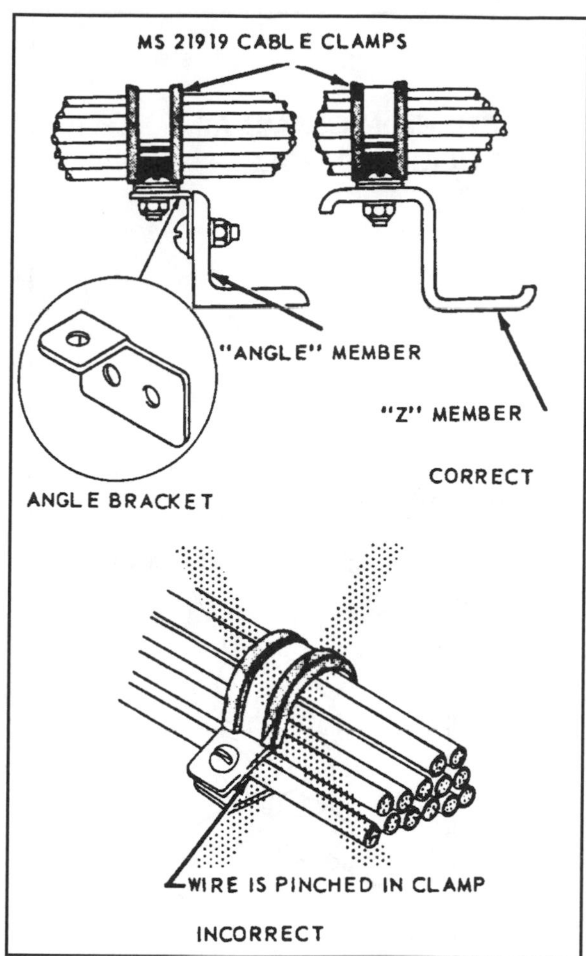

FIGURE 11-13. Installing cable clamp to structure.

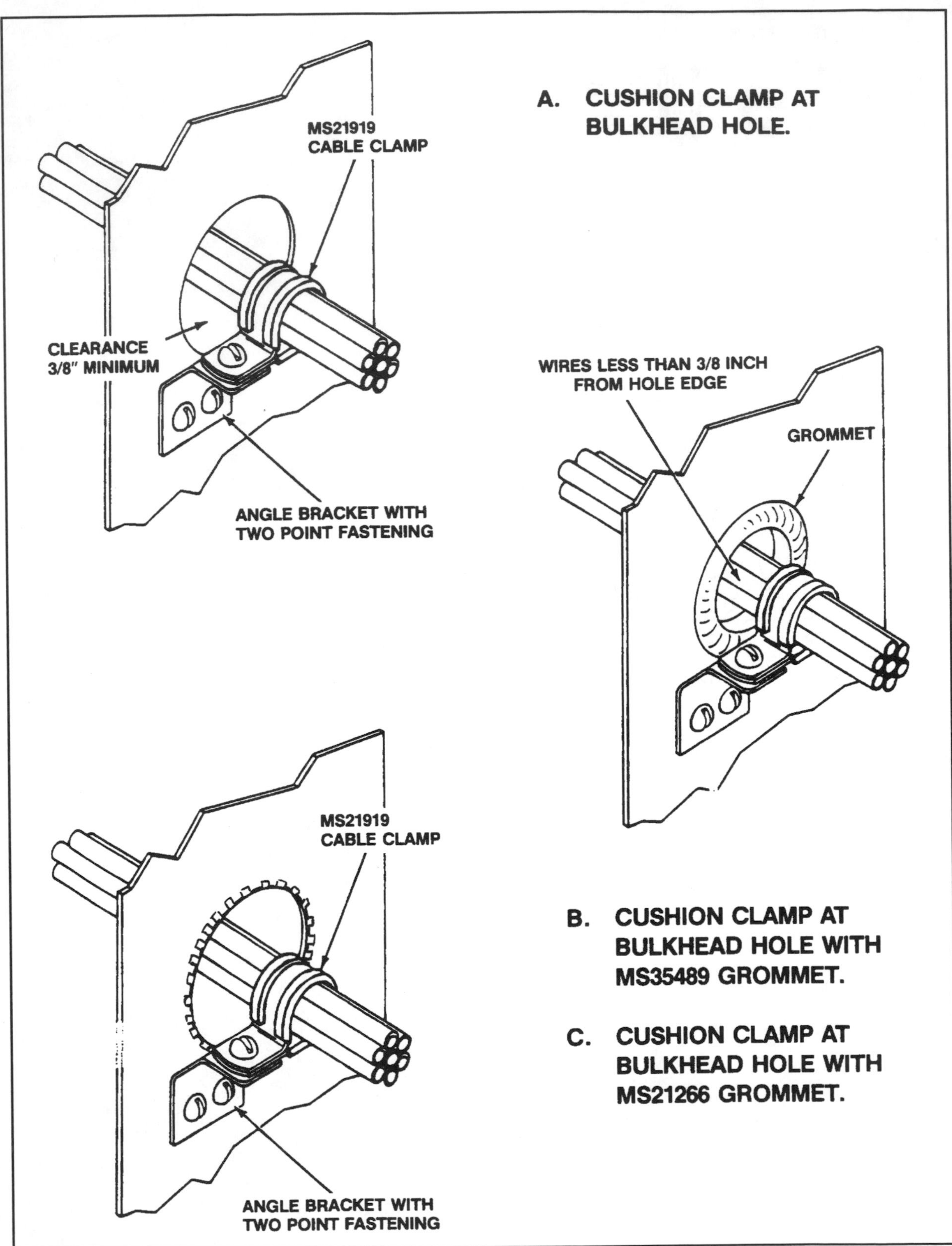

FIGURE 11-14. Clamping at a bulkhead hole.

11-148.—11-154. [RESERVED.]

SECTION 12. WIRE INSULATION AND LACING STRING TIE

11-155. GENERAL. Insulation of wires should be appropriately chosen in accordance with the environmental characteristics of wire routing areas. Routing of wires with dissimilar insulation, within the same bundle, is not recommended, particularly when relative motion and abrasion between wires having dissimilar insulation can occur. Soft insulating tubing (spaghetti) cannot be considered as mechanical protection against external abrasion of wire; since at best, it provides only a delaying action. Conduit or ducting should be used when mechanical protection is needed.

11-156. INSULATION MATERIALS. Insulating materials should be selected for the best combination of characteristics in the following categories:

a. Abrasion resistance.

b. Arc resistance (noncarbon tracking).

c. Corrosion resistance.

d. Cut-through strength.

e. Dielectric strength.

f. Flame resistance.

g. Heat distortion temperature.

h. Impact strength.

i. Mechanical strength.

j. Resistance to fluids.

k. Resistance to notch propagation.

l. Smoke emission.

m. Special properties unique to the aircraft.

n. For a more complete selection of insulated wires refer to SAE AS 4372 Aerospace Wire Performance Requirement and SAE AS 4373 Test Methods for Aerospace Wire.

11-157. STRIPPING INSULATION. Attachment of wire, to connectors or terminals, requires the removal of insulation to expose the conductors. This practice is commonly known as stripping. Stripping may be accomplished in many ways; however, the following basic principles should be practiced.

a. Make sure all cutting tools used for stripping are sharp.

b. When using special wire stripping tools, adjust the tool to avoid nicking, cutting, or otherwise damaging the strands.

c. Damage to wires should not exceed the limits specified in table 11-13.

d. When performing the stripping operation, remove no more insulation than is necessary.

11-158. LACING AND TIES. Ties, lacing, and straps are used to secure wire groups or bundles to provide ease of maintenance, inspection, and installation. Braided lacing tape per MIL-T-43435 is suitable for lacing and tying wires. In lieu of applying ties, straps meeting Specification MS17821 or MS17822 may be used in areas where the temperature does not exceed 120 ▪C. Straps may not be used in areas of SWAMP such as wheel wells, near wing flaps or wing folds. They may not be used in high vibration areas, where failure

TABLE 11-13. Allowable nicked or broken strands.

Maximum allowable nicked and broken strands			
Wire Size	Conductor material	Number of strands per conductor	Total allowable nicked and broken strands
24-14 12-10 8-4 2-1 0-00 000 0000	Copper or Copper Alloy	19 37 133 665-817 1,045-1,330 1,665- 2,109-	2 nicked, none broken 4 nicked, none broken 6 nicked, 6 broken 6 nicked, 6 broken 6 nicked, 6 broken 6 nicked, 6 broken 6 nicked, 6 broken
8-000	Aluminum	All numbers of strands	None, None

of the strap would permit wiring to move against parts which could damage the insulation and foul mechanical linkages or other moving mechanical parts. They also may not be used where they could be exposed to UV light, unless the straps are resistant to such exposure.

a. Lacing. Lace wire groups or bundles inside junction boxes or other enclosures. Single cord-lacing method, shown in figure 11-15, and tying tape, meeting specification MIL-T-43435, may be used for wire groups of bundles 1-inch in diameter or less. The recommended knot for starting the single cord-lacing method is a clove hitch secured by a double-looped overhand knot as shown in figure 11-15, step a. Use the double cord-lacing method on wire bundles 1-inch in diameter or larger as shown in figure 11-16. When using the double cord-lacing method, employ a bowline on a bight as the starting knot.

b. Tying. Use wire group or bundle ties where the supports for the wire are more than 12 inches apart. A tie consists of a clove hitch, around the wire group or bundle, secured by a square knot as shown in figure 11-17.

c. Plastic Ties. Refer to Paragraph 11-220 and table 11-21.

11-159. INSULATION TAPE. Insulation tape should be of a type suitable for the application, or as specified for that particular use. Insulation tape should be used primarily as a filler under clamps and as secondary support. Nonadhesive tape may be used to wrap around wiring for additional protection, such as in wheel wells. All tape should have the ends tied or otherwise suitably secured to prevent unwinding. Tape used for protection should be applied so that overlapping layers shed liquids. Drainage holes should be provided at all trap points and at each low point between clamps. Plastic tapes, that absorb moisture or have volatile plasticizers that produce chemical reactions with other wiring, should not be used. (Reference MIL-W-5088.)

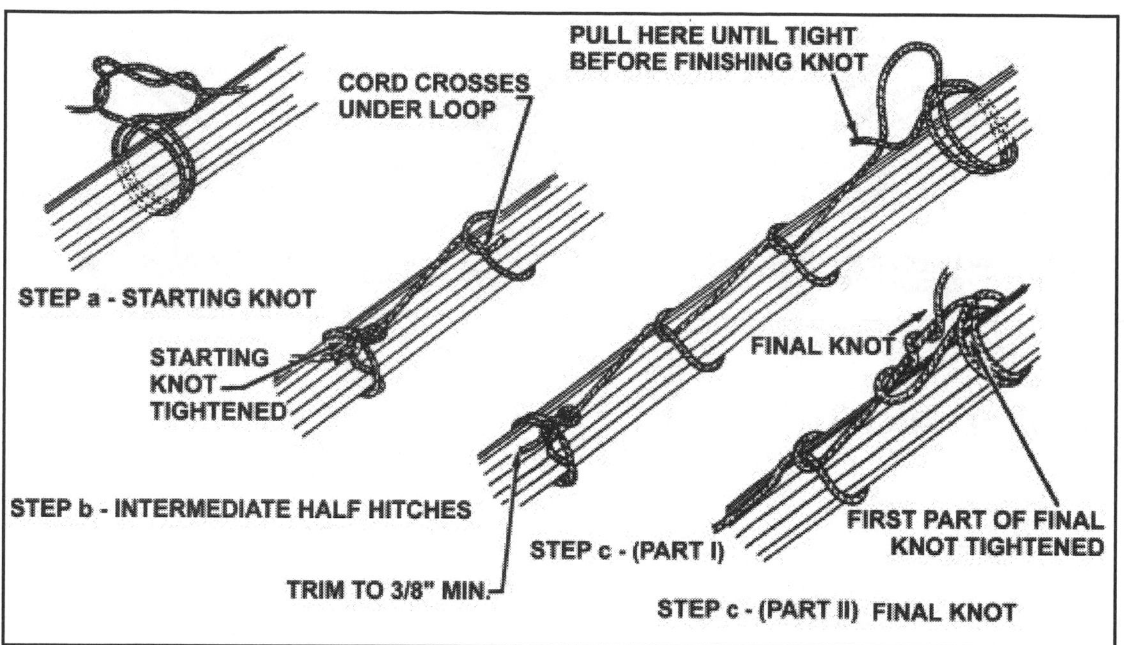

FIGURE 11-15. Single cord lacing.

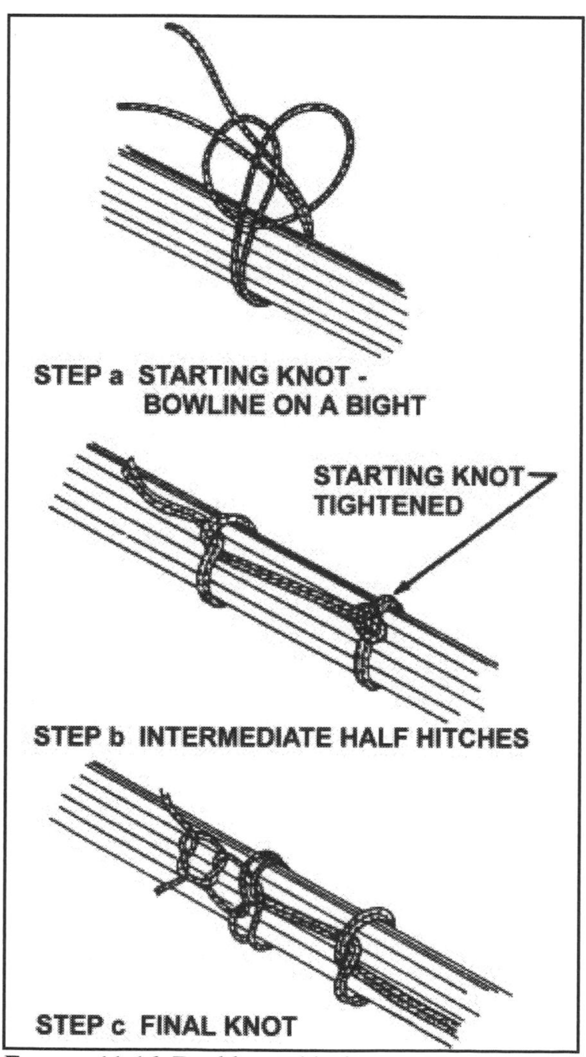

FIGURE 11-16. Double cord lacing.

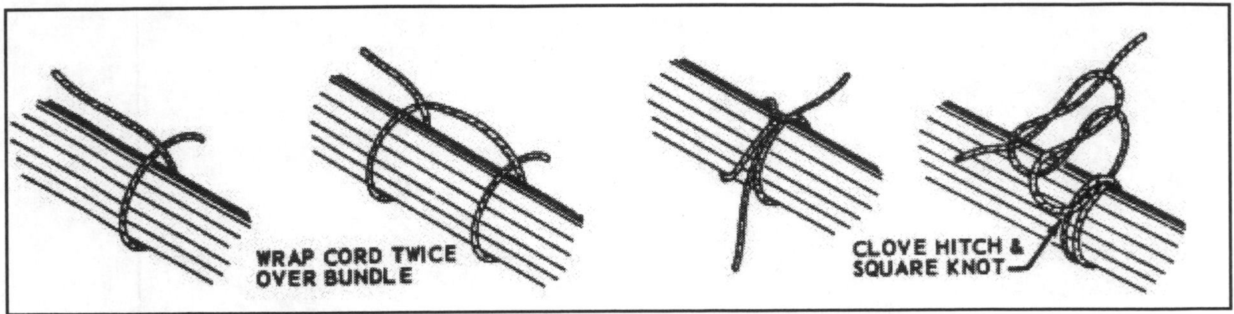

FIGURE 11-17. Making ties.

11-160.—11-166. [RESERVED.]

SECTION 13. SPLICING.

11-167. GENERAL. Splicing is permitted on wiring as long as it does not affect the reliability and the electromechanical characteristics of the wiring. Splicing of power wires, coaxial cables, multiplex bus, and large gauge wire must have approved data.

a. Splicing of electrical wire should be kept to a minimum and avoided entirely in locations subject to extreme vibrations. Splicing of individual wires in a group or bundle should have engineering approval and the splice(s) should be located to allow periodic inspection.

b. Many types of aircraft splice connectors are available for use when splicing individual wires. Use of a self-insulated splice connector is preferred; however, a noninsulated splice connector may be used provided the splice is covered with plastic sleeving that is secured at both ends. Environmentally sealed splices, that conform to MIL-T-7928, provide a reliable means of splicing in SWAMP areas. However, a noninsulated splice connector may be used, provided the splice is covered with dual wall shrink sleeving of a suitable material.

c. There should not be more than one splice in any one wire segment between any two connectors or other disconnect points, except; when attaching to the spare pigtail lead of a potted connector, to splice multiple wires to a single wire, to adjust wire size to fit connector contact crimp barrel size, and to make an approved repair. (Reference MIL-W-5088, now AS50881A, and NAVAIR 01-1A-505.)

d. Splices in bundles must be staggered so as to minimize any increase in the size of the bundle, preventing the bundle from fitting into its designated space, or cause congestion that will adversely affect maintenance. (See figure 11-18.)

e. Splices should not be used within 12 inches of a termination device, except for paragraph f below.

f. Splices may be used within 12 inches of a termination device when attaching to the pigtail spare lead of a potted termination device, or to splice multiple wires to a single wire, or to adjust the wire sizes so that they are compatible with the contact crimp barrel sizes.

g. Selection of proper crimping tool, refer to paragraph 11-178.

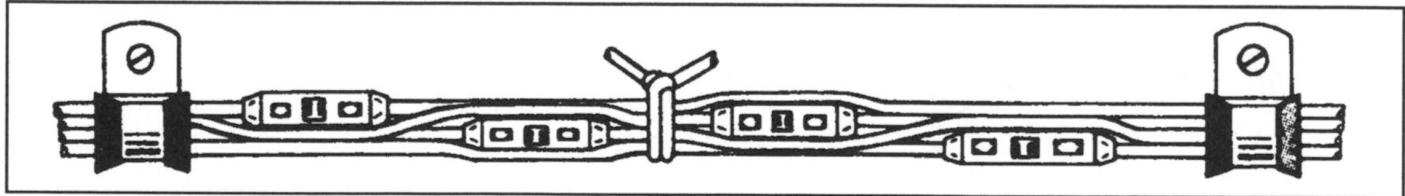

FIGURE 11-18. Staggered splices in wire bundle.

11-168.—11-173. [RESERVED.]

SECTION 14. TERMINAL REPAIRS

11-174. GENERAL. Terminals are attached to the ends of electrical wires to facilitate connection of the wires to terminal strips or items of equipment. The tensile strength of the wire-to-terminal joint should be at least equivalent to the tensile strength of the wire itself, and its resistance negligible relative to the normal resistance of the wire.

a. Selection of Wire Terminals. The following should be considered in the selection of wire terminals.

(1) Current rating.

(2) Wire size (gauge) and insulation diameter.

(3) Conductor material compatibility.

(4) Stud size.

(5) Insulation material compatibility.

(6) Application environment.

(7) Solder/solderless.

Pre-insulated crimp-type ring-tongue terminals are preferred. The strength, size, and supporting means of studs and binding posts, as well as the wire size, should be considered when determining the number of terminals to be attached to any one post. In high-temperature applications, the terminal temperature rating must be greater than the ambient temperature plus current related temperature rise. Use of nickel-plated terminals and of uninsulated terminals with high-temperature insulating sleeves should be considered. Terminal blocks should be provided with adequate electrical clearance or insulation strips between mounting hardware and conductive parts.

b. Terminal Strips. Wires are usually joined at terminal strips. A terminal strip fitted with barriers should be used to prevent the terminals on adjacent studs from contacting each other. Studs should be anchored against rotation. When more than four terminals are to be connected together, a small metal bus should be mounted across two or more adjacent studs. In all cases, the current should be carried by the terminal contact surfaces and not by the stud itself. Defective studs should be replaced with studs of the same size and material since terminal strip studs of the smaller sizes may shear due to overtightening the nut. The replacement stud should be securely mounted in the terminal strip and the terminal securing nut should be tight. Terminal strips should be mounted in such a manner that loose metallic objects cannot fall across the terminals or studs. It is good practice to provide at least one spare stud for future circuit expansion or in case a stud is broken. Terminal strips that provide connection of radio and electronic systems to the aircraft electrical system should be inspected for loose connections, metallic objects that may have fallen across the terminal strip, dirt and grease accumulation, etc. These type conditions can cause arcing which may result in a fire, or system failures.

c. Terminal Lugs. Wire terminal lugs should be used to connect wiring to terminal block studs or equipment terminal studs. No more than four terminal lugs or three terminal lugs and a bus bar should be connected to any one stud. Total number of terminal lugs per stud includes a common bus bar joining adjacent studs. Four terminal lugs plus a common bus bar thus are not permitted on one stud. Terminal lugs should be selected with a stud hole diameter that matches the diameter of the stud. However, when the terminal lugs attached to a stud vary in diameter, the greatest diameter should be placed on the bottom and the smallest diameter on top. Tightening terminal connections should not deform the terminal lugs or the studs. Terminal lugs should be so positioned that bending of the terminal lug is not required to remove the fastening screw or nut, and movement of the terminal lugs will tend to tighten the connection.

d. Copper Terminal Lugs. Solderless crimp style, copper wire, terminal lugs should be used and conform to MIL-T-7928. Spacers or washers should not be used between the tongues of terminal lugs.

e. Aluminum Terminal Lugs. The aluminum terminal lugs conforming to MIL-T-7099 (MS-25435, MS-25436, MS-25437, and MS-25438) should be crimped to aluminum wire only. The tongue of the aluminum terminal lugs or the total number of tongues of aluminum terminal lugs when stacked, should be sandwiched between two MS-25440 flat washers when terminated on terminal studs. Spacers or washers should not be used between the tongues of terminal lugs. Special attention should be given to aluminum wire and cable installations to guard against conditions that would result in excessive voltage drop and high resistance at junctions that may ultimately lead to failure of the junction. Examples of such conditions are improper installation of terminals and washers, improper torsion ("torquing" of nuts), and inadequate terminal contact areas.

f. Class 2 Terminal Lugs. The Class 2 terminal lugs conforming to MIL-T-7928 may be used for installation, provided that in such installations, Class 1 terminal lugs are adequate for replacement without rework of installation or terminal lugs. Class 2 terminal lugs should be the insulated type, unless the conductor temperature exceeds 105 °C. In that case uninsulated terminal lugs should be used. Parts' lists should indicate the appropriate Class 1 terminal lugs to be used for service replacement of any Class 2 terminal lugs installed.

g. Termination of Shielded Wire. For termination of shielded wire refer to MIL-DTL-27500.

11-175. ATTACHMENT OF TERMINALS TO STUDS. Connectors and terminals in aircraft require special attention to ensure a safe and satisfactory installation. Every possibility of short circuits, due to misinstallation, poor maintenance, and service life, should be addressed in the design. Electrical equipment malfunction has frequently been traced to poor terminal connections at terminal boards. Loose, dirty, or corroded contact surfaces can produce localized heating that may ignite nearby combustible materials or overheat adjacent wire insulation. (See paragraph 11-178)

11-176. STUDS AND INSULATORS. The following recommendations concerning studs also apply to other feed-through conductors.

a. Current Carrying Stud Resistance. Due to heat loss arising from wire-to-lug and lug-to-stud voltage drop, the resistance per unit length of a current carrying stud should not be greater than that of the wire.

b. Size of Studs. In designing the stud for a feed-through connection, attention should be given to the higher resistance of brass, as compared to copper. A suggested method of determining the size is to use a current density in the stud equivalent to that of the wire, compensating for the difference of resistance of the metals. Consideration should also be given to mechanical strength.

c. Support for Studs. The main stud support in the feed-through insulation should be independent of the attachment of the lugs to the stud. Therefore, loosening of the insulation support of the stud will not affect the electric contact efficiency. In other words, the contact pressure on the wire lugs should not in any way be affected by the loosening of the stud in the insulator.

d. Support of Wire at Studs. Unless some other positive locking action is provided, the lug or wire should be supported next to the stud to prevent loosening the connection with a side pull on the wire. Torque recommendations for attaching electrical wiring devices to terminal boards or blocks, studs, posts, etc., are normally found in the manufacturer's maintenance instruction manual.

e. Feed-Through Insulator and Stud Design. Feed-through insulator design should be such as to prevent a loose insulator from failing to provide circuit isolation. It should not be able to move from between the stud and the structure, thus allowing the two to come into contact. The assembly should be so designed that it is impossible to inadvertently misassemble the parts so that faults will result. Also, it is desirable to provide means to prevent the feed-through stud from turning while tightening the connection.

11-177. WIRE TERMINALS AND BINDING POSTS. All wire terminals in or on electrical equipment, except case ground, must be firmly held together with two nuts or suitable locking provisions, or should be secured in a positive manner to equipment in such a way that no insulation material is involved in maintaining physical pressure between the various current carrying members of an electrical connection. Terminal studs or binding posts should be of a size that is entirely adequate for the current requirements of the equipment and have sufficient mechanical strength to withstand the torque required to attach the cable to the equipment. All terminals on equipment should have barriers and covers provided by equipment manufacturers.

11-178. CRIMP ON TERMINAL LUGS AND SPLICES (pre-insulated crimp type). The crimp on terminal lugs and splices must be installed using a high quality ratchet-type, crimping tool. We recommend the use of the proper calibrated tool. Aircraft quality crimp tools are manufactured to standards. Such tools are provided with positioners for the wire size and are adjusted for each wire size. It is essential that the crimp depth be appropriate for each wire size. If the crimp is too deep or not deep enough, it may break or cut individual strands, or it may not be tight enough to retain the wire in the terminal or connector. Crimps that are not tight enough are also susceptible to high resistance due to corrosion build-up between the crimped terminal and the wire. MIL-C22520/2 or MIL-T-DTl2250G specification covers in detail the general requirement for crimp tools, inspection gages and tool kits.

a. Hand, portable, and stationary power tools are available for crimping terminal lugs. These tools crimp the barrel to the conductor, and simultaneously from the insulation support to the wire insulation.

b. Crimp tools must be carefully inspected:

(1) Insure that the full cycle ratchet mechanism is tamper-proof so that it cannot be disengaged prior to or during the crimp cycle.

(2) If the tool does not function or faults are found, reject the tool and send the tool to be repaired.

(3) The tool calibration and adjustments are make only by the manufacturer or an approved calibration laboratory.

(4) Suitable gages of the Go/No Go type are available and shall be used prior to

any crimping operation and whenever possible during operation to ensure crimp dimensions.

11-179. LOCK WASHERS FOR TERMINALS ON EQUIPMENT. Where locknuts are used to ensure binding and locking of electrical terminals, they should be of the all metal type. In addition, a spring lock washer of suitable thickness may be installed under the nut to ensure good contact pressure. A plain washer should be used between the spring washer and the terminal to prevent galling. A plain nut with a spring lock washer and a plain washer may be used to provide binding and contact pressure.

11-180.—11-184. [RESERVED.]

SECTION 15. GROUNDING AND BONDING

11-185. GENERAL. One of the more important factors in the design and maintenance of aircraft electrical systems is proper bonding and grounding. Inadequate bonding or grounding can lead to unreliable operation of systems, e.g., EMI, electrostatic discharge damage to sensitive electronics, personnel shock hazard, or damage from lightning strike. This section provides an overview of the principles involved in the design and maintenance of electrical bonding and grounding. SAE ARP-1870 provides for more complete detailed information on grounding and bonding, and the application of related hardware.

11-186. GROUNDING. Grounding is the process of electrically connecting conductive objects to either a conductive structure or some other conductive return path for the purpose of safely completing either a normal or fault circuit.

a. Types of Grounding. If wires carrying return currents from different types of sources, such as signals of DC and AC generators, are connected to the same ground point or have a common connection in the return paths, an interaction of the currents will occur. Mixing return currents from various sources should be avoided because noise will be coupled from one source to another and can be a major problem for digital systems. To minimize the interaction between various return currents, different types of grounds should be identified and used. As a minimum, the design should use three ground types: (1) ac returns, (2) dc returns, and (3) all others. For distributed power systems, the power return point for an alternative power source would be separated. For example, in a two-ac generator (one on the right side and the other on the left side) system, if the right ac generator were supplying backup power to equipment located in the left side, (left equipment rack) the backup ac ground return should be labeled "ac Right". The return currents for the left generator should be connected to a ground point labeled "ac Left"

b. Current Return Paths. The design of the ground return circuit should be given as much attention as the other leads of a circuit. A requirement for proper ground connections is that they maintain an impedance that is essentially constant. Ground return circuits should have a current rating and voltage drop adequate for satisfactory operation of the connected electrical and electronic equipment. EMI problems, that can be caused by a system's power wire, can be reduced substantially by locating the associated ground return near the origin of the power wiring (e.g. circuit breaker panel) and routing the power wire and its ground return in a twisted pair. Special care should be exercised to ensure replacement on ground return leads. The use of numbered insulated wire leads instead of bare grounding jumpers may aid in this respect. In general, equipment items should have an external ground connection, even when internally grounded. Direct connections to a magnesium (which may create a fire hazard) structure must not be used for ground return.

c. Heavy-Current Grounds. Power ground connections, for generators, transformer rectifiers, batteries, external power receptacles, and other heavy-current, loads must be attached to individual grounding brackets that are attached to aircraft structure with a proper metal-to-metal bonding attachment. This attachment and the surrounding structure must provide adequate conductivity to accommodate normal and fault currents of the system without creating excessive voltage drop or damage to the structure. At least three fasteners, located in a triangular or rectangular pattern, must be used to secure such brackets in order to minimize susceptibility to loosening under vibration. If the structure is fabricated of a material such as carbon fiber composite (CFC), which has a higher resistivity than aluminum or copper, it will be necessary to provide an alternative ground path(s) for power return current. Special attention should be considered for composite aircraft.

d. Current Return Paths for Internally Grounded Equipment. Power return or fault current ground connections within flammable vapor areas must be avoided. If they must be made, make sure these connections will not arc, spark, or overheat under all possible current flow or mechanical failure conditions, including induced lightning currents. Criteria for inspection and maintenance to ensure continued airworthiness throughout the expected life of the aircraft should be established. Power return fault currents are normally the highest currents flowing in a structure. These can be the full generator current capacity. If full generator fault current flows through a localized region of the carbon fiber structure, major heating and failure can occur. CFC and other similar low-resistive materials must not be used in power return paths. Additional voltage drops in the return path can cause voltage regulation problems. Likewise, repeated localized material heating by current surges can cause material degradation. Both problems may occur without warning and cause nonrepeatable failures or anomalies.

e. Common Ground Connections. The use of common ground connections for more than one circuit or function should be avoided except where it can be shown that related malfunctions that could affect more than one circuit will not result in a hazardous condition. Even when the loss of multiple systems does not, in itself, create a hazard, the effect of such failure can be quite distracting to the crew.

(1) Redundant systems are normally provided with the objective of assuring continued safe operation in the event of failure of a single channel and must therefore be grounded at well separated points. To avoid construction or maintenance errors that result in connecting such ground at a single point, wires that ground one channel of a redundant system should be incapable of reaching the ground attachment of the other channel.

(2) The use of loop type grounding systems (several ground leads connected in series with a ground to structure at each end) must be avoided on redundant systems, because the loss of either ground path will remain undetected, leaving both systems, with a potential single-point failure.

(3) Electrical power sources must be grounded at separate locations on the aircraft structure. The loss of multiple sources of electrical power, as the result of corrosion of a ground connection or failure of the related fasteners, may result in the loss of multiple systems and should be avoided by making the ground attachments at separate locations.

(4) Bonds to thermally or vibration-isolated structure require special consideration to avoid single ground return to primary structure.

(5) The effect of the interconnection of the circuits when ungrounded should be considered whenever a common ground connection is used. This is particularly important when employing terminal junction grounding modules or other types of gang grounds that have a single attachment point.

f. Grounds for Sensitive Circuits. Special consideration should be given to grounds for sensitive circuits. For example:

(1) Grounding of a signal circuit through a power current lead introduces power current return voltage drop into the signal circuit.

(2) Running power wires too close will cause signal interference.

(3) Separately grounding two components of a transducer system may introduce ground plane voltage variations into the system.

(4) Single point grounds for signal circuits, with such grounds being at the signal source, are often a good way to minimize the effects of EMI, lightning, and other sources of interference.

11-187. BONDING. The following bonding requirements must be considered:

a. Equipment Bonding. Low-impedance paths to aircraft structure are normally required for electronic equipment to provide radio frequency return circuits and for most electrical equipment to facilitate reduction in EMI. The cases of components which produce electromagnetic energy should be grounded to structure. To ensure proper operation of electronic equipment, it is particularly important to conform the system's installation specification when interconnections, bonding, and grounding are being accomplished.

b. Metallic Surface Bonding. All conducting objects on the exterior of the airframe must be electrically connected to the airframe through mechanical joints, conductive hinges, or bond straps capable of conducting static charges and lightning strikes. Exceptions may be necessary for some objects such as antenna elements, whose function requires them to be electrically isolated from the airframe. Such items should be provided with an alternative means to conduct static charges and/or lightning currents, as appropriate.

c. Static Bonds. All isolated conducting parts inside and outside the aircraft, having an area greater than 3 in^2 and a linear dimension over 3 inches, that are subjected to appreciable electrostatic charging due to precipitation, fluid, or air in motion, should have a mechanically secure electrical connection to the aircraft structure of sufficient conductivity to dissipate possible static charges. A resistance of less than 1 ohm when clean and dry will generally ensure such dissipation on larger objects. Higher resistances are permissible in connecting smaller objects to airframe structure.

11-188. BONDING INSPECTION. Inspect for the following:

a. If there is evidence of electrical arcing, check for intermittent electrical contact between conducting surfaces, that may become a part of a ground plane or a current path. Arcing can be prevented either by bonding, or by insulation if bonding is not necessary.

b. The metallic conduit should be bonded to the aircraft structure at each terminating and break point. The conduit bonding strap should be located ahead of the piece of equipment that is connected to the cable wire inside the conduit.

c. Bond connections should be secure and free from corrosion.

d. Bonding jumpers should be installed in such a manner as not to interfere in any way with the operation of movable components of the aircraft.

e. Self-tapping screws should not be used for bonding purposes. Only standard threaded screws or bolts of appropriate size should be used.

f. Exposed conducting frames or parts of electrical or electronic equipment should have a low resistance bond of less than 2.5 millohms to structure. If the equipment design includes a ground terminal or pin, which is internally connected to such exposed parts, a ground wire connection to such terminal will satisfy this requirement. Refer to manufacturer's instructions.

g. Bonds should be attached directly to the basic aircraft structure rather than through other bonded parts.

h. Bonds must be installed to ensure that the structure and equipment are electrically stable and free from the hazards of lightning, static discharge, electrical shock, etc. To ensure proper operation and suppression of radio interference from hazards, electrical bonding of equipment must conform to the manufacturer's specifications.

i. Use of bonding testers is strongly recommended.

j. Measurements should be performed after the grounding and bonding mechanical connections are complete to determine if the measured resistance values meet the basic requirements. A high quality test instrument (AN AN/USM-21A or equivalent) is required to accurately measure the very low resistance values specified in this document. Another method of measurement is the millivolt drop test as shown in figure 11-19.

k. Use appropriate washers when bonding aluminum or copper to dissimilar metallic structures so that any corrosion that may occur will be on the washer.

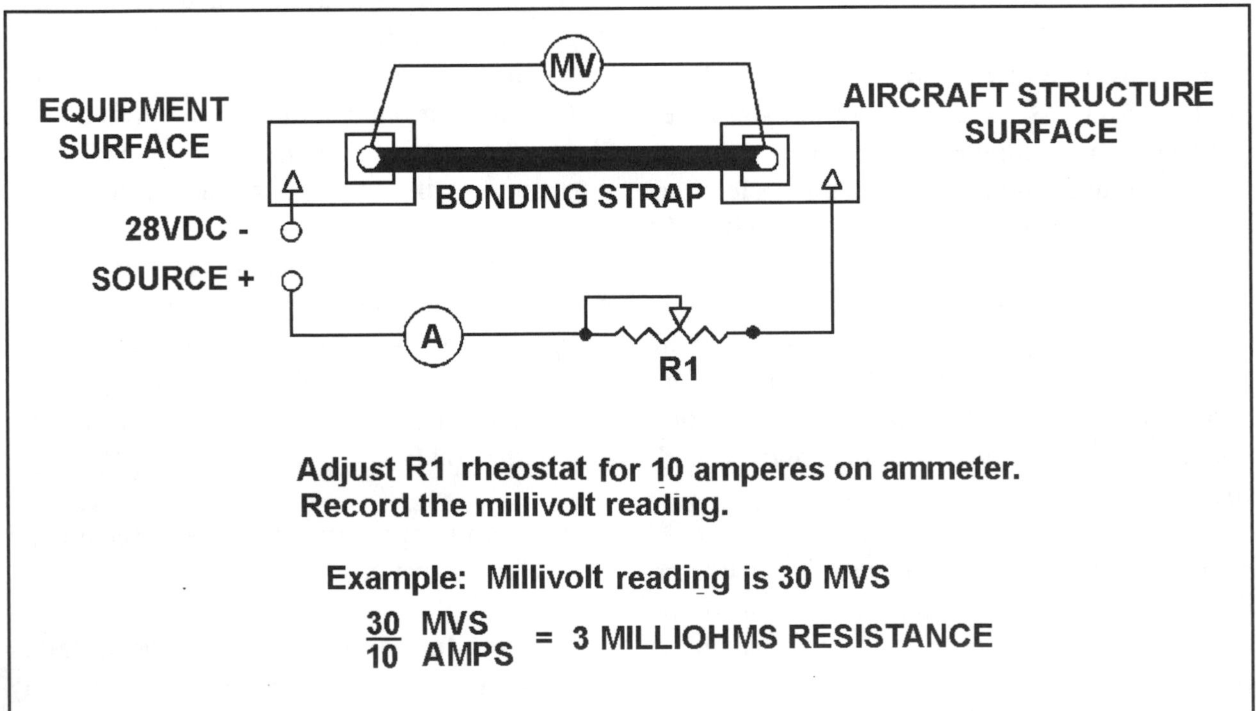

Figure 11-19. Millivolt drop test.

11-189. BONDING JUMPER INSTALLATIONS. Bonding jumpers should be made as short as practicable, and installed in such a manner that the resistance of each connection does not exceed .003 ohm. The jumper should not interfere with the operation of movable aircraft elements, such as surface controls, nor should normal movement of these elements result in damage to the bonding jumper.

a. Bonding Connections. To ensure a low-resistance connection, nonconducting finishes, such as paint and anodizing films, should be removed from the attachment surface to be contacted by the bonding terminal. On aluminum surfaces, a suitable conductive chemical surface treatment, such as Alodine, should be applied to the surfaces within 24 hours of the removal of the original finish. Refer to SAE, ARP 1870 for detailed instructions. Electric wiring should not be grounded directly to magnesium parts.

b. Corrosion Protection. One of the more frequent causes of failures in electrical system bonding and grounding is corrosion. Aircraft operating near salt water are particularly vulnerable to this failure mode. Because bonding and grounding connections may involve a variety of materials and finishes, it is important to protect completely against dissimilar metal corrosion. The areas around completed connections should be post-finished in accordance with the original finish requirements or with some other suitable protective finish within 24 hours of the cleaning process. In applications exposed to salt spray environment, a suitable noncorrosive sealant, such as one conforming to MIL-S-8802, should be used to seal dissimilar metals for protection from exposure to the atmosphere.

c. Corrosion Prevention. Electrolytic action may rapidly corrode a bonding connection if suitable precautions are not taken. Aluminum alloy jumpers are recommended for most cases; however, copper jumpers should be used to bond together parts made of stainless steel, cadmium plated steel, copper, brass, or bronze. Where contact between dissimilar metals cannot be avoided, the choice of jumper and hardware should be such that corrosion is minimized, and the part likely to corrode would be the jumper or associated hardware. Tables 11-14 through 11-16 and figures 11-20 through 11-22 show the proper hardware combinations for making a bond connection. At locations where finishes are removed, a protective finish should be applied to the completed connection to prevent subsequent corrosion.

d. Bonding Jumper Attachment. The use of solder to attach bonding jumpers should be avoided. Tubular members should be bonded by means of clamps to which the jumper is attached. Proper choice of clamp material should minimize the probability of corrosion.

e. Ground Return Connection. When bonding jumpers carry substantial ground return current, the current rating of the jumper should be determined to be adequate and that a negligible voltage drop is produced.

11-190. CREEPAGE DISTANCE. Care should be used in the selection of electrical components to ensure that electrical clearance and creepage distance along surfaces between adjacent terminals, at different potentials, and between these terminals and adjacent ground surfaces are adequate for the voltages involved.

TABLE 11-14. Stud bonding or grounding to flat surface.

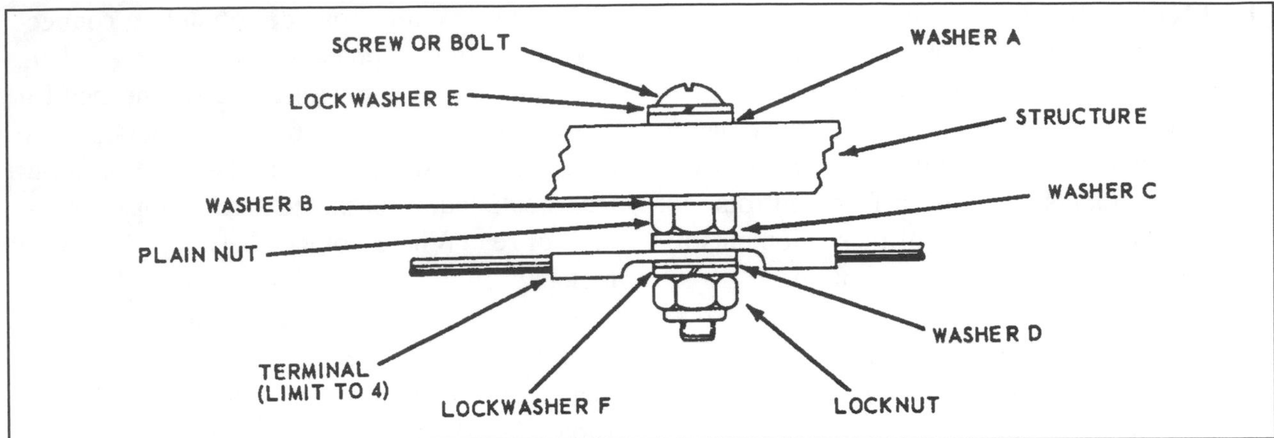

Structure	Screw or Bolt and Lock nut	Plain nut	Washer A	Washer B	Washer C & D	Lock washer E	Lock washer F
Aluminum Terminal and Jumper							
Aluminum Alloys	Cadmium Plated steel	Cadmium Plated Steel	Aluminum Alloy	Aluminum Alloy	Cadmium Plated Steel or Aluminum	Cadmium Plated Steel	Cadmium Plated Steel
Magnesium Alloys	Cadmium Plated Steel	Cadmium Plated Steel	Magnesium Alloy	Magnesium Alloy	Cadmium Plated Steel or Aluminum	Cadmium Plated Steel	Cadmium Plated Steel
Steel, Cadmium Plated	Cadmium Plated Steel	Cadmium Plated Steel	None	None	Cadmium Plated Steel or Aluminum	Cadmium Plated Steel	Cadmium Plated Steel
Steel, Corrosion Resisting	Corrosion Re-sisting Steel	Cadmium Plated Steel	None	None	Cadmium Plated Steel or Aluminum	Corrosion Resist Steel	Cadmium Plated Steel
Tinned Copper Terminal and Jumper							
Aluminum Alloys	Cadmium Plated Steel	Cadmium Plated Steel	Aluminum Alloy	Aluminum Alloy	Cadmium Plated Steel	Cadmium Plated Steel	Cadmium Plated Steel or Aluminum
Magnesium Alloys[1]							
Steel, Cadmium Plated	Cadmium Plated Steel	Cadmium Plated Steel	None	None	Cadmium Plated Steel	Cadmium Plated Steel	Cadmium Plated Steel
Steel, Corrosion Resisting	Corrosion Re-sisting Steel	Corrosion Resisting Steel	None	None	Cadmium Plated Steel	Corrosion Resisting Steel	Corrosion Resisting Steel

[1] Avoid connecting copper to magnesium.

TABLE 11-15. Plate nut bonding or grounding to flat surface.

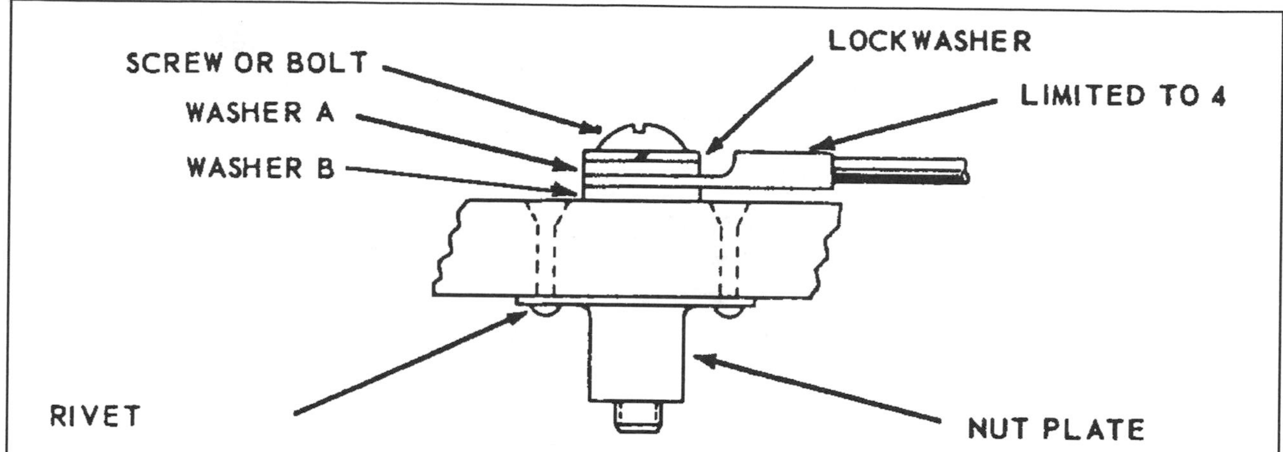

Structure	Screw or bolt and nut plate	Rivet	Lockwasher	Washer A	Washer B
Aluminum Terminal and Jumper					
Aluminum Alloys	Cadmium Plated Steel	Aluminum Alloy	Cadmium Plated Steel	Cadmium Plated Steel or Aluminum	None
Magnesium Alloys	Cadmium Plated Steel	Aluminum Alloy	Cadmium Plated Steel	Cadmium Plated Steel or Aluminum	None or Magnesium Alloy
Steel, Cadmium Plated	Cadmium Plated Steel	Corrosion Resisting Steel	Cadmium Plated Steel	Cadmium Plated Steel or Aluminum	None
Steel, Corrosion Resisting	Corrosion Resisting Steel or Cadmium Plated Steel	Corrosion Resisting Steel	Cadmium Plated Steel	Cadmium Plated Steel or Aluminum	Cadmium Plated Steel
Tinned Copper Terminal and Jumper					
Aluminum Alloys	Cadmium Plated Steel	Aluminum Alloy	Cadmium Plated Steel	Cadmium Plated Steel	Aluminum[2] Alloy
Magnesium Alloys[1]					
Steel, Cadmium Plated	Cadmium Plated Steel	Corrosion Resisting Steel	Cadmium Plated Steel	Cadmium Plated Steel	None
Steel, Corrosion Resisting	Corrosion Resisting Steel	Corrosion Resisting Steel	Cadmium Plated Steel	Cadmium Plated Steel	None

[1] Avoid connecting copper to magnesium.
[2] Use washers having a conductive finished treated to prevent corrosion, suggest AN960JD10L

TABLE 11-16. Bolt and nut bonding or grounding to flat surface.

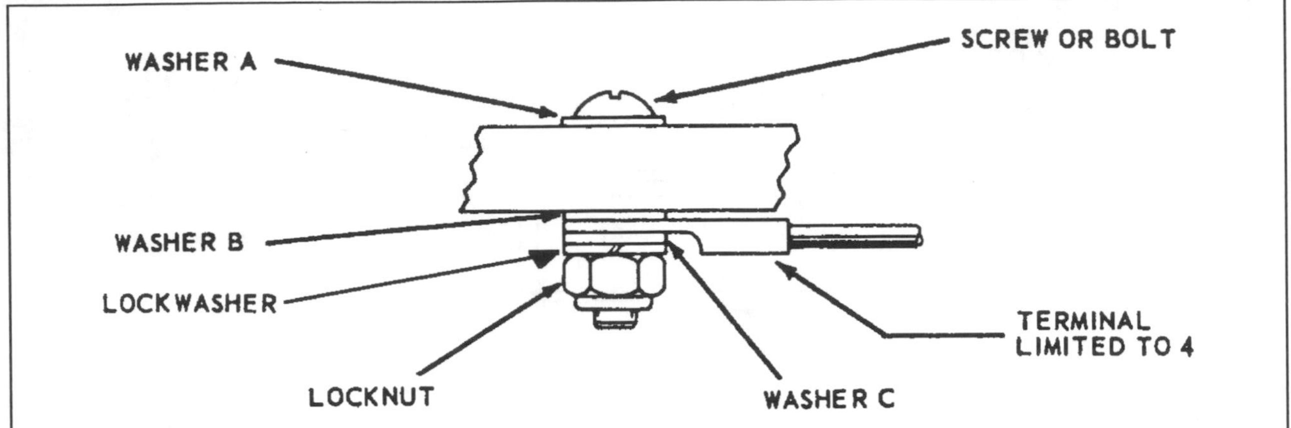

Structure	Screw or bolt and nut plate	Lock-nut	Washer A	Washer B	Washer C
Aluminum Terminal and Jumper					
Aluminum Alloys	Cadmium Plated Steel	Cadmium Plated Steel	Cadmium Plated Steel or Aluminum	None	Cadmium Plated Steel or Aluminum
Magnesium Alloys	Cadmium Plated Steel	Cadmium Plated Steel	Magnesium Alloy	None or Magnesium alloy	Cadmium Plated Steel or Aluminum
Steel, Cadmium Plated	Cadmium Plated Steel	Cadmium Plated Steel	Cadmium Plated Steel	Cadmium Plated Steel	Cadmium Plated Steel or Aluminum
Steel, Corrosion Resisting	Corrosion Resisting Steel or Cadmium Plated Steel	Cadmium Plated Steel	Corrosion Resisting Steel	Cadmium Plated Steel	Cadmium Plated Steel or Aluminum
Tinned Copper Terminal and Jumper					
Aluminum Alloy	Cadmium Plated Steel	Cadmium Plated Steel	Cadmium Plated Steel	Aluminum[2] Alloy	Cadmium Plated Steel
Magnesium Alloy[1]					
Steel, Cadmium Plated	Cadmium Plated Steel	Cadmium Plated Steel	Cadmium Plated Steel	None	Cadmium Plated Steel
Steel, Corrosion Resisting	Corrosion Resisting Steel or Cadmium Plated Steel	Cadmium Plated Steel	Corrosion Resisting Steel	None	Cadmium Plated Steel

[1] Avoid connecting copper to magnesium.
[2] Use washers having a conductive finished treated to prevent corrosion, suggest AN960JD10L

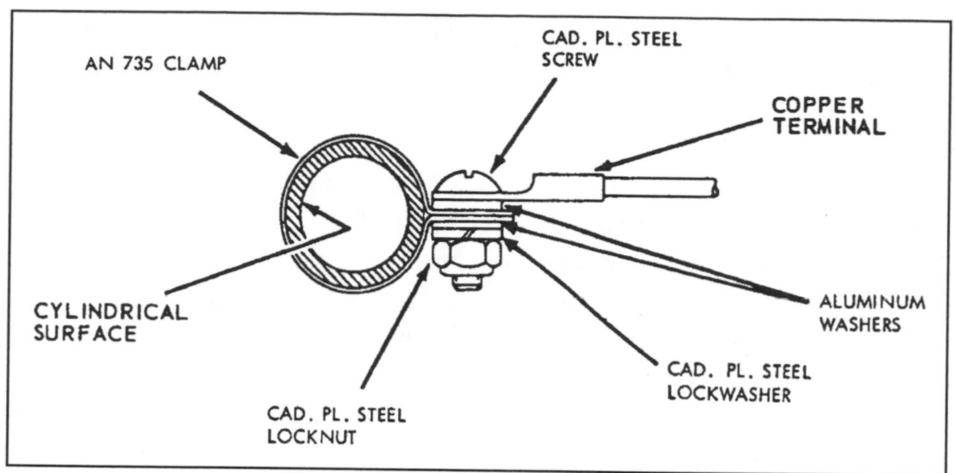

FIGURE 11-20. Copper jumper connector to tubular structure.

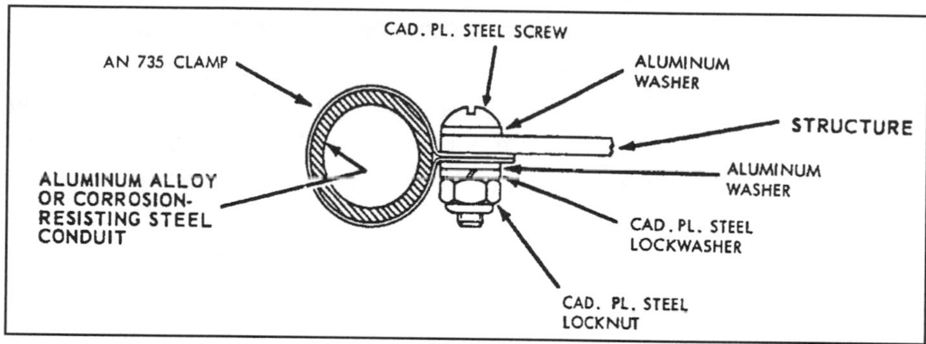

FIGURE 11-21. Bonding conduit to structure.

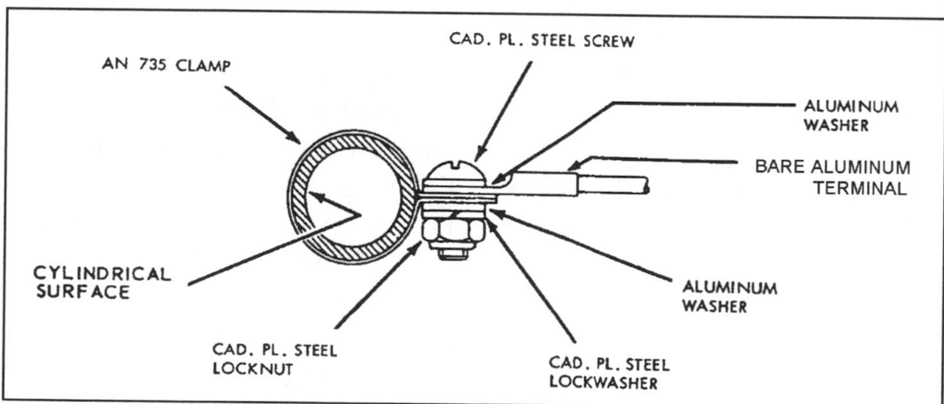

FIGURE 11-22. Aluminum jumper connection to tubular structure.

11-191. FUEL SYSTEMS. Small metallic objects within an aircraft fuel tank, that are not part of the tank structure, should be electrically bonded to the structure so as to dissipate static charges that may otherwise accumulate on these objects. A practical bonding design would use a flexible braided jumper wire or riveted bracket. In such situations, a DC resistance of 1 ohm or less should indicate an adequate connection. Care should be taken, in designing such connections, to avoid creating continuous current paths that could allow lightning or power fault currents to pass through connections not designed to tolerate these higher amplitude currents without arcing. Simulated static charge, lightning, or fault current tests may be necessary to establish or verify specific designs. All other fuel system components, such as fuel line (line to line) access doors, fuel line supports, structural parts, fuel outlets, or brackets should have an electromechanical (bonding strap) secure connector that ensures 1 ohm or less resistance to the structure. Advisory Circular 20-53A Protection of Aircraft Fuel Systems Against Fuel Vapor Ignition Due to Lightning, and associate manual DOT/FAA/ CT-83/3, provide detailed information on necessary precautions.

11-192. ELECTRIC SHOCK PREVENTION BONDING. Electric shock to personnel should be prevented by providing a low resistance path of 1/100 ohm or less between structure and metallic conduits or equipment. The allowable ground resistance should be such that the electric potential of the conduit or equipment housing does not reach a dangerous value under probable fault conditions. The current carrying capacity of all elements of the ground circuit should be such that, under the fault condition, no sparking, fusion, or dangerous heating will occur. Metallic supports usually provide adequate bonding if metal-to-metal contact is maintained.

11-193. LIGHTNING PROTECTION BONDING. Electrical bonding is frequently required for lightning protection of aircraft and systems, especially to facilitate safe conduction of lightning currents through the airframe. Most of this bonding is achieved through normal airframe riveted or bolted joints but some externally mounted parts, such as control surfaces, engine nacelles, and antennas, may require additional bonding provisions. Generally, the adequacy of lightning current bonds depends on materials, cross-sections, physical configurations, tightness, and surface finishes. Care should be taken to minimize structural resistance, so as to control structural voltage rises to levels compatible with system protection design. This may require that metal surfaces be added to composite structures, or that tinned copper overbraid, conduits, or cable trays be provided for interconnecting wire harnesses within composite airframes. Also care must be taken to prevent hazardous lightning currents from entering the airframe via flight control cables, push rods, or other conducting objects that extend to airframe extremities. This may require that these conductors be electrically bonded to the airframe, or that electrical insulators be used to interrupt lightning currents. For additional information on lightning protection measures, refer to DOT/FAA/CT-89-22. Report DOT/FAA/ CT 86/8, April 1987, Determination of Electrical Properties of Bonding and Fastening Techniques may provide additional information for composite materials.

a. Control Surface Lightning Protection Bonding. Control surface bonding is intended to prevent the burning of hinges on a surface that receives a lightning strike; thus causing possible loss of control. To accomplish this bonding, control surfaces and flaps should have at least one 6500 circular mil area copper (e.g. 7 by 37 AWG size 36 strands) jumper across each hinge. In any case, not less than two 6500 circular mil jumpers should be used on each control surface. The installation location of these jumpers should be carefully chosen to provide a low-impedance shunt for lightning current across the hinge to the structure. When jumpers may be subjected to arcing, substantially larger wire sizes of 40,000 circular mils or a larger cross section are required to provide protection against multiple strikes. Sharp bends and loops in such jumpers can create susceptibility to breakage when subjected to the inductive forces created by lightning current, and should be avoided.

b. Control Cable Lightning Protection Bonding. To prevent damage to the control system or injury to flight personnel due to lightning strike, cables and levers coming from each control surface should be protected by one or more bonding jumpers located as close to the control surface as possible. Metal pulleys are considered a satisfactory ground for control cables.

11-194. LIGHTNING PROTECTION FOR ANTENNAS AND AIR DATA PROBES. Antenna and air data probes that are mounted on exterior surfaces within lightning strike zones should be provided with a means to safely transfer lightning currents to the airframe, and to prevent hazardous surges from being conducted into the airframe via antenna cables or wire harnesses. Usually, the antenna mounting bolts provide adequate lightning current paths. Surge protectors built into antennas or installed in coaxial antenna cables or probe wire harnesses will fulfill these requirements. Candidate designs should be verified by simulated lightning tests in accordance with RTCA DO-160C, Section 23.

11-195. STATIC-DISCHARGE DEVICE. Means should be provided to bleed accumulated static charges from aircraft prior to ground personnel coming in contact with an aircraft after landing. Normally, there is adequate conductivity in the tires for this, but if not, a static ground should be applied before personnel come into contact with the aircraft. Fuel nozzle grounding receptacles should be installed in accordance with the manufacturer's specifications. Grounding receptacles should provide a means to eliminate the static-induced voltage that might otherwise cause a spark between a fuel nozzle and fuel tank access covers and inlets. In addition, static discharging wicks are installed on wings and tail surfaces to discharge static changes while in flight.

11-196. CLEANING. In order to ensure proper ground connection conductivity, all paint, primer, anodize coating, grease, and other foreign material must be carefully removed from areas that conduct electricity. On aluminum surfaces, apply chemical surface treatment to the cleaned bare metal surface in accordance with the manufacturer's instructions within 4-8 hours, depending on ambient moisture/contaminate content.

11-197. HARDWARE ASSEMBLY. Details of bonding connections must be described in maintenance manuals and adhered to carefully when connections are removed or replaced during maintenance operations. In order to avoid corrosion problems and ensure long-term integrity of the electrical connection, hardware used for this purpose must be as defined in these documents or at least be equivalent in material and surface. Installation of fasteners used in bonded or grounded connections should be made in accordance with SAE ARP-1870. Threaded fasteners must be torqued to the level required by SAE ARP-1928.

11-198.—11-204. [RESERVED.]

SECTION 16. WIRE MARKING

11-205. GENERAL. The proper identification of electrical wires and cables with their circuits and voltages is necessary to provide safety of operation, safety to maintenance personnel, and ease of maintenance.

a. Each wire and cable should be marked with a part number. It is common practice for wire manufacturers to follow the wire material part number with the five digit/letter C.A.G.E. code identifying the wire manufacturer. Existing installed wire that needs replacement can thereby be identified as to its performance capabilities, and the inadvertent use of a lower performance and unsuitable replacement wire avoided.

b. The method of identification should not impair the characteristics of the wiring.

CAUTION: Do not use metallic bands in place of insulating sleeves. Exercise care when marking coaxial or data bus cable, as deforming the cable may change its electrical characteristics.

11-206. WIRE IDENTIFICATION. To facilitate installation and maintenance, original wire-marking identification is to be retained. The wire identification marks should consist of a combination of letters and numbers that identify the wire, the circuit it belongs to, its gauge size, and any other information to relate the wire to a wiring diagram. All markings should be legible in size, type, and color.

11-207. IDENTIFICATION AND INFORMATION RELATED TO THE WIRE AND WIRING DIAGRAMS. The wire identification marking should consist of similar information to relate the wire to a wiring diagram.

11-208. PLACEMENT OF IDENTIFICATION MARKINGS. Identification markings should be placed at each end of the wire and at 15-inch maximum intervals along the length of the wire. Wires less than 3 inches long need not be identified. Wires 3 to 7 inches in length should be identified approximately at the center. Added identification marker sleeves should be so located that ties, clamps, or supporting devices need not be removed in order to read the identification.

The wire identification code must be printed to read horizontally (from left to right) or vertically (from top to bottom). The two methods of marking wire or cable are as follows:

a. Direct marking is accomplished by printing the cable's outer covering. (See figure 11-23.)

b. Indirect marking is accomplished by printing a heat-shrinkable sleeve and installing the printed sleeve on the wire or cables outer covering. Indirect-marked wire or cable should be identified with printed sleeves at each end and at intervals not longer than 6 feet. The individual wires inside a cable should be identified within 3 inches of their termination. (See figure 11-24.)

11-209. TYPES OF WIRE MARKINGS. The preferred method is to mark directly on the wire. A successful requirement qualification should produce markings that meet the marking characteristics specified in MIL-W-5088 or AS50881A without causing insulation degradation. Teflon coated wires, shielded wiring, multi-conductor cable, and thermocouple wires usually require special sleeves to carry identification marks. There are some wire marking machines in the market that can be used to stamp directly on the type wires mentioned above. Whatever method of marking is used, the marking should be legible and the color should contrast with the wire insulation or sleeve.

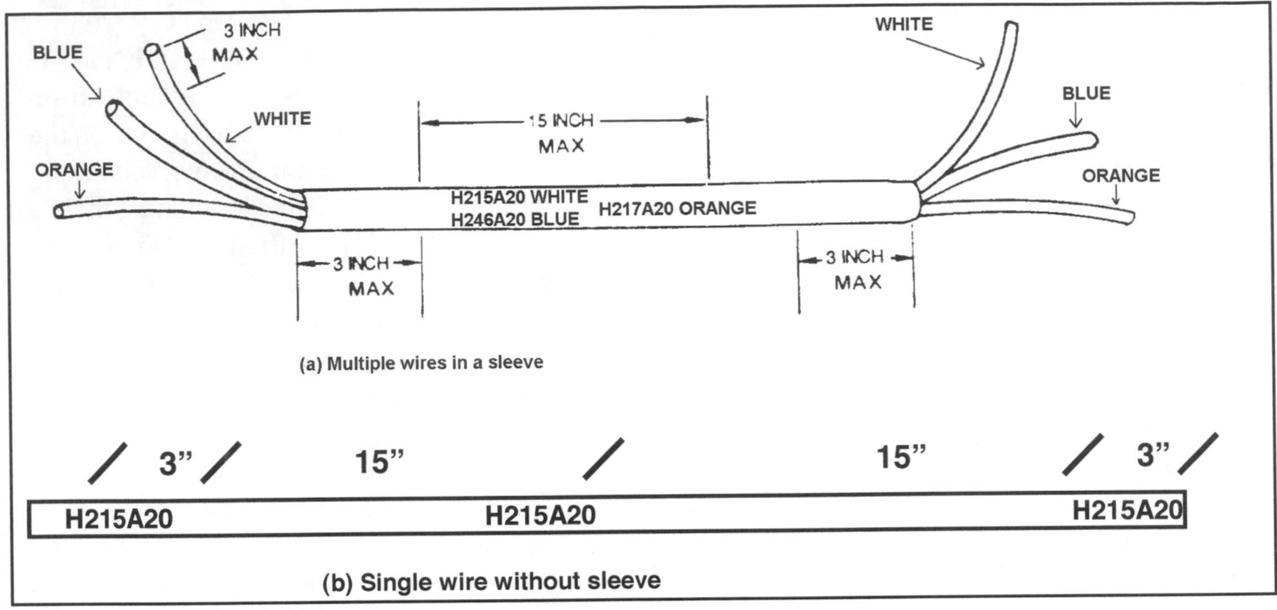

FIGURE 11-23. Spacing of printed identification marks (direct marking).

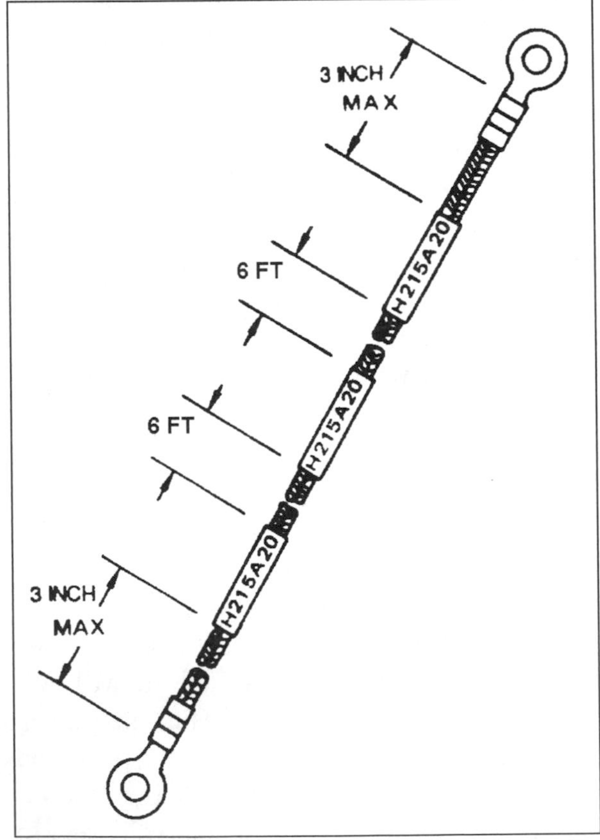

FIGURE 11-24. Spacing of printed identification marks (indirect marking).

a. Extreme care must, therefore, be taken during circuit identification by a hot stamp machine on insulation wall 10 mils or thinner.

b. Alternative identification methods such as "Laser Printing", "Ink Jet", and "Dot Matrix" are preferred. When such modern equipment is not available, the use of stamped identification sleeving should be considered on insulation wall thickness of 10 mils or less.

11-210. HOT STAMP MARKING. Due to widespread use of hot stamp wire marking, personnel should refer to SAE ARP5369, Guidelines for Wire Identification Marking using the Hot Stamp Process, for guidance on minimizing insulation damage. Hot stamp process uses a heated typeface to transfer pigment from a ribbon or foil to the surface of wires or cables. The traditional method imprints hot ink marks onto the wire. Exercise caution when using this method, as it has been shown to damage insulation when incorrectly applied. Typeset characters, similar to that used in printing presses but shaped to the contour of the wire, are heated to the desired temperature. Wire is pulled through a channel directly underneath the characters. The heat of the type set characters transfers the ink from the marking foil onto the wire.

a. Good marking is obtained only by the proper combination of temperature, pressure, and dwelling. Hot stamp will mark wire with an outside diameter of 0.038 to 0.25-inch.

b. Before producing hot stamp wire, it must be assured that the marking machine is properly adjusted to provide the best wire marking with the least wire insulation deterioration. The marking should never create an indent greater than 10 percent of the insulation wall.

CAUTION: The traditional Hot Stamp method is not recommended for use on wire with outside diameters of less than 0.035. (REF. SAE ARP5369). Stamping dies may cause fracture of the insulation wall and penetration to the conductor of these materials. When various fluids wet these opening in service, arcing and surface tracking damage wire bundles. Later in service, when various fluids have wet these openings, serious arcing and surface tracking will have damaged wire bundles.

11-211. DOT MATRIX MARKING. The dot matrix marking is imprinted onto the wire or cable very similar to that of a dot matrix computer printer. The wire must go through a cleaning process to make sure it is clean and dry for the ink to adhere. Wires marked with dot matrix equipment require a cure consisting of an UV curing process, which is normally applied by the marking equipment. This cure should normally be complete 16 to 24 hours after marking. Dot matrix makes a legible mark without damaging the insulation. Depending on equipment configuration, dot matrix can mark wire from 0.037 to 0.5-inch outside diameter. Multi-conductor cable can also be marked.

11-212. INK JET MARKING. This is a "non-impact" marking method wherein ink droplets are electrically charged and then directed onto the moving wire to form the characters. Two basic ink types are available: thermal cure and UV cure.

a. Thermal cure inks must generally be heated in an oven for a length of time after marking to obtain their durability. UV cure inks are cured in line much like dot matrix.

b. Ink jet marks the wire on the fly and makes a reasonably durable and legible mark without damaging the insulation. Ink jets normally mark wire from 0.030 to 0.25-inch outside diameter. Multiconductor cable can also be marked.

11-213. LASER MARKING. Of the variety of laser marking machines, UV lasers are proving to be the best. This method marks into the surface of the wire's insulation without degradation to its performance. One common type of UV laser is referred to as an excimer laser marker. UV laser produces the most durable marks because it marks into the insulation instead of on the surface. However, excimer laser will only mark insulation that contain appropriate percentages of titanium dioxide (TiO_2). The wire can be marked on the fly. UV can mark from 0.030 to 0.25-inch outside diameter. The UV laser makes only gray marks and they appear more legible on white or pastel-colored insulation.

11-214. IDENTIFICATION SLEEVES. Flexible sleeving, either clear or opaque, is satisfactory for general use. When color-coded or striped component wire is used as part of a cable, the identification sleeve should specify which color is associated with each wire identification code. Identification sleeves are normally used for identifying the following types of wire or cable:

a. Unjacketed shielded wire.

b. Thermocouple wire identification is normally accomplished by means of identification sleeves. As the thermocouple wire is usually of the duplex type (two insulated wires within the same casing), each wire at the termination point bears the full name of the conductor. Thermocouple conductors are alumel, chromel, iron, constantan, and copper constantan.

c. Coaxial cable should not be hot stamped directly. When marking coaxial cable, care should be taken not to deform the cable as this may change the electrical characteristics of the cable. When cables cannot be printed directly, they should be identified by printing the identification code (and individual wire color, where applicable) on a nonmetallic material placed externally to the outer covering at the terminating end and at each junction or pressure bulkhead. Cables not enclosed in conduit or a common jacket should be identified with printed sleeves at each end and at intervals not longer than 3 feet. Individual wires within a cable should be identified within 3 inches from their termination.

d. Multiconductor cable normally use identification sleeves for identifying unshielded, unjacketed cable.

e. High-temperature wire with insulation is difficult to mark (such as Teflon and fiberglass).

11-215. IDENTIFICATION TAPE. Identification tape can be used in place of sleeving, in most cases (i.e. polyvinylfluoride).

11-216. OPERATING CONDITIONS. For sleeving exposed to high temperatures (over 400 °F), materials such as silicone fiberglass should be used.

11-217. INSTALLATION OF PRINTED SLEEVES. Polyolefin sleeving should be used in areas where resistance to solvent and synthetic hydraulic fluids is necessary. Sleeves may be secured in place with cable ties or by heat shrinking. The identification sleeving for various sizes of wire is shown in table 11-17.

Table 11-17. Recommended size of identification sleeving.

Wire Size		Sleeving Size	
AN	AL	No.	Nominal ID (inches)
#24		12	.085
#22		11	.095
#20		10	.106
#18		9	.118
#16		8	.113
#14		7	.148
#12		6	.166
#10		4	.208
#8	#8	2	.263
#6	#6	0	.330
#4	#4	3/8 inch	.375
#2	#2	1/2 inch	.500
#1	#1	1/2 inch	.500
#0	#0	5/8 inch	.625
#00	#00	5/8 inch	.625
#000	#000	3/4 inch	.750
#0000	#0000	3/4 inch	.750

11-218. IDENTIFICATION OF WIRE BUNDLES AND HARNESSES. The identification of wire bundles and harnesses is becoming a common practice and may be accomplished by the use of a marked sleeve tied in place or by the use of pressure-sensitive tape as indicated in figure 11-25.

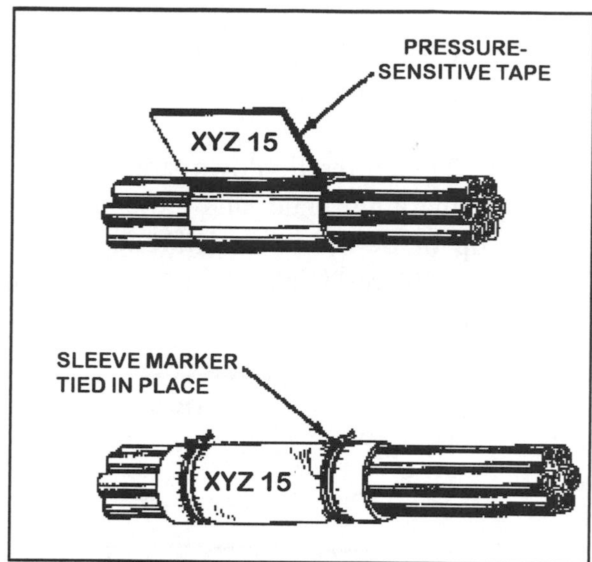

FIGURE 11-25. Identification of wire bundles and harnesses.

a. Wires for which identifications are reassigned after installation, may be remarked on sleeves at the termination of each wire segment. It may be necessary to reidentify such wires throughout their lengths to facilitate ease of maintenance.

b. For high-density harnessed, shielded, and jacketed multiconductor cables and when using nonsignificant wire identification, color coding or its alphanumeric equivalent may be interchanged within the same harnesses. The alphanumeric equivalent of the color code should be as set forth in MIL-STD-681.

11-219. TERMINAL MARKING SLEEVE AND TAGS. Typical cable markers are flat, nonheat-shrinkable tags. Heat-shrinkable marking sleeves are available for marking wires and cables, and should be inserted over the proper wire or cable and heat-shrunk using the proper manufacturer recommended heating tool. (See figures 11-26 and 11-27.)

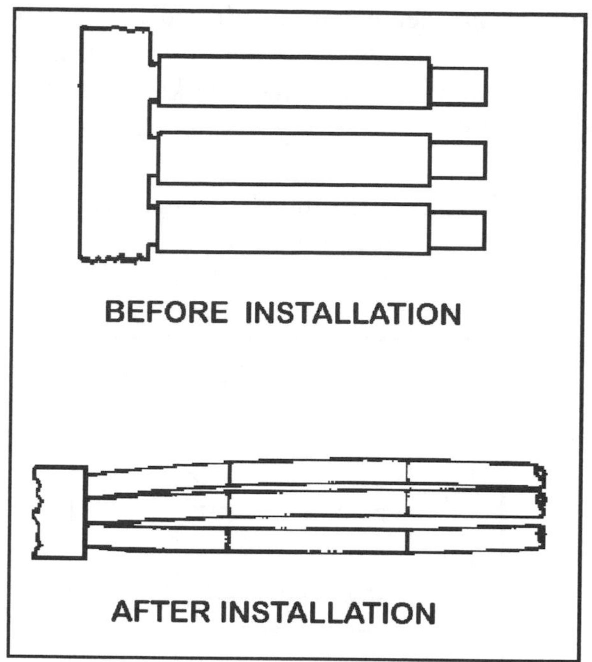

FIGURE 11-26. Standard sleeves (135 °C).

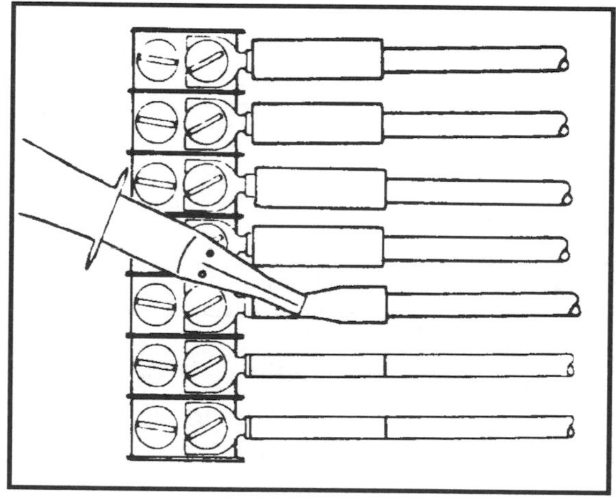

FIGURE 11-27. Installation of heat-shrinkable insulation sleeves.

11-220. SLEEVES AND CABLE MARKERS SELECTION. Sleeves and cable markers must be selected by cable size and operating conditions. (See tables 11-18 through 11-21).

a. Markers are printed using a typewriter with a modified roller. Blank markers on a bandolier are fed into the typewriter, where they are marked in any desired combination of characters. The typed markers, still on bandoliers, are heated in an infrared heating tool that processes the markers for permanency. The typed and heat-treated markers remain on the bandolier until ready for installation.

b. Markers are normally installed using the following procedure:

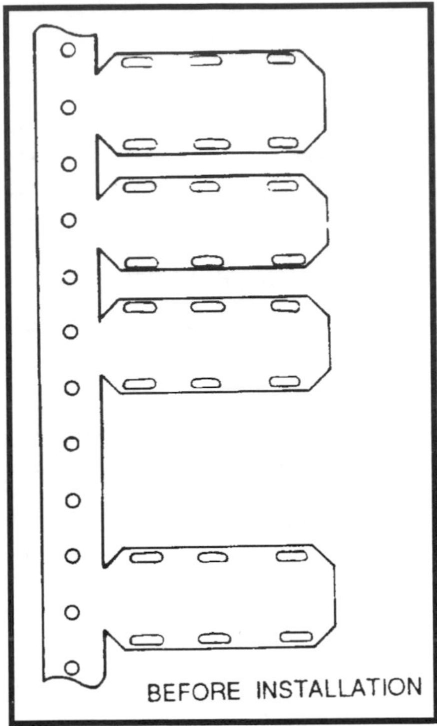

FIGURE 11-28. Cable markers.

(1) Select the smallest tie-down strap that will accommodate the outside diameter of the cable. (See table 11-22.)

(2) Cut the marking plate from the bandolier. (See figure 11-28.)

(3) Thread the tie-down straps through holes in marking plate and around cable. Thread tip of tie-down strap through slot in head. (See figure 11-29.) Pull tip until strap is snug around cable.

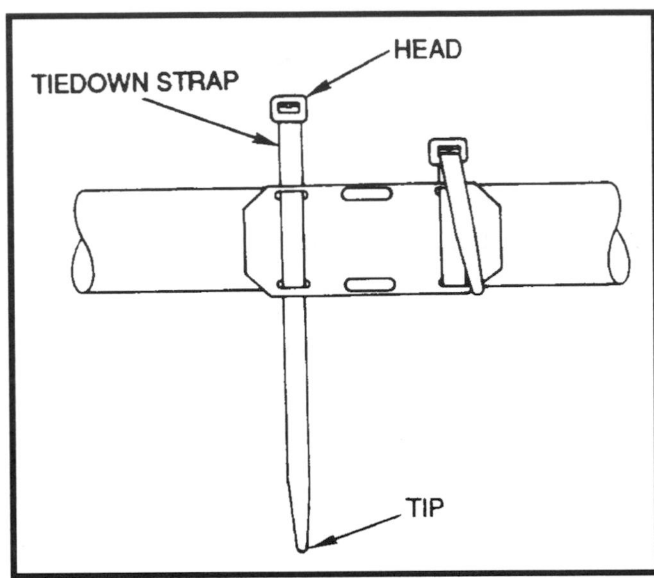

FIGURE 11-29. Tie-down strap installation.

TABLE 11-18. Selection table for standard sleeves.

Wire or Cable Diameter Range. (inches) Min	Max	Markable Length * (inches)	Installed Sleeve Length (nom) (inches)	Installed Wall Thickness (max inches)	As-supplied Inside Diameter (min inches)
0.050	0.080	18	1.5	0.026	0.093
0.075	0.110	18	1.5	0.026	0.125
0.100	0.150	18	1.5	0.028	0.187
0.135	0.215	18	1.5	0.028	0.250
0.200	0.300	18	1.5	0.028	0.375
0.135	0.300	18	1.5	0.028	0.375
0.260	0.450	18	1.5	0.028	0.475

* Based on 12 characters per inch

TABLE 11-19. Selection table for thin-wall sleeves.

Wire or Cable Diameter Range (inches) Min.	Max.	Markable Length * (inches)	Installed Sleeve Length (nom) (inches)	Installed Wall Thickness (max inches)	As-supplied Inside Diameter (min inches)
0.035	0.080	22	1.75	0.020	0.093
0.075	0.110	22	1.75	0.020	0.125
0.100	0.150	21	1.75	0.021	0.187
0.135	0.225	21	1.75	0.021	0.250

* Based on 12 characters per inch

TABLE 11-20. Selection table for high-temperature sleeves.

Wire or Cable Diameter Range (inches) Min.	Max.	Markable Length * (inches)	Installed Sleeve Length (nom) (inches)	Installed Wall Thickness (max inches)	As-supplied Inside Diameter (min inches)
0.035	0.080	18	1.5	0.019	0.093
0.075	0.110	18	1.5	0.016	0.125
0.100	0.150	18	1.5	0.018	0.187
0.135	0.215	18	1.5	0.018	0.250
0.200	0.300	18	1.5	0.018	0.375
0.260	0.450	18	1.5	0.018	0.475

* Based on 12 characters per inch

TABLE 11-21. Selection table for cable markers.

Cable Diameter Range (inches)	Type of Cable Marker	Number of Attachment Holes	Number of Lines of Type	Marker Thickness (nom) (inches)
0.25-0.50	Standard, 135 °C	4	2	0.025
0.25-0.50	High Temperature, 200 °C	4	2	0.020
0.25-0.50	Nuclear, 135 °C	4	2	0.025
0.50-up	Standard, 135 °C	4	3	0.025
0.50-up	Standard, 135 °C	6	3	0.025
0.50-up	High Temperature, 200 °C	4	3	0.020
0.50-up	High Temperature, 200 °C	6	3	0.020
0.50-up	Nuclear, 135 °C	4	3	0.025
0.50-up	Nuclear, 135 °C	6	3	0.025

TABLE 11-22. Plastic tie-down straps (MS3367, Type I, Class 1).

Cable Diameter (inches) Min	Max	Tie-down Strap MS3367-	Strap Identification *	Installation Tool	Tension Setting
1/16	5/8	4-9	Miniature (MIN)	MS90387-1	2
1/16	1¼	5-9	Intermediate (INT)	MS90387-1	4
1/16	4	2-9	Standard (STD)	MS90387-1	6
3/16	8	6-9	Heavy (HVY)	MS90387-2	6

* The specified tool tension settings are for typical cable application. Settings less than or greater than those specified may be required for special applications.

(4) Select the applicable installation tool and move the tension setting to the correct position. (See figure 11-30.)

(5) Slide tip of strap into opening in the installation tool nose piece. (See figure 11-30.)

(6) Keeping tool against head of tie-down strap, ensure gripper engages tie-down strap, and squeeze trigger of installation tool until strap installation is completed as shown in figure 11-31.

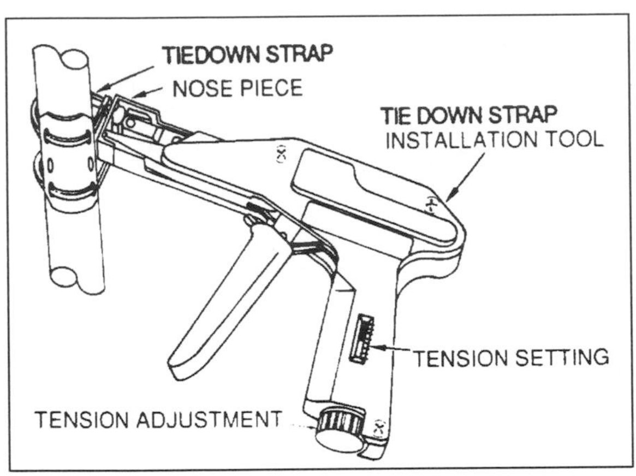

FIGURE 11-30. Tie-down strap installation tool.

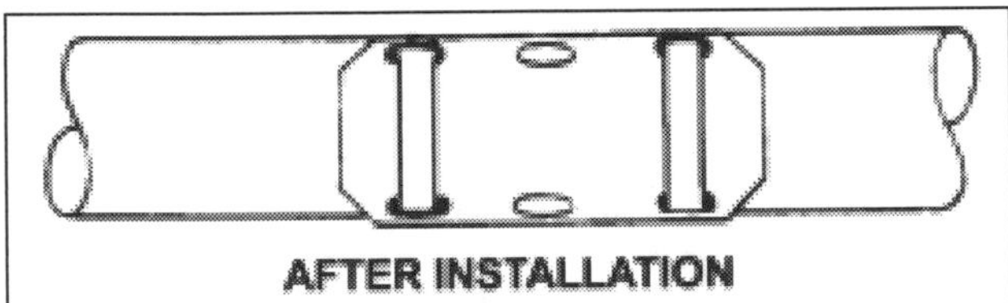

FIGURE 11-31. Completed installation.

11-221. TEMPORARY WIRE AND CABLE MARKING PROCEDURE. A temporary wire marking procedure follows but should be used only with caution and with plans for future permanence. (See figure 11-32.)

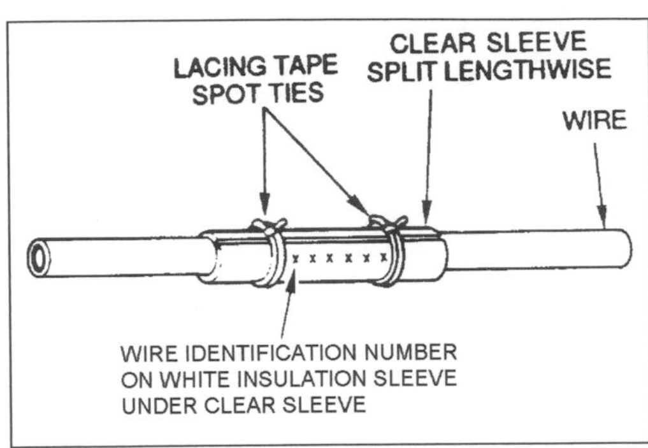

FIGURE 11-32. Temporary wire identification marker.

a. With a pen or a typewriter, write wire number on good quality white split insulation sleeve.

b. Trim excess white insulation sleeve, leaving just enough for one wrap around wire to be marked, with number fully visible.

c. Position marked white insulation sleeve on wire so that shielding, ties, clamps, or supporting devices need not be removed to read the number.

d. Obtain clear plastic sleeve that is long enough to extend 1/4 inch past white insulation sleeve marker edges and wide enough to overlap itself when wrapped around white insulation and wire.

e. Slit clear sleeve lengthwise and place around marker and wire.

f. Secure each end of clear sleeve with lacing tape spot tie to prevent loosening of sleeve.

11-222. MARKER SLEEVE INSTLATION AFTER PRINTING. The following general procedures apply:

a. Hold marker, printed side up, and press end of wire on lip of sleeve to open sleeve. (See figure 11-33.)

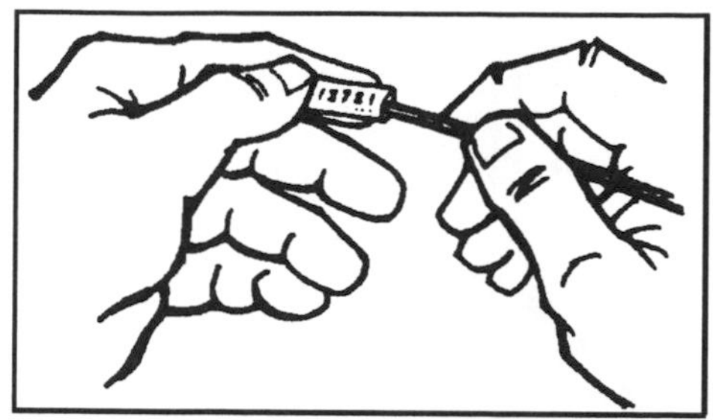

FIGURE 11-33. Inserting wire into marker.

b. If wire has been stripped, use a scrap piece of unstripped wire to open the end of the marker.

c. Push sleeve onto wire with a gentle twisting motion.

d. Shrink marker sleeve, using heat gun with shrink tubing attachment. (See figure 11-34.)

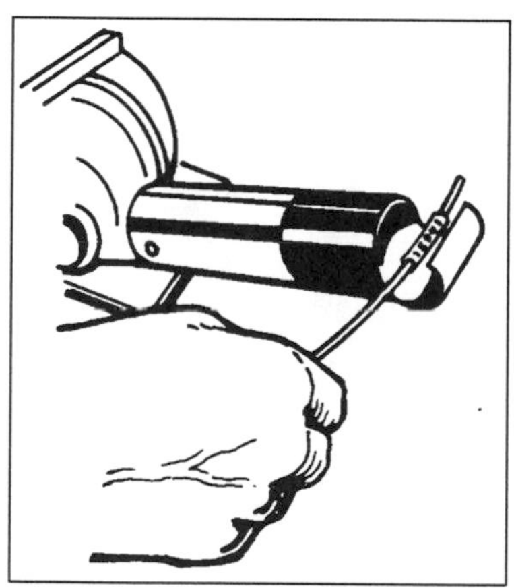

FIGURE 11-34. Shrinking marker on wire.

11-223.—11-229. [RESERVED.]

SECTION 17. CONNECTORS

11-230. GENERAL. There is a multitude of types of connectors. Crimped contacts are generally used. Some of the more common are the round cannon type, the rectangular, and the module blocks. Environmental-resistant connectors should be used in applications subject to fluids, vibration, thermal, mechanical shock, and/or corrosive elements. When HIRF/Lightning protection is required, special attention should be given to the terminations of individual or overall shields. The number and complexity of wiring systems have resulted in an increased use of electrical connectors. The proper choice and application of connectors is a significant part of the aircraft wiring system. Connectors must be kept to a minimum, selected, and installed to provide the maximum degree of safety and reliability to the aircraft. For the installation of any particular connector assembly, the specification of the manufacturer or the appropriate governing agency must be followed.

11-231. SELECTION. . Connectors should be selected to provide the maximum degree of safety and reliability considering electrical and environmental requirements. Consider the size, weight, tooling, logistic, maintenance support, and compatibility with standardization programs. For ease of assembly and maintenance, connectors using crimped contacts are generally chosen for all applications except those requiring an hermetic seal. (Reference SAE ARP 1308, Preferred Electrical Connectors For Aerospace Vehicles and Associated Equipment.) A replacement connector of the same basic type and design as the connector it replaces should be used. With a crimp type connector for any electrical connection, the proper insertion, or extraction tool must be used to install or remove wires from such a connector. Refer to manufacturer or aircraft instruction manual. After the connector is disconnected, inspect it for loose soldered connections to prevent unintentional grounding. Connectors that are susceptible to corrosion difficulties may be treated with a chemically inert waterproof jelly.

11-232. TYPES OF CONNECTORS. Connectors must be identified by an original identification number derived from MIL Specification (MS) or OAM specification. Figure 11-35 provides some examples of MS connector types. Several different types are shown in figures 11-36 and 11-37.

a. Environmental Classes. Environment-resistant connectors are used in applications where they will probably be subjected to fluids, vibration, thermal, mechanical shock, corrosive elements, etc. Firewall class connectors incorporating these same features should, in addition, be able to prevent the penetration of the fire through the aircraft firewall connector opening and continue to function without failure for a specified period of time when exposed to fire. Hermetic connectors provide a pressure seal for maintaining pressurized areas. When EMI/RFI protection is required, special attention should be given to the termination of individual and overall shields. Backshell adapters designed for shield termination, connectors with conductive finishes, and EMI grounding fingers are available for this purpose.

b. Rectangular Connectors. The rectangular connectors are typically used in applications where a very large number of circuits are accommodated in a single mated pair. They are available with a great variety of contacts, which can include a mix of standard, coaxial, and large power types. Coupling is accomplished by various means. Smaller types are secured with screws which hold their flanges together. Larger ones have integral guide pins that ensure correct alignment, or jackscrews that both align and lock the connectors. Rack and panel connectors use integral or rack-mounted pins for alignment and box mounting hardware for couplings.

c. Module Blocks. These junctions accept crimped contacts similar to those on connectors. Some use internal busing to provide a variety of circuit arrangements. They are useful where a number of wires are connected for power or signal distribution.

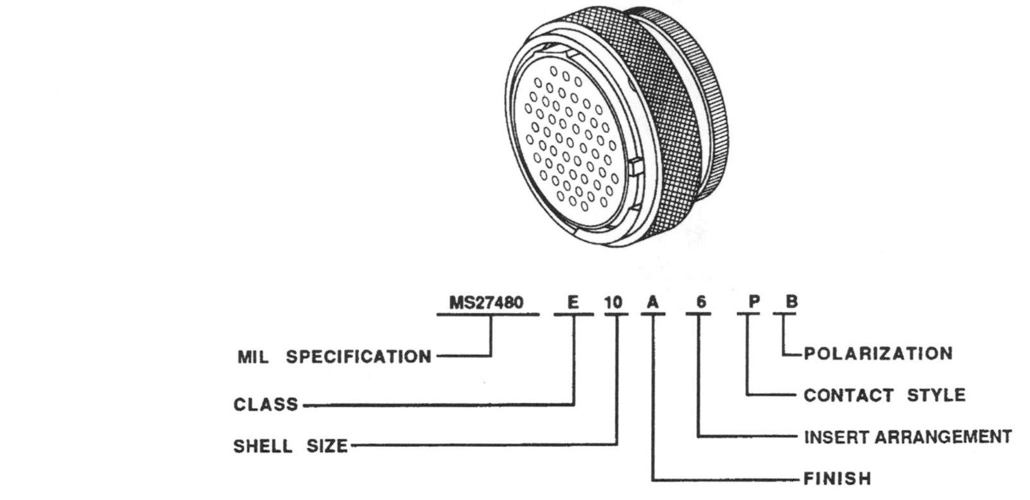

MS27472 WALL MOUNT RECEPTACLE
MS27473 STRAIGHT PLUG
MS27474 JAM NUT RECEPTACLE
MS27475 HERMITIC WALL MOUNT RECEPTACLE
MS27476 HERMETIC BOX MOUNT RECEPTACLE
MS27477 HERMETIC JAM NUT RECEPTACLE
MS27478 HERMETIC SOLDER MOUNT RECEPTACLE
MS27479 WALL MOUNT RECEPTACLE (NOTE 1)
MS27480 STRAIGHT PLUG (NOTE 1)
MS27481 JAM NUT RECEPTACLE (NOTE 1)
MS27482 HERMETIC WALL MOUNT RECEPTACLE (NOTE 1)
MS27483 HERMETIC JAM NUT RECEPTACLE (NOTE 1)
MS27484 STRAIGHT PLUG, EMI GROUNDING
MS27497 WALL RECEPTACLE, BACK PANEL MOUNTING
MS27499 BOX MOUNTING RECEPTACLE
MS27500 90° PLUG (NOTE 1)
MS27503 HERMETIC SOLDER MOUNT RECEPTACLE (NOTE 1)
MS27504 BOX MOUNT RECEPTACLE (NOTE 1)
MS27508 BOX MOUNT RECEPTACLE, BACK PANEL MOUNTING
MS27513 BOX MOUNT RECEPTACLE, LONG GROMMET
MS27664 WALL MOUNT RECEPTACLE, BACK PANEL MOUNTING (NOTE 1)
MS27667 THRU-BULKHEAD RECEPTACLE

NOTE

1. ACTIVE	SUPERSEDES
MS27472	MS27479
MS27473	MS27480
MS27474	MS27481
MS27475	MS27482
MS27477	MS27483
MS27473 WITH MS27507 ELBOW	MS27500
MS27478	MS27503
MS27499	MS27504
MS27497	MS27664

CLASS

E ENVIRONMENT RESISTING-BOX AND THRU-BULKHEAD MOUNTING TYPES ONLY (SEE CLASS T)
P POTTING-INCLUDES POTTING FORM AND SHORT REAR GROMMET
T ENVIRONMENT RESISTING-WALL AND JAM-NUT MOUNTING RECEPTACLE AND PLUG TYPES: THREAD AND TEETH FOR ACCESSORY ATTACHMENT
Y HERMETICALLY SEALED

FINISH

A SILVER TO LIGHT IRIDESCENT YELLOW COLOR CADMIUM PLATE OVER NICKEL (CONDUCTIVE), -65°C TO +150C° (INACTIVE FOR NEW DESIGN)
B OLIVE DRAB CADMIUM PLATE OVER SUITABLE UNDERPLATE (CONDUCTIVE), -65°C TO +175°C
C ANODIC (NONCONDUCTIVE), -65°C TO +175°C
D FUSED TIN, CARBON STEEL (CONDUCTIVE), -65°C TO 150°C
E CORROSION RESISTANT STEEL (CRES), PASSIVATED (CONDUCTIVE), -65°C TO +200°C
F ELECTROLESS NICKEL COATING (CONDUCTIVE), -65°C TO +200°C
N HERMETIC SEAL OR ENVIRONMENT RESISTING CRES (CONDUCTIVE PLATING), -65°C TO +200°C

CONTACT STYLE

A WITHOUT PIN CONTACTS
B WITHOUT SOCKET CONTACTS
C FEED THROUGH
P PIN CONTACTS-INCLUDING HERMETICS WITH SOLDER CUPS
S SOCKET CONTACTS-INCLUDING HERMETICS WITH SOLDER CUPS
X PIN CONTACTS WITH EYELET (HERMETIC)
Z SOCKET CONTACTS WITH EYELET (HERMETIC)

POLARIZATION

A, B NORMAL-NO LETTER REQUIRED
C, OR
D

FIGURE 11-35. Connector information example.

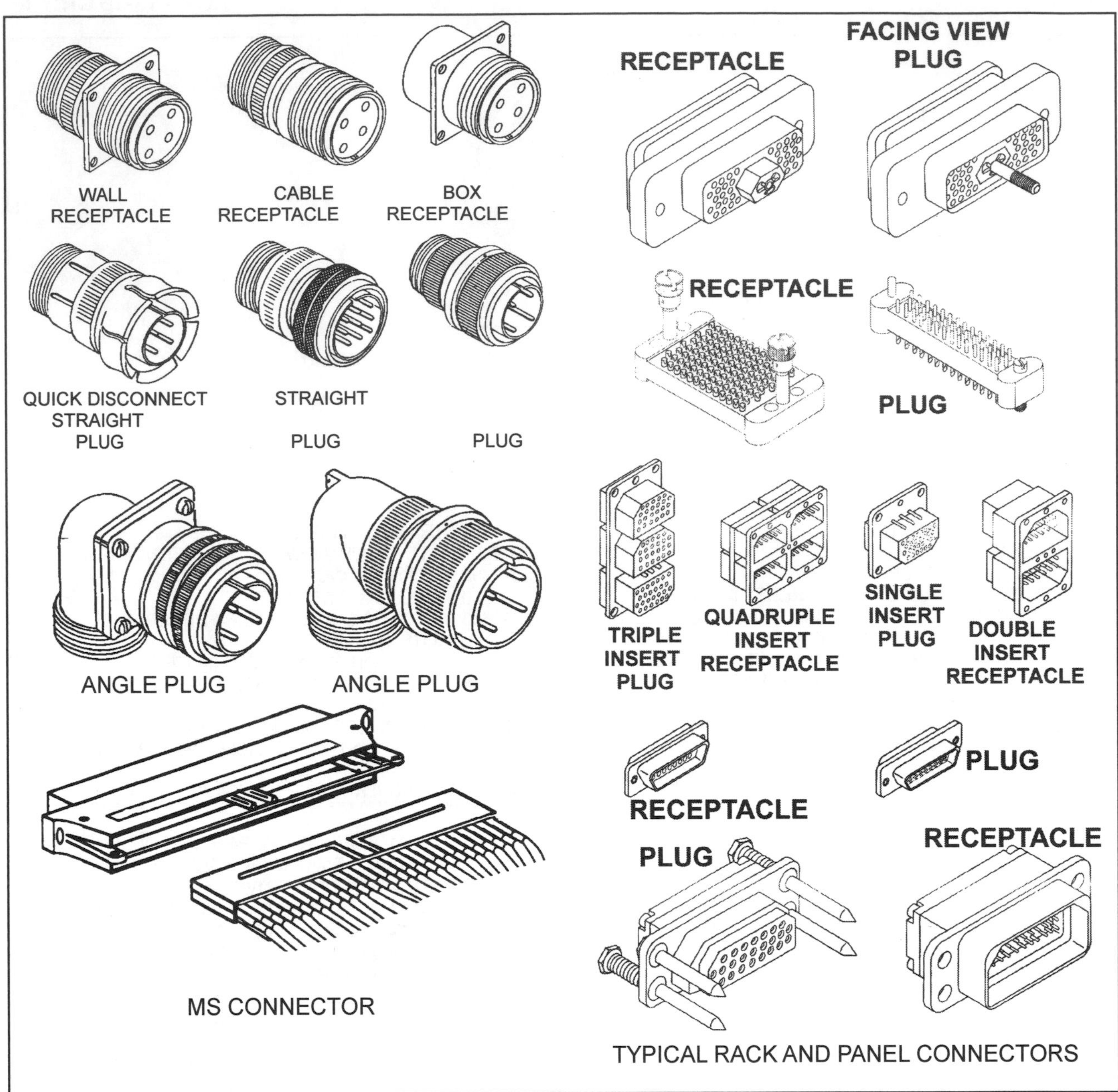

FIGURE 11-36. Different types of connectors.

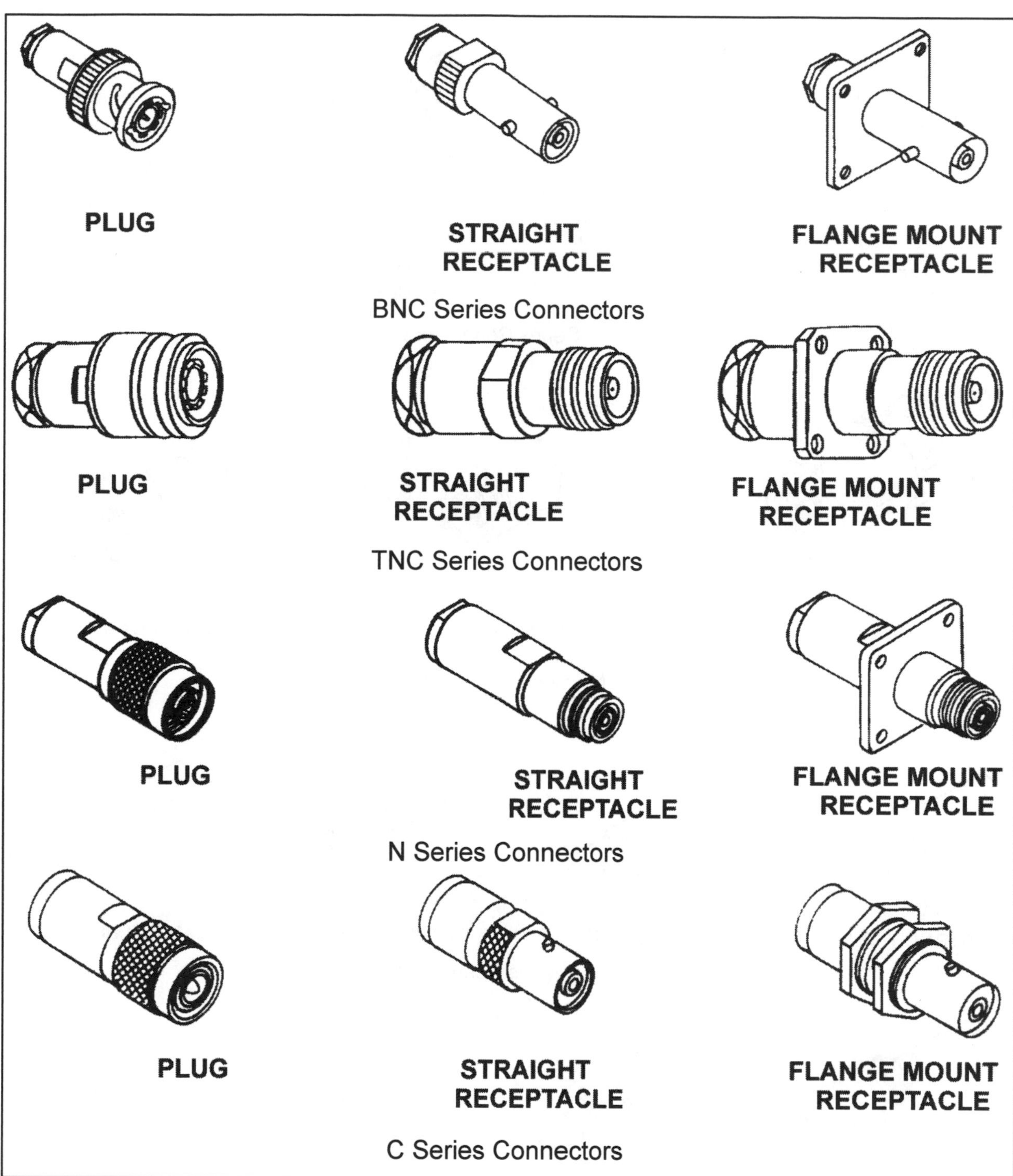

FIGURE 11-37. Coax cable connectors.

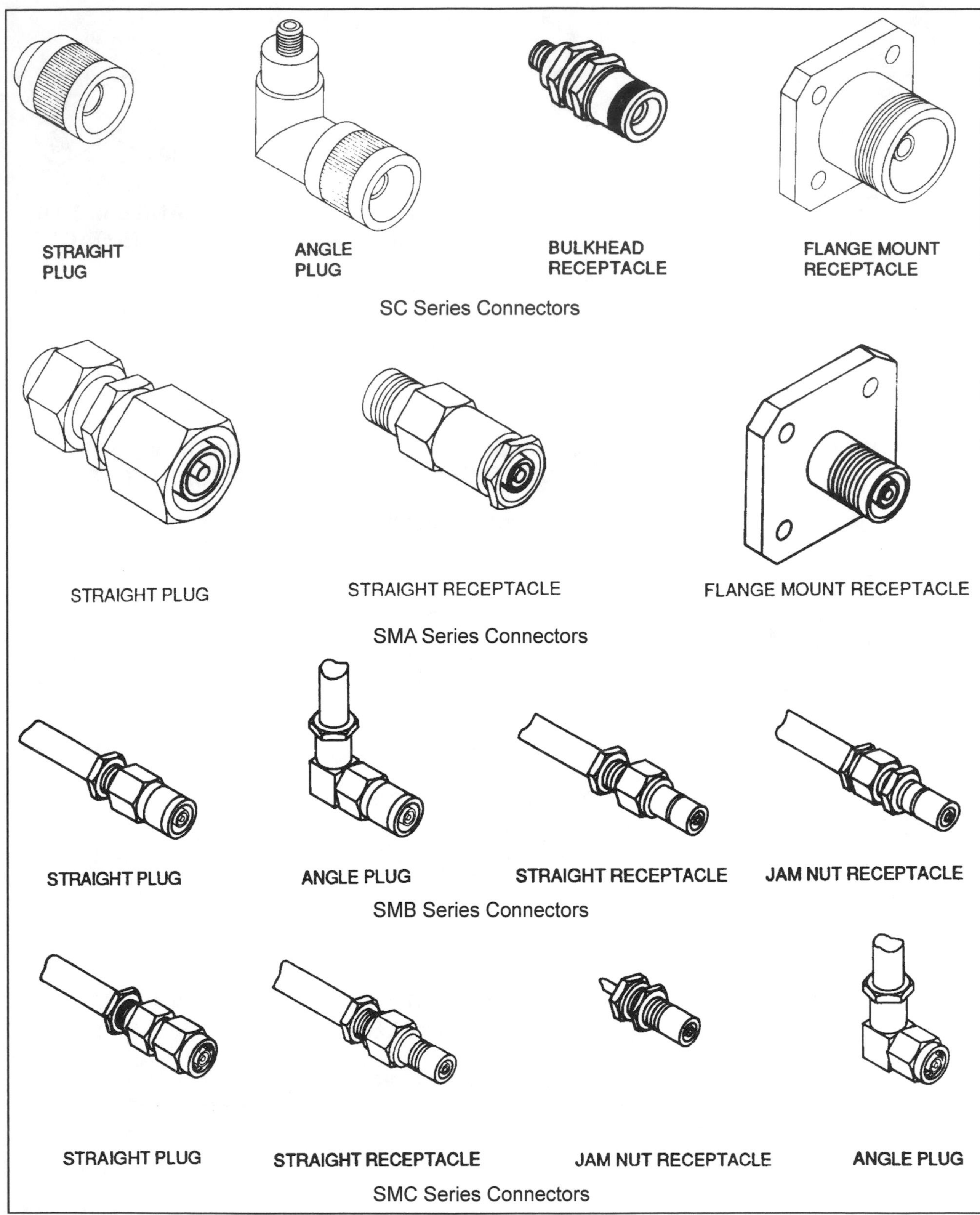

FIGURE 11-37. Coax cable connectors (continued).

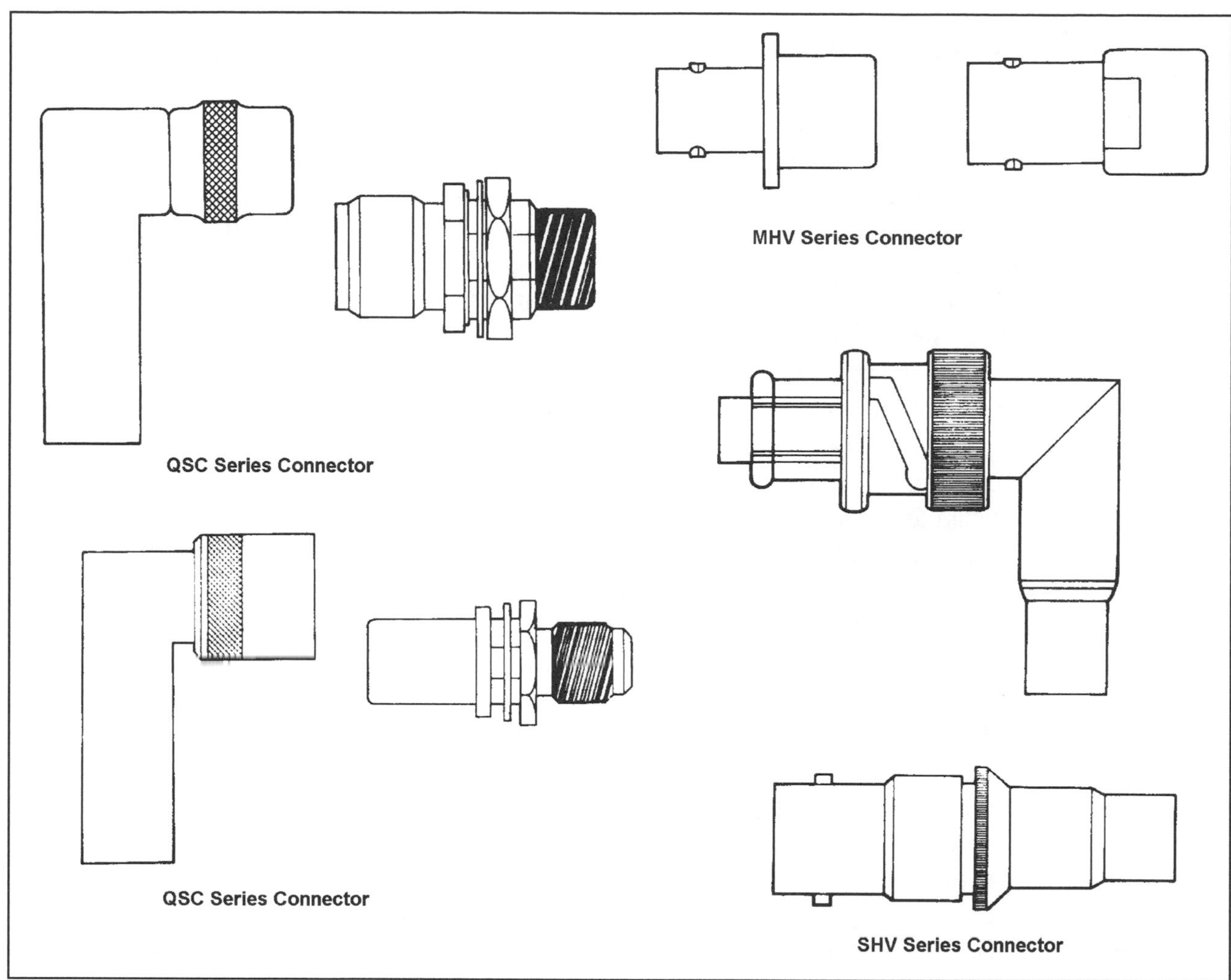

FIGURE 11-37. Coax cable connectors (continued).

When used as grounding modules, they save and reduce hardware installation on the aircraft. Standardized modules are available with wire end grommet seals for environmental applications and are track-mounted. Function module blocks are used to provide an easily wired package for environment-resistant mounting of small resistors, diodes, filters, and suppression networks. In-line terminal junctions are sometimes used in lieu of a connector when only a few wires are terminated and when the ability to disconnect the wires is desired. The in-line terminal junction is environment-resistant. The terminal junction splice is small and may be tied to the surface of a wire bundle when approved by the OAM.

11-233. VOLTAGE AND CURRENT RATING. Selected connectors must be rated for continuous operation under the maximum combination of ambient temperature and circuit current load. Hermetic connectors and connectors used in circuit applications involving high-inrush currents should be derated. It is good engineering practice to conduct preliminary testing in any situation where the connector is to operate with most or all of its contacts at maximum rated current load. When wiring is operating with a high conductor temperature near its rated temperature, connector contact sizes should be suitably rated for the circuit load. This may require an increase in wire size also. Voltage derating is required when connectors are used at high altitude in nonpressurized areas. Derating of the connectors should be covered in the specifications.

11-234. SPARE CONTACTS (Future Wiring). To accommodate future wiring additions, spare contacts are normally provided. Locating the unwired contacts along the outer part of the connector facilitates future access. A good practice is to provide: Two spares on connectors with 25 or less contacts; 4 spares on connectors with 26 to 100 contacts; and 6 spares on connectors with more than 100 contacts. Spare contacts are not normally provided on receptacles of components that are unlikely to have added wiring. Connectors must have all available contact cavities filled with wired or unwired contacts. Unwired contacts should be provided with a plastic grommet sealing plug.

11-235. INSTALLATION.

a. Redundancy. Wires that perform the same function in redundant systems must be routed through separate connectors. On systems critical to flight safety, system operation wiring should be routed through separate connectors from the wiring used for system failure warning. It is also good practice to route a system's indication wiring in separate connectors from its failure warning circuits to the extent practicable. These steps can reduce an aircraft's susceptibility to incidents that might result from connector failures.

b. Adjacent Locations. Mating of adjacent connectors should not be possible. In order to ensure this, adjacent connector pairs must be different in shell size, coupling means, insert arrangement, or keying arrangement. When such means are impractical, wires should be routed and clamped so that incorrectly mated pairs cannot reach each other. Reliance on markings or color stripes is not recommended as they are likely to deteriorate with age.

c. Sealing. Connectors must be of a type that exclude moisture entry through the use of peripheral and interfacial seal that are compressed when the connector is mated. Moisture entry through the rear of the connector must be avoided by correctly matching the wire's outside diameter with the connector's rear grommet sealing range. It is recommended that no more than one wire be terminated in any crimp style contact. The use of heat-shrinkable tubing to build up the wire diameter, or the application of potting to the wire entry area as additional means of providing a rear compatibility with the rear grommet is recommended. These extra means have inherent penalties and should be considered only where other means cannot be used. Unwired spare contacts should have a correctly sized plastic plug installed. (See section 19.)

d. Drainage. Connectors must be installed in a manner which ensures that moisture and fluids will drain out of and not into the connector when unmated. Wiring must be routed so that moisture accumulated on the bundle will drain away from connectors. When connectors must be mounted in a vertical position, as through a shelf or floor, the connectors must be potted or environmentally sealed. In this situation it is better to have the receptacle faced downward so that it will be less susceptible to collecting moisture when unmated.

e. Wire Support. A rear accessory backshell must be used on connectors that are not enclosed. Connectors having very small size wiring, or are subject to frequent maintenance activity, or located in high-vibration areas must be provided with a strain-relief-type backshell. The wire bundle should be protected from mechanical damage with suitable cushion material where it is secured by the clamp. Connectors that are potted or have molded rear adapters do not normally use a separate strain relief accessory. Strain relief clamps should not impart tension on wires between the clamp and contact.

f. Slack. Sufficient wire length must be provided at connectors to ensure a proper drip loop and that there is no strain on termination after a complete replacement of the connector and its contacts.

g. Identification. Each connector should have a reference identification that is legible throughout the expected life of the aircraft.

11-236. FEED-THROUGH BULKHEAD WIRE PROTECTION. Feed-through bushing protection should be given to wire bundles which pass through bulkheads, frames, and other similar structure. Feed through bushings of hard dielectric material are satisfactory. The use of split plastic grommets (nylon) is recommended in lieu of rubber grommets in areas subject to fluids, since they eliminate the unsatisfactory features of rubber grommets and are resistant to fluids usually encountered in aircraft.

11-237. SPECIAL PURPOSE CONNECTOR. Many special-purpose connectors have been designed for use in aircraft applications, such as: subminiature connector, rectangular shell connector, connectors with short body shells, or connector of split-shell construction used in applications where potting is required. Make every attempt to identify the connector part number from the maintenance manual or actual part, and the manufacturer's instruction used for servicing.

11-238. POTTING COMPOUNDS. Many types of potting compounds, both commercial and per military specifications, are available and offer various characteristics for different applications. Carefully consider the characteristics desired to ensure the use of the proper compound. Preparation and storage of potting materials should receive special attention. Careful inspection and handling during all stages of the connector fabrication until the potting compound has fully cured is recommended. Potting compounds selected must not revert to liquid or become gummy or sticky due to high humidity or contact with chemical fluids.

a. Potting compounds meeting Specification MIL-S-8516 are prepared in ready-to-use tube-type dispensers and in the unmixed state, consisting of the base compound and an accelerator packed in paired containers. To obtain the proper results, it is important that the manufacturer's instructions be closely followed.

b. Potting compounds normally cure at temperatures of 70 °F to 76 °F. If the mixed compound is not used at once, the working pot life (normally 90 minutes) can be prolonged by storing in a deep freeze at -20 °F for a maximum of 36 hours. The time factor starts from the instant the accelerator is added to the base compound and includes the time expended during the mixing and application processes.

c. Mixed compounds that are not to be used immediately should be cooled and thawed quickly to avoid wasting the short working life. Chilled compounds should be thawed by blowing compressed air over the outside of the container. Normally the compound will be ready for use in 5 to 10 minutes.

CAUTION: Do not use heat or blow compressed air into the container when restoring the compound to the working temperature.

11-239. POTTING CONNECTORS. Connectors that have been potted primarily offer protection against concentration of moisture in the connectors. A secondary benefit of potting is the reduced possibility of breakage between the contact and wire due to vibration.

a. Connectors specifically designed for potting compounds should be potted to provide environment resistance. An o-ring or sealed gasket should be included to seal the interface area of the mated connector. A plastic potting mold, that remains on the connector after the potting compounds have cured, should also be considered. To facilitate circuit changes, spare wires may be installed to all unused contacts prior to filling the connector with potting compound.

b. Connect wires to all contacts of the connector prior to the application of the potting compound. Wires that are not to be used should be long enough to permit splicing at a later date. Unused wires should be as shown in figure 11-38 and the cut ends capped with heat-shrinkable caps or crimped insulated end caps such as the MS 25274 prior to securing to the wire bundle. Clean the areas to be potted with dry solvent and complete the potting operation within 2 hours after this cleaning. Allow the potting compound to cure for 24 hours at a room temperature of 70 °F to 75 °F or carefully placed in a drying oven at 100 °F for 3 to 4 hours. In all cases follow manufacturer's instructions.

11-240. THROUGH BOLTS. Through bolts are sometimes used to make feeder connections through bulkheads, fuselage skin, or firewalls. Mounting plates for through bolts must be a material that provides the necessary fire barrier, insulation, and thermal properties for the application. Sufficient cross section should be provided to ensure adequate conductivity against overheating. Secure through bolts mechanically and independently of the terminal mounting nuts, taking particular care to avoid dissimilar metals among the terminal hardware. During inspection, pay particular attention to the condition of the insulator plate or spacer and the insulating boot that covers the completed terminal assembly.

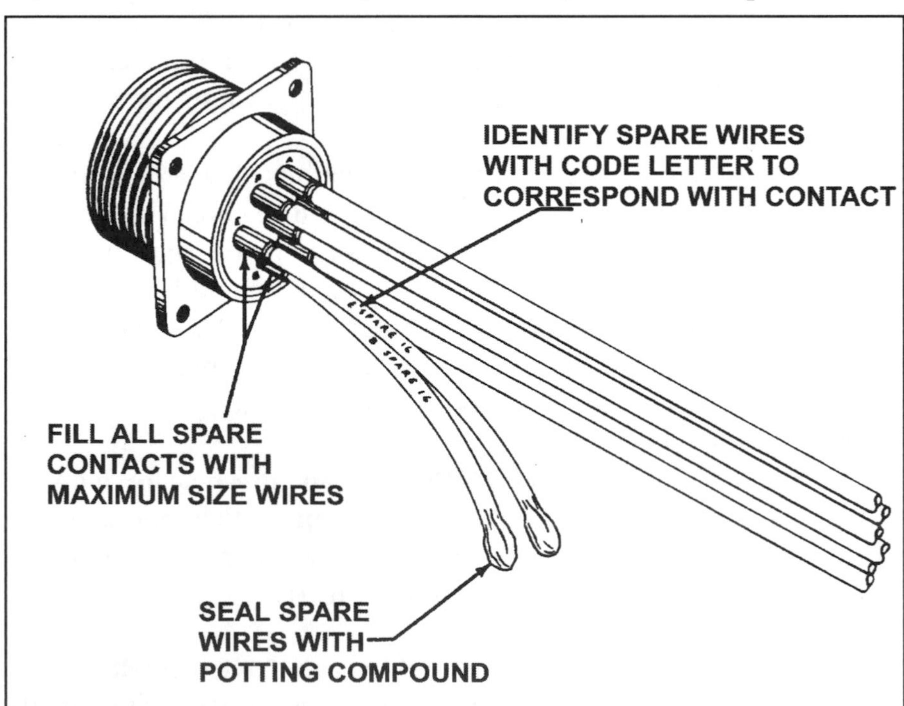

FIGURE 11-38. Spare wires for potting connector.

11-241.—11-247. [RESERVED.]

SECTION 18. CONDUITS

11-248. GENERAL. Conduit is manufactured in metallic and nonmetallic materials and in both rigid and flexible forms. Primarily, its purpose is for mechanical protection of cables or wires. Conduit should be inspected for: proper end fittings; absence of abrasion at the end fittings; proper clamping; distortion; adequate drain points which are free of dirt, grease, or other obstructions; and freedom from abrasion or damage due to moving objects, such as aircraft control cables or shifting cargo.

11-249. SIZE OF CONDUIT. Conduit size should be selected for a specific wire bundle application to allow for ease in maintenance, and possible future circuit expansion, by specifying the conduit inner diameter (I.D.) about 25 percent larger than the maximum diameter of the wire bundle.

11-250. CONDUIT FITTINGS. Wire is vulnerable to abrasion at conduit ends. Suitable fittings should be affixed to conduit ends in such a manner that a smooth surface comes in contact with the wire. When fittings are not used, the end of the conduit should be flared to prevent wire insulation damage. Conduit should be supported by use of clamps along the conduit run.

11-251. CONDUIT INSTALLATION. Conduit problems can be avoided by following these guidelines:

a. Do not locate conduit where passengers or maintenance personnel might use it as a handhold or footstep.

b. Provide drainholes at the lowest point in a conduit run. Drilling burrs should be carefully removed.

c. Support conduit to prevent chafing against structure and to avoid stressing its end fittings.

11-252. RIGID CONDUIT. Conduit sections that have been damaged should be repaired to preclude injury to the wires or wire bundle which may consume as much as 80 percent of the tube area. Minimum acceptable tube bend radii for rigid conduit are shown in table 11-23. Kinked or wrinkled bends in rigid conduits are not recommended and should be replaced. Tubing bends that have been flattened into an ellipse and the minor diameter is less than 75 percent of the nominal tubing diameter should be replaced because the tube area will have been reduced by at least 10 percent. Tubing that has been formed and cut to final length should be deburred to prevent wire insulation damage. When installing replacement tube sections with fittings at both ends, care should be taken to eliminate mechanical strain.

TABLE 11-23. Bend radii for rigid conduit.

Nominal Tube O.D. (inches)	Minimum Bend Radii (inches)
1/8	3/8
3/16	7/16
1/4	9/16
3/8	15/16
1/2	1 1/4
5/8	1 1/2
3/4	1 3/4
1	3
1 1/4	3 3/4
1 1/2	5
1 3/4	7
2	8

11-253. FLEXIBLE CONDUIT. Flexible aluminum conduit conforming to Specification MIL-C-6136 is available in two types: Type I, Bare Flexible Conduit, and Type II, Rubber Covered Flexible Conduit. Flexible brass conduit conforming to Specification MIL-C-7931 is available and normally used instead of flexible aluminum where necessary to minimize radio interference. Also available is a plastic flexible tubing. (Reference MIL-T-8191A.) Flexible conduit may be used where it is impractical to use rigid conduit, such as areas that have motion between conduit ends or where complex bends are necessary. The use of transparent adhesive tape is recommended when cutting flexible tubing with a hacksaw to minimize fraying of the braid. The tape should be centered over the cutting reference mark with the saw cutting through the tape. After cutting the flexible conduit, the transparent tape should be removed, the frayed braid ends trimmed, burrs removed from inside the conduit, and coupling nut and ferrule installed. Minimum acceptable bending radii for flexible conduit are shown in table 11-24.

TABLE 11-24. Minimum bending radii for flexible aluminum or brass conduit.

Nominal I.D. of conduit (inches)	Minimum bending radius inside (inches)
3/16	2 1/4
1/4	2 3/4
3/8	3 3/4
1/2	3 3/4
5/8	3 3/4
3/4	4 1/4
1	5 3/4
1 1/4	8
1 1/2	8 1/4
1 3/4	9
2	9 3/4
2 1/2	10

11-254.—11-259. [RESERVED.]

SECTION 19. UNUSED CONNECTORS AND UNUSED WIRES

11-260. GENERAL. Connectors may have one or more contact cavities that are not used. Depending on the connector installation, unused connector contact cavities may need to be properly sealed to avoid damage to the connector, or have string wire installed. Unused wires can be secured by tying into a bundle or secured to a permanent structure; individually cut with strands even with insulation; or preinsulated closed end connector or 1 inch piece of insulating tubing folded and tied back.

11-261. QUICK REFERENCE CHART. A quick reference chart of unused connector contact cavity requirements is given in table 11-25. These requirements apply to harness manufacturing or connector replacement only.

11-262. UNPRESSURIZED AREA CONNECTORS. Connectors may be installed in unpressurized areas of the aircraft. Unused connector contact cavities installed in unpressurized areas should be properly sealed as follows:

a. Firewall Connectors Installations. Firewall unused connector contact cavities should be filled with spare contacts and stub wires. (See figure 11-39.)

(1) Construct stub wires using high temperature wire (260 °C). Ensure that stub wires are of the same type of wires in the bundle.

(2) Crimp the proper contact, for the connector and cavity being used, onto the wire. Install the crimped contact into the unused cavity.

(3) Extend stub wires beyond the back of the connector clamp from 1.5 to 6 inches. Feather trim stub wires to taper wire bundle.

(4) Secure wire ends with high temperature (greater than 250 °C) lacing cord. Nylon cable ties are not allowed for this installation.

NOTE: Both connectors mating through the engine fire-seal are considered firewall connectors. Connectors mounted on or near, but not through, the engine fire-seal are not considered firewall connectors.

b. Non-firewall Connector Installations. In this type of installation all unused connector cavities must also be filled with spare contacts. It is not required, however, to crimp stub wires on filling contacts.

Fill unused contact cavities with spare contacts and Teflon sealing plugs or rods. (See figure 11-40.) Rods shall be cut so that they extend 1/8 to 1/4 inch beyond the surface of the grommet when bottomed against the end of the spare contact. (See table 11-26 for dimensions.)

11-263. PRESSURIZED AREAS. Connectors installed in pressurized areas of the aircraft may be divided into two main installation categories, sealed and unsealed.

a. Sealed connector installations. Sealed connectors installed in pressurized areas must have their unused contact cavities filled with Teflon sealing plugs or rods. (See figure 11-40.) Installation of spare contacts is optional, except for future wiring addition requirements. (See paragraph 11-234). No stub wires are required.

b. Unsealed Connector Installations. It is not required to fill unused contact cavities of unsealed connectors installed in pressurized areas with Teflon sealing plugs or rods. Installation of spare contacts is optional, except for future wiring addition requirements. (See paragraph 11-234.)

TABLE 11-25. Contact cavity sealing-quick reference.

Sealing Means	Connector Installation Types	
	Unpressurized Area	
	Firewall	Non-Firewall
Sealing Plugs or Teflon Sealing Rods	No	Yes
Stub Wires (Note 2)	Yes	No
Spare Contacts	Yes	Yes
NOTE 1: Sealing plugs may be included with the spare connector and may be used for sealing unused contacts. Sealing rods are procured from stock by the foot. (See table 11-26 for sealing rod dimensions.) NOTE 2: Stub wires must be of the same type as the other wires of the bundle.		

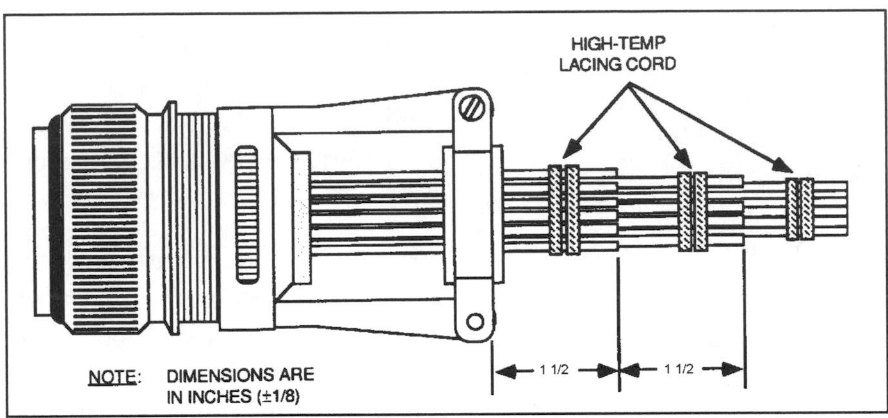

FIGURE 11-39. Stub wire installation.

TABLE 11-26. Sealing rod dimensions.

CONTACT SIZE (AWG)	DIAMETER (INCHES)	ROD LENGTH (INCHES)	
		MIN	MAX
20	1/16	5/8"	3/4"
16	3/32	7/8"	1"
12	1/8	7/8"	1"

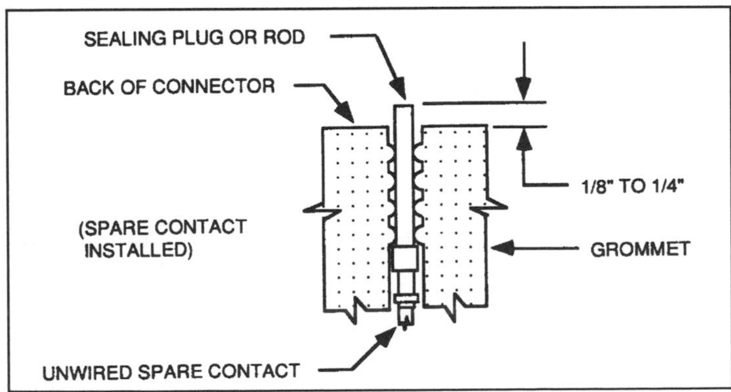

FIGURE 11-40. Sealing unused contact cavities-unpressurized areas-(cut-away view).

11-264.—11-270. [RESERVED.]

SECTION 20. ELECTRICAL AND ELECTRONIC SYMBOLS

11-271. GENERAL. The electrical and electronic symbols shown here are those that are likely to be encountered by the aviation maintenance technician. They are in accordance with ANSI-Y32.2-1975.

11-272. SYMBOLS. Only those symbols associated with aircraft electrical and electronic wiring have been listed in general. Refer to ANSI-Y32.2-1975 for more specific detail on each symbol.

TABLE 11-27. Electronic/Electrical Symbols.

Symbol	Meaning
	Adjustability Variability
	Radiation Indicators
	Physical State Recognition
	Test-Point Recognition
+ −	Polarity Markings
	Direction of Flow of Power, Signal, or Information
	Kind of Current
	Envelope Enclosure
	Shield Shielding
	Special Connector or Cable Indicator

TABLE 11-27. Electronic/Electrical Symbols (continued).

Symbol	Meaning
	Resistor
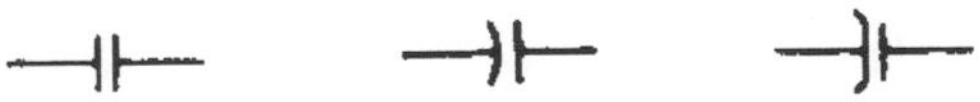	Capacitor
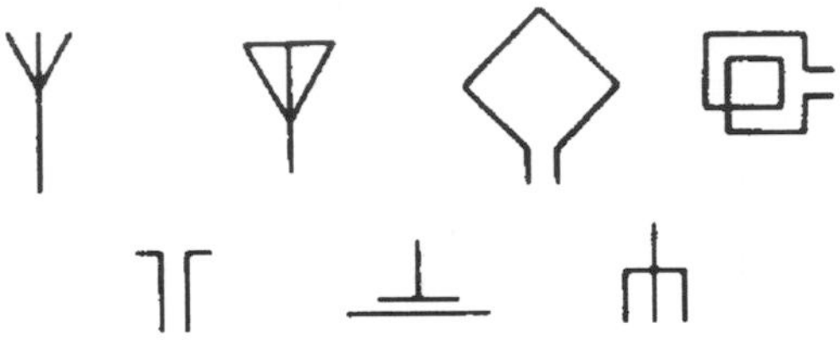	Antenna
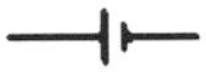	Battery
	Thermal Element Thermomechanical Transducer
	Thermocouple
	Spark Gap Ignitor Gap
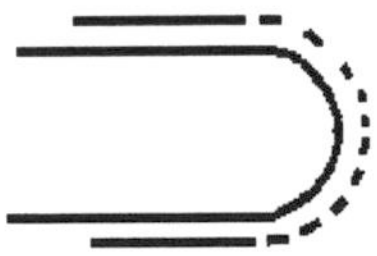	Continuous Loop Fire Detector (Temperature Sensor)
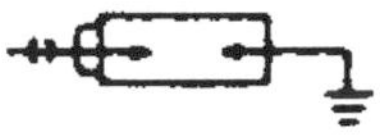	Ignitor Plug

TABLE 11-27. Electronic/Electrical Symbols (continued).

Symbol	Meaning
DEL SPLICE	Transmission Patch Conductor Cable Wiring
F S T V F	Distribution Lines Transmission Lines
	Alternative or Conditioned Wiring
	Associated or Future

TABLE 11-27. Electronic/Electrical Symbols (continued).

Symbol	Meaning
	Intentional Isolation of Direct-Current Path in Coaxial or Waveguide Applications
	Waveguide
	Strip-Type Transmission Line
	Termination
	Circuit Return
	Pressure-Tight Bulkhead Cable Gland Cable Sealing End
	Switching Function
	Electrical Contact

TABLE 11-27. Electronic/Electrical Symbols (continued).

Symbol	Meaning
TC TDC TO TDO	Basic Contact Assemblies
	Magnetic Blowout Coil
	Operating Coil Relay Coil
	Switch
	Pushbutton, Momentary, or Spring-Return

TABLE 11-27. Electronic/Electrical Symbols (continued).

Symbol	Meaning
	Two-Circuit, Maintained, or Not Spring-Return
	Nonlocking Switching, Momentary, or Spring-Return
	Locking Switch
OFF	Combination Locking and Nonlocking Switch
	Key-Type Switch Lever Switch

TABLE 11-27. Electronic/Electrical Symbols (continued).

Symbol	Meaning
	Selector or Multiposition Switch
	Safety Interlock
	Limit Switch Sensitive Switch
TDC TDO TDC TDC	Switches with Time-Delay Feature
	Flow-Actuated Switch

TABLE 11-27. Electronic/Electrical Symbols (continued).

Symbol	Meaning
	Liquid-Level Actuated Switch
	Pressure- or Vacuum-Actuated Switch
	Temperature-Actuated Switch
	Thermostat
	Flasher Self-Interrupting Switch
	Foot-Operated Switch Foot Switch
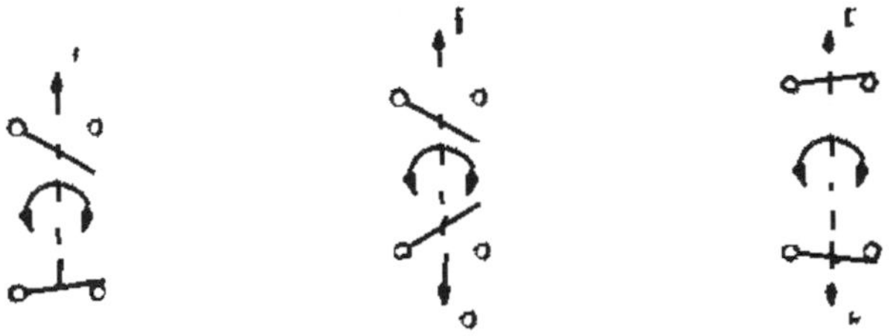	Switch Operated by Shaft Rotation and Responsive to Speed or Direction
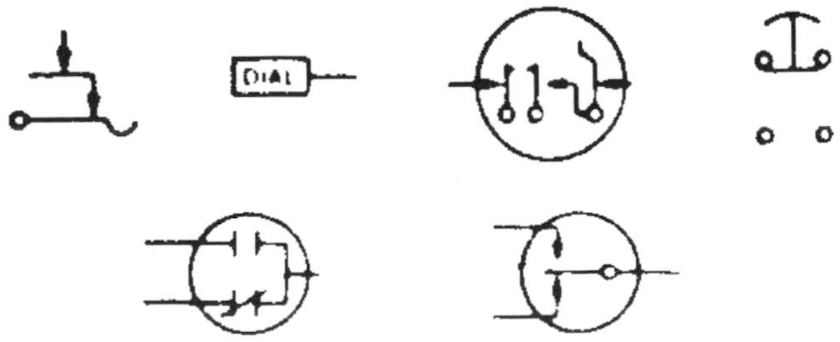 DIAL	Switches with Specific Features

TABLE 11-27. Electronic/Electrical Symbols (continued).

Symbol	Meaning
	Governor Speed Regulator
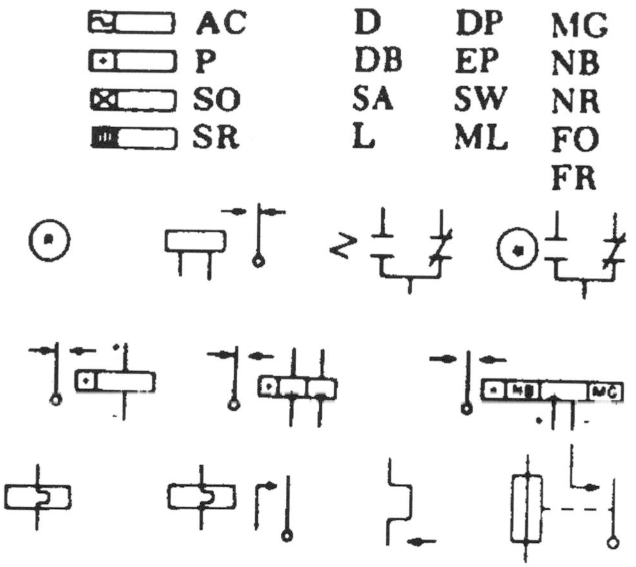 AC P SO SR D DB SA L DP EP SW ML MG NB NR FO FR	Relay
	Inertia Switch
	Mercur Switch
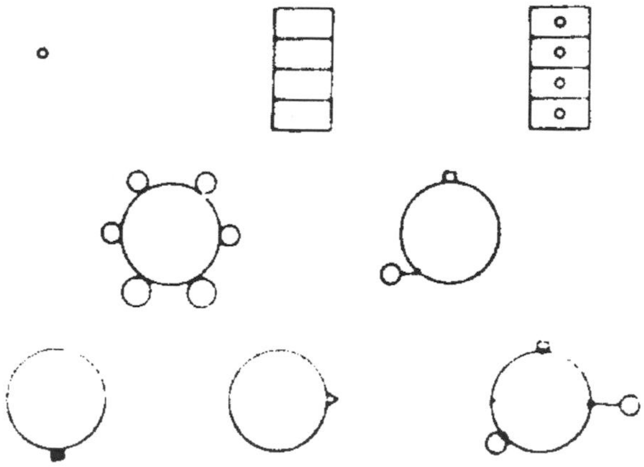	Terminals

TABLE 11-27. Electronic/Electrical Symbols (continued).

Symbol	Meaning
	Cable Termination
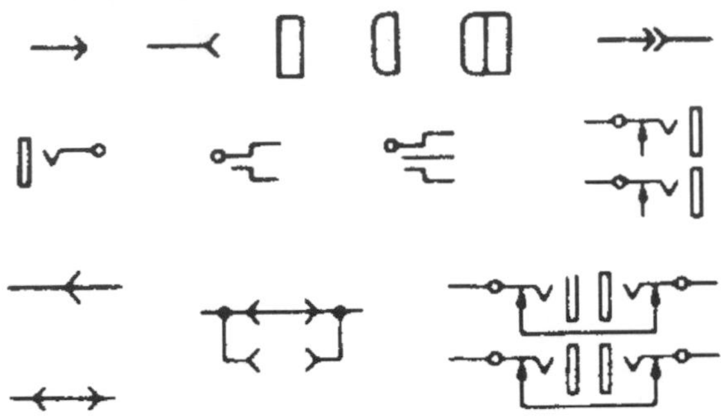	Connector Disconnecting Device
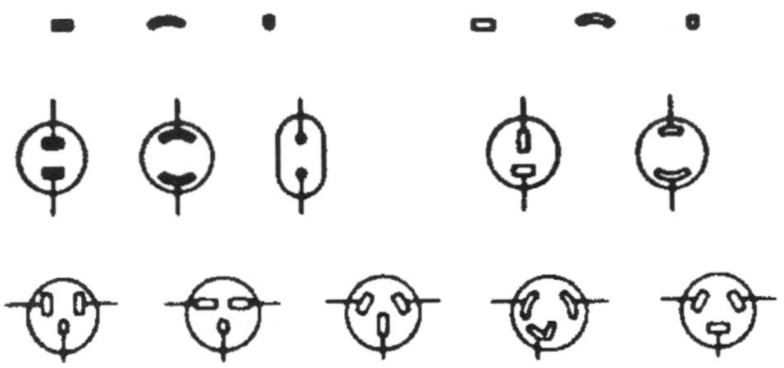	Connectors of the Type Commonly Used for Power-Supply Purposes
	Test Blocks
	Coaxial Connector
	Waveguide Flanges Waveguide Junction

TABLE 11-27. Electronic/Electrical Symbols (continued).

Symbol	Meaning
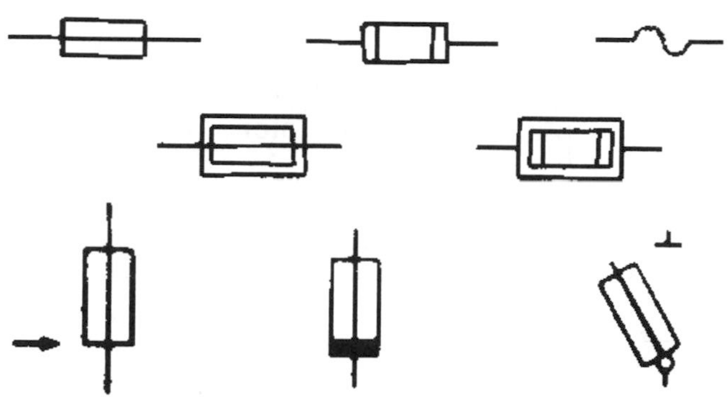	Fuse
	Lightning Arrester Arrester Gap
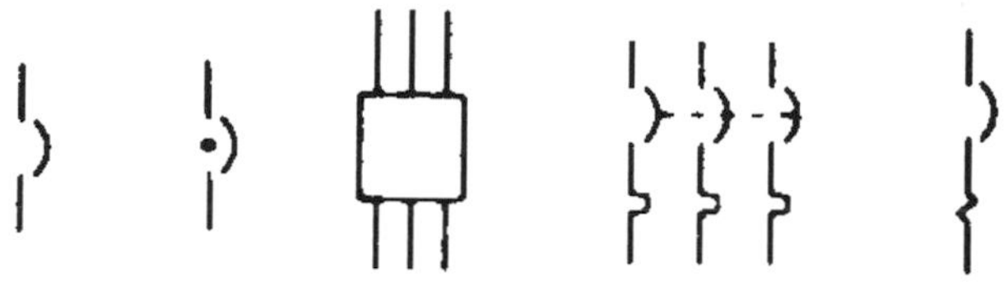	Circuit Breaker
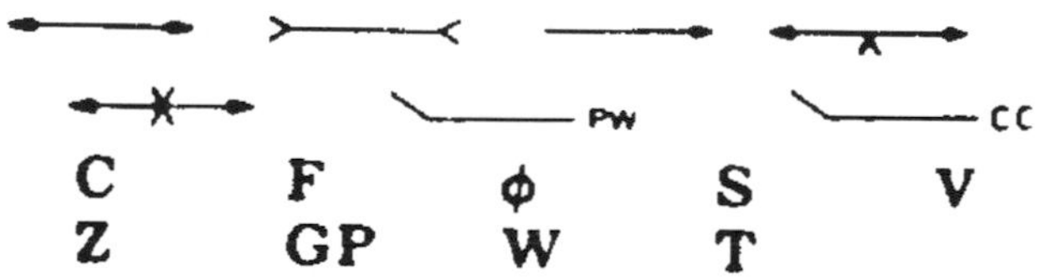 PW CC C F ϕ S V Z GP W T	Protective Relay
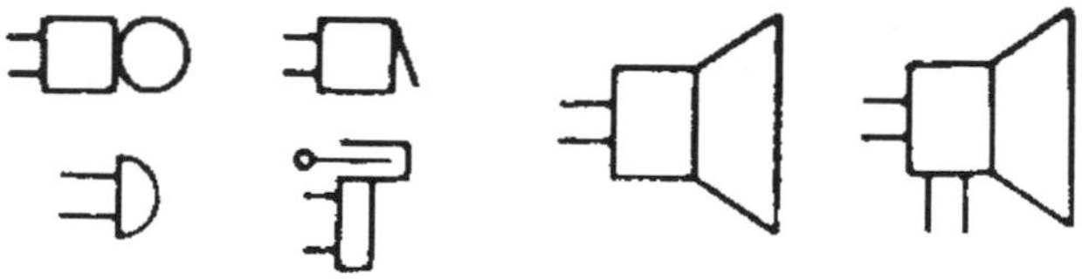	Audible-Signaling Device
	Microphone

TABLE 11-27. Electronic/Electrical Symbols (continued).

Symbol	Meaning
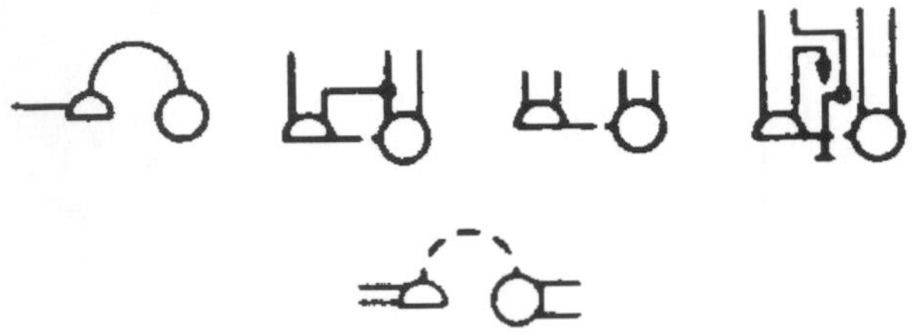	Handset Operator's Set
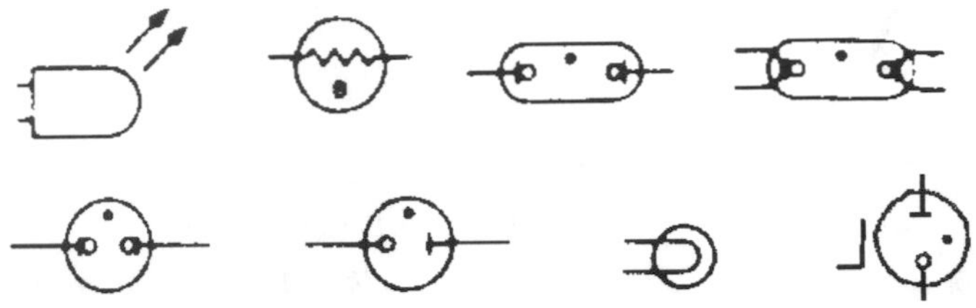	Lamp
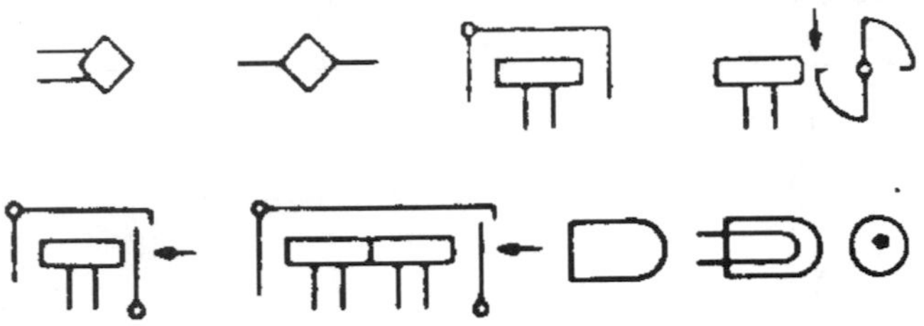	Visual-Signaling Device
	Mechanical Connection Mechanical Interlock
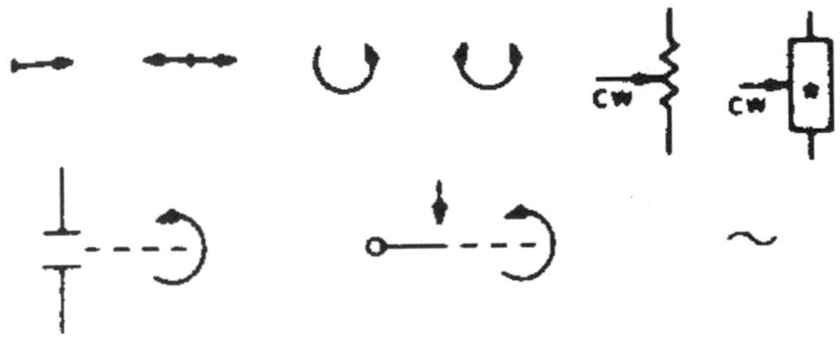 CW CW	Mechanical Motion
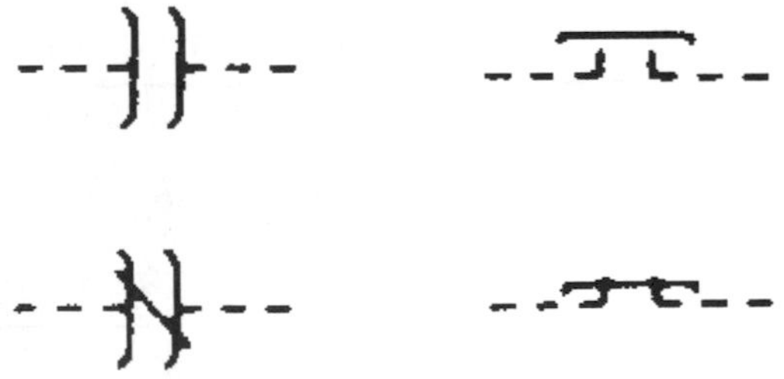	Clutch Brake

TABLE 11-27. Electronic/Electrical Symbols (continued).

Symbol	Meaning
	Manual Control
	Gyro Gyroscope Gyrocompass
	Position Indicator
	Fire Extinguisher Actuator Head
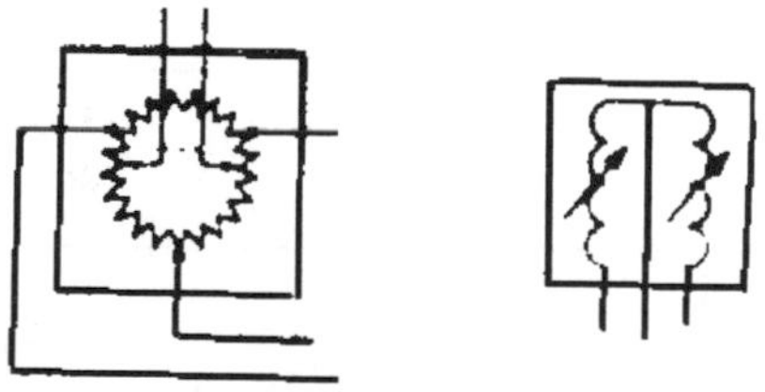	Position Transmitter
	Radio Station
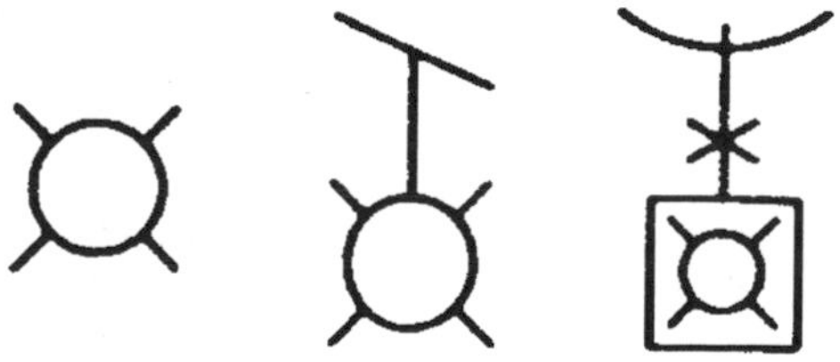	Space Station

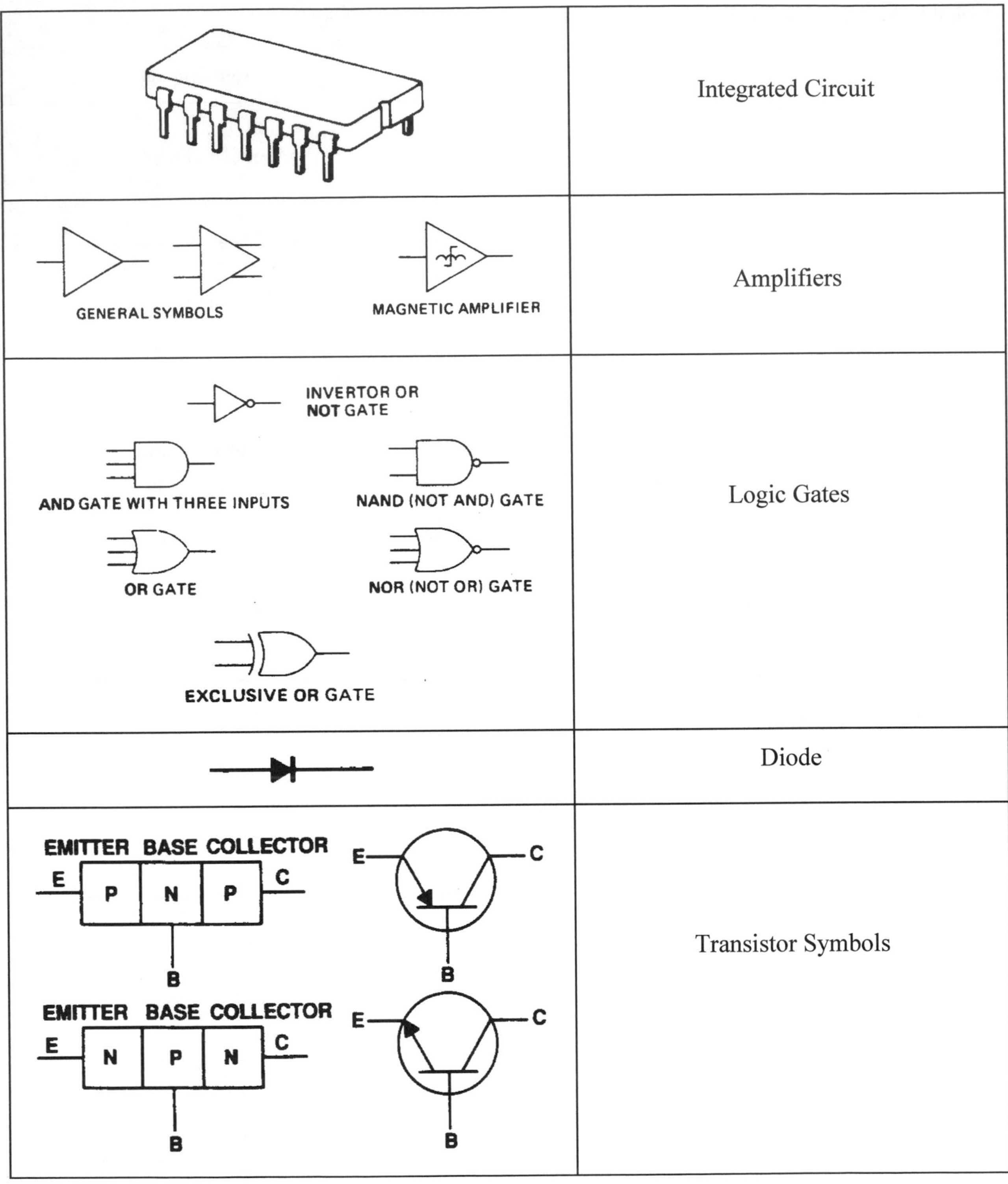
Integrated Circuit
GENERAL SYMBOLS
MAGNETIC AMPLIFIER
Amplifiers
INVERTOR OR NOT GATE
AND GATE WITH THREE INPUTS
NAND (NOT AND) GATE
OR GATE
NOR (NOT OR) GATE
EXCLUSIVE OR GATE
Logic Gates
Diode
EMITTER BASE COLLECTOR
E P N P C
B
E C
B
EMITTER BASE COLLECTOR
E N P N C
B
E C
B
Transistor Symbols

11-273.—11-283. [RESERVED.]

CHAPTER 12. AIRCRAFT AVIONICS SYSTEMS

SECTION 1. AVIONICS EQUIPMENT MAINTENANCE

12-1. GENERAL. There are several methods of ground checking avionics systems.

a. Visual Check. Check for physical condition and safety of equipment and components.

b. Operation Check. This check is performed primary by the pilot, but may also be performed by the mechanics after annual and 100-hour inspections. The aircraft flight manual, the Airman's Information Manual (AIM), and the manufacturer's information are used as a reference when performing the check.

c. Functional Test. This is performed by qualified mechanics and repair stations to check the calibration and accuracy of the avionics with the use of test equipment while they are still on the aircraft, such as the transponder and the static checks. The equipment manufacturer's manuals and procedures are used as a reference.

d. Bench Test. When using this method the unit or instrument is removed from the aircraft and inspected, repaired, and calibrated as required.

e. Electromagnetic Interference (EMI). For EMI tests, refer to chapter 11 paragraph 11-107 of this AC.

12-2. HANDLING OF COMPONENTS. Any unit containing electronic components such as transistors, diodes, integrated circuits, proms, roms, and memory devices should be protected from excessive shocks. Excessive shock can cause internal failures in an of these components. Most electronic devices are subject to damage by electrostatic discharges (ESD).

CAUTION: To prevent damage due to excessive electrostatic discharge, proper gloves, finger cots, or grounding bracelets should be used. Observe the standard procedures for handling equipment containing electrostatic sensitive devices or assemblies in accordance with the recommendations and procedures set forth in the maintenance instructions set forth by the equipment manufacturers.

12-3.—12-7. [RESERVED.]

SECTION 2. GROUND OPERATIONAL CHECKS FOR AVIONICS EQUIPMENT (ELECTRICAL)

12-8. GENERAL. When the operating or airworthiness regulations require a system to perform its intended function, the use of the Technical Standard Order (TSO) equipment or the submission of data substantiating the equipment performance is strongly recommended. An operation check of avionics is the responsibility of the pilot in command. However, it is recommended that after replacement of equipment during 100 hour or annual inspections, an operational check of avionics equipment be performed. The accomplishments of these checks must be done in accordance with the recommendations and procedures set forth in the aircraft's flight manual instructions published by the avionics equipment manufacturers.

12-9. INSPECTION OF AVIONICS SYSTEMS.

a. The inspection shall include the following:

(1) Inspect the condition and security of equipment including the proper security of wiring bundles.

(2) Check for indications of overheating of the equipment and associated wiring.

(3) Check for poor electrical bonding. The bonding requirements are specified by equipment manufacturers. Installation cabling should be kept as short as possible, except for antenna cables which are usually precut or have a specific length called out at installation. Proper bonding on the order of 0.003 ohms is very important to the performance of avionics equipment.

(4) Check to assure that the radios and instruments are secured to the instrument panel.

(5) Check that all avionics are free of dust, dirt, lint, or any other airborne contaminates. If there is a forced air cooling system, it must be inspected for proper operation. Equipment ventilation openings must not be obstructed.

(6) Check the microphone headset plugs and connectors and all switches and controls for condition and operation. Check all avionics instruments for placards. Check lightoning, annunciator lights, and cockpit interphone for proper operation.

(7) The circuit breaker panel must be inspected for the presence of placarding for each circuit breaker installed.

(8) Check the electrical circuit switches, especially the spring-load type for proper operation. An internal failure in this type of switch may allow the switch to remain closed even though the toggle or button returns to the OFF position. During inspection, attention must be given to the possibility that improper switch substitution may have been made.

b. Inspect antennas for:

(1) broken or missing antenna insulators

(2) lead through insulators

(3) springs

(4) safety wires

(5) cracked antenna housing

(6) missing or poor sealant at base of antenna

(7) correct installation

(8) signs of corrosion, and

(9) the condition of paint/bonding and grounding.

(10) Check the bonding of each antenna from mounting base to the aircraft skin. Tolerance: .1 ohm, maximum.

(a) Test Equipment:

1 1502B Metallic Time Domain Reflectometer or equivalent.

2 Thruline Wattmeter.

(b) Perform the antenna evaluation check using the domain reflectometer to determine the condition of the antenna and coax cables. Refer to manufacturer's maintenance procedures.

(c) Use thruline wattmeter as needed for addition evaluation. Refer to manufacturer's maintenance procedures. Check for the following:

1 Resistance.

2 Shorts.

3 Opens.

c. Inspect the static dischargers/wicks for:

(1) physical security of mounting attachments, wear or abrasion of wicks, missing wicks, etc.,

(2) assurance that one inch of the inner braid of flexible vinyl cover wicks extends beyond the vinyl covering,

(3) assurance that all dischargers are present and securely mounted to their base,

(4) assurance that all bases are securely bonded to skin of aircraft in order to prevent the existence in voltage level differences between two surfaces,

(5) signs of excessive erosion or deterioration of discharger tip,

(6) lighting damage as evidenced by pitting of the metal base, and

(7) megohm value of static wick itself as per manufacturer's instructions. It should not be open.

d. Subsequent inspection must be made after a maintenance action on a transponder. Refer to Title 14 of the Code of Federal Regulations (14 CFR) part 91, sections 91.411 and 91.413.

e. Inspection of the emergency locator transmitter operation, condition and date of the battery.

f. Perform a function check of the radio by transmitting a request for a radio check. Perform a function check on navigation equipment by moving the omni bearing selection (OBS) and noting the needle swing and the TO/FROM flag movement.

12-10. COMMUNICATION SYSTEMS. Ground operation of communication systems in aircraft may be accomplished in accordance with the procedures appropriate for the airport and area in which the test is made and the manufacturer's manuals and procedures. Check system(s) for side tone, clarity of transmission, squelch, operations using head phones, speaker(s), and hand microphone. If a receiver or transmitter is found to be defective, it should be removed from the aircraft and repaired.

12-11. VHF OMNI-DIRECTIONAL RANGE (VOR). A VOR operates within the 108.0 to 111.85 MHz, and 112.0 to 117.95 MHz frequency bands. The display usually consists of a deviation indicator and a TO/FROM indicator. The controls consist of a frequency selector for selecting the ground station and an OBS, which is used for course selection. An ON/OFF flag is used to determine adequate field strength and presence of a valid signal. There are numerous configurations when integrated into flight directors and/or when using a slaved compass system, which uses an additional indicator that points continually to the selected omni station regardless of OBS selection. In order to determine the accuracy specified in a functional check, a ground test set must be used in accordance with the manufacturer's specifications. For the purpose of this inspection/maintenance activity, the following operational check can be accomplished to determine if the equipment has the accuracy required for operation in instrument flight rules (IFR) environment. Verify audio identification, OBS operation, flag operation, radio magnetic indicator (RMI) interface, and applicable navigation (NAV) switching functions. The operational check is also published in the AIM, section 1-1-4. This check is required by 14 CFR part 91, section 91.171 before instrument flight operations.

12-12. DISTANCE MEASURING EQUIPMENT (DME). The operation of DME consists of paired pulses at a specific spacing, sent out from the aircraft (this is what is called interrogation), and are received by the ground station, which then responds with paired pulses at the specific spacing sent by the aircraft, but at a different frequency. The aircraft unit measures the time it takes to transmit and then receive the signal, which then is translated into distance. DME operates on frequencies from 962 MHz to 1213 MHz. Because of the curvature of earth, this line-of-sight signal is reliable up to 199 nautical mile (NM) at the high end of the controlled airspace with an accuracy of 1/2 mile or 3 percent of the distance. DME inspection/maintenance on the aircraft is most commonly limited to a visual check of the installation, and if there have been previously reported problems, the antenna must be inspected for proper bonding and the absence of corrosion, both on the mounting surface, as well as the coax connector. Accuracy can be determined by evaluating performance during flight operations, as well as with ground test equipment. If a discrepancy is reported and corrected, it is good practice to make the accuracy determination before instrument flight. Tune the DME to a local station, or use the proper ground test equipment to check audio identification, and DME hold function verify correct display operation.

12-13. AUTOMATIC DIRECTION FINDER (ADF). The ADF receivers are primarily designed to receive nondirectional beacons (NDB) in the 19 to 535 kHz amplitude modulation (AM) broadcast low band. The receivers will also operate in the commercial AM band. The ADF display pointer will indicate the relative bearing to a selected AM band transmitter that is in range. An ADF system must be checked by tuning to an adequate NDB or commercial AM station. Verify proper bearing to station, audio identification and tone/beat frequency oscillator (BFO), correct operation in closed circuit (LOOP) and sense modes. Note the orientation of the selected station to the aircraft using an appropriate chart. Observe the ADF relative bearing reading, and compare to the chart. Slew the needle and observe how fast (or slowly) it returns to the reading. ADF performance may be degraded by lightning activity, airframe charging, ignition noise and atmospheric phenomena.

12-14. INSTRUMENT LANDING SYSTEMS (ILS). The ILS consist of several components, such as the localizer, glide slope, marker beacon, radio altimeter, and DME. Localizer and glide slope receivers and marker beacons will be discussed in this section.

a. Localizer receiver operates on one of 40 ILS channels within the frequency range of 108.10 to 111.95 MHz (odd tens). These signals provide course guidance to the pilot to the runway centerline through the lateral displacement of the VOR/localizer (LOC) deviation indicator. The ground transmitter is sighted at the far end of the runway and provides a valid signal from a distance of 18 NM from the transmitter. The indication gives a full fly left/right deviation of 700 feet at the runway threshold. Identification of the transmitter is in International Morse Code and consists of a three letter identifier preceded by the Morse Code letter I (two dots). The localizer function is usually integral with the VOR system, and when maintenance is performed on the VOR unit, the localizer is also included. The accuracy of the system can be effectively evaluated through normal flight operations if evaluated during visual meteorological conditions. Any determination of airworthiness after reinstallation before instrument flight must be accomplished with ground test equipment.

b. The glide slope receiver operates on one of 40 channels within the frequency range 329.15 MHz, to 335.00 MHz. The glide slope transmitter is located between 750 feet and 1250 feet from the approach end of the runway and offset 250 to 650 feet. In the absence of questionable performance, periodic functional flight checks of the glide slope system would be an acceptable way to ensure continued system performance. The functional flight test must be conducted under visual flight rules (VFR) conditions. A failed or misleading system must be serviced by an appropriately-rated repair station. Ground test equipment can be used to verify glide slope operation.

c. Localizer/Glide Slope (LOC/GS) may have self test function, otherwise the proper ground test equipment must be used. Refer to manufacturer's or aircraft instruction manual.

12-15. MARKER BEACON. Marker beacon receivers operate at 75 MHz and sense the audio signature of each of the three types of beacons. The marker beacon receiver is not tunable. The blue outer marker light illuminates when the receiver acquires a 75 MHz signal modulated with 400 Hz, an amber middle marker light for a 75 MHz signal modulated with 1300 Hz and, a white inner marker light for a 75 MHz signal modulated with 3000 Hz. The marker beacon system must be operationally evaluated in VFR when an ILS runway is available. The receiver sensitivity switch must be placed in LOW SENSE (the normal setting). Marker audio must be adequate. Ground test equipment must be used to verify marker beacon operation. Marker beacon with self test feature, verify lamps, audio and lamp dimming.

12-16. LONG RANGE NAVIGATION (LORAN). The LORAN has been an effective alternative to Rho/Theta R-Nav systems. Hyperbolic systems require waypoint designation in terms of latitude and longitude, unlike original R-Nav (distance navigation) systems, which define waypoints in terms of distance (Rho) and angle (Theta) from established VOR or Tacan facilities. Accuracy is better than the VOR/Tacan system but LORAN is more prone to problems with precipitation static. Proper bonding of aircraft structure and the use of high-quality static wicks will not only produce improved LORAN system performance, but can also benefit the very high frequency

(VHF) navigation and communications systems. This system has an automatic test equipment (ATE).

NOTE: Aircraft must be outside of hangar for LORAN to operate.

Normally self test check units, verification of position, and loading of flight plan will verify operation verification of proper flight manual supplements and operating handbooks on board, and proper software status can also be verified.

12-17. GLOBAL POSITIONING SYSTEM (GPS). The GPS is at the forefront of present generation navigation systems. This space-based navigation system is based on a 24-satellite system and is highly accurate (within 100 meters) for establishing position. The system is unaffected by weather and provides a world-wide common grid reference system. Database updating and antenna maintenance are of primary concern to the GPS user.

NOTE: Aircraft must be outside of hangar for ground test of GPS.

12-18. AUTOPILOT SYSTEMS. Automatic Flight Control Systems (AFCS) are the most efficient managers of aircraft performance and control. There are three kinds of autopilot; two axes, three axes, and three axes with coupled approach capability. Attention must be given to the disconnect switch operation, aural and visual alerts of automatic and intentional autopilot disconnects, override forces and mode annunciation, servo operation, rigging and bridle cable tension, and condition. In all cases the manufacturer's inspection and maintenance instructions must be followed.

12-19. ALTIMETERS. Aircraft conducting operations in controlled airspace under instrument flight rule (IFR) are required to have their static system(s) and each altimeter instrument inspected and tested within the previous 24 calendar months. Frequent functional checks of all altimeters and automatic pressure altitude reporting systems are recommended.

a. The tests required must be performed by:

(1) The manufacturer of the aircraft on which the tests and inspection are to be performed.

(2) A certificated repair station properly equipped to perform those functions and holding:

(a) An instrument rating Class I.

(b) A limited instrument rating appropriate to the make and model of appliance to be tested.

(c) A certified/qualified mechanic with an airframe rating(static system tests and inspections only). Any adjustments shall be accomplished only by an instrument shop certified/qualified person using proper test equipment and adequate reference to the manufacturer's maintenance manuals. The altimeter correlation adjustment shall not be adjusted in the field. Changing this adjustment will nullify the correspondence between the basic test equipment calibration standards and the altimeter. It will also nullify correspondence between the encoding altimeter and its encoding digitizer or the associated blind encoder.

b. Examine the altimeter face for evidence of needle scrapes or other damage. Check smoothness of operation, with particular attention to altimeter performance during decent.

c. Contact an appropriate air traffic facility for the pressure altitude displayed to the controller from your aircraft. Correct the reported altitude as needed, and compare to the reading on the altimeter instrument. The difference must not exceed 125 feet.

12-20. TRANSPONDERS. There are three modes (types) of transponders that can be used on various aircraft. Mode A provides a (non altitude-reporting) four-digit coded reply; Mode C provides a code reply identical to Mode A with an altitude-reporting signal; and Mode S has the same capabilities as Mode A and Mode C and responds to traffic alert and collision avoidance system (TCAS)-Equipped Aircraft.

a. Ground ramp equipment must be used to demonstrate proper operation. Enough codes must be selected so that each switchposition is checked at least once. Low and high sensitivity operation must be checked. Identification operation must be checked. Altitude reporting mode must be demonstrated. Demonstrate that the transponder system does not interfere with other systems aboard the aircraft, and that other equipment does not interfere with transponder operation. Special consideration must be given to other pulse equipment, such as DME and weather radar.

b. All transponders must be tested every 24-calendar months, or during an annual inspection, if requested by the owner. The test must be conducted by an authorized avionics repair facility.

12-21. EMERGENCY LOCATOR TRANS- MITTERS (ELT). The ELT must be evaluated in accordance with TSO-C91a, TSO-C126 for 406 MHz ELT's, or later TSO's issued for ELT's. ELT installations must be examined for potential operational problems at least once a year (section 91.207(d)). There have been numerous instances of interaction between ELT and other VHF installations. Antenna location should be as far as possible from other antennas to prevent efficiency losses. Check ELT antenna installations in close proximity to other VHF antennas for suspected interference. Antenna patterns of previously installed VHF antennas could be measured after an ELT installation. Tests should be conducted during the first 5 minutes after any hour. If operational tests must be made outside of this time frame, they should be coordinated with the nearest FAA Control Tower or FSS. Tests should be no longer than three audible sweeps.

12-22. INSPECTION OF ELT. An inspection of the following must be accomplished by a properly certified person or repair station within 12-calendar months after the last inspection:

a. Proper Installation.

(1) Remove all interconnections to the ELT unit and ELT antenna. Visually inspect and confirm proper seating of all connector pins. Special attention should be given to coaxial center conductor pins, which are prone to retracting into the connector housing.

(2) Remove the ELT from the mount and inspect the mounting hardware for proper installation and security.

(3) Reinstall the ELT into its mount and verify the proper direction for crash activation. Reconnect all cables. They should have some slack at each end and should be properly secured to the airplane structure for support and protection.

b. Battery Corrosion. Gain access to the ELT battery and inspect. No corrosion should be detectable. Verify the ELT battery is approved and check its expiration date.

c. Operation of the Controls and Crash Sensor. Activate the ELT using an applied force. Consult the ELT manufacturer's instructions before activation. The direction for mounting and force activation is indicated on the ELT. A TSO-C91 ELT can be activated by using a quick rap with the palm. A TSO-C91a ELT can be activated by using a rapid forward (throwing) motion coupled by a rapid reversing action. Verify that the ELT can be activated using a watt meter, the airplane's VHF radio communications receiver tuned to 121.5 MHz, or other means (see NOTE 1). Insure that the "G" switch has been reset if applicable.

d. For a Sufficient Signal Radiated From its Antenna. Activate the ELT using the ON or ELT TEST switch. A low-quality AM broadcast radio receiver should be used to determine if energy is being transmitted from the antenna. When the antenna of the AM broadcast radio receiver (tuning dial on any setting) is held about 6 inches from the activated ELT antenna, the ELT aural tone will be heard (see NOTE 2 and 3).

e. Verify that All Switches are Properly Labeled and Positioned.

f. Record the Inspection. Record the inspection in the aircraft maintenance records according to 14 CFR part 43, section 43.9. We suggest the following:

I inspected the Make/Model ______________ ELT system in this aircraft according to applicable Aircraft and ELT manufacturer's instructions and applicable FAA guidance and found that it meets the requirements of section 91.207(d).

Signed: ____________________
Certificate No. ____________________
Date: ____________________

NOTE 1: This is not a measured check; it only indicates that the G-switch is working.

NOTE 2: This is not a measured check; but it does provide confidence that the antenna is radiating with sufficient power to aid search and rescue. The signal may be weak even if it is picked up by an aircraft VHF receiver located at a considerable distance from the radiating ELT. Therefore, this check does not check the integrity of the ELT system or provide the same level of confidence as does the AM radio check.

NOTE 3: Because the ELT radiates on the emergency frequency, the Federal Communications Commission allows these tests only to be conducted within the first five minutes after any hour and is limited in three sweeps of the transmitter audio modulation.

12-23. FLIGHT DATA RECORDER. The flight data recorder is housed in a crush-proof container located near the tail section of the aircraft. The tape unit is fire resistant, and contains a radio transmitter to help crash investigators locate the unit under water. Inspection/Operational checks include:

a. Check special sticker on front of the flight data recorder for the date of the next tape replacement, if applicable.

b. Remove recorder magazine and inspect tape for the following:

(1) broken or torn tape,

(2) proper feed of tape, and

(3) all scribes were recording properly for approximately the last hour of flight.

c. Conditions for tape replacement (as applicable):

(1) There is less than 20 hours remaining in the magazine as read on the *tape remaining* indicator.

(2) Tape has run out.

(3) Broken tape.

(4) After hard landings and severe air turbulence have been encountered as reported by the pilots. After the same tape has been in use 1 year (12 months), it must be replaced.

(5) Ensure that a correlation test has been performed and then recorded in the aircraft records.

d. Refer to the specific equipment manufacturer's manuals and procedures.

e. The state-of-the art Solid-State Flight Data Recorder (SSFDR) is a highly flexible model able to support a wide variety of aeronautical radio, incorporated (ARINC) configurations. It has a Built-In Test Equipment (BITE) that establishes and monitors the mission fitness of the hardware. BITE performs verification after storage (read after write) of flight data and status condition of the memory. These recorders have an underwater acoustic beacon mounted on its front panel which must be returned to their respective manufacturer's for battery servicing. For maintenance information refer to the equipment or aircraft manufacture's maintenance instruction manual.

12-24. COCKPIT VOICE RECORDERS (CVR). CVR's are very similar to flight data recorders. They look nearly identical and operate in almost the same way. CVR's monitors the last 30 minutes of flight deck conversations and radio communications. The flight deck conversations are recorded via the microphone monitor panel located on the flight deck. This panel is also used to test the system and erase the tape, if so desired. Before operating the erase CVR mode, consult the operational manual of the manufacturer for the CVR.

a. Playback is possible only after the recorder is removed from the aircraft.

b. Refer to the specific equipment manufacturer's manuals and procedures.

c. The Solid State Cockpit Voice Recorder system is composed of three essential components a solid state recorder, a control unit (remote mic amplifier), and an area microphone. Also installed on one end of the recorder is an Under water Locator Beacon (ULB). The recorder accepts four separate audio inputs: pilot, copilot, public address/third crew member, and cockpit area microphone and where applicable, rotor speed input and flight data recorder synchronization tone input. For maintenance information refer to the equipment manufacturer's maintenance manual.

12-25. WEATHER RADAR. Ground performance shall include antenna rotation, tilt, indicator brilliance, scan rotation, and indication of received echoes. It must be determined that no objectionable interference from other electrical/electronic equipment appears on the radar indicator, and that the radar system does not interfere with the operation of any of the aircraft's communications or navigation systems.

CAUTION: Do not turn radar on within 15 feet of ground personnel, or containers holding flammable or explosive materials. The radar should never operate during fueling operations. Do not operate radar system when beam may intercept larger metallic objects closer than 150 feet, as crystal damage might occur. Do not operate radar when cooling fans are inoperative. Refer to the specific Ra

dar System equipment manufacturer's manuals and procedures.

12-26. RADOME INSPECTION. Inspection of aircraft having weather radar installations should include a visual check of the radome surface for signs of surface damage, holes, cracks, chipping, and peeling of paint, etc. Attach fittings and fastenings, neoprene erosion caps, and lightening strips, when installed, should also be inspected.

12-27. DATA BUS. Data Buses provide the physical and functional partitioning needed to enable different companies to design different avionics boxes to be able to communicate information to each other. It defines the framework for system(s) intergration. There are several types of data bus analyzers used to receive and review transmitted data or to transmit data to a bus user. Before using an analyzer, make sure that the bus language is compatible with the bus analyzer. For further information refer to ARINC specifications such as 429 Digital Information Transfer System, Mark 33 which offers simple and affordable answers to data communications on aircraft.

12-28. ELECTRIC COMPATABLITY. When replacing an instrument with one which provides additional functions or when adding new instruments, check the following electrical (where applicable) for compatibility:

a. Voltage (AC/DC).

b. Voltage polarity (DC).

c. Voltage phase (s) (AC).

d. Frequency (AC).

e. Grounding (AC/DC).

f. System impedance matching.

g. Compatibility with system to which connected.

12-29.—12-36. [RESERVED.]

SECTION 3. GROUND OPERATIONAL CHECKS FOR AVIONICS EQUIPMENT (NON ELECTRICAL)

12-37. COMPASS SWING must be performed whenever any ferrous component of the system (i.e. flux valve compensator, or Standby Compass) is installed, removed, repaired, or a new compass is installed. The magnetic compass can be checked for accuracy by using a compass rose located on an airport. The compass swing is normally effected by placing the aircraft on various magnetic headings and comparing the deviations with those on the deviation cards. Refer to CFR14, 23.1327, 14 CFR 23.1547, and the equipment or aircraft manufacturer's manual.

a. A compass swing must be performed on the following occasions:

(1) When the accuracy of the compass is suspected.

(2) After any cockpit modification or major replacement involving ferrous metal.

(3) Whenever a compass has been subjected to a shock; for example, after a hard landing or turbulence.

(4) After aircraft has passed through a severe electrical storm.

(5) After lighting strike.

(6) Whenever a change is made to the electrical system.

(7) Whenever a change of cargo is likely to affect the compass.

(8) When an aircraft operation is changed to a different geographic location with a major change in magnetic deviation. (e.g., from Miami, Florida to Fairbanks, Alaska.)

(9) After aircraft has been parked on one heading for over a year.

(10) When flux valves are replaced.

b. Precautions.

(1) The magnetic compass must be checked for accuracy in a location free of steel structures, underground pipes or cables, or equipment that produces magnetic fields.

(2) Personnel engaged in the compensation of the compass shall remove all magnetic or ferrous material from their possession.

(3) Use only nonmagnetic tools when adjusting the compass.

(4) Position the aircraft at least 100 yards from any metal object.

(5) All equipment in the aircraft having any magnetic effect on the compass must be secured in the position occupied in normal flight.

c. Compass Swing Procedures.

(1) Have the aircraft taxied to the NORTH (0°) radial on the Compass Rose. Use a hairline sight compass (a reverse reading compass with a gun sight arrangement mounted on top of it) to place the aircraft in the general vicinity. With the aircraft facing North and the person in the cockpit running the engine(s) at 1000 rpm, a mechanic, standing approximately 30 feet in front of the aircraft and facing South, "shoots" or aligns the master compass with the aircraft center line. Using hand signals, the mechanic signals the person in the cockpit to make additional adjustments to align the aircraft with the master compass. Once aligned on the heading, the person in the cockpit runs the engine(s) to approximately 1,700 rpm to duplicate the aircraft's magnetic field and then the person reads the compass.

NOTE: (1) For conventional gear aircraft, the mechanic will have to position the magnetic compass in the straight and level position or mount the tail of the aircraft on a moveable dolly to simulate a straight and level cruise configuration. (2) Remember the hairline sight compass is only intended to be used as a general piece of test equipment.

(2) If the aircraft compass is not in alignment with the magnetic North of the master compass, correct the error by making small adjustments to the North-South brass adjustment screw with a nonmetallic screw driver (made out of brass stock, or stainless steel welding rod). Adjust the N-S compensator screw until the compass reads North (0°). Turn the aircraft until it is aligned with the East-West, pointing East. Adjust the E-W compensator screw until it reads 90°. Continue by turning the aircraft South 180° and adjust the N-S screw to remove one-half of the South's heading error. This will throw the North off, but the total North-South should be divided equally between the two headings. Turn the aircraft until it is heading West 270°, and adjust the E-W screw on the compensator to remove one-half of the West error. This should divide equally the total E-W error. The engine(s) should be running.

(3) With the aircraft heading West, start your calibration card here and record the magnetic heading of 270° and the compass reading with the avionics/electrical systems on then off. Turn the aircraft to align with each of the lines on the compass rose and record the com pass reading every 30°. There should be not more than a plus or minus 10° difference between any of the compass' heading and the magnetic heading of the aircraft.

(4) If the compass cannot be adjusted to meet the requirements, install another one.

NOTE: A common error that affects the compass' accuracy is the mounting of a compass or instruments on or in the instrument panel using steel machine screws/nuts rather than brass hardware, magnetized control yoke, structural tubing, and improperly routed electrical wiring, which can cause unreasonable compass error.

(5) If the aircraft has an electrical system, two complete compass checks should be performed, one with minimum electrical equipment operating and the other with all electrical accessories on (e.g. radios, navigation, radar, and lights). If the compass readings are not identical, the mechanic should make up two separate compass correction cards, one with all the equipment on and one with the equipment off.

(6) When the compass is satisfactorily swung, fill out the calibration card properly and put it in the holder in full view for the pilot's reference.

d. Standby (wet) Compass. Adjustment and compensation of the Standby Compass may also be accomplished by using the "compass swing" method.

12-38. PNEUMATIC GYROS.

a. Venturi Systems. The early gyro instruments were all operated by air flowing out of a jet over buckets cut into the periphery of the gyro rotor. A venturi was mounted on the outside of the aircraft to produce a low pressure, or vacuum, which evacuated the instrument case, and air flowed into the instrument through a paper filter and then through a nozzle onto the rotor.

(1) Venturi systems have the advantage of being extremely simple and requiring no power from the engine, nor from any of the other aircraft systems; but they do have the disadvantage of being susceptible to ice, and when they are most needed, they may become unusable.

(2) There are two sizes of venturi tubes: those which produce four inches of suction are used to drive the attitude gyros, and smaller tubes, which produce two inches of suction, are used for the turn and slip indicator. Some installations use two of the larger venturi tubes connected in parallel to the two attitude gyros, and the turn and slip indicator is connected to one of these instruments with a needle valve between them. A suction gage is temporarily connected to the turn and slip indicator, and the aircraft is flown so the needle valve can be adjusted to the required suction at the instrument when the aircraft is operated at its cruise speed. (See figure 12-1.)

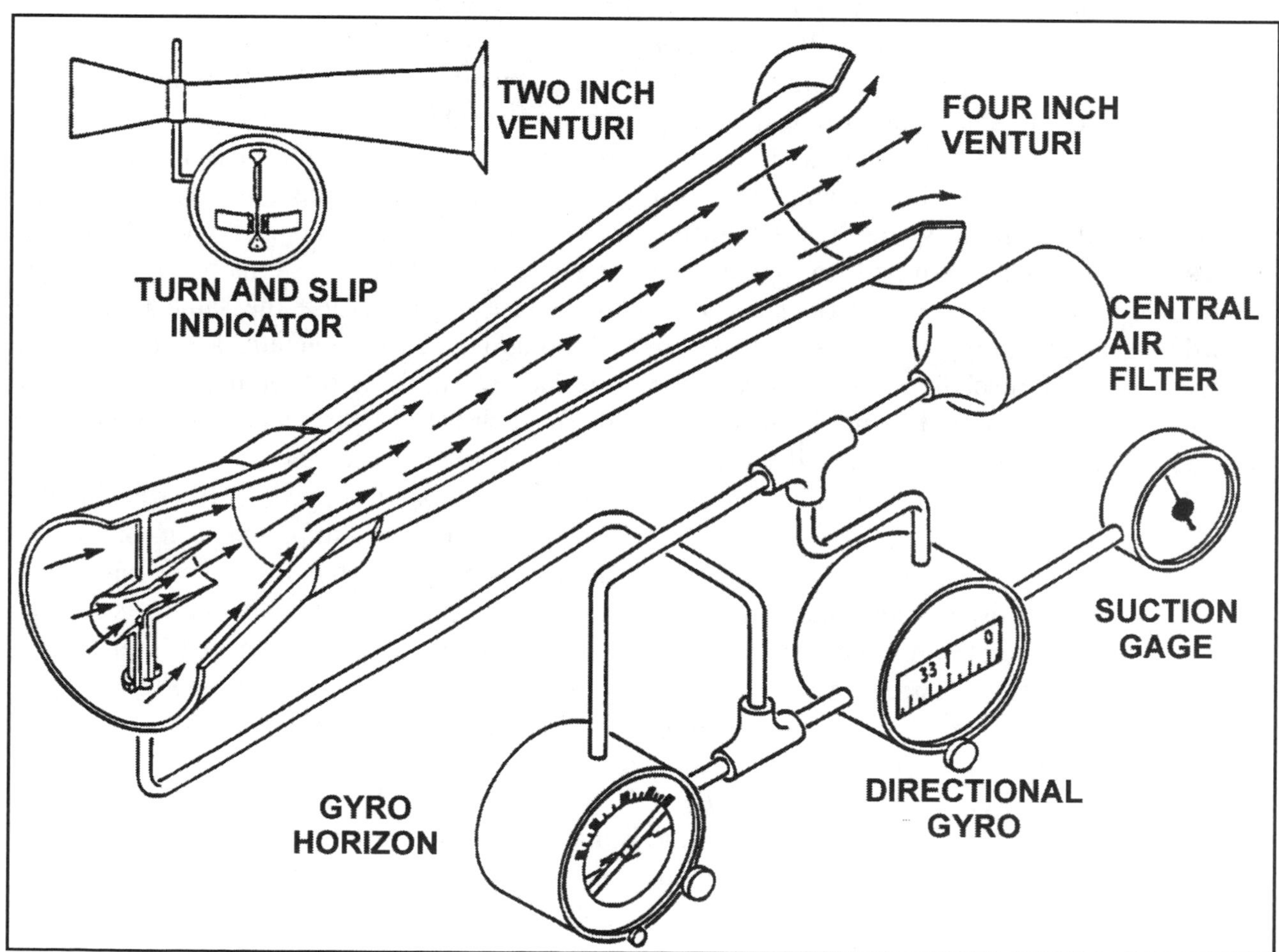

FIGURE 12-1. Venturi system for providing airflow through gyro instruments.

b. Vacuum Pump Systems. In order to overcome the major drawback of the venturi tube, that is, its susceptibility to ice, aircraft were equipped with engine driven vacuum pumps and the gyro instruments were driven by air pulled through the instrument by the suction produced by these pumps. A suction relief valve maintained the desired pressure (usually about four inches of mercury) on the attitude gyro instruments, and a needle valve between one of the attitude indicators and the turn and slip indicator restricted the airflow to maintain the desired 2 inches of suction in its case. Most of the early instruments used only paper filters in each of the instrument cases, but in some installations a central air filter was used to remove contaminants from the cabin air before it entered the instrument case.

(1) The early vacuum pumps were vane-type pumps of what is called the *wet* type-one with a cast iron housing and steel vanes. Engine oil was metered into the pump to provide sealing, lubrication, and cooling, and then this oil, along with the air, was blown through an oil separator where the oil collected on baffles and was returned to the engine crankcase. The air was then exhausted overboard. Aircraft equipped with rubber deicer boots used this discharge air to inflate the boots. But before it could be used, this air was passed through a second stage of oil separation and then to the distributor valve and finally to the boots. (See figure 12-2.)

(2) The airflow through the instruments is controlled by maintaining the suction in the instrument case at the desired level with a suction relief valve mounted between the pump and the instruments. This valve has a spring-loaded poppet that offsets to allow cabin air to enter the pump and maintain the correct negative pressure inside the instrument case.

(3) The more modern vacuum pumps are of the dry type. These pumps use carbon vanes and do not require any lubrication, as the vanes provide their own lubrication as they wear away at a carefully predetermined rate. Other than the fact that they do not require an oil separator, systems using dry air pumps are quite similar to those using a wet pump. One slight difference, however, is in the need for keeping the inside of the pump perfectly clean. Any solid particles drawn into the system through the suction relief valve can damage one of the carbon vanes, and this can lead to destruction of the pump, as the particles broken off of one vane will damage all of the other vanes. To prevent particles entering the relief valve, its air inlet is covered with a filter, and this must be cleaned or replaced at the interval recommended by the aircraft manufacturer.

c. Positive Pressure Systems. Above about 18,000 feet there is not enough mass to the air drawn through the instruments to provide sufficient rotor speed, and, to remedy this problem, many aircraft that fly at high altitude use positive pressure systems to drive the gyros. These systems use the same type of air pump as is used for vacuum systems, but the discharged air from the pump is filtered and directed into the instrument case through the same fitting that receives the filtered air when the vacuum system is used. A filter is installed on the inlet of the pump, and then, before the air is directed into the instrument case, it is again filtered. A pressure regulator is located between the pump and the in-line filter to control the air pressure so only the correct amount is directed into the instrument case.

System Filters. The life of an air-driven gyro instrument is determined to a great extent by the cleanliness of the air that flows over the rotor. In vacuum systems, this air is taken

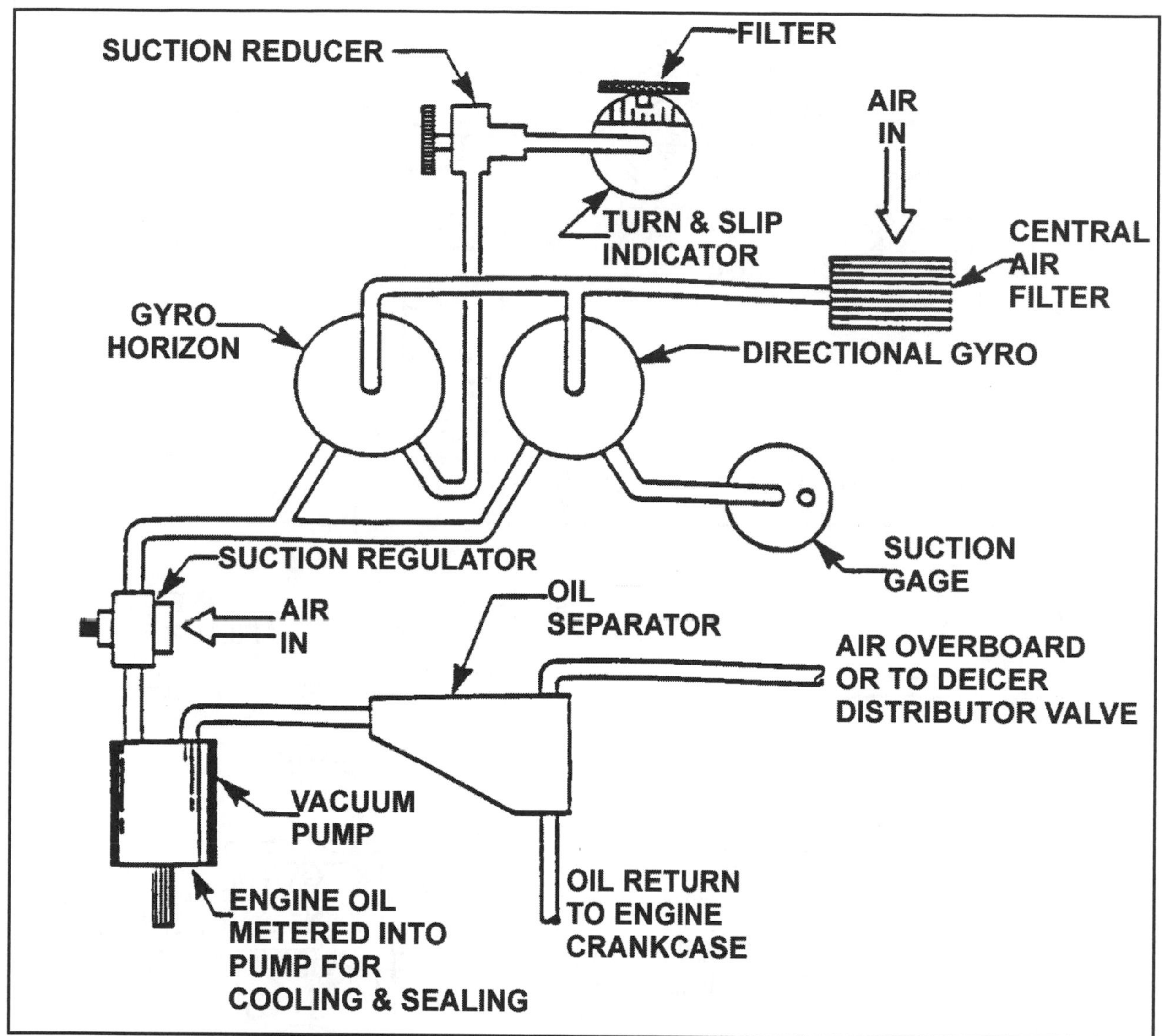

FIGURE 12-2. Instrument vacuum system using a wet-type vacuum pump.

from the cabin where there is usually a good deal of dust and very often tobacco smoke. Unless all of the solid contaminants are removed from the air before it enters the instrument, they will accumulate, usually in the rotor bearings, and slow the rotor. This causes an inaccurate indication of the instrument and will definitely shorten its service life. Dry air pumps are also subject to damage from ingested contaminants, and all of the filters in the system must be replaced on the schedule recommended by the aircraft manufacturer, and more often if the aircraft is operated under particularly dusty conditions, especially if the occupants of the aircraft regularly smoke while flying. (See figures 12-3 and 12-4.)

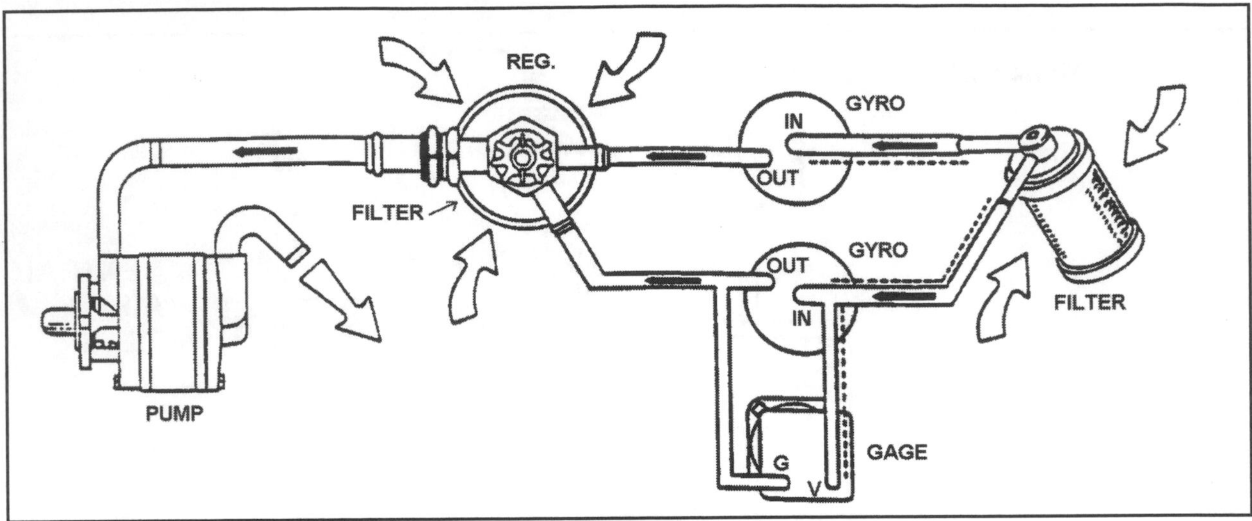

FIGURE 12-3. Instrument vacuum system using a dry-type air pump.

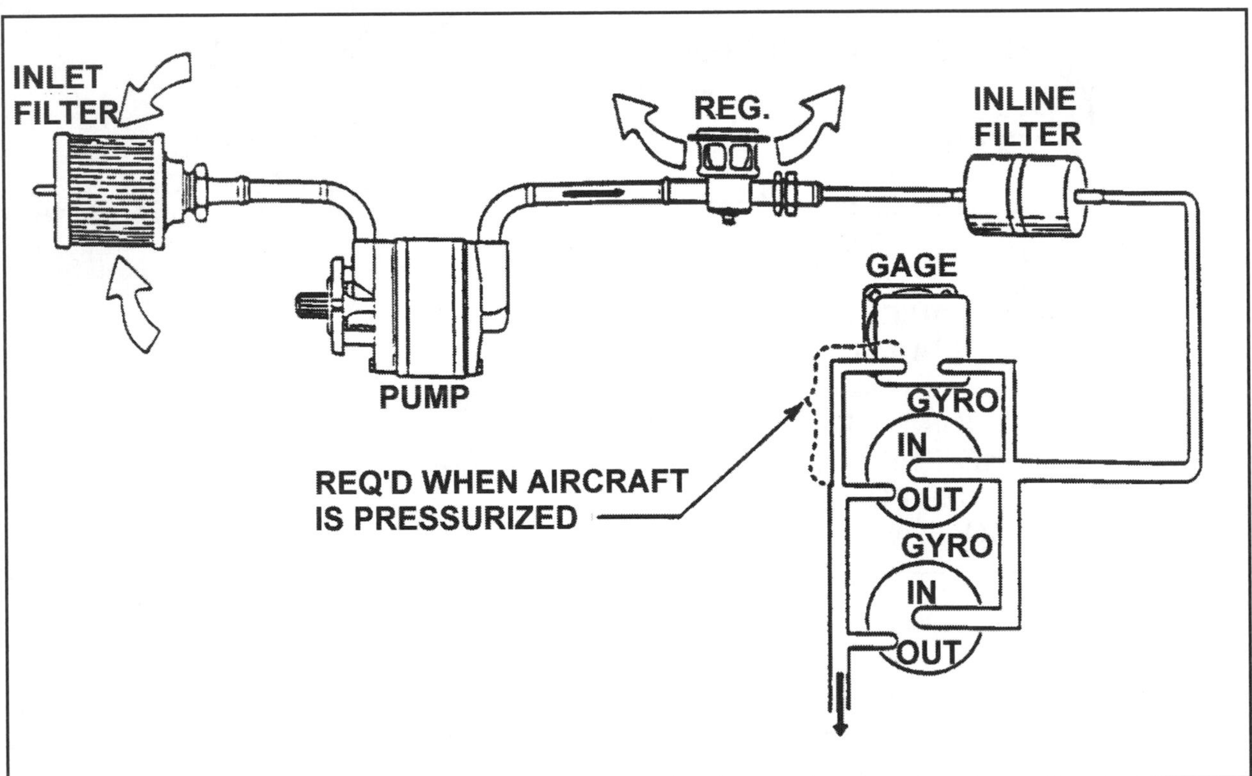

FIGURE 12-4. Instrument pressure system using a dry-type air pump.

12-39.—12-50. [RESERVED.]

SECTION 4. PITOT/STATIC SYSTEMS

12-51. GENERAL. In order for the pitot-static instruments to work properly, they must be connected into a system that senses the impact air pressure with minimum distortion and picks up undisturbed static air pressure.

Pitot pressure is ram air pressure picked up by a small open-ended tube about a ¼-inch in diameter that sticks directly into the air stream that produces a pressure proportional to the speed of the air movement. Static pressure is the pressure of the still air used to measure the altitude and serves as a reference in the measurement of airspeed.

Airspeed requires pitot, altimeter, rate of climb, and transponder-required static.

12-52. SYSTEM COMPONENTS. The conventional design of the pitot system consists of pitot-static tubes or pitot tubes with static pressure parts and vents, lines, tubing, water drains and traps, selector valves, and various pressure-actuated indicators or control units such as the altimeter, airspeed and rate-of-climb indicators, and the encoding altimeter connected to the system. (See figure 12-5.)

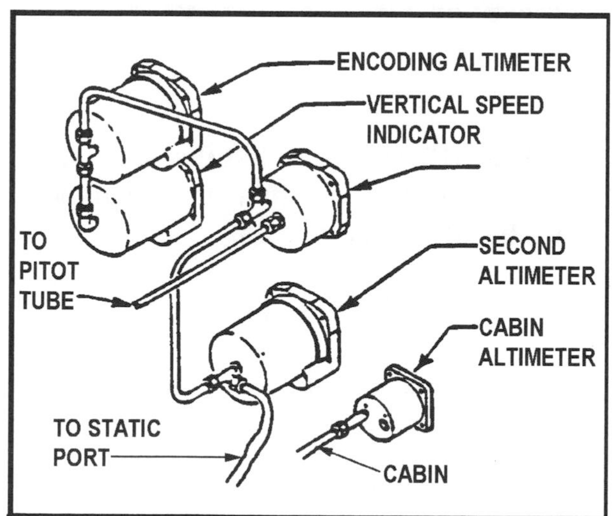

Figure 12-5. Pitot/static system for a small aircraft.

12-53. PITOT/STATIC TUBES AND LINES. The pitot tube (see figure 12-6) is installed at the leading edge of the wing of a single-engine aircraft, outside the propeller slipstream or on the fuselage of a multiengine aircraft with the axis parallel to the longitudinal axis of the aircraft, unless otherwise specified by the manufacturer.

12-54. STATIC PORTS AND VENTS (more modern trend) should be mounted flush with fuselage skin. One port is located on either side of the fuselage, usually behind the cabin.

Inspect for elevation or depression of the port or vent fitting. Such elevation or depression may cause airflow disturbances at high speeds and result in erroneous airspeed and altitude indications.

12-55. HEATER ELEMENTS. A heating element is located within the tube head to prevent the unit from becoming clogged during icing conditions experienced during flight. A switch in the cockpit controls the heater. Some pitot-static tubes have replaceable heater elements while others do not. Check the heater element or the entire tube for proper operation by noting either ammeter current or that the tube or port is hot to the touch. (See figure 12-6.)

12-56. SYSTEM INSPECTION.

a. Inspect air passages in the systems for water, paint, dirt or other foreign matter. If water or obstructive material has entered the system, all drains should be cleaned. Probe the drains in the pitot tube with a fine wire to remove dirt or other obstructions. The bottom static openings act as drains for the head's static chamber. Check these holes at regular intervals to preclude system malfunctioning.

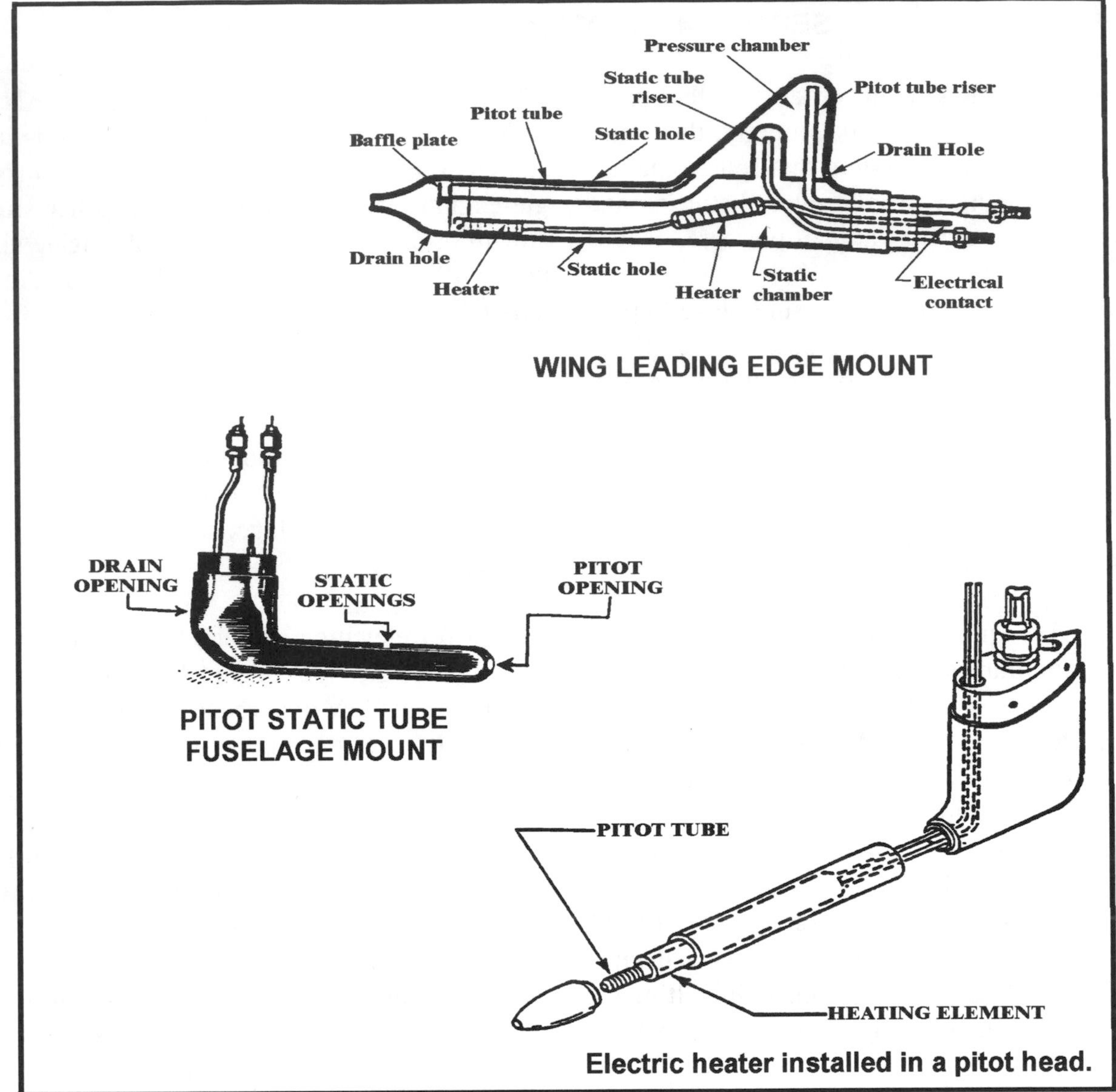

Figure 12-6. Pitot/Static Tube Head

b. Check to ensure the water drains freely. If a problem is experienced with the pitot-static system drainage or freezing at altitude, and the tubing diameter is less than 3/8-inch, replace it with larger tubing.

c. Check the pitot tube for corrosion.

(1) The pitot probe should not have any corrosion within ½-inch of the probe tip.

(2) Make sure there is no flaking which forms pits and irregularities in the surface of the tube.

NOTE: It is essential that the static air system be drained after the airplane has been exposed to rain.

12-57. SYSTEM LEAK TEST.

a. Pitot-static leak tests should be made with all instruments connected to assure that no leaks occur at instrument connections. Such tests should be accomplished whenever a connection has been loosened or an instrument replaced.

b. After the conclusion of the leak test, return the system to its normal flying configuration. Remove tape from static ports and pitot drain holes and replace the drain plug.

12-58. STATIC SYSTEM TESTS must comply with the static system tests required by 14 CFR 91.411 and be performed by an appropriately-rated repair station with the appropriate test equipment.

If the manufacturer has not issued instructions for testing static systems, the following may be used:

a. Connect the test equipment directly to the static ports, if practicable. Otherwise, connect to a static system drain or tee connection and seal off the static ports. If the test equipment is connected to the static system at any point other than the static port, it should be made at a point where the connection may be readily inspected for system integrity. Observe maintenance precautions given in paragraph 12-60 of this section.

b. Do not blow air through the line toward the instrument panel. This may seriously damage the instruments. Be sure to disconnect the instrument lines so no pressure can reach the instruments.

c. Apply a vacuum equivalent to 1,000 feet altitude, (differential pressure of approximately 1.07 inches of mercury or 14.5 inches of water) and hold.

d. After 1 minute, check to see that the leak has not exceeded the equivalent of 100 feet of altitude (decrease in differential pressure of approximately 0.0105 inches of mercury or 1.43 inches of water).

12-59. TEST PITOT SYSTEM in accordance with the aircraft manufacturer's instructions. If the manufacturer has not issued instructions for testing pitot systems, the following may be used:

a. Seal the drain holes and connect the pitot pressure openings to a tee to which a source of pressure and manometer or reliable indicator is connected.

b. Restrain hoses that can whip due to applied pressure.

c. Apply pressure to cause the airspeed indicator to indicate 150 knots (differential pressure 1.1 inches of mercury or 14.9 inches of water), hold at this point and clamp off the source of pressure. After 1 minute, the leakage should not exceed 10 knots (decrease in differential pressure of approximately 0.15 inches of mercury or 2.04 inches of water).

CAUTION: To avoid rupturing the diaphragm of the airspeed indicator, apply pressure slowly and do not build up excessive pressure in the line. Release pressure slowly to avoid damaging the airspeed indicator.

d. If the airspeed indicator reading declines, check the system for leaky hoses and loose connections.

e. Inspect the hoses for signs of deterioration, particularly at bends and at the connection points to the pitot mast and airspeed indicator. Replace hoses that are cracked or hardened with identical specification hoses. Any time a hose is replaced, perform a pressure check.

Warning: Do not apply suction to pitot lines.

12-60. MAINTENANCE PRECAUTIONS. Observe the following precautions in all pitot-static system leak testing:

a. Before any pitot/static system is tested, determine that the design limits of instruments attached to it will not be exceeded during the test. To determine this, locate and identify all instruments attached to the system.

b. A system diagram will help to determine the location of all instruments as well as locate a leak while observing instrument indications. If a diagram is not available, instruments can be located by tracing physical installation.

c. Be certain that no leaks exist in the test equipment.

d. Run full range tests only if you are thoroughly familiar with the aircraft instrument system and test equipment.

e. Make certain the pressure in the pitot system is always equal to, or greater than, that in the static system. A negative differential pressure across an airspeed indicator can damage the instrument.

f. The rate of change or the pressure applied should not exceed the design limits of any pitot or static instruments connected to the systems.

g. When lines are attached to or removed from the bulkhead feed-through fitting or at a union, ensure the line attached to the opposite end is not loose, twisted, or damaged by rotation of the fitting. Such fittings normally are provided with a hex flange for holding the fitting.

12-61. REPLACING LINES. If necessary to replace lines, observe the following installation:

a. Attach lines at regular intervals by means of suitable clamps.

b. Do not clamp lines at end fittings.

c. Maintain the slope of lines toward drains to ensure proper drainage.

d. Check the lines for leaks.

12-62. RELOCATON OF PITOT TUBE. If pitot tube relocation is necessary, perform the relocation in accordance with the manufacturer's recommendations and consider the following:

a. Freedom of aerodynamic disturbances caused by the aircraft.

b. Location protected from accidental damage.

c. Alignment with the longitudinal axis of the aircraft when in cruising flight.

12-63. TROUBLESHOOTING THE PITOT/STATIC PRESSURE SYSTEM.

a. If instruments are inoperative or erratic operation occurs, take the following action:

Table 12-1. Color codes for pitot-static systems.

CODE ABBR.	DEFINITION	COLOR
PP	PITOT PRESSURE	NATURAL
SP	STATIC PRESSURE (PILOT)	RED
	STATIC PRESSURE (CO-PILOT)	GREEN
	STATIC PRESSURE (CABIN)	YELLOW
	STATIC PRESSURE (STANDBY)	BLUE

(1) Check for clogged lines. Drain lines at the valves (especially after aircraft has been exposed to rain). Disconnect lines at the instruments and blow them out with low-pressure air.

(2) Check lines for leaks or looseness at all connections. Repair as required.

b. If the pitot heating element(s) are operative, check the following:

(1) Are circuit breaker(s) tripped?

(2) Reset the circuit breaker to determine if:

(a) The system is OK, or

(b) The circuit breaker trips again, if so:

1. Check the wiring continuity to the ground. If the switch(s) is defective, repair as necessary.

2. Check the heating element; replace it if it is defective.

12-64.—12-69. [RESERVED.]

SECTION 5. AVIONICS TEST EQUIPMENT

12-70 GENERAL. Certificated individuals who maintain airborne avionics equipment must have test equipment suitable to perform that maintenance.

12-71 TEST EQUIPMENT CALIBRATION STANDARDS.

a. The test equipment calibration standards must be derived from and traceable to one of the following:

(1) The National Institute of Standards and Technology.

(2) Standards established by the test equipment manufacturer.

(3) If foreign-manufactured test equipment, the standards of the country, where it was manufactured, if approved by the Administrator.

b. The technician must make sure that the test equipment used for such maintenance is the equipment called for by the manufacturer or equivalent.

(1) Before acceptance, a comparison should be made between the specifications of the test equipment recommended by the manufacturer and those proposed by the repair facility.

(2) The test equipment must be capable of performing all normal tests and checking all parameters of the equipment under test. The level of accuracy should be equal to or better than that recommended by the manufacturer.

(3) For a description of avionics test equipment used for troubleshooting, refer to the equipment or aircraft manufacturing instruction manual.

12-72 TEST EQUIPMENT CALIBRATION. Test equipment such as meters, torque wrenches, static, and transponder test equipment should be checked at least once a year.

c. National Institute of Standards and Technology traceability can be verified by reviewing test equipment calibration records for references to National Institute of Standards and Technology test report numbers. These numbers certify traceability of the equipment used in calibration.

d. If the repair station uses a standard for performing calibration, that calibration standard cannot be used to perform maintenance.

e. The calibration intervals for test equipment will vary with the type of equipment, environment, and use. The accepted industry practice for calibration intervals is usually one year. Considerations for acceptance of the intervals include the following:

(1) Manufacturer's recommendation for the type of equipment.

(2) Repair facility's past calibration history, as applicable.

f. If the manufacturer's manual does not describe a test procedure, the repair station must coordinate with the manufacturer to develop the necessary procedures, prior to any use of the equipment.

12-73 – 12-83. [RESERVED.]

CHAPTER 13. HUMAN FACTORS

13-1. HUMAN FACTORS INFLUENCE ON MECHANIC'S PERFORMANCE. To accomplish any task in aviation maintenance at least three things must be in evidence. A mechanic must have the tools, data, and technical skill to perform maintenance. Only recently has the aviation industry addressed the mechanic job functions, pressures, and stress, by identifying those human factors (HF) that impact the mechanics performance.

13-2. THE FAA AVIATION SAFETY PROGRAM has condensed these HF reports into a personal minimums checklist, which asks the mechanic to answer 10 'yes or no' questions before the maintenance task is begun and 10 'yes or no' questions after the task is completed. If the mechanic answers "NO" to any of the 20 questions, the aircraft should not be returned to service. We have provided the checklist in figure 13-1 for your evaluation and review. A color copy of the checklist is available from any Flight Standards District Office. Just ask for the Airworthiness Safety Program manager.

Airworthiness Aviation
Safety Program
Federal Aviation
Administration

MAINTENANCE
"PERSONAL MINIMUMS" CHECKLIST

√ Before the task

	DO I HAVE THE KNOWLEDGE TO PERFORM THE TASK?
	DO I HAVE THE TECHNICAL DATA TO PERFORM THE TASK?
	HAVE I PERFORMED THE TASK PREVIOUSLY?
	DO I HAVE THE PROPER TOOLS AND EQUIPMENT TO PERFORM THE TASK?
	HAVE I HAD THE PROPER TRAINING TO SUPPORT THE JOB TASK?
	AM I MENTALLY PREPARED TO PERFORM THE JOB TASK?
	AM I PHYSICALLY PREPARED TO PERFORM THE TASK?
	HAVE I TAKEN THE PROPER SAFETY PRECAUTIONS TO PERFORM THE TASK?
	DO I HAVE THE RESOURCES AVAILABLE TO PERFORM THE TASK?
	HAVE I RESEARCHED THE FARíS TO ENSURE COMPLIANCE?

Airworthiness Aviation
Safety Program
Federal Aviation
Administration

√After the task

	DID I PERFORM THE JOB TASK TO THE BEST OF MY ABILITIES?
	WAS THE JOB TASK PERFORMED TO BE EQUAL TO THE ORIGINAL?
	WAS THE JOB TASK PERFORMED IN ACCORDANCE WITH APPROPRIATE DATA?
	DID I USE ALL THE METHODS, TECHNIQUES, AND PRACTICES ACCEPTABLE TO INDUSTRY?
	DID I PERFORM THE JOB TASK WITHOUT PRESSURES, STRESS, AND DISTRACTIONS?
	DID I REINSPECT MY WORK OR HAVE SOMEONE INSPECT MY WORK BEFORE RETURNING TO SERVICE?
	DID I MAKE THE PROPER RECORD ENTRIES FOR THE WORK PERFORMED?
	DID I PERFORM THE OPERATIONAL CHECKS AFTER THE WORK WAS COMPLETED?
	AM I WILLING TO SIGN ON THE BOTTOM LINE FOR THE WORK PERFORMED?
	AM I WILLING TO FLY IN THE AIRCRAFT ONCE IT IS APPROVED FOR THE RETURN TO SERVICE?

FIGURE 13-1. Personal Minimum's Checklist

APPENDIX 1. GLOSSARY

The following words and terms represent some of those that are often encountered in the field of aviation. For a more complete list of definitions, a mechanic or technician should consult an aviation dictionary.

abrasion resistant PTFE—a solid insulation wall of PTFE with hard, nonconductive grit positioned midway in the wall thickness, and significantly improves the resistance of the PTFE material to damage from wear.

acetylene—gas composed of two parts of carbon and two parts of hydrogen. When burned in the atmosphere of oxygen, it produces one of the highest flame temperatures obtainable.

acetylene regulator—manually adjustable device used to reduce cylinder pressure to torch pressure and to keep the pressure constant. They are never to be used as oxygen regulators.

adherend—one of the members being bonded together by adhesive.

Airworthiness Directive—a regulation issued by the FAA that applies to aircraft, aircraft engines, propellers, or appliances, when an unsafe condition exists and that condition is likely to exist or develop in other products of the same type design.

airworthy—is when an aircraft or one of its component parts meets its type design and is in a condition for safe operation.

ambient light—the visible light level measured at the surface of the part.

ampere (A)—the basic unit of current flow. One A is the amount of current that flows when a difference of potential of 1 V is applied to a circuit with a resistance of 1 Ω. One coulomb per second.

antenna—a device designed to radiate or intercept electromagnetic waves.

anti-tear strips—strips of fabric of the same material as the airplane is covered with, laid over the wing rib under the reinforcing tape.

apparent power—the product of volts and amperes in AC circuits where the current and voltage are out of phase.

appliance—any instrument, mechanism, equipment, part, apparatus, appurtenance, or accessory, including communications equipment, that is used or intended to be used in operating or controlling an aircraft in flight, is installed in or attached to the aircraft, and is not part of an airframe, engine or propeller.

arm—a measurement of distance, in inches, feet, etc., used in weight and balance calculations. Normally only the longitudinal arm is of practical importance. The three axial arms are longitudinal arm, lateral arm, and vertical arm.

automatic direction finder (ADF)—a radio receiver utilizing a directional loop antenna that enables the receiver to indicate the direction from which a radio signal is being received; also called a radio compass.

automatic flight control system (AFCS)—a flight control system incorporating an automatic pilot with additional systems such as a VOR coupler, an ILS approach coupler, and an internal navigation system that is fully automatic, so the aircraft can be flown in a completely automatic mode.

avionics—the science and technology of electronics as applied to aviation.

azimuth—angular distance measured on a horizontal circle in a clockwise direction from either north or south.

balance—the condition of stability which exists in an aircraft when all weight and forces are acting in such a way as to prevent rotation about an axis or pivot point.

base metal—the metal to be welded, brazed, soldered, or cut.

black light—electromagnetic radiation in the near ultraviolet range of wavelength.

blade station—is a reference position on a blade that is a specified distance from the center of the hub.

bond—the adhesion of one surface to another, with or without the use of an adhesive as a bonding agent.

bonding—a general term applied to the process of electrically connecting two or more conductive objects. In aircraft, the purpose of bonding (except as applied to individual connections in the wiring and grounding systems) is to provide conductive paths for electric currents. This is accomplished by providing suitable low-impedance connections joining conductive aircraft components and the aircraft structure. Another purpose of bonding is to ensure the safe passage of current caused by lightning or static electricity through the aircraft structure.

borescope—a long, tubular optical instrument designed for remote visual inspection of surfaces.

brashness—a condition of wood characterized by low resistance to shock and by an abrupt failure across the grain without splintering.

braze welding—a welding process variation in which a filler metal, having a liquidus above 450 °C (840 °F) and below the solidus of the base metal is used. Unlike brazing, in braze welding the filler metal is not distributed in the joint by capillary action.

brazing—the joining of two pieces of metal by wetting their surface with molten alloy of copper, zinc, or tin.

bus or bus bar—solid copper strips to carry current between primary and secondary circuits; also used as jumpers.

butt joint—a joint between two members aligned approximately in the same plane.

butyrate dope—a finish for aircraft fabric consisting of a film base of cellulose fibers dissolved in solvents with the necessary plasticizers, solvent, and thinners.

cable—(electrical)—assembly of one or more conductors within an enveloping protective sheath so constructed as to permit use of conductors separately or in a group.

calibration—a set of operations, performed in accordance with a definite document procedure, which compares the measurements performed by an instrument or standard, for the purpose of detecting and reporting, or eliminating by adjustment, errors in the instrument tested.

center of gravity—that point about which the aircraft would balance if suspended. For field weight and balance purposes/control, the center of gravity is normally calculated only along its longitudinal axis (nose to tail), disregarding both the lateral and vertical location.

certification—implies that a certificate is in existence which certifies or states a qualification.

check—a lengthwise separation of the wood, the greater part of which occurs across the rings of annual growth.

chemical conversion coating (Specification MIL-C-81706)—is a chemical surface treatment used on aluminum alloys to inhibit corrosion and to provide a proper surface for paint finishing.

chord—an imaginary straight line joining the leading and trailing edges of an airfoil.

circuit—a closed path or mesh of closed paths usually including a source of EMF.

circuit breaker—a protective device for opening a circuit automatically when excessive current is flowing through it.

close-grained wood—wood with narrow and inconspicuous annual rings. The term is sometimes used to designate wood having small and closely-spaced pores, but in this sense the term "fine-textured" is more often used.

coil shot—production of longitudinal magnetization accomplished by passing current through a coil encircling the part being inspected.

compass—a device used to determine direction on the Earth's surface. A magnetic compass utilizes the Earth's magnetic field to establish direction.

compression wood—identified by its relatively wide annual rings, usually eccentric, and its relatively large amount of summer wood, usually more than 50 percent of the width of the annual rings in which it occurs. Compression wood shrinks excessively lengthwise as compared with normal wood.

conductor—a wire or other material suitable for conducting electricity.

conduit—a rigid metallic or nonmetallic casing, or a flexible metallic casing covered with a woven braid or synthetic rubber used to encase electrical cables.

contact—electrical connectors in a switch, solenoid or relay that controls the flow of current.

control panel—an upright panel, open or closed, where switches, rheostats, meters, etc., are installed for the control and protection of electrical machinery.

corrosion—the electrochemical deterioration of a metal resulting from chemical reaction to the surrounding environment.

crack—is a partial separation of material caused by vibration, overloading, internal stresses, nicks, defective assemblies, fatigue, or rapid changes in temperature.

creepage—is the conducting of electrical current along a surface between two points at different potentials. The current's ability to pass between two points increases with higher voltage and when deposits of moisture or other conductive materials exist on the surfaces.

cross grain—grain not parallel with the axis of a piece. It may be either diagonal or spiral grain or a combination of the two.

cross coat—a double coat of dope or paint. It is sprayed on in one direction, and then immediately after the solvent flash-off, it is sprayed at right angles to the first coat.

cure—to change the properties of a thermosetting resin irreversibly by vulcanization or chemical reaction. May be accomplished by the addition of curing (cross-linking) agents, with or without a catalyst, and with or without heat or pressure.

curing temperature—temperature to which a resin or an assembly is subjected in order to cure the resin.

cutting torch—a device used in gas cutting of metals.

damping—limiting the duration of vibration by either electrical or mechanical means.

data—information that supports and/or describes the original aircraft design, alteration or repair including the following: (1) drawings, sketches, and or photographs; (2) engineering analysis; (3) engineering orders; and (4) operating limitations.

datum—imaginary vertical plane from which all horizontal measurements are made or indicated when the aircraft is in level flight attitude.

derating—is a technique whereby a part is stressed in actual usage at values well below the manufacturer's rating for the part. By decreasing mechanical, thermal, and electrical stresses, the probability of degradation or catastrophic failure is lessened.

direct current electrode negative—the arrangement of direct current arc welding leads in which the work is the positive pole and the electrode is the negative pole of the welding arc.

direct current electrode positive—the arrangement of direct current arc welding leads in which the work is the negative pole and the electrode is the positive pole of the welding arc.

discontinuity—an interruption in the normal physical structure or configuration of a part, such as a crack, lap, seam, inclusion, or porosity.

distal tip—the tip, lens end, of a borescope.

dope—liquid applied to fabric to tauten it by shrinking, strengthen it, and render it airtight by acting as a filler.

Dope-proofing—protecting a surface from the chemicals and chafing qualities of dope and doped fabrics.

drape—the ability of tape and broad goods to conform to a contoured shape.

drip loop—a bundle installation method used to prevent water or other fluid contaminants from running down the wiring into a connector.

dry rot—a term loosely applied to many types of wood decay but especially to that which, when in an advanced stage, permits the wood to be easily crushed to a dry powder. The term is actually a misnomer for any decay, since all fungi require considerable moisture for growth.

dwell time—the total time that a penetrant, emulsifier (or remover), or developer remains on the surface of the test part.

dye penetrant inspection—an inspection method for surface cracks in which a penetrating dye is allowed to enter any cracks present and is pulled out of the crack by an absorbent developer. A crack appears as a line on the surface of the developer.

edge grain—edge-grain lumber has been sawed parallel with the pith of the log and approximately at right angles to the growth rings; that is, the rings form an angle of 45 degrees or more with the surface of the piece.

electricity—one of the fundamental quantities in nature consisting of elementary particles, electrons and protons, which are manifested as a force of attraction or repulsion, and also in work that can be performed when electrons are caused to move; a material agency which, when in motion, exhibits magnetic, chemical, and thermal effects, and when at rest is accompanied by an interplay of forces between associated localities in which it is present.

electromagnet—temporary magnet which is magnetized by sending current through a coil of wire wound around an iron core.

Electromagnetic/Radio Frequency Interference (EMI/RFI)—frequency spectrum of electromagnetic radiation extending from subsonic frequency to X-rays. This term should not be used in place of the term Radio Frequency Interference (RFI). (See radio frequency interference.) Shielding materials for the entire EMI spectrum are not readily available.

electromotive force (EMF)—difference of electrical potential measured in volts.

electron—a negative charge that revolves around the nucleus of an atom; a unit of a negative electrical charge.

electronics—general term that describes the branch of electrical science and technology that treats the behavior and effects of electron emission and transmission.

electron Volt (eV)—a unit of energy equal to the energy aquired by an electron falling though potential differences of one volt, approximately 1.602X 10-19 joule.

emulsion-type cleaner—a chemical cleaner which mixes with water or petroleum solvent to form an emulsion (a mixture which will separate if allowed to stand). It is used to loosen dirt, soot, or oxide films from the surface of an aircraft.

epoxy—one of various usually thermosetting resins capable of forming tight cross-linked polymer structures marked by toughness, strong adhesion, high corrosion, and chemical resistance, used especially in adhesives and surface coating.

epoxy primer—a two-part catalyzed material used to provide a good bond between a surface and a surface coating.

epoxy resin—a common thermosetting resin which exhibits exceptionally good adhesion, low cure shrinkage, and low water-absorption properties.

erosion—loss of metal from metal surfaces by the action of small particles such as sand or water.

ETFE—(Frequently referred to by the trade name, *TEFZEL*) a copolymer of PTFE and polyethylene.

exciter—small generator for supplying direct current to the alternator's field windings.

exfoliation corrosion—a form of intergranular corrosion that attacks extruded metals along their layer-like grain structure.

expandable sleeving—open-weave braided sleeving used to protect wire and cables from abrasion and other hazards (commonly known by trade name *EXPANDO*).

FEP—fluorinated ethylene propylene (commonly known by the trade name, *TEFLON*). A melt extrudable fluorocarbon resin, very similar in appearance and performance to PTFE, but with a maximum temperature rating of 200 °C.

ferrous metal—iron, or any alloy containing iron.

fiberglass—the most common material used to reinforce structures in home-built and experimental aircraft. Available as mat, roving, fabric, etc. It is incorporated into both thermoset and thermoplastic resins. The glass fibers increase mechanical strength, impact resistance, stiffness, and dimensional stability of the matrix.

fill—threads in a fabric that run crosswise of the woven material.

filiform corrosion—a thread, or filament-like corrosion which forms on aluminum skins beneath the finish.

finish—external coating or covering of an aircraft or part.

flat grain—lumber has been sawed parallel with the pith of the log and approximately tangent to the growth rings; that is, the rings form an angle of less than 45 degrees with the surface of the piece.

fluorescent—a substance is said to be fluorescent when it will glow or fluoresce when excited by ultraviolet light. Some types of dye-penetrant material use fluorescent dyes which are pulled from the cracks by a developer and observed under "black" ultraviolet light.

flux—materials used to prevent, dissolve, or facilitate removal of oxides and other undesirable surface substances. Also, the name for magnetic fields.

fretting corrosion—corrosion damage between close-fitting parts which are allowed to rub together. The rubbing prevents the formation of protective oxide films and allows the metals to corrode.

fuse—a protective device containing a special wire that melts when current exceeds the rated value for a definite period.

functional check—this test may require the use of appropriate test equipment.

galvanic corrosion—corrosion due to the presence of dissimilar metals in contact with each other.

gas cylinder—a portable container used for transportation and storage of a compressed gas.

gas tungsten arc welding—(GTAW) an arc welding process which produces coalescence of metals by heating them with an arc between a tungsten (nonconsumable) electrode and the work. Shielding is obtained from a gas or gas mixture. Pressure may or may not be used and filler metal may or may not be used.

generator—a device for converting mechanical energy into electrical energy.

global positioning system (GPS)—a navigation system that employs satellite transmitted signals to determine the aircraft's location.

grain—the direction, size, arrangement, appearance, or quality of the fibers in wood or metal.

grain - diagonal—annual rings in wood at an angle with the axis of a piece as a result of sawing at an angle with the bark of the tree.

grommet—an insulating washer that protects the sides of holes through which wires must pass/or a metal or plastic drain attached to fabric on aircraft.

gross weight—the total weight of the aircraft including its contents.

grounding—the term is usually applied to a particular form of bonding that is the process of electrically connecting conductive objects to either conductive structure or some other conductive return path for the purpose of safely completing either a normal or fault circuit.

harness—a cable harness is a group of cables or wires securely tied as a unit.

honeycomb—manufactured product consisting of a resin-impregnated sheet or metal material which has been corrugated or expanded into hexagon-shaped and other structural-shaped cells. Primarily used as core material for sandwich constructions.

inductance (L)—the ability of a coil or conductor to oppose a change in current flow.

insulator—a material that will not conduct current to an appreciable degree.

integrated circuit—small, complete circuit built up by vacuum deposition and other techniques, usually on a silicon chip, and mounted in a suitable package.

intergranular corrosion—the formation of corrosion along the grain boundaries within a metal alloy.

interlocked-grained wood—wood in which the fibers are inclined in one direction in a number of rings of annual growth, then gradually reverse and are inclined in an opposite direction in succeeding growth rings, then reverse again.

inverter—a device for converting direct current to alternating current.

laminate—a product obtained by bonding two or more laminae of the same material or of different materials.

laminated wood—a piece of wood built up of plies or laminations that have been joined either with glue or with mechanical fastenings. The term is most frequently applied where the plies are too thick to be classified as veneer and when the grain of all plies is parallel.

leakage field—the magnetic field forced out into the air by the distortion of the field within a part, caused by the presence of a discontinuity or change in section configuration.

linter—the short fiber left on the cotton seed after ginning.

localizer—that section of an ILS that produces the directional reference beam.

LORAN (Long-Range Navigation)—a radio navigation system utilizing master and slave stations transmitting timed pulses. The time difference in reception of pulses from several stations establishes a hyperbolic line of position that may be identified on a LORAN chart. By utilizing signals from two pairs of stations, a fix in position is obtained.

magnetic field—the space around a source of magnetic flux in which the effects of magnetism can be determined.

marker beacon—a radio navigation aid used in an instrument approach to identify distance to the runway. As the aircraft crosses over the marker-beacon transmitter, the pilot receives an accurate indication of the airplane's distance from the runway through the medium of a flashing light and an aural signal.

master switch—a switch designed to control all electric power to all circuits in a system.

moisture content of wood—weight of the water contained in the wood usually expressed in percentage of the weight of the kiln-dry wood.

multiconductor cable—consists of two or more cables or wires, all of which are encased in an outer covering composed of synthetic rubber, fabric, or other material.

nick—a sharp notch-like displacement of metal surface.

nomex braid—*NOMEX* is the trade name for a high-temperature polyamide thread that is braided over the larger sizes (# 8 gage and larger) of many of the military specification wires. It can be encountered in either an off-white or black/green color.

normalizing—reforming of the grain structure of a metal or alloy by proper heat treatment to relieve internal stresses.

open circuit—an incomplete or broken electrical circuit.

open-grained wood—common classification of painters for woods with large pores, such as oak, ash, chestnut, and walnut. Also known as "coarse-textured."

operational check—this is an operational test to determine whether a system or component is functioning properly in all aspects in conformance with minimum acceptable manufacture design specifications.

optical fiber—any filament or fiber made of dielectric materials that guides light whether or not it is used to transmit signals.
rifice—opening through which gas or air flows. It is usually the final opening controlled by a valve.

oxidizing—combining oxygen with any other substance. For example, a metal is oxidized when the metal is burned, i.e., oxygen is combined with all the metal or parts of it

oxidizing flame—an oxy-fuel gas flame having an oxidizing effect due to excess oxygen.

oxygen cutting—cutting metal using the oxygen jet which is added to an oxygen-acetylene flame.

oxygen regulator—manually-adjustable device used to reduce cylinder pressure to torch pressure and to keep the pressure constant. They are never to be used as fuel gas regulators.

peel ply—a layer of resin-free material used to protect a laminate for later secondary bonding (sometimes referred to as a release film).

pickling—the treatment of a metal surface by an acid to remove surface corrosion.

pitch—is the distance, in inches, that a propeller section will move forward in one revolution, or the distance a nut will advance in one revolution of the screw in a single thread.

pitch distribution—is the gradual twist in the propeller blade from shank to tip.

pitted—small irregular shaped cavities in the surface of the parent material usually caused by corrosion, chipping, or heavy electrical discharge.

pitting—the formation of pockets of corrosion products on the surface of a metal.

plastic—an organic substance of large molecular weight which is solid in its finished state and, at some stage during its manufacture or its processing into a finished article, can be shaped by flow.

polyester braid—a plastic braiding thread, when used as the outer surface of a wire, provides a cloth-like appearance.

polyimide tape—a plastic film (commonly referred to by the trade name, *KAPTON*). The tape has a dark brown color, and is frequently coated with a polyimide varnish that has a very distinct mustard yellow color. At times, the spiral edge of the outermost tape is apparent under the varnish topcoat. It may be used for wire insulation. Total polyimide tape insulated wire constructions are inactive for new design on military aircraft and are subject to the procedures defined in FAA Advisory Circular AC 29-2A Change 2 Paragraph 29.1359 in Civil Aircraft.

polyimide varnish—a liquid form of polyimide that is applied to the outer surface of a wire through the process of repeated dipping through the varnish bath with subsequent heat curing. The successive layers rarely reach a total buildup of 1 mil.

polymerization—basic processes for making large (high-polymer) molecules from small ones, normally without chemical change; can be by addition, condensation, rearrangement, or other methods.

porosity—cavity-type discontinuities in metal formed by gas entrapment during solidification.

prepreg—a mat, a fabric, or covering impregnated with resin that is ready for lay up and curing.

propeller—is a rotating airfoil that consists of two or more blades attached to a central hub which is mounted on the engine crankshaft.

protractor—is a device for measuring angles.

PTFE Tape (Insulation)—polytetrafluoroethylene tape (commonly known by the trade name, *TEFLON*), wrapped around a conductor and then centered with heat, fusing the layers into a virtually homogeneous mass. It is used both as a primary insulation against the conductor, and as an outer layer or jacket over a shield. Maximum temperature rating is 260 °C.

PVF_2 Polyvinylidine Fluoride—a fluorocarbon plastic, that when used in aircraft wire, is invariably radiation cross-linked and employed as the outer layer.

radar (radio detecting and ranging)—radio equipment that utilizes reflected pulse signals to locate and determine the distance to any reflecting object within its range.

radome—a nonmetallic cover used to protect the antenna assembly of a radar system.

rectifier—a device for converting alternating current to direct current.

reinforcing tape—a narrow woven cotton or polyester tape used over aircraft fabric to reinforce it at the stitching attachments.

relay—an electrically-operated remote-control switch.

resin—vast profusion of natural and increasingly, synthetic materials used as adhesives, fillers, binders and for insulation.

resistance—the opposition a device or material offers to the flow or current.

resonance method (ringing) of ultrasonic inspection—a method of detecting material thickness or indications of internal damage by injecting variable frequency ultrasonic energy into a material. A specific frequency of energy will produce the clearest indication of damage in a given thickness of material. When the equipment is calibrated for a specific thickness, and this thickness changes, an aural or visual alert is given.

resonant frequency—the frequency of a source of vibration that is exactly the same as the natural vibration frequency of the structure.

resonate—a mechanical system is said to resonate when its natural vibration frequency is exactly the same as the frequency of the force applied. When an object resonates at a particular frequency, the amplitude in its vibration will increase immensely as that frequency is reached and will be less on either side of that frequency.

rib—part of primary structure, whose purpose is to maintain profile of airfoil and support fabric or thin wood covering.

sacrificial corrosion—a method of corrosion protection in which a surface is plated with a metal less noble than itself. Any corrosion will attack the plating rather than the base metal.

sandwich construction—a structural panel concept consisting in its simplest form of two relatively thin, parallel sheets (face sheets) of structural material bonded to and separated by a relatively thick, lightweight core. High strength-to-weight ratios are obtained with sandwiched materials.

scarf joint—a joint made by cutting away similar angular segments of two adherents and bonding the adherents with cut areas fitted together.

score—a surface tear or break on a surface that has a depth and length ranging between a scratch and a gouge.

scratch—a superficial small cut on a surface.

semiconductor device—any device based on either preferred conduction through a solid in one direction, as in rectifiers; or on a variation in conduction characteristics through a partially conductive material, as in a transistor.

severe wind and moisture problem (SWAMP) areas—areas such as wheel wells, wing folds, and near wing flaps, and areas directly exposed to extended weather conditions are considered SWAMP areas on aircraft.

silicone rubber—a high temperature (200 °C) plastic insulation that has a substantial silicone content.

soldering—a group of welding processes that produces coalescence of materials by heating them to the soldering temperature and by using a filler metal having a liquidus not exceeding 450 °C (840 °F) and below the solidus of the base metals. The filler metal is distributed between the closely-fitted surfaces of the joint by capillary action.

solenoid—a tubular coil for the production of a magnetic field; electromagnet with a core which is able to move in and out.

spar—main spanwise structural member(s) of an aircraft wing or rotorcraft rotor. A wing may have one or two made into a single strong box to which secondary leading and trailing structures are added.

spiral grain—a type of growth in wood which the fibers take a spiral course about the bole of a tree instead of the normal vertical course. The spiral may extend right-handed or left-handed around the tree trunk.

stator—the part of an AC generator or motor which contains the stationary winding.

stress corrosion—corrosion of the intergranular type that forms within metals subject to tensile stresses which tend to separate the grain boundaries.

surface tape—pinked-edge strips of fabric doped over all seams, rib stitching, and edges of fabric covering (also called finishing tape).

switch—a device for opening or closing an electrical circuit.

tape—a tape or a "narrow fabric" is loosely defined as a material that ranges in width from 1/4 inch to 12 inches.

TCAS—traffic alert and collision avoidance system. An airborne system that interrogates mode A, C, and S transponders in nearby aircraft and uses the replies to identify and display potential and predicted collision threats.

thermocouple—device to convert heat energy into electrical energy.

thermoplastic material—a material that can be repeatedly softened by an increase in the temperature and hardened by a decrease in the temperature with no accompanying chemical change. For example, a puddle of tar on the road in the summer during the heat of day: the tar is soft and fluid; however, when cooler in the evening, it becomes solid again.

thermoset material—a material which becomes substantially infusible and insoluble when cured by the application of heat or by chemical means. A material that will undergo, or has undergone, a chemical reaction (different from a thermoplastics physical reaction) by the action of heat, catalysts, ultraviolet light, etc. Once the plastic becomes hard, additional heat will not change it back into a liquid as would be the case with a thermoplastic.

tip—part of the torch at the end where the gas burns, producing the high-temperature flame.

transceiver—a unit serving as both a receiver and a transmitter.

transformer—a device for raising or lowering AC voltage.

transmitter—an electronic system designed to produce modulated RF carrier waves to be radiated by an antenna; also, an electric device used to collect quantitative information at one point and send it to a remote indicator electrically.

transponder—an airborne receiver-transmitter designed to aid air traffic control personnel in tracking aircraft during flight.

unbonding—adhesive or cohesive failure between laminates. Compare definitions of adhesive, cohesive debond, and disbond.

very high frequency (VHF)—a frequency between 30 and 300 MHz

VHF omnirange (VOR)—an electronic air navigation system that provides accurate direction information in relation to a certain ground station.

videoscope—a type of borescope.

visible light—electromagnetic radiation that has a wavelength in the range from about 3,900 to 7,700 angstroms and that may be seen by the unaided human eye.

visual check—utilizing acceptable methods, techniques, and practices to determine physical condition and safety item.

volt—unit of potential, potential difference, or electrical pressure.

voltage regulator—device used in connection with generators to keep the voltage constant as load or speed is changed.

warp—threads in a fabric that run the length of the woven material as it comes from the mill.

watt—the unit of power; equal to a joule per second.

wattmeter—an instrument for measuring electrical power.

waveguide—a hollow, typically rectangular, metallic tube designed to carry electromagnetic energy at extremely high frequencies.

wavy-grained wood—wood in which the fibers collectively take the form of waves or undulations.

welding—a materials-joining process used in making welds.

welding rod—a form of welding filler metal, normally packaged in straight lengths.
welding torch—the device used in gas welding.

wood decay—disintegration of wood substance through the action of wood-destroying fungi.

wood decay - incipient—the early stage of decay in which the disintegration has not proceeded far enough to soften or otherwise perceptibly impair the hardness of the wood.

wood decay - typical or advanced—the stage of decay in which the disintegration is readily recognized because the wood has become punky, soft and spongy, stringy, pitted, or crumbly.

x-ray—a radiographic test method used to detect internal defects in a weld.

XL-ETFE—A process of radiation cross-linking the polymer chains is used to thermally set the plastic. This prevents the material from softening and melting at elevated temperature.

XL-Polyalkene—an insulation material based on the polyolefin family that has its normally thermomelt characteristic altered by the radiation cross-linking process to that of a nonmelt, therm-set material.

APPENDIX 2. ACRONYMS AND ABBREVIATIONS

The acronyms and abbreviations listed are some of many that are likely to be encountered by the aviation mechanic or technician involved in the maintenance of aircraft.

429—ARINC 429 data bus standard
629—ARINC 629 data bus standard
A/D—analog/digital; analog-to -digital
A/D CONV—analog-to -digital converter
A/L—autoland
AC—Advisory Circular
ac—alternating current
ACARS—ARINC Communication Addressing and Reporting System
ACO—Aircraft Certification Office
AD—Airworthiness Directive
ADC—air-data computer
ADCP—ATC dual-control panel
ADEDS—advanced electronic display system
ADF—automatic direction finder
ADI—attitude-director indicator; air data instrument
AFC—automatic frequency control
AFCS—automatic flight control system
AFDS—autopilot flight director system
AIM—Aeronautical Information Manual
AIRCOM—air/ground communications
AM—amplitude modulation
AMP or **AMPL**—amplifier
AMP—amperes
AMS—Aerospace Material Specification
AN—Army/Navy
AND—Army Navy Design
ANSI—American National Standards Institute
ANT—antenna
AP—autopilot
APB—auxiliary power breaker
APCU—auxiliary power control unit
APU—auxiliary power unit
ARINC—Aeronautical Radio Incorporated
ARNC IO—ARINC I/O error
ARNC STP—ARINC I/O UART data strip error
ASTM—American Society for Testing Materials
ATA—Air Transport Association
ATC—air traffic control
ATCT—ATC transponder
ATCTS—ATC transponder system
AUX—auxiliary
AVC—automatic volume control
AWG—American Wire Gauge
AWS—Air Weather Service
B/CU—battery/charger unit
BAT or **BATT**—battery
BCD—binary-coded decimal
BIT—binary digit; built-in test
BITE—built-in test equipment
BITS—bus interconnect transfer switch
BNR—binary numerical reference; binary
BP—band-pass
BPCU—bus power control unit
BT—bus tie
BTB—bus tie breaker
BTC—before top center
BUS—electrical bus; 429 digital data bus
C.G.—Center of Gravity
CAC—caution advisory computer
CAGE—commercial and government entity code
CAWS—central aural warning system; caution and warning system
CB, C/B, or **CKT/BKR**—circuit breaker
CDI—course-deviation indicator
CDU—central display unit
CFC—carbon fiber composite
CFDIU—centralized fault display interface unit
CFDS—centralized fault display system
CH or **CHAN**—channel
CHGR—charger
CKT—circuit
CLK—clock
CLR—clear
CMCS—central maintenance computer system
CMPTR—computer
CO—carbon monoxide
COAX—coaxial
COP—copper
CP—control panel
CRT—cathode-ray tube; circuit
CSE or **CSEU** —control system electronics unit
CSEUP—control system electronics unit panel
CT—computed tomography
CT—current transformer
CTN—caution
CU—control unit; copper
CVR—cockpit voice recorder
CW—continuous wave
D/A—digital-to-analog
DAC—digital-to analog converter
DADC—digital air-data computer
DBT—dead bus tie
dc—direct current

DCDR—decoder
DDB—digital data bus
DEMOD—demodulator
DEMUX—demultiplexer
DFDR—digital flight data recorder
DG—directional gyro
DGTL—digital
DH—decision height
DISC SOL—disconnect solenoid
DISC—disconnect
DISTR—distribution
DMA—direct memory access
DMB—dead main bus
DMC—display management computer
DME—distance-measuring equipment
DMEA—distance-measuring equipment antenna
DN—down
DU—display unit
E/E—or E & E electrical/electronic
E1-1—first shelf, number 1 equipment rack
E2-2—second shelf, number 2 equipment rack
EADF—electronic automatic direction finder
EADI—electronic attitude-director indicator
EAROM—electrically alterable read-only memory
EC—EICAS computer
ECAM—electronic centralized aircraft monitoring
EDSP—EICAS display select panel
EDU—EICAS display unit
EEC—electronic engine control
EFI—electronic flight instrument
EFIS—electronic flight instrument system
EFISCP—EFIS control panel
EFISCU—EFIS comparator unit
EFISG EFIS—symbol generator
EFISRLS EFIS—remote light sensor
EHSI—electronic horizontal-situation indicator
EHSID—electronic horizontal-situation indicator display
EHSV—electrohydraulic servo value
EICAS—engine indicating and crew alerting system
ELCU—electrical load control unit
ELEC—electric; electronic
ELECT—electrical
ELEX—electronics; electrical
ELT—Emergency Locator Transmitter
EMER GEN—emergency generator
emf—electromotive force
EMFI—electromechanical flight instrument
EMI—Electromagnetic interference
EP AVAIL—external power available
EP—external power
EPC—external power contactor
EPCS—electronic power control switch
EPROM—erasable programmable read-only memory
eV—electron volt
EXCTR—exciter
EXT PWR—external power
FAA—Federal Aviation Administration
FAA-PMA—Federal Aviation Administration Parts Manufacturer Approval
FM—frequency modulation
FM/CW—frequency modulation continuous wave
FMC—flight management computer
FMCD—flight management computer control display unit
FMCS—flight management computer system
FMS—flight management system
FOD—foreign object damage
FREQ—frequency
FSEU—flap/slat electronic unit
FW or FWD—forward
G/S—glide slope
GAL or GALY—galley
GCR—generator control relay auxiliary contact
GCU—generator control unit
GEB—generator circuit breaker
GEN—generator
GLR—galley load relay
GMAW—gas metal arc welding
GMT—Greenwich mean time; cordinated Universal time
GND PWR—ground power
GND RET—ground return
GND SVCE—ground service
GND or **GRD**—ground
GPCU—ground power control unit
GPS—global positioning system
GPSW—gear opposition switch
GPU—ground power unit
GPW—ground proximity warning
GPWS—ground proximity warning system
GSR—ground service relay
GSSR—ground service select relay
GSTR—ground service transfer relay
GTAW—gas tungsten arc welding
GWPC—ground proximity warning computer
H/L—high/low
HEA—high-frequency radio antenna
HF (hf) —high frequency (3 to 30 MHz)
HFCP—high-frequency radio control panel

HI Z—high impedance
HZ—hertz
I.D.—inner diameter
I/O—input/output
IAPS—integrated avionics processor system
IAS—indicated airspeed
IDG—integrated drive generator
IF—intermediate frequency
IFR—instrument flight rules
IGN—ignition
IIS—integrated instrument system
ILS—instrument landing system
INDL—indicator light
INST—instrument
INSTR—instrument
INTCON—interconnect
INTEC—interface
INTER—interrogation
INTPH—interphone
INV—inverter
IR ILS—receiver
kHz—kilohertz
KSI—thousands of pounds per square inch
kV—kilovolts
kVA—kilovoltamperes
kVAR—kilovoltampere reactive
L-Band—radio frequency band (390 to 1550 MHz)
LCD—liquid-crystal display
LD—load
LED—light-emitting diode
LF (lf) —low frequency (30 to 300 kHz)
LO Z—low impedance
LOC—localizer
LRU—line replaceable unit
LS—loudspeaker
LSB—lower sideband
LSPTM—limit switch position transmitter module
LT—light
LTS— lights
MAC—mean aerodynamic chord
MAN/ELEC—manual/electric
MBA—marker-beacon antenna
MCDP—maintenance control and display panel
MCDU—multipurpose control and display unit
MDE—modern digital electronics
MEC—main equipment center; main engine control
MEG or **MEGA**—million
MEK—methylethylketone
MEM—memory
METO—Maximum except-take off
MF—(mf) medium frequency (300 kHz to 3 MHz)
MHz—megahertz
MIC—microphone
MICRO-P—microprocessor
MIG—metal inert gas
MILLI—one one-thousandth (0.001)
MKR BCN—marker beacon
MS—military standard
MSDS—Material Safety Data Sheets
MSEC—(ms) milliseconds
MSG—message
MTBF—mean time-between-failure
MUX—multiplexer
mV—millivolts
NAS—National Aerospace Standard
NAV—navigation
NC—normally closed; not connected; no connection
NDB—nondirectional beacon
NDI—Nondestructive Inspection
NEG—negative
NSEC— (ns) nanoseconds
NTSB—National Transportation Safety Board
NVM—nonvolatile memory
OAM—original aircraft manufacturer
OBS—omni bearing selection
OC—overcurrent
OEM—original equipment manufacturer
OF—over-frequency
OVV or **OV**—overvoltage
OVVCO or **OVCO**—overvoltage cutout
P-S—parallel to series
PA—passenger address; power amplifier
PARA/SER—parallel to serial
PCU—passenger control unit; power control unit
PFD—permanent-magnet generator
PMA—Parts Manufacturer Approval
POS—positive
POT—potentiometer; plan of test
PR—power relay
PRL—parallel
PROM—programmable read-only memory
PROX—proximity
PSEU—proximity switch electronic unit
PSI—pounds per square inch
PWR—power
PWR SPLY—power supply
QPL—Qualified Products List
QTY—quantity
r-t—receiver-transmitter
RA—radio altimeter; radio altitude
RAD—radio

RAIND radio altimeter indicator
RAM—random-access memory
RART—radio altimeter receiver-transmitter
RAT—ram air turbine
RCCB—remote-control circuit breaker
RCL—recall
RCVR—receiver
RCVR/XMTR—receiver/transmitter
RDMI—radio distance magnetic indicator
RF (rf) —radio frequency
RFI—radio-frequency interference
RLS—remote light sensor
RMI—radio magnetic indicator
rpm—revolution per minute
RTV—room temperature vulcanizing
SAE—Society of Automotive Engineers
SAT—static air temperature
SATCOM—satellite communication
SCR—silicon-controlled rectifier
SDI—source destination identifier
SELCAL—selective calling system
SER DL—serial data link
SG—symbol generator
SITA—Société International de Telecommunications Aeronautiques
SMAW—shielded metal arc welding
SMD—surface mounted device
SNR—signal-to-noise ratio
SOL—solenoid
SOLV—solenoid valve
SOM—start of message
SOT—start of transmission
SPKR—speaker
SPR—software problem report
SQL—squelch
SSB—single sideband
SSID—Supplemental Structural Inspection Documents
SSM—sign status matrix
ST—synchro transmitter
STAT INV—static inverter
STBY—standby
STC—Supplemental Type Certificate
SW—switch
SYM GEN—symbol generator
T-R—transformer-rectifier
TAT—true air temperature
TBDP—tie bus differential protection
TC—Type Certificate
TCAS—traffic alert and collision avoidance system
TCDS—Type Certificate Data Sheets
TDC—top dead center
TFR—transfer
TIG—tungsten inert gas
TMC—thrust management computer
TMS—terminal marking sleeve
TMS—thrust management system
TMSP—thrust mode select panel
TRU—transformer-rectifier unit
TSO—Technical Standard Order
TXPDR—transponder
μ—micro
UBR—utility bus relay
UF—underfrequency
UHF—ultrahigh frequency (300 MHz to 3 GHz)
UNDF—underfrequency
UNDV—undervoltage
US—underspeed
USB (us)—upper sideband
USEC—microseconds
UV—undervoltage
UV—utraviolet
V ac, Vac, or **VAC**—volts alternating current
V dc, Vdc, or **VDC** —volts direct current
V—volts; voltage; vertical; valve
VA—volt-amperes
VAR—volt-ampere reactive
VFR—visual flight rules
VHF (vhf) —very high frequency (30 TO 300 MHz)
VLSI—very large-scale integration
VOR—VHF omnirange; visual omnirange
VORTAC—VOR tactical air navigation
VR—voltage regulator
VRMS—volts root means square
W—watts
WARN—warning
WCP—weather radar control panel
WEA—weather
WEU—warning electronics unit power supply
WPT—waypoint
WX (WXR)—weather radar
XCVR—transceiver
XDCR—transducer
XFMR—transformer
XFR—transfer
XMIT—transmit
XMTR—transmitter
XPDR—transponder

APPENDIX 3. METRIC-BASED PREFIXES AND POWERS OF 10

Atto (a)	=	quintillionth of	=	10^{-18} times
Femto (f)	=	quadrillionth of	=	10^{-15} times
Pico (p), or $\mu\mu$	=	trillionth of	=	10^{-12} times
Nano (n), or mμ	=	billionth of	=	10^{-9} times
Micro (μ)	=	millionth of	=	10^{-6} times
Milli (m)	=	thousandth of	=	10^{-3} times`
Centi (c)	=	hundredth of	=	10^{-2} times
Deci (d)	=	tenth of	=	10^{-1} times
		unity	=	$10^{0} = 1$
Deka (da)	=	ten times	=	10 times
Hecto (h)	=	hundred times	=	10^{2} times
Kilo (k)	=	thousand times	=	10^{3} times
Mega (M)	=	million times	=	10^{6} times
Giga (G), or kM	=	billion times	=	10^{9} times
Tera (T)	=	trillion times	=	10^{12} times

U.S. Department of Transportation
Federal Aviation Administration

Advisory Circular

Subject: Acceptable Methods, Techniques, and Practices – Aircraft Alterations

Date: 3/3/08
Initiated by: AFS-300

AC No: 43.13-2B

1. PURPOSE. This advisory circular (AC) contains methods, techniques, and practices acceptable to the Administrator for the inspection and alteration on non-pressurized areas of civil aircraft of 12,500 lbs gross weight or less. This AC is for use by mechanics, repair stations, and other certificated entities. This data generally pertains to minor alterations; however, the alteration data herein may be used as approved data for major alterations when the AC chapter, page, and paragraph are listed in block 8 of FAA Form 337 when the user has determined that it is:

a. Appropriate to the product being altered,

b. Directly applicable to the alteration being made, and

c. Not contrary to manufacturer's data.

2. CANCELLATION. AC 43.13-2A, Acceptable Methods, Techniques, and Practices—Aircraft Alterations, dated January 1, 1977, is canceled.

3. REFERENCE. Title 14 of the Code of Federal Regulations (14 CFR) part 43, § 43.13(a) states that each person performing maintenance, alteration, or preventive maintenance on an aircraft, engine, propeller, or appliance must use the methods, techniques, and practices prescribed in the current manufacturer's maintenance manual or Instructions for Continued Airworthiness prepared by its manufacturer, or other methods, techniques, or practices acceptable to the Administrator, except as noted in § 43.16. FAA inspectors are prepared to answer questions that may arise in this regard. Persons engaged in the inspection and alteration of civil aircraft should be familiar with 14 CFR part 43, Maintenance, Preventive Maintenance, Rebuilding, and Alterations, and part 65, subparts A, D, and E of Certification: Airmen Other than Flight Crewmembers, and applicable airworthiness requirements under which the aircraft was type-certificated.

4. COMMENTS INVITED. Comments regarding this AC should be directed to DOT/FAA: ATTN: Aircraft Maintenance Division, 800 Independence Ave., SW., Washington, DC 20591, FAX (202) 267-5115.

ORIGINAL SIGNED By

James J. Ballough
Director Flight Standards Service

CONTENTS

CHAPTER 1. STRUCTURAL DATA

100. GENERAL. Structural integrity is a major factor in aircraft design and construction. Addition or removal of equipment involving changes in weight could affect the structural integrity, weight, balance, flight characteristics, reliability, or performance of an aircraft. This chapter is generic in nature and meant to assist the aviation maintenance technician in determining structural integrity. It is not meant to circumvent utilizing a Federal Aviation Administration (FAA) engineer or the Aircraft Certification Office (ACO) when necessary.

101. STRUCTURAL DESIGN PROCESS. Structural design processes follows these steps:

a. Determine the overall load factors.

b. Estimate the resulting loads.

c. Distribute these loads over the aircraft.

d. Determine the material, size, and shape of the part.

e. Calculate the resulting stresses in the part.

f. Compare these stresses with the maximum allowable for the material used.

g. Resize the part as necessary.

102. TYPES OF LOADS AND STRESSES.

a. Limit load factors are the maximum load factors which may be expected during service (the maneuvering, gust, or ground load factors established by the manufacturer for type certification).

b. Aircraft parts may be formed out of different types of material and joined together. Each of those parts carries a load and the fastener that brings these parts together has to carry the load from one part to the other.

c. Every aircraft is subject to different types of structural stress. Stress acts on an aircraft whether it is on the ground or in flight. Stress is defined as a load applied to a unit area of material.

d. Tension is a force acting against another force that is trying to pull something apart.

e. Compression is a squeezing or crushing force that tries to make parts smaller.

f. Torsion is a twisting force.

g. Shear stress is when one piece of material slides over another.

h. Bending is a combination of two forces, compression, and tension. During bending stress, the material on the inside of the bend is compressed and the outside material is stretched in tension.

FIGURE 1-1. BENDING OF A BEAM

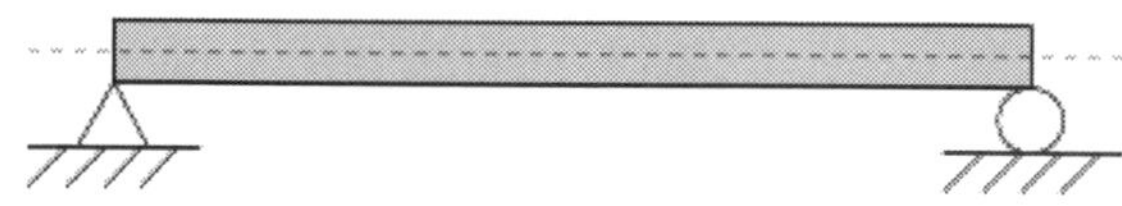

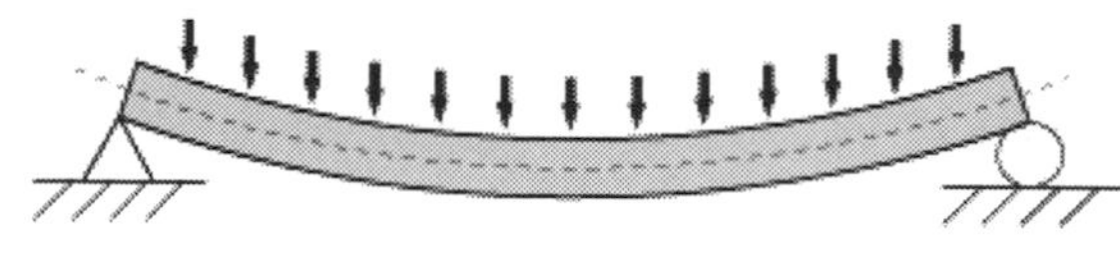

i. An aircraft structure in flight is subjected to variable stresses due to the varying loads that may be imposed. The designer's problem involves anticipating the possible stresses that the structure will have to endure and build the structure strong enough to withstand these stresses.

103. STATIC LOADS. Static loads are loads which do not undergo change in magnitude or direction during a measurement procedure. Load factors are defined as follows:

a. Limit load factors are the maximum load factors which may be expected during service (the maneuvering, gust, or ground load factors established for type certification).

b. Ultimate load factors are the limit load factors multiplied by a prescribed factor of safety. Certain loads, such as the minimum ultimate inertia forces prescribed for emergency landing conditions, are given directly in terms of ultimate loads.

c. Static test load factors are the ultimate loads multiplied by the casting, fitting, bearing, and/or other special factors, when applicable. Where no special factors apply, the static test loads are equal to the ultimate loads.

d. Critical static test load factors are the greater of the maneuvering, gust, ground, and inertia load static test load factors for each direction (up, down, starboard, port, fore, and aft).

FIGURE 1-2. TYPICAL LOAD

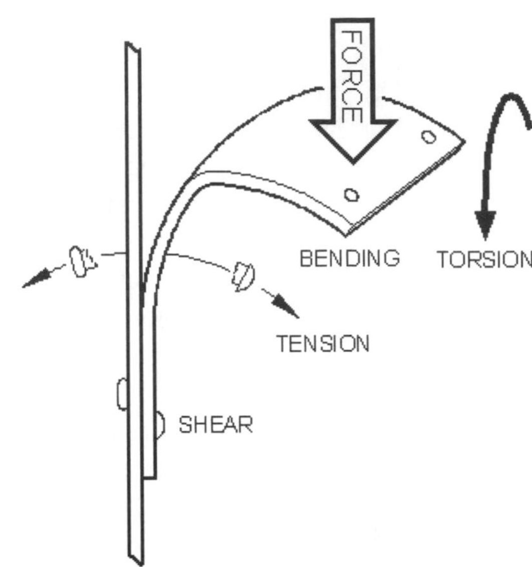

104. STRUCTURAL SIZING AND ANALYSIS. Design and size your load structures, including wing spars, wing attach fittings, stabilizers, landing gear struts, etc.

a. Static tests using the following load factors are acceptable for equipment installations. The alteration needs to comply with the limit load factors as required by the aircraft's certification basis.

TABLE 1-1. LIMIT LOAD FACTORS

Direction of Force Applied	Normal-Utility Occupant 14 CFR part 23 (CAR 3)	Acrobatic Occupant 14 CFR part 23 (CAR 3)	Items of Mass within the cabin 14 CFR part 23 (CAR 3)	Rotorcraft Occupant and Items of Mass within the cabin 14 CFR part 27 (CAR 6)
Sideward	3.0g	1.5g	4.5 g	8.0g
Upward	3.0g	4.5g	3.0 g	4.0g
Forward	9.0g	9.0g	18.0 g	16.0g
Downward	6.6g	9.0g	---	20.0g
Rearward	---	---	---	1.5 g

*When equipment mounting is located externally to one side, or forward of occupants, a forward load factor of 2.0g is sufficient.

**Due to differences among various aircraft designs in flight and ground load factors, contact the aircraft manufacturer for the load factors required for a given model and location. In lieu of specific information, the factors used for part 23 utility category are acceptable for aircraft that never exceed the speed of 250 knots and the factors used for part 23 acrobatic category.

b. The following is an example of determining the static test loads for a 7-pound piece of equipment to be installed in a utility category aircraft (part 23).

TABLE 1-2. SAMPLE LOAD FACTORS

Load Factors (From the above table)	Static Test Loads (Load factor X 7 pounds)
Sideward 1.5g	10.5 pounds
Upward 3.0g	21.0 pounds
Downward 6.0g	42.0 pounds
Forward 9.0g	63.0 pounds

c. When an additional load is to be added to structure already supporting previously installed equipment, determine the capability of the structure to support the total load (previous load plus added load). If the additional load requires access to applicable design data or the capability to reverse engineer the installation, further assistance may be required from FAA engineering or the ACO or an appropriately rated Designated Engineering Representative (DER).

105. STATIC TESTS.

CAUTION: The aircraft and/or equipment can be damaged in applying static loads, particularly if a careless or improper procedure is used. It is recommended, whenever practicable, that static testing be conducted on a duplicate installation in a jig or mockup which simulates the related aircraft structure. Static test loads may exceed the yield limits of the assemblies being substantiated and can result in partially sheared fasteners, elongated holes, or other damage which may not be visible unless the structure is disassembled. If the structure is materially weakened during testing, it may fail at a later date. Riveted sheet metal and composite laminate construction methods especially do not lend themselves to easy detection of such damage. To conduct static tests:

a. Determine the weight and center of gravity position of the equipment item.

b. Install attachment in the aircraft or preferably in a jig using the applicable static test load factors.

c. Determine the critical ultimate load factors for the sideward, upward, downward, and forward directions. A hypothetical which follows steps (1) through (4) below pertains to the example in Figure 1-3, Hypothetical of Determining Static Test Loads.

(1) Convert the gust, maneuvering, and ground load factors obtained from the manufacturer or FAA engineer or DER to determine the ultimate load factors. Unless otherwise specified in the airworthiness standards applicable to the aircraft, ultimate load factors are limit load factors multiplied by a 1.5 safety factor. (See columns 1, 2, and 3 for items A, B, and C.)

(2) Determine the ultimate inertia load forces for the emergency landing conditions as prescribed in the applicable airworthiness standards. (See items D and E, column 3.)

(3) Determine what additional load factors are applicable to the specific seat, litter, berth, or cargo tiedown device installation. The ultimate load factors are then multiplied by these factors to obtain the static test factors.

(4) Select the highest static test load factors obtained in steps 1, 2, and/or 3 for each direction (sideward, upward, downward, and forward). These factors are the critical static test load factors used to compute the static test load. (See column 6.)

d. Apply a load at center of gravity position (of equipment item or dummy) by any suitable means to demonstrate that the attachment and structure are capable of supporting the required loads. When no damage or permanent deformation occurs after 3 seconds of applied static load, the structure and attachments are acceptable. Should permanent deformation occur after 3 seconds, modifications or reinforcements are required to the affected structure. Additional load testing is not necessary.

e. Static tests may need to be reviewed by an FAA Engineer so that appropriate limitations, procedures, checks and balances may be applied to mitigate any risks.

106. MATERIALS AND WORKMANSHIP. Use materials conforming to an accepted Government or industry standard such as Army/Navy and Air Force/Navy (AN) National Aerospace Standards (NAS), Technical Standard Order (TSO), or Military Specifications (MIL-SPEC).

a. Suitability and durability of materials used for parts, the failure of which could adversely affect safety, must:

(1) Be established by experience or tests;

(2) Meet approved specifications that ensure the strength and other properties, assumed in the design data; and

(3) Take into account the effects of environmental conditions, such as temperature and humidity, expected in service.

b. Workmanship must be of a high standard.

107. MATERIAL STRENGTH PROPERTIES AND DESIGN VALUES. Material strength properties must be based on enough tests of material meeting specifications to establish design values on a statistical basis such as Metallic Materials Properties D Specification (MIL-HNDK-5). Design values must be chosen to minimize the probability of structural failure due to material variability. Except as provided in subparagraph e below, compliance with this paragraph must be shown by selecting design values that ensure material strength with the following probabilities:

a. Where applied loads are eventually distributed through a single member within an assembly, the failure of which would result in loss of structural integrity of the component — 99 percent probability with 95 percent confidence.

b. For redundant structure, in which the failure of individual elements would result in applied loads being safely distributed to other load carrying members — 90 percent probability with 95 percent confidence.

c. The effects of temperature on allowable stresses used for design in an essential component or structure must be considered where thermal effects are significant under normal operating conditions.

d. The design of the structure must minimize the probability of catastrophic fatigue failure, particularly at points of stress concentration.

e. Design values greater than the guaranteed minimums required by this paragraph 107 may be used where only guaranteed minimum values are normally allowed. For example, if a "premium selection" of the material is made, in which, a specimen of each item is tested before use to determine if the actual strength properties of that particular item are equal or exceed those used in design.

108. FASTENERS. Use hardware conforming to an accepted Government or industry standard such as AN, NAS, TSO, or MIL-SPEC. Attach equipment in such a way that prevents loosening in service due to vibration.

a. Each removable fastener must incorporate two retaining devices in case one retaining device should fail during flight operations.

b. Fasteners and their locking devices must not be adversely affected by the environmental conditions associated with the particular installation.

c. No self-locking nut may be used on any bolt subject to rotation in operation, unless a non-friction locking device is used in addition to the self-locking device.

109. PROTECTION OF STRUCTURE. Provide protection against deterioration or loss of strength due to corrosion, abrasion, electrolytic action, or other causes. Each part of the structure must:

a. Be suitably protected against deterioration or loss of strength in service due to any cause, including:

(1) Weathering,

(2) Corrosion, and

(3) Abrasion.

b. Havc adequate provisions for ventilation and drainage.

110. ACCESSIBILITY. Provide adequate provisions to permit close examination of equipment or adjacent parts of the aircraft that regularly require inspection, adjustment, lubrication, etc. For each part that requires maintenance, inspection, or other servicing, appropriate means must be incorporated into the aircraft design to allow such servicing to be accomplished.

111. AFFECTS ON WEIGHT AND BALANCE. Assure that the altered aircraft can be operated within the weight and center of gravity ranges listed in the FAA type certificate (TC), data sheet, or Aircraft Listing Aircraft Specification. When adding items of mass to the aircraft, the effect on the empty weight and balance should be considered and documented in the aircraft weight and balance. Determine that the altered aircraft will not exceed maximum gross weight. (If applicable, correct the loading schedule to reflect the current loading procedure.) Consult the current edition of AC 43.13-1, Acceptable Methods, Techniques, and Practices—Aircraft Inspection and Repair, for weight and balance computation procedures.

112. AFFECTS ON SAFE OPERATION. Install equipment in a manner that will not interfere with or adversely affect the safe operation of the aircraft (controls, navigation equipment operation, etc.).

a. The factor of safety prescribed in 14 CFR part 23, § 23.303 must be multiplied by the highest pertinent special factors of safety prescribed in 14 CFR §§ 23.621 through 23.625 for each part of the structure where strength is:

(1) Uncertain,

(2) Likely to deteriorate in service before normal replacement, or

(3) Subject to appreciable variability because of uncertainties in manufacturing processes or inspection methods.

b. Unless otherwise provided, a factor of safety of 1.5 must be used.

113. CONTROLS AND INDICATORS. Locate and identify equipment controls and indicators so they can be operated and read from the appropriate crewmember position.

114. PLACARDING. Label equipment requiring identification and, if necessary, placard operational instructions. Amend weight and balance information as required. Any required placards installed or required by an alteration must be added to the Limitations Section of the Instructions for Continued Airworthiness to ensure that maintenance personnel will know if a required placard is missing in future inspections.

115. THRU 199. RESERVED

FIGURE 1-3. HYPOTHETICAL OF DETERMINING STATIC TEST LOADS

UTILITY CATEGORY AIRCRAFT (14 CFR PART 23)							
Type of load	Direction	LOAD FACTORS					
		1 Limit	2 X Safety	3 = Ultimate	4 X Special	5 Static = Test	6 Critical Static Test
A. Maneuvering	Fwd	(None)		---------------	--------------	-------------	
	Down	6.2g	1.5	9.30g	--------------	9.3g	9.3g
	Side	(None)	---------------	---------------	--------------	-------------	
	Up	-3.8g	1.5	-5.7g	--------------	-5.7g	5.7g
	Aft	1.0g	1.5	1. 5g	--------------	1.5g	
B. Gust (=30 FPS @ KVc)	Fwd	(None)	---------------	---------------	--------------	-------------	
	Down	6.0g	1.5	9.0g	--------------	9.0g	
*For locations aft of fuselage Sta. 73.85.	Down*	6.4g	1.5	9.6g	--------------	9.g	*9.6g
	Side	1.6g	1.5	2.4g	--------------	2.4g	2.4g
	Up	-2.8g	1.5	-4.2g	--------------	-4.2g	
	Aft	(None)	--------------	---------------	--------------	-------------	
C. Ground	Fwd	6.6g	1.5	9.9g	--------------	9.9g	9.9g
	Down	4.0g	1.5	6.0g	--------------	6.0g	
D. Ultimate Inertia Forces for Emergency Landing Condition (Section 23.561).	Fwd	Already Prescribed as Ultimate		9.0g	--------------	-------------	
	Fwd.**			4.5g	--------------	-------------	**4.5g
	Down			(None)	--------------	-------------	
	Side			1.5g	--------------	1.5g	
**For Separate cargo compartments.	Up	Already Prescribed as Ultimate		-3.0g	--------------	-3.0g	
	Aft			(None)	--------------	-------------	

FIGURE 1-3. HYPOTHETICAL OF DETERMINING STATIC TEST LOADS – CONTINUED

UTILITY CATEGORY AIRCRAFT (14 CFR PART 23)							
Type of load	Direction	LOAD FACTORS					
		1 Limit	2 X Safety	3 = Ultimate	4 X Special	5 Static = Test	6 Critical Static Test
E. Ultimate Inertia Forces for Emergency Landing Condition For Seat, Litter, & Berth Attachment to Aircraft Structure (Section 23.785).	Fwd	Already Prescribed as Ultimate		9.0g	1. 33	12.0g	12.0g
	Down			(None)	---------------	--------------	
	Side			1. 5g	1.33	2.0g	
	Up			-3.0g	1.33	-4.0g	
	Aft			(None)	---------------	--------------	

* Asterisks denote special load conditions for the situation shown.

CHAPTER 2. COMMUNICATION, NAVIGATION, AND EMERGENCY LOCATOR TRANSMITTER SYSTEM INSTALLATIONS

200. PURPOSE. This chapter describes installation considerations and requirements for basic stand-alone, installations of communication, navigation, and emergency locator transmitter (ELT) equipment.

NOTE: Stand-alone installations do not depend on other systems or complex interfaces to function.

201. HAZARDS AND WARNINGS.

a. When installing these systems follow the aircraft and equipment manufacturers' instructions as appropriate. Practice a "clean as you go" philosophy. Ensure that equipment and systems function properly and perform their intended function(s).

b. Alterations of aircraft that are performed to accommodate the installation of radio equipment must be evaluated for their impact on aircraft design and operation. Refer to Advisory Circular (AC) 23.1309-1, Equipment, Systems, and Installations in Part 23 Airplanes, (as amended) for additional information concerning the evaluation for equipment, systems, and installations in Title 14 of the Code of Federal Regulations (14 CFR) part 23 airplanes.

c. Frequently an alteration to accommodate the installation of radio equipment will have little impact on the design or operation of an aircraft; however, all potential elements of impact must be considered. One approach is to evaluate each element independently.

d. Consider the impact when weight and balance or structural load limits of an added system exceeds existing installations. Consider the impact when radio frequency such as electromagnetic interference (EMI), high intensity radiated fields (HIRF), or lightning may negatively affect existing systems (e.g., accuracy of the magnetic compass).

e. When evaluating elements of impact consider the before and after states. No further analysis of weight and balance may be required if an object of similar size and weight was previously installed in a location. If mounting attach points were previously substantiated to support a specific load and the same load or less is being installed, the previous analysis may be referenced.

NOTE: Data that is referenced must be available and reviewed.

f. When structures must be fabricated or reinforced, the standard practices approved for repairs if applicable may be employed. AC 43.13-1 (as amended), Acceptable Methods, Techniques, and Practices—Aircraft Inspection and Repair, may provide structural design data for fabrication of mountings and attachments.

g. Ensure that the capacity of the aircraft's charging system is not exceeded, including any required additional allowances.

h. Care should be taken to ensure that cables or wires will not interfere with the aircraft's flight, engine, or propeller controls.

i. When removing older radios/wiring/power supplies and installing newer solid state components weigh the old equipment and perform a new weight and balance calculation. This is important since differences in the location and weight of equipment will shift the center of gravity.

j. Refer to AC 43.13-1 (as amended), chapter 10 and FAA-H-8083-1, Aircraft Weight and Balance Handbook, for additional information on determining of weight and balance.

202. CONSIDERATIONS WHEN INSTALLING AVIONICS EQUIPMENT. When installing radio equipment, use areas or locations designated by the airframe manufacturer and use factory supplied brackets or racks. Follow the aircraft manufacturer's installation instructions. When this information is not available, use locations in the aircraft of known load carrying capabilities. Baggage compartments and cabins or cockpit floors are good mounting platforms provided the floor attachments meet the strength requirements. Another method is to fabricate support racks, brackets, or shelves and attach them to the aircraft structure to provide a mounting that will withstand the inertia forces stipulated in chapter 1.

a. General Considerations. Ensure the following:

(1) There is appropriate air circulation to ensure proper cooling and dissipation of any heat generated or present. Consider the flammability characteristics of all associated elements.

(2) There are appropriate clearances to prevent mechanical damage to other parts of the aircraft or from other parts of the aircraft.

(3) There is protection provided to the component or article from any fluids or fumes that may be expected and that the component or article will not cause any fluids or fumes to be present that may result in damage to the aircraft or its occupants.

(4) That any interference, environmental or operational, to an aircraft or any system of the aircraft is identified and minimized as to not affect airworthiness of the aircraft.

(5) That flight characteristics of the aircraft are not altered unless appropriately identified and the changes are within the certified design limits.

b. Structural Consideration. Consider the following:

(1) Structural requirements of a mounting must be considered (see chapter 1).

FIGURE 2-1. FORCE DIAGRAM NORMAL-UTILITY CATEGORY

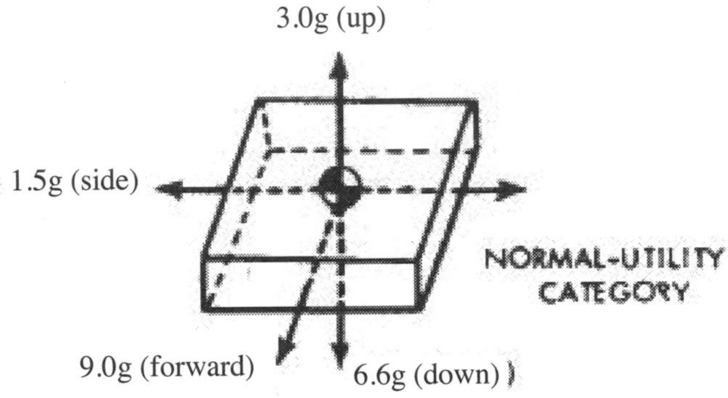

(2) Alterations that include making additional cutouts or enlargements of existing panel cutouts must be evaluated to maintain structural integrity. Some aircraft instrument panels are load bearing structures.

(3) Loads must be determined to be within the structural design limits of the supports.

(4) Instrument panels as well as other panels throughout the aircraft may be structural or nonstructural in design. Structural loads must be adequately transferred to primary airframe members.

(5) Methods and practices described elsewhere in this AC and in AC 43.13-1 (as amended) may be employed for the fabrication of attachments and structure.

FIGURE 2-2. TYPICAL FABRICATED PANEL MOUNTING

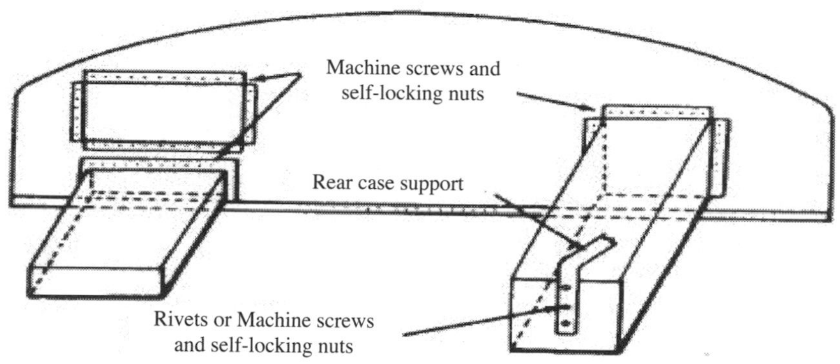

FIGURE 2-3. TYPICAL LAYOUTS

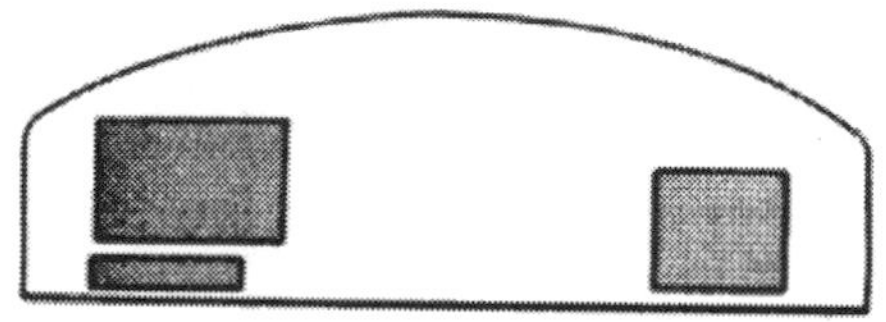

Typical layout older aircraft

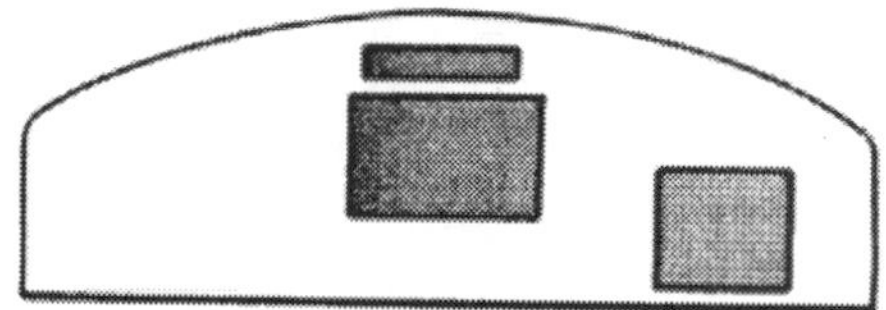

Typical layout newer aircraft

(6) Existing structures may be reinforced or strengthened using methods described in AC 43.13-1 (as amended).

203. INSTRUMENT PANEL MOUNTING. This paragraph is supplemented by AC 43.13-1 (as amended), chapter 2, and is applicable to the installation of radio units in instrument panels.

a. Stationary Instrument Panels—Nonstructural and Structural. The stationary instrument panel in some aircraft is part of the primary structure. Prior to making any additional "cutouts" or enlargements of an existing "cutout," determine if the panel is part of the primary structure. If the panel is structural, make additional "cutouts" or the enlargement of existing "cutouts" in accordance with the aircraft manufacturers' instructions, or substantiate the structural integrity of the altered panel in a manner acceptable to the Administrator. Radius all corners and remove all burrs from "cutout" and drilled holes.

b. Added Equipment Stationary Instrument Panel. When radio equipment is to be installed in a stationary panel already supporting instruments, glove compartments, etc., determine the capability of the panel to support the total load.

c. Case Support. To minimize the load on a stationary instrument panel, whenever practicable, install a support between the rear (or side) surface of the radio case and a nearby structural member of the aircraft (Figure 2-2).

d. Added Equipment—Shock-Mounted Panels. When installing radio equipment designed for use in shock-mounted panels, total accumulated weight of equipment installed must not exceed the weight carrying capabilities of the shock mounts. Determine that the structure to which the shock mounts are connected is satisfactory for supporting the added weight.

e. Existing Factory Fasteners. When possible, use existing plate nuts and machine screws provided by the aircraft manufacturer for attachment of the radio case or rack. If additional fastening is required, use machine screws and elastic stop nuts (preferably plate nuts).

f. Magnetic Direction Indicator. As a function of the radio installation, determine if it is necessary to swing the compass. Install a suitable placard which indicates the compass error with the radio(s) on and off. Maximum acceptable deviation in level flight is 10 degrees on any heading. The following is an example of a typical compass calibration card (refer to current edition of AC 43.13-1, chapter 12, on how to swing a compass).

TABLE 2-1. TYPICAL COMPASS CALIBRATION CARD

FOR	N	30	60	E	120	150
Radio On Steer	4°	35°	63°	93°	123°	154°
Radio Off Steer	358°	27°	58°	88°	118°	148°

FOR	S	210	240	W	300	330
Radio On Steer	183°	214°	244°	274°	304°	337°
Radio Off Steer	178°	208°	238°	268°	293°	327°

204. OTHER MOUNTING AREAS. The following are acceptable methods for installing radio equipment at other than instrument panel locations.

a. Shock-mounted Units.

(1) Wood or Composition Flooring. Secure the shock-mounted base assembly (suitable to radio unit) directly to the floor using machine screws. Add a doubler to the bottom of the floor thereby sandwiching the composition floor between each shock-mount foot and the doubler. Subsequent removal and reinstallation of the shock-mount foot will be facilitated if plate nuts are secured to the doubler. Where practicable, use small retaining screws to keep the doubler in position. Install a ground strap between the radio rack and metal structure of the aircraft.

FIGURE 2-4. TYPICAL SHOCK-MOUNTED BASE

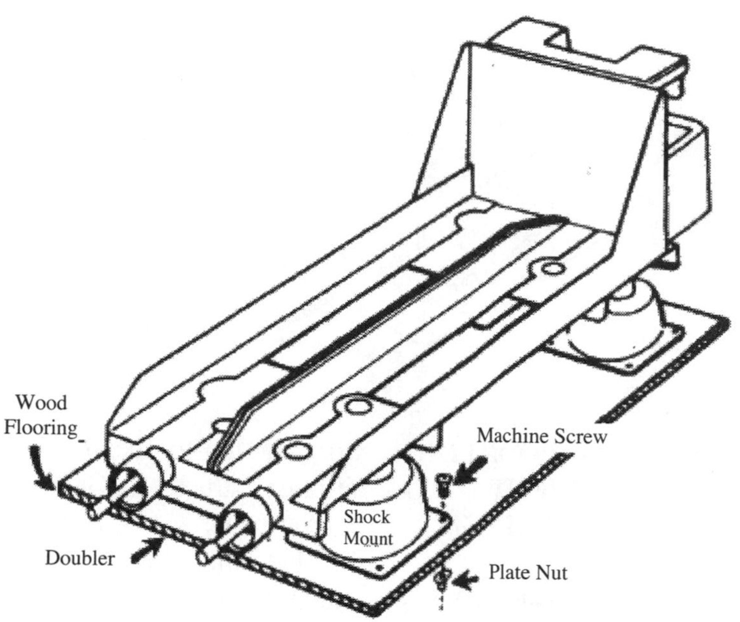

(2) **Metal Flooring.** Secure the shock-mounted base assembly directly to the floor using machine screws, washers, and self-locking nuts. Floor area under and around thc radio mounting bases may require installation of doublers or other reinforcement to prevent flexing and cracking. Installation of plate nuts on the floor or doubler will facilitate removal and installation of the shock mounts. Install a ground strap between the shock mount foot and the radio rack.

FIGURE 2-5. TYPICAL SHOCK-MOUNTED BASE

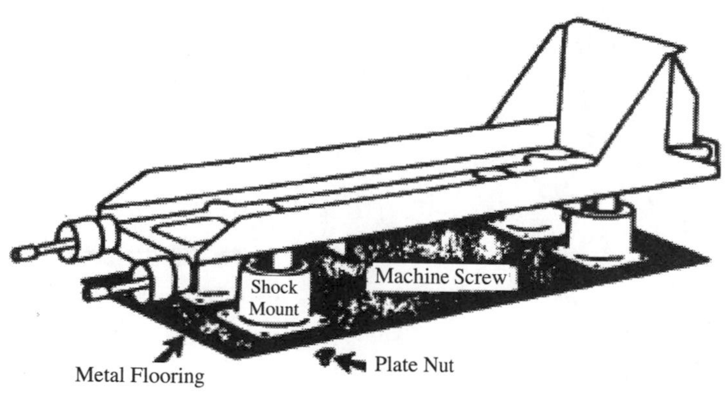

b. Rigid-Mounted Unit Base. Secure radio mounting base plate(s) to the floor (wood, composite, or metal) using machine screws as shown in Figure 2-6. Use a reinforcing plate or large area washers or equivalent under wood or composite flooring. When the mounting base is secured to wood or composite material, install a ground strap between the base and aircraft metal structure.

FIGURE 2-6. TYPICAL RIGID BASE PLATE MOUNT

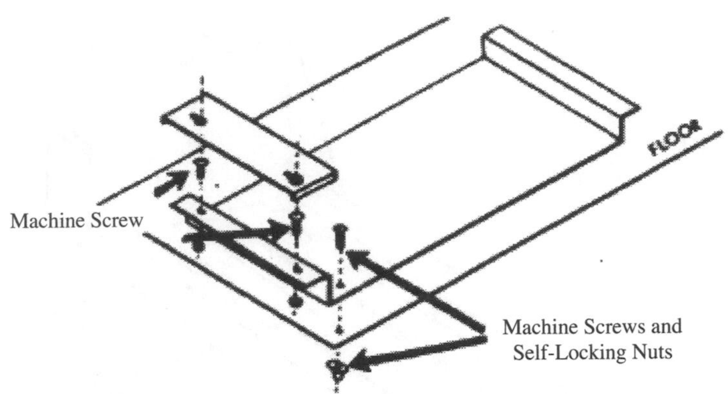

205. FABRICATION OF SUPPORTING BRACKETS FOR ATTACHMENT TO STRUCTURE OTHER THAN FLOORING.

a. Typical supporting brackets usually consist of a shelf or platform upon which the radio unit mounting base assembly can be installed in the same manner as described in applicable paragraph 203.

b. Fabricate bracket in accordance with good aircraft design, layout, assembly practices, and workmanship to obtain results compatible with the airframe structure. Generally, the thickness of bracket material will depend on the size or area of the platform and load it must sustain in accordance with provisions set forth in chapter 1.

c. Use a rivet size and pattern compatible with the aircraft structure to provide the strength needed to assure support of the loads imposed under all flight and landing conditions.

FIGURE 2-7. TYPICAL UNDERSEAT INSTALLATION

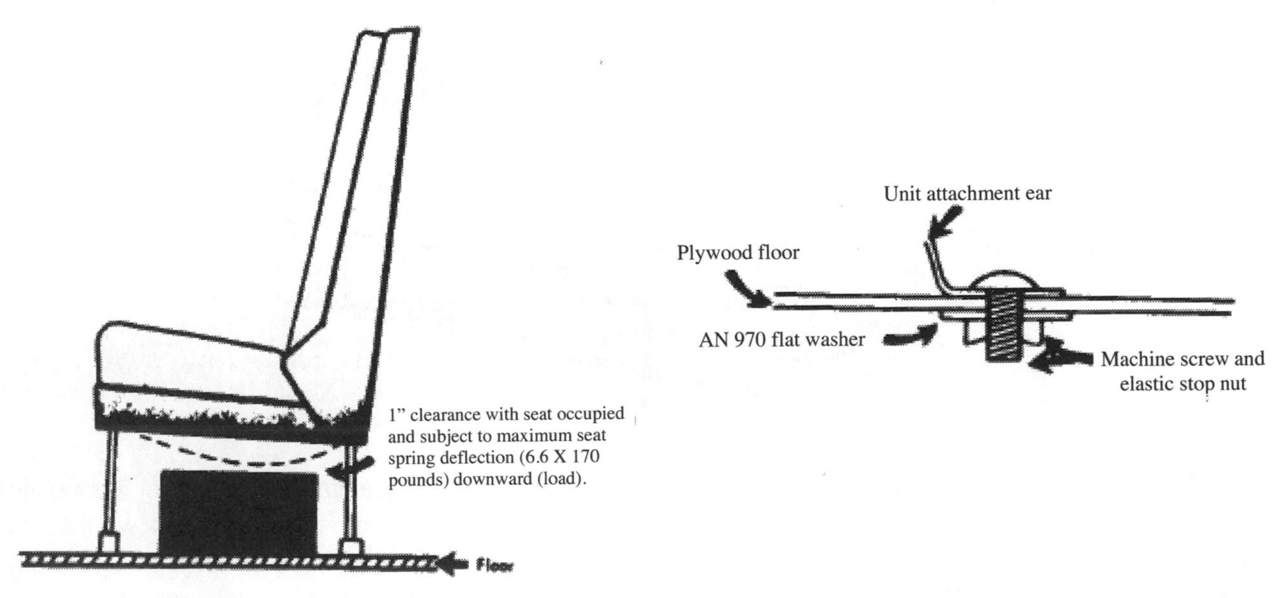

NOTE: To increase the strength of floor attachment points, metal reinforcement may be installed as needed.

206. REINFORCEMENT OF SUPPORTING STRUCTURE.

a. Attach equipment to the supporting structure of the aircraft so that its supported load will be transmitted to aircraft structural members. If direct attachment to the existing structure (bulkheads, horizontal stringers, etc.) is not feasible, add the necessary stringers, doublers, bulkhead flange reinforcements, etc., to provide adequate support and assure load transfer to the primary structure. When attaching to the existing structure ensure that the attachment does not weaken the structure. Alteration to primary structure may require approved engineering data.

b. Placard. Fasten onto the shelf or bracket a permanent placard (as the example below) stating the design load which the installed structure is determined capable of supporting.

"Shelf load not to exceed

__________lbs."

FIGURE 2-8. TYPICAL REMOTE UNIT MOUNTING BASE-VERTICAL OR HORIZONTAL OTHER THAN STRUCTURE TO FLOOR

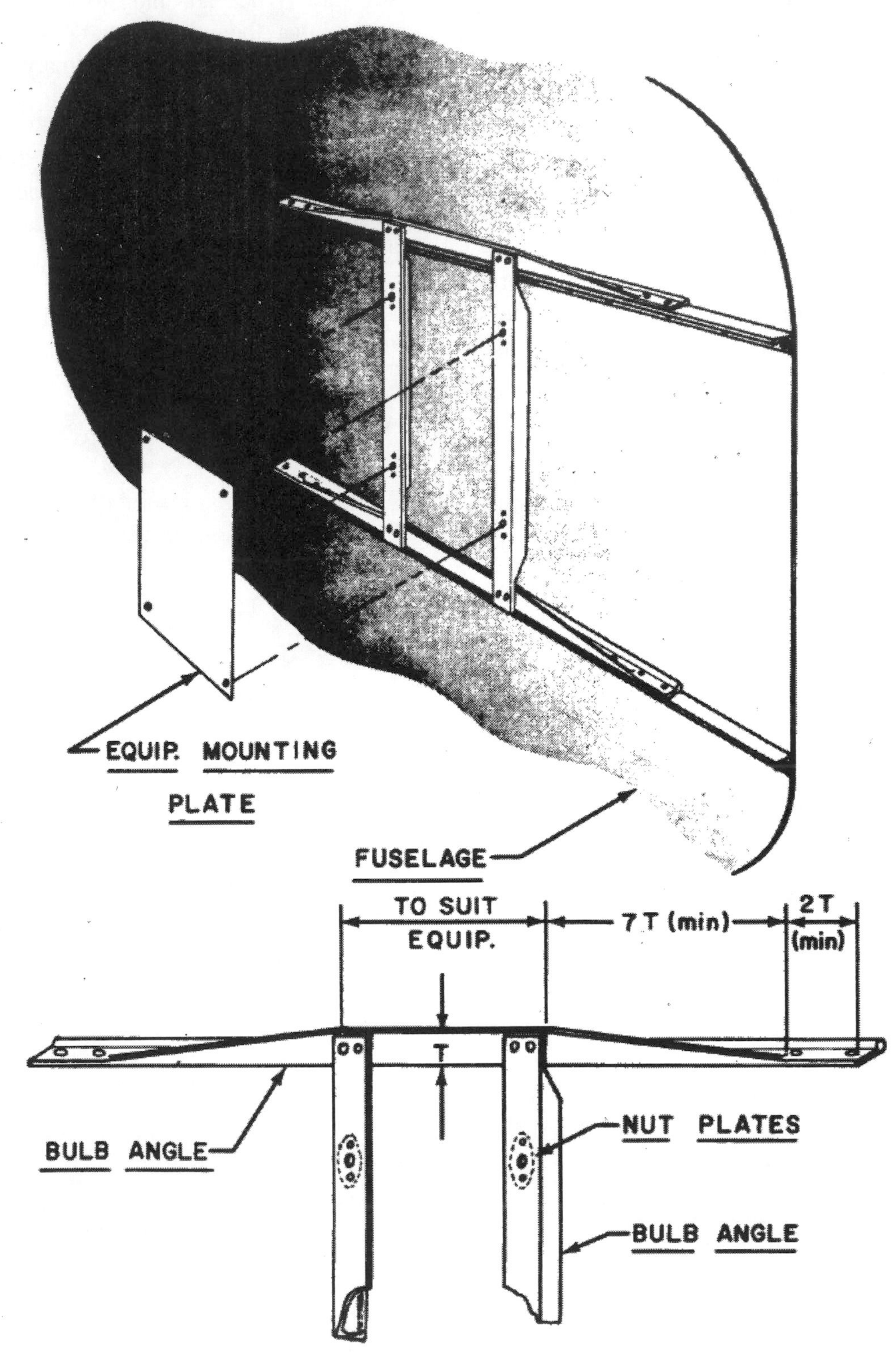

FIGURE 2-9. TYPICAL SHELF INSTALLATION

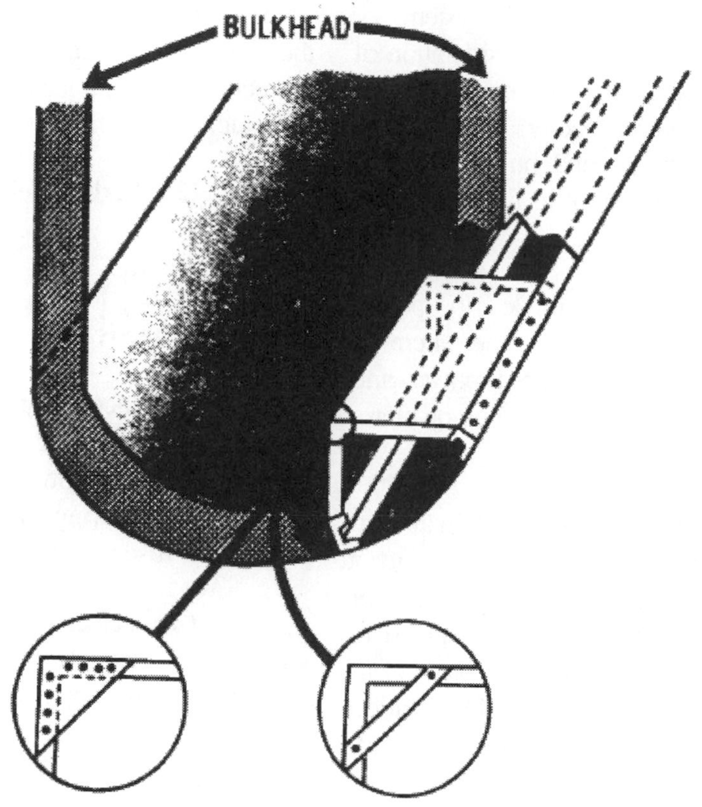

NOTE: Use standard aircraft practices and procedures for fabrication and attachment of the shelf. Reinforce fore and aft corners with gussets or bulb angle.

NOTE: Fabricate a platform using 2017T4(17ST) or equivalent. Apply standard aircraft practices for fabrication and installation.

NOTE: The equipment manufacturer mounting bases that meet load requirements and can be utilized are acceptable.

FIGURE 2-10. TYPICAL ATTACHMENT OF SUPPORT STRUCTURE TO TUBULAR FRAME OTHER THAN STRUCTURE TO FLOOR

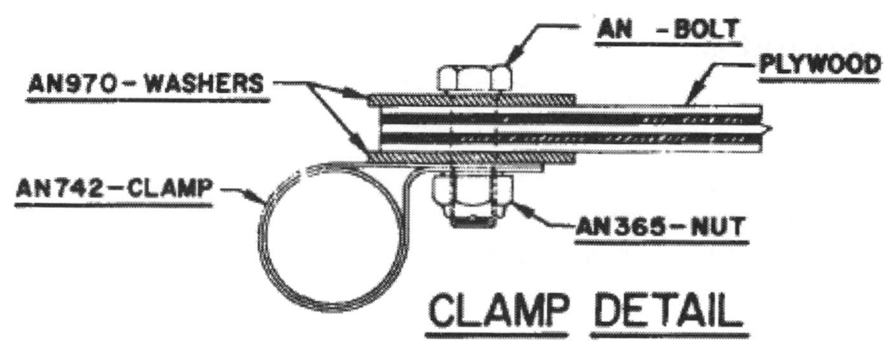

207. ELECTRICAL REQUIREMENTS.

a. Installation of an electrical system or component into an aircraft requires consideration of the electrical load, the appropriate power distribution circuit, and available power capacity. The specific requirements for a system depend on its electrical characteristics and the criticality of its application for use in the operation of the aircraft.

b. The total energy available to power electrical systems is referred to as the aircraft's capacity. It includes available stored power and generated power. This will vary depending on phase of flight or type of operation.

c. The critical distribution circuit of an aircraft is designed to transfer power from source to a system determined critical to the operation or function of the aircraft. This circuit is required to include additional capacity and circuit protection as required by applicable regulations. Distribution systems should be designed to facilitate load-shedding procedures. Power distribution system design includes the following concerns. Reference AC 43.13-1 (as amended), chapter 11, for:

(1) Circuit protection.

(2) Wire selection.

(3) Connectors, switches, and termination devices.

(4) Wire routing.

(5) Wiring/cable support.

(6) Identification.

d. Installation of Wiring.

(1) Use a type and design satisfactory for the purpose intended.

(2) Install in a manner suitably protected from fuel, oil, water, other detrimental substances, oxygen systems, and abrasion damages.

e. Power Sources.

(1) Connect radio electrical systems to the aircraft electrical system at the power source protective device, a terminal strip, or use a plug and receptacle connection.

(2) Radio electrical systems must function properly whether connected in combination or independent.

f. Protective Devices.

(1) Incorporate a "trip free" re-settable type circuit breaker or a fuse in the power supply from the bus. Mount in a manner accessible to a crewmember during flight for circuit breaker resetting or fuse replacement and label.

(2) Select circuit breakers or fuses that will provide adequate protection against overloading of the radio system wiring.

(3) Connect all leads in such a manner that the master switch of the aircraft will interrupt the circuit when the master switch is opened, unless the equipment is intended to be powered when the master switch is open.

(4) Radio system controls are to provide independent operation of each system installed and be clearly labeled to identify their function relative to the unit of equipment they operate.

g. Wire Bundle Separation from Flammable Fluid Lines.

(1) Physically separate radio electric wire bundles from lines or equipment containing oil, fuel, hydraulic fluid, alcohol, or oxygen.

(2) Mount radio electrical wire bundles above flammable fluids lines and securely clamp to the structure. (In no case must radio electrical wire bundles be clamped to lines containing flammable fluids.)

h. Cable Attachment to Shock-Mounted Units. Route and support electrical wire bundles and mechanical cables in a manner that will allow normal motion of equipment without strain or damage to the wire bundles or mechanical cables.

i. Radio Bonding. It is advisable to electrically bond radio equipment to the aircraft in order to provide a low impedance ground and to minimize radio interference from static electrical charges. When electrical bonding is used, observe the following:

(1) Keep bonding jumpers as short as possible.

(2) Prepare bonded surfaces for best contact (resistance of connections should not exceed 0.003 ohm).

(3) Avoid use of solder to attach bonding jumpers. Clamps and screws are preferred.

(4) For bonding aluminum alloy, use aluminum alloy or tinned or cadmium-plated copper jumpers. Use brass or bronze jumpers on steel parts.

(5) When contact between dissimilar metals cannot be avoided, put a protective coating over the finished connection to minimize corrosion.

208. ELECTRICAL LOAD ANALYSIS PROCEDURE.

a. Available Power Supply. To preclude overloading the electric power system of the aircraft when additional equipment is added, perform an electrical load analysis to determine whether the available power is adequate. Radio equipment must operate satisfactorily throughout the voltage range of the aircraft electrical system under taxi, takeoff, slow cruise, normal cruise, and landing operating conditions. Compute the electrical load analysis for the most adverse operating conditions, typically this is for night and/or instrument flight.

b. One method for the analysis may be found in the ASTM International, Standard Guide for Aircraft Electrical Load and Power Source Capacity Analysis, F 2490-05.

c. Applicable elements of a previously performed electrical load analysis if available may be reused.

209. ELECTROMAGNETIC COMPATIBILITY.

a. Electromagnetic Interference (EMI) may disrupt the performance of systems and has varying degrees of consequence. These consequences may be identified as: no safety effect, minor, major, hazardous, or catastrophic. The purpose of electromagnetic compatibility (EMC) analysis and testing is to assure that equipment does not cause interference with any existing aircraft system function, and that existing systems do not cause any interference with the new equipment. (Refer to Table 2-2.)

TABLE 2-2. RELATIONSHIP PROBABILITIES, SEVERITY OF FAILURE CONDITIONS

Classification of Failure Conditions	No Safety Effect	<--Minor-->	<--Major-->	<--Hazardous-->	<--Catastrophic-->
Effect on Airplane	No effect on operational capabilities or safety	Slight reduction in functional capabilities or safety margins	Significant reduction in functional capabilities or safety margins	Large reduction in functional capabilities or safety margins	Normally with hull loss
Effect on Occupants	Inconvenience for passengers	Physical discomfort for passengers	Physical distress to passengers, possibly including injuries	Serious or fatal injury to an occupant	Multiple fatalities
Effect on Flightcrew	No effect on flightcrew	Slight increase in workload or use of emergency procedures	Physical discomfort or a significant increase in workload	Physical distress or excessive workload impairs ability to perform tasks	Fatal Injury or incapacitation

b. When EMC characteristics are known, the need for and extent of EMC testing can be determined by a review of those characteristics. Knowing specific target frequencies, EMC testing can focus on the aircraft systems (and even those susceptible frequencies in the case of tunable systems) likely to be affected by interference. Where sensitive systems or potentially strong sources of EMI are involved, more intensive evaluation will be required.

TABLE 2-3. COMMONLY USED RADIO FREQUENCIES ON AIRCRAFT

Range	Hz	Mode	Function
190-1750	kHz	Rx	ADF Navigation
2-30	MHz	Tx/Rx	HF Communications
75	MHz	Rx	Marker Beacon Receiver
108-112	MHz	Rx	ILS Localizer Receiver
108-118	MHz	Rx	VHF Omnirange (VOR) Receiver
118-137	MHz	Tx/Rx	VHF Communications
243	MHz	Tx	Emergency Locator Xmtr (Satellite)
328.6-335.4	MHz	Rx	ILS Glide Slope Receiver
406.3	MHz	Tx	Emergency Locator Transmitter
960-1215	MHz	Tx/Rx	DME System
1027-1033	MHz	Tx/Rx	Transponder & TCAS Systems
1087-1093	MHz	Tx/Rx	Transponder & TCAS Systems
1575.42	MHz	Rx	GPS Satellite Navigation

c. On-aircraft EMC tests for systems or equipment should be conducted. If lab test data is available it should be used to guide the planning of these tests. If lab test analysis is not available a more comprehensive EMC testing on the aircraft systems and equipment typically needs to be performed.

(1) The aircraft should not be close to large reflecting surfaces such as buildings or other aircraft. Use of ground power is not recommended, as ground power units are not routinely checked for output quality.

(2) All normally closed circuit breakers should be closed and power should be supplied to all normally powered AC and DC distribution busses during testing.

(3) The aircraft should be in flight configuration. Doors and hatches that might be in any interfering signal's path should be in the position they would normally be in during flight.

(4) Aircraft systems being tested should be operated and monitored for indication of interference. (It is essential that systems determined critical for the operation of the aircraft are tested.) The following systems, if installed, should be included in the aircraft EMC test plan.

TABLE 2-4. AIRCRAFT ELECTRICAL AND ELECTRONIC SYSTEMS

System
ADF
Air Data Systems
Altitude Alert System
ATC Transponder
Audio Distribution System
Autopilot/Flight Guidance System
Compass/Directional Gyro Systems
DME
Electronic Flight Control System
Electronic Flight Instrument System (EFIS)
Global Positioning System (GPS)
Marker Receiver System
VHF Communications
VOR/LOC/GS
Newly Installed Electrical/Electronic System

210. FUNCTIONAL HAZARD ASSESSMENT (FHA).

NOTE: Refer to AC 43.1309-1 (current edition) for additional information on FHA.

a. Many older aircraft designs did not provide for all weather operations or potential increases in the pilot's reliance on installed systems and equipment. Requirements to assure design safeguards against hazards have developed as technologies have become available and pilots have increased their reliance on installed systems and equipment. A fundamental analysis to assure design safeguards is accomplished through a functional hazard assessment.

b. Alterations that involve systems or equipment that perform critical functions or that include complex designs that have a high degree of integration, use of new technology, or novel applications of conventional technology, must be assessed to determine the severity of failure conditions. Complexity in itself does not drive the need to perform a system safety analysis but the effect of a failure does. Comparison with similar, previously approved systems is sometimes helpful.

c. Evaluate the system to determine if it is essential or not essential to safe operation. For aircraft of 6,000 pounds or less maximum weight, refer to the regulations incorporated by reference in the type certificate, unless the Administrator has found that the change is significant in an area.

d. Determine if the equipment has any unacceptable, adverse affect when operated.

e. Determine if the operation of the installed equipment has an adverse affect on equipment not essential to safe operation, and if a means exists to inform the pilot of the effect.

f. Determine if a failure or malfunction of the installed equipment could result in unacceptable hazards.

g. Design requirements and methodology of hazard resolution differing upon application and type of aircraft (i.e., single-engine, multiengine, commuter use).

(1) Operation of equipment that has an adverse effect on other equipment essential to safe operation of the aircraft is unacceptable.

(2) Operation of equipment that has an adverse effect on other equipment that is not essential to safe operation of the aircraft may be acceptable if there is a means to inform the pilot of the effect.

(3) If a probable failure or malfunction will result in a hazard in a multiengine aircraft it is unacceptable.

(4) If a probable failure or malfunction will result in a hazard in a single-engine aircraft its impact must be minimized.

211. THRU 299. RESERVED

CHAPTER 3. ANTENNA INSTALLATION

300. PURPOSE. The purpose of this chapter is to describe antenna installation methods and practices. An antenna that is installed on an aircraft must function properly and may not adversely affect other systems or equipment.

301. HAZARDS AND WARNINGS.

a. Follow antenna manufacturer's instructions and recommendations when they are available and appropriate, and not contrary to the instructions of the aircraft manufacturer.

b. Extension of the landing gear or flaps may impact belly-mounted antenna performance.

302. ADDITIONAL REFERENCES. For further information concerning acceptable methods, techniques, and practices concerning alteration involving specific structures refer to the appropriate chapter of Advisory Circular (AC) 43.13-1, Acceptable Methods, Techniques, and Practices—Aircraft Inspection and Repair (as amended), and Civil Aviation Regulation 6, Rotorcraft Airworthiness; Normal Category.

303. STRUCTURAL SUPPORT.

a. The antenna's structural load, plus any required allowances, may not exceed the design capacity of the structure intended to support it. It is important to understand the operational characteristics of the aircraft and consider forces that occur during flight (dynamic loading) as well as those that occur when the aircraft is not in motion (static loading). For example, an aircraft designed without flaps may employ a side slip procedure, to lose altitude, during which the direction of airflow across the fuselage is not in line with the aircraft longitudinal axis. Antenna mountings on these aircraft need to be designed and evaluated for the direction of airflow that occurs during such an operation.

b. Whenever possible, an antenna should be mounted to a flat surface. Minor aircraft skin curvature can be accommodated with the use of an appropriate gasket but if gaps over 0.020" appear between the base plate and mounting surface, use of a mounting saddle is recommended.

c. Since antenna systems typically require a ground plane (this may be a conductive surface that the antenna mounts to) any separation of an antenna from its ground plane may impact performance. Contact the manufacturer for recommendations if a gasket or mounting saddle is needed.

FIGURE 3-1. ANTENNA MOUNT WITH SADDLE

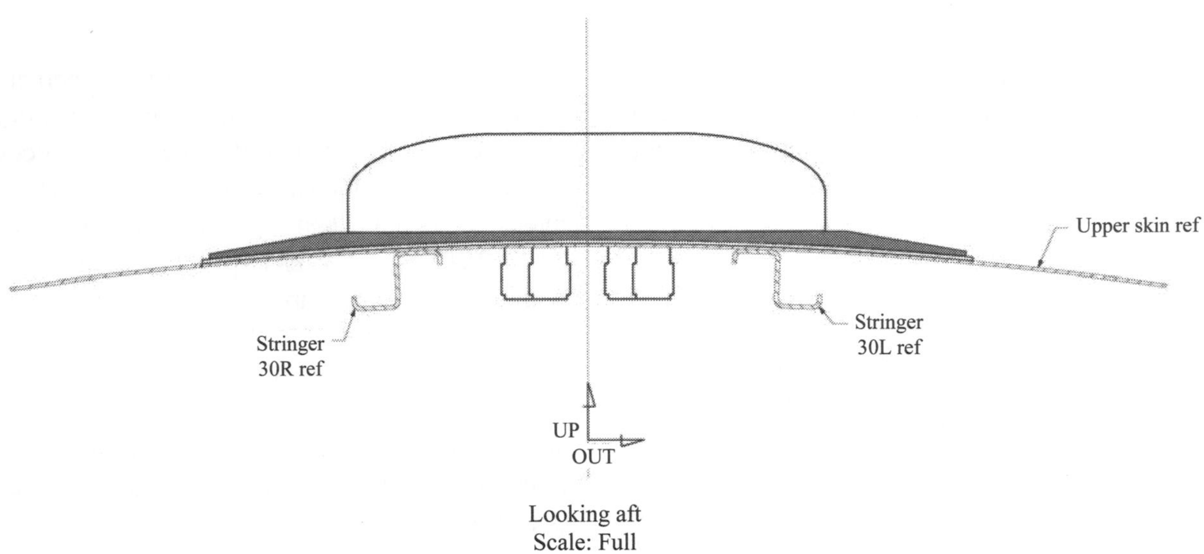

d. Mounting screws must never be over torqued in an attempt to distort aircraft structure to reduce gaps between the antenna base plate and aircraft-mounting surface.

e. Consider the factors of flutter, vibration characteristics, and drag load. The approximate drag load an antenna develops may be determined by the formula:

$$D=0.000327\ AV^2$$

(The formula includes a 90 percent reduction factor for the streamline shape of the antenna.)
D is the drag load on the antenna in lbs.
A is the frontal area of the antenna in sq. ft.
V is the V_{NE} of the aircraft in f.p.s.

Example: Antenna manufacturer specification frontal area = 0.135 sq. ft. and V_{NE} of aircraft is 250 f.p.s.

$$D=0.000327 \times .135 \times (250)^2$$
$$=0.000327 \times .135 \times 62{,}500$$
$$= 2.75 \text{ lbs}$$

f. The above formula may be adapted to determine side load forces by substitution of the apparent frontal area value for A, when the aircraft motion and antenna orientation are not the same.

304. PHYSICAL INTERFERENCE.

a. Antennas should be located where they will not interfere with the operation of the aircraft or other aircraft systems. One such example of interference could be the obstruction of visibility of a navigation position light or beacon.

b. Antennas should be located so that they don't obstruct or limit airflow to areas of the airframe that require airflow. Care should be exercised that an antenna is not located where it will be damaged by heat from engine exhaust, fumes from battery vents or fuel/fluid drains.

c. Antennas may accumulate ice that can then depart and damage areas behind them. Special attention should be paid to areas of the airframe near pitot static ports and sensors and near flight controls, since the antenna may alter airflow characteristics.

d. Antennas should be located in such a manner that they are not susceptible to damage from misuse such as near a door where they might be mistaken for or used as a handhold.

305. ANTENNA SELECTION. The selection of an appropriate antenna will include consideration of system requirements and aircraft characteristics. The size and shape of an antenna varies with frequency, power rating, and maximum design speed of the antenna. See Figures 3-7 through 3-19 for pictures of typical antennas.

306. ANTENNA LOCATION.

a. In general, antenna locations on an aircraft, which provide unobstructed line-of-sight views of the transmitted or received signals, are preferred. Objects located in the path of a signal may cause a blanking of antenna coverage and impact the performance of the system.

NOTE: Global Positioning System (GPS) antennas will not receive a signal if a line-of-sight view of a satellite is not available. Do not mount a GPS antenna on the underside of an aircraft.

b. Acceptable and unacceptable spacing between an antenna and an obstacle or the permissible interval between antennas is dependent upon operating frequency and system characteristics. When in doubt contact the antenna manufacturer or system designer for further information.

c. Antennas should be separated as far as possible from interference sources (other radiating antennas, ignition noise sources, etc.). When known interference sources are present it may be advisable to temporarily position an antenna and check a location for suitability prior to mounting the antenna.

d. VHF Com 1 should be mounted on the top of the aircraft since this will provide the best unobstructed location. VHF Com 2 can also be mounted on the top, provided there is at least 1/2 wavelength (of the antenna operating frequency) distance available between antennas.

e. If Com 2 is mounted under the aircraft, a bent whip may be required to provide ground clearance. Bent whips may not provide the best performance because of proximity to the aircraft skin. Signal reflection and obstruction is more of a problem with such locations. Extension of the landing gear or flaps may also impact belly mounted antenna performance.

f. Antennas need to "see" with a direct line-of-site to the source. Antenna patterns can be disrupted by landing gear or vertical stabilizers as examples. When mounting antennas, try to locate them in areas where line-of-sight view is not obstructed.

g. As a rule of thumb, maintain 36 inches as a minimum distance between antennas. Refer to manufacturer's installation guidelines for specific system limitations and requirements.

h. Antennas should be located such that cable runs between antenna and equipment are as short as practical. Signal loss of a cable is dependent upon cable design, length, and frequency. In some cases, cables must be specific lengths to provide a required capacitance, attenuation, or signal transmission time. VOR/LOC/GS blade or towel bar type antennas require the cables to their coupling assembly to be the exact same length to maintain a phase relationship.

307. ANTENNA BONDING.

a. The electrical bonding of the antenna to the aircraft surface is extremely important. The conductive skin of an aircraft is an electrical part of the antenna system. If an antenna is not properly bonded to the aircraft, its pattern may be distorted and nulls in coverage may appear.

b. The electrical bonding of the antennas to the aircraft skin of a metal aircraft is best accomplished by direct metal-to-metal contact of the antenna base to the skin. A resistance of no more than 0.003 ohms between the antenna base plate and skin should be achieved.

- To achieve this electrical bonding, the aircraft paint in the mounting area will need to be removed and the surface covered with an oxide film (i.e., aluminum conversion coat) to protect aluminum against corrosion in accordance with MIL-C-5541B

c. An alternate method for providing electrical bonding to metal aircraft skin is through the antenna mounting screws, which attach to a backing plate inside the aircraft, making electrical contact with the backside of the skin. To ensure good contact remove any interior paint in the area where the backing plate is placed and coat this area in accordance with MIL-C-5541B to minimize corrosion.

d. Composite or fabric covered aircraft that do not provide a conductive mounting surface generally require fabrication of a conductive surface (ground plane) and bonding through the mounting screws.

e. Antenna performance can be severely degraded from corrosion caused by moisture accumulation where the antenna electrically bonds to its ground plane. It is advisable to apply RTV around the antenna edges to seal the antenna bond; however, always ensure chemical compatibility before using any sealant.

308. ELECTROMAGNETIC INTERFERENCE (EMI).

a. Since the purpose of an antenna is to either receive or transmit RF energy (or both) it is essential to consider EMI.

b. Antenna mounting positions should be selected that are as far as possible from an EMI source. In special cases it may be possible to employ filters or select an antenna that has been specifically designed to be resistant to an EMI.

c. EMI test procedures are found in chapter 2.

309. MECHANICAL INSTALLATION.

a. Mounting Hardware.

(1) Typical antenna installations employ either #8-32 or #10-32 stainless steel mounting screws.

(2) Some designs require a pan head screw. For others, a counter sunk screw is required.

(3) Mounting screw length will vary based on each particular installation requirement.

b. General Practices.

(1) Refer to installation drawing before drilling holes in aircraft skin to determine proper size and spacing.

NOTE: When replacing antennas, it is important to match the original mounting holes. Previous mounting holes that are not reused with appropriate hardware must be repaired and the mounting location returned to its design strength.

(2) Use of a structural backing plate is highly recommended. Backing plates strengthen the immediate point of attachment but if they are not attached to load carrying structure they do not provide structural load support.

(3) Mounting screws should be secured with stainless steel nuts with flat washers and lock washers, or with flat washers and lock nuts to secure the antenna properly.

(4) Sandwich the aircraft skin between the antenna base plate and the internally mounted backing plate. Before securing the antenna to the aircraft make sure that all the cables are connected to the unit and fit through the connector holes in the aircraft.

(5) Gently tighten the mounting hardware so that uniform stress is placed on each side of the antenna. For #8-32 screws DO NOT exceed 20 in•lbs of torque and for #10-32 screws DO NOT exceed 23 in•lbs of torque. Refer to fastener manufacturer's torque guidelines to confirm that these recommended settings do not exceed the chosen fasteners torque limits.

(6) Once the antenna is mounted, any minor gaps between the base plate or gasket and aircraft skin should be filled with RTV silicone adhesive sealant.

(7) Double check that a reading of 0.003 ohms between the antenna base plate and ground has been achieved.

310. GROUND PLANE REQUIREMENT (WOOD/FABRIC AND COMPOSITE AIRCRAFT).

a. When the antenna is not mounted to a conductive surface capable of providing a required ground plane for operation a ground plane must be fabricated.

b. Most antennas require a ground plane size of approximately 24" by 24". While the rule of thumb is to provide a minimum of 1/4 wavelength of the operation frequency, larger is better and ground plane symmetry is critical. Gaps in antenna coverage or performance may occur if a ground plane is not symmetrical.

TABLE 3-1. WAVELENGTH IN FEET = 984 / FREQUENCY IN MEGAHERTZ (MHZ)

Frequency	Wavelength (ft)	1/4 wavelength (in)
75 MHz	13.1	40
125 MHz	7.9	24
1000 MHz	1	3

c. Wire mesh is the best material to use when a solid plate is not practical. Heavy aluminum foil can also be used. In all cases, electrical continuity from ground plane to airframe ground is essential.

d. Be sure the ground plane is well attached to the airframe with cement or epoxy if not otherwise supported. This will prevent noise problems or erratic operation that could occur if the plane moves. Capacitance will occur as an antenna base is separated from its ground plane. This may distort antenna coverage or operation.

FIGURE 3-2. ANTENNA GROUND PLANE FOR NONCONDUCTIVE MOUNT

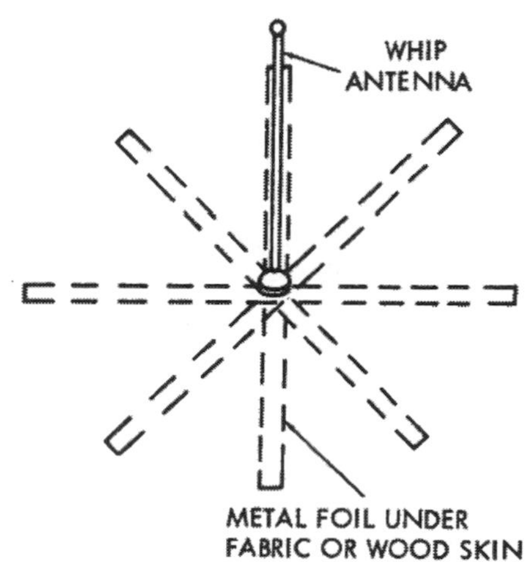

FIGURE 3-3. ONE MEANS TO PROVIDE ADEQUATE ANTENNA BONDING THROUGH A COMPOSITE AIRFRAME

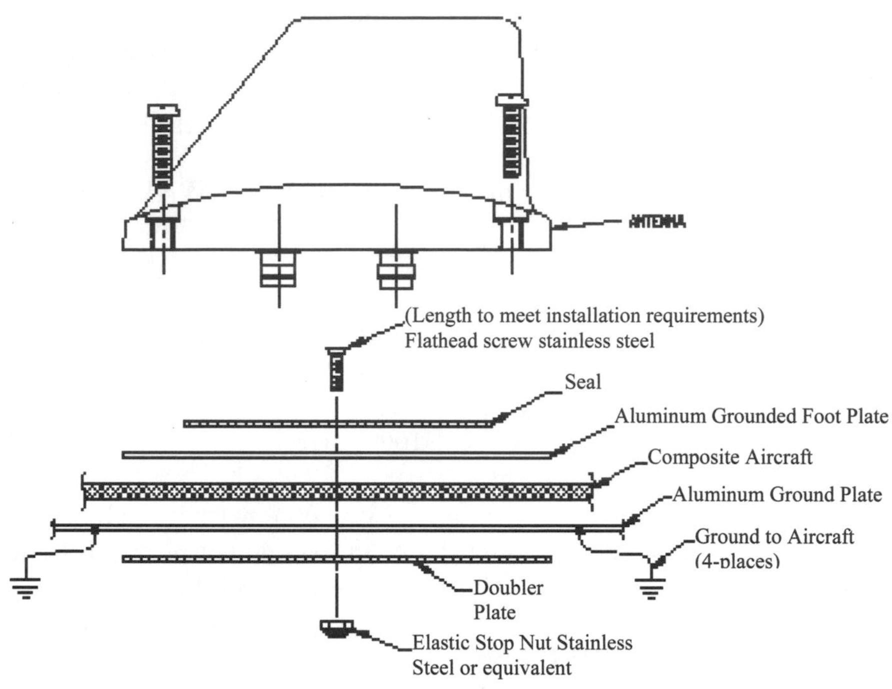

FIGURE 3-4. USE BUSHINGS FOR ALL SCREWS

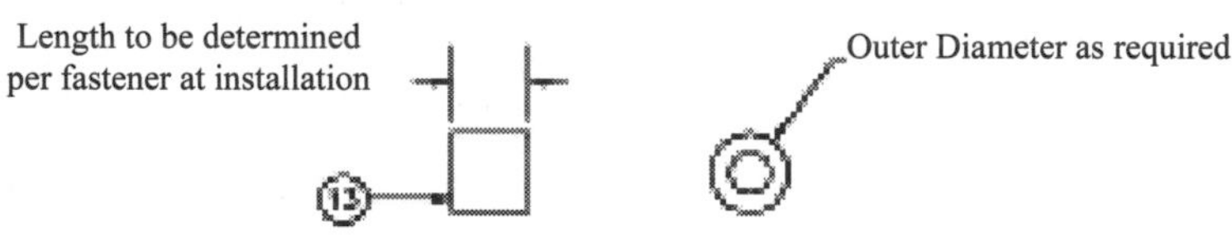

NOTE: Carbon Fiber composite material, while conductive has not been found to be adequate as a ground plane.

e. Refer to AC 43.13-1 (as amended), chapter 3, for acceptable methods, techniques, and practices applicable to fiberglass and plastics.

311. ANTENNA FEED LINE BALUN.

a. Antenna cables (electrical feed lines) may be designed to be electrically balanced or unbalanced. Certain antenna designs incorporate dual elements with a requirement for balanced input. In these cases, standard cables which are unbalanced are generally employed for the cable run and a balancing transformer is located at the antenna feed connection.

b. A balun is a device that converts an unbalanced feed into a balanced input and may include a transformer that matches feed impedance to provide maximum signal transfer. Follow the manufacturer's installation procedures when a balun is required. Some balun designs require that the balun be grounded to the airframe.

c. Refer to AC 43.13-1 (as amended), chapter 11, for bonding practices.

FIGURE 3-5. TYPICAL DIPOLE ANTENNA ASSEMBLY

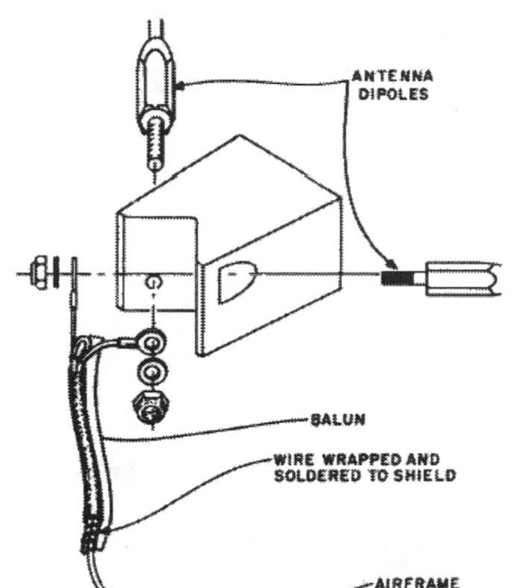

FIGURE 3-6. TYPICAL VOR BALUN

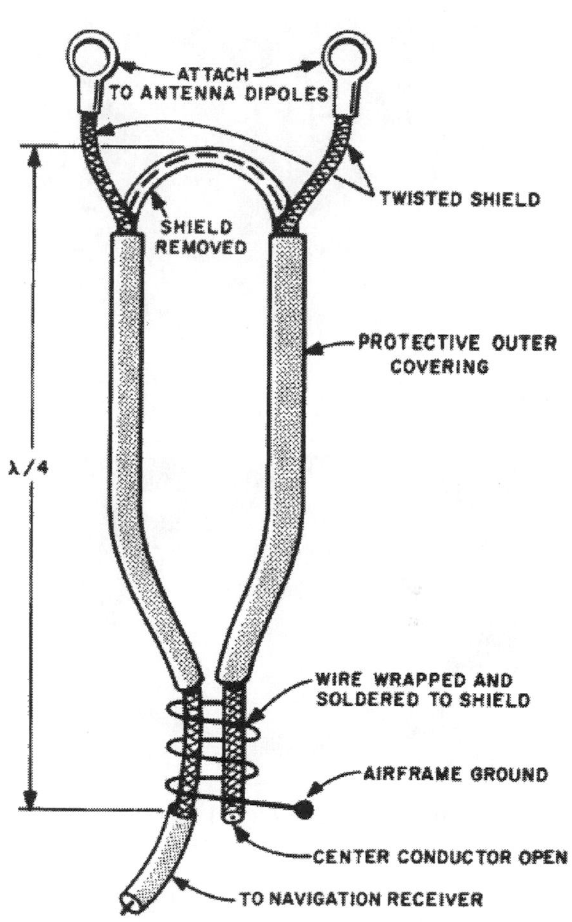

312. ANTENNA REPAIR. Painting an antenna or applying protective coatings or devices that are not approved are not allowed under this AC. Paint is an RF de-tuner. If an antenna is painted in the field, paint type and paint thickness present uncontrolled variables that will affect an antenna's performance, and may result in the antenna no longer meeting its specifications or Technical Standard Order.

313. THRU 399. RESERVED

FIGURE 3-7. ADF LOOP

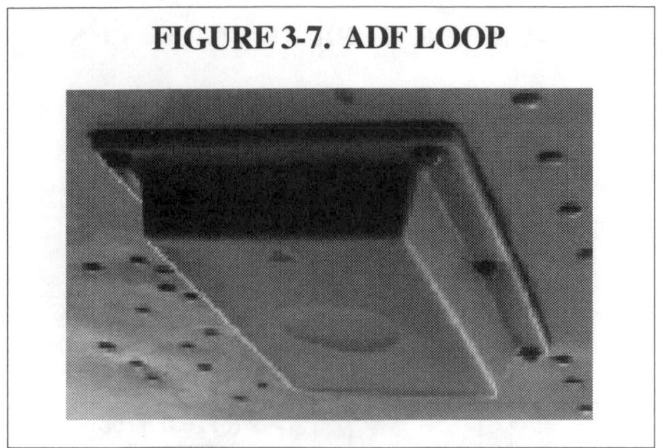

FIGURE 3-8. ADF COMBINED SENSE LOOP

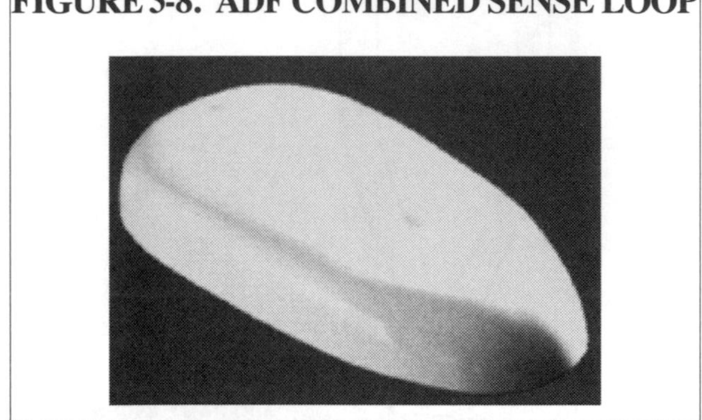

FIGURE 3-9. COM WHIP

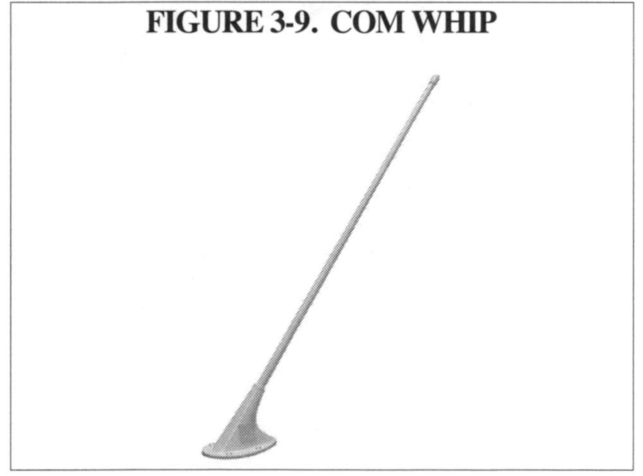

FIGURE 3-10. COM WHIP BENT

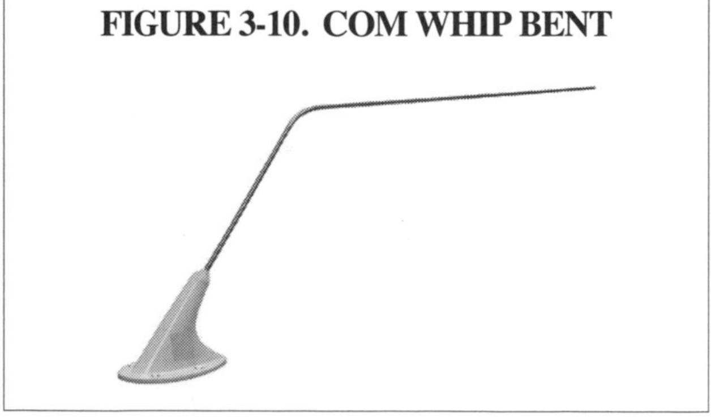

FIGURE 3-11. ELT

FIGURE 3-12. GPS

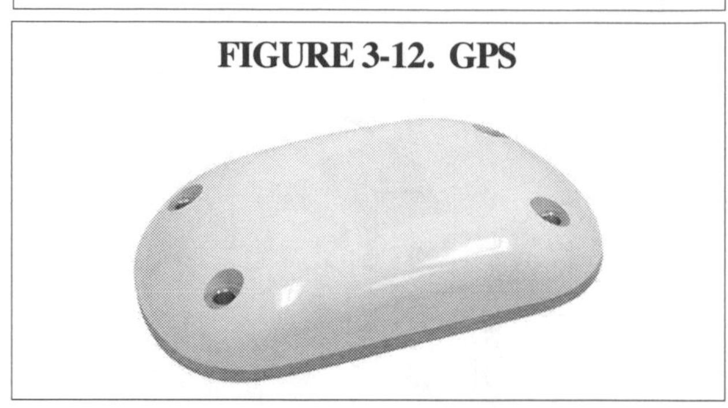

FIGURE 3-13. GLIDESLOPE

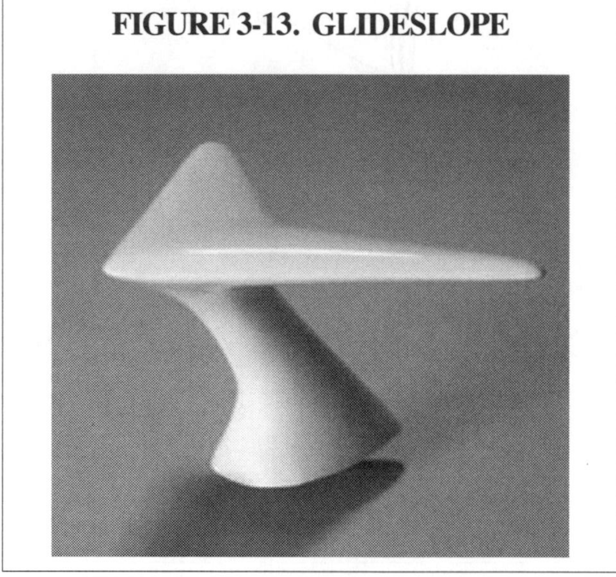

FIGURE 3-14. MARKER

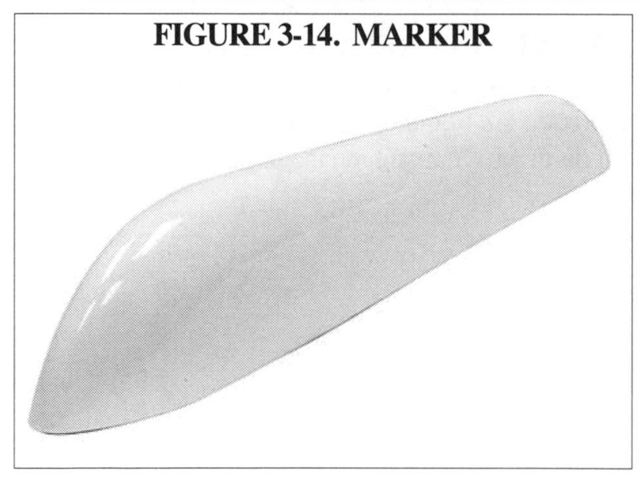

FIGURE 3-15. COMBINED COM/VOR

FIGURE 3-16. VOR RABBIT EAR

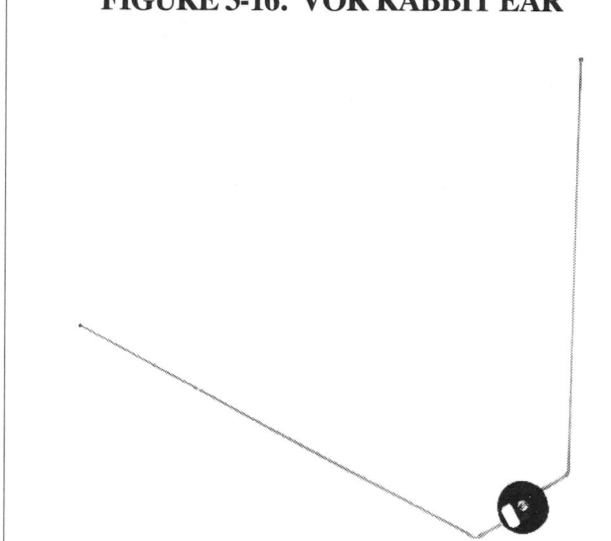

FIGURE 3-17. VOR BLADES

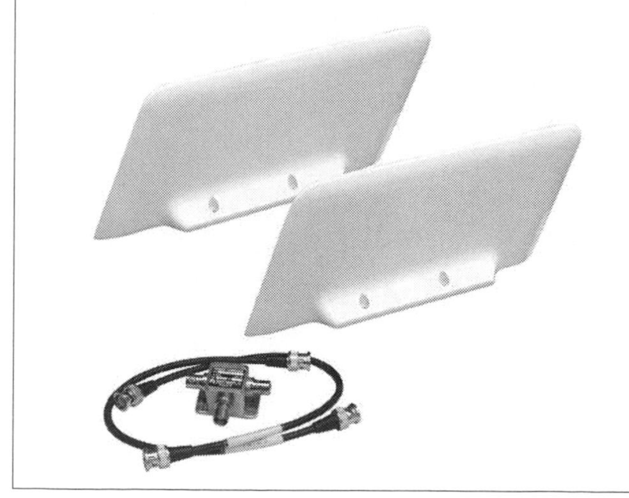

FIGURE 3-18. TRANSPONDER/DME PROBE

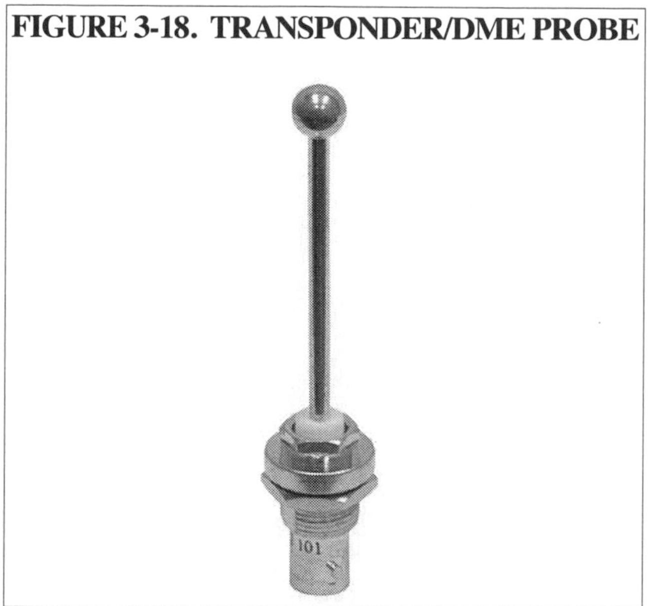

FIGURE 3-19. DME/TRANSPONDER BLADE

CHAPTER 4. ANTICOLLISION AND SUPPLEMENTARY LIGHT INSTALLATION

400. PURPOSE. This chapter gives procedures and standards to be used when replacing older rotating beacon assemblies and wing lights with strobe or other anticollision systems. This chapter assumes that the newer units have FAA approval in the form of a Parts Manufacturer Approval (PMA) or Technical Standard Order (TSO), and not an experimental or aviation unit.

401. HAZARDS AND WARNINGS. When installing anticollison lights take care to ensure the unit is properly grounded, the airframe structure can support the new unit, and the aircraft wiring is of the correct size. Mechanics should take special precautions to protect their eyes when testing the new unit. Strobe lights are especially hazardous in dark or darken hangars when activated.

402. REGULATIONS AND OTHER REFERENCES. The requirements for anticollision lights are included in Title 14 of the Code of Federal Regulations (14 CFR) part 23, § 23.1401 and part 27, § 27.1401 for non-transport category aircraft. For part 23 aircraft certificated after March 11, 1996, § 91.205 are required to have an anticollision light. The night VFR requirements for part 23 certificated on or before August 11, 1971, must have an approved white or red anticollison light. Aircraft for which an application for type certificate was made before April 1, 1957, may conform either to the above regulations or to the following standards: Additional information can be found in AC 20-74.

a. Civil Aviation Regulation (CAR) 6, Rotorcraft Airworthiness; Normal Category.

b. Anticollision lights (when installed) should be installed on top of the fuselage or tail in such a location that the light will not impair the flight crewmembers' vision and will not detract from the conspicuity of the position lights. If there is no acceptable location on top of the fuselage or tail, a bottom fuselage or wing tip installation may be used.

c. The color of the anticollision light must be either aviation red or aviation white in accordance with the specifications of § 23.1397 or § 27.1397, as applicable.

d. The arrangement of the anticollision light system, (i.e., number of light sources, beam width, speed of rotation and other characteristics, etc.) must give an effective flash frequency of not less than 40, nor more than 100, cycles per minute. The effective flash frequency is the frequency at which the aircraft's complete anticollision light system is observed from a distance, and applies to each sector of light including any overlaps that exist when the system consists of more than one light source. In overlaps, flash frequencies may exceed 100 but not more than 180 cycles per minute.

e. The system must consist of enough lights to illuminate the vital areas around the aircraft, considering the physical configuration and flight characteristics of the aircraft. The field of coverage must extend in each direction within at least 75 degrees above and 75 degrees below the horizontal plane of the aircraft. The minimum light intensity and minimum effective intensities are given in §§ 23.1401 and 27.1401 respectively.

f. Supplementary lights may be installed in addition to position and anticollision lights required by applicable regulations; provided that, the required position and anticollision lights are continuously visible and unmistakably recognizable and their conspicuity is not degraded by such supplementary lights.

403. OPERATIONAL CONSIDERATIONS: CREW VISION. Partial masking of the anticollision light may be necessary to prevent direct or reflected light rays from any anticollision or supplementary light from interfering with crew vision. Determine if the field of coverage requirements are met. An acceptable method of preventing light reflection from propeller disc, nacelle, or wing surface is an application of nonreflective paint on surfaces which present a reflection problem. Perform a night flight-check to assure that any objectionable light reflection, sometimes known as flicker vertigo, has been eliminated. Enter a notation to that effect in the aircraft records.

404. INSTALLATION CONSIDERATIONS.

a. Communication and Navigation. Assure that the installation and operation of any anticollision/supplementary light does not interfere with the performance of installed communication or navigation equipment. Capacitor discharge light (strobe) systems may generate radio frequency interference (RFI). This radiated interference can be induced into the audio circuits of communication or navigation systems and is noticeable by audible clicks in the speaker or headphones. The magnitude of the RFI disturbance does not usually disrupt the intelligence of audio reception.

b. Precautions. RFI can be reduced or eliminated by observing the following precautions during installation of capacitor discharge light systems:

(1) Locate the power supply at least 3 feet from any antenna, especially antennas for radio systems that operate in the lower frequency bands.

(2) Assure that the lamp unit (flash tube) wires are separated from other aircraft wiring placing particular emphasis on coaxial cables and radio equipment input power wires.

(3) Make sure that the power supply case is adequately bonded to the airframe.

(4) Ground the shield around the interconnecting wires between the lamp unit and power supply at the power supply end only.

405. MARKINGS AND PLACARDS. Identify each switch for an anticollision/supplementary light and indicate its operation. The aircraft should be flight tested under haze, overcast, and visible moisture conditions to ascertain that no interference to pilot vision is produced by operation of these lights. If found unsatisfactory by test or in the absence of such testing, a placard should be provided to the pilot stating that the appropriate lights be turned off while operating in these conditions.

406. ELECTRICAL INSTALLATION. Install an individual switch for the anticollision light or supplementary light system that is independent of the position light system switch. Data for the installation of wiring, protection device, and generator/alternator limitations is contained in Advisory Circular (AC) 43.13-1B Acceptable Methods, Techniques, and Practices-Aircraft Inspection and Repair, (as amended) chapter 11. Assure that the terminal voltage at each light is within the limits as prescribed by the manufacturer.

407. ALTERATION OF STRUCTURE.

a. The simplest light installation is to secure the light to a reinforced fuselage skin panel. The reinforcement doubler shall be of equivalent thickness, material, and strength as the existing skin. (Install as shown in Figure 4-1.)

FIGURE 4-1. TYPICAL ANTICOLLISION OR SUPPLEMENTARY LIGHT INSTALLATION IN A SKIN PANEL (UNPRESSURIZED)

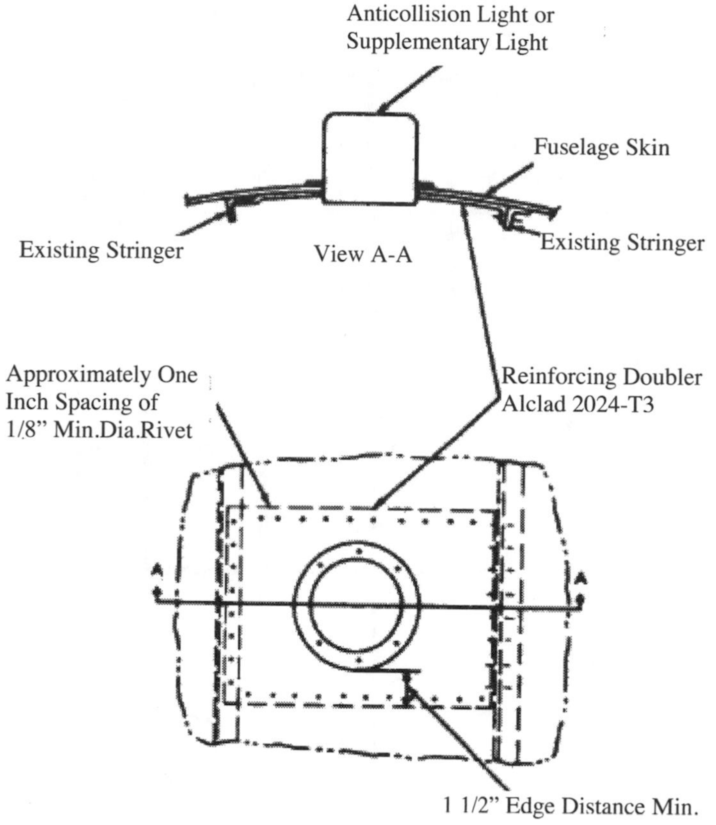

b. When a formed angle stringer is cut and partially removed, position the reinforcement doubler between the skin and the frame. The doubler is to be equivalent to the stringer in thickness and extend lengthwise beyond the adjacent fuselage frames. The distance between the light and the edge of the doubler is to be twice the height of the doubler flange. (See Figure 4-2 for typical installation.)

c. Engineering evaluation is required for installations involving the cutting of complex formed or extruded stiffeners, fuselage frames, or pressurized skin of pressurized aircraft.

d. Vertical stabilizer installations may be made on aircraft if the stabilizer is large enough in cross section to accommodate the light installation, and if aircraft flutter and vibration characteristics are not adversely affected. Locate such an installation near a spar, and add formers as required to stiffen the structure near the light. (A typical installation is shown in Figure 4-3.)

e. Rudder installations are not recommended because of the possible structural difficulties. However, if such installations are considered, a FAA engineering evaluation to determine whether the added mass of the light installation will adversely affect the flutter and vibration characteristics of the tail surfaces must be made.

FIGURE 4-2. TYPICAL ANTICOLLISION OR SUPPLEMENTARY LIGHT INSTALLATION INVOLVING A CUT STRINGER (UNPRESSURIZED)

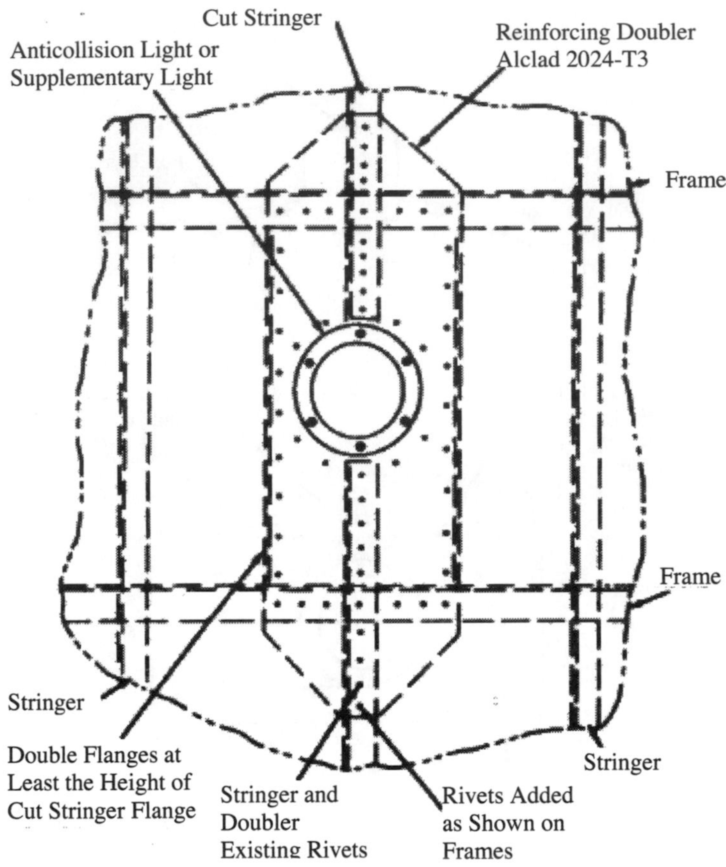

FIGURE 4-3. TYPICAL ANTICOLLISION OR SUPPLEMENTARY LIGHT INSTALLATION IN A FIN TIP

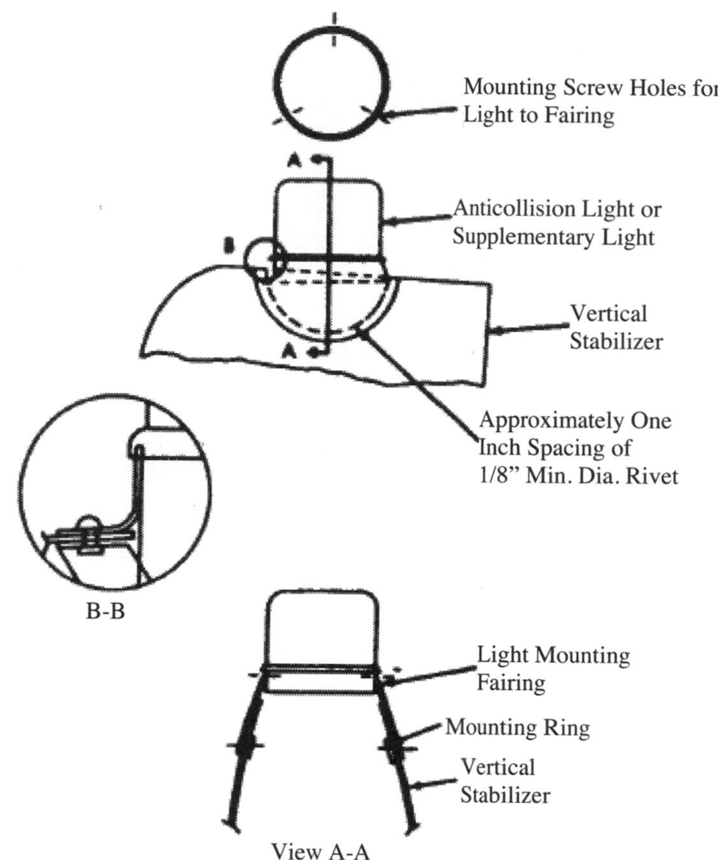

NOTE: Skin thickness of mounting ring and fairing are at least equivalent.

CHAPTER 5. SKI INSTALLATIONS

500. PURPOSE. This chapter provides information for ski installations on small airplane. The information provided for main ski and nose ski installations applies to wheel replacement skis only. Tire-cushioned skis other than tail skis, wheel penetration skis, and hydraulically adjustable or retractable skis involve special considerations and cannot be installed by relying solely on data in this advisory circular (AC).

501. HAZARDS AND WARNINGS. Operation of ski planes exposes the airplane and its occupants to additional risks not associated with wheel-equipped landplanes. The additional weight and surface area of skis impose additional ground and air loads on the airplane. Ground handling, taxiing, takeoff, and landing can place significant side loads and twisting moments to the landing gear and its attachment structure which can cause hidden and/or cumulative damage. Improper rigging and/or weak springs or shock cords can cause the skis to "dump," or rotate nose down in flight, possibly rendering the airplane uncontrollable or causing it to break up in flight. Skis with weak springs or shock cords may rotate nose down and "dig," or penetrate the snow, during takeoff or landing on uneven or drifted snow, which could result in an accident. In-service failure of ski attachment hardware, springs, shock cords, or cables creates a high risk of those parts or a ski itself entering the propeller arc, which has resulted in complete loss of airplanes in flight. For these reasons, proper installation, rigging, periodic inspection, and maintenance of skis and their attaching parts are of utmost importance to safety. Consultation with experienced ski maintenance technicians and operators is strongly recommended when considering any new ski installation or any alteration of an existing ski installation.

502. ADDITIONAL REFERENCE MATERIAL (current editions).

a. Airframe and ski manufacturers' data, if available.

b. AC 43.13-1, Acceptable Methods, Techniques, and Practices—Airplane Inspection and Repair.

c. AC 43-210, Standardized Procedures for Requesting Field Approval of Data, Major Alterations, and Repairs.

d. Civil Aviation Regulation (CAR) 6, Rotorcraft Airworthiness; Normal Category.

e. FAA Order 8110.54, Instructions for Continued Airworthiness.

f. FAA-H-8083-23, Seaplane, Ski plane, and Float/Ski Equipped Helicopter Operations Handbook.

503. INSTALLATION CONSIDERATIONS.

a. Determining Eligibility of an Airplane. Only an airplane approved for operation on skis is eligible for ski installations in accordance with this chapter. Eligibility can be determined by referring to the Aircraft Specifications, type certificate data sheets (TCDS), Aircraft Listing, Summary of Supplemental Type Certificates, or by contacting the manufacturer. Also determine the need for any required alterations to the airplane to make it eligible for ski operations. (See ski plane-specific entries throughout TCDS A4CE on airspeeds, weight and balance limitations and additional placards, and the Required Equipment listing for the first model in Aircraft Specification A-790 for examples.) If the airplane is not approved in a ski plane configuration by type design, then skis cannot be installed by relying solely on data in this AC. Contact FAA engineering for approval or obtain/develop approved data from another source.

b. Identification of Approved Model Skis. Determine that the skis are of an approved model by examining the identification plates or placards displayed on the skis. Skis of approved models will have such plates or placards, and the Technical Standard Order (TSO) number TSO-C28, an Aircraft Component, Accessory, or equipment type certificate (TC) number, or an airplane part number (if the skis have been approved as part of the airplane) will be engraved or imprinted on each plate or placard.

c. Maximum Limit Load Rating.

(1) Known limit landing load factor. Before installation, determine that the maximum limit load rating (L) of the ski as specified on its identification plate or placard is at least equal to the maximum static load on it (S) times the limit landing load factor *(fl)* previously determined from drop tests of the airplane by its manufacturer. This requirement can be expressed by the following equation:

$$L = S \times fl$$

(2) Unknown limit landing load factor. In lieu of a value *fl* determined from such drop tests, a value of *fl* determined from the following formula may be used:

$$\eta = 2.80 + \frac{9000}{(W + 4000)}$$

where "W" is the certificated gross weight of the airplane

d. Oversize Ski Installations. This limitation is to assure that the oversize skis will not adversely affect the performance, stability, controllability, and spin recovery behavior of the airplane or impose excessive loads on it.

e. Landing Gear Moment Reactions: Landing Gear Bending Moments. In order to avoid excessive bending moments on the landing gear and attachment structure, the ski pedestal height measured from the bottom surface of the ski to the axle centerline must not exceed 130 percent of the static rolling radius of the standard tire approved for the airplane, when the tire is installed on the standard wheel at the approved inflation pressure. Do not use oversize or "tundra" tires to determine the static rolling radius.

504. FABRICATION AND INSTALLATION.

a. Hub-Axle Clearance. The pedestal hub should fit the axle to provide a clearance of 0.005" minimum to 0.020" maximum. Hubs may be bushed to adjust for axle size, using any ferrous or nonferrous metal, hard rubber, or fiber. If rubber or fiber bushings are used, use retaining washers of sufficient size on each side to retain the hub if the bushing should slip or fail. (See Figure 5-1.) Field experience has shown that the use of good quality, low-temperature grease; particularly modern synthetic-based grease, improves ski operation and wear protection when used on the axle-to-hub or axle-to-bushing faying surfaces.

FIGURE 5-1. TYPICAL HUB INSTALLATION

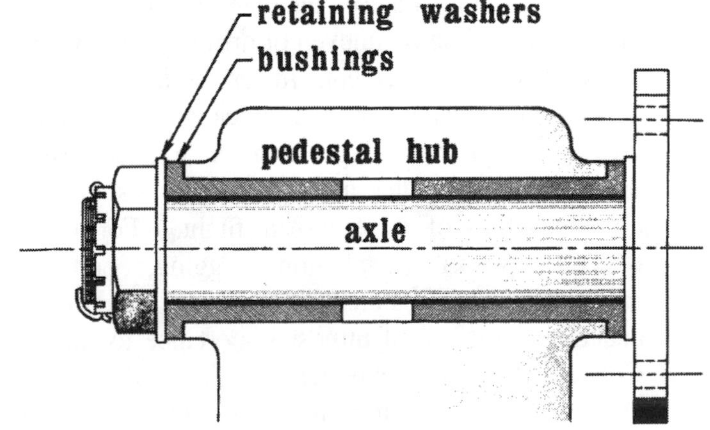

FIGURE 5-2. TYPICAL SKI INSTALLATION

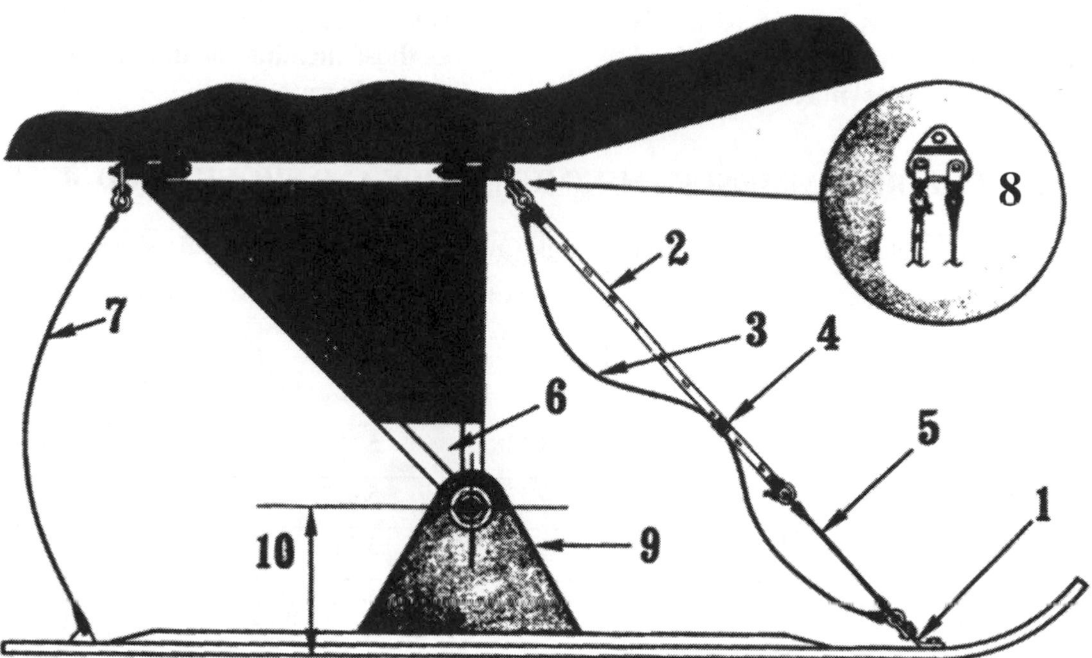

1. Fitting
2. Shock Cord
3. Safety Cable
4. Tape
5. Crust-cutter Cable
6. Fabric removed to facilitate inspection
7. Check Cable
8. Clevis
9. Ski Pedestal
10. Pedestal Height

b. Crust-Cutter Cables. Crust-cutter cables are optional. However, when operating in severe crust conditions, it is advisable to have this cable installed to prevent the shock cord from being cut if the nose of the ski breaks through the crust while taxiing.

c. Cable and Shock Cord Attachment and Attachment Fittings.

(1) Field experience. Service reports indicate that failure of the ski itself is not a predominant factor in ski failures. Rigging (improper tension and terminal attachments) and cast-type pedestal material failures are predominant. Failures of the safety cable and shock cord attachment fittings usually occur at the ski end and not at the fuselage end.

(2) Separating attachment points. It is strongly recommended that tension cords and safety cables be attached to entirely separate fittings at their fuselage ends. Although the attachment fitting detail shown in Figure 5-2 may be adequate for some installations where alternate attachment locations are unavailable, we recommend that each cord and cable be attached to its own fitting (such as the right-hand fitting in Figure 5-3) and attached at separate points on the fuselage when possible. Provide separate means of attaching cables and shock cords at the forward and aft ends of the skis.

(3) Fabrication. Approved skis are normally supplied with cables, shock cord, and fittings. However the specifications in Table 5-1, subparagraphs (a) through (c) below, and Figure 5-3 may be used for fabricating and installing cables, shock cord assemblies, and fuselage fittings.

NOTE: Field experience indicates that accelerated wear and damage can occur to a 1/8" safety or crust-cutting cable and its attachment hardware in normal service on skis having a limit load rating of 1,500 pounds or more. The FAA

recommends a minimum cable size of 5/32" for use in fabricating safety or crust-cutting cables for use with skis of 1,500 pounds or greater limit load rating. 1/8" cables may be suitable for use on airplanes with light-weight skis and maximum certificated weights less than 1,500 pounds, such as those meeting the definition of light sport aircraft.

TABLE 5-1. RECOMMENDED MINIMUM CABLE AND SHOCK CORD SIZES

Ski Limit Load Rating (Pounds)	Single Safety Cable	Double Safety Cable	Single Crust-Cutting Cable	Double Crust-Cutting Cable	Single Shock Cord	Double Shock Cord
Less than 1,500	1/8"	1/8"	1/8"	1/8"	1/2"	1/2"
1,500-3,000	5/32"	5/32"	5/32"	5/32"	1/2"	1/2"
3,000-5,000	Do Not Use	5/32"	5/32"	5/32"	Do Not Use	1/2"
5,000-7,000	Do Not Use	5/32"	5/32"	5/32"	3/4"	3/4"
7,000-9,000	Do Not Use	3/16"	Do Not Use	5/32"	Do Not Use	3/4"

(a) Make check cable, safety cable, and crust-cutting cable ends by the splice, swage, or nicopress methods. Cable clamps may be used if adjustable lengths are desired, but they are not recommended. Use standard airplane hardware only. (Hardware used to attach cables must be compatible with cable size.) Refer to AC 43.13-1, chapter 7, as amended, for more information on cable fabrication.

(b) Shock cord ends may be fabricated by any of the following methods:

1. Make a wrapped splice using a proper size rope thimble and No. 9 cotton cord, 0.041" (minimum) safety wire (ref. National Aerospace Standard NASM20995), 1025 steel, or its equivalent (AISI 4130). Attach with clevis or spring steel snap fastener. (*Do not* use cast iron snaps.)

2. Use approved spring-type shock cord end fasteners, 1025 steel, or its equivalent (AISI 4130).

(c) Fitting (Figure 5-3) Specifications and Installation:

1. Fittings fabricated for 1/8-inch cable or 1/2-inch shock cord must be at least 0.065" 1025 steel or its equivalent.

2. Fittings fabricated for 5/32-inch cable or 3/4-inch shock cord must be at least 0.080" 1025 steel or its equivalent.

3. An improperly installed fitting may impose excessive eccentric loads on the fitting and attach bolts and result in failure of the fitting or bolts.

4. If attaching cables directly to holes in fittings, radius the hole edges to reduce stress concentration and accelerated wear of the thimble. Stainless steel thimbles are recommended for increased wear resistance.

5. If attaching cables to fittings using clevises, clevis bolt castellated nuts should be used, then properly torqued and safetied with cotter pins. Field experience has shown that diaper-pin-style quick-releasing safety devices are more prone to failure during operation, and are not recommended.

FIGURE 5-3. TYPICAL FUSELAGE FITTINGS

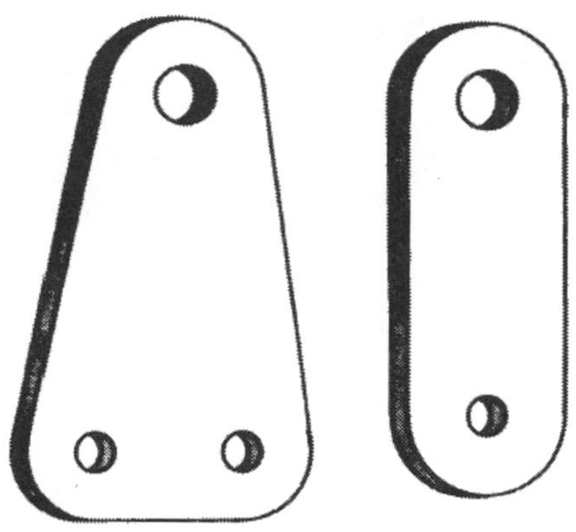

d. Provisions for Inspection. An airplane using fabric-covered landing gear should have at least the lower 4 inches of fabric removed to facilitate inspection of the axle attachment area, and to prevent the entrapment of snow and ice, which can lead to damage and corrosion of the landing gear. (See Item 6 in Figure 5-2.)

505. RIGGING OF SKIS.

a. Location of Attach Fittings on Fuselage or Landing Gear. Locate fittings so the shock cord and cable angles are not less than 20 degrees when measured in the vertical plane with the shock absorber in the fully extended position (see Angle B, Figures 5-4 and 5-5).

NOTE: Do not attach fittings to wing-brace struts, except by special approval (manufacturer or FAA).

b. Main Ski Incidence Angles.

(1) Set cable lengths with the airplane level and no weight on the landing gear.

(2) Adjust length of check cable to provide a ±0- to ±5-degree ski incidence angle (reference Figures 5-4 and 5-6).

(3) Adjust length of safety cable to provide a ±15-degree ski incidence angle (reference Figures 5-5 and 5-6).

FIGURE 5-4. MAIN SKI AT MAXIMUM POSITIVE INCIDENCE (CHECK CABLE TAUT)

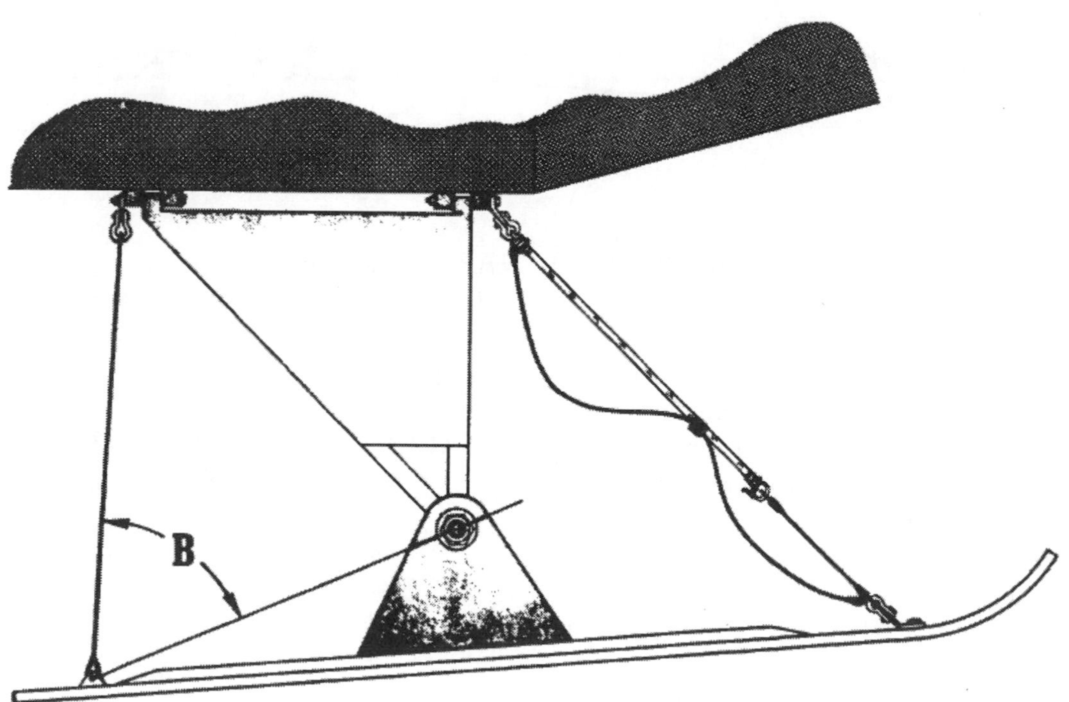

FIGURE 5-5. MAIN SKI AT MAXIMUM NEGATIVE INCIDENCE (SAFETY CABLE TAUT)

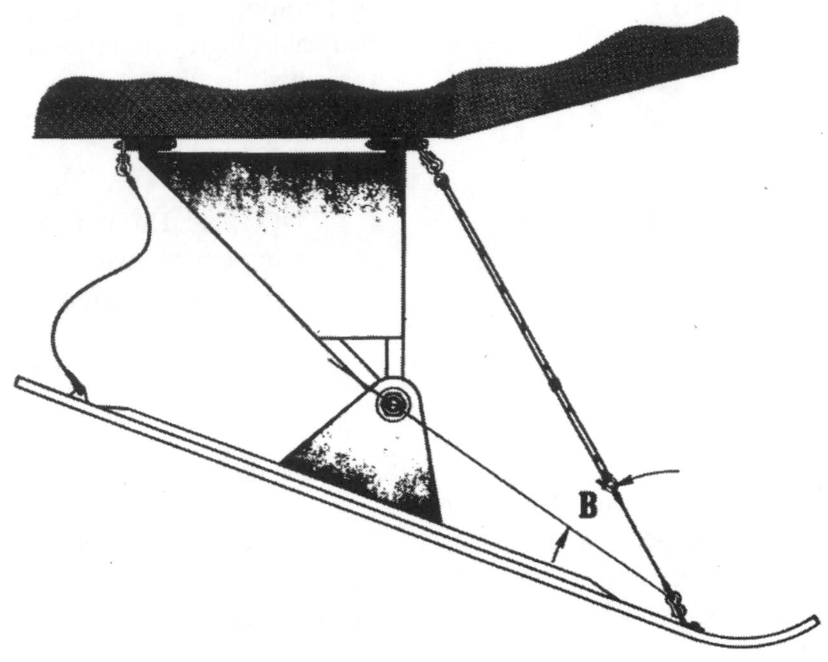

FIGURE 5-6. MAIN SKI INCIDENCE ANGLES

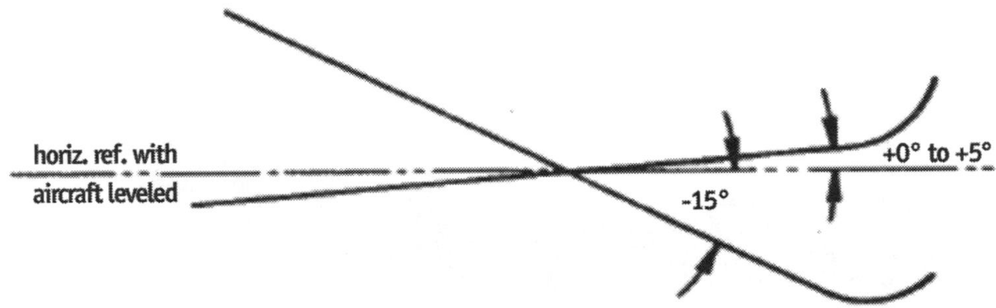

c. Tension Required in Main Ski Shock Cords.

(1) Apply sufficient shock cord tension to the forward ends of the skis to prevent flutter and "dumping" throughout the range of airspeeds and attitudes at which the airplane will operate on skis. Because of the various angles used in attaching the shock cord to the skis, shock cord tension cannot be specified. It is possible to specify the downward force that must be applied to the forward end of the ski in order to overcome the shock cord tension and cause the check cable to slacken when the ski is in the normal flight attitude. That downward force is commonly referred to as the *shock cord tension force,* or simply the *tension force.* In most installations on rigid, truss type landing gear, the tension force should be approximately as listed in Table 5-2.

TABLE 5-2. APPROXIMATE MAIN SKI TENSION FORCES

Ski Limit Load Capacity	*Downward Force (pounds)*
1500-3000	*20-40*
3000-5000	*40-60*
5000-7000	*60-120*
7000-9000	*120-200*

NOTE: Do not rely upon these tension force values for main ski installations on airplanes with spring steel or other flexible landing gear. Shock cord tensions great enough to require the downward forces listed in Table 5-2 to overcome them may produce excessive toe-in of the main skis on such airplanes. Variations in gear leg flexibility make it difficult to establish a generic table of tension forces appropriate for all airplanes with flexible landing gear.

(2) The shock cord tension must also be sufficient to return the skis to the normal flight attitude from their maximum negative incidence at all airspeeds up to the airplane's never-exceed speed with skis installed. In the absence of more precise data, each shock cord must be able to produce a nose-up moment about the ski pedestal bearing centerline of $M = (0.0000036)(W)(V_{NE})2$ ft•lbs, when the ski is at its maximum negative incidence, where W is the maximum certificated gross weight of the airplane and V_{NE} is its never-exceed speed with skis installed.

d. Springs in Place of Shock Cords. If springs are used in place of shock cords to provide rigging tension, they must be able to withstand extreme cold and slight external scratching without premature fatigue failure, and must not cause skis, rigging, or landing gear to experience flutter or objectionable vibration during an airplane flight and dive tests.

e. Nose Ski Installation. Install the nose ski on an airplane with tricycle landing gear in the same manner as the main skis (see Figure 5-7), except:

(1) Adjust length of safety cable to provide ±5- to ±15-degree ski incidence.

(2) Where it is possible for the nose ski rigging to contact the propeller tips due to vibration, install a 1/4-inch shock cord to hold the rigging out of the propeller arc.

FIGURE 5-7. TYPICAL NOSE SKI INSTALLATION

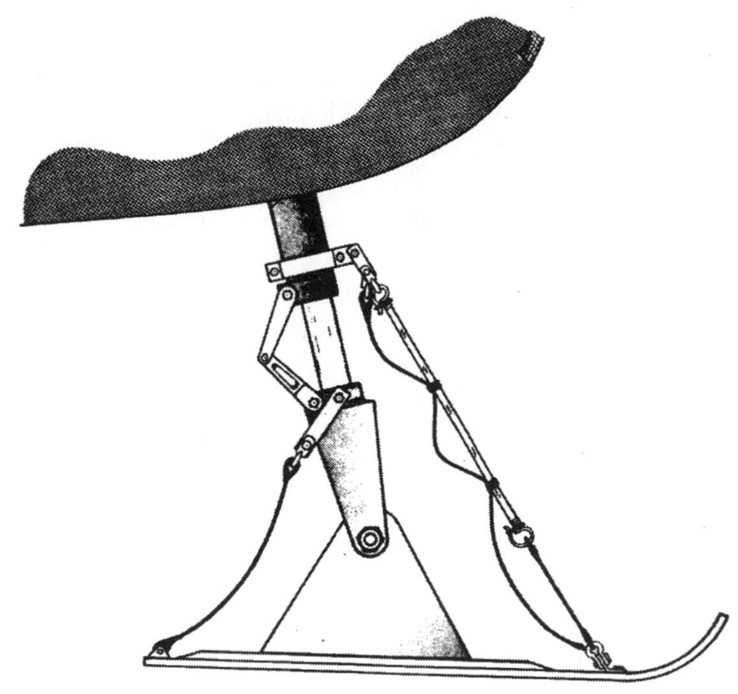

f. Tail Ski Installation.

(1) When installing a tail ski on an airplane with conventional landing gear, use a tail ski that has been approved on an airplane of approximately the same weight and whose tail wheel bears approximately the same fraction of that weight when the airplane is in the three-point attitude (within 10 percent), or select the tail ski as outlined in paragraphs 501 and 503. Some types of tail ski require that the tail wheel be removed to install the rest on its upper surface "ski."

(2) Adjust the length of the limiting cable (reference Figure 5-8) to allow the ski to turn approximately 35 degrees either side of the straight-forward position with the weight of the airplane resting on the ski.

(3) The shock cord (reference Figure 5-8) must be of a length that will hold the ski in the straight-forward position during flight.

FIGURE 5-8. TYPICAL TAIL SKI INSTALLATION

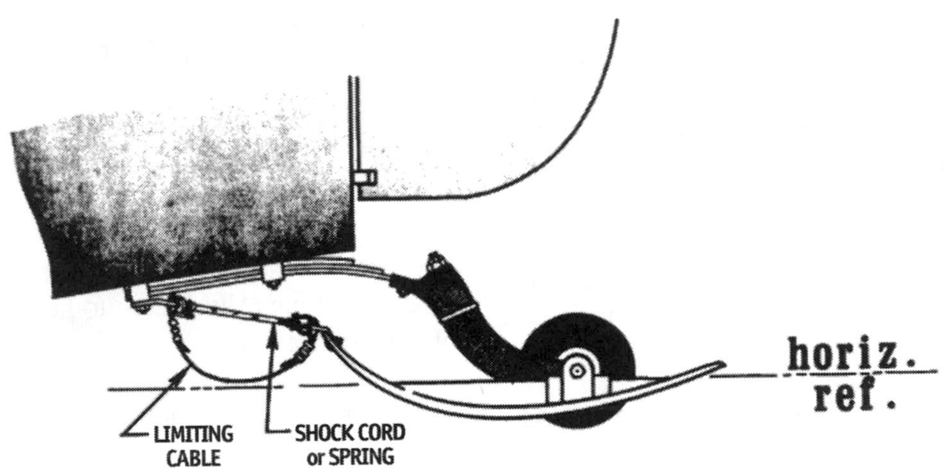

506. DOCUMENTATION.

a. Airplane or Ski Manufacturer's Data. Comply with the requirements for placards, markings, and manuals required to operate the airplane as a skiplane, as listed in the approved or accepted documents discussed in paragraph 503a.

b. Performance Information. The following Paragraphs contain the minimum additional performance data required for airplanes equipped with new or altered ski installations. Consult AC 43-210 (current edition) chapter 4, for additional guidance regarding approved Aircraft Flight Manual (AFM) supplements.

(1) For an airplane that requires an approved AFM, obtain FAA approval for an AFM supplement that adds the following or similar information to the Performance section of the Manual.

(a) Takeoff. Under the most favorable conditions of smoothly packed snow at temperatures approximating 32° F, the skiplane takeoff distance is approximately 10 percent greater than that shown for the landplane.

NOTE: In estimating takeoff distance for other conditions, caution should be exercised as lower temperatures or other snow conditions will usually increase these distances.

(b) Landing. Under the most favorable conditions of smoothly packed snow at temperatures approximately 32° F, the skiplane landing distance is approximately 20 percent greater than that shown for the landplane.

NOTE: In estimating landing distances for other conditions, caution should be exercised as other temperatures or other snow conditions may either decrease or increase these distances.

(c) Climb Performance. In cases where the landing gear is fixed (both landplane and skiplane), where climb requirements are not critical, and the climb reduction is small (30 to 50 feet per minute), the FAA will accept a statement of the approximate reduction in climb performance placed in the performance information section of the AFMS. For larger variations in climb performance, where the minimum requirements are critical, or the landing gear of the landplane is retractable, appropriate climb data should be obtained to determine the changes and new curves, tables, or a note should be incorporated into the AFMS.

(2) For an airplane that does not require an AFM, make the information in paragraph 506b(1) available to the pilot in for form of placards, markings, manuals, or any combination thereof. One type of acceptable manual is an approved Supplementary AFM.

507. FLIGHT AND HANDLING OPERATIONAL CHECKS. Accomplish an operational check in accordance with Title 14 of the Code of Federal Regulations (14 CFR) part 91, § 91.407(b), to determine the takeoff, landing, and ground handling characteristics. Ensure that the ski angles during tail high and tail low landings will not cause the skis to dig in or fail from localized stress. Verify that ground control is adequate to satisfactorily complete a landing run with a turnoff at slow speed. In flight, the skis must ride steady with check cables taut, and must not produce excessive drag or unsatisfactory flight characteristics. Enter a notation of this check in the airplane records.

508. MAINTENANCE (INCLUDING INSPECTION).

a. Inspection and Repair Data Sources. Contact the airplane and ski manufacturers for any specific inspection and maintenance instructions they may have developed. Refer to AC 43.13-1 (as amended), chapter 9, for more information.

b. Instructions for Continued Airworthiness (ICA). The modifier (developer of the ski installation or alteration) must provide instructions for future inspection, maintenance, and repair of the added or altered parts, and is also responsible for assessing the need for any changes to the product-level ICA (changes that affect the airplane as a whole when the skis are installed). For simple airplane/ski combinations where skis of the same model have been approved on similar airplanes with appropriate ICA, it may only be necessary to reference those ICA in the maintenance records of the newly altered airplane and/or in Block 8 of the FAA Form 337 documenting the ski installation. For complex ski installations requiring special considerations, the modifier may need to develop new installation-specific ICA. In either case, the modifier must ensure that adequate and appropriate ICA is available to the skiplane owner or operator. Consult current editions of AC 43-210, chapter 5, and FAA Order 8110.54, for additional guidance regarding ICA.

c. Interchanging of Skis and Wheels. A person appropriately authorized by 14 CFR part 43, § 43.3, must perform a new weight and balance computation when the skis are initially installed. The FAA recommends that the airplane be weighed for this initial computation. After the initial installation, removing the skis and reinstalling the wheels or vice versa is considered a preventive maintenance operation if it does not involve complex assembly operations or a new weight and balance computation (ref. part 43, appendix A, paragraph (b)(4)(c)(18)).

NOTE: During subsequent weight and balance changes to the airplane, be sure to update its weight and

balance records and its equipment list to account for all approved ski, wheel, and float installations.

d. Periodic Inspection Required. Seasonally removed and installed equipment items such as skis should be inspected at installation to comply with §§ 91.407(a) and 91.409(a), and part 43, appendix D, paragraphs (e)(1) and (e)(10), if they were not installed on the airplane at the time of the last inspection. All available data described in this paragraph should be used during the inspection.

509. THRU 599. RESERVED

CHAPTER 6. OXYGEN SYSTEM INSTALLATIONS IN NONPRESSURIZED AIRCRAFT

SECTION 1. GENERAL

600. PURPOSE. This chapter provides data for acceptable means of gaseous oxygen system installations in nonpressurized aircraft. For other oxygen system installations (i.e., liquid oxygen), installers should contact their local Flight Standard District Office (FSDO) for assistance in applying for a Supplemental Type Certificate (STC).

601. HAZARDS AND WARNINGS TO CONSIDER WHEN INSTALLING AN OXYGEN SYSTEM.

a. Oxygen itself does not burn, but materials that burn in air will burn much hotter and more vigorously in an oxygen rich environment.

b. Oil and grease burn with explosive violence in the presence of oxygen.

c. Rapid release of high-pressure oxygen in the presence of foreign particles can cause temperatures sufficient to ignite combustible materials and materials that would not normally burn in air.

d. Pressurized oxygen cylinder failures, particularly aluminum-lined composite cylinders, have the potential of producing violent explosions.

602. ADDITIONAL REFERENCES (current editions).

a. Title 14 of the Code of Federal Regulations (14 CFR) part 23, Airworthiness Standards: Normal, Utility, Acrobatic, and Commuter Category Airplanes.

b. Title 14 CFR part 43, Maintenance, Preventive Maintenance, Rebuilding, and Alteration.

c. Title 14 CFR part 91, General Operating and Flight Rules.

d. Civil Aviation Regulations (CAR) 3, Airplane Airworthiness; Normal, Utility, and Acrobatic Categories.

e. CAR 6, Rotorcraft Airworthiness; Normal Category.

f. Advisory Circular (AC) 27-1, Certification of Normal Category Rotorcraft.

g. AC 43.13-1, Acceptable Methods, Techniques, and Practices—Aircraft Inspection and Repair.

h. Society of Automotive Engineers Aerospace Information Report (SAE AIR) No. 825B, Oxygen Equipment for Aircraft and SAE AIR 822, Oxygen Systems for General Aviation.

i. Handbook Bulletin for Airworthiness (HBAW) 02-01B, Maintenance of Pressure Cylinders in Use as Aircraft Equipment.

j. FAA Order 8310.6, Airworthiness Compliance Check Sheet Handbook.

603. THRU 606. RESERVED

SECTION 2. INSTALLATION OF THE OXYGEN SYSTEM

607. SYSTEM REQUIREMENTS. Gaseous oxygen systems may be a higher pressure system with the oxygen stored at 1850 psi or a low pressure system with the oxygen stored at 425 psi. All oxygen systems contain a storage tank, a regulation system, and a distribution system. The main difference in system type is in the regulation of the oxygen to the user (re: paragraph f below).

a. Cylinders. Install oxygen cylinders conforming to Interstate Commerce Commission (ICC) requirements for gas cylinders which carry the ICC or DOT 3A, 3AA, or 3HT designation followed by the service pressure metal-stamp on the cylinder.

b. Tubing/Lines.

(1) In systems having low pressure, use seamless aluminum alloy or equivalent having an outside diameter of 5/16 inch and a wall thickness of 0.035". Double flare the ends to attach to fittings.

(2) In high-pressure systems (1800 psi), use 3/16-inch O.D., 0.035" wall thickness, seamless copper alloy tubing meeting Specification WWT-779a type N, or stainless steel between the filler valve and the pressure-reducing valve. Silver-solder cone nipples to the ends of the tubing to attach the fittings in accordance with Specification MIL-B-7883.

(3) Use 5/16-inch O.D. aluminum alloy tubing after the pressure-reducer (low-pressure side).

NOTE: Any lines that pass through potential fire zones should be stainless steel.

NOTE: If lines are located behind upholstery or not 100 percent visible during normal operations, they should be solid metal lines or high-pressure flexible lines.

c. Fittings. All fittings must be manufactured from materials that are compatible for use with oxygen systems. Fittings should not be made of mild steel or materials that are prone to corrosion when in contact with another material.

(1) High Pressure. Intercylinder connections are made with regular flared or flareless tube fittings with stainless steel. Usually fittings are of the same material as the lines. Mild steel or aluminum alloy fittings with stainless steel lines are discouraged. Titanium fittings should never be used because of a possible chemical reaction and resulting fire.

(2) Low Pressure. Fittings for metallic low-pressure lines are flared or flareless, similar to high pressure lines. Line assemblies should be terminated with "B" nuts in a similarly manner to a manufactured terminating connection. Universal adapters (AN 807) or friction nipples used in conjunction with hose clamps are not acceptable for use in pressurized oxygen systems.

d. Valves. Each system must contain a slow-opening/closing shutoff valve that is accessible to a flight crewmember to turn on and shut off the oxygen supply at the high pressure source.

e. Regulators. The cylinder or system pressure is reduced to the individual cabin outlets by means of a pressure-reducing regulator that can be manually or automatically controlled. The regulator should be mounted as close as possible to the cylinders and certificated for aviation environment.

f. Types of Regulators. The four basic types of oxygen systems, classified according to the type of regulator employed, are:

(1) Continuous-flow Type. The constant flow type provides the same output pressure or flow regardless of altitude. Continuous-flow oxygen systems provide protection for passengers up to 25,000 feet mean sea level (MSL) and a continuous flow of 100 percent oxygen to the user. They may be automatic or manual in their operation.

(2) Diluter-demand Type. This type dilutes pure oxygen with ambient air and maintains the proper portion of oxygen in the breathing gas depending on altitude. Oxygen concentration is automatically diluted proportionate to the specific altitude's predetermined human oxygen consumption requirement. Such systems only supply oxygen, mixed with cabin air, during inhalation.

(3) Demand Type. This type uses high-pressure compressed oxygen that feeds a supply of oxygen to a 'high-to-low' pressure regulator at the individual crew station. The regulator, after reducing the higher pressure, automatically cycled low-pressure breathing oxygen to the wearer only on demand. Section 23.1441 requires aircraft that are certified to operate above 25,000 feet to be equipped with a demand system to supply required crewmembers.

(4) Pressure-demand Type. This type is not likely to be included on small general-aviation models. Aircraft certified to exceed 40,000 feet must have a pressure-demand system, which delivers pressurized oxygen to pilots such as high altitude Oxygen breathing system (above 40,000 feet) using anthropomorphic facial measurements of aircrew to produce a mask that would satisfactorily contain the pressure required to allow breathing under pressure, while maintaining an airtight face-seal and also remaining relatively comfortable to the wearer.

g. Flow Indicators.

(1) A pith-ball flow indicator, vane, wheel anemometer, or lateral pressure indicator which fluctuates with changes in flow or any other satisfactory flow indicator may be used in a continuous flow-type system.

(2) An Air Force/Navy flow indicator or equivalent may be used in a diluter-demand type system. Each flow indicator should give positive indication when oxygen flow is occurring.

h. Relief Valve.

(1) A relief valve is installed in low-pressure oxygen systems to safely relieve excessive pressure, such as that caused by overcharging.

(2) A relief valve is installed in high-pressure oxygen systems to safely relieve excessive pressure, such as that caused by heating.

i. Gauge. Provide a pressure gauge to show the amount of oxygen in the cylinder during flight.

j. Masks. Only approved masks designed for the particular system should be used.

608. INSTALLATION AND DESIGN CONSIDERATIONS. Oxygen systems present a hazard. Therefore, follow the precautions and practices listed below:

a. Remove oil, grease (including lip salves, hair oil, etc.), and dirt from hands, clothing, and tools before working with oxygen equipment.

b. Prior to cutting the upholstery, check the intended route of the system.

CAUTION: Ensure all system components are kept completely free of oil or grease during installation and locate components so they will not contact or become contaminated by oil or oil lines.

c. Keep open ends of cleaned and dried tubing capped or plugged at all times, except during attachment or detachment of parts. Do not use tape, rags, or paper.

d. Clean all lines and fittings that have not been cleaned and sealed by one of the following methods:

(1) A vapor-degreasing method with stabilized trichlorethylene conforming to Specification MIL-T-7003 or carbon tetrachloride. Blow tubing clean and dry with a stream of clean, dried, water-pumped air, or dry nitrogen (water-vapor content of less than 0.005 milligrams per liter of gas at 700º F and 760 millimeters of mercury pressure).

(2) Flush with naptha conforming to Specification TT-N-95; blow clean and dry off all solvent with water-pumped air; flush with antiicing fluid conforming to Specification MIL-F-5566 or anhydrous cthyl alcohol; rinse thoroughly with fresh water; and dry thoroughly with a stream of clean, dried, water-pumped air, or by heating at a temperature of 250º to 300º F for one-half hour.

(3) Flush with hot inhibited alkaline cleaner until free from oil and grease; rinse thoroughly with fresh water; and dry thoroughly with a stream of clean, dried, water-pumped air, or by heating at a temperature of 250º to 300º F for one-half hour.

e. Install lines, fittings, and equipment above and at least 6 inches away from fuel, oil, and hydraulic systems. Use deflector plates where necessary to keep hydraulic fluids away from the lines, fittings, and equipment.

f. Allow at lcast a 2-inch clearance between the plumbing and any flexible control cable or other flexible moving parts of the aircraft. Provide at least a 1/2-inch clearance between the plumbing and any rigid control tubes or other rigid moving parts of the aircraft.

g. Allow a 6-inch separation between the plumbing and the flight and engine control cables, and electrical lines. When electrical conduit is used, this separation between the plumbing and conduit may be reduced to 2 inches.

h. Route the oxygen system tubing, fittings, and equipment away from hot air ducts and equipment. Insulate or provide space between these items to prevent heating the oxygen system.

i. Mount all plumbing in a manner that prevents vibration and chafing. Support a 3/16-inch O.D. copper line each 24 inches and a 3/16-inch O.D. aluminum each 36 inches with cushioned loop-type line support clamps (AN-742) or equivalent.

j. Locate the oxygen supply valve (control valve) so as to allow its operation by the pilot during flight. The cylinder shutoff valve may be used as the supply control valve, if it is operable from the pilot's seat. Manifold plug-in type outlets, which are incorporated in automatic systems, may be considered oxygen supply valves since the pilot can control the flow of oxygen by engaging and disengaging the plug-in type oxygen mask.

k. Filler connections, if provided, are recommended to be located outside the fuselage skin or isolated in a manner that would prevent leaking oxygen from entering the aircraft. Careful evaluation should also be made of any nearby source of fuel, oil, or hydraulic fluid under normal or malfunction conditions. Each filler connection should be placarded. Additionally, any valve (aircraft or ground servicing equipment) associated with high pressure should be slow acting.

NOTE: Locate the oxygen shutoff valve on or as close as practicable to the cylinder to prevent loss of oxygen due to leakage in the system.

609. EQUIPMENT LOCATION AND MOUNTING. Determine the weight/load factors and center of gravity (CG) limits for the installation prior to commencing the installation.

a. Mount the cylinder in the baggage compartment or other suitable location in such a position that the shutoff valve is readily accessible. Provide access to this valve from inside the cabin so that it may be turned on or off in flight.

b. Fasten the cylinder brackets securely to the aircraft, preferably to a frame member or floorboard using AN bolts with fiber or similar locking nuts. Add sufficient plates, gussets, stringers, cross-bracing, or other reinforcements, where necessary, to provide a mounting that will withstand the inertia forces, stipulated in chapter 1.

c. When cylinders are located where they may be damaged by baggage or stored materials, protect them with a suitable guard or covering.

d. Provide at least 1/2-inch of clear airspace between any cylinder and a firewall or shroud isolating a designated fire zone.

e. Mount the regulator close to the cylinder to avoid long high-pressure lines.

f. Store the masks in such a way that there will be a minimum delay in removing and putting them into use.

610. THREAD COMPOUND. Use anti-seize or thread-sealing compound conforming to Specification MIL-T-5542-B, or equivalent.

a. Do not use compound on aluminum alloy flared tube fittings having straight threads. Proper flaring and tightening should be sufficient to make a flared tube connection leakproof.

b. Treat all male-tapered pipe threads with antiseize and sealing compound (MIL-T-5542-B, or tetrafluroethylene tape MIL-T-27730), or equivalent.

c. Apply the compound in accordance with the manufacturer's recommendation. Make sure that the compounds are carefully and sparingly applied only to male threads, coating the first three threads from the end of the fitting. Do not use compound on the coupling sleeves or on the outside of the tube flares.

611. FUNCTIONAL TEST. Before inspection plates, cover plates, or upholstering are replaced, make a system check including at least the following:

a. Open cylinder valve slowly and observe the pressure gauge.

b. Open supply valve and remove one of the mask tubes and bayonet fittings from one of the masks in the kit. Plug the bayonet into each of the oxygen outlets. A small flow should be noted from each of the outlets. This can be detected by holding the tube to the lips while the bayonet is plugged into an outlet.

c. Check the complete system for leaks. This can be done with a soap solution made only from a mild (castile) soap or by leak-detector solution supplied by the oxygen equipment manufacturer.

d. If leaks are found, close the cylinder shutoff valve and reduce the pressure in the system by plugging a mask tube into one of the outlets or by carefully loosening one of the connections in the system. When the pressure has been reduced to zero, make the necessary repairs. Repeat the procedure until no leaks are found in the system.

WARNING: Never tighten oxygen system fittings with oxygen pressure applied.

e. Test each outlet for leaks at the point where the mask tube plugs in. This can be done by using a soapy solution over each of the outlets. Use the solution sparingly to prevent dogging the outlet by soap. Remove all residue to prevent accumulation of dirt.

f. Examine the system to determine if the flow of oxygen through each outlet is at least equal to the minimum required by the pertinent requirements at all altitudes at which the aircraft is to be operated. This can be accomplished by one of the following methods:

(1) In a continuous flow system when the calibration (inlet pressure vs. flow) of the orifices used at the plug-in outlets is known, the pressure in the low-pressure distribution line can be measured at the point which is subject to the greatest pressure drop. Do this with oxygen flowing from all outlets. The pressure thus measured should indicate a flow equal to or greater than the minimum flow required.

(2) In lieu of the above procedure, the flow of oxygen, through the outlet that is subject to the greatest pressure drop, may be measured with all other outlets open. Gas meters, rotometers, or other suitable means may be used to measure flows.

(3) The measurement of oxygen flow in a continuous flow system which uses a manually adjusted regulator can be accomplished at sea level. However, in a continuous flow system which uses an automatic-type regulator, it may be necessary to check the flow at maximum altitude which will be encountered during the normal operation of the aircraft. The manufacturer of the particular continuous-flow regulator used should be able to furnish data on the operating characteristics of the regulator from which it can be determined if a flight check is necessary.

(4) Checking the amount of flow through the various outlets in a diluter-demand or straight-demand system is not necessary since the flow characteristics of the particular regulator being used may be obtained from the manufacturer of the regulator. However, in such systems the availability of oxygen to each regulator should be checked by turning the lever of the diluter-demand regulator to the "100 percent oxygen" position and inhaling through the tube via the mask to determine whether the regulator valve and the flow indicator are operating.

g. Provide one of the following acceptable means or equivalent to indicate oxygen flow to each user by:

(1) Listening for audible indication of oxygen flow.

(2) Watching for inflation of the rebreather or reservoir bag.

(3) Installing a flow indicator.

612. OPERATING INSTRUCTIONS. Provide instructions appropriate to the type of system and masks installed for the pilot on placards. Include in these instructions a graph or a table which will show the duration of the oxygen supply for the various cylinder pressures and pressure altitudes (Table 6-1).

613. THRU 617. RESERVED

TABLE 6-1. TYPICAL OXYGEN DURATION TABLE

ACTUAL DURATION IN HOURS AT VARIOUS ALTITUDES					
Number of Persons	*8000 Ft.*	*10,000 Ft.*	*12,000 Ft.*	*15,000 Ft.*	*20,000 Ft.*
Pilot only	7.6 hr	7.1 hr	6.7 hr	6.35 hr	5.83 hr
Pilot and 1 Passenger	5.07 hr	4.74 hr	4.47 hr	4.24 hr	3.88 hr
Pilot and 2 Passengers	3.8 hr	3.55 hr	3.36 hr	3.18 hr	2.92 hr
Pilot and 3 Passengers	3.04 hr	2.84 hr	2.68 hr	2.54 hr	2.34 hr
Pilot and 4 Passengers	2.53 hr	2.37 hr	2.24 hr	2.12 hr	1.94 hr
NOTE: The above duration time is based on a fully charged 48 cubic-foot cylinder. For duration using 63 cubic-foot cylinder, multiply any duration by 1.3.					

FIGURE 6-1. TYPICAL FLOOR MOUNTING

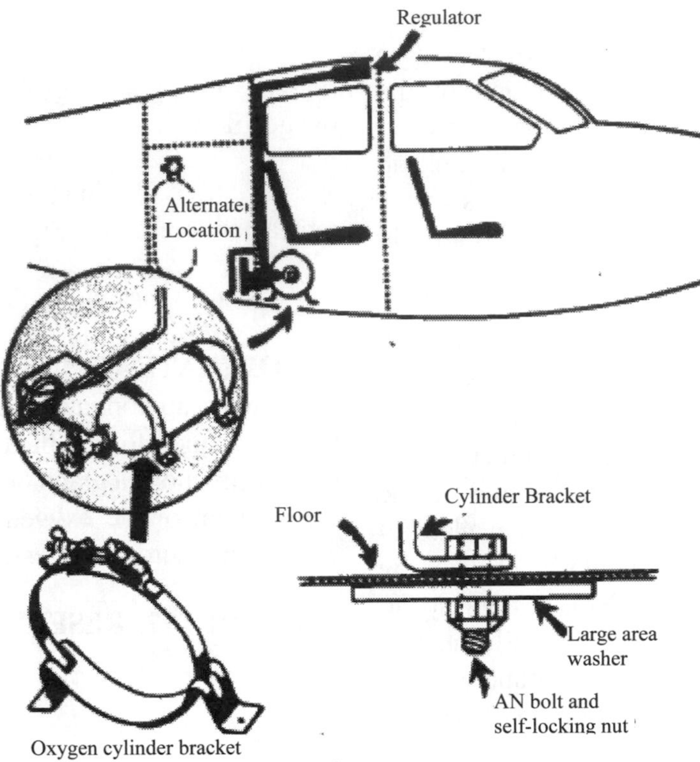

Reinforce floor, if necessary, to withstand the added load.
Like aluminum or plywood of sufficient thickness.

FIGURE 6-2. TYPICAL BAGGAGE COMPARTMENT MOUNTING

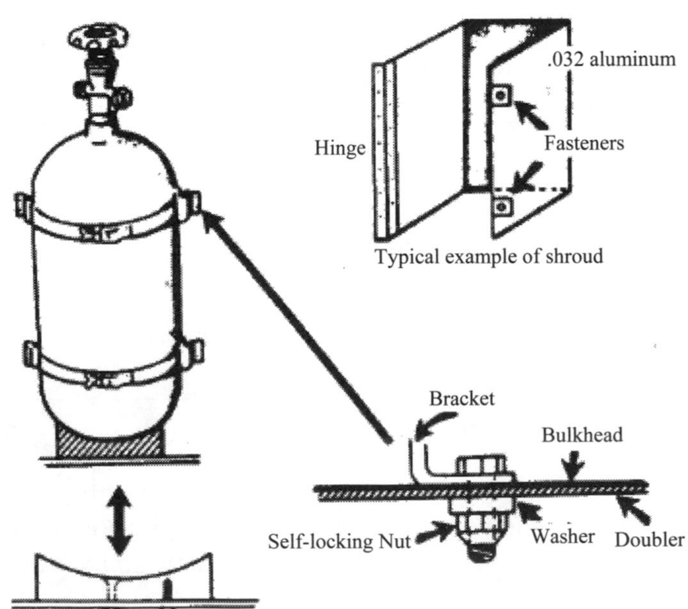

NOTE: Enclose cylinder and valve with shroud to prevent damage from baggage.

FIGURE 6-3. TYPICAL OXYGEN INSTALLATION IN LIGHT TWIN AIRCRAFT

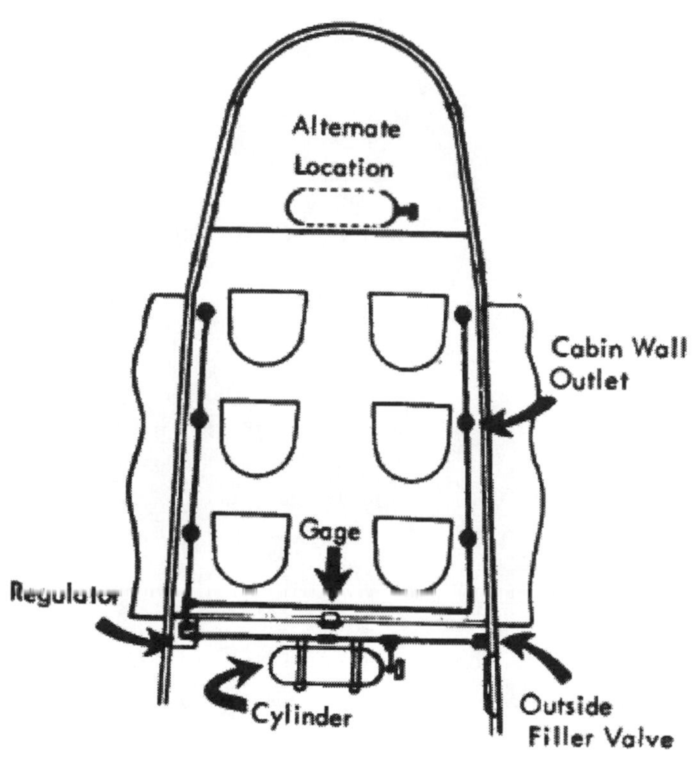

SECTION 3. AIRWORTHINESS COMPLIANCE CHECK SHEET: OXYGEN SYSTEM INSTALLATION IN UNPRESSURIZED AIRCRAFT

618. GENERAL. Oxygen system installations made in accordance with FAA-approved airframe manufacturer, or other FAA-approved installations, may be accepted without further investigation. On other installations, the following points should be checked to determine if the installation is satisfactory.

619. APPLICABLE FEDERAL AVIATION REGULATIONS. Determine if the installation complies with the regulations listed in paragraph 602.

620. STRUCTURAL REQUIREMENTS.

a. If changes or alterations of the aircraft structure are made (mounting of oxygen cylinder), determine if the original strength and integrity of the structure is retained.

b. If gages are added to the instrument panel or an outside filler valve installed on the fuselage, determine if the structural integrity of the panel and airframe or its supporting structure is retained.

c. Determine if the extent of the modification has affected the center of gravity (CG) of the aircraft evaluated.

d. Check whether all lines are properly routed and supported.

621. HAZARDS TO THE AIRCRAFT OR ITS OCCUPANTS. Determine if the design of the oxygen system is evaluated to ensure that the aircraft and its occupants are safe from hazards identified in paragraph 601.

622. OPERATING ASPECTS.

a. When required by the operating rules for the use of supplemental oxygen, determine if the system's capacity is sufficient to supply oxygen to all combinations of crew and passengers.

b. Determine if the oxygen system provides the required flow.

c. Determine if the oxygen regulator controls are accessible to a member of the flightcrew in flight.

d. Determine if there is a means, readily available to the crew in flight, to turn on and shut off the oxygen supply at the high pressure source.

e. Check whether there is a means to allow the crew to readily determine during flight the quantity of oxygen available in each source of supply.

623. DETAIL DESIGN STANDARDS. Determine if:

a. All parts are suitable for use with oxygen.

b. The regulator is located as close as physically possible to the oxygen cylinder and minimizes the use of fittings.

c. No lines are 100 percent visible during normal operation solid metal lines.

d. Each breathing device has a device attached that visually shows the flow of oxygen.

e. The lines that pass through potential fire zones are stainless steel.

f. When oxygen system components are added to the baggage compartments, there are provisions to protect the system components from shifting cargo.

g. Where oxygen components are installed, the compartment is placarded against the storage of oil or hydrocarbons.

h. A smoke detector is installed where oxygen cylinders are installed in a closed, nonaccessible compartment.

i. The cargo area weight limitations placard is updated.

j. All oxygen outlets are placarded.

k. "No Smoking When Oxygen Is In Use" placards and other appropriate placards (i.e., operation instructions) are visible to the crew and occupants of the aircraft.

624. INSTRUCTIONS FOR CONTINUED AIRWORTHINESS. Determine if:

a. There are written instructions concerning system operation, maintenance, and cylinder changing procedures.

b. There are written instructions in the use of the oxygen equipment in the AFM or placards.

NOTE: Any changes to the AFM must be approved by the FAA.

c. There are written inspection and test schedules and procedures.

d. Mechanical drawings and wiring diagrams are available, as required.

e. Written instructions are available concerning oxygen cylinder hydrostatic testing requirements and cylinder replacement requirements.

f. There is a scheduled (annual) check of a constant flow system manifold output pressure for recommended output pressure.

g. The guidance contained in AC 43.13-1 (current edition), paragraphs 9-47 to 9-51 is considered in the design of the oxygen maintenance program.

625. RECORDKEEPING. Determine if:

a. A maintenance record entry has been made. (Reference § 43.9.)

b. The equipment list and weight and balance has been revised. (Reference Order 8310.6, chapter 1.)

626. THRU 699. RESERVED

CHAPTER 7. ROTORCRAFT EXTERNAL-LOAD-DEVICE INSTALLATIONS CARGO SLINGS AND EXTERNAL RACKS

SECTION 1. GENERAL

700. PURPOSE. This section contains structural and design information for the fabrication and installation of a cargo sling used as an external load attaching means for a Class B rotorcraft-load combination operation under Title 14 of the Code of Federal Regulations (14 CFR) part 133. As an external-load attaching means, a "cargo sling" includes a quick-release device (hook) and the associated cables, fittings, etc., used for the attachment of the cargo sling to the rotorcraft. Part 133, § 133.43(d) specifies the requirements for the quick-release device.

701. HAZARDS AND WARNINGS. Particular attention should be paid to the effect of the sling load on the lateral as well as the fore and aft center of gravity (CG) of the rotorcraft. Use TC PMA, T50 or Designated Engineering Representative approved parts.

702. REFERENCES. It is the installer's responsibility to ensure that the latest revisions of any regulations, advisory circulars, manufacturer's data, etc., are used in any cargo sling or rack installation. Reference Title 14 of the Code of Federal Regulations part 27 and Civil Aviation Regulation 6, Rotorcraft Airworthiness; Normal Category.

703. INSTALLATION CONSIDERATIONS.

a. Location of Cargo Release in Relation to the Rotorcraft's CG Limits. An ideal location would be one that allows the line of action to pass through the rotorcraft's CG at all times. (See Figure 7-1, Illustration A.) However, with most cargo sling installations, this ideal situation is realized only when the line of action is vertical or near vertical and through the rotorcraft's CG (See Figure 7-1, Illustration B.)

(1) Whenever the line of action does not pass through the rotorcraft's CG due to the attachment method used, acceleration forces, or aerodynamic forces, the rotorcraft-load combined CG will shift from the rotorcraft's CG position. Depending upon the factors involved, the shift may occur along either or both the longitudinal or lateral axes. The amount of shift is dependent upon the force applied (F) and the length of the arm of the line of action. Their product (F x Arm) yields a moment which can be used to determine the rotorcraft-load combined CG (See Figure 7-1, Illustration C.) If the rotorcraft-load CG is allowed to shift beyond the rotorcraft's approved CG limits, the rotorcraft may become violently uncontrollable.

FIGURE 7-1. LOCATION OF CARGO RELEASE IN RELATION TO THE ROTORCRAFT'S CENTER OF GRAVITY

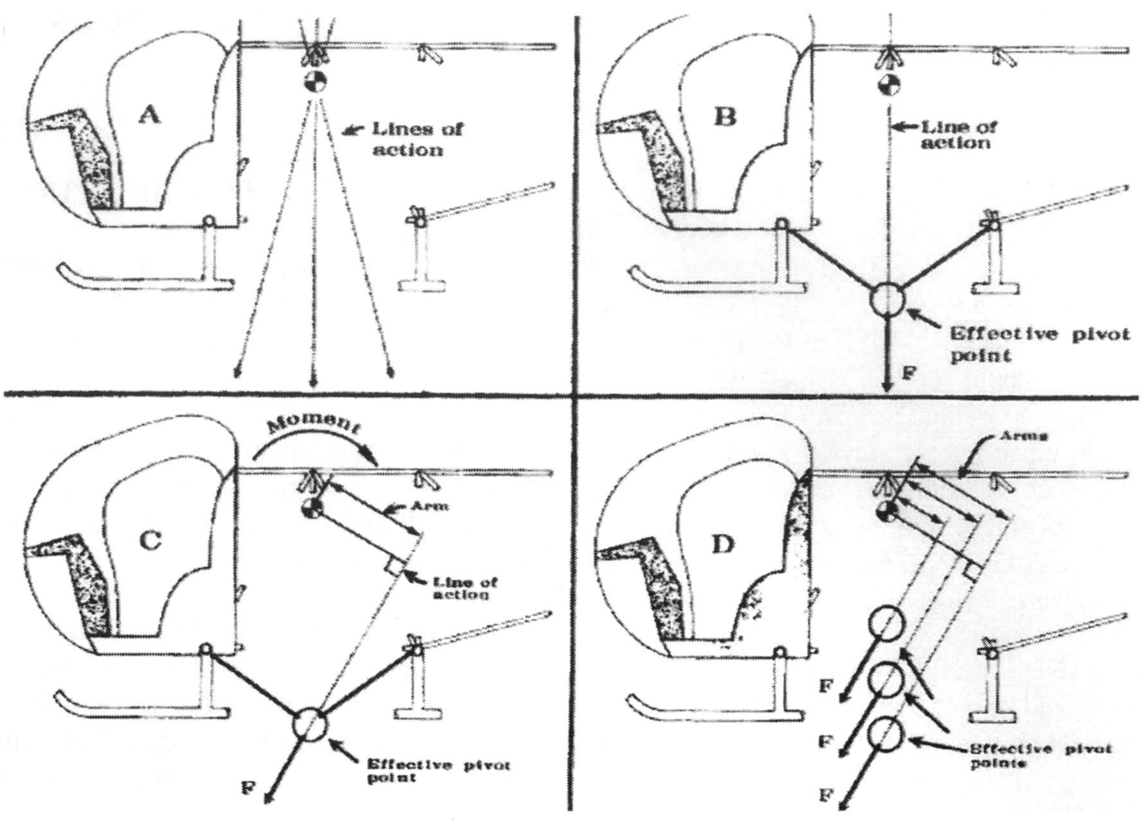

(2) Thus, any attachment method or location which will decrease the length of the arm will reduce the distance that the combined CG will shift for a given load (F) and line of action angle. (See Figure 7-1, Illustration D.)

b. Maximum External Load. The maximum external load (including the weight of the cargo sling) for which authorization is requested may not exceed the rated capacity of the quick-release device.

704. FABRICATION AND INSTALLATION.

a. Static Test. The cargo sling installation must be able to withstand the static load required by § 133.43(a). Conduct the test as outlined in chapter 1. If required during the test, supports may be placed at the landing gear to airframe attach fittings to prevent detrimental deformation of the landing gear due to the weight of the aircraft.

b. Sling-Leg Angles of Cable-Supported Slings. The optimum sling-leg angle (measured from the horizontal) is 45 to 60 degrees. Minimum tension in a sling leg occurs with a sling-leg angle of 90 degrees, and the tension approaches infinity as the angle approaches zero. Thus, larger sling-leg angles are desirable from a standpoint of cable strength requirements. Slings should not be attached in such a manner as to provide sling-leg angles of less than 30 degrees.

c. Minimum Sling-Leg Cable Strength.

(1) An analysis which considered the effects of 30-degree sling angles showed that the minimum cable strength design factor required would be 2.5 times the maximum external load for each leg regardless of the number of legs. Although this is the minimum strength required by part 133, it may be desirable to double this value to allow for deterioration of the sling-leg cables in service. This will result in a cable strength equal to five times the maximum external load.

Example: Maximum external load 850 pounds
Minimum required sling-leg cable
strength 850 x 2.5 = 2125
Minimum desired sling-leg cable
strength 850 x 2.5 x 2 = 4250

(2) A 3/16-inch, nonflexible 19-wire cable (MIL-W-6940*)* provides a satisfactory cable strength. For convenience, the cable sizes desired for various loads have been calculated and are tabulated in Table 7-1 based on a factor of 5:

TABLE 7-1. CABLE LOAD TABLE

Maximum External Load (pounds)	Aircraft Cable Size For Each Cargo Sling Leg		
	MIL-C-5693 and MIL-W-6940	MIL-W-1511	MIL-C-5424
100	1/16	3/32	3/32
200	3/32	1/8	1/8
300	7/64	1/8	1/8
400	1/8	1/8	5/32
500	5/32	5/32	3/16
600	5/32	3/16	3/16
700	3/16	3/16	3/16
800	3/16	3/16	7/32
900	3/16	7/32	7/32
1,000	7/32	7/32	7/32
1,200	7/32	1/4	¼
1,400	¼	1/4	9/32
1,600	1/4	9/32	5/16
1,800	5/16	5/16	5/16
2,000	5/16	11/32	3/8

d. Sling Installation.

(1) Attach the cargo sling to landing gear members or other structure capable of supporting the loads to be carried. Install the quick-release device in a level attitude with the throat opening facing the direction as indicated on the quick-release device. When cables are used to support the quick-release device, make sure the cables are not twisted or allowed to twist in the direction to un-lay the cable.

(2) Some cargo release devices are provided with a fitting to permit installation of a guideline to assist in fully automatic engagement of the load target ring or load bridle. Secure the guideline to the quick-release device with a shear pin of a definite known value which will shear if a load becomes entangled on or over the guideline. Provision should also be made for cable-supported slings to be drawn up against the fuselage into a stowage position to prevent striking or dragging the release on the ground when not in use.

e. Installation of Release Controls. See Figure 7-2 for typical wiring diagram of the electrical controls.

(1) Install a cargo release master switch, readily accessible to the pilot, to provide a means of deactivating the release circuit. The power for the electrical release circuit should originate at the primary bus. The "auto" position of the release master switch on some cargo release units provides for automatic release when the load contacts the ground and the load on the release is reduced to a preset value.

(2) Install the cargo release switch on one of the pilot's primary controls. It is usually installed on the cyclic stick to allow the pilot to release the load with minimum distraction after maneuvering the load into the release position.

FIGURE 7-2. TYPICAL CARGO SLING WIRING DIAGRAM

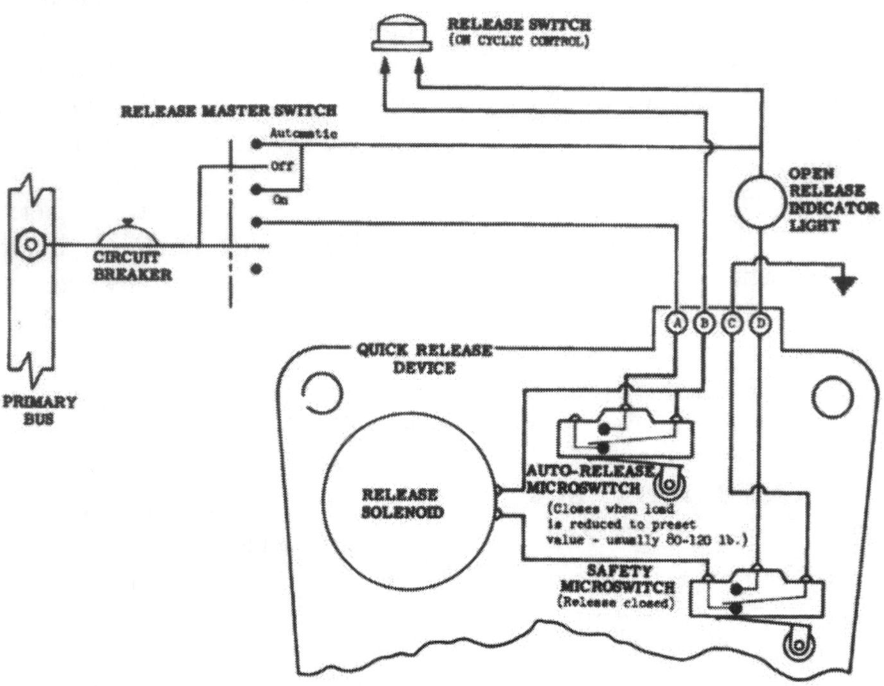

(3) Install the emergency manual release control in a suitable position that is readily accessible to the pilot or other crewmember. Allow sufficient slack in the control cable to permit complete cargo movement without tripping the cargo release.

(4) The manual ground release handle, a feature of some cargo release units, permits opening of the cargo release by ground personnel.

(5) Label or placard all release controls as to each function and operation.

f. Functional Test.

(1) Test the release action of each release control of the quick-release device with various loads up to and including the maximum external load. This may be done in a test fixture or while installed on the rotorcraft, if the necessary load can be applied.

(2) If the quick-release device incorporates an automatic release, the unit should not release the load when the master switch is placed in the "automatic" position until the load on the device is reduced to the preset value, usually 80 to 120 pounds.

FIGURE 7-3. TYPICAL CARGO SLING INSTALLATION NO. 1

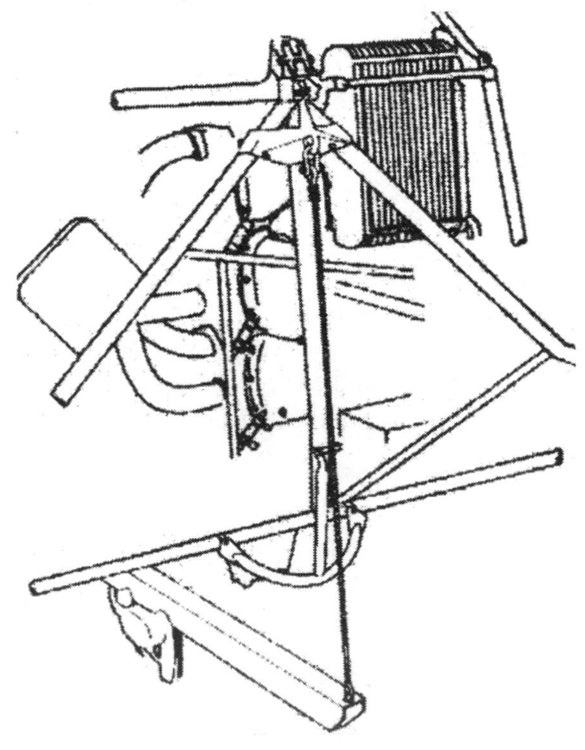

g. Supplemental Flight Information. The aircraft may not be used in part 133 external-load operations until a Rotorcraft-Load Combination Flight Manual is prepared in accordance with § 133.47 of that part. Appropriate entries should also be made in the aircraft's weight and balance data, equipment list, and logbooks. The FAA Form 337, Major Repair and Alteration (Airframe, Powerplant, Propeller, or Appliance), should also be executed as required by part 43, § 43.5(a) and (b).

h. Inspection and Maintenance. Inspection of the complete installation should be accomplished prior to each lift for security and functionality. Maintenance should be accomplished in accordance with the manufacturers instructions.

705. THRU 706. RESERVED

FIGURE 7-4. TYPICAL CARGO SLING INSTALLATION NO. 1 (SHOWING FUSELAGE ATTACHMENT FITTING)

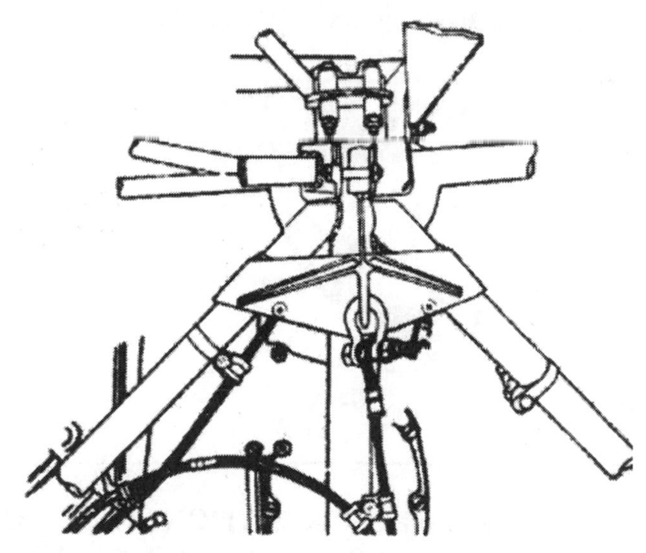

FIGURE 7-5. TYPICAL CARGO SLING INSTALLATION NO. 1 (SHOWING FORE AFT LIMITING STOPS)

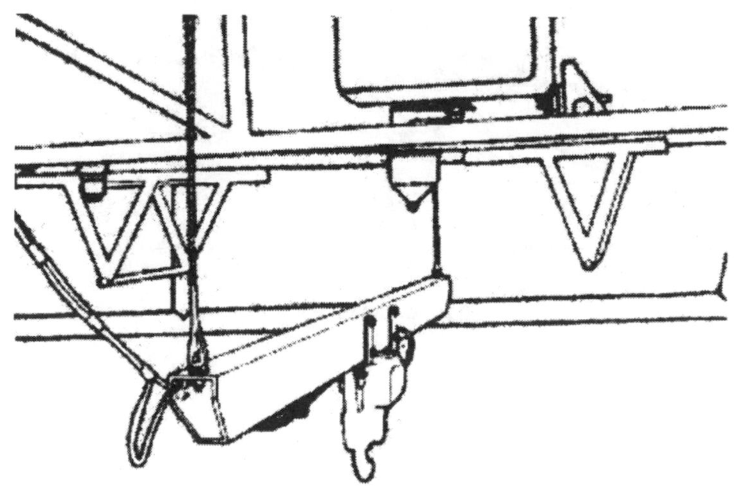

FIGURE 7-6. TYPICAL CARGO SLING INSTALLATION NO. 2 (CARGO HOOK ATTACHED DIRECTLY TO UNDERSIDE OF FUSELAGE)

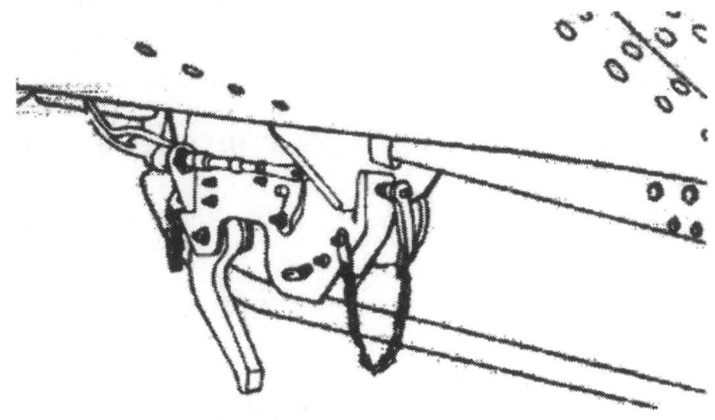

FIGURE 7-7. TYPICAL CARGO SLING INSTALLATION NO. 3 (4-LEG, CABLE SUSPENDED)

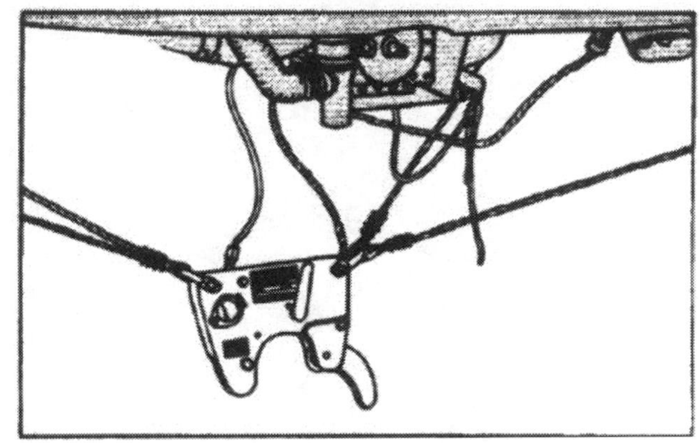

FIGURE 7-8. TYPICAL CARGO SLING INSTALLATION NO. 3 (SHOWING CABLE SLING LEG ATTACHMENT TO LANDING GEAR CROSSTUBE FITTING)

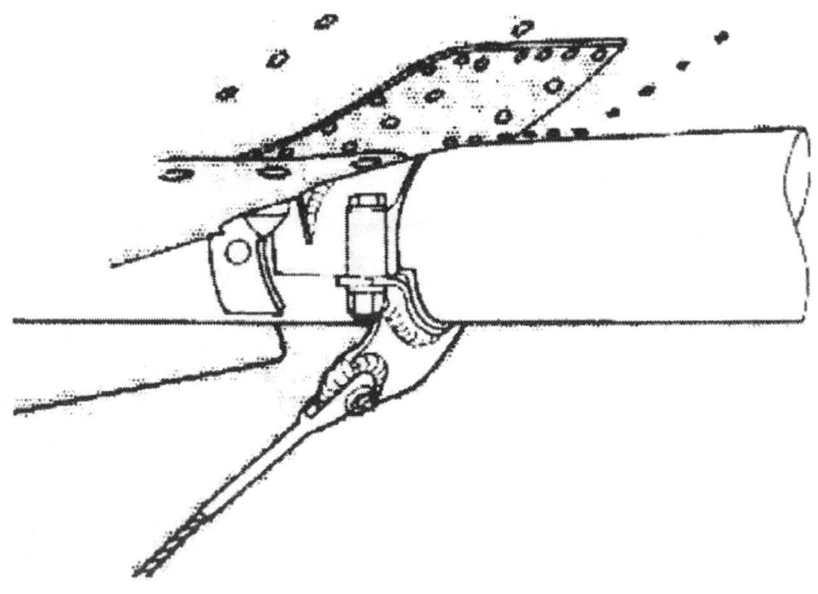

FIGURE 7-9. TYPICAL CARGO SLING INSTALLATION NO. 3 (SHOWING CARGO SLING IN STOWED POSITION)

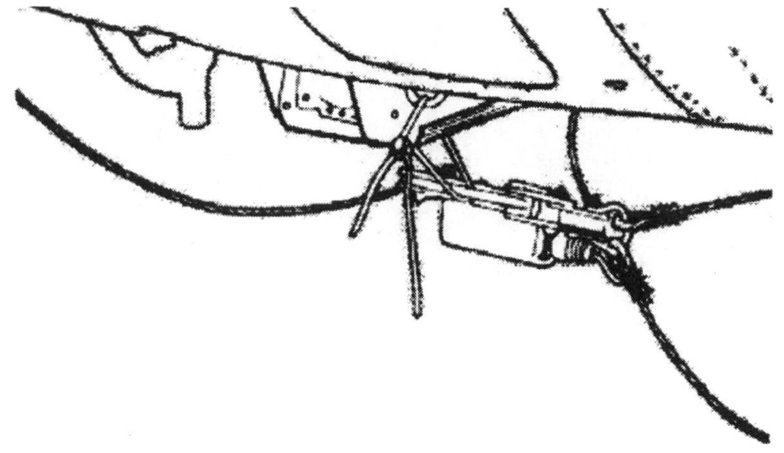

SECTION 2. CARGO RACKS

707. GENERAL. This section contains structural and design information for the fabrication and installation of a cargo rack used as an external-load attaching means for a Class A rotorcraft-load combination operation under part 133.

708. FABRICATION OF CARGO RACKS. The type of construction and method of attachment depends upon the material to be used and the configuration of the rotorcraft involved. Illustrations of typical construction and installation methods are shown in Figures 7-10 through 7-14.

FIGURE 7-10. TYPICAL CARGO RACK INSTALLATION NO. 1

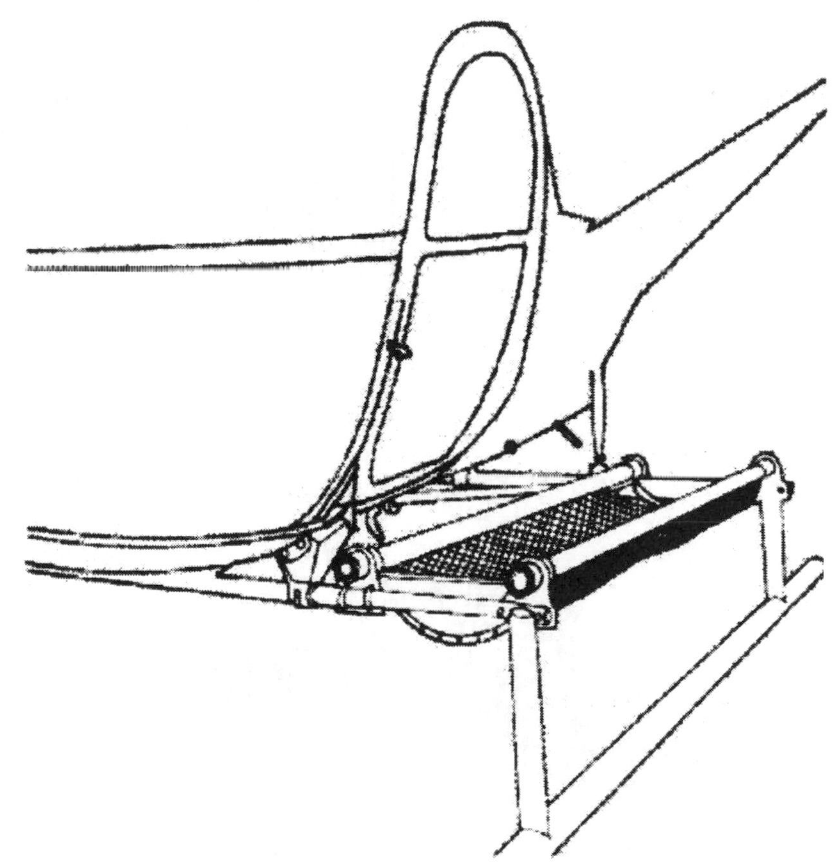

709. STATIC TEST. The cargo rack installation must be able to withstand the static test load required by § 133.43(a). Conduct the test as outlined in chapter 1.

710. SUPPLEMENTAL FLIGHT INFORMATION. The aircraft may not be used in part 133 external-load operations until a rotorcraft-load combination flight manual is prepared in accordance with § 133.47.

711. THRU 799. RESERVED

FIGURE 7-11. TYPICAL CARGO RACK INSTALLATION NO. 1 (SHOWING ATTACHMENT DETAIL)

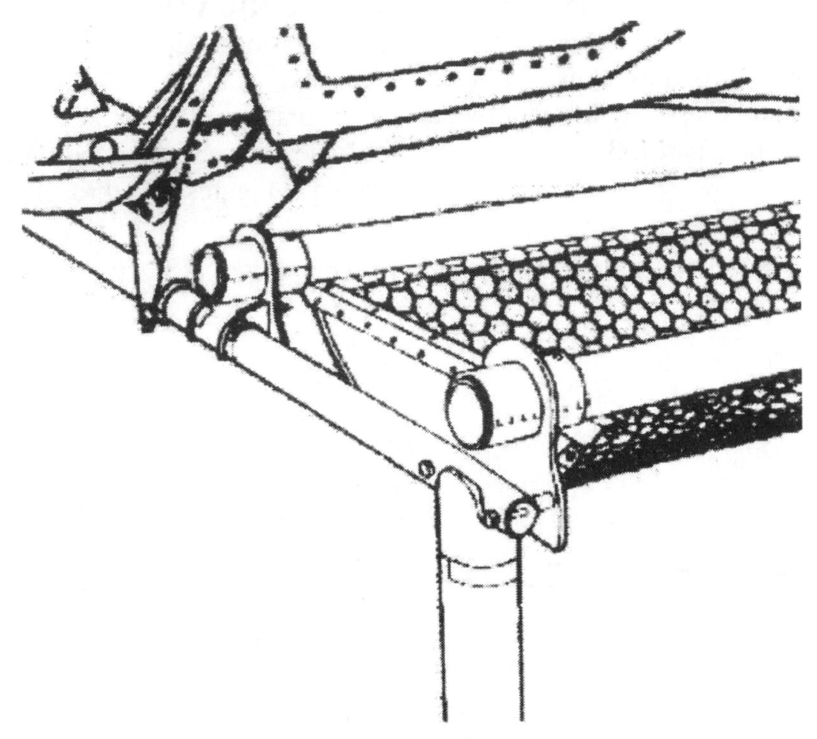

FIGURE 7-12. TYPICAL CARGO RACK INSTALLATION NO. 2

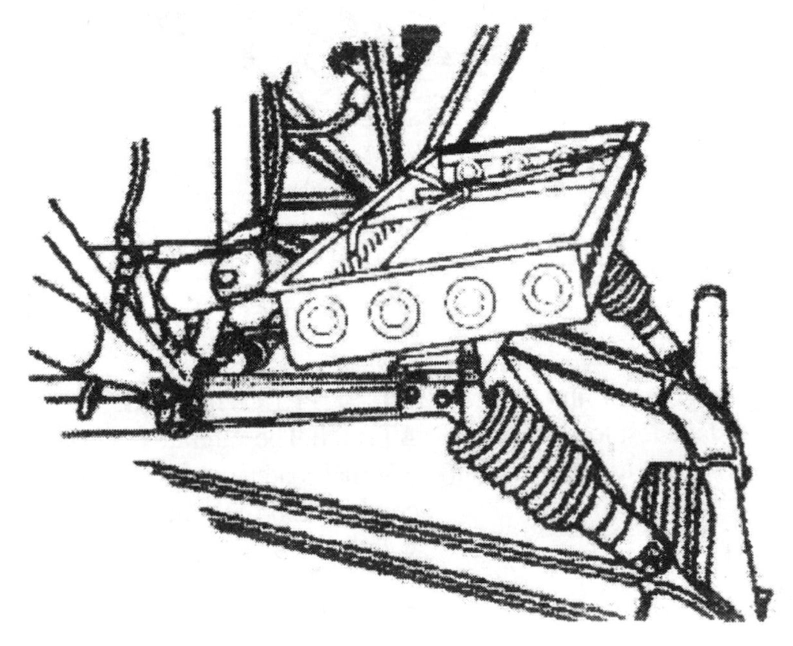

FIGURE 7-13. TYPICAL CARGO RACK INSTALLATION NO. 2 (SHOWING RACK PARTIALLY INSTALLED)

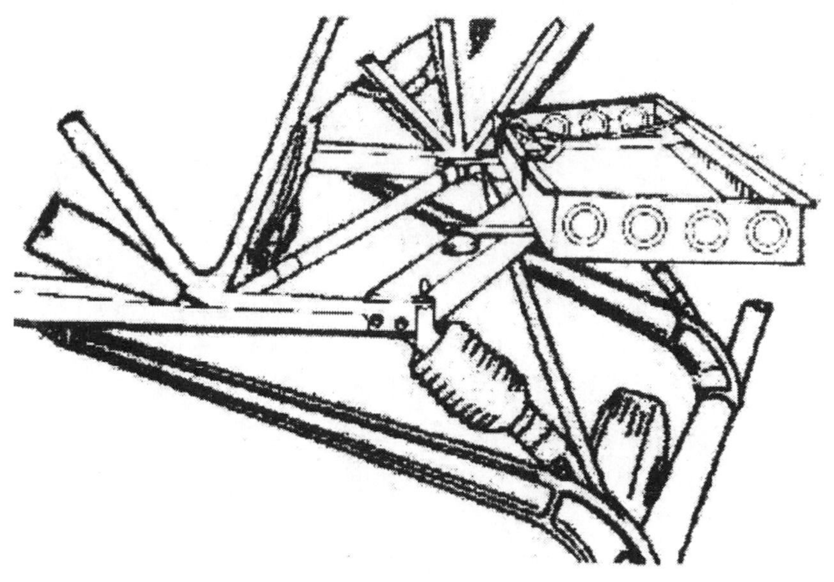

FIGURE 7-14. TYPICAL CARGO RACK INSTALLATION NO. 3

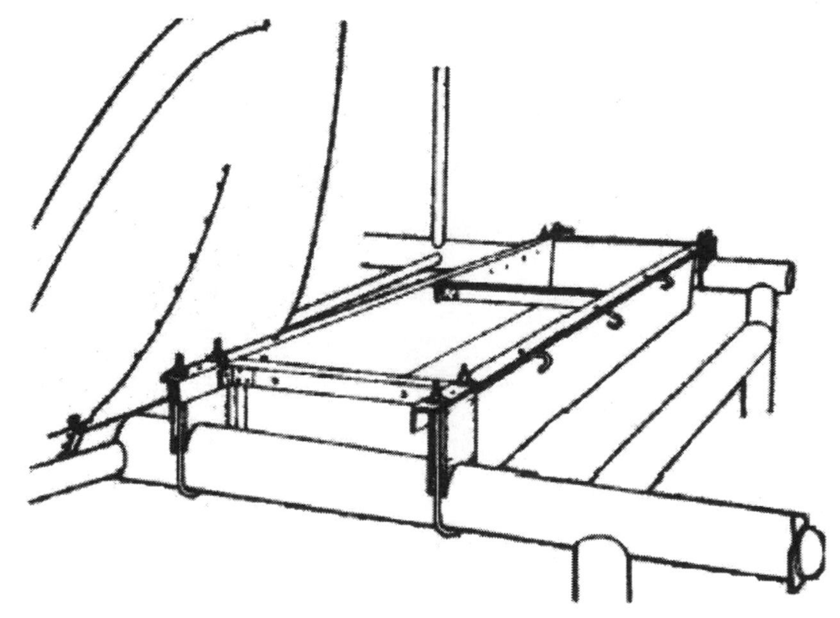

CHAPTER 8. GLIDER AND BANNER TOW-HITCH INSTALLATIONS

800. PURPOSE. This chapter contains design and installation information for banner and glider tow hitches. Guidance for inspection, service, and continuous airworthiness requirements for the hitches are also addressed in this chapter.

801. HAZARDS AND WARNING. The direction and maximum arc of displacement of banner towline loads occur within a more limited rearward cone of displacement than do glider towline loads (see Figure 8-1 and 8-2). Hitches that meet the banner tow criteria of this chapter may not be suitable for glider towing. Due to the basic aerodynamic differences between the two objects being towed, glider and banner tow-hitch installations are treated separately with regard to loading angles.

802. REFERENCES. This chapter will occasionally reference manufacturer's documents, certain parts of Title 14 of the Code of Federal Regulations (14 CFR), and certain FAA advisory circulars (AC). It is the installer's responsibility to ensure the latest revisions of these documents are used as reference material. Refer to Civil Aviation Regulation 6, Rotorcraft Airworthiness; Normal Category, and Order 8900.1, Volume 8, Chapter 5, Section 2, Changes to Special Purpose for Restricted Aircraft.

803. INSTALLATION CONSIDERATIONS.

a. Weight and Balance. In most cases, the weight of the tow-hitch assembly will affect the aft center of gravity (c.g.) location. To assure that the possibility of an adverse effect caused by the installation has not been ignored, enter all pertinent computations in the aircraft weight and balance records, in accordance with the provisions contained in 14 CFR part 43, § 43.5(c). The requirements of § 43.5(a) and (b) should also be addressed, for maintenance record entries and repair and alteration forms.

b. Equipment List. The aircraft equipment list should be updated to reflect any tow equipment installations. Consideration should also be given to adding appropriate revisions to the aircraft's Pilot Operating Handbook (POH), or Flight Manual, as required.

c. Corrosion Protection. Tow hitches are traditionally simple mechanical devices; however, improper care may lead to hazardous conditions for the aircraft operator. The aft, external location of tow hitches exposes them to the elements, and proper corrosion protection methods should be employed to prevent improper operation or malfunction. Reference should be made to the manufacturers documents or current edition of AC 43.13-1, Acceptable Method, techniques, and Practices—Aircraft Inspection and Repair, chapter 6, for some additional corrosion protective measures that may be used.

804. FABRICATION AND INSTALLATION PROCEDURES.

a. Methods. Accomplish the installation of tow hitches using manufacturer's data or that data previously approved by a representative of the Administrator, when available, such as a Supplemental Type Certificate (STC) or a Field Approval. Installations requiring fabrication of brackets, parts, fittings, etc. should be accomplished using data in the form of ACs such as AC 43.13-1 (current edition), to determine material requirements, load requirements, and type and size of hardware used.

b. Structural Requirements. The structural integrity of a tow-hitch installation on an aircraft is dependent upon its intended usage.

c. Attachment Points. Tow-hitch mechanisms are characteristically attached to, or at, tie down points or tail wheel brackets on the airframe. These are points where the design load-bearing qualities may be sufficient for towing loads. Keep the length from the airframe attachment point to the tow hook at a minimum as the loads on the attachment bolts are multiplied by increases in the attachment arm.

d. Glider Tow Hitch Load Testing.

(1) Protection for the tow-plane is provided by requiring use of a towline assembly that will break prior to structural damage occurring to the tow plane. The normal tow load imposed on the hitch rarely exceeds 80 percent of the weight of the glider. Therefore, the towline assembly design load for a 1,000-pound glider could be estimated at 800 pounds. By multiplying the estimated design load by 1.5 (to provide a safety margin), we arrive at a limit load value of 1,200 pounds. The 1,200-pound limit load value is used in static testing or analysis procedures per paragraph 8-2 to prove the strength of the tow hook installation. When the hook and its attachment to the aircraft structure have been proven to withstand the limit load, 1,200 pounds in this example, then the "maximum" breaking strength of the towline assembly is established at the design load of 800 pounds. Thus, the towline will break well before structural damage will occur to the tow-plane.

FIGURE 8-1. GLIDER TOW ANGLE

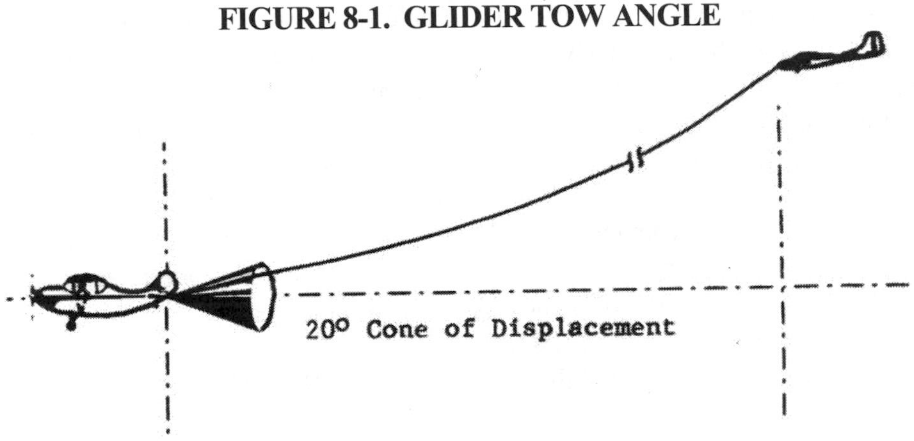

FIGURE 8-2. BANNER TOW ANGLE

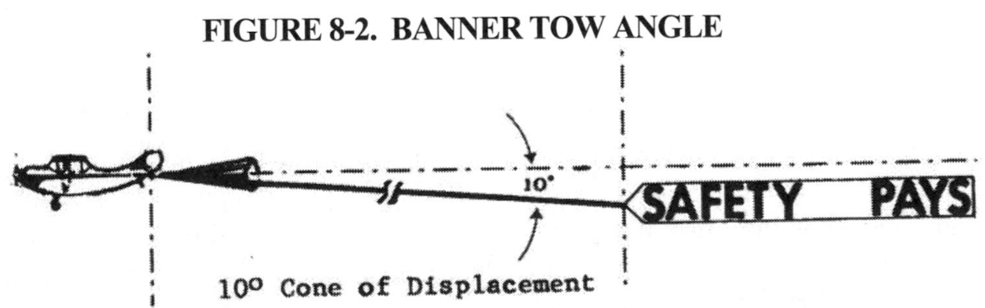

(2) Another approach can be applied if the limit load carrying capabilities of a tow hook and fuselage are known. In this case, the known load value can be divided by 1.5 to arrive at the design load limits. For example, if the tow hook and fuselage limit loads are known to be 1,800 pounds, divide this by 1.5 (1,800 ÷ 1.5 = 1,200) and we arrive at a design load value of 1,200 pounds. Thus, if a towline assembly rated at 1,200 pounds is used it will break before reaching the structural limits of the hook and attaching structure.

(3) When considering tow hook installations, one may establish maximum towline breaking strength by:

(a) Dividing the known limit load capabilities of the fuselage and tow hook installation by 1.5; or

(b) Knowing the design load needs of the towline assembly and multiplying by 1.5 to arrive at a limit load. Then analysis or static testing, determine that the hook and fuselage are capable of towing the load.

(4) Banner Tow Hitches. Install and test the hitch to support a limit load equal to at least two times the operating weight of the banner.

(5) Multiple Hitches. Multiple tow hitches are sometimes used on banner tow aircraft. These installations should be evaluated individually for approval.

805. STRUCTURAL TESTING. When installations are made on an aircraft using brackets that have not been previously approved, some structural testing may be required. Adequacy of the aircraft structure to withstand the required loads can be determined by either static test or structural analysis.

a. Static Testing. When using static tests to verify structural strength, subject the tow hitch to the anticipated limit load. Aircraft tow hitches used for banner towing shall be tested a minimum of 2 times the weight of the heaviest banner to be towed, using the cone angle shown in Figure 8-2. Aircraft towline used for glider towing shall be tested to a minimum load approximately 80 percent of the weight of the heaviest glider to be towed, using the cone angle shown in Figure 8-1. Static testing should to be done in accordance with the procedures in chapter 1, paragraph 106.

b. Structural Analysis. If the local fuselage structure is not substantiated by static test for the proposed tow load, using a method that experience has shown to be reliable, subject the fuselage to engineering analysis to determine that the local structure is adequate. Use a fitting factor of 1.15 or greater in the loads for this analysis.

806. ANGLES OF TOW. Tests should be conducted on the system at various tow angles to insure that:

a. There is no interference with the tail wheel or adjacent structure. Tow-hitches mounted to tail wheel springs or trusses, as in Figures 8-6 and 8-7, which travel up and down with the tail wheel, should be tested under load to ensure they don't contact any control surfaces.

b. The towline clears all fixed and movable surfaces at the maximum lateral and vertical cone of displacement and full surface travel.

c. The tow hitch does not swivel. Experience has shown swiveling could result in fouling both the release line and towline during operations by the tow plane.

d. The opened jaw of the hitch does not strike any portion of the aircraft.

e. The hitch is able to release under load at all tow angles.

807. PLACARDS. A placard should be installed in a conspicuous place in the cockpit to notify the pilot of the structural design limits of the tow system. The following are examples of placards to be installed:

a. For glider tow "Glider towline assembly breaking strength not to exceed _____*______ pounds." (*Value established per paragraph 804d.)

b. For banner tow "Tow hitch limited to banner maximum weight of _____**_____ pounds." (**Banner hitch limitations are one-half the load applied per paragraph 804d.)

808. INSTALLATION PROCEDURES—TYPES OF HITCHES. Two types of glider tow hooks are used in the United States: the American-made Schweizer and the European-made TOST brand, with Schweizer being the most commonly-used in the United States at the time of this publication. The FAA has coordinated with Schweizer in developing detailed inspection procedures and identification of life-limiting parts. These procedures and specifications are identified in subparagraph a. The European-made TOST releases are German-manufactured and approved by the German Civil Aviation Authority. They are available in various types and configurations. Two types of TOST releases can be found on U.S. operated gliders. The "E-type" release mechanism is commonly used as a nose release for sailplanes and as a tail release on towing aircraft. The "G-type" release mechanism is typically used as a center of gravity release for winch launching. TOST has provided installation, inspection, and maintenance instructions for its systems. An overview of these systems is identified in subparagraph b. Regardless of the brand used, all tow hooks should be inspected for proper operation daily, prior to tow activity.

a. Schweizer Hitch: Installation and Maintenance. The Schweizer is a simple over center L-hook type with a rubber tension block to preload the release lever (Figure 8-10). It is eligible for installation on several models of Cessna and Piper aircraft by STC, and has been installed on many other aircraft using the Field Approval process. It uses a tow rope with a single round steel ring attaching to the hook. While this hitch is a simple mechanism, proper maintenance and frequent inspection are necessary to ensure proper operation. All initial installations should be proof tested using the procedures outlined in the latest revision of Schweitzer Aircraft Corp. (SAC) Form F-236. The following additional procedures are recommended as a minimum, and should be performed at each 100-hour annual inspection, unless otherwise stated. All initial installations should be proof-tested using the procedures outlined in the latest revision of SAC Form F-236. This form is available through Schweizer and can be found at the following Web address: http://www.sacusa.com/support/ServiceLetter/ F-236.pdf.

(1) Inspect the entire tow hook system for loose or worn pivot pins, damaged fasteners, elongated holes, cracks, corrosion, surface damage, excessive wear, deformed parts, frayed release cable, rubber block damage, and freedom of operation. The mounting location of the hitches leaves them exposed to sunlight and the elements. Ozone and heat can have a detrimental effect on the rubber block. Look for excessive hardness of the rubber block as well as a permanent indentation caused by the contact with the hook lever.

(2) Perform a closing check by verifying that a sufficient closing force is required to compress the rubber block with the pivot hook. The pivot hook should apply sufficient locking load against the latch arm after the latch arm is engaged. Verify that the movement of the latch arm toward the release position causes additional compression of the rubber block. The original shape of the rubber block must be maintained.

(3) Perform a no-load pull test at the release arm to verify that a load of 4 to 10 pounds of pull is required to release the lever. See SAC Form F-236 for this procedure. If the release load cannot be obtained within the specified range, the rubber block is worn or deformed and should be replaced with a serviceable block.

NOTE: The above procedures, when properly implemented, help to ensure proper operation of the hitch. When the glider under tow operates above a certain angle to the tow plane, the ring may slide upwards on the hook, causing excessive load on the hook, and difficulty in releasing the tow rope ring. The closing check and pull test should be performed with a standard tow ring in the hook.

(4) For a periodic inspection, a closing check should be performed during "each" hookup of the tow rope. Tow plane and glider pilots should follow recommended launch and recovery procedures to help prevent this occurrence.

b. TOST Hitch. The TOST release is constructed using a steel housing which contains the hook mechanism surrounded by a steel ring. The tow rope attaches to a connecting ring pair: an oblong ring and a round ring, looped through each other. This ring pair must meet required specifications. Welded ring pairs are prohibited. The ring surrounding the hook mechanism, along with the double rings on the tow rope, allows ease of tow release at high angles (see Figure 8-9). The life-limiting part is the release spring, with a life expectancy of about 10,000 actuations or 2000 launches. This assumes about five actuations in normal night operations. If more actuations occur per launch, the time between overhaul is reduced accordingly. Once life expectancy is met, the release must be returned to the manufacturer or TOST representative for complete reconditioning and regulatory check. TOST recommends a general overhaul after 4 years: Its safety and operating life can only be guaranteed by keeping the prescribed maintenance intervals. Installation of the TOST release should be accomplished using manufacturer's brackets where possible. Use of any other installation equipment may require additional evaluation. In all cases, the installation, adjustment, maintenance, inspection, and overhaul intervals should be accomplished in accordance with the latest revisions of the TOST Installation and operating manuals for tow releases.

WARNING NOTE: Because of the difference in the size of the steel rings, under no circumstances should the Schweizer single ring rope be used with the TOST hook, nor the TOST double ring rope with the Schweizer hook.

809. TOW RELEASE MECHANISM.

a. Release Lever. A placard indicating the direction of operation should be installed to allay the possibility of confusion or inadvertent operation, and the design of the release lever should provide the following:

(1) Convenience in operation.

(2) Smooth and positive release operation.

(3) Positioned so as to permit the pilot to easily exert a straight pull on the release handle.

(4) Sufficient handle travel to allow for normal slack and stretch of the release cable.

(5) A sufficient handle/lever ratio to assure adequate release force when the tow line is under high loads. (See Figure 8-3.)

(6) Protection of cables from hazards such as:

(a) Wear and abrasion during normal operation.

(b) Binding where cables pass through fairleads, pulleys, etc.

(c) Accidental release.

(d) Interference with or by other aircraft components.

(e) Freezing and moisture accumulation when fixed or flexible tubing guides are used.

FIGURE 8-3. TYPICAL TOW-HITCH RELEASE HANDLE

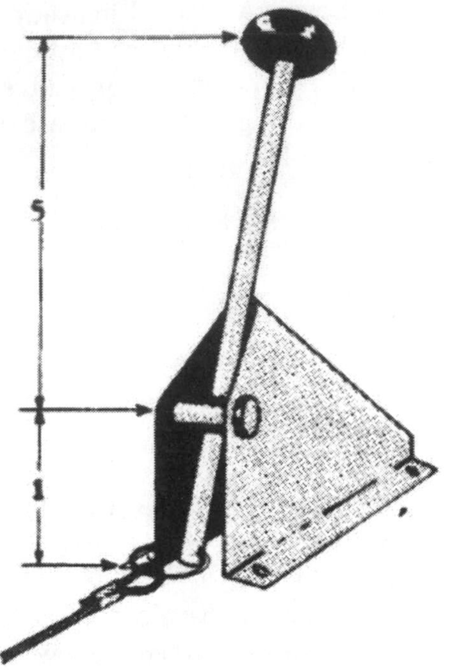

b. Test of Release Lever. Depending on the installation, the Schweizer type hitch is susceptible to excessive release loads when the tow cable is at high positive angles, and should be tested before each tow in accordance with the procedure in paragraph 808.

c. Release Cable. Representative size and strength characteristics of steel release cable are as shown in Table 8-1; however, it is recommended that all internally installed release cables be 1/16-inch or larger.

TABLE 8-1. REPRESENTATIVE STEEL CABLE QUALITIES

Diameter inches	Nonflexible Carbon Steel 1 x 7 and 1 x 19 (MIL-W-6904B)		Flexible Carbon Steel 7 x 7 and 7 x 19 (MIL-W-1511A and MIL-C-5424A)	
	Breaking strength (lbs.)	Pounds 100 ft.	Breaking Strength (lbs.)	Pounds 100 ft.
1/32	185	.25	---	---
3/64	375	.55	---	---
1/16	500	.85	480	.75
5/64	800	1.40	---	---
3/32	1,200	2.00	920	1.60

810. THRU 899. RESERVED

FIGURE 8-4. TRICYCLE GEAR AIRCRAFT

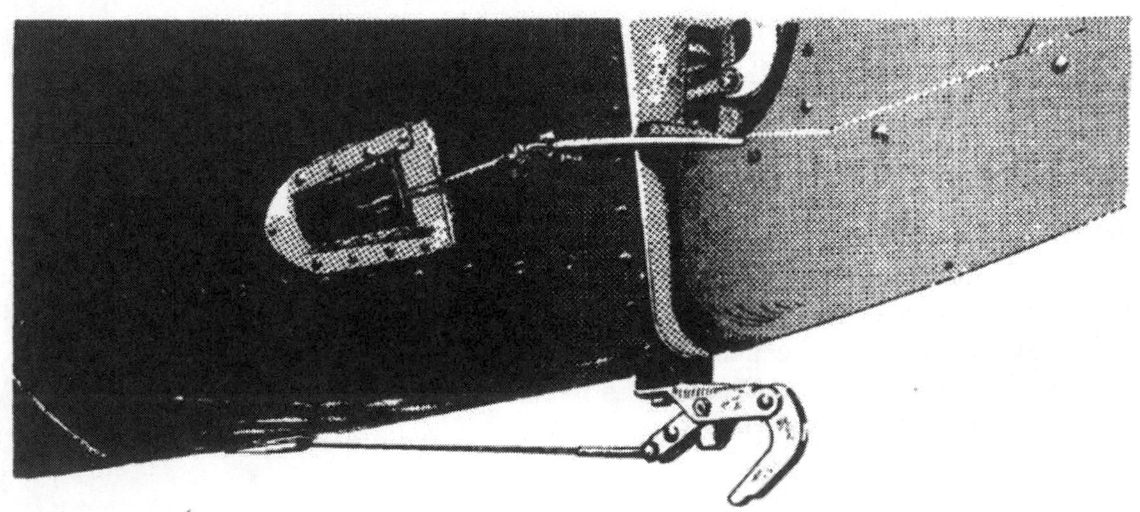

FIGURE 8-5. CONVENTIONAL GEAR AIRCRAFT-LEAF SPRING TYPE TAILWHEEL

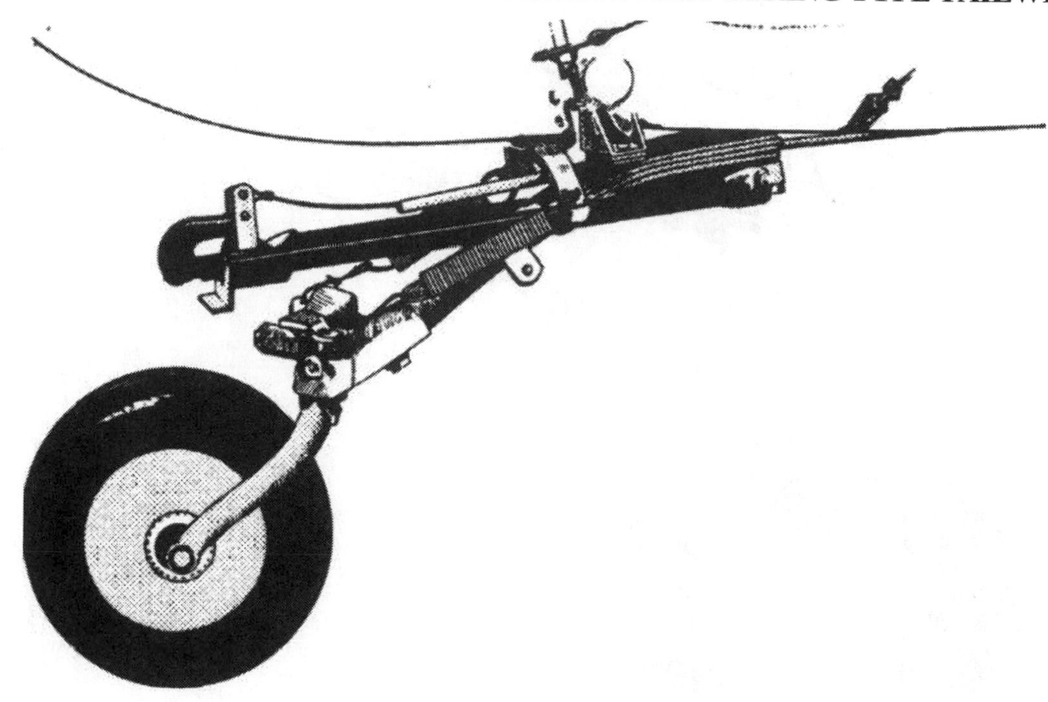

FIGURE 8-6. CONVENTIONAL GEAR AIRCRAFT-SHOCK STRUT TYPE TAILWHEEL

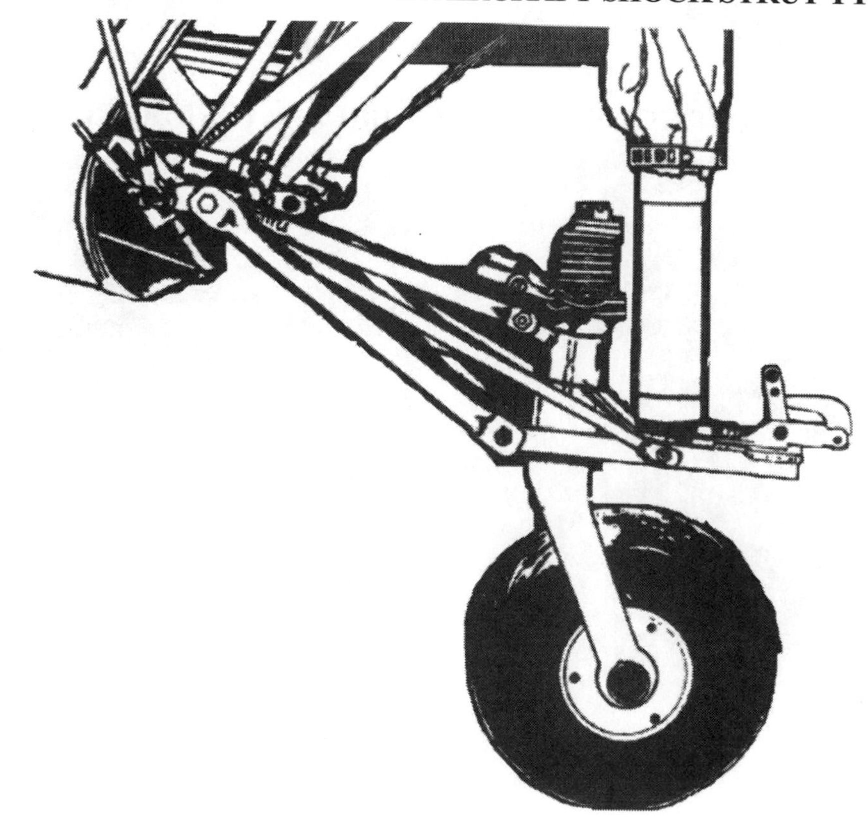

FIGURE 8-7. CONVENTIONAL GEAR AIRCRAFT – TUBULAR SPRING TYPE TAILWHEEL

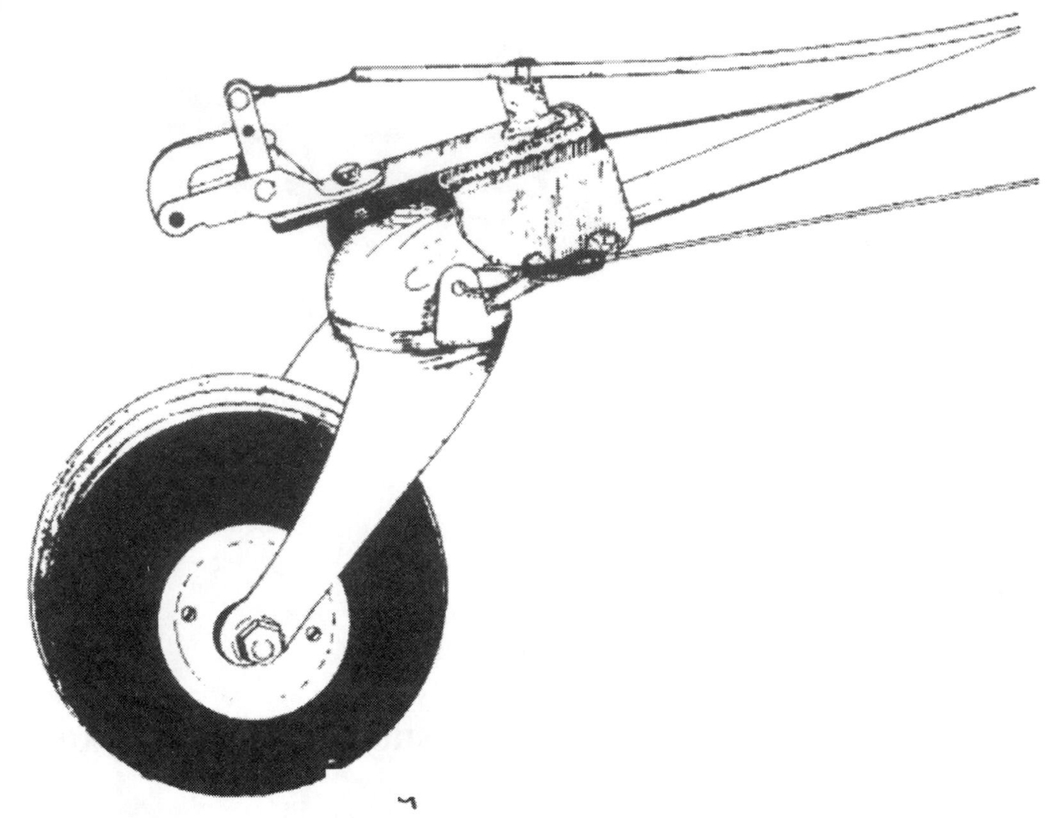

FIGURE 8-8. TYPICAL TOST HITCH

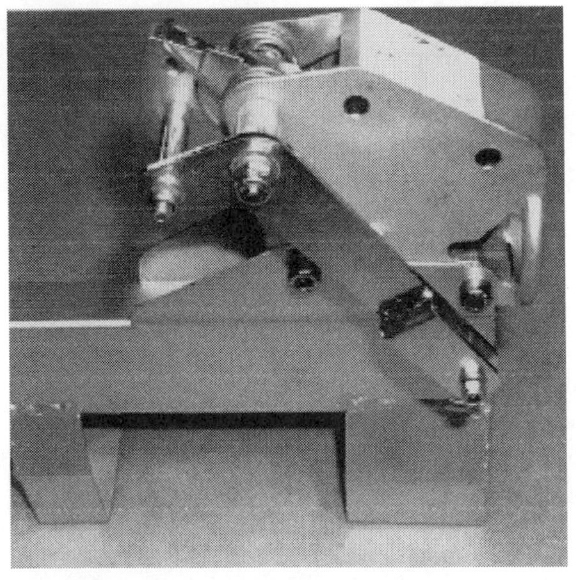

FIGURE 8-9. TOST DOUBLE TOW RINGS

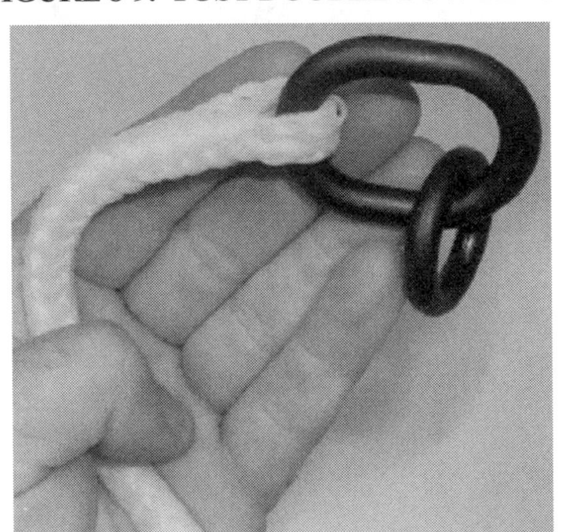

FIGURE 8-10. SCWEIZER WELD ON TYPE HITCH

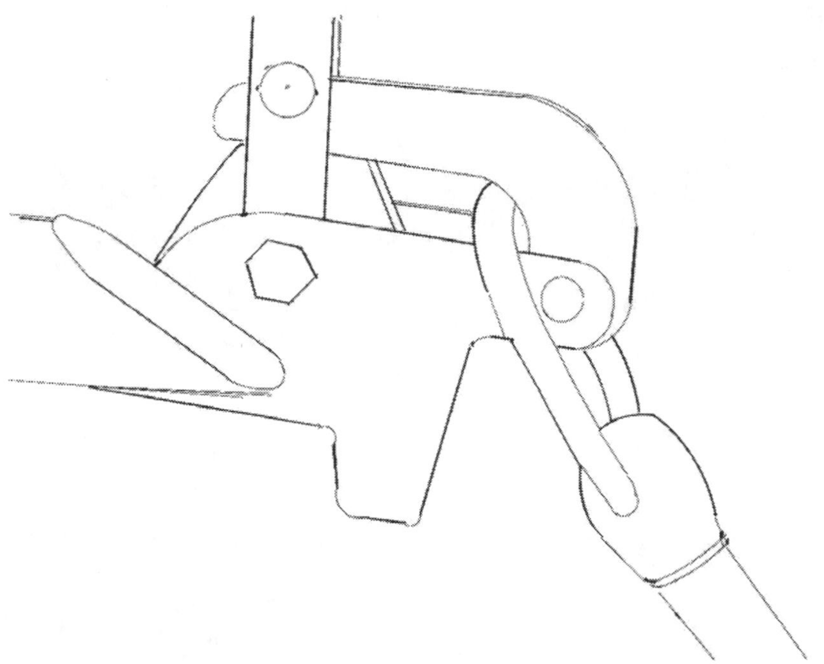

FIGURE 8-11. TYPICAL MULTIPLE HITCH FOR BANNER TOW

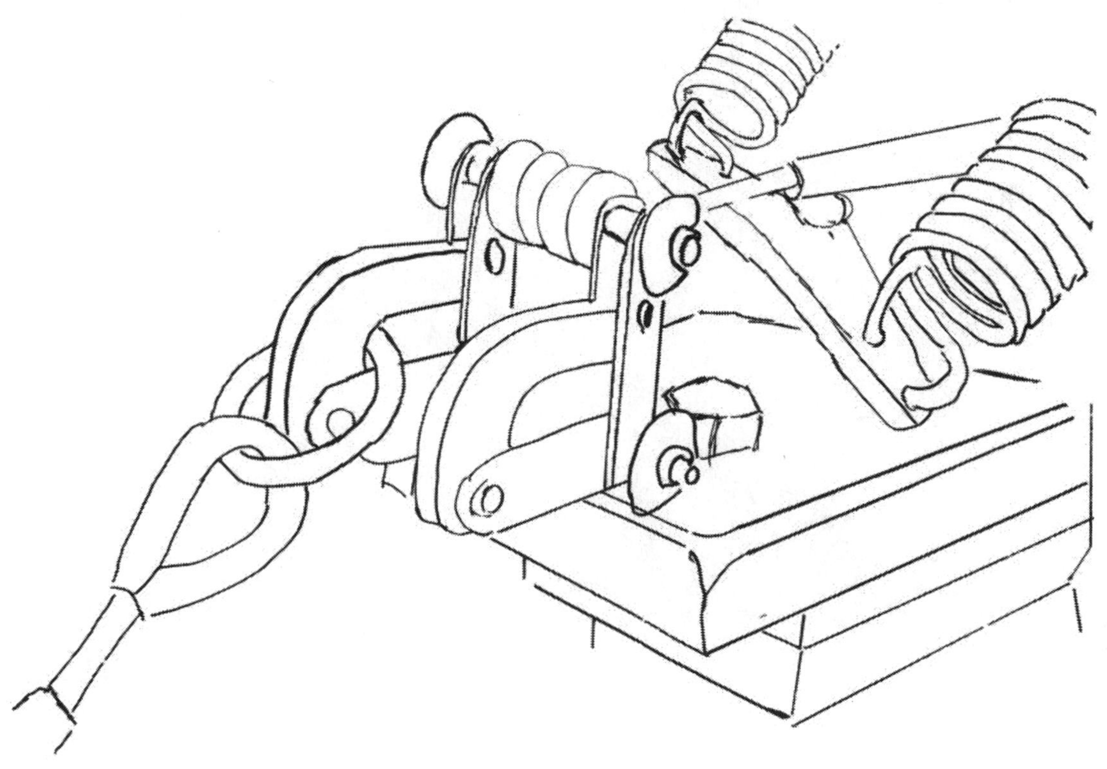

FIGURE 8-12. TYPICAL TOST MOUNT FOR TRICYCLE GEAR AIRCRAFT

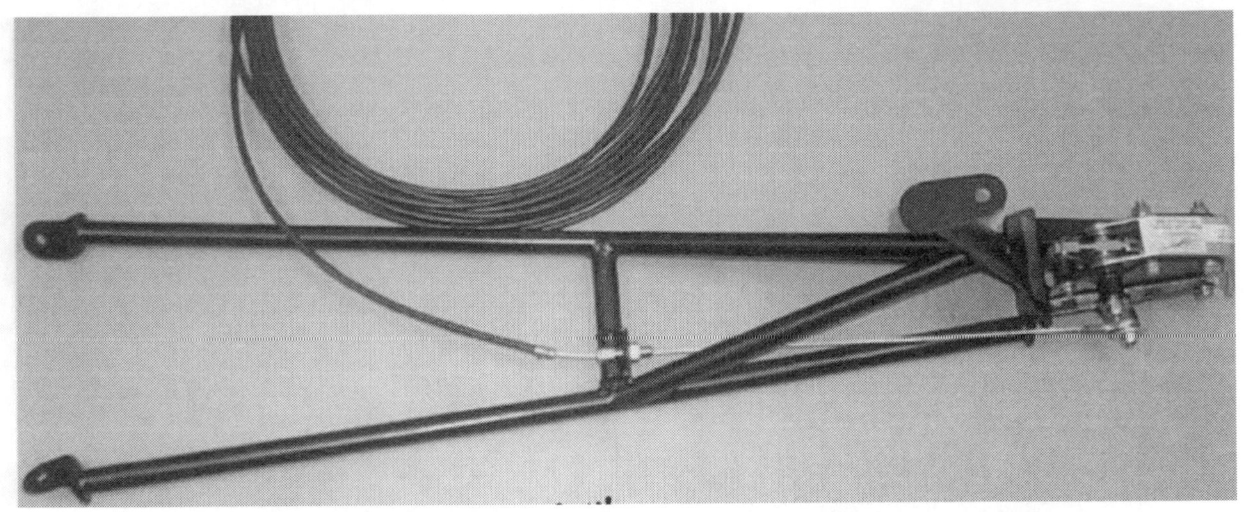

FIGURE 8-13. TYPICAL TOST CONVENTIONAL LEAF SPRING MOUNT

CHAPTER 9. SHOULDER HARNESS INSTALLATIONS

SECTION 1. GENERAL

900. PURPOSE. The purpose of this chapter is to provide guidance for retrofit shoulder harness installations. Information contained herein may be adaptable for the installation of shoulder harnesses in aircraft for which aircraft manufacturer or Supplemental Type Certificate (STC) retrofit installations have not been developed.

901. HAZARDS AND WARNINGS. Installations that do not meet the minimum standards prescribed by regulations are not acceptable. At no time should a retrofit shoulder harness installation perform at less than the static test load requirements specified in Section 3, Table 9-1, Static Test Requirements.

902. ADDITIONAL REFERENCES. The following references (current editions) provide additional information for shoulder harness installations.

a. Advisory Circular (AC) 21-34, Shoulder Harness-Safety Belt Installations.

b. AC 23-17, Systems and Equipment Guide for Certification of Part 23 Airplanes and Airships.

c. AC 91-65, Use of Shoulder Harnesses in Passenger Seats.

d. Civil Aviation Regulation 6, Rotorcraft Airworthiness; Normal Category.

e. TSO-C22, Safety Belts.

f. TSO-C114, Torso Restraint Systems.

g. Aerospace Standard SAE, AS8043, Restraint Systems for Civil Aircraft.

903. INSTALLATION METHODS. Shoulder harness installations can be performed by minor or by major alterations to the type design, depending on the complexity.

a. Minor alterations are limited to those where no change in the aircraft structure is required for mounting the harness. If the installation does not require operations such as drilling holes into or welding brackets onto the primary structure, it could be classified as a minor alteration. (See Figure 9-1.) Two examples of minor alterations for shoulder harnesses are:

(1) Some aircraft manufacturers have included hard-points in the type design, such as nutplates or predrilled holes, for the mounting of harnesses. Some also provide service kits or service instructions that include parts and instructions necessary to install harnesses. If the harness installation does not involve modification of primary structures, it can be returned to service as a minor alteration, unless otherwise specified in the installation instructions. The authorized mechanic needs only to complete a maintenance record entry, and update the equipment list and weight and balance as required.

(2) In some instances, a cable or a bracket can be secured around a structural member, without altering the structure, which will accommodate attachment of the harness. Truss tube construction is most commonly retrofitted with harnesses using this method. After performing static load tests or obtaining stress analysis documentation, the record entries as described above are completed. Refer to chapter 1 to determine design loads.

b. Major alterations can be accomplished by one or more of the following methods and will require completion of the FAA Form 337 using approved data.

(1) STC. There are many STCs issued for installation of shoulder harnesses in a variety of aircraft. The STCs are issued for specific makes and models of aircraft. A listing of STCs can be searched for applicability on the FAA Web site.

(2) Field-Approval. A properly trained and certified FAA airworthiness aviation safety inspector (ASI) can field approve data under certain conditions. ASIs are not engineers, so unless the case for field approval is supported with adequate data to evaluate the installation, the request for field approval may be turned-down. An example of justification for field approval might be, if an STC exists for the same make/model, with a similar mounting configuration, but the STC does not cover the aircraft by year of manufacture or serial number.

(3) Designated Engineering Representatives (DER) Data. DERs can evaluate structural attachments and provide approved data on FAA Form 8110-3. This data can be substituted for static tests, allowing the installation to be approved for return to service on the FAA Form 337 by an appropriately authorized person.

(4) Manufacturer Data. Some manufacturers have developed service kits or service instructions that are FAA-approved for harness retrofit installations. Some manufacturers have developed service kits or service instructions that are FAA-approved for harness retrofit installations. Depending on the complexity, these installations may be performed as major or minor alterations. For example, if the installation consists of affixing harness assemblies to existing hard points such as nutplates, the installation could be classified as minor, with no requirement to complete FAA Form 337. If the kit is FAA-approved but results in modification to the airframe structure, FAA Form 337 must be completed, referencing the approved kit/instructions, with no additional approval required.

(5) Other FAA-Approved Data. As specified in the Introduction, the data contained herein may conditionally be used as approved data. Data such as static tests, attachments, and materials could be used to show that the installation complies with regulations. Previously performed static tests meeting the minimum standards specified in this AC may be applicable for a retrofit installation if adequately documented.

FIGURE 9-1. MAJOR VS. MINOR ALTERATIONS

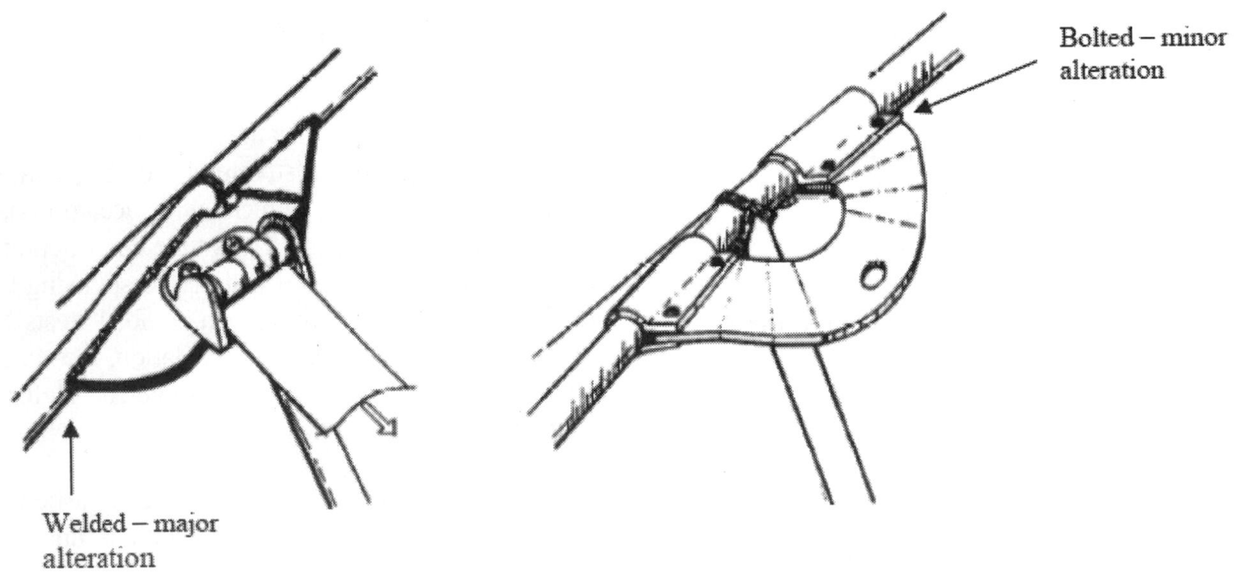

904. RESTRAINT SYSTEM CONFIGURATIONS. Restraint systems incorporating a shoulder harness are available in three configurations:

a. The 3-point system consists of a single shoulder belt that is positioned diagonally across the occupant's upper torso. (See Figure 9-2.)

b. The 4-point system consists of dual shoulder belts with one belt passing over each of the occupant's shoulders. Upper end attachment is accomplished at either two locations aft of the occupant's shoulders or at one location aft of the occupant's head after the belts have been joined together in a "Y." Lower end attachment is accomplished at a buckle centered on the occupant's lap belt or symmetrically at each side of the occupant. (See Figure 9-8.)

c. The 5-point system is similar to the 4-point system except that an additional belt, the negative-G strap, commonly referred to as a "crotch strap", is passed between the occupant's legs, attaching one end at the lap belt, and the other end at the front edge of the seat or to the airframe under the seat. A variation of the 5-point system is the 6-point system where 2 belts pass between the occupant's legs. (See Figure 9-9.)

905. ADVANTAGES OF DIFFERENT CONFIGURATIONS.

a. The 3-point single diagonal shoulder harness in combination with a lap belt is the least-cost, most-simple restraint system, and has been proven to work effectively for longitudinal (forward) decelerations. However, during lateral (sideward) decelerations away from the shoulder harness, an occupant in this type of harness has a tendency to slip out from the harness even when it fits snugly.

b. The 4-point dual shoulder harness works well for both longitudinal and lateral decelerations.

c. The 5-point system, incorporating the negative-G strap, resists the upward motion of the buckle during loading and limits submarining, which is the tendency for the occupant to slide underneath the lap belt during rapid decelerations. The 5-point system has proven to be very effective and has been adopted for many commercial, agricultural, military, and aerobatic operations.

906. MANUFACTURING STANDARDS. There are several standards that aircraft restraint system may be manufactured to.

a. Restraint Systems Produced by or for the Aircraft Manufacturer. These Original Equipment Manufacturer (OEM) harnesses may bear the manufacturer's part number or other identification.

b. Restraint systems produced under a Parts Manufacturing Approval (PMA) with specific aircraft eligibility as listed in the PMA. Restraints will bear the PMA markings required by § 45.15(a).

c. Technical Standard Order (TSO) Restraints. Two TSOs are applicable to the performance standards of restraint systems. These TSOs do not approve the restraint for installation in the aircraft. Restraints approved to a TSO will be marked in accordance with § 21.607(d) and the specific TSO marking instructions.TSO restraints will be marked in accordance with § 21.607(d).

(1) TSO-C22G, Safety Belts, prescribes the minimum performance standards that safety belts must meet in order to be identified with the applicable TSO marking. This TSO applies to the pelvic or lap belt portion of a restraint system. Belts bearing an earlier revision TSO marking (e.g., C22f) are acceptable for continued use if their condition remains satisfactory.

(2) TSO-C114, Torso Restraint Systems, prescribes the minimum performance standards that torso restraint systems must meet in order to be identified with the applicable TSO marking. This TSO applies to pelvic and upper torso restraints and includes the fifth belt of a 5-point system. Harnesses manufactured prior to March 27, 1987, the effective date of this TSO, will not be marked as meeting this TSO.

d. Restraint systems produced under a Military Specification (MIL-SPEC) such as MIL-R-81729. These restraints are marked in accordance with MIL-STD-130. FAA-approved data will need to be obtained for installation of restraints designed to MIL-SPEC standards.

907. COMPLIANCE WITH STANDARDS.

a. Prior to March 27, 1987, the TSO-C114 shoulder harness standards were established. Lacking such standards, harnesses manufactured prior to this date often were not identified with any markings. These harnesses are acceptable for existing installations if they were installed before the effective date of this TSO and remain in satisfactory condition.

b. For harness installations performed under this AC, use only those restraints that are properly marked and traceable to one of the above standards. There are several restraint manufacturers who can custom-build restraint system components that are manufactured to and identified with TSO-C114 markings. There are also several companies that can manufacture restraints under a PMA for specific applications.

c. It is an acceptable practice to replace existing restraints, including lap belts, with OEM, TSO, or PMA units after compatibility has been determined. This can be performed as preventive maintenance, defined under part 43, appendix A, paragraph (c)(14), by the aircraft owner/operator, along with the required maintenance record entry. However, if the aircraft is operated under part 121, 129, or 135, the work must be accomplished by appropriately rated mechanic.

d. Used TSO restraints, typically obtained through salvage companies, must be overhauled by an FAA-approved facility in accordance with an FAA-approved specification prior to installation, as these harnesses may have been exposed to unknown environmental conditions or accident loads.

908. MATERIALS. For a more thorough discussion of restraint assembly materials, refer to AC 21-34, Shoulder Harness—Safety Belt Installations, as amended.

a. Webbing, the woven fabric portion of the restraint, is made from synthetic materials such as nylon or polyester. Minimum breaking strength is determined by the standard under which the restraint was manufactured.

b. Attachment hardware must conform to AN, MS, NAS, or other acceptable industry standards or specifications, and be able to withstand the loads it will be subjected to.

c. Retractors are frequently incorporated into the shoulder harnesses, and sometimes into pelvic restraints. Some current production aircraft incorporate retractors into the harness and the lap belt. Retractors function to provide for adjustment in length and allow the occupant additional freedom of movement when compared to fixed harnesses. They are available in two categories:

(1) Automatic locking retractors provide automatic retraction of webbing for length adjustment and stowage of webbing. Their mechanism permits free webbing extension for coupling of the belt, but the moment any webbing is automatically retracted, the locking mechanism locks to prevent further webbing extension.

(2) Emergency locking retractors are frequently called "inertia reels" because their mechanism provides positive restraint only when inertial forces are experienced. The most common type of inertia reel appropriate for aircraft use is known as the webbing sensitive reel. It produces locking by a change in the rate (acceleration) of webbing withdrawal from the retractor, which is functional for occupant accelerations in any direction producing extension of the webbing. Emergency locking retractors may be equipped with a mechanism that will allow the user to manually lock the reel when a deceleration is anticipated. This feature relieves the possibility of a malfunctioning inertia mechanism.

d. Buckles suitable for shoulder harness installations are defined by their release mechanism and come in three types:

(1) Lift lever,

(2) Push Button, and

(3) Rotary.

909. PARTS PRODUCED BY OWNERS/ OTHERS. Section 21.303(b)(2) allows owners or operators to produce parts for altering their own aircraft under certain conditions. Since approved restraints meeting TSO, PMA, or other standards are readily available, applying this regulation for the production of restraints is not advised, as owner produced restraints would also need to demonstrate proof of compliance with these standards. However, airframe attachment brackets or fittings might be candidates to be produced under this regulation. To qualify, the owner must have participated in controlling the design, manufacture, or quality of the part such as by:

a. Providing the manufacturer with the design or performance data from which to make the part. The owner could provide the manufacturer with a part to be duplicated.

b. Providing the manufacturer with the materials from which to make the part.

c. Providing the manufacturer with fabrication processes or assembly methods to make the part.

d. Providing the quality control procedures to make the part.

e. Personally supervising the manufacture of the part.

(1) An example of this might be if the owner has discovered a desirable harness attachment bracket in an aircraft similar to his, and he creates a drawing to duplicate this bracket, specifying materials and performance standards. He could then either make the part himself or contract out for the manufacture of the part. When a mechanic installs the part, the maintenance record entry would include the installation information as required from the mechanic, and an entry by the owner that the part was produced under § 21.303(b)(2) by the owner for his aircraft. Note that this regulation provides no authority for the owner to install the part. Furthermore, the mechanic will need to show that the installation meets minimum strength standards through static testing or stress analysis.

(2) Parts and kits to install harnesses are sometimes available from parts warehouses or individuals who supply components and instructions for harness installations without FAA approval such as STC, TSO, or PMA. The installer of these parts will need to obtain FAA approval, typically a field approval, for such installations.

910. THRU 912. RESERVED

SECTION 2. GEOMETRY AND ATTACHMENT

913. GENERAL.

a. Harness attachment points physically locate the shoulder harness relative to the occupant being restrained and establish the angles that will impose loads upon the aircraft structure. Careful selection of appropriate attachment points will maximize overall performance of the restraint system.

b. For best results, the restraint system should be anchored to the primary aircraft structure, defined as: "that structure which contributes significantly to resisting or transmitting flight or ground loads or may lead to an unsafe condition if failed."[1] The structural attachment should be designed to spread the suddenly applied impact loads over as large an area of the structure as possible. The shoulder harness may be attached to selected secondary members that will deform slowly or collapse at a limited rate. This will assist in dissipating the high impact "G" loads to a level tolerable to the human body. However, the possibility of secondary members collapsing and creating a new impact hazard for the occupant, or making it difficult for an occupant to exit the aircraft, should not be overlooked.

914. MOUNTING CONFIGURATIONS. The type of shoulder restraint configuration acceptable for installation is dependent upon the attachments available in the aircraft. Basic harness mounting configurations are:

a. Seat mounted.

b. Airframe mounted.

(1) Side.

(2) Ceiling.

(3) Floor.

(4) Directly rearward.

[1] AC 23-15A, Small Airplane Certification Compliance Program, p. 1.

915. BELT LENGTH. In all installations, it is desirable to keep the harness belt lengths as short as practical while still allowing for the required freedom of movement. Belt stretching, which reduces the effectiveness of the restraint by allowing slack during loading, increases as the belt length does. If too much slack is present, the occupant may contact the instrument panel or slide out of the harness during rapid decelerations.

916. ATTACHMENT GEOMETRY. The following are general guidelines for attachment of 3-point and 4/5-point harness configurations:

a. Single Diagonal 3-Point Harness. A proper installation for this type of harness positions the shoulder belt so that it passes over the midpoint of the shoulder, with the lower end fastened well to the opposite side of the occupant's hip as shown in Figure 9-2. The optimum rearward attachment area for this type of harness is within an angle of 30-degrees above the horizontal measured from the midpoint on the occupant's shoulder as shown in Figure 9-3. Upper harness attachments should be located to the rear and outboard of the occupant's neck. This mounting area is shown in Figure 9-4.

(1) Attachment points inboard of this area would allow the harness to impinge on the neck and could result in neck injury during crash impact. (See Figure 9-5.) In addition, the constant rubbing of the strap on the neck would be uncomfortable and, as a result, act as a distraction to the safe operation of the aircraft and a deterrent to use of the harness.

(2) Attachment points forward of this area would reduce the effectiveness of the harness, due to a reduction of contact between the harness and the upper torso of the occupant. (See Figure 9-6.) As a result, the potential for increased forward movement of the torso, increases the likelihood of head impact injuries from the instrument panel. Additionally, the chances for twisting out of the harness are significantly increased.

(3) A retractor can be used with the diagonal harness. It has the added benefit of allowing for more freedom of movement, especially when controls such as fuel selectors are located on the cockpit floor. However, it may be more complicated to mount a retractor and maintain an unrestricted, straight-line entry and exit of the webbing.

b. Double Over-the-Shoulder 4/5-Point Harness. This type of harness should be mounted either directly rearward or to the ceiling. Ideally, the mount should be within the 30-degree vertical angle, or because of the limited number of rearward shoulder harness attachment points in many aircraft, a 5-degree angle below the horizontal is also considered satisfactory, as shown in Figure 9-7. These mounting angles may be used for either the dual independent or the "Y" type belts. Figures 9-8 and 9-9 depict correct harness positioning of 4/5-point harnesses.

(1) If the harness attachment is located more than 5-degrees below the horizontal angle measured from the midpoint on the occupant's shoulder, there is an increased risk of spinal compression caused by the vertical component induced during impact deceleration. (See Figure 9-6.)

(2) For dual independent harnesses, the outboard limit must be established to provide sufficient contact that will prevent the belt from slipping off the shoulder, and the maximum inboard angle is limited to a point that will prevent impingement on the neck. (See Figure 9-5.) Where the mounting structure is incapable of withstanding loads imposed by a "Y" type harness single retractor, two retractors used with dual independent harnesses may spread the load enough to satisfy strength requirements. Dual independent harnesses that are crossed aft of the occupant's head will need careful evaluation to preclude neck impingement.

(3) Retractors are often used with "Y" type and dual independent harnesses. The single retractor used with a "Y" type harness is mounted aft of the center vertical plane of the occupant. (See Figures 9-4 and 9-10.) The fifth belt, if used, is attached to the seat or airframe so that it joins the buckle perpendicular to the lap belt in the centerline of the seat. Figure 9-9 shows a 5-point system.

FIGURE 9-2. THE 3-POINT SINGLE HARNESS POSITIONING

FIGURE 9-3. SIDE MOUNTED SINGLE DIAGONAL TYPE HARNESS

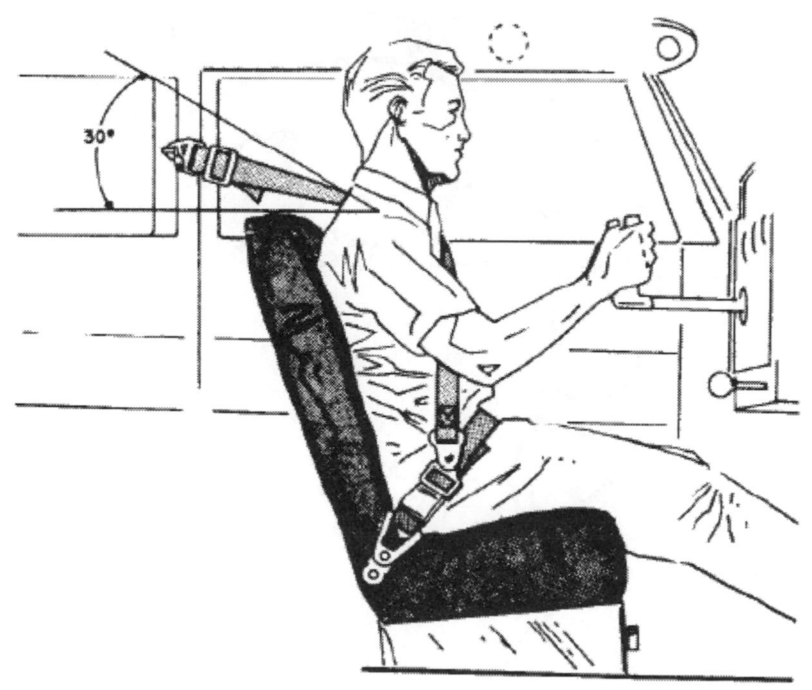

FIGURE 9-4. ACCEPTABLE HARNESS MOUNTING AREAS

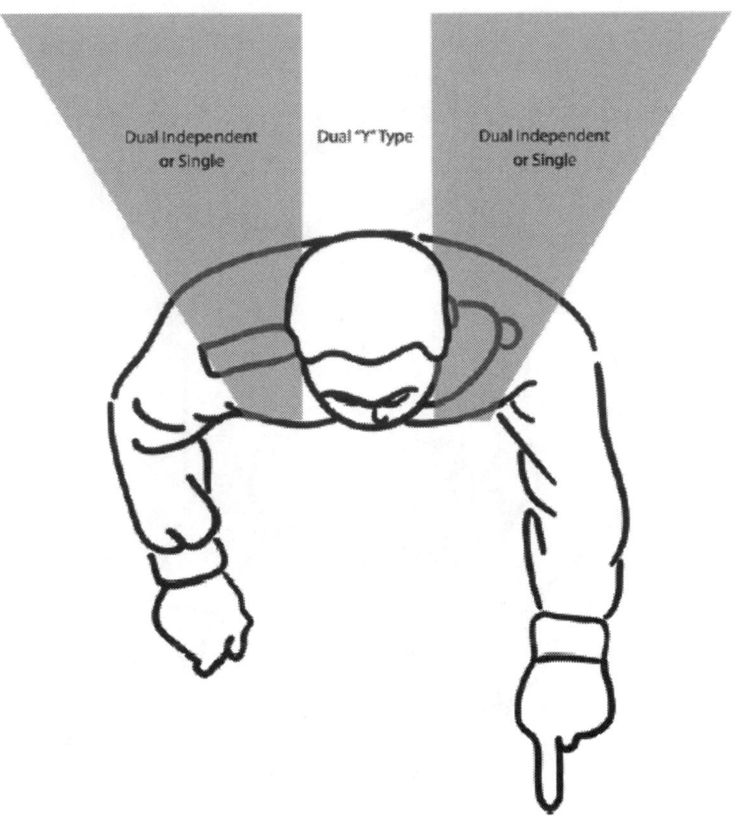

FIGURE 9-5. UNDESIRABLE HORIZONTAL HARNESS POSITIONING

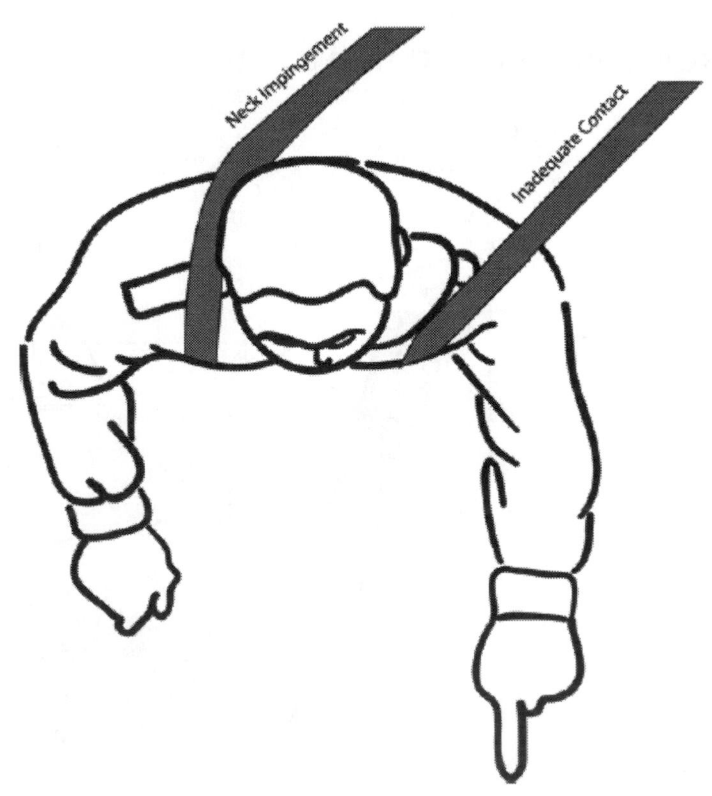

FIGURE 9-6. UNDESIRABLE VERTICAL HARNESS POSITIONING

FIGURE 9-7. CEILING MOUNTED INERTIA REEL—DOUBLE OVER-THE-SHOULDER TYPE HARNESS

FIGURE 9-8. THE 4-POINT INDEPENDENT HARNESSES POSITIONING

FIGURE 9-9. THE 5-POINT HARNESS POSITIONING

FIGURE 9-10. "Y" TYPE RETRACTOR POSITIONING

917. AREA AND ANGLE DEVIATIONS. While the areas and angles given in the above paragraphs are intended to assist in the selection of attachment points, they should be considered the desirable optimum. Area and/or angle deviations could result in a decrease in the overall efficiency of the restraint system; however, they may be necessary in order to permit harness installation in an aircraft that cannot accommodate ideal harness geometry. As discussed in section 3, angles have a significant bearing on static test load requirements.

918. STRUCTURAL ATTACHMENT. This chapter presents only a few generic examples of structural attachment of harnesses that may be determined to be acceptable for a specific application. Refer to section 3 for strength requirements of the attachment.

a. Floor and Seat Attachments. The dual over-the-shoulder or Y type harness may be used with either floor or seat mounting points. Typical installations are illustrated in Figures 9-11, 9-12, and 9-13. Several factors need to be considered that may make this configuration undesirable:

(1) The floor, seat structure, and anchorages must be capable of withstanding the additional "G" loads imposed upon them by the restraints.

(2) The height of the seat back should at least be equal to the shoulder height of the seated occupant to reduce the possibility of spinal compression injuries.

(3) Harness guides may be necessary to maintain proper harness position over the occupant's shoulders.

(4) Seat back strength is critical to performance of these installations. Folding seat backs must have a locking mechanism that can withstand the imposed loads; however, a locked seat back may impede emergency egress of other occupants and create an impact hazard for occupants seated aft of the locked seat back.

FIGURE 9-11. FLOOR MOUNTED INERTIA REEL—DOUBLE OVER-THE-SHOULDER TYPE HARNESS

FIGURE 9-12. TYPICAL FLOOR MOUNTED INERTIA REEL INSTALLATION

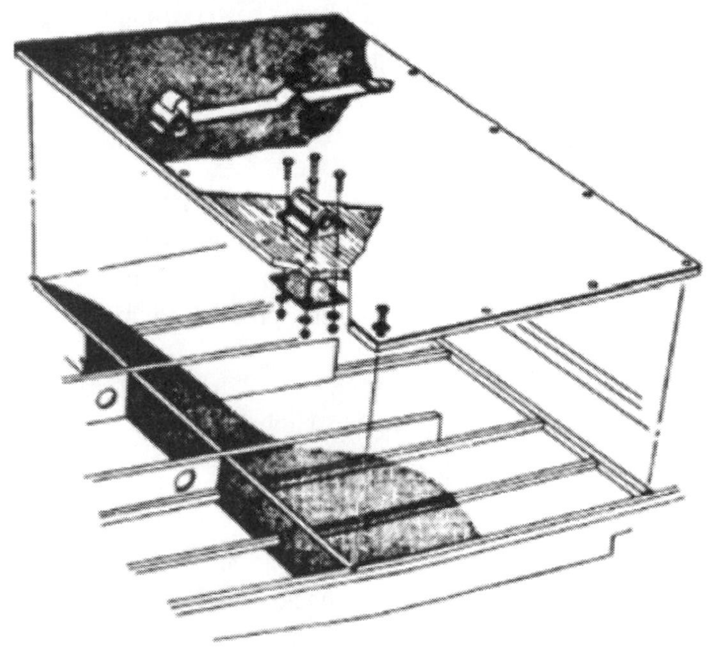

FIGURE 9-13. TYPICAL SEAT MOUNTED INERTIA REEL INSTALLATION

b. Airframe Attachments. The method used for the attachment of shoulder harness anchorages is dependent upon the construction features of the aircraft involved. When selecting a point of attachment, careful consideration should be given to the static strength and testing requirements found in section 3.

(1) Monocoque/Semimonocoque Type Constructions. Illustrations of typical aircraft members and installation methods are shown in Figures 9-14 through 9-18. Intercostal doublers and stiffeners are frequently added to provide increased strength. AC 43.13-1, Acceptable Methods, Techniques, and Practices-Aircraft Inspection and Repairs, chapter 4 (as amended), provides useful information on fabrication and installation of sheet metal repairs that may be applicable to doubler and stiffiner installations.

(2) Tube Type Construction. Various typical methods of attaching shoulder harness anchorages are shown in Figure 9-19. Attachment should be accomplished at the intersection of tubular members and not at the center of single unsupported tubes. When aircraft cable is used as a component in a shoulder harness anchorage, swage the cable terminals in accordance with the procedures contained in AC 43.13-1, chapter 7, as amended.

c. Structural Repair Instructions. In some instances, structural repair instructions are provided in the aircraft manufacturer's maintenance manual. While these instructions are primarily intended for use in repairing defective or damaged structure, they may also be used as reinforcement methods for shoulder harness attach fittings.

d. Flexible Attachments. Various aircraft are designed so that fuselage members and/or skin will flex or "work." This type of structure should not be heavily reinforced for the purpose of attaching shoulder harnesses, as this would defeat the design purpose. In these cases, use a localized reinforcement such as that shown in Figure 9-18, at the attachment point. This will allow the fuselage to flex while still maintaining a collapsible structure to absorb the loads encountered in a crash.

919. THRU 922. RESERVED

FIGURE 9-14. TYPICAL WING CARRY-THROUGH INSTALLATION

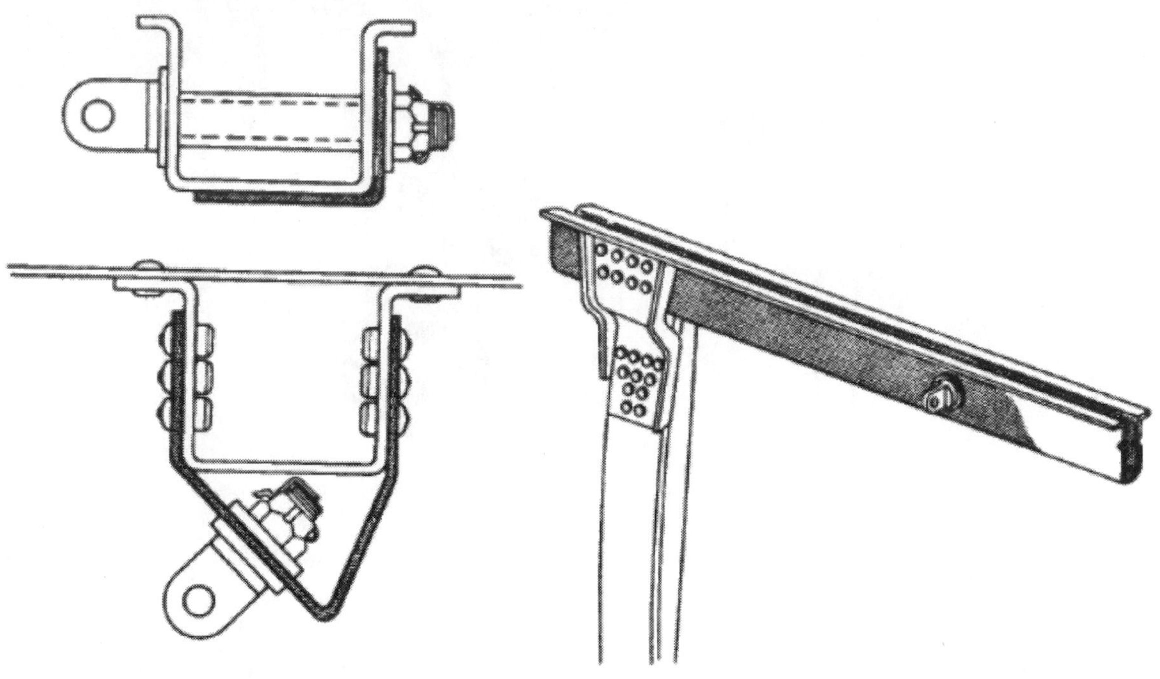

FIGURE 9-15. TYPICAL HAT SECTION REINFORCEMENT INSTALLATION

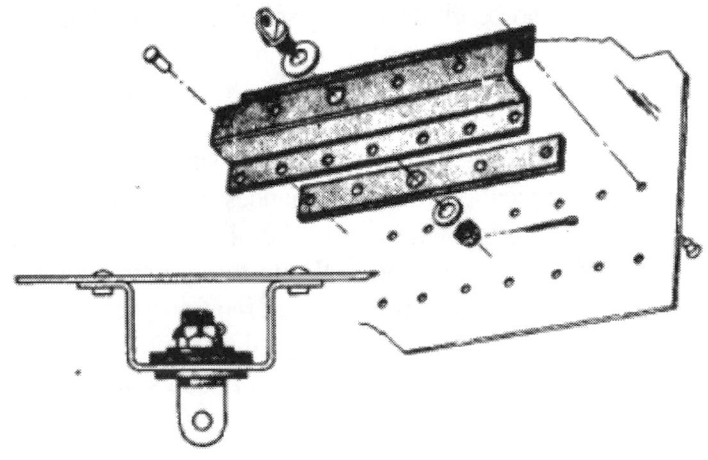

FIGURE 9-16. TYPICAL BULKHEAD REINFORCEMENT INSTALLATION

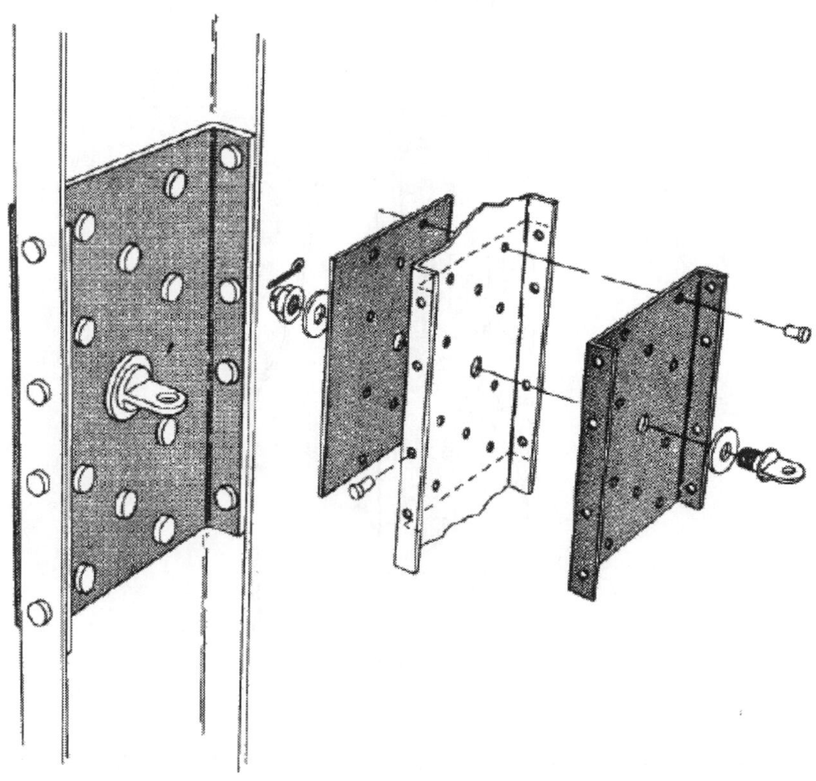

FIGURE 9-17. TYPICAL STRINGER SECTION REINFORCEMENT INSTALLATION

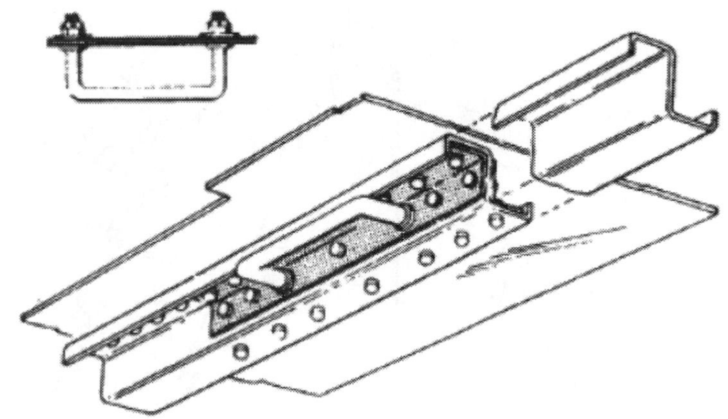

FIGURE 9-18. TYPICAL LOCALIZED STRINGER SECTION REINFORCEMENT INSTALLATION

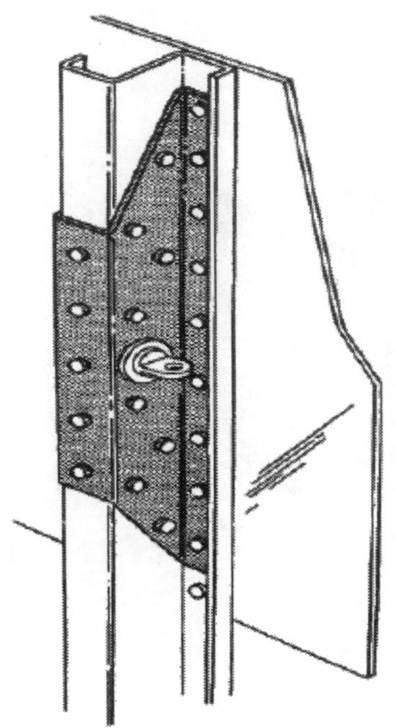

FIGURE 9-19. TYPICAL ATTACHMENTS TO TUBULAR MEMBERS

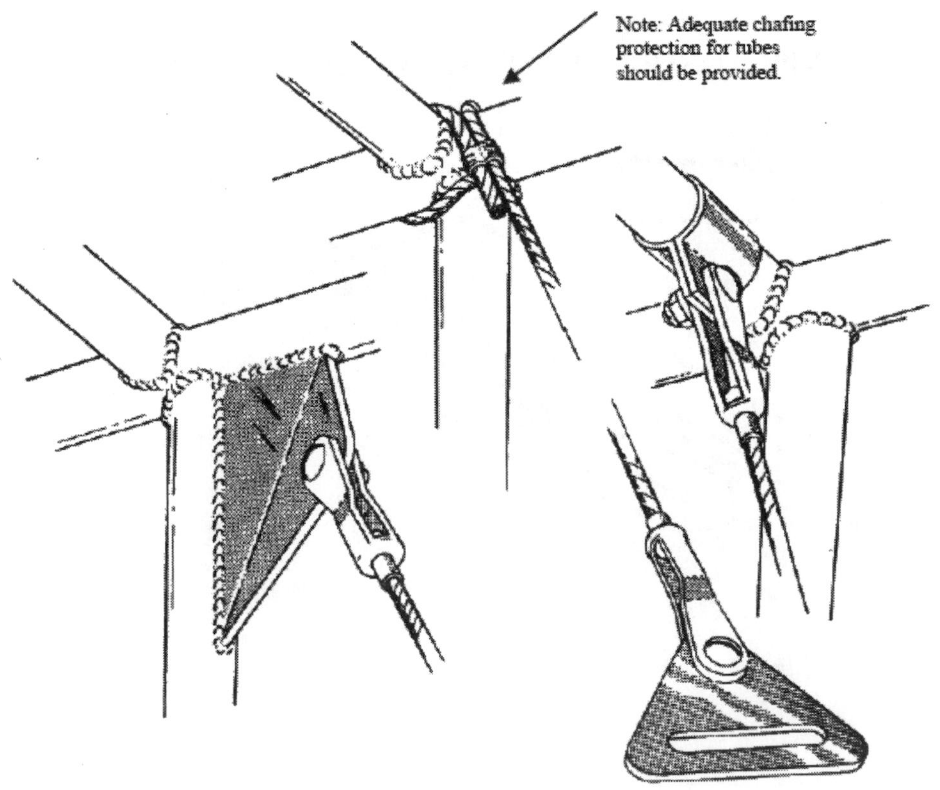

Note: Adequate chafing protection for tubes should be provided.

SECTION 3. STATIC STRENGTH AND TESTING

923. PROOF OF COMPLIANCE. Retrofit harness installations must be proven to meet minimum strength requirements applicable to the aircraft certification basis; otherwise, their ability to provide adequate restraint under accident decelerations is undetermined. Static strength requirements can be demonstrated by static test or stress analysis.

a. Static tests are accomplished by application of the ultimate load to the harness attachment point. Since TSO and PMA restraints have already been shown to comply with strength requirements, static tests are accomplished to substantiate the airframe attachment. Static testing in operational aircraft is undesirable because there is the risk of airframe damage; however, static testing in a conforming but unserviceable fuselage or cabin section of the same make and model aircraft is an acceptable alternative.

b. Stress analysis is accomplished through engineering data developed for the specific attachment point. This data can be developed by FAA Designated Engineering Representatives (DER) with aircraft structural approval authority. The DER will perform the analysis, prepare a report, and complete FAA Form 8110-3, Statement of Compliance with the Federal Aviation Regulations, which demonstrates that a specific regulation has been met. The DER will list on FAA Form 8110-3 the data needed to show the structural adequacy of the installation of the harness. Since the DER is only approving the structural aspects of harness attachment, approval for return to service for the installation as a whole is accomplished by the authorized individual or agency on FAA Form 337. To locate an appropriately authorized DER in your locality, contact the FAA Flight Standards District Office or Aircraft Certification Office having jurisdiction in your geographic area.

NOTE: It is up to the installer to determine which method will be the most efficient. For simple installations, it is possible that the DER could perform stress analysis in just a few hours. The DER may also be able to assist in the design of attachment points.

924. LOAD AND DISTRIBUTION — AIRPLANES. Table 9-1 provides a reference to determine minimum static test loads based upon certification date, category, standard occupant weight, fitting factors, and harness factors. The numbers in each line are multiplied together to obtain the static test load minimum standard.

a. Load. For airplanes type-certificated prior to September 14, 1988, occupant weights were established as 170 pounds for normal category and 190 pounds for utility and acrobatic category airplanes. The additional 20 pounds accounts for a parachute. For aircraft type-certificated on or after this date, 215 pounds is the established weight for the 3 categories.

b. Distribution. In the assessment of a combined shoulder harness-safety belt restraint system, a forward static test load distribution of 40 percent to the shoulder harness and 60 percent to the safety belt has been an acceptable combined static test load distribution. Therefore, demonstration of harness attachment static strength is accomplished by applying 40 percent of the ultimate restraint system load to a single or "Y" type harness attachment, or 20 percent of the load simultaneously to each attachment of a dual independent harness. Static strength test load requirements for the fifth belt of a 5-point system have not been established for aircraft.

c. Factor. The airplane must be designed to protect each occupant during emergency landing conditions. The critical ultimate static load is established at 9.0 G's in the forward direction. If the attachment can sustain this load, it is assumed the lesser loads in upward, sideward, and downward directions will be accommodated.

d. Fitting Factors. Regulations prescribe multiplying factors of safety, fitting factors, that structural attachments must be subjected to in order to prove minimum load bearing capabilities. A 1.15 fitting factor for restraint attachments in small aircraft type-certificated prior to September 14, 1969, must be used. For aircraft type-certificated on or after this date, a fitting factor of 1.33 must be used.

925. LOAD AND DISTRIBUTION — NORMAL CATEGORY HELICOPTERS.

a. Load. For helicopters type-certificated in the normal category, occupant weights are established as 170 pounds.

b. Distribution. In the assessment of a combined shoulder harness-safety belt restraint system, for helicopters type-certificated prior to December 13, 1989, a forward static test load distribution of 40 percent to the shoulder harness and 60 percent to the safety belt is the required combined static test load distribution.

c. G Factor. For helicopters type-certificated prior to December 13, 1989, the critical ultimate static load is established at 4.0 G's in the forward direction. If the attachment can sustain this load, it is assumed the loads in upward, sideward, and downward directions will be accommodated.

NOTE: Due to increased G factors and limited applicability for retrofit harnesses installations, helicopters type-certificated on or after December 13, 1989, are not addressed in this chapter. Additionally, airplanes seat/restraint systems type-certificated after September 14, 1988, must undergo dynamic testing, as prescribed by § 23.562, which is not covered in this chapter.

926. DEMONSTRATING STATIC LOADS. Two methods are available to demonstrate compliance with static load requirements. One method involves the fabrication of test blocks and application of the ultimate load to the blocks that are being restrained by the harness. The other method involves use of an equation to calculate and simulate the ultimate load at the harness attachment fitting, compensating for horizontal and vertical angles as a result of restraint attachment geometry.

a. Test Blocks. Although AC 23-4, Static Strength Substantiation of Attachment Points for Occupant Restraint System Installations, was cancelled on January 27, 2003, it is still available in various archives and can be used as an acceptable method for fabricating test blocks and applying static loads to restraints. Using this method, deceleration loads imposed upon the restraint by the occupant are accurately duplicated, and the load figures in Table 9-1 can be applied directly to the test blocks. Because of the time-consuming nature of fabricating test blocks for this procedure, it may be desirable to use the second method described below that, in effect, replaces the test blocks with an equation.

b. Calculation. The alternate method is to perform a mathematical calculation to account for the angles that the attachment points are subjected to during decelerations. Increases in angles can result in a significant increase in the load that must be applied to simulate belt loading during occupant decelerations. It is not uncommon for a harness to impose both vertical and horizontal angles that must be compensated for by use of the equation. (See Figures 9-20 and 9-21.) In the case of a "Y" type harness, the horizontal angle is eliminated as long as the attachment is located along the vertical centerline of the occupant.

(1) The equation used to perform the calculation is:

Test Load = [Static Test Minimum]
[1/Cosine(vertical angle)]
[1/Cosine(horizontal angle)]

(2) Table 9-2 provides 1/Cosine numbers for various angles. These numbers can be inserted into the equation to determine the static load that needs to be applied. For example, using Table 9-1 and Table 9-2, if the airplane is normal category, post-September 14, 1969, pre-September 14, 1988, the test load is 814 lbs. If the horizontal angle is 10° and the vertical angle is 15°, the belt load is calculated as follows.

Test Load = [814][1/Cos(15)][1/Cos(10)]
= [814][1.035][1.015]
= 855 lbs.

This is not a large increase, but if both angles were 30°, the belt load would be 1086 lbs.
[814][1.155][1.155] = 1086

If there is no angle present in one of the directions, that portion of the equation is eliminated. For an airplane type-certificated in the normal category prior to September 14, 1969, with a vertical angle of 25 degrees, the equation would be: [704][1.103] = 777 lbs.

c. After obtaining the test load value, the load is applied for a minimum of 3 seconds, forward (horizontally) when using test blocks, or in the direction of the restraint angles when applying the load to the attachment point(s).

d. Equipment used for measuring test loads must be calibrated to a standard acceptable to the FAA. Load-cells are capable of performing these measurements; however, other equivalent equipment as determined by the user may be acceptable.

927. THRU 930. RESERVED

TABLE 9-1. STATIC TEST REQUIREMENTS

TC Basis Airplanes	Category*	G Factor	Weight Factor (lbs)	Fitting Factor	Harness Factor (40%)	Static Test Minimum Load (lbs)
Effective 09/14/88 and on	N, U, A	9	215	1.33	.4	1029
Effective 09/14/69	N	9	170	1.33	.4	814
	U, A	9	190	1.33	.4	910
Pre 09/14/69	N	9	170	1.15	.4	704
	U, A	9	190	1.15	.4	787
Helicopter Pre 12/16/84	N	4	170	1.15	.6	469
Helicopter Post 12/16/84 Pre 12/13/89	N	4	170	1.33	.6	543

- N=Normal, U=Utility, A=Acrobatic
- ** Airplane seat/restraint systems type certificated after September 14, 1988, must undergo dynamic testing, as prescribed by § 23.562, which is not covered in this chapter.

TABLE 9-2. CALCULATED 1/COSINE VALUES

Degrees	5	10	15	20	25	30	35	40	50	60
1/Cos Multiplier	1.004	1.015	1.035	1.064	1.103	1.155	1.221	1.305	1.556	2.0

FIGURE 9-20. VERTICAL ANGLE

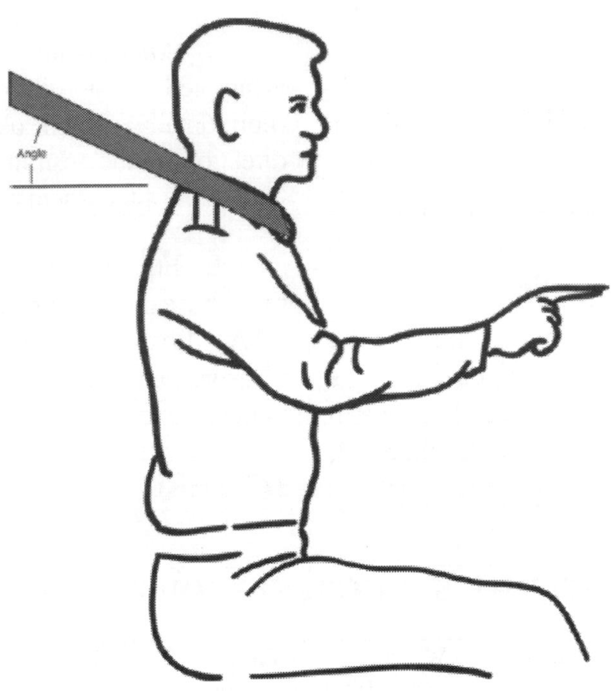

FIGURE 9-21. HORIZONTAL ANGLE

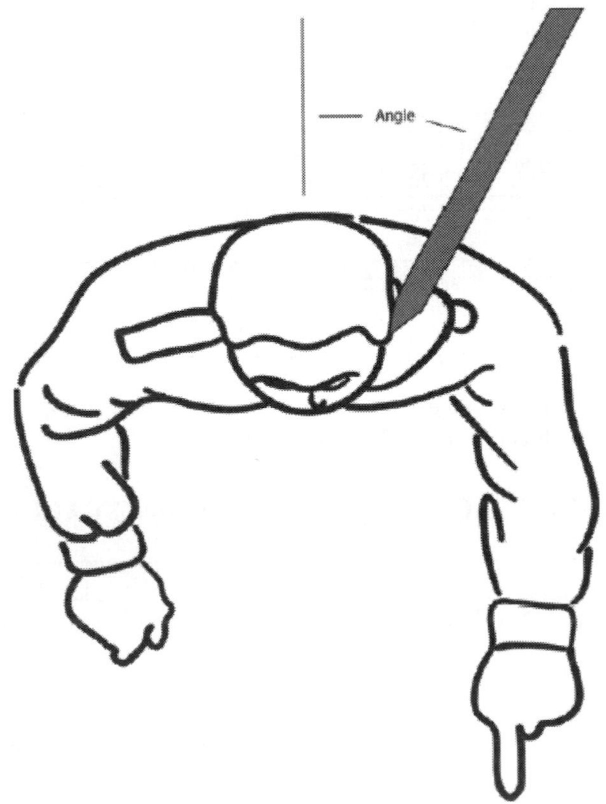

SECTION 4. INSTALLATION AND INSPECTION CHECKLISTS

931. GENERAL. The following checklists are not all-inclusive, but may provide a quick reference for factors to consider when installing retrofit shoulder harnesses and for establishing instructions for continued airworthiness of retrofit harness installations. If available, manufacturer's instructions take precedence over this AC.

a. Shoulder Harness Installation Checklist.

(1) Locate potential attach points.

(2) Evaluate the geometry of attach points in relation to the occupant and determine the best harness configuration. Short belt lengths are desirable.

(3) Ensure that the configuration will allow unimpeded egress for all occupants. Single-point release is mandatory. There should be a means to secure belts and harnesses when not in use to avoid interfering with operation of the airplane or egress from it.

(4) Restraints must allow crewmembers to perform all necessary flight operation functions while seat belts and harnesses are fastened.

(5) Utility and acrobatic category airplane restraints must accommodate an occupant wearing a parachute.

(6) If retractors will be used, ensure that mounting will provide straight-line entry and exit of webbing to prevent binding or frictional drag. Retractor loading should not impose bending forces upon retractor mounting brackets.

(7) If harness installation will impose loads on the seat back or seat attachment, additional evaluation will be needed for structural integrity.

(8) Refer to the aircraft type certificate to find the certification date and basis to establish minimum static load requirements. Determine the feasibility of performing static tests or stress analysis. Static testing on operational aircraft is not recommended.

(9) Select only restraints that meet OEM, TSO, PMA, or other established industry standards or specifications.

(10) Install restraints using AN, MS, NAS, or other acceptable aircraft hardware with adequate strength properties.

(11) Perform a check to ensure all components function properly.

(12) Complete record entries as required, including FAA Form 337, logbook, weight and balance, and equipment list.

b. Shoulder Harness Inspection Checklist. Inspect restraint system for condition and function at each annual or each required inspection of cabin or cockpit equipment. If questions arise regarding any of the conditions listed below, contact the restraint manufacturer for specific limits.

(1) Inspect stitching on webbing for broken or missing stitches.

(2) Inspect webbing for fraying, fading or cuts. Fraying that causes binding in the retractor is excessive. Fading caused by exposure to sunlight or chemicals may indicate a reduction in strength.

(3) Ensure that TSO, PMA, OEM, or other required identification tags are present and legible on each belt assembly. Tags may not be required for harnesses manufactured prior to March 27, 1987. Contact the aircraft or restraint manufacturer for specific requirements.

(4) If so equipped, check the harness post on the lap belt to make sure the nylon bushing or grommet is present and functional to provide positive harness end fitting engagement. Do not replace the bushing with nylon bundle ties. Contact the belt manufacturer for replacement bushings/grommets and instructions.

(5) Check the belt buckle for latching and release functions.

(6) Check the retractors to ensure that locking mechanisms engage when webbing is positioned at the normal operating length. Inertia reels should lock when the webbing is accelerated quickly out of the reel. Automatic locking retractors should lock at approximately one-inch increments as the webbing retracts back into the reel.

(7) Inspect buckles, connectors, and fittings for corrosion, cracks, or other damage. Check mounting hardware for security and ensure that airframe attachment of end fittings self-align and do not bind.

(8) Inspect quick release end fittings for cotter pins.

(9) If equipped with manual locking inertia reel, check for proper operation and condition.

932. THRU 999. RESERVED

CHAPTER 10. AIRCRAFT BATTERY INSTALLATIONS

SECTION 1. GENERAL

1000. PURPOSE. This chapter contains structural and design considerations for the fabrication of aircraft battery installations.

1001. HAZARDS AND WARNINGS: HANDLING PRECAUTIONS. Serious injury can result from carelessness while handling and working with batteries. Failure to heed these warnings could result in serious injury or death.

a. All tools must be insulated.

b. Care must be taken with all metal items to include clothing items such as belt buckles, zippers, metal fasteners and wallet chains, as well as jewelry items such as rings, watches, bracelets, and necklaces. All metal or conductive articles should be removed from your person when handling batteries.

c. Wear protective clothing and eye protection. The electrolyte can cause burns if in contact with skin or eyes. Do not touch eyes, nose, or mouth after handling batteries or acid.

d. Do not smoke or hold naked flames near batteries on charge. If allowed to accumulate in a confined space, the gases emitted during charge could cause an explosion. To prevent the accumulation of hydrogen gas in the manifold, do not charge a flooded electrolyte or vented battery on the bench with the cover on.

e. Do not service flooded or vented lead-acid and nickel-cadmium batteries in the same shop area, as cross contamination of acid and alkaline electrolytes may happen.

f. Always pour acid into water, NEVER pour water into acid.

g. Do not use petroleum spirits, trichloroethylene, or other solvents.

h. Know the location and use of emergency eyewash and shower nearest the battery charging area.

1002. ADDITIONAL REFERENCES (current editions).

a. AC 20-106, Aircraft Inspection for the General Aviation Aircraft Owner.

b. AC 43-4, Corrosion Control for Aircraft.

c. AC 120-27, Aircraft Weight and Balance Control.

d. Civil Aviation Regulation 6, Rotorcraft Airworthiness; Normal Category.

e. Federal Aviation Administration (FAA)-H-8083-1, Aircraft Weight and Balance Handbook.

f. FAA-H-8083-19, Plane Sense General Aviation Information.

1003. LOCATION REQUIREMENTS. The battery installation and/or its installation should provide:

a. Accessibility for Battery Maintenance and Removal. The installation should ensure that the battery could be easily installed or removed and serviced without removing seats, fairings, etc.

b. Protection from Engine Heat. If installed in the engine compartment the battery should be protected from extreme heat both during engine operation and after the engine has been shut down. This kind of protection can be provided by a source of cooling air to the battery box or additional thermal protection around the battery. Care should be taken not to interfere with the flow of engine-cooling air.

c. Protection from Mechanical Damage. Vibration and other shock loads are a major cause of short battery life. Install the battery in a location that will minimize damage from airframe vibration and prevent accidental damage by passengers or cargo.

d. Passenger Protection. Insure that the battery is enclosed within a container/box so that passengers/crew are protected from any fumes or electrolytes that may be spilled as a result of battery overheating, minor crash, or un-intentional inverted flight.

e. Airframe Protection. To minimize damage to adjacent metal structures, fabric covering or electrical equipment can be accomplished by properly locating battery drains and vent discharge lines, and adequately venting the battery compartment. To protect the airframe structure and fluid lines apply asphaltic or rubber-based paint to the areas adjacent to and below the battery or battery box.

1004. AIRCRAFT STORAGE BATTERY DESIGN AND INSTALLATION.

a. Lead Acid.

(1) Each aircraft storage battery, whether approved to a Technical Standards Order (TSO) or not, must be designed as required by regulation and installed as prescribed by the manufacturer.

(2) No explosive or toxic gases emitted by any battery in normal operation, or as the result of any probable malfunction in the charging system or battery installation, may accumulate in hazardous quantities within the airplane.

(3) Corrosive fluids or gases that may escape from the battery may damage surrounding structures or adjacent essential equipment.

b. Nickel Cadmium.

(1) Each aircraft storage battery, whether approved to a TSO or not, must be designed as required by regulation and installed as prescribed by the manufacturer.

(2) Safe cell temperatures and pressures must be maintained during any probable charging and discharging condition. No uncontrolled increase in cell temperature may result when the battery is recharged (after previous complete discharge).

(a) At maximum regulated voltage or power;

(b) During a flight of maximum duration; and

(c) Under the most adverse cooling condition likely to occur in service.

(3) Compliance with paragraph 1004b(2) must be shown by tests unless experience with similar batteries and installations has shown that maintaining safe cell temperatures and pressures presents no problem.

(4) No explosive or toxic gases emitted by any battery in normal operation, or as the result of any probable malfunction in the charging system or battery installation, may accumulate in hazardous quantities within the airplane.

(5) Corrosive fluids or gases that may escape from the battery may damage surrounding structures or adjacent essential equipment.

1005. DUPLICATION OF THE MANUFACTURER'S INSTALLATION. The availability of readymade parts and attachment fittings may make it desirable to consider the location and/or type of installation selected and designed by the airframe manufacturer. Appreciable savings in time and work may be realized if previously approved data and/or parts are used.

1006. OTHER INSTALLATIONS. If the battery installation has not been previously approved, or if the battery is to be installed or relocated in a manner or location other than provided in previously approved data, perform static tests on the completed installation as outlined in chapter 1. Because of the concentrated mass of the battery, the support structure should also be rigid enough to prevent undue vibration or undue shock, which may lead to early structural failure.

1007. DELIVERY INSPECTION. When the battery is unpacked, a thorough inspection should be made to ensure that no damage occurred during shipment. Inspect the shipping container as well as the battery. Before putting the battery into service, perform a safety check by following these points carefully.

a. Damage. See if any liquid has spilled into the shipping container. This may indicate that a cell is damaged. Check for dented, cracked, or discolored areas on the sides and bottom of the battery case. Check for cracked cell cases or covers. Do not place a damaged battery into service.

b. Shorting Straps. Some nickel-cadmium batteries are shipped with shorting devices across the main power receptacle output terminals. Before subjecting a battery to electrical service this device must be removed.

c. Electrical Connections. Test all terminal hardware to ensure tightness. Poor electrical contact between mating surfaces may reduce discharge voltage, cause local overheating and damage the battery.

NOTE: Before charging the battery read and become familiar with the manufacturer's charge procedures.

1008. BATTERY INSTALLATION AND REMOVAL. The following instructions are generic. See the airframe manufacturer's maintenance manuals or STC for instructions specific to a particular aircraft model.

a. Removal.

(1) Set master switch to the OFF position and tag the switch.

(2) Disconnect any external power supply.

(3) Open battery compartment access panels.

(4) Disconnect battery quick disconnect plug or remove terminal bolts and disconnect battery cables from battery terminals. Always disconnect the ground cable first and install the ground cable last.

(5) Disconnect battery ventilation tubes, if any.

(6) Unlock battery hold down clamps or remove battery hold down bars. Disengage battery.

(7) Carefully remove battery.

WARNING: Batteries are heavy. Use appropriate lifting devices or equipment. Use battery handles where provided.

b. Installation.

(1) Inspect the battery for damage. Cracks in metal or plastic containers are not permitted. Dents in metal containers that impinge on the interior plastic container are not acceptable.

(2) Set master switch to the OFF position and tag (explain what should be on the tag "Do not turn on master switch").

(3) Disconnect any external power supply and tag (explain what should be on the tag "Do not connect external power").

(4) Open battery compartment access panels.

(5) Ensure the battery container or tray is clean and dry. Treat and paint any corrosion areas.

(6) Install battery in battery container or tray.

WARNING: Batteries are heavy. Use appropriate lifting devices or equipment. Use battery handles where provided.

(7) Engage battery hold down hardware, torque and safety wire per airframe manufacturer's maintenance manual.

(8) Connect battery vent tubes.

(9) Connect battery quick disconnect plug, any auxiliary connector or for ring terminals, install with bolt and lock washer. Torque terminal bolts as recommended by the manufacturer.

(10) Replace electrical compartment access panel.

(11) Perform an operational test.

(12) Update aircraft weight and balance data, if necessary.

(13) Update equipment list, if applicable.

(14) Make a log book entry with battery serial number and date of installation.

1009. THRU 1012. RESERVED

FIGURE 10-1. TYPICAL BATTERY INSTALLATION IN THE AIRCRAFT

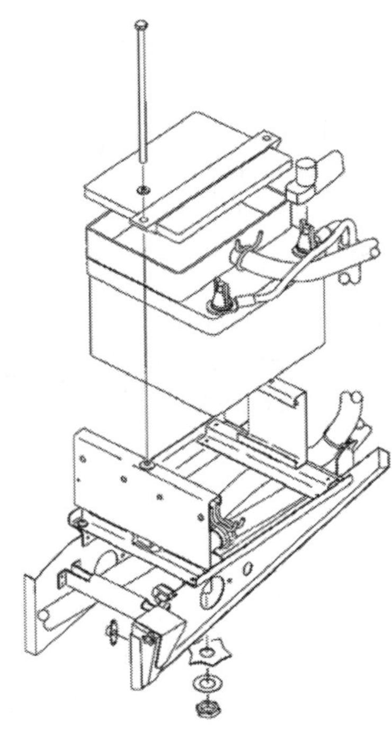

SECTION 2. LEAD ACID BATTERY INSTALLATIONS

1013. GENERAL. In a lead acid battery the voltage will slowly drop as opposed to a nickel-cadmium battery. These batteries are typically less expensive, do not require temperature sensor monitoring, require virtually no maintenance, and when unable to meet the manufacturer's capacity requirements, are simply removed and replaced.

1014. BATTERY BOX. The battery box should have an open drain in case the electrolyte overflows. The box should be vented to prevent an accumulation of flammable hydrogen gas.

1015. SECURING THE BATTERY. Install the battery in such a manner as to hold the battery securely in place without subjecting it to excessive localized pressure, which may distort or crack the battery case. Apply paralketone, heavy grease, or other comparable protective coating to battery cables terminal nuts/connectors. Ensure that proper torque is applied to the terminal nuts/connectors. Do not over tighten terminal nuts, which may result in fracturing of the terminal posts. Provide adequate clearance between the battery and any bolts and/or rivets which may protrude into the battery box or compartment.

WARNING: When installing or removing a battery, wear safety glasses and take special care to ensure that no sparks are created by tools, or loose jewelry that provide a short to ground. Always remove the ground cable first and install it last. If possible, attach the ground cable to the frame of the battery compartment. Do not lift the battery by their vent tubes, receptacles or terminals.

1016. SUMP JAR. Lead acid batteries are often installed with a sump jar in the exhaust vent that neutralizes vented acid fumes to protect the airframe from corrosive battery acid. If installed, the sump jar should have a capacity of approximately one pint. The jar should contain a 1/2" think pad saturated with a 5-percent solution of sodium bicarbonate (baking soda) in water or about 3/8" of dry sodium bicarbonate. The inlet tube carrying fumes to the sump should extend into the jar about 1" from the lid. (See Figure 10-2.)

FIGURE 10-2. TYPICAL BATTERY INSTALLATION WITH SUMP JAR

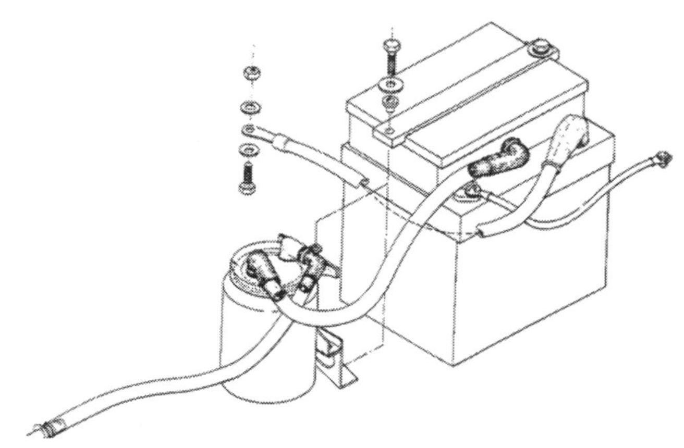

1017. VENTING. Provide suitable venting to the battery compartment to prevent the accumulation of the hydrogen gas expelled during operation.

> **NOTE: Valve regulated lead acid batteries can use the same ventilation system as the original nickel-cadmium battery.**

a. Manifold Type. In this type of venting, one or more batteries are connected, via the battery manifold(s) or battery box vents, to a hose or tube manifold system as shown in Figure 10-3. Fasten such hoses securely to prevent shifting and maintain adequate bend radii to prevent kinking.

(1) The upstream side of the system is connected to a positive pressure point on the aircraft, and the downstream side is usually discharged overboard to a negative pressure area. It is advisable to install a battery sump jar in the downstream side to neutralize any corrosive vapors that may be discharged.

(2) When selecting these pressure points, select points that will always provide the proper direction of airflow through the manifold system during all normal operating attitudes. Reversals of flow within the vent system should not be permitted when a battery sump jar is installed, as the neutralizing agent in the jar may contaminate the electrolyte within the battery.

FIGURE 10-3. BATTERY VENTILATION SYSTEM

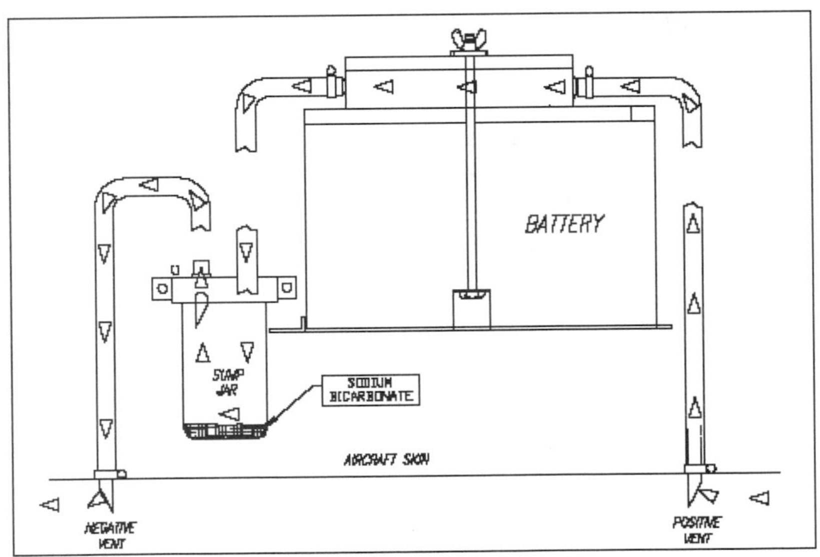

b. Free Airflow Type. Battery cases or boxes that contain louvers may be installed without an individual vent system, provided that:

(1) The compartment in which the battery is installed has sufficient airflow to prevent the accumulation of explosive mixtures of hydrogen;

(2) Noxious fumes are directed away from occupants; and

(3) Suitable precautions are taken to prevent corrosive battery fluids or vapors from damaging surrounding structure, covering, equipment, control cables, wiring, etc.

1018. DRAINS. Position battery compartment drains so that they do not allow spillage to come in contact with the aircraft during either ground or flight attitudes. Route the drains so they have a positive slope without traps. Drains should be at least 1/2" in diameter to prevent clogging.

1019. ELECTRICAL INSTALLATION.

a. Electrical equipment, controls, and wiring must be installed so that operations of any one unit or system of units will not adversely affect the simultaneous operation of any other electrical unit or system essential to safe operation. Any electrical interference likely to be present in the airplane must not result in hazardous effects upon the airplane or its systems.

b. Cables/Connectors. Use cables and/or connectors that are adequately rated for the current demand and are properly installed. (See AC 43.13-1, Acceptable Methods, Techniques, and Practices-Aircraft Inspection and Repair (as amended), chapter 11.) Cable size can also be selected by using the same gage as used on a previously approved production aircraft with the same battery.

(1) The cables should be of sufficient length to prevent undue strain on the battery connector or terminals.

(2) Clamp and protect cables, including the bus, in a secure manner. Since the batteries are not generally fused, any fault in the battery feeder cable could cause loss of the battery electrical system in addition to a possible fire hazard.

(3) Route cables so that cable or terminals cannot short to the battery case or to the hold-down frame.

(4) Route cables outside the battery box whenever practicable to prevent corrosion by acid fumes. When internal routing is unavoidable, protect the cable inside the box with acid-proof tubing.

(5) Assure that cables will not be inadvertently reversed on the battery terminals either by proper cable lengths and clamps or, if this is not practical, use conspicuous color coding.

c. Cable installation must be designed and installed as follows:

(1) Means of permanent identification must be provided for electrical cables, connectors, and terminals.

(2) Electrical cables must be installed and secured so that the risk of mechanical damage and/or damage caused by fluids, vapors, or sources of heat, is minimized.

d. When installing lead acid batteries in place of nickel-cadmium batteries some airframes require deactivation or removal of the temperature monitoring systems. Generally this alteration requires a flight manual supplement to override the emergency procedures regarding battery overheating.

NOTE: FAA field approval or STC is required for this kind of alteration.

e. Battery Cutoff. Install a battery cutoff relay to provide a means of isolating the battery from the aircraft's electrical system. An acceptable battery cutoff circuit is shown in Figure 10-4. Mount the relay so that the cable connecting the relay to the battery is as short as feasible to reduce the possibility of a fire occurring because of a short within this section of cable.

FIGURE 10-4. TYPICAL BATTERY CUTOFF AND GENERATOR ALTERNATOR CONTROL CIRCUIT

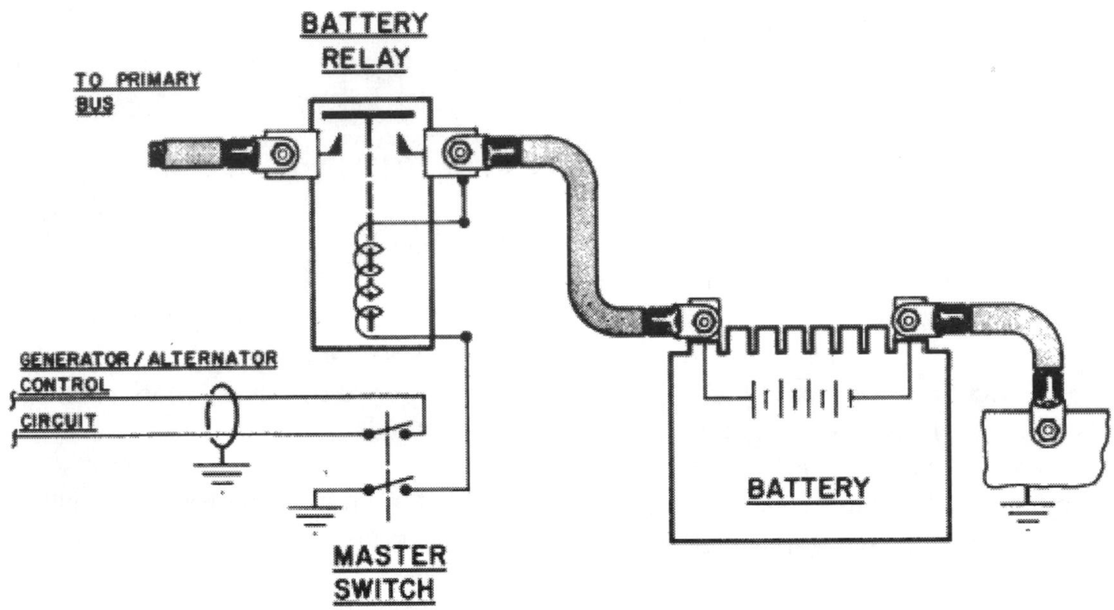

1020. QUICK DISCONNECT. Look for and replace the terminal pins when:

a. Excessive pitting or corrosion cannot be removed.

b. Signs of burning or arcing.

c. Cracked part or housing.

d. Excessive wear on contact pins, socket lock pins, or worm screw.

e. Large deposits form on contacts or plastic is discolored.

f. Excessively loose handle and locking assembly.

NOTE: Most manufacturers sell or provide dimensions for tools to check the fit of the quick disconnect sockets.

1021. WEIGHT AND BALANCE. After installation or alteration with the replacement battery the weight and balance of the aircraft should be recomputed if:

a. The weight of the replacement battery is different from that of the original battery.

b. The location of the battery is different from that of the original battery.

NOTE: Weight and balance procedures for aircraft are contained in AC 43.13-1 (as amended), chapter 10.

1022. THRU 1024. RESERVED

SECTION 3. NICKEL-CADMIUM BATTERY INSTALLATIONS

1025. GENERAL. Nickel-cadmium batteries fulfill a need for a power source that will provide large amounts of current, fast recharge capability, and a high degree of reliability. Nickel-cadmium batteries produce a constant voltage and can operate at lower temperatures. They are generally more expensive to purchase.

1026. ELECTRICAL ANALYSIS. The ampere-hour capacity of a nickel-cadmium battery is selected to accommodate the aircraft load requirements. When making this selection, the following items should be considered:

a. The low internal resistance permits it to recharge very quickly. This high recharge rate can exceed the generator rated capacity and deprive essential circuits of necessary operating current. Total system load (battery recharging plus system loads) must not exceed the pre-established electrical capacity of the generator system.

b. Compare the discharge characteristics curves of the batteries to make sure a reduced capacity nickel-cadmium battery is adequate regarding the following:

(1) Ability to provide engine starting or cranking requirements. Some turbine engines require an initial surge of approximately 1200 amperes, which tapers off within 10 seconds to approximately 800 amperes cranking current. Reciprocating engines require approximately 100 to 200 amperes cranking current.

(2) Ability to provide sufficient capacity for low temperature starting. Nickel-cadmium batteries deliver their rated capacity when the ambient temperature range is 70°F to 90°F. For best engine cranking, replacement batteries with increased capacity will offset the lower power or reduced capacity available when the batteries are cold soaked.

(3) Some nickel-cadmium batteries deliver greater power at temperature extremes than comparable rated lead acid batteries; take care not to overload the cables and connectors.

1027. MAINTENANCE CONSIDERATIONS. To provide for ease of inspection and because nickel-cadmium batteries are generally not serviced in the aircraft, it is important that the battery be located where it can easily be inspected, removed, and installed. Some battery cases are designed with view ports on each side of the case for visual monitoring of the cell electrolyte level. If this type of case is to be used, carefully consider the location of the battery compartment to accommodate this feature.

1028. STRUCTURAL REQUIREMENTS. Most lead-acid battery compartments provide adequate structure attachment for the installation of nickel-cadmium batteries. However, cantilever supported battery boxes/compartments may not be suitable for nickel-cadmium battery installations unless modified to compensate for an increased over-hang moment. This may be caused by a change in battery shape and center of gravity (CG) location even though the replacement battery may weigh less than the original lead-acid battery. Whenever the total installation weight and/or the overhang moment exceed those of the original installation, perform a static test as outlined in chapter 1. If the battery compartment is to be relocated, follow the location requirement procedures outlined in paragraph 3.

1029. ISOLATION OF BATTERY CASE. Because of the material from which nickel-cadmium battery cases are generally made (stainless or epoxy coated steel), it is desirable to electrically isolate the case from the aircraft structure. This will eliminate the potential discharge current produced when spillage or seepage of the electrolyte provides a current path between the cell terminal or connector and the exposed metal of the battery case.

NOTE: Epoxy coated nickel cadmium battery cases serve to isolate the battery from the airframe thus eliminating electrical leakage to ground. Some batteries use a series of liners that are inside the battery. This isolates the battery from the airframe and helps eliminate electrical leakage to ground.

1030. VENTILATION. During the charging process, nickel-cadmium batteries produce hydrogen and oxygen gases. This occurs near the end of the charging cycle when the battery reaches what is called the gassing potential. To avoid a buildup of these gases, and possible accidental ignition, ventilation should be provided to evacuate this gas from the aircraft. There are two types of nickel-cadmium battery cases, one with vent nozzles and one with viewports.

a. The vent nozzle type utilizes vent hoses to evacuate the gas overboard by use of forced air or by venturi effect.

b. Battery cases with viewports or louvers must have airflow sufficient to keep the mixture of air and hydrogen below 4 precent. The gases from this type of case are evacuated into the battery compartment. Regardless of the ventilation system used, the airflow should be provided at a minimum rate of 0.040 cubic feet per minute (CFM), this equates to 1.13 liters per minute (lpm).

1031. PRE-INSTALLATION REQUIREMENTS. Inspect the replacement battery for possible damage incurred during shipment or storage. Give particular attention to signs of spilled liquid within the shipping container, as it may indicate a damaged cell. Follow procedures outlined in section 2 for battery venting and electrical connections.

a. Pre-installation Battery Servicing. Check the following in accordance with the battery manufacturer's instructions:

(1) Remove the shipping plugs (if used) and clean and install the filler cap vent plugs.

(2) Check the tightness of terminal hardware including each cell connector strap to the proper torque values.

(3) Check the polarity of each cell to be sure they are connected in the proper series or sequence.

(4) Prepare the battery for installation in accordance with the manufacturer's requirements.

b. Compartments or battery boxes which have previously housed lead-acid batteries must be washed out, neutralized with ammonia or a baking soda solution, allowed to dry thoroughly, and painted with alkaline-resistant paint. Remove all traces of sulfuric acid and its corrosive products from the battery vent system to prevent contamination of the potassium hydroxide electrolyte and/or possible damage to the battery case material. Replace those parts of the vent system, which cannot be thoroughly cleansed (hoses, etc.).

1032. NICKEL CADMIUM BATTERY INSTALLATION. Each installation must have provisions to prevent any hazardous effects on structure or essential systems that may be caused by the maximum amount of heat the battery can generate during a short-circuit of the battery or individual cells.

a. Nickel-cadmium battery installations must have:

(1) A system to control the charging rate of the battery automatically to prevent battery overheating;

(2) A battery temperature sensing and over-temperature warning system with a means for disconnecting the battery from its charging source in the event of an over-temperature condition; or

(3) A battery failure sensing and warning system with a means for disconnecting the battery from its charging source in the event of battery failure.

b. In the event of a complete loss of the primary electrical power generating system, the battery must be capable of providing at least 30 minutes of electrical power to those loads that are essential to continue safe flights and landing. The 30-minute time period includes the time needed for the pilots to recognize the loss of generated power and take appropriate load shedding action.

1033. SECURING THE BATTERY. Follow the procedures outlined in section 1. Make certain that the hold down bolts are not drawn up too tightly. Ensure that the case to cover seal is installed so that the battery case/cover does not become distorted.

CAUTION: In installations where care has been taken to isolate the battery cases, inadvertent grounding may occur through improper or careless use of safety wire.

1034. QUICK DISCONNECT. Look for and replace the terminal pins when:

a. Excessive pitting or corrosion that cannot be removed.

b. Signs of burning or arcing.

c. Cracked part or housing.

d. Excessive wear on contact pins, socket lock pins, or worm screw.

e. Large deposits form on contacts or plastic is discolored.

f. Excessively loose handle and locking assembly.

NOTE: Most manufacturers sell or provide dimensions for tools to check the fit of the quick disconnect sockets.

1035. VOLTAGE AND CURRENT REGULATION. It is essential that the charging voltage and current be checked and, if necessary, the voltage regulator reset to meet the requirements of the nickel-cadmium battery being installed.

IMPORTANT: Improper charging current or voltage can destroy a battery in a short period of time.

1036. WEIGHT AND BALANCE. After installation of the nickel-cadmium battery the weight and balance of the aircraft should be recomputed if:

a. The weight of the nickel-cadmium battery is different from that of the original battery.

b. The location of the nickel-cadmium battery is different from that of the original battery.

NOTE: Weight and balance procedures for aircraft are contained in AC 43.13-1 (as amended), chapter 10.

1037. THRU 1040. RESERVED.

SECTION 4. BATTERY INSTALLATION CHECKLIST

1041. STRUCTURAL REQUIREMENTS.

a. Determine if the battery is installed in such a manner that it can withstand the required loads. The effect on other structure (primary or secondary) should be considered.

b. Determine whether suitable materials are used in the construction, including standard fasteners, confirm that the method of fabrication will result in a consistently sound structure.

c. If a mounting bracket is used, determine if the method used in its fabrication will produce a consistently sound structure.

d. If the equipment is mounted either on the existing structure or on a bracket attached to the existing structure, confirm whether all of the structure (including the bracket, if used) is adequate to support the required loads. This answer can be determined by either of two methods:

(1) By direct comparison with an existing approved installation having the same or similar (approximately the same weight and size) equipment installed.

(2) By structural analysis or static test. Such installations do not lend themselves readily to analysis, but are normally adaptable to a static test. In conducting a static test, the following procedure may be used:

(a) Determine the weight and CG position of the equipment item.

(b) Mount the equipment in its position in the airplane or simulate the equipment with a dummy so that the required loads can be applied at the CG position of the actual equipment.

(c) The required loads should then be applied by any suitable means. If the equipment is light in weight, the inspector could use his own strength and/or weight to determine if the installation will withstand the required loads.

NOTE: All items of mass likely to injure the passengers or crew in a minor crash landing should have their supporting structure designed to the crash load requirements of Title 14 of the Code of Federal Regulations (14 CFR) part 23, § 23.561, insofar as the forward, upward, and sideward directions are concerned. The applicable downward load factor shall be the critical flight or landing load factor specified in §§ 23.341 and 23.473, whichever is greater.

(3) In lieu of a calculated determination of the down load factor, the ultimate factors of 6.6, 6.6, and 9.0 may be used for the normal, utility, and acrobatic categories, respectively. For equipment location not covered by § 23.561, the required loads (ref. § 23.301) are the flight and landing load factors of §§ 23.337, 23.341, and 23.473. In lieu of a calculated determination of these loads, the down load factors referenced above may be used.

(4) Supporting structure of other mass items should be designed to the critical flight or landing load factors of § 23.321, 23.471, 27.321, or 27.471. The values shown in § 23.561 or 27.561 may be used in lieu of determination of these values.

e. Determine if the equipment is installed so that it does not adversely affect another structure (either primary or secondary).

f. Confirm whether means are provided to permit proper inspections of the installation and related adjacent parts as components.

1042. HAZARDS TO THE AIRCRAFT AND ITS OCCUPANTS.

a. Confirm whether the parts of the airplane adjacent to the battery are protected against corrosion from any products likely to be emitted by the battery during servicing or flight.

NOTE: Methods that may be used to obtain protection include: acid-proof paint that will resist corrosive action by emitted electrolyte, drain to discharge corrosive liquids clear of the aircraft, positive pressure vents to carry corrosive fumes and flammable gases outside the aircraft, enclosed battery cases that would contain any amount of electrolyte that might be spilled, or combination of these methods.

b. Determine whether the battery container or compartment is vented in such a manner that any explosive gases released by the battery during charging or discharging are carried outside the airplane.

c. Confirm that the battery container or compartment is vented in such a manner that any noxious gases emitted by the battery are directed away from the crew and passengers.

d. Verify whether the battery connector terminals or other exposed parts are protected against electrical contact with the battery container or compartment.

e. Determine if adequate provision is made for the drainage of spilled or excess battery fluid.

1043. OPERATING ASPECTS. If a battery is the only source of electrical power, determine if the battery has sufficient capacity to supply the electrical power necessary for dependable operation of all electrical equipment essential to the safe operation of the airplane.

1044. DETAIL DESIGN STANDARDS. Verify that the battery is accessible for inspection or servicing on the ground.

1045. RECORDKEEPING.

a. Confirm that a maintenance record entry has been made.

b. Determine if the equipment list and weight and balance has been revised.

1046. THRU 1048. RESERVED.

SECTION 5. INSTRUCTIONS FOR CONTINUED AIRWORTHINESS

1049. LEAD-ACID BATTERIES.

a. Airworthiness Limitations.

(1) Battery Inspection. To ensure continued airworthiness, the battery should be removed and capacity tested. Follow the battery manufacturer's recommended instructions for continued airworthiness (ICA) to determine service periods.

(2) Connector/Wiring Inspection. Check for mechanical integrity, resiliency, pitted, or corroded mating surfaces, burn marks, condition, and type of wiring.

(3) Electrolyte Levels. Electrolyte levels must be maintained just over the plates at all times. Replenish consumed water with distilled or demineralized water.

(4) Sump Jar Maintenance. Inspect the electrolyte levels and the sump jar every 100-flight hours.

b. Capacity Test. The capacity test should be performed as follows:

(1) Check for proper battery installation per Supplemental Type Certificate (STC) or manufacturer's ICA when performing annual and 100-hour inspections and when replacing the battery after a capacity test.

(2) Stabilize the battery at 15°C (59°F) or higher. The battery should be at temperature for at least 24 hours.

(3) Remove the battery from the aircraft and charge it according to the recommended charging instructions. Allow the battery to stand on open circuit for 1 hour.

(4) Connect the fully charged battery to a capacity tester that incorporates a load resistance, ammeter, voltmeter, and a timer.

(5) Discharge the battery at the C1 rate to 1.75 volts per cell (10 volts for a 12-volt battery and 20-volts for a 24-volt battery). Note the discharge time.

(6) The battery is considered airworthy if it meets 80 percent of its C1 (1 hour) capacity rating. However it is recommended to return batteries to service when their capacity is above the minimum; i.e., 85 percent minimum or 51 minutes to end point voltage.

(7) If the battery fails to meet the minimum runtime, continue by using the constant current C1 method in the manufacturer's ICA. Allow the battery to stand on open circuit for 1 hour.

(8) Repeat the discharge test as indicated. If the failure persists, replace the battery.

(9) If the battery is found to be airworthy, it must be recharged with constant potential (CP) prior to re-installing it in the aircraft.

1050. NICKEL-CADMIUM BATTERIES.

a. Airworthiness Limitations. To ensure continued airworthiness, the battery should be removed and inspected per the manufacturer's recommendations.

(1) Connector/Wiring Inspection. Check for mechanical integrity, resiliency, pitted or corroded mating surfaces, burn marks, condition, and type of wiring.

(2) Voltage Regulator. Periodic checks to correct out-of-tolerance regulators and replacement of defective units will reduce the possibility of inadvertent increases in charging voltage with the resultant rise in charge current and battery temperature and water consumption.

(3) Battery. Inspect can and cover for dents, damage, epoxy coating separation, vent tube obstruction, latch function, and cover seal condition.

Remove the battery cover and clean top of cells and connectors with a nylon brush. Verify torque on every intercell connection. If disassembly is required, discharge the battery first.

(4) Electrolyte Levels. Electrolyte levels should be adjusted during the last 15 minutes of the topping charge and while the current is still flowing, because the cells are at their most uniform electrolyte level at this time. Replenish electrolyte levels with distilled, deionized, or demineralized water only. Insure that the proper nozzle and syringe assembly are used to level the cells by referring to the component maintenance manual for the syringe/nozzle specifications. Using the incorrect nozzle may impact battery serviceability and longevity.

(5) Electrical Leakage. Determine if external leakage is of such a magnitude as to require a complete battery cleaning. Follow the manufacturer's recommended procedures.

(6) Sensor Assembly. Inspect the battery for proper placement of thermostats, heaters, thermistors or other sensor elements. Inspect wiring and receptacle for insulation damage, corrosion, and crimping or other defects. If the sensor/harness assembly fails testing or is damaged, it must be replaced. Perform a functional test on the temperature sensor assembly at least once each calendar year.

b. Capacity Test. The capacity test must be performed in accordance with the manufacturer's recommendations.

1051. THRU 1099. RESERVED.

CHAPTER 11. ADDING OR RELOCATING INSTRUMENTS

1100. PURPOSE. This chapter contains structural and design guidance to consider when aircraft alterations are to be accomplished by the addition or relocation of instruments.

1101. HAZARDS AND WARNINGS. The rapid advance of technical progress in the aviation industry has resulted in a virtual explosion of high-tech aftermarket instrumentation. In many instances, these innovations are marketed without the support of a proper certification process. As a result, much of the equipment purported to be the most advanced may not be certificated or even certificable for installation on aircraft for which uninformed purchasers have chosen the equipment for installation.

NOTE: The burden of provision of and compliance with approved data falls entirely on the technician approving the aircraft for return to service.

1102. ADDITIONAL REFERENCES. Before initiating an alteration involving the addition or relocation of instruments, the regulatory basis of the aircraft must be considered. The introduction page of this document provides guidance to be considered on the subject of certification basis. For this chapter, the following additional references are provided:

a. Department of Commerce, Aeronautics Branch, Aeronautics Bulletin 7a, section 73(A) through (H) provides regulatory requirements for electrical equipment applicable to the 24 makes and 115 models of aircraft certificated under the provisions of that document. Section 75(B) of the same document provides additional regulatory requirements for instrumentation to be installed on the aircraft listed therein.

NOTE: Exercise care in the use of Bulletin 7a as certification basis proof data. Subsequent changes in ownership and production of some makes and models may have also resulted in changes of certification basis.

b. Department of Commerce, Civil Aeronautics Administration Bureau of Regulation Inspection Handbook, as revised to January 29, 1947, chapter XVII provides a listing of approved type certificated and 609 Group 2 aircraft under those categories. The Group 2 memoranda are identified and briefly described but complete text documentation is not provided. As of this publication no known repository of complete Group 2 memoranda has been identified.

c. Civil Aeronautics Regulation (CAR) 18 and the related Civil Aeronautics Manual (CAM) 18 established and maintained the standards and practices for all maintenance, repair, and alteration of aircraft applicable under the provisions of the CAR. That document remained in effect until the advent of the systemic changes dictated by the Federal Aviation Act of 1958 and the resultant documentary changes.

d. CAR 6, Rotorcraft Airworthiness; Normal Category.

1103. PREPARATION. Before initiating any alteration involving the addition or relocation of instruments the regulatory basis of the aircraft must be considered. For the purposes of this chapter the following references are provided:

- Civil Air Regulation (CAR) 3.661 through 3.676 provides the regulatory basis for installation of instruments in CAR 3 airplanes
- CAR 4a532 through 4a537 provide the regulatory basis for supplemental

variations for installation of instruments in CAR 4 non-air carrier (NAC) airplanes

- Title 14 of the Code of Federal Regulations (14 CFR) part 23, § 23.1321 provides the regulatory basis for the arrangement and visibility of instruments in part 23 airplanes

a. Structure. Chapter 1 provides guidance by which structural integrity may be determined. Chapter 2, paragraphs 202 and 203, provides information pertinent to instrument panel installations.

b. Location. In the absence of specific regulatory requirements, for installation of instruments required for operation under Instrument Meteorological Conditions (IMC), the recommended configuration is in the form of the basic "T" (Figure 11.1).

FIGURE 11-1. THE BASIC "T" VMC INSTRUMENT CONFIGURATION

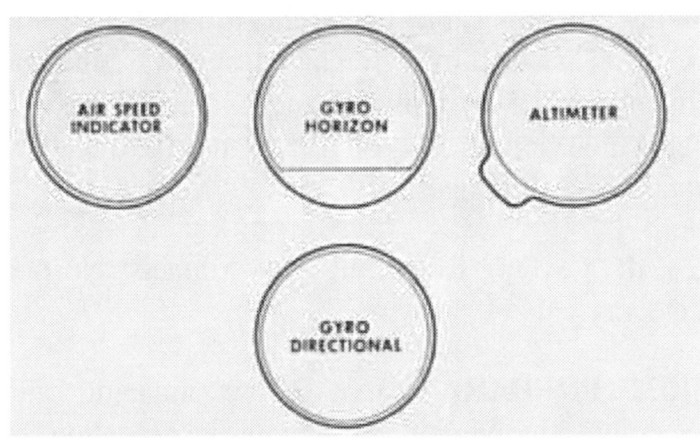

(1) The aircraft attitude indicator is located at the top center of the installation.

(2) The air speed indicator is located adjacent to and left of the attitude indicator.

(3) The altimeter is located adjacent to and to the right of the attitude indicator.

(4) The directional indicator is located adjacent to and immediately below the attitude indicator.

NOTE: As instrument panel installations have become more complex, the basic "T" has become more difficult to accomplish. With the relocation of the directional indicator, the relationship of the ASI-ATT-AI combination is assumed.

1104. INSTALLATION. Throughout the development of the complexity of aircraft the requirements for the mounting of all instruments has remained the same. All instruments must be mounted so they are visible to the crewmember primarily responsible for their use.

a. Structure. Before initiating changes to instrument panel installations, determine the load bearing requirements of the component. In some aircraft the instrument panel is stressed as the primary structure; with the majority, the panel is treated as the secondary structure with load bearing responsibilities limited to instruments and equipment installed. Regardless of the structural nature, the altering technician is responsibility for the installation to its original or properly altered state.

(1) In all cases, where available, refer to the manufacturer's instructions for continued airworthiness (ICA) when considering alterations to any structure. For aircraft manufactured before the regulatory requirement for the manufacturer to provide such information, refer to AC 43.13-1, Acceptable Methods, Techniques, and Practices (as amended), chapter 4, section 4 and/or chapter 2, of this AC for methods and techniques of retaining structural integrity.

(2) Failing availability or applicability of those sources we recommend that the altering individual have a Designated Engineering Representative (DER) approve the data before accomplishing of the task.

b. Instrument Plumbing. The majority of CAR 3 and CAR 4 general aviation aircraft use instrumentation identified as "wet" gauges. This term has nothing to do with what is being measured by the gauge, but rather the material to be measured is delivered directly to the gauge. Typical "wet" systems are fuel pressure, engine oil pressure and, when so equipped, hydraulic pressure. While not usually considered "wet" systems, the airspeed and vacuum systems use this same system. The tubing used is generally thin walled seamless aluminum or stainless steel. However, flexible rubber and/or neoprene lines are prevalent in airspeed and vacuum sensing lines.

(1) The most reliable source of information on the material used in a particular aircraft is the manufacturer's ICA. If that source is not available, AC 43.13-1 (as amended), chapter 8 provides inspection and maintenance guidance on fuel lines, while chapter 9 provides the same level of information on hydraulic systems.

(2) The installation of remote sensing systems per part 23 has replaced the "wet" systems with system pressures being remotely measured by transducers and electrically transmitted to the cockpit indicators.

(3) Aircraft with long histories of alteration may contain a mixture of mechanical and/or electrical analogue instruments and digital presentations.

c. Venturi Vacuum Source. A venturi is a relatively low-cost means of producing the vacuum to operate gyroscopic instruments such as the turn and bank, directional gyro, and artificial horizon. It is mounted on the exterior of the fuselage, parallel with the longitudinal axis of the aircraft. As the aircraft moves through the air, an area of reduced pressure, a partial vacuum, is created in the throat of the venturi. The venturi throat is connected by a tube to the gyro instrument case, resulting in a reduction of pressure within the case. Ambient air, entering the instrument through the inlet port of the case, passes over the gyro rotor, causing it to spin rapidly and causes the instrument to activate. Venturis are available in sizes providing 2", 4", and 9" Hg. of vacuum.

(1) The vacuum requirement for the operation of each instrument is generally provided on the data plate attached to its case. If it is not, obtain the data from the manufacturer or another acceptable source, such as AN and MS standards.

(2) If the vacuum available exceeds the requirements of the installation it will be necessary to install an in-line regulator to adjust the flow within requirements.

d. Pumped Vacuum Source. Current aviation technology has produced durable light-weight, mechanically-driven, pump and control systems for providing instrument operating vacuum. Selection of the correct pump remains dependent on the vacuum requirements of the system being driven. Control is provided by either the system itself or an in-line regulator. Production and aftermarket standby vacuum systems are available to provide operating capabilities in the event of failure of the primary mechanically-driven system.

e. Calculating Vacuum Loads. When a venturi vacuum source is selected, do not assume the venturi selected will provide sufficient flow and negative pressure to operate the instrument package. Even within the make and model of the venturi selected, tolerance may be insufficient to meet the requirements of the system selected. Therefore, it is essential that the vacuum load requirements be carefully evaluated.

(1) Gyroscopic instruments require optimum value of airflow to produce their rated rotor speed. For instance, a specific bank and pitch indicator required approximately 2.30 cubic feet per minute (CFM) flow and a resistance, or pressure drop, of 4" Hg. If the altering technician has selected a 2" Hg. Venturi, the resultant vacuum would be insufficient to drive the instrument.

(2) The following vacuum driven items are examples for the purposes of calculation:

TABLE 11-1. CFM/VACUUM VALUES

instrument	*flow*	*vacuum*
Bank and Pitch Indicator	2.3 cubic feet per minute	4.0" Hg
Directional Gyro Indicator	1.3 cubic feet per minute	4.0" Hg
Turn and Bank Indicator	.5 cubic feet per minute	2.0" Hg
Total flow required	4.10 cubic feet per minute	

The above listed instruments are listed in Tables 11-2 and 11-4. Optimum values are shown in Table 11-4. The negative pressure air source must deliver not only the optimum value of vacuum for the instruments, but must also have sufficient volume capacity to accommodate the total flow requirements of the various instruments it serves.

NOTE: The example components listed above and in Tables 11-2 and 11-4 are accepted as viable and the operating parameters related to them as accurate. The nomenclature and the properties related have no effect on the resulting computations.

TABLE 11-2. PROVIDES INSTRUMENT AIR CONSUMPTION FOR AN EXAMPLE VACUUM DRIVEN AUTOPILOT AND INSTRUMENT INSTALLATION

Instrument	Air consumption at sea level	
	Differential drop in. Hg suction (Optimum)	Cubic feet/per minute
Automatic Pilot System (Type A-2, A-3, & A-3A)		
Directional gyro control unit across mount assembly	5.00	2.15*
Bank & climb gyro control unit across mount assembly	5.00	3.85*
Total	—	6.00*
Automatic Pilot System (Type A-4)		
Directional gyro control unit	5.00	3.50*
Bank & climb gyro control unit	5.00	5.00*
Total	—	8.50*
Bank & pitch indicator	4.00	2.30
Directional gyro indicator	4.00	1.30
Turn & bank indicator	2.00	.50
(*) NOTE.— Includes air required for operations of pneumatic relays.		

TABLE 11-3. PROVIDES THE EQUIVALENT STRAIGHT TUBE LINE DROPS FOR THE 90-DEGREES ELBOWS INSTALLED IN ANY GIVEN SYSTEM (BY O.D.)

Tubing size			Pressure drop in a 90° elbow in terms of length of straight tube equivalent to a 90° elbow
O.D inch		Wall thickness inch	Feet
1/4	X	0.035	0.28
3/8	X	0.035	0.46
1/2	X	0.042	0.62
5/8	X	0.042	0.81
3/4	X	0.049	0.98
1	X	0.049	1.35

TABLE 11-4. PROVIDES THE DIFFERENTIAL PRESSURE ACROSS THE INSTRUMENT INLET AND OUTLET OF THE EXAMPLE INSTRUMENT PACKAGE

Instrument	Suction in inches of Mercury (Hg)		
	Minimum	Optimum	Maximum
Automatic Pilot System (Type A-2, A-3, & A-3A)			
Directional gyro control unit across mount assembly	4.75	5.00	5.25
Bank & climb gyro control unit across mount assembly	4.75	5.00	5.25
Gauge reading (differential gauge in B & C control unit)	3.75	4.00	4.25
Automatic Pilot System (Type A-4)			
Directional gyro control unit	3.75	5.00	5.00
Bank & climb gyro control unit	3.75	5.00	5.00
Bank & pitch indicator	3.75	4.00	5.00
Directional gyro indicator	3.75	4.00	5.00
Turn & bank indicator	1.80	2.00	2.20

(3) Calculation of Equivalent Straight Line Pressure Drop Due to Routing. In addition to the effects of the instrumentation itself consideration must be given to the parasitic resistance to flow provided by the routing of the tubing providing the source pressure to the instruments. For this problem, assume the example system has four right-angle elbows and 20 feet of 1/2-inch O.D. X 0.042" tubing.

(4) Solution to the Stated Problem (Step-by-Step).

(a) Accept the flow requirements of the example instruments listed in paragraph 1104e(2) as 4.10 CFM. The pressure drop for one 90-degree 1/2-inch O.D. elbow is equivalent to 0.62 feet of straight tubing. Therefore, the pressure drop of the four 90-degree elbows is the equivalent to 2.48 feet of tubing. (Ref. Table 11-3.)

(b) Determine the pressure drop through 22.48 feet (20 feet plus the above 2.48 feet) of 1/2-inch O.D. X 0.42 inch tubing at 4.10 CFM flow. (See Figure 11-2.)

FIGURE 11-2. PRESSURE DROP DATA FOR SMOOTH TUBING

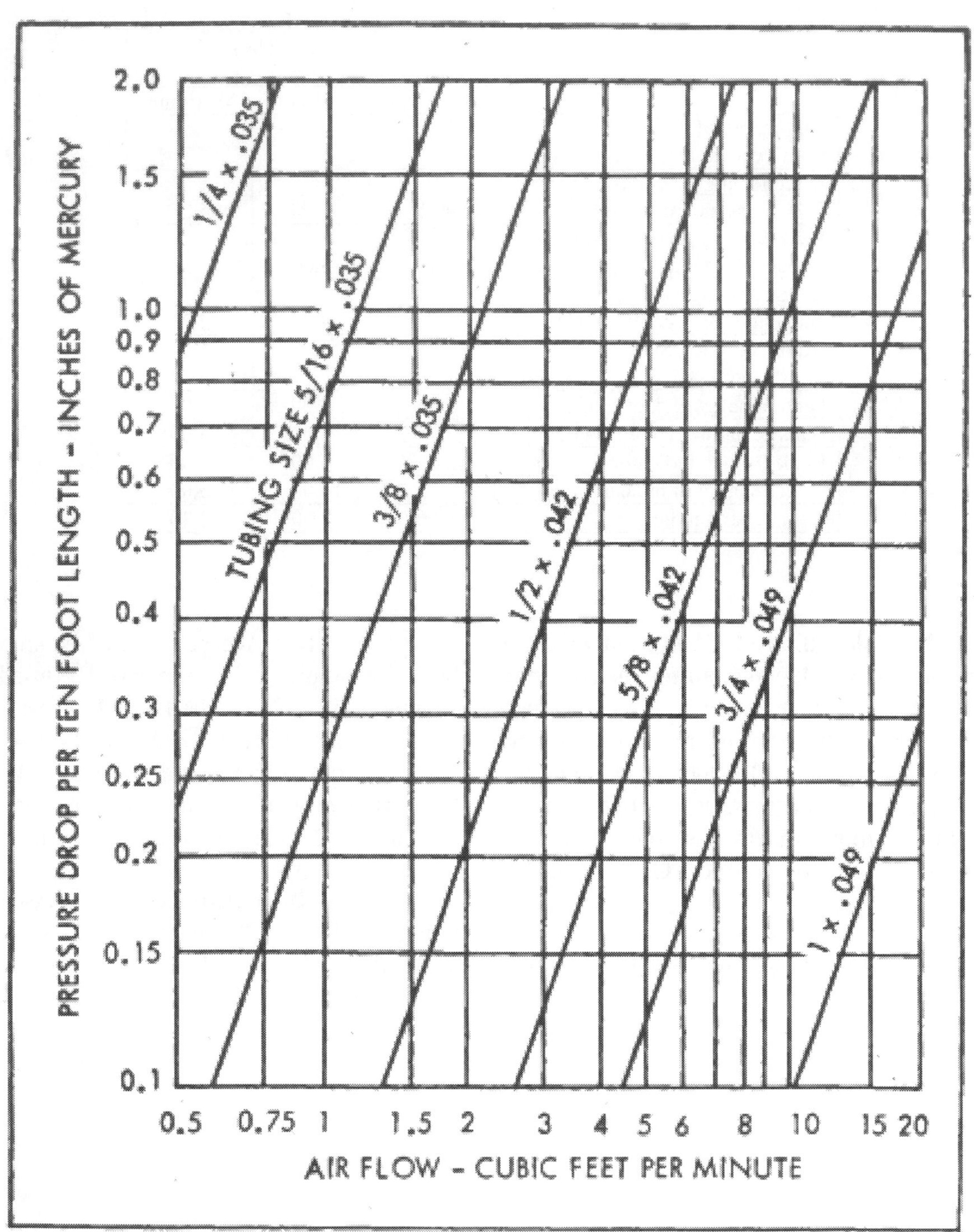

1. The pressure drop for each 10-foot length of that tube is 0.68" Hg.

2. Divide 22.48 feet of tubing to determine the number of 10-foot lengths (i.e., 22.48 divided by 10 equals 2.248).

3. Multiply the number of sections (2.248) by 0.68" Hg to obtain the pressure drop through the system (0.68 X 2.248 = 1.53" Hg).

4. The pump must therefore be capable of producing a minimum pressure differential of 5.63" Hg (i.e., 4.10" Hg) for maximum instrument usage + 1.53" Hg (determined) at a flow of 4.10 CFM.

(c) Filters are used to prevent dust, lint, or other foreign matter from entering the instrument and vacuum system. Filters may be located at the instrument intake port or the manifold intake port when instruments are interconnected. Determine if the flow capacity of the filter is equal to or greater than the flow capacity of the vacuum system. If it is not, the restriction will create a pressure drop in the system. AC 43.13-1 (as amended), chapter 12, paragraph 38a through d provides additional guidance on the installation and maintenance of venturi and engine-driven vacuum and instrument systems.

(d) Electrical supply for instruments. AC 43.13-1 (as amended), chapter 11 provides 16 sections of text on the inspection and installation of electrical systems.

(e) Instrument lighting. The regulatory requirements for instrument lighting have changed little as certification specifications have developed.

1. CAR 3.696 and 3.697 provide two paragraphs simply stating that (1) instrument light installations should be safe, (2) provide sufficient illumination to make instruments and controls easily readable, and (3) shall be installed in such a manner as not to shine in the pilot's eyes.

2. CAR 4a577 adds that instrument lighting shall be equipped with a rheostat control for dimming unless it can be shown a non-dimming light is satisfactory.

3. Section 23.1381 consolidates the language of the earlier regulatory requirements with no appreciable changes.

(f) Magnetic Direction Indicator. The magnetic compass is commonly referred to as the whiskey compass. The maximum deviation limitations of magnetic compasses have changed little since 1928.

1. CAR 3.666 specifies that the Magnetic Direction Indicator must be installed that its accuracy is not excessively affected by the airplane's vibration or magnetic field. After compensating for this in the installation, the deviation level in flight must not exceed 10 degrees on any heading. CAR 3.758 provides and requires the installation and maintenance of the Compass Deviation Card.

2. CAR 4a562 refers to dampening and compensation of the installation and acknowledges the effects of electrical disturbances resulting from the increase in proliferation of aircraft electrical systems. As a result, specific aircraft required to meet the provisions of CAR 4a may be required to display two compass correction cards, one for operation with electrical power off, and one for electrical power on operation.

3. Section 23.1327 provides location and deviation considerations also provided for under CAR 3.666 and CAR 4a562. This section additionally provides for more than 10 degrees deviation of the non-stabilized magnetic compass due to the operation of adjacent high draw electrical components: if either a magnetic stabilized indicator, not having a deviation of greater than 10 degrees on any heading, or a gyroscopic direction indicator is installed.

(g) Alternative installations to liquid-filled Magnetic Direction Indicators. With the development of the vertical reading dry compass, it is practical to replace the liquid-filled compass with a viable and approved alternative.

1. Vertical reading dry compasses provide the pilot with a true relationship of the aircraft to azimuths as opposed to the reverse reading requirements of the liquid filled compass.

2. The vertical reading dry compass does not leak and requires no periodic refilling or cleaning to make it stable and readable.

3. The vertical reading compass provides no relief from the requirement for magnetic correction compensation. Depending on the manufacturer and individual installation, the unit may even require supplemental compensation to meet the maximum deviation requirements.

4. Vertical reading compasses are available on the aftermarket in both Technical Standard Order (TSO) and non-TSO versions. The altering technician must be aware of the limitations and certification responsibilities of the unit selected.

1105. TESTING, MARKING, AND PLACARDING.

a. Testing the Venturi Tube-Powered Systems. At normal in-flight cruise speed, or an accurately generated representative airflow, check the venturi tube-powered system to assure that the required vacuum is being supplied to the system.

b. Testing the Vacuum Pump-Powered System. When the system is powered by either engine or auxiliary driven vacuum pumps, check the system for proper output at their rated RPM. The output should be measured at the point of delivery to the instrument.

c. Testing of Altimeters and Static Systems. Before performing an altimeter or static system test, determine that the system is free of contaminating materials such as dirt and water. With all instruments disconnected from the system, purge the plumbing with low pressure dry filtered air or nitrogen. Part 43, appendix E provides guidance and practical guidance on altimeter and static systems tests and inspections.

NOTE: Altimeter tests in accordance with part 43, appendix E must be accomplished by a properly certificated repair agency.

d. Testing Instrument Electrical Supply. Subsequent to major repairs or alterations that results in addition, replacement, or rearrangement of instrument electrical circuitry, verify continuity and current availability before connecting the instruments. With the individual instruments isolated from the power circuits, determine if the current available is in accordance with the manufacturer's requirements.

e. Fuel, Oil, and Hydraulic Fluid Supply (Wet Instruments). Verify that the fluid transmission lines are free of residual material, dirt, and water before connecting them to the instruments. Purge them using a low pressure application of dry filtered air or nitrogen.

(1) On many CAR 3 and CAR 4a aircraft, common-sized fluid connections make it possible to incorrectly connect fluid lines to the wrong instruments. Be careful to assure delivery of fluids to the correct instrument.

NOTE: Fuel, Oil, and Hydraulic Fluid Supply (Wet Instruments), subparagraph (1) speaks to line fittings. Note that these wet instruments require a restricted fitting where the line attaches to the engine pressure outlet port. The restricted fitting is necessary to prevent fuel/oil/etc. from being sprayed into the cockpit during an instrument malfunction. There have been cases where this restricted fitting was removed and a normal fitting was installed, a fatal error for some personnel and airplane.

(2) Verify fluid pressures at both the source and instrument to confirm the absence of restrictions or blockage before connection to the instrument.

f. Fuel, Oil, and Hydraulic Fluid Supply (Dry Instruments). Use the same care exercised on the verification of security, source, and hygiene of wet instrument systems when checking dry systems.

(1) The primary difference is the delivery of the material to be measured to a transducer or pressure transmitter, rather than to the back of an instrument. Use of the wrong fluid can damage an instrument beyond repair.

(2) The additional difference between the two instrument systems is the attention required to provide the correct electrical circuitry and current between the transmitter and the instrument. (See subparagraph d.)

g. Instrument Markings and Placards.

(1) When additional instruments are installed, they must be appropriately marked. Refer to the applicable CAR and 14 CFR for specific instrument marking and placard requirements.

(2) Especially when the instrument panel was replaced, the altering individual should refer to the applicable ATC, TC, Group 2, Bulletin 7A, or TCDS of the aircraft to assure proper installation and placement of the required placards and limitations.

1106. ELECTRONIC DISPLAY INSTRUMENT SYSTEMS OR ELECTRONIC DISPLAY INDICATORS. The installation of these systems, regardless of the certification basis of the airplane into which they are being installed, are defined and specified under the provisions of § 23.1311.

a. Electrostatic Discharges.

(1) With new technologies come the requirements to learn new skills. While a certain amount of care and attention to detail while handling mechanical and electrical instruments has always been required, the hazards have been based on circumstances that could be seen and felt. With the glass cockpit, a different kind of hazard has surfaced as a real threat to airworthiness of instrumentation. That threat is called Electrostatic Discharges (ESD).

(2) ESD is not a new phenomena. It has been with the industry a long time. However, with the advent of the electronic display instrument system and its multiple presentations, the problem can now disrupt entire display systems as a result of one event. Any unit containing electronic components such as diodes, transistors, integrated circuits, programmable read-only memory (ROM), ROM, and memory devices must be protected from ESD. The simple act of improperly carrying an electronic device across a room without adequate protection can render it unairworthy.

CAUTION: To prevent damage due to excessive electrostatic discharge, use proper gloves, finger cots, or grounding bracelets. Observe the standard procedures for handling equipment containing electrostatic sensitive devices or assemblies in accordance with the recommendations in the manufacturer's maintenance instructions.

b. Electronic Display Instrument Systems Provide No Relief from the "Basic T". Section 23.1311(a)(5) requires systems using electronic displays to have independent backup systems to provide basic IMC reference in case electrical power is lost.

(1) Subparagraph 5 requires an independent magnetic indicator and either an independent secondary mechanical altimeter, airspeed indicator, and attitude instrument; or

(2) Individual electronic display indicators for altitude, airspeed, and attitude that are independent from the airplane's primary electrical system.

(3) These secondary instruments may be installed in panel positions that are displaced from the primary positions as specified by § 23.1321(d), but must be located where they meet the pilot's visibility requirements of § 23.1321(a).

c. Advisory Circular (AC) 23.1311-1, Installation of Electronic Display in Part 23 Airplanes (as amended), paragraph 3.0, provides valuable interface references relating to the relationships between the CAR and 14 CFR regulatory requirements installation of this technology to older and current technology in airplanes.

1107. ENVIRONMENTAL CONDITIONS.

a. General. The equipment environmental limits established by the manufacturer should be compatible with the operating environment of the airplane. When evaluation of the equipment installation, consider such factors as the maximum operating altitude of the airplane and whether the equipment is located within a temperature- and pressure-controlled area. Applicable methods for testing the performance characteristics of the equipment for specific environmental conditions are provided in the current edition of AC 21-16, RTCA, Inc. Document RTCA/DO-160E, Environmental Conditions and Test Procedures for Airborne Equipment. Either test or analysis, or both, ensures the compatibility between the operational environment and the environmental equipment category of the laboratory tests.

b. Temperature. An electronic system's reliability is strongly related to the temperature of the solid-state components in the system. Component temperatures depend on the internal thermal design and external cooling. In evaluating the temperature requirements, consider the additional heat generated by the equipment, especially in an area where air flow is restricted. To determine if adequate cooling is provided, the evaluation must make maximum use of previous data from compatible installations. This will assist in limiting the ground and/or flight tests of those installations that cannot be verified by other means. When the equipment operating environment cannot be verified from previous experience or from evaluation of temperature values in that equipment location, a cooling test must be conducted.

c. Attitude Information. Attitude information should continue to be presented for a minimum of 30 minutes after the in-flight loss of cooling for the primary instrument when in the normal operating environment (temperature/altitude). If proper performance of the flight instrument functions is adversely affected due to loss of in-flight cooling, such conditions must be annunciated. Consider incorporation of an over-temperature shut-down of the system in case of cooling system failure. If such systems are used, AFM documentation should be established, requiring subsequent pilot actions. Additionally, applicable placards must be provided for pilot situational awareness of the critical condition. These actions should include procedures to allow possible recovery of a system that has had an over-temperature shutdown condition.

d. Annunciation. Annunciation of in-flight loss of cooling or fan monitors may not be required if shown by a safety analysis or test demonstration that a hazardous or catastrophic condition is not indicated. The safety analysis should consider the reliability of the fans, redundancies of functions, reversionary features (such as the ability to transfer critical functions), the enunciation of over-temperature and its response time, and the availability of other flight instrumentation. In some systems, cooling fans may be installed to improve the operating environment of the components and reduce the possibility of a failure condition or shutdown of the equipment. With supplementary installations, fan monitoring or additional temperature sensors may not be required. If cooling fans are needed to prevent a hazardous or catastrophic failure condition, installation of fan monitoring or other methods of determining the status of the cooling fan must be provided prior to flight.

1108. THRU 1199. RESERVED

CHAPTER 12. CARGO TIEDOWN DEVICE INSTALLATIONS

1200. PURPOSE. This chapter provides data for making acceptable cargo tiedown device installations in non-pressurized areas of civil aircraft of 12,500 lbs gross weight or less. Engineering assistance is required for floor/attach fittings load analysis and material burn testing.

1201. HAZARDS AND WARNINGS.

a. Structural failure may occur if aircraft floor loading limits are exceeded.

b. Fire hazards may exist if materials do not meet flame resistant specifications.

c. Exceeding manufacturer's weight and balance limitations create unsafe flight conditions.

1202. INSTALLATION CONSIDERATIONS.

a. Assure that the altered aircraft can be operated within the permissible weight and center of gravity (CG) ranges.

b. Determine that there will be unobstructed access to all equipment and controls essential to the proper operation of the aircraft, required emergency exits, and emergency equipment.

c. Use only materials that are at least flame resistant for covering of floors and webbing material. Refer to the applicable airworthiness standards for the aircraft involved to determine the required flame-resistant qualities. For aircraft in air taxi or other commercial operations, refer to the applicable operating rule for special requirements regarding fire protection, cargo bins, location of cargo with respect to passengers, cargo compartment, or aisle width.

1203. FABRICATION AND INSTALLATION.

a. Cargo Tiedown Devices.

(1) Cargo tiedown devices may be assembled from webbing, nets, rope, cables, fittings, or other material that conforms to a FAA-PMA, TSO, NAS, AN, or MIL-SPEC standards. Use snaps, hooks, clamps, buckles, or other acceptable fasteners rather than relying upon knots for securing cargo. Install tensioning devices or other acceptable means to provide a method of tightening and adjusting the restraint system to fit the cargoes to be carried.

(2) Provide covers or guards where necessary to prevent damage to or jamming of the aircraft's equipment, structure, or control cables.

(3) Straps and nets manufactured with MIL-SPEC webbing and thread must be evaluated to determine that the working load requirements are met. All tiedown assemblies are only as strong as the weakest component in the system, including the point of attachment.

NOTE: The owner/operator is responsible for ensuring that a basis of approval/acceptance is obtained for the tiedown device before use on aircraft. This is accomplished by providing substantiating engineering data of the devices being used, including aircraft floor load limits.

b. Structural Attachment. Commercially-available seat tracks, rails, or other types of anchor plates may be used for structural attachment, provided they conform to a NAS, AN, or MIL-SPEC standard. This type of hardware permits a ready means of mounting a wide variety of quick-disconnect fittings for cargo tiedown. Typical examples of such fittings and their attachments are shown in Figures 12-1 through 12-5.

(1) When installing these fittings, reinforce the existing floorboards and/or other adjacent structure to obtain the necessary load carrying capacity. Seat tracks installed longitudinally across lateral floor beams generally require full-length support for adequate strength and rigidity between beam attach points (see Figure 12-4).

(2) Consider the inherent flexibility of the aircraft structure and install any reinforcement in a manner that will avoid localized stress concentrations in the structural members/areas. Give specific attention to the size, shape, and thickness of the reinforcement, fastener size and pattern, and the effects of any adhesives used.

(3) Fittings used for cargo tiedown attachment need not be substantiated by static tests if it can be shown that the fitting's rated minimum breaking strength would not be exceeded by the applicable static test loads. Existing racks, rails, or other points used for attachment may be verified by static tests, analysis, or a written statement by the aircraft manufacturer attesting to its adequacy to withstand the necessary loads.

FIGURE 12-1. EXTRUDED TRACK, ANCHOR PLATES, AND ASSOCIATED FITTINGS

EXTRUDED TRACK

ANCHOR PLATE

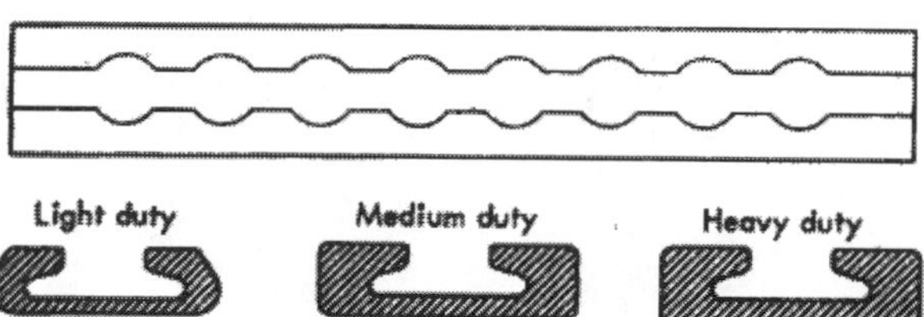

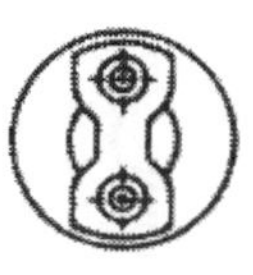

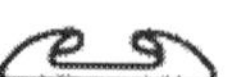

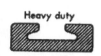

Extruded track and anchor plates are available in several different styles and load capacities and will accommodate a wide variety of quick attachment fittings.

SINGLE PIN TYPE
HOLD DOWN FITTINGS

These types of fittings are suitable for litter or berth attachment to the extruded track and anchor plate styles shown above.

SINGLE PIN TYPE
CARGO TIE DOWN FITTINGS

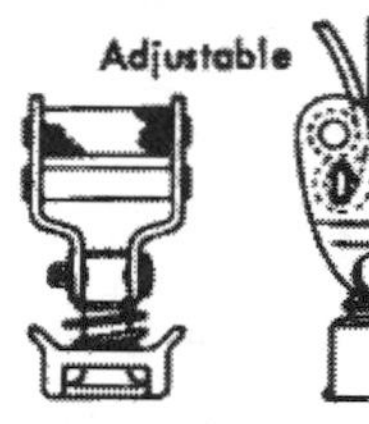

These types of fittings are suitable for cargo tie down attachment to the extruded track and anchor plate styles shown above.

DUAL PIN TYPE CARGO TIE FITTINGS

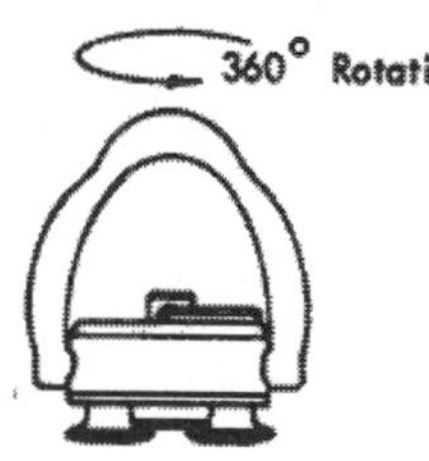

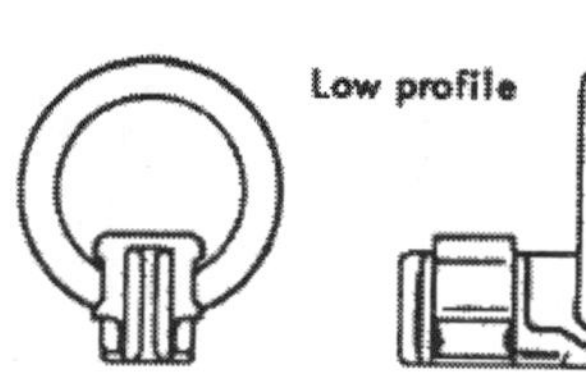

These types of cargo tie down fittings are of greater capacity than the single pin types and are suitable for use with the extruded track style shown above.

FIGURE 12-2. MISCELLANEOUS LITTER, BERTH, AND CARGO TIEDOWN FITTINGS

PAN FITTINGS

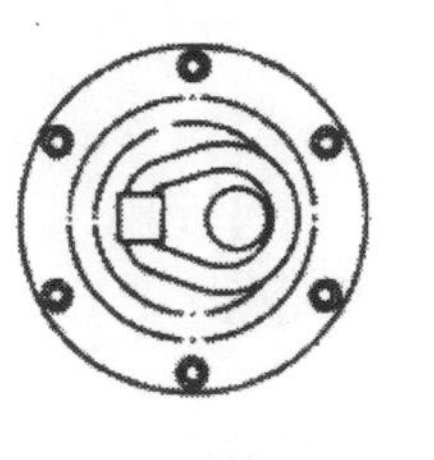

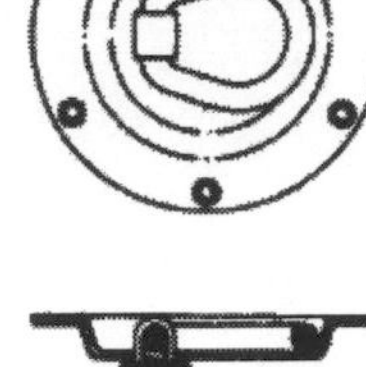
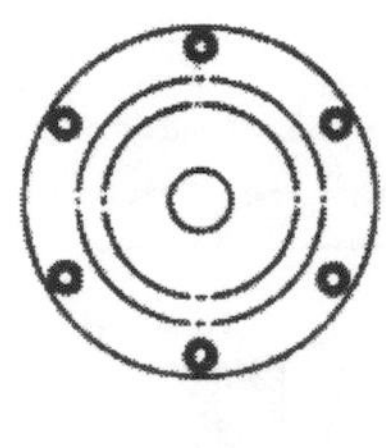

Stud & Cargo ring | Cargo ring only | Stud only

SINGLE STUD FITTINGS

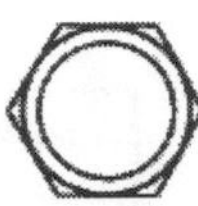
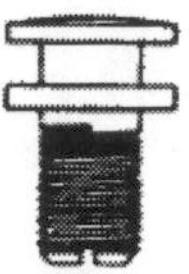
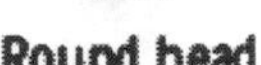

Round head | Hex head

SINGLE STUD CARGO TIE DOWN FITTING

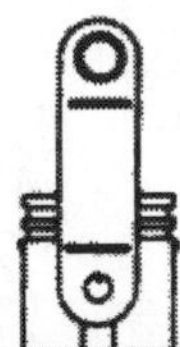
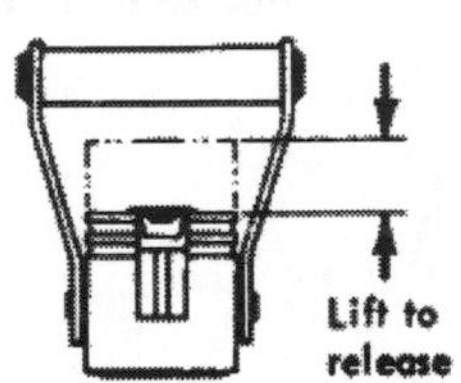

These types of fittings are suitable for cargo tie down attachment to the single stud fittings or stud equipped pan fittings shown above.

SINGLE STUD HOLD DOWN FITTINGS

These types of fittings are suitable for litter or berth attachment to the single stud fittings or stud equipped pan fittings shown above.

STUD/RING

EYE BOLT

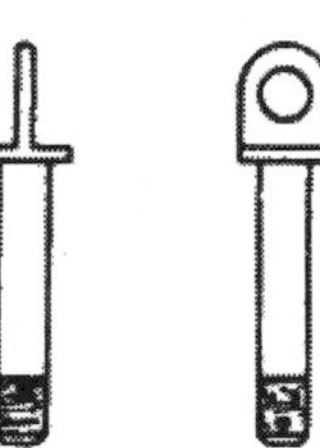

These types of fittings are suitable for litter, berth, and/or cargo tie down attachment directly to the aircraft structure.

FIGURE 12-3. TYPICAL ATTACHMENT OF FITTINGS TO HONEYCOMB STRUCTURES

A. Attachment method utilizing a honeycomb doubler.

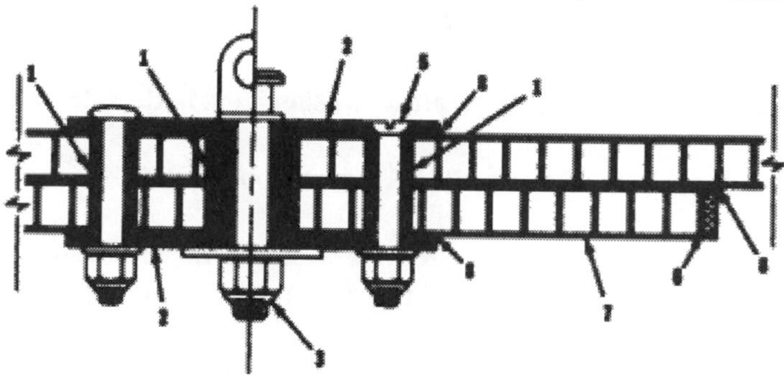

Single Studs or Eye Bolts.

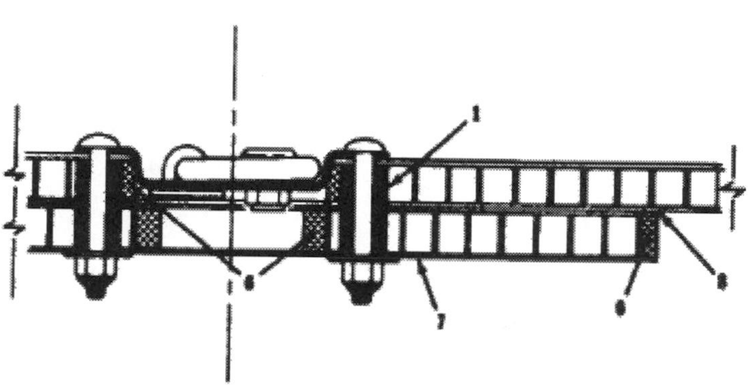

Pan Fittings.

B. Attachment methods utilizing reinforcing plates.

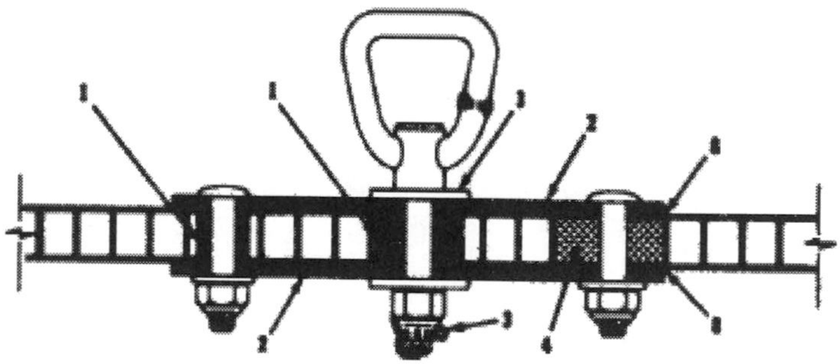

Stud/Rings.

FIGURE 12-3. TYPICAL ATTACHMENT OF FITTINGS TO HONEYCOMB STRUCTURES – CONTINUED

1. Bed all inserts and spacers in a suitable potting compound.
2. Reinforcing plate.
3. Where fitting is subject to rotation, place washers on both sides and use a positive safety means.
4. (Alternate method in lieu of spacers) Undercut honeycomb, inject potting compound, and drill through when set.
5. Countersink if required for clearance or if desired for appearance.
6. Undercut all open edges of honeycomb 1/16" and seal with potting compound.
7. Honeycomb doubler.
8. Use epoxy or other suitable adhesive to attach doubler and reinforcing plates.

FIGURE 12-4. INSTALLATION OF UNDERFLOOR SUPPORT FOR EXTRUDED TRACK

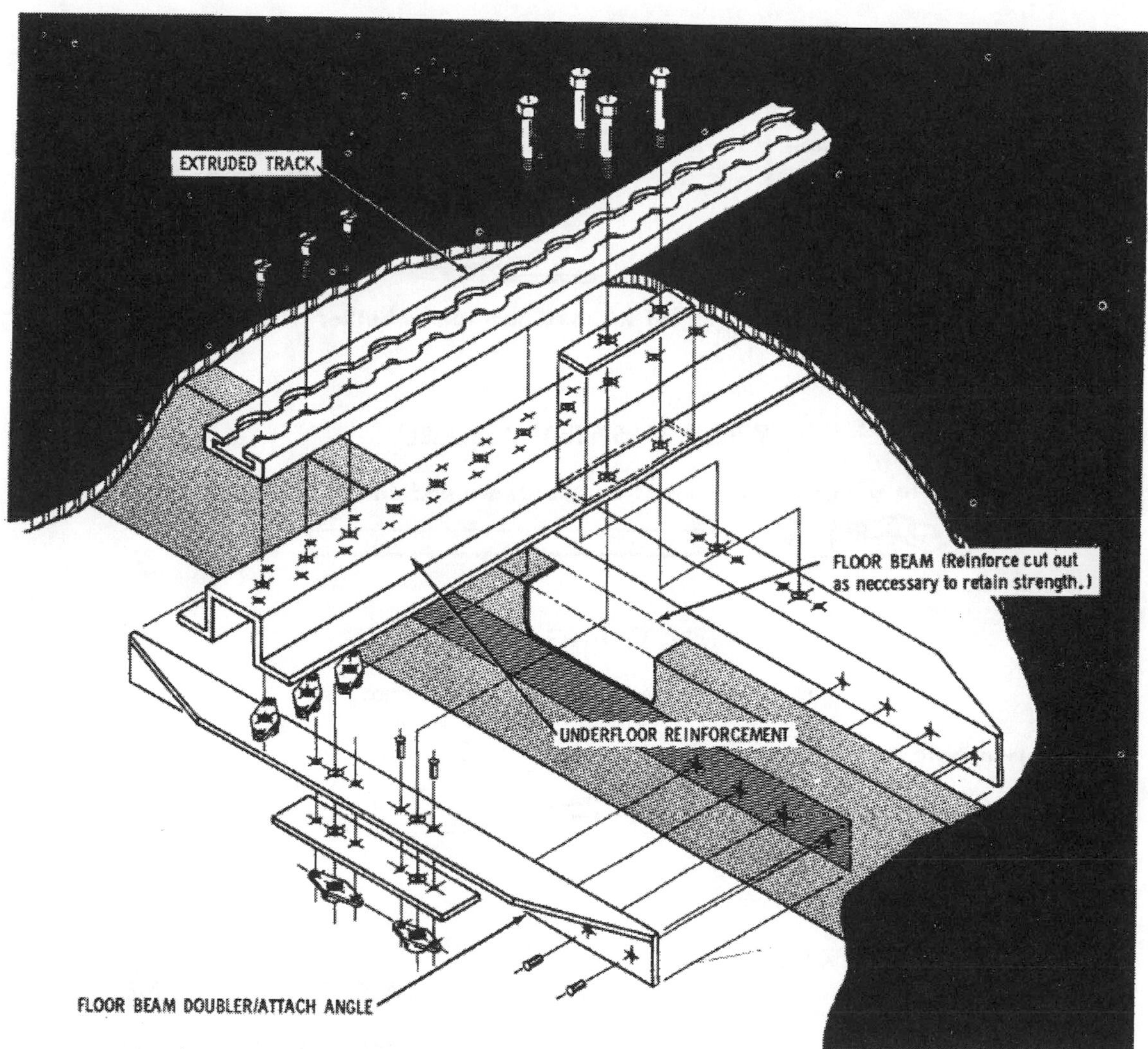

FIGURE 12-5. TYPICAL CARGO TIEDOWN STRAPS AND CARGO NETS

THREE BAR TYPE SLIDE

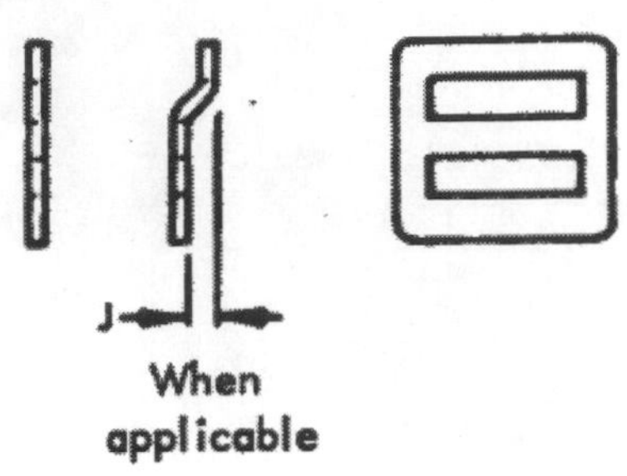

Rigging for easiest adjustment and moderate loads.

Rigging for maximum load whether slide is joggled or not.

TYPICAL NAS STRAP ASSEMBLY

Available with various types of end hardware and up to 5000# capacity.

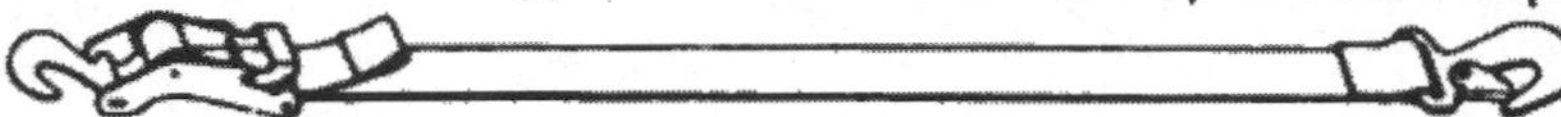

TENSIONING SLIDE

Used to preload cargo tie down straps.

CARGO BARRIER NET

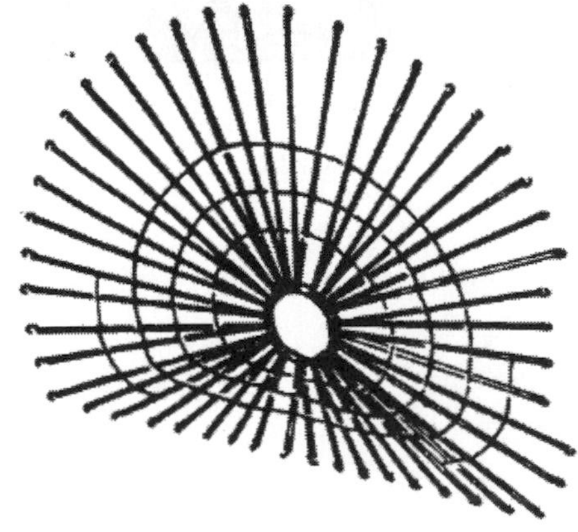

CARGO TIE DOWN NET

Commonly used to restrain bulky or composite cargo.

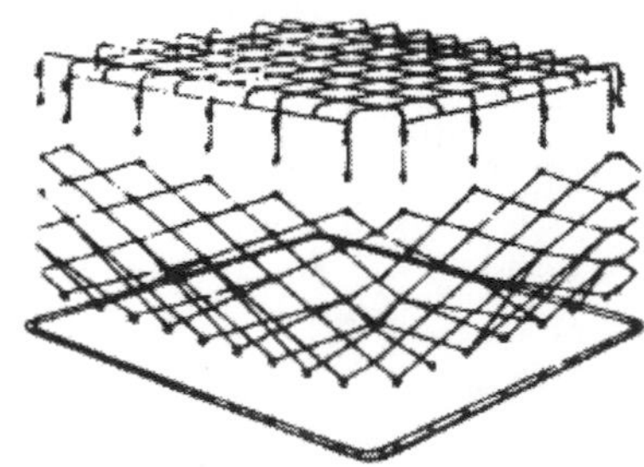

c. Load Factors.

(1) Use the load factor established by the aircraft manufacturer for type certification as the basis for substantiating the cargo tiedown devices and attachments to the aircraft structure. Refer to the applicable operating rules for any additional load factor requirements if the aircraft is to be used for air taxi or other commercial operations.

(2) The critical load factors to which the installation is to be substantiated are generally available from the holder of the aircraft's type-certificate (TC). When the TC holder is no longer active, contact the certificate management Aircraft Certification Office (ACO).

(3) The maximum loadings are a requirement to which the aircraft manufacturer must adhere. Aircraft manufacturer floor loading limitations take precedence over the load rating of the net, fitting, and tiedown devices.

d. Static Tests.

(1) It is recommended that static testing be conducted on a duplicate installation in a jig or mockup that simulates the related aircraft structure. Refer to chapter 1, paragraph 3 for static test information.

(2) If the actual installation is used for static testing, inspect both the aircraft and the cargo tiedown device installation thoroughly before releasing to service. Check all members and fittings for cracks, distortion, wrinkles, or elongated holes. Replace all bolts and threaded fittings that are not inspected by magnetic particle or other acceptable Nondestructive Testing (NTD) inspection process. Inspect riveted joints for tipped rivet heads and other indications of partially sheared rivets or elongated holes.

(3) All cargo tiedown installations must be tested to the critical ultimate load factor. Refer to chapter 1 of this AC for computation and testing procedures.

(4) When the cargo compartment is separated from the cockpit by a bulkhead that is capable of withstanding the inertia forces of emergency conditions, a forward load factor of 4.5 g may be used. All other applications require the use of a 18 g forward load factor.

(5) Each cargo tiedown fitting installation must be static tested under forward, side, and up load conditions. Individual fittings may be tested by applying a single pull of 12.6 g forward load at an angle of 18.5° up and 9.5° to the left or right (as applicable) of the aircraft longitudinal axis. For example, assuming a 5,000-lb static pull (rating of a typical tiedown fitting) is applied as described and divided by the g load factor, we find the fitting installation will be capable of restraining a 397-lb load under emergency conditions.

9 g x 1.33 = 12.0

(6) When a cargo-restraining net or cargo container with multiple attachments is used, the static load requirements for each tiedown fitting may be divided equally between the fittings. For example, if the maximum cargo load to be carried is 1,800 lbs and 10 tiedown fittings are to be used, the static load requirement for each fitting is approximately 2,155 lbs.

Example: static load for each tiedown fitting
9 g x 1.33 x 1,800/10 = 2,154.6
Placard individual tiedowns for the maximum weight to be secured.

1204. OPERATING LIMITATIONS, LOADING INSTRUCTIONS, AND PLACARDS.

a. General. Revisions or supplements to the approved portions of the Aircraft's Flight Manual (AFM) regarding markings, placards, or other operating limitations require FAA engineering approval. Submit the requested changes and supporting data to the local FAA Flight Standards District Office for review and processing.

b. Operating Limitations and Loading Instructions.

(1) Prepare revisions or supplements to the AFM or operating limitations, weight and balance records, and equipment list changes as necessitated by the installation of the cargo tiedown systems.

(2) Provide instructions covering the installation and use of the cargo restraint system. For aircraft that require a flight manual, incorporate these instructions as a supplement. On other aircraft, provide a placard that references the appropriate instruction. In the instructions, cover such items as removal and reinstallation of seats or other equipment exchanged for cargo restraint systems, use of cargo nets, barrier nets, number and positioning of tiedown straps, maximum load for each compartment or tiedown area, permissible load per square foot, number of tiedown points allowable per foot of track, and maximum height of the load's CG above the floor.

c. Placards: Cargo Area Placards. Install placards or other permanent markings to indicate the maximum allowable cargo load and weight per square foot limitation for each cargo area. Placard seat tracks as to number of tiedown points permissible per foot of track. Attach a permanent label or other marking on each cargo net, barrier net, and at cargo tiedowns to indicate the maximum cargo weight that the net or attachment will restrain when installed according to the loading instructions.

1205. AIRWORTHINESS COMPLIANCE CHECK SHEET: CARGO TIEDOWN DEVICE INSTALLATIONS.

a. General. Cargo tiedown device installations that are the same as those made by the manufacturer, or other installations which are already approved, may be accepted without further investigation. On other installations, the following points should be checked to determine that the installation is satisfactory.

b. Applicable Civil Aviation Regulations (CAR).

(1) CAR 3.390 - Seats and Berths.

(2) CAR 6.355 – Seats and Berths.

c. Applicable Title 14 of the Code of Federal Regulations (14 CFR).

(1) Part 21, § 21.303—Replacement and Modification Parts.

(2) Part 23, § 23.785—Seats, Berths, Litters, Safety Belts, and Shoulder Harnesses.

(3) Part 23, § 23.787—Baggage and Cargo Compartments.

(4) Part 27, § 27.785—Seats, Berths, Litters, Safety Belts, and Shoulder Harnesses.

(5) Part 27, § 27.787—Cargo and Baggage Compartments.

(6) Part 29, § 29.785—Seats, Berths, Litters, Safety Belts, and Shoulder Harnesses.

(7) Part 29, § 29.787—Cargo and Baggage Compartments.

d. Structural Requirements.

(1) If the aircraft structure is changed or altered, determine if the original strength and integrity of the structure is retained. (Ref. AC 43.13-2B, chapter 1 and § 23.561.)

(2) Determine if the extent to which the modification affects the aircraft CG has been evaluated. (Section 23.1589.)

(3) If the equipment is mounted either on the existing structure or on a bracket attached to the existing structure, confirm that all of the structure (including the bracket, if used) is adequate to support the required loads. (Ref. §§ 23.307, 23.613, 23.561, 25.307, 25.613, 25.561, 27.307, 27.613, 27.561, 29.307, 29.613, and 29.561.)

(4) Verify that the equipment is installed so that it does not adversely affect other structures (either primary or secondary).

(5) Confirm that means are provided to permit proper inspections of the installation and related adjacent parts as components. (Ref. § 23.611.)

e. Hazards to the Aircraft or Its Occupants. Determine whether the:

(1) Modification creates any projections that may cause injury by human impact.

(2) Fabric used in the modification complies with flame-resistant requirements.

(3) Modifications adversely affect the accessibility of the exits and doors.

f. Detail Design Standards.

(1) Determine if suitable materials are used in the construction, including standard fasteners, and if the method of fabrication will result in a consistently sound structure. (Ref. §§ 21.305, 23.603, 23.605, 23.607, 23.613, 27.603, 27.605, 27.607, and 27.613.)

(2) Verify that cargo tiedown devices conform to an acceptable standard.

g. Instructions for Continued Airworthiness. Determine whether:

(1) There are written procedures concerning equipment installation and removal procedures.

(2) Written equipment serviceability requirements are available.

(3) Placards are installed. (Ref. paragraph 1204.)

(4) Revisions or supplements are provided for the AFM or operating limitations, if required. (Ref. paragraph 1204.)

(5) Written scheduled inspection requirements are available to ensure the aircraft structure, tiedown devices, nets, and fittings are in serviceable condition.

(6) Drawings are available. (Ref. Figure 12-6.)

h. Recordkeeping. Verify whether:

(1) A maintenance record entry has been made. (Ref. § 43.9.)

(2) The equipment list and weight and balance has been revised. (Ref. Order 8310.6, chapter 1.)

(3) FAA Form 337, Major Repair and Alteration (Airplane, Powerplant, Propeller, or Appliance), and Instructions for Continued Airworthiness have been completed and accepted by the FAA

1206. THRU 1299. RESERVED

FIGURE. 12-6. TYPICAL ALLOWABLE CARGO LOADING DIAGRAM

AirDesign	report 490-1	sheet E3
1906 Conard Circle	prepared by	H.Wells
Austin, Texas 78734	checked by	H. Wells Howard
(512) 266-5250 fax (512) 266-5052	revision	G

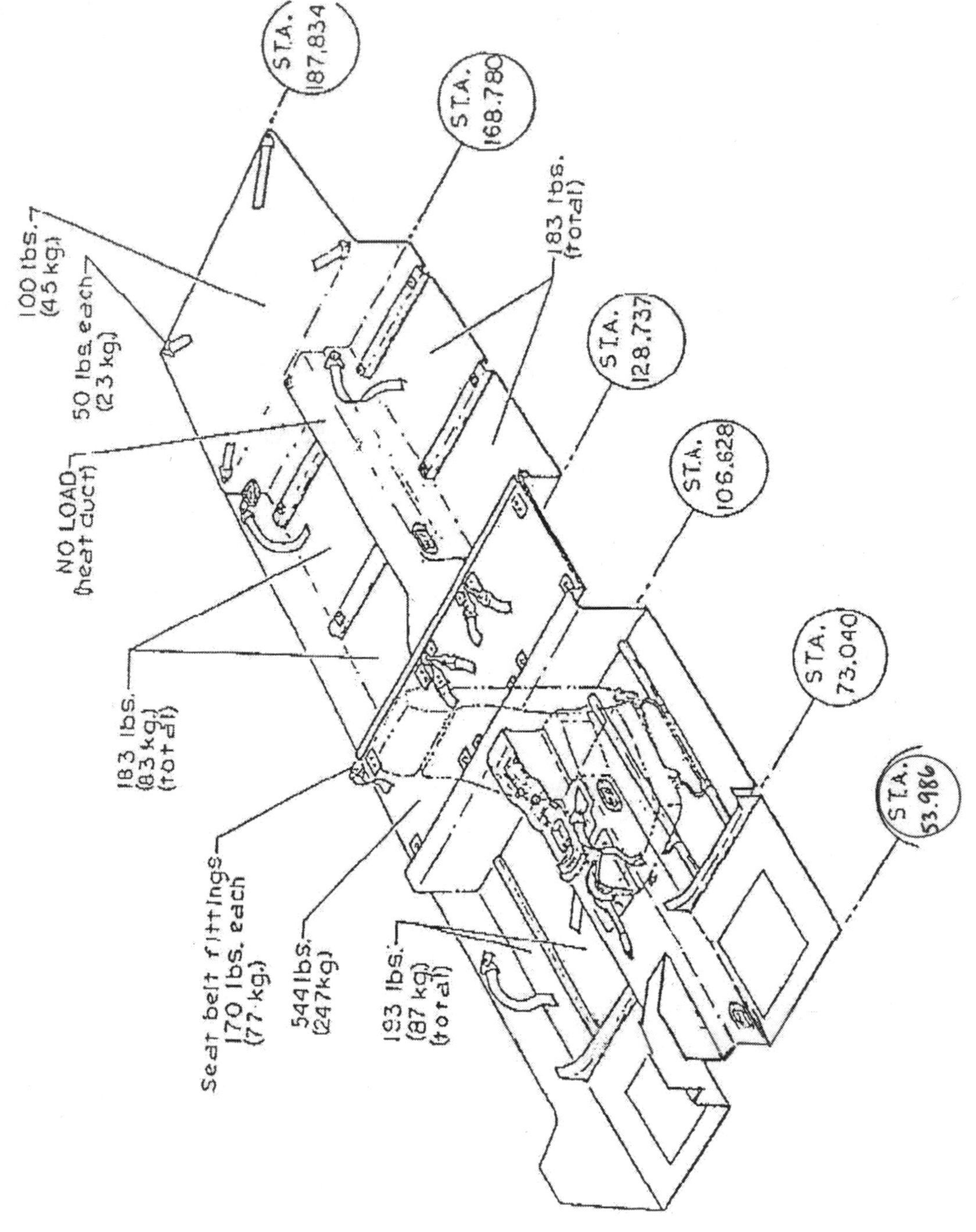